─ ra‿

MW00326059

Neka ti ovaj
rječnik bude mali
podsjetnik na naša
što češća viđanja
u godinama koje
dolaze, a i Johnu
poticaj da nas bolje
razumije.

Od srca,
mala obitelj _____

ENGLISH-CROATIAN AND CROATIAN-ENGLISH DICTIONARY

ENGLESKO-HRVATSKI I HRVATSKO-ENGLESKI RJEČNIK

ENGLISH-CROATIAN
AND
CROATIAN-ENGLISH
DICTIONARY

Editor-in-chief
DAMIR KALOGJERA

Editors
NATA ČENGIĆ
VOJO MICAK
NATAŠA PAVLOVIĆ

ISBN 953-6088-03-7

ENGLESKO-HRVATSKI
I
HRVATSKO-ENGLESKI
RJEČNIK

U redakciji
DAMIRA KALOGJERE

Sastavili
NATA ČENGIĆ
VOJO MICAK
NATAŠA PAVLOVIĆ

Editing and proofs
Redaktura i korektura

BLANKA PEČNIK-KROFLIN

Contents – Sadržaj

Introduction

The intention of the authors has been to compile a small-size dictionary with maximum information. The user of the dictionary will realize this after using it for a period of time. The following instructions should contribute to its more efficient use.

The authors have followed a descriptive approach and introduced words from every style and register of English and Croatian. Words felt to belong to special functional styles have been so marked: *form* (formal), *coll* (colloquial), *sl* (slang), *vulg* (vulgar), *tab* (taboo) etc. Within the limited space, the plan has been to register modern English and Croatian vocabulary including Croatian neologisms and older words in use again, particularly in the formal and official styles.

A list of all abbreviations used in the Dictionary with reference to style, word classes, gender, number etc. has been given under the title **Abbreviations used in the dictionary**.

WHEN THE USER OF THE DICTIONARY IS UNABLE TO LOCATE A WORD WHERE IT SHOULD APPEAR IN ALPHABETICAL ORDER, HE/SHE SHOULD LOOK IT UP WITHIN THE ENTRY WHERE THE ROOT OF THE WANTED WORD IS THE HEADWORD.

Thus **istodoban, istoimen, istoznačan** are to be sought under the entry **isti**.

Space saving has been effected by means of the symbol ~ which stands for the first part of the entry (to the vertical line): **mrt|av** *adj* dead... **~vac** *nm* corpse... **~vački** *adj* deadly... **~vačnica** *nf* morgue.

In order to register a greater number of different meanings of entries and their derivatives, some obvious derivatives have not been registered if they are regular and retain the meaning of the root as eg. Croatian nouns ending in -ost: **spor-sporost** (slow-slowness). However, when a new meaning is found in the derivative as in the case: **naklon-naklonost** (in English bow-favour) such derivatives are registered. The decision whether to register a certain derivative often depends on the equivalent in the other language.

A more general survey of word-formation in both languages can be found in the basic grammars of Croatian and English and in the lists of suffixes in both languages.

Different words having the same form are marked with numbers (1), (2) and make up separate entries. When a single word has different meanings each one is marked with numbers **1,2,...** In such cases the area of their meaning is suggested by words in brackets as eg. **vedar**... **1** (nebo) clear... **2** (osoba) cheerful...

If a phrase has several meanings they have been marked with letters **a. b. c.**

When an entry of the same form belongs to two different word classes eg. **istaknuti** as a verb and **istaknuti** as an adjective, this is marked by the black point (•): **istaknuti** *v* point out...• *adj* prominent.

A similar case within a single entry is marked with a circle ○ eg. **zdrav** *adj* healthy ~**o** *adv* healthily ○ *int* hello.

The movable **a** sound in Croatian (see Croatian grammar) is marked by the symbol *a*.

Phrases within entries are written in **bold letters** and examples of use in *italics*.

The sound values of the Croatian letters have been illustrated with comparable sounds in English (see **Basic Croatian Grammar**). The English pronunciation is marked by the International Phonetic Alphabet.

More data on Croatian and English words have been given in the following lists:

Common abbreviations in both languages
Irregular English verbs
Religious holidays
Chemical elements
Planets
Military ranks
Weights and measures
Geographical names.

We are grateful to the members of Nightingale Hall SCR and of the Department of Slavonic Studies in the University of Nottingham who in 1993-1994 stoically endured and patiently answered the Editor's countless queries about English words.

The authors

Predgovor

Namjera autorâ je bila sastaviti rječnik malog formata s najvećom mogućom količinom obavijesti. Korisnik će se u to uvjeriti kad rječnik upozna, a upoznat će ga u prvom redu duljom upotrebom. Ovih nekoliko uvodnih uputa trebale bi također tome pridonijeti.

Rječnik je opisne vrste što znači da bilježi riječi iz svih slojeva vokabulara (kako engleskog tako i hrvatskoga), od tzv. formalnoga (*form*), preko razgovornog (*coll*) do slanga (*sl*) i vulgarnog (*vulg*, *tab*) stila, što se po potrebi i označuje navedenim kraticama. U okviru opisnoga pristupa, ali i ograničenoga prostora, nastojalo se unijeti suvremeni vokabular oba jezika uključivši i hrvatske novotvorine ili obnovljene starije riječi koje su danas dio formalnog i službenoga stila.

Sve kratice upotrijebljene u rječniku, kako za stil tako za vrste riječi, rod, broj i dr., dane su zajedno u posebnom popisu pod naslovom **Kratice u rječniku**.

KAD KORISNIK RJEČNIKA NE NAĐE RIJEČ NA MJESTU GDJE BI SE PO ABECEDNOM REDU MORALA NALAZITI, TREBA JE POKUŠATI NAĆI U OKVIRU IZVEDENICA OD KORIJENA TE TRAŽENE RIJEČI.

Tako će se **istodoban, istoimen, istoznačan** naći pod natuknicom **isti** i sl.

Unutar natuknice prostor se štedjelo znakom ~ koji zamjenjuje prvi dio natuknice (do uspravne crte): **mrt|av** *adj* dead... **~vac** *nm* corpse... **~vački** deadly... **~vačnica** *nf* morgue.

Da bi se obuhvatilo što više različitih značenja jedne natuknice i njezinih izvedenica, neke očigledne izvedenice nisu zabilježene ako su pravilne i ne odstupaju od značenja osnove, kao primjerice hrvatske imenice na -ost: **spor-sporost**. Međutim kad se pri tvorbi dobiva novo značenje kao u primjeru **naklon-naklonost** (što se vidi i u engleskom prijevodu **bow-favour**) takvi se slučajevi navode. Ekvivalent u drugom jeziku često je utjecao na navođenje izvedenice; **mladost** prema **mlad** je navedena jer je u engleskom ekvivalentu tvorba posebna: **young-youth**. Suprotan je primjer **vjeran** gdje ne navodimo **vjernost** jer je i u engleskom tvorba predvidljiva: **faithful-faithfulness**.

Općenitija pravila i primjeri tvorbe riječi u hrvatskom i engleskom mogu se naći u kratkim gramatikama engleskoga i hrvatskog jezika pridodanim rječniku kao i u popisu sufiksa za oba jezika koji se nalaze u Dodatku pod naslovom **Tvorba riječi - Word formation**.

Manje izvedenica iz jednog korijena koje ne donose nova značenja stvorilo je mjesta za značenjski zanimljivije izvedenice i složenice.

Pozornost treba obratiti na neke znakove koji olakšavaju snalaženje.

Homonimi, riječi koje se jednako pišu a imaju drukčije podrijetlo i značenje, označeni su brojevima (l), (2) i tvore posebne natuknice. Kad je u pitanju polisemija, jedna riječ koja ima više značenja, pojedina značenja obilježena su brojevima 1,2. U takvim slučajevima, po potrebi, opseg njihova značenja sugeriraju riječi u zagradama, npr. **vedar** l (nebo) clear...2 (osoba) cheerful.

Ako fraza ima više značenja, ta su označena malim slovima **a. b. c**. Kad jedna natuknica u istom obliku pripada dvjema vrstama riječi npr. *istaknuti* kao glagol i *istaknuti* kao pridjev, to se označuje crnom točkom (•): **istaknuti** *v* point out...• *adj*   prominent...

Kad imamo sličnu pojavu među podnatuknicama, unutar jedne natuknice, tada se služimo praznom točkom o, npr. **zdrav** *adj* healthy ~o *adv* healthily o *int* hello.

Unutar natuknice izričaji (fraze) istaknuti su masnim, a primjeri uporabe kosim slovima.

Korisniku engleske strane izgovor je označen novom verzijom međunarodne fonetske abecede (International Phonetic Alphabet) i može se usvojiti iz priloženoga popisa. Korisniku hrvatske strane dane su glasovne vrijednosti hrvatskih slova.

Podatke o hrvatskim i engleskim riječima nadopunjuju popisi. Pored kratkih pregleda engleske i hrvatske gramatike i najvažnijih tvorbenih sufiksa oba jezika korisnik će naći :

Uobičajene svakodnevne kratice u oba jezika,
Nepravilne engleske glagole,
Vjerske blagdane,
Kemijska počela,
Planete,
Vojničke činove,
Mjere,
Zemljopisna imena.

Posebno zahvaljujemo članovima Nightingale Halla i Odsjeka za slavenske studije na Sveučilištu u Nottinghamu koji su stoički izdržali i odgovarali na bezbrojna pitanja urednika o engleskim riječima.

Autori

Abbreviations used in the Dictionary
Kratice u Rječniku

A	*accusative*	akuzativ
abbrev	*abbreviation*	kratica
adj	*adjective*	pridjev
adv	*adverb*	prilog
arch	*archaic*	zastarjelo
attrib	*attributive use*	samo u službi atributa
aux	*auxiliary*	pomoćni
bibl	*biblical*	biblijski pojam
chem	*chemistry*	kemija
coll	*colloquial*	razgovorno
collect	*collective*	zbirna imenica
comm	*commerce*	trgovina
comp	1 *comparative* 2 *computer*	1 komparativ 2 kompjutor
conj	*conjunction*	veznik
D	*dative*	dativ
defect	*defective*	defektivni gl.
derog	*derogatory*	pogrdno
dial	*dialectal*	dijalektalno
dim	*diminutive*	umanjenica
eccl	*ecclesiastical*	crkveni izraz
econ.	*economy/economics*	gospodarstvo
etc.	*and so on*	i tako dalje
euph	*euphemistic*	eufemizam, ublažen izraz
f	*feminine gender*	ženski rod
fig	*figurative*	preneseno značenje
form	*formal*	formalan izraz
G	*genitive*	genitiv
GB	*British word/expression*	britanska riječ/izraz
gram	*grammar*	gramatika
hist	*history*	povijesni izraz/pojam
I	*instrumental*	instrumental
I	*first person*	prvo lice
II	*second person*	drugo lice
III	*third person*	treće lice
imper	*imperative*	imperativ
int	*interjection*	uzvik
Ir	*Irish*	irski
irreg	*irregular*	nepravilni (glagol)
joc	*jocularly*	u šali
L	*locative*	lokativ
legal	*legal term*	pravni izraz
lit	*literary*	knjiški izraz
m	*masculine*	muški rod
math	*mathematics*	matematika
med	*medicine*	medicina
mod	*modifier*	imenica u službi pridjeva
modal	*modal*	modalni glagol
mus	*music*	glazba

n	*noun*	imenica
nf	*noun, feminine*	imenica ženskog roda
nm	*noun, masculine*	imenica muškog roda
num	*cardinal number*	glavni broj
num ord	*ordinal number*	redni broj
pass	*passive*	trpni
pers	*personal*	osobni/osobna
pl	*plural*	množina
poet	*poetic*	pjesnički izraz
poss	*possessive*	posvojni/posvojna
pp	*past participle*	glagolski pridjev prošli
pred	*predicative use*	samo u službi predikata
prefix	*prefix*	prefiks
prep	*preposition*	prijedlog
pres	*present prezent*	sadašnje vrijeme
pron	*pronoun*	zamjenica
prov	*proverb*	poslovica
pt	*preterite, Past Simple*	prošlo vrijeme
reflex	*reflexive*	povratni/povratna
sb	*somebody*	ko, koga, komu
Scot	*Scottish*	škotski
sg	*singular*	jednina
sl	*slang*	slang izraz
sport	*sports*	šport
sth	*something*	što, čega, čemu
suffix	*suffix*	sufiks
sup	*superlative*	superlativ
swh	*somewhere*	(ne)gdje
tab	*taboo*	društveno neprihvatljivo
tech	*technical*	stručni naziv
TM	*trade mark*	zaštitni znak
US	*American word/expression*	amerikanizam
v	*verb*	glagol
vi	*intransitive verb*	neprijelazni glagol
vt	*transitive verb*	prijelazni glagol
vulg	*vulgar*	nepristojno

Special symbols
Posebni znakovi

- *same word as entry, different part of speech*
  ista riječ kao u natuknici, druga vrsta riječi

- *same word as the last subentry, different part of speech*
  ista riječ kao posljednja podnatuknica, druga vrsta riječi

- *α* *"movable" a sound (see Basic Croatian Grammar)*
  nepostojano a (vidi dodatak Osnove hrvatske gramatike)

0 *intransitive verb*
   neprijelazni glagol

1, 2 various meanings of entry
   različita značenja natuknice

a.,b.,c. various meanings of a phrase
   različita značenja izričaja

/ **or**
   ili

¶ *note on usage*
   upozorenje o uporabi

+ **and**
   i

→ *see*
   vidi

Pronunciation key
Transkripcija

Vowels - Samoglasnici

i: *bee* /biː/ dugo i
ɪ   *sit* /sɪt/ kratko i
e   *bet* /bet/ kratko e
æ   *cat* /kæt/ glas između e i a
ɑ: *part* /pɑːt/ dugo a
ɒ   *lot* /lɒt/ kratko o
ɔ: *draw* /drɔː/ dugo o
ʊ   *pull* /pʊl/ kratko u
u: *fool* /fuːl/ dugo u
ʌ   *sun* /sʌn/ kratko a
ə   *afraid* /əˈfreɪd/ glas sličan onome što se čuje uz suglasnike kad ih
   naglasimo: d /də/
ɜ: *learn* /lɜːn/ u hrvatskom se sličan glas čuje kad tko zapinje pri govoru

Diphthongs - Dvoglasi (kombinacije gorenavedenih samoglasnika)

eɪ	*rave* /reɪv/	
əʊ	*home* /həʊm/	
aɪ	*drive* /draɪv/	
aʊ	*house* /haʊs/	
ɔɪ	*boy* /bɔɪ/	
ɪə	*fear* /fɪə(r)/	
eə	*bare* /beə(r)/	
ʊə	*poor* /pʊə(r)/	

Triphthongs - Troglasi

aʊə hour /aʊə/
aɪə fire /faɪə/

Consonants - Suglasnici

ʃ *shine* /ʃaɪn/ slično hrvatskom š
ʒ *measure* /'meʒə(r)/ slično hrvatskom ž
θ *thin* /θɪn/ izgovara se kao glas t, ali s jezikom između zuba
ð *they* /ðeɪ/ izgovara se kao glas d, ali s jezikom između zuba
ŋ *sing* /sɪŋ/ glas g ne izgovori se do kraja
ʃ *chair* /tʃeə(r)/ slično hrvatskom č
dʒ jack /dʒæk/ slično hrvatskom dž

Symbol ' is placed before the stressed syllable
Znak ' nalazi se ispred naglašenoga sloga

Symbol ˌ marks secondary stress
Znak ˌ nalazi se ispred drugonaglašenoga sloga

(r) means r is heard only if the next word begins with a vowel
Glas r čuje se samo ako iduća riječ počinje samoglasnikom

¶ *To save space, only standard British English pronunciation is given.*
  Poradi uštede prostora naveden je samo standardni britanski izgovor.

ENGLISH – CROATIAN DICTIONARY

ENGLESKO – HRVATSKI RJEČNIK

A

A, a /ei/ **1** prvo slovo engl. abecede; a **2** ocjena odličan; pet

a- *prefix* ne-, a-

a /ə, ei/ **an** /ən, æn/ neodređeni član **1** upotrebljava se kad se imenica spominje prvi put, samo s brojivim imenicama u jednini **2** neki ¶ u hrv. se rijetko prevodi

aback /ə'bæk/ *adv* be taken ~ zaprepastiti se

abandon /ə'bændən/ *vt* **1** napustiti, ostaviti **2** odustati od ~ **oneself to** prepustiti se **~ed** *adj* **1** napušten, ostavljen **2** raskalašen • *n* **with ~** divlje

abase /ə'beis/ *vt* ~ **oneself** poniziti se

abashed /ə'bæʃt/ *adj* smeten/posramljen

abate /ə'beit/ *vt, vi* jenjati, popustiti

abattoir /'æbətwɑ:(r)/ *n* klaonica

abbess /'æbes/ *n* nadstojnica samostana, časna majka **abbey** /'æbi/ *n* opatija **abbot** /'æbət/ *n* opat, gvardijan

abbreviate /ə'bri:vieit/ *vt* skratiti **abbreviation** *n* kratica

abdicate /'æbdikeit/ *vi, vt* odreći se, abdicirati

abdomen /'æbdəmən/ *n med* abdomen **abdominal** *adj* trbušni, u trbuhu

abduct /æb'dʌkt/ *vt* ugrabiti **~ion** *n* otmica

aberration /ˌæbə'reiʃn/ *n* **1** odstupanje, skretanje (+ *fig*) **2** pogreška

abet /ə'bet/ *vt leg* podsticati, potpomagati **aid and ~ leg** sudjelovati u zločinu **~tor** *n* sukrivac

abhor /əb'hɔ:(r)/ *vt* mrziti **~rence** *n* mržnja, gađenje

abide /ə'baid/ *vt, vi irreg* **1** ~ **by** *form* pridržavati se, poštovati **law-abiding** *adj* pošten **2** podnijeti **abiding** *adj* trajan

ability /ə'biləti/ *n* **1** sposobnost **2** pamet **3** vještina, talent

abject /'æbdʒekt/ *adj* bijedan; ponizan

ablaze /ə'bleiz/ *adj, adv* u plamenu, sjajan (+ *fig*)

able /'eibl/ *adj* **1** sposoban, u stanju be ~ **to do sth** moći što učiniti → **can**, **could 2** sposoban, spretan, vješt

abnormal /æb'nɔ:ml/ *adj* nenormalan

Abo /'æbəʊ/ *n derog* aboridžin

aboard /ə'bɔ:d/ *adv, prep* **1** na brod/avion/US vlak/US autobus **2** na brodu/u avionu/u vlaku/u autobusu

abode /ə'bəʊd/ *n* **1** *arch* dom, stan **2** *leg* prebivalište **of/with no fixed ~** bez stalnog prebivališta

abode *v irreg* → **abide**

abolish /ə'bɒliʃ/ *vt* ukinuti **abolition** *n* ukidanje, abolicija **abolitionist** *n* protivnik ropstva

abominable /ə'bɒminəbl/ *adj* **1** mrzak, gadan **2** *coll* neugodan, grozan **abomination** *n* **1** gnušanje **2** grozota, gadost

aboriginal /ˌæbə'ridʒənl/ *adj* starosjedilački • *n* starosjedilac **Aborigine** *n* australski starosjedilac, aboridžin

abort /ə'bɔ:t/ *vt, vi* **1** izjaloviti se **2** prekinuti, odustati od **3** pobaciti **~ion** *n* abortus **~ive** *adj* propali, neuspjeli

abound /ə'baʊnd/ *vi* ~ **in/with** obilovati čime

about /ə'baʊt/ *prep, adv* **1** o, oko, unaokolo, posvuda **2** što se tiče, o **How/What ~ ...?** a. Što je s...? b. Kako bi bilo da ...? **up and ~** na nogama

above /ə'bʌv/ *prep, adv* nad (kim, čim), iznad (koga, čega), gore, više od ~ **all** iznad svega **~mentioned** gorenavedeni

abrasive /ə'breisiv/ *adj* **1** abrazivan **2** *fig* grub, oštar • *n* abrazivno sredstvo

abrasion n 1 abrazija 2 ozljeda

abreast /ə'brest/ adv usporedo

abridge /ə'brɪdʒ/ vt skratiti ~**ment**, **abridgment** n skraćena verzija

abroad /ə'brɔːd/ adv 1 u inozemstvu, vani 2 nadaleko, posvuda

abrupt /ə'brʌpt/ adj 1 nagao, iznenadan 2 nesuvisao 3 prijek, nagao 4 strm

absence /'æbsəns/ n 1 odsutnost 2 izbivanje 3 izostanak 4 pomanjkanje, nepostojanje **absent** adj 1 (from) odsutan, nenazočan 2 odsutan duhom **absentee** n odsutna osoba **absenteeism** n često izostajanje **absent-minded** adj rastresen o /'æbsənt/ vt (oneself from) biti odsutan

absolute /'æbsəluːt/ adj apsolutan, potpun ~**ly** adv apsolutno, sasvim, nedvojbeno **absolutism** n apsolutizam

absolve /əb'zɔlv/ vt (from) odriješiti **absolution** n odrješenje

absorb /əb'sɔːb/ vt 1 upiti, apsorbirati 2 zaokupiti ~**ent** adj koji upija o n sredstvo koje upija **absorption** n 1 apsorpcija 2 zaokupljenost, zadubljenost

abstain /əb'steɪn/ vi (from) uzdržati se od, apstinirati ~**er** n apstinent

abstention /əb'stenʃn/ n 1 (from) uzdržavanje (od glasovanja) 2 uzdržani glas

abstinence /'æbstɪnəns/ n (from) apstinencija

abstract /'æbstrækt/ adj apstraktan • vt /əb'strækt/ (from) odijeliti ~**ed** adj odsutan, rastresen ~**ion** n 1 rastresenost 2 apstraktna zamisao

absurd /əb'sɜːd/ adj apsurdan, nerazuman, smiješan ~**ity** n apsurd, glupost

abundance /ə'bʌndəns/ n obilje **abundant** adj 1 obilan 2 ~ **in** koji obiluje čime **abundantly** adv obilato, izdašno, i više nego dovoljno

abuse /ə'bjuːs/ n 1 (of) zloupotreba **drug** ~ narkomanija 2 nepravda 3 psovke, kletve pl • /ə'bjuːz/ vt 1 zlorabiti 2 psovati, ocrnjivati 3 zlostavljati **abusive** adj uvredljiv, pogrdan

abysmal /ə'bɪzməl/ adj 1 bez dna 2 fig, coll najdublji, totalan, krajnji

abyss /ə'bɪs/ n bezdan, ponor (+ fig)

academic /ˌækə'demɪk/ adj 1 akademski 2 teoretski, puka teorija • n sveučilišni nastavnik, znanstvenik **academy** /ə'kædəmɪ/ n akademija /əˌkædə'mɪʃn/ n akademik

accede /æk'siːd/ vi form (to) 1 pristati 2 stupiti na

accelerate /ək'seləreɪt/ vt, vi ubrzati (se) **acceleration** n ubrzanje, akceleracija **accelerator** n 1 gas coll 2 phys akcelerator

accent /'æksənt/ n naglasak, akcent (+ fig) • vt /æk'sent/ izgovoriti s naglaskom, naglasiti (+ fig)

accept /ək'sept/ vt, vi 1 prihvatiti 2 priznati, uzeti u obzir ~**able** adj prihvatljiv, poželjan ~**ance** n 1 prihvaćanje 2 odobravanje

access /'ækses/ n 1 prilaz 2 mod prilazni 3 pristup, uvid ~**ible** adj (to) dostupan, pristupačan • vt comp uči u

accessary (**accessory** US) /ək'sesərɪ/ adj leg sukrivac

accession /æk'seʃn/ n (to) 1 stupanje (na), prelazak (u) 2 povećanje, prirast 3 prinova

accessory /ək'sesərɪ/ n 1 → **accessary** 2 pl pribor; modni detalji

accident /'æksɪdənt/ n 1 slučaj **by** ~ slučajno 2 nesretan slučaj, nesreća, nezgoda ~**al** adj slučajan, neočekivan ~ **death** smrt nesretnim slučajem

acclaim /ə'kleɪm/ vt 1 oduševljeno pozdraviti, klicati 2 aklamacijom proglasiti • n ovacije **acclamation** /ˌæklə'meɪʃn/ n 1 aklamacija 2 pl ovacije

accolade /'ækəleɪd/ n fig pohvala

accommodate /ə'kɒmədeɪt/ vt 1 primiti, pružiti smještaj 2 ~ **sb** (with sth) izaći ususret 3 ~ **sth to** prilagoditi **accommodating** adj uslužan **accommodation** n 1 GB smještaj 2 pl US smještaj, stan i hrana 3 udobnost, pogodnost

accompany /ə'kʌmpənɪ/ vt pratiti, popratiti

accomplice /ə'kʌmplɪs/ n suučesnik, sudrug, sukrivac

accomplish /ə'kʌmpliʃ/ *vt* postići, izvršiti, ispuniti **an ~ed fact** svršeni čin **~ed** *adj* 1 vješt 2 dobro odgojen **~ment** *n* izvršenje, uspjeh, dostignuće

accord /ə'kɔːd/ *n* 1 **of one's own ~** svojom voljom **with one ~** jednoglasno 2 *n* (between, with) sporazum • *vi,vt* 1 (with) složiti se, biti u skladu s 2 *form* dodijeliti **~ance** *n* in **~ance with** u skladu s, po, prema **~ing to** *prep* a. po b. prema, u skladu s **~ingly** *adv* 1 stoga 2 u skladu s tim

accordion /ə'kɔːdɪən/ *n* (**piano ~**) harmonika

account /ə'kaʊnt/ *n* 1 *comm* račun **settle one's ~** platiti; srediti račune (+ *fig*) **balance/square ~s with sb** srediti račune (+ *fig*) 2 korist, probitak **turn/put sth to (good) ~** dobro iskoristiti **work on one's own ~** raditi sam/za svoju korist 3 iskaz, izvještaj, prikaz **by/from all ~s** svi se slažu da... 4 važnost **be of some/small ~** biti (od) određene/male važnosti 5 obzir **take sth into ~/take ~ of sth** uzeti u obzir **take no ~ of sth** prijeći preko čega 6 razlog **on ~ of** zbog **on this ~** stoga **on no/not on any ~** ni u kom slučaju, ni iz kojeg razloga, nipošto **call/bring sb to ~** pozvati na odgovornost, zahtijevati objašnjenje **give a good ~ of oneself** dobro se ponijeti, iskazati se • *vt,vi* 1 **~ for** objasniti, obrazložiti, opravdati 2 **~ for** pobiti, likvidirati, uhvatiti 3 smatrati **~able** *adj* odgovoran

accountancy /ə'kaʊntənsɪ/ *n* računovodstvo **accountant** *n* računovoda

accredit /ə'kredɪt/ *vt* 1 akreditirati 2 pripisati komu što **~ed** *adj* 1 službeno priznat 2 općeprihvaćen 3 zajamčene kvalitete

accrue /ə'kruː/ *vi* izrasti, rasti **~d interest** narasle kamate

accumulate /ə'kjuːmjʊleɪt/ *vt,vi* nagomilati (se), nakupiti (se), skupiti (se), akumulirati (se), zgrnuti **accumulation** *n* nakupina, hrpa, mnoštvo, zbirka **accumulator** /ə'kjuːmjʊleɪtə(r)/ *n* GB akumulator

accurate /'ækjʊrət/ *adj* točan, precizan

accuracy *n* preciznost

accusation /ˌækjuː'zeɪʃn/ *n* optužba **bring an ~ of** optužiti za **be under an ~ of** biti optužen za **accuse** /ə'kjuːz/ *vt* (sb of sth) optužiti koga zbog čega/za što **the accused** *n* optuženik

accustom /ə'kʌstəm/ *vt* ~ (oneself) **to** naviknuti (se) na **become/get/be ~ed to** naviknuti se **~ed** *adj* uobičajen

ace /eɪs/ *n* 1 as (u kartama), jedinica (na kocki) 2 *coll* (pilotski, trkački) as

acerbity /ə'sɜːbətɪ/ *n* gorčina, zagrižljivost

ache /eɪk/ *n* bol **head~** glavobolja • *vi* 1 boljeti *my head ~s* boli me glava *I ~ all over* sve me boli 2 (for) čeznuti

achieve /ə'tʃiːv/ *vt* postići, polučiti **~ment** *n* uspjeh, dostignuće

acid /'æsɪd/ *adj* 1 kiseo 2 *fig* oštar, sarkastičan • *n* 1 kiselina **~ test** *n fig* konačna kušnja 2 *coll* LSD

acknowledge /ək'nɒlɪdʒ/ *vt* 1 priznati 2 potvrditi 3 odati priznanje **~ment**, **acknowledgment** *n* priznanje, potvrda, zahvala

acne /'æknɪ/ *n* akne

acolyte /'ækəlaɪt/ *n* ministrant (+ *fig*)

acorn /'eɪkɔːn/ *n* žir

acoustic /ə'kuːstɪk/ *adj* akustičan • **~s** *n* 1 (+ *sing*) *phys* akustika 2 (+ *pl*) akustika, akustičnost

acquaint /ə'kweɪnt/ *vt* 1 upoznati (se) s 2 **be ~ed** poznavati se **~ance** 1 poznavanje **make sb's ~/make the ~ of sb** upoznati se s 2 poznanik 3 krug poznanstva

acquiesce /ˌækwɪ'es/ *vi* 1 složiti se 2 ~ **in** pristati na, pomiriti se s **~nce** *n* pristanak

acquire /ə'kwaɪə(r)/ *vt* steći **an ~ed taste** stečena sklonost

acquisition /ˌækwɪ'zɪʃn/ *n* 1 prinova 2 *fig* dobitak **acquisitive** *adj* gramzljiv

acquit /ə'kwɪt/ ~ **sb** (of/on sth) osloboditi koga optužbe za što **~tal** *n* oslobađajuća presuda

acre /'eɪkə(r)/ *n* jutro, ral **God's A~** crkveno groblje **~age** *n* površina

acrid /'ækrɪd/ *adj* oštar, jedak (+ *fig*)

acrimonious /ˌækrɪ'məʊnɪəs/ *adj* ljut, ogorčen

acrobat /'ækrəbæt/ *n* akrobat
across /ə'krɒs/ *adv* 1 preko, širom, po širini 2 vodoravno (u križaljci) • *prep* preko, s druge strane **~-the-board** *adj* sveobuhvatni
act /ækt/ *n* 1 čin, djelo **A~ of God** viša sila 2 zakon 3 *theat* čin 4 točka, šou 5 pretvaranje, gluma **put on an ~** *coll* pretvarati se • *vt,vi* 1 djelovati, stupiti u akciju 2 ponašati se, postupati ~ **(up)on** postupiti u skladu s, poslušati 3 funkcionirati 4 vršiti svoju dužnost ~ **as** biti ~ **for/on behalf of** predstavljati 5 glumiti ~ **up** *coll* gnjaviti, zadavati glavobolju **~ing** *adj* vršitelj dužnosti **~ing** partner aktivni **partner** ○ *n* gluma **~ion** *n* 1 djelovanje, djela *pl* **take ~ion** poduzeti korake/mjere **~ions speak louder than words** valja prijeći s riječi na djela 2 mehanizam 3 kretanje, pokreti 4 parnica **bring an ~ion against sb** pokrenuti parnicu protiv koga 5 *mil* borba, akcija **~ion radius** borbeni radijus ~ **stations** vatreni položaji **~ive** *adj* aktivan, živahan, radin, djelatan **~ivate** *vt* aktivirati **~ivist** *n* aktivist **~ivity** /æk'tɪvəti/ *n* aktivnost, aktivni život, djelatnost, bavljenje poslom **~or** *n* 1 glumac 2 protagonist **~ress** *n* glumica
actual /'æktʃʊəl/ *adj* stvaran, pravi, točan **~ly** *adv* 1 u biti, zapravo 2 stvarno, doista
acute /ə'kjuːt/ *adj* 1 oštar, jak 2 akutan
ad /'æd/ *n coll* oglas
adamant /'ædəmənt/ *adj* tvrd, nepopustljiv, odlučan
adapt /ə'dæpt/ *vt,vi* prilagoditi (se), adaptirati **~er, ~or** *n tech* adaptor **~able** *adj* prilagodljiv **~ation** *n* (of sth) (for/to sth) prilagodba, adaptacija
add /æd/ *vt,vi* 1 (to/and) zbrojiti 2 pridodati, dodati, nadovezati se ~ **sth in** uključiti ~ **to** povećati ~ **sth up** zbrojiti ~ **up** (to) a. iznositi b. *coll* značiti, svoditi se na c. imati smisla **~ition** /ə'dɪʃn/ *n* 1 zbrajanje **in ~ition to** uz to, osim 2 prinova, novi član **~itional** *adj* dodatni, dopunski, daljnji **~itive** /'ædɪtɪv/ *n* aditiv, dodatak

adder /'ædə(r)/ *n* guja
addict /ə'dɪkt/ *n* ovisnik • *vt* **be ~ed to** biti ovisan o **~ive** /ə'dɪktɪv/ *adj* koji stvara ovisnost
addle /'ædl/ *vt* pomutiti **~d egg** mućak • *adj* zbrkan, pomućen **~-brained** *adj* pošemerio
address /ə'dres/ *n* 1 adresa, naslov 2 govor **public ~ system** razglas 3 obraćanje **~ee** /ˌædre'siː/ *n* naslovnik • *vt* 1 održati govor 2 osloviti 3 nasloviti ~ **sth to** uputiti **~oneself to** *form* posvetiti se
adept /'ædept/ *adj* vješt • *n* stručnjak
adequate /'ædɪkwət/ *adj* primjeren, adekvatan, odgovarajući
adhere /əd'hɪə(r)/ *vi* (to) 1 prianjati 2 držati se **~nt** *n* pristaša **adhesion** /əd'hiːʒn/ *n* 1 prianjanje 2 podrška **adhesive** *adj* ljepljiv ○ *n* ljepilo
adjacent /ə'dʒeɪsnt/ *adj* susjedni, priležni
adjective /'ædʒɪktɪv/ *n gram* pridjev
adjoin /ə'dʒɔɪn/ *vt,vi* (to) biti uz **~ing** *adj* susjedni
adjourn /ə'dʒɜːn/ *vt,vi* 1 odgoditi 2 prekinuti suđenje **~ment** *n* prekid, odgoda
adjust /ə'dʒʌst/ *vt* (to) prilagoditi, namjestiti, regulirati **well-~ed** *adj* prilagođen **~ment** *n* 1 prilagođavanje, regulacija 2 kontrole *pl*
ad lib /ˌæd 'lɪb/ *adv coll* slobodno • *vi coll* improvizirati • *adj* improviziran
administer *vt,vi* 1 upravljati 2 primjenjivati 3 dati, dijeliti 4 nanijeti **administration** /ədˌmɪnɪ'streɪʃn/ *n* 1 uprava, administracija 3 primjena, dodjela **administrative** /əd'mɪnɪstrətɪv/ *adj* administrativan, upravni **administrator** /əd'mɪnɪstreɪtə(r)/ *n* 1 administrator 2 dobar organizator 3 *leg* izvršitelj oporuke
admiral /'ædmərəl/ *n* admiral **~ty** *n* 1 čin admirala 2 admiralitet
admire /əd'maɪə(r)/ *vt* 1 diviti se **~r** *n* obožavatelj **admiring** *adj* pun divljenja **admirable** /'ædmərəbl/ *adj* divan, zadivljujući **admiration** /ˌædmə'reɪʃn/ *n* divljenje
admission /əd'mɪʃn/ *n* 1 upis, pristup, primanje u članstvo, ulaz 2 priznanje

admit /əd'mɪt/ *vt,vi* **1** pustiti unutra, propustiti, uvesti, upisati, primiti **2** imati mjesta za **3** (to) priznati što **~tedly** *adv* **1** po općem mišljenju **2** moram/moraš/mora se itd. priznati **~tance** *n* pristup, ulaz **no ~tance** ulaz zabranjen

admonish /əd'mɒnɪʃ/ *vt form* upozoriti, opomenuti

ado /ə'du:/ *n arch* buka, okapanje

adobe /ə'dəʊbɪ/ *n* ćerpič

adolescence /,ædə'lesns/ *n* mladost

adopt /ə'dɒpt/ *vt* **1** posvojiti **2** usvojiti, prihvatiti **~ion** *n* usvajanje **~ive** *adj* adoptivan, koji je posvojio

adore /ə'dɔ:(r)/ *vt* štovati, obožavati **adorable** *adj* divan **adoration** *n* obožavanje, štovanje **adoring** *adj* pun obožavanja

adorn /ə'dɔ:n/ *vt* ukrasiti (se), krasiti

adroit /ə'drɔɪt/ *adj* (at/in) spretan, vješt

adult /'ædʌlt/ *adj* **1** odrastao, zreo **2** *coll* pornografski • *n* odrasla osoba **~hood** *n* odraslo doba, zrelo doba

adulterate /ə'dʌltəreɪt/ *vt* patvoriti

adultery /ə'dʌltərɪ/ *n* preljub **adulterer** *n* preljubnik **adulteress** preljubnica **adulterous** *adj* preljubnički, grešan

advance /əd'vɑns/ *n* **1** napredak, napredovanje **in ~** (of) unaprijed, ispred, prije **2** predujam **~ booking** rezervacija • *vi,vt* **1** napredovati **2** rasti **3** pomaknuti unaprijed, odgoditi **4** promaknuti **5** podići **6** isplatiti predujam/akontaciju **~d** *adj* **1** uznapredovao **2** napredan **~ level (A level)** *GB* ocjena koja omogućava upis na fakultet **~ment** *n* promicanje, unapređivanje

advantage /əd'vɑntɪdʒ/ *n* **1** prednost **2** korist **take ~ of sb** prevariti, zloupotrijebiti **to ~** u najboljem svjetlu, na najbolji način, u (čiju) korist **3** prednost (tenis) **~ous** /,ædvən-'teɪdʒəs/ *adj* probitačan, povoljan

advent /'ædvənt/ *n* **1** pojava **2** A**~** Došašće, Advent **3** Kristov dolazak

adventure /əd'ventʃə(r)/ *n* pustolovina, avantura **~r** *n* avanturist, pustolov **~ss** *n* pustolovka **adventurous** *adj* pustolovan

adverb /'ædvɜ:b/ *n gram* prilog

adversary /'ædvəsərɪ/ *n* protivnik, neprijatelj

adverse /'ædvɜ:s/ *adj* nepovoljan, loš, protivan, neprijateljski raspoložen

adversity /əd'vɜ:sətɪ/ *n* nevolja, nedaća, nesreća

advertise /'ædvətaɪz/ *vt,vi* oglasiti **advertising** *n* propaganda **~ment** /əd'vɜ:tɪsmənt/ *n* **1** reklama **2** *mod* reklamni **3** oglas, reklama

advice /əd'vaɪs/ *n* savjet **a piece of ~** (jedan) savjet **take legal ~** zatražiti pravno mišljenje

advise /əd'vaɪz/ *vt,vi* **1** savjetovati, preporučiti **~ against** opomenuti **2** izvijestiti **advisable** *adj* mudar, preporučljiv **~r** *n* savjetnik **ill-~d** *adj* nerazborit **~ly** *adv* promišljeno **advisory** *adj* savjetodavni

advocate /'ædvəkət/ *n* zagovornik • /'ædvəkeɪt/ *vt* zalagati se za **advocacy** /'ædvəkəsɪ/ *n* (of) zagovaranje, obrana

(a)egis /'i:dʒɪs/ *n* zaštita, pokroviteljstvo

aerial /'eərɪəl/ *adj* zračni, iz zraka • *n* antena

aeroplane /'eərəpleɪn/ *n* zrakoplov

aerospace /'eərəʊspeɪs/ zračni prostor (uključuje i svemir) **the ~ industry** avioindustrija i svemirska istraživanja

(a)esthete /'i:sθi:t/ *n* estet **(a)esthetic** *adj* estetski ○ *n* estetika

affable /'æfəbl/ *adj* prijazan **affability** /,æfə'bɪlətɪ/ *n* (to/towards) prijaznost

affair /ə'feə(r)/ *n* **1** stvar, briga **2** *pl* poslovi, stvari **Secretary of State for Foreign/Home A~s** ministar vanjskih/unutarnjih poslova **3** (ljubavna) veza

affect (1) /ə'fekt/ *vt* **1** (nepovoljno) utjecati na **2** pogoditi, ticati se **3** djelovati na, dirnuti **4** zahvatiti **~ing** *adj* dirljiv

affect (2) *vt* **1** hiniti, izigravati **2** biti sklon, voljeti **~ed** *adj* afektiran, usiljen **~ation** *n* **1** afektacija **2** hinjenje

affection /ə'fekʃn/ *n* naklonost, ljubav **~ate** *adj* (to) pun ljubavi, nježan (prema)

affiliate /ə'filieit/ *vt,vi* (to, with) pridružiti (se), udružiti (se), biti članom **~d company** podružnica **affiliation** *n* pripojenje, udruženje, udruga **affiliation order** *GB leg* utvrđivanje očinstva

affinity *n* /ə'finəti/ 1 (between, to) bliskost, srodstvo, veza, povezanost 2 (for) afinitet; naklonost prema

affirm /ə'fɜ:m/ *vt,vi* ustvrditi, potvrditi **~ation** *n* potvrda, tvrdnja **~ative** *adj* potvrdan o *n* potvrdan odgovor

affix /ə'fiks/ *vt* (to) *form* staviti, udariti (pečat), nalijepiti (marku)

afflict /ə'flikt/ *vt* mučiti **~ion** *n* 1 nesreća, nevolja 2 jadi *pl*

affluence /'æfluəns/ *n* bogatstvo **affluent** *adj* bogat

afford /ə'fɔ:d/ *vt* 1 priuštiti sebi 2 *form* pružiti

aflame /ə'fleim/ *adj poet* u plamenu, goreći (+ *fig*)

afloat /ə'fləut/ *adj* 1 na moru, na brodu 2 pod vodom 3 solventan **get sth ~** pokrenuti

afoot /ə'fut/ *adj* koji je u pripremi, koji se sprema

afraid /ə'freid/ *adj* prestrašen **be ~ (of)** bojati se *I'm ~ I don't know* nažalost, ne znam

afresh /ə'freʃ/ *adv* iznova

after /'ɑ:ftə(r)/ *adv* kasnije • *conj* nakon (što) • *prep* 1 poslije (čega) **the day ~ tomorrow** prekosutra 2 iza (čega), nakon (čega) 3 u stilu 4 za **be ~ sb** biti kome za petama **accident ~ accident** nesreća za nesrećom **~ all** usprkos svemu, na kraju (krajeva), ipak • **after-** *prefix* koji ostaje nakon, koji je posljedica **~birth** /'ɑ:ftə:θ/ posteljica **~effect** /'ɑ:ftəri'fekt/ *n* posljedica **~life** /'ɑ:ftəlaif/ *n* (**the ~**) život poslije smrti **~math** /'ɑ:ftə(r)mæθ/ *n* 1 otava 2 *fig* posljedice *pl* **~taste** /'ɑ:ftəteist/ *n* okus u ustima **~thought** /'ɑ:ftəθɔ:t/ *n* naknadna misao **~noon** /'ɑ:ftə'nu:n/ *n* 1 poslijepodne **in/during the ~noon** poslije podne **on Sunday ~noon** u nedjelju p.p. 2 *mod* poslijepodnevni **~s** /'ɑ:ftəz/ *n pl coll* desert **~wards** /'ɑ:ftəwədz/ *adv* kasnije,

poslije

again /ə'gen/ *adv* 1 ponovno, još jednom, iznova 2 opet 3 (+ *neg*) (nikad) više 4 još (jednom) (toliko) **now and ~** ponekad **~ and ~/ time and (time) ~** stalno **then ~** no s druge strane

against /ə'genst/ *prep* 1 protiv 2 po, u 3 na pozadini od 4 za 5 uz

age /eidʒ/ *n* 1 starost, životna dob *what's his ~* ? koliko mu je godina? *at the ~ of 5* sa 5 godina *when I was your ~* u tvojim godinama **~-group** dobna skupina **old ~** starost **be/come of ~** biti/postati punoljetan **under ~** maloljetan 2 doba, vijek 3 *coll* (cijela) vječnost • *vt,vi* 1 stariti, postarati (se) **~d** *adj* 1 u dobi od 2 star **aging, ~ing** *n* starenje o *adj* postariji **~less** *adj* vječan **~-long, ~-old** *adj* stoljetni

agency /'eidʒənsi/ 1 agencija, predstavništvo 2 djelovanje

agent o *n* 1 agent 2 posrednik 3 sredstvo

agenda /ə'dʒendə/ *n* dnevni red

aggravate /'ægraveit/ *vt,vi* 1 pogoršati (se) 2 *coll* nervirati, ići na živce **aggravation** *n* 1 pogoršanje 2 ljutnja 3 gnjavaža

aggregate /'ægrigət/ *n* 1 skup, cjelina **in the ~** u cjelini 2 pijesak, šljunak

aggression /ə'greʃn/ *n* (on/upon) agresija, napad na/protiv **aggressive** *adj* 1 agresivan 2 ofenzivan

aggro /'ægrəu/ *n GB sl* agresivno ponašanje

aghast /ə'gɑ:st/ *adj* zaprepašten

agile /'ædʒail/ *adj* hitar, okretan **agility** *n* hitrina; spretnost

agitate /'ædʒiteit/ *vt,vi* 1 uznemiriti, uzbuditi 2 **~ for** agitirati za **~d** *adj* uznemiren, uzbuđen **agitation** *n* 1 uzbuđenje, strepnja 2 raspra 3 gibanje, previranje

aglow /ə'gləu/ *adj* (with) rumen, zažaren

agnostic /æg'nɒstik/ *n* agnostik

ago /ə'gəu/ *adv* prije **a year ~** prije godinu dana

agog /ə'gɒg/ *adj* u napetom očekivanju, uzbiban

agony /'ægəni/ *n* agonija, patnja **~ col-**

umn rubrika povjerljivo **agonized** *adj* bolan, pun patnje **agonizing** *adj* izluđujući, mučan

agree /ə'gri:/ *vi,vt* **1** (to) složiti se s čim, pristati na što **2** složiti se, dogovoriti se **3** (with) poklapati se sa **4** odobriti ~ **with** prijati, odgovarati *the food didn't ~ with me* bilo mi je loše od hrane ~**able** *adj* **1** ugodan **2** (to) sporazuman s ~**ment** *n* **1** suglasnost **2** sporazum **come to/arrive at/make/reach an** ~**ment** postići sporazum

agriculture /'ægrɪkʌltʃə(r)/ *n* poljoprivreda **agricultural** *adj* poljoprivredni

ahead /ə'hed/ *adj, adv* (of) ispred, naprijed

aid /eɪd/ *vt* pomagati • *n* **1** pomoć **2** pomagalo **hearing-**~ *n* slušni aparat

AIDS /eɪdz/ *n* stečeni sindrom gubitka imuniteta; sida *coll*

ail /eɪl/ *vt,vi* **1** mučiti **2** pobolijevati ~**ing** *adj* boležljiv ~**ment** *n* bolest

aim /eɪm/ *vt,vi* (at) **1** ciljati na; uperiti **2** smjerati, planirati • *n* **take** ~ naciljati cilj, svrha ~**less** *adj* besciljan

air /eə(r)/ *n* **1** zrak by ~ zrakoplovom **2** *mod* zračni **3** vjetrić **4** melodija, arija **5** držanje, izgled **6** *pl* afektirano ponašanje **give oneself/put on** ~**s** praviti se važan ~**s and graces** afektiranje **7** *radio* eter **on the** ~ u eteru **come/go on the** ~ početi emitirati ~**bed** *n* zračni jastuk ~**borne** *adj* a. zrakoplovni b. u zraku c. *mil* zračnodesantni ~**conditioning** *n* klimauređaj ~**craft** *n* (*pl* ~) zrakoplov ~ **drop** *n* doprema (ljudstva, tehnike) padobranima ~**field** *n* (vojni) aerodrom **(an/the)** ~ **force** *n* (+ *sing/pl*) ratno zrakoplovstvo ~ **hostess** *n* stjuardesa ~**lift** *n* zračni most ~**line** *n* **a.** zračna linija **b.** aviokompanija ~**liner** *n* putnički zrakoplov ~**mail** *n* zračna pošta ~**man** *n* avijatičar, pilot ~**plane** *n* *US* zrakoplov, avion ~**port** *n* zračna luka, aerodrom ~**raid** *n* zračni napad ~**raid warning** zračna uzbuna ~ **space** *n* zračni prostor ~**strip** *n* pista ~**tight** *adj* hermetički zatvoren ~**way** *n* **a.** zračni

koridor **b.** *pl* zrakoplovna tvrtka ~**to**~ **missile** raketa zrak-zrak • *vt* **1** prozračiti **2** otvoreno pokazivati/iskazivati ~**ing** *n* izlaganje ~**y** *adj* **1** zračan **2** prozračan, eteričan **3** površan, bez osnove

aisle /aɪl/ *n* **1** crkvena lađa **2** *US* prolaz među sjedalima **3** *mod* kod prolaza

ajar /ə'dʒa:(r)/ *adj* pritvoren, odškrinut

akimbo /ə'kɪmbəʊ/ *adv* podbočen

akin /ə'kɪn/ *adj* (to) srodan

alacrity /ə'lækrətɪ/ *n* spremnost **with** ~ objeručke, spremno

alarm /ə'la:m/ *n* **1** uzbuna, znak za uzbunu, sirena za uzbunjivanje **give/raise/sound the** ~ podići uzbunu, dati znak za uzbunu ~**(clock)** budilica **2** panika, uzrujanost • *vt* uzbuniti, prestrašiti ~**ing** *adj* alarmantan

alas /ə'læs/ *int* jao!

albeit /,ɔ:l'bi:ɪt/ *conj form* iako

album /'ælbəm/ *n* album

alchemy /'ælkɪmɪ/ *n* alkemija **alchemist** *n* alkemičar

alcohol /'ælkəhɒl/ *n* alkohol ~**ic** *adj* alkoholni ○ alkoholičar

ale /eɪl/ *n* (tamno) pivo

alert /ə'lɜ:t/ *adj* **1** budan, oprezan **2** živahan, spreman • *n* **1** oprez **on the** ~ **for/against** na oprezu **2** uzbuna **3** stanje pripravnosti • *vt* uzbuniti, biti u stanju pripravnosti

alga /'ælgə/ *n* (*pl* ~e) alga

alias /'eɪlɪəs/ *n* drugo/lažno ime • *adv* alijas

alibi /'ælɪbaɪ/ *n* alibi

alien /'eɪlɪən/ *n* **1** *leg* stranac, strani državljanin **2** svemirac • *adj* (to) tuđ, stran ~**ate** /'eɪlɪəneɪt/ *vt* (from) **1** odvratiti **2** otuđiti se **3** preuzeti, prenijeti, otuđiti (vlasništvo)

alight (1) /ə'laɪt/ *adj* u plamenu, upaljen, koji gori (+ *fig*)

alight (2) *vi* sići, sjahati, sletjeti ~ **on** *form* naletjeti na

align /ə'laɪn/ *vt,vi* **1** svrstati **2** poravnati (po) **3** (with) priključiti se kome ~**ment** *n* **1** vrsta, poravnanje **2** poredak

alike /ə'laɪk/ *adj* sličan, nalik • *adv* **1** na isti način **2** kako .... tako, i i

alimentary /ˌælɪ'mentərɪ/ adj 1 prehrambeni 2 probavni

alimony /'ælɪmənɪ/ n alimentacija

alive /ə'laɪv/ adj 1 živ, živući 2 živahan ~ **to** svjestan čega ~ **with** pun

alkali /'ælkəlaɪ/ n baza, lužina **~ne** adj lužnat

all /ɔːl/ adj sav, svaki, sve, svi, cijeli • adv 1 potpuno, sasvim ~ **alone** sam samcat ~ **along a.** duž **b.** coll od samog početka ~ **for** coll bezrezervno za ~ **the same** pa ipak **it is** ~ **the same/one to me** svejedno mi je ~ **in a.** coll iscrpljen **b.** sveobuhvatan **~-out** coll totalan, bespoštedan ~ **over a.** posvuda, po cijelom **b.** gotovo ~ **right, alright** US u redu, dobro **he is not ~ there** coll nisu mu sve na broju coll ~ **told** sve u svemu • n sve • pron sve ~ **of us** svi mi **we** ~ svi mi **Not at** ~ Nema na čemu **at** ~ uopće **not at** ~ uopće ne **for** ~ **I care** što se mene tiče **for ~ I know** koliko ja znam **once (and) for** ~ jednom zauvijek

all- prefix piše se s crticom sve- **~-powerful** svemoćan **~-embracing** sveobuhvatan, **~-metal** sav od metala **~-round** svestran **~-time high/low** n coll najviši/najniži (broj, rezultat i sl.) svih vremena

allay /ə'leɪ/ vt ublažiti

allege /ə'ledʒ/ vt ustvrditi, navesti **~d** adj navodni **~dly** adv navodno **allegation** /ˌælɪ'geɪʃn/ n (nedokazana) tvrdnja, navod

allegiance /ə'liːdʒəns/ n lojalnost, vjernost

allegory /'ælɪgərɪ/ n alegorija

allergy /'ælədʒɪ/ n alergija **allergic** /ə'lɜːdʒɪk/ adj (to) alergičan na (+ fig)

alleviate /ə'liːvɪeɪt/ vt ublažiti

alley /'ælɪ/ n 1 (~way) prolaz, uličica **~-cat a.** mačka olučarka **b.** fig uličar **blind** ~ slijepa ulica (+ fig) 2 kuglačka staza

alliance /ə'laɪəns/ n 1 povezanost **in** ~ **with** zajedno sa, u suradnji sa 2 savez, udruženje

alligator /'ælɪgeɪtə(r)/ n aligator ~ **pear** avokado

allocate /'æləkeɪt/ (to/for) raspodijeliti, dodijeliti, namijeniti **allocation** n raspodjela

allot /ə'lɒt/ vt (to) dodijeliti, podijeliti, odrediti **~ment** n 1 raspodjela 2 dio

allow /ə'laʊ/ vt,vi 1 dopustiti **not ~** zabraniti **not be ~ed** ne smjeti 2 dati 3 odobriti 4 priznati ~ **for** uzeti u obzir ~ **of** ostaviti mjesta **~ance** n 1 džeparac, doplatak, naknada 2 popust **make ~ance(s) for** uzeti u obzir/kao olakšavajuću okolnost

alloy /'ælɔɪ/ n 1 slitina, legura 2 mod s primjesama • vt 1 legirati 2 fig pokvariti, onečistiti

allude /ə'luːd/ vi ~ **to** aludirati na, spomenuti **allusion** n (to) aluzija, spominjanje

allure /ə'lʊə(r)/ vt dovoditi u napast, mamiti • n zamamnost **alluring** adj privlačan, zamaman

ally /ə'laɪ/ vt 1 ~ (oneself) **with/to** udružiti se, povezati se, sklopiti savezništvo 2 **be allied with** biti povezan/srodan s • n saveznik

almighty /ɔːl'maɪtɪ/ adj svemoćan • n **the A~** Bog

almond /'ɑːmənd/ n badem **~-shaped** adj bademast

almost /'ɔːlməʊst/ adv skoro, gotovo

aloft /ə'lɒft/ adv visoko

alone /ə'ləʊn/ adj sam, usamljen, na osami • adv samo, jedino **let** ~ kamoli **let/leave sb/sth** ~ ostaviti na miru

along /ə'lɒŋ/ prep duž, uz, niz **~side** adv, prep uz, pokraj, kraj

aloof /ə'luːf/ adv po strani **stand/keep/hold** (oneself) ~ (from) držati se rezervirano • adj rezerviran, nepristupačan

aloud /ə'laʊd/ adv 1 naglas 2 glasno, na sav glas

alphabet /'ælfəbet/ n abeceda **~ical** /ˌælfə'betɪkl/ adj abecedni

alpine /'ælpaɪn/ adj alpski, planinski

already /ɔːl'redɪ/ adv već

alright → **all right**

Alsatian /æl'seɪʃn/ n njemački ovčar

also /'ɔːlsəʊ/ adv također, i **~-ran** n fig neuspješni sudionik (u natjecanju), bezveznjaković

altar /'ɔ:ltə(r)/ n oltar, žrtvenik

alter /'ɔ:ltə(r)/ vt,vi 1 preinačiti, izmijeniti (se) 2 prepraviti ~ation n izmjena, preinaka ~nate /ɔ:l'tɜ:nət/ adj naizmjeničan, čas....čas...., s 2 sve u svemu gi /'ɔ:ltəneɪt/ vt,vi biti čas.... čas...., izmjenjivati (se) ~ between kolebati se, biti naizmjence ~ with izmjenjivati se ~nating current n izmjenična struja ~native /ɔ:l'tɜ:nətɪv/ adj alternativni ○ n alternativa ~natively adv u suprotnom, ili

although /ɔ:l'ðəʊ/ conj iako, premda

altitude /'æltɪtju:d/ n (nadmorska) visina

alto /'æltəʊ/ n alt

altogether /,ɔ:ltə'geðə(r)/ adv 1 u cijelosti, sasvim 2 sve u svemu

aluminium /,æljʊ'mɪnɪəm/ (aluminum /ə'lu:mɪnəm/ US) n aluminij

alumna /ə'lʌmnə/ n bivša učenica/studentica alumnus /ə'lʌmnəs/ n bivši učenik/student

always /'ɔ:lweɪz/ adv uvijek, stalno

am /əm/ → be

amalgam /ə'mælgəm/ n amalgam ~ate vt,vi spojiti, združiti, amalgamirati (se)

amass /ə'mæs/ vt nagomilati, zgrnuti

amateur /'æmətə(r)/ n 1 amater, diletant ¶ obratno od amateur je professional 2 ljubitelj 3 mod amaterski ~ish adj amaterski, neznalački

amatory /'æmətərɪ/ adj form, joc ljubavni, ljubavnički

amaze /ə'meɪz/ vt zaprepastiti, začuditi amazing adj zapanjujući, izvanredan; fantastičan coll ~ment n iznenađenje, šok

ambassador /æm'bæsədə(r)/ n 1 (to) veleposlanik/ambasador u 2 posebni izaslanik 3 službeni predstavnik

amber /'æmbə(r)/ n 1 jantar 2 mod od jantara 3 mod žut

ambience /'æmbɪəns/ n ambijent, ozračje

ambiguity /,æmbɪ'gju:ətɪ/ n dvosmislenost ambiguous /æm'bɪgjʊəs/ adj dvosmislen

ambition /æm'bɪʃn/ n 1 ambicioznost, častohleplje 2 ambicija ambitious adj ambiciozan

ambivalent /æm'bɪvələnt/ adj ambivalentan ambivalence n ambivalentnost

amble /'æmbl/ vi lagano šetati, šetkati se • n polagani hod

ambulance /'æmbjʊləns/ n kola hitne pomoći

ambush /'æmbʊʃ/ n zasjeda • vt napasti iz zasjede

amen /ɑ:'men/ int amen

amenable /ə'mi:nəbl/ adj (to) 1 povodljiv, popustljiv 2 leg odgovoran pred 3 koji se može riješiti, za koji vrijedi

amend /æ'mend/ vt,vi 1 poboljšati, ispraviti, popraviti 2 izmijeniti ~ment n 1 poboljšanje 2 amandman ~s n pl naknada make ~ (to sb) (for sth) nadoknaditi (komu što)

amenity /ə'mi:nətɪ/ n 1 pl prednosti, pogodnosti, blagodati 2 kurtoazija 3 sing ugodnost

amiable /'eɪmɪəbl/ adj prijazan, ljubazan, mio

amid(st) /ə'mɪd(st)/ prep među, posred

amiss /ə'mɪs/ adj pogrešan • adv loše, po zlu

amity /'æmətɪ/ n prijateljstvo

ammonia /ə'məʊnɪə/ n amonijak

ammunition /,æmjʊ'nɪʃn/ n municija, streljivo

amnesia /æm'ni:zɪə/ n amnezija

amnesty /'æmnəstɪ/ n amnestija

amoeba /ə'mi:bə/ n ameba

amok, amuck /ə'mɒk/ adv run ~ pomahnitati

among /ə'mʌŋ/, amongst /ə'mʌŋst/ prep među, između

amorous /'æmərəs/ n zaljubljen, pun ljubavnog žara

amount /ə'maʊnt/ vi ~ to 1 iznositi, dostići vrijednost/iznos od, vrijediti 2 svoditi se, biti isto što • n 1 iznos, svota 2 količina

amp /æmp/ n coll pojačalo

amphibian /æm'fɪbɪən/ n 1 vodozemac 2 amfibijsko vozilo amphibious adj amfibijski

ample /'æmpl/ adj 1 prostran 2 bogat, obilan 3 dovoljan

amplify /'æmplɪfaɪ/ vt 1 proširiti 2 pojačati, povećati amplifier n pojačalo

amputate /'æmpjuteɪt/ *vt* amputirati **amputee** *n* osoba s amputiranim udom

amuse /ə'mju:z/ *vt* (at) zabaviti (se) čime/na račun koga **amusing** *adj* zabavan **~ment** *n* zabava, razonoda **~ment arcade** igračnica **~ment park/grounds** lunapark

an → **a, an**

anachronism /ə'nækrənɪzəm/ *n* anakronizam **anachronistic** /ə,nækrə'nɪstɪk/ *adj* anakronistčan

anaemia /ə'ni:mɪə/ (**anemia** US) *n med* anemija, slabokrvnost **anaemic** *adj* slabokrvan: anemičan (+ *fig*)

anaesthesia (**anesthesia** US) /,ænɪs'θi:zɪə/ *n* anestezija **anaesthetic** /,ænɪs'θetɪk/ *n* anestetik **anaesthetize** /ə'ni:sθətaɪz/ *vt* dati anesteziju

anal /'eɪnl/ *adj* analni

analgesic /,ænæl'dʒi:sɪk/ *n* analgetik

analogous /ə'næləgəs/ *adj* (with) analogan komu/čemu **analogue** (**analog**) *n* surogat **~ computer** *n* analogni kompjuter **analogy** *n* analogija **draw an ~ between** povući paralelu **by/from ~; on the ~ of** analogijom, po analogiji

analyse (**analyze** US) /'ænəlaɪz/ *vt* analizirati, raščlaniti **analysis** /ə'næləsɪs/ *n* analiza **analytic(al)-**/,ænə'lɪtɪkl/ *adj* analitički **analyst** /'ænəlɪst/ *n* analitičar

anarchy /'ænəkɪ/ *n* anarhija

anatomy /ə'nætəmɪ/ *n* anatomija **anatomical** *adj* anatomski

ancestor /'ænsestə(r)/ *n* predak **ancestry** *n* preci, podrijetlo **ancestral** /æn'sestrəl/ *adj* djedovski

anchor /'æŋkə(r)/ *n* sidro **let go/drop/cast the ~** baciti sidro **weigh ~** dići sidro **lie/ride/be at ~** biti čvrsto usidren **~man** *n TV, radio* koordinator ekipe • *vt* usidriti (se) **~age** *n* sidrište

anchovy /'æntʃəvɪ/ *n* inčun

ancient /'eɪnʃənt/ *adj* 1 drevni, stari 2 prastar

ancillary /æn'sɪlərɪ/ *adj* 1 (to) pomoćni 2 sporedan

and /ən, ənd/ *conj* i

anecdote /'ænɪkdəʊt/ *n* anegdota

anew /ə'nju:/ *adv* iznova

angel /'eɪndʒl/ *n* anđeo (+ *fig*) **~ic** /æn'dʒlɪk/ *adj* anđeoski **A~us** /'ændʒɪləs/ *n* Pozdravljenje

anger /'æŋgə(r)/ *n* (at sth) ljutnja, srdžba • *vt* razljutiti **angry** /'æŋgrɪ/ *adj* 1 (with sb/at sth/about sth) ljutit, bijesan (na koga, zbog čega) 2 upaljen 3 olujan

angle (1) /'æŋgl/ *n* 1 kut **~-park** *vt,vi* parkirati (se) ukoso 2 *fig* kut gledanja, gledište • *vt* prikazati iz (određenog) kuta

angle (2) *vi* pecati **~ for** *fig* loviti, mamiti **~r** *n* ribič **angling** *n* pecanje

Anglican /'æŋglɪkən/ *n* Anglikanac • *adj* anglikanski

anglicize /'æŋglɪsaɪz/ *vt* poengleziti

Anglo- *prefix* englesko- **~Indian** *n, adj* 1 Britanac koji živi u Indiji 2 osoba miješane britanske i indijske krvi **~Saxon** *n, adj* 1 Anglosas, anglosaski 2 (osoba) s engleskog govornog područja, britanski i američki

angst /æŋst/ *n* tjeskoba

anguish /'æŋgwɪʃ/ *n* strepnja, tjeskoba, muka **~ed** *adj* tjeskoban, napaćen

angular /'æŋgjulə(r)/ *adj* 1 kutni 2 uglat 3 krut, ukočen

animal /'ænɪml/ *n* 1 životinja 2 *mod* tjelesni

animate /'ænɪmət/ *adj* živ, živahan • *vt* /'ænɪmeɪt/ (to/with sth) oživjeti, udahnuti život, potaknuti **~d cartoon** *n* crtani film **animation** /,ænɪ'meɪʃn/ *n* živahnost, živost, interes

animosity /,ænɪ'mɒsɪtɪ/ *n* (against/towards/between) netrpeljivost (prema/među)

ankle /'æŋkl/ *n* gležanj

annals /'ænlz/ *n pl* 1 ljetopis *sing* 2 anali **annalist** *n* ljetopisac

annex /ə'neks/ *vt* 1 anektirati 2 (to) dodati, pridružiti **~ation** *n* aneksija • (**annexe**) *n* (to) 1 depandansa 2 aneks

annihilate /ə'naɪəleɪt/ *vt* (totalno) uništiti

anniversary /,ænɪ'vɜ:sərɪ/ *n* godišnjica, proslava godišnjice

annotate /'ænəteɪt/ *vt* popratiti bilješkama, komentirati **annotation** *n* bilješka, komentar

announce /ə'naʊns/ *vt* **1** objaviti, priopćiti, izjaviti **2** najaviti ~**ment** *n* objava, priopćenje ~**r** *n* najavljivač; spiker *coll*

annoy /ə'nɔɪ/ *vt* **1** ići na živce, iritirati **2 be** ~**ed** (with sb/at sth/about sth) razljutiti se na koga/zbog čega ~**ing** *adj* koji smeta/nervira/ide na živce ~**ance** *n* **1** ljutnja **2** gnjavaža

annual /'ænjʊəl/ *adj* **1** godišnji **2** jednogodišnji • *n* **1** jednogodišnja biljka **2** godišnjak

annuity /ə'nju:əti/ *n* anuitet, renta

annul /ə'nʌl/ *vt* poništiti

annunciation /ə,nʌnsi'eiʃn/ *n* objava **the A~** Navještenje Gospodinovo

anodyne /'ænədain/ *n* lijek *fig* • *adj* mlitav, isprazan

anoint /ə'nɔint/ *vt* pomazati

anomalous /ə'nɒmələs/ *adj* nepravilan **anomaly** *n* anomalija

anonymity /,ænə'nɪmətɪ/ *n* anonimnost **anonymous** /ə'nɒnɪməs/ *adj* anoniman

anorak /'ænəræk/ *n* skijaška jakna

another /ə'nʌðə(r)/ *pron, adj* još jedan, (neki) drugi

answer /'ɑ:nsə(r)/ *n* (to) **1** odgovor **2** rješenje • *vt,vi* **1** odgovoriti ~ **a question** odgovoriti na pitanje ~ **the door/the bell** otvoriti vrata ~ **the telephone** javiti se ~ (sb) **back** odgovarati **2** odgovarati ~**able** *adj* **1** koji ima odgovor **2** (to sb) odgovoran komu

ant /ænt/ *n* mrav ~**-eater** mravojed ~**-hill** mravinjak **white** ~ termit

antagonism /æn'tægənizəm/ *n* (for/toward/between) antagonizam prema/među **antagonist** *n* protivnik **antagonize** • *vt,vi* učiniti koga neprijateljem, antagonizirati, izazvati

ante /'ænti/ *n* ulog **raise the** ~ podići ulog

ante- *prefix* ante-, prije-

antecedent /,ænti'si:dnt/ *adj* (to) koji čemu prethodi • *n* **1** događaj, slučaj i sl. koji prethodi čemu **2** *pl* preci, prethodnici **antecedence** *n* prednost

antechamber /'æntitʃeimbə(r)/ *n*

predsoblje

antedate /,ænti'deit/ *vt* **1** antedatirati **2** prethoditi

antediluvian /,æntidɪ'lu:viən/ *n* pretpotopni (+ *fig*)

antelope /'æntiləʊp/ *n* antilopa

antenna /æn'tenə/ *n* **1** ticalo **2** *US* antena

anterior /æn'tɪərɪə(r)/ *adj form* prethodni

anteroom /'æntirʊm/ *n* predsoblje, čekaonica

anthem /'ænθəm/ *n* crkvena himna **national** ~ (državna) himna

anthology /æn'θɒlədʒɪ/ *n* antologija

anthrax /'ænθræks/ *n* bedrenica, crni prišt

anthropoid /'ænθrəpɔid/ *adj* čovjekolik

anthropology /,ænθrə'pɒlədʒɪ/ *n* antropologija

anti- /,ænti/ *prefix* anti-, protu- ~**-aircraft** *adj* protuzračni –**biotic** /,æntibai'ɒtik/ *n* antibiotik ○ *adj* antibiotski ~**body** /'æntibɒdi/ *n* protutijelo ~**-clockwise** /ænti'klɒkwaiz/ *adv* u smjeru suprotnom od kazaljke na satu ~**dote** /'æntidəʊt/ *n* protuotrov ~**freeze** /'æntifri:z/ *n* antifriz ~**-personnel** *adj* nagazni ~**-Semite** /,ænti'si:mait/ *n* antisemit ~**-Semitic** *adj* antisemitski ~**septic** /,ænti'septik/ *adj* antiseptički ○ *n* antiseptik ~**thesis** /æn'tiθəsis/ *n* (of sth to sth/between) antiteza, suprotstavljanje, suprotnost

antics /'æntiks/ *n pl* ludovanje, mahnitanje

anticipate /æn'tisipeit/ *vt* **1** unaprijed/prijevremeno učiniti **2** učiniti prije, preteći **3** predvidjeti **4** očekivati **anticipatory** /æn,tisi'peitəri/ *adj* **1** prijevremen, preuranjen **2** očekivan, predviđen **3** u očekivanju **anticipation** /an,tisi'peiʃn/ *n* očekivanje, iščekivanje

antipathy /æn'tipəθi/ *n* (to/towards/against/between) antipatija prema/između **antipathetic** /,æntipə'θetik/ *adj* nesklon komu/čemu

antipodes /æn'tipədi:z/ *n pl* (**the** ~) antipodi

antiquarian /ˌænti'kweəriən/ *adj* antikvarski • *n* antikvar

antiquary /'æntikwəri/ *n* antikvar

antique /æn'ti:k/ *adj* antikni • *n* antikni komad namještaja, antikvitet, starina **the ~** antika, antički stil **antiquity** /æn'tikwəti/ *n* starina, daleka prošlost **Classical Antiquity** klasična starina, antika

antler /'æntlə(r)/ *n* 1 rog (jelena) 2 parožak

anvil /'ænvil/ *n* nakovanj (+ *anat*)

anxiety /æŋ'zaiəti/ *n* 1 nemir, tjeskoba, zabrinutost 2 briga 3 žudnja, velika želja **anxious** /'æŋkʃəs/ *adj* 1 (about/for/at) zabrinut zbog čega/za što 2 **~ to/for/about/that** željan

any /'eni/ *adj* bilo koji, bilo kakav, ikakav, ikoji, svaki, svakakav, nikoji, nikakav, nijedan **in ~ case, at ~ rate** u svakom slučaju, ionako • *adv* imalo, nimalo

anybody /'enibɒdi/ *n, pron* 1 bilo tko, itko, svatko, nitko 2 netko, važna osoba, netko

anyhow /'enihaʊ/ *adv* → **anyway**

anyone /'eniwʌn/ → **anybody**

anyplace /'enipleis/ *adv* → **anywhere**

anything /'eniθiŋ/ *n, pron* bilo što, išta, svašta, ništa

anyway /'eniwei/ *adv* 1 bilo kako, ikako, na bilo koji način 2 nemarno 3 u svakom slučaju, bilo kako bilo ¶ česta poštapalica

anywhere /'eniweə(r)/ *adv* bilo gdje, igdje, svagdje, nigdje (-kamo, -kuda)

apart /ə'pɑ:t/ *adv* 1 daleko 2 na stranu, postrance **set/put ~** (from) a. staviti na stranu, odrediti za, sačuvati za b. činiti posebnim 3 razmaknuto, razdvojeno **~ from** osim **tell/know ~** razlikovati

apartment /ə'pɑ:tmənt/ *n* 1 apartman 2 *US* stan **~ house** stambena zgrada

apathy /'æpəθi/ *n* apatija **apathetic** /ˌæpə'θetik/ *adj* apatičan

ape /eip/ *n* 1 (čovjekoliki) majmun (+ *fig*) 2 imitator **play the ~** oponašati • *vt* oponašati

aperture /'æpətʃə(r)/ *n* otvor **lens ~** otvor leće; blenda *coll*

apex /'eipeks/ *n* (*pl* **apices** /'eipisi:z/)

vrhunac, vrh

aphrodisiac /ˌæfrə'diziæk/ *n* afrodizijak • *adj* afrodizijački

apiece /ə'pi:s/ *adv* po komadu, po osobi

aplomb /ə'plɒm/ *n* samouvjerenost

apogee /'æpədʒi:/ *n fig* vrhunac

apologetic /əˌpɒlə'dʒetik/ *adj* 1 pokajnički **be ~ about/for** ispričavati se zbog **apologize** *vi* (to sb) (for sth) ispričati se **apology** *n* 1 isprika **offer/make an apology** ispričati se 2 obrana

apoplectic /ˌæpə'plektik/ *adj coll* 1 crven u licu 2 jarostan

apostle /ə'pɒsl/ *n* apostol **apostolic** /ˌæpə'stɒlik/ *adj* apostolski

apostrophe /ə'pɒstrəfi/ *n* apostrof

appal (appall *US*) /ə'pɔ:l/ *vt* užasnuti, zgroziti **~ling** *adj* užasan, zastrašujući

apparatus /ˌæpə'reitəs/ *n* 1 uređaj(i), aparat 2 organi, sustav **the state ~** državni aparat

apparent /ə'pærənt/ *adj* 1 očit, jasan, siguran 2 prividan **~ly** *adv* 1 očito 2 naizgled

apparition /ˌæpə'riʃn/ *n* 1 pojava 2 prikaza

appeal /ə'pi:l/ *vi* (to sb) (against/for/from sth) 1 apelirati (na koga za što) 2 uložiti priziv 3 prosvjedovati (protiv) 4 biti privlačan • *n* 1 apel 2 priziv 3 prosvjed 4 privlačnost 5 molba **~ing** *adj* 1 dirljiv 2 privlačan

appear /ə'piə(r)/ *vi* 1 pojaviti se 2 nastupiti 3 izaći 4 izgledati, djelovati 5 ispasti **~ance** *n* 1 nastup 2 dolazak **make an ~** doći, pojaviti se **put in an ~ance** osobno prisustvovati 3 vanjština, izgled **keep up ~ances** sačuvati formu

appease /ə'pi:z/ *vt* utažiti (žeđ), utoliti (glad), zadovoljiti (znatiželju), smiriti (gnjev) **~ment** *n* ustupak, popuštanje

append /ə'pend/ *vt* (to) *form* dopuniti, dodati **~ix** *n* 1 dodatak 2 slijepo crijevo **~icitis** *n* upala slijepog crijeva **~ectomy** *n* operacija slijepog crijeva

appetite /'æpitait/ *n* 1 apetit, tek 2 *fig*

želja **appetizer** n pikantno predjelo
appetizing adj ukusan, tečan; primamljiv (+ fig)
applaud /ə'plɔːd/ vi,vt 1 pljeskati 2 odobravati **applause** n pljesak
apple /'æpl/ n jabuka **the ~ of one's eye** zjenica oka **~-polish** vt coll laskati; uvlačiti se coll
appliance /ə'plaɪəns/ n aparat, naprava, sredstvo **household ~s** kućanski aparati
apply /ə'plaɪ/ vt,vi 1 podnijeti molbu, natjecati se 2 primijeniti 3 (to sth) vrijediti, moći se primijeniti **~ oneself/one's mind** (to sth/to doing sth) prionuti na što **applied** adj primijenjen **applicable** /'æplɪkəbl/ adj (to) primjenjiv, koji vrijedi **applicant** /'æplɪkənt/ n (for) natjecatelj, molitelj **application** /ˌæplɪ'keɪʃn/ n 1 (to sb/for sth) zahtjev, molba **application form** obrazac za molbu 2 (of sth/to sth) primjena, upotreba 3 oblog 4 zalaganje
appoint /ə'pɔɪnt/ vt 1 (for sth) odrediti 2 (sb to sth/sb sth) imenovati (koga čime), postaviti (koga za što) 3 ustanoviti **~ed** adj uređen, opremljen **~ment** n 1 dogovor, ugovoreni termin 2 imenovanje
appraise /ə'preɪz/ vt procijeniti **appraisal** n procjena **appraising** adj ocjenjivački
appreciate /ə'priːʃɪeɪt/ vt,vi 1 cijeniti, znati cijeniti; uživati u 2 biti zahvalan 3 shvaćati, uviđati 4 dobiti na vrijednosti **appreciable** /ə'priːʃəbl/ adj primjetan **appreciation** n 1 procjena 2 uživanje, poznavanje 3 zahvalnost 4 rast vrijednosti **appreciative** adj zahvalan
apprehend /ˌæprɪ'hend/ vt 1 shvaćati 2 leg uhititi **apprehension** n 1 shvaćanje 2 strah, strepnja 3 leg uhićenje **apprehensive** adj zabrinut, u brizi
apprentice /ə'prentɪs/ n šegrt, naučnik **~ship** n šegrtovanje, nauk
apprise /ə'praɪz/ vt (of) obavijestiti o
approach /ə'prəʊtʃ/ vt,vi 1 (pri)bližiti se 2 obratiti se, pristupiti • n pristup (+ fig) **make ~es to sb a.** prilaziti,

pristupati **b.** udvarati se
approbation /ˌæprə'beɪʃn/ n form odobrenje
appropriate /ə'prəʊprɪət/ adj (for/to sth) prikladan, odgovarajući
appropriation /əˌprəʊprɪ'eɪʃn/ n 1 prisvajanje 2 dotacija
approve /ə'pruːv/ vt,vi (of sth/sb) odobriti, složiti se sa, potvrditi **approval** n 1 odobravanje 2 odobrenje **meet with sb's approval** naići na odobravanje
approximate /ə'prɒksɪmət/ adj (to) približan • /ə'prɒksɪmeɪt/ vi,vt **~ to** približavati se, doći/biti nadomak **approximation** n približna procjena/iznos i sl.
apricot /'eɪprɪkɒt/ n marelica
April /'eɪprəl/ n travanj **~ fool** osoba koja nasjedne na prvotravanjsku šalu; budala
apron /'eɪprən/ n 1 pregača 2 platforma zračne luke
apt /æpt/ adj 1 (at doing sth) sposoban, koji brzo shvaća 2 zgodan, umjestan 3 koji naginje, sklon **~ to break** lako lomljiv **~ly** adv prikladno, pravo **~itude** n (for) dar
aqualung /'ækwəlʌŋ/ n ronilačka oprema
aquarium /ə'kweərɪəm/ n akvarij
Aquarius /ə'kweərɪəs/ n astrol Vodenjak
aquatic /ə'kwætɪk/ adj vodeni
aquiline /'ækwɪlaɪn/ adj orlovski
Arab /'ærəb/ n Arap(in) **street a~** n uličnjak
arable /'ærəbl/ adj obradiv
arbitrary /'ɑːbɪtrərɪ/ adj proizvoljan; samovoljan
arbitrate /'ɑːbɪtreɪt/ vt,vi (between) presuditi **arbitration** n arbitraža
arbour /'ɑːbə(r)/ (-or US) n sjenica
arc /ɑːk/ luk **~-lamp, ~-light** lučna svjetiljka
arcade /ɑː'keɪd/ n arkada **shopping-~** n trgovački centar
arcane /ɑː'keɪn/ adj tajanstven
arch (1) /ɑːtʃ/ n luk, svod, slavoluk **~way** nadsvođen prolaz **~ support** ortopedski uložak • vt,vi saviti u luk, savijati se u luku

arch (2) *adj* nestašan

arch- *prefix* arhi-, nad-, glavni

archaeology /ˌaːkɪˈɒlədʒɪ/ *n* arheologija archaeologist *n* arheolog

archaic /aːˈkeɪɪk/ *adj* 1 arhaičan, zastario 2 star, drevan

archangel /ˈaːkeɪndʒl/ *n* arkanđeo

archbishop /ˌaːtʃˈbɪʃəp/ *n* nadbiskup

archdiocese /ˌaːtʃˈdaɪəsɪs/ *n* nadbiskupija

archduke /ˌaːtʃˈdjuːk/ *n* nadvojvoda

archer /ˈaːtʃə(r)/ *n* strijelac ~y *n* streličarstvo

archetype /ˈaːkɪtaɪp/ *n* arhetip archetypal *adj* arhetipski

archipelago /ˌaːkɪˈpelɪgəʊ/ *n* arhipelag

architect /ˈaːkɪtekt/ *n* arhitekt (+ *fig*) ~ure *n* arhitektura ~ural *adj* arhitektonski

archives *n* /ˈaːkaɪvz/ *n pl* arhiv archivist *n* arhivar

ardent /ˈaːdnt/ *adj* gorljiv, žarki ardour (-or *US*) *n* gorljivost, žar

arduous /ˈaːdjʊəs/ *adj* 1 naporan 2 strm

are /ə(r)/ → be

area /ˈeərɪə/ *n* 1 površina 2 područje ~ code *US* → dialling code

arena /əˈriːnə/ *n* arena, poprište

argue /ˈaːgjuː/ *vi,vt* 1 (about/over sth) svađati se oko čega, raspravljati o čemu 2 (for/against/that) tvrditi, dokazivati (da nešto jest/nije) ~ sb into/out of doing sth nagovoriti koga na što/odgovoriti koga od čega arguble *adj* diskutabilan

argument *n* 1 (about/over sth) svađa, prepirka 2 rasprava 3 (for/against) argument 4 kratki sadržaj argumentative *adj* svadljiv

arid /ˈærɪd/ *adj* 1 suh, sušan 2 suhoparan

Aries /ˈeəriːz/ *n astrol* Ovan

arise /əˈraɪz/ *vi irreg* 1 pojaviti se ~ from proizići 2 *arch* ustati

arisen *v irreg* → arise

aristocracy /ˌærɪˈstɒkrəsɪ/ *n* plemstvo aristocrat /ˈærɪstəkræt/ *n* plemić aristocratic /ˌærɪstəˈkrætɪk/ *adj* aristokratski

arithmetic /əˈrɪθmətɪk/ *n* aritmetika

ark /aːk/ *n* 1 arka, korablja 2 A~ of the Covenant kovčeg zavjetni

arm (1) /aːm/ *n* 1 ruka carry/take sb/sth in sb's ~s nositi u naručju/uzeti u naručje baby/child/infant in ~s dojenče keep sb at ~'s length držati koga na udaljenosti with open ~s objeručke, oduševljeno ~-in-~ ruku pod ruku ~chair naslonjač ~pit pazuho 2 rukav 3 grana 4 rukavac

arm (2) *vt vi* (with) naoružati (se) čime (+ *fig*) the ~ed forces/services oružane snage ~ament /ˈaːməmənt/ *n* 1 *pl* oružane snage 2 *pl* naoružanje 3 naoružavanje ~s /aːmz/ *n pl* 1 oružje, naoružanje ~s-race *n* utrka u naoružanju fire~s vatreno oružje small ~s lako/pješačko naoružanje lay down ~s položiti oružje take up ~s, rise up in ~s podići se na oružje (+ *fig*) (be) up in ~s (about/over) nakostriješiti se (+ *fig*) 2 grb coat of ~s grb ~y /ˈaːmɪ/ *n* (+ *sing/pl*) vojska

armature /ˈaːmətʃʊə(r)/ *n el* kotva

armistice /ˈaːmɪstɪs/ *n* primirje

armorial /aːˈmɔːrɪəl/ *adj* heraldički, grboslovni

armour /ˈaːmə(r)/ (-or *US*) *n* oklop ~-plate *n* oklop ~ed *adj* 1 oklopljen 2 oklopni ~er *n* oružar ~y *n* oružarnica

aroma /əˈrəʊmə/ *n* aroma, miris (+ *fig*) ~tic *adj* aromatičan

arose *v irreg* → arise

around /əˈraʊnd/ *adv* 1 (all ~) naokolo, odasvuda, posvuda 2 u blizini he has been ~ iskusio je svašta • *prep* 1 (all ~) po cijelom 2 oko

arouse /əˈraʊz/ *vt* 1 pobuditi 2 potaknuti 3 uzbuditi

arrange /əˈreɪndʒ/ *vt,vi* 1 aranžirati, posložiti, dovesti u red, pobrinuti se za, srediti 2 dogovoriti, ugovoriti 3 (for) napraviti aranžman 4 riješiti ~ment *n* 1 raspored 2 dogovor 3 aranžman 4 *pl* planovi make ~ment → arange

array /əˈreɪ/ *n* 1 poredak 2 (of) izbor, prikaz

arrears /əˈrɪəz/ *n pl* zaostatak, dugovanje be in/fall into ~ (with) kasniti s plaćanjem

arrest /ə'rest/ vt 1 uhititi 2 zaustaviti ~ sb's attention/eyes privući čiju pozornost/pogled itd. • n 1 uhićenje **under ~** uhićen **place/put under ~** uhititi 2 prestanak rada, zatajenje **~ing** adj koji privlači pozornost, frapantan

arrive /ə'raɪv/ vi (0/at/in) doći, stići ~ **at a decision** odlučiti se **arrival** n 1 dolazak 2 novopridošli(ca), prinova

arrogant /'ærəgənt/ adj arogantan **arrogance** n arogancija

arrow /'ærəʊ/ n strijela, strelica **~head** n šiljak strelice

arse /ɑːs/ n tab 1 guzica, dupe tab 2 glupan **~hole** n 1 šupak vulg 2 fig budala

arsenal /'ɑːsənl/ n arsenal

arsenic /'ɑːsnɪk/ n arsen

arson /'ɑːsn/ n palež, podmetanje požara **~ist** n podmetač požara

art /ɑːt/ n 1 umjetnost; likovna umjetnost **the fine ~s** lijepa umjetnosti a **work of ~** umjetničko djelo 2 mod umjetnički, ... umjetnosti **~ school** škola za primijenjenu umjetnost 3 umjetnička snaga/vrijednost 4 **~s** humanističke znanosti **Bachelor of ~s** diplomirani profesor **Master of ~s** magistar znanosti **Faculty of ~s** filozofski fakultet 5 lukavost, vještina, trik **the black ~** crna magija **~ful** adj pun trikova, lukav **~ist** n umjetnik **~iste** /ɑː'tiːst/ n artist **~istic** adj 1 umjetnički 2 dobrog ukusa, s ukusom, sa stilom **~istry** n umjetnost, vještina umjetnika **~less** adj prirodan, bezazlen **~y** adj coll pretenciozan

artery /'ɑːtərɪ/ n 1 arterija 2 fig prometna žila kucavica **arterial** adj 1 arterijski 2 glavni

artichoke /'ɑːtɪtʃəʊk/ n artičoka

article /ɑː'tɪkl/ n 1 artikl, predmet 2 članak 3 leg članak, uvjet 4 gram član

articulate /ɑː'tɪkjʊlət/ adj artikuliran, razgovijetan, jasan • /ɑː'tɪkjʊleɪt/ vt,vi 1 artikulirati, razgovijetno izgovoriti, izreći 2 (+ pass) biti povezan zglobom **~d vehicle/truck** vozilo/kamion s prikolicom articu-

lation n 1 artikulacija 2 zglob

artifact, artefact /'ɑːtɪfækt/ n proizvod, artefakt

artifice /'ɑːtɪfɪs/ n 1 umješnost 2 lukavost, lukavstvo **~r** /ɑː'tɪfɪsə(r)/ n rukotvorac, tvorac **artificial** /ɑːtɪ'fɪʃl/ adj umjetni, lažni

artillery /ɑː'tɪlərɪ/ n topništvo, artiljerija

as /əz/ conj 1 dok, kad, kako 2 budući da, kako • adv kao (što) **as tall as I** visok (isto) kao ja **not so/as big as** ne tako velik kao **such as** kao naprimjer, poput **as if/though** kao da **as for** što se tiče **as to** što se tiče **so as to a.** da bi b. tako da **be as good as one's word** ispuniti obećanje **as long as** dokle god **as well** također

asbestos /æz'bestəs/ n azbest

ascend /ə'send/ vt,vi uspeti se (na što) ~ **the throne** doći na prijestolje **~ancy, ~ency** n 1 prevlast 2 vladajuća klasa **~ent** adj in **the ~** u usponu **ascension** /ə'senʃn/ n uspon **the Ascension** Uzašašće **ascent** /ə'sent/ n uspon

ascertain /ˌæsə'teɪn/ vt ustanoviti

ascetic /ə'setɪk/ adj asketski • n asket

ascribe /ə'skraɪb/ vt ~ to pripisati, pridati

ash (1) /æʃ/ n grab

ash (2) /æʃ/ n (**~es** pl) pepeo **A~ Wednesday** Pepelnica **~-bin, ~-can** n kanta za smeće **~-tray** n pepeljara **~en** adj pepeljast

ashamed /ə'ʃeɪmd/ adj posramljen **be ~ to/of/that** sramiti se

ashore /ə'ʃɔː(r)/ adv na obali, na obalu, na kopno

aside /ə'saɪd/ adv na stranu • n aparte

ask /ɑːsk/ vt,vi 1 pitati (za) ~ **a question** postaviti pitanje ~ **after** raspitivati se o komu/čemu 2 tražiti što od koga, zahtijevati 3 pozvati ~ **for trouble** izazivati (nevolje) ~ **for it** sam tražiti, sam sebi biti kriv **~ing price** početna cijena

askew /ə'skjuː/ adv, adj ukoso, nakrivo

asleep /ə'sliːp/ adv, adj u snu, zaspao **fall ~** zaspati

asparagus /ə'spærəgəs/ n šparoga

aspect /'æspekt/ n 1 izgled, držanje 2 vid, aspekt

aspen /'æspən/ n jasika

asperity /æ'sperətɪ/ n form oštrina, oštra riječ

asphalt /'æsfælt/ n asfalt • vt asfaltirati

aspic /'æspɪk/ n hladetina

aspire /ə'spaɪə(r)/ vi (to/after) težiti, hlepiti za čim **aspiration** /,æspə'reɪʃn/ n (for/after) (to do/be) aspiracija, težnja

ass (1) /æs/ n magarac (+ fig)

ass (2) US → **arse**

assail /ə'seɪl/ vt (with) napasti, obuzeti, mučiti ~**ant** n napadač

assassin /ə'sæsɪn/ n ubojica, atentator ~**ate** vt izvršiti atentat ~**ation** n atentat

assault /ə'sɔːlt/ n (on/upon) napad, juriš ~ **and battery** leg tvorni napadaj **indecent** ~ leg bludna radnja ~ **craft** desantni čamac • vt izvršiti napad, jurišati na

assemble /ə'sembl/ vt,vi 1 sakupiti (se) 2 složiti, sastaviti

assembly n 1 montaža **assembly hall a.** dvorana za sastanke **b.** montažna hala ~ **line** tekuća vrpca 2 skupština, zbor

assent /ə'sent/ n (to) pristanak, odobrenje • vt (to) odobriti, pristati na što

assert /ə'sɜː/ vt 1 pozivati se na, insistirati na, zahtijevati 2 tvrditi ~ **oneself** autoritativno/samouvjereno ~**ion** n 1 traženje svojih prava 2 tvrdnja ~**ive** n samouvjeren, koji se zna nametnuti

assess /ə'ses/ vt procijeniti ~ **the taxes** razrezati porez ~**ment** n procjena ~**or** n 1 procjenitelj 2 prisjednik

asset /'æset/ n 1 pl aktiva, imovina 2 prednost **he is an** ~ na veliku je korist

assiduous /ə'sɪdjʊəs/ adj marljiv, uporan

assign /ə'saɪn/ vt 1 (sth to sb/sth) dodijeliti, zadati 2 utvrditi 3 (sb to/to do) postaviti, odrediti ~**ment** n doznaka, dodjela, položaj, posao, domaća zadaća, zadatak

assimilate /ə'sɪmɪleɪt/ vt,vi 1 apsor-

birati (se) 2 (to) asimilirati (se)

assist /ə'sɪst/ vt,vi (sb) (with sth/in doing sth/to do sth) pomoći (komu u čemu/da što učini) ~**ance** n pomoć ~**ant** n pomoćnik, asistent **shop-~ant** n prodavač

associate /ə'səʊʃɪət/ n suradnik, partner • /ə'səʊʃɪeɪt/ vt,vi ~ **with 1** udružiti se, povezati (se) 2 asocirati, povezivati 3 družiti se **association** n 1 (with) druženje, suradnja 2 udruga, savez 3 asocijacija

assorted /ə'sɔːtɪd/ adj miješani **assortment** n asortiman, izbor

assume /ə'sjuːm/ vt 1 pretpostaviti, uzeti zdravo za gotovo, smatrati 2 preuzeti 3 poprimiti, uzeti, zauzeti **assumption** /ə'sʌmpʃn/ n 1 pretpostavka **on the assumption that** pod pretpostavkom da 2 (of) preuzimanje 3 (of) hinjenje 4 **the Assumption** Velika Gospa

assurance /ə'ʃʊərəns/ n 1 (self-~) sigurnost, samosvijest 2 uvjerenje, jamstvo 3 GB osiguranje **life-~** životno osiguranje 4 drskost 5 (in) povjerenje u **assure** vt 1 uvjeravati 2 osigurati, jamčiti 3 osigurati se **rest ~assured** budi uvjeren **assuredly** adv sigurno, sa sigurnošću

asthma /'æsmə/ n astma **asthmatic** adj astmatičan

astir /ə'stɜː(r)/ adv, adj u pometnji, uskomešan(o)

astonish /ə'stɒnɪʃ/ vt zapanjiti ~**ing** adj zapanjujući, šokantan ~**ment** n iznenađenje, šok

astound /ə'staʊnd/ vt zatraviti

astray /ə'streɪ/ adv, adj na stranputici, na stranputicu

astride /ə'straɪd/ adv zajahavši, jašući

astrology /ə'strɒlədʒɪ/ n astrologija **astrologer** n astrolog

astronaut /'æstrənɔːt/ n astronaut

astronomy /ə'strɒnəmɪ/ n astronomija **astronomer** n astronom **astronomical** adj astronomski (+ fig)

astute /ə'stjuːt/ n prepreden, pronicav

asunder /ə'sʌndə(r)/ adv 1 razdvojeno **drive** ~ razdvojiti 2 na komadiće

asylum /ə'saɪləm/ n 1 azil, utočište 2 umobolnica

at /ət/ *prep* u, na **look at sth** pogledati što at **2 o'clock** u 2 sata **at (the age of) 12** sa 12 godina **at first** isprva **at last** konačno **at work** na poslu **good at acting** dobar glumac **at war** u ratu, zaraćen **at full speed** punom brzinom **at great cost** skupo **at one's best** najbolje moguće **at least** najmanje, barem

ate *v irreg* → **eat**

atheism /'eɪθɪɪzəm/ *n* ateizam **atheist** *n* ateist

athlete /'æθliːt/ *n* športaš, atlet **athletic** *adj* športski, atletski **athletics** /æθ'letɪks/ *n pl* (+ *sing*) 1 bavljenje športom 2 atletika

atmosphere /'ætməsfɪə(r)/ *n* 1 (the ~) atmosfera 2 zrak 3 *fig* atmosfera, ozračje

atom /'ætəm/ *n* atom ~**ic** *adj* atomski ~**izer** *n* raspršivač

atone /ə'təʊn/ *vi* (for) nadoknaditi, okajati ~**ment** *n* nadoknada, okajanje

atop /ə'tɒp/ *adv* (of) *US* povrh, na vrhu

atrocious /ə'trəʊʃəs/ *adj* okrutan; grozan (+ *fig coll*) **atrocity** /ə'trɒsətɪ/ *n* 1 okrutnost, zloća 2 strahota, zločin

atrophy /'ætrəfɪ/ *n* atrofija • *vi* atrofirati, odumrijeti

attach /ə'tætʃ/ *vt,vi* 1 pričvrstiti 2 pridati, pripisati 3 priložiti 4 **be** ~**ed** biti privržen 5 ~ **oneself to** priključiti se ~**ment** *n* 1 privrženost 2 nastavak, priključak

attache /ə'tæʃeɪ/ *n* ataše ~ **case** torba za spise

attack /ə'tæk/ *n* (against/on) napad na **come under** ~ pretrpjeti napad **heart** ~ infarkt • *vt* napasti, napadati

attain /ə'teɪn/ *vt,vi* (to) postići ~**able** *adj* dostižan ~**ment** *n* 1 uspjeh 2 dostignuće

attainder /ə'teɪndə(r)/ *n leg* gubitak građanskih prava

attempt /ə'tempt/ *vt* pokušati, latiti se • *n* ~ **to do sth/at** (doing) **sth** pokušaj, nastojanje ~ **on/upon** napad **an** ~ **on sb's life** atentat

attend /ə'tend/ *vt,vi* 1 (to) pratiti 2 (to) usredotočiti se na 3 (to) služiti 4 (on/upon) brinuti o, njegovati, služiti 5 pohađati ~**ance** *n* 1 pratnja, njega 2 pohađanje 3 publika ~**ant** *n* 1 sluga, pratilac 2 *pl* pratnja • *adj* 1 popratan 2 koji njeguje/poslužuje

attention /ə'tenʃn/ *n* 1 pozornost **pay** ~ obratiti pozornost 2 *pl* znak pažnje 3 *mil* stav "pozor" **stand at** ~ stati u "pozoru" **attentive** *adj* (to) pažljiv (prema), koji pazi **attentively** *adv* pažljivo, pozorno

attenuate /ə'tenjʊeɪt/ *vt* istanjiti, oslabiti, smanjiti

attest /ə'test/ *vt,vi* 1 dokazati 2 atestirati, ovjeriti 3 zakleti (se) ~ **to** svjedočiti o

attic /'ætɪk/ *n* potkrovlje

attire /ə'taɪə(r)/ *n lit* odjeća

attitude /'ætɪtjuːd/ *n* držanje, stav (+ *fig*) **strike an** ~ zauzeti pozu

attorney /ə'tɜːnɪ/ *n* 1 opunomoćenik **letter/warant of** ~ pisana punomoć **power of** ~ punomoć 2 odvjetnik **district** ~ okružni tužitelj **A~ General** državni odvjetnik

attract /ə'trækt/ *vt* privući (+ *fig*) ~**ion** *n* 1 privlačnost 2 atrakcija ~**ive** *adj* privlačan

attribute /ə'trɪbjuːt/ *vt* ~ **to** pripisivati • /'ætrɪbjuːt/ *n* atribut

attrition /ə'trɪʃn/ *n* trošenje **war of** ~ taktika iscrpljivanja

attune /ə'tjuːn/ *vt* ~ **to** 1 ugoditi, uskladiti 2 navikanuti

aubergine /'əʊbəʒiːn/ *n* patlidžan

auburn /'ɔːbən/ *adj* crvenkast, zlaćanosmeđ, kestenjast

auction /'ɔːkʃn/ *n* dražba, aukcija • *vt* (off) prodati na dražbi ~**eer** *n* dražbovatelj

audacious /ɔː'deɪʃəs/ *adj* 1 odvažan 2 drzak **audacity** /ɔː'dæsətɪ/ *n* smionost, drskost

audible /'ɔːdəbl/ *adj* čujan **audibly** *adv* (dovoljno) glasno

audience /'ɔːdɪəns/ *n* 1 publika, auditorij, slušateljstvo, čitateljstvo 2 audijencija

audio- /'ɔːdɪəʊ/ *prefix* audio-

audit /'ɔːdɪt/ *n* revizija (poslovnih knjiga) • *vt* izvršiti reviziju ~**or** *n* revizor

audition /ɔː'dɪʃn/ *n* 1 audicija 2 sluh • *vt* 1 ići na audiciju 2 napraviti audiciju **auditory** /ˈɔːdɪtrɪ/ adj slušni

augment /ɔːgˈment/ vt,vi povećati (se) **~ation** n povećanje, dodatak

augur /ˈɔːgə(r)/ vi,vt predskazivati ~ **well/ill** (for sb/sth) biti dobar/loš znak za budućnost **~y** n znamen, predznak

august /ɔːˈgʌst/ adj uzvišen, veličanstven

August /ˈɔːgəst/ n kolovoz

auld lang syne /ˌɔːld læŋ ˈsaɪn/ n dobra stara vremena

aunt /ɑːnt/ n teta **~ie/~y** n teta, tetica **A~ Sally** fig predmet pogrde

au pair /ˌəʊˈpeə(r)/ n strana dadilja

aural /ˈɔːrəl/ adj ušni

aureole /ˈɔːrɪəʊl/ n aureola

auspices /ˈɔːspɪsɪz/ n pl 1 okrilje 2 ozračje **auspicious** /ɔːˈspɪʃəs/ adj povoljan, sretan

Aussie /ˈɒzɪ/ n sl Australac

austere /ɔːˈstɪə(r)/ adj 1 strog 2 jednostavan **authentic** /ɔːˈθentɪk/ adj autentičan **~ity** /ˌɔːθənˈtɪsətɪ/ n autentičnost, izvornost **~ate** vt utvrditi/potvrditi autentičnost

author /ˈɔːθə(r)/ n 1 autor, pisac 2 tvorac, stvoritelj **~ship** n 1 autorstvo 2 (književno) stvaralaštvo

authoritarian /ɔːˌθɒrɪˈteərɪən/ adj autoritaran • n pristaša autoritarne politike **authoritative** /ɔːˈθɒrɪtətɪv/ adj 1 autoritativan 2 ovlašten 3 provjeren

authority /ɔːˈθɒrətɪ/ n 1 autoritet, utjecaj 2 (for sth/to do sth) ovlast 3 pl vlasti, organi vlasti, uprava 4 autoritet, stručnjak 5 izvor **authorize** /ˈɔːθəraɪz/ vt autorizirati, ovlastiti **authorization** n autorizacija, ovlaštenje, ovlast

auto /ˈɔːtəʊ/ n US coll auto

auto- /ˌɔːtəʊ/ prefix auto-, samo-

autobiography /ˌɔːtəbaɪˈɒgrəfɪ/ n autobiografija

autocue /ˈɔːtəkjuː/ n TV "idiot", blesimetar coll

autograph /ˈɔːtəgrɑːf/ n autogram, vlastoručni potpis • vt dati autogram, potpisati

automatic /ˌɔːtəˈmætɪk/ adj automatski • n automatik **automation** n automatizacija

automobile /ˈɔːtəməbiːl/ n automobil

autonomous /ɔːˈtɒnəməs/ adj autonoman **autonomy** n autonomija

autumn /ˈɔːtəm/ n 1 jesen **in ~** ujesen 2 mod jesenski **~al** adj jesenski

auxiliary /ɔːgˈzɪlɪərɪ/ adj pomoćni • n 1 pomoćni glagol 2 pl pomoćne trupe

avail /əˈveɪl/ vt,vi koristiti **~ oneself of** iskoristiti, okoristiti se • n korist **of no/little ~** nikakva/mala korist **be of no ~** ne uroditi plodom **without/to no ~** bez rezultata, bezuspješno **~able** adj 1 koji se može dobiti/nabaviti, raspoloživ, slobodan 2 valjan 3 dostupan, pristupačan

avalanche /ˈævəlɑːnʃ/ n lavina (+ fig)

avant-garde /ˌævɒnˈgɑːd/ n 1 avangarda 2 mod avangardni

avarice /ˈævərɪs/ n škrtost, pohlepa

avenge /əˈvendʒə/ vt (sth on/upon sb for sth) osvetiti (se za što) **~r** n osvetnik

avenue /ˈævənjuː/ n 1 aleja 2 avenija 3 (to) fig put do

average /ˈævərɪdʒ/ n 1 prosjek **on (an/the) ~** u prosjeku • adj prosječan • vt,vi 1 izračunati prosjek 2 u prosjeku iznositi

averse /əˈvɜːs/ adj **~ from/to** protivan, nesklon **aversion** n 1 ~ to averzija 2 predmet mržnje

avert /əˈvɜːt/ vt 1 (from) odvratiti (od) 2 spriječiti

aviation /ˌeɪvɪˈeɪʃn/ n letenje, zrakoplovstvo **~ spirit** kerozin

avid /ˈævɪd/ adj **~ for** željan čega, lakom za čim **~ity** n lakomost

avoid /əˈvɔɪd/ vt izbjeći **~ance** n izbjegavanje

avow /əˈvaʊ/ vt form priznati, očitovati **~al** n priznanje, očitovanje **~edly** adv po vlastitom priznanju, otvoreno

await /əˈweɪt/ vt 1 očekivati 2 čekati

awake /əˈweɪk/ vi irreg probuditi se **~ to** postati svjestan čega, shvatiti • adj budan **~ to** svjestan

awaken /əˈweɪkn/ vt probuditi **~ sb to sth** učiniti koga svjesnim **~ing** n buđenje, osvještavanje

award /əˈwɔːd/ vt (sb sth) nagraditi

koga čime, dodijeliti komu što • *n* nagrada

aware /ə'weə(r)/ *adj* ~ **of/that** svjestan čega/da ~**ness** *n* svijest o čemu

awash /ə'wɒʃ/ *adj* pod vodom, u vodi

away /ə'weɪ/ *adv* **1** daleko **two miles** ~ dvije milje odavde **2** dalje **3** *sport* u gostima **right/straight** ~ odmah, iz ovih stopa

awe /ɔ:/ *n* strahopoštovanje • *vt* **1** uliti strahopoštovanje **2** *pass* biti obuzet strahopoštovanjem ~**inspiring** *adj* koji ulijeva strahopoštovanje ~**stricken/struck** *adj* pun strahopoštovanja ~**some** *adj* strašan, silan (+ *fig*)

awful /'ɔ:fl/ *adj* strašan, grozan ~**ly** *adv coll* vrlo; užasno

awhile /ə'waɪl/ *adv* neko vrijeme, nakratko

awkward /'ɔ:kwəd/ *adj* **1** nespretan, nezgrapan **2** neugodan, nezgodan, nelagodan **an** ~ **customer** *coll* nezgodan svat

awning /'ɔ:nɪŋ/ *n* tenda

awoke, awoken *v irreg* → **awake**

awry /ə'raɪ/ *adv, adj* nakrivo, naopako **go** ~ poći naopako

ax(e) /æks/ sjekira **apply the** ~ **to** *fig* potkresati **have an** ~ **to grind** imati vlastiti interes **get the** ~ *coll* dobiti nogu *coll* • *vt coll* **1** skresati (troškove, broj zaposlenih) **2** otpustiti

axis /'æksis/ *n* **1** os **2** politička osovina

axle /'æksl/ *n* osovina

aye, ay /aɪ/ *int Scot* da • *n pl* glasovi "za"

B

B, b /biː/ *n* 1 drugo slovo engl. abecede; be 2 (ocjena) vrlo dobar

babble /ˈbæbl/ *vi,vt* 1 brbljati 2 žuboriti

baby /ˈbeɪbɪ/ *n* 1 dijete, beba 2 mladunče • *vt coll* tetošiti ~**sit** *vi irreg* (→ **sit**) čuvati djecu

bachelor /ˈbætʃələ(r)/ *n* neženja **B~ of Arts/B~ of Science** diplomirani profesor

back /bæk/ *n* 1 leđa 2 poleđina, stražnja strana 3 naslon **at the ~ of/in ~ of** *US* iza **at the ~ of one's mind** u podsvijesti **at/in the ~ of** beyond Bogu iza leđa **like the ~ of one's hand** *coll* kao svoj džep • *adv* 1 natrag, unatrag, straga 2 prije, nekada c. opet, iznova **be ~** vratiti se **~ and forth** amo-tamo • *vt,vi* 1 ići/voziti unatrag 2 podržati 3 kladiti se na ~ **down/off** *US* odreći se; uzmaknuti ~ **out** odustati ~ **up** podupirati, podržati, pomoći ~**bencher** običan zastupnik u parlamentu ~**biting** *n* ogovaranje ~**bone** *n* kičma (+ *fig*) ~**breaking** *adj* težak, naporan ~**drop/cloth** *GB* a. kulisa b. *fig* pozadina ~**date** *vt* antedatirati ~**fire** *vi* a. prerano paliti (motor) b. *fig* izjaloviti se, osvetiti se ~**ground** *n* a. pozadina, podloga b. situacija 3 odgoj, obrazovanje, iskustvo; porijeklo, pripadnost ~**ing** *n* pomoć, potpora, podrška ~**lash** reakcija ~**log** zaostali posao, zaostaci ~ **number/copy/issue** stari broj novina/časopisa ~**pack** *US* naprtnjača ~ **seat** stražnje sjedalo **take a ~ seat** *fig* povući se u sjenu ~**side** stražnjica ~**stage** *adv* iza pozornice ○ *adj coll* zakulisan, tajan ~**stroke** ledno plivanje ~**track** *vi* vratiti se istim putem ~**up** *n* a. podrška b. *comp* rezervna

kopija ~**ward** *adj* 1. prema natrag, unatrag 2 zaostao, nerazvijen ~**wards/ward** *US adv* 1 natraške, natrag 2 obrnuto, naopako 3 nagore, unatrag ~**water** a. ustajala voda u riječnom rukavcu b. *fig* mrtvilo ~**yard** stražnje dvorište

bacon /ˈbeɪkən/ *n* slanina **bring home the ~** *coll* zarađivati za kruh

bacteria /bækˈtɪərɪə/ *n pl* bakterije

bad /bæd/ *adj* (*comp* **worse**, *sup* **worst**) 1 loš 2 zao 3 slab 4 loše kvalitete **go ~** pokvariti se (**it's/that's**) **too ~** *coll* šteta • *n* 1 zlo 2 manjak, gubitak; propast ~**lands** *US* neplodna područja ~**ly** *adv* 1 loše 2 teško 3 prijeko potrebno, nužno **bad-mouth** *vt US sl* olajavati, opanjkati

bade *v irreg* → **bid**

badge /bædʒ/ *n* 1 značka 2 obilježje

badger /ˈbædʒə(r)/ *n* jazavac • *vt* gnjaviti, salijetati

baffle /ˈbæfl/ *vt* 1 zbuniti 2 osujetiti

bag /bæg/ *n* 1 torb(ic)a, vreć(ic)a 2 lovina ~**gy** *adj* vrećast, širok • *vt,vi* strpati u torbu/vreću

baggage /ˈbægɪdʒ/ *n US* prtljaga

bagpipes /ˈbægpaɪps/ *n pl* gajde

bail /beɪl/ *n* jamčevina **go/put in/stand ~ for sb** položiti jamčevinu za koga **released on ~** pušten na slobodu uz jamčevinu **grant sb ~** pustiti uz jamčevinu • *vt* (**out**) 1 osloboditi koga uz jamčevinu 2 izbaciti vodu iz čamca 3 izvući *fig* 4 *US* → **bale out**

bailiff /ˈbeɪlɪf/ *n* 1 *GB leg* ovrhovoditelj 2 *GB* upravitelj imanja, nadstojnik 3 *US* sudski nadzornik 4 *US* šerifov pomoćnik

bait /beɪt/ *n* mamac, meka (+ *fig*) • *vt,vi* 1 (with) namamiti 2 izazivati, dražiti

bake /beɪk/ *vt,vi* 1 (is)peći (se) 2 *fig* peći se, kuhati se (na suncu) ~r *n* pekar ~r's (**shop**) pekara ~r's **dozen** trinaest komada ~**ry** *n* pekara **baking powder** prašak za pecivo

balaclava /ˌbæləˈklɑːvə/ *n* vunena kapa s prorezima za oči i usta

balance /ˈbæləns/ *n* 1 ravnoteža, protuteža (+ *fig*) 2 vaga 3 *comm* bilanca, saldo 4 ostatak, višak **tip the** ~ prevagnuti **on** ~ uzevši sve u obzir, sve u svemu ~ **of trade/payments** trgovinska/platna bilanca ~ **of power** ravnoteža snaga ~ **sheet** bilanca, zaključni račun • *vt,vi* 1 vagati 2 držati ravnotežu 3 uravnotežiti 4 poravnati (prihode i rashode) 5 (against) *fig* usporediti

balcony /ˈbælkənɪ/ *n* balkon

bald /bɔːld/ *adj* 1 ćelav 2 ogolio 3 *fig* gol

bale (1) /beɪl/ *n* bala

bale (2) *vi* (out) skočiti padobranom

baleful /ˈbeɪlfʊl/ *adj* zlokoban, poguban

ball (1) /bɔːl/ *n* 1 lopta; kugla 2 očna jabučica, jagodica palca 3 metak 4 ~s *tab sl* jaja; sranje; drskost; petlja *coll* ~ **bearing** kuglični ležaj ~-**point** (**pen**) kemijska olovka

ball (2) *n* 1 bal 2 *coll* sjajan provod ~**room** plesna dvorana

ballet /ˈbæleɪ/ *n* balet ~ **dancer** balerina, baletan

ballocks → **bollocks**

balloon /bəˈluːn/ *n* 1 balon 2 "oblačić" (s tekstom u stripu)

ballot /ˈbælət/ *n* 1 glasački listić 2 tajno glasovanje 3 broj glasova ~ **box** glasačka kutija **take a** ~ glasovati • *vi,vt* (for) tajno glasovati, izabrati

ballyhoo /ˌbælɪˈhuː/ *n coll* bučna reklama, galama

balmy /ˈbɑːmɪ/ *adj* blag, ugodan

bamboo /bæmˈbuː/ *n* bambus

bamboozle /bæmˈbuːzl/ *vt* (sb into/out of doing sth) *coll* prevariti, nasamariti

ban /bæn/ *vt* (sth; sb from doing sth) zabraniti (komu što) • *n* zabrana

banal /bəˈnɑːl/ *adj* banalan, običan,

otrcan

banana /bəˈnɑːnə/ *n* banana

band /bænd/ *n* 1 vrpca; obruč; povez; prsten 2 banda, četa, družba 3 muzički orkestar, grupa 4 valna dužina • *vi* udružiti se

bandage /ˈbændɪdʒ/ *n* povez, zavoj • *vt* (up) povezati, zaviti (ranu)

bandaid /ˈbændeɪd/ *n US TM* flaster

bandit /ˈbændɪt/ *n* razbojnik, bandit

bandwagon /ˈbændwægən/ *n* **climb/jump/get on the** ~ pridružiti se većini

bandy (1) /ˈbændɪ/ *adj* kriv, svinut ~-**legged** krivonog

bandy (2) *vt* 1 dobacivati (riječi), izmjenjivati (poglede), primati i davati (udarce) 2 prepirati se

bang /bæŋ/ *n* 1 udarac, tresak, prasak, pucanj 2 ~**s** šiške *coll* • *vt,vi* 1 (za)lupiti, tresnuti 2 tući, udariti 3 eksplodirati, prasnuti, pucati 4 *tab* ševiti • *adv* ~ **in the middle** točno u sredinu • *inter* bum!

bangle /ˈbæŋgl/ *n* narukvica

banish /ˈbænɪʃ/ *vt* 1 prognati 2 otjerati, odagnati

banister(s) /ˈbænɪstə(r)/ *n* ograda stubišta

bank (1) /bæŋk/ *n* 1 banka 2 ulog u kartanju ~ **account** bankovni račun ~**book** bankovna knjižica ~ **card/~er's card** *GB* čekovna kartica ~**er** *n* bankar ~**note** novčanica ~ **rate** *comm* eskontna stopa ~ **statement** izvod s računa • *vt,vi* 1 položiti (novac) u banku 2 baviti se bankarstvom 3 (with) imati račun (u banci) 4 (on/upon) računati, osloniti se na ~**ing** *n* bankarstvo

bank (2) *n* 1 obala (rijeke) 2 nasip • *vt,vi* 1 (up) nagomilati (se); zgrnuti (vatru) 2 naginjati se

bankrupt /ˈbæŋkrʌpt/ *adj* bankrot(iran), nelikvidan **become/go** ~ bankrotirati, pasti pod stečaj • *vt* dovesti pod stečaj, upropastiti ~**cy** /ˈbæŋkrəpsɪ/ *n* 1 stečaj 2 *fig* neuspjeh, propast **file** ~ najaviti/ zatražiti stečaj ~**cy proceedings** stečajni postupak

banner /ˈbænə(r)/ *n* 1 stijeg 2 transparent ~ **headline** novinski naslov preko cijele (naslovne) stranice

banquet /'bæŋkwɪt/ n banket, gozba

banter /'bæntə(r)/ vt,vi zadirkivati, bockati • n zadirkivanje

baptism /'bæptɪzəm/ n krštenje ~ **of fire** vatreno krštenje **baptize** vt krstiti

bar /baː/ n 1 šipka; poluga; rešetka 2 rebro (čokolade), komad (sapuna) 3 zabrana 4 lokal, bar; šank 5 sud; optuženička klupa 6 takt 7 pruga, crta **the B~** 1 odvjetnici, odvjetničko zvanje **be called to the B~** postati odvjetnik ~**maid** pipničarka, šankerica ~**tender** US pipničar • vt 1 navući zasun 2 zapriječiti; zabraniti • (~**ring**) prep osim, izuzev

barb /baːb/ n kukica (na udici/strelici) ~**ed wire** bodljikava žica

barbaric /baːˈbærɪk/ adj barbarski, divljački

barbecue /'baːbɪkjuː/ n 1 roštilj 2 piknik s roštiljem

barber /'baːbə(r)/ n brijač

bare /beə(r)/ adj 1 gol 2 prazan 3 puki **lay ~** (raz)otkriti (tajnu) ~**faced** adj drzak ~**foot(ed)** adj, adv bosonog ~**headed** adj, adv gologlav ~**ly** adv 1 jedva, tek, samo 2 oskudno, bijedno • vt (raz)otkriti, razgoliti, pokazati

bargain /'baːgɪn/ n 1 pogodba, posao 2 jeftina kupnja; rasprodaja **make/strike a** ~ pogoditi se, sklopiti posao • vt,vi cjenkati se, pogoditi se

barge (1) /baːdʒ/ n teglenica ~ **pole** čaklja

barge (2) vi 1 (into/against) zaletjeti se 2 (in/into) upasti, uletjeti, nahrupiti 3 (about) teturati, glavinjati

bark (1) /baːk/ vi,vt 1 (at) lajati (na) 2 izderati se ~ **up the wrong tree** fig krivo optužiti • n lavež

bark (2) n kora drveta

barley /'baːlɪ/ n ječam

barmy /'baːmɪ/ adj coll luckast

barn /baːn/ n štagalj

baron /'bærən/ n 1 barun 2 fig magnat ~**ess** /'bærənɪs/ n barunica

barracks /'bærəks/ n pl vojarna

barrage /'bærɑːʒ/ n mil zaprečna paljba

barrel /'bærəl/ n 1 bačva 2 cijev (puške i sl.)

barren /'bærən/ n neplodan, suh; jalov (+ fig)

barricade /ˌbærɪˈkeɪd/ n zapreka • vt zaprijeičiti

barrier /'bærɪə(r)/ n 1 ograda 2 brklja 3 prepreka, zapreka **sound ~** zvučni zid

barrister /'bærɪstə(r)/ n pravni zastupnik, odvjetnik

barrow /'bærəʊ/ n 1 (**wheel~**) tačke 2 kolica

barter /'baːtə(r)/ vt,vi 1 razmijeniti, trampiti 2 fig prodati • n razmjena robe, trampa

base /beɪs/ n 1 osnova, temelj, baza (+ fig) 2 postolje, podnožje ○ vt (on/upon) zasnivati, temeljiti ~**d in** sa sjedištem u • adj 1 podao, nizak 2 neplemenit (kovina) 3 krivotvoren (kovani novac) **basic** /'beɪsɪk/ adj 1 osnovni, temeljni 2 coll elementaran **basically** adv u osnovi, u biti **basis** /'beɪsɪs/ n (pl **bases**) (of/for) fig osnova, temelj

basement /'beɪsmənt/ n 1 podrum 2 suteren

bash /bæʃ/ vt 1 coll lupiti, odalamiti 2 GB coll verbalno napasti • n coll snažan udarac

bashful /'bæʃfl/ adj sramežljiv

basil /'bæzl/ n bosiljak

basin /'beɪsn/ n 1 GB zdjela 2 (**wash~**) umivaonik; lavor 3 dok; zaljev 4 riječni sliv

bask /baːsk/ vi (in) 1 sunčati se 2 fig uživati

basket /'baːskɪt/ n košar(ic)a, koš ~**ball** sport košarka

bass /beɪs/ n bas

bassoon /bəˈsuːn/ n fagot

bastard /'baːstəd/ n 1 derog vanbračno dijete, kopile 2 sl gad, svinja **lucky ~!** sretnik! **poor ~!** jadnik!

baste /beɪst/ vt,vi 1 labavo zašiti, jemčiti; heftati coll 2 zalijevati pečenku

bastion /'bæstɪən/ n bastion (+ fig)

bat (1) /bæt/ n palica • vt,vi udariti loptu

bat (2) n šišmiš, slijepi miš **he has ~s**

in the belfry *coll* fali mu daska u glavi

bat (3) *vt* namignuti **not ~ an eyelid** *coll* ne trepnuti okom

batch /bætʃ/ *n* 1 količina ispečenog kruha/kolača 2 grupa, garnitura, serija, kolekcija

bated /'beɪtɪd/ *adj* **with ~ breath** suspregnuvši/zadržavši dah

bath /bɑːθ/ *n* 1 kada 2 kupanje, kupka 3 **~s** *GB* (zatvoreno) kupalište **have/take a ~** kupati se **run a ~** pustiti vodu u kadu **~robe** kupaći ogrtač **~room** kupaonica **~tub** *US* kada **~e** /beɪð/ *vi,vt* 1 *GB* kupati se (u moru) 2 *US* kupati se (u kadi) 3 ispirati **~er** *n* kupač **~ing costume/suit** kupaći kostim **~ing trunks** *pl GB* kupaće gaćice

baton /'bætən/ *n* 1 pendrek, palica 2 dirigentski štapić

battalion /bə'tæliən/ *n mil* bataljun

batter /'bætə(r)/ *vt,vi* lupati, udarati, razbiti **~ing ram** ovan za probijanje bedema • *n* tijesto za palačinke

battery /'bætəri/ *n* 1 električna baterija 2 akumulator 3 *mil* baterija 4 *fig* niz **assault and ~** *leg* tvorni napad **~ farm** peradarska farma

battle /'bætl/ *n* bitka, boj, borba (+ *fig*) **fight a ~** voditi bitku **pitched ~** prava bitka, žestoki okršaj **~field** bojno polje, bojište **~ship** bojni brod

bawdy /'bɔːdɪ/ *adj* prost, razvratan

bawl /bɔːl/ *vt,vi* 1 (out) (za)urlati 2 plakati, derati se **~sb out** *US coll* izgrditi

bay (1) /beɪ/ *n* zaljev

bay (2) *n* (~ **tree**) lovor

bay (3) *n* 1 udubljenje u zidu, niša 2 odio, poseban prostor; pregradak 3 (~ **window**) erker 4 (**sick~**) brodska bolnica

bay (4) *vi* zavijati • *n* dubok lavež **keep/hold sb at** ~ ne dopustiti kome da se približi, držati koga podalje od sebe **bring/drive to** ~ natjerati u tjesnac, stjerati uza zid

bay (5) *n* konj riđan, dorat

bazaar /bə'zɑː(r)/ *n* 1 prodaja u dobrotvorne svrhe 2 bazar 3 jeftin dućan

be /biː/ *vi, aux irreg* 1 biti, postojati, živjeti 2 nalaziti se **the be-all and end-all** (of sth) glavni smisao, cilj, svrha **mother-to-be** buduća majka ~ **that as it may** bilo kako bilo **for the time being** za sada **being** /'biːɪŋ/ *n* 1 postojanje 2 biće, stvor **bring/call sth into being** stvoriti **come into being** nastati, postati, ostvariti se

beach /biːtʃ/ *n* pješčana obala, plaža

beacon /'biːkən/ *n* 1 svjetlosni signal 2 svjetionik 3 *fig* zvijezda vodilja

bead /biːd/ *n* 1 kuglica, zrno 2 kap, graška (znoja) 3 mušica (na puški)

beak /biːk/ *n* 1 (kukast) kljun 2 *sl* nosina, kljuka

beaker /'biːkə(r)/ *n* 1 pokal, pehar 2 plastična čaša

beam /biːm/ *n* 1 greda 2 zraka, trak, snop • *vt,vi* 1 zračiti 2 odašiljati (radio-signale) 3 sjati od zadovoljstva

bean /biːn/ *n* 1 grah; bob 2 zrno kave **broad ~s** bob **French/green/runner/string ~s** mahune **~sprouts** klice (za salatu) **spill the ~s** izbrbljati, izlanuti

bear (1) /beə(r)/ *n* 1 medvjed 2 burzovni špekulant, besist 3 neotesanac, grubijan

bear (2) *vt,vi irreg* 1 nositi 2 dopustiti; izdržati; podnijeti, trpjeti 3 roditi 4 gajiti, osjećati (ljubav, mržnju) 5 (oneself) držati se, ponašati se ~ **a resemblance to** nalikovati kome ~ **witness** to sth/for sb) (po)svjedočiti ~ (to the) **right** držati se desne strane ~ **in mind** imati na umu ~ **fruit** uroditi plodom ~ **down** a. nadjačati, pobijediti, poraziti, svladati b. pritiskati ~ **down on/upon** navaliti, obrušiti se ~ **on/upon** odnositi se na, ticati se, utjecati na **bring pressure to** ~ **on** izvršiti pritisak na ~ **out** potvrditi; podržati ~ **up** hrabro se držati ~ **with** imati strpljenja **~able** *adj* podnošljiv **~er** *n* 1 nosač; nositelj 2 *comm* donositelj **~ing** *n* 1 ponašanje, držanje 2 (on) utjecaj; veza 3 (**ball ~**) (kuglični) ležaj 4 kut, smjer (kompasa) 5 **~ings** orijentacija

beard /bɪəd/ *n* brada (dlake) **~ed** *adj* bradat

beast /biːst/ *n* životinja; zvijer (+ *fig*) ~ **of burden** tegleća životinja ~ **of prey** grabežljivac ~**ly** *adj*, *adv* coll odvratan, loš

beat /biːt/ *vt*, *vi* *irreg* 1 tući, udarati, lupati 2 šibati (vjetar/kiša); žariti (sunce) 3 kucati (srce) 4 kovati 5 mahati (krilima) 6 pobijediti, poraziti; oboriti (rekord) 7 (sb to sth) prestići koga 8 utrti (put) ~ **about the bush** okolišati ~ **it!** *sl* briši! **it** ~**s me** pojma nemam ~ **off** odbiti ~ **up** *coll* premlatiti • *n* 1 udarac 2 ritam 3 patrolna ruta policajca • *adj* **dead** ~ *coll* mrtav umoran

beaten *v irreg* → **beat**

beautician /bjuːˈtɪʃn/ *n* kozmetičar

beautiful /ˈbjuːtɪfl/ *adj* lijep, krasan **beauty** /ˈbjuːtɪ/ *n* 1 ljepota 2 ljepotica **beauty parlour/salon** kozmetički salon **beauty spot a.** kraj s prekrasnom prirodom **b.** madež

beaver /ˈbiːvə(r)/ *n* dabar **eager** ~ nadobudna osoba

became *v irreg* → **become**

because /bɪˈkɒz/ *conj* 1 jer, zato što 2 budući da ~ **of** uslijed, zbog

beck /bek/ *n* mig, znak **he's at my** ~ **and call** kud ja okom, tud on skokom

beckon /ˈbekən/ *vt*, *vi* pozvati koga, dati kome znak, domahnuti

become /bɪˈkʌm/ *vt*, *vi* *irreg* 1 postati 2 pristajati 3 dolikovati, priličiti **becoming** *adj* (to) 1 pristao, odgovarajući 2 doličan

bed /bed/ *n* 1 krevet, ležaj 2 dno, korito 3 podloga, postolje 4 gredica 5 sloj ~ **and breakfast** pansion ~**ridden** *adj* prikovan uz krevet ~**room** spavaća soba ~**side manner** liječnikovo ophođenje s bolesnicima ~**sit(ter)** *GB* minijaturni stan, sobičak ~**spread** ukrasni pokrivač za krevet ~**time** vrijeme za spavanje • *vt* 1 (in) usaditi 2 presaditi 3 (down) primiti na prenočište, pripremiti postelju; leći 4 (sb) spavati s kim

bedlam /ˈbedləm/ *n* 1 *arch* ludnica 2 *fig coll* luda kuća

bedraggled /bɪˈdrægld/ *adj* mokar, blatan

bee /biː/ *n* pčela **have a** ~ **in one's**

bonnet imati fiksnu ideju **spelling** ~ natjecanje u pravopisu ~**hive** košnica (+ *fig*) **the** ~**'s knees** *GB coll* savršen, idealan **make a** ~**line for** *coll* uputiti se ravno prema

beech /biːtʃ/ *n* bukva

beef /biːf/ *n* 1 govedina 2 *coll* snaga 3 *coll* žalba ~**steak** biftek ~**y** *adj coll* 1 krupan, jak, mišićav 2 gojazan • *vi*, *vt* 1 (about) *coll* derog žaliti se, buniti se 2 (up) *coll* pojačati

been *v irreg* → **be**

beer /bɪə(r)/ *n* pivo

beet /biːt/ *n* repa **red** ~/~**root** cikla **sugar/white** ~ šećerna repa

beetle /ˈbiːtl/ *n* 1 kukac, kornjaš 2 *coll* Volkswagen; buba *coll*

before /bɪˈfɔː/ *adv* prije, ranije; već • *conj* prije nego; radije nego • *prep* prije; pred, ispred ~ **long** ubrzo, uskoro ~ **one's eyes** naočigled ~**hand** *adv* unaprijed; prethodno

beg /beg/ *vt*, *vi* 1 prositi, prosjačiti 2 (za)moliti *I* ~ **your pardon** oprostite! ~ **to differ** ne slagati se ~ **the question a.** izbjegavati srž problema, okolišati **b.** uzeti zdravo za gotovo ~ **off** izvući se, ispričati se ~**gar** *n* 1 prosjak 2 jadnik, siroman

began *v irreg* → **begin**

begin /bɪˈgɪn/ *vt*, *vi* *irreg* (za)početi **to** ~ **with** kao prvo, ponajprije ~**ner** *n* početnik ~**ning** *n* početak at the ~**ning of** na početku, početkom **in the** ~**ning** u početku

begun *v irreg* → **begin**

behalf /bɪˈhɑːf/ *n* korist, probitak **on/in** *US* ~ **of** u ime, u korist

behave /bɪˈheɪv/ *vi* 1 ponašati se, vladati se 2 (oneself) pristojno se ponašati **behaviour** (-vor *US*) /bɪˈheɪvɪə(r)/ *n* ponašanje, vladanje; ophođenje

behead /bɪˈhed/ *vt* odrubiti glavu

beheld *v irreg* → **behold**

behind /bɪˈhaɪnd/ *adv* 1 otraga, straga 2 u zakašnjenju/zaostatku ~ kasniti • *prep* iza **we are** ~ **them** zaostajemo za njima • *n coll* stražnjica

behold /bɪˈhəʊld/ *vt irreg arch*, *lit* vidjeti, ugledati **lo and** ~! gle! vidi!

beholden /bɪˈhəʊldən/ *adj* **be** ~ **to sb**

dugovati komu

beige /beɪʒ/ *n* bež (tkanina); drap, bež (boja)

belated /bɪ'leɪtɪd/ *adj* zakasnio

belch /beltʃ/ *vi,vt* 1 podrignuti se 2 kuljati, rigati

beleaguer /bɪ'li:gə(r)/ *vt* 1 opsjedati 2 *fig* dodijavati

belfry /'belfrɪ/ *n* zvonik

belie /bɪ'laɪ/ *vt form* kositi se s

belief /bɪ'li:f/ *n* (in) 1 vjera 2 povjerenje 3 uvjerenje **believe** /bɪ'li:v/ *vt,vi* 1 (in) vjerovati 2 misliti, smatrati **believer** *n* vjernik

belittle /bɪ'lɪtl/ *vt* umanjivati, omalovažavati

bell /bel/ *n* 1 zvono 2 čaška (cvijeta) **that rings a ~** zvuči poznato

belligerent /bɪ'lɪdʒərənt/ *adj* 1 ratoboran 2 zaraćen • *n* zaraćena strana

bellow /'beləʊ/ *vt,vi* 1 rikati 2 derati se, urlati

bellows /'beləʊz/ *n pl* mijeh

belly /'belɪ/ *n* 1 *coll* trbuh; želudac 2 *fig* utroba, trup **~ button** *coll* pupak • *vi,vt* (out) nabreknuti, napuhnuti (se)

belong /bɪ'lɒŋ/ *vi* (to) pripadati; spadati; biti član **~ings** *n pl* imovina

beloved /bɪ'lʌvɪd/ *adj* drag, ljubljen, voljen • *n* ljubljeni, ljubljena

below /bɪ'ləʊ/ *adv* dolje, ispod, niže **from ~** odozdo • *prep* ispod, pod

belt /belt/ *n* remen; pojas (+ *fig*) • *vt* 1 (up) opasati, pripasati (pojas) 2 istući 3 *GB sl* juriti 4 (out) *coll* glasno pjevati **~way** *US* obilaznica

bemused /bɪ'mju:zd/ *adj* zbunjen, smeten

bench /bentʃ/ *n* 1 klupa 2 sudac; suci; sud 3 poslanička klupa

bend /bend/ *vt,vi irreg* 1 saviti (se); napeti (luk) 2 (down) sagnuti se 3 (forward/over) nagnuti se 4 skretati 5 (to) popustiti pred **~one's mind** to usredotočiti se na • **over backwards** dati sve od sebe • *n* 1 zavoj 2 svijanje; svinutost **the ~s** *coll* kesonska bolest **round the ~** *coll* lud **bent** *adj* 1 svinut, zakrivljen 2 *sl* nepošten; podmitljiv; ukraden (roba); homoseksualan **be bent on doing sth** čvrsto odlučiti što o *n* naginjanje,

sklonost

beneath /bɪ'ni:θ/ *adv* dolje, niže • *prep* ispod, pod

benediction /ˌbenɪ'dɪkʃn/ *n* blagoslov

benefactor /'benɪfæktə(r)/ *n* dobročinitelj

beneficial /ˌbenɪ'fɪʃl/ *adj* koristan, blagotvoran

benefit /'benɪfɪt/ *n* 1 korist, prednost, dobrobit; pogodnost, povlastica 2 novčana potpora 3 dobrotvorna priredba **give sb the ~ of the doubt** vjerovati komu dok se ne dokaže suprotno • *vt,vi* 1 koristiti, biti od koristi komu 2 (from/by) imati koristi od

benevolent /bɪ'nevələnt/ *adj* (to) dobrohotan, blagonaklon

benign /bɪ'naɪn/ *adj* 1 dobrostiv 2 povoljan 3 *med* dobroćudan

bent *v irreg* → **bend**

bequest /bɪ'kwest/ *n form* ostavština

bereaved /bɪ'ri:vd/ *adj* ožalošćen, ucviljen

bereft /bɪ'reft/ *adj* (of) lišen čega

beret /'bereɪ/ *n* beretka

berk /bɜ:k/ *n GB sl* budala

berry /'berɪ/ *n* boba, bobica, jagoda, zrno

berserk /bə'sɜ:k/ *adj* **go ~** (with) podivljati, pomahnitati

berth /bɜ:θ/ *n* 1 pristanište; vez 2 ležaj **give sb/sth a wide ~** *coll* zaobilaziti koga/što u velikom luku

beseech /bɪ'si:tʃ/ *vt irreg form*, *lit* preklinjati

beset /bɪ'set/ *vt irreg* 1 mučiti, opsjedati, pritisnuti 2 napadati, opkoliti

beside /bɪ'saɪd/ *prep* 1 (po)kraj, pored, uz, mimo 2 u usporedbi s **be ~ one-self with** biti izvan sebe od **~ the point** nebitan **~s** *adv* 1 osim toga, uz to 2 nadalje, povrh toga o *prep* 1 osim, pored, uz 2 osim što

besiege /bɪ'si:dʒ/ *vt* 1 *mil* opkoliti, opsjedati 2 okružiti 3 (with) *fig* mučiti, salijetati

besought *v irreg* → **beseech**

best /best/ *adj sup* (→ **good**) najbolji, najveći **the ~ part of** najveći dio, većina **~ man** vjenčani kum **~ before/by** rok upotrebe do • *adv* najbolje, najviše • *n* najbolji, ono najbolje **do one's** ~ dati sve od sebe, učiniti najbolje **to the** ~ **of my knowledge** koliko mi je poznato **to the** ~ **of my ability** najbolje što mogu **at (the)** ~ u najboljem slučaju **at my/your/his** etc. ~ u najboljem raspoloženju/izdanju/formi • *vt coll* nadmašiti; pobijediti

bestow /bɪˈstəʊ/ *vt* (sth on/upon sb) *form* dati, podariti komu što

bet /bet/ *vt,vi irreg* (on sth; that) (o)kladiti se *I ~ you a fiver* kladimo se u pet funti *I ~* siguran sam *you ~!* sigurno! • *n* (on) oklada **lay/make/put a** ~ kladiti se ~**ter**, ~**tor** *n* kladitelj

betray /bɪˈtreɪ/ *vt* 1 izdati 2 odati, otkriti ~**al** *n* 1 izdaja 2 otkrivanje

better /ˈbetə(r)/ *adj comp* (→ **good**) bolji, prikladniji, veći **the** ~ **part of** veći dio • adv bolje, više **be** ~ **off** biti imućniji, bolje stajati *we'd be* ~ *off without them* bilo bi nam bolje bez njih *I should have known* ~ trebao sam biti pametniji **think** ~ **of (doing) sth** predomisliti se *you had* ~ *leave* bolje da odeš **so much the** ~ tim bolje • *n* ono što je bolje **my** ~**s** moji pretpostavljeni **get the** ~ **of** nadvladati, nadmudriti **for** ~ **or for worse** i u dobru i u zlu • *vt form* 1 poboljšati, popraviti, unaprijediti 2 nadmašiti

between /bɪˈtwiːn/ *prep* između, među *they had 10 pounds* ~ *them* zajedno su imali 10 funti • *adv* između toga **in** ~ između, u sredini

beverage /ˈbevərɪdʒ/ *n form* piće, napitak

bevy /ˈbevɪ/ *n* 1 društvo, skup (djevojaka) 2 jato 3 stado

beware /bɪˈweə(r)/ *vi,vt* paziti, čuvati se, biti na oprezu ~ **of the dog** oštar pas

bewilder /bɪˈwɪldə(r)/ *vt* zbuniti, smesti

beyond /bɪˈjɒnd/ *adv* 1 s one strane, preko, ondje 2 tamo dalje, iza • *prep* 1 preko, iznad, izvan (dosega), dalje od 2 s one strane, onkraj 3 poslije 4 osim ~ **doubt** bez sumnje ~ **recognition** neprepoznatljiv *it's* ~ *me* ne

mogu shvatiti • *n* ono nepoznato, drugi svijet **at/in the back of** ~ u zabiti, Bogu iza leđa

bias /ˈbaɪəs/ *n* 1 sklonost 2 pristranost, predrasuda **on the** ~ ukoso • *vt* (towards/against) 1 utjecati na 2 naginjati ukoso

bib /bɪb/ *n* 1 dječji podbradnik 2 gornji dio pregače

Bible /ˈbaɪbl/ *n* Biblija (+ *fig*)

bicarbonate of soda, bicarb *coll* /ˌbaɪˈkɑːbənət/ *n* soda bikarbona

bicker /ˈbɪkə(r)/ *vi* prepirati se, rječkati se

bicycle /ˈbaɪsɪkl/ *n* bicikl **ride (on) a** ~ voziti (se na) bicikl(u) **on one's** ~**/by** ~ biciklom • *vi* voziti se biciklom

bid /bɪd/ *vt,vi irreg* 1 (for) ponuditi na dražbi 2 (for) pokušati osvojiti (vlast), nastojati pridobiti 3 (for) natjecati se, nadmetati se 4 zapovjediti; reći, zamoliti 5 zaželjeti • *n* 1 ponuda 2 natječaj **make a** ~ for nastojati domoći se čega **in a** ~ **to** u nastojanju da

bidden *v irreg* → **bid**

bide /baɪd/ *vt* ~ **one's time** čekati povoljnu priliku

bifocals /ˌbaɪˈfəʊklz/ *n pl* bifokalne naočale

big /bɪg/ *adj* 1 velik, visok 2 debeo, krupan; odrastao 3 važan 4 ohol, hvalisav **talk** ~ praviti se važan **B~ Dipper a.** *US* Veliki medvjed **b.** veliki tobogan na tračnice ~ **shot** utjecajna osoba; velika zvjerka *coll*

bigot /ˈbɪgət/ *n* slijepi pobornik ~**ed** *adj* zadrt ~**ry** *n* zadrtost

bike /baɪk/ *n coll* bicikl

bile /baɪl/ *n* 1 žuč 2 *fig* gorčina, gnjev

bill (1) /bɪl/ *n* 1 račun 2 prijedlog zakona 3 *US* novčanica 4 plakat **foot the** ~ platiti račun **fill the** ~ udovoljavati zahtjevima ~**board** reklamni pano ~**fold** *US* lisnica • *vt* 1 poslati kome račun 2 (as) najaviti, oglasiti

bill (2) *n* kljun

billet /ˈbɪlɪt/ *n* konačište za vojnike (u privatnim kućama) • *vt* (on) ukonačiti, smjestiti

billion /ˈbɪlɪən/ *n* 1 *GB* bilijun 2 *US* milijarda

bimbo /'bɪmbəʊ/ *ns/* glupača

bin /bɪn/ *n* kutija, kanta **dust~** kanta za smeće **litter~** koš za smeće **~liner** *GB* vreća za smeće

bind /baɪnd/ *vt,vi irreg* **1** vezati (+ *fig*); zavezati, pričvrstiti, spojiti **2** (up) svezati (kosu), oviti (ranu), uvezati (knjigu) **3** (with) obrubiti **4** (up/together) vezati se, stvrdnuti se **5** (by) (ob)vezati **~ing** *n* uvez ○ *adj* (on) obvezujući • *n* veza, spoj

binge /bɪndʒ/ *n sl* pijančevanje, tulumarenje **eating** ~ prežderavanje

bingo /'bɪŋgəʊ/ *n* bingo (vrsta tombole) • *int* pun pogodak!

binoculars /bɪ'nɒkjʊləz/ *n pl* dalekozor,

biochemistry /,baɪəʊ'kemɪstrɪ/ *n* biokemija

biography /baɪ'ɒgrəfɪ/ *n* biografija, životopis

biology /baɪ'ɒlədʒɪ/ *n* biologija **biological** /,baɪə'lɒdʒɪkl/ *adj* biološki

bipartisan /,baɪpɑː'tɪˈzæn/ *adj* dvostranački

birch /bɜːtʃ/ *n* breza

bird /bɜːd/ *n* **1** ptica **2** *GB sl* djevojka **3** *coll* čovjek, tip **4** *sl* zatvor **a ~ in the hand is worth two in the bush** bolje vrabac u ruci nego golub na grani **kill two ~s with one stone** ubiti dvije muhe jednim udarcem **~s of a feather flock/stick together** svaka ptica svome jatu leti **give sb the ~** *sl* izviždati koga **~'s-eye view** ptičja perspektiva **~ watching** promatranje ptica u prirodi

biro /'baɪərəʊ/ *n GB TM* kemijska olovka

birth /bɜːθ/ *n* **1** rođenje; porod; stvaranje **2** podrijetlo **give ~ to** roditi, donijeti na svijet **~ certificate** krsni list, izvod iz matične knjige rođenih **~ control** kontracepcija **~day** rođendan

biscuit /'bɪskɪt/ *n* **1** *GB* keks **2** *US* pogačica

bisect /baɪ'sekt/ *vt* raspoloviti

bishop /'bɪʃəp/ *n* **1** biskup **2** (šah) lovac

bit (1) /bɪt/ *n* **1** komad(ić), djelić **2** zalogaj, gutljaj **~ by ~/a ~ at a time** malo-pomalo, postupno **every ~ as ... as** baš kao, isto kao **it's a ~ much/thick** to je malo previše **not a ~** nimalo **fall/go to ~s** raspasti se u komadiće **do one's ~** *coll* uraditi svoj dio (posla)

bit (2) *n* **1** žvale **2** *comp* bit

bit (3) *v irreg* → **bite**

bitch /bɪtʃ/ *n* **1** kuja; ženka **2** *derog* kučka, kurva a **~ of a** problem *sl* gadan problem **~y** *adj* pakostan • *vi sl* (about) **1** gunđati **2** biti pakostan

bite /baɪt/ *vt,vi irreg* **1** (za)gristi **2** ubosti, ugristi **3** peći **4** nagrizati **5** štipati **once bitten twice shy** tko se jednom opeče i na hladno puše **~ sb's head off** *coll* izderati se na koga **~ the dust** *coll* poginuti; propasti • *n* **1** ugriz, zagriz; ubod **2** griz, zalogaj **3** oštrina, britkost, jetkost, prodornost, oštroumnost

bitten *v irreg* → **bite**

bitter /'bɪtə(r)/ *adj* gorak, opor, oštar (+ *fig*) • *n* **1** gorčina **2** *GB* gorko pivo

blab /blæb/ *vi,vi coll* (out) izlanuti

black /blæk/ *adj* **1** crn; mračan, taman; prljav **2** , tužan **3** opasan, zao **4** mrk, mrzovoljast **~ and blue** pun modrica **~berry** kupina **~bird** kos **~board** školska ploča **~currant** crni ribizl **~en** *vt,vi* **1** zacrniti **2** ocrniti **~ eye** modrica; šljiva *coll* **~head** sujedica **~mail** *n* ucjena ○ *vt* (sb into doing sth) ucjenjivati **~market** crna burza; šverc *coll* **~out** *n* **a.** zamračenje **b.** kratkotrajna nesvjestica **~ pudding** krvavica **~smith** kovač, potkivač **~** **1** crna boja **2** crnina **3** crnac **in the ~** *comm* s pozitivnim saldom; u plusu *coll* • *vt* **1** obojiti u crno **2** laštiti

bladder /'blædə(r)/ *n* (mokraćni) mjehur

blade /bleɪd/ *n* **1** oštrica **2** (razor ~) britvica; žilet *coll* **3** lopatica vesla, krilo propelera **4** vlat

blame /bleɪm/ *vt* (sb for sth/sth on sb) **1** okriviti **2** predbaciti, zamjerati • *n* krivnja, odgovornost **bear/take the ~** (for sth) snositi odgovornost, preuzeti krivicu **put/lay the ~ on sb** (for sth) pripisati/svaliti krivicu na

bland /blænd/ *adj* **1** bezukusan, bljutav

2 učtiv 3 blag 4 *fig* bezličan

blank /blæŋk/ *adj* 1 prazan, neispisan, neispunjen 2 bezizražajan, nezainteresiran ~ **cartridge** manevarski metak ~ **cheque** bjanko ček • *n* 1 praznina 2 neispunjen obrazac 3 rupa u sjećanju 4 manevarski metak

blanket /'blæŋkɪt/ *n* 1 pokrivač 2 *fig* zavjesa, pokrivač **wet** ~ *coll* osoba koja kvari raspoloženje

blare /bleə(r)/ *vi,vt* (out) trubiti, treštati

blasé /'blaːzeɪ/ *adj* blaziran

blast /blæːst/ *n* 1 udar, nalet 2 eksplozija (at) **full** ~ punom parom • *vt* 1 minirati, dići u zrak; bombardirati 2 (away at) gađati, pucati na 3 ofuriti (mraz), spaliti (grom), uništiti ~**-off** *n* polijetanje, lansiranje (rakete)

blatant /'bleɪtnt/ *adj* bezočan

blaze /bleɪz/ *n* 1 plamen 2 požar 3 sjaj 4 izljev, provala 5 rafalna pucnjava • *vi,vt* 1 (away) plamtjeti, buktjeti (+ *fig*) 2 sjati, svijetliti ~ **a trail a.** markirati put **b.** *fig* prokrčiti/utrti put

blazer /'bleɪzə(r)/ *n* športska jakna; kaputić

bleach /bliːtʃ/ *vt,vi* 1 (iz)bijeliti (platno) 2 izbijeliti, posvijetliti • *n* bjelilo

bleak /bliːk/ *adj* 1 hladan, tmuran 2 ogolio, pust 3 sumoran ~ **prospects** loši izgledi

bleary-eyed /ˌblɪərɪ'aɪd/ *adj* mutnih očiju

bleat /bliːt/ *vi* blejati, meketati

bled *v irreg* → **bleed**

bleed /bliːd/ *vi,vt irreg* 1 krvariti 2 *coll* opelješiti 3 puštati krv

blemish /'blemɪʃ/ *vt* nagrditi; okaljati • *n* 1 greška, mrlja, mana, nedostatak 2 ljaga, sramota

blend /blend/ *vt,vi* 1 miješati 2 (with) slagati se 3 (in with) uklapati se 4 (into) stapati se ~**er** *n* mikser • *n* 1 mješavina 2 spoj, kombinacija

blent *v irreg* → **blend**

bless /bles/ *vt irreg* blagosloviti; posvetiti ~ **you!** nazdravlje! (pri kihanju) ~ **me/(God)** ~ **my soul!** za Boga miloga! ~**ed** /blest/ *adj* 1 blagoslovljen, posvećen 2 sretan, blažen **the B~ed Virgin** Blažena Djevica ~**ing** *n* (on/upon) 1

blagoslov (+ *fig*) 2 sreća, blagodat ~**ing in disguise** sreća u nesreći **count one's** ~**ings** cijeniti ono što čovjek ima

blest *v irreg* → **bless**

blew *v irreg* → **blow**

blight /blaɪt/ *n* 1 snijet 2 poguban utjecaj 3 propast, uništenje • *vt* uništiti, pokvariti **B~y** /'blaɪtɪ/ *n mil sl* Engleska, dom, zavičaj

blimey /'blaɪmɪ/ *int GB sl* ti boga! ti bokca! bogati!

blind (1) /blaɪnd/ *adj* slijep; zaslijepljen (+ *fig*) **go** ~ oslijepiti **turn a** ~ **eye to** zažmiriti na jedno oko, progledati kroz prste ~ **corner** mrtvi kut ~ **date** sastanak na neviđeno ~**fold** *n* povez preko očiju ∘ *vt* staviti povez preko očiju, zavezati oči ∘ *adv* zavezanih očiju ~ **man's buff** igra slijepog miša ~ **spot a.** slijepa točka u oku **b.** mrtvi kut, nepregledan dio ceste **c.** rupa u znanju • *vt* oslijepiti (+ *fig*)

blind (2) *n* 1 zavjesa; roleta 2 *fig* paravan 3 *US* lovačka promatračnica

blink /blɪŋk/ *vi,vt* 1 treptati, žmirkati 2 svjetlucati 3 *US* dati žmigavac • *n* treptaj, mig ~**ers** *n pl* 1 *GB* konjski naočnjaci 2 *US* žmigavci

bliss /blɪs/ *n* blaženstvo, radost, sreća

blister /'blɪstə(r)/ *n* žulj, plik; mjehurić • *vt,vi* dobiti žuljeve; osuti se mjehurićima

blithe /blaɪð/ *adj lit* radostan

blitz /blɪts/ *n* iznenadni zračni napad, bombardiranje • *vt* napasti iz zraka, bombardirati

blizzard /'blɪzəd/ *n* mećava, snježna oluja

bloated /'bləʊtɪd/ *adj* natečen, podbuo, napuhan (+ *fig*)

blob /blɒb/ *n* 1 kapljica 2 *fig* mrvica, točkica

bloc /blɒk/ *n* blok *fig*

block /blɒk/ *n* 1 veliki komad, gromada 2 zgrada ~ **of flats** stambena zgrada 3 *US* blok zgrada 4 blokada, smetnja, zapreka, začepljenje 5 panj, klada **road~** barikada, zapreka na cesti • *adj* ~**buster** *coll* veliki hit ~ **letters/capitals** velika tiskana slova

~ **vote** predstavnički glas • *vt* 1 (up/off) zakrčiti, zapriječiti, začepiti 2 spriječiti, ometati ~**ade** /blʊˈkeɪd/ *n* blokada ○ *vt* blokirati ~**age** /ˈblʊkɪdʒ/ *n* blokada, smetnja, zapreka

bloke /bləʊk/ *n GB coll* čovjek, tip, frajer

blond /blɒnd/ *adj, n* plavokos (muškarac) ~**e** *adj, n* plavokos (žena); plavuša

blood /blʌd/ *n* 1 krv 2 krvno srodstvo, rod 3 *mod* krvni 4 narav in **cold** ~ hladnokrvno ~**bath** krvoproliće, pokolj ~ **group/type** krvna grupa ~**shed** krvoproliće ~**shot** *adj* podliven krvlju, zakrvavljen ~**stream** krvotok ~**thirsty** krvožedan ~**y** *adj* 1 krvav 2 *GB coll tab* proklet

bloom /bluːm/ *n* cvat, cvijet (+ *fig*) **in (full)** ~ u (punom) cvatu • *vi* cvjetati, cvasti (+ *fig*)

bloomer /ˈbluːmə(r)/ *n GB sl* glupa pogreška, kiks *sl*

blossom /ˈblɒsəm/ *n* cvijet (voćke) **in** ~ u cvatu • *vi* 1 cvasti, (pro)cvijetati 2 (out into) razviti se u

blot /blɒt/ *n* 1 mrlja 2 *fig* ljaga • *vt* 1 umrljati, zapackati 2 (sth out) prekriti, sakriti ~**ting paper** bugačica

blotchy /ˈblɒtʃɪ/ *adj* mrljav; pjegav

blouse /blaʊz/ *n* bluza

blow /bləʊ/ *vi,vt irreg* puhati ~ **one's nose** ispuhati nos ~ **one's top/stack** razljutiti se ~ **it** uprskati • *n* udarac **at one/a single** ~ jednim udarcem **come to** ~**s** potući se ~**dry** *vt* fenirati (kosu) ○ *n* 1 fen frizura 2 *US sl* kokain ~ **job** *sl tab* fellatio; pušenje *tab sl* ~**lamp/torch** *US* lemilica, let lampa ~ **out a.** ugasiti (se) **b.** pregorjeti **c.** puknuti ~ **over a.** proći **b.** pasti u zaborav ~ **up a.** eksplodirati, odletjeti u zrak **b.** rasrditi se **c.** napuhati (+ *fig*) **d.** uvećati (fotografiju)

blown *v irreg* → **blow**

bludgeon /ˈblʌdʒn/ *n* toljaga

blue /bluː/ *adj* 1 plav 2 *coll* tužan, potišten 3 nepristojan **once in a** ~ **moon** jednom u sto godina ~**bottle** muha zunzara ~**collar** *adj* radnički ~ **film** porno film ~**print** nacrt, plan • *n* 1 plava boja 2 ~**s** *coll* tuga, potištenost **out of the** ~ kao grom iz vedra neba

bluff (1) /blʌf/ *vt,vi* blefirati • *n* blef, varka; lažna prijetnja **call sb's** ~ natjerati koga da otkrije karte

bluff (2) *adj* grub ali srdačan

bluff (3) *n* strma stjenovita obala

blunder /ˈblʌndə(r)/ *n* glupa pogreška; kik *sl* • *vi,vt* 1 zabrljati 2 posrtati, bauljati

blunt /blʌnt/ *adj* 1 tup 2 grub, bezobziran; netaktičan • *vt* otupiti

blur /blɜː(r)/ *n* zamagljenost, nejasni obrisi, mrlja • *vt,vi* zamrljati; zamagliti, učiniti nejasnim

blurb /blɜːb/ *n* kratak sadržaj knjige na ovitku

blurt /blɜːt/ *vt* (out) izbrbljati, izlanuti

blush /blʌʃ/ *vi* 1 pocrvenjeti od stida 2 stidjeti se • *n* crvenilo ~**er** *n* rumenilo za lice

blustery /ˈblʌstərɪ/ *adj* vjetrovit, olujan

boar /bɔː(r)/ *n* 1 nerast 2 vepar

board /bɔːd/ *n* 1 daska; drvena ploča 2 odbor, komisija; ministarstvo ~ **and lodging/bed and** ~ stan i hrana **full/half** ~ pansion/polupansion ~ **of directors** upravni odbor ~**er** *n* 1 gost u pansionu 2 učenik u internatu ~**ing card** ukrcajna karta ~**inghouse** pansion ~**ing school** internat ~ **room** dvorana za sastanke **go/get on** ~ ukrcati se na **take on** ~ prihvatiti • *vt,vi* 1 (up) prekriti daskama 2 ukrcati se na 3 primiti na stan i hranu 4 (with/at) stanovati (hraniti se) kod

boast /bəʊst/ *vt,vi* 1 hvali(sa)ti se, ponositi se

boat /bəʊt/ *n* 1 čamac 2 *coll* brod 3 zdjelica (za umak) ~**swain** /ˈbəʊsn/ *n* voda palube, nostromo

bob (1) /bɒb/ *vi* 1 poskakivati, ljuljati se 2 (up) iskrsnuti 3 nakloniti se • *n* 1 poskakivanje, ljuljanje 2 naklon

bob (2) *vt* podšišati kosu

bob (3) /bɒb/ *n GB coll arch* šiling

bobbin /ˈbɒbɪn/ *n* kalem

bobby /ˈbɒbɪ/ *n GB coll* policajac

bobsleigh, bobsled /ˈbɒbsleɪ, ˈbɒbsled/ *n sport* bob

bode /bəud/ *vt,vi lit* ~ **well/ill** (for) slutiti na dobro/zlo

bodice /'bɒdɪs/ *n* 1 prsni dio haljine 2 *arch* steznik

body /'bɒdɪ/ *n* 1 tijelo 2 leš, truplo 3 trup 4 glavni/središnji dio; 5 količina; masa 6 tijelo, organ 7 (~**work**) karoserija 8 jačina ~ **count** broj mrtvih/poginulih ~**guard** tjelohranitelj; straža **bodily** /'bɒdɪlɪ/ *adj* tjelesni, fizički ○ *adv* osobno

bog /bɒg/ *n* 1 močvara 2 *GB sl* zahod • *vt,vi* **get ~ged down** zaglibiti (+ *fig*)

boggle /bɒgl/ *vi* (at) 1 oklijevati, kolebati se 2 zabezeknuti se

bogus /'bəugəs/ *adj* lažan, izmišljen, patvoren

boil (1) /bɔɪl/ *vi,vt* 1 kipjeti, vreti 2 *fig* planuti ~ **down to** svoditi se na ~ **over** prekipjeti ~**er** *n* parni kotao ~**er suit** *GB* radnički kombinezon ~**ing point** vrelište • *n* **be on the ~** ključati, vreti **bring sth to the ~** pustiti da zakipi **come to the ~** zakipjeti

boil (2) *n* gnojni čir

boisterous /'bɔɪstərəs/ *adj* bučan, neobuzdan

bold /bəuld/ *adj* 1 hrabar 2 drzak 3 jasan, izrazit 4 mastan (slova) ~**face** masno tiskana slova

bollard /'bɒləd/ *n* 1 *GB* stupić uz cestu 2 stup za vezanje broda

bollocks /'bɒləks/ *n pl GB tab sl* jaja, muda ~! sranje!

boloney /bə'ləunɪ/ *n US sl* glupost, besmislica

bolster /'bəulstə(r)/ *n* dugačak jastuk • *vt* (up) poduprijeti, pojačati, povećati

bolt /bəult/ *n* 1 vijak 2 zasun, kračun 3 munja, grom 4 bala (tkanine), smotak (tapete) • *vt,vi* 1 pojuriti, pobjeći; uplašiti se, poskočiti 2 (down) naglo gutati 3 zakračunati • *adv* ~ **upright** sasvim uspravno

bomb /bɒm/ *n* bomba • *vt,vi* 1 bombardirati (iz aviona) 2 *US coll* pasti na ispitu; doživjeti neuspjeh ~**er** *n* bombarder ~**shell** 1 šok, neugodno iznenađenje 2 ljepotica; komad *coll* ~**ard** /bɒm'bɑ:d/ *vt* (with) 1 tući top-

ničkom paljbom 2 *fig* obasipati

bond /bɒnd/ *n* 1 veza, spona, spoj; vez 2 ugovor, obveza, jamstvo 3 obveznica ~**age** /'bɒndɪdʒ/ *n* 1 *lit* ropstvo 2 sadomazohizam

bone /bəun/ *n* kost ~ **of contention** kamen smutnje, jabuka razdora **have a ~ to pick with sb** imati s kime što raščistiti **make no ~s about** (doing) **sth** ne ustezati se ~**dry** *adj* cоli suh kao barut ~**idle** *adj* lijen kao trut **bony** /'bəunɪ/ *adj* 1 mršav, suhonjav 2 pun kostiju 3 koščat • *vt* 1 izvaditi kosti 2 (up on sth) *coll* naštrebati

bonfire /'bɒnfaɪə(r)/ *n* krijes

bonk /bɒŋk/ *vt,vi* 1 lupiti; kresnuti *coll* 2 ševiti (se)

bonkers /bɒŋkəz/ *adj GB sl* lud

bonnet /'bɒnɪt/ *n* 1 dječja kapica 2 poklopac motora automobila; hauba *coll*

bonus /'bəunəs/ *n* 1 doplatak, dodatak 2 *coll* prednost; plus *coll*

boo /bu:/ *int* ua! • *vi,vt* zviždati, izviždati

booby trap /'bu:bɪtræp/ *n* mina iznenađenja • *vt* minirati

book /buk/ *n* 1 knjiga 2 blok 3 tekst, libreto **the B~** Biblija **by the ~** po pravilima ~**keeping** računovodstvo ~**let** *n* brošura ~**maker/bookie** *coll* kladioničar ~**shop/store** *US* knjižara • *vt,vi* 1 (up) rezervirati 2 angažirati ~**ing** *n* rezervacija

boom /bu:m/ *vt,vi* 1 (out) tutnjiti, grmjeti 2 *fig* cvjetati, napredovati • *n* 1 tutnjava, grmljavina 2 nagli razvoj, porast

boon /bu:n/ *n form* velika korist

boost /bu:st/ *vt* 1 dignuti, gurnuti uvis 2 povećati, pojačati, podići 3 *US coll* reklamirati, poboljšati prodaju • *n* 1 podizanje 2 poticaj 3 porast

boot /bu:t/ *n* 1 čizma, visoka cipela 2 *GB* prtljažnik **get/give the ~** dobiti/dati nogu *coll* **to ~** uz to • *vt* 1 udariti (nogom) 2 (out) otpustiti, najuriti

booth /bu:ð/ *n* 1 kabina 2 odjeljak

bootleg /'bu:tleg/ *vt,vi* krijumčariti alkoholna pića • *adj* ~ **records** piratske ploče

booty /'bu:tɪ/ n (ratni) plijen

booze /bu:z/ vi sl lokati coll • n sl cuga sl ~r n sl 1 pijanac 2 GB birc coll

border /'bɔ:də(r)/ n 1 rub 2 gredica 3 granica ~**land** granično područje (+ fig) ~**line** granica (+ fig) ~**line case** fig granični slučaj • vt,vi 1 omeđiti 2 (with) porubiti 3 (on/upon/at) graničiti (+ fig)

bore (1) v irreg → **bear**

bore (2) /bɔ:(r)/ n 1 dosadnjaković 2 gnjavaža ~**dom** n dosada • vt dosađivati I'm ~d with it dosta mi je toga **boring** adj dosadan

bore (3) vt,vi (iz)bušiti • n 1 (~**hole**) bušotina, rupa 2 promjer cijevi, kalibar

born /bɔ:n/ v irreg **bear** • adj rođen ~ **again** preporođen

borne /bɔ:n/ v irreg → **bear** water-**diseases** bolesti koje se prenose vodom it was ~ **in on us** shvatili smo, postalo nam je jasno

borough /'bʌrə/ n gradska općina

borrow /'bɒrəʊ/ vt 1 (from) posuditi od koga 2 preuzeti ~**ing** n gram posuđenica

bosom /'bʊzəm/ n 1 prsa, njedra, grudi 2 fig srce, duša ~ **friend** bliski prijatelj

boss /bɒs/ n coll gazda, šef ~**y** adj koji voli šefovati • vt (about/around) zapovijedati, šefovati

bosun /'bəʊsn/ n → **boatswain**

botany /'bɒtənɪ/ n botanika

botch /bɒtʃ/ vt (up) pokvariti, zabrljati, sprtljati

both /bəʊθ/ adj, adv, pron oba, obadva, obje, obadvije, oboje ~ ... **and** i ... i

bother /'bɒðə(r)/ vt,vi 1 gnjaviti, smetati, uznemiravati 2 (about/with) brinuti se, truditi se, uzbuđivati se • n 1 briga, gnjavaža, muka 2 (**a spot of** ~) GB coll tučnjava, gužva, nered ~**some** adj dosadan, neugodan

bottle /'bɒtl/ n 1 boca, flaša 2 GB sl hrabrost; petlja coll **hot-water** ~ termofor ~ **bank** GB kontejner za stakleni otpad ~**feed** vt irreg (→ **feed**) hraniti na bočicu ~**neck** fig usko grlo ~**opener** otvarač za boce • vt puniti

boce ~ **sth up** potiskivati

bottom /'bɒtəm/ n 1 dno; podloga; podnožje 2 stražnji dio; kraj 3 stražnjica ~ **up** naopačke, naglavce ~**s up!** coll naiskap! na eks! **pyjama** ~**s** pl donji dio pidžame • adj donji, najniži, posljednji **the** ~ **line a.** konačna aktiva **b.** osnovna stvar, bit • vi (out) comm pasti

bough /baʊ/ n grana

bought v irreg → **buy**

boulder /'bəʊldə(r)/ n veliki kamen, gromada

boulevard /'bu:ləva:d/ n bulevar

bounce /baʊns/ vi,vt (od)skočiti, poskakivati, odbi(ja)ti se ~ **back** oporaviti se **the check** ~**d** ček nije imao pokrića ~**r** n coll izbacivač, redar • n 1 odskok 2 coll živost, energija

bound (1) v irreg → **bind**

bound (2) /baʊnd/ adj 1 obvezan 2 uvezan (knjiga) 3 (up in) zaokupljen/ zauzet čime **it's** ~ **to happen** to će se sigurno dogoditi

bound (3) n skok **by/in leaps and** ~**s** neočekivano brzo • vi skakati, poskakivati; odskočiti, odbiti se

bound (4) adj (for) na putu za a London-bound train vlak za London

boundary /'baʊndrɪ/ n granica (+ fig)

bounds /baʊndz/ n pl fig granice **know no** ~ nemati/ne poznati granice **put a place out of** ~ **to** zabraniti pristup komu/čemu

bouquet /bʊ'keɪ/ n 1 kita cvijeća, buket 2 miris vina, buké

bourgeois /'bʊəʒwa:/ adj buržujski, (malo)građanski • n buržuj

bout /baʊt/ n 1 kratko razdoblje 2 napadaj (bolesti) 3 boks meč

boutique /bu:'ti:k/ n butik

bovine /'bəʊvaɪn/ adj kravlji

bow (1) /baʊ/ vi,vt 1 (down to/before) klanjati se 2 pognuti 3 (down with) saviti se 4 (down to) pokoriti se, popustiti 5 (out of) povući se • n naklon **take a** ~ pokloniti se pred publikom

bow (2) /bəʊ/ n 1 luk 2 gudalo 3 čvor ~**legged** adj krivonog ~ **tie** leptirkravata

bow(s) (3) /baʊ(s)/ n pramac

bowel /'baʊəl/ *n* 1 crijevo 2 *pl* utroba (+ *fig*)

bowl (1) /bəʊl/ *n* 1 zdjela 2 WC školjka 3 stadion

bowl (2) /bəʊl/ *n* 1 kugla 2 *pl* kuglanje, boćanje • *vi,vt* 1 kuglati, baciti kuglu/lopticu 2 kotrljati se 3 (along) juriti ~ **over** a. oboriti, srušiti b. ugodno iznenaditi ~**er** *n* 1 kuglaš 2 bacač (kriket) 3 (~ **hat**) *GB* policilindar ~**ing** *n* kuglanje ~**ing alley** kuglana ~**ing green** teren za kuglanje

box (1) /bɒks/ *n* 1 kutija; kovčeg; sanduk 2 loža 3 *sl* televizija (**tele**)**phone** ~ telefonska govornica ~ **office bea** ~ **office success/hit** doživjeti financijski uspjeh blagajna (kina) • *vt* 1 staviti u kutiju 2 (in/up) zatvoriti, nagurati, zbiti

box (2) *vt,vi* boksati ~ **sb's ears** *coll* dati kome zaušnicu ~**ing** *n* boks

box (3) *n* šimšir

Boxing Day /'bɒksɪŋ deɪ/ *n* drugi dan Božića, Stjepanje

boy /bɔɪ/ *n* dječak, dečko, mladić ~**friend** dečko ~**ish** *adj* dječački • *int US coll* Bože!

boycott /'bɔɪkɒt/ *vt* bojkotirati • *n* bojkot

bra /brɑː/ *n* grudnjak

brace /breɪs/ *n* 1 spona; potporanj; remen 2 *pl GB* naramenice 3 ~**s** aparat za zube 4 vitičasta zagrada • *vt,vi* 1 poduprijeti, spojiti, učvrstiti, napeti 2 (oneself for) pripremiti se za **bracing** *adj* okrepljujući

bracelet /'breɪslɪt/ *n* narukvica

bracken /'brækn/ *n* paprat

bracket /'brækɪt/ *n* 1 zagrada 2 kategorija, skupina 3 nosač, potporanj • *vt* 1 staviti u zagradu 2 svrstati zajedno

brag /bræg/ *vi* hvalisati se

braid /breɪd/ *n* 1 ukrasna vrpca, obrub 2 *US* pletenica • *vt* (is)plesti; obrubiti

brain /breɪn/ *n* 1 mozak 2 *mod* moždani 3 (+ *pl*) glava, pamet, razum, mozak **beat/rack one's** ~**(s)** (about sth) razbijati glavu zbog čega **have sth on the** ~ misliti samo na ~**child** *coll* ideja, zamisao, umotvo-

rina ~ **drain** odljev mozgova ~**wash** *vt* ispirati mozak ~**wave** *GB coll* iznenadna sjajna ideja ~**y** *adj* pametan, bistar

braise /breɪz/ *vt* pirjati

brake (1) /breɪk/ *n* kočnica • *vt,vi* (za)kočiti

brake (2) *n* paprat; šipražje

bramble /'bræmbl/ *n* kupina (grm)

bran /bræn/ *n* mekinje, posije *pl*

branch /brɑːntʃ/ *n* 1 grana 2 rukavac; odvojak 3 (~ **office**) podružnica • *vi* 1 (out) (raz)granati se, rašljati se 2 (off from) odvajati se 3 (out into) razgranati (se)

brand /brænd/ *n* 1 *comm* zaštitni znak, marka; vrsta (robe) 2 žig 3 *lit* ugarak • *vt* 1 obilježiti žigom 2 *fig* ostaviti trag, usjeći se (u pamćenje) 3 javno optužiti, ocrniti ~**-new** potpuno nov, nov novcat

brandish /'brændɪʃ/ *vt* mahati, vitlati

brandy /'brændɪ/ *n* rakija, vinjak, konjak

brash /bræʃ/ *adj* 1 bezobziran, drzak 2 nagao; odvažan 3 upadljiv

brass /brɑːs/ *n* 1 mjed, mesing 2 (**the** ~) duhački instrumenti 3 mjedena pločica 4 *coll* drskost, odvažnost 5 *GB sl* lova *coll* **top** ~ visoki časnici ~ **band** limena glazba **get down to** ~ **tacks** *coll* prijeći na stvar

brassiere /'bræsɪə(r)/ *n GB form, US* → **bra**

brat /bræt/ *n derog* derište

bravado /brə'vɑːdəʊ/ *n* razmetanje hrabrošću, nepotrebno izlaganje opasnosti

brave /breɪv/ *adj* hrabar • *vt* hrabro se suprotstaviti, prkositi (komu/čemu) • *n* indijanski ratnik ~**ry** *n* hrabrost, junaštvo, srčanost

brawl /brɔːl/ *n* galama, svađa, tučnjava

brawn /brɔːn/ *n* 1 mišići; snaga, mišićavost 2 *GB* hladetina

bray /breɪ/ *vi* 1 njakati, revati 2 grohotom se smijati

brazen /'breɪzn/ *adj* 1 besraman, bezočan 2 mjeden; metalan (zvuk) • *vt* ~ **it out** praviti se kao da ništa nije bilo

brazier /'breɪzɪə(r)/ *n* žeravnik

breach /bri:tʃ/ *n* **1** prekid, raskid, kršenje, narušavanje **2** pukotina, rupa **3** razilaženje, razdor **~ of contract** kršenje ugovora **~ of the peace** remećenje javnog reda i mira **in ~ of u** suprotnosti s • *vt* **1** prodrijeti, probiti **2** prekršiti, narušiti, povrijediti

bread /bred/ *n* **1** kruh **2** *sl* novac; lova *coll* **~crumbs** *pl* mrvice **on the ~line** jako siromašan **~winner** uzdržavatelj obitelji

breadth /'bretθ/ *n* širina (+ *fig*) **~ways/~wise** *adj, adv* po širini, u širinu

break /breɪk/ *vi,vt* *irreg* **1** slomiti, razbiti, prekinuti **2** oboriti (rekord) **3** prekršiti, raskinuti **4** ukrotiti, dresirati **~ away** (from) a. otrgnuti se, pobjeći b. napustiti, odvojiti se, odcijepiti se **~ down** a. srušiti; skršiti, slomiti, uništiti b. pokvariti se (stroj) c. propasti, izjaloviti se d. slomiti se (od boli, tuge) e. razgraditi, rastvoriti, raščlaniti **~down** *n* a. kvar; prekid b. neuspjeh c. slom živca d. raščlamba, analiza **~er** *n* veliki val **~ even** pokriti troškove, biti na nuli **~ free** osloboditi se **~ in** provaliti, upasti **~in** *n* provala, upad **~ing and entering** *leg* provala **~ into** a. provaliti b. prasnuti (u smijeh), dati se u **~ loose** osloboditi se, oteti se **~ off** a.prekinuti b. odlomiti (se) **~ open** otvoriti **~ out** izbiti **~ out of** pobjeći iz **~ out in** osuti se čime; planuti **~ through** a. probiti se b. ostvariti napredak, svladati poteškoće **~through** *n* a. značajan napredak, pomak b. *mil* proboj **~ up** a. razbiti (se) b. rastaviti (se) c. prekinuti **~up** *n* raspad, razlaz, prestanak • *n* **1** kidanje, lom **2** prekid, prijelom **3** raskid **4** pukotina **5** odmor, stanka **6** (dobra) prilika **7** bijeg **give me a ~** a. pusti me na miru b. drugom ti se **~age** /'breɪkɪdʒ/ *n* **1** lom; prekid **2** **~s** *comm* šteta (od loma)

breakfast /'brekfəst/ *n* doručak • *vi* (on) doručkovati

breakwater /'breɪkwɔːtə(r)/ *n* gat, lukobran

breast /brest/ *n* dojka; grudi, prsa *pl* **make a clean ~ of** sve priznati **~feed** *vi,vt* *irreg* (→ feed) dojiti (na prsa) **the ~stroke** *n* prsno plivanje

breath /breθ/ *n* **1** dah; udisaj, izdisaj **2** dašak **3** tračak, nagovještaj **4** čas, tren **bad ~** zadah iz usta **out of/short of ~** bez daha, zadihan **take a deep ~** duboko udahnuti **take sb's ~ away** iznenaditi, zadiviti koga **~less** *adj* **1** bez daha, zadihan **2** napet, pun iščekivanja **3** bez daška vjetra, sparan **~taking** *adj* zapanjujući **~ test** *GB* alkotest

breathalyser/breathalizer *US* /'breθəlaɪzə(r)/ *n coll* alkotest; balon *coll*

breathe /bri:ð/ *vi,vt* **1** disati **2** piriti (vjetar) **3** tiho govoriti, šaputati **~ in** udahnuti **~ into** *fig* udahnuti **~ out** izdahnuti **~ a sigh of relief** odahnuti **don't ~ a word of it** nikom ni riječi **~r** *n* predah

bred *v irreg* → **breed**

breed /bri:d/ *vi,vt* *irreg* **1** razmnožavati se, kotiti se **2** uzgajati **3** izazvati, prouzročiti, rađati **4** odgojiti **~er** *n* uzgajivač **~ing** *n* **1** razmnožavanje **2** uzgajanje, uzgoj **3** odgoj, kultura • *n* pasmina, rod, vrsta

breeze /bri:z/ *n* **1** lahor, povjetarac **breezy** *adj* **1** vjetrovit, svjež **2** bezbrižan, vedar

brethren /'breðrən/ *n pl* braća

brevity /'brevəti/ *n form* **1** kratkoća **2** jezgrovitost, sažetost

brew /bru:/ *vt,vi* **1** variti (pivo) **2** skuhati (čaj/kavu) **3** *fig* zakuhati **4** spremati se (nevrijeme) **~ery** /'bru:əri/ *n* pivovara • *n* piće, napitak

bribe /braɪb/ *vt* podmititi, potkupiti • *n* mito **~ry** *n* podmićivanje

bric-a-brac /'brɪk ə bræk/ *n* drangulije, tričarije *pl*; starudija

brick /brɪk/ *n* **1** cigla, opeka **2** četvrtast predmet **3** **~s** dječje kocke **~layer** *n* zidar

bride /braɪd/ *n* mladenka **bridal** *adj* svadbeni **~groom** *n* mladoženja **~smaid** *n* djeveruša

bridge /brɪdʒ/ *n* most (+ *fig*) • *vt* premostiti (+ *fig*)

bridle /'braɪdl/ n uzda • vt,vi zauzdati, obuzdati (+ fig)

brief /briːf/ adj 1 kratak 2 jezgrovit, sažet in ~ ukratko ~**case** aktovka ~**ly** adv nakratko ~**s** n pl gaćice • n 1 sažetak sudskog postupka za odvjetnika 2 GB upute, instrukcije **hold no** ~ **for** ne podržavati (koga/što) • vt (sb on sth) izvijestiti, dati upute ~**ing** n davanje uputa, upoznavanje sa činjenicama press/news ~**ing** konferencija za tisak

brigade /brɪ'geɪd/ n mil brigada **the fire** ~ vatrogasci **brigadier** /,brɪ-gə'dɪə(r)/ n brigadir

bright /braɪt/ adj 1 svijetao, sjajan 2 jarki 3 radostan, vedar 4 bistar, pametan ~**en** vt,vi (up) osvijetliti (se), razvedriti (se)

brilliant /'brɪlɪənt/ adj 1 sjajan, blistav 2 briljantan, izvrstan • n briljant

brim /brɪm/ n 1 rub 2 obod • vi 1 (with) biti vrhom pun (čega) 2 (over) prelijevati se

brine /braɪn/ n 1 rasol 2 (the ~) lit more

bring /brɪŋ/ vt irreg 1 donijeti; dovesti 2 izazvati, prouzročiti, proizvesti 3 podići (tužbu) ~ **sth to an end/a close/a stop** okončati ~ **sb/oneself to do sth** navesti, nagovoriti, natjerati (se) da ~ **about** izvršiti, izazvati, prouzročiti, proizvesti, postići ~ **down** a. oboriti, srušiti; spustiti b. smanjiti, sniziti ~ **forward** a. iznijeti, predložiti, pokazati b. pomaknuti ranije ~ **in** a. unijeti; privesti b. predložiti nacrt zakona c. donositi zaradu d. donijeti ~ **off** uspješno izvesti, ostvariti ~ **on** a. dovesti do b. poboljšati, pospješiti na vidjelo; istaknuti, naglasiti ~ **over** → ~ **round** (a) ~ **round/around** a. pridobiti b. dozvati k svijesti ~ **to** → ~ **round** (b) ~ **up** a. odgojiti, othraniti b. pokrenuti (pitanje)

brink /brɪŋk/ n 1 rub (+ fig) ~**manship** n politiziranje do same granice sukoba

brisk /brɪsk/ adj 1 živahan, žustar 2 svjež

bristle /'brɪsl/ n čekinja, oštra dlaka •

vi 1 (up) nakostriješiti se 2 fig razljutiti se 3 (with) biti načičkan čime

brittle /'brɪtl/ adj krhak, lomljiv (+ fig)

broach /brəʊtʃ/ vt načeti (+ fig)

broad /brɔːd/ adj 1 širok, prostran 2 općenit 3 naglašen ~**cast** vt,vi irreg (→ cast) 1 emitirati 2 razglasiti ○ n radio/TV emisija, prijenos ~**en** vt,vi (pro)širiti, raširiti (se) ~ **jump** US skok udalj ~**ly** adv 1 široko 2 općenito ~**minded** adj širokih pogleda • n US derog sl ženska

broccoli /'brɒkəlɪ/ n brokula

brochure /'brəʊʃə(r)/ n brošura, prospekt

broil /brɔɪl/ vt,vi US peći na roštilju/žaru

broke /brəʊk/ v irreg → **break** • adj coll (**stony/flat** ~) bez prebite pare

broken /'brəʊkən/ v irreg → **break** • adj ~ **English** loš engleski

broker /'brəʊkə(r)/ n mešetar, posrednik

brolly /'brɒlɪ/ n GB coll kišobran

bronchitis /brɒŋ'kaɪtɪs/ n bronhitis

bronze /brɒnz/ n 1 bronca 2 mod brončan • vt,vi potamnjeti

brooch /brəʊtʃ/ n broš

brood /bruːd/ n 1 leglo, jato 2 coll djeca, potomstvo ~ **hen** kvočka ~ **mare** rasplodna kobila • vi 1 sjediti na jajima 2 (on/over/about) duboko razmišljati 3 (over) nadviti se (oblaci)

brook /brʊk/ n potok

broom /bruːm/ n 1 metla 2 žutilovka

broth /brɒθ/ n mesna juha

brothel /'brɒθl/ n bordel, javna kuća

brother /'brʌðə(r)/ n 1 brat 2 (pl **brethren**) brat (redovnik) ~**in-law** (pl **brethren**) brat (redovnik) ~**in-law** šogor, šurjak ~**s in arms** braća po oružju

brought /brɔːt/ v irreg → **bring**

bouhaha /bruː'haːhaː/ n coll halabuka, strka

brow /braʊ/ n 1 (eye~) obrva 2 čelo **knit one's** ~**s** namrštiti se

brown /braʊn/ adj 1 smeđ 2 preplanuo ~ **bread** crni kruh ~**ie** n 1 dobri kućni duh 2 US čokoladni kolač s orasima 3 US izviđač ~**ie point** nagrada za dobro djelo • vt,vi posmeđiti, potamnjeti

browse /braʊz/ *vi* 1 (through) prebirati po knjigama 2 pasti, brstiti

bruise /bru:z/ *n* modrica, masnica • *vt,vi* 1 udariti; isprebijati 2 *fig* povrijediti (osjećaje)

brunch /brʌntʃ/ *n coll* kasni doručak

brunette, brunet US /bru:'net/ *n* brineta

brunt /brʌnt/ *n* glavnina napada **bear the ~ of** podnijeti najveći teret

brush (1) /brʌʃ/ *n* 1 četka; kist 2 lagani dodir 3 (with) kratak susret; okršaj • *vt,vi* (o)četkati, (po)čistiti, (po)mesti; prati (zube) ~ **aside** prijeći preko čega ~ **off** odbiti, odbaciti **give sb the ~-off** grubo odbiti ~ **past/against** očešati se o ~ **up** osvježiti, obnoviti (znanje)

brush (2) *n* 1 (~**wood**) pruće, šiblje 2 šipražje

brusque /bru:sk/ *adj* otresit

Brussels sprouts /ˌbrʌsəlz 'spraʊts/ *n pl* prokulice

brute /bru:t/ *n* životinja; zvijer (+ *fig*) • *adj* životinjski; sirov *fig* **brutal** *adj* brutalan, okrutan, surov

bubble /'bʌbl/ *n* mjehurić, balon ~ **and squeak** GB kuhani krumpir i zelje ~ **gum** guma za žvakanje **bubbly** *adj* 1 pjenušav 2 živahan ○ *n coll* pjenušac • *vi* 1 pjeniti se, kipjeti 2 (away) žuboriti

buck /bʌk/ *n* 1 srndać 2 mužjak 3 antilopa 4 US *coll* dolar **a quick/fast ~-pas the ~ (to sb)** *coll* prebaciti odgovornost na drugog US *coll* laka zarada ~**toothed** zubat, isturenih zuba • *vi,vt* 1 propinjati se, ritati se 2 (off) zbaciti jahača 3 *coll* boriti se protiv, odupirati se, suprotstaviti se ~ **up** *coll* **a.** poboljšati **b.** požuriti (se) **c.** odobrovoljiti (se), živnuti

bucket /'bʌkɪt/ *n* kabao, vedro **kick the ~** *coll* otegnuti papke

buckle /'bʌkl/ *n* kopča, spona • *vt,vi* 1 (on) zakopčati, opasati 2 svinuti se ~ **to/down to** latiti se, prionuti na

bud /bʌd/ *n* pupoljak **nip in the ~** ugušiti/uništiti u zametku • *vi* pupati ~**ding** *adj* nadobudni

buddy /'bʌdɪ/ *n coll* prijatelj, kolega

budge /bʌdʒ/ *vt,vi* 1 pomaknuti, pokrenuti (se) 2 *fig* odstupiti

budgerigar /'bʌdʒərɪgɑ:(r)/ *n* papigica

budget /'bʌdʒɪt/ *n* proračun • *vi* (for) predvidjeti/napraviti proračun, planirati

budgie /'bʌdʒɪ/ *n coll* → **budgerigar**

buff /bʌf/ *n* 1 kravlja koža 2 *mod* žućkast 3 *coll* poklonik, obožavatelj • *vt* (up) kožom polirati kovinu

buffalo /'bʌfələʊ/ *n* 1 bivol 2 bizon

buffer /'bʌfə(r)/ *n* 1 odbojnik 2 *comp* međumemorija podataka ~ **state** tampon država • *vt* ublažiti, zaštititi

buffet (1) /'bʌfɪt/ *vt* 1 udariti, tući 2 šibati (kiša/vjetar) • *n* udarac (šakom)

buffet (2) /'bʌfeɪ/ *n* hladni narezak ~-**car** GB vagon-restoran

bug /bʌg/ *n* 1 stjenica 2 US kukac 3 *coll* klica, virus 4 *sl* prisluškivač 5 *coll* (po)greška, kvar, smetnja 6 *coll* mušica • *vt sl* 1 prisluškivati skrivenim uređajima; ozvučiti *coll* 2 gnjaviti, ići na živce

bugbear /'bʌgbeə(r)/ *n* bauk

bugger /'bʌgə(r)/ *vt,vi* GB *tab sl* ~ **about/with** zajebavati ~ (**it**) jebi ga ~ **off** odjebi ~ **up** sjebati, upropastiti ~**y** *n* GB *tab sl*, *leg* sodomija ○ *n* GB *tab sl* 1 kreten; gad 2 peder

bugle /'bju:gl/ *n* vojnička truba

build /bɪld/ *vt,vi irreg* (iz)graditi, (sa)zidati, napraviti, podići, stvoriti ~ **in/into** ugraditi **built-in** *adj* ugraden ~ **on a.** nadograditi **b.** osloniti se na ~ **up a.** pojačati, povećati (se); gomilati (vojsku) **b.** poboljšati, ojačati **c.** promovirati **built-up area** naseljeno područje ~**er** *n* graditelj, građevinar ~**ing** *n* 1 gradnja 2 građevina, zgrada ~**ing site** gradilište ~**ing society** stambena zadruga, štedionica ~ **industry** građevinarstvo • *n* građa tijela, stas

built *v irreg* → **build**

bulb /bʌlb/ *n* 1 gomolj, lukovica 2 žarulja

bulge /bʌldʒ/ *n* 1 ispupčenje, izbočina, nateklina 2 porast • *vi,vt* (out) izbočiti se **bulging** *adj* 1 debeo 2 izbuljen

bulk /bʌlk/ *n* 1 opseg, veličina 2 velika

masa/količina **3** većina, glavnina **in ~ naveliko**; bez ambalaže, u rinfuzi **~head** nepropusna pregrada **~y** *adj* **1** krupan, debeo **2** glomazan, masivan; nespretan

bull /bʊl/ *n* **1** bik **2** mužjak **3** *comm* hosist **4** *coll* → **bull's eye 5** (papinska) bula **6** *sl* glupost ~ **in the china shop** slon u staklani **take the ~ by the horns** uhvatiti se u koštac s teškoćama **~dozer** jaružalo; buldožer *coll* **~ock** /'bʊlək/ *n* vol **~ring** arena za borbu s bikovima **~'s eye** središte mete **~shit** *n tab sl* glupost; sranje *tab* ○ *vi,vt* lupetati gluposti **~y** *n* nasilnik, razbijač ○ *vt* tiranizirati, zastrašivati **~y sb into sth** prisiliti koga na što

bullet /'bʊlit/ *n* metak **~proof vest** neprobojan prsluk

bulletin /'bʊlətin/ *n* bilten, kratko izvješće, dnevni pregled

bullion /'bʊliən/ *n* zlato/srebro u polugama

bum /bʌm/ *n* **1** *GB sl* stražnjica; guzica *coll* **2** *US sl* skitnica, propalica • *vt,vi sl* **1** žicati *sl* **2** skitati (se)

bumblebee /'bʌmblbi:/ *n* bumbar

bump /bʌmp/ *vt,vi* **1** udariti, zaletjeti se **2** truckati se **3** (into) *coll* naletjeti na **4** (off) *sl* ubiti • *n* **1** udarac, tresak **2** čvoruga **3** izbočina, grba **~er** *n* branik, odbojnik ○ *adj* obilan, rekordan **~y** *adj* neravan

bumptious /'bʌmptʃəs/ *adj* napuhan, uobražen, umišljen

bun /bʌn/ *n* **1** kolačić s grožđicama **2** punđa **have a ~ in the oven** biti u drugom stanju

bunch /bʌntʃ/ *n* **1** snop, svežanj; kita; grozd **2** *coll* skupina, gomila; društvo; družina • *vt,vi* (up/together) **1** skupiti (se), stisnuti (se) **2** nabrati (se) **3** svezati u snop

bundle /'bʌndl/ *n* **1** svežanj, snop, zavežljaj **2** *sl* mnogo novaca **be a ~ of nerves** biti jako živčan • *vt,vi* **1** (up/together) svezati, zamotati, zapakirati **2** (into) pobacati, strpati **3** (off) otpraviti, otpremiti **4** (off/-out/away) odjuriti, pokupiti se

bunged up /bʌnd 'ʌp/ *adj coll* zače-

pljen

bungalow /'bʌŋgələʊ/ *n* kuća prizemnica

bungle /'bʌŋgl/ *vt* zabrljati **~r** *n* nespretnjaković, šeprtlja

bunk /bʌŋk/ *n* **1** ležaj **2** *sl* glupost **~ beds** kreveti na kat • *vi* **1** (down) *coll* leći **2** (off) *GB sl* markirati *sl*

bunker /'bʌŋkə(r)/ *n* **1** spremište ugljena **2** *mil* bunker

bunny /'bʌni/ *n* zečić, zeko

bunting /'bʌntiŋ/ *n* **1** zastav(ic)e **2** tkanina za zastave

buoy /bɔi/ *n* plutača **life ~** pojas za spasavanje • *vt* **1** označiti plutačama **2** (up) držati na površini, održavati (+ *fig*) **3** hrabriti, poticati **~ant** *adj* **1** koji pluta, plutajući **2** *fig* vedar **3** rastući

burden /'bɜ:dn/ *n* **1** breme, teret (+ *fig*) **2** nosivost (broda) **3** (the ~) bit • *vt* natovariti, opteretiti

bureau /'bjʊərəʊ/ *n* (pl **~x/-z/**) **1** *GB* pisaći stol **2** *US* komoda **3** ured; zavod; uprava **~cracy** /bjʊə'rɒkrəsi/ *n* birokracija **~crat** /'bjʊərəkræt/ *n* birokrat

burger /'bɜ:gə(r)/ *n coll* hamburger

burglar /'bɜ:glə(r)/ *n* provalnik **~y** provala, provalna krađa **burgle/burglarize** *US vt* provaliti, opljačkati

burial /'beriəl/ *n* pogreb, pokop

burly /'bɜ:li/ *adj* jak, snažan, kršan

burn /bɜ:n/ *vt,vi irreg* **1** gorjeti, plamtjeti **2** peći, (s)paliti, zapaliti **3** zagorjeti; opeći **4** (with) izgarati od ~ **away** a. gorjeti b. izgorjeti, sagorjeti ~ **down** a. spaliti, izgorjeti (do temelja) b. dogorjeti ~ **low** dogorjevati ~ **off** (s)paliti ~ **out** a. dogorjeti, ugasiti se b. pregorjeti **be ~ed out** izgorjeti ~ **up** a. rasplamsati (se) b. izgorjeti **~er** *n* plamenik, žižak **put sth on the back ~er** odgoditi **~ing** *adj* gorući (+ *fig*) • *n* opekotina

burnt *v irreg* → **burn**

burp /bɜ:p/ *vi coll* podrignuti

burr (1) /bɜ:(r)/ *n* **1** brujanje, zujanje (stroja) **2** grleni izgovor glasa "r"

bur(r) (2) *n* čičak

burrow /'bʌrəʊ/ *n* rupa, jazbina • *vi,vt* **1** iskopati (rupu) **2** priviti se, ugnijezditi se 3 pretraživati, rovati

bursar /'bɜːsə(r)/ n školski/sveučilišni blagajnik ~y 1 školska/sveučilišna blagajna 2 stipendija

burst /bɜːst/ vi,vt irreg 1 pr(a)snuti, pući, eksplodirati 2 provaliti, probiti 3 izbiti (pupoljak) ~ **in** on/upon prekinuti, zateći, banuti ~ **into flames** buknuti, planuti ~ **into laughter** prasnuti u smijeh ~ **into song** zapjevati ~ **into tears** briznuti u plač ~ **into** banuti ~ **out laughing** prasnuti u smijeh ~ **out** uskliknuti, uzviknuti ~ **open** naglo (se) otvoriti be ~ing **to** izgarati od želje da be ~ing **with a.** prepun, krcat **b.** fig pucati od • n 1 prasak, eksplozija 2 pukotina, raspuklina 3 fig napad, provala 4 rafal; puškaranje

bury /'berı/ vt 1 pokopati 2 zakopati; pokriti, sakriti 3 zariti

bus /bʌs/ n autobus ~ station autobusni kolodvor ~ **stop** stajalište autobusa miss the ~ coll propustiti priliku, zakasniti

bush /buʃ/ n 1 grm(lje) 2 (the ~) divljina **beat about the** ~ obilaziti kao mačak oko vruće kaše, okolišati ~y adj 1 grmovit 2 čupav, gust, kitnjast

business /'bıznıs/ n 1 poslovanje, trgovina, biznis 2 posao, djelatnost 3 dućan, lokal, poduzeće 4 dužnost, zadaća 5 stvar be away on ~ biti na poslovnom putovanju do ~ with poslovati s get down to ~ prijeći na stvar it's none of your ~ to te se ne tiče mean ~ misliti ozbiljno mind one's own ~ gledati svoja posla on ~ poslovno ~ hours uredovno vrijeme the ~ end of a gun cijev pištolja ~like adj poslovan, praktičan, metodičan, sistematičan ~man poslovni čovjek

busker /'bʌskə(r)/ n GB coll ulični svirač

bust (1) /bʌst/ n 1 bista, poprsje 2 obujam grudi

bust (2) vt,vi irreg 1 coll razbiti, razlupati 2 sl privesti, uhititi 3 sl izvršiti raciju 4 US coll skinuti čin, degradirati 5 (up) coll prekinuti 6 (up) US pokvariti, upropastiti ~-**up** n sl 1

bučna svađa 2 raskid (braka) • n 1 sl racija, pretres 2 US potpun promašaj, neuspjeh • adj coll pokvaren, potrgan go ~ propasti, bankrotirati

bustle /'bʌstl/ vi (about) ushodati se, ustrčati se, žuriti se • n žurba, strka, jurnjava, vreva

busy /'bızı/ adj 1 (with sth/doing sth) zaposlen, zauzet čime 2 marljiv, vrijedan 3 aktivan, živ, prometan 4 US zauzet (tel. linija, WC) ~**body** njuškalo, znatiželjnik **busily** adv marljivo, radišno • vt ~ **oneself with** zaokupiti se čime

but /bʌt/ conj 1 ali, ipak, no, uza sve to 2 nego 3 osim da 4 a da ne • prep osim it's nothing ~ to je baš the **last** ~ **one** predzadnji **all** ~ gotovo, skoro, praktički • adv samo, jedino, tek he's ~ **a child** on je još dijete • n prigovor, zamjerka no ~s **about it**/~ me no ~s nema tu nikakvog ali

butcher /'butʃə(r)/ n 1 mesar 2 fig krvolok • vt 1 ubiti, zaklati 2 masakrirati

butler /'bʌtlə(r)/ n batler, glavni sluga

butt (1) /bʌt/ vt,vi udariti/zaletjeti se glavom/rogovima ~ **in** sl prekidati, upadati • n udarac glavom/rogovima

butt (2) n predmet ismijavanja, cilj

butt (3) n 1 kundak 2 opušak 3 sl guzica

butter /'bʌtə(r)/ n maslac ~**cup** ljutić ~**milk** sirutka • vt namazati maslacem ~ **sb up** coll laskati, ulagivati se

butterfly /'bʌtəflaı/ n 1 leptir 2 (~ stroke) leptir **have butterflies in one's stomach** coll osjećati nervozu

buttocks /'bʌtəks/ n pl guzica, stražnjica

button /'bʌtn/ n 1 gumb, dugme 2 US bedž ~**hole** n zapučak • vt,vi ~ **up** zakopčati ~ **up!** sl zaveži!

buttres /'bʌtrıs/ n 1 potpornjak 2 fig oslonac, potpora • vt (up) poduprijeti (+ fig)

buxom /'bʌksəm/ adj jedar, stasit (žena)

buy /baı/ vt,vi irreg 1 kupiti 2 sl povjerovati, nasjesti ~**er** n kupac; nabavljač ~ **in** nakupovati ~ **off** potplatiti ~ **out** otkupiti ~ **up** pokupovati; otkupiti • *n coll* kupovina, kupnja

buzz /bʌz/ *vi,vt* **1** zujati **2** (with) odzvanjati od **3** (for) pozvati interfonom **3** *coll* nisko nadlijetati ~ **off!** briši! ~**er** *n* zvonce; zujalo; telefon • *n* **1** zujanje **2** galama, žamor **give sb a** ~ *coll* nazvati telefonom ~**word** pomodna riječ

buzzard /'bʌzəd/ *n* **1** *GB* škanjac **2** *US* lešinar

by /baɪ/ *prep* blizu, kraj, kod, pored, pri *I was attacked* ~ *a dog* napao me je pas ~ *car/train* autom/vlakom ~ *name* po imenu ~ *sight* iz viđenja *a picture* ~ *Picasso* Picassova slika ~ *tomorrow* do sutra *play* ~ *the rules* igrati po pravilima ~ **9** *percent* za 9 posto *he led her* ~ *the hand* vodio ju je za ruku *sell* ~ *the metre* prodavati na metre *little* ~ *little* malo-pomalo ~ *accident* slučajno ~ **heart** napamet (**all**) ~ **oneself** (potpuno) sam ~ **the**

way usput rečeno • *adv* pokraj, pored; blizu ~ **and large** sve u svemu, općenito

bye(-bye) /'baɪ(baɪ)/ *int coll* doviđenja! bok! pa-pa!

by(e)-election /'baɪɪlekʃn/ *n GB* naknadni/dopunski izbori *pl*

bygone /'baɪgɒn/ *adj* prošao; bivši; zastario • *n* **let** ~**s be** ~**s** što je bilo, bilo je

bylaw /'baɪlɔ:/ *n* lokalni zakon

byline /'baɪlaɪn/ *n* redak s imenom autora novinskog članka

bypass /'baɪpæs/ *n* obilaznica • *vt* **1** zaobići **2** *med* bajpas *fig* izbjeći

by-product /'baɪprɒdʌkt/ *n* nusproizvod, sporedni proizvod (+ *fig*)

bystander /'baɪstændə(r)/ *n* pasivni promatrač, slučajni prolaznik

byte /baɪt/ *n comp* bajt

byway /'baɪweɪ/ *n* **1** sporedni put **2** *fig* slabo poznato područje

byword /'baɪwɜ:d/ *n* primjer čega, sinonom za što

C

C, c /si:/ 3. slovo engl. abecede; ce
cab /kæb/ *n* 1 taksi 2 vozačka kabina
cabbage /'kæbɪdʒ/ *n* kupus, zelje
cabin /'kæbɪn/ *n* 1 koliba 2 kabina
cabinet /'kæbɪnɪt/ *n* 1 ormarić **filing ~** o. za spise **(china)** ~ vitrina **~–maker** *n* majstor za izradu namještaja 2 *pol* kabinet
cable /'keɪbl/ *n* 1 uže 2 kabel, žica **~–car, ~ railway** uspinjača **~ television** kabelska televizija 3 **(~gram)** brzojav • *vt,vi* brzojaviti
cache /kæʃ/ *n* skrivene zalihe (hrane, oružja) *pl* • *vt* sakriti zalihe
cachet /'kæʃeɪ/ *n* dokaz kvalitete
cackle /'kækl/ *vi* 1 kokodakati 2 kreštavo se smijati • *n* kokodakanje, kreštav smijeh
cactus /'kæktəs/ *n* (*pl* **cacti**) kaktus
cad /kæd/ *n* bezobraznik **~dish** *adj* bezobrazan
cadet /kə'det/ *n* kadet
cadge /kædʒ/ *vt,vi* (from) žicati *coll* **~er** *n* žicar
Caesarian /sɪ'zeərɪən/ *adj* ~ **(section)** *n* carski rez
café /'kæfeɪ/ *n* 1 kafić 2 *(GB)* zdravljak
cafeteria /ˌkæfɪ'tɪərɪə/ *n* restoran-samoposluživanje, kantina
caffein(e) /'kæfi:n/ *n* kofein
cage /keɪdʒ/ *n* kavez (+*fig*) • *vt* staviti u kavez
cagey /'keɪdʒɪ/ *adj coll* nepovjerljiv
cajole /kə'dʒəʊl/ *vt* (sb into/out of doing sth) (laskanjem) nagovoriti koga na što; natentati *coll* **~ry** *n* 1 tentanje *coll* 2 vještina nagovaranja, laska
cake /keɪk/ *n* 1 kolač, torta a **piece of** ~ *sl* ništa lakša **have one's** ~ **and eat it** *prov* vuk sit a koza cijela **sell like hot** ~**s** prodavati se kao alva **take the** ~ *coll* nadmašiti sve 2 komad **a** ~ **of**

soap • *vt,vi* prekriti skorenom masom (blatom i sl.)
calamity /kə'læmətɪ/ *n* katastrofa, nesreća
calcium /'kælsɪəm/ *n* kalcij
calculate /'kælkjʊleɪt/ *vt,vi* 1 kalkulirati, izračunati, proračunati 2 *pass* (to) biti smišljen (da) 3 (on) *US* računati na **calculating** *adj* proračunat
calculus /'kælkjʊləs/ (*pl* **calculi**) *n* 1 *mat* račun 2 *med* (bubrežni i sl.) kamenac
calendar /'kælɪndə(r)/ *n* 1 kalendar 2 *mod* kalendarski
calf (1) /ka:f/ *n* (*pl* **calves** /ka:vz/) 1 tele 2 mlado tuljana/kita 3 **(~skin)** teleća koža
calf (2) *n* list (noge)
calibre /'kælɪbə(r)/ *n* kalibar (+*fig*)
call /kɔ:l/ *n* 1 poziv ~ **girl** kolgerla *coll* 2 zov 3 posjet **pay/make a** ~ navratiti **port of** ~ luka pristajanja 4 zahtjev (za isplatu novca) **~loan, ~money, money payable at/on** ~ kredit/novac koji se mora vratiti na prvi poziv • *vt* 1 pozvati ~ **out** oglasiti se, kriknuti 2 (on sb/at a place) navratiti kod koga **~er** *n* posjetitelj 3 (sb sth) nazvati koga kako/čime, nazivati se, smatrati (se) ~ **sb names** vrijeđati 4 nazvati, telefonirati XY ~**ing** ovdje XY 5 sazvati ~**ing** *n* poziv, zanimanje ~**ing card** *n US* posjetnica ~ **for** a. zahtijevati b. *pass* biti primjeren ~ **sth off** otkazati, prekinuti ~ **on sb** a. navratiti kod koga b. obratiti se komu ~ **sb/sth up** a. telefonirati b. prisjetiti se c. pozvati u vojsku
callisthenics /ˌkælɪs'θenɪks/ *n pl* (+ *sing*) gimnastika
callous /'kæləs/ *adj* 1 otvrdnuo, žuljevit 2 *fig* (to) neosjetljiv (na)

callow /'kæləʊ/ *adj* mlad i neiskusan

calm /kɑːm/ *n* **1** mir **2** bonaca • *adj* miran • *vt, vi* (down) smiriti se **~ness** *n* smirenost, mirnoća

Calor gas /'kælə gæs/ *n TM* butan

calorie /'kælərɪ/ *n* kalorija **low—** *adj* niskokaloričan

calumny /'kæləmnɪ/ *n form* kleveta

calve /kɑːv/ *vi* oteliti se

calyx /'keɪlɪks/ *n* (*pl* **calices**) lap (cvijeta)

cam /kæm/ *n mot* bregasta osovina

camaraderie /ˌkæmə'rɑːdərɪ/ *n* prijateljstvo, zajedništvo

came → *v irreg* **come**

camel /'kæml/ *n* deva **~hair** *n* devina dlaka; kamelhar *coll*

cameo /'kæmɪəʊ/ *n* **1** kameja **2** sporedna uloga koju tumači poznati glumac

camera /'kæmərə/ *n* kamera **~man** *n* snimatelj; kamerman *coll*

camomile, chamomile /'kæməmaɪl/ *n* kamilica

camouflage /'kæməflɑːʒ/ *n* **1** mimikrija **2** kamuflaža **3** maskirna odora • *vt* kamuflirati, maskirati se

camp (1) /kæmp/ *n* **1** logor **~fire** logorska vatra **2** tabor (+ *fig*) **3** kamp **4** *mod* poljski, sklopivi **~er** *n* **1** kamper **2** kamp–vozilo **~(ing) site** *n* kampiralište, kamp • *vi* logorovati, kampirati **go ~ing** kampirati

camp (2) /kæmp/ *adj* **1** ženskast; homoseksualan **2** kičast

campaign /kæm'peɪn/ *n* kampanja • *vi* sudjelovati u kampanji **old ~er** *n* džomba *coll*

campus /'kæmpəs/ *n* **1** zgrade i prostor fakulteta **2** fakultet

can (1) /kæn/ *n* **1** kanta **2** limenka, konzerva **~ opener** *n* otvarač za konzerve **3** *US sl* zatvor **4** *sl* zahod • *vt* pakirati u limenke

can (2) *modal v* (*neg* **cannot, can't** *pret* **could**) **1** moći, biti u stanju (ostala vremena **be able to**) **2** *coll* smjeti; moći *coll* **cannot** ne smjeti **could I?** da li bih mogao? **3** znati (*pret* **could**)

canal /kə'næl/ *n* kanal

canary /kə'neərɪ/ *n* **1** (**~ bird**) kanarinac **2** *fig* izdajnik, koji je

"propjevao"

cancel /'kænsl/ *vt, vi* **1** (out) poništiti **2** otkazati **3** ukinuti **~lation** *n* otkaz, odustajanje, ukinuće

cancer /'kænsə(r)/ *n* **1** rak **2** *fig* rak–rana **C~** *n astrol* Rak

candid /'kændɪd/ *adj* iskren **~ camera** skrivena kamera

candidate /'kændɪdət/ *n* kandidat **candidature** /'kændɪdətʃə(r)/ *n* kandidatura

candle /'kændl/ *n* svijeća **~light** *n* svjetlo svijeća **~stick** *n* svijećnjak

candour (**–or** *US*) /'kændə(r)/ *n* iskrenost

candy /'kændɪ/ *n* **1** *US* bombon **2** kandirani šećer **~floss** *n GB* šećerna vata • *vt* kandirati, šećeriti

cane /keɪn/ *n* **1** trska **2** *mod* od trske **3** štap **4** šiba • *vt* šibati

canine /'keɪnaɪn/ *adj* pasji **~ tooth** *n* očnjak

canister /'kænɪstə(r)/ *n* kanistar

canker /'kæŋkə(r)/ *n* **1** *med* rak, čir **2** *bot* snijet **3** *fig* rak–rana

cannabis /'kænəbɪs/ *n* kanabis

cannibal /'kænɪbl/ *n* kanibal **~ism** *n* kanibalizam **~istic** *adj* kanibalski

cannon /'kænən/ *n* **1** top **~ball** *n* topovska kugla **2** (**~s**) topništvo **~fodder** *n fig* topovsko meso

cannot → **can**

canny /'kænɪ/ *adj* bistar, lukav, promućuran

canoe /kə'nuː/ *n* kanu **~ist** *n* kanuist

canon /'kænən/ *n* **1** kanon **2** kanonik **canonize** *vt* proglasiti svetim; kanonizirati (+ *fig*)

canopy /'kænəpɪ/ *n* baldahin (+ *fig*)

cant /kænt/ *n* **1** licemjerni govor **2** žargon

cantankerous /kæn'tæŋkərəs/ *adj* svadljiv

canteen /kæn'tiːn/ *n* **1** kantina **2** kutija za jedaći pribor **3** *mil* čuturica; vojnička porcija

canter /'kæntə(r)/ *n* laki galop • *vi* lagano galopirati

cantilever /'kæntɪliːvə(r)/ *n* isturena greda **~ bridge** most s potpornim stupovima

canvas /'kænvəs/ *n* **1** šatorsko krilo,

jedrenina 2 (slikarsko) platno **under** ~ **a.** pod šatorom **b.** pod jedrima

canvass /ˈkænvəs/ *vt* **1** (for) agitirati **2** pretresti

canyon /ˈkænjən/ *n* kanjon

cap /kæp/ *n* **1** kapa, kapica **2** poklopac **3** kruna (na zubu) • *vt* **1** poklopiti (+ *fig*) **2** prekriti; staviti krunu

capability /ˌkeɪpəˈbɪləti/ *n* **1** (of doing sth/to do sth) sposobnost **2** *pl* potencijal *sing* **capable** /ˈkeɪpəbl/ *adj* **1** sposoban **2** ~ **of** (doing) **sth** u stanju učiniti

capacity /kəˈpæsəti/ *n* **1** kapacitet, obujam **2** položaj, svojstvo, ovlast

cape (1) /keɪp/ *n* pelerina

cape (2) /keɪp/ *n* rt

caper /ˈkeɪpə(r)/ *vi* skakutati

capital /ˈkæpɪtl/ *n* **1** glavni grad **2** (~ **letter**) veliko slovo **3** kapital **4** glavni ~ **expenditure** investicijska potrošnja ~ **gain** povećanje vrijednosti imovine ~ **gains tax** → **tax** ~ **goods** *n pl* investicijska dobra ~ **levy** porez na imovinu **fixed** ~ fiksni k. **floating** ~ roba **make** ~ **of** sth iskoristiti što ~**ism** *n* kapitalizam ~**ist** *n* **1** kapitalist ∘ *adj* kapitalistički ~**ize** *vt, vi* **1** ispisati velikim slovima **2** pretvoriti u kapital (+ *fig*) **3** ~ **on** okoristiti se čime, profitirati na ~**ization** *n* kapitalizacija • *adj* ~ **punishment** smrtna kazna

capitulate /kəˈpɪtʃuleɪt/ *vi* kapitulirati

capricious /kəˈprɪʃəs/ *adj* hirovit

caprice /kəˈpriːs/ *n* kapric, hir

Capricorn /ˈkæprɪkɔːn/ *n astrol* Jarac

capsize /kæpˈsaɪz/ *vt, vi* prevrnuti (se)

capsule /ˈkæpsjuːl/ *n* kapsula

captain /ˈkæptɪn/ *n* **1** kapetan **2** vođa **3** *mil* satnik

caption /ˈkæpʃn/ *n* potpis pod slikom

captivate /ˈkæptɪveɪt/ *vt* očarati

captive /ˈkæptɪv/ *adj* **1** u zarobljeništvu/zatočeništvu **take/hold** ~ zarobiti **2** ~ **audience** publika koja mora slušati silom prilika; publika koja pomno prati **captivity** *n* zatočeništvo

capture /ˈkæptʃə(r)/ *vt* uhvatiti, zarobiti ~ **the attention** privući pozornost • *n* zarobljavanje, uhićenje

car /kɑː(r)/ *n* **1** automobil **2** *GB* putnič-

ki vagon **3** *US* putnički/teretni vagon

caramel /ˈkærəmel/ *n* **1** karamel **2** lijevani bombon **toffee** ~ karamela

carat /ˈkærət/ *n* karat 24-~ **gold/gold of** 24 ~**s** 24-karatno zlato

caravan /ˈkærəvæn/ *n* **1** karavan **2** karavan–vozilo, kamp-kućica

caraway /ˈkærəweɪ/ *n* kumin

carbohydrate /ˌkɑːbəʊˈhaɪdreɪt/ *n* ugljikohidrat

carbon /ˈkɑːbən/ *n* **1** ugljik **2** (~ **paper**) karbon (papir) ~ **copy** *n* kopija ~**ated** *adj* gaziran ~**ize** *vt* karbonizirati

carburettor (**carburetor** *US*) /ˌkɑːbjʊˈretə(r)/ *n* rasplinjač

carcass, carcase /ˈkɑːkəs/ *n* **1** strvina, truplo **2** zaklana životinja ~ **meat** svježe meso

card /kɑːd/ *n* kartica; karta; iskaznica **visiting** ~ *n* posjetnica Christmas-/birthday ~ božićna/rođendanska čestitka ~ **index** katalog **on the** ~**s** vjerojatan

cardboard /ˈkɑːdbɔːd/ *n* karton

cardiac /ˈkɑːdɪæk/ *adj* srčani

cardigan /ˈkɑːdɪɡən/ *n* džemper na kopčanje

cardinal /ˈkɑːdɪnl/ *adj* kardinalan, glavni ~ **number** glavni broj • *n* kardinal

care /keə(r)/ *n* **1** briga, pažnja, mar **take** ~ paziti, paziti na što, poklanjati pozornost **2** čuvanje, paska, skrb **in sb's care/under the** ~ **of** sb na čuvanju kod, pod čijom paskom ~ **of** (c/o) XY–a kod ¶ u adresiranju pisama **take into** ~ uzeti u skrb (dijete) **take** ~ **of** *coll* pobrinuti se za, riješiti ~**taker** *n* domar ~**taker Government** prijelazna vlada **3** briga ~**free** *adj* bezbrižan ~**worn** *adj* zabrinut • *vi* **1** (about) brinuti se zbog čega/za što **I don't** ~ nije me briga **2** ~ **for** brinuti za koga, skrbiti **3** ~ **for** biti raspoložen za **4** ~ **for** voljeti ~**ful** *adj* oprezan, na oprezu, pažljiv **caring** *adj* skrban, pun ljubavi i pažnje ~**less** *adj* nepažljiv, bezobziran, neoprezan

career /kəˈrɪə(r)/ *n* **1** životni put **2** karijera

caress /kə'res/ *vt* milovati, gladiti • *n* milovanje, nježan dodir **~ing** *adj* nježan

cargo /'ka:gəʊ/ *n* 1 teret 2 *mod* teretni

caricature /'kærɪkətjʊə(r)/ *n* karikatura • *vt* karikirati

caries /'keəri:z/ *n med* karijes

carnage /'ka:nɪdʒ/ *n* pokolj

carnal /'ka:nl/ *adj* puteni, tjelesni ~ **knowledge (of)** spolno općenje (sa)

carnation /ka:'neɪʃn/ *n* karanfil

carnival /'ka:nɪvl/ *n* karneval, mesopust

carnivore /'ka:ni:vɔ:(r)/ *n* mesožder

carol /'kærəl/ *n* (**Christmas ~**) božićna pjesma

carp /ka:p/ *n* šaran

carpenter /'ka:pɪntə(r)/ *n* stolar, drvodjelac **carpentry** stolarija

carpet /'ka:pɪt/ *n* tepih; prekrivač (+ *fig*) • *vt* postaviti tepih

carriage /'kærɪdʒ/ *n* 1 kočija **~way** *GB* vozna traka, kolnik 2 *GB* vagon 3 transport 4 troškovi transporta 5 postolje (strojnice i sl.) 6 valjak (pisaćeg stroja) ~ **return** povratnica 7 *fig* držanje

carrier /'kærɪə(r)/ *n* 1 prijevoznik 2 prijenosnik 3 držač prtljage 4 *mil* transporter **aircraft** ~ *mil* nosač aviona ~ **bag** vrećica ~ **pigeon** golub listonoša

carrot /'kærət/ *n* mrkva **the stick and the** ~ prijetnje i nagrade

carry /'kærɪ/ *vt,vi* 1 prenositi 2 nositi 3 nositi, držati 4 nositi sa sobom 5 usvojiti 6 držati se 7 pronositi se, dosezati **get carried away** zanijeti se ~ **off** osvojiti ~ **on a.** voditi, održavati **b.** raditi kravale *coll* **c.** (with) nastaviti ~ **out** izvesti, ostvariti

cart /ka:t/ *n* kola **~wheel** zvijezda (okret) • *vt* 1 prevoziti 2 *coll fig* vući

cartilage /'ka:tɪlɪdʒ/ *n* hrskavica

carton /'ka:tn/ *n* kutija od ljepenke ~ **of milk** mlijeko u tetrapaku ~ **of cigarettes** *coll* šteka cigareta

cartoon /ka:'tu:n/ *n* 1 karikatura 2 crtani film **~ist** *n* karikaturist

cartridge /'ka:trɪdʒ/ *n* 1 čahura 2 patrona, naboj 3 glava gramofonske

ručice 4 *US* → **casette**

carve /ka:v/ *vt,vi* 1 (out of sth/in sth/from sth) izrezbariti 2 urezati 3 razrezati (meso) **carving knife**, **~r** *n* nož za rezanje mesa **carving** *n* rezbarija

cascade /kæ'skeɪd/ *n* vodopad • *vi* slijevati se

case (1) /keɪs/ *n* 1 primjer, slučaj **just in** ~ za svaki slučaj **in** ~ **of** u slučaju da **in any** ~ u svakom slučaju ~ **history** povijest bolesti 2 *leg* slučaj, parnica 3 *gram* padež

case (2) /n 1 kutija 2 (**suit~**) kovčeg **glass** ~ vitrina **pillow** ~ jastučnica **upper/lower** ~ velika/mala slova

casement /'keɪsmənt/ *n* višekrilni prozor

cash /kæʃ/ *n* 1 gotovina ~ **crops** *pl* poljoprivredne kulture za prodaju ~ **dispenser** bankomat ~ **flow** gotovinski promet ~ **down/on delivery** pouzećem ~ **register** blagajna (u trgovini) **~ier** /kæ'ʃɪə(r)/ *n* 1 blagajnik, blagajna 2 novac • *vt* 1 unovčiti 2 ~ **in (on)** okoristiti se

cashew /'kæʃu:/ *n* indijski oraščić

cashmere /kæʃ'mɪə(r)/ *n* kašmir(ska vuna)

cask /ka:sk/ *n* bačvica

casket /'ka:skɪt/ *n* 1 kutijica 2 *US* → **coffin**

casserole /'kæsərəʊl/ *n* 1 vatrostalna posuda 2 složenac

cassette /kə'set/ *n* 1 kaseta 2 smotak filma

cassock /'kæsək/ *n* reverenda, sutana, mantija

cast /ka:st/ *n* 1 bacanje 2 lijev, kalup **plaster** ~ gipsani ovoj 3 glumačka postava • *vt*, *vi irreg* 1 baciti, spustiti ~ **a vote** glasovati **~ing vote** *n* odlučujući glas ~ **one's eye/a glance** baciti pogled 2 lijevati ~ **iron** *n* lijevano željezo **~iron** *adj* **a.** od lijevanog željeza **b.** *fig* čvrst; čeličan *fig* ~ **aside** odbaciti ~ **off a.** otploviti **b.** odbaciti **~off** *adj* odbačen **~ing** *n* odljevak, lijevana roba 3 dati ulogu

castaway /'ka:stəweɪ/ *n* brodolomac

caste /ka:st/ *n* kasta

castle /'ka:sl/ *n* 1 dvorac, zamak 2

kula (u šahu)

castor, caster /ˈkɑːstə(r)/ n 1 kotačić 2 posipaljka ~ **sugar** šećer u prahu

castor oil /ˌkɑːstər ˈɔɪl/ n ricinusovo ulje

castrate /kæˈstreɪt/ vt uškopiti, kastrirati

casual /ˈkæʒʊəl/ adj 1 slučajan, usputan, nehotičan 2 prigodan, neredovit, sezonski 3 ležeran, neformalan; športski (odjeća) 4 nemaran

casualty /ˈkæʒʊəltɪ/ n 1 nesreća **C~ Ward/Department** hitni odjel traumatologije 2 žrtva **casualties** pl poginuli i ranjeni, gubici

cat /kæt/ n 1 mačka 2 (~**o'-nine--tails**) bič ~**call** n zvižduk ○ vt izviždati ~**fish** n som ~**nap** drijem ~**walk** 1 uzak nogostup 2 modna pista ~**ty** adj zloban

catalogue /ˈkætəlɒɡ/ n katalog • vt katalogizirati

catapult /ˈkætəpʌlt/ n 1 praćka 2 katapult • vt katapultirati

catastrophe /kəˈtæstrəfɪ/ n katastrofa

catch /kætʃ/ vt irreg 1 uhvatiti 2 uloviti (+ fig) 3 zapeti 4 čuti, shvatiti 5 dobiti, navući (bolest) ~ **sb's eye** skrenuti pozornost ~ **sight of** ugledati ~ **fire** zapaliti se ~ **one's breath** zadržati dah ~ **sb up**, ~ **up** (with sb) dostići nekog ~**ing** adj zarazan ~**y** adj 1 lako pamtljiv; zarazan 2 varljiv ~**phrase** popularna fraza/slogan ~**word a.** izvlaka **b.** glavna riječ • n 1 lovina, plijen 2 zamka; kvaka fig 3 zapon

categorical /ˌkætɪˈɡɒrɪkl/ adj kategoričan

category /ˈkætɪɡərɪ/ n kategorija

cater /ˈkeɪtə(r)/ vi 1 ~ **for** dobavljati/pripremati hranu 2 ~ **for/to** podilaziti ~**er** n ugostitelj, dobavljač hrane ~**ing** n ugostiteljstvo

caterpillar /ˈkætəpɪlə(r)/ n gusjenica

cathedral /kəˈθiːdrəl/ n katedrala

catholic /ˈkæθəlɪk/ adj 1 opći, širok, liberalan 2 **C~** katolički **Roman C~** n rimokatolik ○ adj rimokatolički **C~ism** /kəˈθɒləsɪzəm/ n katoličanstvo

cattle /ˈkætl/ n pl stoka sing

caucus /ˈkɔːkəs/ n 1 izborni odbor, rukovodstvo stranke 2 sastanak i.o./r.s.

caught → irreg **catch**

cauldron /ˈkɔːldrən/ n kotao

cauliflower /ˈkɒlɪflaʊə(r)/ n cvjetača

cause /kɔːz/ n 1 uzrok 2 razlog 3 stvar • vt prouzročiti

causeway /ˈkɔːzweɪ/ n cestovni nasip

caustic /ˈkɔːstɪk/ adj jedak (+ fig)

caution /ˈkɔːʃn/ n 1 oprez 2 upozorenje • vt (against) upozoriti, opomenuti **cautious** /ˈkɔːʃəs/ adj oprezan

cavalier /ˌkævəˈlɪə(r)/ adj blaziran

cavalry /ˈkævlrɪ/ n konjaništvo

cave /keɪv/ n pećina ~**man** n pećinski čovjek (+ fig) ~ **in** urušiti se

cavern /ˈkævən/ n lit pećina ~**ous** adj fig upao (o očima)

caviar(e) /ˈkævɪɑː(r)/ n kavijar

cavity /ˈkævətɪ/ n šupljina, rupa

cavort /kəˈvɔːt/ vi coll skakutati, đipati

cayenne /keɪˈen/ n ljuta paprika

cease /siːs/ vt, vi form prestati ~ **fire** obustaviti vatru ~**-fire** n obustava vatre, primirje ~**less** adj neprestan

cedar /ˈsiːdə(r)/ n 1 cedar 2 cedrovina

ceiling /ˈsiːlɪŋ/ n 1 strop **hit the ~** coll pobjesniti 2 gornja granica

celebrate /ˈselɪbreɪt/ vt slaviti ~**d** adj slavan **celebration** n slavlje, proslava **celebrity** /sɪˈlebrətɪ/ n slavna osoba, zvijezda

celery /ˈselərɪ/ n celer

celestial /sɪˈlestɪəl/ adj 1 nebeski 2 fig božanstven

celibacy /ˈselɪbəsɪ/ n celibat **celibate** /ˈselɪbət/ n nevjenčana osoba

cell /sel/ n 1 ćelija, sobica 2 biol stanica 3 el galvanski članak 4 pol ćelija ~**ular** /ˈseljʊlə(r)/ adj stanični ~**(ular) phone** n mobitel **cellulose** /ˈseljʊləʊs/ n celuloza

cellar /ˈselə(r)/ n podrum

cello /ˈtʃeləʊ/ n (violon)čelo **cellist** n čelist

Celsius /ˈselsɪəs/ n Celzij

cement /sɪˈment/ n 1 cement ~ **mixer** mješalica 2 vezivno sredstvo • vt cementirati

cemetery /ˈsemətrɪ/ n groblje

censor /ˈsensə(r)/ n 1 cenzor • vt cen-

zurirati ~**ship** n cenzura
censure /'senʃə(r)/ vt (for) koriti • n
kritika **vote of** ~ glasovanje o nepovjerenju ¶ cenzura = **censorship**
census /'sensəs/ n popis stanovništva
cent /sent/ n cent **per** ~ posto
centenarian /ˌsentɪ'neərɪən/ n stogodišnjak
centenary /sen'ti:nərɪ/ adj stogodišnji
• n stogodišnjica
centennial /sen'tenɪəl/ → **centenary**
center US → **centre**
centigrade /'sentɪɡreɪd/ adj stupnjeva
Celzija **100 degrees** ~ 100 °C
centimetre /'sentɪˌmi:tə(r)/ n centimetar
centipede /'sentɪpi:d/ n stonoga
centre /'sentə(r)/ n središte, centar • vt,
vi 1 staviti u središte, centrirati 2 ~
on/upon usredotočiti (se) **central**
/'sentrəl/ adj 1 središnji 2 glavni,
ključni **central heating** centralno
grijanje **centralize** /'sentrəlaɪz/ vt
centralizirati
centrifugal /sen'trɪfjʊɡl/ adj centrifugalni
century /'sentʃərɪ/ n stoljeće **in the**
20th ~ u 20. st.
ceramic /sɪ'ræmɪk/ adj keramički,
lončarski ~**s** n 1 (+ v sing) keramika
2 (+ v pl) predmeti od keramike;
keramika
cereal /'sɪərɪəl/ n žitarica (breakfast)
~**s** pl žitne pahuljice
cerebral /'serɪbrəl/ adj 1 moždani 2 fig
misaoni
ceremony /'serɪmənɪ/ n 1 obred, ceremonija **Master of Ceremonies** n
voditelj svečanosti 2 formalnost **ceremonial** /ˌserɪ'məʊnɪəl/ adj ceremonijalni, svečani • n ceremonijal,
obred **ceremonious** /ˌserɪ'məʊnɪəs/
adj ceremonijalan, ukočen
certain /'sɜ:tn/ adj 1 siguran 2 uvjeren
3 pouzdan 4 izvjestan, neki 5
određen **make** ~ **a.** provjeriti **b.** osigurati ~**ly** adv 1 sasvim sigurno, nesumnjivo 2 naravno ~**ty** n 1 (nešto)
sigurno 2 sigurnost, izvjesnost 3 sigurna stvar
certificate /sə'tɪfɪkət/ n uvjerenje,
potvrda, svjedodžba **marriage** ~

vjenčani list **birth** ~ izvod iz matične
knjige rođenih ~**d** adj kvalificiran
certify /'sɜ:tɪfaɪ/ vt, vi potvrditi, posvjedočiti ~ **(as) insane** proglasiti ludim
certifiable /ˌsɜ:tɪ'faɪəbl/ adj coll zreo
za ludnicu **certified** adj ovlašten
cervix /'sɜ:vɪks/ n med grlić maternice
cervical adj grlića maternice
cessation /se'seɪʃn/ n form prestanak,
prekid
cesspit /'sespɪt/ n septička jama
chafe /tʃeɪf/ vi,vt 1 nažuljati 2 **at/under** fig ljutiti se • n nažuljano mjesto
chaff /tʃɑ:f/ n pljeva
chagrin /'ʃæɡrɪn/ n jad, zlovolja • vt
(pass) biti ozlojeđen
chain /tʃeɪn/ n 1 lanac 2 mod lančani ~
store n niz (lanac) prodavaonica ~
saw n motorna pila • vt vezati
lancem
chair /tʃeə(r)/ n 1 stolica 2 **the** ~
položaj predsjedatelja, predsjedatelj
be in/take the ~ predsjedati 3 profesura 4 katedra • vt predsjedati
~**man/woman/person** n predsjedatelj/predsjedateljica
chalet /'ʃæleɪ/ n planinska drvena
kućica
chalice /'tʃælɪs/ n kalež
chalk /tʃɔ:k/ n kreda ~ **and cheese** dvije potpuno različite stvari, • vt upisati/označiti (kredom) ~**y** adj kredast
challenge /'tʃælɪndʒ/ n izazov • vt 1
(sb to) izazvati (koga na) 2 dovesti u
pitanje ~**er** n izazivač
chamber /'tʃeɪmbə(r)/ n 1 arch soba
~**maid** sobarica ~**pot** noćna posuda 2
mod komorni 3 dom (parlamenta),
komora ~ **of commerce** gospodarska
komora 4 klijetka, šupljina 5 ležište
metka
champ /tʃæmp/ n coll šampion, majstor
champagne /ʃæm'peɪn/ n pjenušac,
šampanjac
champion /'tʃæmpɪən/ n 1 šampion,
pobjednik 2 pobornik ~**ship** n prvenstvo
chance /tʃɑ:ns/ n 1 slučaj 2 mod slučajan 3 mogućnost 4 prilika **chancy**
adj opasan • vi,vt 1 ~ **on/upon**
nabasati 2 slučajno se zateći, zadesiti

se; potrefiti se *coll* 3 riskirati

chancellor /ˈtʃɑːnsələ(r)/ *n* 1 kancelar 2 počasni rektor ~ **of the Exchequer** *n GB* ministar financija

chandelier /ˌʃændəˈlɪə(r)/ *n* 1 svijećnjak 2 luster

change /tʃeɪndʒ/ *n* 1 promjena **for a** ~ za promjenu ~ **of life** *n* menopauza 2 rezervna odjeća 3 sitniš • *vt,vi* 1 promijeniti (se) 2 presvući (se) 3 (trains) presjesti 4 razmijeniti, usitniti (novac) 5 zamijeniti se za 6 prijeći (sa nečega na nešto) ~ **one's mind** predomisliti se **~able** *adj* promjenjiv

channel /ˈtʃænl/ *n* 1 kanal, tjesnac **the English C~** La Manche 2 *fig* kanal, put 3 *radio*, *TV* kanal, program • *vt* 1 napraviti kanal 2 *fig* kanalizirati

chant /tʃɑːnt/ *n* 1 napjev 2 navijačka pjesma • *vi,vt* 1 pjevati, pojati 2 skandirati

chaos /ˈkeɪɒs/ *n* kaos, zbrka **chaotic** /keɪˈɒtɪk/ *adj* kaotičan

chap (1) /tʃæp/ (1) *n coll GB* momak

chap (2) *vi, vt* ogrubjeti, ispucati (se)

chapel /ˈtʃæpl/ *n* kapelica

chaperon /ˈʃæpərəʊn/ *n* gardedama (+ *fig*) • *vt* pratiti, nadzirati

chaplain /ˈtʃæplɪn/ *n* kapelan, duhovnik

chapter /ˈtʃæptə(r)/ *n* 1 poglavlje (+ *fig*) ~ **and verse** točan izvor podataka 2 kaptol

char (1) /tʃɑː(r)/ *vt* pougljeniti

char (2) *vi* čistiti po kućama **~lady/woman** *n* čistačica

character /ˈkærəktə(r)/ *n* 1 karakter, značaj **act in/out of** ~ ponašati se uobičajeno/neuobičajeno 2 karakternost 3 lik 4 čudak 5 znak **~istic** *adj* svojstven, karakterističan ○ *n* karakteristika, značajka **~ize** *vt* karakterizirati

charade /ʃəˈrɑːd/ *n* igra pantomime; šarada (+ *fig*)

charcoal /ˈtʃɑːkəʊl/ *n* drveni ugljen

charge /tʃɑːdʒ/ *n* 1 optužba 2 navala, juriš 3 trošak, cijena **free of** ~ besplatno 4 naboj 5 odgovornost **be in** ~ biti glavni, biti zadužen **take** ~ **of** preuzeti • *vt, vi* 1 (with) optužiti 2 navaliti 3 (for) naplatiti 4 to/up/up to

teretiti, staviti na (račun) 5 napuniti (oružje) 6 ~ **with** povjeriti što, dati u zadatak

chargé d'affaires /ˌʃɑːʒeɪ dæˈfeə(r)/ *n* otpravnik poslova

charity /ˈtʃærəti/ *n* 1 milostinja 2 dobrotvorna ustanova 3 dobrota **charitable** /ˈtʃærɪtəbl/ *adj* 1 milosrdan 2 dobrotvoran

charm /tʃɑːm/ *n* 1 privlačnost, draž 2 šarm 3 srećonoša ~ **bracelet** *n* narukvica s privjescima • *vt,vi* 1 privući 2 očarati **~ing** *adj* dražestan, čaroban **~er** *n* šarmer, zavodnik, zavodnica

chart /tʃɑːt/ *n* 1 karta, zemljovid 2 dijagram, grafikon

charter /ˈtʃɑːtə(r)/ *n* 1 isprava, povelja 2 najam 3 *mod* unajmljeni; čarter *coll* • *vt* 1 izdati povelju 2 unajmiti (brod, avion)

chase /tʃeɪs/ *vt,vi* goniti, progoniti • *n* hajka, lov

chasm /ˈkæzm/ *n* ponor, jaz (+ *fig*)

chastity /ˈtʃæstəti/ *n* 1 čistoća, nevinost, krepost ~ **belt** *n* pojas nevinosti 2 jednostavnost **chaste** /tʃeɪst/ *adj* 1 nevin, čist, krepostan 2 jednostavan

chat /tʃæt/ *n* razgovor, ćaskanje • *vi, vt* ćaskati, brbljati ~ **sb up** *coll* upucavati se *coll* **~up line** uvod u upucavanje *coll* **~ty** *adj* brbljav

chatter /ˈtʃætə(r)/ *vi* 1 brbljati 2 cvokotati • *n* 1 žagor 2 cvokot **~box** *n* brbljavac

chauffer /ˈʃəʊfə(r)/ *n* osobni vozač **~ed car** auto s vozačem

chauvinism /ˈʃəʊvɪnɪzəm/ *n* šovinizam **chauvinist** *n* šovinist *adj* šovinistički

cheap /tʃiːp/ *adj* 1 jeftin (+ *fig*) 2 plitak **~ness** *n* jeftinoća **~ly** *adv* jeftino **~en** *vt,vi* pojeftiniti, sniziti cijenu

cheat /tʃiːt/ *vi,vt* 1 (in/at sth) varati (na/u) 2 sb (out of sth) prevariti koga (za što) 3 ~ **on sb** varati koga (u braku) • *n* varalica

check (1) /tʃek/ *vt, vi* 1 provjeriti, pregledati ~ **up on sb** ispitati čiju prošlost **~sth/up/up on sth/sth out** *US* **a.** provjeriti **b.** *sl* pogledati, obratiti pozornost 2 zaustaviti, us-

poriti **3** šahirati **4** susprezati, obuzdati **~in** prijaviti se (u hotel, tvornicu, aerodrom) **~-in (desk)** *n* recepcija; ček in *coll* ~ **out** odjaviti se
~out *n* blagajna • *n* **1** kontrola, provjera **~list** *n* kontrolni popis **~point** *n*
kontrolna točka **~up** kontrolni pregled **hold in ~** zadržavati **2** priznanica **3** *US* → **cheque-mate** *n* šah–mat
(+ *fig*) *vt* matirati

check (2) *n* **1** karirani uzorak **2** kari-
rana tkanina **~ed** *adj* kariran

cheek /tʃi:k/ *n* **1** obraz **2** drskost **have
the ~** imati obraza **~y** *adj* drzak, bezobrazan

cheer /tʃɪə(r)/ *vt, vi* **1** (up) razveseliti
(se), obodriti (se) **2** klicati **3** (on)
navijati, bodriti • *n* navijanje, klica-
nje (hura) **~s!** *int* živio! **~ful** *adj*
veseo, vedar, sretan **~io** *int coll* bog!
~less *adj* tmuran, beživotan

cheese /tʃi:z/ *n* sir

cheetah /tʃi:tə/ *n* gepard

chef /ʃef/ *n* kuhar

chemical /ˈkemɪkl/ *adj* kemijski • *n*
kemikalija

chemist /ˈkemɪst/ *n* **1** kemičar **2**
ljekarnik **~ry** *n* kemija

cheque /tʃek/ *n* ček

chequered /ˈtʃekə(r)d/ *adj* **1** kariran,
šaren **2** *fig* buran

cherish /ˈtʃerɪʃ/ *vt* **1** voljeti **2** njegovati,
gajiti (nadu i sl.)

cherry /ˈtʃerɪ/ *n* trešnja • *adj* rumen

cherub /ˈtʃerəb/ *n* kerubin, anđeo

chess /tʃes/ *n* šah **~man** *n* šahovska
figura

chest /tʃest/ *n* **1** škrinja **~ of drawers**
n komoda **2** grudni koš, prsa **get sth
off one's ~** *coll* olakšati si dušu

chestnut /ˈtʃesnʌt/ *n* kesten **sweet ~**
pitomi kesten **horse ~** divlji kesten •
adj kestenjast

chew /tʃu:/ *vt, vi* žvakati **~ sth
over/upon sth** *coll fig* prežvakavati
~ing gum *n* guma za žvakanje

chic /ʃi:k/ *n, adj* šik

chick /tʃɪk/ *n* **1** pile **2** *US sl* cura; komad *sl* **~pea** slanutak

chicken /ˈtʃɪkɪn/ *n* **1** pile **count one's
~s before they are hatched** *prov*
praviti ražanj dok je zec u šumi **~pox**

n vodene kozice **2** piletina **3** *sl*
kukavica • *adj sl* kukavički • *vi* **~ out**
izgubiti petlju *coll*

chicory /ˈtʃɪkərɪ/ *n* cikorija

chief /tʃi:f/ *n* **1** vođa, glavar **2** voditelj,
šef **3** poglavica **~in-~** *adj* glavni,
vrhovni **editor–in–~** • *adj* **1** glavni **2**
vrhovni **~ly** *adv* **1** prvenstveno,
poglavito **2** uglavnom, većinom

chieftain /ˈtʃi:ftən/ *n* poglavica

chilblain /ˈtʃɪlbleɪn/ *n* ozeblina

child /tʃaɪld/ *n* (*pl* **children** /ˈtʃɪldrən/)
dijete **~bearing** *n* rađanje **~hood** *n*
djetinjstvo **~ish** *adj* djetinjast **~like**
adj jednostavan, djetinji

chill /tʃɪl/ *n* **1** hladnoća, studen **2** po-
kunjenost, malodušje **3** prehlada • *vt,
vi* **1** ohladiti **2** prozepsti **~y** *adj* leden
(+ *fig*)

chilli /ˈtʃɪlɪ/ *n* **1** čili paprika **2** ljuti gulaš

chime /tʃaɪm/ *n* zvonjava • *vi,vt* **1**
zvoniti **2 ~ in** ubaciti se (u razgovor)
~ (in) with poklapati

chimney /ˈtʃɪmnɪ/ *n* dimnjak **~ sweep**
n dimnjačar

chimpanzee /ˌtʃɪmpænˈzi:/ *n* čimpanza

chin /tʃɪn/ *n* brada *she has a jutting ~*
ona ima isturenu bradu

china /ˈtʃaɪnə/ *n* **1** porculan **2** porculanski servis **3** *mod* porculanski

chink (1) /tʃɪŋk/ *n* pukotina

chink (2) *n* zveckanje

chip /tʃɪp/ *n* **1** krhotina, iver **~board** *n*
iverica **~ off the old block** *prov*
jabuka ne pada daleko od stabla
have a ~ on one's shoulder biti
ogorčen **2** *pl GB* prženi krumpirići,
pomfrit *coll* **3** *US* čips **4** *comp* čip **5**
žeton • *vt,vi* **1** okrhnuti, odlomiti **2 ~
in** dati novčani prilog

chiropodist /kɪˈrɒpədɪst/ *n* pediker

chirp /tʃɜ:p/ *vi* cvrčati; cvrkutati (+ *fig*)

chisel /ˈtʃɪzl/ *n* dlijeto • *vt* klesati **~led**
adj fig (kao) isklesan

chit /tʃɪt/ *n* zadužnica, potvrda

chitchat /ˈtʃɪtʃæt/ *n* ćaskanje, brbljanje

chivalry /ˈʃvlrɪ/ *n* **1** viteštvo **2** galant-
nost **chivalrous** *adj* galantan, viteški

chive /tʃaɪv/ *n* vlasac

chocolate /ˈtʃɒklət/ *n* **1** čokolada **hot ~**
čokolada (napitak) **2** *mod* čokoladni

choice /tʃɔɪs/ *n* izbor • *adj* probran, izvrstan

choir /'kwaɪə(r)/ *n* 1 zbor 2 kor (u crkvi)

choke /tʃəʊk/ *vt,vi* 1 gušiti (se) (+ *fig*) 2 (up) (with) začepiti (se) (čime) 3 ~ **sth back/down** susprezati • *n* prigušnik; čok *coll*

choose /tʃuːz/ *vt,vi irreg* 1 izabrati 2 odlučiti 3 htjeti, sviđati se **choosy** *adj coll* izbirljiv

chop /tʃɒp/ *vt,vi* (up/into) sjeći, rezati • *odrezak* ~**per** *n* 1 (mesarska) sjekira 2 *coll* helikopter

choppy /'tʃɒpi/ *adj* 1 valovit, uzburkan 2 promjenjiva smjera

chopsticks /'tʃɒpstɪks/ *n pl* štapići za jelo

choral /'kɔːrəl/ *adj* zborni, koralni

chord /kɔːd/ *n* 1 akord 2 *geom* tetiva 3 žica (+ *fig*)

chore /tʃɔː(r)/ *n* 1 kućanski posao 2 mrska dužnost

choreography /ˌkɒrɪ'ɒgrəfi/ *n* koreografija **choreographer** *n* koreograf

chortle /'tʃɔːtl/ *n* zadovoljno smijuljenje • *vi* smijuljiti se

chorus /'kɔːrəs/ *n* 1 zbor (pjevača, plesača) 2 refren 3 mnoštvo glasova

chose, chosen *v irreg* → **choose**

Christ /kraɪst/ Krist

christen /'krɪsn/ *vt* krstiti ~**ing** *n* krštenje **C~dom** /'krɪsndəm/ *n* kršćani, kršćanstvo

Christian /'krɪstʃən/ *adj* kršćanski ~ **name** krsno ime • *n* kršćanin ~**ity** /ˌkrɪstɪ'ænəti/ *n* kršćanstvo

Christmas /'krɪsməs/ *n* 1 Božić 2 *mod* božićni

chromium /'krəʊmɪəm/ *n* krom ~**plated** *adj* kromiran

chronic /'krɒnɪk/ *adj* kronični

chronicle /'krɒnɪkl/ *n* kronika

chronological /ˌkrɒnə'lɒdʒɪkl/ *adj* kronološki **chronology** /krə'nɒlədʒɪ/ *n* kronologija

chrysanthemum /krɪ'sænθəməm/ *n* krizantema

chubby /'tʃʌbɪ/ *adj* punašan, bucmast

chuck /tʃʌk/ *vt coll* 1 izbaciti 2 odbaciti

chuckle /'tʃʌkl/ *n* hihot, smijuljenje •

vi smijuljiti se

chum /tʃʌm/ *n* prijatelj • *vi* ~ **up with sb** združiti se; skompati se *coll*

chunk /tʃʌŋk/ *n* komadina, debeli komad ~**y** *adj* kratak i debeo

church /tʃɜːtʃ/ *n* crkva ~**yard** groblje **the C~ of England** Anglikanska crkva **the C~ of Ireland** A. c. u Irskoj

churn /tʃɜːn/ *n* bućkalica • *vt, vi* 1 bućkati 2 (up) uzburkati (+ *fig*) 3 ~ **out** proizvoditi u masovnim količinama

chute /ʃuːt/ *n* 1 kosina 2 odvod, tobogan 3 *coll* padobran

cider /'saɪdə(r)/ *n* jabukovača

cigar /sɪ'gɑː(r)/ *n* cigara

cigarette /ˌsɪgə'ret/ *n* cigareta ~ **case** *n* tabakera ~**holder** *n* cigaretnik

cinder /'sɪndə(r)/ *n* 1 ugljevlje 2 troska **C~ella** *n* Pepeljuga

cinema /'sɪnəmə/ *n* 1 *GB* kino 2 kinematografija

cinnamon /'sɪnəmən/ *n* cimet

cipher /'saɪfə(r)/ *n* 1 šifra 2 nula, ništica (+ *fig*) • *vt, vi* šifrirati

circle /'sɜːkl/ *n* 1 krug (+ *fig*) 2 prsten 3 mezanin 4 ciklus • *vt,vi* obići, kružiti, cirkulirati

circuit /'sɜːkɪt/ *n* 1 puni krug 2 strujni krug ~**ous** /sɜː'kjuːɪtəs/ *adj* zaobilazan

circular /'sɜːkjʊlə(r)/ *adj* 1 kružni 2 okrugao ~ (**letter**) *n* okružnica ~ **saw** *n* cirkularna pila **circulate** *vi,vt* 1 kružiti, kolati 2 staviti u optjecaju, biti u optjecaju **circulation** *n* 1 kruženje 2 optok, cirkulacija 3 optjecaj 4 naklada

circumcise /'sɜːkəmsaɪz/ *vt* obrezati **circumcision** /ˌsɜːkəm'sɪʒn/ *n* obrezivanje

circumference /sə'kʌmfərəns/ *n* opseg

circumspect /'sɜːkəmspekt/ *adj* oprezan

circumstance /'sɜːkəmstəns/ *n* 1 okolnost, činjenica **in/under the ~s** u tim okolnostima 2 *pl* prilike **circumstantial** /ˌsɜːkəm'stænʃl/ *adj* 1 detaljan 2 zasnovan na indicijama

circus /'sɜːkəs/ *n* 1 cirkus 2 okrugli trg

cistern /'sɪstən/ *n* 1 cisterna, čatrnja 2

vodokotlić

cite /saɪt/ vt 1 citirati 2 US pohvaliti za ratne zasluge 3 pozvati na sud **citation** n 1 citat 2 pohvala

citizen /'sɪtɪzn/ n 1 građanin 2 građanin, državljanin **~ship** n državljanstvo

citric /'sɪtrɪk/ adj limunski

citrus /'sɪtrəs/ n agrum

city /'sɪtɪ/ n 1 grad **the C~** poslovni dio Londona 2 mod gradski

civic /'sɪvɪk/ adj gradski, građanski **~s** n pl (+ sing) znanost o društvenom uređenju

civil /'sɪvl/ adj 1 građanski 2 civilni 3 uljudan **~ engineering** n građevinarstvo **~ service** n državna služba **~ian** adj civilni, građanski ○ n **civil ~lity** n uljudnost **~ization** /ˌsɪvəlaɪˈzeɪʃn/ n civilizacija, kultura, uljudba **~ize** vt civilizirati, uljuditi

clad v irreg → **clothe**

claim /kleɪm/ n 1 zahtjev 2 pravo, povlastica 3 pretenzija, polaganje prava, svojatanje 4 udio, parcela 5 odšteta • vt, vi 1 zahtijevati (svoje), tražiti, svojatati 2 tvrditi **~ant** n tražitelj, tužitelj

clairvoyant /kleəˈvɔɪənt/ n vidovnjak

clam /klæm/ n školjka • vi **~ up** coll naglo zašutjeti

clamber /'klæmbə(r)/ vi uzverati se

clammy /'klæmɪ/ adj vlažan, ljepljiv

clamour (–or US) /'klæmə(r)/ n buka, povika • vi, vt dići poviku **~ for** glasno zahtijevati

clamp /klæmp/ n stezaljka, steg • vt, vi 1 stegnuti, pritegnuti 2 **~ down** (on) coll fig pojačati kontrolu/pritisak **~down** n uvođenje oštrijih mjera

clan /klæn/ n klan

clandestine /klæn'destɪn/ adj tajni

clang /klæŋ/ vt, vi zazvečati • n zveket

clap (1) /klæp/ vt, vi 1 pljeskati, aplaudirati 2 pljesnuti 3 fig nabiti • n pucanj

clap (2) n sl gonoreja; triper coll

claret /'klærət/ n (francusko) crveno vino

clarify /'klærɪfaɪ/ vt, vi 1 razjasniti 2 razbistriti **clarification** /ˌklærɪfɪ-'keɪʃn/ n razjašnjenje **clarity** n jas-

noća

clash /klæʃ/ n 1 zveket 2 sukob 3 nesklad (boja) • vi 1 zveketati 2 sukobiti se 3 biti u neskladu

clasp /klɑːsp/ n 1 kopča **~knife** n nož na sklapanje 2 stisak • vt, vi 1 stiskati 2 zakopčati **~ hands** sklopiti ruke

class /klɑːs/ n 1 klasa, razred, red, skupina 2 stalež 3 razred **~ room** n učionica 4 vrsnost, stil **~ify** /'klæsɪfaɪ/ vt klasificirati **~ification** n klasifikacija, razvrstavanje **~ified** adj 1 klasificiran **~ified advertisements** n pl mali oglasnik 2 tajni **~y** adj coll pun stila, šik

classic /'klæsɪk/ adj 1 klasičan 2 uzoran, izvrstan • n 1 klasik 2 pisac iz klasične starine 3 the **~s** klasična filologija **~al** /'klæsɪkl/ adj 1 klasični **~ music, ~ studies** 2 nedostavan

clatter /'klætə(r)/ n zveket • vi, vt zveketati **~ down** srušiti se uz zveket

clause /klɔːz/ n 1 rečenica 2 klauzula, točka

claw /klɔː/ n 1 pandža, kandža 2 štipaljka **~s** pl kliješta pl • vt **~ at** 1 grepsti 2 fig hvatati se zubima i noktima

clay /kleɪ/ n 1 glina 2 mod glinen

clean /kliːn/ adj čist (+ fig) • adv potpuno; čisto coll **~cut** adj jasan, oštrih crta **~shaven** adj glatko izbrijan • vt, vi očistiti **~ up** počistiti, pospremiti **~er** n čistač(ica)

cleanly /'klenlɪ/ adj čist **cleanliness** n čistoća

cleanse /'klenz/ vt očistiti **ethnic cleansing** n etničko čišćenje

clear /klɪə(r)/ adj 1 bistar; čist (+ fig), jasan (+ fig) do I make myself **~**? da li razumijete? je li vam jasno? 2 prohodan, prazan (put) • adv 1 jasno **loud and ~** jasno i glasno **~cut** adv izrazit 2 potpuno **~ of** podalje (od) • vt, vi 1 (of/from) očistiti (od), ukloniti (što) 2 osloboditi sumnje 3 ostvariti čistu zaradu 4 proći kroz **~ up** raščistiti (se) (+ fig) **~ance** n 1 raščišćavanje 2 slobodni prostor 3 dozvola **~ing** n čistina **~ly** /'klɪəlɪ/ jasno, očigledno

cleave /kliːv/ vt, vi irreg rasjeći, kalati

(se) **cleft palate** vučje ždrijelo **cleavage** n dekolte

clef /klef/ n mus ključ

cleft v irreg → **cleave**

clemency /'klemənsı/ n blagost

clench /klentʃ/ vt stisnuti

clergy /'klɜːdʒı/ n (+ pl) svećenstvo **~man** n svećenik

clerical /'klerıkl/ adj 1 svećenički 2 činovnički

clerk /klɑːk/ n 1 činovnik 2 US prodavač

clever /'klevə(r)/ n 1 pametan 2 spretan 3 lukav

cliche /'kliːʃeɪ/ n kliše **~d** adj otrcan

click /klık/ n škljocaj • vi škljocnuti, lupnuti

client /'klaɪənt/ n 1 stranka 2 kupac **~ele** n kupci, gosti

cliff /klıf/ n klisura

climate /'klaımıt/ n klima (+ fig)

climax /'klaımæks/ n vrhunac • vi postići vrhunac, doći do vrhunca

climb /klaım/ vi, vt 1 (up) penjati se 2 (down) spustiti se • n uspon **~er** n penjač

clinch /klıntʃ/ vt, vi 1 zaključiti (posao, raspravu) 2 zgrabiti (u klinč)

cling /klıŋ/ vi irreg (to/together) 1 pribiti/držati se uz, ne dati se odvojiti od 2 prianjati, pripijati se uz ~ **film** plastična folija (za kućanstvo)

clinic /'klınık/ n klinika **~al** adj 1 klinički 2 hladan, bešćutan

clink /klıŋk/ n zveket

clip (1) /klıp/ n (paper ~) spajalica 2 kvačica, spona 3 mil magazin 4 video-spot • vt pričvrstiti spajalicom

clip (2) vt 1 podrezati, strići, šišati **~ped speech** odsječan govor 2 poništiti (kartu) **~per** n 1 **~s** pl šišalica, grickalica 3 naut kliper **~ping** n izrezak iz novina

clique /kliːk/ n klika

cloak /kləʊk/ n ogrtač **~room** n garderoba • vt fig zastrti

clock /klɒk/ n sat **~wise** adv u smjeru kazaljke na satu **~work** n mod na navijanje • vt, vi ~ **in/out** otkucati karticu na ulasku/izlasku

clog (1) /klɒg/ n klompa

clog (2) vt začepiti

cloister /'klɔɪstə(r)/ n 1 trijem 2 samostan **~ed** adj samotan

close /kləʊs/ adj 1 blizak (+ fig); prisan 2 podroban, poman 3 tijesan (+ fig) 4 zatvoren (+ fig) 5 zagušljiv 6 škrt **~up** n krupni plan **~ly** adv pomno, izbliza **~ness** n bliskost; zagušljivost • adv 1 tik uz 2 čvrsto ~ **on/upon** skoro, gotovo **~fitting** adj uzak • n 1 kraj **draw/bring sth to a ~** dovršiti 2 slijepa ulica • vt, vi 1 zatvoriti 2 zaključiti 3 zbiti ~ **down** zatvoriti ~ **in** skraćivati se ~ **on/upon** približavati se

closet /'klɒzıt/ n 1 sobica 2 spremnica 3 mod prikriveni, potajni • vt **be ~ed with sb** sastati se iza zatvorenih vrata; šurovati

closure /'kləʊʒə(r)/ n zatvaranje

clot /klɒt/ n ugrušak • vt, vi zgrušati (se), slijepiti (se)

cloth /klɒθ/ n 1 tkanina 2 krpa

clothe /kləʊð/ vt irreg odijevati **clad** odjeven; oklopljen **~s** n pl odjeća **bed ~** n posteljina ~ **peg/pin** kvačica **clothing** n odjeća

cloud /klaʊd/ n oblak (+ fig) • vi, vt (over) 1 naoblačiti se 2 fig zamutiti, pomutiti **~y** adj 1 naoblačen 2 mutan

clove (1) /kləʊv/ n klinčić

clove (2) n česan

clove, cloven v irreg → **cleave**

clover /'kləʊvə(r)/ n djetelina **four–leaf~** četverolisna d.

clown /klaʊn/ n klaun • vi glupirati se

cloying /'klɔɪıŋ/ adj prezasićen, otužan

club /klʌb/ n 1 toljaga 2 palica 3 tref 4 klub • 1 vt udariti toljagom 2 vi ~ **together** udružiti se ~ **foot** n čopava noga

cluck /klʌk/ vi kvocati

clue /kluː/ n indicija, ključ rješenja **not have a ~** coll nemati pojma

clump /klʌmp/ n skupina

clumsy /'klʌmzı/ adj nespretan, nezgrapan

clung → v irreg **cling**

cluster /'klʌstə(r)/ n 1 grozd, skupina, nakupina • vi (together/round) okupljati se, ovijati se, gomilati se

clutch /klʌtʃ/ vt, vi ščepati, zgrabiti • n

1 *pl fig* ralje, šake **2** spojka
clutter /'klʌtə(r)/ *vt* prenatrpati • *n* nered
coach (1) /kəʊtʃ/ *n* **1** (međugradski) autobus **2** vagon **3** kočija
coach (2) *n* trener • *vt* trenirati
coagulate /kəʊ'ægjʊleɪt/ *vt,vi* zgrušati (se)
coal /kəʊl/ *n* ugljen ~ **gas** *n* rasvjetni plin ~ **mine/pit** *n* ugljenokop
coarse /kɔːs/ *adj* **1** grub (+ *fig*) **2** običan, prost
coast /kəʊst/ *n* obala ~ **line** *n* obala • *vi, vt* **1** ploviti uz obalu **2** spuštati se ne okrećući pedale ~**al** *adj* obalni ~**er** *n* podložak za čašu
coat /kəʊt/ *n* **1** kaput **2** dlaka, krzno **3** premaz ~ **of arms** *n* grb ~ **hanger** *n* vješalica • *vt* **1** zaodjenuti **2** prekriti, premazati, prevući ~**ing** *n* sloj, premaz
coax /'kəʊks/ *vt, vi* **1** (from) izmamiti **2** (into/out of) laskanjem nagovoriti/odgovoriti
cob /kɒb/ *n* klip
cobble /'kɒbl/ *vt* popločati kockama
cobbler /'kɒblə(r)/ *n* postolar
cobweb /'kɒbweb/ *n* paučina
cocaine /kəʊ'keɪn/ *n* kokain
cock /kɒk/ *n* **1** pijevac ~**–a–doo-dle–doo** /,kɒk ə ,duːdl'duː/ *int* kukuriku **2** ventil **3** oroz **4** *tab* kurac *tab* • *vt* (up) **1** podići ~ **one's ears** naćuliti uši **2** napeti oroz ~ **up** *sl* zeznuti stvar *sl* ~**up** *sl* propala stvar ~**eyed** *adj* škiljav; iskrivljen
cockatoo /,kɒkə'tuː/ *n* kakadu
cockerel /'kɒkərəl/ *n* pjetlić
cockle /'kɒkl/ *n* školjka
cockney /'kɒknɪ/ *n, mod* pravi Londonac
cockpit /'kɒkpɪt/ *n* pilotska kabina
cockroach /'kɒkrəʊtʃ/ *n* žohar
cockscomb /'kɒkskəʊm/ *n* **1** kresta **2** ludina kapa
cocktail /'kɒkteɪl/ *n* koktel ~ **dress** popodnevna haljina
cocoa /'kəʊkəʊ/ *n* kakao
coconut /'kəʊkənʌt/ *n* kokosov orah
cocoon /kə'kuːn/ *n* čahura
cod /kɒd/ *n* bakalar ~**liver oil** *n* riblje ulje

code /kəʊd/ *n* **1** kodeks **2** šifra, kod • *vt* šifrirati
coeducational (**coed** *coll*) /,kəʊ,edʒʊ-'keɪʃənl/ *adj* mješovit
coerce /kəʊ'ɜːs/ *vt* prisiliti **coercion** *n* prisila **coercive** *adj* prisilan
coexistence /,kəʊɪg'zɪstəns/ *n* suživot
coffee /'kɒfɪ/ *n* kava (biljka, prah, napitak)
coffer /'kɒfə(r)/ *n* škrinja ~**s** *pl* trezor
coffin /'kɒfɪn/ *n* lijes
cog /kɒg/ *n* zubac ~**wheel** *n* zupčanik
coherent /kəʊ'hɪərənt/ *adj* smislen, jasan **coherence** *n* smislenost
cohesion /kəʊ'hiːʒn/ *n* kohezija
coiffure /kwɑː'fjʊə(r)/ *n* frizura
coil /kɔɪl/ *vt,vi* uvijati (se), smotati (se), namotati • *n* **1** viguja, navoj, uvojak **2** *coll* spirala *coll*
coin /kɔɪn/ *n* kovanica • *vt* **1** kovati novac **2** izmisliti/iskovati (novu riječ)
coincide /,kəʊɪn'saɪd/ *vi* (with) podudarati se, poklapati se, slagati se ~**nce** *n* koincidencija
coke /kəʊk/ *n* **1** koks **2** C~ *coll* Coca–Cola **3** *sl* kokain; koka *sl*
colander /'kʌləndə(r)/ *n* cjedilo
cold /kəʊld/ *adj* **1** hladan (+ *fig*) **2** suzdržan **3** odbojan **have ~ feet** strahovati **in ~ blood** hladnokrvno ~**blooded** *adj* hladnokrvan ~ **steel** hladno oružje ~ *n* **1** hladnoća **out in the ~** *fig* zanemaren **2** prehlada ~**ly** *adv fig* hladno ~**ness** *n* hladnoća
collaborate /kə'læbəreɪt/ *vi* (on sth/with sb) surađivati na čemu/s kim **collaboration** *n* suradnja **collaborator** *n* suradnik **collaborationist** *n* kolaboracionist
collapse /kə'læps/ *vi* **1** srušiti se, propasti **2** malaksati **3** sklopiti ~**able/~ible** *adj* na sklapanje
collar /'kɒlə(r)/ *n* **1** ovratnik **2** ogrlica ~**bone** ključna kost
collateral /kə'lætərəl/ *adj* sekundaran, dodatni ~ **security** imovina kao jamstvo plaćanja • *n* jamstvo plaćanja
colleague /'kɒliːg/ *n* kolega
collect /kə'lekt/ *vt,vi* **1** (up/together) sakupiti (se) **2** skupljati ~ **stamps** **3** pokupiti, podići **4** sabrati (se) • *adj, adv US* **call** ~ → reverse charges ~**ed**

adj sabran ~**ion** *n* 1 zbirka 2 skupljanje 3 skupljanje milodara ~**ive** *adj* zajednički, skupan ~**or** *n* sakupljač

college /ˈkɒlɪdʒ/ *n* 1 koledž, visoka/viša/srednja škola 2 zbor

collide /kəˈlaɪd/ *vi* (with) 1 sudariti se 2 sukobiti se

collier /ˈkɒlɪə(r)/ *n* rudar ~**y** *n* ugljenokop

collision /kəˈlɪʒn/ *n* sudar, sukob

colloquial /kəˈləʊkwɪəl/ *adj* kolokvijalan, razgovoran

collusion /kəˈluːʒn/ *n* doslu h

colon (1) /ˈkəʊlən/ *n* dvotočka

colon (2) *n* med debelo crijevo

colonel /ˈkɜːnl/ *n* brigadir

colonial /kəˈləʊnɪəl/ *adj* kolonijalni • *n* kolon ~**ism** *n* kolonijalizam **colonize** /ˈkɒlənaɪz/ *vt* kolonizirati **colony** /ˈkɒlənɪ/ *n* kolonija

colour (–**or** *US*) /ˈkʌlə(r)/ *n* 1 boja —**blind** slijep za boje 2 *mod* u boji ~ *TV* 3 ton *local* ~ 4 *pl* mar, mil zastava (+ *fig*) **come through with flying** ~**s** postići veliki uspjeh 5 rasa ~ **bar** rasna segregacija • *vt, vi* 1 obojiti 2 porumeniti ~**ed** *adj* obojen ~**ing** *n* boja ~**ful** *adj* živ, jasan

colt /kəʊlt/ *n* ždrijebe

column /ˈkɒləm/ *n* 1 stup 2 kolona 3 stupac 4 kolumna ~**ist** *n* kolumnist

coma /ˈkəʊmə/ *n* koma

comb /kəʊm/ *n* češalj • *vt, vi* 1 češljati 2 *fig* pročešljati 3 ~ **out** *fig* pročistiti

combat /ˈkɒmbæt/ *n* 1 borba 2 *mod* borbeni 3 *mod* vojnički • *vt, vi* (θ/against/with) boriti se s/protiv

combination /ˌkɒmbɪˈneɪʃn/ *n* kombinacija ~ **lock** *n* šifrirana brava **combine** /kəmˈbaɪn/ *vt, vi* (with) spojiti, sjediniti *n* 1 trust, udruga 2 (~ **harvester**) kombajn

combustion /kəmˈbʌstʃən/ *n* sagorijevanje

come /kʌm/ *vi irreg* 1 (to/from) doći 2 *coll* svršiti ~ **of age** postati punoljetan **how** ~? kako to? **coming** *n* dolazak ∘ *adj* sljedeći ~ **about** dogoditi se ~ **across** naići ~ **along** pridružiti se, doći ~ **apart** raspasti se ~ **back** vratiti se ~**back** *n* povratak ~ **by sth** dokopati se, doći do ~

down pasti ~ **down with** oboljeti od ~ **from** biti iz ~ **in** ući, stići ~ **into** naslijediti ~ **off a.** odigrati se **b.** uspjeti **c.** otpasti, izbrisati se **d.** pasti, sići ~ **on!** *int* a. hajde! **b.** ma daj! ~**on a.** doći za kime **b.** napredovati **b.** nailaziti ~ **out a.** izići **b.** pojaviti se **c.** ispasti ~ **over a.** doći **b.** spopasti ~ **through a.** izvući (se (fig) **b.** stići (vijest i sl.) **c.** preživjeti ~ **to** osvijestiti se ~ **up a.** izići (sunce) **b.** doći na dnevni red **c.** pojaviti se, iskrsnuti ~ **up against** suočiti se ~ **up with** pronaći

comedian /kəˈmiːdɪən/ *n* komičar **comedienne** /kəˌmiːdɪˈen/ *n* komičarka **comedy** /ˈkɒmədɪ/ *n* komedija

comeuppance /ˌkʌmˈʌpəns/ *n* zaslužena kazna

comfort /ˈkʌmfət/ *n* 1 udobnost, komocija ~**s** *pl* komfor 2 utjeha • *vt* tješiti ~**able** /ˈkʌmftəbl/ *adj* 1 udoban **make oneself** ~**able** raskomotiti se 2 pristojan *fig* ~**er** *n* 1 *GB* vuneni šal 2 *GB* duda varalica 3 *US* poplun

comic /ˈkɒmɪk/ *adj* komičan • *n* 1 komičar 2 (~ **strip**) strip

comma /ˈkɒmə/ *n* zarez

command /kəˈmɑːnd/ *n* 1 zapovijed 2 zapovjedništvo **have/take** ~ **of** preuzeti z. 3 (of) poznavanje 4 vlast, kontrola 5 *mil* stožer • *vt, vi* 1 zapovijedati 2 raspolagati 3 vladati 4 zasluživati ~**ing** *adj* zapovjednički ~**ing officer,** ~**ant,** ~**er** *n* zapovjednik ~**er–in–Chief** vrhovni zapovjednik ~**eer** /ˌkɒmənˈdɪə(r)/ *vt* rekvirirati ~**ment** *n* zapovijed ~**o** *n* komandos

commemorate / kəˈmeməreɪt/ *vt* obilježiti uspomenu, komemorirati

commence /kəˈmens/ *vt, vi* početi ~**ment** *n* početak

commend /kəˈmend/ *vt* 1 (on sth) pohvaliti zbog čega 2 ~ **sth to** povjeriti što kome 3 ~ **oneself to sb** svidjeti se kome ~**able** *adj* hvalevrijedan

comment /ˈkɒment/ *n* komentar, primjedba • *vi* (on/upon) primijetiti, komentirati što ~**ary** /ˈkɒməntrɪ/ 1 komentar (Biblije i sl.) 2 komentar (utakmice i sl.) **running** ~**ary** prijenos ~**ator** *n* komentator, izvjestitelj(ica)

commerce /'kɒmɜ:s/ n trgovina **commercial** /kə'mɜ:ʃl/ adj 1 trgovački 2 komercijalni • n TV/radio reklama **commercialize** vt komercijalizirati

commiserate /kə'mɪzəreɪt/ vi ~ with suosjećati s

commission /kə'mɪʃn/ n 1 ovlast 2 narudžba, ugovor 3 provizija 4 odbor, povjerenstvo • vt (sb to do sth) naručiti od, angažirati ~**aire** n portir ~**er** n povjerenik **The UN High ~er for Refugees** visoki povjerenik UN za izbjeglice

commit /kə'mɪt/ vt 1 počiniti 2 (to) smjestiti (u zatvor), staviti 3 (oneself to) preuzeti na sebe, obvezati se ~**ment** n 1 zatvor 2 obveza ~**tee** n odbor

commodity /kə'mɒdətɪ/ n roba

common /'kɒmən/ adj 1 zajednički 2 običan 3 uobičajen 4 vulgaran ~ **ground** n fig zajednički nazivnik ~ **sense** n zdrav razum ~ **law** n običajno pravo ~–**law wife** n nevjenčana supruga ~**place** adj običan **C~ Market** n EEZ ~**wealth** n zajednica naroda ~**er** n pučanin ~**ly** adv obično • n 1 javni park 2 **have in** ~ (with) dijeliti, imati zajedničko **out of the** ~ neobično 3 **the (House of) C~s** n pl GB Donji dom

commotion /kə'məʊʃn/ n komešanje

commune /'kɒmju:n/ n 1 općina 2 komuna • vi /kə'mju:n/ (with) komunicirati/razgovarati (s) **communal** /'kɒmjunl/ adj komunalni, zajednički

communicate /kə'mju:nɪkeɪt/ vt,vi 1 priopćiti 2 komunicirati s **communication** /kə,mju:nɪ'keɪʃn/ n priopćenje, komunikacija, komunikacije **communicative** /kə'mju:nɪkətɪv/ adj otvoren **communicable** /kə'mju:nɪkəbl/ adj prenosiv

communion /kə'mju:nɪən/ n zajedništvo, općenje **(Holy) C~** Sveta pričest

communique /kə'mju:nɪkeɪ/ n priopćenje

communism /'kɒmjunɪzəm/ n komunizam

community /kə'mju:nətɪ/ n 1 zajedni-ca 2 zajedništvo

commute /kə'mju:t/ vt,vi 1 smanjiti kaznu 2 putovati na posao ~**r** n stanovnik predgrađa koji putuje u grad na posao ~ **train** n prigradski vlak

compact /kəm'pækt/ adj gust, kompaktan, nabijen • n 1 puderijera 2 mali auto

companion /kəm'pænɪən/ n 1 suputnik 2 drug, drugarica, pratilac, pratilja 3 partner 4 priručnik ~**ship** n drugarstvo

company /'kʌmpənɪ/ n 1 društvo **keep** (sb) ~ praviti komu društvo 2 gosti 3 poduzeće 4 družina 5 mil četa

compare /kəm'peə(r)/ vt,vi (with/to) usporediti (sa) **comparable** /'kɒmpərəbl/ adj usporediv **comparative** adj 1 komparativan 2 razmjerni **comparison** n usporedba **by/in comparison** ako se usporedi **bear/stand comparison with** moći se usporedivati

compartment /kəm'pɑ:tmənt/ n 1 odjeljak 2 kupe ~**alize** vt klasificirati

compass /'kʌmpəs/ n 1 kompas 2 ~**es** pl šestar

compassion /kəm'pæʃn/ n smilovanje, suosjećajnost ~**ate** adj sućutan

compatible /kəm'pætəbl/ adj (with) 1 spojiv 2 comp kompatibilan **IBM ~** kompatibilan s IBM

compel /kəm'pel/ vt (to) prisiliti na

compensate /'kɒmpenseɪt/ vt 1 odštetiti 2 (for) nadoknaditi (koga/što) **compensation** n odšteta

compere /'kɒmpeə(r)/ n najavljivač

compete /kəm'pi:t/ vi (in/with) natjecati se **competition** /,kɒmpə'tɪʃn/ n 1 natjecanje 2 konkurencija **competitive** /kəm'petətɪv/ adj 1 natjecateljski 2 konkurentan **competitor** /kəm-'petɪtə(r)/ n natjecatelj, konkurent

competence /'kɒmpɪtəns/ n 1 sposobnost, mogućnost 2 nadležnost, jurisdikcija **competent** adj sposoban, kvalificiran, nadležan

compile /kəm'paɪl/ vt prikupiti, sastaviti **compilation** /,kɒmpɪ'leɪʃn/ n kompilacija, zbirka

complacence, complacency /kəm-

'pleısnsı/ *n* samozadovoljstvo **complacent** *adj* samozadovoljan

complain /kəm'pleın/ *vi* (to sb about sth/sb) tužiti se (komu na što/koga), žaliti se ~t *n* 1 žalba, tužba 2 boljka

complaisance /kəm'pleızəns/ *n* popustljivost **complaisant** *adj* popustljiv

complement /'kɒmplımənt/ *n* 1 dopuna 2 popuna • *vt* dopunjavati ~ary *adj* dopunski

complete /kəm'pli:t/ *adj* 1 potpun 2 dovršen ~ly *odv* potpuno, sasvim • *vt* dovršiti, popuniti, ispuniti **completion** /kəm'pli:ʃn/ *n* dovršenje, istek

complex /'kɒmpleks/ *adj* složen • *n* kompleks ~ity *n* složenost 1 pl začkoljice

complexion /kəm'plekʃn/ *n* ten

compliance /kəm'plaıəns/ 1 povodljivost 2 udovoljavanje **in ~ with** u skladu s

complicate /'kɒmplıkeıt/ *vt* zakomplicirati

complicity /kəm'plısıtı/ *n* (in) suučesništvo

compliment /'kɒmplımənt/ *n* 1 kompliment **pay a ~** udijeliti k. 2 *pl* pozdravi • *vt* (on sth) čestitati na čemu, pohvaliti što ~ary /,kɒmplı'mentrı/ *adj* 1 pohvalan 2 besplatan

comply /kəm'plaı/ *vt* (with) pridržavati se (čega), postupati prema (čemu), pokoriti se (čemu)

component /kəm'pəʊnənt/ *adj* sastavni • *n* sastavni dio

compose /kəm'pəʊz/ *vt,vi* 1 sastaviti 2 **be ~ed** (of) sastojati se od 3 napisati, skladati 4 složiti 5 smiriti se ~**r** *n* kompozitor, skladatelj

composite /'kɒmpəzıt/ *adj* sastavljen od više dijelova **composition** /,kɒmpə'zıʃn/ *n* 1 skladba 2 sastav **compositor** /kəm'pɒzıtə(r)/ *n* slagar ¶ kompozitor = **composer composure** /kəm'pəʊʒə(r)/ *n* spokojstvo, staloženost

compound /'kɒmpaʊnd/ *adj* složen ~ **interest** kamate na kamate • *n* 1 spoj, složenica 2 kompleks (zgrada)

comprehend /,kɒmprı'hend/ *vt* 1 shvatiti 2 obuhvaćati **comprehen-**

sion *n* razumijevanje **comprehensive** /,kɒmprı'hensıv/ *adj* opsežan, sveobuhvatan **~ (school)** *n* srednja škola

compress /kəm'pres/ *vt* 1 stisnuti 2 sažeti • *n* /'kɒmpres/ ovoj

comprise /kəm'praız/ *vt* sastojati se od

compromise /'kɒmprəmaız/ *n* kompromis, nagodba • *vt, vi* 1 nagoditi se 2 kompromitirati 3 ugroziti

compulsive /kəm'pʌlsıv/ *adj* prisilan **compulsory** *adj* obavezan **compulsion** *n* prisila

computer /kəm'pju:tə(r)/ *n* kompjutor, računalo ~ize *vt* kompjuterizirati

comrade /'kɒmreıd/ *n* drug ~ship *n* drugarstvo

con /kɒn/ *vt* prevariti ~man *n* prevarant

conceal /kən'si:l/ *vt* (from) sakriti, tajiti (pred kim) ~ment *n* skrivanje

concede /kən'si:d/ *vt* 1 priznati 2 ustupiti

conceit /kən'si:t/ *n* taština ~ed *adj* umišljen

conceive /kən'si:v/ *vt,vi* 1 zamisliti 2 začeti

concentrate /'kɒnsntreıt/ *vt,vi* 1 koncentrirati (se) 2 (on/upon) usredotočiti se, skoncentrirati se **concentration** *n* ~ **camp** *n* koncentracijski logor

concept /'kɒnsept/ *n* pojam ~ion *n* 1 koncepcija 2 začeće

concern /kən'sɜ:n/ *vt* 1 ticati se koga/čega, odnositi se na koga/što 2 (oneself with/in/about) baviti se 3 **be ~ed** (about/for) brinuti zbog koga/čega • *n* 1 briga 2 posao 3 udio, interes ~**ed** *adj* zabrinut ~**ing** *prep* glede, s obzirom na

concert /'kɒnsət/ *n* 1 koncert 2 sloga **in ~** (with) zajedno s ~**ed** *adj* zajednički

concertina /,kɒnsə'ti:nə/ *n* harmonika

concession /kən'seʃn/ *n* 1 ustupak 2 koncesija

concise /kən'saıs/ *adj* sažet

conclude /kən'klu:d/ *vt,vi* 1 zaključiti 2 sklopiti 3 dovršiti, završiti **conclusion** *n* 1 zaključak 2 okončanje **conclusive** *adj* konačan, nedvojben concoct /kən'kɒkt/ vt 1 smiješati 2 fig smisliti ~ion n mješavina

concourse /'kɒŋkɔ:s/ n 1 skup, stjecaj 2 dvorana, predvorje

concrete (1) /'kɒŋkri:t/ adj konkretan, stvaran

concrete (2) n 1 beton 2 mod betonski

concur /kən'kɜ:(r)/ vi 1 slagati se 2 podudarati se

concussion /kən'kʌʃn/ n potres (mozga)

condemn /kən'dem/ vt 1 (for) osuditi koga zbog čega 2 (to) osuditi na ~ed cell ćelija osuđenika na smrt ~ed building zgrada za rušenje

condense /kən'dens/ vt,vi 1 kondenzirati (se) 2 fig sažeti ~r n kondenzator

condensation /,kɒnden'seɪʃn/ n kondenzacija

condescend /,kɒndɪ'send/ vi (to) 1 biti tako ljubazan da 2 udostojiti se iron ~ing adj 1 ljubazan 2 snishodljiv

condition /kən'dɪʃn/ n 1 uvjet on ~ pod uvjetom 2 stanje, kondicija 3 pl okolnosti • vt 1 uvjetovati 2 dovesti do čega 3 staviti regenerator; omekšivač i sl. ~ed reflex uvjetovani refleks ~al adj 1 uvjetan 2 gram pogodben ~er n regenerator, omekšivač

condolence /kən'dəʊləns/ n sućut offer ~s izjaviti sućut

condom /'kɒndəm/ n prezervativ

condo(minium) /,kɒndə'mɪnɪəm/ n US zgrada u etažnom vlasništvu

condone /kən'dəʊn/ vt prijeći preko, tolerirati

conduct /'kɒndʌkt/ n 1 ponašanje 2 vođenje • /kən'dʌkt/ vt, vi 1 voditi 2 upravljati 3 el provodvima 4 ponašati se ~or n 1 dirigent 2 kondukter 3 el vodič

cone /kəʊn/ n 1 stožac 2 kornet 3 češer

confection /kən'fekʃn/ n 1 slatkiš ~er slastičar ~ery n 1 slatkiši 2 slastičarnica

confer /kən'fɜ:(r)/ vt,vi 1 (on/upon) dodijeliti 2 (with/on/about) vijećati, savjetovati se ~ence /'kɒnfərəns/ n sastanak, konferencija

confess /kən'fes/ vt,vi 1 (0, to) priznati 2 (to sb) ispovjediti ~ion

/kən'feʃn/ n 1 priznanje 2 ispovijed 3 vjeroispovijest ~ional n ispovjedaonica

confide /kən'faɪd/ vt,vi 1 ~ to povjeriti se 2 ~ in imati povjerenja confidant /'kɒnfɪdænt/ n pouzdanik ~nce /'kɒnfɪdəns/ n 1 povjerenje 2 tajna 3 pouzdanje, vjera con(fidence) trick n prevara con(fidence) man n prevarant ~nt /'kɒnfɪdənt/ adj (of) pun pouzdanja, uvjeren ~ntial /,kɒnfɪ'denʃl/ adj 1 povjerljiv 2 tajni ~ntiality n tajnost

confine /kən'faɪn/ vt 1 (to) ograničiti na 2 zatočiti ~ment n 1 zatvor solitary ~ment n samica 2 porod 3 pl granice

confirm /kən'fɜ:m/ vt 1 potvrditi 2 ratificirati 3 krizmati, firmati ~ation /,kɒnfə'meɪʃn/ n (of) 1 potvrda 2 Sv. potvrda, krizma

confiscate /'kɒnfɪskeɪt/ vt konfiscirati

conflict /'kɒnflɪkt/ n 1 sukob 2 proturječje • vi (with) biti u proturječnosti s ~ing adj proturječan

conform /kən'fɔ:m/ vi,vt (to) 1 pridržavati se, postupati u skladu s 2 prilagoditi (se) ~ist n konformist

confound /kən'faʊnd/ vt 1 smesti 2 (with) pobrkati

confront /kən'frʌnt/ vt 1 ~ sb with suočiti koga s čim 2 ispriječiti se pred ~ation n konfrontacija

confuse /kən'fju:z/ vt (with) 1 smesti, zbuniti 2 pobrkati ~dly adv smeteno confusion n 1 pometnja, metež 2 zabuna

congeal /kən'dʒi:l/ vi,vt 1 zalediti (se) 2 zgrušati (se)

congenial /kən'dʒi:nɪəl/ adj srodan, ugodan

congenital /kən'dʒenɪtl/ adj prirođen

congested /kən'dʒestɪd/ adj 1 zagušen 2 pun krvi congestion n 1 zagušenje 2 navala krvi

conglomerate /kən'glɒmərət/ n konglomerat conglomeration n /kən,glɒmə'reɪʃn/ n konglomeracija

congratulate /kən'grætʃʊleɪt/ vt (on) čestitati na congratulation /kən,grætʃʊ'leɪʃn/ n čestitka congratulations int čestitam!

congregate /'kɒŋgrɪgeɪt/ vi skupiti se
congregation n kongregacija, skup
congress /'kɒŋgres/ n 1 zbor, skup, kongres 2 C~ pol Kongres **~man/woman** n član(ica) Kongresa
conical /'kɒnɪkl/ adj stožast, šiljat
conifer /'kɒnɪfə(r)/ n crnogorica **~ous** /kə'nɪfərəs/ adj crnogoričan
conjecture /kən'dʒektʃə(r)/ n pretpostavka, nagađanje • vt, vi nagađati **conjectural** adj zasnovan na indicijama
conjugal /'kɒndʒʊgl/ adj bračni
conjugate /'kɒndʒʊgeɪt/ vt gram sprezati
conjunction /kən'dʒʌŋkʃn/ n 1 gram veznik 2 povezanost **in ~ with** zajedno s
conjure /'kʌndʒə(r)/ vi, vt 1 izvoditi mađioničarske trikove 2 **~ up** dočarati 3 **~ up** dozvati/stvoriti čarolijom **~r** n mađioničar, čarobnjak
conk /kɒŋk/ vi **~ out** coll krepati, riknuti coll
connect /kə'nekt/ vt, vi 1 (with/to) povezati (se), priključiti (se) 2 (with) udariti o **~ion, connexion** n 1 veza 2 spoj, priključak 3 klijentela, poslovne veze
connive /kə'naɪv/ vi, vt **~ at** gledati kroz prste **~ with** šurovati s
connoisseur /ˌkɒnə'sɜː(r)/ n znalac
connote /kə'nəʊt/ vt 1 konotirati 2 ukazivati na
conquer /'kɒŋkə(r)/ vt 1 osvojiti 2 pobijediti **~or** n osvajač **conquest** n 1 osvajanje 2 osvojena zemlja i sl.
conscience /'kɒnʃəns/ n savjest **conscientious** /ˌkɒnʃi'enʃəs/ adj savjestan **~ objection** prigovor savjesti **~ objector** osoba koja odbija služiti vojni rok
conscious /'kɒnʃəs/ adj 1 (of/that) svjestan čega/da 2 samosvjestan **~ly** adv svjesno **~ness** n svijest **lose/regain ~** onesvijestiti/osvijestiti se
conscript /'kɒnskrɪpt/ n novak **~ion** n novačenje
consecrate /'kɒnsɪkreɪt/ vt posvetiti
consecutive /kən'sekjʊtɪv/ adj konzekutivan; uzastopni; sljedeći

consensus /kən'sensəs/ n suglasnost
consent /kən'sent/ vi (to) suglasiti se, pristati na što • n 1 suglasnost 2 pristanak **age of ~** punoljetnost
consequence /'kɒnsɪkwəns/ n 1 posljedica **in ~ of** uslijed 2 važnost **person of ~** važna osoba **consequent** adj (on) koji je posljedica čega **~ly** adv odatle
conservation /ˌkɒnsə'veɪʃn/ n čuvanje, zaštita
conservative /kən'sɜːvətɪv/ adj 1 oprezan, suzdržljiv 2 konzervativan **the C~ Party** GB Konzervativna stranka • n konzervativac
conservatory /kən'sɜːvətrɪ/ n 1 staklenik 2 konzervatorij
conserve /kən'sɜːv/ vt 1 sačuvati 2 konzervirati • n džem
consider /kən'sɪdə(r)/ vt 1 razmisliti 2 uzeti u obzir **all things ~ed** sve u svemu 3 smatrati **~able** adj priličan, značajan **~ate** adj obziran, pažljiv **~ation** /kənˌsɪdə'reɪʃn/ n 1 razmatranje **take into ~** uzeti u obzir 2 pažnja, obzir 3 moment, čimbenik **~ing** prep s obzirom na
consign /kən'saɪn/ vt otpremiti, predati **~ment** n pošiljka
consist /kən'sɪst/ vi 1 (of) sastojati se od 2 (in) ležati u
consistent /kən'sɪstənt/ adj dosljedan **~ with** u skladu s **consistency** n 1 dosljednost 2 konzistencija
console (1) /kən'səʊl/ vt tješiti **consolation** /ˌkɒnsə'leɪʃn/ n utjeha **~ prize** n utješna nagrada
console (2) /'kɒnsəʊl/ n konzola
consolidate /kən'sɒlɪdeɪt/ vt, vi 1 učvrstiti 2 ujediniti
consomme /kən'sɒmeɪ/ n bistra juha
consonant /'kɒnsənənt/ n suglasnik
consort /'kɒnsɔːt/ n supruga, suprug • vi (with) družiti se
conspicuous /kən'spɪkjuəs/ adj 1 jasan, očit 2 upadljiv
conspire /kən'spaɪə(r)/ vi, vt (to/with/against) kovati urotu, rotiti se **everything ~d against me** sve se urotilo protiv mene **conspiracy** /kən'spɪrəsɪ/ n urota **conspirator** /kən'spɪrətə(r)/ n urotnik

constable /'kʌnstəbl/ n pozornik **constabulary** /kən'stæbjʊlərɪ/ n policija

constant /'kɒnstənt/ adj 1 stalni 2 postojan **constancy** n postojanost, vjernost

constellation /ˌkɒnstə'leɪʃn/ n konstelacija (+ fig)

constipated /'kɒnstɪpeɪtɪd/ adj koji pati od zatvora **constipation** n zatvor (stolice)

constituency /kən'stɪtjʊənsɪ/ n 1 izborni okrug 2 birači 3 fig interesna sfera **constituent** adj sastavni • n 1 birač 2 sastavni dio

constitution /ˌkɒnstɪ'tju:ʃn/ n 1 ustav 2 tjelesni ustroj **~al** adj ustavni **constitute** /'kɒnstɪtju:t/ vt 1 (us)postaviti 2 tvoriti

constrain /kən'streɪn/ vt nagnati, prisiliti **~ed** adj usiljen **~t** n 1 prisila 2 suzdržanost

constricted /kən'strɪktɪd/ adj fig uzak, uskogrudan

construct /kən'strʌkt/ vt graditi, konstruirati **~ion** n 1 izgradnja 2 građevina, konstrukcija 3 tumačenje **~ive** adj konstruktivan

construe /kən'stru:/ vt,vi tumačiti

consul /'kɒnsl/ n konzul

consult /kən'sʌlt/ vt,vi konzultirati (se), savjetovati se **~ant** n konzultant, savjetnik

consume /kən'sju:m/ vt,vi 1 konzumirati, pojesti, trošiti 2 fig proždrijeti fig **time-consuming** adj koji odnosi puno vremena **~r** n potrošač **~r goods** pl roba široke potrošnje **~r society** potrošačko društvo **~rism** n zaštita potrošača

consummate /'kɒnsəmeɪt/ vt konzumirati (brak); postići • adj vrhunski

consumption /kən'sʌmpʃn/ n 1 potrošnja 2 TBC

contact /'kɒntækt/ n dodir, susret, veza, kontakt **make ~ with** stupiti u kontakt **~ lense** n kontaktna leća • vt doći u dodir

contagion /kən'teɪdʒən/ n zaraza **contagious** adj zarazan

contain /kən'teɪn/ vt 1 sadrža(va)ti 2 zadržati **~er** n 1 posuda 2 kontejner

contaminate /kən'tæmɪneɪt/ vt zagadi-

ti **contamination** n zagađenje

contemplate /'kɒntempleɪt/ vt,vi 1 razmatrati 2 razmišljati (o)

contemporary /kən'temprərɪ/ adj suvremeni • n suvremenik

contempt /kən'tempt/ n prezir, neobaziranje **~ of court** neodazivanje pozivu na sud **~ible** adj prezira vrijedan **~uous** adj preziran

contend /kən'tend/ vt,vi 1 boriti se 2 sporiti se **~er** n suparnik

content (1) /kən'tent/ adj zadovoljan **be ~ to do sth** učiniti sa zadovoljstvom • n zadovoljstvo **to one's heart's ~** do mile volje • vt zadovoljiti **~ed** adj zadovoljan **~ment** n zadovoljstvo

content (2) /'kɒntent/ n 1 sadržaj **(table of) ~s** sadržaj (knjige) **fat ~** količina masti 2 zapremina

contention /kən'tenʃn/ n 1 prepirka 2 argument **contentious** adj svadljiv

contest /kən'test/ vt 1 pobijati 2 boriti se za, natjecati se • n natjecanje

context /'kɒntekst/ n kontekst

continent /'kɒntɪnənt/ n 1 kontinent 2 GB (ostala) Europa **~al** adj kontinentalan

contingency /kən'tɪndʒənsɪ/ n 1 mogućnost 2 pl nepredviđene okolnosti 3 mod rezervni

contingent /kən'tɪndʒənt/ n kontingent

continue /kən'tɪnju:/ vi,vt 1 nastaviti (se) 2 zadržati se, nastaviti s, ostati **continual** adj stalan, učestao **continuation** /kən,tɪnjʊ'eɪʃn/ n nastavak **continuity** /ˌkɒntɪ'nju:ətɪ/ n kontinuitet **continuous** /kən'tɪnjʊəs/ adj neprekidan

contort /kən'tɔ:t/ vt iskriviti

contour /'kɒntʊə(r)/ n obris **~ line** n izohipsa

contraband /'kɒntrəbænd/ n 1 krijumčarenje 2 mod krijumčaren

contraception /ˌkɒntrə'sepʃn/ n kontracepcija **contraceptive** adj, n kontracepcijski, kontraceptiv

contract /'kɒntrækt/ n ugovor **enter into/make a. ~** sklopiti ugovor • vi,vt /kən'trækt/ sklopiti ugovor 2 zaraziti se, dobiti 3 stegnuti (se), skupiti (se)

~ion n 1 kontrakcija, stezanje 2 skraćeni oblik ~or n poduzetnik

contradict /ˌkɒntrəˈdɪkt/ vt proturječiti ~ion n 1 proturječje 2 suprotstavljanje ~ory /ˌkɒntrəˈdɪktərɪ/ adj proturječan

contraption /kənˈtræpʃn/ n coll naprava

contrary /ˈkɒntrərɪ/ adj suprotan ~ to u suprotnosti • n the ~ suprotnost on the ~ baš suprotno

contrast /ˈkɒntrɑːst/ n 1 kontrast 2 razlika • /kənˈtrɑːst/ vt, vi 1 usporediti 2 razlikovati se

contravene /ˌkɒntrəˈviːn/ vt 1 prekršiti 2 pobijati 3 sukobiti se contravention /ˌkɒntrəˈvenʃn/ n kršenje act in contravention of kršiti

contribute /kənˈtrɪbjuːt/ vt, vi (to) pridonijeti, dati/slati priloge contributor n suradnik (novina) contribution /ˌkɒntrɪˈbjuːʃn/ n 1 doprinos 2 prilog

contrive /kənˈtraɪv/ vt, vi 1 smisliti 2 srediti, naći načina

control /kənˈtrəʊl/ n 1 kontrola, nadzor 2 pl kontrolni uređaji • vt 1 kontrolirati, nadzirati, pregledavati 2 obuzdavati ~ler n kontrolor, nadzornik

controversy /ˈkɒntrəvɜːsɪ/ n kontroverzija, sporna tema controversial /ˌkɒntrəˈvɜːʃl/ adj kontroverzan

convalesce /ˌkɒnvəˈles/ vi ozdraviti ~nce n ozdravljenje

convene /kənˈviːn/ vt, vi 1 sazvati 2 sastati se

convenience /kənˈviːnɪəns/ n 1 praktičnost, prednost, dobra strana at your ~ kad ti bude odgovaralo 2 pl komfor all mod(ern) con(venience)s potpun komfor public ~ GB javni zahod convenient adj 1 koji odgovara, dobar, pogodan 2 praktičan

convent /ˈkɒnvənt/ n samostan

convention /kənˈvenʃn/ n konvencija (skupština, ugovor, običaj) ~al adj konvencionalan

converge /kənˈvɜːdʒ/ vi (at/on/upon) stjecati se, približavati se

conversation /ˌkɒnvəˈseɪʃn/ n razgovor ~al adj 1 razgovoran 2 zabavan

converse /kənˈvɜːs/ vi razgovarati

convert /kənˈvɜːt/ vt (from/to/into) 1 pretvoriti 2 obratiti • /ˈkɒnvɜːt/ n obraćenik conversion n obraćenje; konverzija ~ible n kabriolet

convey /kənˈveɪ/ vt 1 (from/to) prevoziti, voditi, (pre)nositi 2 (to) prenijeti fig ~er-belt n tekuća vrpca ~ance n prijenos, prijevoz

convict /ˈkɒnvɪkt/ n kažnjenik • /kənˈvɪkt/ vt (sb of sth) osuditi, proglasiti krivim ~ion n 1 osuda 2 uvjerljivost 3 uvjeravanje 4 uvjerenost

convince /kənˈvɪns/ vt uvjeriti

convoy /ˈkɒnvɔɪ/ n 1 konvoj 2 pratnja

convulse /kənˈvʌls/ vt be ~d with grčiti se u, potresati convulsion n 1 grč 2 potres

coo /kuː/ vi, vt gukati (+ fig)

cook /kʊk/ vt, vi kuhati, pripremati (jelo) ~ up izmisliti • n kuhar ~er n štednjak ~ery n kulinarstvo ~(ery) book kuharica ~ing n kuhanje ~y n US keks

cool /kuːl/ adj 1 prohladan 2 fig hladan 3 miran 4 sl odličan • n coll mirnoća • vt, vi rashladiti ~ down/off ohladiti se

coop /kuːp/ n kokošinjac • vt ~ up staviti u krletku (+ fig)

co-op /kəʊ ɒp/ n coll → cooperative society (shop)

cooperate /kəʊˈɒpəreɪt/ vi (with/in doing/to do) suradivati s kim na čemu cooperation /kəʊˌɒpəˈreɪʃn/ n suradnja cooperative /kəʊˈɒpərətɪv/ adj voljan suradivati cooperative society zadruga

coordinate /kəʊˈɔːdənət/ vt koordinirati, uskladiti

cop (1) /kɒp/ n coll policajac, murjak

cop (2) vi ~ out (of) sl dići ruke od

cope /kəʊp/ vi (with) boriti se, savladati (teškoće i sl.), uspijevati, izlaziti na kraj s

copious /ˈkəʊpɪəs/ adj obilan

copper /ˈkɒpə(r)/ n 1 bakar 2 mod bakren 3 (bakreni) novčić 4 coll murjak

copy /ˈkɒpɪ/ n 1 kopija ~cat n sl imitator 2 primjerak good ~ zanimljiva vijest **~right** n autorsko pravo **~writer** n pisac reklama • vt, vi 1 kopirati 2 oponašati 3 prepisivati

cord /kɔːd/ n uzica **vocal ~s** glasnice **spinal ~** ledna moždina

cordial /ˈkɔːdɪəl/ adj srdačan • n osvježavajuće piće

cordon /ˈkɔːdn/ n pojas • vt **~ off** okružiti

corduroy /ˈkɔːdərɔɪ/ n 1 samt 2 mod samtast

core /kɔː(r)/ n jezgro, srž (+ fig)

cork /kɔːk/ n 1 pluto 2 čep **~screw** n vadičep

corn (1) /kɔːn/ n 1 zrno 2 žitarica 3 US kukuruz **~cob** n klip kukuruza 4 mod kukuruzni

corn (2) n kurje oko

corn (3) vt usoliti

cornea /ˈkɔːnɪə/ n rožnica

corner /ˈkɔːnə(r)/ n 1 kut, ugao **cut ~s** fig skratiti postupak **~stone** kamen temeljac (+ fig) 2 zakutak • vt, vi 1 stjerati u kut 2 stvoriti monopol na tržištu

corny /ˈkɔːnɪ/ adj coll bezvezan, sladunjav

coronary /ˈkɒrənrɪ/ n coll infarkt

coronation /ˌkɒrəˈneɪʃn/ n krunidba

coroner /ˈkɒrənə(r)/ n mrtvozornik

coronet /ˈkɒrənət/ n kruna

corporal (1) /ˈkɔːpərəl/ adj tjelesni

corporal (2) n mil desetnik

corporate /ˈkɔːpərət/ adj 1 (od) korporacije, korporacijski 2 grupni **corporation** /ˌkɔːpəˈreɪʃn/ n 1 korporacija, pravna osoba 2 US → **limited liability company**

corps /kɔː(r)/ n mil korpus

corpse /kɔːps/ n leš

corpuscle /ˈkɔːpʌsl/ n tjelešce

corral /kɒˈrɑːl/ n obor

correct /kəˈrekt/ adj 1 ispravan, točan 2 doličan • vt ispraviti **~ion** n ispravljanje, ispravak

correspond /ˌkɒrɪˈspɒnd/ vi 1 (with/to) odgovarati, podudarati se 2 dopisivati se **~ing** adj odgovarajući **~ence** n 1 dodirna točka 2 dopisivanje **~ence course** dopisni tečaj **~ent** n dopisnik

corridor /ˈkɒrɪdɔː(r)/ n hodnik

corroborate /kəˈrɒbəreɪt/ vt potkrijepiti

corrode /kəˈrəʊd/ vt, vi izjedati **corrosion** /kəˈrəʊʒn/ n korozija **corrosive** /kəˈrəʊsɪv/ adj koji nagriza (+ fig)

corrugated /ˈkɒrəgeɪtɪd/ adj nabran **~ iron** n valoviti lim

corrupt /kəˈrʌpt/ adj pokvaren, korumpiran • vt, vi 1 iskvariti 2 potkupiti **~ion** n 1 raspadanje 2 korupcija

corsage /kɔːˈsɑːʒ/ n buketić cvijeća

cortege /kɔːˈteɪʒ/ n pogrebna povorka

cosmetic /kɒzˈmetɪk/ adj kozmetički • n kozmetički preparat

cosmic /ˈkɒzmɪk/ adj svemirski

cosmopolitan /ˌkɒzməˈpɒlɪtən/ adj svjetski, kozmopolitski • n kozmopolit

cosmos /ˈkɒzmɒs/ n svemir

cosset /ˈkɒsɪt/ vt razmaziti

cost /kɒst/ n 1 cijena **at all ~s** po svaku cijenu 2 trošak, troškovi **~ effective** adj ekonomičan • vi irreg koštati, stajati **~ly** adj skup

co-star /ˌkəʊ ˈstɑː(r)/ vi (with) igrati s (u filmu)

costume /ˈkɒstjuːm/ n nošnja, odjeća **~ jewellery** n bižuterija

cosy /ˈkəʊzɪ/ adj udoban **cosily** adv **cosiness** n • n (**tea ~**) prekrivač za čajnik

cot /kɒt/ n kolijevka

cottage /ˈkɒtɪdʒ/ n kućica **~ cheese** n svježi kravlji sir

cotton /ˈkɒtn/ n 1 pamuk 2 pamučni **~ wool** n vata

couch (1) /kaʊtʃ/ n kauč

couch (2) vi (in) izraziti se

cougar /ˈkuːgə(r)/ n puma

cough /kɒf/ n kašalj • vi, vt kašljati **~ sth up a.** iskašljati **b.** sl ispljunuti (novac) sl

council /ˈkaʊnsl/ n 1 savjet 2 vijeće **~ flat/house** stan/kuća u općinskom vlasništvu (za socijalno ugrožene) **~lor** n vijećnik

counsel /ˈkaʊnsl/ n 1 savjet 2 odvjetnik **~lor** n 1 savjetnik 2 US odvjetnik

count (1) /kaʊnt/ n 1 brojanje, račun 2 točka optužnice **~able** adj brojiv **~er** n brojač **~less** adj bezbrojan • vt, vi 1 brojati, izbrojati 2 računati 3 držati **~**

among; ~ **sb/sth among** ubrajati (se) u ~ **down** odbrojavati ~**down** n ~ **in a.** ubrajati **b.** računati na ~ **on/upon** računati na ~ **out a.** izbrojati **b.** ne računati na

count (2) n grof ~**ess** n grofica

countenance /'kauntɪnəns/ n 1 izraz lica 2 potpora • vt podržati

counter (1) /'kauntə(r)/ n pult **over–the–**~ adj bez recepta **under the** ~ ispod pulta

counter (2) adv ~ **to** suprotno

counter (3) vt, vi (with) odgovoriti na napad s, parirati

counter– prefix protu–, kontra–

counteract /,kauntər'ækt/ vt neutralizirati

counterfeit /'kauntəfɪt/ adj krivotvoren • vt krivotvoriti

counterpart /'kauntəpa:t/ n par, dopuna; kolega

counterpoint /'kauntəpɔɪnt/ n kontrapunkt

countersign /'kauntəsaɪn/ n supotpisati

country /'kʌntrɪ/ n 1 zemlja 2 domovina 3 ~**side** selo, priroda 4 mod seoski; sa sela • (+ derog) 5 kraj ~**man/woman** n 1 seljak/seljakinja 2 zemljak(inja)

county /'kauntɪ/ n 1 GB grofovija 2 kotar, okrug

coup /ku:/ n 1 uspjeh 2 državni udar

couple /'kʌpl/ n par • vt spojiti, spariti, pariti se

courage /'kʌrɪdʒ/ n hrabrost ~**ous** adj hrabar

courier /'kurɪə(r)/ n kurir, dostavljač

course /kɔ:s/ n 1 tok, tijek **of** ~ naravno 2 trkalište, teren (za golf) 3 tečaj, (školski) predmet; 4 naut kurs 5 jelo 6 med tretman

court /kɔ:t/ n 1 sud ~**–martial** n vojni sud ○ vt izvesti pred vojni sud 2 dvor 3 igralište 4 (~**yard**) dvorište • vt, vi 1 udvarati se 2 izazivati ~**eous** /'kɜ:tɪəs/ adj uljudan ~**esy** n ljubaznost, dobrota ~ **of** zahvaljujući ~**ship** n udvaranje

cousin /'kʌzn/ n bratić; sestrična; rođak

cove /kəuv/ n uvala

cover /'kʌvə(r)/ vt 1 pokriti, prekriti 2 pokrivati 3 prikriti 4 **be** ~**ed** biti obuzet 5 izvješćivati s 6 štititi 7 držati na nišanu 8 čuvati 9 namiriti 10 obraditi 11 odnositi se na 12 prevaliti ~**up** n prikrivanje • n 1 poklopac 2 prekrivač 3 omot 4 zaklon **take** ~ zakloniti se **under** ~ **a.** u zaklonu, pod zaštitom/okriljem **b.** (of) pod krinkom 5 pokriće ~**age** n izvještavanje **live** ~ izvještavanje uživo

covert /'kʌvət/ adj skrovit

covet /'kʌvɪt/ vt hlepiti za

cow (1) /kau/ n 1 krava 2 ženka (slona, kita i sl.)

cow (2) vt zastrašiti

coward /'kauəd/ n kukavica ~**ly** adj kukavički ~**ice** n kukavičluk

cower /'kauə(r)/ vi šćućuriti se, skupiti se

coxswain /'kɒksn/ n kormilar

coy /kɔɪ/ adj plah, sramežljiv

coyote /kɔɪ'əut/ n kojot

crab /kræb/ n rak

crack /kræk/ n 1 napuklina **the** ~ **of dawn** praskozorje 2 pucanj 3 **wise~** sl dosjetka; fora sl 4 sl pokušaj 5 mod elitni 6 (droga) **crack** • vt, vi 1 napući; razbiti (se) (+ fig) ~ **open** razvaliti 2 pucnuti, opaliti 3 (o glasu) promuknuti 4 provaliti (šifru) ~ **a joke** izvaliti štos coll ~ **down on** pooštriti mjere protiv ~ **sb/sth up** hvaliti ~ **up** doživjeti živčani slom

cracker /'krækə(r)/ n 1 kreker 2 žabica, petarda

crackle /'krækl/ vi pucketati

crackling /'kræklɪŋ/ n hrskava kožica (pečenja)

cradle /'kreɪdl/ n kolijevka

craft /kra:ft/ n 1 zanat, obrt 2 (pl ~) plovilo, letjelica 3 lukavost ~**y** adj lukav, vješt ~**sman** n zanatlija, obrtnik ~**smanship** n zanatstvo

crag /kræg/ n greben

cram /kræm/ vt, vi 1 (into/up/with) natrpati 2 nabubati

cramp (1) /kræmp/ n grč

cramp (2) vt 1 stjesniti, nagurati 2 fig sprečavati ~ **one's style** coll kvariti dojam ~**ed** adj sitnih slova

cranberry /'krænbərı/ n brusnica
crane /kreın/ n 1 ždral 2 kran • vt ~ one's neck iskrenuti/ispružiti vrat
crank (1) /kræŋk/ n ručica ~shaft n kurbla • ~ up vt pokrenuti ručkom
crank (2) n čudak
crap /kræp/ vi tab srati tab • n 1 tab govno 2 sl sranje, glupost
crash /kræʃ/ n 1 prasak, tresak, lom 2 sudar, pad (aviona) 3 propast, slom ~ course n intenzivni tečaj ~ helmet n zaštitna kaciga ~ -land vi,vt prisilno sletjeti • vt,vi 1 udariti, pasti, srušiti (se) 2 probiti se 3 propasti
crass /kræs/ adj 1 krajnji (glupost i sl.) 2 prostački
crate /kreıt/ n gajba
crater /'kreıtə(r)/ n krater
cravat /krə'væt/ n vratna marama
crave /kreıv/ vt,vi (sth/for sth) čeznuti za
crawl /krɔ:l/ vi 1 puzati (+ fig) 2 gmizati, miljeti ~ with vrvjeti kime/čime 3 ježiti se • n kraul
crayfish /'kreıfıʃ/ n riječni rak
crayon /'kreıɒn/ n bojica
craze /kreız/ n ludilo, manija fig ~d adj izluđen, luđački
crazy /'kreızı/ adj 1 (about) lud za fig 2 lud
creak /kri:k/ vi škripati • n škripa ~y adj škripav
cream /kri:m/ n 1 (slatko) vrhnje 2 krema, pasta cold ~ krema za lice 3 fig elita, krema • adj žućkast ~y adj poput kreme, mekan (+ fig), gust; žućkast
crease /kri:s/ vt 1 zgužvati se 2 nabrati se • n nabor
create /kri:'eıt/ vt stvoriti creation n 1 stvaranje 2 stvor 3 djelo, kreacija creative adj kreativan, stvaralački creator n stvoritelj, stvaratelj creature /'kri:tʃə(r)/ n stvor ~ comforts pl užici
creche /kreıʃ/ n jaslice
cred → credibility
credence /'kri:dns/ n give ~ to povjerovati
credentials /kri'denʃlz/ pl 1 vjerodajnice 2 svjedodžbe
credible /'kredəbl/ adj 1 vjerodostojan

2 vjerojatan credibly adv iz pouzdanih izvora credibility /,kredı-'bılətı/ n vjerodostojnost, povjerenje
credit /'kredıt/ n 1 kredit ~ rating n bonitet 2 potraživanje 3 čast, zasluga 4 vjerovanje 5 vjerodostojnost • vt (with sth) 1 pripisivati 2 knjižiti u korist ~or n vjerovnik
creed /kri:d/ n vjera the C~ Vjerovanje
creek /kri:k/ n 1 uvala 2 US rječica
creep /kri:p/ vi irreg 1 (us)puzati 2 fig miljeti 3 obuzeti 4 ježiti se • sl gnjida he gives me the ~s od njega mi se ježi koža ~er n penjačica ~y adj jeziv
cremate /krı'meıt/ vt kremirati
crepe /kreıp/ n 1 krep 2 (~ rubber) sirova guma
crept → v irreg creep
crescent /'kresnt/ n polumjesec
cress /kres/ n dragušac
crest /krest/ n 1 kresta 2 kruna, grb 3 vrh ~ -fallen adj pokunjen
cretin /'kretın/ n kreten
crevasse /krı'væs/ n duboka raspuklina
crevice /'krevıs/ n pukotina
crew /kru:/ n 1 momčad 2 posada ~ -cut n "jež" frizura ~ -neck n okrugli izrez (džempera i sl.)
crib /krıb/ n 1 jasle pl 2 kolijevka 3 šalabahter coll • vt prepisati
cricket /'krıkıt/ n cvrčak 2 kriket
cried → cry
crime /kraım/ n 1 zločin 2 kriminal criminal /'krımınl/ adj 1 zločinački 2 krivični o n kriminalac
crimson /'krımzn/ adj grimizan • n grimiz
cringe /krındʒ/ vi 1 (at) zguriti se pred 2 fig ropski se ponašati
crinkle /'krıŋkl/ n nabor • vt,vi naborati (se), nabrati
cripple /'krıpl/ n bogalj • vt 1 osakatiti 2 fig sputati
crisis /'kraısıs/ n (pl crises) kriza
crisp /krısp/ adj 1 hrskav 2 oštar, svjež 3 odlučan • n pl GB čips
criss-cross /'krıskrɒs/ iskrižan • adv ukriž • vi, vt iskrižati
criterion /kraı'tıərıən/ (pl criteria) n

kriterij

critic /'krıtık/ n kritičar ¶ kritika = review, criticism ~al adj kritičan criticism /'krıtısızəm/ n kritika

criticize /'krıtısaız/ vt,vi kritizirati

croak /krəuk/ n graktanje, kreket • vt,
vi fig 1 biti zloguk prorok 2 sl crknuti

crock /krɒk/ n ćup ~ery n zemljano
posuđe

crocodile /'krɒkədaıl/ n krokodil

crocus /'krəukəs/ n šafran

crone /krəun/ n vještica fig

crony /'krəunı/ n prisni prijatelj, kom-
panjon

crook /krʊk/ n 1 kuka 2 zavoj 3 coll
varalica, lopov • vt svinuti ~ed adj 1
svinut 2 coll pokvaren

crop (1) /krɒp/ n 1 usjev 2 ljetina 3
mnoštvo

crop (2) /krɒp/ vt,vi 1 popasti 2
podšišati 3 ~ up iskrsnuti

croquet /'krəukeı/ n kroket

cross /krɒs/ n 1 križ (+ fig) 2 križić 3
križanje uk križanac on the ~ ukoso •
vt,vi 1 prijeći ~ one's mind pasti na
pamet 2 presjeći 3 prekrižiti ~
swords ukrstiti mačeve keep one's
fingers ~ed držati fige ~ oneself
prekrižiti se 4 mimoići se 5 osujetiti
6 križati ~ out prekrižiti • adj coll
ljut ~bow n samostrel ~breed n
mješanac ~check n provjera ~
country n kros ~examine vt unak-
rsno ispitati ~eyed adj razrok ~
fire n unakrsna vatra ~sing n 1
prelazak, prijelaz 2 raskrižje ~
legged adj prekriženih nogu ~ref-
erence n višestruka uputnica ~
roads n (+ sing) raskrižje (+ fig),
križanje ~section n presjek ~word
n križaljka

crotch /krɒtʃ/ n prepone pl

crouch /krautʃ/ vi (down) čučnuti

crow (1) /krəu/ n vrana

crow (2) /krəu/ vi irreg 1 kukurikati 2
gukati (beba)

crow–bar /'krəuba:(r)/ n željezna
poluga; pajser coll

crowd /kraud/ n 1 mnoštvo, svjetina 2
društvo • vi, vt 1 nagrnuti na ~ round
sjatiti se oko 2 nagurati, nagomilati,

nabiti ~ed adj prenapučen, prepun,
krcat

crown /kraun/ n 1 kruna 2 mod GB
kraljevski ~ prince(ss) pri-
jestolonasljednik/-a ~ witness
krunski svjedok 3 kruna (novac) 4
vrh, vrhunac • vt 1 okruniti (+ fig) to
~ it all i povrh svega 2 staviti krunu

crucial /'kru:ʃl/ adj odlučujući, ključni

crucifix /'kru:sıfıks/ n raspelo ~ion n
raspeće crucify /'kru:sıfaı/ vt raspeti

crude /kru:d/ adj nepriređen; sirov (+
fig) ~ly adv fig grubo

cruel /kruəl/ adj okrutan, surov ~ty n
okrutnost

cruise /kru:z/ vi 1 krstariti ~ speed/al-
titude ekonomična brzina/visina
(auta, aviona) 2 sl brijati sl • n
krstarenje ~r n naut krstarica; krstaš

crumb /krʌm/ n 1 mrvica (+ fig) 2 sredina kruha

crumble /'krʌmbl/ vt,vi 1 mrviti, drobiti 2 raspasti se crumbly adj
mrvljiv; trošan

crumpet /'krʌmpıt/ n 1 čajni kolačić 2
sl dobra ženska coll

crumple /'krʌmpl/ vt,vi zgužvati (se)

crunch /krʌntʃ/ vt,vi 1 hrskati 2 škripati, drobiti (uz škripu) • n škripa,
drobljenje when it comes to the ~
kada dođe stani–pani

crusade /kru:'seıd/ n križarski rat (+
fig); kampanja • vi (for/against)
povesti borbu za/protiv ~r n 1 križar
2 borac (za pravdu i sl.)

crush /krʌʃ/ vt,vi 1 smrviti, zgnječiti,
zgaziti 2 nabiti 3 zgužvati ~ing adj
totalan • n 1 stiska, gužva 2 voćni
sok 3 zacopanost coll have a ~ on
sb biti zateleban u koga

crust /krʌst/ n korica, kora, naslaga ~y
adj 1 hrskav 2 otresit

crutch /krʌtʃ/ n 1 štaka 2 fig potpora

crux /krʌks/ n bit

cry /kraı/ vi,vt 1 plakati 2 (~ out)
kriknuti 3 vikati, derati se ~ off odustati • n 1 krik, povik a far/long cry
from ni blizu 2 slogan 3 plakanje
~baby n plačljivac

crypt /krıpt/ n kripta

cryptic /'krıptık/ adj zagonetan

crystal /'krıstl/ n kristal ~line

/'krɪstəlaɪn/ adj kristalan **~lize** vt, vi 1 (is)kristalizirati (se) 2 ušećeriti

cub /kʌb/ n 1 mladunče 2 (~ **scout**) izvidač

cubby–hole /'kʌbɪ həʊl/ n sobičak; rupa

cube /kju:b/ n 1 kocka 2 treća potencija • vt 1 izrezati na kocke 2 dići na treću potenciju **cubic** adj kubični

cubicle /'kju:bɪkl/ n kabina

cuckold /'kʌkəʊld/ n prevareni muž, rogonja • vt nabiti rogove

cuckoo /'kʊku:/ n kukavica

cucumber /'kju:kʌmbə(r)/ n krastavac **cool as a ~** mrtav hladan

cuddle /'kʌdl/ vt, vi 1 grliti 2 ~ **up** privinuti se, stisnuti se • n zagrljaj **cuddly** adj 1 mazan 2 mekan, plišan

cue (1) /kju:/ n 1 theat štihvort 2 mig **take one's ~ from sb** oponašati koga

cue (2) n biljarski štap, tak

cuff /kʌf/ n 1 orukvica **~link** n puce, gumb za manšetu 2 US → **turn–up** 3 pl coll lisice • vt ćušnuti

cuisine /kwɪ'zi:n/ n kuhinja

cul–de–sac /'kʌl də sæk/ n slijepa ulica

culinary /'kʌlɪnərɪ/ adj kulinarski

cull /kʌl/ vt 1 brati 2 probirati

culminate /'kʌlmɪneɪt/ vi kulminirati u **culmination** n vrhunac

cult /kʌlt/ n 1 štovanje, kult 2 mod kultni

cultivate /'kʌltɪveɪt/ vt 1 obrađivati 2 njegovati **~d** adj kultiviran

culture /'kʌltʃə(r)/ n 1 kultura 2 uzgoj **~d** adj kulturan, kultiviran **~d pearl** n uzgojeni biser **cultural** adj kulturni

culvert /'kʌlvət/ n propust (kanal)

cumbersome /'kʌmbəsəm/ adj nezgrapan, trom

cunning /'kʌnɪŋ/ adj lukav • n lukavština

cunt /kʌnt/ n tab pička tab; pizda (+ fig)

cup /kʌp/ n 1 šalica **it's my ~ of tea** baš mi je po volji 2 kalež 3 pehar **~–final** n završna utakmica • vt 1 skupiti ruke 2 poduhvatiti šakom

cupboard /'kʌbəd/ n ormar

curable /'kjʊərəbl/ adj izlječiv

curate /'kjuərət/ n kapelan

curator /kjuə'reɪtə(r)/ n kustos

curb /kɜ:b/ n 1 žvala, uzda **put a ~ on** fig obuzdavati 2 → **kerb** • vt obuzdati (+ fig)

curd /kɜ:d/ n gruševina **lemon ~** krema od limuna

curdle /'kɜ:dl/ vi, vt zgrušati ~ **one's blood** slediti krv u žilama **blood-curdling** adj jeziv

cure /kjuə(r)/ n 1 lijek 2 ozdravljenje • vt, vi 1 (sb of sth/sth) izliječiti koga od čega, liječiti što (+ fig) 2 soliti, sušiti, dimiti (meso)

curfew /'kɜ:fju:/ n redarstveni sat

curiosity /,kjʊərɪ'ɒsətɪ/ n 1 radoznalost 2 kuriozitet **curious** adj 1 radoznao 2 čudnovat

curl /kɜ:l/ n uvojak, kovrča • vt, vi 1 kovrčati se 2 navorati (se) 3 sklupčati se **~er** n uvijač **~y** adj kovrčav

currant /'kʌrənt/ n 1 ribiz 2 grožđica

currency /'kʌrənsɪ/ n 1 raširenost, korištenje 2 novac **hard ~** devize pl

current /'kʌrənt/ n 1 struja 2 tok • adj 1 važeći, u optjecaju, koji se (trenutačno) koristi, sadašnji 2 tekući **~ly** adv trenutačno, sada

curriculum /kə'rɪkjʊləm/ n nastavni plan **~ vitae** n životopis

curry (1) /'kʌrɪ/ n 1 curry 2 začinjeno jelo

curry (2) vt **~favour** (with sb) ulagivati se kome

curse /kɜ:s/ n 1 kletva, psovka 2 prokletstvo **be under a ~** biti prokleti 3 **the ~** coll menstruacija • vt, vi 1 (at) proklinjati 2 psovati 3 **be ~ed with** trpjeti zbog

curt /kɜ:t/ adj kratak (odgovor i sl.)

curtail /kɜ:'teɪl/ vt 1 skratiti 2 ograničiti

curtain /'kɜ:tn/ n zavjesa, zastor (+ theat, +fig) • vt postaviti zastor ~ **off** odijeliti zastorom

curtsey /'kɜ:tsɪ/ n naklon; kniks • vi (to) nakloniti se komu

curve /kɜ:v/ n 1 krivulja 2 zavoj • vt, vi vijugati, savijati (se)

cushion /'kʊʃn/ n jastuk • vt 1 obložiti 2 (against) zaštititi od, ublažiti što

custard /'kʌstəd/ *n cul* šodo
custodian /kʌ'stəʊdɪən/ *n* čuvar, skrbnik
custody /'kʌstədɪ/ *n* 1 starateljstvo 2 čuvanje 3 pritvor
custom /'kʌstəm/ *n* 1 običaj 2 stalne mušterije 3 ~s *pl* carina 4 *mod* po narudžbi ~ary *adj* uobičajen ~er *n* mušterija, kupac
cut /kʌt/ *n* 1 rez 2 sniženje **power ~** nestanak struje, redukcija 3 odrezak 4 kroj **short ~** prečac **be a ~ above** *coll* nadmašivati • *vt, vi irreg* 1 (in) zarezati, porezati, podrezati, (off) odrezati, (up, out) izrezati, (up) razrezati, (down) prerezati, (up) urezati 2 sjeći ¶ sa svim prefiksima kao i rezati 3 markirati 4 sniziti ~ **corners** *fig* ići prečicom ~**ting** *adj* britki ○ *n* 1 isječak 2 prosjek ~ **back** smanjiti ~**back** *n* redukcija, rez ~ **down** a. posjeći, pokositi b. (on) smanjiti ~ **in** ubaciti se ~ **off** *fig* a. odsjeći b. isključiti c. obustaviti ~

out a. zatajiti b. krojiti ~ **it out** prestani ~**out** *n* kroj
cute /kju:t/ *adj* zgodan, sladak
cutlery /'kʌtlərɪ/ *n* jedaći pribor
cutlet /'kʌtlɪt/ *n* kotlet
cutthroat /'kʌtθrəʊt/ *n* ubojica • *adj fig* bezobziran, razbojnički
cuttle–fish /'kʌtlfɪʃ/ *n* sipa
cyanide /'saɪənaɪd/ *n* cijanid
cycle /'saɪkl/ *n* 1 ciklus 2 *coll* bicikl • *vi* voziti bicikl **cyclic(al)** *adj* ciklični **cyclist** *n* biciklist
cyclone /'saɪkləʊn/ *n* ciklon
cygnet /'sɪgnɪt/ *n* labudić
cylinder /'sɪlɪndə(r)/ *n* valjak
cymbal /'sɪmbl/ *n* činela
cynic /'sɪnɪk/ *n* cinik ~**al** *adj* ciničan ~**ism** /'sɪnɪsɪzəm/ *n* cinizam
cypher → **cipher**
cypress /'saɪprəs/ *n* čempres
cyst /sɪst/ *n* cista
czar /zɑ:(r)/ *n* ruski car ~**ina** /zɑ:'riːnə/ *n* ruska carica

D

D, d /di:/ četvrto slovo engl. abecede; de

dab /dæb/ *vt,vi* (at) 1 tapkati 2 nanijeti • *n* 1 nanos/mrlja boje 2 lagani dodir, tapkanje

dabble /'dæbl/ *vt,vi* 1 praćakati se, prskati 2 ~ **at/in** baviti se amaterski

dad /dæd/ *n coll* tata *coll* ~**dy** *n* tata

daffodil /'dæfədɪl/ *n* sunovrat, narcis

daft /dɑːft/ *adj coll* bedast

dagger /'dægə(r)/ *n* bodež

daily /'deɪlɪ/ *adj* (svaki)dnevni, svaki-dašnji • *adv* (svako)dnevno, svakoga dana • *n coll* dnevni list

dainty /'deɪntɪ/ *adj* 1 delikatan, profinjen; fin; loman 2 razmažen, izbirljiv 3 ukusan • *n* poslastica

dairy /'deərɪ/ *n* 1 mljekara, mljekarstvo 2 *mod* mljekarski, mliječni ~**-maid** *n* mljekarica

daisy /'deɪzɪ/ *n* tratinčica

dale /deɪl/ *n* dolina

dally /'dælɪ/ *vi* 1 (with) poigravati se 2 (over) gubiti vrijeme

dam /dæm/ *n* brana, nasip • *vt* (up) 1 zagraditi branom, zajaziti 2 *fig* zauzdati

damage /'dæmɪdʒ/ *n* 1 (to) šteta 2 *pl leg* odšteta • *vt* oštetiti

damn /dæm/ *vt* 1 prokleti 2 osuditi; pokopati *coll* 3 *coll* ići/poslati do vraga ~ (**it**)! *int* k vragu! ~ **you**! vrag te odnio! • *n* **not give/care a** ~ **about** fućkati se (komu za što) *coll* • *adj, adv coll* 1 vraški, proklet(o) 2 užasno; veoma ~**ation** *n* prokletstvo, propast ~**ed** *adj* proklet

damp /dæmp/ *adj* vlažan • *n* vlaga • *vt,vi* 1 navlažiti (se) 2 (~**en**) ugušiti 3 ~ **down** zapretati 4 ~ **off** istruliti

dance /dɑːns/ *n* 1 ples 2 *mod* plesni • *vi,vt* 1 plesati 2 poigravati, poskakivati ~**r** *n* plesač **dancing** *n* 1 ples

mod plesni

dandelion /'dændɪlaɪən/ *n* maslačak

dandruff /'dændrʌf/ *n* prhut

dandy /'dændɪ/ *n* gizdelin, šminker • *adj sl* izvrstan, super

Dane /deɪn/ *n* 1 Danac 2 (**great ~**) danska doga **Danish** *adj* danski ○ *n* (~ **pastry**) slatko pecivo

danger /'deɪndʒə(r)/ *n* opasnost ~**ous** *adj* (to/for) opasan

dangle /'dæŋgl/ *vt,vi* 1 visiti, klatiti se 2 mahati (čime) 3 *fig* mamiti (koga čime)

dare /deə(r)/ *v anom* usuditi se

dare /deə(r)/ *vt* 1 usuditi se 2 suočiti se 3 ~ **sb to do sth** izazvati • *n* izazov **daring** *adj* smion, odvažan *n* smionost, odvažnost

dark /dɑːk/ *n* mrak, tama (+ *fig*) **keep sb/be in the ~** držati koga/živjeti u neznanju • *adj* 1 mračan, taman ~**-room** tamna komora 2 *fig* skriven, skrovit 3 mračan, žalostan 4 neprosvijetljen ~**en** *vt,vi* zamračiti (se) ~ **horse** (konj) autsajder

darling /'dɑːlɪŋ/ *n* 1 dragi 2 *mod* drag, sladak

darn /dɑːn/ *vt,vi* 1 krpati 2 *euph* **damn**

dart /dɑːt/ *n* 1 nagli pokret 2 strelica za pikado ~**s** pikado ~**board** *n* meta za pikado • *vi,vt* naglo (se) pokrenuti, jurnuti, baciti (se)

dash /dæʃ/ *n* 1 juriš, trk 2 polet 3 mrvica, kapljica 4 crtica • *vt,vi* 1 razbiti (se), razbijati (se) 2 juriti, žuriti ~ **off/away** odjuriti 3 pljusnuti, zapljusnuti ~**ing** *adj* poletan; odvažan; pristao

dashboard /'dæʃbɔːd/ *n* ploča s instrumentima

data /'deɪtə/ *n pl* podaci ~ **base** *n* baza podataka

date /deɪt/ *n* 1 datum 2 razdoblje **be/go**

out of ~ zastarjeti, izaći iz mode **out-of-~** *adj* staromodan, zastario **be/bring sth up to** ~ **a.** osuvremeniti **b.** upotpuniti **up-to-~** *adj* ažuran, suvremen **to** ~ **do** danas **3** *coll* sastanak; spoj *coll* **blind** ~ sastanak s nepoznatom osobom **double** ~ sastanak učetvero **4** *coll* partner (za izlazak) • *vt,vi* **1** staviti datum, datirati **2** odrediti starost **3** ~ **from/back to** datirati iz, biti iz **4** zastarijevati **5** izlaziti s kim

daughter /'dɔ:tə(r)/ *n* kći **~-in-law** *n* snaha

daunt /dɔ:nt/ *vt* obeshrabriti **~less** *adj* neustrašiv

dawdle /'dɔ:dl/ *vi,vt* (away) gubiti vrijeme

dawn /dɔ:n/ *n* zora, osvit (+ *fig*) • *vi* svitati ~ **on/upon sb** sinuti (komu) *fig*

day /deɪ/ *n* **1** dan **by** ~ danju ~ **in,** ~ **out** stalno **the other** ~ neki dan **some** ~ jednoga dana **one of these** ~**s** uskoro **one of those** ~**s** loš dan **that'll be the** ~ *iron* to se nikad neće dogoditi **he's fifty if he is a** ~ ima najmanje pedeset godina **call it a** ~ prestati, prekinuti (s radom) ~ **off** slobodan dan **2** vrijeme **the present** ~ danas **present-**~ *adj* današnji ~**break** osvit ~ **care** dnevni boravak ~**dream** sanjariti ~**long** cjelodnevni ~**time** dan ~**light a.** dnevno svjetlo **in broad** ~**light** usred bijela dana **b.** zora

daze /deɪz/ *vt* omamiti • *n* omama, ošamućenost

dazzle /'dæzl/ *vt* zaslijepiti, zabljesnuti • *n* bljeskavilo **dazzling** *adj* blistav

de- *prefix* od-, raz-, de- (*defrost, deice* uikloniti led, odmrznuti)

deacon /'di:kən/ *n* đakon

dead /ded/ *adj* **1** mrtav ~ **march** posmrtni marš **in the** ~ **of the night** u gluho doba noći ~ **end** slijepa ulica (+ *fig*) **2** neživ **3** obamro ~ **to** neosjetljiv na ~ **to the world** u dubokom snu ~ **calm** grobna tišina ~ **loss** nenadoknadiv gubitak **the** ~ **centre** točna sredina **4** potrošen, ugašen **go** ~ prestati raditi; crknuti

coll **5** bez sjaja, mutan ~**line** krajnji rok ~**lock** pat pozicija, mrtva točka ~**pan** *coll* mrtav-hladan • *adv* sasvim, potpuno ~ **drunk** mrtav pijan ~ **certain** sasvim siguran ~ **slow** vrlo sporo ~**en** *vt* umrtviti, ugušiti, ugasiti, prigušiti ~**ly** *adj* **1** smrtonosan **2** smrtni **3** mrtvački **4** *coll* super *coll*

deaf /def/ *adj* gluh (+ *fig*), nagluh ~ **mute** gluhonijema osoba **turn a** ~ **ear to** oglušiti se ~**en** *vt* zaglušiti ~**ening** *adj* zaglušni

deal (1) /di:l/ *n* **a** (good/great) ~ **of sth** mnogo

deal (2) *vt,vi irreg* (**out**) (po)dijeliti ~ **sb a blow** zadati udarac (+ *fig*) ~ **in sth** prodavati, trgovati čime ~ **with a.** poslovati **b.** imati posla **c.** raspravljati, baviti se, obrađivati **e.** riješiti • *n* posao **it's a** ~ dogovoreno je **a fair/square** ~ pošten posao **a raw/rough** ~ loš postupak ~**er** *n* trgovac **authorized** ~**er** zastupnik ~**ing** *n pl* poslovi, poslovanje

dealt *v irreg* → **deal**

dean /di:n/ *n* **1** dekan **2** doajen ~**ery** *n* dekanat

dear /dɪə(r)/ *adj* **1** (to) drag **D~ Mr Jones**, Štovani g. Jones! **D~ Sirs**, Štovana gospodo!/Štovani! **hold sb/sth** ~ voljeti **3** skup **3** mio, dragocjen • *adv* skupo • *n* **1** mila osoba, zlato **2** (~**est**) dragi, draga • *int* zaboga! ~**ly** *adv* **1** vrlo **2** skupo ~**ness** *n* skupoća

dearth /dɜ:θ/ *n* (of) oskudica

death /deθ/ *n* **1** smrt **at** ~'**s door** na samrti **to** ~ nasmrt, do smrti **put sb to** ~ pogubiti **be the** ~ **of sb** doći glave ~'**s head** mrtvačka glava **2** *mod* ~ **sentence** smrtna kazna ~ **roll** popis poginulih ~ **toll** broj poginulih ~ **warrant a.** nalog za izvršenje smrtne osude **b.** *fig* smrtna osuda ~**bed** smrtna postelja ~**blow** smrtni/konačni udarac (+ *fig*) ~**less** *adj* besmrtan ~**like** *adj* grobni, mrtvački ~**ly** *adj* mrtvački ○ *adv* samrtno

deb /deb/ *n coll* → **debutante**

debase /dɪ'beɪs/ *vt* pokvariti, iskvariti, poniziti, smanjiti vrijednost

debate /dɪ'beɪt/ n rasprava, debata • vi, vt 1 (on/upon/about) raspravljati (što, o čemu) 2 razmatrati **debatable** adj prijeporan, sporan

debauch /dɪ'bɔ:tʃ/ vt upropastiti, navesti na razvrat **~ery** n razvrat **~ee** n razvratnik

debit /'debɪt/ n dug, dugovanje (u knjigovodstvu) • vt **~** (sth/against/to sb) knjižiti na teret **~** (sb/with sth) zadužiti

debrief /,di:'bri:f/ vt izvući informacije

debris /'deɪbrɪ:/ n sing otpaci, krhotine n pl

debt /det/ n dug **get into/out of ~** zadužiti se/isplatiti dugove **National D~** javni dug **~or** n dužnik

debug /,di:'bʌg/ vt coll 1 ukloniti probleme 2 ukloniti prislušne uređaje

debut /'deɪbju:/ n 1 ulazak u društvo (djevojke) 2 debi, prvi nastup **~ante** n djevojka koja ulazi u društvo

decade /'dekeɪd/ n desetljeće

decadence /'dekədəns/ n dekadencija **decadent** adj dekadentan

decaffeinated /dɪ'kæfɪneɪtɪd/ adj bez kofeina

decanter /dɪ'kæntə/ n bokal

decapitate /dɪ'kæpɪteɪt/ vt odrubiti glavu

decay /dɪ'keɪ/ vi propadati, truliti, raspadati se (+ fig) • n trulež, propadanje, raspadanje **tooth ~** karijes

deceased /dɪ'si:st/ adj, n pokojni(k)

deceit /dɪ'si:t/ n 1 lažljivost, himba 2 laž, prijevara **~ful** adj lažljiv, prijevaran **deceive** /dɪ'si:v/ vt 1 prevariti 2 (sb into) navesti koga na 3 (oneself) zavaravati (se)

December /dɪ'sembə(r)/ n prosinac

decency /'di:snsɪ/ n pristojnost **decent** /'di:snt/ adj 1 pristojan 2 odjeven

deceptive /dɪ'septɪv/ adj varljiv **~ly** adv varljivo, samo naizgled **deception** n prijevara, varka

decide /dɪ'saɪd/ vt,vi 1 (between/for/in favour of/against) odlučiti se, donijeti odluku, presuditi 2 (on) zaključiti 3 nagnati na odluku **~d** adj 1 jasan 2 odlučan **~dly** adv decidirano, nesumnjivo

deciduous /dɪ'sɪdjʊəs/ adj bjelo-

goričan

decimal /'desɪml/ adj decimalan **the ~ point** decimalni zarez

decimate /'desɪmeɪt/ vt desetkovati

decipher /dɪ'saɪfə(r)/ vt dešifrirati

decision /dɪ'sɪʒn/ n 1 odluka **reach/come to/arrive at/take/make a ~** donijeti odluku 2 odlučnost **decisive** /dɪ'saɪsɪv/ adj 1 odlučujući 2 odlučan

deck /dek/ n 1 paluba **~ hand** n član posade broda 2 US snop (karata); špil coll 3 kat (autobusa)

declare /dɪ'kleə(r)/ vt,vi 1 objaviti, proglasiti, navijestiti 2 izjaviti **~ one-self** (for/against) deklarirati se, izjasniti se, opredijeliti se (za/protiv) 3 prijaviti **declarable** adj koji se mora prijaviti na carini **declaration** /,deklə'reɪʃn/ n deklaracija; proglas; izjava

declension /dɪ'klenʃn/ n gram deklinacija, sklanjanje

declination /,deklɪ'neɪʃn/ n otklon deklinacija

decline /dɪ'klaɪn/ vt,vi 1 odbiti 2 propadati, slabiti, opadati 3 gram deklinirati • n pad, propast, opadanje

decode /,di:'kəʊd/ vt dešifrirati

decompose /,di:kəm'pəʊz/ vt,vi 1 raspadati se, trunuti 2 razbiti, odijeliti **decomposition** /,di:kɒmpə'zɪʃn/ n raspadanje

decontaminate /,di:kən'tæmɪneɪt/ vt dekontaminirati

decor /'deɪkɔ:(r)/ n dekor **~ate** /'dekəreɪt/ vt 1 (with) ukrasiti čime 2 urediti (prostoriju) 2 (for) odlikovati **~ator** /'dekəreɪtə(r)/ n ličilac, soboslikar **~ation** /,dekə'reɪʃn/ n 1 ukrašavanje, ukras, dekoracija 3 odlikovanje **~ative** /'dekərətɪv/ adj ukrasan

decoy /'di:kɔɪ/ n mamac (+ fig) • vt namamiti

decrease /dɪ'kri:s/ vt,vi smanjiti, sniziti • n /'di:kri:s/ smanjenje, pad

decree /dɪ'kri:/ n 1 dekret, odluka, proglas **issue a ~** donijeti dekret 2 presuda, rješenje • vt donijeti dekret, odrediti

decrepit /dɪ'krepɪt/ adj oronuo

decry /dɪ'kraɪ/ *vt* ocrniti

dedicate /'dedɪkeɪt/ *vt* (to) posvetiti **dedication** *n* 1 predanost, žar 2 posveta ~**d** *adj* predan, odan

deduce /dɪ'dju:s/ *vt* (from) izvesti zaključak

deduct /dɪ'dʌkt/ *vt* odbiti, oduzeti ~**ion** *n* 1 odbitak 2 dedukcija, zaključak

deed /di:d/ *n* 1 djelo, čin 2 povelja, isprava

deem /di:m/ *vt form* smatrati, držati

deep /di:p/ *adj* 1 dubok **ankle-~** do gležnja **in ~ water(s)** u škripcu 2 taman 3 nedokučiv 4 tajanstven 5 temeljit • *adv* duboko **Still waters run ~** *prov* tiha voda brijege dere ~-**laid** *adj* pažljivo isplaniran ~-**rooted** duboko ukorijenjen ~-**seated** duboko usađen • *vt,vi* produbiti (se) ~**ly** *adv* duboko **deer** /dɪə(r)/ *n* (*pl* ~) jelen

deface /dɪ'feɪs/ *vt* nagrditi

defamatory /dɪ'fæmətrɪ/ *adj* klevetnički **defame** /dɪ'feɪm/ *vt* ocrniti

default /dɪ'fɔ:lt/ *vi* ne pojaviti se (pred sudom, na natjecanju), ne izvršiti (obvezu) • *n* neizvršenje obveze, nepojavljivanje, oglušba **to win by ~** pobijediti zato što protivnička strana nije pristupila natjecanju **~ value** *comp* unaprijed zadani parametar/ vrijednost ~**er** *n* dezerter

defeat /dɪ'fi:t/ *vt* 1 poraziti 2 spriječiti • *n* poraz

defect (1) /'di:fekt/ *n* greška, nedostatak, mana ~**ive** *adj* 1 loš, s greškom, manjkav, defektan 2 *gram* nepotpun

defect (2) /dɪ'fekt/ *vi* (from) (to) prebjeći ~**or** *n* prebjeg, odmetnik ~**ion** *n* 1 prelazak (na drugu vjeru, u drugu stranku) 2 bijeg iz zemlje (iz političkih razloga)

defence (**defense** *US*) /dɪ'fens/ *n* obrana **self-~** samoobrana ~**less** *adj* nezaštićen **defensive** *adj* 1 defenzivan, obrambeni 2 narogušen o *n* defenziva

defend /dɪ'fend/ *vt* (against/from) štititi, braniti (se), stati u obranu ~**er** *n* 1 branitelj 2 branič ~**ant** *n* optuženik

defer /dɪ'fɜ:(r)/ *vi* ~ **to** popustiti, poko-

riti se ~**ence** /'defərəns/ *n* pokornost, smjernost, poštovanje **in ~ence to** iz poštovanja prema ~**ential** /ˌdefə'renʃl/ *adj* pristojan, pokoran, pun poštovanja

defiance /dɪ'faɪəns/ *n* prkos, neposluh **in ~ of** prkoseći **defiant** *adj* prkosan, nepokoran

deficiency /dɪ'fɪʃnsɪ/ *n* 1 nedostatak, nestašica, pomanjkanje **vitamin ~** pomanjkanje vitamina 2 mana, nedostatak **deficient** *adj* (in) manjkav, kojem nedostaje čega

deficit /'defɪsɪt/ *n* deficit

defile /dɪ'faɪl/ *vt* uprljati, zagaditi, oskvrnuti ~**ment** *n* zagađenje, oskvrnuće

define /dɪ'faɪn/ *vt* definirati, odrediti **definite** /'defɪnət/ *adj* jasan, konačan ~ **article** *n gram* određeni član ~**ly** *adj* 1 definitivno, konačno 2 sigurno **definition** *n* 1 definicija 2 oštrina (slike)

deflate /dɪ'fleɪt/ *vt* 1 ispuhati 2 *fig* srezati 2 poduzeti mjere za smanjivanje inflacije **deflation** *n* 1 ispuhavanje, splašnjavanje 2 deflacija

deflect /dɪ'flekt/ *vt,vi* (from) skrenuti s putanje

deform /dɪ'fɔ:m/ *vt* izobličiti, deformirati ~**ed** *adj* 1 deformiran 2 izopačen ~**ity** *n* izobličenost, deformacija

defrost /ˌdi:'frɒst/ *vt* odmrznuti ~**er** *n* odmrzivač

deft /deft/ *adj* vješt, spretan

defunct /dɪ'fʌŋkt/ *adj* 1 preminuo, pokojan 2 ništetan

defuse /ˌdi:'fju:z/ *vt* 1 ukloniti upaljač, dezaktivirati 2 *fig* smiriti (krizu i sl.)

defy /dɪ'faɪ/ *vt* prkositi, opirati se ~ **sb to do sth** izazvati koga da što učini

degenerate /dɪ'dʒenəreɪt/ *vi* (into) izroditi se, izopačiti se, degenerirati • /dɪ'dʒenərət/ *adj* izopačen, degeneriran • *n* degenerik

degrade /dɪ'greɪd/ *vt* 1 degradirati, lišiti čina 2 srozati se

degree /dɪ'gri:/ *n* 1 stupanj **by ~s** postupno **to a ~** *coll* **a.** u najvećoj mjeri **b.** u određenoj mjeri **first ~** *adj* prvog stupnja **third ~** *n* maltretiranje ispitanika **murder in the first ~**

ubojstvo s predumišljajem **2** položaj, rang **3** akademski stupanj, diploma **take one's ~** diplomirati

dehydrate /ˌdiː'haɪdreɪt/ vt dehidrirati **~d** adj sušen

deign /deɪn/ vi (to do sth) udostojiti se

deity /'diːɪtɪ/ n božanstvo

dejected /dɪ'dʒektɪd/ adj snužden **dejection** /dɪ'dʒekʃn/ n tuga

delay /dɪ'leɪ/ vt,vi **1** odugovlačiti, oklijevati **2** kasniti **3** zadržati **4** odgoditi • n oklijevanje, odgađanje, kašnjenje **without ~** odmah

delectable /dɪ'lektəbl/ adj ugodan, mio, šarmantan, poželjan

delegate /'delɪgət/ n izaslanik, delegat • /'delɪgeɪt/ vt (sth/sb, sth to) delegirati **delegation** n izaslanstvo

delete /dɪ'liːt/ vt izbrisati, izbaciti

deli /'delɪ/ n coll trgovina delikatesama

deliberate /dɪ'lɪbərət/ adj **1** namjeran **2** promišljen • /dɪ'lɪbəreɪt/ vt,vi (over/on/upon) razmatrati, promišljati **deliberation** /dɪˌlɪbə'reɪʃn/ n **1** razmatranje **2** promišljenost **deliberative** /dɪ'lɪbərətɪv/ adj za razmatranje

delicacy /'delɪkəsɪ/ n **1** delikatnost, nježnost, krhkost **2** delikatesa **delicate** /'delɪkət/ adj **1** nježan, mek **2** profinjen **3** osjetljiv, krhak (+ fig) **4** delikatan, pipav **5** istančan, precizan **6** obazriv **delicatessen** n trgovina delikatesama; delikatesa

delicious /dɪ'lɪʃəs/ adj **1** ukusan, slastan **2** zabavan

delight /dɪ'laɪt/ n užitak, zadovoljstvo, radost **take ~ in** uživati u • vt,vi oduševiti, pružiti užitak, razveseliti **~ in** uživati u **~ful** adj divan

delinquency /dɪ'lɪŋkwənsɪ/ n delinkvencija, prijestup **juvenile ~** maloljetnička delinkvencija **delinquent** n prijestupnik

delirious /dɪ'lɪrɪəs/ adj (with) u deliriju (od) (+ fig) **delirium** n bunilo; delirij (+ fig)

deliver /dɪ'lɪvə(r)/ vt **1** dostaviti **2 ~ from** arch izbaviti **3** održati (govor) **4** roditi **5** (up/over/to) predati, izručiti **6** zadati **7** izvršiti (obećano) **~ance** n (from) izbavljenje (od) **~y** n **1** is-

poruka, dostava **on ~y** kod isporuke **take ~y of** primiti **2** način govora **3** porod

dell /del/ n udolina

delude /dɪ'luːd/ vt **~ sb with sth/into doing sth** zavarati, zavesti **delusion** /dɪ'luːʒn/ n zavaravanje, varka, zabluda **delusion of grandeur** megalomanija **delusive** adj varljiv

deluge /'deljuːdʒ/ n poplava (+ fig), potop • vt (with) preplaviti, zasuti

delve /delv/ vt **1** arch kopati **2 ~ into** kopati, rovati po čemu (+ fig)

demand /dɪ'mɑːnd/ n (for) **1** zahtjev **on ~** na zahtjev **2** potražnja **in ~** tražen • vt zahtijevati, tražiti

demarcate /'diːmɑːkeɪt/ vt razgraničiti

demean /dɪ'miːn/ vt **~ oneself** poniziti se

demeanour /dɪ'miːnə(r)/ n ponašanje, držanje

demented /dɪ'mentɪd/ adj umno poremećen

demijohn /'demɪdʒɒn/ n pletenka, demižon

demilitarize /ˌdiː'mɪlɪtəraɪz/ vt demilitarizirati

demise /dɪ'maɪz/ n leg smrt

demo /'deməʊ/ n coll **1** demonstracija **2** (~-tape) demo-snimka coll

demob /ˌdiː'mɒb/ vt GB coll demobilizirati • n demobilizacija **~ilize** /dɪ'məʊbəlaɪz/ vt demobilizirati

democracy /dɪ'mɒkrəsɪ/ n demokracija **democrat** /'deməkræt/ n demokrat, pristaša demokracije **democratic** adj demokratski **democratically** adv demokratizirati **democratize** vt demokratizirati

demography /dɪ'mɒgrəfɪ/ n demografija **demographic** adj demografski

demolish /dɪ'mɒlɪʃ/ vt demolirati, uništiti **demolition** /ˌdemə'lɪʃn/ n uništenje; rušenje (stare zgrade)

demon /'diːmən/ n demon, zloduh **~ic** /diː'mɒnɪk/ adj demonski

demonstrate /'demənstreɪt/ vt,vi **1** pokazati, izvršiti demonstraciju, dokazati **2** demonstrirati **demonstration** /ˌdemən'streɪʃn/ n **1** pokazivanje, prezentacija **2** iskazivanje **3** demonstracije *pl* **demonstrative** /dɪ'mɒn-strətɪv/ *adj* 1 koji iskazuje (svoje) osjećaje 2˜ otvoren, demonstrativan **demonstrator** /'demənstreɪtə(r)/ *n* 1 demonstrant 2 demonstrator

demote /ˌdi:'məʊt/ *vt* lišiti čina, degradirati

demur /dɪ'mɜ:(r)/ *vi* (at/to) *form* prigovarati, sustezati se • *n* 1 sustezanje 2 prigovor **without ˜** bez pogovora

demure /dɪ'mjʊə(r)/ *adj* ozbiljan, koji se pravi ozbiljnim

den /den/ *n* 1 brlog, leglo, jazbina (+ *fig*) 2 radna soba

denial /dɪ'naɪəl/ *n* (of) poricanje, nijekanje, odbijanje

denim /'denɪm/ *n* 1 traper (platno) 2 *pl* traperice, traper jakna itd.

denizen /'denɪzn/ *n* stanovnik

denomination /dɪ,nɒmɪ'neɪʃn/ *n* 1 vjera 2 denominacija **˜al** *adj* konfesionalni **denominator** /dɪ'nɒmɪneɪtə(r)/ *n* nazivnik **lowest common denominator** najniži zajednički nazivnik

denote /dɪ'nəʊt/ *vt* označavati

denouement /ˌdeɪ'nu:mɒːŋ/ *n* rasplet

denounce /dɪ'naʊns/ *vt* 1 denuncirati, prokazati 2 otkazati, prekršiti

dense /dens/ *adj* 1 gust 2 *coll* glup, tup **˜ly** *adv* **˜ness**, **density** *n* gustoća; glupost

dent /dent/ *n* 1 ulubljenje 2 *fig* udarac **a ˜ in one's armour** slabost • *vt, vi* ulubiti (se)

dental /'dentl/ *adj* zubni **˜ surgeon** zubni liječnik **˜ plate** zubalo **˜ work** zubna proteza

dentist /'dentɪst/ *n* zubar **˜ry** *n* zubarstvo

denture /'dentʃə(r)/ *n* zubalo

deny /dɪ'naɪ/ *vt* 1 poricati, nijekati 2 odreći se, zanijekati 3 odbiti, uskratiti

deodorant /di:'əʊdərənt/ *n* dezodorans

depart /dɪ'pɑ:t/ *vi* 1 (from) otići, krenuti, otputovati **˜ (from) this life** napustiti ovaj svijet 2 **˜ from** odstupiti od **˜ed** *adj* prošli **the ˜ed** *n* pokojnici **˜ure** *n* (from) 1 odlazak 2 odstupanje od **a new ˜ure** novi pravac

department /dɪ'pɑ:tmənt/ *n* 1 resor 2 odsjek 3 odjel **˜ store** robna kuća 4 ministarstvo **the State D˜** *US* Ministarstvo vanjskih poslova 5 departman, kotar

depend /dɪ'pend/ *vi* **˜ on/upon** 1 ovisiti o, zavisiti od 2 osloniti se, pouzdati se **˜ upon it** možeš biti siguran **˜able** *adj* pouzdan **˜ant**, **˜ent** *n* štićenik, uzdržavani član obitelji **˜ence** *n* 1 zavisnost, ovisnost 2 pouzdanje 3 uvjetovanost **˜ent** *adj* **˜ on/upon** ovisan

depict /dɪ'pɪkt/ *vt* prikazati, opisati

depilatory /dɪ'pɪlətrɪ/ *n* sredstvo za depilaciju • *adj* za depilaciju

deplete /dɪ'pli:t/ *vt* (of) isprazniti, iscrpsti **depletion** *n* iscrpljenje, smanjivanje

deplorable /dɪ'plɔ:rəbl/ *adj* žalostan, za svaku osudu

deploy /dɪ'plɔɪ/ *vt, vi* mil 1 rasporediti (se), razviti (se) (duž bojišnice) 2 *fig* upotrijebiti, angažirati **˜ment** *n* raspored vojske

deport /dɪ'pɔ:t/ *vt* deportirati, protjerati

depose /dɪ'pəʊz/ *vt* svrgnuti

deposit /dɪ'pɒzɪt/ *vt* 1 položiti, odložiti 2 deponirati, uložiti 3 predujmiti 4 nataložiti • *n* 1 predujam 2 ulog **˜ account** štedni račun **safe ˜ (box)** sef u banci 3 naslaga, talog **˜or** *n* ulagač **˜ory** *n* 1 spremište, skladište 2 riznica (+ *fig*)

depot /'depəʊ/ *n* 1 spremište, depo 2 remiza 3 *US* kolodvor

depraved /dɪ'preɪvd/ *adj* izopačen **depravity** /dɪ'prævətɪ/ *n* izopačenost

deprecating /'deprəkeɪtɪŋ/ *adj* preziran

depreciate /dɪ'pri:ʃɪeɪt/ *vt, vi* spustiti cijenu, obezvrijediti, podcijeniti **depreciation** /dɪ,pri:ʃɪ'eɪʃn/ *n* pad vrijednosti, deprecijacija

depress /dɪ'pres/ *vt* 1 pritisnuti 2 potlačivati 3 deprimirati 4 smanjiti se, sniziti cijenu/vrijednost **˜ion** *n* 1 depresija, potištenost 2 uleknuće 3 kriza 4 polje niskog tlaka **˜ive** *adj* depresivan, koji izaziva/potiče depresiju

deprive /dɪ'praɪv/ *vt* ~ **of** lišiti čega ~**d** *adj* siromašan **deprivation** /,deprɪ'veɪʃn/ *n* lišavanje, oskudica, gubitak

depth /depθ/ *n* dubina (+ *fig*) **in-~** *adj* temeljit ○ *adv* temeljito

deputy *n* /,depjʊ'tɪ/ 1 zamjenik 2 zastupnik, poslanik, deputat

derail /dɪ'reɪl/ *vt* 1 izbaciti vlak iz tračnica 2 **be ~ed** iskočiti iz tračnica

derange /dɪ'reɪndʒ/ *vt* smutiti, poremetiti (**mentally**) ~**d** *adj* umno poremećen

derby /'dɑːbɪ/ *n* 1 **The D~** konjske trke u Epsomu 2 *US* godišnja konjska utrka 3 važna utakmica; derbi *coll* 4 *US* cilindar

derelict /'derəlɪkt/ *adj* napušten, zapušten ~**ion** /,derə'lɪkʃn/ *n* 1 opustošenje 2 zapuštanje ~**ion of duty** zanemarivanje dužnosti

derision /dɪ'rɪʒn/ *n* ismijavanje, sprdnja **derisive** /dɪ'raɪsɪv/ *adj* posprdan

de rigueur /də rɪ'gɜː(r)/ *adj* obvezatan

derivation /,derɪ'veɪʃn/ *n* porijeklo, izvođenje, derivacija **derivative** /dɪ'rɪvətɪv/ *n* 1 izvedenica 2 derivat • *adj* 1 izveden, deriviran 2 neoriginalan **derive** /dɪ'raɪv/ *vt,vi* ~ **from** 1 *form* izvlačiti, 2 potjecati

derogatory /dɪ'rɒgətrɪ/ *adj* (to) podcjenjivački, preziran

derrick /'derɪk/ *n* bušaći toranj ~ **crane** kran, dizalica

derv /dɜːv/ *n* diesel gorivo

descale /,diː'skeɪl/ *vt* očistiti od vapnenca

descend /dɪ'send/ *vi,vt* 1 *form* sići niz 2 ~ **from** (+ *pass*) potjecati od 3 prijeći nasljedstvom 4 ~ **on/upon a.** napasti **b.** *fig* nenajavljeno posjetiti 5 ~ **to** srozati se do ~**ant** *n* potomak

descent /dɪ'sent/ *n* 1 silazak, spuštanje 2 padina, spust 3 podrijetlo 4 ~ **on/upon** napad, nenajavljeni posjet 5 nasljeđivanje

describe /dɪ'skraɪb/ *vt* 1 opisati ~ **sb/sth as** reći za koga/što da je 2 nacrtati, opisati **description** /dɪ'skrɪpʃn/ *n* opisivanje, opis **descriptive** /dɪ'skrɪptɪv/ *adj* opisan, deskriptivan

desecrate /'desɪkreɪt/ *vt* oskvrnuti

desegregate /,diː'segrɪgeɪt/ *vt* ukinuti (rasnu) segregaciju ~**d school** škola za djecu svih rasa

desert (1) /dɪ'zɜːt/ *vt,vi* 1 napustiti, ostaviti (na cjedilu), iznevjeriti 2 dezertirati ~ **ed** *adj* napušten, pust ~**er** *n* dezerter ~**ion** *n* 1 napuštanje 2 dezertiranje

desert (2) /'dezət/ *n* pustinja • *adj* 1 neplodan 2 nenastanjen, pust

deserts /dɪ'zɜːts/ *n pl* zasluga

deserve /dɪ'zɜːv/ *vt,vi* zaslužiti ~**d** *adj* zaslužen, pravedan **deserving** *adj* (of) vrijedan, dostojan, zaslužan

design /dɪ'zaɪn/ *n* 1 nacrt, projekt 2 dizajn 3 konstrukcija 4 uzorak, šara 5 nakana, plan **have ~s on/against** kovati podle planove protiv • *vt,vi* izraditi nacrt, dizajnirati, projektirati ~**ed for sb/for sth/to do sth** namijenjen, predviđen za ~**er** *n* 1 dizajner 2 modni kreator 3 *mod* poznatog kreatora 4 *mod coll* šminkerski ~**ing** *adj* koji spletkari

designate /'dezɪgneɪt/ *adj* budući (koji je već imenovan) • /'dezɪgneɪt/ *vt* 1 obilježiti, imenovati 2 imenovati, postaviti za **designation** /,dezɪg'neɪʃn/ *n* 1 imenovanje 2 ime, naziv

desire /dɪ'zaɪə(r)/ *n* (for) želja, žudnja za • *vt form* 1 željeti 2 umoljavati **desirable** *adj* poželjan

desk /desk/ *n* 1 radni stol 2 recepcija ~ **clerk** *n US* recepcionar

desolate /'desələt/ *adj* 1 zapušten, pust 2 ucviljen, očajan **desolation** /,desə'leɪʃn/ *n* opustošenje, pustoš; čamotinja

despair /dɪ'speə(r)/ *n* očaj, beznađe • *vi* (of) izgubiti svaku nadu da, pasti u očaj zbog ~**ing** *adj* očajan

despatch → **dispatch**

desperate /'despərət/ *adj* 1 očajan 2 spreman na sve, očajnički ~ **remedies** ljuta trava 3 opasan **desperation** /,despə'reɪʃn/ *n* očajanje, spremnost na sve

despicable /dɪ'spɪkəbl/ *adj* prezira vrijedan

despise /dɪ'spaɪz/ *vt* prezirati

despite /dɪ'spaɪt/ *prep* usprkos komu/čemu

dessert /dɪ'zɜ:t/ n desert

destination /ˌdestɪ'neɪʃn/ n odredište

destine /'destɪn/ vt be ~d (for) I was ~d for bilo mi je suđeno da **destiny** n usud, sudbina

destitute /'destɪtju:t/ adj siromašan **destitution** n oskudica

destroy /dɪ'strɔɪ/ vt 1 uništiti, razoriti 2 ubiti ~er n 1 uništavač 2 mil razarač

destruction /dɪ'strʌkʃn/ n 1 uništenje 2 propast **destructive** adj koji uništava, razoran, destruktivan

detach /dɪ'tætʃ/ vt 1 (from) otkvačiti, odvojiti 2 mil izdvojiti ~ed adj 1 nepristran 2 ravnodušan 3 odvojen, samostalan ~ed house obiteljska, samostojeća kuća ~ment n 1 nepristranost, ravnodušnost, hladnoća 2 mil odred

detail /'di:teɪl/ n 1 pojedinost, detalj in ~ detaljno 2 mil odred s posebnim zadatkom • vt 1 detaljno opisati 2 mil dodijeliti zadatak

detain /dɪ'teɪn/ vt 1 zadržati 2 zadržati u pritvoru, pritvoriti ~ee /ˌdi:teɪ'ni:/ n (politički) zatvorenik

detect /dɪ'tekt/ vt pronaći, otkriti ~or n detektor ~ion n otkrivanje, detekcija ~ive n detektiv, istražitelj

detente /ˌdeɪ'tɑ:nt/ n detant, popuštanje

detention /dɪ'tenʃn/ n 1 dulji ostanak u školi za kaznu 2 pritvor **hold in** ~ držati u pritvoru ~ **camp** zatočenički logor ~ **centre** popravni dom

deter /dɪ'tɜ:(r)/ vt (from) odvratiti, zastrašiti ~rence n zastrašivanje ~rent n, adj sredstvo zastrašivanja

detergent /dɪ'tɜ:dʒənt/ n detergent chem

deteriorate /dɪ'tɪərɪəreɪt/ vt,vi pogoršati se, pokvariti se

determine /dɪ'tɜ:mɪn/ vt,vi 1 odrediti 2 ~ **to do sth/on/upon sth** odlučiti (se za) što 3 ~ **sb to sth** nagnati koga na što 4 ~ **against sth** odgovoriti od čega **determinate** /dɪ'tɜ:mɪnət/ adj određen, ograničen **determination** /dɪˌtɜ:mɪ'neɪʃn/ n 1 određivanje 2 (to do sth) odlučnost

detest /dɪ'test/ vt mrziti ~able adj

mrzak, odvratan

detonate /'detəneɪt/ vt,vi eksplodirati, izazvati eksploziju **detonator** n upaljač, detonator

detour /'di:tʊə(r)/ n skretanje, obilazni put • vt ići obilaznim putem, skrenuti

detract /dɪ'trækt/ vi ~ **from** umanjiti (što)

detriment /'detrɪmənt/ n šteta **to the** ~ **of** na štetu ~al /ˌdetrɪ'mentl/ adj škodljiv, štetan

detritus /dɪ'traɪtəs/ n 1 nanos (šljunka, pijeska i sl.) 2 fig ostaci, krhotine

deuce /dju:s/ n 1 dvojka (u kartama i kocki) 2 tennis izjednačenje

devalue /ˌdi:'vælju:/, **devaluate** /ˌdi:'væljʊeɪt/ vt devalvirati **devaluation** n devalvacija

devastate /'devəsteɪt/ vt opustošiti, poharati ~d adj fig skrhan

develop /dɪ'veləp/ vt,vi 1 razviti (se) ~ing **countries** zemlje u razvoju 2 razviti (film) 3 pojaviti se 4 izgraditi ~er n 1 graditelj, graditeljsko poduzeće 2 razvijač ~ment n 1 razvoj, izgradnja 2 razvoj događaja, događaji

deviate /'di:vɪeɪt/ vi ~ **from** zastraniti, skrenuti s **deviation** n 1 odstupanje 2 devijacija

device /dɪ'vaɪs/ n 1 naprava 2 plan, osnova, lukavština **leave sb to one's own** ~s ostaviti koga da se sam snalazi 3 znak, simbol

devil /'devl/ n 1 vrag (+ fig) 2 (**poor** ~) jadnik, bijednik **what the** ~... koga vraga... **he is a** ~ **of a skier** odlično skija • vt,vi 1 peći s jakim začinima 2 (for) volontirati (u odvjetničkoj kancelariji) ~-**may-care** adj nehajan ~ish adj vraški, paklenski ~ment, ~ry n 1 opačina 2 nestašnost, živahnost

devious /'di:vɪəs/ adj 1 okolni, okolišni 2 fig nepošten

devise /dɪ'vaɪz/ vt smisliti

devoid /dɪ'vɔɪd/ adj (of) lišen (čega)

devolution /ˌdi:və'lu:ʃn/ n decentralizacija (vlasti)

devote /dɪ'vəʊt/ vt ~ **oneself/sth to** posvetiti (se/što) ~d adj predan, odan ~e n 1 ljubitelj 2 fanatični pristaša

devotion *n* 1 (for) ljubav 2 (to) posvećenost 3 pobožnost **devotional** *adj* molitveni

devour /dɪ'vaʊə(r)/ *vt* 1 proždrijeti 2 be ~ed with *fig* žderati se od

devout /dɪ'vaʊt/ *adj* 1 pobožan 2 odan

dew /dju:/ *n* rosa ~**y** *adj* orošen

dexterity /dek'sterɪtɪ/ *n* spretnost **dexterous, dextrous** /'dekstrəs/ *adj* spretan

diabetes /,daɪə'bi:ti:z/ *n med* dijabetes, šećerna bolest **diabetic** *n* dijabetičar

diabolic(al) /,daɪə'bɒlɪk(l)/ *adj* vraški

diagnose /'daɪəgnəʊz/ *vt* dijagnosticirati **diagnosis** /,daɪəg'nəʊsɪs/ *n* 1 dijagnostika 2 dijagnoza, nalaz

diagonal /daɪ'ægənl/ *n* dijagonala • *adj* dijagonalan

diagram /'daɪəgræm/ *n* dijagram

dial /daɪəl/ *n* 1 brojčanik **radio** ~ skala radija • *vt* nazvati, okrenuti (broj) ~**ling code** pozivni broj ~**ling tone** znak slobodne linije

dialect /'daɪəlekt/ *n* narječje, dijalekt

dialectic, dialectics /,daɪə'lektɪk/ *n* (+ *sing*) dijalektika

dialogue (dialog US**)** /'daɪəlɒg/ *n* dijalog

diameter /daɪ'æmɪtə(r)/ *n* dijametar **diametrically** /,daɪə'metrɪklɪ/ *adv* dijametralno

diamond /'daɪəmənd/ *n* 1 dijamant 2 *mod* dijamantni 3 karo

diaper /'daɪəpə(r)/ *n* US pelena

diaphanous /daɪ'æfənəs/ *adj* prozračan, proziran

diaphragm /'daɪəfræm/ *n* 1 dijafragma; ošit 2 membrana

diarrhoea, diarrhea /,daɪə'rɪə/ *n med* proljev

diary /'daɪərɪ/ *n* dnevnik **diarist** *n* osoba koja piše dnevnik

dice /daɪs/ *n pl (sing* **die)** kocke **to play** ~ kockati se **the die is cast** kocka je bačena • *vi,vt* 1 kockati se 2 nasjeckati na kockice ~**y** /'daɪsɪ/ *adj coll* opasan, riskantan

dick /dɪk/ *n coll tab* pimpek *coll tab* ~**head** *n coll tab* glupan, seronja

dictate /dɪk'teɪt/ *vt,vi* 1 (to) diktirati 2 ~ **to** nalagati, određivati • *n* diktat, nalog **dictation** /dɪk'teɪʃn/ *n* diktat

dictator /dɪk'teɪtə(r)/ *n* diktator ~**ship** *n* diktatura

dictionary /'dɪkʃənrɪ/ *n* rječnik

dictum /'dɪktəm/ *n* izreka

did *v irreg* → **do**

didactic /dɪ'dæktɪk/ *adj* poučan, didaktičan ~**s** *n* (+ *sing*) didaktika

die (1) /daɪ/ *n* 1 dice 2 kalup, matrica ~-**cast** *adj* lijevan

die (2) *vi* 1 umrijeti 2 **be dying for sth/to do sth** umirati od želje za čim/da se što učini 3 nestati ~-**hard** *n, mod* a. konzervativac b. koji se ne da, žilav ~ **away** zamrijeti, splasnuti, stišati se ~ **down** trnuti, slabiti ~ **off** poumirati ~ **out** izumrijeti

diesel /'di:zl/ *n, mod* dizel, na dizel pogon

diet (1) /'daɪət/ *n* 1 prehrana 2 dijeta • *vt,vi* biti na dijeti ~**ary** *adj* prehrambeni, dijetni, dijetetski

diet (2) *n* sabor

differ /'dɪfə(r)/ *vi* 1 (from) razlikovati se (od) 2 ~ **from sb** (about/on sth) biti drugog mišljenja ~**ence** *n* (between) 1 razlika 2 neslaganje **settle the** ~**ences** pomiriti se ~**ent** *adj* 1 (from/to/than US) različit 2 drugi ~**ential** *adj* diferencijalan ∘ *n* diferencijal, mjenjač ~**entiate** *vt* 1 (from) razlikovati 2 (between) različito se odnositi

difficult /'dɪfɪkəlt/ *adj* težak *fig* ~**y** *n* poteškoća

diffident /'dɪfɪdənt/ *adj* plah, nesiguran **diffidence** *n* plahost, nesigurnost

diffuse /dɪ'fju:z/ *vt,vi* 1 širiti (+ *fig*) 2 miješati se • /dɪ'fju:s/ *adj* 1 preopširan 2 difuzan ~**ness, diffusion** *n* 1 širenje 2 difuzija

dig /dɪg/ *vt,vi irreg* 1 kopati (+ *fig*) 2 *sl* uživati; furati se na *sl* 3 *sl* razumjeti; kužiti *sl* • *n* 1 udarac, ubod (+ *fig*) 2 *pl GB coll* iznajmljena soba ~**ger** *n* 1 kopač 2 rovokopač

digest /'daɪdʒest/ *n* sažetak, skraćena verzija • /dɪ'dʒest/ *vt,vi* 1 probaviti 2 shvatiti ~**ion** *n* probava ~**ive** *adj* probavni

digit /'dɪdʒɪt/ *n* 1 brojka, znamenka 2 prst ~**al** *adj* digitalan

dignified /'dɪgnɪfaɪd/ *adj* dostojanstven

dignity /'dɪgnətɪ/ *n* dostojanstvo **1 beneath one's ~** ispod časti **2** titula, čast **dignitary** *n* dostojanstvenik

digress /daɪ'gres/ *vi* (from) skrenuti s, zastraniti **~ion** *n* digresija

dike, dyke /daɪk/ *n* **1** jarak **2** nasip **3** *tab* derog *sl* muškobanjasta lezbijka

dilapidated /dɪ'læpɪdeɪtɪd/ *adj* ruševan, trošan

dilate /daɪ'leɪt/ *vi,vt* raširiti (se) **dilation** *n* širenje; dilatacija *med*

dilemma /dɪ'lemə/ *n* dilema

diligence /'dɪlɪdʒəns/ *n* marljivost **diligent** *adj* marljiv

dill /dɪl/ *n* kopar

dilute /daɪ'lju:t/ *vt* (with) razblažiti, razrijediti, oslabiti • *adj* razvodnjen, razblažen, razrijeđen

dim /dɪm/ *adj* **1** mutan, nejasan, prigušen, zamućen **take a ~ view of** *coll* gledati prijekim okom **2** *coll* glup • *vt,vi* prigušiti, potamniti, zasjeniti

dime /daɪm/ *n* **1** (novčić od) 10 centi **2** *fig* para **~ novel** petparački roman

dimension /dɪ'menʃn/ *n* dimenzija **two/three/~al** *adj* dvo/trodimenzionalan

diminish /dɪ'mɪnɪʃ/ *vt,vi* smanjiti (se)

diminutive /dɪ'mɪnjutɪv/ *adj* majušan • *n gram* deminutiv

dimple /'dɪmpl/ *n* rupica (na bradi/obrazu)

din /dɪn/ *n* velika buka • *vi,vt* bučiti, odzvanjati

dine /daɪn/ *vt, vi* **1** večerati **~ out** izaći na večeru **2** prirediti svečanu večeru (za koga) **dining-car** vagon-restoran **dining-room** blagovaonica **~r** *n* **1** uzvanik/gost na večeri **2** → **dining-car 3** *US* restorančić

dinghy /'dɪŋgɪ/ *n* mali čamac

dingy /'dɪndʒɪ/ *adj* prljav

dinner /'dɪnə(r)/ *n* ručak, večera (glavni dnevni obrok) **have/eat ~** večerati **ask sb to ~** pozvati na večeru **~ jacket** smoking

dinosaur /'daɪnəsɔ:(r)/ *n* dinosaur

dint /dɪnt/ *n* **1** → **dent 2** by **~ of** zahvaljujući, putem, pomoću

diocese /'daɪəsɪs/ *n* biskupija

dip /dɪp/ *vt,vi* **1 ~ in/into** umočiti, uroniti **2** obrušiti se **3** spustiti **~ the headlights** oboriti svjetla • *n* **1** uranjanje, umakanje **2** *coll* kupanje **take/have a ~** bućnuti se *coll* **3** nizbrdica; pad *fig* **4** umak

diploma /dɪ'pləumə/ *n* diploma

diplomacy /dɪ'pləuməsɪ/ *n* diplomacija **diplomat** /'dɪpləmæt/ *n* diplomat **diplomatic** /,dɪplə'mætɪk/ *adj* diplomatski

dipper /'dɪpə(r)/ *n* kutlača **the Big/Little D~** *US* Veliki/Mali medvjed

dipsomaniac /,dɪpsə'meɪnɪək/ *n* pijanac

dire /'daɪə(r)/ *adj* **1** strašan **2** krajnji in **~ straits** u velikoj nevolji

direct /dɪ'rekt/ *adj* izravan, neposredan, direktan; ravan **~ current** istosmjerna struja **~ speech** *gram* upravni govor • *vt,vi* **1 ~** (sb to) uputiti **2 ~** (sth to) nasloviti na **3 ~** (sth to sb) odnositi se na, uputiti **4** upravljati **5** režirati, biti redatelj **6** (to/towards) usmjeriti, upraviti **7** narediti **~ion** /dɪ'rekʃn/ *n* **1** smjer **2** *pl* upute **3** uprava, direkcija **~ly** *adv* **1** izravno, neposredno, direktno **2** odmah **3** ubrzo, začas • *conj coll* čim **~or** *n* **1** direktor, član upravnog odbora **Board of D~ors** *US* upravni odbor **2** redatelj

directory /dɪ'rektərɪ/ *n* **1** (telefonski) imenik **2** *comp* direktorij

dirt /dɜ:t/ *n* **1** prljavština (+ *fig*) **2** prašina **~-road** *US* neasfaltirani put **treat sb like ~** svinjski se odnositi prema kome **~ cheap** veoma jeftin **~y** *adj* prljav (+ *fig*), gadan • *vt,vi* uprljati (se)

dis- *prefix* ne-, od- (označava gubitak)

disable /dɪs'eɪbl/ *vt* onesposobiti, isključiti **~d** *adj* invalidan **~d person** invalid **disability** /,dɪsə'bɪlətɪ/ *n* nesposobnost (za rad), invalidnost

disadvantage /,dɪsəd'vɑ:ntɪdʒ/ *n* **1** loša strana, nedostatak **be at a ~** biti u nepovoljnom položaju **2** šteta **~ous** /,dɪs,ædvən'teɪdʒəs/ *adj* (to) štetan, loš po

disaffection /,dɪsə'fekʃn/ *n* (političko) nezadovoljstvo

disagree /ˌdɪsəˈgriː/ vi 1 (with) ne složiti se (s) 2 ~ **with sb** ne ići u tek **the food** ~s **with me** od hrane mi je pozlilo ~**able** adj neugodan, neljubazan ~**ment** n 1 neslaganje 2 spor, svađa

disappear /ˌdɪsəˈpɪə(r)/ vi nestati ~**ance** n nestanak

disappoint /ˌdɪsəˈpɔɪnt/ vt 1 razočarati 2 ne ispuniti ~**ed** (in/at sth) razočaran (u kome, u što) ~**ment** n razočaranje

disapprove /ˌdɪsəˈpruːv/ vi,vt (of) ne odobravati **disapproval** n neslaganje, neodobravanje **disapproving** adj prijekoran

disarm /dɪsˈɑːm/ vi,vt (+ fig) razoružati ~**ament** n razoružanje

disarray /ˌdɪsəˈreɪ/ n metež, zbrka • vt uzrokovati metež, pobrkati

disaster /dɪˈzɑːstə(r)/ n katastrofa **disastrous** adj katastrofalan

disband /dɪsˈbænd/ vt,vi raspustiti, raspasti se

disbelief /ˌdɪsbɪˈliːf/ n nevjerica **in** ~ s nevjericom

disc, disk /dɪsk/ n 1 okrugla ploča, kolut ~ **brakes** n disk-kočnice 2 comp disk 3 comp disketa 4 coll gramofonska ploča ~ **jockey** (DJ) n diskdžokej **compact** ~ (CD) n kompakt disk 5 međukralješčani kolut

discard /dɪsˈkɑːd/ vt odbaciti

discern /dɪˈsɜːn/ vt razabrati ~**ing** adj oštrovidan, oštrouman ~**ible** adj vidljiv ~**ment** n moć rasuđivanje

discharge /dɪsˈtʃɑːdʒ/ vt 1 istovariti 2 izbacivati 3 izlijevati (se) 4 ispražniti 5 ispaliti 6 raspustiti, otpustiti, pustiti 7 ispustiti 8 isplatiti • /ˈdɪstʃɑːdʒ/ n 1 istovar 2 izlijevanje, pražnjenje, ispuštanje 3 otpust 4 izlazak (iz)vršenje 5 isplata 6 iscjedak

disciple /dɪˈsaɪpl/ n učenik, sljedbenik, apostol

discipline /ˈdɪsɪplɪn/ n 1 stega, disciplina 2 znanstvena disciplina 3 metoda 4 kazna • vt 1 disciplinirati, zavesti red 2 kazniti **disciplinary** /ˈdɪsɪplɪnərɪ/ adj disciplinski

disclaim /dɪsˈkleɪm/ vt zanijekati, odreći se ~**er** n demanti, ograđivanje

disclose /dɪsˈkləʊz/ vt (to) otkriti, ob-

javiti **disclosure** n otkriće

disco /ˈdɪskəʊ/ n coll disko (klub)

discolour /dɪsˈkʌlə(r)/ vt,vi promijeniti boju, potamniti **discoloration** n promjena boje, mrlja

discomfort /dɪsˈkʌmfət/ n 1 neugoda, nelagoda 2 neugodnost, poteškoća

discomposure /ˌdɪskəmˈpəʊʒə(r)/ n uznemirenost, nemir

disconcert /ˌdɪskənˈsɜːt/ vt uznemiriti, uzrujati

disconnect /ˌdɪskəˈnekt/ vt (from) isključiti, rastaviti, prekinuti ~**ed speech** nesuvisao govor

disconsolate /dɪsˈkɒnsələt/ adj neutješan

discontent /ˌdɪskənˈtent/ n nezadovoljstvo • vt 1 izazvati nezadovoljstvo 2 **be** ~**ed** (with) biti nezadovoljjan (kime, čime)

discontinue /ˌdɪskənˈtɪnjuː/ vt,vi prekinuti, prestati, završiti **discontinuous** adj isprekidan, nepovezan

discord /ˈdɪskɔːd/ n 1 nesloga, razdor, svađa 2 nesklad ~**ance** /dɪsˈkɔːdəns/ n razilaženje ~**ant** /dɪsˈkɔːdənt/ adj 1 koji se ne slaže 2 neskladan

discotheque /ˈdɪskətek/ n diskoteka, disko-klub

discount /ˈdɪskaʊnt/ n popust • /dɪsˈkaʊnt/ vt primiti s rezervom

discourage /dɪsˈkʌrɪdʒ/ vi 1 obeshrabriti 2 ~ **sb from doing sth** pokušati spriječiti, odvraćati ~**ment** n obeshrabrenost, nešto što obeshrabruje

discourse /ˈdɪskɔːs/ n govor, predavanje, propovijed, rasprava, diskurs • /dɪsˈkɔːs/ vi (upon) form raspravljati, pričati, propovijedati

discover /dɪsˈkʌvə(r)/ vt otkriti ~**y** n otkriće

discredit /dɪsˈkredɪt/ vt 1 ne držati vjerodostojnim 2 diskreditirati • n 1 diskreditacija, nepovjerenje 2 **a** ~ **to** sramota za 3 sumnja, nevjerica ~**able** adj sramotan

discreet /dɪsˈkriːt/ adj oprezan, razborit, uviđavan

discrepancy /dɪsˈkrepənsɪ/ n nesrazmjer, nesuglasnost

discrete /dɪsˈkriːt/ adj zaseban, diskretan

discretion /dɪ'skreʃn/ n oprez, razboritost **years/age of** ~ punoljetnost ~**ary** adj diskrecioni, neograničen

discriminate /dɪ'skrɪmɪneɪt/ vt,vi 1 razlikovati 2 (against) provoditi diskriminaciju **discriminating** adj 1 istančan 2 koji vrši diskriminaciju **discrimination** n 1 razlikovanje 2 dobar ukus, izbirljivost 3 diskriminacija

discursive /dɪ'skɜːsɪv/ adj 1 opširan 2 razvučen

discus /'dɪskəs/ n sport disk **the ~ throw** bacanje diska

discuss /dɪ'skʌs/ vt (sth) raspravljati o čemu, razmatrati (što) ~**ion** n rasprava, diskusija

disdain /dɪs'deɪn/ vt prezirati ~**ful** adj prezіran

disease /dɪ'ziːz/ n bolest ~**d** adj bolestan

disembark /ˌdɪsɪm'bɑːk/ vt,vi (from) iskrcati se ~**ation** n iskrcavanje

disembowel /ˌdɪsɪm'baʊəl/ vt rasporiti utrobu

disengage /ˌdɪsɪn'geɪdʒ/ vt,vi (from) 1 odvojiti (se) 2 povući se ~**d** adj slobodan ~**ment** n povlačenje

disentangle /ˌdɪsɪn'tæŋgl/ vt,vi (from) 1 razmrsiti, raspetljati (+ fig) 2 iskobeljati se, osloboditi se

disfigure /dɪs'fɪgə(r)/ vt unakaziti, nagrditi

disgorge /dɪs'gɔːdʒ/ vt izbljuvati, izbaciti

disgrace /dɪs'greɪs/ n sramota **bring ~ on oneself** osramotiti se **be in ~** biti u nemilosti ~**ful** adj sramotan • vt 1 osramotiti 2 **be ~d** pasti u nemilost

disgruntled /dɪs'grʌntld/ adj (at sth/with sb) ogorčen

disguise /dɪs'gaɪz/ vt 1 prerušiti (se), maskirati (se) 2 prikriti • n 1 prerušavanje, prikrivanje **in ~** prerušen 2 maska

disgust /dɪs'gʌst/ n (at sth/with sb) gađenje, gnušanje • vt zgaditi, izazvati gađenje ~**ing** adj gnjusan, odvratan ~**ed** adj zgađen

dish /dɪʃ/ n 1 tanjur 2 **the ~es** posuđe

do the ~es oprati posuđe ~**washer** stroj za pranje posuđa 3 jelo 4 satelitska antena; tanjur coll 5 sl dobra ženska, komad sl ~**y** adj sl zgodan • vt 1 ~ **sth up** servirati, pripraviti (+ fig) 2 ~ **sth out** razdijeliti

dishabille /ˌdɪsæ'biːl/ n negliže

dishearten /dɪs'hɑːtn/ vt obeshrabriti

dishevelled /dɪ'ʃevld/ adj raskuštran, neuredan

dishonest /dɪs'ɒnɪst/ adj nepošten ~**y** n nepoštenje

dishonour /dɪs'ɒnə(r)/ n sramota • vt 1 osramotiti, obeščastiti 2 ne iskupiti (mjenicu) ~**able** adj nečastan, sramotan

disillusion /ˌdɪsɪ'luːʒn/ vt osloboditi iluzija **be ~ed** razočarati se • (~**ment**) n gubitak iluzija, razočaranje

disinfect /ˌdɪsɪn'fekt/ vt dezinficirati ~**ant** adj za dezinfekciju • n sredstvo za dezinfekciju

disinfest /ˌdɪsɪn'fest/ vt dezinficirati i deratizirati, uništiti gamad

disinherit /ˌdɪsɪn'herɪt/ vt razbaštiniti ~**ance** n razbaštinjenje

disintegrate /dɪs'ɪntɪgreɪt/ vt,vi razbiti, dezintegrirati

disinterested /dɪs'ɪntrəstɪd/ adj 1 nepristran 2 nezainteresiran

disjointed /dɪs'dʒɔɪntɪd/ adj nepovezan

disk → **disc**

dislike /dɪs'laɪk/ vt ne voljeti **I ~ him** ne svida mi se, mrzak mi je • n antipatija, mržnja **have a ~ of/for sth/sb** mrziti koga/što **take a ~ to sb** zamrziti

dislocate /'dɪsləkeɪt/ vt 1 iščašiti 2 poremetiti **dislocation** n 1 iščašenje 2 poremetnja

dislodge /dɪs'lɒdʒ/ vt (from) pomaknuti, izbaciti, odbaciti

dismal /'dɪzməl/ adj tužan, žalostan, turoban

dismantle /dɪs'mæntl/ vt isprazniti, poskidati, rastaviti

dismay /dɪs'meɪ/ n očaj, užas • vt užasnuti

dismember /dɪs'membə(r)/ vt rastrgati; raskomadati (+ fig)

dismiss /dɪs'mɪs/ vt (from) **1** otpustiti **2** raspustiti **3** napustiti, ostaviti se **~al** n otpust, otpuštanje **~ed!** mil otpust!

dismount /dɪs'maʊnt/ vt,vi **1** (from) sjahati, sići (s bicikla) **2** skinuti s postolja **3** srušiti s konja

disobedience /ˌdɪsə'biːdɪəns/ n (to) neposluh (prema) **disobedient** adj neposlušan

disobey /ˌdɪsə'beɪ/ vt ne poslušati, ne poštovati (zakon)

disorder /dɪs'ɔːdə(r)/ n **1** nered, zbrka **2** neredi, pobuna **3** smetnja, poremećaj • vt izazvati pometnju, nered, zbrku **~ly** adj **1** neuredan **2** razuzdan, buntovan

disorientate /dɪs'ɔːrɪənteɪt/ vt dezorijentirati, zbuniti

disown /dɪs'əʊn/ vt odreći se

disparaging /dɪ'spærɪdʒɪŋ/ adj omalovažavajući, preziran

disparity /dɪ'spærətɪ/ n razlika, disparitet

dispassionate /dɪ'spæʃənət/ adj nepristran, hladnokrvan

dispatch /dɪ'spætʃ/ n **1** otpremanje, otprema **2** izvještaj, depeša **3** hitrina • vt **1** (to) otpremiti, odaslati, poslati **2** obaviti (na brzinu) **3** ubiti

dispel /dɪ'spel/ vt rastjerati (+ fig)

dispensation /ˌdɪspen'seɪʃn/ n **1** dijeljenje, izdavanje **2** upravljanje, djelovanje **3** dispenzacija **dispense** vi,vi (to) dijeliti **2** pripremati lijekove, izdavati lijekove **dispensing chemist** apoteka(r) **3** ~ **with a.** moći bez, ne trebati **b.** učiniti nepotrebnim **dispensary** /dɪ'spensərɪ/ n ambulanta, dispanzer **dispenser** /dɪ'spensə/ n **1** djelitelj **2** apotekar **3** držač, automat

disperse /dɪ'spɜːs/ vt,vi rastjerati, raspršiti (se), razbježati se **dispersal** n rastjerivanje, bijeg, raspršivanje **dispersion** n disperzija svjetla **the Dispersion** dijaspora

dispirit /dɪ'spɪrɪt/ vt obeshrabriti

displace /dɪs'pleɪs/ vt **1** raseliti **~d person** (DP) prognanik **2** doći na mjesto, zamijeniti **~ment** n **1** zamjena **2** deplasman

display /dɪ'spleɪ/ n **1** izlaganje, prikazivanje **2** otvoreno/pretjerano iskazivanje **3** ekran **on** ~ prikazan, izložen • vt izložiti, prikazati, pokazati

displease /dɪs'pliːz/ vt **1** izazvati nezadovoljstvo **2 be ~d** biti nezadovoljan **displeasing** adj (to) neugodan **displeasure** /dɪs'pleʒə(r)/ n nezadovoljstvo

disposal /dɪ'spəʊzl/ n (of) **1** uništavanje, rješavanje, odvoz **2** raspoređivanje **3** upravljanje, raspolaganje **at one's** ~ na raspolaganju komu

dispose vi,vt **1** ~ **of** riješiti se **2** raspo   rediti **3** ~ **sb to do sth** nagnati, navesti **~d** adj (to) voljan, raspoložen da/za **disposable** adj za jednokratnu upotrebu **disposition** /ˌdɪspə'zɪʃn/ n **1** raspored **2** ćud, narav **3** sklonost **4** raspoloženje **5** pravo raspolaganja

disproportion /ˌdɪsprə'pɔːʃn/ n nesrazmjer **~ate** adj (to) nesrazmjeran

disprove /ˌdɪs'pruːv/ vt opovrgnuti, pobiti

dispute /dɪ'spjuːt/ n **1** rasprava **beyond/past (all)** ~ nedvojben(o) **2** sukob, spor • vi,vi **1** (with/against sb) **1** raspravljati, prepirati se (s kim) **2** osporavati **3** boriti se za pobjedu

disqualify /dɪs'kwɒlɪfaɪ/ vt (for sth/from doing sth) **1** diskvalificirati **2** učiniti nesposobnim

disquiet /dɪs'kwaɪət/ n nemir, strepnja • vt uznemiriti **~ing** adj uznemirujući **~ude** n nemir

disregard /ˌdɪsrɪ'gaːd/ vt zanemariti, ne obazirati se • n nehaj, zanemarivanje, nedostatak poštovanja

disrepair /ˌdɪsrɪ'peə(r)/ n zapuštenost **be in/fall into** ~ propasti (zgrada i sl.)

disreputable /dɪs'repjʊtəbl/ adj **1** na zlu glasu **2** sumnjiva izgleda ~ **to** koji sramoti **disrepute** n zao glas, ozloglašenost

disrespect /ˌdɪsrɪ'spekt/ n nepristojnost, nedostatak poštovanja **~ful** adj nepristojan, bez poštovanja

disrupt /dɪs'rʌpt/ vt razbiti, slomiti, izazvati razdor **~ion** n prekid, slom, razdor **~ive** adj razoran

dissatisfaction /'dɪsˌsætɪs'fækʃn/ n

(with sb/sth/at doing sth) nezadovoljstvo **dissatisfy** /dɪˈsætɪsfaɪ/ *vt* 1 ne zadovoljiti 2 **be dissatisfied** biti nezadovoljan

dissect /dɪˈsekt/ *vt* 1 secirati 2 *fig* potanko raščlaniti **~ion** *n* seciranje, analiza

dissemble /dɪˈsembl/ *vt,vi form* hiniti **~r** *n* varalica

disseminate /dɪˈsemɪneɪt/ *vt* širiti **dissemination** *n* širenje

dissension /dɪˈsenʃn/ *n* svađa, žučljiva prepirka

dissent /dɪˈsent/ *n* neslaganje • *vi* 1 **~ from** ne slagati se 2 (from) odvojiti se od Anglikanske crkve **~er** *n* 1 koji se ne slaže, protivnik 2 **D~** nonkonformistički protestant

dissertation /ˌdɪsəˈteɪʃn/ *n* disertacija

disservice /dɪsˈsɜːvɪs/ *n* (to) medvjeđa usluga

dissident /ˈdɪsɪdənt/ *adj* koji se ne slaže, drugačiji • *n* disident

dissimilar /dɪˈsɪmɪlə(r)/ *adj* (from/to) različit **~ity** /ˌdɪsɪmɪˈlærəti/ *adj* različitost

dissipate /ˈdɪsɪpeɪt/ *vt,vi* 1 rastjerati 2 rasipati, spiskati **~d** *adj* razuzdan, raspusan **dissipation** *n* razuzdanost

dissociate /dɪˈsəʊʃɪeɪt/ *vt* (from) 1 razlučiti, razdvojiti 2 ograditi se

dissolute /ˈdɪsəljuːt/ *adj* razuzdan, nemoralan **dissolution** /ˌdɪsəˈluːʃn/ *n* (of) raspad, prekid; raspuštanje

dissolve /dɪˈzɒlv/ *vt,vi* 1 rastopiti (se) 2 (in) rastopiti (se) u 3 nestati, izgubiti se u 4 prekinuti **to ~ Parliament** raspustiti parlament

dissuade /dɪˈsweɪd/ *vt* (from sth/from doing sth) odgovoriti, odvratiti koga od čega **dissuasion** *n* odvraćanje

distance /ˈdɪstəns/ *n* 1 udaljenost **keep one's ~** držati se rezervirano **long-~** *adj* a. na duge pruge b. međugradski 2 vremenska distanca • *vt* (from) držati/biti na udaljenosti **distant** *adj* 1 (from) udaljen **distant view of X** pogled na X u daljini 2 dalek 3 suzdržan, na distanci

distaste /dɪsˈteɪst/ *n* (for) averzija prema **~ful** *adj* (to) neugodan, mrzak

distemper /dɪˈstempə(r)/ *n* štenećak

feline ~ mačičak

distend /dɪˈstend/ *vt,vi* nateći, proširiti se, naduti se

distil /dɪˈstɪl/ *vt, vi* 1 destilirati 2 peći 3 izlučivati **~lation** *n* 1 destilacija 2 destilat **~ler** *n* proizvođač žestokih alkoholnih pića **~lery** *n* tvornica žestokih alkoholnih pića

distinct /dɪˈstɪŋkt/ *adj* 1 jasan, razgovijetan, vidljiv, očit 2 (from) različit **~ion** *n* 1 razlikovanje, lučenje 2 razlika 3 čast, odlikovanje, naslov **~ive** *adj* 1 razlikovni 2 osobit, specifičan, svojstven

distinguish /dɪˈstɪŋgwɪʃ/ *vt,vi* 1 (one thing from another/between two things) razlikovati (jedno od drugog/dvije stvari) 2 razabrati 3 **~ from** razlikovati, činiti različitim 4 **~ oneself** iskazati se **~ed** *adj* slavan, poznat, istaknut

distort /dɪˈstɔːt/ *vt* izobličiti, iskriviti **~ion** *n* izobličenje

distract /dɪˈstrækt/ *vt* **~ from** odvratiti pozornost od, dekoncentrirati **~ed** *adj* (with/by) izbezumljen, izvan sebe **~ion** *n* 1 dekoncentracija, rastresenost 2 smetnja 3 zabava, zanimljivost 4 izbezumljenost **to ~ion** bezumno

distraught /dɪˈstrɔːt/ *adj* (with) izbezumljen, izvan sebe od

distress /dɪˈstres/ *n* 1 jad, bol, nevolja, neimaština 2. opasnost • *vt* rastužiti, uzrujati **~ful, ~ing** *adj* uznemirujući, bolan

distribute /dɪˈstrɪbjuːt/ *vt* 1 (to/among) razdijeliti, podijeliti, raspodijeliti 2 distribuirati 3 (into) klasificirati 4 **be ~d** biti rasprostranjen **distribution** /ˌdɪstrɪˈbjuːʃn/ *n* 1 distribucija 2 podjela, dioba 2 rasprostranjenost **distributor** /dɪˈstrɪbjuːtə(r)/ *n* distributer, prodavač

district /ˈdɪstrɪkt/ *n* 1 područje, kraj 2 okrug

distrust /dɪsˈtrʌst/ *n* (of) nepovjerenje • *vt* sumnjati, nemati povjerenja u **~ful** *adj* nepovjerljiv

disturb /dɪˈstɜːb/ *vt* poremetiti, uznemiriti (se), uzrujati (se) **~ance** *n* metež, izgred, nemir

disuse /dɪs'ju:s/ *n* nekorištenje **fall into ~** izaći iz upotrebe **~d** *adj* koji se više ne koristi

ditch /dɪtʃ/ *n* jarak • *vt,vi* 1 kopati/čistiti jarke 2 baciti u jarak **~ the plane** prisilno sletjeti u more 3 *fig sl* odbaciti (plan); nogirati (partnera) *sl*

dither /'dɪðə(r)/ *vi coll* oklijevati, omuhavati se • *n coll* nervoza

ditto /'dɪtəu/ *n* isto

dive /daɪv/ *n* 1 skok 2 *coll* prčvarnica *coll* • *vi irreg* (off/from/into) 1 skočiti u vodu 2 zaroniti, roniti 3 ponirati, obrušiti se 4 zarinuti **~r** *n* ronilac **diving** *n* 1 ronjenje 2 skokovi u vodu 3 *mod* **diving-board** daska za skakanje **diving-dress/suit** ronilačko odijelo

diverge /daɪ'vɜ:dʒ/ *vi* (from) razilaziti se, skrenuti, odvojiti se **~nce** *n* odstupanje **~nt** *adj* koji odstupa

diverse /daɪ'vɜ:s/ *adj* različit, raznolik, razan **diversify** *vt* 1 učiniti raznolikim 2 diverzificirati, proširiti poslovanje/asortiman **diversification, diversity** *n* raznolikost

diversion /daɪ'vɜ:ʃn/ *n* 1 skretanje 2 zabava 3 *mil, fig* diverzija, akcija za odvraćanje pozornosti **divert** *vt* (from) 1 skrenuti 2 zabaviti 3 odvratiti pozornost **diverting** *adj* zabavan

divide /dɪ'vaɪd/ *vt,vi* 1 ~ (sth up/out; sth between/among sb; into) razdijeliti, podijeliti 2 (sth from sth) odijeliti 3 (by/into) dijeliti sa • *n* razvođe, razmeđa **~nd** /'dɪvɪdend/ *n* 1 djeljenik 2 dividenda

division /dɪ'vɪʒn/ *n* 1 podjela 2 *math* dijeljenje 3 odjel 4 granica, crta koja dijeli 5 spor 6 *mil* divizija **divisible** /dɪ'vɪzəbl/ *adj* djeljiv **divisive** /dɪ'vaɪsɪv/ *adj* sporan

divine /dɪ'vaɪn/ *vt,vi* pogoditi, predvidjeti, dokučiti

divine (2) *adj* 1 božanski **D~ Service** služba Božja 2 *coll* sjajan, divan **divinity** /dɪ'vɪnəti/ *n* 1 božanstvo 2 teologija **the divinity school** bogoslovni fakultet

divorce /dɪ'vɔ:s/ *n* (from) 1 *leg* rastava braka 2 razdvajanje • *vt* 1 (from) rastaviti se od 2 (oneself from) *fig* napustiti, ograditi se **~e** /dɪ,vɔ:'si:/ *n* rastavljena osoba

divulge /daɪ'vʌldʒ/ *vt* (to) razglasiti, odati

dizzy /'dɪzɪ/ *adj* 1 kojem se vrti u glavi 2 *fig* omamljen, zbunjen 3 vrtoglav • *vt* izazvati vrtoglavicu **dizziness** *n* vrtoglavica

do /də/ (1) *v aux irreg* 1 tvori upitne i negativne oblike gl. vremena *present simple* i *preterite* 2 u potvrdnom obliku ovih vremena služi za naglašavanje 3 zamjenjuje već spomenuti glavni glagol ili glavni izraz u usporednim reč., *tag questions*, odgovorima

do (2) *vt,vi* 1 raditi *what are you ~ing? I'm ~ing my lessons* **~gooder** *n coll* derog Samaritanac *gl.* vremena **~it-yourself** (DIY) *n, mod* uradi sam ~ **one's best/utmost** dati sve od sebe, učiniti sve 2 baviti se čime *what does he ~ for a living? what are you ~ing?* 3 studirati *she's ~ing science* 4 *she ~es wonders in the kitchen* 5 napraviti *have you done your homework?* 6 obaviti, izvršiti ~ *your duty* **~ the dishes** oprati posuđe **~ the cooking** skuhati 7 izračunati **~ the sum** 8 urediti, aranžirati **~ one's hair** napraviti frizuru 9 prevaliti *we did 60 miles* 10 ispeći, skuhati *the steak is not done* odrezak je sirov *done to a turn* ispečeno/skuhano baš kako treba 11 *sl tab* (*seks*) obraditi; okrenuti 12 **~ sb well** ugostiti 13 **~ oneself well** udovoljiti sebi 14 **~ sb** (out of sth) prevariti 15 (for) poslužiti svrsi, odgovarati **make sth ~/make ~** (with sth) zadovoljiti se s 16 uspijevati/ne uspijevati *the flower is ~ing well/is not ~ing well* 17 osjećati se *how are you ~ing?* kako si? *how ~ you ~?* dragi mi je ¶ formula pri upoznavanju 18 ići *the car was ~ing 60 miles an hour* 19 igrati ulogu *he did Macbeth well* **have to ~ with** imati veze **~er** *n* čovjek od djela **~ing** *n pl coll* poslovi **~ away with** riješiti se, ukinuti **~ in** *sl* ubiti **~ sth up** a. renovirati b. preurediti c. zapakirati d. zakopčati e.

izmoriti ~ **with** tolerirati **can/could ~ with** trebati *I could ~ with a drink* dobro bi mi došlo jedno piće ~ **without sb/sth** biti bez čega

doc /dɒk/ *n coll* doktor

docile /ˈdəʊsaɪl/ *adj* poslušan, pokoran **docility** /dəʊˈsɪlətɪ/ *n* poslušnost

dock (1) /dɒk/ *n* 1 dok **dry/graving ~** suhi dok 2 *pl* luka **~-yard** *n* brodogradilište 3 *US* pristanište, vez **~er** *n* lučki radnik

dock (2) *n* optuženička klupa

doctor /ˈdɒktə(r)/ *n* 1 liječnik, doktor (medicine) 2 doktor (znanosti) • *vt* 1 *coll* liječiti 2 *coll* kastrirati 3 patvoriti 4 ubaciti drogu u 5 krivotvoriti **~al** *adj* doktorski **~ate** *n* doktorat

doctrine /ˈdɒktrɪn/ *n* doktrina

document /ˈdɒkjʊmənt/ *n* dokument, spis, isprava • *vt* potkrijepiti (dokumentima), dokumentirati **~ation** /ˌdɒkjʊmenˈteɪʃn/ *n* dokumentacija **~ary** /ˌdɒkjʊˈmentrɪ/ *adj* dokumentaran **~ary (film)** *n* dokumentarni film, dokumentarac

dodge /dɒdʒ/ *n* 1 izmicanje 2 *coll* prijevara 3 *coll* (lukav) plan • *vt,vi* 1 izmaknuti se 2 izvući se 3 izbjegavati **~r** *n* zabušant, varalica **fare ~r** švercer (u javnom prometu) **draft ~r** osoba koja izbjegava novačenje **dodgy** *adj* 1 prepreden 2 riskantan; zeznut *coll*

doe /dəʊ/ *n* 1 košuta 2 zečica, ženka kunića **~skin** jelenska koža

does *v irreg* → do

dog /dɒg/ *n* pas (+ *fig* o osobi, značenje ovisno o kontekstu) **~ eat ~** bezobzirne metode **dressed like a ~'s dinner** obučen po posljednjoj modi **go to the ~s** otići k vragu **let sleeping ~s lie** *prov* pusti lava dok spava **top ~** glavni šef **the ~s** utrke pasa **~-biscuits** pseći keksi **~-collar** *coll* svećenikova ogrlica **~-days** pasje vrućine **~-eared** s magarećim ušima **~-fish** manji morski pas **~'s body** koji radi kao pas **~ tooth** riblja kost kao pas **~-like** *adj* poput psa **~gy**, **~gie** *n* psić • *vt* biti za petama, pratiti (+ *fig*)

dogged /ˈdɒgɪd/ *adj* tvrdoglav

dogma /ˈdɒgmə/ *n* dogma, dogme **dogmatic** *adj* dogmatski (+ *fig*)

doldrums /ˈdɒldrəmz/ *n pl* loše raspoloženje **in the ~** u depresiji

dole /dəʊl/ *vt* **~ out** dijeliti • *n* 1 milostinja 2 **the ~** naknada za nezaposlene **be/go on the ~** biti na burzi, primati naknadu za nezaposlene

doleful /ˈdəʊlfl/ *adj* tužan, turoban

doll /dɒl/ *n* lutka (+ *fig*) • *vt,vi* **~ up** urediti (se) **~y** *n* 1 lutka, lutkica (+ *fig*) 2 transportna kolica

dollar /ˈdɒlə(r)/ *n* dolar **get top ~** biti vrhunski plaćen

dolphin /ˈdɒlfɪn/ *n* dupin

domain /dəʊˈmeɪn/ *n* domena (+ *fig*)

dome /dəʊm/ *n* kupola **~d** *adj* u obliku kupole, okrugao, izbočen

domestic /dəˈmestɪk/ *adj* 1 domaći, kućni 2 unutarnji, domaći, tuzemni 3 domaći, pitom 4 kućna pomoćnica **~ate** *vt* pripitomiti

dominant /ˈdɒmɪnənt/ *adj* 1 dominantan, glavni, najvažniji 2 koji nadvisuje što/dominira **dominance** *n* prevlast **dominate** /ˈdɒmɪneɪt/ *vt,vi* (over) 1 dominirati (kime, čime), nadvladati 2 nadvisivati **domination** *n* dominacija

domineer /ˌdɒmɪˈnɪə(r)/ *vi* (over) tiranizirati **~ing** *adj* tiranski

dominion /dəˈmɪnɪən/ *n* 1 (over) vlast (nad) 2 teritorij pod vlašću 3 dominion

domino /ˈdɒmɪnəʊ/ *n* 1 pločica za domino 2 *pl* (+ *sing*) domino 3 krinka, domino

don (1) /dɒn/ *n GB* sveučilišni nastavnik **~nish** *adj* profesorski

don (2) *vt arch* odjenuti

donate /dəʊˈneɪt/ *vt* (to) pokloniti, dati u dobrotvorne svrhe **donation** *n* prilog

done *v irreg* → do

donkey /ˈdɒŋkɪ/ *n* magarac

donor /ˈdəʊnə(r)/ *n* 1 donator 2 davalac **blood ~** dobrovoljni davalac krvi

doodle /ˈduːdl/ *vi coll* črčkati

doom /duːm/ *vt* 1 propast, smrt, zla sudbina 2 (**Doomsday**) smak svijeta, sudnji dan • vt **1** ~ **to** osuditi (na) **2** propasti

door /dɔ:(r)/ n vrata ~-**to**~ **salesman** pokućarac **out of** ~**s** na svježem zraku, na otvorenom ~**bell** kućno zvono ~**knob/handle** kvaka ~**man** vratar ~ **mat** otirač (+ fig) ~-**post** dovratak ~**step** prag ~**way** vrata

dope /dǝʊp/ n **1** lak **2** coll droga; **dop** sl **3** coll budala • vt drogirati, dopingirati ~**y** adj sl blesav

dorm /dɔ:m/ coll → **dormitory**

dormant /'dɔ:mǝnt/ adj uspavan, mrtav, pritajen

dormitory /'dɔ:mɪtrɪ/ n **1** spavaonica **2** studentski dom

dormouse /'dɔ:maʊs/ n (pl **dormice** /'dɔ:maɪs/) puh

dose /dǝʊs/ n **1** doza (+ fig) **2** sl spolna bolest • vt dati dozu lijeka/lijek **dosage** n doziranje

dossier /'dɒsɪeɪ/ n dosje

dot /dɒt/ n točkica on the ~ coll točno, na dlaku • vt označiti točkama, staviti točke, posuti (točkama i sl.) ~**ted** adj točkast ~**ted line** coll mjesto potpisa

dotage /'dǝʊtɪdʒ/ n senilnost **dotard** n senilni starac

dote /dǝʊt/ vi ~ **on/upon** obožavati, ludo voljeti **doting** adj lud za

double /'dʌbl/ adj dvostruk • adv dvostruko • n **1** dvojnik **2** dubler **3** igra parova on the ~ iz ovih stopa • vt,vi **1** podvostručiti **2** (up/over/-across) presavinuti (se), savinuti (se) **3** (back) naglo skrenuti **4** (as) igrati dvije uloge, istovremeno raditi kao ~-**barrelled** adj a. dvocijevni b. dvosmislen c. dvostruk ~-**bass** n kontrabas ~-**check** vt dva puta provjeriti ~-**cross** vt prevariti • n prijevara ~-**decker** dvokatni autobus ~-**dutch** coll a. nerazumljivi govor b. preskakivanje preko užeta ~-**dyed** adj premazan svim mastima ~-**edged** adj dvosjekli ~-**entry** dvostruko knjigovodstvo ~-**faced** adj dvoličan ~-**park** parkirati uz već parkirani auto ~-**quick** vrlo brzo ~ **room** dvokrevetna soba ~-**talk** laganje **doubly** adv (+ adj) dvostruko

doubt /daʊt/ n dvojba, sumnja **when in** ~ kad ne znaš što bi • vt (**if/whether**) sumnjati (da li) ~-**ful** adj **1** (about/if) nesiguran, u sumnji, u dvojbi **2** sumnjiv ~**less** adv najvjerojatnije

douche /du:ʃ/ n **1** ispiranje **2** sprava za ispiranje

dough /dǝʊ/ n **1** tijesto **2** US sl novac; lova coll ~**nut** n uštipak

douse, dowse /daʊs/ vt **1** baciti u vodu, politi vodom **2** coll ugasiti (svjetlo)

dove /dʌv/ n **1** golubica ~-**cote** n golubarnik **2** fig coll miroljubiva osoba; "golub" coll

dove v irreg US → **dive**

dovetail /'dʌvteɪl/ n užljebljenje • vt,vi **1** užlijebiti (se) **2** fig (with) uklapati se u, poklapati se s

dowdy /'daʊdɪ/ adj otrcan

down (1) /daʊn/ n paperje ~**y** adj paperjast

down (2) n brežuljak

down (3) adv **1** dolje **2** (sve) do **3** from .... ~ **to** od .... (uključivo) do **4** coll u depresiji **money/cash** ~ platiti odmah ~ **payment** učešće **be** ~ **and out** coll a. biti nesposoban za nastavak boks-meča b. fig propasti ~-**and-out** n propalica ~ **on one's luck** coll loše sreće ~-**to-earth** adj praktičan, realan **D**~ **Under** coll Australija • int ~ **with** .... Dolje .... • prep **1** niz **2** tijekom • vt coll srušiti ~ **a pint/glass** iskapiti čašu • n **ups and** ~**s** promjenjiva sreća, uspjesi i neuspjesi

downbeat /'daʊnbɪ:t/ n realističan, neuljepšan

downcast /'daʊnkɑ:st/ adj **1** utučen **2** spušten

downfall /'daʊnfɔ:l/ n **1** pljusak **2** fig propast, pad

downhearted /,daʊn'hɑ:tɪd/ adj utučen

downhill /,daʊn'hɪl/ adv nizbrdo

Downing Street /'daʊnɪŋ stri:t/ n sjedište britanskog premijera, britanska vlada

downpour /'daʊnpɔ:(r)/ n pljusak

downright /'daʊnraɪt/ adj **1** otvoren,

pošten 2 čist, potpun • *adv* potpuno

downstairs /daʊn'steəz/ *adv* 1 niza stube 2 kat niže

downtown /'daʊntaʊn/ *n* 1 gradsko središte 2 *mod* u centru grada

downward /'daʊnwəd/ *adj* koji se spušta, pada, opada • ~(s) *adv* (prema) dolje

dowry /'daʊərɪ/ *n* miraz

dowse /daʊs/ → **douse**

doze /dəʊz/ *vi* drijemati ~ **off** zadrijemati • *n* drijemež

dozen /'dʌzn/ *n* 1 tuce *a* ~ **eggs, three** ~ **eggs** 2 desetak ~**s of** deseci, na desetke, mnoštvo

drab /dræb/ *adj* 1 tamnosmeđ 2 *fig* nezanimljiv, jednoličan

draft /drɑːft/ *n* 1 koncept 2 *mod* grub, početan 3 nacrt, skica, mjenica, nalog za isplatu 4 *US* novačenje 4 *US* → **draught** • *vt* 1 izraditi koncept 2 *US* novačiti ~**ee** /ˌdrɑː'ftiː/ *n* novak

draftsman /'drɑːftsmən/ *n* tehnički crtač

drafty *US* → **draughty**

drag /dræg/ *n* 1 (~**net**) koča 2 drljača 3 *coll* davež, gnjavaža, teret 4 *sl* **in** ~ u ženskoj odjeći ~ **queen** *sl* transvestit 5 *sl* dim (cigarete) • *vt,vi* vući (se), izvlačiti, povlačiti ~ **one's feet** *fig* odugovlačiti, zatezati 2 ~ **out** razvući (se) 3 pretraživati dno (rijeke, mora i sl.)

dragon /'drægən/ *n* zmaj (+ *fig*) ~**fly** vilin konjic

drain /dreɪn/ *n* 1 (~**pipe**) odvodna cijev **go down the** ~ otići k vragu 2 *pl* kanalizacija 3 *fig* teret, nešto što iscrpljuje **brain**-~ odljiv stručnjaka • *vt,vi* 1 ~ **away/off** otjecati, isušiti 2 (away/off); (of) *fig* nestajati, istjecati 3 (is)cijediti, ocijediti 4 ispiti (do dna) ~**age** *n* 1 isušivanje, odvođenje voda 2 kanalizacija 3 otpadne vode ~**age-basin** sliv rijeke

drake /dreɪk/ *n* patak

drama /'drɑːmə/ *n* drama (+ *fig*) ~**tic** /drə'mætɪk/ *adj* 1 dramski 2 dramatičan ~**tics** *n* (+ *sing*) 1 dramska umjetnost 2 dramatičan nastup, dramatiziranje ~**tist** *n* dramatičar ~**tize** *vt* 1 adaptirati za pozornicu 2 praviti

dramu od

drank *v irreg* → **drink**

drape /dreɪp/ *vt* 1 (round/over) namjestiti nabore 2 (with) prekriti, ukrasiti 3 (round/over) nemarno prebaciti • *n* *US* draperija, zavjesa ~**r** *n* *GB* suknar, trgovac tekstilom ~**ry** *n* 1 trgovina tekstilom 2 ukrasne tkanine 3 draperija

drastic /'dræstɪk/ *adj* drastičan

draught /drɑːft/ *n* 1 propuh 2 izvlačenje mreže 3 gaz 4 gutljaj 5 ~**s** *sing* dama (igra) ~ **beer/beer on** ~ pivo na čaše, točeno pivo • *vt* → **draft** ~**-horse** tegleći konj ~**sman** *n* pločica (u igri dame) ~**y** *adj* izložen propuhu, pun propuha

draw /drɔː/ *n* 1 ždrijeb, izvlačenje 2 neodlučan rezultat 3 mamac ~**er** /drɔː(r)/ *n* 1 ladica 2 *pl* gaće 3 /'drɔːə(r)/ crtač ~**ing** *n* 1 crtanje 2 crtež, nacrt ~**ing-board** crtaća daska **on the** ~**ing-board** u početnoj fazi ~**ing-pin** čavlić • *vt,vi irreg* 1 povući, privući, izvući, navući, svući, vući 2 podizati 3 potegnuti 4 izmamiti 5 bližiti se 6 crtati, ocrtati (+ *fig*) 7 ispisati 8 gaziti 9 odigrati neodlučno 10 točiti (pivo) ~ **back** *fig* skanjivati se ~ **in a.** bližiti se kraju **b.** postajati kraći ~ **on** bližiti se ~ **on sth/sb** poslužiti se ~ **sb on** privlačiti ~ **out** postajati dužim ~ **sth out** izdužiti, oduljiti ~ **sb out** namamiti ~ (sth/sb) **up a.** stati **b.** sastaviti **c.** rasporediti

drawback /'drɔːbæk/ *n* 1 nedostatak 2 povrat carine

drawbridge /'drɔːbrɪdʒ/ *n* most na spuštanje

drawing-room /'drɔːɪŋ rʊm/ *n* primaća soba, salon

drawl /drɔːl/ *vi,vt* razvlačiti u govoru • *n* razvlačenje

drawn *v irreg* → **draw**

dread /dred/ *n* užas, strah • *vt,vi* užasavati se ~**ed** *adj* strašan ~**ful** *adj* grozan

dream /driːm/ *n* san ~**like** *adj* kao u snu • *vt,vi irreg* (about/of) sanjati (o čemu/što) **ni u snu** ~ **away** protratiti ~ **up** *coll* smisliti ~**er** *n* sanjar ~**y** *adj*

1 sanjarski 2 nestvaran, kao u snu 3 umirujući, uspavljujajući

dreamt *v irreg* → **dream**

dreary /'drɪərɪ/ *adj* sumoran, turoban

dredge /dredʒ/ *vt* (up) izvući na površinu, iskopati (+ *fig*) • *n* jaružalo

dregs /dregz/ *n pl* 1 talog **drink/drain to the ~** ispiti do dna 2 *fig* dno

drench /drentʃ/ *vt* promočiti **~ in** natopiti čime

dress /dres/ *n* 1 haljina 2 odjeća **~ circle** mezanin **~ coat** frak **~ maker** krojačica **~ rehearsal** generalna proba **evening ~** svečana odjeća **full ~** svečano odijelo/odora • *vt,vi* 1 odjenuti get **~ed** odjenuti se **~ up a.** preodjenuti se **b.** napadno se odjenuti **~ down** odjenuti se neupadljivo 2 svečano se odjenuti 3 odijevati se 4 učiniti, uštaviti 5 začiniti 6 pripremiti 7 urediti, počešljati, iščetkati 8 obraditi (ranu) 9 dekorirati 10 svrstati **~er** *n* 1 kostimer 2 kuhinjski ormar 3 *US* toaletni stolić **~ing** *n* 1 odijevanje, uredivanje, obrađivanje itd. **~ing-case** neseser **~ing-gown** kućna haljina **~ing-room** garderoba **~ing-table** toaletni stolić 2 zavoj, oblog 3 začini 4 apretura **~y** *adj coll* koji se lijepo odijeva

drew *v irreg* → **draw**

dribble /'drɪbl/ *vt,vi* 1 curiti, kapati 2 sliniti 3 driblati • *n* kap

drift /drɪft/ *n* 1 struja 2 zanošenje (zbog struje) **~net** vrša 3 nanos, zapuh, naplavina 4 *fig* tok, smjer **get the ~** shvaćati 5 *fig* pasivnost • *vi,vt* 1 biti nošen, plutati 2 besciljno lutati 3 nanositi **~er** *n* 1 čistač mina 2 lutalica

drill (1) /drɪl/ *n* bušilica • *vt,vi* bušiti

drill (2) *n* vježba • *vt,vi* vježbati, drilati

drink /drɪŋk/ *n* 1 piće 2 alkoholno piće **be the worse for ~** biti pijan **take to ~** propiti se • *vt,vi irreg* 1 piti 2 (in/up) upiti (+ *fig*) 3 (to) nazdraviti **~ing-water** voda za piće

drip /drɪp/ *vi,vt* kapati • *n* 1 kapanje 2 *sl* dosadnjaković

dripping /'drɪpɪŋ/ *n* mast od pečenja

drive /draɪv/ *n* 1 vožnja 2 (**~way** *US*) prilaz 3 polet 4 kampanja 5 turnir 6 pogon **front/rear/four-wheel ~** prednji/stražnji pogon/pogon na sva četiri kotača 7 nagon • *vt,vi irreg* 1 tjerati 2 voziti (se) **driving** (driver's *US*) **licence** vozačka dozvola **driving school** auto-škola **~in** *n, mod* kino u kojem se film gleda iz auta 3 povesti 4 *pass* biti na pogon **driving-wheel** pogonski kotač 5 goniti, tjerati, nagoniti 6 juriti, šibati 7 **~ sth in/sth into sth** zabiti 8 dovesti do **~ sth home** *fig* utuviti u glavu **~ sb crazy/mad** izluditi **~ a hard bargain** biti nepopustljiv u pregovorima 9 **~ at** *fig* ciljati na što 10 odlagati **~r** *n* 1 vozač 2 gonič stoke 3 zamašnjak

drivel /'drɪvl/ *vi* gluparati, blebetati • *n* blebetanje, lupetanje

driven *v irreg* → **drive**

drizzle /'drɪzl/ *vi* sipiti • *n* kišica

drone /drəʊn/ *n* 1 trut (+ *fig*) 2 zujanje 3 monotoni govor 4 dosadnjaković • *vi,vt* 1 zujati 2 monotono govoriti, mrmljati

drool /druːl/ *vi* (over) sliniti (+ *fig*)

droop /druːp/ *vi,vt* 1 ovjesiti se; klonuti (+ *fig*) 2 poniknuti • *n* ovješenost, klonulost **~ing** *adj* klonuo, ovješen, svinut prema dolje

drop /drɒp/ *n* 1 kap(ljica) (+ *fig*) 2 *pl* kapi **nose ~s** kapi za nos 3 kapljica (alkohola) 4 (nagli) pad **at the ~ of a hat** bez oklijevanja 5 ono što se spušta, ubacuje i sl. • *vt,vi* 1 kapati 2 ispustiti 3 ne izgovarati; gutati *fig* 4 oslabiti, spustiti (glas) 5 pasti, klonuti 6 spustiti **~ anchor** spustiti sidro **~ a hint** natuknuti **~ a few lines/a postcard** poslati par redaka/razglednicu 7 iskrcati 8 prestati 9 ostaviti se **let's ~ the subject** promijenimo temu **~pings** *n pl* izmet **~ back** zaostati **~ behind** zaostati **~ in on/~ by/in/over/round** navratiti **~ off a.** otpasti, smanjiti se **b.** zaspati **~ sth/sb off** (at sth) dovesti, iskrcati **~ out a.** ispasti iz natjecanja/momčadi **b.** napustiti školovanje **c.** povući se iz društva **~out** *n* propali student

dross /drɒs/ *n* drozga, šljaka 2 *fig* otpad, šljam

drought /draʊt/ *n* suša

drove *v irreg* → **drive**

drove /drəʊv/ *n* stado (+ *fig*) ~**r** *n* gonič stoke

drown /draʊn/ *vt,vi* 1 udaviti (se), utopiti (se) 2 (out) ugušiti, nadjačati

drowse /draʊs/ *vi,vt* (away) drijemati • *n* drijemež, polusan **drowsy** *adj* sanjiv, u polusnu, uspavljujući

drudgery /'drʌdʒeri/ *n* težak i dosadan posao

drug /drʌg/ *n* 1 lijek ~**store** *n US* dragstor 2 (opojna) droga • *vt* 1 ubaciti uspavljujuće sredstvo/drogu 2 drogirati ~**gist** *n* 1 *GB* ljekarnik, apotekar 2 drogerist

drum /drʌm/ *n* 1 bubanj, zvuk bubnja ~**fire** rafalna paljba iz teškog oružja ~**stick a.** bubnjarska palica **b.** batak 2 bačva • *vt,vi* svirati bubnjeve, bubnjati ~ **up** smoći, iskopati ~ **sth into sb/into sb's head** utuviti komu što u glavu ~**mer** *n* 1 bubnjar 2 (*US*) trgovački putnik

drunk *v irreg* → **drink**

drunk /drʌŋk/ *adj* pijan **get** ~ napiti se ~ **with sth** *fig* opijen • *n* pijanac ~**ard** *n* pijanac ~**en** *adj* pijan

dry /drai/ *adj* 1 suh 2 sušan 3 presušen, presušio 4 suh ~ **martini** 5 žedan, koji izaziva žeđ 6 suhoparan 7 *fig* hladan, opor 8 neuljepšan ~**cleaning** kemijsko čišćenje ~**clean** *vt* dati na kemijsko čišćenje ~ **nurse** dadilja ~ **rot** *n* **a.** suha trulež **b.** *fig* trulež ~ **run** *n coll* proba **drily** *adv* ~**ness** *n* • *vt,vi* 1 (out) (o)sušiti ~ **up** presušiti, isušiti (+ *fig*) 2 sušiti **dried fruit** suho voće ~**er, drier** *n* sušilo

dual /'dju:əl/ *adj* dvojni, dvostruki ~ **carriageway** cesta s dvije vozne trake

dub /dʌb/ *vt* 1 dodijeliti vitešku čast 2 nadjenuti nadimak 3 sinkronizirati

dubious /'dju:biəs/ *adj* 1 (of/about) sumnjičav, koji sumnja, nesiguran 2 sumnjiv

duchess /'dʌtʃis/ *n* vojvotkinja, kneginja **duchy** *n* vojvodstvo

duck (1) /dʌk/ *n* 1 patka **like water off a ~'s back** bez ikakvih posljedica 2 (~**y**) *coll* zlato, milo ~**ling** *n* pače **ugly ~ling** ružno pače

duck (2) *vt,vi* 1 sagnuti (se), izmaknuti (se) 2 zaroniti • *n* 1 izmicanje 2 zaranjanje

duct /dʌkt/ *n* vod, kanal **air** ~ odvod za ventilaciju

dud /dʌd/ *n* neeksplodirana bomba, nevažeća novčanica i sl. • *adj* bezvrijedan, lažan

dude /dju:d/ *n* 1 *US* frajer *coll* 2 šminker ~ **ranch** *n* ranč za turiste

due /dju:/ *adj* 1 (to) koji dospijeva na naplatu 2 odgovarajući, primjeren, pravovremen 3 koji treba doći, koji se očekuje, koji je predviđen ~ **to** *conj* zbog, uslijed • *adv* ravno prema • *n* 1 ono što komu pripada, što se mora dati/priznati 2 *pl* pristojbe, članarina

duel /'dju:əl/ *n* dvoboj • *vi* izaći na dvoboj

duffle /'dʌfl/ *adj* ~ **bag** mornarska/vojnička vreća

dug *v irreg* → **dig**

dug-out /'dʌg aʊt/ *n mil* zemunica, gnijezdo

duke /dju:k/ *n* vojvoda, knez ~**dom** *n* vojvodstvo

dull /dʌl/ *adj* 1 mutan, taman, tmuran 2 tup (+ *fig*) 3 dosadan 4 mrtav ~**ard** *n* tupan

duly /'dju:li/ *adv* valjano, pravovremeno

dumb /dʌm/ *adj* 1 nijem; mutav *derog* **deaf and** ~ gluhonijem **go** ~ zanijemiti **strike** ~ zapanjiti 2 glup ~ **show** pantomima ~**bell** *n* bučica, uteg

dumbfound /dʌm'faʊnd/ *vt* zapanjiti

dumbwaiter /ˌdʌm'weitə(r)/ *n* 1 kolica za posluživanje 2 *US* **food-lift**

dummy /'dʌmi/ *n* 1 lutka 2 duda varalica 3 statist *fig* 4 *mod* lažni ~ **run** proba

dump /dʌmp/ *n* 1 smetlište 2 *mil* skladište 3 *sl derog* rupa • *vt* 1 izbaciti, istovariti 2 *coll* odbaciti 3 izvoziti po nižim cijenama ~**ing** *n* damping, izvoz po niskim cijenama ~**ing ground** smetlište

dumpling /'dʌmpliŋ/ *n* valjušak

dumps /dʌmps/ *n pl* (down) **in the** ~ *coll* u depresiji

dumpy /'dʌmpɪ/ *adj* bucmast

dunce /dʌns/ *n* glupi učenik, glupan ~'s **cap** magareća klupa

dune /dju:n/ *n* dina

dung /dʌŋ/ *n* balega, gnoj ~**hill** *n* gnojište

dungarees /ˌdʌŋgə'ri:z/ *n pl* hlače s naramenicama

dungeon /'dʌndʒən/ *n* tamnica

dupe /dju:p/ *vt* nasamariti • *n* žrtva prijevare, glupan

duplex /'dju:pleks/ *n* dvoetažni stan

duplicate /'dju:plɪkeɪt/ *vt* **1** izraditi u duplikatu, umnožiti **2** podvostručiti • *n* **1** duplikat **in** ~ u dva primjerka **2** *mod* u duplikatu ~ **keys** rezervni ključevi **duplication** *n* umnažanje

duplicity /dju:'plɪsətɪ/ *n* himba

durable /'djʊərəbl/ *adj* trajan **durability** *n* trajnost

duration /dju'reɪʃn/ *n* trajanje

duress /djʊ'res/ *n* prisila, pritisak

during /'djʊərɪŋ/ *prep* za vrijeme, tijekom

dusk /dʌsk/ *n* sumrak ~**y** *adj* **1** taman, nejasan **2** crnomanjast

dust /dʌst/ *n* **1** prašina **bite the** ~ *sl* zaglaviti ~**bowl** isušeni predio ~**jacket/wrapper** ovitak knjige ~**pan** lopatica za smeće ~**sheet** prekrivač za namještaj **2** *GB* ~**bin** kanta za smeće ~**cart** smetlarska kola ~**man** smetlar **3** *arch, poet* prah (pokojnika) • *vt* **1** (down/off) obrisati prašinu ~**up** svada, tučnjava **2** naprašiti, posipati ~**er** *n* krpa za prašinu ~**y** *adj* prašnjav

Dutch /dʌtʃ/ *adj* **1** nizozemski **2** *coll* ~ **treat** izlazak kod kojeg svatko plaća za sebe **go** ~ (with sb) podijeliti troškove

dutiful /'dju:tɪfl/ *adj* (to) poslušan

duty /'dju:tɪ/ *n* **1** (to) dužnost, obaveza (prema) **on/off** ~ službujući/slobodan **do** ~ **for** poslužiti kao ~ **call** posjet iz kurtoazije **2** (on) carina, porez ~**free** *adj* na koji se ne plaća carina, bescarinski ○ *adv* bez carine

duvet /'dju:veɪ/ *n* **1** perina, poplun **2** *mod* od perja ~ **jacket** skijaška jakna

dwarf /dwɔ:f/ *n* **1** patuljak **2** *mod* patuljast • *vt* **1** spriječiti u rastu **2** učiniti da se doima malenim

dwell /dwel/ *vi irreg* **1** ~ **in/at** stanovati **2** ~ **on/upon** razmatrati, razglabati ~**er** *n* stanovnik **town**~**er** *n* građanin ~**ing** *n* prebivalište, stan

dwelt *v irreg* → **dwell**

dwindle /'dwɪndl/ *vi* postupno se smanjivati/izumirati/nestajati

dye /daɪ/ *vt,vi* **1** bojati ~**d-in-the-wool** *adj fig* zadrt **2** primati boju **3** bojiti, obojiti • *n* boja (za tkaninu) **of the deepest** ~ najgore vrste ~**stuff** boja

dyke → **dike**

dynamic /daɪ'næmɪk/ *adj* dinamičan (+ *fig*) • *n* **1** pokretačka snaga **2** ~**s** (+ *sing*) dinamika **dynamism** *n* polet, energija

dynamite /'daɪnəmaɪt/ *n* dinamit • *vt* dići u zrak dinamitom

dynasty /'dɪnəstɪ/ *n* dinastija

E

E, e /iː/ n peto slovo engl. abecede; c

each /iːtʃ/ adj, adv, pron svaki, svaki
pojedini ~ **other** jedan drugoga,
među sobom, uzajamno **they kissed**
~ **other** poljubili su se

eager /ˈiːɡə(r)/ adj željan, nestrpljiv,
revan

eagle /ˈiːɡl/ n orao

ear /iə(r)/ n 1 uho 2 sluh 3 klas (žita)
be all ~**s** sav se pretvoriti u uho
~**drum** bubnjić ~**mark** vt (for)
odrediti/odvojiti sredstva ~**phones**
slušalice ~**ring** naušnica ~**shot** do-
mašaj/doseg zvuka ~**splitting** za-
glušujući ~**wig** uholaža

earl /ɜːl/ n grof (u Britaniji)

early /ˈɜːlɪ/ adj, adv 1 rani; rano 2 na
početku, početkom 3 skori **earlier
on** ranije, prije **as ~ as May** već u
svibnju **be ~** uraniti ~ **bird/riser** ranoranilac **the ~ bird catches the
worm** prov tko rano rani dvije sreće
grabi

earn /ɜːn/ vt,vi 1 zaraditi 2 zaslužiti,
steći 3 donijeti ~**ings** n pl 1 zarada,
dohodak 2 prihodi

earnest /ˈɜːnɪst/ adj ozbiljan, odlučan;
marljiv; iskren • n **in** ~ ozbiljno

earth /ɜːθ/ n 1 (**the/** E~) Zemlja 2 svijet 3 zemlja, tlo 4 GB uzemljenje
why/how on ~ zašto/kako zaboga
~**enware** n zemljano/glineno posuđe
~**ly** adj ovozemaljski ~**quake** potres
~**worm** glista ~**y** adj 1 zemljan 2 zemaljski 3 grub • vt GB uzemljiti

ease /iːz/ n 1 lakoća 2 udobnost, opu-
štenost, lagodnost **at one's** ~ ugodno, opušteno, udobno **ill at** ~
nelagodno, neugodno (**stand**) **at** ~
mil na mjestu odmor • vt,vi 1 (off)
olakšati, ublažiti 2 umiriti (savjest) 3
(off/up) popustiti, smanjiti se 4 polako ući/izaći i sl. **easy** adj 1 lak; la-

gan 2 lagodan, udoban 3 neusiljen
easygoing adj 1 blag, tolerantan 2
bezbrižan, nemaran ○ adv **take
it/things easy** opusti se **easy does it**
samo polako, bez žurbe **go easy on
sb** blago/pažljivo postupati s kime
easy come easy go kako došlo, tako
prošlo **easily** adv 1 lako, bez muke 2
nesumnjivo 3 lako moguće

easel /ˈiːzl/ n slikarski stalak

east /iːst/ n istok **the Far** E~ Daleki
istok **the Middle** E~ Srednji istok
the Near E~ Bliski istok • adj istočni • adv istočno, na istok ~**bound**
adv prema istoku ~**erly** adj istočni, s
istoka ○ adv istočno, na istok ○ n istočni vjetar, istočnjak ~**ern** adj istočni, istočnjački ~**ward** adj u smjeru istoka ~**ward(s)** adv prema istoku

Easter /ˈiːstə(r)/ n Uskrs

eat /iːt/ vt,vi irreg 1 jesti 2
(away/into/through) nagrizati 3 fig
gristi, mučiti ~ **one's heart out**
požderati se ~ **one's words** priznati
krivnju

eavesdrop /ˈiːvzdrɒp/ vi (on sb) prisluškivati

ebb /eb/ n 1 (~**tide**) oseka 2 fig
(o)padanje, smanjivanje **the ~ and
flow** oseka i plima **be at a low** ~
stagnirati • vi 1 otjecati 2 (away) fig
smanjiti se, (o)padati

ebony /ˈebənɪ/ n 1 ebanovina 2 mod
crn

eccentric /ɪkˈsentrɪk/ adj 1 neobičan,
čudan 2 ekscentričan • n čudak, ekscentrik

ecclesiastical /ɪˌkliːzɪˈæstɪkl/ adj
crkveni

echo /ˈekəʊ/ n jeka, odjek • vi,vt 1
odjekivati, odzvanjati; odbijati/vra-
ćati jeku 2 mehanički ponavljati

eclipse /ɪˈklɪps/ n pomrčina • vt 1

pomračiti 2 *fig* zasjeniti, nadmašiti

ecology /i:ˈkɒlədʒi/ *n* ekologija

economic /ˌiːkəˈnɒmɪk/ *adj* 1 ekonomski, gospodarski 2 rentabilan, profitabilan **~al** *adj* ekonomičan, štedljiv, racionalan **~s** *n pl* 1 ekonomija (znanost) 2 ekonomika, racionalnost

economist *n* ekonomist; gospodarstvenik **economize** /iˈkɒnəmaɪz/ *vi* (on) biti ekonomičan, štedjeti

economy /iˈkɒnəmi/ *n* 1 štedljivost, ekonomičnost, ušteda 2 gospodarstvo, privreda 3 gospodarsko uređenje ○ *adj* jeftin

ecstasy /ˈekstəsɪ/ *n* zanos, ekstaza **ecstatic** *adj* oduševljen

eddy /ˈedɪ/ *n* vir, vrtlog

edelweiss /ˈeɪdlvaɪs/ *n* runolist

edge /edʒ/ *n* 1 oštrica 2 brid; rub 3 britkost, oštrina (+ *fig*) **on ~** na iglama **fig have the ~ on/over sb** *coll* biti u maloj prednosti nad **take the ~ off sth** ublažiti • *vt, vi* 1 (with) obrubiti, omeđiti 2 (na)oštriti, (na)brusiti 3 primicati se, progurati se **edgy** *adj* nervozan, razdražljiv

edible /ˈedɪbl/ *adj* jestiv; neotrovan

edict /ˈiːdɪkt/ *n* proglas, ukaz

edifice /ˈedɪfɪs/ *n form* zdanje

edit /ˈedɪt/ *vt* 1 uređivati, redigirati, priređivati, pripremiti 2 montirati (film) **~ion** /ɪˈdɪʃn/ *n* izdanje, naklada **~or** *n* 1 (glavni) urednik, redaktor 2 (filmski) montažer **~or-in-chief** glavni urednik **~orial** *adj* urednički **the ~orial staff** uredništvo (osoblje) ○ *n* uvodnik, uvodni članak

educate /ˈedʒʊkeɪt/ *vt* odgojiti, obrazovati, školovati; podučavati, izučiti, uvježbati **education** *n* odgoj i obrazovanje, školovanje, školstvo **educational** *adj* odgojni, obrazovni, prosvjetni

eel /iːl/ *n* jegulja

eerie /ˈɪərɪ/ *adj* tajanstven, stravičan, jeziv

effect /ɪˈfekt/ *n* (on/upon) 1 djelovanje, utjecaj 2 učinak, posljedica, rezultat 3 dojam, utisak 4 **~s** vlasništvo, osobna imovina, pokretnine **in ~ a.** na snazi **b.** u stvari, zapravo **to this/that ~ a.** za tu svrhu **b.** u tom smislu

bring/carry/put sth into ~ izvršiti, provesti **come into ~** stupiti na snagu **take ~ a.** stupiti na snagu **b.** početi djelovati **~ive** *adj* 1 učinkovit, efikasan 2 efektan 3 stvaran, postojeći, efektivan **become ~ive** stupiti na snagu

effeminate /ɪˈfemɪnət/ *adj derog* ženskast

effervescent /ˌefəˈvesnt/ *adj* 1 pjenušav 2 *fig* ushićen

efficacy /ˈefɪkəsɪ/ *n* djelotvornost **efficacious** /ˌefɪˈkeɪʃəs/ *adj* djelotvoran

efficiency /ɪˈfɪʃnsɪ/ *n* 1 sposobost 2 djelotvornost, efikasnost, uspješnost **efficient** /ɪˈfɪʃnt/ *adj* 1 sposoban 2 djelotvoran, uspješan

effigy /ˈefɪdʒɪ/ *n* lik, lutka, kipić

effort /ˈefət/ *n* 1 nastojanje, napor, trud 2 pothvat, akcija **make an ~ (to do sth)** uložiti napor **~lessly** *adv* lako, bez muke

egg /eg/ *n* 1 jaje 2 jajašce **~head** *derog* intelektualac, teoretičar **~plant** *US* patlidžan **~shell** ljuska od jajeta **~whisk** pjenjača • *vt* (sb on to do sth) ohrabriti, nagovoriti, nahuškati

ego /ˈegəʊ/ *n* 1 (**the ~**) ego, (svoje/vlastito) ja 2 uobraženost **~ism** /ˈegəʊɪzəm/ *n* egoizam, sebičnost, samoživost **~ist** *n* egoist, sebičnjak **~tism** /ˈegəʊtɪzm/ *n* samoljublje, samodopadnost

eiderdown /ˈaɪdədaʊn/ *n GB* perina

eight /eɪt/ *n* 1 osam (8) 2 osmerac **~een** /ˌeɪˈtiːn/ *num* osamnaest (18) **~h** /eɪtθ/ *num ord* osmi **~ieth** /ˈeɪtɪəθ/ *num ord* osamdeseti **~y** *num* osamdeset (80) **the ~ies** osamdesete godine

either /ˈaɪðə(r)/ *adj, pron* 1 oba, oboje, jedan ili drugi 2 jedan (bilo koji) od dvoje **on ~ side** na obje strane • *adv, conj* 1 *haven't been there ~* ni ja nisam bio tamo **~ ... or** ili ... ili

eject /ɪˈdʒekt/ *vt, vi* (from) 1 izbaciti 2 ispuštati

eke /iːk/ *vt* **~ out a living** krpati kraj s krajem

elaborate /ɪˈlæbərət/ *adj* 1 razrađen, pomno izrađen 2 složen 3 izvještačen • *vt, vi* /ɪˈlæbəreɪt/ 1 razraditi u tančine 2 (on) dati podrobnije podatke o, obrazložiti

elapse /ɪ'læps/ vi proći, prolaziti

elastic /ɪ'læstɪk/ adj 1 elastičan, rastezljiv, savitljiv 2 fig fleksibilan • n gumilastika, guma ~ **band** GB gumica (za kosu i sl.)

elated /ɪ'leɪtɪd/ adj (at/by) oduševljen, ushićen

elbow /'elbəʊ/ n 1 lakat 2 tech koljeno 3 pregib, ugao, zavoj, okuka • vt gurnuti laktom, munuti ~ **one's way through** prograti se (laktovima)

elder (1) /'eldə(r)/ adj stariji ~**ly** adj postariji **eldest** adj, n najstariji • n stariji; starješina

elder (2) n bazga

elect /ɪ'lekt/ vt 1 birati, izabrati (glasovanjem) 2 odlučiti se za ~**ion** /ɪ'lekʃn/ n 1 biranje, izbor 2 izbori 3 mod izborni ~**ion campaign** (pred)izborna kampanja **call a pre-term** ~**ion** raspisati prijevremene izbore ~**ioneering** /ɪˌlekʃə'nɪərɪŋ/ n predizborna agitacija ~**or** n birač, glasač ~**oral** /ɪ'lektərəl/ adj izborni, birački ~**oral roll/register** popis birača ~**orate** /ɪ'lektərət/ n biračko tijelo, birači

electric /ɪ'lektrɪk/ adj električan; na struju ~ **fire** električna peć ~**al** adj električan ~**al apparatus/appliance** električni aparat ~**al engineering** elektrotehnika **electrician** /ɪˌlek'trɪʃn/ n električar **electricity** /ɪˌlek'trɪsəti/ n elektricitet, električna struja ~**s** n pl GB coll električne instalacije **electrify** /ɪ'lektrɪfaɪ/ vt 1 elektrizirati (+ fig) 2 elektrificirati **electrocute** /ɪ'lektrəkjuːt/ vt 1 ubiti el. strujom 2 smaknuti na el. stolici

electronic /ˌɪlek'trɒnɪk/ adj elektronski; elektronički ~**s** n pl elektronika

elegance /'elɪɡəns/ n elegancija, otmjenost, profinjenost **elegant** adj 1 elegantan, otmjen, fin 2 jednostavan, domišljat

element /'elɪmənt/ n 1 element, (pra)počelo 2 fig čimbenik 3 ~**s** derog pojedinci ~**ary** /ˌelɪ'mentrɪ/ adj elementaran, osnovni ~**ary school** US osnovna škola

elephant /'elɪfənt/ n slon

elevate /'elɪveɪt/ vt form 1 podići, povisiti 2 promaknuti, uzvisiti **elevation** /ˌelɪ'veɪʃn/ n 1 promaknuće 2 uzvišenost (stila) 3 nadmorska visina 4 **front elevation** nacrt; **side elevation** bokocrt 5 form uzvisina 6 mil uzdignuće **elevator** /'elɪveɪtə(r)/ n 1 US lift 2 teretno dizalo 3 silos

eleven /ɪ'levn/ num jedanaest (11) ~**th** num ord jedanaesti **at the** ~**th hour** u posljednji čas

elf /elf/ n (pl **elves**) vilenjak ~**in** adj vilenjački

elicit /ɪ'lɪsɪt/ vt (from) izvući, izmamiti

eligible /'elɪdʒəbl/ adj (for) odgovarajući, prikladan, poželjan, koji ispunjava uvjete

eliminate /ɪ'lɪmɪneɪt/ vt ukloniti, izbaciti, isključiti

elite /eɪ'liːt/ n elita

elm /elm/ n brijest

elongated /'iːlɒŋɡeɪtɪd/ adj izdužen, istegnut, rastegnut

elope /ɪ'ləʊp/ vi (with) pobjeći

eloquence /'elɒkwəns/ n rječitost, izražajnost, elokvencija **eloquent** adj 1 rječit 2 snažan, uvjerljiv, izražajan

else /els/ adv 1 još, drugi 2 inače, ili, ako ne **somebody** ~ netko drugi **nothing** ~ ništa više ~**where** drugamo, drugdje

elude /ɪ'luːd/ vt izbjeći, izmaknuti, izigrati **elusive** /ɪ'luːsɪv/ adj neuhvatljiv

emaciated /ɪ'meɪʃieɪtɪd/ adj omršavio, oslabio, izmožden

emanate /'eməneɪt/ vi (from) form 1 izlaziti, izbijati, istjecati 2 fig potjecati iz

emancipate /ɪ'mænsɪpeɪt/ vt (from) osloboditi; emancipirati

embankment /ɪm'bæŋkmənt/ n nasip; (zidana) obala

embargo /ɪm'bɑːɡəʊ/ n zabrana, embargo **lift/raise/remove an** ~ **from** ukinuti embargo **place/lay sb/sth under (an)** ~/**put an** ~ **on** uvesti embargo na • vt staviti zabranu na, uvesti embargo

embark /ɪm'bɑːk/ vi,vt 1 ukrcati se 2 (on/upon) upustiti se (u) ~**ation**

/ɪmbə'keɪʃn/ n ukrcavanje, utovar

embarrass /ɪm'bærəs/ vt dovesti u neugodan položaj, posramiti; smesti, zbuniti *she was ~ed* bilo joj je neugodno **~ing** adj neugodan, nezgodan **~ment** n 1 neugodan položaj, neprilika, sramota 2 novčana neprilika, škripac

embassy /'embəsɪ/ n ambasada, veleposlanstvo

embed /ɪm'bed/ vt (in) ukopati, usaditi, ugraditi

embellish /ɪm'belɪʃ/ vt (with) ukrasiti, uljepšati (+ fig)

embers /'embəz/ n pl žar, žeravica

embezzle /ɪm'bezl/ vt pronevjeriti (novac)

embitter /ɪm'bɪtə(r)/ vt ogorčiti, zagorčiti, ozlojediti

embody /ɪm'bɒdɪ/ vt (in) 1 utjeloviti 2 uključiti, sadržavati, obuhvatiti **embodiment** n utjelovljenje

emboss /ɪm'bɒs/ vt (with) ispupčiti, ukrasiti ispupčenim motivom

embrace /ɪm'breɪs/ vt,vi 1 zagrliti 2 prihvatiti; iskoristiti (priliku) 3 obuhvatiti, sadržavati, uključiti • n zagrljaj

embroider /ɪm'brɔɪdə(r)/ vt,vi (in/with) 1 (iz)vesti 2 fig ukrasiti, uljepšati **~y** n vez(enje), ukras

emerald /'emərəld/ n smaragd

emerge /ɪ'mɜːdʒ/ vi 1 izroniti, isplivati, izaći na površinu 2 pojaviti se, (pro)izaći, nastati **~nce** n pojavljivanje, nastanak **~ncy** n hitan slučaj, opasnost, nužda **~ncy exit** izlaz za nuždu **~ncy meeting** izvanredni sastanak **state of ~ncy** izvanredno stanje

emery /'emərɪ/ n smirak

emigrant /'emɪgrənt/ n iseljenik **emigrate** /'emɪgreɪt/ vi iseliti se, emigrirati **emigration** /ˌemɪ'greɪʃn/ n iseljenje, emigracija **émigré** /'emɪgreɪ/ n politički emigrant

eminence /'emɪnəns/ n visok položaj, slava, ugled **eminent** adj 1 istaknut, ugledan 2 izrazit; izvanredan, osobit **eminently** adv form nadasve

emission /ɪ'mɪʃn/ n form odašiljanje, ispuštanje, zračenje **emit** /ɪ'mɪt/ vt

odašiljati, ispuštati, isijavati, zračiti, emitirati

emotion /ɪ'məʊʃn/ n emocija, osjećaj **~al** adj emocionalan, osjećajan

emperor /'empərə(r)/ n car

emphasis /'emfəsɪs/ n naglašavanje, naglasak, isticanje, važnost **lay/place/put (great) ~ on** naročito istaknuti **emphasize** /'emfəsaɪz/ vt istaknuti, naglasiti **emphatic** /ɪm'fætɪk/ adj 1 istaknut, naglašen 2 jasan, nedvosmislen

empire /'empaɪə(r)/ n carstvo

empirical /ɪm'pɪrɪkl/ adj empirijski, iskustven

emplacement /ɪm'pleɪsmənt/ n mil topničko gnijezdo

employ /ɪm'plɔɪ/ vt 1 uposliti, zaposliti 2 iskoristiti **~ee** n namještenik **~er** n poslodavac **~ment** n posao • in form **in sb's ~/in the ~ of** u službi kod

emporium /ɪm'pɔːrɪəm/ n form velika trgovina

empower /ɪm'paʊə(r)/ vt (sb to do sth) ovlastiti, dati pravo, opunomoćiti

empress /'emprɪs/ n carica

empty /'emptɪ/ adj 1 prazan 2 isprazan, besmislen **empties** n pl coll ambalaža **emptiness** n 1 praznina 2 ispraznost, besmislenost • vt,vi 1 (out) isprazniti (se) 2 isprazniti, istresti, izliti 3 (into) ulijevati se, utjecati

emulate /'emjʊleɪt/ vt oponašati koga

enable /ɪ'neɪbl/ vt (sb/sth to do sth) omogućiti; ovlastiti; osposobiti

enact /ɪ'nækt/ vt 1 ozakoniti, donijeti zakon, propisati 2 form glumiti, igrati, predstavljati

enamel /ɪ'næml/ n 1 glazura, emajl 2 lak boja 3 zubna caklina • vt emajlirati, glazirati, pocakliti, lakirati

encased /ɪn'keɪst/ adj (in) zatvoren, obložen, oklopljen

enchant /ɪn'tʃɑːnt/ vt 1 očarati, oduševiti 2 lit općiniti **~ing** adj čaroban

encircle /ɪn'sɜːkl/ vt okružiti, opkoliti; obujmiti

enclose /ɪn'kləʊz/ vt (with) 1 obzidati, ograditi, opasati 2 priložiti (pismu) **enclosure** /ɪn'kləʊʒə(r)/ n 1 ograđeni prostor **2** ograđivanje **3** prilog (u pismu)

encompass /ɪnˈkʌmpəs/ *vt* **1** obuhvaćati, sadržavati, uključivati **2** okružiti, opkoliti

encore /ˈɒŋkɔː(r)/ *int* bis! još! • *n* poziv na bis; izlazak na bis

encounter /ɪnˈkaʊntə(r)/ *vt form* (sth/sb) **1** doživjeti, naići na (nevolje, otpor) **2** naletjeti na, susresti se sa **3** sukobiti se sa • *n* (with) **1** susret **2** sukob, okršaj

encourage /ɪnˈkʌrɪdʒ/ *vt* (sb in sth/to do sth) hrabriti, bodriti, poticati ~ment *n* ohrabrenje; poticaj; podrška **encouraging** *adj* ohrabrujući, obećavajući

encroach /ɪnˈkrəʊtʃ/ *vi* (on/upon) (za)dirati u (prava, slobode)

encyclop(a)edia /ɪnˌsaɪkləˈpiːdɪə/ *n* enciklopedija

end /end/ *n* **1** kraj, konac, svršetak **2** okrajak, ostatak **3** svrha, namjera, cilj **at an** ~/**at the** ~ **of** pri kraju, na kraju **in the** ~ konačno, na kraju **for hours on** ~ satima on ~ uspravno **bring sth to an** ~/**make an** ~ **of sth**/**put an** ~ **to sth** okončati što **come to an** ~ završiti **draw to an** ~ bližiti se kraju **make (both)** ~s **meet** sastavljati kraj s krajem **for/to this** ~, **with this** ~ **in view** u tu svrhu ~ **product** krajnji/finalni proizvod ~**ing** *n* **1** kraj, svršetak **2** *gram* nastavak, dočetak ~**less** *adj* beskrajan • *vi,vt* završiti, dovršiti, dokrajčiti, okončati ~ **up in** završiti u

endanger /ɪnˈdeɪndʒə(r)/ *vt* ugroziti

endearing /ɪnˈdɪərɪŋ/ *adj* drag, simpatičan **endearment** *n* ljubav, nježnost, nježna riječ

endeavour (-**vor** *US*) /ɪnˈdevə(r)/ *n form* nastojanje, pokušaj, trud • *vi* nastojati, pokušati

endorse /ɪnˈdɔːs/ *vt* **1** odobriti, potvrditi, prihvatiti, usvojiti **2** indosirati, prenijeti ~**ment** *n* odobrenje, potvrda, pristanak

endow /ɪnˈdaʊ/ *vt* **1** novčano pomagati, subvencionirati, darivati **2** prirodno obdariti

endurance /ɪnˈdjʊərəns/ *n* izdržljivost;

podnošenje; trajanje **past/beyond** ~ neizdrživ **endure** /ɪnˈdjʊə(r)/ *vt,vi* **1** podnijeti; (pre)trpjeti, (pre)patiti **2** izdržati; trajati **enduring** *adj* trajan

enemy /ˈenəmɪ/ *n* neprijatelj; protivnik

energetic /ˌenəˈdʒetɪk/ *adj* energičan; odlučan **energy** /ˈenədʒɪ/ *n* **1** energija; snaga **2** (+ *pl*) napor(i), sposobnost

enforce /ɪnˈfɔːs/ *vt* **1** (on/upon) provoditi (zakone); nametnuti, uvesti **2** potkrijepiti

engage /ɪnˈgeɪdʒ/ *vt,vi* **1** privući/zaokupiti (pozornost) **2** zakvačiti se (zupčanici); staviti u pogon, pritisnuti (kvačilo), ubaciti u (brzinu) **3** napasti, zapodjenuti bitku **4** uzeti u službu, unajmiti, angažirati **5** *GB* rezervirati **6** (in) sudjelovati u, baviti se **7** (in) uvući u (razgovor) ~**d** *adj* **1** (to) zaručen **2** zauzet ~**ment** *n* **1** zaruke *pl* **2** dogovor, sastanak; obaveza; angažman **3** bitka, borba

engender /ɪnˈdʒendə(r)/ *vt* izazvati, prouzročiti, rađati

engine /ˈendʒɪn/ *n* **1** stroj, motor **2** lokomotiva ~ **driver** strojovođa ~**er** /ˌendʒɪˈnɪə(r)/ *n* **1** inženjer **2** strojar **3** *US* strojovođa **4** *mil* inženjerac **civil/chemical/electrical/mechanical/mining** ~**er** inženjer građevine/kemije/elektrotehnike/strojarstva/rudarstva ∘ *vt,vi* **1** organizirati, planirati **2** graditi, konstruirati ~**ering** *n* **1** strojarstvo, strojogradnja **2** inženjering

engraving /ɪnˈgreɪvɪŋ/ *n* graviranje; gravura, rezbarija

engrossed /ɪnˈgrəʊst/ *adj* zaokupljen, zadubljen

engulf /ɪnˈgʌlf/ *vt* (in) *fig* progutati

enhance /ɪnˈhɑːns/ *vt* povećati, povisiti, pojačati

enjoy /ɪnˈdʒɔɪ/ *vt* **1** uživati u **2** svidjeti se, voljeti **3** *form* imati, uživati **4** (oneself) dobro se zabavljati ~**able** *adj* ugodan, zabavan

enlarge /ɪnˈlɑːdʒ/ *vt,vi* **1** povećati **2** (on/upon) opširno/detaljno opisati ~**ment** *n* **1** uvećana fotografija **2** povećanje

enlighten /ɪnˈlaɪtn/ *vt* (on) prosvijetliti, razjasniti **the E~ment** *n* prosvjetiteljstvo

enlist /ɪnˈlɪst/ *vi,vt* **1** (in) dobrovoljno se javiti u vojsku **2** unovačiti **3** (in/for) pridobiti, steći

enmity /ˈenmɪtɪ/ *n* neprijateljstvo, mržnja

enormity /ɪˈnɔːmɪtɪ/ *n* **1** grozota, strahota, užas **2** veličina, težina **enormous** /ɪˈnɔːməs/ *adj* golem, ogroman

enough /ɪˈnʌf/ *adj* dovoljan, dostatan • *adv* dovoljno, dosta, prilično; dovoljno sasvim • *n* dovoljnost, dostatnost

enquire /ɪnˈkwaɪə(r)/ → **inquire**

enrage /ɪnˈreɪdʒ/ *vt* razbjesniti, razjariti

enrich /ɪnˈrɪtʃ/ *vt* (with) obogatiti (+ *fig*)

enrol(l) /ɪnˈrəʊl/ *vt,vi* (in/at/as) upisati (se), staviti na popis

en route /ˌɒn ˈruːt/ *adv* putem, na putu

ensign /ˈensən/ *n* **1** zastava (na brodu) **2** (čin) zastavnik

enslave /ɪnˈsleɪv/ *vt* porobiti, podjarmiti

ensue /ɪnˈsjuː/ *vi* (from) slijediti, proizlaziti, nastati

ensure (**insure** *US*) /ɪnˈʃʊə(r)/ *vt* osigurati, jamčiti

entail /ɪnˈteɪl/ *vt* (on) **1** tražiti, zahtijevati **2** nametnuti; povlačiti za sobom **3** *leg* ostaviti u neotuđivu baštinu

entangle /ɪnˈtæŋgl/ *vt* (in/with) zaplesti, zamrsiti

enter /ˈentə(r)/ *vt,vi* **1** ući, ulaziti **2** stupiti u; upisati se, postati članom **3** (for) kandidirati se, prijaviti (se) **4** (in) unijeti (podatke) **5** (up/in) proknjižiti **~ into** započeti (pregovore) **~ on/upon one's duties** stupiti na dužnost

enterprise /ˈentəpraɪz/ *n* **1** pothvat **2** poduzetnost, hrabrost **3** poduzeće **enterprising** *adj* poduzetan, hrabar

entertain /ˌentəˈteɪn/ *vt* **1** (with) zabavljati **2** (to) ugostiti, imati goste **~er** *n* (profesionalni) zabavljač **~ment** *n* **1** zabava **2** javna priredba, predstava **3** primanje, doček **~ment expenses/allowance** izdaci za reprezentaciju

enthral(l) /ɪnˈθrɔːl/ *vt* očarati, fascinirati

enthusiasm /ɪnˈθjuːzɪæzəm/ *n* (for/about) oduševljenje, zanos, žar **enthusiast** *n* zanesenjak, entuzijast **enthusiastic** *adj* (about/over) zanesen, oduševljen **enthuse** *vi* (about/over) oduševljavati se

entice /ɪnˈtaɪs/ *vt* namamiti, privući, navesti **enticing** *adj* primamljiv, zamaman

entire /ɪnˈtaɪə(r)/ *adj* cijeli, čitav, potpun, sav **~ly** *adv* potpuno, u cijelosti **~ty** *n* potpunost, cjelovitost **in its ~ty** u potpunosti, u cjelini

entitle /ɪnˈtaɪtl/ *vt* **1** ovlastiti koga, dati pravo na **2 be ~d to sth/to do sth** imati pravo na/da **3** nasloviti

entity /ˈentɪtɪ/ *n* bit(nost), suština; entitet, biće, cjelina **legal ~** pravna osoba

entourage /ˌɒntʊˈrɑːʒ/ *n* pratnja, svita

entrails /ˈentreɪlz/ *n pl* utroba; crijeva

entrance (1) /ˈentrəns/ *n* **1** (to) ulaz, vrata **2** ulazak, ulaženje **~ exam** prijemni ispit **~ fee** ulaznina **~ hall** predsoblje, predvorje

entrance (2) /ɪnˈtrɑːns/ *vt* oduševiti, ushititi, zanijeti

entreat /ɪnˈtriːt/ *vt* (usrdno) moliti, preklinjati

entrenched /ɪnˈtrentʃɪt/ *adj* **1** ustaljen, uvriježen **2** *mil* ukopan, u rovovima

entrepreneur /ˌɒntrəprəˈnɜː(r)/ *n* poduzetnik **~ial** *adj* poduzetnički

entrust /ɪnˈtrʌst/ *vt* povjeriti komu što, zadužiti koga čime

entry /ˈentrɪ/ *n* **1** (into) ulazak, ulaženje **2** ulaz, ulazna vrata; pristup **3** stavka; natuknica **4** kandidat, natjecatelj **make an ~** proknjižiti **~ visa** ulazna viza **~ form** pristupnica

enumerate /ɪˈnjuːməreɪt/ *vt* nabrojati, pobrojati

enunciate /ɪˈnʌnsɪeɪt/ *vt,vi* **1** jasno izgovarati **2** izložiti

envelop /ɪnˈveləp/ *vt* (in) omotati, oviti, zaviti, okružiti **envelope** /ˈenvələp/ *n* **1** kuverta **2** omot, ovoj, ovitak

enviable /ˈenvɪəbl/ *adj* zavidan (uspjeh) **envious** /ˈenvɪəs/ *adj* (of) zavidan (kome)

environment /ɪn'vaɪərənmənt/ *n* okolina, okoliš; okruženje, sredina **~al** *adj* ekološki **~alist** *n* ekolog **environs** *n pl* okolica

envisage /ɪn'vɪzɪdʒ/ *vt* predvidjeti; zamišljati

envision /ɪn'vɪʒən/ *US* → **envisage**

envoy /'envɔɪ/ *n* izaslanik

envy /'envɪ/ *n* zavist • *vt* zavidjeti na

ephemeral /ɪ'femərəl/ *adj* kratkotrajan, prolazan

epic /'epɪk/ *n* epska pjesma, ep • *adj* 1 epski 2 *coll* herojski, impresivan

epidemic /,epɪ'demɪk/ *n* epidemija, zaraza • *adj* epidemijski, zarazan

epilepsy /'epɪlepsɪ/ *n* epilepsija, padavica **epileptic** *adj* epileptičan **epileptic fit** napadaj padavice o *n* epileptičar, padavičar

episode /'epɪsəud/ *n* 1 događaj; zgoda 2 epizoda

epistle /ɪ'pɪsl/ *n* epistola, poslanica

epitome /ɪ'pɪtəmɪ/ *n* 1 izvadak, kratak sadržaj, sažetak 2 oličenje; tipičan primjer **epitomize** /ɪ'pɪtəmaɪz/ *vt* 1 sažeti 2 biti oličenje/tipičan primjer

epoch /'iːpɒk/ *n* epoha, razdoblje **~making** epohalan, značajan

equal /'iːkwəl/ *adj* jednak, isti; ravnopravan **be ~ to doing sth** biti dorastao/sposoban za **~ rights** ravnopravnost **~ in my ~s** meni ravni **without ~** bez premca • *vt* 1 biti jednak; izjednačiti 2 iznositi 3 mjeriti se s, biti ravan; konkurirati **~ity** /i'kwɒlɪtɪ/ *n* jednakost, ravnopravnost **~ize** *vt* 1 izjednačiti, ujednačiti 2 *sport* izjednačiti, poravnati **~izer** *n sport* izjednačenje **~ly** *adv* 1 jednako 2 na isti način, isto tako

equanimity /,ekwə'nɪmətɪ/ *n* smirenost, staloženost

equate /ɪ'kweɪt/ *vt* izjednačavati **equation** /i'kweɪʒn/ *n* 1 jednadžba 2 (with/between) izjednačenje, ravnoteža

equator /ɪ'kweɪtə(r)/ *n* ekvator, polutnik

equilibrium /,iːkwɪ'lɪbrɪəm/ *n* ravnoteža

equinox /'iːkwɪnɒks/ *n* ekvinocij,

ravnodnevnica

equip /ɪ'kwɪp/ *vt* (with/for) opremiti, opskrbiti **~ment** *n* 1 oprema 2 opremanje

equitable /'ekwɪtəbl/ *adj* pravičan, pravedan, pošten, razuman **equity** *n* pravednost, pravičnost, nepristranost

equities *n pl* osnovne/temeljne dionice

equivalent /ɪ'kwɪvələnt/ *adj* (to) istovrijedan, istoznačan • *n* ekvivalent

equivocal /ɪ'kwɪvəkl/ *adj* 1 dvosmislen 2 sumnjiv, dvojben

era /'ɪərə/ *n* era, doba, razdoblje

eradicate /ɪ'rædɪkeɪt/ *vt* iskorijeniti

erase /ɪ'reɪz/ *vt* izbrisati; uništiti **~r** *n* gumica; brisalo

erect /ɪ'rekt/ *vt* 1 (po)dignuti, izgraditi, postaviti **~ion** /ɪ'rekʃn/ *n* 1 (po)dizanje; izgradnja 2 erekcija

ermine /'ɜːmɪn/ *n* hermelin, zerdav

erotic /ɪ'rɒtɪk/ *adj* erotski, erotičan **~ism** /ɪ'rɒtɪsɪzəm/ *n* erotika

err /ɜː(r)/ *vi form* (po)griješiti **~ on the side of caution** biti pretjerano oprezan

errand /'erənd/ *n* poruka, nalog; posao **go on/run ~s (for sb)** obavljati sitne poslove izvan kuće; (raz)nositi vijesti/poruke **~ boy** dostavljač, potrčko

erratic /ɪ'rætɪk/ *adj* 1 nepravilan, nejednak 2 nepostojan; prevrtljiv

error /'erə(r)/ *n* pogreška, omaška, zabuna **human ~** ljudska pogreška

ersatz /'eəzæts/ *adj* umjetni, lažni • *n* nadomjestak

erupt /ɪ'rʌpt/ *vi* buknuti, izbiti **~ion** /ɪ'rʌpʃn/ *n* erupcija, provala; izbijanje

escalate /'eskəleɪt/ *vt,vi* pojačati (se), povećati (se), zaoštriti (se)

escalator /'eskəleɪtə(r)/ *n* pokretne stepenice *pl*

escape /ɪ'skeɪp/ *vt,vi* (from) 1 pobjeći, spasiti se 2 izbjeći, izmaknuti 3 istjecati, izlaziti • *n* 1 bijeg 2 izlaz **fire ~** protupožarne stube *pl* **make one's ~** pobjeći, umaknuti **have a narrow ~** za dlaku izbjeći

escort /'eskɔːt/ *n* pratnja, pratilac, zaštita • /ɪ'skɔːt/ *vt* (ot)pratiti

especially /ɪ'speʃəlɪ/ *adv* naročito,

osobito, posebno

espionage /'espiənɑːʒ/ *n* špijunaža, uhođenje

essay /'eseɪ/ *n* 1 sastavak; esej 2 pokušaj • /e'seɪ/ *vt form* pokušati

essence /'esns/ *n* 1 bit, srž, suština 2 ekstrakt **essential** /ɪ'senʃl/ *adj* (to/for sth) bitan, prijeko potreban, nužan, osnovni, važan

establish /ɪ'stæblɪʃ/ *vt* 1 osnovati, utemeljiti; uspostaviti 2 (oneself as/in) afirmirati se, učvrstiti svoj položaj 3 smjestiti; namjestiti, postaviti 4 ustanoviti, utvrditi, dokazati, konstatirati **~ment** *n* 1 osnivanje, utemeljenje 2 poduzeće, tvrtka, ustanova; kućanstvo; hotel; vojska 3 posluga; osoblje **the E~ment** vladajući krugovi, vlast, sistem, sustav

estate /ɪ'steɪt/ *n* 1 posjed, imanje 2 *leg* imovina, imetak; ostavština ~ **agent** *GB* posrednik za nekretnine ~ **car** *GB* karavan **industrial** ~ industrijska zona **real** ~ nekretnine *pl*

esteem /ɪ'stiːm/ *vt* 1 cijeniti, (po)štovati 2 držati, smatrati • *n* (po)štovanje, ugled **hold sb in high** ~ visoko cijeniti

esthetic /ˌiːs'θetɪk/ *US* → **aesthetic**

estimate /'estɪmeɪt/ *vt,vi* 1 prosuditi, ocijeniti 2 (for) procijeniti, proračunati • /'estɪmət/ *n* procjena, sud; proračun **rough** ~ slobodna procjena **estimation** /ˌestɪ'meɪʃn/ *n* procjena; sud, mišljenje

estrange /ɪ'streɪndʒ/ *vt* (from) otuđiti, odvojiti, udaljiti **be ~d** razići se

estuary /'estʃuərɪ/ *n* estuarij

etcetera /ɪt'setərə/ *adv* (*abbrev* etc.) i tako dalje, itd.

etching /'etʃɪŋ/ *n* bakropis

eternal /ɪ'tɜːnl/ *adj* vječan **eternity** /ɪ'tɜːnətɪ/ *n* vječnost (+ *fig*)

ethical /'eθɪkl/ *adj* 1 etički, moralan 2 (moralno) ispravan **ethics** *n pl* 1 (+ *sing v*) etika, znanost o ćudoređu 2 (+ *pl v*) moralnost, etičnost

ethnic /'eθnɪk/ *adj* etnički

euphemism /'juːfəmɪzəm/ *n* eufemizam, ublažen izraz

evacuate /ɪ'vækjʊeɪt/ *vt* 1 evakuirati 2

form isprazniti (crijeva) **evacuation** /ɪˌvækjʊ'eɪʃn/ *n* 1 evakuacija 2 pražnjenje

evade /ɪ'veɪd/ *vt* izbjeći, izbjegavati, izigrati (propise), izvući se od, umaknuti, zaobići **evasion** /ɪ'veɪʒn/ *n* 1 izbjegavanje 2 izgovor, izlika, okolišanje **tax evasion** utaja poreza **evasive** /ɪ'veɪsɪv/ *adj* okolišan, neodređen

evaluate /ɪ'væljʊeɪt/ *vt* (pr)ocijeniti

evaporate /ɪ'væpəreɪt/ *vt,vi* ispariti, ishlapiti (+ *fig*)

eve /iːv/ *n poet* večer **on the** ~ **of** uoči **Christmas E~** Badnjak **New Year's E~** Stara godina, Silvestrovo

even (1) /'iːvn/ *adj* 1 ravan; gladak; jednak, jednolik 2 ujednačen, uravnotežen, ravnomjeran 3 miran, staložen 4 isti 5 paran (broj) **be** ~ **with sb** izravnati račune **get** ~ **with sb** vratiti kome milo za drago ~ **odds** podjednaki izgledi **~-handed** pravedan, nepristran • *vt,vi* ~ **out** izjednačiti (se), izravnati, uravnotežiti ~ **up** izjednačiti, izravnati (račune)

even (2) *adv* čak, štoviše, dapače; uopće ~ **as** baš kada ~ **if/though** čak i da, sve da i, pa makar i, pa da i ~ **so** pa ipak

evening /'iːvnɪŋ/ *n* večer **this** ~ večeras **in the** ~ navečer

event /ɪ'vent/ *n* 1 događaj 2 *sport* disciplina, natjecanje 3 priredba, manifestacija **in any** ~ u svakom slučaju **in the** ~ **of** u slučaju **~ful** *adj* zanimljiv, uzbudljiv; važan, značajan **~ual** /ɪ'ventʃʊəl/ *adj* konačan, krajnji, zaključan **~uality** /ɪˌventʃuæ'lɒtɪ/ *n* (nepredviđena) mogućnost, slučaj **~ually** *adv* konačno, na koncu/kraju (¶ eventualno)

ever /'evə(r)/ *adv* ikad(a), uopće **for** ~ zauvijek **hardly** ~ gotovo nikad ~ **since** otada **~green** *adj* zimzelen o *n* zimzelen **~lasting** *adj* 1 vječan 2 neprestan

every /'evrɪ/ *adj* svaki (pojedini); sav **~body/one** *pron* svatko, svi **~day** *adj* svakodnevni, svakidašnji, uobičajen **~thing** *n* sve **~where** *adv* svugdje, (po)svuda, svukud(a), svakamo

evict /ɪ'vɪkt/ vt (from) deložirati, izbaciti ~**ion** /ɪ'vɪkʃn/ n deložacija

evidence /'evɪdəns/ n 1 dokaz(i), dokazni materijal 2 sudski iskaz 3 znak, trag, nagovještaj, indicija 4 očiglednost **be in** ~ biti očit, prisutan **call sb in** ~ pozvati za svjedoka • vt dokazati, pokazati **evident** adj jasan, očit, bjelodan

evil /'i:vl/ adj (comp **worse,** sup **the worst**) 1 zao, loš, opak 2 pokvaren, nemoralan; štetan 3 zloban, pakostan ~**doer** zlotvor ~ **eye** urokljiv pogled ~**-minded** zlonamjeran, pakostan • n 1 zlo 2 grijeh, opačina 3 šteta; nesreća

evoke /ɪ'vəʊk/ vt evocirati, buditi (uspomene)

evolution /ˌi:və'lu:ʃn/ n 1 evolucija 2 razvoj, razvitak **evolve** /ɪ'vɒlv/ vt,vi (from/in/into) razvijati/razviti (se), izgraditi, stvoriti, nastati

ewe /ju:/ n ovca

ex /eks/ n coll bivši, bivša • **ex-** prefix bivši

exact /ɪg'zækt/ adj 1 točan, ispravan, pravi, precizan 2 savjestan, pedantan ~**ly** adv točno; upravo, sasvim • vt (from) 1 iznuditi (obećanje), utjerivati (porez) 2 zahtijevati, inzistirati 3 iziskivati ~**ing** adj strog; zahtjevan, naporan

exaggerate /ɪg'zædʒəreɪt/ vt,vi pretjerivati, preuveličati

exam /ɪg'zæm/ n coll ispit

examination /ɪgˌzæmɪ'neɪʃn/ n 1 ispitivanje, istraživanje 2 med pregled, pretraga 3 leg preslušavanje 4 ispit, test znanja 5 provjera; revizija, pregled **examine** /ɪg'zæmɪn/ vt 1 (for) ispitati, istražiti, pregledati, pretražiti, razmotriti 2 leg preslušati 3 (in/on) ispitati **examiner** n 1 ispitivač 2 istraživatelj 3 revizor

example /ɪg'zɑ:mpl/ n 1 primjer; uzor 2 uzorak 3 opomena **for** ~ na primjer **make an** ~ **of sb** kazniti koga za opomenu **set an** ~ biti uzor

exasperate /ɪg'zæspəreɪt/ vt ozlojediti, razljutiti, razbjesniti **exasperating** adj ozlojeđujući **exasperation**

/ɪgˌzæspə'reɪʃn/ n ljutnja, ogorčenje

excavate /'ekskəveɪt/ vt iskopati, otkopati

exceed /ɪk'si:d/ vt 1 nadilaziti, nadmašiti, premašiti 2 prekoračiti, prijeći mjeru, pretjerati ~**ingly** adv krajnje

excel /ɪk'sel/ vi,vt (in/at) 1 nadmašiti 2 isticati se, odlikovati se ~**lence** /'eksələns/ n (in/at) kvaliteta, vrsnoća ~**lent** adj odličan, izvrstan, izvanredan

except /ɪk'sept/ prep osim ~ **for** izuzevši • vt (from) izuzeti, isključiti ~**ion** /ɪk'sepʃn/ n 1 iznimka, izuzetak 2 prigovor 3 izuzimanje **make an** ~**ion** (of sb/sth) učiniti izuzetak **an** ~**ion to the rule** iznimka od pravila **take** ~ (to sth) **a.** zamjeriti **b.** staviti prigovor na **c.** protiviti se ~**ionable** adj prijeporan, sporan ~**ional** adj izniman, izuzetan, izvanredan

excerpt /'eksɜ:pt/ n izvadak

excess /ɪk'ses/ n 1 višak, preobilje 2 prekomjernost, pretjeranost, neumjerenost 3 ~**es** krajnosti, ispadi **in** ~ **of** više od, preko **to** ~ pretjerano, previše • /'ekses/ adj dodatan, suvišan ~**ive** /ɪk'sesɪv/ adj pretjeran

exchange /ɪks'tʃeɪndʒ/ n 1 izmjena, razmjena, zamjena 2 burza, tržište 3 (oružani/verbalni) obračun 4 kratak razgovor **in** ~ **for** u zamjenu za ~ **rate/rate of** ~ devizni tečaj **foreign** ~ devize **the Stock E~** burza dionica **telephone** ~ telefonska centrala • vt mijenjati, razmjenjivati, zamijeniti

exchequer /ɪks'tʃekə(r)/ n državna blagajna, riznica **the E~** britansko ministarstvo financija **the Chancellor of the E~** ministar financija

excise /ɪk'saɪz/ n trošarina

excite /ɪk'saɪt/ vt 1 uzbuditi; uzrujati 2 razdražiti 3 pobuditi, izazvati 4 nadražiti, podražiti ~**ment** n uzbuđenje; uzrujavanje **exciting** adj uzbudljiv

exclaim /ɪk'skleɪm/ vt,vi uskliknuti, (uz)viknuti, kriknuti **exclamation** /ˌeksklə'meɪʃn/ n usklik, uzvik **exclamation mark/point** US uskličnik

exclude /ɪk'sklu:d/ vt (from doing sth) isključiti, izostaviti, odbaciti; zabraniti (ulaz/pristup) **excluding** prep isključujući, izuzevši **exclusion** /ɪk'sklu:ʒn/ n isključenje, izuzimanje **exclusive** /ɪk'sklu:sɪv/ adj 1 isključujući 2 isključiv 3 ekskluzivan, skup 4 jedini **exclusively** adv jedino, isključivo, samo

excommunicate /,ekskə'mju:nɪkeɪt/ vt eccl izopćiti

excrement /'ekskrəmənt/ n izmet

excruciating /ɪk'skru:ʃɪeɪtɪŋ/ adj bolan, mučan; oštar

excursion /ɪk'skɜ:ʃn/ n izlet

excuse /ɪk'skju:s/ n isprika, izgovor, izlika, opravdanje **make ~s** ispričavati se • /ɪk'skju:z/ vt 1 (for) ispričati, opravdati, oprostiti 2 (from) osloboditi (obaveze) **~ me** oprostite, ispričavam se

ex-directory /,eksdɪ'rektərɪ/ adj koji se ne nalazi u telefonskom imeniku

execute /'eksɪkju:t/ vt 1 izvršiti, izvesti, ostvariti, provesti 2 leg učiniti pravovaljanim; ovjeriti 3 pogubiti, smaknuti 4 izvesti, odglumiti, odsvirati **execution** /,eksɪ'kju:ʃn/ n 1 izvedba, izvršenje 2 način izvedbe, stil 3 smaknuće **executioner** n krvnik **executive** /ɪg'zekjʊtɪv/ adj izvršni ○ n 1 **(the)** izvršna vlast 2 izvršni organ, direktor, rukovoditelj **executor** n izvršitelj oporuke

exemplify /ɪg'zemplɪfaɪ/ vt 1 pokazati na primjeru, služiti se primjerima 2 služiti kao primjer

exempt /ɪg'zempt/ adj (from) osloboden, izuzet, pošteden • vt osloboditi, poštedjeti, izuzeti **~ from tax** osloboditi plaćanja poreza **~ion** /ɪg'zempʃn/ n oslobođenje

exercise /'eksəsaɪz/ n 1 vježba; vježbanje 2 primjena, upotreba, (iz)vršenje, obnašanje 3 zadaća, zadatak 4 **~s** vojne vježbe **~ book** bilježnica **take ~** kretati se • vt, vi 1 vježbati, kretati se, razgibati se 2 vršiti, obnašati 3 primijeniti, upotrijebiti, koristiti

exert /ɪg'zɜ:t/ vt 1 (on/upon) primijeniti, upotrijebiti, izvršiti; napregnuti

(oneself) naprezati se, nastojati, potruditi se **~ion** /ɪg'zɜ:ʃn/ n 1 primjena, upotreba 2 napor

exhale /eks'heɪl/ vt, vi (from) izdahnuti

exhaust /ɪg'zɔ:st/ vt iscrpsti, istrošiti, isprazniti **~ed** adj iscrpljen, umoran **~ing** adj iscrpljujući, naporan, zamoran **~ion** /ɪg'zɔ:stʃən/ n iscrpljenost, umor **~ive** adj iscrpan • n 1 **(~ pipe)** ispušna cijev 2 ispušni ventil 3 ispuh

exhibit /ɪg'zɪbɪt/ vt, vi 1 izložiti, izlagati 2 pokazati, • n 1 izložak, eksponat 2 US izložba 3 leg dokazni materijal **~ion** /,eksɪ'bɪʃn/ n 1 izložba, izlaganje 2 pokazivanje, ispoljavanje **exhilarating** /ɪg'zɪləreɪtɪŋ/ adj razveseljavajući, vesco

exhort /ɪg'zɔ:t/ vt form nagovarati, poticati, savjetovati, uvjeravati **exile** /'eksaɪl/ n 1 izgon, progon(stvo) 2 prognanik • vt prognati

exist /ɪg'zɪst/ vi 1 postojati 2 (on) živjeti **~ence** n 1 postojanje 2 život **come into ~ence** nastati, postati **~ing** adj postojeći, sadašnji

exit /'eksɪt/ n 1 izlaz 2 izlazak; odlazak • vi izaći, otići

exorbitant /ɪg'zɔ:bɪtənt/ adj pretjeran

exotic /ɪg'zɒtɪk/ adj egzotičan, neobičan

expand /ɪk'spænd/ vt, vi 1 proširiti (se), povećati (se); razviti (se) 2 prostirati se 3 (on/upon) razraditi 4 orasploložiti se **expanse** /ɪk'spæns/ n prostranstvo **expansion** /ɪk'spænʃn/ n (pro)širenje, povećanje **expansive** adj dobre volje

expatriate /eks'pætrɪət/ n emigrant, iseljenik

expect /ɪk'spekt/ vt 1 očekivati, iščekivati, nadati se 2 coll misliti, pretpostavljati **~ancy** n očekivanje, iščekivanje, nada(nje) **life ~ancy** (prosječan) životni vijek **~ant** adj pun nade **~ant mother** buduća majka **~ation** /,ekspek'teɪʃn/ n 1 očekivanje, iščekivanje, nada 2 **~ations** izgledi **~ing** adj u drugom stanju, trudna

expedient /ɪk'spi:dɪənt/ adj koristan, svrsishodan, uputan • n nužna mjera, sredstvo, izlaz, način **expediency**, **expedience** n svrsishodnost, uputnost; probitačnost

expedition /ˌekspɪ'dɪʃn/ n 1 ekspedicija, putovanje, pohod 2 brzina, hitrina

expel /ɪk'spel/ vt (from) istjerati, izbaciti, prognati

expend /ɪk'spend/ vt utrošiti ~iture /ɪk'spendɪtʃə(r)/ n trošenje, potrošnja, izdatak, rashod

expense /ɪk'spens/ n 1 trošak; potrošnja 2 ~s izdaci **at the ~ of/at sb's ~** na račun, na štetu ~ **account** putni troškovi **expensive** adj skup, skupocjen

experience /ɪk'spɪərɪəns/ n 1 iskustvo 2 doživljaj • vt iskusiti, doživjeti, osjetiti, proživjeti ~d adj (at/in) iskusan; spretan, vješt

experiment /ɪk'sperɪmənt/ n (on) pokus • vi (on/with) vršiti pokuse ~al adj pokusni

expert /'ekspɜ:t/ n (at/in/on) stručnjak, vještak, ekspert • adj stručan, iskusan, vješt ~**ise** /ˌekspɜ:'ti:z/ n 1 stručna procjena, vještačenje, ekspertiza 2 stručno znanje, stručnost

expire /ɪk'spaɪə(r)/ vi 1 isteći (rok), prestati vrijediti 2 lit izdahnuti, preminuti **expiry** /ɪk'spaɪərɪ/ n istek

explain /ɪk'spleɪn/ vt (sth to sb) objasniti ~ **oneself a.** biti jasniji **b.** obrazložiti svoje postupke ~ **sth away** opravdavati **explanation** /ˌeksplə'neɪʃn/ n (of/for) objašnjenje, razjašnjenje, tumačenje **explanatory** /ɪk'splænətrɪ/ adj koji objašnjava

explicit /ɪk'splɪsɪt/ adj izričit, određen

explode /ɪk'spləʊd/ vi,vt 1 eksplodirati 2 aktivirati (bombu) 3 fig prasnuti ~ **into/with laughter** prasnuti u smijeh, puknuti od smijeha ~d adj tech shematski prikazan

exploit (1) /ɪk'splɔɪt/ vt iskorištavati, eksploatirati ~**ation** /ˌeksplɔɪ'teɪʃn/ n iskorištavanje, eksploatacija

exploit (2) /'eksplɔɪt/ n podvig, pothvat

explore /ɪk'splɔ:(r)/ vt 1 istraži(va)ti 2 ispitati ~**r** n istraživač

explosion /ɪk'spləʊʒn/ n 1 eksplozija, prasak 2 provala (smijeha) 3 (nagli) porast **explosive** /ɪk'spləʊsɪv/ adj 1

eksplozivan 2 nagao 3 osjetljiv (pitanje) ○ n eksploziv

exponent /ɪk'spəʊnənt/ n 1 pobornik, predstavnik, zagovornik 2 math eksponent

export /ɪk'spɔ:t/ vi,vt izvoziti • /'ekspɔ:t/ n 1 izvoz 2 ~s izvezena roba ~**er** n izvoznik

expose /ɪk'spəʊz/ vt (to) 1 izložiti, izvrgnuti (opasnosti) 2 (raz)otkriti, prijaviti 3 osvijetliti, eksponirati 4 napustiti, ostaviti (dijete) ~**d** adj izložen, nezaštićen **exposure** /ɪk'spəʊʒə(r)/ n 1 izlaganje, izloženost 2 (raz)otkrivanje 3 ekspozicija **die of exposure** umrijeti od hladnoće

expound /ɪk'spaʊnd/ vi,vt (on/to) form razložiti, iznijeti

express /ɪk'spres/ vt 1 izraziti, izreći 2 GB poslati ekspresno • n 1 (~ **train**) ekspresni vlak 2 GB ekspresna pošiljka • adv ekspresno • adj 1 ekspresni, brz, hitan 2 form izričit, jasan; osobit ~**ly** adv 1 izričito, jasno 2 naročito, posebno ~**ion** /ɪk'spreʃn/ n 1 izražavanje 2 izraz 3 izražajnost ~**ionless** adj bezizražajan ~**ive** adj izražajan

expulsion /ɪk'spʌlʃn/ n izbacivanje, isključenje, izgon, protjerivanje

exquisite /'ekskwɪzɪt/ adj 1 fin, istančan, profinjen 2 izuzetan, odličan, savršen 3 form oštar, snažan (bol, osjećaj)

extend /ɪk'stend/ vi,vt 1 produžiti (se), prostirati se, proširiti (se) 2 (is)pružiti (ruku); raširiti (krila) 3 (sth to sb) pružiti, iskazati 4 **be** ~**ed** napregnuti se **extension** /ɪk'stenʃn/ n 1 produljenje, produžetak; proširenje; nastavak, dodatak 2 kućni telefonski broj **extensive** adj opsežan, opširan, velik, znatan

extent /ɪk'stent/ n 1 duljina, širina, površina, veličina 2 opseg; stupanj; mjera 3 granica **to a certain** ~/**to some** ~ donekle **to such an** ~ **that** u tolikoj mjeri da, toliko da **to the** ~ **of** do (iznosa od) **to what** ~ u kojoj mjeri

extenuating /ɪk'stenjʊeɪtɪŋ/ adj ~ **circumstances** olakotne okolnosti

exterior /ɪk'stɪərɪə(r)/ *adj* (to) vanjski • *n* **1** vanjština, vanjski izgled **2** eksterijer

exterminate /ɪk'stɜ:mɪneɪt/ *vt* iskorijeniti, istrijebiti

external /ɪk'stɜ:nl/ *adj* (to) vanjski; inozemni ~**s** *n pl* vanjski izgled

extinct /ɪk'stɪŋkt/ *adj* **1** izumro **2** ugasli (vulkan) ~**ion** /ɪk'stɪŋkʃn/ *n* **1** izumiranje, propast **2** gašenje (vatre, nade)

extinguish /ɪk'stɪŋgwɪʃ/ *vt form* **1** ugasiti, utrnuti **2** uništiti (**fire**) ~**er** *n* protupožarni aparat

extort /ɪk'stɔ:t/ *vt* (from) iznuditi ~**ion** /ɪk'stɔ:ʃn/ *n* iznuđivanje; ucjena ~**ionate** *adj* pretjeran (cijena)

extra /'ekstrə/ *adj* dodatni, poseban • *adv* dodatno, posebno • *n* **1** dodatak, dodatna naplata/pristojba **2** filmski statist **3** posebno izdanje

extract /ɪk'strækt/ *vt* (from) **1** izvući, izvaditi **2** iznamiti, iznuditi **3** iscijediti, istisnuti • /'ekstrækt/ *n* **1** izvadak (iz knjige) **2** ekstrakt

extracurricular /,ekstrəkə'rɪkjʊlə(r)/ *adj* izvannastavni ~ **activities** slobodne aktivnosti

extradite /'ekstrədaɪt/ *vt* izručiti (kriminalca)

extramarital /,ekstrə'mærɪtl/ *adj* izvanbračni

extramural /,ekstrə'mjʊərəl/ *adj* GB izvansveučilišni, izvanškolski, izvanredan

extraordinary /ɪk'strɔ:dnrɪ/ *adj* **1** neobičan **2** izuzetan, nesvakidašnji, osobit **3** izvanredan (sastanak) **4** poseban, specijalan

extravagant /ɪk'strævəgənt/ *adj* **1** rasipan, rastrošan **2** raskošan **3** raskalašen, razuzdan **4** neumjeren **extravagance** *n* **1** rasipnost **2** raskošnost **3** neumjerenost; ekstravagancija

extreme /ɪk'stri:m/ *adj* krajnji, vrlo velik; najdalji; dubok (starost); najteži (kazna); ekstreman ~**ly** *adv* krajnje, izuzetno, vrlo • *n* krajnost; najviši stupanj **in the** ~ krajnje, do krajnosti **go to** ~**s** ići u krajnosti **extremity** /ɪk'stremətɪ/ *n* **1** krajnost, krajnja granica **2** velika nevolja **extremities** *n pl* **1** udovi **2** krajnje mjere

extricate /'ekstrɪkeɪt/ *vt* raspetljati; ispetljati, izvući ~ **oneself from** iskobeljati se iz

extrovert /'ekstrəvɜ:t/ *n* ekstrovertirana osoba

exuberant /ɪg'zju:bərənt/ *adj* **1** živ(ahan), nesputan **2** bujan

exude /ɪg'zju:d/ *vi,vt* **1** ispuštati, istjecati, curiti, kapati **2** *fig* zračiti

eye /aɪ/ *n* **1** oko **2** vid; pogled **3** ušica igle **4** središte (uragana) **set** ~ **on** ugledati **have an** ~ **to** imati što u vidu **keep an** ~ **on** držati na oku **make** ~**s at** očijukati **in the** ~**s of/in one's** ~**s** u očima, po mišljenju **private** ~ *US sl* privatni detektiv ~**ball** očna jabučica ~**brow** obrva ~**catching** upadljiv ~**lash** trepavica ~**lid** očni kapak, vjeđa **it was an** ~**opener to me** bi mi je otvorilo oči ~**sight** vid ~**sore** *coll* ruglo; šaka u oko *coll* ~**tooth** očnjak ~**wash** *coll* zavaravanje, mazanje očiju ~**witness** očevidac • *vt* gledati, promatrati

F

F, f /ef/ 6. slovo engl. abecede; cf
fab *adj coll* → **fabulous**
fable /'feɪbl/ *n* 1 basna, bajka 2 legenda 3 izmišljotina
fabric /'fæbrɪk/ *n* 1 tkanina 2 građa; tkivo *fig* 3 građevina, tvorevina ~**ate** *vt* 1 stvoriti, izraditi, proizvesti, konstruirati 2 izmisliti, krivotvoriti, skovati ~**ation** *n* 1 izrada 2 izmišljotina, krivotvorina
fabulous /'fæbjʊləs/ *adj* 1 *coll* fantastičan 2 basnoslovan, čaroban
façade /fə'sɑːd/ *n* 1 pročelje; fasada (+ *fig*)
face /feɪs/ *n* 1 lice ~ **to** ~ licem u lice; u četiri oka 2 *mod* za lice **come ~ to ~ with** suočiti se **s in (the)** ~ **of** a. pred čime b. unatoč **fly in the ~ of** sth prkositi 3 izraz lica **straight ~** ozbiljno lice **long ~** kiselo lice **make/pull a ~** kreveljiti se 4 obraz *fig* 5 izgled, pojava, vanjština **put a brave ~ on** sth hrabro podnijeti **on the ~ of it** naizgled 6 prednja/prava strana 7 površina 8 fasada, faseta ~ **of the clock** brojčanik sata ~ **value** a. nominalna vrijednost b. vanjski dojam • *vt,vi* 1 biti licem u lice/nasuprot/pred, gledati (prema, na) 2 suprotstaviti se, prkositi 3 suočiti se, priznati 4 naći se oči u oči ~ **the music** hrabro se suočiti s posljedicama ~ **up to** sth suočiti se s čime 5 (with) prevući, optočiti **facial** /'feɪʃl/ *adj* za lice, ... lica, lični o *n* kozmetički tretman
facetious /fə'siːʃəs/ *adj* u šali, neozbiljan
facile /'fæsaɪl/ *adj* 1 lagan, bez muke 2 okretan 3 površan, olak **facilitate** /fə'sɪlɪteɪt/ *vt* olakšati, pripomoći, omogućiti **facility** /fə'sɪlɪtɪ/ *n* 1 lakoća, spretnost 2 *pl* objekti, sredstva

fact /fækt/ *n* 1 činjenica **the ~s of life** *coll* istina o seksu 2 čin, djelo 3 stvarnost **in ~, as a matter of ~** ustvari, zapravo; štoviše ~**ual** *adj* činjenični, istinski, stvaran
faction /'fækʃn/ *n* frakcija
factor /'fæktə(r)/ *n* čimbenik, faktor
factory /'fæktərɪ/ *n* 1 tvornica 2 *mod* tvornički
faculty /'fækltɪ/ *n* 1 sposobnost, dar, snaga, moć 2 fakultet 3 nastavničko osoblje
fad /fæd/ *n* 1 modna ludost 2 hir
fade /feɪd/ *vt,vi* (away, out) blijedjeti, mutiti (se), tamniti, stišati (se), polako iščezavati, venuti, zamirati
fag /fæg/ *n* 1 *GB sl* cigareta 2 *US derog tab* peder *derog tab* ~**-end** *coll* 1 opušak; čik *coll* 2 škart
faggot *n* (fagot *US*) 1 svežanj pruća 2 *US derog tab* peder *derog tab*
fail /feɪl/ *vt,vi* 1 (in) propasti, ne uspjeti, izjaloviti se 2 pasti (ispit) 3 rušiti na ispitu 4 zatajiti, pokvariti se 5 uzmanjkati, presušiti, podbaciti 6 iznevjeriti 7 propustiti, ne učiniti ~**-safe** *adj* pouzdan • *n* 1 negativna ocjena 2 **without ~** sigurno ~**ing** *n* slabost, mana ~**ure** /'feɪljə(r)/ *n* 1 neuspjeh, propast, promašaj 2 propalica, propala stvar 3 podbacivanje, kvar, zatajenje 4 ~**ure to appear/write** etc. nedolazak/nepisanje
faint /feɪnt/ *adj* 1 slab, nejasan, neodređen, dalek, blag, slabašan, jedva primjetan; blijed; mlitav; neuvjerljiv **to have not the ~est idea** nemati pojma 2 klonuo, iscrpljen • *vi* 1 onesvijestiti se 2 malaksati
fair (1) /feə(r)/ *adj* 1 pošten, nepristran, pravedan, korektan 2 pristojan, dobar 3 po-voljan, lijep 4 čist 5 plav(okos); svi-

jetle puti **6** *arch* lijep **the ~ sex** ljepši spol • *adv* **1** pošteno, nepristrano, pravedno **2** u čisto **~ enough** *coll* u redu, može **~ly** *adv* **1** prilično **2** pošteno, pravedno **3** *coll* sasvim, potpuno

fair (2) *n* sajam, velesajam **~ground** sajmište

fairy /'feərɪ/ *n* **1** vila **2** *mod* vilinski, čaroban **~ lamps/lights** lampioni **~tale** bajka (+ *fig*) **2** *derog* peder *derog*

faith /feɪθ/ *n* **1** (in sb/sth) vjera, povjerenje **2** vjera, religija **3** zadana riječ **4** odanost, vjernost **~ful** *adj* (to) **1** vjeran, odan **2** vjeran, vjerodostojan, točan **the ~ful** vjernici

fake /feɪk/ *n* **1** falsifikat, imitacija, krivotvorina **2** *mod* lažan, krivotvoren **3** prevarant • *vt* (up) krivotvoriti, glumiti

falcon /'fɔ:lkən/ *n* sokol

fall /fɔ:l/ *n* **1** pad, sniženje, spuštanje, opadanje **2** spust, nizbrdica **3** propast, slom, poraz, pad **4** (~s) vodopad **5** *US* jesen • *vi irreg* **1** (down, over) pasti, padati **2** propasti **~ short of** nemati/ne skupiti dovoljno **~ in love** (with) zaljubiti se (u) **~ back** povući se **~ behind** zaostati **~ for** podleći; pasti na *coll* **~ in** urušiti se **~ off** a. opasti b. otpasti **~ on** napasti **~ out** posvaditi se **~ through** propasti

fallacy /'fæləsɪ/ *n* logička pogreška, zabluda

fallen *v irreg* → **fall**

fallible /'fæləbl/ *adj* pogrešiv

false /fɔ:ls/ *adj* **1** lažan **2** pogrešan **3** nevjeran **4** krivotvoren **5** umjetan, lažan **by/on/under ~** pretences na prijevaru **~hood** *n* laž **falsies** *n pl* *coll* lažne grudi **falsify** *vt* **1** krivotvoriti, falsificirati **2** lažno predstaviti, iskriviti

falter /'fɔ:ltə(r)/ *vi,vt* **1** spoticati se, teturati **2** oklijevati **3** pentati, propentati

fame /feɪm/ *n* **1** slava, ugled **2** glas **good/ill ~** dobar/zao glas **~d** *adj* (for) slavan, glasovit (zbog čega)

familiar /fə'mɪlɪə(r)/ *adj* **1** (with) u-

pućen u što **2** (to) poznat **3** običan, svakidašnji, uobičajen **4** prisan, prijateljski, familijaran **~ity** *n* /fə,mɪlɪ'ærətɪ/ **1** (with/to) dobro poznavanje, vladanje **2** prisnost, familijarnost **~ize** /fə'mɪlɪəraɪz/ *vt* **1** (sb/oneself with) upoznati (se) približe s čime **2** upoznati, odomaćiti

family /'fæməlɪ/ *n* **1** obitelj **2** porodica, skupina **3** *mod* kućni, obiteljski **family name** prezime **in the family way** *coll* trudna

famine /'fæmɪn/ *n* glad

famish /'fæmɪʃ/ **1** *vi* umirati od gladi **2** *vt* izgladnjivati, moriti glađu **3** be **~ed** *coll* umirati od gladi

famous /'feɪməs/ *adj* slavan, čuven, poznat

fan (1) /fæn/ *n* **1** lepeza **2** ventilator • *vi,vt* hladiti (se) lepezom; raspirivati (+ *fig*)

fan (2) *n* obožavatelj, ljubitelj, navijač

fanatic /fə'nætɪk/ *n* fanatik • (**~al**) *adj* fanatičan **~ism** /fə'nætɪsɪzəm/ *n* fanatizam, zanos

fancy /'fænsɪ/ *n* **1** mašta **2** utvara **3** (for) sklonost, želja **take a ~ to** zavoljeti • *adj* **1** šaren, ukrašen, luksuzan, šminkerski, ekstravagantan **2** neobičan **~ dress ball** maskenbal • *vt* **1** zamisliti **2** imati dojam, smatrati **3** željeti **I ~ him** sviđa mi se

fang /fæŋ/ *n* očnjak

fanny /'fænɪ/ *n* *US sl* guza

fantasize /'fæntəsaɪz/ *vt* (about) maštati, fantazirati o komu/čemu **fantastic** /fæn'tæstɪk/ *adj* **1** čudesan **2** nemoguć, apsurdan **3** *coll* fantastičan **fantasy** /'fæntəsɪ/ *n* **1** mašta **2** maštarija

far /fɑ:(r)/ *adj* (*comp* farther, further *sup* farthest, furthest) dalek **a ~ cry from** daleko od **the ~ end** drugi kraj/strana • *adv* **1** daleko **by ~** nadaleko **go ~** uspjeti, daleko dogurati **go too ~** pretjerati **~ and near/wide** posvuda, nadaleko **so ~** zasad, dosad **So ~ so good** Zasad je sve u redu **as/so ~ as** a. do b. koliko **~ and away** daleko **~away** *adj* **a.** dalek **b.** (o pogledu) izgubljen **~-fetched** *adj* nategnut, pretjeran

~-off *adj* udaljen **~-reaching** *adj* dalekosežan **~-sighted** *adj* dalekovidan (+ *fig*)

farce /fɑ:s/ *n* farsa (+ *fig*)

fare (1) /feə(r)/ *n* 1 cijena putne karte 2 mušterija (taksista)

fare (2) *n* poslužena hrana **bill of ~** jelovnik

fare (3) *vi* 1 napredovati 2 *arch* ići, putovati

farewell /ˌfeəˈwel/ *int* zbogom • *n* 1 oproštaj 2 *mod* oproštajni

farm /fɑ:m/ *n* farma **~hand** težak • *vt,vi* obrađivati zemlju, uzgajati stoku **~er** *n* farmer; seljak

farrow /ˈfærəʊ/ *vi* oprasiti se • *n* leglo prasadi

fart /fɑ:t/ *vi vulg* prdnuti, prdjeti *vulg* • *n* 1 prdac 2 stari šajser

farther /ˈfɑ:ðə(r)/ *adv comp* dalje, dublje • *adj comp* dalji

farthest /ˈfɑ:ðɪst/ *adv sup* najdalje **at (the) ~ a.** najviše **b.** najkasnije • *adj sup* najdalji

fascinate /ˈfæsɪneɪt/ *vt* očarati, fascinirati **fascinating** *adj* očaravajući, fascinantan

fascism /ˈfæʃɪzəm/ *n* fašizam **fascist** *adj* fašistički o *n* fašist

fashion /ˈfæʃn/ *n* 1 način **after/in a ~** kako-tako **after the ~ of** u stilu 2 moda **set the ~** diktirati modu **man/woman of ~** osoba iz mondenog svijeta **~ plate** modna fotografija **~-show** modna revija • *vt* oblikovati **~able** *adj* moderan, pomodan, eleganatan

fast (1) /fɑ:st/ *adj* 1 brz **my watch is ~** sat mi ide naprijed **~ lane** brza traka na auto-putu **live in the ~ lane** živjeti u brzom ritmu 2 čvrst, trajan, pouzdan • *adv* 1 brzo 2 čvrsto **~en** /ˈfɑ:sn/ *vi,vt* 1 (up, down) učvrstiti (se), pričvrstiti (se), vezati 2 **~en on/upon** prikvačiti (nadimak), prikrpati (se), uprijeti (pogled), uhvatiti se **~ener** *n* kopča, zatvarač

fast (2) *vi* postiti • *n* post

fastidious /fəˈstɪdɪəs/ *adj* sitničav, pedantan

fat /fæt/ *adj* mastan; debeo; utovljen; plodan **a ~ lot** *sl* nimalo **~-head** *n*

glupan • *n* mast, salo, ulje **chew the ~** trabunjati **live off/on the ~ of the land** živjeti kao bubreg u loju • *vt* toviti **~ten** *vi,vt* (up) udebljati (se), utoviti (se) **~ty** *adj* mastan

fate /feɪt/ *n* 1 sudbina, usud 2 smrt, kraj • *vt* **be ~d** biti suđeno (komu) **~ful** *adj* 1 sudbonosan, koban 2 proročki **fatal** *adj* 1 smrtonosan 2 koban, sudbonosan **fatality** /fəˈtælətɪ/ *n* 1 nesreća, smrtni slučaj 2 usud, kob, fatalna slučajnost 3 poginuli; žrtva

father /ˈfɑ:ðə(r)/ *n* 1 otac 2 predak 3 pater **~-in-law** tast, punac, svekar **~hood** *n* očinstvo **~land** *n* domovina **F~ Christmas** Djed Božićnjak **Our F~** Očenaš **like ~ like son** kakav otac, takav *sin* • *vt* postati/biti otac; biti začetnik/autor; stvoriti

fathom /ˈfæðəm/ *n* mjera za dubinu vode (1,8 m) • *vt fig* dokučiti **~less** *adj* bez dna; nedokučiv

fatigue /fəˈti:g/ *n* 1 umor, zamor (metala) 2 *mil* zanimanje 3 *pl* radna uniforma

fatuous /ˈfætʃʊəs/ *adj* isprazan, samozadovoljan

faucet /ˈfɔ:sɪt/ *n US* slavina

fault /fɔ:lt/ *n* 1 mana, nedostatak, slabost **to a ~** pretjerano **find ~** (with) prigovarati 2 pogreška 3 krivnja 4 rasjelina **~y** *adj* pokvaren, neispravan

favour (**favor** *US*) /ˈfeɪvə(r)/ *n* 1 naklonost **be in/out of ~** (with sb) biti u čijoj milosti/nemilosti 2 pomoć, podrška **in ~ of a.** za, na strani **b.** u korist 3 pristranost 4 usluga • *vt* 1 štititi, ići na ruku, biti sklon 2 pretpostavljati, biti pristran 3 potpomoći, omogućiti, olakšati 4 sličiti na koga **~able** *adj* povoljan **~ite** *n* 1 ljubimac 2 povlaštena osoba **the ~ite** o *adj* omiljen, najmiliji **~itism** *n* pristranost, protekcija

fawn (1) /fɔ:n/ *n* lane, srnče • *adj* žućkastosmeđ

fawn (2) *vt* (on) mahati repom, ulagivati se kome

fax /fæks/ *n coll* faks • *vt* poslati faks(om)

fear /fɪə(r)/ *n* strah; bojazan; strahopoštovanje **for ~ (that/lest)** da ne bi • *vi,vt* bojati se, strepiti, strahovati (od, za) **~ful** *adj* 1 zastrašujući, strašan 2 uplašen, zabrinut **~less** *adj* neustrašiv

feasible /ˈfiːzəbl/ *adj* izvediv, moguć; *coll* vjerojatan **feasibility** /ˌfiːzəˈbɪlətɪ/ *n* izvedivost **feasibility study** prethodno ispitivanje

feast /fiːst/ *n* 1 blagdan **movable ~** pomična svetkovina 2 gozba, svečanost • *vi,vt* 1 svetkovati, slaviti, gostiti se **~ on** naslađivati se **~ one's eyes** napasati oči

feat /fiːt/ *n* podvig, pothvat

feather /ˈfeðə(r)/ *n* pero; *pl* perje **birds of a ~ flock together** *prov* svaka ptica svome jatu leti **~bed** *vt* tetošiti; štititi **~-brained** *adj* glup • *vt* okititi/prekriti/napuniti perjem **~ one's nest** napuniti vlastite džepove

feature /ˈfiːtʃə(r)/ *n* 1 lice, crte lica, obličje 2 obilježje, osebujnost 3 glavni članak u novinama; atrakcija, senzacija **~-film** cjelovečernji igrani film • *vt* **the film ~s XY** u filmu igra XY

February /ˈfebruərɪ/ *n* veljača

feckless /ˈfeklɪs/ *adj* beskoristan, isprazan, neodgovoran

fed *v irreg* → **feed**

federal /ˈfedərəl/ *adj* savezni, federalni **federation** /ˌfedəˈreɪʃn/ *n* federacija, savez

fee /fiː/ *n* honorar; pristojba; troškovi; školarina; ulaznina; kotizacija

feeble /ˈfiːbl/ *adj* slab, nemoćan, iscrpljen **~-minded** slabouman

feed /fiːd/ *n* hrana, obrok **~back a.** povratna sprega **b.** povratne informacije • 1 *vt* (on) hraniti (se) (čime) **~ up** toviti, nasititi **I'm fed up** (with) *coll* dosta mi je, puna mi je kapa 2 *vi* jesti, hraniti se 3 *vt* opskrbiti, ubaciti

feel /fiːl/ *n* opip, pipanje, dodir • *vi,vt irreg* 1 pipati, dirati, doticati **~ one's way** oprezno napredovati (+ *fig*) 2 (about for) pokušati napipati, mašiti se 3 osjetiti **~ sb out** pokušati procijeniti 4 osjećati (se); uzeti k srcu, proživljavati **~ for/with** suosjećati s

5 smatrati 6 biti svjestan **~ like** biti raspoložen za što **~ up to** osjećati se sposobnim za **~er** *n* 1 pipak, ticalo 2 prijedlog **put out ~ers** diskretno ispitati teren **~ing** *n* 1 sposobnost osjeta 2 osjećaj, dojam **no hard ~ings** nemojte zamjeriti 3 razumijevanje 4 **bad/ill ~ing** bijes, ogorčenost o *adj* osjećajan, sućutan

feet /fiːt/ → *n pl* **foot**

feign /feɪn/ *vt* hiniti, glumiti

feint /feɪnt/ *n* 1 hinjenje, lukavština 2 zavaravanje, lažni napad, finta • *vi* (at, upon, against) izvesti lažni napad

felicity /fəˈlɪsətɪ/ *n* 1 sreća, zadovoljstvo 2 umjesnost, prikladnost

feline /ˈfiːlaɪn/ *adj* mačji

fell (1) *v irreg* → **fall**

fell (2) /fel/ *vt* oboriti, sasjeći

fellow /ˈfeləʊ/ *n* 1 *coll* momak, čovjek 2 kolega, partner **~-citizen** sugrađanin **~-traveller** suputnik; komunistički simpatizer **~-countryman** zemljak 3 član (nastavničkog zbora/znanstvenog društva), stipendist **~-feeling** osjećaj zajedništva **~ship** *n* 1 zajednica, bratstvo, udruga 2 zajedništvo 3 nastavnički zbor sveučilišta 4 stipendija

felon /ˈfelən/ *n* zločinac, počinitelj zločina **~y** *n* težak zločin, krivično djelo

felt (1) *v irreg* → **feel**

felt (2) /felt/ *n* 1 pust, filc 2 *mod* pusten **~-tip pen** flomaster

female /ˈfiːmeɪl/ *adj* ženski • *n* 1 ženka 2 *derog* ženska feminina / *adj* 1 ženski 2 ženstven **femininity** *n* ženskost, ženstvenost **feminism** /ˈfemɪnɪzəm/ *n* feminizam **feminist** *n* feminist(kinja) o *adj* feministički

fence (1) /fens/ *n* ograda, plot **sit/be on the ~** biti neutralan • *vt* (in) ograditi

fence (2) *vi* 1 mačevati se 2 *fig* parirati (argumentima i sl.) **~r** *n* mačevalac **fencing** *n* mačevanje

fend /fend/ *vi,vt* 1 **~ off** braniti (se), odbiti, odvratiti, odupirati se 2 **~ for oneself** brinuti se sam za sebe, uzdržavati se **~er** *n* US branik, odbojnik, blatobran **~er-bender** manji sudar

fennel /'fenl/ n anis, komorač

feral /'fiərəl/ adj divlji, nepripitomljen, surov

ferment /fə'ment/ n kvasac, ferment **in a ~ u** previranju • vt, vi **1** fermentirati **2** fig vreti, biti u previranju

fern /fɜːn/ n paprat

ferocious /fə'rəuʃəs/ adj okrutan, oštar

ferret /'ferɪt/ n afrički tvor (sličan lasici) • vt, vi ~ **sth out** iščeprkati ~ **about** njuškati

ferroconcrete /,ferəu'kɒŋkriːt/ n armirani beton

ferry /'feri/ n trajekt; skela ~**-boat** trajekt • vt, vi prevoziti preko vode

fertile /'fɜːtaɪl/ adj plodan **fertility** /fə'tɪlətɪ/ n plodnost **fertilize** /'fɜːtəlaɪz/ vt **1** oplođivati **2** gnojiti **fertilizer** n gnojivo **fertilization** n oplodnja

fervent /'fɜːvənt/ adj gorljiv, revan **fervid** /'fɜːvɪd/ adj vatren fig **fervour** (**-vor** US) /'fɜːvə(r)/ n fig žar, žestina

fester /'festə(r)/ vi **1** gnojiti se, upaliti se **2** fig zatrovati se

festival /'festɪvl/ n **1** slavlje, svetkovina, festival **2** mod svečan, praznični **festive** adj svečan, praznični, veseo **festivity** /fe'stɪvətɪ/ n svetkovina, svečanost

fetch /fetʃ/ vt, vi **1** (otići i) donijeti, dovesti, otići po koga/što **2** izmamiti, izazvati ~ **a high price** postići visoku cijenu ~ **sb a slap** coll opaliti pljusku, prilijepiti zaušnicu ~**ing** coll privlačan, zgodan

fete /feɪt/ n svečanost

fetid /'fetɪd/ adj smrdljiv

fetter /'fetə(r)/ n puto, lanci pl (+ fig) • vt sputati, sapeti (+ fig)

fettle /'fetl/ n **in fine/good ~** u dobroj formi, kondiciji

feud /fjuːd/ n zavada, svađa

feudal /'fjuːdl/ adj feudalni, feudalistički

fever /'fiːvə(r)/ n groznica, vrućica; temperatura coll ~**ed** adj grozničav, uzbuđen ~**ish** adj **1** grozničav (+ fig) **2** malaričan

few /fjuː/ adj **1** (+ pl n) malobrojni,

malo (njih), rijetki **2 a ~** nekoliko (njih), nekolicina **a good ~; quite a ~; not a ~** nemali broj **3 the ~** manjina, šačica • pron ~ **of** malo (koga, čega) **a ~ of** nekoliko (koga, čega), neki od

fiancé /fi'ɒnseɪ/ n zaručnik ~**e** n zaručnica

fib /fɪb/ n coll (sitna) laž • vi lagati, pričati izmišljotine

fibre (**-ber** US) /'faɪbə(r)/ n **1** vlakno ~**board** n (+ mod) iverica ~**glass** n (+ mod) fiberglas **2** srž **3** celuloza **fibrous** /'faɪbrəs/ adj vlaknast

fickle /'fɪkl/ n nestalan, prevrtljiv

fiction /'fɪkʃn/ n **1** izmišljotina, neistina, proizvod mašte **2** proza, beletristika

fictitious /fɪk'tɪʃəs/ adj izmišljen, fiktivan

fiddle /'fɪdl/ n **1** violina, gusle **fit as a ~** zdrav kao drijen ~**-stick** gudalo **2** prijevara, pronevjera **be on the ~** varati • vt **1** svirati violinu **2** (about, with) poigravati se, petljati **3** pronevjeriti ~**r** n **1** violinist **2** pronevjeritelj **fiddling** adj coll trivijalan, beznačajan

fidelity /fɪ'delətɪ/ n (to) vjernost, odanost; točnost, preciznost

fidget /'fɪdʒɪt/ vi, vt (about, with) poigravati se, vrpoljiti se • n (the ~**s**) nemir, nervoza ~**y** adj nemiran, nervozan

field /fiːld/ n **1** polje **2** površina, teren **3** nalazište **4** područje (+ fig) ~ **day** dan parade (+ fig) **have a ~ day** slaviti, trijumfirati • vt, vi **1** zaustaviti loptu **2** spretno odgovoriti (na teško pitanje)

fiend /fiːnd/ n **1** vrag, zlobnik **2** coll strastveni ljubitelj, ovisnik ~**ish** adj demonski, vraški, okrutan

fierce /fɪəs/ adj divlji, okrutan, bijesan **2** žestok, strastven **fiery** /'faɪərɪ/ adj gorući, vatren, plamen (+ fig), žestok, strastven

fifth /fɪfθ/ num ord peti ~ **column** peta kolona, petokolonaši

fifty /'fɪftɪ/ num pedeset (50) **the fifties** pedesete (godine)

fig /fɪg/ n smokva

fight /faɪt/ n 1 borba, bitka, tučnjava; svada **put up a (good/poor)** ~ boriti se (srčano/malodušno) 2 borbenost • vi,vt irreg (sb/sth/with/against) boriti se protiv/sa, tući se sa ~ **shy of** ustezati se ~ **back** (sb/at) uzvratiti napad ~**er** n borac ~**ing** n borbe pl

figment /'fɪgmənt/ n izmišljotina, proizvod mašte

figurative /'fɪgjərətɪv/ adj slikovit, figurativan, metaforičan

figure /'fɪgə(r)/ n 1 brojka 2 slika, prikaz 3 lik ~-**head a.** lik na pramcu broda **b.** samo figura 4 obličje, obris, pojava **keep one's** ~ paziti na liniju 5 ličnost, značajna pojava • vt,vi 1 zamisliti 2 (on) računati (na), smatrati ~ **in** odigrati ulogu, pojaviti se ~ **sth/sb out a.** izračunati **b.** coll prokljuviti

filament /'fɪləmənt/ n vlakno, nit

filch /fɪltʃ/ vt ukrasti; zdipiti sl

file (1) /faɪl/ n strugalica • vt strugati **filings** n pl strugotine

file (2) n 1 registrator, fascikl 2 dosje 3 comp datoteka • vt 1 odložiti u dosje, arhivirati 2 podnijeti, uručiti

file (3) n red, stroj, vrsta, kolona **the rank and** ~ obični vojnici (+ fig) • vi ići/stupati u vrsti po jedan

filial /'fɪlɪəl/ adj sinovski, kćerinski

filibuster /'fɪlɪbʌstə(r)/ n opstrukcionaš, filibustjer • vi ometati rad parlamenta

fill /fɪl/ vi,vt 1 (with) ispuniti, napuniti ~ **in** dopuniti, (is)puniti ~ **out** popuniti (se) ~ **up** napuniti (se) 2 zauzeti mjesto, obavljati posao ~ **the bill** coll zadovoljiti 3 izvršiti, udovoljiti • n **drink one's** ~ napiti se do mile volje **cry one's** ~ isplakati se **I have my** ~ (of sth) coll dosta mi je ~**ing** n 1 nadjev 2 punjenje, plomba ~**ing station** benzinska crpka o adj zasitan

fillet /'fɪlɪt/ n odrezak bez kostiju, file • vt očistiti kosti

filly /'fɪlɪ/ n ždrebica

film /fɪlm/ n 1 tanki sloj 2 film, rola filma • vt,vi 1 snimiti 2 (over) prekriti (se) tankim slojem

filter /'fɪltə(r)/ n filtar, prečistač • vt,vi 1 filtrirati (se) 2 fig probijati (se),

procuriti **filtrate** /fɪl'treɪt/ vt,vi filtrirati

filth /fɪlθ/ n prljavština; fig nemoral ~**y** adj prljav; fig besraman, nemoralan ~**y rich** coll vrlo bogat

fin /fɪn/ n 1 peraja 2 fig stabilizator, krilce

final /'faɪnl/ adj 1 krajnji, posljednji, zaključni, završni 2 definitivan, konačni • n (pl) završnica natjecanja, završni ispiti ~**ly** adv 1 na kraju 2 konačno, definitivno ~**ity** /faɪ'nælətɪ/ n konačnost, neopozivost, odlučnost

finance /'faɪnæns/ n financije pl **the Minister of F**~ ministar financija ~ **house/company** novčarsko poduzeće ~**s** novčano stanje • vt financirati **financial** /faɪ'nænʃl/ adj financijski, novčani **the financial year** budžetska godina **financier** /faɪ'nænsɪə(r)/ n financijer, novčar, kapitalist

find /faɪnd/ n nalaz, otkriće • vt irreg 1 pronaći, naći, zateći ~ **oneself** naći se 2 otkriti, iznaći 3 nalaziti, smatrati 4 (out) saznati ~ **sb out** razotkriti 5 donijeti presudu, proglasiti (**view**)- ~**er** tražilo kamere ~**ings** n pl 1 rezultati istrage/istraživanja 2 odluka porote

fine (1) /faɪn/ n globa, kazna • vt (for) globiti, kazniti globom

fine (2) adj 1 lijep; vedar; ugodan 2 nježan, fin 3 sitan 4 tanak, zašiljen 5 (o metalima) čist, pročišćen 6 profinjen, uglađen **I feel** ~ dobro sam • adv coll odlično ~-**spoken** laskav ~**ly** adv 1 lijepo, krasno 2 na sitne komadiće ~**ry** n svečano ruho, svečan izgled

finesse /fɪ'nes/ n rafinman, uglađenost

finger /'fɪŋgə(r)/ n 1 prst (na ruci) ¶ palac = thumb **index** ~/**fore**~ kažiprst **middle** ~ srednjak **ring** ~ prstenjak **little** ~ mali prst **have green** ~**s** biti spretan vrtlar, znati s biljkama **lay a** ~ **on** taknuti **lay/put one's** ~ **on** točno odrediti **not lift a** ~ **to help sb** ne maknuti malim prstom **put the** ~ **on sb** sl potkazati **slip through one's** ~**s** ispustiti iz šaka ~**print** otisak prsta ~**tip** vrh prsta

have sth **at** one's **~tips** imati u malom prstu 2 keks; odrezak • *vt* dirati, poigravati se

finish /'fɪnɪʃ/ *vt,vi* 1 dovršiti, završiti, dokrajčiti (+ *fig*) ~ **sb off** *sl* dotući ~ **sth off/up** pojesti ~ **with sb/sth** biti gotov s kim/čim 2 dovršiti, usavršiti, dotjerati **~ing school** škola za mlade djevojke iz otmjenih obitelji • *n* 1 *sport* finiš **fight to the ~** borba do kraja 2 obrada 3 finoća, uglađenost

finite /'faɪnaɪt/ *adj* ograničen

fir /fɜ:(r)/ *n* jela, jelovina

fire /'faɪə(r)/ *n* 1 vatra **be on ~** gorjeti **set sth on ~/set ~ to sth** zapaliti, potpaliti **take/catch ~** zapaliti se **make up a ~** podstaći vatru **electric/gas ~** električna/plinska grijalica 2 požar 3 paljba, vatra **open/cease ~** (on/at) otvoriti/prekinuti vatru 4 *fig* vatrenost, strast **~arm(s)** vatreno oružje **~brand a.** ugarak **b.** *fig* smutljivac, pobunjenik **~brick** šamotna opeka **~brigade** vatrogasni odred **~bug** *sl* piroman **~cracker** petarda, žabica **~damp** praskavi plin **~engine** vatrogasna kola **~escape** požarne stepenice **~extinguisher** aparat za gašenje požara **~fighter** vatrogasac **~fly** krijesnica **~irons** *pl* mašice, lopatica, žarač **~light** svjetlost s ognjišta **~lighter** nažigač **~man** vatrogasac **~place** kamin ~ **plug** hidrant **~power** vatrena moć **~proof** otporan na vatru, vatrostalan **the ~side** ognjište; *fig* dom, toplina doma **~wood** drvo za potpalu **~work(s)** vatromet • *vi,vt* 1 zapaliti, potpaliti, podmetnuti požar 2 peći, paliti 3 raspaliti, podjariti ~ **sb with sth** oduševiti koga za što 4 (at/into/on/upon) opaliti, ispaliti, pucati ~ **away a.** nastaviti pucati **b.** početi, dati se u što **firing-line** prva borbena linija **firing-squad/party** streljački stroj 5 *coll* dati kome otkaz, otpustiti

firm (1) /fɜ:m/ *adj* 1 čvrst, tvrd 2 nepokolebljiv, strog 3 odlučan, siguran • *adv* čvrsto, pouzdano, nepokolebljivo

firm (2) *n* tvrtka, firma

first /fɜ:st/ *num ord* prvi **at ~ sight** na prvi pogled **in the ~ place** u prvom redu ~ **thing** najprije ~ **things ~** počnimo od najvažnijeg **not to know the ~ thing about** sth nemati pojma o čemu ~ **aid** prva pomoć ~ **class** prva klasa **~-class** *adj* prvoklasan ~ **cost** cijena koštanja **~-fruits** rano voće; *fig* prvi rezultati **~-hand** *adj* iz prve ruke **at ~ hand** neposredno ~ **name** ime ~ **night** premijera ~ **mate** prvi oficir **~ offender** osoba koja do sada nije bila osuđivana **~-rate** *adj* prvorazredan **~-ly** *adv* kao prvo, u prvom redu **• *adv* 1** prvo, kao prvo ~ **of all/~ and foremost** u prvom redu, kao prvo ~ **and last** u cjelini uzevši 2 (po) prvi put 3 prvo, prije čega drugog 4 prije, radije • *n* **at ~** spočetka, isprva **from the ~** od samog početka **~born** *n* prvorođenac o *adj* prvorođen

fiscal /'fɪskl/ *adj* fiskalni, porezni ~ **year** budžetska godina

fish /fɪʃ/ *n* (*pl* ~/~es) riba **have other ~ to fry** imati važnijeg posla ~ **and chips** pohani riblji odresci i prženi krumpirići ~ **finger** (~ **stick** *US*) pohani riblji štapić **~monger** trgovac ribom **~wife** *coll* prostakuša **~y** *adj* 1 (koji ima okus, miris i sl.) po ribi 2 *coll* sumnjiv • *vt,vi* 1 loviti ribu ~ **in troubled waters** loviti u mutnom 2 *fig* pokušavati se dokopati, iznuđivati ~ **up/out** (of/from) izvući, iskopati **~ing** *n* ribolov, ribarstvo **~ing-line** povraz **~ing-rod** štap za pecanje **~ing tackle** pribor za ribolov **~erman** *n* ribar **~ery** *n* lovište ribe, ribolovno područje **deep-sea ~eries** oceanski ribolov **in-shore ~eries** priobalni ribolov

fissure /'fɪʃə(r)/ *n* pukotina, rascjep, fisura

fist /fɪst/ *n* (stisnuta) šaka, pest

fit (1) /fɪt/ *adj* 1 (for) prikladan, valjan, dobar 2 u redu, koji se pristoji **think/see ~** (to do sth) odlučiti se (za što) 3 u dobroj kondiciji, zdrav **~ness** *n* 1 prikladnost 2 zdravlje; dobra kondicija **~ness club** vježbaonica • *vt,vi* 1 odgovarati, pristajati 2 (on) isprobati (odjeću) **3** (on) namjestiti, postaviti **4** (for) osposobiti za što/koga **5 in** (with) uklopiti se ~ **sb/sth out/up** opremiti koga/što za što • *n* kroj, stil ~**ter** *n* **1** krojač **2** monter ~**ting** *adj* prikladan, ispravan, odgovarajući ○ *n* **1** proba (kod krojača) **2** *(pl)* instalacije u zgradi **3** *(pl)* oprema

fit (2) *n* **1** napad **have a** ~ *coll* pobjesniti **2** izljev **by/in** ~**s and starts** na mahove ~**ful** *adj* neredovit, hirovit

five /faɪv/ *num* pet (5) ~**r** *n* **1** *coll* GB novčanica od 5 funti; petak *coll*

fix /fɪks/ *vt, vi* **1** učvrstiti, pričvrstiti, fiksirati **2** privući ~ **one's eyes/attention** on usmjeriti pogled/pozornost na **3** odrediti, uglaviti **4** *sl* podmititi **5** *sl* srediti, obračunati se sa **6** *coll* urediti, pripraviti, popraviti ~ **sb up** (with sth)/~ **sth up** (with sb) srediti, urediti ~ **on/upon** odlučiti se za ~**ed** *adj* učvršćen; fiksan, nepromjenjiv, nepomičan, netremičan ~**edly** *adv* netremice • *n* **1** dilema, neugodna situacija **2** *sl* injekcija droge; fiks *sl* ~**ate** *vt* **1** fiksirati pogledom **2 be** ~**ated** (on) *coll* biti opsjednut čime ~**ation** *n* **1** fiksiranje **2** (on) fiksacija, opsesija, opsjednutost

fixture /'fɪkstʃə(r)/ *n* **1** inventar (+ *fig coll*) **2** datum natjecanja, natjecanje

fizz /fɪz/ *vi* šištati, pjenušati se, muzirati • *n* **1** šištanje **2** mjehurići, pjenušavost ~**y** *adj* pjenušav, gaziran

fizzle /'fɪzl/ *vi* šištati, pištati, cvrčati ~ **out** *fig* ugasiti se, izjaloviti se

flabbergast /'flæbəgɑːst/ *vt coll* zaprepastiti, izbezumiti

flabby /'flæbɪ/ *adj* mlohav

flag (1) /flæg/ *n* zastava, stijeg, barjak F~**Day** *US* Dan zastave, 14. lipnja ~ **officer** admiral ~**ship** admiralski brod ~**staff** jarbol • *vt* **1** ukrasiti/označiti zastavama **2** (down) mahanjem zaustaviti

flag (2) *vi* klonuti, malaksati, oslabiti

flag (3) *vt* popločati ~**stone** kamen za popločavanje

flagrant /'fleɪɡrənt/ *adj* otvoren, očit, flagrantan

flail /fleɪl/ *n* mlatilo • *vt fig* lomatati

flair /fleə(r)/ *n* urođena sposobnost, dar, osjećaj

flak /flæk/ *n* paljba iz protuavionskog oružja; *fig* kritika ~ **jacket** *n* pancirka *coll*

flake /fleɪk/ *n* pahuljica, ljuskica • *vi* (off) ljuštiti se **flaky** *adj* ljuskav

flamboyant /flæm'bɔɪənt/ *adj* sjajan, blistav, kićen, pretjeran

flame /fleɪm/ *n* **1** plamen ~**thrower** *n* bacač plamena **2** sjaj, žar **3** strast, žar **4** ljubav(nik, -nica) • *vi* gorjeti, plamtjeti **flaming** *adj* **1** gorući, plamteći **2** *euph* proklet

flammable /'flæməbl/ *adj* zapaljiv

flan /flæn/ *n* voćna pita

flank /flæŋk/ *n* **1** bok; slabine *pl* **2** strana, krilo, obronak **3** *mil* krilo, bok • *vt* **1** nalaziti se postrance, uz bok, na krilu **2** zaobići bok, napasti s boka

flannel /'flænl/ *n* **1** flanel **2** *pl* športske ljetne hlače

flap /flæp/ *n* **1** udarac, packa **2** poklopac, zaklopac, preklop **3** jezik (cipele) **4** zakrilce **be in/get into a** ~ uzrujati se • *vt, vi* **1** lepršati, mlatarati **2** pljesnuti ~ **away/off** udarcem otjerati **3** uzrujati se

flare (1) /fleə(r)/ *vi* plamtjeti ~ **up a.** buknuti **b.** *fig* razbjesniti se • *n* **1** svjetlost, bljesak **2** baklja, signalna raketa

flare (2) *vi* širiti se zvonoliko, širiti se prema dnu • *n* širenje, izbočenje ~**s** *coll* trapez-hlače

flash /flæʃ/ *n* **1** bljesak (+ *fig*) **in a** ~ u tren oka ~ **in the pan** uspjeh kratka vijeka ~**back** vraćanje radnje u prošlost ~**bulb** bljeskalica, fleš ~**light a.** reflektor **b.** *US* baterijska svjetiljka **2** (news~) kratka vijest **3** *mod coll* upadljiv • *vi, vt* **1** bljesnuti, sijevnuti **2** sinuti, pasti na pamet **3** prohujati, projuriti **4** odaslati, signalizirati ~**y** *adj* kričav, upadljiv; moderan

flat (1) /flæt/ *n* stan ~**let** *n* garsonijera

flat (2) *adj* **1** plosnat, ravan, vodoravan, gladak ~**fish** iverak ~ **feet** ravna stopala **2** *coll* odlučan; neopoziv **3** plitak **4** jednoličan, beživotan; bljutav 5 *mus* snižen • *n* 1 the ~ (of) plosnata strana (mača i sl.) 2 (*pl*) nizina 3 snižena nota, snizilica 4 *US* puknuta guma • *adv* 1 ravno, plosnato **sing** ~ pjevati pogrešno 2 pljoštimice, svom dužinom i širinom 3 potpuno, sasvim ~ **broke** *coll* bez prebite pare ~ **out a.** iz sve snage **b.** iscrpljen **~ly** *adv* odlučno, bezuvjetno, odrješito **~ten** *vt* (out) spljoštiti, izravnati, stanjiti, ispružiti

flatter /'flætə(r)/ *vt* 1 laskati 2 goditi 3 prikazati ljepšim nego što jest 4 ljepo pristajati ~ **oneself** utvarati sebi

flatulence /'flætjʊlʊns/ *n* nadutost, nadimanje; *fig* umišljenost, taština **flatulent** *adj* nadut (+*fig*)

flaunt /flɔ:nt/ *vt* razmetati se čime, šepiriti se

flavour (**flavor** *US*) /'fleɪvə(r)/ *n* okus, aroma, začin • *vt* začiniti **~ing** *n* aroma

flaw /flɔ:/ *n* 1 mana, pogreška 2 pukotina, rasjelina **~less** *adj* savršen

flax /flæks/ *n* lan **~en** *adj* lanen, boje lana, svjetložut

flay /fleɪ/ *vt* oguliti kožu; *fig* oštro kritizirati

flea /fli:/ *n* buha **send sb off with a ~ in his ear** očitati komu bukvicu **~-bitten** *adj* šaren, točkast

fleck /flek/ *n* 1 pjegica, mrlja 2 komadić, čestica • *vt* poprskati, prošarati

fled *v irreg* → **flee**

fledged /fledʒd/ *adj* **fully-~** *adj fig* potpuno razvijen **fledg(e)ling** *n* mladi ptić; *fig* žutokljunac

flee /fli:/ *vi,vt irreg* pobjeći iz, bježati od, izbjegavati

fleece /fli:s/ *n* runo, runasta kosa • *vt coll* opljačkati; odrati *coll*

fleet /fli:t/ *n* 1 flota 2 vozni park

Fleet Street *n GB fig* novinstvo, tisak

fleeting /'fli:tɪŋ/ *adj* kratkotrajan, prolazan

flesh /fleʃ/ *n* 1 meso ~ **wound** laka ozljeda 2 the ~ put, tijelo

flew *v irreg* → **fly**

flex (1) /fleks/ *n* žica

flex (2) *vt* savijati, napinjati (mišiće) ~ **one's muscles** demonstrirati silu

~ible *adj* fleksibilan, elastičan, savitljiv, prilagodljiv **~itime** klizno radno vrijeme

flick /flɪk/ *n* 1 lak udarac, čvrga 2 trzaj **~knife** nož skakavac 3 *film* the **~s** *coll* film(ska umjetnost) • *vt* lako udariti, lupnuti ~ **sth away/off** otresti

flicker /'flɪkə(r)/ *vi* svjetlucati, treperiti, palucati • *n* svjetlucanje, trepet; bljesak

flight (1) /flaɪt/ *n* 1 let **in-~** za vrijeme leta ~ **recorder** crna kutija 2 jato (ptica), tuča (strelica i sl.) 3 uzlet, izljev 4 stubište 5 eskadrila

flight (2) /flaɪt/ *n* bijeg, uzmak **take ~/take to ~** pobjeći **~y** *adj* nestalan, kolebljiv

flimsy /'flɪmzɪ/ *adj* 1 lagan, tanak, krhak 2 tanak, neuvjerljiv • *n* pelir papir

flinch /flɪntʃ/ *vi* (from) ustuknuti pred čim, trgnuti se

fling /flɪŋ/ *vt,vi irreg* 1 baciti, hitnuti 2 baciti se, mahati 3 srnuti, odjuriti • *n* afera

flint /flɪnt/ *n* kremen

flip /flɪp/ *vt, vi* baciti, hitnuti, zvrcnuti • *n* lagani udarac • *adj coll* olak **the ~ side** *coll* B-strana (gramofonske ploče)

flippant /'flɪpənt/ *adj* površan; neozbiljan, lakomislen

flipper /'flɪpə(r)/ *n* peraja (ne u riba)

flirt /flɜ:t/ *vi* (with) 1 očijukati, flertati 2 poigravati se, razmatrati **~ation** *n* flert **~atious** *adj* koketan

float /fləʊt/ *n* 1 plovak, plutača 2 otvoreni kamionet • *vi,vt* 1 plutati, lebdjeti 2 odsukati 3 pokrenuti (posao), financijski potpomoći 4 uvesti plutajući tečaj valute 5 pustiti u optjecaj, širiti **~ing** *adj* kolebljiv, nestalan **~ing debt** kratkoročni zajam **~ation** (**flotation**) *n* pokretanje poduzeća

flock /flɒk/ *n* 1 jato (ptica) 2 stado (ovaca, koza; vjernika *fig*) 3 gomila 4 stado (vjernika) • *vi* okupljati se, gomilati se

flog /flɒg/ *vt* 1 bičevati, šibati ~ **a dead horse** soliti more 2 *sl* prodati; utrapiti *sl*

flood /flʌd/ *n* **1** poplava (+ *fig*) **2** (~**tide**) plima ~**gate** brana, ustava ~**lights** reflektori • *vt,vi* poplaviti, preplaviti (+ *fig*)

floor /flɔː(r)/ *n* **1** pod **2** kat **ground** ~ *GB* prizemlje **first** ~ **a.** *US* prizemlje **b.** *GB* prvi kat

flop /flɒp/ *vi,vt* **1** bacakati se, praćakati se, skljokati se, pljusnuti ~ **down** tresnuti (na pod) **2** propasti • *n* **1** (nespretan, težak) pad **belly-**~ *n* skok na trbuh **2** fijasko, neuspjeh ~**py** *adj* opušten, koji visi ~**py disk** *comp* disketa

floral /flɔːrəl/ *adj* cvjetni, cvjetast

florid /flɒrɪd/ *adj* **1** kićen **2** rumene puti

florist /flɒrɪst/ *n* cvjećar

floss /flɒs/ *n* svilene niti *pl* **dental** ~ zubna svila

flotsam /flɒtsəm/ *n* olupina broda ~ **and jetsam** *fig* žrtve

flounder /flaʊndə(r)/ *vi* **1** koprcati se, posrtati **2** *fig* zapinjati

flour /flaʊə(r)/ *n* brašno • *vt* pobrašniti

flourish /flʌrɪʃ/ *vi,vt* **1** cvasti, napredovati **2** razmahivati se, vitlati **3** biti na vrhuncu • *n* **1** ukrasna vitica (potpisa) **2** tuš, fanfare

flout /flaʊt/ *vt* prezreti, ne obazirati se na

flow /fləʊ/ *vi* **1** teći **2** padati • *n* pritjecanje; bujica; lepršanje

flower /flaʊə(r)/ *n* cvijet (+ *fig*) **in** ~ u cvatu ~**bed** lijeha ~**pot** lonac za cvijeće ~**ed** *adj* cvjetast ~**y** *adj* **1** cvjetan, pun cvijeća **2** kićen

flown *v irreg* → **fly**

flu /fluː/ *n coll* gripa

fluent /fluːənt/ *adj* tečan, koji tečno govori **fluency** *n* dobro vladanje

fluff /flʌf/ *n* **1** paperje **2** neuspio pokušaj • *vt* **1** (out) našušuriti se, razrahliti **2** *coll* upropastiti, zabrljati ~**y** *adj* pahuljast, mucast

fluid /fluːɪd/ *adj* **1** tekuć **2** *fig* mekan (pokret) • *n* tekućina ~**ity** /fluːˈɪdətɪ/ *n* **1** tekuće stanje **2** mekoća (pokreta)

fluke /fluːk/ *n* sretan slučaj, slučajnost

flung *v irreg* → **fling**

flunk /flʌŋk/ *vt,vi* (out) pasti (ispit),

rušiti (na ispitu)

fluorine /flʊəriːn/ *n* fluor

flurry /flʌrɪ/ *n* **1** nalet vjetra, nagli pljusak i sl. **2** *fig* pometnja

flush (1) /flʌʃ/ *adj* (with) **1** poravnat, u ravnini **2** pun čega

flush (2) *n* **1** mlaz vode, ispiranje **2** navala krvi u lice, rumenjenje **3** uzbuđenje **4** (**first** ~) procvat, obilje, sjaj • *vi,vt* **1** zarumeniti se **2** natjerati krv u lice **3** isprati, isplahnuti ~ **the toilet** pustiti vodu u zahodu **4** preplaviti, šiknuti ~ **out/from** istjerati iz zaklona

fluster /flʌstə(r)/ *vt* zbuniti, uznemiriti • *n* zbunjenost, nervoza

flute /fluːt/ *n* flauta ~ **glass** šampanjska čaša

flutter /flʌtə(r)/ *vi,vt* lepršati, lepetati, uskomešati se, ustrčati se, lupati (srce) • *n* **1** lepet **2** nervoza, usplahirenost

fluvial /fluːvɪəl/ *adj* riječni

flux /flʌks/ *n* **1** stalna mijena **2** protjecanje

fly (1) /flaɪ/ *n* muha ~**blown** zagađen od muha, pokvaren ~**fish** pecati na mušicu ~**trap** muholovka ~**weight** boksač muha kategorije

fly (2) *vi,vt irreg* **1** letjeti **2** prevoziti zrakom **3** *fig* poletjeti, zaletjeti se, žuriti (se) ~ **at sb** napasti ~ **into a rage/passion/temper** ražestiti se **4** puštati u zrak (zmaja), vijati (zastavu) **5** pobjeći iz ~**er** (**flier**) *n* **a.** letač **b.** letak ~**ing** *adj* leteći ~**ing boat** hidroavion ~**ing colours** izvješene zastave **come through/off with** ~**ing colours** trijumfirati ~**ing saucer** leteći tanjur ~**ing visit** kratki posjet

fly (3) *n* rasporak; šlic *coll*

flyleaf /flaɪliːf/ *n* čisti list na početku ili kraju knjige

flyover /flaɪəʊvə(r)/ *n GB* nadvožnjak

foal /fəʊl/ *n* ždrijebe

foam /fəʊm/ *n* **1** pjena **2** (~**rubber**) pjenasta guma • *vi* pjeniti se, zapjeniti se (+ *fig*) ~**y** *adj* pjenušav, pjenast, zapjenjen

fob /fɒb/ *vt* ~ **sth off on sb** / ~ **sb off with sth** **1** uvaliti (komu nešto) bezvrijedno) **2** lažno obećavati, umirivati lažnim obećanjima

focus /'fəukəs/ *n* fokus, žarište (+*fig*) • *vt,vi* **1** (on) fokusirati **2** ~ **on** baviti se

focal *adj* **1** fokusni **2** u žarištu, glavni

fodder /'fɒdə(r)/ *n* stočna hrana

foe /fəu/ *n* neprijatelj

foetus (fetus) /'fi:təs/ *n* fetus, plod

foetal *adj* fetusni, fetalni

fog /fɒg/ *n* magla **in a ~** *fig* zbunjen, u neznanju ~**lamp** maglenka • *vt* **1** prekriti maglom **2** *fig* zbuniti, zamutiti ~**gy** *adj* **1** maglovit **2** nejasan, zbrčkan

fog(e)y /'fəugɪ/ *n* derog (old ~) konzervativac

foible /'fɔɪbl/ *n* slabost, slaba strana

foil (1) /fɔɪl/ *n* **1** folija **2** kontrast

foil (2) *n* floret

foil (3) *vt* pokvariti, pomrsiti

fold (1) /fəuld/ *vt,vi* savinuti (se), presaviti (se), sklopiti (se), složiti ~ (up) *fig coll* propasti • ~ **one's arms** prekrižiti ruke • *n* nabor ~**er** *n* fascikl

fold (2) *n* **1** obor **2** *fig* vjernici **return to the** ~ vratiti se domu/vjeri

foliage /'fəulɪɪdʒ/ *n* lišće

folk /fəuk/ *n* **1** *collect pl* ljudi **2** narod **3** *mod* narodni **4** *pl coll* obitelj

follow /'fɒləu/ *vt,vi* **1** slijediti, dolaziti/ići/biti iza ~ **through** izvršiti (zadaću, obećanje) **2** ići dalje, nastaviti istim putem **3** *fig* pratiti (govor i sl.) **4** povoditi se za ~ **suit** slijediti čiji primjer **5** (from) proizlaziti iz ~ **sth up** nastaviti raditi na ~**er** *n* sljedbenik ~**ing** *adj* sljedeći, idući o *n* sljedbeništvo, pristaše

folly /'fɒlɪ/ *n* ludost

foment /fəu'ment/ *vt fig* podjarivati

fond /fɒnd/ *adj* **1 be ~ of** voljeti **2** nježan, pun ljubavi **3** slijepo zaljubljen **4** pust (snovi i sl.) ~**ly** *adv* **1** s ljubavlju **2** naivno

fondle /'fɒndl/ *vt* maziti, milovati, gladiti

font /fɒnt/ *n* **1** krstionica **2** *comp* tip slova

food /fu:d/ *n* **1** hrana **fast ~** hrana koja se jede s nogu **2** namirnice ~**-stuffs** prehrambeni proizvodi

fool /fu:l/ *n* **1** budala, glupan **2** (dvor-

ska) luda **All F~s' Day** 1. travnja • *vi,vt* **1** (around/about) glupirati se; zezati se *coll* **2** (sb out of sth) prevariti, nasamariti koga za što ~**ery** *n* budalaština ~**hardy** *adj* ludo odvažan ~**ish** *adj* glup, budalast ~**proof** *adj* stoposto provjeren

foot /fut/ *n* (*pl* **feet**) **1** stopalo **2** noga **on** ~ pješice **have feet of clay** biti kukavica/slabić **put one's ~ down** *coll* prosvjedovati, ustrajati **put one's ~ in it** *coll* zabrljati, izvaliti glupost **put one's best ~ forward** raditi iz sve snage **sweep sb off his feet** oboriti s nogu **3** korak **4** podnožje **5** stopa ~**-and-mouth disease** slinavka i šap ~**ball** nogometna lopta; nogomet ~**bridge** pješački most ~**fall** korak ~**fault** *sport* prijestup ~**hold** uporište ~**lights** svjetla na rubu pozornice **the ~lights** *fig* glumačka profesija ~**loose (and fancy free)** slobodan kao ptica na grani ~**man** sluga, lakaj ~**note** bilješka u dnu stranice; fusnota *coll* ~**print** otisak stopala ~**rule** ravnalo ~**step** korak **follow in sb's ~steps** ići nečijim stopama ~**wear** obuća • *vt, vi* ~ **it** *coll* ići pješice ~ **the bill** *coll* platiti račun ...~**ed** *adj* (u složenicama) ... nogu/stopala/koraka ~**age** *n* metraža (filma i sl.) ~**ing** *n* **1** uporište **2** status, položaj **be/get on a friendly** etc. ~**ing** (with) biti u prijateljskim itd. odnosima sa

for /fə(r), fɔː(r)/ *prep* **1** prema, za **2** radi **go ~ a walk** otići u šetnju **what is it ~?** čemu to služi? **take sb ~ sb** zamijeniti koga s kime, smatrati ~ **all that** unatoč svemu **stand ~** predstavljati, značiti **3** zbog, od **4** unatoč **5 ~ two days** dva dana ~ **good** zauvijek **6 ~ miles** miljama • *conj* jer, zato što

forage /'fɒrɪdʒ/ *n* stočna hrana • *vi* ~ **for** ići u potragu za (hranom i sl.)

forasmuch as /ˌfɔːrəz'mʌtʃ əz/ *conj* budući da

foray /'fɒreɪ/ *n* pljačkaški pohod, napad • *vi* krenuti u (pljačkaški) pohod

forbade *v irreg* → **forbid**

forbear (1) /fɔː'beə(r)/ *vt,vi irreg*

(from) ustegnuti se **~ance** n strpljenje, samokontrola

forbear (2) n predak

forbid /fə'bɪd/ vt irreg zabraniti **~ding** adj strog, odbojan, prijeteći

forbidden v irreg → **forbid**

forbore, forborne v irreg → **forbear**

force /fɔːs/ n 1 snaga, moć **in** ~ u velikom broju 2 sila, snaga **armed ~s** pl vojska 3 energija 4 valjanost, djelovanje (zakona) **in/into** ~ na snazi • vt 1 natjerati, prisiliti, nametnuti 2 prodrijeti, silom ući/otvoriti **~d landing** prisilno slijetanje **~d march** usiljeni marš » **sb's hand** natjerati koga na djelovanje 3 forsirati **~d** adj usiljen **~-feed** vt hraniti silom, šopati (+ fig) **~ful** adj snažan, prodoran

forcible /'fɔːsəbl/ adj 1 nasilan, pod prijetnjom sile 2 uvjerljiv

ford /fɔːd/ n gaz

fore- /fɔː(r)/ prefix označava da je glavni dio složenice prednji, prvi, prije

fore /fɔː(r)/ adj prednji • n **to the ~** na čelu

forearm /ˌfɔːr'ɑːm/ n podlaktica

forebode /fɔː'bəʊd/ vt 1 ukazivati na, nagovješćivati 2 slutiti, predosjećati **foreboding** n zla slutnja

forecast /'fɔːkɑːst/ vt irreg prognozirati • n prognoza

forefather /'fɔːfɑːðə(r)/ n pl predak

forefinger /'fɔːfɪŋɡə(r)/ n kažiprst

forefoot /'fɔːfʊt/ n prednja noga

forefront /'fɔːfrʌnt/ n **the ~** prvi plan, prvi red, prvi (bojni) redovi

forego /fɔː'ɡəʊ/ vi,vt irreg → **go** prethoditi **~ing** adj gorespomenuti, navedeni **foregone conclusion** očit zaključak

foreground /'fɔːɡraʊnd/ n prednji/prvi plan (+ fig)

forehand /'fɔːhænd/ n sport forhend

forehead /'fɒrɪd/ n čelo

foreign /'fɒrən/ adj 1 stran, inozemni **the F~ Office** GB ministarstvo vanjskih poslova **F~ Secretary** GB ministar vanjskih poslova **~ exchange** devize pl 2 (to) tuđ, neprirodan 3 stran **~er** n stranac

foreleg /'fɔːleɡ/ n prednja noga

forelock /'fɔːlɒk/ n šiške **touch one's ~** ponizno pozdraviti

foreman /'fɔːmən/ n 1 predradnik 2 predsjednik porote

foremost /'fɔːməʊst/ adj prvi, glavni, najistaknutiji **first and ~** u prvom redu, ponajprije

forename /'fɔːneɪm/ n ime

forensic /fə'rensɪk/ adj sudski

foreplay /'fɔː(r)pleɪ/ n (seksualna) predigra

forerunner /'fɔːrʌnə(r)/ n 1 glasnik, navještač 2 preteča, prethodnik

foresee /fɔː'siː/ vt irreg (→ **see**) predvidjeti **~able** adj predvidiv **the ~able future** dogledno vrijeme

foresight /'fɔːsaɪt/ n moć predviđanja, dalekovidnost

foreskin /'fɔːskɪn/ n kožica na vršku penisa

forest /'fɒrɪst/ n 1 šuma (+ fig) 2 mod šumski **~er** n šumar **~ry** n šumarstvo

forestall /fɔː'stɔːl/ vt preduhitriti

foretaste /'fɔːteɪst/ n (of) navještaj

foretell /fɔː'tel/ vt irreg (→ **tell**) proricati, najaviti

forethought /'fɔːθɔːt/ n predumišljaj, smotrenost

forever /fə'revə(r)/ adv zauvijek, vječito

foreword /'fɔːwɜːd/ n predgovor

forfeit /'fɔːfɪt/ vt 1 zaplijeniti, oduzeti 2 proigrati, izgubiti vlastitom krivnjom • n zalog

forgave v irreg → **forgive**

forge (1) /fɔːdʒ/ n 1 kovačnica 2 talionica • vt 1 iskovati (+ fig) 2 krivotvoriti **~er** n krivotvoritelj **~ry** n krivotvorenje, krivotvorina

forge (2) vi ~ **ahead** napredovati, probiti se na čelo

forget /fə'ɡet/ vt,vi irreg (→ **get**) 1 (about) zaboraviti, ne sjetiti se, smetnuti s uma — **it!** ništa od toga! **~-me-not** potočnica 2 zanemariti **~ful** adj zaboravan

forgive /fə'ɡɪv/ vt,vi irreg (→ **give**) 1 ~ **sb** (sth/for doing sth) oprostiti 2 otpustiti (dug) **forgiving** adj pomirljiv, blag **~ness** n oprost

forgo /fɔː'ɡəʊ/ vt irreg (→ **go**) odreći

se

fork /fɔːk/ *n* **1** vilica ~ **lunch/supper** švedski stol **2** vile **3** vilica kotača **4** račvanje putova ~**lift truck** viljuškar • *vt,vi* **1** nositi, premetati i sl. vilama **2** račvati se **3** skrenuti ~**ed** *adj* račvast

forlorn /fɔˈlɔːn/ *adj poet* nesretan, napušten

form /fɔːm/ *n* **1** oblik **2** lik, oblik, obličje **3** forma, oblik **4** oblik, vid, vrsta **5** formalnost, etiketa **6** formular **7** forma, kondicija **8** *GB* razred • *vt,vi* **1** oblikovati (se), (s)tvoriti, formirati **2** graditi, razvijati, stvarati **3** organizirati (se) **4** nastajati, javiti se, roditi se ~**al** *adj* **1** formalan, služben, svečan **2** pravilan, simetričan **3** vanjski, pojavan ~**ality** *n* **1** uštogljenost **2** formalnost ~**at** *n* format, oblik, stil, način provođenja o *vt comp* oblikovati; formatirati *comp* ~**ation** *n* **1** oblikovanje, formiranje **2** formacija, stroj, poredak **3** *geol* sastav

former /ˈfɔːmə(r)/ *adj* **1** nekadašnji, bivši, prijašnji **2** (+ *pron*) the ~ prvi (od dvoje) ~**ly** nekad, prije

Formica /fɔːˈmaɪkə/ *n TM* ultrapas

formidable /ˈfɔːmɪdəbl/ *adj* **1** strašan, zastrašujući **2** impresivan, golem, koji ulijeva strahopoštovanje

formula /ˈfɔːmjʊlə/ *n* (*pl* ~**s/**~**e**) formula ~**te** *vt* formulirati

fornication /ˌfɔːnɪˈkeɪʃn/ *n* blud, razvrat

forsake /fəˈseɪk/ *vt irreg* ostaviti (na cjedilu), napustiti, odreći se

forsaken *v irreg* → **forsake**

forswear /fɔːˈsweə(r)/ *vt irreg* (→ **swear**) ostaviti se ~ **oneself** krivo se zakleti

fort /fɔːt/ *n* utvrda ~**ify** *vt* (against) utvrditi, učvrstiti položaje, ojačati, okrijepiti, oboružati se (+ *fig*) ~**ification** *n* utvrđenje ~**ress** *n* tvrđava

forte /ˈfɔːteɪ/ *n* jaka strana

forth /fɔːθ/ *adv* **1** *arch* van **2** *form* nadalje **and so** ~ i tako dalje **back and** ~ tamo i natrag, amo-tamo ~**coming** *adj* **1** predstojeći, idući **2** uslužan ~**right** *adj* otvoren, izravan ~**with** *adv* odmah, smjesta

fortitude /ˈfɔːtɪtjuːd/ *n* hrabrost, odvažnost

fortnight /ˈfɔːtnaɪt/ *n GB* dva tjedna ~**ly** *adv* svaka dva tjedna

fortuitous /fɔːˈtjuːɪtəs/ *adj form* slučajan

fortune /ˈfɔːtʃuːn/ *n* **1** slučaj, sudbina **2** sreća (dobra, loša), sretan slučaj **try one's** ~ okušati sreću **tell sb his** ~ gatati ~**teller** gatara **3** uspjeh, blagostanje, bogatstvo, velik imetak **come into a** ~ naslijediti imetak **make a** ~ zaraditi mnogo novaca ~ **hunter** lovac na miraz **soldier of** ~ plaćenik **fortunate** *adj* sretan, povoljan **fortunately** *adv* nasreću, srećom

forward /ˈfɔːwəd/ *adj* **1** prednji, koji kreće i sl. (u)naprijed **2** napredan **3** preuzetan, nagao, drzak **4** ekstreman, pretjeran • *vt* **1** potpomoći **2** poslati, odaslati ~**ing agent** *n* otpremnik, špediter **3** poslati (pismo) na novu adresu ~**ing address** nova adresa • (~**s**) *adv* **1** naprijed **2** nadalje, ubuduće **bring** ~ skrenuti pozornost na, ukazati na

foster /ˈfɒstə(r)/ *vt* njegovati, brinuti se za; gajiti ~**brother/sister** brat/sestra po mlijeku ~**child** posvojče ~ **parent** skrbnik, staratelj ~**mother** pomajka

fought *v irreg* → **fight**

foul /faʊl/ *adj* **1** odvratan; kužan, zagađen **2** zao, pokvaren, prostački, ružan ~ **play a.** *sport* prekršaj; faul **b.** zločin **fall** ~ **of** *fig* doći u sukob s • *n sport* prekršaj • *vt,vi* (up) **1** zagaditi, onečistiti **2** sudariti se, sukobiti se, zaplesti se **3** *sport* počiniti prekršaj

found (1) *v irreg* → **find**

found (2) /faʊnd/ *vt* **1** utemeljiti, osnovati, ustanoviti **2** ~ **sth on/upon** zasnovati na ~**ation** *n* **1** utemeljenje, osnutak **2** ustanova, zavod, zaklada, fondacija **3** (*pl*) temelji ~**ation-stone** kamen temeljac **4** osnova, načelo, polazište ~**ation cream** podloga za šminku ~**er** *n* osnivač, utemeljitelj

foundling /ˈfaʊndlɪŋ/ *n* nahoče

foundry /ˈfaʊndrɪ/ *n* ljevaonica

fountain /'fauntɪn/ n 1 izvor, vrelo (+ *fig*) 2 vodoskok, fontana ~**pen** nalivpero ~-**head** *fig* izvor

four /fɔː(r)/ *num* četiri (4) ~-**letter word** prosta riječ **on all** ~**s** četveronoške

four- *prefix* četvero- ~**poster** krevet s baldahinom

fowl /faʊl/ n 1 perad 2 kokoš 3 *arch* ptica **wild** ~ divljač (ptice)

fox /fɒks/ n lisica ~-**glove** n naprstak, digitalis ~**hole** rov ~**hound** pas lisičar ~**hunt** lov na lisice ~**y** *adj* lukav; prefrigan *coll* • *vt* prevariti, zbuniti

foyer /'fɔɪeɪ/ n predvorje, foaje

fracas /'fræka:/ n bučna svađa

fraction /'frækʃn/ n 1 djelić, mrvica 2 razlomak

fracture /'fræktʃə(r)/ n (prije)lom, fraktura

fragile /'frædʒaɪl/ *adj* loman, krhak

fragment /'frægmənt/ n fragment, ulomak, krhotina ~**ation** /,frægmen'teɪʃn/ n ~**ation bomb** rasprskavajuća bomba

fragrant /'freɪgrənt/ *adj* mirisan **fragrance** n miomiris, parfem

frail /freɪl/ *adj* slabašan, krhak ~**ty** n 1 krhkost 2 (moralna) slabost, mana

frame /freɪm/ n 1 okosnica, konstrukcija, kostur 2 okvir 3 tijelo ~ **of mind** stanje duha ~**work** sistem, struktura, okosnica • *vt, vi* 1 uobličiti, zamisliti, stvoriti 2 uokviriti 3 razvijati (se), obećavati 4 *sl* lažno okriviti ~**up** *sl* zavjera

franchise /'fræntʃaɪz/ n 1 **the** ~ pravo glasa 2 koncesija • *vt* dati koncesiju

frank /fræŋk/ *adj* iskren, otvoren

frantic /'fræntɪk/ *adj* mahnit, pomaman

fraternal /frə'tɜːnl/ *adj* bratski **fraternity** n 1 bratstvo, osjećaj bratstva 2 bratstvo, udruženje 3 *US* studentsko udruženje **fraternize** /'frætənaɪz/ *vi* (with) bratimiti se, sprijateljiti se

fraud /frɔːd/ n 1 prijevara, podvala ~**ulent** /'frɔːdjʊlənt/ *adj* prijevaran, lažan

fraught /frɔːt/ *adj* pun

fray (1) /freɪ/ n sukob

fray (2) *vt, vi* izlizati (se), otrcati (se) ~**ed nerves** slabi živci

freak /friːk/ n 1 ćud, mušica, hir 2 *mod* neočekivan, neuobičajen 3 nakaza, hir prirode • *vt, vi* ~ **out** *sl* **a.** biti pod utjecajem droge; otkačiti se *sl* **b.** pobjesnjeti ~**ish**, ~**y** *adj* abnormalan, neprirodan

freckle /'frekl/ n pjegica • *vt, vi* osuti (se) pjegicama

free /friː/ *adj* 1 slobodan 2 oslobođen, na slobodi **feel** ~ **to ask** slobodno pitajte **allow sb/give sb a** ~ **hand** dati odriješene ruke ~ **enterprise** slobodno poduzetništvo ~-**handed** darežljiv ~**hold** neograničeno vlasništvo ~**holder** vlasnik nekretnine ~-**labour** radnici koji nisu članovi sindikata ~-**lance** *vi* raditi honorarno/kao vanjski suradnik ~**lancer** slobodnjak, nezavisni pisac/novinar i sl. ~-**range chicken/eggs** domaći pilići/jaja ~ **speech** sloboda govora ~-**spoken** otvoren ~-**way** autoput ~ **will** slobodna volja ~ **from** bez 3 besplatan ~ **of charge** besplatan, besplatno **for** ~ *coll* besplatno ~ **on board** franko-brod 4 obilan, bogat (čime), koji ne škrtari 5 nepristojan • *vt* (from/of) osloboditi ~**dom** n 1 sloboda 2 slobodna uporaba, pravo na uporabu **give sb/receive the** ~ **of a town/city** postati počasni građanin ~**dom fighter** borac za slobodu

freeze /friːz/ *vt, vi irreg* 1 (over, up) zalediti (se), smrznuti (se), zamrznuti (se) **freezing point** ledište **make one's blood** ~ prestraviti **frozen food** zamrznuta hrana 2 ukipiti se ~! *int* stoj! • n 1 mraz, velika hladnoća 2 zamrzavanje plaća, cijena itd. **deep-** ~ duboko zamrzavanje ~**r** n hladnjak za duboko zamrzavanje

freight /freɪt/ n 1 transport robe morem (*US* i kopnom) 2 vozarina ~**liner** brzi teretni vlak ~ **train** *US* teretni vlak • *vt, vi* ~ (with) 1 tovariti, ukrcati robu 2 otpremiti robu ~**er** n teretni avion/brod

French /frentʃ/ *adj* francuski **take** ~ **leave** otići bez pozdrava ~ **bread/loaf/stick** francuski kruh;

francuz *coll* ~ **dressing** ulje i ocat ~ **fries** *US* pomfrit

frenzy /'frenzɪ/ *n* ludilo, mahnitost

frequent /frɪ'kwent/ *vt* biti čest gost, često ići • /'friːkwənt/ *adj* čest, uobičajen **frequency** /'friːkwənsɪ/ *n* 1 učestalost 2 frekvencija

fresh /freʃ/ *adj* 1 svjež ~**man** brucoš ~**water** slatka voda 2 nov; drugačiji 3 svjež, prohladan, čist 4 živ, zdrav 5 *coll* drzak, bezobrazan • (~**ly**) *adv* svježe, netom, nedavno ~**-picked**, ~*ly* *picked* ~**er** brucoš ~**en** *vt,vi* (up) osvježiti, oživjeti, ojačati

fret /fret/ *vi,vt* 1 brinuti se, uzrujavati se, biti loše volje 2 izgristi, izjesti ~*n* uzrujanost, razdražljivost ~**ful** *adj* uzrujan, razdražljiv, srdit

Freudian /'frɔɪdɪən/ *adj* frojdovski ~ **slip** *coll* slučajna pogreška koja otkriva podsvjesne želje

friar /'fraɪə(r)/ *n* fratar

friction /'frɪkʃn/ *n* 1 trenje 2 trvenje, sukob

Friday /'fraɪdɪ/ *n* petak **man** ~ vjerni sluga, pomagač

fridge /frɪdʒ/ *n coll* hladionik, frižider

friend /frend/ *n* 1 prijatelj **be** ~**s with** biti nečiji prijatelj **make** ~**s/make** ~**s with/make a** ~ **of** sprijateljiti se, postati nečiji prijatelj 2 pomagač ~**ly** *adj* srdačan, prijateljski raspoložen, prijateljski **be on** ~**ly terms** biti u prijateljskim odnosima ~**liness** *n* srdačnost, naklonost ~**ship** *n* prijateljstvo

frigate /'frɪgət/ *n* 1 *hist* fregata 2 *GB* fregata, eskortni razarač 3 *US* bojni brod srednje veličine

fright /fraɪt/ *n* 1 strah, užas **take** ~ **at sth** prestrašiti se nečeg **give sb a** ~ prestrašiti 2 *coll* strašilo, nakaza ~**en** *vt* prestrašiti ~ **sb into/out of doing sth** zastrašivanjem natjerati nekoga da nešto učini/ne učini ~**ened** *adj* (of/at) *coll* prestrašen ~**ening** *adj* zastrašujući ~**ful** *adj* 1 strašan, grozan 2 *coll* velik; strašan *coll*

frigid /'frɪdʒɪd/ *adj* 1 hladan (+ *fig*) 2 frigidan

frill /frɪl/ *n* 1 nabor, čipkasti ukras na odjeći 2 *pl* afektiran govor, pretje-

rana kićenost ~**y** *adj* 1 čipkast, nabran 2 *coll* pretjerano kićen

fringe /frɪndʒ/ *n* 1 obrub, rese na obrubu 2 rub, kraj ~ **area** rubno područje; *fig* područje od marginalnog značenja ~ **benefits** dodatne beneficije ~ **group** marginalna skupina ~ **theatre/medicine** alternativna medicina/kazalište 3 šiške *pl* • *vt* obrubiti

frisk /frɪsk/ *vi,vt* 1 skakutati, poskakivati 2 pretražiti, izvršiti osobnu pretragu ~**y** *adj* živahan, nestašan

fritter /'frɪtə(r)/ *vt* ~ **sth away** rasipati, protratiti

frivolous /'frɪvələs/ *adj* neozbiljan, isprazan, frivolan

fro /frəʊ/ *adv* **to and** ~ amo-tamo, naprijed-natrag, tamo i natrag

frock /frɒk/ *n* 1 haljina 2 redovnička halja

frog /frɒg/ *n* 1 žaba ~**man** ronilac, čovjek-žaba ~**march** grubo vući 2 kopča

frolic /'frɒlɪk/ *vi* skakutati, zbijati šalu, igrati se • *n* zabava, veselje, obijest

from /frəm; frɒm/ *prep* 1 od 2 iz, na temelju – ... **to** ... od ... do, s ... na, iz ... u ~ **above** odozgo

front /frʌnt/ *n* 1 **the** ~ prednji dio, prednjica, čelo 2 *mod* prednji, prvi, ... sprijeda **come to the** ~ dospjeti u prvi plan, istaći se **in** ~**/in** ~ **of** naprijed, ispred ~ **runner** favorit ~**man** vođa 3 *meteor* fronta 4 *mil* bojišnica 5 fasada, maska *fig* **have the** ~ **to do sth** imati obraza nešto učiniti **put on/show/present a bold** ~ hrabro se suočiti **shirt**~ prednjica košulje • *vt,vi* gledati na ~**al** *adj* frontalni

frontier /'frʌntɪə(r)/ *n* 1 granica 2 granica civilizacije i divljine; Divlji zapad 3 *mod* pogranični, graničarski

frost /frɒst/ *n* 1 studen ~**bite** ozeblina ~**bound** zamrznut 2 mraz, inje **black** ~ studen bez mraza • *vt, vi* 1 (over, up) prekriti (se) mrazom 2 uništiti mrazom 3 posuti šećerom ~**ed glass** mliječno staklo ~**y** *adj* 1 studen *fig* hladan

froth /frɒθ/ *n* 1 pjena 2 isprazne misli/riječi • *vi* pjeniti se

frown /fraun/ *vi* (at) mrštiti se
~**on/upon** poprijeko gledati • *n*
mrštenje, mrk pogled

froze, frozen *v irreg* → **freeze**

frugal /ˈfruːgl/ *adj* (of) štedljiv, skroman

fruit /fruːt/ *n* 1 voće ~**cake** kolač sa
sušenim voćem ~**fly** (vinska) mušica ~ **salad** *GB* voćna salata; *US* puding s voćem 2 plod (+ *fig*) ~**machine** *GB coll* automat za kockanje,
jednoruki jack • *vi* donijeti ploda
~**erer** *n* prodavač voća ~**ful** *adj* plodan (+ *fig*) ~**less** *adj* neplodan, besplodan, uzaludan ~**y** *adj* 1 voćni 2
coll pikantan ~**ion** /fruːˈɪʃn/ *n* ostvarenje, oživotvorenje

frump /frʌmp/ *n* strašilo, neukusno
odjevena osoba

frustrate /frʌˈstreɪt/ *vt* spriječiti **frustration** *n* frustracija, razočaranje,
poraz

fry (1) /fraɪ/ *vt,vi* pržiti ~**ing pan** tava
out of the ~**ing pan and into the
fire** iz zla u gore

fry (2) *n pl* riblja mlad **small** ~
bezveznjakovići, nevažne osobe

fuck /fʌk/ *vt,vi sl tab* jebati (se) *tab* ~
(**it**)! *int sl tab* jebi ga! *tab* ~ **off**! *int sl*
tab jebi se! *tab* ~ **sth up** zajebati ~**ed
up** zajeban ~**up** *n* zajeb ~**all** ništa
~**er** kreten

fuddle /ˈfʌdl/ *vt* ošamutiti, opiti

fudge /fʌdʒ/ *n* karamela • *vt* muljati,
vrdati

fuel /ˈfjuːəl/ *n* gorivo **add** ~ **to the
flames** dolijevati ulje na vatru • *vt*
opskrbiti gorivom, tankirati

fugitive /ˈfjuːdʒətɪv/ *n* 1 (from) bjegunac (od) 2 *mod* u bijegu • *adj* prolazan

fulfil (**fulfill** US) /fulˈfil/ *vt* ispuniti,
izvršiti ~**ment** *n* ispunjenje, ostvarenje, izvršenje, udovoljenje

full /ful/ *adj* 1 (of) pun (čega) ~ **up** *coll*
dupkom pun, sit do grla 2 ~ **of** prepun, ispunjen **be** ~ **of shit** *tab* srati
fig tab 3 punašan, popunjen 4 širok,
komotan (o odjeći) 5 pun, čitav 6
cjelovit, detaljan **in** ~ **career** u
punom zamahu **to the** ~ do kraja
~**blooded** punokrvan ~**blown** u

punom cvatu ~ **dress** svečana odora
~**dress rehearsal** generalna proba
~ **face** odnaprijed ~ **house** puno
kazalište ~ **marks** najviše ocjene
~**page** preko cijele stranice ~**scale**
u naravnoj veličini; *coll* potpun ~
stop točka **come to a** ~ **stop** zaustaviti se ~**time** s punim radnim vremenom, stalno zaposlen **a** ~**time
job a.** stalni posao **b.** *fig* stvar/osoba
koja oduzima mnogo vremena i
snage ~**y** *adv* potpuno, u potpunosti

fulsome /ˈfulsəm/ *adj* pretjeran,
neiskren (o hvali)

fumble /ˈfʌmbl/ *vi,vt* 1 pipati, petljati
oko 2 šeprtljati, loše obaviti posao

fume /fjuːm/ *n* 1 (*pl*) dim, para, isparavanje 2 ushit • *vt, vi* 1 (at) isparavati,
dimiti se 2 *fig* pušiti se od bijesa 3
dimiti

fumigate /ˈfjuːmɪgeɪt/ *vt* raskuživati
dimom, prašiti

fun /fʌn/ *n* 1 zabava, šala, igra **have** ~
zabavljati se ~**fair** lunapark **make** ~
of/poke ~ **at** zadirkivati nekog, izrugivati se iz nekog **for/in** ~ u šali 2
mod zabavan, za zabavu, šaljiv ~**ny**
adj 1 zabavan, šaljiv 2 čudan

function /ˈfʌŋkʃn/ *n* 1 funkcija, uloga
2 priredba, svečanost • *vi* funkcionirati, raditi, vršiti ulogu ~**al** *adj* 1
funkcionalan 2 koji funkcionira ~**ary**
n derog funkcionar; foteljaš *derog*

fund /fʌnd/ *n* 1 (*pl*) novčani fond **be
short of** ~**s** *coll* biti bez novaca 2 *fig*
obilje • *vt* financirati

fundamental /ˌfʌndəˈmentl/ *adj* (to)
temeljni, ključni, osnovni **the** ~**s** osnovna načela ~**ism** *n* fundamentalizam

funeral /ˈfjuːnərəl/ *n* 1 pogreb, ukop 2
mod pogrebni **funereal** /fjuːˈnɪərɪəl/
adj pogrebni, žalobni, mračan

funicular /fjuːˈnɪkjʊlə(r)/ *adj* ~ **railway** uspinjača

funk /fʌŋk/ *n* 1 strah, prestravljenost 2
kukavica • *vt,vi* preplašiti se ~**y** *adj*
karakterističan za *funk* glazbu

funnel /ˈfʌnl/ *n* 1 lijevak 2 dimnjak (na
brodu, lokomotivi i sl.) • *vt,vi fig*
preusmjeravati, ubacivati (novac i
neki pothvat i sl.)

fur /fɜ:(r)/ n 1 krzno 2 mod krznen **~ry** adj krznen, poput krzna, prekriven krznom, dlakav **~rier** n krznar

furbish /'fɜ:bɪʃ/ vt ulaštiti, očistiti, osvježiti, obnoviti

furious /'fjʊərɪəs/ adj divlji, bijesan, nasilan, nekontroliran **fast and ~** divlji, buran

furl /fɜ:l/ vt,vi smotati, sklopiti, zatvoriti

furlong /'fɜ:lɒŋ/ n 220 jardi (201 m), osmina milje

furlough /'fɜ:ləʊ/ n dopust

furnace /'fɜ:nɪs/ n peć

furnish /'fɜ:nɪʃ/ vt opskrbiti, opremiti, namjestiti **~ings** n pl oprema, namještaj

furniture /'fɜ:nɪtʃə(r)/ n namještaj

furore /fjʊ'rɔ:rɪ/ n senzacija, halabuka

furrow /'fʌrəʊ/ n brazda, bora • vt izborati

further /'fɜ:ðə(r)/ adv, adj 1 dalje (→ **farther**) 2 više, još, daljnji **until ~ notice** do daljnjega, do opoziva 3 (**~more**) nadalje, štoviše • vt promicati **~ education** GB daljnje školovanje (izvan fakulteta) **~ance** n promičba **~most** adj najdalji

furthest /'fɜ:ðɪst/ → **farthest**

furtive /'fɜ:tɪv/ adj potajni, učinjen krišom **~ly** adv krišom, kradomice

fury /'fjʊərɪ/ n bijes, gnjev, srdžba

furze /fɜ:z/ n štipavac, žutilovka

fuse /fju:z/ n 1 fitilj 2 (**fuze** US) detonator, upaljač **time-~** tempirani upaljač 3 osigurač • vt,vi 1 rastaliti se 2 pregorjeti 3 fig stopiti se u jedno 4 staviti detonator

fuselage /'fju:zəlɑ:ʒ/ n trup aviona

fusilade /,fju:zɪ'leɪd/ n puškaranje, pucnjava

fusion /'fju:ʒn/ n fuzija, stapanje, koalicija

fuss /fʌs/ n prekomjerna/nepotrebna galama, uzrujavanje; frka coll **make a ~** dići galamu, uzrujavati se • vt,vi (over) uzrujavati se oko, gnjaviti, zanovijetati, obasipati koga pažnjom **~y** adj 1 sitničav, pedantan 2 nervozan, uzrujan 3 afektiran

fustian /'fʌstɪən/ n 1 bombastičnost 2 mod bombastičan

fusty /'fʌstɪ/ adj pljesniv (+ fig)

futile /'fju:taɪl/ adj uzaludan, neuspio, jalov, površan, beskoristan **futility** /fju:'tɪlətɪ/ n ispraznost, jalovost

future /'fju:tʃə(r)/ n 1 budućnost, sutrašnjica, sutra 2 mod budući **for the ~** za ubuduće, za sutra **in ~** ubuduće 3 pl com još neproizvedena roba koja se prodaje i plaća po sadašnjoj cijeni

futurity /fju:'tjʊərətɪ/ n budućnost

fuze US →**fuse**

fuzz /fʌz/ n malje, paperje **~y** adj 1 maljast, kovrčav, vunast 2 nejasan, zamrljan

G

G, g /dʒi:/ 7. slovo engl. abecede; ge
gab /gæb/ vi coll brbljati • n brbljanje
gabbie /'gæbl/ vi,vt 1 blebetati 2 gakati
gable /'geɪbl/ n zabat ~ **end** bočni zid
gad /gæd/ vi (about/around) lutati, skitati ~**about** n coll vjetrogonja
gadfly /'gædflaɪ/ n 1 obad 2 fig dosadnjaković
gadget /'gædʒɪt/ n naprava, spravica ~**ry** n collect razne naprave
Gael /geɪl/ n Škot/Irac; Kelt ~**ic** adj gelski ○ n gelski (irski/škotski) jezik
gaff (1) /gæf/ n harpun; osti **blow the** ~ sl odati tajnu
gaff (2) GB sl stan
gaffer /'gæfə(r)/ n 1 film majstor rasvjete 2 GB coll šef; poslovođa 3 coll stari
gag /gæg/ vt začepiti usta (+ fig); ušutkati • n šala, geg
gaga /'gɑ:gɑ:/ adj luckast; senilan
gage US → **gauge**
gaggle /'gægl/ n jato gusaka
gaiety /'geɪətɪ/ n 1 veselje, dobro raspoloženje 2 arch zabava, svečanost
gain /geɪn/ n 1 dobit, dobitak 2 korist, probitak 3 povećanje, porast 4 (~s) zarada, profit **ill-gotten** ~s nepošteno stečen novac ~**ful** adj unosan • vt,vi 1 dobiti, dobivati ~ **entry** ući ~ **ground** napredovati, osvajati; širiti se ~ **strength** ojačati ~ **the upper hand** nadjačati ~ **victory** pobijediti ~ **weight** udebljati se 2 steći, zaraditi, profitirati 3 povećati 4 (on/upon) (do)stići; doći do 5 (sat) ići naprijed
gainsay /ˌgeɪn'seɪ/ vt arch, form poreći, nijekati
gait /geɪt/ n način hoda; hod
gal /gæl/ dial, coll → **girl**
gala /'gɑ:lə/ n 1 svečanost, proslava 2 mod svečan, sjajan 3 GB športsko natjecanje
galaxy /'gæləksɪ/ n 1 galaktika 2 (**the G~**) Mliječna staza 3 fig zvijezde **galactic** /gə'læktɪk/ adj galaktički
gale /geɪl/ n 1 snažan vjetar 2 fig provala, bura (smijeha)
gall (1) /gɔ:l/ n 1 med žuč (+ fig) 2 mod žučni ~ **stone** žučni kamenac 3 fig pakost 4 drskost
gall (2) vt jediti
gallant /'gælənt/ adj 1 lit srčan, odvažan, plemenit 2 (+ /gə'lænt/) udvoran; galantan • n arch udvarač; kavalir ~**ry** n 1 srčanost 2 udvornost 3 udvaranje
gallery /'gælərɪ/ n 1 galerija 2 publika s galerije 3 dugačka prostorija **shooting** ~ streljana 4 hodnik (u rudniku)
galley /'gælɪ/ n 1 galija ~ **slave** galijot 2 brodska kuhinja 3 (~ **proof**) ogledni otisak; špalta coll
Gallic /'gælɪk/ adj galski; francuski
gallivant /ˌgælɪ'vænt/ vi coll skitati, lutati
gallon /'gælən/ n galon
gallop /'gæləp/ n galop • vi,vt 1 galopirati ~**ing inflation** galopirajuća inflacija 2 fig juriti
gallows /'gæləʊz/ n pl 1 (~**tree**) vješala 2 (**the** ~) smrtna kazna vješanjem
galore /gə'lɔ:(r)/ adv u izobilju, napretek
galvanize /'gælvənaɪz/ vt 1 pocinčati 2 (into) potaknuti (na) **galvanic** /gæl'vænɪk/ adj 1 galvanski 2 silan, snažan, iznenadan
gambit /'gæmbɪt/ n 1 otvaranje 2 fig početni potez
gamble /'gæmbl/ vi,vt 1 kockati se, igrati na sreću; riskirati 2 (away) proigrati, prokockati • n igra na sreću, kocka, rizik ~**r** n kockar

gambling *n* kockanje **gambling den/house** kockarnica

game (1) /geɪm/ *n* **1** (društvena/sportska/dječja) igra (+ *fig*) **2** natjecanje, utakmica; partija **3** gem **4** pribor za igru **5** tajni plan **the ~ is up** plan je otkriven **make ~ of sb** ismijavati koga **6** divljač **~keeper** lovočuvar **7** *fig* lovina, plijen **fair ~ a.** dopuštena lovina **b.** *fig* osoba koju je dopušteno napadati/ kritizirati; laka meta **be on the ~** *GB sl* prostituirati se

game (2) *adj* **1** borben, srčan, odlučan **2** (for) spreman, voljan

game (3) *v* → **gamble**

game (4) *adj* → **gammy**

gammon /ˈɡæmən/ *n* usoljena/dimljena/sušena šunka

gammy /ˈɡæmɪ/ *adj GB coll* hrom

gamut /ˈɡæmət/ *n* dijapazon; lepeza (*fig*)

gander /ˈɡændə(r)/ *n* gusak **have/take a ~ at** *coll* pogledati

gang /ɡæŋ/ *n* **1** družba; banda **~-bang** *sl* (naglas) **vulg** *sl* **2** skupina (radnika, zatvorenika) **chain ~** kažnjenici na prisilnom radu **3** skupina prijatelja; škvadra *sl* • *vi* ~ **up on/against sb** urotiti se protiv koga

gangling /ˈɡæŋɡlɪŋ/ *adj* štrkljast

gangway /ˈɡæŋweɪ/ *n* **1** most (na brodu) **2** *GB* prolaz (između redova sjedala)

gaol, jail /dʒeɪl/ *n* zatvor; zatvorska kazna **~-bird** (stari) zatvorenik • *vt* zatvoriti; strpati u zatvor **~er** *n* zatvorski čuvar, tamničar

gap /ɡæp/ *n* **1** procijep, pukotina **2** razmak **3** praznina, rupa (+ *fig*) **4** prekid **5** razlika; jaz **generation ~** jaz između generacija **credibility ~** neuvjerljivost; nesrazmjer između riječi i djela **6** prijevoj, klanac

gape /ɡeɪp/ *vi* **1** buljiti u čudu; zinuti **2** otvoriti se, zjapiti

garage /ˈɡærɑːʒ, ɡəˈrɑːʒ/ *n* **1** garaža **2** *GB* mehaničarska radionica, benzinska crpka, salon automobila • *vt* garažirati

garb /ɡɑːb/ *n lit* odora

garbage /ˈɡɑːbɪdʒ/ *n* **1** otpaci **2** *US* smeće **~ can** kanta za smeće

garble /ˈɡɑːbl/ *vt* iskriviti; pogrešno prenijeti/prikazati

garda /ˈɡɑːdə/ *n Ir* **1** G~ redarstvo **2** (*pl* gardaí /ˈɡɑːdiː/) redarstvenik

garden /ˈɡɑːdn/ *n* **1** vrt **lead sb up the ~ path** prevariti, nasamariti **2** *mod* vrtni **3** (**kitchen ~**) povrtnjak **4** park; perivoj **~ing** *n* vrtlarstvo **~er** *n* vrtlar

gargle /ˈɡɑːɡl/ *vi* grgljati, ispirati grlo • *n* **1** tekućina za ispiranje grla **2** *sl* alkoholno piće

garish /ˈɡeərɪʃ/ *adj* kričav, napadan, kičast

garland /ˈɡɑːlənd/ *n* vijenac • *vt* ukrasiti vijencima; ovjenčati

garlic /ˈɡɑːlɪk/ *n* češnjak

garment /ˈɡɑːmənt/ *n* **1** odjevni predmet **2 ~s** odjeća

garnish /ˈɡɑːnɪʃ/ *vt* obložiti; garnirati • *n* prilog; garnirung *coll*

garret /ˈɡærət/ *n* potkrovlje, tavan

garrison /ˈɡærɪsn/ *n mil* posada • *vt* razmjestiti posadu; čuvati

garter /ˈɡɑːtə(r)/ *n* **1** podvezica **2** (**~ belt**) *US* halter coll

gas /ɡæs/ *n* **1** plin **~-meter** plinomjer **~works** plinara **natural ~** zemni plin **tear-~** suzavac **2** *US* benzin **~ station** benzinska crpka **step on the ~** ubrzati **3** *coll* isprazno blebetanje **~-bag** brbljavac **4** *coll* nešto zabavno/super/genijalno • *vt,vi* **1** otrovati plinom **2** *coll* brbljati **~eous** /ˈɡæsɪəs/ *adj* plinovit **~sy** *adj* **1** plinovit **2** isprazan; tašt

gash /ɡæʃ/ *n* posjekotina, rasjeklina • *vt* posjeći, rasjeći

gasoline, gasolene /ˈɡæsəliːn/ *n US* benzin

gasp /ɡɑːsp/ *vi,vt* **1** dahtati, teško disati **2** ostati bez daha ~ **out** protisnuti • *n* dahtaj

gastric /ˈɡæstrɪk/ *adj* želučani ~ **ulcer** čir na želucu

gate /ɡeɪt/ *n* **1** vrata **~-crash** *vi,vt* ući nepozvan **~keeper** *n* vratar **~post** dovratak **2** izlaz (u zračnoj luci) **3** prijevoj, klanac **4** vratnice **~way** *n* **1** ulaz, izlaz, prolaz **2** put (do čega); vrata (*fig*)

gateau /ˈɡætəʊ/ *n* kolač; torta

gather /ˈɡæðə(r)/ *vi,vt* **1** skupiti (se),

okupiti (se) ~ **speed** dobiti na brzini 2 (u)brati 3 shvatiti; zaključiti 4 nabrati ~**ing** n skup

gauche /gəʊʃ/ adj nespretan, netaktičan

gaudy /'gɔ:dɪ/ adj kričav, napadan, neukusan

gauge (**gage** US) /geɪdʒ/ n 1 mjerilo 2 promjer; kalibar 3 standardna mjera • vt 1 (iz)mjeriti 2 procijeniti

Gaul /gɔ:l/ n 1 Galija 2 Gal

gaunt /gɔ:nt/ adj 1 mršav, suhonjav 2 pust, sumoran

gauntlet /'gɔ:ntlɪt/ n 1 (željezna/zaštitna) rukavica 2 špalir batinama naoružanih ljudi 3 fig napad, kritika

gauze /gɔ:z/ n 1 gaza 2 US zavoj

gave v irreg → **give**

gavel /'gævl/ n čekić

gawk /gɔ:k/ vi buljiti, blejati ~**y** adj nespretan; krakat

gawp /gɔ:p/ vi GB buljiti, piljiti, zuriti

gay /geɪ/ n homoseksualac, homoseksualka • adj 1 homoseksualan 2 veseo; živih boja

gaze /geɪz/ vi zagledati se, zuriti • n dug/netremičan pogled

gazette /gə'zet/ n glasnik, vjesnik; službene novine ~**er** /ˌgæzə'tɪə(r)/ n indeks (abecedni popis)

gear /gɪə(r)/ n 1 pogonski uređaj; zupčanici pl 2 stupanj prijenosa; brzina coll ~ **shift/lever/stick** mjenjač brzina **out of ~ a.** izvan brzine; u leru coll **b.** neispravan 3 oprema, pribor 4 odjeća, obuća • vt,vi prilagoditi ~ **up** pripremiti se

gee /dʒi:/ int (~ **whiz**) US coll euph Isuse!

geese /gi:s/ n pl → **goose**

geezer /'gi:zə(r)/ n sl tip, frajer

gel /dʒel/ n žele, gel (za kosu)

gelatine /ˌdʒelə'ti:n/ n želatina

geld /geld/ vt irreg uškopiti ~**ing** n uškopljena životinja (ob. konj)

gelt v irreg → **geld**

gem /dʒem/ n 1 (polu)dragi kamen; dragulj 2 fig blago, dragocjenost

Gemini /'dʒemɪni/ n astrol Blizanci

gen /dʒen/ n GB coll informacija

gender /'dʒendə(r)/ n rod ~**-bender** sl androgina osoba

gene /dʒi:n/ n gen ~**tic** /dʒɪ'netɪk/ adj genetski ~**tics** n genetika ~**ticist** /dʒɪ'netɪsɪst/ n genetičar

genealogy /ˌdʒi:nɪ'ælədʒɪ/ n 1 genealogija; rodoslovlje 2 rodoslovno stablo

general /'dʒenrəl/ adj 1 opći, sveopći; uobičajen **in ~** uglavnom; većinom **as a ~ rule** u pravilu **in ~ terms** općenito **the ~ alert** opća opasnost ~ **delivery** US poste restante ~ **practicioner** (**GP**) liječnik opće prakse ~ **public** javnost 2 približan **have a ~ idea** znati osnovno 3 glavni; generalni **Secretary-General** glavni tajnik ~ **staff** glavni stožer ~**ly** adv općenito; u pravilu; uglavnom ~**ity** n 1 općenita tvrdnja 2 većina ~**ize** vi,vt /'dʒenrəlaɪz/ poopćiti ~**ization** n uopćavanje, opći zaključak • n general **Major-General** general-bojnik

generate /'dʒenəreɪt/ vt proizvesti, stvoriti, izazvati; generirati **generation** /ˌdʒenə'reɪʃn/ n 1 naraštaj; generacija 2 stvaranje, generiranje

generic /dʒɪ'nerɪk/ adj opći; generički

generous /'dʒenərəs/ adj 1 darežljiv, velikodušan; plemenit 2 obilan, bogat **generosity** /ˌdʒenə'rɒsɪtɪ/ n darežljivost, velikodušnost; plemenitost

genesis /'dʒenəsɪs/ n 1 postanak; geneza 2 **G~** bibl Knjiga postanka

genial /'dʒi:nɪəl/ adj veseo, društven, prijazan, ljubazan; topao, blag

genie /'dʒi:ni/ n duh

genital /'dʒenɪtl/ adj spolni; genitalni ~**s** n pl vanjski spolni organi

genius /'dʒi:nɪəs/ n 1 (pl ~**es**) genij; genijalnost; dar 2 (pl genii) duh **evil ~** zloduh, demon

genocide /'dʒenəsaɪd/ n genocid

genre /'ʒɑ:nrə/ n književna vrsta; žanr

gent /dʒent/ n 1 coll → **gentleman** ~**s** n sg GB muški WC

genteel /dʒen'ti:l/ adj 1 afektiran 2 arch otmjen, iz visoka društva

gentility /dʒen'tɪlətɪ/ n otmjenost, finoća

gentle /'dʒentl/ adj 1 blag, nježan; umjeren; pitom 2 arch plemenita porijekla ~**folk(s)** n arch gospoda

~man /'dʒentlmən/ n 1 častan čovjek; džentlmen; kavalir **gentlemen's agreement** usmena pogodba koju veže čast 2 gospodin **~woman** n arch dama, gospođa

gentry /'dʒentri/ **the** ~ n pl (niže) plemstvo **landed** ~ vlastela **gentrification** n pretvaranje siromašnih četvrti u elitne

genuflect /'dʒenjuflekt/ vi klecnuti

genuine /'dʒenjuɪn/ adj 1 pravi, nepatvoren; autentičan, originalan 2 iskren

geography /dʒɪ'ɒgrəfi/ n 1 zemljopis 2 raspored

geology /dʒɪ'ɒlədʒɪ/ n geologija, zemljoznanstvo

geometry /dʒɪ'ɒmətrɪ/ n geometrija, mjerništvo

Geordie /'dʒɔːdɪ/ n GB žitelj Newcastla i okolice

Georgian /'dʒɔːdʒən/ adj 1 iz vremena kralja Georgea (Đure) 2 iz amer. države Georgie 3 gruziju

geriatric /,dʒerɪ'ætrɪk/ adj 1 gerijatrijski 2 derog (pra)star, beskoristan **~s** n (+ sing) gerijatrija

germ /dʒɜːm/ n 1 klica, zametak (+ fig) 2 mikrob, uzročnik bolesti ~ **warfare** biološki rat **~inate** vi,vt (pro)klijati; niknuti (+ fig)

German /'dʒɜːmən/ adj njemački ~ **measles** rubeola • n Nijemac

germane /dʒɜ'meɪn/ adj (to) povezan (s čime); relevantan (za što)

gerrymander /,dʒerɪ'mændə(r)/ vi,vt podijeliti u izborne jedinice tako da se osigura pobjeda neke stranke

gestation /dʒe'steɪʃn/ n 1 trudnoća 2 fig razvoj zamisli/plana

gesticulate /dʒe'stɪkjuleɪt/ vi gestikulirati; mahati rukama

gesture /'dʒestʃə(r)/ n 1 kretnja, znak kretnjom 2 gesta, znak, postupak

get /ɡet/ vt,vi irreg 1 dobiti; primiti; uzeti 2 **have got** imati 3 **have got to** morati 4 doći, stići 5 razumjeti, shvatiti; (dobro) čuti; doznati 6 postati 7 → **have** (3) ~ **dressed** obući se ~ **drunk** opiti se ~ **excited** uzbuditi se ~ **even with sb** osvetiti se kome ~ **going** (po)krenuti **it got home to**

him shvatio je ~ **to know** upoznati, saznati ~ **lost** izgubiti se ~ **married** oženiti/udati se ~ **a move on!** požuri ~ **ready** spremiti se, pripremiti ~ **tired** umoriti se ~ **used** (to) naviknuti se (na) ~ **well** ozdraviti ~ **wet** smočiti se **I got you!** ulovio sam te (u neznanju, na djelu) **you got me (there)** ne znam ~ **about** a. ponovno ustati (nakon bolesti) b. širiti se ~ **across** prenijeti ~ **ahead of sb** prestići koga ~ **along** a. napredovati b. (with sb) slagati se (s kim) ~ **at** a. dohvatiti; dočepati se b. ciljati (fig) ~ **away** a. pobjeći b. (with sth) nekažnjeno se izvući ~ **back** a. vratiti se b. (at sb) osvetiti se ~ **by** provući se, izvući se; preživjeti ~ **down** a. potištiti b. progutati **c.** zabilježiti **d.** (to sth) prihvatiti se (čega) ~ **in** a. ući; stići b. biti izabran **c.** nabaviti ~ **off** a. krenuti b. (with sb) coll ljubakati/spetljati se (s kim) ~ **on** a. napredovati b. popeti se **c.** (with sb) slagati se (s kim) ~ **out** a. izaći b. saznati se **c.** izdati, objaviti **d.** ~ **sth out of sb** izvući iz ~ **over** preboljeti, zaboraviti ~ **round sb** nagovoriti, pridobiti ~ **round to sth** konačno se primiti čega ~ **through** a. dobiti vezu b. provući se **c.** (to sb) ukazati, dati do znanja ~ **up** ustati; dignuti se

geyser /'ɡiːzə(r)/ n 1 gejzir 2 GB plinski bojler

ghastly /'ɡɑːstlɪ/ adj 1 sablastan; blijed kao smrt 2 grozan, užasan, loš, neugodan

gherkin /'ɡɜːkɪn/ n kiseli krastavac

ghetto /'ɡetəʊ/ n geto

ghost /ɡəʊst/ n duh **a** ~ **of a smile** blijedi smiješak ~ **town** napušteni grad **~writer** osoba koja piše članke/teze/književna djela za drugoga **the Holy Ghost** Duh Sveti **give up the** ~ izdahnuti **~ly** adj sablastan

ghoul /ɡuːl/ n 1 duh koji se hrani lešinama; mrtvožder 2 osoba morbidnih sklonosti/odvratnih navika **~ish** adj odvratan, gnjusan

giant /'dʒaɪənt/ n 1 div 2 mod divovski 3 fig velikan

gibberish /ˈdʒɪbərɪʃ/ n nerazumljiv govor; nesuvislost, besmislica

gibbous /ˈdʒɪbəs/ adj (Mjesec) u posljednjoj četvrti

gibe, jibe /dʒaɪb/ n ruganje, sprdnja • vi (at) rugati se (komu)

giddy /ˈgɪdɪ/ adj 1 koji osjeća vrtoglavicu 2 vrtoglav 3 neozbiljan, lakomislen, površan

gift /gɪft/ n dar **don't/never look a ~ horse in the mouth** prov darovanu konju zube se ne gleda **~ed** adj darovit, nadaren

gig /gɪg/ n 1 coll (pop) koncert 2 lagana kočija

gigantic /dʒaɪˈgæntɪk/ adj divovski, golem

giggle /ˈgɪgl/ vi smijuljiti se, hihotati se • n hihot(anje), smijuljenje

gild /gɪld/ vt irreg 1 pozlatiti 2 fig ukrasiti, uljepšati, zasladiti **~ing** n pozlata

gill /gɪl/ n (~s) škrge pl **green/white about the ~s** coll blijed od straha/mučnine

gill /dʒɪl/ n mjera za tekućinu, četvrt pinte (0.14 l)

gilt /gɪlt/ n pozlata **~-edged shares** državne dionice koje donose malu, ali sigurnu dobit

gimlet /ˈgɪmlɪt/ n svrdlo **~ eye** prodoran pogled

gimme v coll → give me

gimmick /ˈgɪmɪk/ n coll trik, lukavstvo, majstorija

gin /dʒɪn/ n džin

ginger /ˈdʒɪndʒə(r)/ n 1 đumbir **~ ale/beer** gazirano bezalkoholno piće s dodatkom đumbira **~bread/nut** paprenjak 2 coll živahnost, polet • adj rid • vt **~ up** oživjeti, potaknuti na aktivnost **~ly** adj oprezno

gipsy, gypsy /ˈdʒɪpsɪ/ n (G~) ciganin, ciganka

giraffe /dʒɪˈrɑːf/ n (pl ~s, ~) žirafa

gird /gɜːd/ vt irreg lit pripasati **~ up one's loins** pripremiti se za akciju

girder /ˈgɜːdə(r)/ n greda

girdle /ˈgɜːdl/ n 1 steznik 2 pojas (+ fig) • vt okružiti

girl /gɜːl/ n 1 djevojka; djevojčica; cura coll 2 kći 3 spremačica **~friend**
a. djevojka b. prijateljica **~ Friday** uredska djevojka za sve **~ guide/scout** pripadnica izviđačke organizacije **~hood** djevojaštvo **~ish** adj djevojački **~ie/~y** adj koji prikazuje obnažene djevojke

giro /ˈdʒaɪərəʊ/ n žiro

girt v irreg → gird

girth /gɜːθ/ n 1 opseg 2 kolan

gist /dʒɪst/ n bit, srž

git /gɪt/ n GB sl derog budala

give /gɪv/ vt, vi irreg dati, predati, zadati; darovati **I'll ~ him that** to mu priznajem **~ birth** (to) roditi (koga) **~ rise to** prouzročiti, izazvati **~ or take** manje ili više **~ way** (to) a. dati prednost prolaza, propustiti b. povući se c. popustiti (pred); prepustiti se **~ away** odati **~ back** vratiti **~ in** (to sb) predati (se); popustiti **~ out** popustiti, biti na izmaku **~ over** prestati **~ up** odustati (od čega); prestati; prepustiti **~ oneself up** predati se • n elastičnost; popustljivost **~ and take** kompromis

given v irreg → give

glacial /ˈgleɪsɪəl/ adj leden (+ fig)

glacier /ˈglæsɪə(r)/ n ledenjak

glad /glæd/ adj 1 zadovoljan **(I'm) ~ to meet you** drago mi je **I'll be ~ to help you** rado ću ti/vam pomoći 2 veseo, radostan **~ly** adv rado, drage volje

glade /gleɪd/ n lit čistina, proplanak

Glagolitic /ˌglægəˈlɪtɪk/ adj **~ alphabet** glagoljica

glamour /ˈglæmə(r)/ n 1 čar, privlačnost; blistava ljepota; blještavilo, sjaj **~ous** adj čaroban, privlačan, (pre)krasan, blistav **~ize** vt uljepšati, učiniti privlačnijim

glance /glɑːns/ n kratak, letimičan pogled **at a ~** odmah **at first ~** na prvi pogled • vi, vt 1 (at/over/-/through/round) letimice pogledati; preletjeti pogledom; baciti pogled (na/prema) 2 **~ off** odbiti se/odskočiti (od čega); okrznuti (što)

gland /glænd/ n žlijezda **~ular** /ˈglændjʊlə(r)/ adj žlijezdani **~ular fever** zarazna mononukleoza

glare /gleə(r)/ n 1 jako/neugodno/zasljepljujuće svjetlo **in the (full)** ~ **of publicity** izvrgnut pogledu javnosti **2** bijesan/ustrajan pogled • *vi* **1** blještati; bosti u oči (*fig*) **2** bijesno gledati; zuriti **glaring** *adj* **1** blještav; kričav; upadljiv

glass /glɑːs/ *n* **1** staklo **2** *mod* staklen ~**house** staklenik ~**ware** staklena roba ~**works** staklarna **3** **drinking** ~ čaša **4** ~**es** naočale; dalekozor **5** **looking** ~ zrcalo **6** **magnifying** ~ povećalo **7** barometar • *vt* ~ (in) zastakliti ~**y** *adj* **1** staklast; gladak, sjajan **2** *fig* beživotan, bezizražajan

glaze /gleɪz/ *vi,vt* **1** ~ (in) zastakliti **2** prekriti glazurom **3** (over) zabuljiti se u prazno; zamutiti se (oči) • *n* glazura; caklina **gleam** /gliːm/ *n* **1** zraka svjetlosti **2** *fig* bljesak • *vi* svjetlucati; bljesnuti

glean /gliːn/ *vt* **1** skupljati; pabirčiti **2** saznati

glee /gliː/ *n* radost

glen /glen/ *n Sc, Ir* dolina

glib /glɪb/ *n* rječit; brz na jeziku

glide /glaɪd/ *vi* **1** kliziti; lagano se kretati **2** letjeti bez motora; jedriti ~**r** *n* jedrilica

glimmer /ˈglɪmə(r)/ *n* **1** slaba/treperava svjetlost **2** *fig* tračak • *vi* svjetlucati, treperiti, tinjati

glimpse /glɪmps/ *n* kratak/letimičan pogled **get/catch a** ~ **of sb/sth** slučajno ugledati, na trenutak opaziti

glint /glɪnt/ *vi* svjetlucati, sjajiti, ljeskati se • *n* (od)sjaj

glisten /ˈglɪsn/ *vi* blistati, sjajiti (se)

glitter /ˈglɪtə(r)/ *vi* sjajiti, svjetlucati, blistati • *n* sjaj, bljeskavilo (+ *fig*)

glitzy /ˈglɪtsɪ/ *adj sl* glamurozan, monden

gloat /gləʊt/ *vi* likovati, zlurado uživati, nasladivati se

globe /gləʊb/ *n* **1** globus **2** zemaljska kugla ~ **trotter** *sl* svjetski putnik **3** kugla (svjetiljke) **global** *adj* svjetski; globalan

gloom /gluːm/ *n* **1** polumrak, tmina **2** sjeta, potištenost ~**y** *adj* **1** mračan, tmuran **2** sjetan, potišten

glory /ˈglɔːrɪ/ *n* **1** slava; čast; ponos, dika **2** divota **3** blaženstvo • *vi* ~ **in**

uživati (u) **glorify** /ˈglɔːrɪfaɪ/ *vt* **1** slaviti; (u)veličati **glorious** *adj* slavan, častan; veličanstven; divan

gloss (1) /glɒs/ *n* **1** sjaj; sjajna/ulaštena površina **2** lažni/vanjski sjaj **3** (~ **paint**) uljana boja **4** **lip** ~ sjajilo za usne • *vt* (~ **over**) uljepšati; zataškati, prijeći preko čega; površno se dotaknuti čega ~**y** *adj* sjajan, gladak

gloss (2) *n* glosa, bilješka • *vt* popratiti glosama ~**ary** *n* pojmovnik

glove /glʌv/ *n* rukavica **fit like a** ~ pristajati kao saliveno **be hand in** ~ biti usko povezan (s kime)

glow /gləʊ/ *vi* žariti se, sjati, rumenjeti se • *n* žar; rumenilo ~**worm** krijesnica ~**ing** *adj* **1** oduševljen, ushićen **2** žarke boje

glower /ˈglaʊə(r)/ *vi* (at) mrko/prijeteći gledati (koga); sijevati očima

glucose /ˈgluːkəʊs/ *n* glukoza

glue /gluː/ *n* ljepilo ~**sniffing** drogiranje ljepilom; snifanje *sl* ~**y** *adj* ljepljiv • *vt* **1** zalijepiti **2** *fig* prikovati

glum /glʌm/ *adj* tmuran, potišten

glut /glʌt/ *n* (pre)zasićenje, višak, preobilje • *vi,vt* (oneself) (pre)zasititi (se), (pre)natrpati ~**ton** /ˈglʌtn/ *n* **1** proždrljivac; žrjelica ~**tony** *n* neumjerenost u jelu i piću; proždrljivost ~**tonous** *adj* proždrljiv, pohlepan

G-man /ˈdʒiː mæn/ *n US coll* istražitelj FBI-a

gnarled /nɑːld/ *adj* kvrgav

gnash /næʃ/ *vt* škrgutati

gnat /næt/ *n* mušica

gnaw /nɔː/ *vi,vt* (at) **1** glodati **2** (iz)gristi, izjedati (+ *fig*)

gnome (1) /nəʊm/ *n* patuljak

gnome (2) *n* izreka

go /gəʊ/ *vi irreg* **1** ići; otići **2** kretati se, krenuti **one, two, three,** ~! tri, četiri, sad! **ready, steady,** ~! priprema, pozor, sad! **here** ~**es!** počinjem/krećem! **3** postati ~ **mad** poludjeti **4** popustiti; propasti **5** *euph* umrijeti **dead and** ~**ne** mrtav **6** **am/are/is** ~**ing to** + *infinitive gram* izražava budućnost/plan/namjeru ~ **about sth a.** baviti se čime **b.** postupati ~ **after sb/sth** trčati za (kim), pokušavati osvojiti (koga, što) ~

ahead napredovati; nastaviti (se) ~ **ahead!** samo izvoli(te) **~ahead** *n* dozvola, zeleno svjetlo ◦ *adj* napredan ~ **along** nastaviti ~ **along with sb** a. otpratiti b. složiti se ~ **at** napasti ~ **away** otići ~ **back** vratiti se ~ **back on one's word** pogaziti zadanu riječ ~ **before** prethoditi **~between** *n* posrednik ~ **beyond sth** prijeći granicu ~ **by** prolaziti ~ **by sth** a. držati se ~ **by the book** strogo se držati propisa b. suditi (na temelju čega) ~ **down** a. potonuti b. otići na sveučilišta c. stišati se; smanjiti se d. biti zabilježen ~ **down in history** ući u povijest ~ **for** a. napasti; boriti se ~ **for it!** samo naprijed! b. odnositi se na koga, što ~ **in** a. ući b. zanimati se za što, baviti se čime ~ **into** istražiti, razmotriti ~ **off** a. eksplodirati b. (hrana) pokvariti se, ukiseliti se c. izgubiti zanimanje za (koga, što), ohladiti se prema (komu) d. izaći, otići ~ **on** a. događati se **goings-on** *n* događaji b. nastaviti **on-going** koji se nastavlja/razvija, koji traje c. ponašati se d. (about sth) stalno o čemu pričati, gnjaviti ~ **out** a. izaći b. (with) hodati/izlaziti s kime c. ugasiti se ~ **over sth** ispitati; pregledati; provjeriti ~ **round** biti dostatan za sve ~ **through** a. proći, biti odobreno/zaključen b. pretražiti c. doživjeti d. (with sth) obaviti/završiti planirano ~ **under** a. potonuti b. bankrotirati ~ **up** a. podignuti se b. eksplodirati c. otići na sveučilište **it ~es without saying** podrazumijeva se • *n* 1 red 2 pokušaj **have a ~** pokušati 3 energija, životna snaga **on the ~** u pokretu

goad /gəʊd/ *n* 1 štap za tjeranje stoke 2 *fig* poticaj • *vt* (na)tjerati; potaknuti

goal /gəʊl/ *n* 1 cilj 2 *sport* zgodlitak; gol *coll* **score a ~** postići zgodlitak 3 *sport* vrata; gol *coll* **~ keeper**, **~ie** vratar; golman *coll* **~post** stativa

goat /gəʊt/ *n* 1 (she~, **nanny ~**) koza; (he~, **billy ~**) jarac **get sb's ~** *coll* razbjesniti (koga) **~ee** /gəʊ'tiː/ *n* kozja bradica **~herd** pastir 2 razvratnik, pohotnik

gob (1) /gɒb/ *n GB sl derog* gubica *sl derog*

gob (2) *n coll* 1 hrpa 2 ispljuvak

gobbet /'gɒbɪt/ *n coll* komad (hrane), grumen

gobble (1) /'gɒbl/ *vi,vt* (up) progutati; baciti u sebe; smazati *sl*; proždrati *derog, fig*

gobble (2) *vi* glasati se kao puran **~r** *n US coll* puran

goblet /'gɒblɪt/ *n* 1 čaša na stalku 2 *arch* pehar, kupa

goblin /'gɒblɪn/ *n* ružni, zločesti patuljak iz bajke, bauk

god /gɒd/ *n* 1 bog **~dess** božica **~head** božanstvo 2 **G~ Bog My G~!** God~ Almighty! Good G~! Moj Bože, Bože dragi **for G~'s sake** za ime Boga, za Boga miloga **G~ forbid** ne daj Bože **G~ willing/please** ako Bog da **G~speed** neka te Bog čuva **G~ damn it!** kvragu, dovraga, prokletstvo **~child/son/daughter** kumče **~father** kum **~mother** kuma ~ **fearing** *adj* pobožan, bogobojazan ~ **forsaken** *adj* zabačen, napušten, zapušten **~send** *n* iznenadna sreća **~like** *adj* božanski, božanstven **~ly** pobožan 3 **~s** balkon (u kazalištu)

goffer /'gəʊfə/ *n US* potrčko *coll*

goggle /'gɒgl/ *vi* (at) buljiti, zabuljiti se • *n* **~s** 1 zaštitne naočale; naočale za plivanje; maska za ronjenje 2 *coll* naočale **~eyed** *adj* buljook

goitre (-**ter** *US*) /'gɔɪtə(r)/ *n med* guša

gold /gəʊld/ *n* 1 zlato (+ *fig*); zlatna boja 2 *mod* zlatan; zlatne boje ~ **plate** a. zlatno posuđe b. pozlata ~ **rush** zlatna groznica **~smith** zlatar **~en** /'gəʊldən/ *adj* 1 zlatan (+ *fig*); pozlaćen; zlatne boje, zlaćan ~ **goose** koka koja nese zlatna jaja ~ **handshake** novac koji se poklanja pri umirovljenju 2 zlata vrijedan, važan; uspješan

golf /gɒlf/ *n* golf ~ **club** a. palica za golf b. golf-klub

gone *v irreg* → **go**

goner /'gɒnə(r)/ *n sl* **he's a ~** otpisan je, gotov je

gong /gɒŋ/ *n* 1 gong 2 *GB sl* medalja, odlikovanje

gonna /'gɒnə/ v coll → **going to**

goo /gu:/ n sl 1 ljepljiva, vlažna tvar 2 fig sladunjavost **~ey** adj ljepljiv, slatkast; sladunjav

good /gud/ adj 1 dobar as ~ as kao (da) ~ **book** Biblija a ~ **few/many** velik broj, vrlo mnogo G~ **Friday** Veliki petak **~-looking** adj zgodan **make ~ a.** uspjeti **b.** nadoknaditi the G~ **People** vile(njaci) **put in a ~ word for sb** reći što komu u prilog 2 ugodan; ljubazan ~ **night** laku noć **have a ~ time** lijepo se provesti 3 prikladan **all in ~ time** sve u svoje vrijeme 4 ~ **for** vrijedan; sposoban; zdrav **~-for-nothing** ništarija; niškoristi coll • n dobro; dobrobit **do more harm than ~** učiniti više štete nego koristi **for ~** zauvijek **~ on you!** bravo, živio **what ~ is...?** koja je korist (od)...? **~s** roba **worldly ~s** zemaljska dobra **~ness** n dobrota ○ int G~**ness!** nebesa! Bože! **~y** n coll nešto fino/lijepo

goodbye /ˌgud'baɪ/ int doviđenja, zbogom **say ~** pozdraviti se, oprostiti se

goof /gu:f/ n 1 budala 2 US glupa pogreška • vi 1 zabrljati 2 ~ **off** besposličariti; zabušavati **~y** adj blesav, glup G~**y** Šiljo

goon /gu:n/ n 1 glupan, komedijaš 2 US coll plaćeni zločinac

goose /gu:s/ n (pl **geese**) 1 guska (+ fig) **~flesh/pimples** naježena koža, žmarci **~step** mil paradni korak **~berry** n ogrozd **play ~berry** držati svijeću fig

gore (1) /gɔ:(r)/ vt probosti rogovima

gore (2) n krv **gory** adj krvav

gorge /gɔ:dʒ/ n 1 kanjon; ždrijelo (+ anat) 2 sadržaj želuca **it made my ~ rise** dignuo mi se želudac • vi,vt ~ **oneself on/with** žderati, preždravati se (čime)

gorgeous /'gɔ:dʒəs/ adj (pre)krasan, (pre)divan, (pre)lijep

gorilla /gə'rɪlə/ n gorila (+ fig)

gory → **gore** (2)

gosh /gɒʃ/ int euph coll Isuse! Bože!

gosling /'gɒzlɪŋ/ n guščić, gušče

gospel /'gɒspl/ n 1 G~ Evanđelje G~ **according to St Luke** E. po Luki 2

(~ **truth**) nedvojbena istina

gossamer /'gɒsəmə(r)/ n 1 tanka paučina 2 mod lagan, prozračan

gossip /'gɒsɪp/ n 1 ogovaranje; trač coll; naklapanje the ~ **column** tračrubrika 2 nevezan razgovor, čavrljanje 3 (~ **monger**) tračer(ica) • vi ogovarati; tračati coll; naklapati; čavrljati

got v irreg → **get**

Gothic /'gɒθɪk/ adj 1 archit gotski ~ **novel** roman strave 2 print gotički 3 darkerski sl

gotta /'gɒtə/ v coll → **have got to**

gotten v irreg → **get**

gouache /gu'a:ʃ/ n gvaš

gouge /gaʊdʒ/ n (poluokruglo) dlijeto • vt ~ **out** izdubiti; iskopati

gourd /gʊəd/ n tikva

gourmand /'gʊəmənd/ n ljubitelj hrane i pića; izjelica

gourmet /'gʊəmeɪ/ n poznavatelj hrane i pića, gurman

gout /gaʊt/ n kostobolja

govern /'gʌvn/ vt 1 vladati, upravljati 2 odrediti 3 obuzdati 4 be **~ed by** povoditi se (za), slijediti, slušati **~ing** adj vladajući, upravni **~ess** n guvernanta **~ment** n vlada; vladavina **~mental** adj vladin; državni

governor /'gʌvənə(r)/ n 1 namjesnik, guverner 2 član upravnog odbora 3 regulator 4 GB coll šef, gazda; gospon

gown /gaʊn/ n 1 (svečana) haljina **evening ~** večernja haljina **night ~** spavaćica **dressing ~** kućni ogrtač 2 halja; odora; toga; talar

grab /græb/ vt 1 zgrabiti, ugrabiti, uhvatiti 2 na brzinu što učiniti 3 ~ **at sth** posegnuti (za čime)

grace /greɪs/ n 1 lakoća, ljupkost, dražest, gracioznost, elegancija 2 (Božja) milost **in sb's good ~s** u milosti **fall from ~** pasti u nemilost **Your G~** Vaša Milosti 3 molitva prije/poslije jela 4 pristojnost, čast, poštenje **with a good/bad ~** drage volje/nevoljko • vt počastiti, uveličati; ukrasiti **~ful** adj 1 skladan, lagan, graciozan 2 pristojan, pošten, častan **gracious** /'greɪʃəs/ adj 1 ljubazan, uljudan, velikodušan **2** milostiv **3** raskošan

grade /greɪd/ *n* **1** stupanj, razina, klasa **2** *US* razred ~ **school** osnovna škola **3** *US* ocjena **make the ~** uspjeti • *vt* stupnjevati; bodovati, razvrstati po kakvoći **gradation** /grəˈdeɪʃn/ *n* stupanj, nijansa; gradacija **gradient** /ˈgreɪdɪənt/ *n* nagib **gradual** /ˈgrædʒʊəl/ *adj* postupan

graduate /ˈgrædʒʊeɪt/ *vi,vt* **1** *GB, US* diplomirati **2** *US* maturirati **3** obilježiti, stupnjevati • /ˈgrædʒʊət/ *n* **1** *GB* diplomac **2** *US* maturant **graduation** /ˌgrædʒʊˈeɪʃn/ *n* **1** predaja diploma, promocija **2** gradacija

graffiti /grəˈfiːtɪ/ *n pl* grafiti

graft (1) /grɑːft/ *n* cijep, mladica **2** presađeno tkivo • *vt* cijepiti (biljku); presaditi; transplantirati

graft (2) *n US* mito, korupcija, veze

graft (3) *n GB* rad, trud • *vi* marljivo raditi

grain /greɪn/ *n* **1** zrno; zrnce (+ *fig*) **go against the ~** postupati protiv svoje naravi **2** žito **3** mjera za težinu (0.0648 g)

grammar /ˈgræmə(r)/ *n* gramatika ~ **school** *GB* gimnazija **~ian** *n* gramatičar **grammatical** /grəˈmætɪkl/ *adj* gramatički (točan)

gram(me) /græm/ *n* gram

granary /ˈgrænərɪ/ *n* žitnica (+ *fig*)

grand (1) /grænd/ *adj* **1** veličanstven, divan, krasan, sjajan; velik, važan **~child/daughter/son** unuk(a) **~dad/father/pa** djed **~ma/mother** baka **~father clock** veliki drveni sat ~ **piano** klavir **~stand** tribina **2** ohol **~eur** /ˈgrændʒə(r)/ *n* veličina, veličanstvenost

grand (2) *n sl* tisuća

grant /grɑːnt/ *vt* odobriti; dati; ispuniti (želju); pristati; dopustiti; priznati **take sb/sth for ~ed a.** uzeti zdravo za gotovo **b.** zanemarivati, ne cijeniti dovoljno • *n* stipendija; novčana pomoć

granulated /ˈgrænjʊleɪtɪd/ *adj* ~ **sugar** kristalni šećer

grape /greɪp/ *n* grožđe *n collect;* zrno grožđa **a bunch of ~s** grozd **~vine**

loza **on/through ~vine** putem glasina

grapefruit /ˈgreɪpfruːt/ *n* grejpfrut; grejp *coll*

graph /grɑːf / *n* grafikon **~ic** /ˈgræfɪk/ *adj* **1** grafički **2** zoran, živopisan ○ *n* grafika

graphite /ˈgræfaɪt/ *n* grafit

grapple /ˈgræpl/ *vi* (with) **1** hrvati se, boriti se (s) **2** *fig* uhvatiti se u koštac

grasp /grɑːsp/ *vt,vi* **1** čvrsto držati; ugrabiti, zgrabiti, uhvatiti **2** shvatiti **3** ~ **at** posegnuti za • *n* **1** zahvat **in my** ~ u rukama **within** ~ nadohvat ruke **2** shvaćanje, razumijevanje **~ing** *adj* pohlepan, lakom

grass /grɑːs/ *n* **1** trava (+ marihuana) **~hopper** *n* skakavac **~land** pašnjak, livada ~ **roots** obični ljudi, puk **~y** *adj* travnat **2** *GB sl* doušnik

grate (1) /greɪt/ *n* rešetka (kamina)

grate (2) *vt* **1** ribati **~r** *n* ribež **2** strugati; škripati ~ **on sb's nerves** piliti živce **grating** *adj* prodoran, oštar

grateful /ˈgreɪtfl/ *adj* zahvalan

gratify /ˈgrætɪfaɪ/ *vt* nagraditi; zadovoljiti **gratification** /ˌgrætɪfɪˈkeɪʃn/ *n* nagrada, zadovoljenje

gratitude /ˈgrætɪtjuːd/ *n* zahvalnost

gratuitous /grəˈtjuːɪtəs/ *adj* nezaslužen, nepotreban, bezrazložan

gratuity /grəˈtjuːətɪ/ *n form* napojnica; novčana nagrada

grave (1) /greɪv/ *adj* ozbiljan, zabrinjavajući **gravitate** /ˈgrævɪteɪt/ *vi* (to/towards) **1** kretati se (prema); gravitirati; **2** padati, tonuti **gravitation** *n* **1** sklonost **2** sila teža; gravitacija **gravity** /ˈgrævətɪ/ *n* **1** sila teža **2** težina **3** ozbiljnost

grave (2) *n* grob **~digger** grobar **~yard** groblje

gravel /ˈgrævl/ *n* šljunak • *vt* pošljunčati

gravy /ˈgreɪvɪ/ *n* umak; sok od pečenke **~boat** posuda za umak ~ **train** izvor lake zarade

graze (1) /greɪz/ *vi,vt* **1** pasti **2** napasati

graze (2) *vt* **1** oguliti, oderati **2** okrznuti; lagano dodirnuti • *n* ogrebotina

gray *US* → **grey**

grease /griːs/ *n* **1** mast **2** *mech* ulje,

mazivo 3 briljantin • *vt* nauljiti, namazati; podmazati ~ **sb's palm** podmititi koga ~**y** *adj* 1 mastan 2 sklizak 3 *fig* ljigavo udvoran ~**y spoon** *sl* prčvarnica *sl*

great /greɪt/ *adj* 1 velik; važan; sjajan, odličan **a ~ deal/many** mnogo ~! super! **the G~ Wall** Kineski zid **the G~ War** prvi svjetski rat 2 ~ pra- ~**grandfather** pradjed **G~er** *adj* 1 koji uključuje šire gradsko područje 2 *pol* velik ~**ly** *adv* uvelike

Grecian /'griːʃn/ *adj* (staro)grčki

greed /griːd/ *n* pohlepa ~**y** *adj* pohlepan

Greek /griːk/ *adj* grčki

green /griːn/ *adj* 1 zelen (+ *fig*) ~ **beans** *n pl* mahune ~**ery** ukrasno bilje ~**grocer's (shop)** voćarna ~**horn** žutokljunac ~ **pepper** paprika ~**s** zelenje 2 *fig* zavidan, ljubomoran **the ~-eyed monster** ljubomora • *n* 1 zelena boja 2 park; zelene površine *pl* 3 ~**s** zeleni, okolišari

greet /griːt/ *vt* 1 pozdraviti ~**ing** pozdrav ~**ings** čestitke, želje

gregarious /grɪˈgeərɪəs/ *adj* društven

grenade /grɪˈneɪd/ *n* 1 **hand ~** ručna bomba 2 **rifle ~** granata

grew *v irreg* → **grow**

grey /greɪ/ *adj* 1 siv (+ *fig*) ~**hound** hrt 2 sijed • *n* siva boja • *vi* sijedjeti ~**ing** *adj* prosijed

grid /grɪd/ *n* 1 rešetka ~**iron a.** gradele *n pl* **b.** *US* nogometno igralište 2 *GB* električna mreža 3 koordinate

grief /griːf/ *n* žalost, tuga **come to ~** (pro)pasti

grieve /griːv/ *vi,vt* 1 (for) žaliti (za), tugovati 2 (o)žalostiti, rastužiti **grievance** *n* pritužba **grievous** *adj* vrlo težak, ozbiljan **grievous bodily harm** *GB leg* teška tjelesna ozljeda

grill /grɪl/ *n* roštilj; gril • *vi,vt* 1 peći 2 *fig* pržiti se 3 *coll* ispitivati

grille /grɪl/ *n* rešetka

grim /grɪm/ *adj* mračan; strog, oštar; ozbiljan; crn *fig* **the ~ reaper** *fig* smrt

grimace /grɪˈmeɪs/ *n* izraz lica, grimasa • *vi* praviti grimase

grime /graɪm/ *n* nečistoća, prljavština;

čađa **grimy** *adj* prljav; čađav

grin /grɪn/ *n* širok osmijeh • *vi* (at) široko se osmjehivati ~ **and bear it** podnijeti teškoće sa smiješkom

grind /graɪnd/ *vt,vi irreg* 1 mljeti 2 škrgutati (zubima) 3 brusiti ~**stone** *n* brus 4 ~ **down** tlačiti, ugnjetavati 5 ~ **away at** mučiti se; znojiti se *fig* ~**er** *n* 1 mlinac 2 brus(ač) 3 kutnjak

grip /grɪp/ *vt* 1 čvrsto stisnuti, zgrabiti, uhvatiti 2 *fig* obuzeti • *n* 1 stisak **come/get to ~s** uhvatiti se u koštac 2 *sport* zahvat 3 vještina 4 držak ~**ping** *adj* zanimljiv, uzbudljiv

gripe /graɪp/ *vi coll* gunđati, prigovarati • *n* prigovor

gripes /graɪps/ *n pl* grčevi u želucu

grisly /'grɪzlɪ/ *adj* užasan, grozan, jeziv

gristle /'grɪsl/ *n* hrskavica

grit /grɪt/ *n* 1 pijesak 2 hrabrost, odlučnost • *vt* posuti pijeskom ~ **one's teeth** stisnuti zube *fig*

grizzly /'grɪzlɪ/ *n* (~ **bear**) grizli

groan /grəʊn/ *vi* stenjati, ječati; gunđati • *n* uzdah, stenjanje

grocer /'grəʊsə(r)/ *n* trgovac živežnim namirnicama ~**'s** trgovina živežnim namirnicama ~**ies** *pl* namirnice

groggy /'grɒgɪ/ *adj coll* slab, malaksao

groin /grɔɪn/ *n* prepone *pl*

groom /gruːm/ *n* 1 konjušar 2 (**bride~**) ženik • *vt,vi* 1 timariti (konja) 2 dotjerivati, uređivati se 3 (for) pripremati, trenirati

groove /gruːv/ *n* 1 brazda, žlijeb 2 kalup *fig*, kolotečina **groovy** *adj sl* perfa *sl*

grope /grəʊp/ *vi,vt* 1 (na)pipati, tapkati (u mraku) (+ *fig*) 2 *sl* šlatati *sl*, drpati *derog sl*

gross (1) /grəʊs/ *adj* 1 ukupan, brutto 2 grub; očigledan 3 debeo, tust 4 prost; odvratan; neugodan • *vt* zaraditi ukupno

gross (2) *n* 12 tuceta, 144 komada

grotesque /grəʊˈtesk/ *n* groteska • *adj* groteskan

grotty /'grɒtɪ/ *adj GB coll* ružan, grozan

grouch /graʊtʃ/ *vi coll* prigovarati, gunđati • *n* 1 gunđanje 2 gunđalo

ground (1) /graʊnd/ n 1 tlo, zemlja ~ **floor** *GB* prizemlje 2 kopno ~ **troops** kopnene snage 3 morsko dno 4 područje, teren, igralište **lose/give** ~ *mil* povući se s bojnog položaja **get off the** ~ **a.** uzletjeti **b.** početi **go to** ~ sakriti se **stand one's** ~ ne popustiti, ne povući se 5 ~**s** osnova, razlog, temelj **on the** ~**s of** na temelju ~**work** osnova; kostur *fig* 6 podloga, pozadina 7 ~**s** talog • *vi,vt* 1 nasukati se 2 zabraniti polijetanje; *coll* zabraniti izlazak **be** ~**ed on sth** temeljiti se (na) **be well** ~**ed in sth** biti dobro potkovan (u čemu) *fig*

ground (2) *v irreg* → **grind**

group /gru:p/ *n* skupina; grupa • *vi,vt* skupiti (se); razvrstati, grupirati

grouse (1) /graʊs/ *vi coll* (about) gunđati, prigovarati

grouse (2) *n* lještarka

grove /grəʊv/ *n lit* gaj, lug **olive** ~ maslinik

grovel /ˈgrɒvl/ *vi* (to sb) puzati/gmizati pred kim

grow /grəʊ/ *vi,vt irreg* 1 (na)rasti; uspijevati 2 uzgajati; puštati (korijenje, bradu) 3 postati ~ **old** ostariti ~ **away** (from) udaljiti se (od) ~ **out of sth** prerasti (što) ~ **up** odrasti ~**n-up** *n* odrasla osoba ~**ing** *adj* sve veći ~**th** *n* 1 (po)rast; razvoj; povećanje 2 izraslina

growl /graʊl/ *vi* (at) režati (na) (+ *fig*) • *n* režanje

grown *v irreg* → **grow**

grub /grʌb/ *n* 1 ličinka 2 *sl* klopa *sl*

grubby /ˈgrʌbɪ/ *adj* prljav

grudge /grʌdʒ/ *vt* ne priznati; nevoljko dati/učiniti **grudging** *adj* škrt **grudgingly** *adv* nevoljko • *n* zamjerka; ljutnja; mržnja; zavist **have/bear a** ~ **against sb** zamjerati, ljutiti se na koga

gruel /ˈgru:əl/ *n* kaša ~**ling** *adj* iscrpljujući, naporan

gruesome /ˈgru:səm/ *adj* jeziv, strašan, grozan, odvratan

gruff /grʌf/ *adj* grub, opor; osoran

grumble /ˈgrʌmbl/ *vi* 1 gunđati 2 tutnjati, grmiti

grumpy /ˈgrʌmpɪ/ *adj* čangrizav, mr-

zovoljan

grunt /grʌnt/ *vi,vt* 1 (svinja) roktati 2 (osoba) (pro)gunđati • *n mil* guščer *mil sl*

G-string *n* sićušne gaćice *pl*

guarantee /ˌgærənˈti:/ *n* jamstvo; garancija • *vt* jamčiti **guarantor** /ˌgærənˈtɔ:(r)/ *n* jamac **guaranty** /ˈgærəntɪ/ *n leg* jamstvo

guard /gɑ:d/ *n* 1 stražar; čuvar; redarstvenik 2 straža; garda ~**sman** gardist **keep/stand/mount** ~ (over) stražariti; čuvati (koga, što) 3 štitnik 4 oprez, budnost **off** ~ nespreman; na spavanju *fig* • *vt* 1 čuvati 2 ~ **against** štititi (od) ~**ed** *adj* oprezan; suzdržan ~**ian** /ˈgɑ:dɪən/ *n* 1 čuvar 2 skrbnik 3 gvardijan

guerilla /gəˈrɪlə/ *n* 1 gerilac 2 *mod* gerilski

guess /ges/ *vt,vi* 1 pogoditi; nagađati 2 *coll* pretpostaviti • *n* 1 pogodak **have/take/make a** ~ pogađati, pogoditi 2 pretpostavka **your** ~ **is as good as mine** znam koliko i ti, mogu samo nagađati ~**timate** *n coll* gruba procjena ~**work** *n* nagađanje

guest /gest/ *n* gost; posjetitelj ~**house** konačište, hotel ~ **worker** radnik na privremenom radu u inozemstvu

guide /gaɪd/ *n* 1 vodič 2 pokazatelj • *vt* voditi; povoditi se (za čime); upravljati ~**d missile** navođeni projektil ~**lines** *n pl* upute **guidance** *n* 1 poduka 2 vođenje; *mil* navođenje

guild /gɪld/ *n* gilda

guile /gaɪl/ *n* lukavstvo, prijevara ~**less** *adj* bezazlen

guillotine /ˈgɪləti:n/ *n* 1 giljotina 2 stroj za rezanje papira

guilt /gɪlt/ *n* krivnja; osjećaj krivnje ~**y** *adj* (of) kriv (za) ~**y conscience** nečista savjest

guinea /ˈgɪnɪ/ *n* gvineja (1.05 funti)

guinea-pig /ˈgɪnɪ pɪg/ *n* 1 zamorac 2 *fig* pokusni kunić

guise /gaɪz/ *n fig* ruho; krinka

guitar /gɪˈtɑ:(r)/ *n* gitara

gulf /gʌlf/ *n* 1 zaljev **G~ Stream** Golfska struja **the G~ War** rat u Zaljevu 2 *fig, lit* ponor

gull /gʌl/ *n* (**sea~**) galeb

gullet /'gʌlɪt/ *n* **1** jednjak **2** *fig, coll* grlo

gullible /'gʌləbl/ *adj* lakovjeran

gully /'gʌlɪ/ *n* klanac

gulp /gʌlp/ *vi,vt* (down/back) (pro)-gutati • *n* (velik) gutljaj; gutanje

gum (1) /gʌm/ *n* **1** smola ~**tree** eukaliptus **up a** ~**tree** *coll* u škripcu **2** guma **3** ljepilo • *vt* zalijepiti ~**my** *adj* ljepljiv

gum (2) ~**s** *n pl* desni *pl*; zubno meso

gumption /'gʌmpʃn/ *n coll* pribranost, snalažljivost

gun /gʌn/ *n* **1** vatreno oružje; puška; pištolj **at** ~**point** pod prijetnjom oružja ~**boat** *n* topovnjača ~**boat diplomacy** zveckanje oružjem *fig* ~**fire** pucnjava **hired** ~ plaćeni ubojica **machine** ~ strojnica ~**man** naoružani napadač ~**ner** vojnik u topništvu ~**powder** barut ~**runner** krijumčar oružjem ~**shot a.** hitac, pucanj **b.** domet

gurgle /'gɜːgl/ *vi* žuboriti, klokotati; gugutati • *n* žubor

gush /gʌʃ/ *vi,vt* briznuti, šiknuti, navaliti; (iz)lijevati • *n* izljev, navala, provala (+ *fig*) ~**ing** *adj* pretjerano/neiskreno oduševljen

gust /gʌst/ *n* **1** udar **2** *fig* provala, bura ~**y** *adj* olujan

gut /gʌt/ *n* **1** crijevo ~ **reaction/feeling** instinktivna reakcija/osjećaj **hate sb's** ~**s** *coll* mrziti koga iz dna duše **2** ~**s** *coll* hrabrost, odvažnost **3** ~**s** *coll* snaga; bit • *vt* **1** izvaditi iznutrice; rasporiti utrobu **2** uništiti unutrašnjost (zgrade)

gutter /'gʌtə(r)/ *n* **1** žlijeb, oluk **2** jarak, kanal **3** *fig* ulica, blato, bijeda ~ **press** *derog* žuta štampa *coll*

guttural /'gʌtərəl/ *adj* grlen

guv, guv'nor → **governor 4**

guy (1) /gaɪ/ *n coll* **1** tip, dečko, momak, frajer, čovjek **2** *US* dečko, cura **3** (**G~ Fawkes**) lutka koja se pali **5.** studenoga

guy (2) *n* uže

guzzle /'gʌzl/ *vi,vt derog* (down) (po)žderati; lokati

gym /dʒɪm/ *n coll* **1** (**gymnasium**) gimnastička dvorana **2** (**gymnastics**) tjelovježba, gimnastika

gyn(a)ecology /,gaɪnɪ'kɒlədʒɪ/ *n* ginekologija **gynaecologist** *n* ginekolog

gypsy → **gipsy**

H

H, h /eɪtʃ/ 1 8. slovo engl. abecede; ha
2 **H** *sl* heroin

habeas corpus /ˌheɪbɪəs 'kɔːpəs/ *n leg*
sudski nalog

haberdashery /'hæbədæʃərɪ/ *n* poza-
menterija

habit /'hæbɪt/ *n* 1 navika **~ual**
/hə'bɪtʃʊəl/ *adj* uobičajen *he's a ~ual
liar* često laže 2 halja

habitat /'hæbɪtæt/ *n* stanište **~ion**
/ˌhæbɪ'teɪʃn/ *n* 1 stanovanje 2 nastamba **habitable** /'hæbɪtəbl/ *adj* prikladan za stanovanje

hack (1) /hæk/ *vi,vt* (at) (ras)komadati
~ing cough jak suh kašalj **~saw** *n*
pila za rezanje

hack (2) *n* 1 najamni konj 2 piskaralo •
vi,vt jahati

hackles /'hæklz/ *n pl* perje na vratu pi-
jevca **with one's ~ up** ljutit, na-
kostriješen

hackney /'hæknɪ/ *n* konj **~ carriage** fi-
jaker, kočija **~ed** /'hæknɪd/ *adj* otrcan

had *v irreg* → **have**

haddock /'hædək/ *n* bakalar

haemorrhage, hemorrhage /'heməʳ-
rɪdʒ/ *n* krvarenje

haft /haːft/ *n* držak

hag /hæg/ *n* vještica (+ *fig*)

haggard /'hægəd/ *adj* ispijen, oronuo

haggle /'hægl/ *vi* cjenkati se

hail (1) /heɪl/ *n* tuča **~stone** zrno tuče •
vi,vt **1** *it ~s* pada tuča **2** (sth down on
sb) zasuti (koga čime)

hail (2) *vt,vi* 1 pozdraviti **the H~**
Mary Zdravomarija 2 pozvati 3 ~ **from** dolaziti iz

hair /heə(r)/ *n* 1 kosa 2 dlaka **keep
your ~ on** *coll* ne uzrujavaj se **split
~s** cjepidlačiti **~cloth** kostrijet **~cut/-
do/style** frizura **~dresser/stylist** frizer **~drier** sušilo za kosu; fen *coll*

~pin ukosnica **~pin bend** višestruki
zavoj **~y** *adj* dlakav

hale /heɪl/ *adj* ~ **and hearty** zdrav i
čio

half /haːf/ *n* 1 polovina 2 *sport* polu-
vrijeme • *adj* polovičan • *adv* napola
~ **an hour** pola sata ~ *(past) four*
4:30, pola pet **by** ~ jako, previše
~caste *n* mješanac **go off at ~cock**
istrčati pred rudo **go halves** podijeliti
trošak **~hearted** bezvoljan **~way** *adj*
a. na pola puta **b.** polovičan **~wit** *n*
slaboumnik; glupan

hall /hɔːl/ *n* 1 predsoblje 2 aula 3 dvorana 4 blagovaonica **city ~** gradska
vijećnica **~way** veža

hallmark /'hɔːlmaːk/ *n* 1 zlatarski žig 2
fig obilježje

hallow /'hæləʊ/ *vt* posvetiti • *n* **All
H~'s Day/H~mas** Svi sveti **H~e'en**
31. listopada

hallucination /hə,luːsɪ'neɪʃn/ *n* priviđenje; halucinacija **halucinate**
/hə'luːsɪ,neɪt/ *vi* imati priviđenja; ha-
lucinirati

halo /'heɪləʊ/ *n* halo; aureola

halt (1) /hɔːlt/ *n* 1 zastoj, stanka **call a
~ to/bring to a ~** zaustaviti **come to
a ~** zaustaviti se, zastati 2 *GB*
lokalna željeznička postaja • *vi,vt*
zaustaviti; stati ~! *int* stoj!

halt (2) *v* oklijevati; kolebati se

halter /'hɔːltə(r)/ *n* 1 ular, podvodac 2
uže s omčom 3 majica otvorenih leđa

halve /haːv/ *vt* 1 raspoloviti 2 umanjiti
za pola

ham /hæm/ *n* 1 but 2 šunka 3 ~ **radio
operator** radio-amater 4 *coll derog*
amater, loš izvođač

hamlet /'hæmlɪt/ *n* zaselak

hammer /'hæmə(r)/ *n* 1 čekić 2 *sport*
kladivo 3 kokot puške ~ **and tongs**
svom silinom **be/come under the ~**

prodavati se (na dražbi) • *vi,vt* **1** udarati, nabijati, lupati **2** pribiti, zakucati **3** potući ~ **out** a. izravnati; *fig* izgladiti **b.** iskovati (+ *fig*) ~ **at sth** truditi se oko čega

hammock /ˈhæmək/ *n* mreža, ležaljka

hamper (1) /ˈhæmpə(r)/ *vt* smetati, kočiti, otežavati

hamper (2) *n* košara

hamster /ˈhæmstə(r)/ *n* hrčak

hamstring /ˈhæmstrɪŋ/ *n* tetiva koljena • *vt fig* onesposobiti

hand /hænd/ *n* **1** ruka; šaka **at** ~ nadohvat ruke; blizu **at sb's** ~**s** od koga ~ **to**-~ **fighting** borba prsa o prsa **give/lend sb a** ~ pomoći kome **get/gain the upper** ~ steći prednost, nadjačati **free** ~ odriješene ruke ~**s off!** prste k sebi! ~**s up!** ruke uvis! **not lift a** ~ ni prstom ne mrdnuti **on one's** ~**s and knees** na sve četiri **out of** ~ bez odlaganja **get out of** ~ izmaknuti nadzoru **with a heavy/high** ~ diktatorski, surovo **lay one's** ~**s on** sth dočepati se čega **shake** ~**s with sb/shake sb's** ~ rukovati se s kime **win** ~**s down** s lakoćom pobijediti **change** ~**s** promijeniti vlasnika **on the one** ~... **on the other** ~ s jedne strane... s druge strane **right/left** ~ **side** desna/lijeva strana ~**bag** *n* torbica ~**book** priručnik ~**cuffs** *pl* lisice ~**ful** a. pregršt b. šačica, nekoliko **c.** *coll* nemirno/zločesto dijete ~**craft** *n* (ručni) obrt; rukotvorine *pl* ~**work** *n* ručni rad ~**kerchief** rupčić ~**me-down** odjeća starije braće ~**s-on** *adj* praktičan ~**shake** *n* rukovanje ~**stand** *sport* stoj na rukama **2** (~**writing**) rukopis **3** potpis **4** kazaljka **5** pljesak **6** radnik, pomoćnik; mornar **7** podijeljene karte • *vt* **1** uručiti, predati, dodati ~ **sth down to sb** prenositi, ostaviti u baštinu ~ **in** predati ~ **out** a. podijeliti b. udijeliti milostinju ~**out** *n* a. tiskani/umnoženi materijal b. milostinja ~ **over** izručiti predati ~ **it to sb** *coll* odati komu priznanje ~**y** *adj* praktičan, zgodan; pri ruci; spretan **come in** ~**y** dobro doći ~**yman** *n* majstor za sve

handicap /ˈhændɪkæp/ *n* teškoća,

smetnja; hendikep • *vt* otežati; hendikepirati ~**ped** *adj* hendikepiran

handle /ˈhændl/ *n* kvaka; ručka; držak ~**bars** *pl* upravljač bicikla; guvernal *coll* • *vt* **1** rukovati čime; dirati, držati u rukama **2** *fig* postupiti (prema) **3** vladati (situacijom), izaći na kraj ~ **with care** lomljivo! ~**r** *n* dreser

handsome /ˈhænsəm/ *adj* **1** pristao, naočit, zgodan **2** velikodušan

hang /hæŋ/ *vi,vt irreg* ¶ *pp* **hung** za predmete, **hanged** za osobe **1** visiti, biti objesen **2** vjesati, objesiti ~ *wallpaper* lijepiti tapete ~**man** *n* krvnik ~**over** mamurnost ~ **about/around** besposleno se zadržavati; visiti *sl* ~ **back** oklijevati ~ **on** držati, izdržati, ustrajati ~ **on!** čekaj! stani! ~ **on to** sth čvrsto se čega držati ~ **out** a. izvjesiti b. zalaziti, izlaziti ~**out** *n* mjesto za izlaske ~ **together** držati se zajedno ~ **up** spustiti slušalicu, prekinuti vezu **be hung up a.** zadržati se b. *coll* biti iskompleksiran, inhibiran ~**up** *coll* n kompleks ~**er** *n* vješalica ~**ing 1** vješanje **2** *pl* draperije, zavjese ~**nail** zanoktica • **get the** ~ **of sth** *coll* shvatiti (bit čega; kako što radi)

hank /hæŋk/ *n* navoj, kolut

hanker /ˈhæŋkə(r)/ *vi* (after/for) žudjeti (za) ~**ing** *n* žudnja

hanky → **handkerchief** (hand 1)

hansom /ˈhænsəm/ *n* (~ **cab**) fijaker/kočija na dva kotača

haphazard /hæpˈhæzəd/ *adj* slučajan, nasumičan

happen /ˈhæpən/ *vi* dogoditi se, zbiti se *I* ~ *to know* slučajno znam *he* ~*ed to be there* slučajno se tamo zatekao **as it** ~**s** slučajno ~ **(up)on** slučajno naići, naletjeti (na) ~**ing** *n* događaj, događanje

happy /ˈhæpɪ/ *adj* **1** sretan *I'll be* ~ *to* bit će mi drago, rado ću ~**-go-lucky** *adj* bezbrižan **2** prikladan, dobro odabran **happiness** *n* sreća

harass /ˈhærəs/ *vt* mučiti, gnjaviti, uznemirivati, napadati ~**ment** *n* uznemirivanje, salijetanje

harbinger /ˈhɑːbɪndʒə(r)/ *n* navjestitelj, glasnik

harbour (-bor *US*) /'ha:bə(r)/ *n* 1 luka ~ **dues** lučke pristojbe 2 *fig* utočište • *vt* 1 pružiti utočište; zaštititi; sakriti, skloniti 2 gajiti (misli) ~**age** *n* sklonište, zaklon

hard /ha:d/ *adj* 1 tvrd 2 težak 3 strog; oštar; tvrda srca; grub 4 žilav, čvrst ~**back/cover** tvrd uvez ~**board** lesonit • **cash** gotovina *fig* ~**core** *adj fig* tvrd ~ **facts** nepobitne činjenice **no** ~ **feelings** bez uvrede ~**fisted** *adj* škrt ~**headed** *adj* praktičan, racionalan ~**hearted** nemilosrdan ~ **luck** nesreća ~ **of hearing** nagluh ~**ship** *n* nedaća ~ **shoulder** zaustavna traka ~**ware** *n* a. željezna roba **b**. vojna oprema **c**. *comp* hardware ~ **work** naporan/težak posao ~**worker** marljiv radnik ~**y** *adj* 1 snažan, otporan 2 hrabar ~**ly** *adv* 1 jedva; tek što ~ **ever** gotovo nikad 2 teško • *adv* naporno; jako; puno; teško **be** ~ **up** biti bez novca **be** ~ **up for sth** nemati čega ~**boiled** *adj* **a**. tvrdo kuhan **b**. *fig* nesmiljen ~**bitten** *adj* prekaljen ~ **by** blizu **run sb** ~ u stopu pratiti ~**en** *vt* 1 otvrdnuti 2 (pre)kaliti ~**ened criminal** okorjeli zločinac

hare /heə(r)/ *n* zec **run with the ~ and hunt with the hounds** sjediti na dvije stolice ~**bell** *n* plavi zvončić ~**brained** *adj* nepromišljen, budalast ~ **lip** zečja usna

harlot /'ha:lət/ *n arch* bludnica

harm /ha:m/ *n* šteta, povreda; zla namjera **do sb** ~ nauditi, učiniti (komu) nažao • *vt* nauditi (komu); ozlijediti; oštetiti ~**ful** *adj* štetan ~**less** *adj* bezopasan, bezazlen, neškodljiv

harmonica /ha:'mɒnɪkə/ *n* usna harmonika **harmonious** /ha:'məʊnɪəs/ *adj* skladan; složan **harmonize** /'ha:mənaɪz/ *vi,vt* 1 uskladiti 2 slagati se **harmony** /'ha:mənɪ/ *n* sloga; sklad

harness /'ha:nɪs/ *n* orma **in** ~ upregnut • *vt* upregnuti (+ *fig*)

harp /ha:p/ *n* harfa • *vi* svirati harfu ~ **on sth** stalno pjevati istu pjesmu

harpoon /ha:'pu:n/ *n* harpun

harpy /'ha:pɪ/ *n* 1 *myth* harpija 2 *fig* rospija

harridan /'hærɪdən/ *n* stara vještica; babetina

harrier /'hærɪə(r)/ *n* 1 pas zečar 2 trkač 3 sokol

harrow /'hærəʊ/ *n* drljača ~**ing** *adj fig* potresan

harry /'hærɪ/ *vt* 1 pljačkati; pustošiti; napadati 2 gnjaviti, mučiti

harsh /ha:ʃ/ *adj* hrapav; grub; oštar; strog

hart /ha:t/ *n* jelen

harum-scarum /,heərəm 'skeərəm/ *adv coll* nepromišljeno, bezglavo

harvest /'ha:vɪst/ *n* 1 žetva 2 *fig* plodovi rada • *vi,vt* žeti, ubirati ~**er** *n* 1 žetelac (osoba) 2 žetelica (stroj) **combine** ~**er** kombajn

has /hæz/ *v irreg* → **have** ~**been** *n* osoba/predmet čije je vrijeme prošlo

hash /hæʃ/ *vt* (~ **up**) kosati • *n* 1 jelo od kosana mesa 2 *US coll* klopa *sl* 3 *coll* hašiš

hasp /ha:sp/ *n* preklopac (lokota)

hassle /'hæsl/ *n coll* 1 teškoća; gnjavaža 2 svađa • *vt* gnjaviti, dosađivati

hassock /'hæsək/ *n* jastučić za klečanje

haste /heɪst/ *n* žurba, hitnja **make** ~ žuriti se, hitati **more** ~ **less speed** *prov* polako, ali sigurno ~**n** *vi,vt* 1 žuriti se 2 požurivati **hasty** *adj* užurban, prenagljen **hastily** *adv* na brzinu

hat /hæt/ *n* šešir **send the** ~ **round** skupljati priloge **I take my** ~ **to** *fig* skidam kapu ~**ter** *n* klobučar **as mad as a** ~**ter** potpuno lud

hatch (1) /hætʃ/ *n* prozorčić; otvor

hatch (2) *vi,vt* 1 (iz)leći (se) **don't count your chickens before they're** ~**ed** *prov* ne pravi ražanj dok je zec u šumi 2 *fig* smisliti, skovati ~**ery** *n* 1 inkubator (za piliće) 2 mrijestilište

hatchet /'hætʃɪt/ *n* sjekirica **bury the** ~ zakopati ratnu sjekiru ~ **man** plaćeni ubojica

hate /heɪt/ *n* mržnja • *vt* mrziti ~**ful** *adj* mrzak; odvratan **hatred** /'heɪtrɪd/ *n* mržnja

haughty /'hɔ:tɪ/ *adj* ohol, gord

haul /hɔ:l/ *vt* 1 vući, dovlačiti; tegliti; prevoziti 2 promijeniti smjer • *n* 1 vučenje, tegljenje 2 ulov ~age n prijevoz ~ier, ~er n prijevoznik

haunch /hɔ:ntʃ/ n bok

haunt /hɔ:nt/ vt progoniti, ne dati mira **the castle is ~ed** u zamku ima duhova ~ing adj koji progoni, ne da mira • n omiljeno mjesto, boravište

have /hæv/ vt irreg 1 (~ got) imati ~ a **bath/shower** okupati/istuširati se ~ **breakfast/lunch** doručkovati/ručati ~ **a drink** popiti nešto ~ **sth to eat** pojesti nešto ~ **fun** zabaviti se ~ **a go at sth** pokušati ~ **a good time** dobro se provesti ~ **a look** pogledati **I won't ~ it** neću to dopustiti **we've had it** sl propali smo, gotovi smo ~ **(sth) on** imati (što) na sebi ~ **a rest** odmoriti se **rumour has it** priča se ~ **tea** piti čaj **you'll ~ it back** vratit ću ti 2 ~ **to** morati 3 ~ **sth done** dati napraviti *I had my car repaired* dao sam popraviti automobil 4 aux pomoćni glagol pri tvorbi perfekta (~ + past participle) *I ~ gone* otišao sam • n **the ~s and the ~-nots** bogati i siromašni

haven /heɪvn/ n 1 luka 2 fig utočište **safe ~** zaštićena zona

haversack /hævəsæk/ n ranac; ruksak

havoc /hævək/ n 1 katastrofa; velike štete pl; opustošenje **play ~ with/among, make ~ of** uništiti, razoriti, opustošiti, poharati

haw /hɔ:/ n glog (plod) ~**thorn** glog (grm, drvo)

hawk /hɔ:k/ n 1 jastreb 2 sokol ~**eyed** adj oka sokolova

hay /heɪ/ n sijeno **make ~ of sth** razbacati, unijeti pomutnju **make ~ while the sun shines** prov željezo se kuje dok je vruće ~**cock/rick/stack** stog/plast sijena ~ **fever** peludna groznica ~**fork** vile pl **go ~wire** sl skrenuti; poremetiti se **a roll in the ~** euph ljubakanje

hazard /hæzəd/ n 1 pogibelj, opasnost, rizik **smoking is a ~** pušenje šteti zdravlju 2 kocka(nje) • vt 1 izložiti pogibelji, riskirati, staviti na kocku 2 usuditi se reći/učiniti

haze (1) /heɪz/ n 1 izmaglica 2 fig nesigurnost; zbunjenost

haze (2) vt ponižavati; mučiti

hazel /heɪzl/ n 1 ljeska ~**nut** lješnjak 2 boja lješnjaka

he /hi:/ pron on • prefix mužjak ~**goat** jarac ~**man** iron muškarčina, snagator

head /hed/ n 1 glava **at the ~ of** na čelu **be ~ and shoulders above sb** fig biti znatno bolji **bite sb's ~ off** izgalamiti se na koga **give ~** tab sl popušiti **tab sl ~ over heels** a. naglavačke b. fig do ušiju (zaljubljen); do grla (u dugovima) **hit the nail on the ~** pogoditi u sridu **lose one's ~** izgubiti živce, razbjesniti se **I can't make ~ or tail of it** uopće to ne razumijem *we must put our ~s together* moramo se dogovoriti ~**on collision** izravni sudar **scream one's ~ off** vrištati iz petnih žila ~**s or tails?** glava ili pismo? **talk one's ~ off** previše pričati ~**ache** glavobolja ~**light** prednje svjetlo ~**line** a. novinski naslov b. TV-najava glavne vijesti ~**long** adv naglavce; bezglavo, nepromišljeno ~**master** ravnatelj ~**phones** slušalice ~**piece** a. kaciga b. fig mozak, pamet ~**quarters** glavni stožer ~**stone** nadgrobni kamen ~**strong** adj samovoljan; tvrdoglav ~**way** napredak ~**word** natuknica ~y adj a. samovoljan; nepromišljen b. opojan (+ fig) 2. poglavlje 3 predsjednik **H~ of State** predsjednik, šef države/vlade 4 (~**land**) rt 5 pjena (piva) • vt,vi 1 predvoditi, biti na čelu 2 (for) uputiti se, kretati prema *he's ~ing for disaster* srlja u propast 3 udariti glavom ~**er** n a. skok na glavu b. udarac glavom ~**ing** n naslov; zaglavlje

heal /hi:l/ vi,vt 1 zacijeliti 2 (iz)liječiti **time ~s all sorrows** prov vrijeme liječi sve rane **faith ~er** n iscjelitelj

health /helθ/ n 1 zdravlje ~**food** zdrava (pre)hrana **drink sb's ~** nazdraviti kome ~**ful** adj zdrav, ljekovit ~y adj zdrav 2 zdravstvo **the Department of H~ and Social Security** GB Ministarstvo zdravstva i socijalne skrbi

heap /hi:p/ n gomila, hrpa (+ fig);

mnoštvo; *coll* puno • *vt* ~ **up 1** naslagati; nagomilati; zgrnuti; natrpati **2** obasuti

hear /hɜ(r)/ *vi,vt* 1 čuti *I can't* ~ *you* ne čujem te *do you* ~ *from him*? javlja li ti se? ~**say** *n* rekla-kazala **2** *leg* saslušati ~ *me out* saslušaj me do kraja **3** H~, ~! (+ *iron*) bravo! tako je! ~**ing** *n* **1** sluh ~**ing aid** slušni aparat ~**ing-impaired** *adj* oštećena sluha **2** *leg* saslušanje

heard *v irreg* → **hear**

hearse /hɜ:s/ *n* mrtvačka kola

heart /hɑ:t/ *n* srce (+ *fig*) **at** ~ u duši **from the bottom of one's** ~ od sveg srca **in one's** ~ **of** ~s u dubini duše **by** ~ napamet **have a change of** ~ promijeniti mišljenje/stav ~ **to** ~ iskren, otvoren **have one's** ~ **set on** žarko željeti **lose** ~ obeshrabriti se **lose one's** ~ **to sb** zaljubiti se u koga **wear one's** ~ **on one's sleeve** pokazivati osjećaje ~**ache** *n* tuga ~**attack** srčani udar, infarkt ~**breaking/rending** *adj* tužan; srcedrapajući *coll* ~**burn** *n* žgaravica ~**burning** *n* zavist, ogorčenje ~**failure** popuštanje srca **faint-~ed** *adj* malodušan, kukavica *n* ~**felt** *adj* iskren ~**sick** potišten ~**strings** *pl* najdublji osjećaji ~**less** *adj* bezosjećajan, nemilosrdan ~**en** *vt* ohrabriti; razv6eseliti ~**y** *adj* iskren; srdačan **2** *fig* središte; bit, srž, jezgra **3** (karte) srce; herc *coll*

hearth /hɑ:θ/ *n* ognjište (+ *fig*)

heat /hi:t/ *n* 1 vrućina; toplina ~**stroke** toplinski udar **2** *fig* žar **3** (kvalifikacijsko) natjecanje, utrka **4** *zoo* tjeranje **5** *sl* policija; murija *sl* • *vt* (~ **up**) zagrijati; podgrijati ~**ed** *adj fig* vatren, žestok, usijan ~**er** *n* grijalica; peć **immersion** ~**er** bojler **fan** ~**er** kaloriser *coll* ~**ing** *n* grijanje

heath /hi:θ/ *n* 1 pustopoljina, vriština **2** vrijes

heathen /'hi:ðn/ *n* 1 poganin; nekrst **2** *fig* divljak, barbarin ~**dom** *n* poganske zemlje

heather /'heðə(r)/ *n* vrijesak

heave /hi:v/ *v irreg* **1** dignuti **2** dizati se i spuštati; nadimati se **3** *coll* izbaciti ~ **a sigh** uzdahnuti **4** (at/on sth)

vući ~ **to** zaustaviti se

heaven /'hevn/ *n* 1 (H) raj (+ *fig*) nebesa **3** (**the ~s**) nebo, nebeski svod **H~ forbid!** ne daj Bože, sačuvaj Bože! **for H~'s sake!** zaboga! (**good**) **H~s!** nebesa! ~**ly** *adj* 1 rajski, bajan, prekrasan **2** nebeski ~**ly bodies** nebeska tijela

heavy /'hevɪ/ *adj* 1 težak **2** spor, dosadan, zamoran; usporen, trom ~ **casualties** teški gubici, puno žrtava ~ **crops** obilan urod ~**duty** *adj* otporan ~ **fire** žestoka vatra ~**handed** *adj* nespretan ~**hearted** *adj* sjetan ~ **rain** jaka kiša ~ **sky** tmurno nebo ~ **sleep** dubok san ~ **smoker/drinker** osoba koja puno puši/pije ~ **tidings** loše vijesti ~ **traffic** gust promet ~**weight** teška kategorija • *adv* teško ~**ly** *adv* teško

Hebrew /'hi:bru:/ *n* 1 hebrejski jezik **2** Židov; Izraelac • *adj* hebrejski, židovski

heck /hek/ *n coll euph* → **hell**

heckle /'hekl/ *vi,vt* upadicama i pitanjima ometati govornika

hectare /'hektɛə(r)/ *n* hektar

hectic /'hektɪk/ *adj* 1 crven; sušičav; grozničav (+ *fig*) **2** *coll* uzbudljiv

hector /'hektə(r)/ *vt* terorizirati

hedge /hedʒ/ *n* 1 živica ~**hog** *n* jež ~**hop** *vi* nisko letjeti **2** *fig* zaštita, ograda • *vt,vi* 1 ograditi živicom **2** ograditi se *fig*; izbjegavati odgovor **3** *fig* osigurati se

heed /hi:d/ *vt form* obratiti pozornost na; hajati • *n* pozornost **pay/give** ~ (**to**); **take** ~ (**of**) obratiti pozornost (na); hajati

hee-haw /'hi:hɔ:/ *n* 1 njakanje **2** *fig* grohot

heel /hi:l/ *n* peta; potpetica **at/to sb's** ~ za petama **bring to** ~ pokoriti **down at** ~ a. iznošen b. *fig* otrcan **head over** ~s a. naglavce; bezglavo b. potpuno; do ušiju **kick one's** ~s besposleno čekati **take to one's** ~s dati petama vjetra **well-~ed** *adj* bogat

hefty /'heftɪ/ *adj* snažan, kršan

hegemony /hɪ'gemənɪ/ *n* hegemonija

heifer /'hefə(r)/ *n* junica

height /haɪt/ n 1 visina 2 uzvisina 3 vrhunac **~en** vt,vi povisiti; povećati (se); istaknuti

heir /eə(r)/ n nasljednik **~ apparent** prijestolonasljednik **~ess** n nasljednica **~loom** baština

held v irreg → **hold**

helicopter /'helɪkɒptə(r)/ n helikopter

hell /hel/ n pakao (+ fig) **~!** int kvragu! dovraga! **a/one ~ of a** puno, jako **what the ~** kog vraga **come ~ or high water** kud puklo da puklo **for the ~ of it** coll iz puke zabave **like ~!** vraga! **run like ~** juriti **play ~ with** pomutiti **raise ~** razgalamiti se **~ish** adj paklenski **~-bent on sth** coll tvrdoglavo odlučan

hello /hə'ləʊ/ int 1 zdravo **say ~** pozdraviti 2 halo

Hellenic /he'liːnɪk/ adj (staro)grčki

helm /helm/ n 1 kormilo (+ fig) 2 arch kaciga **~sman** n kormilar

helmet /'helmɪt/ n kaciga

help /help/ n 1 pomoć **~!** upomoć! **be of ~** pomoći 2 pomoćnik **~ful** adj od pomoći, uslužan **~less** adj bespomoćan **~ing** n porcija • vi,vt pomoći, pomagati **may I ~ you?** izvolite? **I can't ~ it** ne mogu ja tu ništa **if I can ~ it** ako ja to mogu spriječiti **~ out** pripomoći **~ yourself** (to sth) poslužite se (čime) **give someone a ~ing hand** pomoći kome u nevolji

helter-skelter /ˌheltə 'skeltə(r)/ adv navrat-nanos

hem /hem/ n (po)rub • vt porubiti **~med in** u okruženju

hemisphere /'hemɪsfɪə(r)/ n polutka; hemisfera

hemorrhage /'hemərɪdʒ/ n krvarenje

hemp /hemp/ n konoplja

hen /hen/ n 1 kokoš **~-house** kokošinjac **~ party** iron ženska zabava **~peck** vt držati koga pod papučom 2 n ženka ptice

hence adv form 1 stoga, zato 2 odavde; odsad **~forth** adv odsad nadalje, ubuduće

henchman /'hentʃmən/ n slijepi sljedbenik

henna /'henə/ n kana

her /hɜː/ poss adj njezin **~s** poss pron njezino • pers pron → **she ~self** pron 1 reflex sebe, se; sebi, si (**all**) **by ~ self** (potpuno) sama 2 emph ona sama, ona osobno

herald /'herəld/ n 1 glasnik 2 fig navjestitelj **~ry** n heraldika

herb /hɜːb/ n 1 biljka 2 ljekovita biljka **~al** adj biljni

herd /hɜːd/ n 1 stado; krdo; jato 2 fig svjetina, rulja • vi,vt skupiti (se) na gomilu

here /hɪə(r)/ adv 1 ovdje; tu 2 **~ we are** evo nas **~ you are!** izvoli! **~'s to you!** u tvoje zdravlje! **~ and there** svugdje **~abouts** adv ovdje/tu negdje **~after** adv odsad nadalje **~by** form ovime

hereditary /hɪ'redɪtrɪ/ adj nasljedni **heredity** n nasljeđivanje

heresy /'herəsɪ/ n krivovjerje; hereza **heretic** /'heretɪk/ n krivovjernik; heretik

heritage /'herɪtɪdʒ/ n baština; nasljeđe

hermit /'hɜːmɪt/ n pustinjak **~age** n pustinjakova nastamba

hero /'hɪərəʊ/ n 1 junak; heroj **~ worship** obožavanje, idoliziranje **~ine** n junakinja **~ism** junaštvo **~ic** adj junački

heroin /'herəʊɪn/ n heroin

heron /'herən/ n čaplja

herring /'herɪŋ/ n haringa **~-bone** riblja kost **red ~ a.** dimljena haringa **b.** namjerna digresija

hesitate /'hezɪteɪt/ vi oklijevati **hesita-'tion** /ˌhezɪ'teɪʃn/ n oklijevanje, neodlučnost **hesitant** /'hezɪtənt/ adj neodlučan

heterogenous /ˌhetərə'dʒiːnɪəs/ adj raznovrstan, heterogen

hew /hjuː/ vt irreg 1 (sa)sjeći, (is)cijepati 2 prokrčiti (+ fig)

hewn v irreg → **hew**

hey /heɪ/ int hej!

hey-day /'heɪ deɪ/ n vrhunac, zlatno doba

hi /haɪ/ int coll bok!

hiatus /haɪ'eɪtəs/ n prekid

hibernate /'haɪbəneɪt/ vi spavati zimski san

hiccup, hiccough /'hɪkʌp/ vi štucati • (**the ~s**) n štucavica

hid, hidden v irreg → hide
hide (1) /haɪd/ vi,vt irreg sakriti (se); skrivati se **~and-seek** n igra skrivača **hiding-place** n skrovište • (**~out, ~away**) n skrovište
hide (2) n koža **tan sb's ~/give a good hiding** nalupati/ namlatiti koga **~bound** adj zadrt
hideous /'hɪdɪəs/ adj strašan, grozan, odvratan
hierarchy /'haɪərɑːkɪ/ n hijerarhija
high /haɪ/ adj 1 visok 2 drogiran; pijan **~ and dry a.** nasukan **b.** fig ostavljen na cjedilu **~brow** adj iron visokoparan **H~ Church** dio Anglikanske crkve najsličniji katoličkoj **~class** adj prvoklasan (¶ → **upper**) **~flier/flyer** n pretjerano ambiciozna osoba; karijerist coll the **~ jump** sport skok uvis **~land** n planinski kraj **the H~lands** n pl Škotsko visočje **~lander** n gorštak **~ life** život na visokoj nozi **~light** n a. najistaknutiji dio **b.** najznačajniji događaj **c.** (posvijetljeni) pramen **~ mass** svečana misa **~ priest a.** vrhovni svećenik **b.** fig najutjecajnija osoba **~profile** adj istaknut **~rise** (**building**) neboder **~ school** US srednja škola **~sounding** adj pompozan **~spirited** adj živahan **~(ly-)strung** adj napet, preosjetljiv **~ tea** GB večera **~ tech** adj supermoderan o n visoka tehnologija **~ tide** plima **~ time** krajnje vrijeme **~ treason** veleizdaja **~way** n glavna (međugradska) cesta **~wayman** n hist razbojnik • adv visoko **fly ~ a.** visoko letjeti **b.** fig biti vrlo ambiciozan **~ly** adv 1 vrlo, izuzetno 2 visoko **think ~ly** of imati visoko mišljenje o **~ness** n visina **Your/Her H~ness** Vaša Visosti
hijack /'haɪdʒæk/ vt oteti (zrakoplov, automobil) • (**~ing**) n otmica (zrakoplova)
hike /haɪk/ vi,vt 1 pješačiti 2 naglo dignuti • n šetnja, pješačenje
hilarious /hɪ'leərɪəs/ adj bučno veseo; zabavan
hill /hɪl/ n brijeg; brdo **~side** n obronak **~ock** n brežuljak **~y** adj brdovit **~bil-**

ly n derog seljak
hilt /hɪlt/ n držak
him /hɪm/ → he
himself /hɪm'self/ pron 1 reflex sebe, se; sebi, si (**all**) **by ~** (potpuno) sam 2 emph on sam, on osobno
hind (1) /haɪnd/ adj stražnji **~sight** n vremenska perspektiva
hind (2) /haɪnd/ n košuta
hinder /'hɪndə(r)/ vt (s)priječiti, otežati **hindrance** /'hɪndrəns/ n prepreka, smetnja
hinge /hɪndʒ/ n šarka • vi **~ on/upon** ovisiti o
hint /hɪnt/ vi,vt 1 neizravno dati do znanja 2 **~ at** aludirati na • n znak, aluzija **drop/give a ~** neizravno dati do znanja, natuknuti
hinterland /'hɪntələnd/ n zaleđe
hip (1) /hɪp/ n bok; bedro; kuk
hip (2) n šipak
hip (3) adj sl u trendu coll
hippo /'hɪpəʊ/, **hippopotamus** /,hɪpə-'pɒtəməs/ n vodeni konj
hire /'haɪə(r)/ vt 1 unajmiti **~ out** iznajmiti 2 zaposliti • n najam **~ purchase** kupnja na otplatu **~ling** n derog plaćenik; prodana duša
his /hɪz/ poss 1 pron njegov 2 adj njegovo
hiss /hɪs/ vi,vt 1 siktati (zmija); puhati (mačka) 2 (i)zviždati
history /'hɪstrɪ/ n povijest; (**ancient**) ~ fig davna prošlost, bilo pa prošlo **make ~** ući u povijest **natural ~** prirodopis **historian** /hɪ'stɔːrɪən/ n povjesničar, historičar **historic(al)** /hɪ'stɒrɪk/(hɪ'stɒrɪkl) adj povijesni
hit /hɪt/ vt, vi irreg 1 udariti 2 pogoditi **~ it off** složiti, sprijateljiti se **~ the road** coll put pod noge **~ the roof** eksplodirati od bijesa **~ back** uzvratiti **~ on/upon** nabasati, naletjeti • n 1 udarac 2 hit coll; veliki uspjeh 3 sl plaćeno ubojstvo **~ list** popis osoba koje treba ukloniti **~ man** sl plaćeni ubojica
hitch /hɪtʃ/ vt,vi 1 coll (**~ a ride**) autostopirati **~hike** vi autostopirati **~hiker** n auto-stopist 2 povući, potegnuti 3 pričvrstiti; zakvačiti **get ~ed** coll vjenčati se • n 1 trzaj, povlačenje

2 zastoj

hive /haɪv/ n 1 košnica (+ fig) • vt, vi ~
off 1 odvojiti 2 nestati

hoard /hɔ:d/ n 1 (tajna) zaliha • vt, vi
stvarati zalihe; skupljati; zgrtati

hoarding /'hɔ:dɪŋ/ n 1 ograda 2 oglasna ploča

hoarfrost /hɔ:(r)frɒst/ n inje

hoarse /hɔ:s/ adj promukao; grub

hoax /həʊks/ n podvala; varka • prevariti; nasamariti

hobble /'hɒbl/ vi, vt 1 hramati 2 sapeti
noge (konju)

hobby /'hɒbɪ/ n hobi ~horse n a. konjić za njihanje b. fig omiljena tema

hobnob /'hɒbnɒb/ vi družiti se

hobo /'həʊbəʊ/ n US skitnica

hockey /'hɒkɪ/ n (field ~) hokej na
travi ice ~ hokej na ledu

hoe /həʊ/ n motika

hog /hɒg/ n prasac, svinja (+ fig) • vt
coll uzurpirati (fig)

Hogmanay /'hɒgmənɪ/ n (u Škotskoj)
doček nove godine

hoist /hɔɪst/ vt (po)dignuti • n dizalo

hold /həʊld/ vt, vi irreg 1 držati,
zadržati (se); izdržati; održati 2 smatrati 3 biti vlasnik 4 zauzimati
položaj; obnašati dužnost ~ (the
line) ostati na vezi ~ one's breath
zadržati dah ~ your fire! ne pucajte!
~ your tongue! jezik za zube! ~ it
(right there)! ne miči se! ~ talks
voditi razgovore (not) ~ water (ne)
biti uvjerljiv ~ one's ground obraniti
položaj; ne povući se cigarette-~er
cigaretnik ~-all n putna torba ~ sth
against sb uzeti za zlo ~ back a. oklijevati b. priječiti c. zadržati za sebe
~ in obuzdati ~ on a. izdržati b.
on! stani, čekaj! ~ on to držati se za,
ne pustiti ~ out izdržati, odoljeti ~
over odgoditi ~ up zadržati ~up n
oružana pljačka • n 1 držanje get ~ of
uhvatiti, zgrabiti, dokopati se 2 nadzor; utjecaj 3 stisak 4 oslonac 5 zahvat no ~s barred bez ograničenja
~ing n holding

hole /həʊl/ n 1 rupa (+ fig) pick ~s
nalaziti pogreške a square peg in a
round ~ neprikladna osoba 2 coll
neprilika 3 duplja • vi, vt izbu-

šiti/pogoditi rupu

holiday /'hɒlədeɪ/ n 1 praznik; blagdan
bank ~ GB neradni dan 2 (~s)
(godišnji) odmor; (školski) praznici
~**maker** n izletnik; turist

holiness /'həʊlɪnɪs/ n svetost

holler /'hɒlə(r)/ vi, vt US sl vikati

hollow /'hɒləʊ/ adj 1 šupalj; prazan (+
fig); isprazan ~ **cheeks** upali obrazi •
vt (~ **out**) izdubiti

holly /'hɒlɪ/ n božikovina

holocaust /'hɒləkɔ:st/ n holokaust

holster /'həʊlstə(r)/ n futrola

holy /'həʊlɪ/ adj 1 svet the H~ **Office**
Inkvizicija ~ **war** vjerski rat H~
Week Veliki tjedan 2 pobožan; sve-
tački

homage /'hɒmɪdʒ/ n izraz štovanja
pay ~ **to** izraziti štovanje

home /həʊm/ n 1 dom; kuća; obitelj
(fig) **at** ~ a. doma; kod kuće b. dobro upućen; siguran 2 mod domaći;
iz zemlje ~ **front** pozadina ~ **guard**
domobrani ~**land** n domovina ~
made/grown domaći the H~ **Office**
GB Ministarstvo unutarnjih poslova
the H~ Secretary GB Ministar unutarnjih poslova H~ **Rule** samouprava
~**sick** adj nostalgičan the ~ **team** domaća momčad ~ **town** rodni grad
~**work** n domaća zadaća; priprema ~
truth bolna istina • adv 1 doma; kući
2 do kraja **drive the point** ~ poanti-
rati ~**less** adj bez doma; beskućnik n
homing device naprava za (samo)
navođenje ~**ly** adj 1 jednostavan; domaći 2 US neugledan

homicide /'hɒmɪsaɪd/ n 1 ubojstvo 2
ubojica

homogeneous /,hɒmə'dʒi:nɪəs/ adj
homogen; istovrstan

homosexual /,hɒmə'sekʃʊəl/ adj homoseksualan • n homoseksualac; homoseksualka

honest /'ɒnɪst/ adj pošten; iskren;
otvoren ~**ly** adv iskreno (govoreći);
doista ~**y** n poštenje; iskrenost

honey /'hʌnɪ/ n 1 med ~**bee** pčela
~**comb** saće ~**moon** medeni mjesec
~**suckle** kozja krv 2 coll dušo

honk /hɒŋk/ vi 1 zatrubiti 2 (guska)
gaknuti

honorary /'ɒnərərɪ/ *adj* 1 počasni 2 ne-plaćeni

honour (-**nor** *US*) /'ɒnə(r)/ *n* 1 (po)čast **guard of ~** počasna straža **a man of ~** častan čovjek **a point of ~** pitanje časti *I have the ~ to* čast mi je **Your H~** Časni suče 2 *mod* počasni • *vt* 1 počastiti 2 isplatiti; ispoštovati **~able** *adj* častan **H~able (Hon)** plemeniti

hood /hʊd/ *n* 1 kapuljača 2 *US* pokrov motora; hauba *coll* 3 (**~loom**) *sl* razbojnik, gangster

hoof /hu:f/ *n* (*pl* ~s, **hooves**) kopito

hook /hʊk/ *n* 1 kuka 2 udica (+ *fig*) 3 srp **by ~ or by crook** milom ili silom • *vt* zakvačiti; svinuti; upecati (+ *fig*) **be ~ed (on)** biti ovisan (o) **~er** *n sl* prostitutka

hooky /'hʊkɪ/ *adj* **play ~** markirati

hooligan /'hu:lɪgən/ *n* huligan **football ~ism** izgredi nogometnih navijača

hoop /hu:p/ *n* obruč; metalni prsten

hooray /hu:'reɪ/ *int* hura!

hoot /hu:t/ *vi,vt* 1 (sova) hukati 2 trubiti 3 izvižđati **~er** *n* sirena; truba

hoover /'hu:və(r)/ *n TM coll* usisač • *vt* (o)čistiti usisačem

hop (1) /hɒp/ *n* (~s) hmelj

hop (2) *vi,vt* skakutati; skakati; preskočiti • *n* skok ~, **skip/step and jump** *sport* troskok **~scotch** *n* školica

hope /həʊp/ *n* nada • *vi,vt* nadati se **~ against ~** nadati se unatoč beznadnosti situacije **~ful** *adj* koji ima/daje nade; koji obećava **~fully** *adv* nadajući se, u nadi *fully I'll see him tomorrow* nadam se da ću ga sutra vidjeti **~less** *adj* beznadan

hopper /'hɒpə(r)/ *n* 1 lijevak 2 kukac koji skače

horde /hɔ:d/ *n* horda (+ *fig*); mnoštvo

horizon /hə'raɪzn/ *n* 1 obzor; horizont 2 granica (*fig*) **~tal** /hɒrɪ'zɒntl/ *adj* vodoravan

horn /hɔ:n/ *n* 1 rog (+ *mus*) **~pipe** *n* mornarski ples **~ed** *adj* rogat **~y** *sl* uzbuđen, pohotan, naranjen *sl* 2 *mod* rožnat **~-rimmed glasses** naočale s rožnatim okvirom 3 truba

hornet /'hɔ:nɪt/ *n* stršljen **stir up a ~'s**

nest dirnuti u osinjak

horrendous /hɒ'rendəs/ *adj coll* strašan, užasan

horrible /'hɒrəbl/ *adj* 1 strašan 2 *coll* grozan; očajan

horrid /'hɒrɪd/ *adj* 1 strašan, užasan 2 *coll* odvratan

horrify /'hɒrɪfaɪ/ *vt* prestraviti; užasnuti

horror /'hɒrə(r)/ *n* strava; užas; grozota, strahota ~ **film** film strave **~-struck/stricken** *adj* prestravljen, užasnut

horse /hɔ:s/ *n* 1 konj 2 konjica ~ **and foot** konjica i pješaštvo **a ~ of another colour** drugi par rukava **flog a dead ~** uzalud se truditi **get on one's high ~** praviti se važan **straight from the ~'s mouth** iz prve ruke **on ~back** na konju **~fly** *n* obad **~man** *n* konjanik, jahač **~power (hp)** konjska snaga **~radish** *n* hren **~shoe** *n* potkova • *vi* ~ **around** *sl* zafrkavati se; zbijati neslane šale

horticulture /'hɔ:tɪkʌltʃə(r)/ *n* vrtlarstvo

hose (1) /həʊz/ *n* gumena/platnena cijev **~pipe** cijev za polijevanje, crijevo; šmrk *coll*

hose (2) *n* čarape **panty-~** *US* hulahopke *coll*

hospice /'hɒspɪs/ *n* konačište

hospitable /hɒ'spɪtəbl/ *adj* gostoljubiv

hospital /'hɒspɪtl/ *n* bolnica **~ize** *vt* primiti/smjestiti u bolnicu

hospitality /ˌhɒspɪ'tælətɪ/ *n* gostoprimstvo; gostoljubivost

host (1) /həʊst/ *n* 1 domaćin, voditelj emisije **~ess** domaćica **air ~ess** stjuardesa 2 gostioničar • *vt* ugostiti; voditi

host (2) 1 *arch* vojska 2 mnoštvo

Host (3) *n* **the ~** hostija

hostage /'hɒstɪdʒ/ *n* talac

hostel /'hɒstl/ *n* prenoćište **youth ~** hostel

hostile /'hɒstaɪl/ *adj* neprijateljski, odbojan **hostility** /hɒs'tɪlətɪ/ *n* neprijateljstvo **~ties** *n pl* sukobi, borbe

hot /hɒt/ *adj* 1 vruć *I am ~* vruće mi je **get into ~ water** upasti u nepriliku **get ~ under the collar** raspaliti se, planuti ~ **air** isprazne riječi, prazna obećanja ~**bed** *fig* leglo ~**blooded** *adj* strastven ~**headed** *adj* usijane glave, nepromišljen ~**house** *n* staklenik ~ **news** najnovija/senzacionalna vijest ~**plate** ploča štednjaka; grijalo ~ **potato** neugodan problem **the ~ seat** električna stolica; *fig* neugodan položaj ~ **spot** krizno područje ~**water-bottle** termofor **2** ljut, začinjen, papren **3** *fig* žestok, nagao, vatren **have ~s for sb** biti zagrijan za koga **4** *sl* ukraden • *vt,vi* ~ **up** zagrijati (se) ~**ly** *adv* gorljivo, zagrijano, žestoko

hotchpotch /'hɒtʃpɒtʃ/ *n* zbrka; mišmaš *coll*

hotel /həʊ'tel/ *n* hotel

hound /haʊnd/ *n* lovački pas • *vt* proganjati

hour /'aʊə(r)/ *n* **1** sat **by the ~** na sat **for ~s** satima **in an ~** za 1 sat **at the eleventh ~** *coll* u pet do dvanaest ~**glass** *n* pješčani sat **2** razdoblje **3** doba dana **opening ~s**, **office ~s** radno vrijeme **after ~s** nakon radnog vremena **rush ~** špica *coll* ~**ly** *adv* **1** svaki sat; po satu **2** svakog trenutka

house /haʊs/ *n* (*pl* ~**s** /'haʊzɪz/) **1** kuća; dom ~ **of cards** *fig* kula od karata **on the ~** kuća časti **move ~** preseliti se **keep ~** voditi domaćinstvo **H~ of Commons** (*GB*, *Can*), **H~ of Representatives** (*US* etc.), **Lower H~** Donji dom **H~ of Lords** (*GB*), **Upper H~** Gornji dom **2** dinastija **3** gledateljstvo **bring the ~ down** dobiti veliki pljesak ~**hold** *n* kućanstvo; ukućani ~**hold name** svima poznato ime ~**keeper** *n* domaćica **housing** *n* stanovanje ~**wife** *n* domaćica • *vt* smjestiti

hove *v irreg* → **heave**

hovel /'hʌvl/ *n* šupa; rupa *fig*

hover /'hɒvə(r)/ *vi* **1** lebdjeti **2** (~ **round**) *fig* vrzmati se ~**craft** *n* lebdjelica

how /haʊ/ *adv* kako *and ~ about you?* a ti? ~ **are you?** ~ **is it going?** ~ **are you doing?** kako si/ste? ~ **come?** kako to? ~ **do you do** drago mi je ~ **much/many** koliko ~ **long** koliko

dugo ~ **old is he?** koliko mu je godina? ~**dy**, ~**ya** *int* bok! ~**ever** *adv* **1** međutim **2** kako god, koliko god, ma kako, bilo kako

howitzer /'haʊɪtsə(r)/ *n* haubica

howl /haʊl/ *n* zavijanje; urlik • *vi* zavijati; urlati ~ **down** ušutkati ~**ing** *adj coll* velik

hub /hʌb/ *n* **1** glavčina **2** *fig* središte, stožer ~**cap** ratkapa

hubbub /'hʌbʌb/ *n* buka, graja

hubby /'hʌbɪ/ *n coll* mužić

huddle /'hʌdl/ *vi,vt* (~ up/together) stisnuti se, skupiti se • *n* gomila

hue (1) /hju:/ *n* **1** nijansa **2** *fig* boja

hue (2) *n* ~ **and cry** vika i povika

huff /hʌf/ *vi* **1** (us)puhati (se) **2** razljutiti se • *n* ljutnja ~**y** *adj* uvredljiv

hug /hʌg/ *vt* **1** (za)grliti; prigrliti; držati u rukama **2** ići uz; držati se • *n* zagrljaj

huge /hju:dʒ/ *adj* golem

hulk /hʌlk/ *n* **1** olupina broda **2** gromada (od čovjeka)

hull (1) /hʌl/ *n* trup

hull (2) *n* lupina, ljuska • *vt* oljuštiti

hullabaloo /ˌhʌləbə'lu:/ *n* metež

hum /hʌm/ *vi,vt* **1** zujati ~**mingbird** *n* kolibri ~ **and ha(w)** *coll* brundati, mrmljati **2** pjevušiti • *n* zujanje; žamor

human /'hju:mən/ *adj* **1** ljudski ~ **rights** ljudska prava ~**kind**, ~ **race** čovječanstvo, ljudski rod **2** čovječan; human ~ *n* čovjek, ljudsko biće ~**e** /hju:'meɪn/ *adj* čovječan ~**ity** *n* **1** čovječanstvo **2** čovječnost ~**ities** *n pl* humanističke znanosti ~**itarian** *adj* humanitarni

humble /'hʌmbl/ *adj* **1** skroman; smjeran **2** ponizan **eat a ~ pie** ponizno priznati pogrešku • *vt* poniziti

humblebee /'hʌmbl,bi:/ *n* bumbar

humbug /'hʌmbʌg/ *n* **1** besmislica **2** prijevara

humdrum /'hʌmdrʌm/ *adj* jednoličan, dosadan, monoton

humid /'hju:mɪd/ *adj* vlažan ~**ity** /hju:'mɪdətɪ/ *n* vlažnost

humiliate /hju:'mɪlɪeɪt/ *vt* poniziti **humiliation** *n* poniženje **humility** /hju:'mɪlətɪ/ *n* poniznost

humour (-mor *US*) /'hju:mə(r)/ *n* 1 humor; šaljivost 2 raspoloženje • *vt* ugoditi (komu) **~ous** *adj* šaljiv

hump /hʌmp/ *n* 1 grba 2 *coll* zlovolja • *vi,vt* 1 pogrbiti se 2 vući, teglili 3 *tab sl* ševiti (se) *tab sl*

hunch /hʌntʃ/ *n* 1 predosjećaj 2 grba **~back** *n* grbavac

hundred /'hʌndrəd/ *num* sto (100) **~th** *num ord* stoti • *n* stotina **~s** stotine **~weight** engleska centa (50,8 kg)

hung *v irreg* → **hang**

hunger /'hʌngə(r)/ *n* glad (+ *fig*) **~strike** štrajk glađu • *vi* 1 *arch* gladovati 2 žudjeti **hungry** /'hʌngrɪ/ *adj* gladan

hunk /hʌnk/ *n* 1 komad(ina) 2 *coll iron* snagator

hunt /hʌnt/ *vt,vi* 1 loviti 2 proganjati **~ down** naći, uloviti **~er** *n* lovac • *n* 1 lov (+ *fig*) 2 *collect* lovci 3 lovište **the happy ~ing ground** vječna lovišta

hurdle /'hɜ:dl/ *n* 1 *sport* prepona 2 *fig* zapreka

hurl /hɜ:l/ *vt* baciti, hitnuti, nabaciti se (čime)

hurly-burly /'hɜ:lɪ bɜ:lɪ/ *n* vreva

hurrah /hʊ'rɑ:/, **hurray** /hʊ'reɪ/ *int* hura!

hurricane /'hʌrɪkn/ *n* uragan

hurry /'hʌrɪ/ *n* 1 žurba, hitnja *I'm in a ~* žuri mi se • *vt,vi* 1 žuriti se 2 požurivati **~ up!** požuri **hurried** *adj* učinjen na brzinu, zbrzan **hurriedly** *adv* na brzinu, u žurbi

hurt /hɜ:t/ *vt,vi irreg* 1 ozlijediti 2 povrijediti; učiniti nažao 3 boljeti 4 štetiti • *n* ozljeda; povreda; šteta **~ful** *adj* 1 (to) štetan (za) 2 bolan, uvredljiv

hurtle /'hɜ:tl/ *vi* tresnuti, stropoštati se, strovaliti se

husband /'hʌzbənd/ *n* suprug, muž • *vt* štedjeti **~ry** *n* uzgoj, gospodarstvo

hush /hʌʃ/ *n* tišina • *int* tiho! • *vi,vt* zašutjeti; utišati **~ up** zataškati **~~** *adj coll* tajnovit

husk /hʌsk/ *n* 1 ljuska • *vt* oljuštiti **~y** *adj* 1 promukao, hrapav 2 *coll* snažan

hustle /'hʌsl/ *vt,vi* 1 gurnuti; požuriti (koga/se) 2 (**~ into**) natjerati 3 *US sl* prostituirati se **~r** *n* 1 prostitutka 2 varalica • *n* (**~ and bustle**) gužva, vreva

hut /hʌt/ *n* koliba

hyacinth /'haɪəsɪnθ/ *n* 1 zumbul 2 hijacint

hydrofoil /'haɪdrəfɔɪl/ *n* hidrogliser

hydrogen /'haɪdrədʒən/ *n* 1 vodik 2 *mod* vodikov **~ bomb** (**H-bomb**) hidrogenska bomba

hydrophobia /ˌhaɪdrə'fəʊbɪə/ *n* bjesnilo

hydroplane /'haɪdrəpleɪn/ *n* hidrogliser

hyena, hyaena /haɪ'i:nə/ *n* hijena

hygiene /'haɪdʒi:n/ *n* higijena **hygienic** *adj* higijenski

hymen /'haɪmən/ *n* djevičnjak, himen

hymn /hɪm/ *n* himan • *vt* slaviti, hvaliti

hype /haɪp/ *vt coll* razvikati, napuhati **~d up** *adj coll* uzbuđen; nervozan

hyper /'haɪpə(r)/ *adj coll* pun energije; mahnit

hyper- *prefix* hiper-

hyphen /'haɪfn/ *n* crtica (-) **~ate** *vt* spojiti/odvojiti crticom

hypnosis /hɪp'nəʊsɪs/ *n* hipnoza

hypocrisy /hɪ'pɒkrəsɪ/ *n* licemjerje **hypocrite** /'hɪpəkrɪt/ *n* licemjer **hypocritical** /ˌhɪpə'krɪtɪkl/ *adj* licemjeran

hypodermic /ˌhaɪpə'dɜ:mɪk/ *adj* potkožni • *n* šprica *coll*

hypothesis /haɪ'pɒθəsɪs/ *n* pretpostavka; hipoteza **hypothetical** /ˌhaɪpə'θetɪkl/ *adj* koji se temelji na pretpostavci

hysteria /hɪ'stɪərɪə/ *n* histerija **hysterical** /hɪ'sterɪkl/ *adj* 1 histeričan 2 *coll* jako smiješan **hysterics** *n* 1 napad histerije 2 napadaj smijeha

I

I /aɪ/ 9. slovo engl. abecede; i
I /aɪ/ *pron* ja
ice /aɪs/ *n* 1 led 2 glazura, preljev • *vt,
vi* zalediti (se) (~ up/over) preliti
šećerom, glazurom ~ **age** ledeno
doba ~**berg** ledeni brijeg ~**box** hladnjak ~**breaker** ledolomac ~ **cream**
sladoled ~ **lolly** sladoled na štapiću
icy *adj* 1 leden 2 zaleđen 3 hladan (+
fig)
icicle /ˈaɪsɪkl/ *n* siga
icing /ˈaɪsɪŋ/ *n* glazura, preljev
idea /aɪˈdɪə/ *n* 1 ideja, (za)misao 2 pojam, predodžba 3 plan 4 pret-
postavka **ideal** /aɪˈdɪəl/ *adj* 1 idealan,
savršen 2 uzoran ○ *n* 1 ideal 2 uzor
~**list** *n* idealist ~**listic** *adj* idealistički
identical /aɪˈdentɪkl/ *adj* (to/with) is-
tovjetan, identičan
identify /aɪˈdentɪfaɪ/ *vt* 1 identificirati,
prepoznati 2 poistovjetiti se **identifi-
cation** /aɪˌdentɪfɪˈkeɪʃn/ *n* 1 identi-
fikacija, prepoznavanje 2 poisto-
vjećivanje **identikit** /aɪˈdentɪkɪt/ *n*
foto-robot **identity** /aɪˈdentɪtɪ/ *n* 1
identitet, ličnost, osobnost 2 istovje-
tnost **identity card** osobna karta/
iskaznica
ideology /ˌaɪdɪˈɒlədʒɪ/ *n* ideologija
ideological *adj* ideološki
idiocy /ˈɪdɪəsɪ/ *n* 1 idiotizam 2
slaboumnost **idiot** /ˈɪdɪət/ *n* 1 idiot 2
glupan **idiotic** *adj* 1 idiotski 2 glup
idiom /ˈɪdɪəm/ *n* 1 fraza, izraz 2 narječje
idiosyncrasy /ˌɪdɪəˈsɪŋkrəsɪ/ *n* oso-
benost
idle /ˈaɪdl/ *adj* 1 besposlen 2 neisko-
rišten 3 lijen 4 beskoristan, uzaludan
5 prazan 6 u praznom hodu, u
međuhodu • *vi,vt* 1 ljenčariti 2 biti u
međuhodu/u leru *coll* 3 (~ **away**)
tratiti vrijeme
idol /ˈaɪdl/ *n* idol (+ *fig*) ~**ize** *vt* ido-

lizirati, obožavati
idyll /ˈɪdɪl/ *n* idila ~**ic** *adj* idiličan
if /ɪf/ *conj* 1 ako, (u slučaju) da, kad 2
da li
ignite /ɪgˈnaɪt/ *vt,vi* upaliti (se), zapaliti (se) **ignition** /ɪgˈnɪʃn/ *n* 1 zapalje-
nje 2 paljenje **switch on/off the ignition** upaliti/ugasiti motor **ignition
key** ključ za paljenje
ignorance /ˈɪgnərəns/ *n* 1 (of) neznanje, nepoznavanje, neupućenost (u) 2
coll bezobraština **ignorant** *adj* 1
neobrazovan, neuk, neupućen 2 *coll*
bezobrazan **be ignorant** ne znati
ignore /ɪgˈnɔː(r)/ *vt* ignorirati, ne uzimati u obzir, ne obazirati se na
ill /ɪl/ *adj* 1 bolestan 2 zao, loš • *adv*
loše, slabo, teško, jedva • *n* 1 zlo 2
nesreća, nevolja **be taken ~/ fall ~**
razboljeti se ~ **at ease** nelagodno
~**advised** nesmotren, nerazborit;
~**bred** neodgojen ~**fated** nesretan,
koban ~ **feeling** ljutnja, zlovolja
~**mannered** neodgojen, neučtiv
~**natured** neodgojen ~**timed** u
zao čas ~**treat** zlostavljati ~ **will**
mržnja, neprijateljstvo ~**ness** *n*
bolest
illegal /ɪˈliːgl/ *adj* nezakonit
illegible /ɪˈledʒəbl/ *adj* nečitljiv
illegitimacy /ˌɪlɪˈdʒɪtɪməsɪ/ *n* neza-
konitost, nelegitimnost 2 izvan-
bračnost **illegitimate** *adj* 1 nezakonit, protupravan 2 izvanbračan
illicit /ɪˈlɪsɪt/ *adj* nezakonit, nedo-
pušten
illiterate /ɪˈlɪtərət/ *adj* 1 nepismen 2
neobrazovan **illiteracy** *n* nepis-
menost
illogical /ɪˈlɒdʒɪkl/ *adj* nelogičan
illuminate /ɪˈluːmɪneɪt/ *vt* 1 osvijetliti,
rasvijetliti 2 razjasniti 3 oslikati **illu-
minating** *adj* poučan

illusion /ɪˈluːʒn/ n 1 privid 2 varka, opsjena be **under the ~** zavaravati se **illusory, illusive** /ɪˈluːsɪv/ adj prividan, nestvaran, iluzoran

illustrate /ˈɪləstreɪt/ vt 1 razjasniti, objasniti 2 ilustrirati **illustration** /ˌɪləˈstreɪʃn/ n 1 objašnjenje 2 ilustracija

illustrious /iˈlʌstrɪəs/ adj čuven, glasovit, slavan

image /ˈɪmɪdʒ/ n 1 slika 2 kip 3 lik 4 odraz 5 predodžba 6 poredba, metafora 7 ugled be **the very/spitting ~ of** biti čija slika i prilika **~ry** n slike, simboli pl

imaginary /iˈmædʒɪnərɪ/ adj izmišljen, nestvaran, prividan **imagination** /ɪˌmædʒɪˈneɪʃn/ n mašta, fantazija **imaginable** adj zamisliv **imaginative** adj domišljat **imagine** vt 1 zamisliti, predočiti 2 zamišljati

imbue /ɪmˈbjuː/ vt (**be ~d with**) fig prožeti

imitate /ˈɪmɪteɪt/ vt 1 oponašati, imitirati 2 ugledati se **imitation** /ˌɪmɪˈteɪʃn/ n 1 oponašanje 2 patvorina **imitation leather** umjetna koža

immaculate /ɪˈmækjʊlət/ adj 1 čist, neokaljan 2 besprijekoran **the I~ Conception** Bezgrešno začeće

immaterial /ˌɪməˈtɪərɪəl/ adj 1 nevažan, nebitan 2 bestjelesan, nestvaran

immature /ˌɪməˈtjʊə(r)/ adj nezreo **immaturity** /ˌɪməˈtjʊərətɪ/ n nezrelost

immediate /ɪˈmiːdɪət/ adj 1 bezodvlačan, trenutačan 2 sadašnji 3 skori 4 najbliži 5 direktan, izravan, neposredan **~ly** adv odmah

immense /ɪˈmens/ adj ogroman, golem **~ly** adv veoma, silno

immerse /ɪˈmɜːs/ vt umočiti, uroniti be **~d in** fig utonuti u (misli)

immersion heater /ɪˈmɜːʃn hiːtə/ n (GB) uronjivi električni grijač

immigrant /ˈɪmɪgrənt/ n useljenik **immigrate** /ˈɪmɪgreɪt/ vi useliti se (u stranu zemlju) **immigration** /ˌɪmɪˈgreɪʃn/ n useljavanje, imigracija

imminent /ˈɪmɪnənt/ adj neposredan, predstojeći, neizbježiv

immobile /ɪˈməʊbaɪl/ adj 1 nepokretan

2 učvršćen **immobilize** /ɪˈməʊbəlaɪz/ vt 1 učiniti nepokretnim 2 učvrstiti

immoral /ɪˈmɒrəl/ adj nećudoredan, nemoralan, razvratan

immortal /ɪˈmɔːtl/ adj besmrtan **~ity** /ˌɪmɔːˈtælɪtɪ/ n besmrtnost **~ize** /ɪˈmɔːtəlaɪz/ vt učiniti besmrtnim

immune /ɪˈmjuːn/ adj 1 (to) otporan, imun na 2 (from) izuzet, oslobođen, siguran od **immunity** /ɪˈmjuːnətɪ/ n 1 leg, med imunitet 2 povlastica **immunize** /ˈɪmjʊnaɪz/ vt (against) učiniti imunim na

imp /ɪmp/ n vragolan, nestaško **~ish** adj vragoljast, nestašan

impact /ˈɪmpækt/ n 1 sudar, udarac 2 (on) utjecaj **on ~** pri udarcu

impair /ɪmˈpeə(r)/ vt 1 umanjiti, naškoditi, oslabiti 2 oštetiti

impale /ɪmˈpeɪl/ vt (on) nabiti, nabosti

impart /ɪmˈpɑːt/ vt 1 dati, pridavati 2 priopćiti, reći, kazati

impartial /ɪmˈpɑːʃl/ adj nepristran, objektivan, pravedan

impasse /æmˈpɑːs/ n fig slijepa ulica, mrtva točka

impassive /ɪmˈpæsɪv/ adj bezosjećajan, bešćutan, ravnodušan

impatience /ɪmˈpeɪʃns/ n nestrpljivost **impatient** adj nestrpljiv

impeach /ɪmˈpiːtʃ/ vt 1 posumnjati u 2 leg optužiti, okriviti 3 US pozvati na odgovornost (drž. činovnika)

impeccable /ɪmˈpekəbl/ adj nepogrešiv; bezgrešan; besprijekoran

impede /ɪmˈpiːd/ vt (s)priječiti, ometati **impediment** /ɪmˈpedɪmənt/ n 1 zapreka, teškoća 2 smetnja **speech impediment** govorna mana

impending /ɪmˈpendɪŋ/ adj predstojeći, prijeteći

impenetrable /ɪmˈpenɪtrəbl/ adj 1 neprohodan, neprobojan, nepristupačan 2 nedokučiv

imperative /ɪmˈperətɪv/ adj 1 hitan, prijeko potreban, nužan 2 zapovjednički • n imperativ (+ fig)

imperceptible /ˌɪmpəˈseptəbl/ adj neprimjetan, nezamjetan

imperfect /ɪmˈpɜːfɪkt/ adj nesavršen, nepotpun, manjkav **~ion** n nesavršenost, manjkavost

imperial /ɪmˈpɪərɪəl/ *adj* 1 carski; imperijalan 2 britanske jedinice mjere **~ism** *n* imperijalizam

impermeable /ɪmˈpɜːmɪəbl/ *adj* nepropustan, nepromočiv

impersonal /ˌɪmˈpɜːsənl/ *adj* bezličan

impersonate /ɪmˈpɜːsəneɪt/ *vt* 1 utjeloviti, personificirati 2 imitirati, glumiti 3 izdavati se za

impertinence /ɪmˈpɜːtɪnəns/ *n* nepristojnost, drskost, bezobraština **impertinent** *adj* nepristojan, drzak, bezobrazan

impervious /ɪmˈpɜːvɪəs/ *adj* 1 nepropustan, neprobojan 2 (to) *fig* nedostupan, nepristupačan, neosjetljiv, koji se ne obazire na

impetuous /ɪmˈpetʃʊəs/ *adj* nagao, nepromišljen

impetus /ˈɪmpɪtəs/ *n* 1 zamah 2 poticaj, poriv

implacable /ɪmˈplækəbl/ *adj* nepomirljiv, neumoljiv, nesmiljen

implant /ɪmˈplɑːnt/ *vt* (in/into) *fig* usaditi

implement /ˈɪmplɪmənt/ *n* alat, oruđe, pribor, sprava • *vt* provesti, izvršiti, ostvariti **~ation** /ˌɪmplɪmenˈteɪʃn/ *n* provedba, izvršenje, ostvarenje, primjena

implicate /ˈɪmplɪkeɪt/ *vt* (in) uplesti, umiješati, uvući **implication** /ˌɪmplɪˈkeɪʃn/ *n* 1 upletenost, umiješanost 2 dublji smisao **what are the implications of** što podrazumijeva **by implication** prešutno, indirektno **implicit** /ɪmˈplɪsɪt/ *adj* 1 prešutan, indirektan, koji se podrazumijeva 2 slijep, bezuvjetan (vjera)

implore /ɪmˈplɔː(r)/ *vt* (for) moliti, preklinjati

imply /ɪmˈplaɪ/ *vt* 1 podrazumijevati, značiti 2 nagovijestiti, dati naslutiti

impolite /ˌɪmpəˈlaɪt/ *adj* nepristojan, neuljudan

import /ɪmˈpɔːt/ *vt* (from/into) 1 uvesti 2 *form* značiti, kazivati • /ˈɪmpɔːt/ *n* 1 uvoz 2 uvozna roba 3 *form* značenje; važnost **~er** *n* uvoznik

importance /ɪmˈpɔːtns/ *n* važnost **important** *adj* važan

impose /ɪmˈpəʊz/ *vt,vi* 1 (on) namet-

nuti, uvesti 2 (on sb) nametati se 3 (upon sth) iskorištavati, zlorabiti **imposing** *adj* velik, impozantan **imposition** /ˌɪmpəˈzɪʃn/ *n* 1 nametanje, uvođenje (poreza) 2 namet, porez **be an imposition on sb** biti kome na teret

impossible /ɪmˈpɒsəbl/ *adj* 1 nemoguć 2 nepodnošljiv

impostor /ɪmˈpɒstə(r)/ *n* varalica

impotent /ˈɪmpətənt/ *adj* 1 nemoćan 2 impotentan

impound /ɪmˈpaʊnd/ *vt* zaplijeniti

impoverished /ɪmˈpɒvərɪʃt/ *adj form* osiromašen

impractical /ɪmˈpræktɪkl/ *adj* nepraktičan

impregnable /ɪmˈpregnəbl/ *adj* 1 nesavladiv, neosvojiv 2 neoboriv

impregnate /ˈɪmpregneɪt/ *vt* (with) 1 oploditi 2 zasititi, natopiti 3 prožeti

impress /ɪmˈpres/ *vt* (on/upon/with) 1 utisnuti, otisnuti 2 dojmiti se, usjeći se • /ˈɪmpres/ *n* otisak, biljeg (+ *fig*) **~ion** /ɪmˈpreʃn/ *n* 1 otisak 2 kopija 3 naklada 4 dojam **be under the ~ion that** imati dojam da **~ionable** /ɪmˈpreʃənəbl/ *adj* prijemljiv, osjetljiv, podložan utjecajima **~ive** *adj* dojmljiv, impresivan

imprint /ɪmˈprɪnt/ *vt* (with/on) 1 utisnuti, otisnuti 2 *fig* urezati se • /ˈɪmprɪnt/ *n* 1 otisak, trag (+ *fig*) 2 naziv izdavača

imprison /ɪmˈprɪzn/ *vt* utamničiti, zatvoriti **~ment** *n* zatvor, zatvorska kazna

improbable /ɪmˈprɒbəbl/ *adj* nevjerojatan

impromptu /ɪmˈprɒmptjuː/ *adj, adv* bez pripreme, improviziran(o) • *n* improvizacija

improper /ɪmˈprɒpə(r)/ *adj* 1 neprimjeren 2 netočan, pogrešan, kriv 3 nepristojan

improve /ɪmˈpruːv/ *vt,vi* 1 poboljšati (se), napredovati 2 usavršiti (se) **~ment** *n* poboljšanje

improvise /ˈɪmprəvaɪz/ *vt* improvizirati **improvisation** /ˌɪmprəvaɪˈzeɪʃn/ *n* improvizacija

impudent /ˈɪmpjʊdənt/ *n* drzak, bezobrazan, besraman

impulse /'ɪmpʌls/ *n* 1 poticaj 2 nagon, poriv **on (an)** ~ spontano, nagonski, bez razmišljanja **impulsive** /ɪm'pʌl-sɪv/ *adj* impulzivan, nagao

impunity /ɪm'pju:nətɪ/ *n* nekažnjenost **with** ~ nekažnjeno

impure /ɪm'pjʊə(r)/ *adj* 1 nečist 2 pokvaren, bludan

in /ɪn/ *adv* **be** ~ 1 u kući, kod kuće; u uredu 2 stići na odredište (avion, brod, vlak) 3 skupiti (usjeve) 4 u sezoni (voće) 5 u modi 6 na vlasti; izabran 7 gorjeti **he is** ~ **for sth a.** čeka ga, sprema mu se (nešto neugodno) **b.** kandidirao se za, sudjeluje u (natjecanju) **have it** ~ **for sb** željeti se kome osvetiti, imati koga na zubu, imati pik na koga **be** ~ **for it** nadrljati **be** ~ **on sth** sudjelovati u čemu, upoznati se s čime **be (well)** ~ **with sb** biti s kim u dobrim odnosima **day** ~, **day out** dan za danom **all** ~ *coll* iscrpljen, umoran • *prep* u; na **London** u Londonu ~ **the US** u SAD ~ **the street** na ulici ~ **1993** godine 1993. ~ **May** u svibnju ~ **(the) spring** u proljeće ~ **the morning/afternoon/evening** ujutro, popodne, navečer ~ **6 months** za šest mjeseci **I haven't seen him** ~ **years** nisam ga vidio godinama ~ **the rain** po kiši ~ **the sun** na suncu ~ **dozens/hundreds** na desetke/stotine 8 **metres** ~ **length** 8 metara u duljinu 1 **soldier in** 10 svaki deseti vojnik **have a one** ~ **five chance of success** imati mogućnost uspjeha jedan prema pet **cry out** ~ **pain** kriknuti od boli **cut sth** ~ **two** prerezati nadvoje/popola **speak** ~ **English** govoriti engleski ~ **writing** napismeno ~ **capital letters** velikim slovima ~ **my opinion** po mome mišljenju ~ **a loud voice** glasno **the desease is common** ~ **children** bolest je uobičajena u djece ~ **all** ukupno, sve zajedno ~ **that** utoliko, time, jer ~ **as/so far as** utoliko što ○ *n* **the ~s and (the) outs a.** stranka na vlasti i oporba **b.** pojedinosti čega

inability /ˌɪnə'bɪlətɪ/ *n* (to do sth) nesposobnost, nemoć

inaccessible /ˌɪnæk'sesəbl/ *adj* (to) form nepristupačan

inaccuracy /ɪn'ækjərəsɪ/ *n* netočnost **inaccurate** /ɪn'ækjərət/ *adj* netočan, neispravan

inactivity /ˌɪnæk'tɪvətɪ/ *n* neaktivnost **inadequate** /ɪn'ædɪkwət/ *adj* 1 neprimjeren 2 nedostatan 3 nedorastao

inadmissible /ˌɪnəd'mɪsəbl/ *adj* neprihvatljiv, nedopustiv

inadvertent /ˌɪnəd'vɜːtənt/ *adj form* 1 nepažljiv, nesmotren 2 nehotičan

inadvisable /ˌɪnəd'vaɪzəbl/ *adj* nepreporučljiv

inalienable /ɪn'eɪlɪənəbl/ *adj form* neotuđiv

inane /ɪ'neɪn/ *adj* besmislen, budalast, prazan

inanimate /ɪn'ænɪmət/ *adj* neživ, beživotan, mrtav (+ *fig*)

inapplicable /ɪn'æplɪkəbl/ *adj* (to) 1 neprimjenjiv 2 neprikladan

inappropriate /ˌɪnə'prəʊprɪət/ *adj* (to) 1 neumjestan 2 neprikladan

inapt /ɪn'æpt/ *adj* 1 nesposoban, nespretan 2 nepodesan 3 neprikladan

inarticulate /ˌɪnɑː'tɪkjʊlət/ *adj* nerazgovijetan, nejasan, neartikuliran

inasmuch as /ˌɪnəz'mʌtʃəz/ *adv* 1 jer, budući da 2 ukoliko

inaudible /ɪn'ɔːdəbl/ *adj* nečujan

inaugural /ɪ'nɔːgjʊrəl/ *adj* nastupni, uvodni **inaugurate** /ɪ'nɔːgjʊreɪt/ *vt* 1 svečano otvoriti 2 svečano uvesti u dužnost 3 *fig* označiti početak **inauguration** /ɪˌnɔːgjʊ'reɪʃn/ *n* svečano otvorenje; uvođenje u dužnost

inborn /ˌɪn'bɔːn/ *adj* prirođen, urođen **inbred** /ˌɪn'bred/ *adj* prirođen, urođen; čiji preci su u bliskom srodstvu

incalculable /ɪn'kælkjʊləbl/ *adj* 1 neizračunljiv 2 neprocjenjiv 3 nepredvidiv

incapable /ɪn'keɪpəbl/ *adj* (of doing sth) nesposoban

incapacitate /ˌɪnkə'pæsɪteɪt/ *vt* (sb for/from) 1 onesposobiti 2 diskvalificirati

incapacity /ˌɪnkə'pæsətɪ/ *n* (for sth/for doing sth/to do sth) 1 nesposobnost 2 nemoć

incarcerate /ɪnˈkɑːsəreɪt/ *vt form* utamničiti

incarnate /ɪnˈkɑːneɪt/ *adj* utjelovljen **incarnation** /ˌɪnkɑːˈneɪʃn/ *n* utjelovljenje, inkarnacija

incendiary /ɪnˈsendɪərɪ/ *n* 1 palikuća 2 huškač 3 zapaljiva bomba

incense (1) /ˈɪnsens/ *n* tamjan

incense (2) /ɪnˈsens/ *vt* raspaliti, razjariti, razljutiti

incentive /ɪnˈsentɪv/ *n* (to) poticaj, pobuda

incessant /ɪnˈsesnt/ *adj* neprestan, neprekidan

incest /ˈɪnsest/ *n* incest, rodoskvrnuće **~uous** /ɪnˈsestjuəs/ *adj* rodoskvrni

inch /ɪntʃ/ *n* 1 inč, palac (2,54 cm) 2 *fig* sitnica **be within an ~ of** na milimetar od, za dlaku izbjeći **not give/budge/yield an ~** ne uzmaknuti ni za pedalj **by ~es** za dlaku, za milimetar **~ by ~** malo-pomalo, postupno **every ~** od glave do pete, u svakom pogledu

incidence /ˈɪnsɪdəns/ *n* 1 rasprostranjenost, stopa, broj 2 djelovanje, utjecaj

incident /ˈɪnsɪdənt/ *n* 1 događaj, slučaj 2 nemio događaj, izgred **~al** /ˌɪnsɪˈdentl/ *adj* (to) 1 prateći, popratan, sporedan, usputan 2 slučajan, uzgredan **~ally** *adv* 1 slučajno 2 usput, uzgred (rečeno)

incinerate /ɪnˈsɪnəreɪt/ *vt* spaliti, pretvoriti u pepeo **incinerator** /ɪnˈsɪnəreɪtə(r)/ *n* peć za spaljivanje (smeća)

incision /ɪnˈsɪʒn/ *n* (in/into) urezivanje, (u)rez **incisive** /ɪnˈsaɪsɪv/ *adj* 1 oštar, rezak 2 proniciljiv; zajedljiv **incisor** /ɪnˈsaɪzə(r)/ *n* sjekutić

incite /ɪnˈsaɪt/ *vt* (to) poticati, hrabriti

inclination /ˌɪnklɪˈneɪʃn/ *n* (to sth/to do sth) 1 naklon 2 nagib 3 sklonost

incline /ɪnˈklaɪn/ *vt,vi* (to/towards sth) 1 nagnuti, sagnuti, pognuti (se) 2 *fig* navoditi; biti sklon; biti raspoložen za što; naginjati čemu **~d** *adj* sklon, voljan, raspoložen **I'm ~d to get tired easily** lako se umaram

include /ɪnˈkluːd/ *vt* uključi(va)ti, obuhvaćati, sadržavati, uračunati **in-**

cluding *prep* uključujući **inclusion** /ɪnˈkluːʒn/ *n* uključivanje **(all–) inclusive** /ɪnˈkluːsɪv/ *adj* koji (sve) uključuje **inclusive of** uključivo

incoherent /ˌɪnkəʊˈhɪərənt/ *adj* 1 nesuvisao, nepovezan 2 nedosljedan **incoherence** /ˌɪnkəʊˈhɪərəns/ *n* 1 nesuvislost, nepovezanost 2 nedosljednost

income /ˈɪŋkʌm/ *n* prihod, dohodak ~ **tax** porez na dohodak

incoming /ˈɪnˈkʌmɪŋ/ *adj* koji (na)dolazi, nastupa, ulazni **the ~ president** predsjednik koji preuzima dužnost **the ~ tide** nadolazeća plima

incomparable /ɪnˈkɒmprəbl/ *adj* (to/with) neusporediv

incompatible /ˌɪnkəmˈpætəbl/ *adj* (with) nespojiv, neuskladiv

incompetent /ɪnˈkɒmpɪtənt/ *adj* 1 nesposoban 2 nenadležan **incompetence** *n* nesposobnost

incomplete /ˌɪnkəmˈpliːt/ *adj* nepotpun

incomprehensible /ɪnˌkɒmprɪˈhensəbl/ *adj* nerazumljiv, neshvatljiv

inconceivable /ˌɪnkənˈsiːvəbl/ *adj* nepojmljiv, nezamisliv, nevjerojatan

incongruous /ɪnˈkɒŋgruəs/ *adj* (with) koji se ne podudara s, neskladan, neprimjeren

inconsistent /ˌɪnkənˈsɪstənt/ *adj* (with) 1 koji nije u skladu s 2 protuslovan 3 nestalan, nepostojan

inconspicuous /ˌɪnkənˈspɪkjuəs/ *adj* neupadljiv, neprimjetan

incontinent /ɪnˈkɒntɪnənt/ *adj med* inkontinentan **incontinence** *n med* inkontinencija

inconvenience /ˌɪnkənˈviːnɪəns/ *n* neugodnost, (po)teškoća, neprilika, neudobnost **inconvenient** *adj* neugodan, nepriličan, nezgodan

incorporate /ɪnˈkɔːpəreɪt/ *vt,vi* (in/into/with) 1 pripojiti, uključiti, primiti kao člana 2 udružiti se, spojiti se **~d company** US dioničko društvo

incorrect /ˌɪnkəˈrekt/ *adj* nepravilan, netočan

increase /ˈɪŋkriːs/ *n* (po)rast, povećanje, povišenje **on the ~** u porastu • *vt,* *vi* /ɪnˈkriːs/ (po)rasti, povećati (se), povisiti **increasing** /ɪnˈkriːsɪŋ/ *adj* u porastu, sve veći

incredible /ɪnˈkredəbl/ *adj* nevjerojatan

incredulous /ɪnˈkredjʊləs/ *adj* sumnjičav **~ly** *adv* s nevjericom

incriminate /ɪnˈkrɪmɪneɪt/ *vt* okriviti, optužiti, teretiti

incur /ɪnˈkɜː(r)/ *vt* navući na sebe (mržnju), natovariti na sebe (dugove), izložiti se, pretrpjeti (gubitke), snositi (troškove)

incurable /ɪnˈkjʊərəbl/ *adj* 1 neizlječiv 2 *fig* nepopravljiv (optimist i sl.)

incursion /ɪnˈkɜːʃn/ *n* (neprijateljski) upad, napad, najezda

indebted /ɪnˈdetɪd/ *adj* (to) dužan, zahvalan

indecent /ɪnˈdiːsnt/ *adj* 1 nepristojan, bestidan 2 nepriličan **~ assault** prekršaj protiv ćudorednosti **~ exposure** ekshibicionizam **indecency** *n* 1 nepristojnost, bestidnost 2 nepriličnost

indecisive /ˌɪndɪˈsaɪsɪv/ *adj* neodlučan, koleblijv

indeed /ɪnˈdiːd/ *adv* zaista, uistinu, u stvari, svakako, doduše

indefensible /ˌɪndɪˈfensəbl/ *adj* neobranjiv, neodrživ

indefinite /ɪnˈdefɪnət/ *adj* 1 nejasan 2 neodređen

indelible /ɪnˈdeləbl/ *adj* neizbrisiv

indemnify /ɪnˈdemnɪfaɪ/ *vt* 1 (sb from/against) osigurati 2 (sb for sth) nadoknaditi štetu **indemnity** /ɪnˈdemnəti/ *n* 1 osiguranje 2 odšteta, naknada štete

indent /ɪnˈdent/ *vt,vi* 1 nazupčati, urezati, usjeći 2 uvući redak 3 (on sb/for sth) *comm* naručiti, izdati nalog **~ed coastline** razvedena obala

independent /ˌɪndɪˈpendənt/ *adj* 1 neovisan 2 samostalan **independence** *n* 1 neovisnost 2 samostalnost

indestructible /ˌɪndɪˈstrʌktəbl/ *adj* neuništiv

index /ˈɪndeks/ *n* (*pl* **~es, indices**) 1 kazalo 2 imenik, popis, registar 3 pokazatelj **~ finger** kažiprst

Indian /ˈɪndɪən/ *adj* 1 indijski 2 indi-

janski **in ~ file** u koloni po jedan **~ summer** bablje ljeto **Red ~** Indijanac

indicate /ˈɪndɪkeɪt/ *vt* pokazati, ukazivati na, naznačiti **indication** /ˌɪndɪˈkeɪʃn/ *n* naznaka **be indicative of** ukazivati na **indicator** /ˈɪndɪkeɪtə(r)/ *n* 1 pokazatelj 2 žmigavac *coll*

indict /ɪnˈdaɪt/ *vt* (for) optužiti **~ment** *n* optužba; optužnica **bring in an ~ment against sb** podići optužnicu protiv

indifferent /ɪnˈdɪfrənt/ *adj* 1 (to/towards) ravnodušan, nemaran 2 neutralan 3 osrednji **indifference** *n* ravnodušnost

indigestion /ˌɪndɪˈdʒestʃən/ *n* probavne smetnje *pl*, loša probava

indignant /ɪnˈdɪgnənt/ *adj* (at/with) ljut, ogorčen, srdit na **indignation** /ˌɪndɪgˈneɪʃn/ *n* ljutnja, ogorčenje, srdžba

indignity /ɪnˈdɪgnəti/ *n* uvreda, poniženje

indirect /ˌɪndɪˈrekt/ *adj* neizravan, posredan, zaobilazan **~ speech** *n gram* neupravni govor

indiscreet /ˌɪndɪˈskriːt/ *adj* 1 nepromišljen, nesmotren 2 netaktičan **~ion** /ˌɪndɪˈskreʃn/ *n* (mladenačka) avantura

indiscriminate /ˌɪndɪˈskrɪmɪnət/ *adj* koji ne pravi razlike, nekritičan **~ly** *adv* bez razlike, odreda

indispensable /ˌɪndɪˈspensəbl/ *adj* (to) nužan

indisposed /ˌɪndɪˈspəʊzd/ *adj* 1 koji se loše osjeća 2 (for/to do sth) nesklon, neraspoložen

indisputable /ˌɪndɪˈspjuːtəbl/ *adj* neosporan, nepobitan, neprijeporan

indistinct /ˌɪndɪˈstɪŋkt/ *adj* nejasan, nerazgovijetan

individual /ˌɪndɪˈvɪdʒʊəl/ *adj* 1 pojedini, pojedinačan 2 karakterističan, svojstven • *n* osoba, pojedinac **~ity** /ˌɪndɪˌvɪdʒʊˈæləti/ *n* osobnost

indoor /ˈɪndɔː(r)/ *adj* kućni, sobni, unutarnji, zatvoren **~ sports** dvoranski sportovi **~s** /ˌɪnˈdɔːz/ *adv* unutra, u kući

induce /ɪnˈdjuːs/ *vt* 1 (sb to do sth)

potaknuti, navesti, nagovoriti (koga na što) **2** izazvati **~ment** *n* povod, poticaj, motiv

induct /ɪn'dʌkt/ *vt* (to/into/as) uvesti u dužnost, ustoličiti, primiti u članstvo **~ion** /ɪn'dʌkʃn/ *n* **1** uvođenje u dužnost **2** indukcija

indulge /ɪn'dʌldʒ/ *vt,vi* **1** udovoljavati (željama), ugađati, popuštati **2** (in) priuštiti sebi, prepustiti se, odati se **~nce** /ɪn'dʌldʒəns/ *n* **1** popuštanje, ugađanje **2** (in) uživanje **3** oprost **~nt** *adj* blag, popustljiv

industrial /ɪn'dʌstrɪəl/ *adj* industrijski **~ action** štrajk **~ estate** industrijsko područje **~ist** *n* industrijalac **industry** /'ɪndəstrɪ/ *n* **1** industrija **2** marljivost, radinost

inedible /ɪn'edɪbl/ *adj* nejestiv

ineffective /ˌɪnɪ'fektɪv/ *adj* nedjelotvoran

ineffectual /ˌɪnɪ'fektʃʊəl/ *adj* neučinkovit, neuspješan

inefficient /ˌɪnɪ'fɪʃnt/ *adj* nedjelotvoran; nesposoban **inefficiency** *n* nedjelotvornost; nesposobnost

inept /ɪ'nept/ *adj* nespretan, neprimjeren

inequality /ˌɪnɪ'kwɒlətɪ/ *n* nejednakost

inert /ɪ'nɜːt/ *adj* trom, nepokretan, spor, tup **~ia** /ɪ'nɜːʃɛ/ *n* tromost, tupost

inescapable /ˌɪnɪ'skeɪpəbl/ *adj* neizbježan

inevitable /ɪn'evɪtəbl/ *adj* neizbježan, neminovan

inexcusable /ˌɪnɪk'skjuːzəbl/ *adj* neoprostiv

inexhaustible /ˌɪnɪg'zɔːstəbl/ *adj* neiscrpan

inexorable /ɪn'eksərəbl/ *adj* nepopustljiv, nesmiljen

inexperience /ˌɪnɪk'spɪərɪəns/ *n* neiskustvo **~d** *adj* neiskusan

inexplicable /ˌɪnɪk'splɪkəbl/ *adj* neobjašnjiv

inextricable /ˌɪnɪk'strɪkəbl/ *adj* nerazmrsiv

infallible /ɪn'fæləbl/ *adj* nepogrešiv

infamous /'ɪnfəməs/ *adj* sram(ot)an, nečastan, ozloglašen

infancy /'ɪnfənsɪ/ *n* **1** rano djetinjstvo

2 *leg* maloljetnost, malodobnost **3** *fig* počeci, povoji *pl* **infant** *n* **1** dojenče, malo dijete **2** *leg* maloljetnik **infant prodigy** čudo od djeteta

infantry /'ɪnfəntrɪ/ *n mil* pješaštvo **~man** *n* pješak

infatuated /ɪn'fætʃʊeɪtɪd/ *adj* (with/by) zaluđen čime/kime

infect /ɪn'fekt/ *vt* (with) zaraziti (+ *fig*) **~ion** /ɪn'fekʃn/ *n* zaraza **~ious** /ɪn'fekʃəs/ *adj* zarazan (+ *fig*)

infer /ɪn'fɜː(r)/ *vt* zaključiti **~ence** /'ɪnfərəns/ *n* zaključak

inferior /ɪn'fɪərɪə(r)/ *adj* (to) **1** podređen, niži **2** slab(iji), loš(iji) **~ity** /ɪnˌfɪərɪ'ɒrətɪ/ *n* podređenost, niži položaj

inferno /ɪn'fɜːnəʊ/ *n* pakao (+ *fig*) **infernal** /ɪn'fɜːnl/ *adj* **1** paklenski **2** vražji, proklet, užasan

infest /ɪn'fest/ *vt* (be **~ed with**) vrvjeti čime

infidelity /ˌɪnfɪ'delətɪ/ *n* (to) nevjera

infiltrate /'ɪnfɪltreɪt/ *vt,vi* **1** promočiti **2** prodrijeti, uvući se u

infinite /'ɪnfɪnət/ *adj* beskrajan, neograničen, neizmjeran **infinity** /ɪn'fɪnətɪ/ *n* **1** beskraj **2** neograničen/beskonačan broj

infinitive /ɪn'fɪnətɪv/ *n gram* infinitiv

infirmary /ɪn'fɜːmərɪ/ *n* **1** bolnica **2** ambulanta

inflame /ɪn'fleɪm/ *vt,vi* **1** upaliti se **2** *fig* raspaliti, razjariti **inflammable** /ɪn'flæməbl/ *adj* **1** zapaljiv **2** *fig* nagao **inflammation** /ˌɪnfʰlə'meɪʃn/ *n med* upala **inflammatory** /ɪn'flæmətrɪ/ *adj fig* podstrekački

inflate /ɪn'fleɪt/ *vt* (with) napuhnuti (+ *fig*) **inflation** /ɪn'fleɪʃn/ *n* inflacija

inflexible /ɪn'fleksəbl/ *adj* **1** nesavitljiv **2** *fig* nepopustljiv

inflict /ɪn'flɪkt/ *vt* (sth on/upon) **1** zadati, nanijeti **2** dosuditi (kaznu) **3** nametnuti

inflow /'ɪnfləʊ/ *n* pritjecanje, dotok, priljev

influence /'ɪnflʊəns/ *n* (over/on/upon) utjecaj • *vt* utjecati, imati utjecaja **influential** /ˌɪnflʊ'enʃl/ *adj* utjecajan

influenza /ˌɪnflʊ'enzə/ *n form* gripa

influx /'ɪnflʌks/ → **inflow**

info /'ɪnfəʊ/ coll → information

inform /ɪn'fɔːm/ vt,vi 1 (sb of sth/that) obavijestiti, izvijestiti (koga o čemu) 2 (against/on sb) leg prijaviti, potkazati well-~ed adj dobro obaviješten, upućen ~ant n izvor informacija ~ation /ˌɪnfə'meɪʃn/ n (on/about) obavještavanje, obavijest a piece/bit of ~ation obavijest, informacija, podatak ~ative /ɪn'fɔːmətɪv/ adj informativan, poučan ~er n doušnik, prokazivač

informal /ɪn'fɔːml/ adj 1 neslužben 2 neusiljen, neobavezan

infrastructure /'ɪnfrə'strʌktʃə(r)/ n infrastruktura

infuriate /ɪn'fjʊərɪeɪt/ vt razbjesniti

infuse /ɪn'fjuːz/ vt,vi form 1 (into/with) uliti u, ispuniti s 2 preliti vrućom vodom infusion /ɪn'fjuːʒn/ 1 ulijevanje; priljev fig 2 oparak; čaj coll 3 med infuzija

ingenious /ɪn'dʒiːnɪəs/ adj domišljat, dovitljiv, genijalan, originalan ingenuity /ˌɪndʒɪ'njuːətɪ/ n dovitljivost, domišljatost, genijalnost

ingot /'ɪŋɡət/ n šipka, poluga

ingrained /ˌɪn'ɡreɪnd/ adj ukorijenjen, urođen

ingratiate /ɪn'ɡreɪʃɪeɪt/ vt (oneself with sb) ulagivati se komu, dodvoravati se

ingratitude /ɪn'ɡrætɪtjuːd/ n nezahvalnost

ingredient /ɪn'ɡriːdɪənt/ n sastojak, sastavni dio

ingrowing /'ɪnɡrəʊɪŋ/ adj an ~ nail nokat koji urasta u meso

inhabit /ɪn'hæbɪt/ vt nastanjivati, stanovati, živjeti u ~ant n stanovnik

inhale /ɪn'heɪl/ vt,vi udisati ~r n med inhalator

inherent /ɪn'hɪərənt/ adj (in) 1 svojstven, prirođen 2 neodvojiv, tijesno povezan

inherit /ɪn'herɪt/ vt,vi (from) naslijediti (+ fig) ~ance n nasljedstvo

inhibit /ɪn'hɪbɪt/ vt (s)priječiti, kočiti, obuzda(va)ti ~ion /ˌɪnɪ'bɪʃn/ n inhibicija ~ed adj sputan

inhospitable /ˌɪnhɒ'spɪtəbl/ adj negostoljubiv (+ fig)

inhuman /ɪn'hjuːmən/ adj 1 nečovječan, okrutan 2 neljudski

inhumane /ˌɪnhjuː'meɪn/ adj nečovječan, nehuman

inimitable /ɪ'nɪmɪtəbl/ adj form jedinstven, neponovljiv, bez premca

iniquity /ɪ'nɪkwətɪ/ n form 1 nepravda 2 porok

initial /ɪ'nɪʃl/ adj početni, prvotni ~ly adv na početku, isprva ~ n početno slovo ~s inicijali ~ vt parafirati

initiate /ɪ'nɪʃɪeɪt/ vt 1 (za)početi, pokrenuti 2 uvesti, uputiti u 3 primiti (u članstvo)

initiative /ɪ'nɪʃɪətɪv/ n 1 prvi potez, prvi korak 2 poduzetnost 3 poticaj take the ~ preuzeti inicijativu

inject /ɪn'dʒekt/ vt 1 ubrizgati 2 fig uliti, unijeti ~ion /ɪn'dʒekʃn/ n med injekcija

injunction /ɪn'dʒʌŋkʃn/ n sudski nalog; sudska zabrana

injure /'ɪndʒə(r)/ vt 1 ozlijediti, raniti 2 povrijediti 3 nanijeti štetu injury /'ɪndʒərɪ/ n 1 ozljeda 2 šteta 3 fig uvreda, povreda do sb an injury nauditi kome

injustice /ɪn'dʒʌstɪs/ n nepravda do sb an ~ nanijeti kome nepravdu

ink /ɪŋk/ n tinta, crnilo

inkling /'ɪŋklɪŋ/ n (of sth) nagovještaj, slutnja

inlaid /ˌɪn'leɪd/ adj 1 (in/into) umetnut 2 (with) ukrašen umecima od

inland /'ɪnlənd/ adj 1 unutrašnji, kontinentalan 2 domaći the I~ Revenue GB Uprava prihoda

in-laws /ɪn lɔːz/ n pl coll rodbina po ženidbi, svojta

inmate /'ɪnmeɪt/ n 1 zatvorenik 2 pacijent

inmost /'ɪnməʊst/ → innermost

inn /ɪn/ n krčma, svratište ~-keeper n krčmar

innate /ɪ'neɪt/ adj urođen, prirodan

inner /'ɪnə(r)/ adj unutarnji ~ city gradski geto ~most adj najdublji (+ fig) ~ circle fig uži krug

innocent /'ɪnəsnt/ adj 1 (of) nevin, nedužan 2 bezazlen 3 prostodušan

innocuous /ɪ'nɒkjʊəs/ adj neškodljiv, bezazlen, bezopasan

innovation /ˌɪnəˈveɪʃn/ n novina, novost, promjena

innuendo /ˌɪnjuːˈendəʊ/ n aluzija, insinuacija

innumerable /ɪˈnjuːmərəbl/ adj bezbrojan

inoculate /ɪˈnɒkjʊleɪt/ vt (sb with sth/against sth) 1 cijepiti 2 fig zadojiti

inoffensive /ˌɪnəˈfensɪv/ adj 1 bezopasan, bezazlen 2 dobronamjeran

inopportune /ɪnˈɒpətjuːn/ adj nezgodan, neprikladan

inorganic /ˌɪnɔːˈgænɪk/ adj 1 neorganski 2 anorganski

in-patient /ɪn ˈpeɪʃnt/ n bolesnik koji se liječi u bolnici

input /ˈɪnpʊt/ n 1 comp ulaz podataka 2 fig ulaganja pl

inquest /ˈɪnkwest/ n (on) istraga (o uzroku smrti)

inquire (enquire) /ɪnˈkwaɪə(r)/ vt,vi 1 (sth of sb) pitati koga što 2 raspitivati se 3 (after) pitati kako je netko 4 (for) (za)tražiti, zamoliti 5 (into) ispitati, istražiti **inquiring** adj ispitivački, radoznao **inquiry (enquiry)** /ɪnˈkwaɪərɪ/ n 1 upit 2 istraga **make inquiries about sb or sth** raspitati se o **on inquiry** na zahtjev, na upit **court of inquiry** istražni sud

inquisitive /ɪnˈkwɪzətɪv/ adj radoznao

insane /ɪnˈseɪn/ adj 1 lud, umobolan 2 fig ludački **insanity** /ɪnˈsænətɪ/ n 1 ludilo 2 bezumnost

insatiable /ɪnˈseɪʃəbl/ adj nezasitan

inscribe /ɪnˈskraɪb/ vt (on/in/with) upisati, zapisati **inscription** /ɪnˈskrɪpʃn/ n natpis

inscrutable /ɪnˈskruːtəbl/ adj 1 nedokučiv 2 tajnovit, zagonetan

insect /ˈɪnsekt/ n kukac

insecure /ˌɪnsɪˈkjʊə(r)/ adj nesiguran, nepouzdan **insecurity** n nesigurnost

insemination /ɪnˈsemɪˈneɪʃn/ n oplodnja

insensible /ɪnˈsensəbl/ adj 1 bez svijesti, u nesvijesti 2 (of) nesvjestan čega 3 (to) neosjetljiv 4 bezosjećajan, bešćutan

insensitive /ɪnˈsensətɪv/ adj (to) neosjetljiv prema

inseparable /ɪnˈseprəbl/ adj (from) nerazdvojiv, nerazdvojan

insert /ɪnˈsɜːt/ vt umetnuti, ubaciti, uvrstiti • /ˈɪnsɜːt/ n umetak **~ion** /ɪnˈsɜːʃn/ n umetanje, umetak

in–service /ˈɪn sɜːvɪs/ adj ~ **training** izobrazba uz rad

inset /ˈɪnset/ n 1 dodatak, prilog 2 umetak • /ˌɪnˈset/ adj (with) s umecima od

inshore /ˌɪnˈʃɔː(r)/ adj (pri)obalni

inside /ɪnˈsaɪd/ n 1 unutrašnjost, unutrašnji dio, unutrašnja strana 2 coll (+ pl) trbuh, utroba **turn sth ~ out a.** izvrnuti, preokrenuti **b.** isprevrtati **know sth ~ out** coll imati što u malom prstu • /ˈɪnsaɪd/ adj unutrašnji, unutarnji **~ information** povjerljiva informacija (podatak dobiven iz same organizacije) • adv 1 unutra, iznutra 2 GB sl u zatvoru **~ of a.** coll za manje od **b.** US u, unutar • prep u, unutar **~ two hours** coll za manje od dva sata

insidious /ɪnˈsɪdɪəs/ adj podmukao, neprimjetan

insight /ˈɪnsaɪt/ n (into sth) 1 pronicavost 2 predodžba, slika

insignia /ɪnˈsɪgnɪə/ n pl 1 znakovi, simboli 2 mil oznake

insignificant /ˌɪnsɪgˈnɪfɪkənt/ adj nevažan, beznačajan

insincere /ˌɪnsɪnˈsɪə(r)/ adj neiskren

insinuate /ɪnˈsɪnjʊeɪt/ vt 1 (oneself) uvlačiti se 2 (to sb that) natuknuti, aludirati

insipid /ɪnˈsɪpɪd/ adj 1 neukusan, bljutav 2 fig dosadan

insist /ɪnˈsɪst/ vi,vt (on/that) 1 isticati, uporno tvrditi 2 zahtijevati, tražiti **~ent** adj ustrajan, uporan; hitan

in so far as /in as far as/ US **insofar as** /ˌɪnsəˈfɑː(r)/ adv utoliko što, u toj mjeri da, koliko

insolent /ˈɪnsələnt/ adj drzak, bezobrazan

insoluble /ɪnˈsɒljubl/ adj 1 ne(ras)topiv, nerastvoriv 2 nerješiv

insolvent /ɪnˈsɒlvənt/ adj insolventan, nelikvidan

insomnia /ɪnˈsɒmnɪə/ n nesanica **~c** /ɪnˈsɒmnɪæk/ n bolesnik od nesanice

insomuch /ˌɪnsəʊˈmʌtʃ/ adv ~ as utoliko što, ukoliko ~ **that** toliko da, u tolikoj mjeri da

inspect /ɪnˈspekt/ vt 1 pregledati 2 nadgledati, nadzirati **~ion** /ɪnˈspekʃn/ n 1 pregled(avanje) 2 nadzor, kontrola **~or** n nadzornik, inspektor, kontrolor

inspire /ɪnˈspaɪə(r)/ vt nadahnuti koga, potaknuti, pobuditi u komu što, uliti što u koga **inspiration** /ˌɪnspəˈreɪʃn/ n nadahnuće, poticaj

instability /ˌɪnstəˈbɪlətɪ/ n nestabilnost, nestalnost

install /ɪnˈstɔːl/ vt (sb/sth in sth) 1 postaviti (na položaj) 2 uvesti (struju) 3 (sb/oneself in) smjestiti (se) **~ation** /ˌɪnstəˈleɪʃn/ n 1 postavljanje, uvođenje 2 uređaj, instalacija 3 mil postrojenje, baza

instalment /ɪnˈstɔːlmənt/ n 1 nastavak 2 obrok, rata 3 postavljanje, uvođenje **in ~s** u nastavcima **by ~s** na otplatu, na rate ~ **plan** US kupovanje na kredit

instance /ˈɪnstəns/ n 1 primjer 2 slučaj **for** ~ na primjer

instant /ˈɪnstənt/ adj 1 trenutačan, brz 2 hitan, nuždan 3 instant **~ly** adv odmah, smjesta • n tren(utak), čas **this ~/on the** ~ odmah, smjesta

instead /ɪnˈsted/ adv umjesto toga ~ **of** prep umjesto (koga, čega)

instep /ˈɪnstep/ n svod stopala

instigate /ˈɪnstɪɡeɪt/ vt (sth/sb to do sth) poticati **instigation** /ˌɪnstɪˈɡeɪʃn/ n poticaj **at sb's instigation** na nečiji poticaj

instil /ɪnˈstɪl/ vt (sth into sb) fig usaditi, uli(jeva)ti

instinct /ˈɪnstɪŋkt/ n nagon **~ive** /ɪnˈstɪŋktɪv/ adj nagonski

institute /ˈɪnstɪtjuːt/ n zavod, institut • vt 1 ustanoviti, utemeljiti 2 pokrenuti (postupak) 3 uvesti (ograničenje) 4 (sb to) imenovati na položaj **institution** /ˌɪnstɪˈtjuːʃn/ n 1 ustanovljavanje 2 institucija (zakon, običaj) (+ fig) 3 zavod, ustanova 4 ludnica; staračački dom; sirotište **institutionalize** /ˌɪnstɪˈtjuːʃənəlaɪz/ vt 1 učiniti dijelom društvenog sustava, instituciona-

lizirati 2 staviti u ludnicu/dom

instruct /ɪnˈstrʌkt/ vt 1 podučavati, instruirati 2 uputiti, dati upute 3 obavijestiti **~ion** /ɪnˈstrʌkʃn/ 1 poduka, podučavanje 2 pl upute, nalozi, naredbe **~ive** adj poučan **~or** n instruktor

instrument /ˈɪnstrʊmənt/ n 1 sprava, uređaj 2 glazbalo 3 leg dokument **~al** /ˌɪnstrʊˈmentl/ adj instrumentalan **be ~al in doing sth** pripomoći, posredovati u **~alist** /ˌɪnstrʊˈmentəlɪst/ n glazbenik

insubordinate /ˌɪnsəˈbɔːdɪnət/ adj neposlušan **insubordination** /ˌɪnsəˌbɔːdɪˈneɪʃn/ n neposlušnost

insubstantial /ˌɪnsəbˈstænʃl/ adj 1 fig krhak, slab 2 netvaran, nematerijalan, netjelesan; nestvaran

insufferable /ɪnˈsʌfrəbl/ adj nepodnošljiv, nesnosan

insufficient /ˌɪnsəˈfɪʃnt/ adj nedovoljan, nedostatan

insular /ˈɪnsjʊlə(r)/ adj 1 otočan 2 fig uskogrudan, ograničen

insulate /ˈɪnsjʊleɪt/ vt (from/against) 1 izolirati 2 odvojiti, udaljiti, (za)štititi **insulation** /ˌɪnsjʊˈleɪʃn/ n izolacija **insulating tape** izolacijska vrpca, izolirband coll

insult /ˈɪnsʌlt/ n uvreda • /ɪnˈsʌlt/ vt uvrijediti **~ing** /ɪnˈsʌltɪŋ/ adj uvredljiv, pogrdan

insuperable /ɪnˈsjuːprəbl/ adj nesavladiv

insure /ɪnˈʃʊə(r)/ vt (against) osigurati **the ~d** n osiguranik **the ~r** n osiguravatelj **insurance** /ɪnˈʃʊərəns/ (against/on) n 1 osiguranje 2 osigurnina **insurance company** osiguravajuće društvo **insurance policy** polica osiguranja **life insurance** životno osiguranje

insurgent /ɪnˈsɜːdʒənt/ n pobunjenik, ustanik • adj pobunjen, ustanički **insurrection** /ˌɪnsəˈrekʃn/ n pobuna, ustanak

insurmountable /ˌɪnsəˈmaʊntəbl/ adj nesavladiv

intact /ɪnˈtækt/ adj nedirnut, netaknut, neoštećen

intake /ˈɪnteɪk/ 1 priljev, pritjecanje, unošenje, primanje 2 dovodni otvor, ulaz

intangible /ɪnˈtændʒəbl/ *adj* 1 neopipljiv 2 *fig* neshvatljiv

integer /ˈɪntɪdʒə(r)/ *n* cijelo, cijeli broj

integral /ˈɪntɪgrəl/ *adj* 1 sastavni 2 cijeli, potpun ~ **calculus** integralni račun **integrate** /ˈɪntɪgreɪt/ *vt* (with/into) 1 upotpuniti, sastaviti 2 uklopiti **integration** /ˌɪntɪˈgreɪʃn/ *n* 1 upotpunjavanje 2 uklapanje **integrity** /ɪnˈtegrəti/ *n* 1 poštenje, čestitost 2 cjelovitost, potpunost

intellect /ˈɪntəlekt/ *n* 1 razum 2 um, u-man čovjek ~**ual** /ˌɪntəˈlektʃuəl/ *adj* (raz)uman, duhovan, intelektualan ○ *n* intelektualac

intelligence /ɪnˈtelɪdʒəns/ *n* 1 inteligencija, snalažljivost, oštroumnost, brzo shvaćanje 2 vijesti, novosti; podaci 3 obavještavanje, špijunaža; obavještajna služba **intelligent** /ɪnˈtelɪdʒənt/ *adj* razborit, pametan, inteligentan **the intelligentsia** /ɪnˌtelɪˈdʒentsɪə/ *n* inteligencija

intelligible /ɪnˈtelɪdʒəbl/ *adj* razumljiv, shvatljiv

intemperate /ɪnˈtempərət/ *adj* neumjeren, neobuzdan

intend /ɪnˈtend/ *vt* 1 (to do/doing sth) namjeravati, naumiti, htjeti 2 (for) namijeniti, predvidjeti, odrediti za 3 (by) *arch* misliti, htjeti kazati **that was ~ed as a joke** to je trebalo shvatiti kao šalu **my ~ed** *coll* moj budući, moja buduća

intense /ɪnˈtens/ *adj* 1 jak, žestok 2 revan, strastven, vatren **intensify** /ɪnˈtensɪfaɪ/ *vt,vi* pojača(va)ti (se) **intensity** *n* jačina **intensive** *adj* 1 pojačan, intenzivan 2 temeljit **intensive care** *med* intenzivna skrb

intent /ɪnˈtent/ *adj* 1 napet, pažljiv, skoncentriran 2 (on/upon sth/doing sth) usredotočen na, zaokupljen čime; čvrsto odlučiti ○ *n* 1 namjera, nakana 2 *leg* predumišljaj **with good/evil** ~ dobronamjerno/ zlonamjerno **to all ~s and purposes** u svakom pogledu, praktički ~**ion** /ɪnˈtenʃn/ *n* namjera **without ~** ne-

namjerno **with the ~ion of doing sth** s namjerom da **well-~ed** dobronamjeran **ill-~ed** zlonamjeran ~**ional** /ɪnˈtenʃənl/ *adj* namjeran

inter /ɪnˈtɜ:(r)/ *vt form* pokopati

interact /ˌɪntərˈækt/ *vi* (with) međusobno djelovati ~**ion** /ˌɪntərˈækʃn/ *n* (between/with) međusobno djelovanje

intercede /ˌɪntəˈsiːd/ *vi* (with sb/for sb/on sb's behalf) posredovati kod, zauzeti se za

intercept /ˌɪntəˈsept/ *vt* presresti, uhvatiti, spriječiti, zaustaviti ~**ion** /ˌɪntəˈsepʃn/ *n* presretanje

interchange /ˌɪntəˈtʃeɪndʒ/ *vt* 1 razmijeniti (gledišta, pisma) 2 zamijeniti (stvari) ~**able** zamjenjiv • *n* 1 izmjena, razmjena, zamjena 2 petlja (cesta)

intercourse /ˈɪntəkɔːs/ *n form* općenje

interest /ˈɪntrəst/ *n* 1 zanimanje, interes 2 korist, dobrobit 3 udio, kapital 4 kamate **take an ~ in** zanimati se za **be of ~ to** biti zanimljiv za (koga), biti od značenja za **to sb's ~** u čijem interesu **in the ~(s) of humanity** za dobrobit čovječanstva **have an ~ in** imati udio u čemu **in rate of ~/~ rate** kamatna stopa **the business ~s** poslovni krugovi **with ~** *fig* s kamatama, dvostruko • *vt* (sb in sth) zanimati, pobuditi čije zanimanje, ticati se **be ~ed in** zanimati se za što ~**ed** *adj* 1 zainteresiran 2 pristran ~**ing** *adj* zanimljiv

interface /ˈɪntəfeɪs/ *n* 1 (between) mjesto dodira 2 *comp* međusklop, sučelje

interfere /ˌɪntəˈfɪə(r)/ *vi* 1 (in sth/between) miješati se, upletati se 2 (with) dirati što, prčkati po 3 (with) ometati, smetati, sprečavati ~**nce** /ˌɪntəˈfɪərəns/ *n* 1 miješanje, upletanje 2 radiosmetnje; interferencija

interim /ˈɪntərɪm/ *n* **in the ~** u međuvremenu • *adj* privremen, prijelazni

interior /ɪnˈtɪərɪə(r)/ *adj* 1 unutarnji 2 unutrašnji 3 domaći • *n* unutrašnjost, interijer **the ~** unutarnji poslovi

interjection /ˌɪntəˈdʒekʃn/ *n* uzvik

interlace /ˌɪntəˈleɪs/ *vt,vi* (with) ispreplesti (se), protkati

interlock /ˌɪntə'lɒk/ vt,vi međusobno spojiti, zakvačiti; spojiti se, zakvačiti se

interlocutor /ˌɪntə'lɒkjʊtə(r)/ n sugovornik

interloper /'ɪntələʊpə(r)/ n nametljivac, uljez

interlude /'ɪntəlu:d/ n 1 međurazdoblje 2 međuigra, interludij

intermarry /ˌɪntə'mærɪ/ vi (with) ženiti se s pripadnicama drugih naroda/rasa, međusobno sklapati brakove

intermediary /ˌɪntə'mi:dɪərɪ/ adj 1 prijelazni 2 posredni • n 1 (between) posrednik 2 prijelazni oblik

intermediate /ˌɪntə'mi:dɪət/ adj srednji, prijelazni, posredni ~ **courses** tečajevi srednjeg stupnja ~**-range ballistic missile** projektil srednjeg dometa

interminable /ɪn'tɜ:mɪnəbl/ adj beskrajan, beskonačan

intermission /ˌɪntə'mɪʃn/ n prekid, stanka **intermittent** /ˌɪntə'mɪtnt/ adj isprekidan, povremen

intern /ɪn'tɜ:n/ vt internirati ~**ment** n internacija • /'ɪntɜ:n/ n US med stažist

internal /ɪn'tɜ:nl/ adj 1 unutarnji, unutrašnji 2 domaći ~ **revenue** prihod od poreza ~ **combustion** unutarnje izgaranje ~ **bleeding** unutarnje krvarenje

international /ˌɪntə'næʃnəl/ adj međunarodni

interplay /'ɪntəpleɪ/ n (of/between) međusobno djelovanje

interpose /ˌɪntə'pəʊz/ vt,vi 1 (oneself between/~ in) postaviti se između, posredovati 2 ubaciti (primjedbu), uložiti (veto) 3 prekinuti, upasti u riječ, uplesti se

interpret /ɪn'tɜ:prɪt/ vt,vi 1 (pro)tumačiti, objasniti 2 izvesti, prikazati, tumačiti (ulogu) 3 usmeno prevesti ~**er** n tumač, prevoditelj ~**ation** /ɪn,tɜ:prɪ'teɪʃn/ n tumačenje; prevođenje

interregnum /ˌɪntə'regnəm/ n (pl ~**s**, ~**na**) međuvlađe

interrelation /ˌɪntərɪ'leɪʃn/ n (of/between) međusobna povezanost

interrogate /ɪn'terəgeɪt/ vt ispitivati, saslušavati **interrogation** /ɪn,terə'geɪʃn/ n ispitivanje, saslušavanje **interrogation mark/point** n upitnik (?) **interrogative** /ˌɪntə'rɒgətɪv/ adj upitni o n gram upitni oblik; upitna riječ

interrupt /ˌɪntə'rʌpt/ vt,vi 1 prekinuti 2 upasti u riječ ~**ion** /ˌɪntə'rʌpʃn/ n prekid(anje)

intersect /ˌɪntə'sekt/ vt,vi (pre)sjeći, presijecati (se) ~**ion** /ˌɪntə'sekʃn/ n 1 presijecanje 2 raskrižje; sjecište

intersperse /ˌɪntə'spɜ:s/ vt 1 (among/between/in/throughout) razasuti, posuti 2 (with) prošarati, protkati (+ fig)

interstate /ˌɪntə'steɪt/ adj međudržavni (u SAD) • n US autocesta koja povezuje savezne države

intertwine /ˌɪntə'twaɪn/ vt,vi ispreplesti (se)

interval /'ɪntəvl/ n 1 (between) razmak 2 stanka, pauza 3 interval **at short** ~**s** u kratkim razmacima **at** ~**s of 10 feet** u razmacima od 10 stopa

intervene /ˌɪntə'vi:n/ vi 1 (in/between) umiješati se, posredovati 2 iskrsnuti, nastupiti 3 pro(te)ći (o vremenu) **intervention** /ˌɪntə'venʃn/ n miješanje, posredovanje, uplitanje (+ mil)

interview /'ɪntəvju:/ n 1 intervju 2 razgovor za posao ~**ee** /ˌɪntəvju:'i:/ n ispitanik ~**er** /'ɪntə,vju:ə/ n ispitivač, koji intervjuira • vt intervjuirati

interweave /ˌɪntə'wi:v/ vt irreg (with) isprepletsi, protkati (+ fig)

intestine /ɪn'testɪn/ n med crijevo **large/small** ~ debelo/tanko crijevo **intestinal** adj crijevni

intimacy /'ɪntɪməsɪ/ n 1 prisnost, intimnost 2 prijateljstvo 3 euph spolni odnos **on terms of** ~ **with** u prisnim odnosima s **intimate** /'ɪntɪmət/ adj 1 blizak, prisan 2 intiman, osoban **on intimate terms with** u prisnim odnosima s **have an intimate knowledge of sth** dobro/temeljito poznavati što o n prisan prijatelj **intimate** /'ɪntɪmeɪt/ vt (sth to sb; to sb that) dati do znanja, natuknuti

intimidate /ɪn'tɪmɪdeɪt/ vt (sb into doing sth) zastraši(va)ti

into /'ɪntʊ/; /'ɪntʊ:/ *prep* (kretanje, smjer) u **come ~ the room/garden** ući u sobu/vrt **jump ~ the water** skočiti u vodu **get ~ trouble** zapasti u nevolje **the rain changed ~ snow** kiša se pretvorila u snijeg **collect sth ~ heaps** skupiti što u hrpe **he scared them ~ silence** toliko ih je uplašio da su ušutjeli **5 ~ 25 goes 5** pet u 25 ide 5 puta **be ~ sth** *coll* baviti se čime, zanimati se za, obožavati što

intolerable /ɪn'tɒlərəbl/ *adj* nepodnošljiv, nesnosan **intolerance** /ɪn-'tɒlərəns/ *n* netrpeljivost, nesnošljivost **intolerant** *adj* netrpeljiv, nesnošljiv

intoxicated /ɪn'tɒksɪkeɪtɪd/ *adj* 1 pijan 2 *fig* opijen

intractable /ɪn'træktəbl/ *adj* nepopustljiv, neukrotiv, tvrdoglav

intransigent /ɪn'trænsɪdʒənt/ *adj form* beskompromisan (u politici)

intransitive /ɪn'trænsətɪv/ *adj gram* neprelazan (glagol)

intravenous /ˌɪntrə'vi:nəs/ *adj med* intravenozan

in–tray *n* pretinac za neobrađene spise

intrepid /ɪn'trepɪd/ *adj* neustrašiv

intricate /'ɪntrɪkət/ *adj* zamršen, zakučast

intrigue /ɪn'tri:g/ *vi,vt* 1 (with sb/against sb) spletkariti 2 pobuditi zanimanje/radoznalost, fascinirati **intriguing** *adj* fascinantan, zanimljiv ○ *n* spletka(renje)

intrinsic /ɪn'trɪnsɪk/ *adj* (to) unutarnji, istinski, pravi, stvaran

introduce /ˌɪntrə'dju:s/ *vt* 1 (sb to sb) predstaviti, upoznati 2 (in/into) donijeti, unijeti, uvesti 3 uvesti zakon 4 (into) umetnuti, utaknuti; potaknuti, pokrenuti (temu) **introduction** /ˌɪntrə'dʌkʃn/ *n* 1 uvođenje 2 upoznavanje 3 uvod; predgovor 4 početnica **introductory** /ˌɪntrə-'dʌktərɪ/ *adj* uvodni

introspective /ˌɪntrə'spektɪv/ *adj* sklon samopromatranju, introspektivan

introvert /'ɪntrəvɜ:t/ *n* povučena/-zatvorena osoba **introverted** *adj* povučen u sebe, zatvoren

intrude /ɪn'tru:d/ *vt,vi* (oneself) **on/-upon sb**; (oneself/sth) **into sth** 1 nametnuti (se), ugurati (se), smetati 2 nametati, naturati (svoje mišljenje) **~r** *n* nametljivac, nezvan gost, uljez

intrusion /ɪn'tru:ʒn/ *n* nametanje, nedopušteno ulaženje, upadanje, smetanje

intuition /ˌɪntju:'ɪʃn/ *n* intuicija

inundate /'ɪnʌndeɪt/ *vt* (with) 1 poplaviti 2 preplaviti (+ *fig*)

invade /ɪn'veɪd/ *vt* 1 *mil* napasti, upasti u 2 *fig* navaliti u velikom broju, preplaviti; obuzeti, spopasti (misli) 3 pokvariti, upropastiti 4 kršiti, povrijediti (prava) **invasion** /ɪn'veɪʒn/ *n* 1 *mil* upad, najezda, navala, invazija (+ *fig*) 2 *leg* kršenje, povreda

invalid /ɪn'vælɪd/ *adj* 1 nevažeći, bez zakonske valjanosti 2 /'ɪnvəlɪd/ boležljiv, slab; nesposoban; invalidski ○ *n* invalid; boležljiva osoba ○ *vt* (sb out of the army) poslati kući kao invalida

invaluable /ɪn'væljʊəbl/ *adj* (to) neprocjenjiv, dragocjen

invariable /ɪn'veərɪəbl/ *adv* nepromjenljiv, stalan, postojan

invent /ɪn'vent/ *vt* 1 izumiti, pronaći 2 izmisliti, smisliti **~ion** /ɪn'venʃn/ *n* 1 izum, pronalazak 2 izmišljotina **~ive** *adj* 1 izumiteljski, pronalazački 2 domišljat **~or** *n* izumitelj, pronalazač **~ory** /'ɪnvəntrɪ/ *n* 1 popis inventara 2 *US* inventar

invert /ɪn'vɜ:t/ *vt* 1 obrnuti, (pre)okrenuti **~ed commas** navodnici **inversion** /ɪn'vɜ:ʃn/ *n* 1 obrtanje, (pre)okretanje, obrnuti (po)red(ak) 2 *gram* inverzija

invertebrate /ɪn'vɜ:tɪbreɪt/ *n* beskičmenjak (+ *fig*)

invest /ɪn'vest/ *vt,vi* 1 (in) uložiti; *coll* kupiti 2 (with) (za)odjenuti; dati, dodijeliti (ovlasti); pridavati (važnost) 3 *arch mil* opkoliti, okružiti **~iture** /ɪn'vestɪtʃə(r)/ *n* ustoličenje, svečano uvođenje u službu **~ment** *n* ulaganje, investicija **~or** *n* ulagač

investigate /ɪn'vestɪgeɪt/ *vt* istražiti, ispitati **investigation** /ɪn,vestɪ'geɪʃn/ *n* istraživanje, istraga **investigator** *n* istražitelj

inveterate /ɪnˈvetərət/ *adj* okorio, nepopravljiv (lažac, pušač)

invidious /ɪnˈvɪdɪəs/ *adj* nepravedan, uvredljiv

invigilate /ɪnˈvɪdʒɪleɪt/ *vi* nadzirati pismeni ispit

invigorate /ɪnˈvɪɡəreɪt/ *vt* ojačati, okrijepiti, osvježiti

invincible /ɪnˈvɪnsəbl/ *adj* nepobjediv

inviolable /ɪnˈvaɪələbl/ *adj form* nepovrediv, neprekršiv (pravo, zakon, zakletva) **inviolate** /ɪnˈvaɪələt/ *adj* nepovrijeđen, neokrnjen, nedirnut

invisible /ɪnˈvɪzəbl/ *adj* (to) nevidljiv ~ **exports/imports** izvoz/uvoz usluga

invite /ɪnˈvaɪt/ *vt* (to) **1** pozvati **2** zamoliti, zatražiti **3** izazivati, poticati, ohrabrivati, mamiti **inviting** *adj* **1** koji poziva **2** privlačan, primamljiv, zamaman **invitation** /ˌɪnvɪˈteɪʃn/ *n* poziv; pozivnica

invoice /ˈɪnvɔɪs/ *n* faktura • *vt* **1** fakturirati **2** (sb for) izdati fakturu

invoke /ɪnˈvəʊk/ *vt form* **1** poz(iv)ati se na **2** prizivati, zazivati **3** zatražiti pomoć **4** dozivati (duhove)

involuntary /ɪnˈvɒləntrɪ/ *adj* nehotičan, nenamjeran, nesvjestan, automatski, nekontroliran

involve /ɪnˈvɒlv/ *vt* (be/become/get ~d in sth/with sb) **1** uvlačiti, uplitati, umiješati **2** zahtijevati, podrazumijevati, povlačiti za sobom **3** obuhvaćati, sadržavati, uključivati **be deeply ~d in debt** pasti u velike dugove ~d *adj* zakučast, kompliciran ~**ment** *n* upletenost, umiješanost

invulnerable /ɪnˈvʌlnərəbl/ *adj* (to) **1** neranjiv, nepovrediv **2** *fig* neosjetljiv (na kritike) **3** neosvojiv, neuništiv (utvrda)

inward /ˈɪnwəd/ *adj* **1** unutarnji, unutrašnji **2** okrenut prema unutra ~**ly** *adv* u sebi ~(s) *adv* (prema) unutra ~**-looking** okrenut sebi, povučen u sebe, zatvoren

iodine /ˈaɪədiːn/ *n* jod

ion /ˈaɪən/ *n* ion

iota /aɪˈəʊtə/ *n* **1** jota, grčko slovo **2** *fig*

(of) mrvica, trunka

irascible /ɪˈræsəbl/ *adj form* razdražljiv, raspaljiv, nagao

irate /aɪˈreɪt/ *adj form* bijesan, ljutit, srdit

iridescent /ˌɪrɪˈdesnt/ *adj* koji se prelijeva u bojama

iris /ˈaɪərɪs/ *n* **1** perunika **2** šarenica oka

irk /ɜːk/ *vt* dosađivati, gnjaviti, ljutiti, živcirati **it ~s me to admit** muka mi je priznati ~**some** /ɜːksəm/ *adj* neugodan, mrzak, dosadan, zamoran

iron /ˈaɪən/ *n* **1** željezo **2** glačalo **3** *pl* okovi, lanci **wrought** ~ kovano željezo **cast** ~ lijevano željezo **scrap** ~ staro željezo **strike while the** ~ **is hot** kuj željezo dok je vruće **the I~ Age** željezno doba **the** ~ **curtain** željezna zavjesa **~ lung** aparat za umjetno disanje ~**monger** željezar, trgovac željeznom robom ~**mongery** željezarija ~**ware** željezna roba ~**works** ljevaonica željeza • *vt* glačati ~ **out** a. izglačati b. *fig* izgladiti **do the** ~**ing** glačati ~**ing board** daska za glačanje

irony /ˈaɪərənɪ/ *n* ironija **the** ~ **of fate** ironija sudbine **ironic(al)** /aɪˈrɒnɪk; aɪˈrɒnɪkl/ *adj* ironičan, podrugljiv

irrational /ɪˈræʃənl/ *adj* nerazuman

irreconcilable /ɪˌrekənˈsaɪləbl/ *adj* (with) **1** nepomirljiv **2** nespojiv, neuskladiv

irrefutable /ˌɪrɪˈfjuːtəbl/ *adj* nepobitan, neoboriv, neosporan

irregular /ɪˈreɡjələ(r)/ *adj* **1** (+ *gram*) nepravilan; nepropisan, neispravan **2** neredovit **3** neujednačen, nejednolik; neravan • *n* (*pl*) *mil* neregularne jedinice ~**ity** /ɪˌreɡjəˈlærətɪ/ *n* nepravilnost

irrelevant /ɪˈreləvənt/ *adj* nevažan, sporedan

irreparable /ɪˈrepərəbl/ *adj* nenadoknadiv, nepopravljiv, nepovratan

irreplaceable /ˌɪrɪˈpleɪsəbl/ *adj* nenadoknadiv, nenadomjestiv, nezamjenjiv

irrepressible /ˌɪrɪˈpresəbl/ *adj* nezaustavljiv, nesusprežljiv, nezatomljiv

irresistible /ˌɪrɪˈzɪstəbl/ *adj* neodoljiv

irresolute /ɪ'rezəluːt/ adj neodlučan, kolebljiv

irrespective /ˌɪrɪ'spektɪv/ adj ~ of bez obzira na

irresponsible /ˌɪrɪ'spɒnsəbl/ adj 1 neodgovoran 2 neuračunljiv

irreverent /ɪ'revərənt/ adj neuljudan, bez poštovanja

irrevocable /ɪ'revəkəbl/ adj neopoziv

irrigate /'ɪrɪgeɪt/ vt 1 navodnjavati 2 med ispirati **irrigation** /ˌɪrɪ'geɪʃn/ n 1 navodnjavanje 2 med ispiranje

irritable /'ɪrɪtəbl/ adj razdražljiv **irritate** /'ɪrɪteɪt/ vt 1 (raz)dražiti, (raz)-ljutiti, ići na živce 2 med nadraživati, smetati **irritation** /ˌɪrɪ'teɪʃn/ n razdraženost, ljutnja, iritiranje (+ med)

Islam /ɪz'lɑːm/ n islam ~**ic** adj islamski, muslimanski

island /'aɪlənd/ n otok (+ fig) **a traffic ~** otok za pješake ~**er** n otočanin

isle /aɪl/ n otok (u imenima) ~**t** /'aɪlɪt/ n otočić

isolate /'aɪsəleɪt/ vt (from) izdvojiti, odvojiti, izolirati

isolation /ˌaɪsə'leɪʃn/ n odvajanje, odvojenost, samoća, izoliranost

isosceles triangle /aɪ'sɒsəliːz 'traɪ-æŋgl/ n istokračan trokut

issue /'ɪʃuː/ vi,vt 1 izda(va)ti; objaviti 2 pustiti u optjecaj, emitirati (novac) 3 (sb with sth/sth to sb) mil opskrbiti, opremiti, podijeliti 4 (out/forth/from) istjecati, izbijati, izlaziti • n 1 pitanje, problem, predmet 2 primjerak, izdanje, broj (novina), serija (maraka) 3 izdavanje (priopćenja, naredbi), dijeljenje (opreme, streljiva); 4 emisija (novca) 5 curenje, istjecanje, izlaženje, izljev 6 ishod, posljedica, rezultat 7 arch, leg potomstvo **join/take ~ with sb on sth** stati se prepirati oko čega **the point/matter at ~** sporno pitanje **at ~** u pitanju **make an ~ of sth** napraviti problem od

čega, svađati se oko čega

isthmus /'ɪsməs/ n prevlaka

it /ɪt/ pers pron to, ono (često se ne prevodi) **Who is ~? I~'s Mary.** Tko je? Ja, Mary. **I like ~ here** svida mi se ovdje **I find ~ hard to say** teško mi je reći **~ doesn't matter** nije važno ~**'s raining** pada kiša, kiši ~**'s hot** vruće ~ **seems** čini se ~**'s my mother I'm worried about** u stvari se brinem za majku • n ono nešto **she really thinks she's** ~ ona stvarno misli da je nešto ~**s** /ɪts/ poss adj njegov, njegova, njegovo; svoj, svoja, svoje (za životinje i neživa pojmove) ~**self** reflex pron 1 sebe, se, sebi, sobom 2 ono samo **by** ~**self** samo od sebe, samo po sebi **in** ~**self** samo po sebi

italics /ɪ'tælɪks/ n pl kurziv **italic type** kurziv **italic handwriting** kosi rukopis **italicize** vt staviti u kurziv, tiskati u kurzivu

itch /ɪtʃ/ vi svrbjeti **I'm** ~**ing all over** sve me svrbi **be** ~**ing for sth/to do sth** coll jedva čekati, izgarati od želje • n 1 svrbež, svrab 2 (have an ~/one's ~ for sth/to do sth) čežnja, velika želja **have/suffer from the ~/an ~** svrbjeti ~**y** adj 1 svrbljiv 2 željan, nestrpljiv od želje

item /'aɪtəm/ n (pojedina) točka, stavka, predmet, stvar **an ~ of clothing** odjevni predmet **an interesting ~ of news/news** ~ zanimljiva vijest ~**ize** /'aɪtəmaɪz/ vt detaljno nabrojiti, navesti, popisati

itinerant /aɪ'tɪnərənt/ adj putujući (glazbenik, propovjednik)

itinerary /aɪ'tɪnərəri/ n plan puta/puto-vanja

ivory /'aɪvəri/ n 1 bjelokost, slonova kost 2 (pl) predmeti od bjelokosti ~ **tower** kula bjelokosna

ivy /'aɪvɪ/ n bršljan

J

J, j /dʒeɪ/ deseto slovo engl. abecede; je

jab /dʒæb/ *vt, vi* 1 ~ **at** bosti, podbosti 2 ~ **into** zabosti • *n* 1 ubod, udarac 2 injekcija, cijepljenje

jabber /ˈdʒæbə(r)/ *vt,vi* 1 blebetati 2 frfljati

jack /dʒæk/ *n* 1 dizalica 2 bulin **every man J~** svatko **the Union J~** britanska zastava **~-o'lantern** izdubljena bundeva s upaljenom svijećom ~ **of all trades** majstor za sve • *vt* ~ **sth up** podići dizalicom

jackal /ˈdʒækɔːl/ *n* šakal

jackass /ˈdʒækæs/ *n* magarac (+ *fig*)

jackboot /ˈdʒæk buːt/ *n* jahaća čizma

jackdaw /ˈdʒækdɔː/ *n* svraka

jacket /ˈdʒækɪt/ *n* 1 kaputić, jakna, sako 2 omotač 3 kora

jack-knife /ˈdʒæk naɪf/ *n* nož na sklapanje • *vi* presaviti se

jackpot /ˈdʒækpɒt/ *n* glavni dobitak

Jacobean /ˌdʒækəˈbɪən/ *adj* iz razdoblja Jamesa I.

Jacobite /ˈdʒækəbaɪt/ *n* pristaša Jamesa II.

jade (1) /dʒeɪd/ *n* žad

jade (2) *n* kljuse **~d** *adj* 1 izmoren 2 oguglao

jag /dʒæg/ *n* hrid • *vt* nazupčati **~ged** *adj* nazubljen

jaguar /ˈdʒægjʊə(r)/ *n* jaguar

jail → **gaol**

jam (1) /dʒæm/ *n* pekmez, džem

jam (2) *vt* 1 (in/under/between etc.) stisnuti, pritijesniti, zgnječiti 2 (on) zaglaviti (se) 3 nagurati, natiskati 4 ometati • *n* 1 gužva **traffic~** zastoj prometa 2 zakočenje 3 *sl* škripac

jamboree /ˌdʒæmbəˈriː/ *n* 1 veselica 2 zbor (izviđača)

jangle /ˈdʒæŋgl/ *vt,vi* 1 zveketati 2 neugodno se dojmiti, imati neugodan prizvuk 3 svađati se • *n* zveket

janitor /ˈdʒænɪtə(r)/ *n* 1 vratar 2 kućepazitelj

January /ˈdʒænjʊərɪ/ *n* siječanj

jar (1) /dʒɑː(r)/ *n* 1 štropot 2 udarac, potres (+ *fig*) • *vi, vt* 1 ~ **against/on** udarati o, štropotati o 2 potresti 3 ~ **on** vrijeđati koga/što 4 (with) ne slagati se, sukobiti se **~ring** *adj* oštar, nesladan

jar (2) *n* vrč, lonac, čaša, staklenka

jaundice /ˈdʒɔːndɪs/ *n* 1 žutica 2 *fig* jal

jaunt /dʒɔːnt/ *n* izlet • *vi* otići na izlet

jaunty /ˈdʒɔːntɪ/ *adj* objestan, živahan

javelin /ˈdʒævlɪn/ *n* *sport* koplje

jaw /dʒɔː/ *n* 1 **lower/upper** ~ gornja/donja vilica **~breaker** *n* riječ koju je teško izgovoriti 2 donja vilica, brada 3 *pl* ralje 3 *pl* *fig* ždrijelo, grotlo 4 *pl* čeljusti (alata)

jay /dʒeɪ/ *n* šojka

jay-walk *vi* neoprezno prelaziti cestu **~er** *n* neoprezni pješak

jazz /dʒæz/ *n* džez • *vt* 1 svirati/plesati džez **~ sth up** *fig* *coll* oživjeti, razbuditi

jealous /ˈdʒeləs/ *adj* 1 ljubomoran 2 (of sb/sth) zavidan zbog 3 (of sb/sth) brižan, budan **~y** *n* ljubomora

jeans /dʒiːns/ *n* *pl* (blue ~) traperice

jeep /dʒiːp/ *n* džip, terensko vozilo

jeer /dʒɪə(r)/ *vi,vi* (at sb) izrugivati se komu, ismijavati koga • *n* poruga, podsmijeh; prosvjed

jelly /ˈdʒelɪ/ *n* 1 želatina 2 žele 3 hladetina **jellied** *adj* u hladetini **~fish** *n* meduza **Jell-O** *n* TM voćni puding

jeopardize /ˈdʒepədaɪz/ *vt* izvrgnuti opasnosti, riskirati

jeopardy *n* opasnost **be/put/place in** ~ izvrgnuti opasnosti

jerk /dʒɜːk/ *n* 1 trzaj 2 grč 3 *sl* budala,

kreten • *vt, vi* 1 trgnuti (se), trzati (se), pokrenuti (se) uz trzaj 2 *sl tab* (off/out) drkati *sl tab*

jerry-building /'dʒerɪ 'bɪldɪŋ/ *n* nesolidna gradnja

jersey /'dʒɜːzɪ/ *n* 1 ~-wool žersej 2 džemper 3 športski dres **yellow** ~ *sport* žuta majica

jest /dʒest/ *n* 1 šala 2 predmet šale • *vi* (with) šaliti se (sa) ~ing *adj* šaljiv, sklon šali (**court**) ~er *n* dvorska luda

Jesus /'dʒiːzəs/ *n* Isus

jet (1) /dʒet/ *n* 1 mlaz ~-**propulsion** mlazni pogon 2 (~ aircraft/airliner/fighter/plane) mlažnjak **the** ~ **set** mondeno društvo, džet set 3 pipac, mlaznica • *vt,vi* ispuštati mlazeve, izbijati u mlazevima

jet (2) *n* crni jantar ~-**black** crn-crncat

jetsam /'dʒetsəm/ *n* naplavljeni predmeti

jettison /'dʒetɪsən/ *vt* 1 baciti preko palube 2 *fig* odbaciti

jetty /'dʒetɪ/ *n* molo

Jew /dʒuː/ *n* Židov ~**ess** *n* Židovka ~**ish** *adj* židovski

jewel /'dʒuːəl/ *n* dragulj, dragi kamen (+ *fig*) ~**ler** *n* draguljar ~**ry**, ~**lery** *n* nakit

jibe /dʒaɪb/ *US* → gibe

jiffy /'dʒɪfɪ/ *vi coll* tren

jig /dʒɪg/ *n* 1 živahni ples • *vi,vt* 1 živahno plesati 2 poskakivati, drmati (se)

jigsaw /'dʒɪgsɔː/ *n* strojna pilica za rezbarenje ~ **puzzle** a. slagalica b. *fig* složena stvar/situacija

jilt /dʒɪlt/ *vt* odbaciti

jingle /'dʒɪŋgl/ *n* 1 zvecket 2 najava; džingl *coll* • *vt,vi* 1 zveckati, zveckati 2 biti zvučan/lako pamtvis

jingo /'dʒɪŋgəu/ *n* šovinist ~**ism** *n* šovinizam ~**ist** *n* šovinist

jitters /'dʒɪtəz/ *n pl* (**the** ~) *sl* nervoza **jittery** *adj* nervozan, ustrašen

jive /dʒaɪv/ *n* 1 (**hand**-~) ples 2 *sl* šatrovački govor; spika *sl* • *vi* 1 plesati ~ 2 govoriti šatrovački; bacati spiku *sl*

job /dʒɒb/ *n* posao **do a good** ~ dobro obaviti posao ~ **centre** burza rada 2 *sl* špekulacija 3 *sl* krađa • *vt,*

vi 1 obavljati povremene poslove 2 mešetariti na burzi 3 *coll* zloupotrijebiti položaj ~**ber** *n* 1 mešetar 2 radnik koji obavlja povremene poslove ~**bery** *n* zloupotreba položaja

jockey /'dʒɒkɪ/ *n* jahač, džokej • *vt,vi* varati

jockstrap /'dʒɒkstræp/ *n* suspender

jocular /'dʒɒkjulə(r)/ *adj* šaljiv, duhovit

jog /dʒɒg/ *vt,vi* 1 gurnuti, protresti ~ **sb's memory** nastojati ga podsjetiti 2 ~ **along/on** polako napredovati 3 *coll* trčati • *n* 1 gurkanje 2 trčakaranje, kas ~**ger** *n* trkač ~**ging** *n* rekreativno trčanje; džoging *coll*

joggle /'dʒɒgl/ *vt, vi* protresti, prodrmati • *n* drmanje

john /dʒɒn/ *n sl* 1 zahod 2 *sl* mušterija (prostitutke)

John Bull /ˌdʒɒn 'bul/ *n* engleska nacija, tipični Englez

join /dʒɔɪn/ *vt, vi* 1 (sth to sth) sastaviti, spojiti (što s čime) ~ **battle** upustiti se u bitku ~ **hands** dati si ruke, udružiti se 2 ulijevati se 3 spajati (se) 4 pridružiti se, uključiti se ~ **up** stupiti u vojsku • *n* spoj

joiner /'dʒɔɪnə(r)/ *n* stolar ~**y** *n* stolarija

joint /dʒɔɪnt/ *adj* zajednički, udružen ~ **stock company** dioničko društvo • *n* 1 spoj 2 utor 3 zglob **out of** ~ iščašen 4 koljenica; plećka; komad mesa 5 *sl* jazbina 6 *sl* cigareta s marihuanom/hašišem; džoint *sl* • *vt* uzglobiti, spojiti zglobovima

joke /dʒəuk/ *n* šala, vic **practical** ~ neslana šala • *vi* šaliti se, zezati se ~**r** *n* 1 zafrkant 2 džoker

jolly /'dʒɒlɪ/ *adj* 1 veseo, dobre volje 2 pod gasom **J**~ **Roger** gusarska zastava • *adv GB coll* vrlo

jolt /dʒəult/ *vt, vi* tresti (se), drmusati (se) • *n* 1 trzaj, udarac 2 *fig* šok

jostle /'dʒɒsl/ *vt,vi* gurati (se)

jot (1) /dʒɒt/ *n* šala ~ **not a** ~ ni malo

jot (2) *vt* ~ **sth down** pribilježiti ~**ter** *n* blok (za bilješke) ~**tings** *n pl* bilješke

journal /'dʒɜːnl/ *n* 1 dnevni list 2 časopis 3 dnevnik 4 poslovna knjiga ~**ese** /ˌdʒɜːnə'liːz/ *n* novinarski jezik

~ism n novinarstvo **~ist** n novinar
journey /'dʒɜ:nɪ/ n put • vt putovati
journeyman /'dʒɜ:nɪmən/ n 1 kalfa 2 solidan zanatlija
joust /dʒaʊst/ n hist viteški turnir • vi boriti se kopljem
Jove /dʒəʊv/ n Jupiter **By ~**! Tako mi svega!
jovial /'dʒəʊvɪəl/ adj veseo, žovijalan
jowl /dʒaʊl/ n donja vilica, brada
joy /dʒɔɪ/ n 1 radost, veselje, sreća 2 veselje **~-ride** n sl vožnja ukradenim automobilom **~-stick** comp komandna palica **~ful** adj sretan, veseo **~ous** adj sretan
jubilant /'dʒu:bɪlənt/ adj koji slavi, trijumfalan
jubilation /,dʒu:bɪ'leɪʃn/ n proslava **jubilee** /'dʒu:bɪli:/ n jubilej
Judaism /'dʒu:deɪɪzm/ n židovstvo **Judaic** /dʒu:'deɪk/ adj židovski
Judas /'dʒu:dəs/ n Juda; izdajnik
judge /dʒʌdʒ/ n 1 sudac 2 stručnjak, poznavalac • vt, vi 1 suditi 2 ocjenjivati 3 procijeniti, prosuditi **~ment** n 1 suđenje sit in ~ment on a case suditi parnicu pass a **~ment** on sb donijeti presudu **the Day of J~ment, J~ment Day** Sudnji dan 2 presuda 3 ocjena, procjena 4 sposobnost prosuđivanja 5 kazna (Božja) 6 mišljenje
judicial /dʒu:'dɪʃl/ adj 1 sudbeni, sudski **the ~ bench** suci **take/bring ~ preceedings against sb** pokrenuti sudski postupak protiv koga **~ murder** pravno umorstvo 2 nepristran 3 kritičan
judiciary /dʒu:'dɪʃərɪ/ n 1 sudstvo 2 sudska vlast
judicious /dʒu:'dɪʃəs/ adj form razborit
jug /dʒʌg/ n 1 vrč 2 sl zatvor • vt coll zatvoriti
juggernaut /'dʒʌgənɔ:t/ n 1 sila koja uništava sve pred sobom 2 coll gigantski kamion
juggle /'dʒʌgl/ vi,vt 1 (with) žonglirati 2 varati, manipulirati 3 istovremeno raditi **~r** n žongler; varalica
jugular /'dʒʌgjʊlə(r)/ adj vratni • n **the ~** vratna žila **go for the ~** htjeti za-

dati smrtni udarac
juice /dʒu:s/ n 1 sok 2 coll gorivo, struja **juicy** adj 1 sočan 2 coll sočan, pikantan
juke-box /'dʒu:k bɒks/ n džuboks
julep /'dʒu:lɪp/ n US koktel s metvicom
July /dʒu:'laɪ/ n srpanj
jumble /'dʒʌmbl/ vi,vt (up) pomiješati • n zbrka **~-sale** n prodaja svega i svačega/starudije
jumbo /'dʒʌmbəʊ/ adj golem
jump /dʒʌmp/ n 1 skok **the long/high ~** skok uvis/udalj 2 trzaj **give sb a ~** prestrašiti koga 3 nagli porast, skok **~y** adj nervozan • vi,vt 1 skakati, skočiti 2 poskočiti 3 preskočiti 4 natjerati da preskoči **~ at** baciti se na **~ into** uskočiti **~ out of** iskočiti **~ over** preskočiti **~ down sb's throat** napasti koga **~ to conclusions** prebrzo donositi zaključke **~ to one's feet** skočiti na noge **~ to it** učiniti smjesta **~ing-off place** start **~ed-up** adj coll skorojevićki **~ the gun** prerano startati **~ the queue** preguravati se **~er** n 1 skakač 2 džemper 3 US pregača, kuta
junction /'dʒʌŋkʃn/ n 1 spajanje, susret 2 prometno čvorište
June /dʒu:n/ n lipanj
jungle /'dʒʌŋgl/ n 1 **the ~(s)** džungla, prašuma (+ fig)
junior /'dʒu:nɪə(r)/ adj, n 1 mlađi 2 **years my ~** 2 godine mlađi od mene 2 niži 3 US učenik trećeg razreda srednje škole, student treće godine
juniper /'dʒu:nɪpə(r)/ n borovica
junk /dʒʌŋk/ n 1 smeće, starudija 2 mod loše kvalitete **~ food** bezvrijedna hrana; smeće coll **~-shop** staretinarnica
junkie, junky /'dʒʌŋkɪ/ n sl narkoman
Jupiter /'dʒu:pɪtə(r)/ n (planet) Jupiter
jurisdiction /,dʒʊərɪs'dɪkʃn/ n 1 jurisdikcija, sudska nadležnost 2 sudstvo, vršenje pravde
juror /'dʒʊərə(r)/ n porotnik
jury /'dʒʊərɪ/ n 1 porota 2 žiri **~man** n → **juror**
just (1) /dʒʌst/ adj 1 pravedan 2 opravdan

just (2) *adv* 1 baš, upravo ~ **as a.** isto **b.** baš kad ~ **now a.** upravo (u ovom času) **b.** malo prije **(only)** ~ za dlaku, jedva 2 samo

justice /ˈdʒʌstɪs/ *n* 1 pravda **in** ~ **to** da bi se zadovoljila pravda **do** ~ **to** pravedno postupiti prema 2 suđenje, dijeljenje pravde **bring sb to** ~ suditi komu 3 sudac (vrhovnog suda) **4 J**~ **of the Peace** (JP) mirovni sudac **Department of** ~ Ministarstvo pravosuđa

justify /ˈdʒʌstɪfaɪ/ *vt* 1 opravdati, opravdavati 2 poravnati tekst po marginama **justifiable** /ˌdʒʌstɪˈfaɪ-əbl/ *adj* opravdan **justification** /ˌdʒʌstɪfɪˈkeɪʃn/ *n* opravdanje

jut /dʒʌt/ *vt* ~ **out** stršiti

jute /dʒuːt/ *n* juta

juvenile /ˈdʒuːvənaɪl/ *n* maloljetnik • *adj* maloljetnički, mladenački, za mlade

juxtapose /ˌdʒʌkstəˈpəʊz/ *vt* staviti jedno uz drugo, jukstaponirati

K

K, k /keɪ/ 1 11. slovo engl. abecede; ka
2 *coll* tisuću

kangaroo /ˌkæŋɡə'ru:/ *n* klokan ~
court *derog* samozvani sud

kebab /kə'bæb/ *n* ćevap; ražnjić

keel /ki:l/ *n* kobilica (broda) **on an
even** ~ stabilan • *vt,vi* preokrenuti
(brod) ~ **over** prevrnuti se

keen (1) /ki:n/ *adj* 1 (**be** ~ **on**) (biti)
oduševljen (čime), zainteresiran (za);
silno željeti, jako voljeti 2 oštar (+
fig) 3 jak, dubok

keen (2) *n Ir* naricaljka • *vi* naricati

keep /ki:p/ *vt,vi* 1 zadržati; održati;
izdržati; uzdržavati 2 (sa)čuvati 3
voditi (knjige, dnevnik, dućan) 4 uzgajati 5 (~ **on**) nastaviti; stalno, često
raditi ~ **an eye on sth** držati što na
oku ~ **in mind** zapamtiti ~ **from
doing sth** spriječiti koga ~ **to oneself**
biti povučen ~ **at sth** ustrajati u
čemu ~ **away/out** ne prilaziti ~
down a. obuzdati, suzbiti **b.** zadržati
u želucu, ne povratiti (hranu) **c.**
držati u pokornosti, tlačiti ~ **off**
držati (se) podalje ~ **off the grass** ne
gazi travu ~ **under** obuzdati, suzbiti,
disciplinirati ~ **up** (with) držati korak, ići ukorak (s) ~ **up appearances**
održavati vanjsku formu • *n* 1 stan i
hrana; uzdržavanje 2 toranj, kula 3
for ~s *coll* zauvijek ~**sake** sitnica za
uspomenu **in ~ing with** u skladu s
~**er** *n* čuvar

keg /keg/ *n* bačva, bure **powder** ~ *fig*
bure baruta

kelp /kelp/ *n* morska trava

kennel /'kenl/ *n* pseća kućica ~**s** *pl* šte-
narnik

kerb (curb) /kɜ:b/ *n* rub pločnika

kerchief /'kɜ:tʃɪf/ *n* rubac

kernel /'kɜ:nl/ *n* sjemenka; jezgra (+
fig)

kerosene, kerozine /'kerəsi:n/ *n US,
Austr* petrolej, kerozin

ketchup /'ketʃəp/ *n* umak od rajčica

kettle /'ketl/ *n* kotao, posuda za grijanje vode **put the** ~ **on** pristaviti vodu
za čaj

kettledrum /'ketldrʌm/ *n* timpan

key /ki:/ *n* 1 ključ (+ *fig*) ~**hole**
ključanica ~**stone** *fig* ključno načelo
2 rješenje, objašnjenje 3 tipka
~**board a.** klavijatura **b.** tipkovnica 4
mod ključni • *vt* ugoditi; prilagoditi

khaki /'ka:kɪ/ *adj* žućkastosmeđ, kaki •
n kaki boja

kick /kɪk/ *vt,vi* 1 udariti (nogom); šut-
nuti *coll* ~ **against the pricks** bosti
se s rogatim ~ **the bucket** *sl* odapeti
sl ~ **up a fuss/row/stink** *coll* izazvati
gužvu 2 (oružje) trznuti • *n* 1 udarac
(nogom) 2 užitak, uzbuđenje 3 jakost
~**off** *n* početni udarac ~**back** *n sl*
postotak, mito

kid (1) /kɪd/ *n* 1 *coll* dijete; klinac 2
mod mladi 3 jarić 4 jareća koža **with**
~**gloves** *fig* u rukavicama, nježno

kid (2) *vt,vi coll* 1 prevariti; zafrkavati
(se) 2 ~ **oneself** zavaravati se

kidnap /'kɪdnæp/ *vt* oteti ~**per** *n* oti-
mač

kidney /'kɪdnɪ/ *n* bubreg ~ **bean** crveni
grah

kike /kaɪk/ *n US sl tab* Židov

kill /kɪl/ *vt,vi* 1 ubiti (+ *fig*); usmrtiti
be/get ~**ed** poginuti ~ **two birds
with one stone** ubiti dvije muhe jednim udarcem 2 uništiti • *n* 1 ubojstvo
2 lovina, ulov ~**er** *n* ubojica

kiln /'kɪln/ *n* peć (za grnčariju);
sušionica

kilo /'ki:ləʊ/ **kilogram(me)** /'kɪləgræm/
n kilogram

kilometre (-ter *US*) /'kɪləmi:tə(r)/ *n*

kilometar

kilt /kɪlt/ n kilt, škotska suknja

kin /kɪn/ n rodbina; rođaci **next of ~** najbliža rodbina

kind /kaɪnd/ adj pažljiv, ljubazan, uljudan *it's very ~ of you* vrlo ste ljubazni **~ly** adv **1** pažljivo, ljubazno **2** rado **3** *will you ~ly...?* hoćete li biti tako dobri; hoćete li, molim vas,... • n vrsta *nothing of the ~* ništa slično **a ~ of** nekakav, **~ of/~a** coll nekako, pomalo, na neki način, recimo **two of a ~** jednaki **in ~ a.** u robi/uslugama **b.** istom mjerom

kindergarten /'kɪndəga:tn/ n dječji vrtić

kindle /'kɪndl/ vt,vi zapaliti (se), raspaliti (+ fig) **kindling** n trješće za potpaljivanje vatre

kindred /'kɪndrɪd/ n rodbina, rodbinske veze • adj srodni

kinetic /kɪ'netɪk/ n kinetički **~s** n kinetika

king /kɪŋ/ n kralj **~fisher** vodomar **~pin** fig ključna osoba **~-size** veći/duži od uobičajenog **~dom** n kraljevstvo **~dom come** coll onaj svijet the **animal/vegetable ~dom** životinjsko/biljno carstvo

kink /kɪŋk/ n **1** uzao, petlja **2** coll nastranost **~y** adj nastran, ekscentričan

kiosk /'ki:ɒsk/ n **1** kiosk **2** GB telefonska govornica

kip /kɪp/ vi GB sl spavati • n Ir mjesto; rupa (fig)

kipper /'kɪpə(r)/ n soljena dimljena haringa

kirk /kɜ:k/ n Sc crkva

kiss /kɪs/ n poljubac **~ of life** umjetno disanje usta na usta **French ~** filmski poljubac • vt,vi (po)ljubiti (se) **~ goodbye** oprostiti se; pozdraviti se (fig) **~ and tell** hvaliti se svojim ljubavnim uspjesima

kit /kɪt/ n **1** oprema; pribor; alat **2** sastavni dijelovi

kitchen /'kɪtʃɪn/ n **1** kuhinja **2** mod kuhinjski **~ garden** povrtnjak **~-sink drama** GB drama iz života nižih staleža **~ette** čajna kuhinja

kite /kaɪt/ n **1** (papirnati) zmaj **2** lunja crvenkasta

kitsch /kɪtʃ/ n kič

kitten /'kɪtn/ n mačić **have ~s** GB coll dobiti mlade fig

kitty /'kɪtɪ/ n **1** novčani ulog **2** kasica **3** maca; mica

kiwi /'ki:wi:/ n **1** kivikalac novozelandski (ptica) **2** (~ **fruit**) kivi **3** coll Novozelanđanin

kleenex /'kli:neks/ n TM papirna maramica

kleptomaniac /,kleptə'meɪnɪæk/ n kleptoman

knack /næk/ n coll spretnost, sposobnost; grif sl **get the ~ of sth** uvježbati se **~ered** adj GB coll mrtav umoran

knapsack /'næpsæk/ n naprtnjača; ruksak

knave /neɪv/ n **1** podlac, hulja, nitkov **~ry** n lopovluk **2** dečko (u kartama)

knead /ni:d/ vt **1** mijesiti **2** masirati

knee /ni:/ n koljeno **~cap** meniskus o vt raznijeti (komu) koljeno (metkom)

kneel /ni:l/ vi irreg klečati **~ down** kleknuti

knell /nel/ n **1** posmrtno/pogrebno zvono **2** fig nagovještaj kraja

knelt v irreg → **kneel**

knew v irreg → **know**

knickers /'nɪkəz/ n pl ženske gaćice

knife /naɪf/ n nož **on a ~-edge** na iglama • vt ubosti nožem

knight /naɪt/ n **1** vitez **2** plemić **3** (šah) skakač, konj • vt dodijeliti viteški/plemićki naslov **~hood** n viteštvo; viteški/plemićki naslov

knit /nɪt/ vt,vi irreg **1** (is)plesti **2** spojiti, sastaviti, povezati **~ one's brows** namrštiti se **~ting** n **a.** pletenje **b.** pletivo **~wear** pletena roba

knob /nɒb/ n **1** (okrugla) kvaka **2** dugme **3** kvrga **4** grudica

knock /nɒk/ n **1** kucanje **2** udarac, lupanje • vt,vi **1** kucati **2** udariti, lupiti **~-kneed** adj koji ima ikserice sl **~er** n alka (na vratima) **~ sth back** sl popiti **~ down** udariti; oboriti; srušiti; rastaviti na dijelove **~ it off!** coll prestani! **~ out a.** sport nokautirati; eliminirati **b.** zapanjiti **~ sb up** vulg sl napumpati vulg sl

knot /nɒt/ n **1** uzao; čvor **2** pundža **3** skupina, gomila

know /nəʊ/ *vt,vi irreg* **1** znati; poznavati; prepoznati; raspoznati, razlikovati **you should ~ better** trebao bi biti razumniji **~(-it)-all** *n* sveznalica **~how** *n* praktično iskustvo, znanje, tehnologija **make ~n** objaviti • *n* **in the ~** upućen **~ing** *adj* lukav, pametan, bistar **~ingly** *adv* **a.** hotimice **b.** lukavo, bistro **~ledge** /ˈnɒlɪdʒ/ *n* **1** znanje **2** razumijevanje, shvaća-

nje **to the best of my ~ledge** koliko ja znam **it has come to my ~ledge** obaviješten sam **~ledgeable** *adj* **a.** upućen **b.** obrazovan

knuckle /ˈnʌkl/ *n* **1** zglob prsta **2** *cul* koljenica • *vi* **~ down to** prionuti **~duster** *n* (metalni) bokser

kudos /ˈkjuːdɒs/ *n GB* **1** velika pohvala, slava **2** prestiž

L

L, l /el/ 12. slovo engl. abecede; el
lab /læb/ n coll laboratorij
label /'leɪbl/ n naljepnica; oznaka • vt 1 označiti (naljepnicom) 2 fig nazvati; etiketirati coll
laboratory /lə'bɒrətrɪ/ 1 laboratorij 2 mod laboratorijski
labour (-bor US) /'leɪbə(r)/ n 1 (težak, naporan, mukotrpan) rad **hard ~** prisilni rad 2 radnici; radna snaga **L~ Exchange** zavod za zapošljavanje **the L~ Party** Laburistička stranka **L~ Day** praznik rada **labor union** US sindikat 3 trudovi pl • vi (teško, naporno, mukotrpno) raditi; mučiti se; naprezati se **~er** n radnik, tl'žak **~ed** adj spor; naporan; tegoban; mučan
labyrinth /'læbərɪnθ/ n labirint (+ fig)
lace /leɪs/ n 1 čipka 2 (**shoe~**) vezica • vt 1 (**~ up**) zavezati 2 **~ with sth** dodati što (u piće) **~lacy** adj čipkast
lacerate /'læsəreɪt/ vt rastrgati (+ fig)
lachrimal /'lækrɪml/ adj suzni **lachrimose** /'lækrɪməʊs/ adj 1 plačljiv 2 derog tugaljiv
lack /læk/ vt nemati (dovoljno) **he ~s courage** nedostaje mu hrabrosti • n nedostatak, pomanjkanje **~ing** adj (in) nedovoljan, manjkav **~lustre** adj **a.** mutan **b.** coll dosadan
lackey /'lækɪ/ n 1 lakaj 2 fig udvorica
lacquer /'lækə(r)/ n lak; pokost • vt lakirati
lad /læd/ n momak; dječak
ladder /'lædə(r)/ n 1 ljestve pl 2 fig ljestvica 3 GB spuštena očica • vi poderati se (očica)
laden /'leɪdn/ adj (with) 1 natovaren, opterećen 2 fig pun
ladies → **lady**
ladle /'leɪdl/ n kutljača
lady /'leɪdɪ/ n 1 gospođa 2 dama 3 (u

naslovima) ledi **ladies (room)** ženski WC **young ~** gospodica **L~ Day** Blagovijest **Our L~** Gospa **~bird** (**~bug** US) bubamara **~-in-waiting** dvorska dama **ladies' man** muškarac omiljen kod žena **~-killer** coll iron Casanova **~like** adj damski **Your L~ship** Vaše gospodstvo
lag (1) /læg/ vi (**~ behind**) zaosta(ja)ti • n zaostatak **jet ~** umor zbog vremenske razlike (nakon leta zrakoplovom)
lag (2) vt toplinski izolirati **~ging** n toplinska izolacija
lager /'lɑːgə(r)/ n svijetlo pivo
lagoon /lə'guːn/ n laguna
laid v irreg → **lay**
lain v irreg → **lie**
lair /leə(r)/ n brlog; jazbina (+ fig)
lake /leɪk/ n jezero
lamb /læm/ n 1 janje (+ fig) **the L~ of God** Jaganjac Božji 2 janjetina
lame /leɪm/ adj 1 hrom 2 fig slab; neuvjerljiv ~ **duck a.** US politički dužnosnik pred istekom mandata **b.** poduzeće (osoba) koje loše posluje
lament /lə'ment/ vt,vi (for) oplakivati, žaliti (za); jadati se • n tužaljka **~able** /'læməntəbl/ adj očajan, grozan
lamp /læmp/ n svjetiljka ~ **post** stup svjetiljke **~shade** sjenilo
lampoon /læm'puːn/ n satirični članak
lance /lɑːns/ n koplje • vt razrezati
lancet /'lɑːnsɪt/ n skalpel
land /lænd/ n 1 zemlja; zemljište 2 kopno ~ **forces** kopnena vojska **~lady** gazdarica **~lord** gazda **~locked** adj bez izlaza na more **~mark** n **a.** međaš (+ fig); prekretnica **b.** orijentir **~mine** nagazna mina **~owner** zemljoposjednik **~scape** krajolik **~slide a.** odron **b. ~slide victory** pobjeda golemom većinom

glasova • *vi,vt* 1 sletjeti, prizemljiti se, pristati 2 dospjeti, naći se 3 dobiti ~**ing** *n* 1 slijetanje 2 *mil* iskrcavanje 3 odmorište

lane /leɪn/ *n* 1 put 2 uličica 3 a. prometna traka b. športska staza 4 koridor, ruta

language /'læŋgwɪdʒ/ *n* jezik **mind your ~** pazi kako se izražavaš

languid /'læŋgwɪd/ *adj* trom, malaksao, bezivotan; spor **languish** /'læŋgwɪʃ/ *vi* venuti *(fig)*; klonuti, slabiti; (for) čeznuti (za) **languor** /'læŋgə(r)/ *n* slabost; čeznutljivost

lank /læŋk/ *adj* 1 tanak, ravan (o kosi) 2 ~**y** visok i mršav

lantern /'læntən/ *n* svjetiljka

lap (1) /læp/ *n* krilo

lap (2) *n* krug (utrke)

lap (3) *vt,vi* 1 laptati 2 zapljuskivati

lapel /lə'pel/ *n* suvratak; rever *coll*

lapse /læps/ *n* 1 pogreška, zabuna 2 pad *fig* 3 protjecanje 4 *leg* zastara • *vi* 1 pasti, posrnuti *fig* 2 *leg* zastarjeti

larceny /'la:sənɪ/ *n* *leg* krađa

lard /la:d/ *n* svinjska mast • *vt* iskititi

larder /'la:də(r)/ *n* smočnica

large /la:dʒ/ *adj* 1 velik 2 širok *fig* **at ~** a. na slobodi b. iscrpno c. općenito d. nasumce ~**ly** *adv* 1 općenito 2 velikodušno

lark (1) /la:k/ *n* *zoo* ševa

lark (2) *n* zabava, šala

lascivious /lə'sɪvɪəs/ *adj* pohotan, požudan

laser /'leɪzə(r)/ *n* 1 laser 2 *mod* laserski

lash /læʃ/ *vt,vi* 1 šibati, bičevati (+ *fig*) 2 (~ **out**) *fig* žestoko napasti 3 pljustati 4 *coll* spiskati ~**ings** *n pl coll* golema količina • *n* 1 švigalo biča; udarac bičem/šibom **the ~ bičevanje** 2 (**eye~**) trepavica

lass /læs/, **lassie** /'læsɪ/ *n* *Scot, Ir* djevojka

last (1) /la:st/ *adj* zadnji; posljednji ~ **but not least** zadnje, ali ne najmanje važno ~ **but one** predzadnji 2 prošli; prethodni ~ **night** sinoć • *adv* zadnji (put) **at (long)** ~ konačno ~**ly** *adv* na kraju

last (2) *vi* 1 (po)trajati 2 izdržati ~**ing** *adj* trajan

latch /lætʃ/ *n* zasun (brave) • *vt,vi* zatvoriti (se) zasunom ~ **on(to)** *coll* shvatiti ~ **onto** *sb coll* zalijepiti se za koga *fig*

late /leɪt/ *adj* 1 kasni **be ~** (za)kasniti 2 pokojni 3 bivši 4 nedavni **the ~st** zadnji, najnoviji • *adv* kasno **as ~ as** tek **of ~**; ~**ly** u zadnje vrijeme

lather /'la:ðə(r)/ *n* pjena; sapunica • *vi* (za)pjeniti se

Latin /'lætɪn/ *adj, n* 1 latinski (jezik) 2 romanski

latitude /'lætɪtju:d/ *n* 1 (zemljopisna) širina 2 sloboda

latter /'lætə(r)/ *adj* 1 zadnji, kasniji 2 potonji, drugi ~**ly** *adv* nedavno ~-**day** *adj* moderni, našeg doba

lattice /'lætɪs/ *n* rešetka

laud /lɔ:d/ *vt* slaviti, hvaliti ~**able** *adj* hvalevrijedan

laugh /la:f/ *vi,vt* 1 (at) smijati se (komu, čemu) 2 ismijati ~ **sth away/off** umanjiti ozbiljnost čega ~ *n* smijeh ~**ter** *n* smijeh ~**able** *adj* smiješan ~**ingstock** *n* ruglo, predmet ismijavanja

launch (1) /lɔ:ntʃ/ *vt* 1 porinuti (brod) 2 lansirati (letjelicu) 3 ispaliti (projektil) 4 početi (napad) 5 *fig* pokrenuti ~ **out** (into) upustiti se ~**ing pad** lansirna/raketna rampa

launch (2) *n* motorni čamac

launder /'lɔ:ndə(r)/ *vt* prati ~**ette** /lɔ:n'dret/ *n* javna praonica rublja **laundry** /'lɔ:ndrɪ/ *n* 1 praonica 2 rublje **do the laundry** oprati rublje

laureate /'lɒrɪət/ *adj* laureat *n* **the Poet L~** *GB* dvorski pjesnik

laurel /'lɒrəl/ *n* lovor **rest on one's ~s** spavati na lovorikama

lavatory /'lævətrɪ/ *n* WC

lavender /'lævəndə(r)/ *n* lavanda; boja lavande

lavish /'lævɪʃ/ *adj* 1 izdašan 2 rastrošan 3 luksuzan • *vt* (**up)on** 1 obasuti 2 potrošiti

law /lɔ:/ *n* 1 zakon **break the ~** (pre)kršiti zakon ~**ful** *adj* zakonit ~**less** *adj* protuzakonit ~ **and order** red i mir ~ **suit** *n* parnica 2 pravo ~**yer** *n* *GB* pravnik; *US* odvjetnik 3 pravilo, propis

lawn /lɔːn/ n tratina ~mower kosilica

lax /læks/ adj nemaran, opušten, raspušten; blag, popustljiv; slab

lay (1) /leɪ/ vt,vi irreg 1 položiti; uložiti; postaviti ~ aside odložiti ~by ugibalište brick-~er n zidar ~ down the law zapovijedati, određivati ~ down dati ostavku ~ off a. odmoriti se b. prestati c. staviti na čekanje; otpustiti ~out n plan, nacrt ~ sth on the line riskirati ~ oneself open to izložiti se čemu ~ up stvarati zalihe ~ waste uništiti, opustošiti 2 nesti (jaja) 3 sl tab povaliti vulg • n an easy ~ derog laka roba fig

lay (2) v irreg → lie

lay (3) adj svjetovni; laički; nestručan ~man n nestručnjak, laik

lazy /leɪzɪ/ adj lijen ~bones coll lijenčina laze vi lijenčariti

lead (1) /liːd/ vt,vi irreg (pred)voditi, odvesti, dovesti ~ sb on zafrkavati, vući za nos coll ~er n čelnik, voda ~ing adj vodeći, glavni ~ing article uvodnik • n 1 vodstvo 2 uzica 3 glavna uloga; glavni glumac/glumica

lead (2) /led/ n 1 olovo swing the ~ coll zabušavati 2 (black ~) grafit ~en adj olovan; težak

leaf /liːf/ n list • vi ~ through listati ~y adj lisnat ~let /ˈliːflɪt/ n letak

league (1) /liːg/ n savez, liga

league (2) n mjera za udaljenost (oko 4.8 km)

leak /liːk/ vi,vt (pro)curiti (+ fig); propuštati ~age n 1 curenje 2 fig otkrivanje tajni • n 1 pukotina 2 tekućina koja curi, plin koji je ispušten take a ~ sl pomokriti se 3 fig otkrivanje tajni

lean (1) /liːn/ adj mršav (+ fig); vitak 2 (meso) nemastan, krt

lean (2) vi,vi 1 nagnuti se 2 (~ towards) fig naginjati ~ing n 3 nasloniti (se) 4 ~ (up)on fig oslanjati se ~ing n sklonost

leap /liːp/ vi,vt irreg 1 (pre)skočiti, skakati look before you ~ prov ispeci pa reci 2 ~ at objeručke prihvatiti • n skok (+ fig) ~frog dječja igra preskakivanja ~ year prijestupna godina

leapt v irreg → leap

learn /lɜːn/ vt,vi irreg 1 (na)učiti (što) 2 (of, about) saznati (za) ~ed adj učen ~ing n znanje; učenost

learnt v irreg → learn

lease /liːs/ n 1 zakup, najam 2 ugovor o zakupu ~holder n zakupac • vt 1 dati/uzeti u zakup 2 posuditi

leash /liːʃ/ n uzica

least /liːst/ adv najmanje not ~ dobrim dijelom • adj najmanji at ~ bar to say the ~ najblaže rečeno

leather /ˈleðə(r)/ n 1 koža 2 mod kožni ~ette n skaj

leave (1) /liːv/ vi,vt irreg 1 otići (iz, s) 2 napustiti, ostaviti (koga, što) 3 prepustiti leftovers n pl ostaci ~ me alone pusti/ostavi me na miru ~ him be pusti ga ~ sth behind zaboraviti ponijeti ~ for krenuti/otići prema/u ~ off prestati ~ sth/sb out a. izostaviti b. izdvojiti ~ it out! coll prestani!

leave (2) n 1 dopuštenje 2 ~ of absence mil dopust sick ~ bolovanje take one's ~ of sb oprostiti se s kim take ~ of one's senses poludjeti

lecher /ˈletʃə(r)/ n pohotnik, razvratnik ~ous adj pohotan, razvratan ~y n pohota, blud

lecture /ˈlektʃə(r)/ n predavanje • vi,vt 1 predavati 2 (o)držati prodiku ~r n predavač

led v irreg → lead

ledge /ledʒ/ n 1 prozorska daska 2 polica 3 greben

ledger /ˈledʒə(r)/ n poslovna knjiga

lee /liː/ n zavjetrina ~ward adv, adj niz vjetar; u zavjetrini ~way n fig (slobodni) prostor za manevriranje

leech /liːtʃ/ n 1 pijavica 2 fig krvopija, parazit

leek /liːk/ n poriluk

leer /lɪə(r)/ n podmukao/zloban/pohotan pogled/smijeh • vi ~ at zlobno/pohotno gledati; ceriti se

left /left/ adj 1 lijevi ~-hand side lijeva strana ~-handed adj ljevoruk 2 (~-wing) pol ljevičarski ~ist n ljevičar • adv lijevo • n 1 lijeva strana 2 (~ wing, the ~) pol ljevica

left v irreg → leave

leg /leg/ n 1 noga not have a ~ to

stand on biti neutemeljen **pull sb's ~**
coll zafrkavati **on one's last ~s a.**
premoren **b.** pred smrt **2** nogavica
~ings *pl* nazuvci **3** *sport* etapa • *vi ~*
it *coll* trčati; bježati
legacy /'legəsı/ *n* 1 nasljedstvo **2** *fig*
nasljeđe
legal /'li:gl/ *adj* **1** zakonit **2** zakonski **~**
tender zakonito sredstvo plaćanja
~ize *vt* ozakoniti
legation /lı'geıʃn/ *n* diplomatsko predstavništvo
legend /'ledʒənd/ *n* legenda **~ary** *adj*
legendarni
legible /'ledʒəbl/ *adj* čitljiv
legion /'li:dʒən/ *n* 1 legija **~ary, le-**
gionnaire legionar; pripadnik Legije
stranaca **2** mnoštvo
legislate /'ledʒısleıt/ *vi* donijeti zakon
legislation *n* zakon, skup zakona
legislative /'ledʒıslətıv/ *adj* zakono-
davni **legislature** /'ledʒısleıtʃə(r)/ *n*
zakonodavno tijelo
legit /'ledʒıt/ *adj sl* zakonit
legitimate /lı'dʒıtımət/ *adj* **1** zakonit **2**
opravdan **legitimize** *vt* ozakoniti
leisure /'leʒə(r)/ *n* slobodno vrijeme
~ly *adv* bez žurbe
lemon /'lemən/ *n* 1 limun **2** boja limuna **~ade** limunada
lend /lend/ *vt* 1 posuditi **~ an ear**
poslušati **~ a hand** pomoći **2** dati,
pridonijeti **3 ~ itself to** biti prikladan
za
length /leŋθ/ *n* 1 dužina **2** duljina, trajanje **at ~ a.** nadugačko **b.** napokon
go to any/great ~(s) učiniti sve, biti
spreman na sve **the ~ and breadth**
of uzduž i poprijeko (čega) **~y** *adj*
(po)dugačak **~en** *vt,vi* produljiti (se)
lenient /'li:nıənt/ *adj* blag, popustljiv
lens /lenz/ *n* 1 leća **2** staklo naočala
lent *v irreg* → **lend**
Lent /lent/ *n* korizma **~en** *adj* koriz-
meni
lentil /'lentl/ *n bot* leća
Leo /'li:əʊ/ *n astrol* Lav
leopard /'lepəd/ *n* leopard
leper /'lepə(r)/ *n* gubavac (+ *fig*) **lep-**
rosy /'leprəsı/ *n* guba
leprechaun /'leprəkɔːn/ *n Ir* patuljak
lesbian /'lezbıən/ *n* lezbijka

lesion /'li:ʒn/ *n* rana, ozljeda
less /les/ *adj, adv* manje **none the ~**
unatoč tome, ipak **~en** *vt,vi* umanjiti
(se) **~er** *adj* manji, minoran
lesson /'lesn/ *n* 1 lekcija; sat **2** *fig* pouka
lest /lest/ *conj form* da ne, kako ne
let /let/ *vt,vi* **1** (do)pustiti **~ alone** a da
ne spominjemo **~ sb/sth be/alone**
pustiti na miru **~ go of sb/sth** pustiti
~ loose osloboditi **~ oneself go** prepustiti se **2** *1. lice množine* i *3. lice*
imperativa **~ us** (~'s) go idemo **~**
him go neka ide **3** iznajmiti **~ down**
a. produljiti **b.** spustiti **c.** razočarati,
ostaviti na cjedilu **~ sth in** suziti **~**
oneself in(to) a. otkljucati vrata i ući
(u) **b.** upustiti se **~ sb into** uputiti u **~**
off a. pustiti **b.** ispaliti **~ on** *coll*
otkriti tajnu **~ out a.** proširiti **b.** ispustiti **~ out at sb** udariti, napasti
(+*fig*) **~ up** popustiti
lethal /'li:θl/ *adj* smrtonosan
letter /'letə(r)/ *n* 1 slovo **capital ~** veliko slovo **to the ~** doslovno **~ing** *n*
vrsta slova; natpis **2** pismo **~box**
poštanski sandučić **3** (~s) književnost; učenost
lettuce /'letıs/ *n* (zelena) salata
levee /'levı/ *n US* nasip
level /'levl/ *adj* 1 ravan **2** izjednačen;
ujednačen **~-headed** *adj* razborit •
vt,vi **1** sravniti; izravnati (se) **2** izjednačiti (se) • *n* razina **on the ~** *coll*
pošten, iskren
lever /'li:və(r)/ *n* poluga (+ *fig*) **~age**
utjecaj
leviathan /lı'vaıəθən/ *n* 1 *bibl* morska
neman **2** *fig* grdosija
levity /'levətı/ *n* lakoumnost; neoz-
biljnost
levy /'levı/ *vt* 1 nametnuti; ubirati **2** novačiti **~ war upon/against** objaviti
rat kome **3** *leg* konfiscirati • *n* ubi-
ranje poreza
lewd /lju:d/ *n* besraman; pohotan
lexical /'leksıkl/ *adj* leksički **lexico-**
graphy /,leksı'kɒgrəfı/ *n* leksiko-
grafija
liable /'laıəbl/ *adj* **1** (~ **for**) odgovoran
(za) **2** ~ (**to sth**) podložan (čemu) **3** ~
(**to do sth**) sklon (čemu) **liability**

/ˌliaiˈbɪlətɪ/ n 1 odgovornost 2 podlijeganje, podložnost 3 (~ties) pasiva **limited liability company** GB društvo s ograničenom odgovornošću

liaison /lɪˈeɪzn/ n veza ~ **officer** časnik za vezu

liar /ˈlaɪə(r)/ n lažac, lažljivac

lib /lɪb/ n coll oslobođenje **women's** ~ pokret za oslobođenje i prava žena

libel /ˈlaɪbl/ n kleveta

liberal /ˈlɪbərəl/ adj 1 liberalan; slobodouman 2 široke ruke • n liberal

liberate /ˈlɪbəreɪt/ vt osloboditi **liberator** n osloboditelj **liberty** /ˈlɪbətɪ/ n 1 sloboda 2 pretjerana prisnost

Libra /ˈliː brə/ n astrol Vaga

library /ˈlaɪbrərɪ/ n knjižnica **librarian** knjižničar

lice /laɪs/ pl → **louse**

licence (**license** US) /ˈlaɪsns/ n 1 odobrenje, dopusnica ~**plate** registarska tablica **on-**~ odobrenje za točenje alkoholnih pića **off-**~ odobrenje za prodaju alkoholnih pića; prodavaonica alkoholnih pića 2 razuzdanost **poetic** ~ pjesnička sloboda **license** vt dati dopuštenje, ovlastiti ~**d premises** lokal u kojem se smije točiti alkohol

licentious /laɪˈsenʃəs/ adj razuzdan

licit /ˈlɪsɪt/ adj zakonit; dopušten

lick /lɪk/ vt 1 lizati 2 coll pobijediti, potući; izmlatiti ~**ing** n poraz • n lizanje **at full** ~ velikom brzinom

lid /lɪd/ n 1 poklopac 2 (**eye**~) kapak

lie (1) /laɪ/ n laž, neistina • vi irreg lagati

lie (2) vi irreg 1 ležati, leći ~ **in** duže odspavati **lying-in hospital** rodilište 2 biti smješten, nalaziti se; prostirati se ~ **low** pritajiti se **let sleeping dogs** ~ prov ne diraj lava dok spava ~ **heavy a.** teško pasti **b.** tištiti **find out how the land** ~**s** izvidjeti kako stvari stoje **it** ~**s with you** tvoja je dužnost

lieu /luː/ n **in** ~ **of** umjesto

lieutenant /lefˈtenənt/ GB, luːˈtenənt US/ n mil poručnik

life /laɪf/ n 1 život **not on your** ~ coll ni govora **true to** ~ vjerno, kao u stvarnom životu, zbiljski **larger than** ~ nestvaran, kao iz filma ~**belt/boat** pojas/čamac za spasavanje ~**guard a.** spasilac **b.** tjelohranitelj 2 sl doživotna kazna ~**er** kažnjenik koji izdržava doživotnu kaznu 3 životopis ~**like** adj životan, stvaran ~**long** doživotan ~**sized** u prirodnoj veličini ~**span** n životni vijek ~**time** život **the chance of a** ~**time** jedinstvena prilika

lift /lɪft/ vt,vi 1 (po)dignuti (se) ~ **off** uzletjeti 2 prekinuti, ukinuti • n 1 dizalo; lift coll 2 prijevoz **give sb a** ~ povesti

light (1) /laɪt/ n 1 svjetlo; svjetlost; o-svjetljenje ~ **year** svjetlosna godina ~**house** svjetionik 2 svjetiljka 3 (**traffic**) ~**s** pl semafor 4 coll vatra (šibica, upaljač) (**cigarette**) ~**er** upaljač 5 prozor • vt, vi irreg 1 zapaliti 2 osvijetliti ~ **up a.** upaliti b. fig ozariti se c. pripaliti cigaretu • adj svijetao ~**en** vt, vi osvijetliti (se)

light (2) / adj lagan **make** ~ **of sth** umanjivati značenje/ozbiljnost ~**headed** adj **a.** mamuran **b.** lakomislen ~**hearted** veseo; neozbiljan ~**weight** laka kategorija ~**en** vt,vi olakšati; postati lakši • adv bez prtljage

lightning /ˈlaɪtnɪŋ/ n munja, grom ~ **conductor/rod** gromobran

like (1) /laɪk/ adj sličan ~ **father,** ~ **son** prov kakav otac, takav sin • conj kao, poput **what is he** ~? kakav je? **what does he look** ~? kako izgleda? **feel** ~ **sth** biti raspoložen za što ~**n** vt prispodobiti ~**ness** n 1 sličnost 2 arch slika ~**wise** adv isto tako, na isti način • n **the** ~ **of which** kakav **and the** ~ i slično **the** ~**s of us** ljudi poput nas

like (2) vt voljeti; sviđati se I ~ **music/skiing** volim glazbu/skijanje I ~ **him** sviđa mi se, simpatičan mi je I **would** ~ volio bih, želio bih if you ~ ako hoćeš, ako želiš **liking** n sklonost, ljubav **to one's liking** po volji

likely /ˈlaɪklɪ/ adj vjerojatan; uvjerljiv; prikladan **he is** ~ **to win** vjerojatno će pobijediti **most** ~ najvjerojatnije **not** ~! ni govora! **likelihood** n vjerojatnost **in all likelihood** najvjerojatnije

lilac /ˈlaɪlək/ *n* **1** jorgovan **2** blijedoljubičasta boja; lila *coll*

lilt /lɪlt/ *n* **1** ritmična pjesma **2** pjevuckanje pri govoru

lily /ˈlɪlɪ/ *n* ljiljan ~ **of the valley** đurđica ~**-white** *adj* **a.** sniježnobijel **b.** *fig* besprijekorna karaktera

limb /lɪm/ *n* ud **out on a** ~ bez podrške

Limbo /ˈlɪmbəʊ/ *n* **1** čistilište **2** l~ *fig* neizvjesnost

lime (1) /laɪm/ *n* vapno, **quick**~ živo vapno ~**stone** vapnenac ~**light** publicitet; središte pozornosti

lime (2) (~**-tree**) *n* lipa

lime (3) /n limeta; sok od limete ~**y** *US sl* Englez

limerick /ˈlɪmərɪk/ *n* šaljiva pjesmica

limit /ˈlɪmɪt/ *n* granica, ograničenje • *vt* ograničiti

limousine /ˈlɪməziːn/, **limo** /ˈlɪməʊ/ *n coll* limuzina

limp (1) /lɪmp/ *adj* mlitav, opušten, klonuo

limp (2) *vi* hramati

limpet /ˈlɪmpɪt/ *n* priljepak (+ *fig*)

limpid /ˈlɪmpɪd/ *adj lit* bistar, proziran

linden /ˈlɪndən/ → **lime** (2)

line (1) /laɪn/ *n* **1** crta **2** granica; Ekvator **3** uže **4** telefonska žica; veza **5** tračnica **6** obiteljska loza **7** ~**s** bore (lica) **8** (brodska, zrakoplovna) linija ~ *n* (putnički) brod; zrakoplov **9** red **the front** ~ prvi borbeni redovi in ~ **with** u skladu s **out of** ~ u suprotnosti s **on the** ~ u opasnosti, u pitanju *drop me a* ~ *coll* piši mi nekoliko riječi **along those** ~**s** u tom smislu **marriage** ~**s** vjenčani list **10** stih **11** tekst (glumca) **12** zanimanje **13** način djelovanja, stav **take a tough** ~ zauzeti oštar stav **hard-**~ *adj* beskompromisan, tvrdokoran **14** podatak, informacija • *vt,vi* **1** iscrtati **2** naborati **3** ~ **up** poredati ~**-up** *n* **a.** poredak **b.** *sport* startna lista **4** ~ **up** organizirati, pripremiti

line (2) *vt* **1** podstaviti **2** obložiti **lining** *n* podstava **every cloud has a silver lining** *prov* u svakom zlu ima nešto dobro **bin** ~**r** vreća za smeće **panty** ~**r** higijenski uložak

lineage /ˈlɪnɪdʒ/ *n* obiteljska loza

linen /ˈlɪnɪn/ *n* **1** lan(ena tkanina); platno **2** posteljina, stolnjaci **dirty** ~ *fig* prljavo rublje

linger /ˈlɪŋgə(r)/ *vi* **1** zadržati se **2** ~ (on) trajati ~**ing** *adj* dugačak; polagan ~**ing hopes/doubts** posljednji ostaci nade/sumnje

lingerie /ˈlænʒəriː/ *n* žensko rublje

lingo /ˈlɪŋgəʊ/ *n sl joc or derog* jezik, govor

linguist /ˈlɪŋgwɪst/ *n* **1** lingvist, jezikoslovac **2** poznavatelj stranih jezika ~**ics** *n* lingvistika

link /lɪŋk/ *n* **1** karika **2** veza **cuff** ~ manžeta • *vt,vi* vezati; povezivati

lino /ˈlaɪnəʊ/ **linoleum** /liˈnəʊlɪəm/ *n* linoleum

lion /ˈlaɪən/ *n* **1** lav ~**ess** lavica **2** znamenita osoba

lip /lɪp/ *n* **1** usna, usnica **give/pay** ~**-service** isprazno/licemjerno govoriti **keep a stiff upper** ~ ne pokazati osjećaje/strah ~**-read** čitati s usana ~**stick** ruž za usne **2** bezobrazluk **3** rub

liqueur /lɪˈkjʊə(r)/ *n* liker

liquid /ˈlɪkwɪd/ *n* tekućina • *adj* **1** tekući **2** vlažan **3** bistar **4** *com* likvidan ~**ate** /ˈlɪkwɪdeɪt/ *vt,vi* **1** (+ *com*) likvidirati **2** podmiriti dug ~**izer** *n* mikser

liquor /ˈlɪkə(r)/ *n* (žestoko) alkoholno piće

liquorice /ˈlɪkərɪs/ *n* slatki korijen, gospino bilje

lisp /lɪsp/ *n* pogrešan izgovor glasa /s/, fufljanje

list (1) /lɪst/ *n* popis; lista **price**~ cjenik **short**~ kandidati koji su ušli u uži izbor • *vt* popisati; staviti na popis; nabrojiti

list (2) *vi* naginjati se • *n* nagib (broda)

listen /ˈlɪsn/ *vi* slušati; poslušati ~**er** *n* slušatelj *she's a good* ~*er* zna slušati

listless /ˈlɪstlɪs/ *adj* trom, malaksao

lit *v irreg* → **light**

liter *US* → **litre**

literacy /ˈlɪtərəsɪ/ *n* pismenost

literal /ˈlɪtərəl/ *adj* **1** doslovan ~**ly** *adv* doslovno **2** (osoba) nemaštovit • *n* tiskarska pogreška

literary /'lɪtərərɪ/ *adj* knjiški; knjiški ~ **property** autorska prava

literate /'lɪtərət/ *adj* 1 pismen 2 obrazovan; načitan

literature /'lɪtrɪtʃə(r)/ *n* 1 književnost 2 (stručna) literatura 3 tiskani materijal

lithe /laɪð/ *adj* savitljiv, gibak

litigate /'lɪtɪɡeɪt/ *vi,vt leg* povesti parnicu **litigation** *n* parničenje

litmus /'lɪtməs/ *n* lakmus

litre (-ter *US*) /'liːtə(r)/ *n* litra

litter /'lɪtə(r)/ *n* 1 otpaci, smeće **cat** ~ mački nužnik 2 leglo 3 nosila • *vt* 1 onečistiti; razbacati 2 okotiti

little /'lɪtl/ *adj* (*comp* **less**, *sup* **least**) 1 malen **the** ~ **people** *Ir* patuljci, vile 2 malo *adv* **a** ~ malo, ponešto • *adv* malo ~ **did they suspect** nisu ni sumnjali ~ **by** ~ malo-pomalo **make** ~ **of** ne pridavati veliku važnost

live /lɪv/ *vi,vt* živjeti; preživjeti; doživjeti **Long** ~...! Živio...! **you** ~ **and learn** čovjek uči dok je živ ~ **and let** ~ biti snošljiv ~ **up to** ispuniti očekivanja **living** *adj* živ **the living image of** isti; pljunuti *coll* (u sredstva za) život; način života **living room** *n* dnevna soba

live /laɪv/ *adj* 1 živ ~ **transmission/broadcast** izravan prijenos 2 neeksplodiran 3 pod naponom • *adv* izravno, uživo ~**ly** /'laɪvlɪ/ *adj* 1 živahan, živ 2 uzbudljiv; opasan ~**lyhood** *n* sredstva za život **liven up** *vi* oživjeti

liver /'lɪvə(r)/ *n* jetra

livery /'lɪvərɪ/ *n* 1 livreja 2 *fig* plašt, ogrtač ~ **company** londonska gilda ~ **stable** konjušnica

livestock /'laɪvstɒk/ *n* stoka, blago

livid /'lɪvɪd/ *adj* 1 plavičast, sivoplav 2 bijesan

lizard /'lɪzəd/ *n* gušter

load /ləʊd/ *n* teret, opterećenje (+ *fig*); tovar *it was a great* ~ *off my mind* pao mi je kamen sa srca **loads of/a load of** *coll* puno, hrpa • *vt* 1 (na)tovariti; utovariti, ukrcati 2 napuniti (oružje) 3 staviti (film) u fotoaparat ~**ed** *adj* 1 pristran 2 *sl* pun novca ~ napunjen (oružje)

loaf (1) /ləʊf/ *n* 1 hljeb, štruca 2 *GB sl*

glava **use your** ~ mućni glavom

loaf (2) *vi* gubiti vrijeme, ljenčariti, zabušavati

loan /ləʊn/ *n* posudba; zajam, kredit **on** ~ posuđen ~**word** *n* posuđenica • *vt* posuditi; iznajmiti

loath, loth /ləʊθ/ *adj* nesklon, neodlučan

loathe /ləʊð/ *vt* mrziti; gaditi se **loathsome** *adj* odvratan **loathing** *n* gađenje, mržnja

lob /lɒb/ *vt* baciti (loptu) u visokom luku • *n* tako bačena lopta

lobby /'lɒbɪ/ *n* 1 predvorje 2 *pol* lobi • *vt,vi* vršiti pritisak

lobe /ləʊb/ *n* 1 (**ear**~) resica uha 2 (plućno) krilo; strana mozga

lobster /'lɒbstə(r)/ *n* jastog

local /'ləʊkl/ *adj* 1 mjesni; lokalni 2 obližnji • *n* mještanin ~**ly** *adv* 1 u blizini, nedaleko 2 mjestimice ~**ity** /ləʊ'kælətɪ/ *n* mjesto; područje; četvrt ~**ize** /'ləʊkəlaɪz/ *vt* ograničiti; dovesti (požar) pod nadzor ~**ism** *n* 1 lokalpatriotizam 2 lokalni izraz

locate /ləʊ'keɪt/ *vt* odrediti mjesto/položaj; smjestiti **location** *n* 1 mjesto, smještaj, položaj 2 *film* lokacija

loch /lɒx/ *n Sc* 1 jezero 2 zaljev

lock (1) /lɒk/ *n* uvojak

lock (2) *n* 1 brava; lokot ~**smith** bravar 2 ustava 3 zastoj 4 zatvarač puške ~, **stock and barrel** sve, u cijelosti • *vt,vi* 1 zaključati (se) 2 (~ **up**) zatvoriti ~**up** *n* zatvor 3 zaglaviti (se) 4 čvrsto zagrliti ~**er** *n* ormarić ~**er room** svlačionica

locket /'lɒkɪt/ *n* medaljon

locomotion /ˌləʊkə'məʊʃn/ *n* pokret, kretanje **locomotive** *adj* pokretan **n** lokomotiva

locust /'ləʊkəst/ *n* skakavac

lodge /lɒdʒ/ *vi,vt* 1 stanovati 2 smjestiti (se) 3 (~ **in**) zaglaviti se 4 podnijeti (žalbu, prosvjed...) 5 pohraniti • *n* 1 kućica, kuća 2 soba, stan, nastamba 3 (masonska) loža ~**r** *n* podstanar **lodgings** *n pl* (unajmljen) stan/soba

loft /lɒft/ *n* 1 potkrovlje **hay**~ sjenik 2 galerija (u crkvi) ~**y** *adj* 1 uzvišen 2 umišljen, gord **3** visok

log /lɒg/ *n* **1** cjepanica, klada **2** (**~book**) **a.** (brodski) dnevnik **b.** prometna dozvola

logic /'lɒdʒɪk/ *n* logika **~al** *adj* logičan **~ian** *n* logičar

logistics /lə'dʒɪstɪks/ *n* logistika **logistic** *adj* logistički

loins /lɔɪns/ *n pl* slabine

loiter /'lɔɪtə(r)/ *vi* skitati; zastajkivati, vući se **~ing** *n leg* skitnja

loll /lɒl/ *vi* objesiti se, opustiti se

lollipop /'lɒlɪpɒp/ *n* lizalica **~ (wo)man** osoba koja zaustavlja promet da djeca mogu prijeći ulicu

lone /ləʊn/ *adj* usamljen

lonely /'ləʊnlɪ/ *adj* **1** usamljen **2** samotan

lonesome /'ləʊnsəm/ *adj* **1** usamljen **2** samotan

long (1) /lɒŋ/ *adj* dugačak; dug; dugotrajan ~ **time no see** *coll* dugo se nismo vidjeli **~term** *adj* dugoročan **~distance** *adj* međugradski **~hand** *n* običan rukopis (za razliku od stenografije/strojopisa) **the ~ jump** *sport* skok udalj ~ **odds** mali izgledi **~range** *adj* **a.** dalekometan **b.** dugoročan **~sighted** *adj* dalekovidan **~term** *adj* dugoročan **in the ~ run** na kraju, kao ishod, na duge pruge **~standing** *adj* dugotrajan • *adv* dugo **as/so ~ as** pod uvjetom da **no ~er/not any ~er** (ne) više **so ~** *US* doviđenja **before ~** uskoro

long (2) *vi* čeznuti **~ing** *n* čežnja *adj* čeznutljiv

longevity /lɒn'dʒevətɪ/ *n* **1** dugovječnost **2** životni vijek

longitude /'lɒndʒɪtjuːd/ *n* (zemljopisna) dužina

loo /luː/ *n GB coll* WC

look /lʊk/ *vi,vt* **1** (at) gledati; razmotriti ~ **sharp**! požuri! ~ **sb up and down** odmjeriti koga **~ing-glass** zrcalo **2** izgledati **~s like/~s as if** izgleda, čini se **3** (~ **for**) tražiti **~ after** čuvati, paziti, brinuti se ~ **back** osvrtati se ~ **down on sb** prezirati **~ forward to sth** željno što iščekivati, veseliti se čemu ~ **into sth** ispitati ~ **on** promatrati ~ **out**! pazi! ~ **to sth** (pri)pa-

ziti (na) ~ **up a**. popravljati se **b.** potražiti, provjeriti ~ **up to sb** cijeniti, štovati • *n* **1** pogled **have a ~** pogledati **2** izraz lica **3** (**~s**) izgled

loom (1) /luːm/ *n* tkalački stan

loom (2) *vi* nazirati se, nadvijati se (prijeteći)

loony /'luːnɪ/ *n sl* luđak ~ **bin** *sl joc* ludnica

loop /luːp/ *n* **1** omča, petlja, prsten **~hole** rupa (*fig*) **2** luping

loose /luːs/ *adj* **1** slobodan; labav, opušten, klimav; komotan **break** ~ pobjeći, osloboditi se **turn/let** ~ osloboditi ~ **bowels** proljev **come** ~ odvezati se, otkopčati se **he has a screw** ~ nisu mu sve na broju **2** (pre)slobodan, nemoralan • (**~n**) *vt,vi* osloboditi; olabaviti, opustiti, rasklimati (se)

loot /luːt/ *vt,vi* pljačkati, otimati • *n* pljačka, otimačina

lop /lɒp/ *vt* ~(**away, off**) podrezati, obrezati **~eared** *adj* klempavih (ovješenih) ušiju **~sided** *adj* **1** nagnut, kos, nesimetričan **2** *fig* pristran

lord /lɔːd/ *n* **1** (naslov) lord **my/m' lord** milorde **his ~ship** njegovo gospodstvo **2** gospodar, vladar, vlastelin **3** L~ Gospod, Gospodin **the L~'s Prayer** Očenaš **4** moćna i utjecajna osoba **war ~s** lokalni vojskovođe • *vt* ~ (over sb) gospodariti, zapovijedati **~ly** *adj* **1** ohol; drzak **2** veličanstven

lore /lɔː(r)/ *n* znanje iz predaje

lorry /'lɒrɪ/ *n GB* kamion

lose /luːz/ *v irreg* **1** (iz)gubiti **be/get lost** izgubiti se ~ **one's head** izgubiti vlast nad sobom ~ **one's nerve** izgubiti hrabrost ~ **one's temper** planuti, naljutiti se **~r** *n* gubitnik **a good/bad ~r** osoba koja dobro/loše podnosi poraz **2** (sat) kasniti

loss /lɒs/ *n* gubitak **at a ~** u nedoumici

lost *v irreg* → **lose**

lot /lɒt/ *n* **1 ~s of/a ~ of** mnogo **2 the whole ~** sve, svi **3** ždrijeb **4** predmet na dražbi; zbirka predmeta; skupina ljudi **5** *fig* sudbina **6** zemljište, parcela **parking ~** parkiralište

lotion /'ləʊʃn/ *n* losion

lottery /'lɒtərɪ/ n lutrija

loud /laʊd/ adj 1 glasan ~**speaker** zvučnik 2 bučan 3 kričave boje

lough /lɒk/ n Ir jezero

lounge /laʊndʒ/ n salon • vi besposličariti, ljenčariti

louse /laʊs/ n (pl lice) uš (+ fig) **lousy** /'laʊzɪ/ adj 1 coll grozan, odvratan, bezvezan 2 prepun, natrpan 3 ušljiv

lout /laʊt/ n klipan, neotesanac, prostak

love /lʌv/ n 1 ljubav **give/send sb one's ~** poslati pozdrave **for ~ or money** nikako in ~ **with sb** zaljubljen u koga **fall in ~ with sb** zaljubiti se u koga **make ~** voditi ljubav ~**affair** ljubavna veza ~**child** vanbračno dijete ~**lorn** adj koji vene od ljubavi 2 dragi/draga; ljubavi; dušo 3 sport nula ~ **all** 0:0 • vt 1 voljeti, ljubiti 2 obožavati **lovable** /'lʌvəbl/ adj drag, dražestan, mio ~**ly** /'lʌvlɪ/ adj lijep, divan, ljubak ~**r** /'lʌvə(r)/ n 1 ljubavnik 2 zaljubljenik

loving /'lʌvɪŋ/ adj pun ljubavi; nježan

low /ləʊ/ adj 1 nizak **we're getting ~ on sth** ponestaje nam čega ~ **fat** dijetalan ~ **tide/water** oseka ~**er class** niži stalež L~ **Church** crkva s minimalno pompe **lie ~** pritajiti se ~**lands** n nizinski kraj L~ **Latin** vulgarni latinski 2 tih 3 (ton) dubok 4 potišten

loyal /'lɔɪəl/ adj odan, vjeran; lojalan ~**ist** n osoba odana režimu na vlasti ~**ty** n odanost, privrženost

lozenge /'lɒzɪndʒ/ n 1 med pastila 2 math romb

lubricant /'lu:brɪkənt/ n sredstvo za podmazivanje **lubricate** /'lu:brɪkeɪt/ vt podmazati (+ fig)

lucid /'lu:sɪd/ adj 1 jasan, razumljiv 2 lucidan 3 lit bistar, proziran

luck /lʌk/ n sreća **bad/hard ~** nesreća **good ~!** sretno! **just my ~** takve sam ja sreće ~**y** adj sretan ~**ily** adv nasreću

lucrative /'lu:krətɪv/ adj unosan **lucre** /'lu:kə(r)/ n derog novac, zarada

ludicrous /'lu:dɪkrəs/ adj smiješan; apsurdan

lug /lʌg/ vt vući, teglити

luggage /'lʌgɪdʒ/ n GB prtljaga

lukewarm /,lu:k'wɔ:m/ adj mlak, mlačan (+ fig)

lull /lʌl/ vt,vi uljuljkati, umiriti (se) • n zatišje ~**aby** /'laləbaɪ/ n uspavanka

lumber (1) /'lʌmbə(r)/ n 1 US (građevno) drvo ~**jack** drvosječa 2 GB stari (drveni) predmeti, ropotarija • vt zakrčiti, natrpati

lumber (2) vi tromo hodati

luminary /'lu:mɪnərɪ/ n fig lučonoša

luminous /'lu:mɪnəs/ adj svijetleći

lump /lʌmp/ n 1 gruda, grumen **in the ~ u cijelosti ~ sum** svota novca plaćena odjednom ~ **in one's throat** knedl u grlu coll 2 kvržica 3 čvoruga • vi,vt zgrudati se; staviti na gomilu ~**ish** nespretan; glup ~**y** adj grudast

lunatic /'lu:nətɪk/ n derog luđak, budala ~ **asylum** tab ludnica **lunacy** /'lu:nəsɪ/ n ludilo; ludost **lunar** /'lu:nə(r)/ adj mjesečev

lunch /lʌntʃ/ (**luncheon** /'lʌntʃən/ form) n ručak • vi,vt ručati

lung /lʌŋ/ n pluća pl

lunge /lʌndʒ/ vi (at/towards) navaliti, nasrnuti • n nasrtaj

lurch /lɜ:tʃ/ vi teturati, naginjati se • n **leave sb in the ~** ostaviti koga na cjedilu

lure /lʊə(r)/ n mamac, privlačnost • vt mamiti, vabiti, privući

lurid /'lʊərɪd/ adj 1 žarke boje, plamen 2 fig grozan, jeziv

lurk /lɜ:k/ vi vrebati (+ fig), čekati u zasjedi, skrivati se

luscious /'lʌʃəs/ adj sočan, slastan

lush /lʌʃ/ adj 1 bujan 2 fig raskošan • n US sl pijanac

lust /lʌst/ n 1 pohota, požuda 2 ~ **for** žudnja • vi ~ (for/after) željeti; žudjeti (za) ~**ful** adj pohotan, požudan

lustre (-**ter** US) /'lʌstə(r)/ n 1 sjaj 2 fig slava, ugled

lusty /'lʌstɪ/ adj snažan, krepak, jedar

luxury /'lʌkʃərɪ/ n 1 raskoš, obilje, sjaj 2 luksuz ~ **items** luksuzna roba **luxuriant** /lʌg'ʒʊərɪənt/ adj 1 bujan 2 kićen **luxurious** /lʌg'ʒʊərɪəs/ adj bogat, skup, raskošan **luxuriate** /lʌg'ʒʊərɪeɪt/ vi (in) uživati (u)

lynch /lɪntʃ/ n linč

lynx /lɪŋks/ *n* ris
lyric /'lɪrɪk/ *adj* lirski • *n* lirska pjesma ~s tekst pjesme **~al** *adj* veseo, oduševljen, osjećajan **~ist** *n* tekstopisac

M

M, m /em/ 13. slovo engl. abecede; em
ma, Ma /mɑː/ *n coll* mama
mace (1) /meɪs/ *n* 1 žezlo 2 buzdovan
Mace (2) *n US TM* suzavac
machinations /ˌmækɪˈneɪʃnz/ *n pl*
spletke, , makinacije
machine /məˈʃiːn/ *n* 1 stroj 2 *fig*
mašinerija 3 auto, motor, avion,
kompjuter **~gun** strojnica **~ tool** alatni stroj **~ry** *n* 1 strojevi 2 *fig* mehanizam, sustav, ustrojstvo **machinist**
n strojar
macho /ˈmætʃəʊ/ *n derog* muškarčina,
frajerčina
mackerel /ˈmækrəl/ *n* skuša
mac(k)intosh, mac(k) /ˈmækɪntɒʃ/ *n
GB* kišna kabanica
mad /mæd/ *adj* 1 lud 2 *coll* (about)
lud, pošašavio za 3 *US* (about/-
at/with) ljut na 4 bijesan (pas)
drive/send sb ~ izluđivati **~ as a**
March hare/as a hatter potpuno lud
be/go ~ poludjeti (+ *fig*) **~house** *coll*
ludnica **~man/~woman** luđak,
luđakinja **~ness** *n* 1 ludilo; mahnitost; bijes 2 ludost **~den** *vt* izluđivati,
razbjesniti, razljutiti
madam /ˈmædəm/ *n* 1 gospođa 2 *GB
derog* milostiva 3 vlasnica bordela
made *v irreg* → **make**
mag /mæg/ *coll* → **magazine**
magazine /ˌmægəˈziːn/ *n* 1 časopis 2
magazin (puške) 3 skladište oružja
maggot /ˈmægət/ *n* crv
magic /ˈmædʒɪk/ *n* 1 čarolija, magija 2
fig čar **~(al)** *adj* čaroban **~ wand**
čarobni štapić **~ian** /məˈdʒɪʃn/ *n*
mađioničar
magistrate /ˈmædʒɪstreɪt/ *n* 1 sudac
za prekršaje 2 mirovni sudac
magnanimous /mægˈnænɪməs/ *adj*
velikodušan **magnanimity** /ˌmægnə-
ˈnɪmətɪ/ *n* velikodušnost

magnesium /mægˈniːzɪəm/ *n* magnezij
magnet /ˈmægnɪt/ *n* magnet
magnificent /mægˈnɪfɪsnt/ *adj* veličanstven
magnify /ˈmægnɪfaɪ/ *vt* 1 uvećati 2 *fig*
pretjer(iv)ati, uveliča(va)ti **~ing**
glass povećalo **magnitude** /ˈmægnɪ-
tjuːd/ *n form* veličina; važnost
magpie /ˈmægpaɪ/ *n* svraka
mahogany /məˈhɒɡənɪ/ *n* mahagonij;
boja mahagonija
maid /meɪd/ *n* 1 kućna pomoćnica 2 *lit*
djevojka, djev(ic)a **old ~** usidjelica **~
of honour** 1 vjenčana kuma 2 dvorska dama *US* prva djeveruša **~en** *n lit*
(neudata) djevojka, djev(ic)a ◇ *adj* 1
djevojački 2 *fig* prvi 3 neudata **~en**
name djevojačko prezime **~en**
speech nastupni govor (u parlamentu)
mail (1) /meɪl/ *n* oklop (od pletene žice
ili pločica)
mail (2) *n* 1 poštanska služba 2 pošta,
poštanske pošiljke **~box** *US* poštanski sandučić **~man** *US* poštar **~ or-**
der poštanska narudžba • *vt US*
poslati poštom **~ing list** popis adresa
korisnika
maim /meɪm/ *vt* osakatiti
main /meɪn/ *adj* glavni **~frame** *comp*
glavni/središnji kompjutor **~land**
kopno **~spring** 1 glavna opruga
(sata) 2 *fig* pokretačka sila **~stay**
glavno uporište **~stream** *n* 1 glavna
struja (+ *fig*) 2 *mod* umjeren **~ly** *adv*
uglavnom, većinom • *n* **the ~s** 1
glavna (vodovodna ili plinska) cijev;
glavni električni vod 2 struja **a ~s**
set/radio radio na struju **in the ~**
uglavnom, većinom; u cijelosti
mainframe veliko (središnje) računalo
mainline /ˈmeɪnlaɪn/ *vt,vi* ubrizgati

drogu u venu

maintain /meɪnˈteɪn/ *vt* 1 održavati, nastaviti 2 zadržati (cijene) 3 održavati (strojeve, ceste) 4 tvrditi 5 uzdržavati (novčano) **maintenance** /ˈmeɪntənəns/ *n* 1 održavanje 2 uzdržavanje

maisonette /ˌmeɪzəˈnet/ *n* dvoetažni stan u kući

maize /meɪz/ *n GB* kukuruz

majestic /məˈdʒestɪk/ *adj* veličanstven **majesty** /ˈmædʒəstɪ/ *n* veličanstvo **Your Majesty!** Vaše visočanstvo!

major /ˈmeɪdʒə(r)/ *adj* 1 glavni, veći, važniji, značajniji 2 dur • *n* 1 *mil* bojnik; **~general** general bojnik 2 *US* glavni predmet studija 3 *leg* punoljetan • *vi US* (in sth) studirati kao glavni predmet **~ity** /məˈdʒɒrəti/ *n* 1 većina 2 punoljetnost

make /meɪk/ *vt, vi irreg* 1 (na)praviti, (na)činiti; izraditi, izgraditi, proizvoditi; stvoriti 2 izazvati, prouzročiti 3 dati učiniti, natjerati, naložiti, prisiliti; nagnati, ponukati 4 zaraditi, steći, postići 5 stići do; uspjeti; prevaliti (udaljenost); ići određenom brzinom 6 prikazati, opisati kao, navoditi da 7 biti, postati, pokazati se kao 8 ukupno iznositi; tvoriti 9 imenovati, postaviti, proglasiti 10 procijeniti ~ **believe** pretvarati se, praviti se ~ **do** (with/without sth) zadovoljiti se (čime/bez čega) ~ **like** *coll* praviti se ~ **it** a. stići na vrijeme b. uspjeti ~ **one's living** (as/at/by/from) zarađivati ~ **or break/mar** sve ili ništa *he made as if to hit me* htio me udariti ~ **away a.** (with oneself) ubiti se b. (with sth) ukrasti što ~ **for sb/sth a.** uputiti se, krenuti prema b. navaliti, zaletjeti se, pojuriti prema c. omogućiti, pridonijeti, služiti čemu ~ **sth/sb into sth** preraditi, preurediti, pretvoriti u ~ **sth of sb/sth** misliti, razumjeti, shvaćati, tumačiti ~ **off** odjuriti, pobjeći ~ **sth out a.** sastaviti (popis); ispuniti, ispisati (ček) b. razabrati ~ **out that/**~ **sb out** to be tvrditi/prikazati koga kao ~ **sb out**

shvatiti, razumjeti ~ **it out** shvatiti, (pro)tumačiti, odgonetnuti, doći do zaključka ~ **out with sb** napredovati ~ **out a case for** zalagati se za što, govoriti u prilog čemu, zagovarati, argumentirati ~ **sth over a.** (into) izmijeniti, pretvoriti b. (to) *leg* prepisati na, prenijeti imetak ~ **sth up a.** izmisliti b. pripremiti; složiti c. sastaviti, sačinjavati, činiti, tvoriti d. skrojiti, sašiti, izraditi ~ **sb/oneself up** našminkati (se) ~ **up one's mind** odlučiti se ~ **up for sth** nadoknaditi ~ **up to sb** ulagivati se ~ **it up** (with sb) pomiriti se (nakon svađe) ~ **it up to sb** (for sth) odužiti se komu, nadoknaditi komu što • *n* marka proizvoda ~**believe** *n* prividnost, opsjena, varka, pretvaranje ~**er** *n* izrađivač, proizvođač, tvorac ~**shift** *adj* privremen, provizoran, improviziran ~**up** *n* 1 šminka 2 sastav, građa 3 narav, temperament **making** *n* izrada, pravljenje, proizvodnja, stvaranje **in the making** u nastajanju **be the making of** pridonijeti boljitku/razvoju, dobro doći komu, biti razlog čijeg uspjeha **have the makings of** imati sva potrebna svojstva/odlike za

malaise /mæˈleɪz/ *n* osjećaj tjelesne slabosti/nelagode/potištenosti

malcontent /ˈmælkəntent/ *n* nezadovoljnik (društvenom situacijom)

male /meɪl/ *adj* muški • *n* 1 muško, muškarac 2 mužjak

malefactor /ˌmælɪˈfæktə(r)/ *n* zločinac, krivac

malevolent /məˈlevələnt/ *adj* pakostan, zloban, zlonamjeran

malformed /ˌmælˈfɔːmd/ *adj* deformiran, izobličen

malfunction /ˌmælˈfʌŋkʃn/ *n* kvar

malice /ˈmælɪs/ *n* 1 pakost, zloba 2 zlonamjernost **malicious** /məˈlɪʃəs/ *adj* 1 zloban 2 zlonamjeran

malignant /məˈlɪgnənt/ *adj* 1 zao, zlonamjeran, zlurad 2 *med* zloćudan

malinger /məˈlɪŋgə(r)/ *vi* pretvarati se bolesnim, simulirati

mall /mɔːl/ *n US* veliki trgovački centar

malnutrition /ˌmælnju:'trɪʃn/ n neishranjenost, slaba prehrana

malpractice /ˌmæl'præktɪs/ n 1 zanemarivanje dužnosti 2 zloupotreba položaja 3 med nesavjestan postupak

malt /mɔ:lt/ n slad

maltreat /ˌmæl'tri:t/ vt zlostavljati ~ment n zlostavljanje

mammal /'mæml/ n sisavac

mammoth /'mæmɔθ/ n mamut • adj fig divovski, golem

man /mæn/ n (pl men) 1 muškarac 2 čovjek 3 muž 4 pl ljudstvo to a ~/the last ~ svi do jednoga/do posljednjeg čovjeka the ~ in the street običan čovjek ~ about town društvena osoba • vt 1 postaviti ljude/posadu 2 opsluživati; držati položaj ~eater ljudožder ~handle vt 1 pokretati ljudskom snagom, ručno prenijeti 2 grubo postupati s ~hole otvor u pločniku; šaht coll ~hood 1 muževno doba, zrelost 2 form muškarci, muško stanovništvo 3 muškost (+ fig) ~kind čovječanstvo ~-made adj umjetan, sintetički ~power ljudstvo; radna snaga ~slaughter ubojstvo iz nehata

manacles /'mænəklz/ n pl 1 lisičine 2 okovi

manage /'mænɪdʒ/ vt,vi 1 (ruko)voditi, upravljati; 2 (to do sth) uspjeti, izvesti, izaći nakraj, provesti u djelo, snaći se 3 fig držati na uzdi ~able /'mænɪdʒəbl/ adj 1 prikladan za rukovanje, kojim se lakše upravlja, koji se lakše kontrolira 2 izvediv ~ment n 1 upravljanje, (ruko)vođenje 2 uprava, rukovodstvo ~r n upravitelj, direktor, ravnatelj ~ress n upraviteljica, direktorica ~rial /ˌmænɪ'dʒɪərɪəl/ adj direktorski managing /'mænɪdʒɪŋ/ adj rukovodeći managing director direktor

mandarin /'mændərɪn/ n mandarin

mandate /'mændeɪt/ n 1 ovlaštenje, punomoć 2 nalog, naredba, zadatak • vt 1 dati ovlaštenje/nalog 2 staviti zemlju pod čiju upravu mandatory /'mændətrɪ/ adj koji nalaže/ovlašćuje; obvezatan

mane /meɪn/ n griva

maneuver /mə'nu:və(r)/ US → manoeuvre

mange /meɪndʒ/ n šuga mangy /'meɪndʒɪ/ adj 1 šugav (pas) 2 fig izlizan

manger /'meɪndʒə(r)/ n jasle

mangle /'mæŋgl/ vt 1 raskomadati, smrskati 2 fig upropastiti

mania /'meɪnɪə/ n (for) 1 ludilo, mahnitost 2 fig manija, pomama ~c n manijak ~cal adj mahnit manic /'mænɪk/ adj manijakalni

manifest /'mænɪfest/ adj form jasan, očit • n brodski manifest • vt 1 očitovati 2 (jasno) pokaz(iva)ti ~ation /ˌmænɪfes'teɪʃn/ n iskaz, izraz ~o /ˌmænɪ'festəʊ/ n manifest, proglas

manifold /'mænɪfəʊld/ adj mnogostruk; brojan; raznolik

manil(l)a /mə'nɪlə/ n (~ paper) pakpapir

manipulate /mə'nɪpjʊleɪt/ vt rukovati, upravljati; manipulirati (čime)

mannequin /'mænɪkɪn/ n 1 krojačka lutka 2 arch maneken(ka)

manner /'mænə(r)/ n 1 način 2 stil, manira 3 ponašanje, nastup 4 pl običaji, navike; lijepo ponašanje in a ~ donekle, u neku ruku in a ~ of speaking moglo bi se reći, da tako kažem(o) ~ed adj izvještačen good-~ed pristojan, uljudan bad-~ed nepristojan ~ism /'mænərɪzəm/ n 1 derog karakteristična osobina/navika 2 manirizam

manoeuvre /mə'nu:və(r)/ n 1 mil pl manevri 2 fig (vješt/promišljen) potez, varka • vi, vt 1 mil imati vojne vježbe 2 manevrirati, izvesti, pomaknuti, ubaciti, probijati se, spretnošću postići

manor /'mænə(r)/ n (plemićki) posjed lord of the ~ vlastelin

mansion /'mænʃn/ n vila (kuća)

mantelpiece /'mæntlpi:s/ n polica iznad kamina

mantle /'mæntl/ n 1 ogrtač, pelerina 2 fig pokrivač, pokrov, plašt

manual /'mænjʊəl/ adj ručni ~ labour/work fizički rad • n priručnik

manufacture /ˌmænju'fæktʃə(r)/ vt proizvoditi, izrađivati • n proizvodnja ~**d goods** tvornička roba ~**r** n proizvođač (tvornica)

manure /mə'njʊə(r)/ n gnoj(ivo)

manuscript /'mænjʊskrɪpt/ n rukopis, manuskript

many /'menɪ/ adj (comp **more**, sup the **most**) mnogo • n mnogi, mnoštvo **a great~** mnoštvo, velik broj **a good ~** priličan broj **how ~**? koliko? **as ~ as** 20 people čak 20 ljudi **be one too ~ for** nadmudriti/nadvladati koga ~-**sided** adj mnogostran

map /mæp/ n (of) zemljopisna karta, zemljovid **off the ~ a.** zabačen, nepristupačan **b.** fig nevažan **wipe sth off the ~** zbrisati s lica zemlje **put sth on the ~** učiniti što poznatim • vt 1 ucrtati, unijeti u zemljovid 2 (sth out) fig zacrtati, isplanirati

maple /'meɪpl/ n javor

mar /mɑ:(r)/ vt (po)kvariti, (po)remetiti, štetiti

marathon /'mærəθɒn/ n maraton

maraud /mə'rɔ:d/ vi pljačkati ~**er** n pljačkaš

marble /'mɑ:bl/ n 1 mramor 2 špekula **lose one's ~s** coll pošašaviti

March (1) /mɑ:tʃ/ n ožujak

march (2) /mɑ:tʃ/ n,vt 1 mil stupati 2 hodati, koračati 3 (sb away/off) odvesti koga • n 1 marš 2 koračnica 3 hod(anje) 4 fig tijek (događanja) **forced ~** forsirani marš ~ **past** počasni mimohod **dead ~** posmrtni marš

Mardi Gras /,mɑ:dɪ 'grɑ:/ n zadnji dan karnevala

mare /meə(r)/ n kobila, magarica

margarine /,mɑ:dʒə'ri:n/ n margarin

marge /mɑ:dʒ/ n coll margarin

margin /'mɑ:dʒɪn/ n 1 margina 2 rub; granica 3 comm marža 4 fig prostor; luft coll ~ **of error** dopuštena pogreška, dopušteno odstupanje **by a narrow ~** za dlaku **win by a huge ~** pobijediti (na izborima) golemom razlikom ~**al** adj 1 rubni, marginalan 2 osvojen neznatnom većinom glasova

marigold /'mærɪgəʊld/ n neven

marijuana, marihuana /,mærɪ'wɑ:nə/ n marihuana

marinate /'mærɪneɪt/ vt marinirati

marine /mə'ri:n/ adj 1 morski 2 pomorski; brodski; mornarički **the M~ Corps** mil mornarička pješadija, marinci • n mornarica **merchant/-mercantile ~** trgovačka mornarica

marital /'mærɪtl/ adj bračni

maritime /'mærɪtaɪm/ adj 1 pomorski 2 primorski

mark /mɑ:k/ n 1 mrlja, trag, otisak, ogrebotina, ožiljak 2 znak, oznaka, biljeg, žig 3 madež 4 ocjena 5 cilj, meta 6 njemačka marka (valuta) **wide of the ~** neprecizan **beside the ~** fig nebitan, nevažan vt 1 (sth on/with sth) označiti, obilježiti; zabilježiti 2 ocijeniti 3 paziti, pozorno slušati, zapamtiti ~ **sth off** razgraničiti ~ **sb out for sth** odrediti, odabrati ~**ed** adj jasan, izrazit, očit, vidljiv ~**ings** n pl oznake; šare ~**sman** dobar strijelac

market /'mɑ:kɪt/ n 1 tržnica; sajam 2 tržište **on the ~** na prodaju, na tržištu **be in the ~ for sth** zainteresiran za kupnju čega **play the ~** špekulirati na burzi ~ **gardening** povrćarstvo ~**place** tržnica • vt,vi 1 staviti u prodaju, prodavati ~**able** adj koji se može prodati ~**ing** n tržišno poslovanje, marketing

marmalade /'mɑ:məleɪd/ n marmelada

maroon (1) /mə'ru:n/ vt 1 iskrcati na pustom otoku 2 fig ostaviti, napustiti

maroon (2) adj kestenjast, smeđ

marquee /mɑ:'ki:/ n veliki šator

marriage /'mærɪdʒ/ n 1 svadba, vjenčanje 2 brak **take sb in ~** uzeti za muža/ženu **marry** /'mærɪ/ vt,vi udati (se), oženiti (se), vjenčati (se) **get married** oženiti se, udati se, vjenčati se

marrow (1) /'mærəʊ/ n koštana srž **to the ~** fig do srži

marrow (2) n tikvica

marsh /mɑ:ʃ/ n močvara; močvarno tlo ~**y** adj močvaran

marshal /'mɑ:ʃl/ n 1 mil maršal 2 majstor ceremonija 3 US šerif • vt 1 postrojiti; poredati, svrstati 2 (svečano) uvesti

martial /'mɑ:ʃl/ adj ratni, ratnički ~ **law** 1 prijeki sud 2 opsadno/ratno stanje **court-~** vojni sud

martyr /'mɑ:tə(r)/ n 1 mučenik; patnik 2 *derog* žrtva ~**dom** /'mɑ:tə(r)dəm/ n mučeništvo

marvel /'mɑ:vl/ n čudo, divota **do/work** ~**s** činiti čuda ~**lous** *adj* čudesan, divan • *vi* 1 (at) diviti se 2 (that) čuditi se, pitati se

mascot /'mæskət/ n maskota

masculine /'mæskjulɪn/ *adj* 1 muški (+ *gram*) 2 muževan; poput muškarca, muškarački

mash /mæʃ/ n *GB coll* pire krumpir • *vt* (z)gnječiti, (z)drobiti

mask /mɑ:sk/ n 1 krinka, maska; krabulja 2 zaštitni povoj, zaštitna maska **gas** ~ zaštitna maska • *vt* 1 staviti masku, maskirati, zakrinkati 2 prikriti, sakriti

mason /'meɪsn/ n 1 zidar 2 slobodni zidar ~**ic** /mə'sɒnɪk/ *adj* masonski ~**ry** /'meɪsnrɪ/ n 1 zidarstvo; zidna konstrukcija 2 masonerija

masquerade /,mɑ:skə'reɪd/ n 1 krabuljni ples, bal pod maskama 2 *fig* pretvaranje, farsa • *vi* (as) maskirati se, zakrabuljiti se, predstaviti se kao

mass (1) /mæs/ n masa, gomila, hrpa, mnoštvo; većina the ~**es** *coll* (široke narodne) mase, gomila, mnoštvo ~ **communications/media** n *pl* sredstva javnog priopćavanja ~ **production** masovna/serijska proizvodnja ~**produce** serijski proizvoditi • *vt, vi* 1 nagomilati (se), nakupiti se, okupiti (se), skupiti (se) 2 *mil* gomilati snage ~**ive** *adj* 1 masivan, krupan, velik 2 jak, težak, znatan

Mass (2) /mæs/ n misa

massacre /'mæsəkə(r)/ n pokolj, masakr • *vt* masakrirati

massage /'mæsɑ:ʒ/ n masaža • *vt* 1 masirati 2 *fig* lažirati (podatke)

mast /mɑ:st/ n jarbol ~**head** vrh jarbola

master /'mɑ:stə(r)/ n 1 gospodar, gazda 2 učitelj 3 kapetan trgovačkog broda 4 majstor 5 glavna snimka, matrica, original **M~ of Arts** magistar humanističkih znanosti **M~ of Science** magistar prirodnih znanosti ~**'s** (**degree**) magisterij **M~ of Ceremonies** majstor ceremonija,

ceremonijar, voditelj programa **be ~ of sth** vladati čime • *adj* 1 majstorski, stručni 2 glavni, najvažniji, najveći **the ~ bedroom** glavna spavaća soba • *vt* svladati, naučiti, usvojiti ~**ful** *adj* zapovjednički, koji voli naređivati ~**mind** n organizator; mozak *coll* ○ *vt coll* smisliti, razraditi, organizirati, upravljati ~**piece** remek-djelo ~**stroke** majstorski potez ~**y** n (over/of) 1 vlast, nadmoć 2 vladanje, znanje

masturbate /'mæstəbeɪt/ *vi, vt* masturbirati

mat /mæt/ n 1 otirač 2 prostirač 3 podmetač

match (1) /mætʃ/ n žigica, šibica ~**wood** iverje **strike a** ~ zapaliti šibicu

match (2) n 1 utakmica 2 (for) par 3 brak **be a/no ~ for** biti/ne biti dorastao komu ~**less** *adj* bez premca ~ **point** odlučujući bod (u tenisu) • *vt, vi* 1 odgovarati, pristajati jedan drugome, slagati se, biti par; uskladiti, spariti 2 mjeriti se, biti ravan kome **not ~ up to/with sth** iznevjeriti (nadanja)

mate /meɪt/ n 1 prijatelj, kolega; frend *coll* 2 mužjak, ženka, partner 3 časnik trgovačke mornarice 4 pomoćnik • *vt, vi* (with) pariti se, (s)pariti se **mating season** doba parenja

material /mə'tɪərɪəl/ *adj* 1 materijalan; stvaran 2 tjelesni 3 bitan, značajan 3 (to) od (velike) važnosti za ~ n građa, materijal; tkanina ~**ize** /mə'tɪərɪəlaɪz/ *vi, vt* 1 poprimiti ili dati tjelesan oblik 2 pojaviti se 3 ostvariti se, ispuniti se

maternal /mə'tɜ:nl/ *adj* majčinski

maternity /mə'tɜ:nətɪ/ n majčinstvo ~ **dress** haljina za trudnice ~ **hospital** rodilište ~ **leave** porodiljni dopust

mathematics /,mæθə'mætɪks/ (*US* **math** /mæθ/; *GB coll* **maths** /mæθs/) n matematika **mathematical** /,mæθə'mætɪkl/ *adj* matematički **mathematician** /,mæθəmə'tɪʃn/ n matematičar

matinée /'mætɪneɪ/ n matineja

matins /'mætɪnz/ n jutrenja

matriculate /mə'trɪkjuleɪt/ *vt, vi* upisati

matriculation /mə,trɪkju'leɪʃn/ n upis na sveučilište

matrimony /'mætrɪmənɪ/ n brak matrimonial /,mætrɪ'məʊnɪəl/ adj bračni

matrix /'meɪtrɪks/ n (pl matrices, ~es) matrica; kalup

matron /'meɪtrən/ n 1 glavna medicinska sestra 2 GB voditeljica internata 3 upraviteljica ženskog zatvora 4 starija gospoda ~ly adj dostojan starije gospode, ozbiljan

matted /'mætɪd/ adj isprepleten, zamršen

matter /'mætə(r)/ n 1 pitanje, predmet, problem, stvar; posao 2 tvar, materija 3 the subject ~ sadržaj reading ~ štivo as a ~ of fact u stvari for that ~ što se toga tiče no ~ the ~ of s obzirom na no ~ who/what tko/što god it's a ~ of few pounds radi se o nekoliko funti what's the ~? što je? ~-of-course adj sam po sebi razumljiv, naravan ~-of-fact adj realistčan, trijezan, suhoparan • vi značiti, biti važno it doesn't ~ to me nije mi važno, ne smeta mi

mattress /'mætrɪs/ n 1 madrac 2 strunjača

mature /mə'tjʊə(r)/ vt,vi 1 dozreti, sazoriti 2 učiniti zrelim 3 comm dospjeti • adj 1 zreo, odrastao 2 sazreo maturity /mə'tjʊərɪtɪ/ n zrelost

maudlin /'mɔːdlɪn/ adj plačljiv, sentimentalan

maul /mɔːl/ vt 1 teško ozlijediti, oderati 2 biti grub prema; tući, udarati, mlatiti 3 fig napasti, oštro iskritizirati

mausoleum /,mɔːsə'liːəm/ n mauzolej

mauve /məʊv/ adj svjetloljubičast

maverick /'mævərɪk/ n 1 US nežigosano tele 2 pol slobodan strijelac, samopouzdana osoba

maxim /'mæksɪm/ n načelo, geslo

maximum /'mæksɪməm/ n maksimum • adj maksimalan, najveći, najviši maximize /'mæksɪmaɪz/ vt maksimalno povećati/iskoristiti

may (1) /meɪ/ v modal smjeti he ~ come možda dođe ~ I come in? smijem li ući? ~ you be happy! sretno ti/vam bilo! come what ~ što god se

dogodilo

May (2) n svibanj ~ Day prvi svibnja

maybe /'meɪbiː/ adv možda

mayday /'meɪdeɪ/ n poziv u pomoć

mayhem /'meɪhem/ n metež, nered, pometnja, zbrka

mayonnaise /,meɪə'neɪz/ n majoneza

mayor /meə(r)/ n gradonačelnik ~ess n gradonačelnica

maze /meɪz/ n 1 labirint (+ fig) 2 zbrka

me /miː/ pron 1 mene, me 2 meni, mi he saw ~ vidio me je it's ~ ja sam, to sam ja

meadow /'medəʊ/ n livada

meagre (-ger US) /'miːgə(r)/ adj 1 mršav, suh 2 slab, oskudan, siromašan

meal (1) /miːl/ n obrok, jelo have a ~ jesti, ručati

meal (2) n grubo mljeveno brašno ~y adj brašnjav, brašnast ~y-mouthed adj slatkorječiv

mean (1) /miːn/ adj 1 škrt, sebičan 2 bezobziran, odvratan, gadan, podao, nizak, zao 3 US sl sjajan he's no ~ cook odličan je kuhar

mean (2) vt irreg 1 značiti 2 (by) misliti; htjeti kazati 3 namjeravati, kaniti, naumiti 4 (for) namijeniti kome što ~ business misliti ozbiljno, ne šaliti se ~ mischief imati zle namjere ~ well by sb htjeti kome dobro ~ing n 1 značenje 2 smisao 3 namjera well-~ing dobronamjeran ~ingful adj značajan ~ingless adj beznačajan; besmislen

mean (3) n sredina, prosjek the happy/golden ~ zlatna sredina • adj srednji, prosječan

meander /mɪ'ændə(r)/ vi 1 vijugati (rijeka) 2 besciljno lutati

means /miːnz/ n pl 1 sredstvo, način 2 novčana sredstva, imetak ~ to an end put do cilja the end justifies the ~ cilj opravdava sredstvo by ~ of pomoću by all ~ svakako by no ~ nikako, nipošto man of ~ bogat čovjek

meant v irreg → mean

meantime /'miːntaɪm/ adv, n (in the) ~ u međuvremenu, međutim

meanwhile /'miːnwaɪl/ adv 1 u međuvremenu **2** dok, za vrijeme

measles /'mi:zlz/ *n med* ospice

measly /'mi:zli/ *adj coll* bijedan, jadan

measure /'meʒə(r)/ *vt,vi* (iz)mjeriti; uzeti mjeru ~ **one's length** pasti koliko je tko dug i širok *the room* ~*s ten metres across* soba je široka deset metara ~**d** *adj* odmjeren, pažljiv, promišljen • *n* mjera; mjerilo; mjerica **made to** ~ po mjeri **in some** ~ donekle **take (strong)** ~**s** poduzeti (oštre) mjere ~**ment** *n* **1** mjerenje **2** *pl* mjere, dimenzije

meat /mi:t/ *n* meso ~**y** *adj* **1** mesni, mesnat **2** *fig* sadržajan

mechanic /mɪ'kænɪk/ *n* mehaničar, strojar ~**al** *adj* **1** mehanički, strojni **2** *fig* automatski, mehanički ~**al engineering** strojarstvo ~**s** *n pl* mehanika **mechanism** /'mekənɪzəm/ *n* mehanizam

medal /'medl/ *n* medalja, odličje ~**list** (~**ist** *US*) *n* dobitnik medalje ~**lion** /mɪ'dælɪən/ *n* medaljon

meddle /'medl/ *vt* **1** (in sth) miješati se, pačati se, uplitati se **2** (with sth) dirati u što, prčkati po čemu ~**some** *adj* radoznao, nametljiv

media /'mi:dɪə/ *n pl* (the ~) sredstva javnog priopćavanja, mediji

mediaeval /ˌmedɪ'i:vl/ → **medieval**

mediate /'mi:dɪeɪt/ *vi, vt* **1** (between/in) posredovati **2** ishoditi, postići posredovanjem **mediator** /'mi:dɪeɪtə(r)/ *n* posrednik

medical /'medɪkl/ *adj* medicinski; liječnički ~ **practicioner** liječnik • *n* liječnički pregled **Medicare** /'medɪkeə(r)/ *n US* zdravstveno osiguranje **medicated** /'medɪkeɪtəd/ *adj* medicinski **medication** /ˌmedɪ'keɪʃn/ *n* **1** liječenje **2** raskuživanje **3** *US* lijek **medicinal** /mɪ'dɪsɪnl/ *adj* **1** medicinski **2** ljekovit **medicine** /'medsn/ *n* **1** lijek **2** medicina **medicine man** vrač

medieval /ˌmedɪ'i:vl/ *adj* srednjovjekovni

mediocre /ˌmi:dɪ'əʊkə(r)/ *adj* osrednji

medium /'mi:dɪəm/ *adj* srednji; prosječan • *n* **1** sredstvo **2** sredina **3**

vodič 4 medij

medley /'medli/ *n* mješavina, šarenilo **400-metre** ~ *sport* 400 m mješovitim stilom

meek /mi:k/ *adj* krotak, popustljiv, ponizan, strpljiv

meet /mi:t/ *vt, vi irreg* **1** susresti se, sresti (se); dočekati **2** upoznati se s kim **3** okupiti se, sakupiti se **4** spajati se, sastajati se **5** dodirnuti se, dotaknuti se **6** (with) doživjeti, iskusiti, pretrpjeti; naići na; sastati se s ~ *US* **7** udovoljiti, zadovoljiti (potražnju), ispuniti (očekivanja) **8** suprotstaviti se; odgovoriti na (kritiku) **9** namiriti (račun) **make (both) ends** ~ sastavljati kraj s krajem ~**ing** /'mi:tɪŋ/ *n* **1** sastanak; susret **2** *sport* susret, natjecanje

megaphone /'megəfəʊn/ *n* megafon

melancholy /'melənkɒlɪ/ *n* tuga, sjeta, nujnost • *adj* **melancolic** *lit* sjetan

melee /'meleɪ/ *n* gužva, gungula, metež

mellow /'meləʊ/ *adj* **1** zreo, sočan, slastan, mekan **2** blag, nježan, topao (boja) **3** zreo *fig* **4** pripit **5** *coll* dobre volje • *vt,vi* **1** sazreti, dozreti **2** omekšati, smekšati (se), postati blaži

melodrama /'melədra:mə/ *n* melodrama (+ *fig*) ~**tic** *adj* melodramski; melodramatičan, patetičan

melody /'melədɪ/ *n* melodija, napjev **melodious** /mɪ'ləʊdɪəs/ *adj* milozvučan, skladan

melon /'melən/ *n* dinja **water**~ lubenica

melt /melt/ *vt,vi irreg* **1** (ras)topiti (se), (ras)taliti (se) **2** *fig* ganuti, smekšati (se) ~ **away a.** otapati se, rastapati se **b.** *fig* nestajati, rasplinuti se, razići se ~ **sth down** rastopiti, rastaliti (kovinu) ~ **into** stopiti se s ~**down** *n* taljenje atomske jezgre ~**ing** *adj* nježan, umiljat; ganutljiv ~**ing point** talište ~**ing pot 1** lonac za taljenje **2** *fig* zemlja u kojoj se useljenici asimiliraju

member /'membə(r)/ *n* **1** (of) član, pripadnik **2** ud ~**ship** *n* članstvo; članovi

membrane /'membreɪn/ *n* opna

memento /mɪ'mentəʊ/ *n* znak sjećanja, uspomena

memoirs /'memwɑː(r)z/ *n pl* memoari

memorable /'memərəbl/ *adj* (for) znamenit, značajan, vrijedan pamćenja, nezaboravan

memorandum /,memə'rændəm/ *n* 1 (**memo**) poslovni dopis (unutar tvrtke) 2 bilješka, podsjetnik 3 memorandum

memorial /mɪ'mɔːrɪəl/ *n* (to) spomenik ~ **tablet** spomen-ploča ~ **service** misa zadušnica

memorize /'meməraɪz/ *vt* naučiti napamet, zapamtiti

memory /'memərɪ/ *n* 1 pamćenje 2 sjećanje 3 uspomena 4 *comp* memorija **commit sth to** ~ naučiti napamet, (za)pamtiti **speak from** ~ govoriti napamet/iz glave **in** ~ **of sb/to the** ~ **of sb** u sjećanje na, u spomen koga

menace /'menəs/ *n* 1 (to) prijetnja, opasnost 2 *coll* prava napast, gnjavator • *vt* prijetiti, ugrožavati

mend /mend/ *vt, vi* 1 popraviti, zakrpati 2 poboljšati; ispraviti 3 oporaviti se • *n* zakrpa, zakrpano mjesto **be on the** ~ *coll* ići nabolje

menfolk /'menfəʊk/ *n coll* muškarci (u obitelji)

menial /'miːnɪəl/ *adj* nizak (posao) • *n* derog sluga, služavka

menopause /'menəpɔːz/ *n med* menopauza, klimakterij

men's room *n US* muški WC

menstruation /,menstrʊ'eɪʃn/ *n med* menstruacija **menstrual** /'menstrʊəl/ *adj* menstruacijski **menstrual period** *form* menstruacija

mental /'mentl/ *adj* umni, duševni ~ **deficiency** slaboumnost ~ **home/hospital** bolnica za duševne bolesti **make a** ~ **note** (of sth) zapamtiti što, zapisati u glavi

mention /'menʃn/ *vt* spomenuti, napomenuti **don't** ~ **it** molim! nema na čemu! **not to** ~ da i ne spominjemo • *n* 1 spominjanje 2 pohvala

menu /'menjuː/ *n* jelovnik; meni (+ *comp*)

mercantile /'mɜːkəntaɪl/ *adj* trgovački

~ **marine** *US* trgovačka mornarica

mercenary /'mɜːsɪnərɪ/ *adj* plaćenički • *n* plaćenik

merchandise /'mɜːtʃəndaɪz/ *n* trgovačka roba

merchant /'mɜːtʃənt/ *n* trgovac (na veliko) ~ **ships** trgovački brodovi **the** ~ **navy/service/marine** trgovačka mornarica

mercury /'mɜːkjʊrɪ/ *n* živa

mercy /'mɜːsɪ/ *n* 1 milost; milosrđe 2 *coll* blagoslov, sreća **at the** ~ **of** na milost i nemilost (koga/čega) **show** ~ **to/have** ~ **on sb** smilovati se komu **show no** ~ biti nemilosrdan **merciful** *adj* (to) milosrdan, samilostan; milostiv **merciless** *adj* nemilosrdan

mere /mɪə(r)/ *adj* puki **he's a** ~ **child** on je tek dijete ~**ly** *adv* samo, jedino, tek

merge /mɜːdʒ/ *vt, vi* 1 (in/into/with) *comm* udružiti (se), integrirati (se), fuzionirati (se) 2 (into) stopiti (se), sjediniti (se), pretvoriti se, prelaziti u ~**r** *n* 1 *comm* integracija 2 stapanje

meringue /mə'ræŋ/ *n* puslica (kolačić)

merit /'merɪt/ *n* 1 zasluga 2 odlika, vrlina; vrijednost **judge sth on its (own)** ~**s** suditi nešto po vrijednosti same stvari **the** ~**s and demerits of sth** prednosti i nedostaci čega • *vt form* zaslužiti, zavrijediti

mermaid /'mɜːmeɪd/ *n* (morska) sirena

merry /'merɪ/ *adj* 1 veseo, radostan 2 zabavan, šaljiv 3 *GB coll* pripit **make** ~ veseliti se, zabavljati se ~**-go-round** vrtuljak ~**making** veselje, zabava

mesh /meʃ/ *n* 1 oko, očica (mreže) 2 (+ *pl*) mreža (+ *fig*) • *vt, vi* 1 uhvatiti u mrežu 2 (with) zahvaćati se (zupčanici) 3 *fig* slagati se

mesmerize /'mezməraɪz/ *vt* hipnotizirati, opčiniti

mess /mes/ *n* 1 nered, zbrka; svinjac *coll* 2 neprilika, nevolja, škripac; sos *coll* 3 (~**room**) *mil* kantina 4 *euph* životinjski izmet **make a** ~ **of** .upropastiti, pokvariti ~**y** *adj* neuredan, prljav • *vi, vt* 1 (about/around) bespsličariti, dangubiti, motati se 2 gluparati, lupetati, glupirati se 3 (about/around with) prčkati, prtljati po **4** motati *coll* maltretirati *coll* **5** (with) *US* spetljati se s kim **6** *Ir* zafrkavati se ~ **sth up** pobrkati, poremetiti, pokvariti; zaprljati ~**up** *n coll* zbrka, nesporazum

message /'mesɪdʒ/ *n* poruka **get the ~** *coll* shvatiti, razumjeti

messenger /'mesɪndʒə(r)/ *n* glasnik; kurir, dostavljač, raznosač

met *v irreg* → **meet**

metal /'metl/ *n* **1** kovina, metal **2** *mod* metalan ~**lic** *adj* metalan

metaphor /'metəfə(r)/ *n* metafora

mete /mi:t/ *vt* (out) odmjeriti, odrediti (kaznu), dodijeliti (nagradu)

meteorology /,mi:tɪə'rɒlədʒɪ/ *n* meteorologija

meter /'mi:tə(r)/ *n* **1** brojilo, mjerilo **2** *US* → **metre** **read the ~** očitati brojilo

method /'meθəd/ *n* **1** metoda, način, postupak **2** red, sustav ~**ical** /mɪ'θɒdɪkl/ *adj* metodički ~**ology** /,meθə'dɒlədʒɪ/ *n* metodologija

methylated spirit (meths *coll*) /'meθɪleɪtɪd 'spɪrɪt/ *n* metilni alkohol

meticulous /mɪ'tɪkjʊləs/ *adj* (in) poman, brižan, pedantan

metre (-ter *US*) /'mi:tə(r)/ *n* metar **metric** *adj* metrički **metrical** *adj* u stihovima

metropolis /mə'trɒpəlɪs/ *n* glavni grad, metropola

metropolitan /,metrə'pɒlɪtən/ *adj* **1** prijestolnički; velegradski **2** matični (zemlja) **the M~ Police** londonska policija o *n* **M~ bishop** nadbiskup

mettle /'metl/ *n* srčanost, borbenost, vatrenost, žar **be on one's ~** dati sve od sebe **put sb on his ~** potaknuti koga da se iskaže

mew /mju:/ *n* mijau • *vi* mijaukati

mews /mju:z/ *n pl GB coll* nekadašnje staje preuređene u stanove/garaže

mezzanine /'mezəni:n/ *n* **1** međukat **2** *US* mezanin

mice /maɪs/ → **mouse**

mickey /'mɪkɪ/ *n GB coll* **take the ~ out of sb** zafrkavati, zezati

microfilm /'maɪkrəʊfɪlm/ *n* mikrofilm • *vt* snimiti na mikrofilmu

microphone /'maɪkrəfəʊn/ *n* mikrofon

microscope /'maɪkrəskəʊp/ *n* mikroskop, sitnozor

microwave /'maɪkrəʊweɪv/ *n* (~ **oven**) mikrovalna pećnica

mid /mɪd/ *adj* srednji **in ~ air** u zraku

midday /,mɪd'deɪ/ *n* podne *at* ~ u podne

middle /'mɪdl/ *n* sredina **in the ~ of** usred, u sredini *I was in the ~ of reading when* baš sam čitao kad **in the ~ of nowhere** u zabiti, Bogu iza leđa ~**aged** srednjih godina **the M~ Ages** srednji vijek **the M~ East** Srednji istok ~ **finger** srednjak ~**man** *comm* posrednik ~ **name** drugo/srednje ime ~**of-the-road** umjeren ~ **course** *fig* srednji put **middling** /'mɪdlɪŋ/ *adj, adv coll* (o)srednji, prosječan

midge /mɪdʒ/ *n* mušica

midget /'mɪdʒɪt/ *n* patuljak, kepec • *adj* malen, patuljast, minijaturni

midland /'mɪdlənd/ *adj* kontinentalni, središnji, unutrašnji

midnight /'mɪdnaɪt/ *n* ponoć **at** ~ u ponoć **burn the ~ oil** raditi do kasno u noć

midriff /'mɪdrɪf/ *n* **1** ošit **2** *coll* trbuh

midst /mɪdst/ *n lit* **in the ~** of u sredini, usred **in our/your/their ~** među nama/vama/njima

midsummer /,mɪd'sʌmə(r)/ *n* **1** sredina ljeta **2** ljetna suncostaja **M~ Day** Ivanje

midway /,mɪd'weɪ/ *adj* srednji • *adv* ~ (between) na pola puta

midwife /'mɪdwaɪf/ *n* primalja

miffed /mɪft/ *adj coll* ozlojeđen, uvrijeđen, naduren

might (1) /maɪt/ *v irreg* → **may**

might (2) *n* moć, sila, snaga **with all one's ~** svom snagom ~ **is right** tko jači, taj kvači ~**y** *adj* moćan, silan, snažan; velik, golem, **high and ~y** *coll* napuhan, uobražen o *adv coll* jako, vrlo, silno

migraine /'mi:greɪn/ *n* migrena

migrate /maɪ'greɪt/ *vi* (from/to) seliti se; putovati **migration** /maɪ'greɪʃn/ *n* seoba

mike /maɪk/ *n coll* mikrofon

milch cow /mɪltʃ/ *n* krava muzara (+ *fig*)

mild /maɪld/ *adj* blag, ugodan, lagan **to put it ~ly** blago rečeno

mildew /'mɪldju:/ *n* snijet; plijesan

mile /maɪl/ *n* 1 milja 2 *pl coll* vrlo, jako, mnogo **~age** *n* 1 daljina u miljama 2 kilometraža 3 potrošnja goriva **~stone** *n* 1 miljokaz 2 *fig* prekretnica

military /'mɪlɪtrɪ/ *adj* vojni, vojnički **~ service** odsluženje vojnog roka **~ police** vojna policija • *in the ~* vojska **militate against sth** ići na štetu čega, raditi protiv **militia** /mɪ'lɪʃə/ *n* (the **~**) paravojska, milicija

milk /mɪlk/ *n* 1 mlijeko 2 *mod* mliječni **~ and water** *fig* luk i voda **~man** mljekar **~ shake** frape **~ tooth** mliječni zub **~y** *adj* 1 mliječan 2 mutan **the Milky Way** Mliječna staza • *vt, vi* 1 musti; davati mlijeko 2 *fig* (iz)musti, izvlačiti (novac, informacije)

mill /mɪl/ *n* 1 mlin 2 tvornica 3 mlinac, žrvanj **cotton ~** predionica pamuka **paper ~** tvornica papira **~er** *n* mlinar • *vt* 1 (sa)mljeti 2 valjati, obrađivati kovinu 3 zupčati kovani novac **~ about/around** *coll* miljeti, razmiliti se

millennium /mɪ'lenɪəm/ *n* (*pl* **-nia**, **~s**) tisućljeće

millet /'mɪlɪt/ *n* proso

milligram(me) /'mɪlɪgræm/ *n* miligram

millimetre (**-meter** *US*) /'mɪlɪ, mi:tə(r)/ milimetar

milliner /'mɪlɪnə(r)/ *n* kitničarka, modistica **~ry** *n* kitničarstvo

million /'mɪlɪən/ *n* milijun **feel/look like a ~ dollars** *coll* osjećati se/izgledati sjajno **~aire** /,mɪlɪə'neə(r)/ *n* milijunaš

mime /maɪm/ *n* 1 mimika; pantomima 2 pantomimičar • *vi, vt* glumiti/objasniti mimikom/pantomimom, oponašati **mimic** /'mɪmɪk/ *n* mimičar, imitator ○ *vt* 1 oponašati, imitirati 2 nalikovati na što ○ *adj* lažan, tobožnji **~ry** *n* 1 oponašanje, imitiranje 2 mimikrija

mince /mɪns/ *vt* 1 (i)sjeckati, kosati,

mljeti, faširati 2 prenemagati se, prenavljati se; hodati sitnim koracima **~d meat** mljeveno meso **a mincing machine/a ~r** stroj za mljevenje mesa **not to ~ matters/one's words** govoriti otvoreno/bez uvijanja, nemati dlake na jeziku • *n* 1 *GB* mljeveno meso 2 *US* **~mincemeat** *n* miješano sušeno voće za kolač **make ~meat of** *fig* samljeti *coll*

mind /maɪnd/ *n* 1 pamet, misli 2 um, razum 3 pamćenje, sjećanje 4 pozornost 5 namjera, nakana, volja, želja 6 mišljenje 7 duh, duša **be on one's ~** biti na umu **to my ~** po mom mišljenju **be/go out of one's ~** sići s uma, poludjeti, skrenuti **bring/call sth to ~** (pri)sjetiti se **bear/keep in ~** držati/imati na umu **change one's ~** predomisliti se **make up one's ~** odlučiti **frame of ~** raspoloženje **absence/presence of ~** odsutnost/prisutnost duha **in one's ~'s eye** u mislima, pred očima **speak one's ~** otvoreno reći *I'll give him a piece of my ~* očitat ću mu bukvicu **evil~ed** opak, zloban **high~ed** plemenit, velikodušan **strong~ed** odlučan, jake volje **~er** *n* pazitelj; tjelohranitelj, osobni čuvar **~less** *adj* 1 (of) koji ne obraća pozornost na 2 besmislen, nerazuman • *vt, vi* 1 paziti (na što), obraćati pozornost na, mariti 2 brinuti se za (koga/što) 3 protiviti se; zamjeriti, prigovarati *I don't* **~** nemam ništa protiv *never* **~** ništa za to **~** *your own business* gledaj svoja posla *do you* **~** *if I smoke/do you* **~** *my smoking?* smeta li vam ako pušim?

mine (1) /maɪn/ *poss pron* moj **that book is ~** to je moja knjiga **a friend of ~** jedan moj prijatelj

mine (2) *n* 1 rudnik 2 *fig* neiscrpan izvor 3 *mil* mina **~ disposal** razminiravanje **~field** minsko polje **~sweeper** minolovac • *vt, vi* 1 (for) kopati/vaditi rudu 2 *mil* minirati; dići u zrak **~er** *n* 1 rudar 2 *mil* miner **mining** /'maɪnɪŋ/ *n* rudarstvo

mineral /'mɪnərəl/ *n* 1 mineral 2 *pl GB* osvježavajuća pića • *adj* mineralni, rudni **~ water** mineralna voda

mingle /'mɪŋgl/ vt, vi (with) (po)miješati (se), izmiješati (se); družiti se

miniature /'mɪnɪtʃə(r)/ n minijatura **in ~ u malome** • adj minijaturan

minicab /'mɪnɪkæb/ n GB privatni taksi (naručuje se telefonom)

minimal /'mɪnɪml/ adj minimalan

minimize /'mɪnɪmaɪz/ vt umanjiti

minimum /'mɪnɪməm/ n najmanji iznos, donja granica **minimum wage** najniži zajamčeni dohodak

minion /'mɪnɪən/ n derog sljedbenik, pristaša, poslušnik

miniskirt /'mɪnɪskɜ:t/ n mini-suknja; minica coll

minister /'mɪnɪstə(r)/ n 1 ministar 2 svećenik 3 izaslanik, predstavnik **~ial** /,mɪnɪ'stɪərɪəl/ adj ministarski • vi (to) brinuti se o, pomagati; zadovoljiti

ministry /'mɪnɪstrɪ/ n 1 ministarstvo 2 svećenstvo **the M~ of Defence/-Finance** Ministarstvo obrane/financija

mink /mɪŋk/ n zerdav, nerc

minnow /'mɪnəʊ/ n 1 klen 2 fig sitna riba

minor /'maɪnə(r)/ adj 1 manji, manje važan 2 malen, neznatan 3 mol • n leg maloljetnik **~ity** /maɪ'nɒrətɪ/ n 1 manjina 2 leg maloljetnost **in a/the minority** u manjini

mint (1) /mɪnt/ n 1 metvica 2 pepermint

mint (2) n kovnica novca **earn/make a ~ (of money)** zarađivati brdo novca **in ~ condition** kao nov, savršeno očuvan

minus /'maɪnəs/ prep 1 manje 2 coll bez • n 1 minus 2 manjak 3 nedostatak

minuscule /'mɪnəskju:l/ adj sitan, sićušan, vrlo malen

minute (1) /'mɪnɪt/ n 1 minuta 2 coll tren, čas 3 pl zapisnik **in a ~ odmah take ~s** voditi zapisnik

minute (2) /maɪ'nju:t/ adj 1 sićušan, sitan 2 iscrpan, podroban, poman **minutiae** /maɪ'nju:ʃɪː/ n pl pojedinosti, potankosti, detalji

miracle /'mɪrəkl/ n čudo **miraculous** /mɪ'rækjʊləs/ adj čudesan

mirage /'mɪrɑ:ʒ/ n fatamorgana, iluzija

mire /'maɪə(r)/ n blato, glib, mulj, kaljuža **drag sb/sb's name through the ~** (javno) blatiti

mirror /'mɪrə(r)/ n ogledalo, zrcalo • vt odražavati

mirth /mɜ:θ/ n veselje, smijeh, radost **~less** adj neveseo

misadventure /,mɪsəd'ventʃə(r)/ n nesreća; nezgoda

misanthrope, misanthropist /'mɪsnθrəʊp, mɪs'ænθrəpɪst/ n čovjekomrzac

misapprehension /,mɪsæprɪ'henʃn/ n pogrešno shvaćanje; nesporazum **be under a ~** biti u zabludi

miscalculate /,mɪs'kælkjʊleɪt/ vt, vi 1 pogrešno (pro)računati 2 pogrešno prosuditi/ocijeniti

miscarriage /,mɪs'kærɪdʒ/ n 1 pobačaj 2 neuspjeh

miscellaneous /,mɪsə'leɪnɪəs/ adj mješovit, (po)miješan, razni

mischance /,mɪs'tʃɑ:ns/ n nesreća, nesretan slučaj, slučajnost

mischief /'mɪstʃɪf/ n 1 nevaljalština, nepodopština, nestašluk, vragolija 2 pakost, zloba 3 form šteta; nesreća, nedaća, zlo 4 coll nestaško, vragolan **mischievous** /'mɪstʃɪvəs/ adj 1 nestašan, vragolast 2 pakostan, zloban 3 štetan

misconception /,mɪskən'sepʃn/ n pogrešno shvaćanje

misconduct /,mɪs'kɒndʌkt/ n 1 prijestup 2 loše upravljanje 3 preljub

misconstrue /,mɪskən'stru:/ vt pogrešno shvatiti/(pro)tumačiti, iskriviti

misdeed /,mɪs'di:d/ n nedjelo, zlodjelo; prekršaj, prijestup

misdemeanour /,mɪsdɪ'mi:nə(r)/ n leg prekršaj

miser /'maɪzə(r)/ n škrtac **~ly** adj škrt; poput škrca

miserable /'mɪzrəbl/ adj bijedan, jadan, nesretan **misery** /'mɪzərɪ/ n 1 bijeda, jad, nevolja 2 patnja, muka **put sb out of ~ misery** skratiti muke

misfire /,mɪs'faɪə(r)/ vi 1 zatajiti (oružje, motor) 2 coll poći krivo, ne upaliti (šala, plan)

misfit /'mɪsfɪt/ n (društveno) neprilagođena osoba, autsajder

misfortune /,mɪs'fɔːtʃuːn/ n nesreća, nezgoda, nevolja, peh

misgiving /,mɪs'gɪvɪŋ/ n bojazan, nepovjerenje, sumnja

misguided /,mɪs'gaɪdɪd/ adj zaveden, pogrešan

mishandle /,mɪs'hændl/ vt 1 pogrešno/nespretno rukovati (čime) 2 grubo postupati (s kime)

mishap /'mɪshæp/ n nezgoda

misinform /,mɪsɪn'fɔːm/ vt loše obavijestiti

misinterpret /,mɪsɪn'tɜːprɪt/ vt pogrešno (pro)tumačiti

misjudge /,mɪs'dʒʌdʒ/ vt pogrešno procijeniti/(pro)suditi

mislaid v irreg → mislay

mislay /,mɪs'leɪ/ vt irreg zametnuti

mislead vt irreg zavesti, zavarati ~**ing** adj koji navodi na pogrešno mišljenje

misled v irreg → mislead

misnomer /,mɪs'nəʊmə(r)/ n pogrešan naziv

misplace /,mɪs'pleɪs/ vt 1 zametnuti 2 (po)staviti na krivo mjesto your trust in him is ~d on ne zaslužuje tvoje povjerenje

misprint /,mɪs'prɪnt/ n tiskarska pogreška

miss (1) /mɪs/ vt,vi 1 previdjeti, ne opaziti; ne čuti; ne shvatiti 2 promašiti; izbjeći 3 nedostajati (komu); primijetiti da tko ili što nedostaje 4 propustiti (priliku, sastanak) 5 zakasniti na (autobus, avion, vlak) ~ **sb/sth out** izostaviti, ispustiti, preskočiti ~ **out on sth** propustiti (što zabavno) ~**ing** adj koji nedostaje **be** ~**ing** nedostajati **the dead, wounded and missing** mil poginuli, ranjeni i nestali **the** ~**ing link** fig karika koja nedostaje, nepoznata karika • n promašaj; neuspjeh **give sth a** ~ GB coll propustiti, preskočiti

Miss (2) n gospođica

misshapen /,mɪs'ʃeɪpən/ adj izobličen, deformiran, kriv

missile /'mɪsaɪl/ n projektil, raketa

guided ~ navođena raketa

mission /'mɪʃn/ n 1 zadatak, zadaća, uloga 2 mil borbeni zadatak, let 3 izaslanstvo 4 misija ~ **in life** životni cilj, životni poziv ~**ary** /'mɪʃənrɪ/ n misionar ○ adj misionarski

misspell /,mɪs'spel/ vt irreg pogrešno napisati

misspelt v irreg → misspell

misspend /,mɪs'spend/ vt irreg protratiti, rasipati

misspent /,mɪs'spent/ v irreg → misspend

missus, missis /'mɪsɪz/ n coll, (the, my, his, your ~) žena (supruga)

mist /mɪst/ n (su)maglica; zamagljenost • vt,vi (over) zamagliti (se) ~**y** adj 1 maglovit; zamagljen 2 mutan, nejasan

mistake /mɪ'steɪk/ n pogreška; zabuna **by** ~ zabunom, greškom **and no** ~ coll nema sumnje **make a** ~ pogriješiti • vt,vi irreg 1 pogriješiti, zabuniti se, pogrešno shvatiti 2 (sb/sth for sb/sth) zamijeniti (koga/što s kim/čim) **be** ~**n** (about sth) varati se, biti u zabludi

mistaken v irreg → mistake

mister /'mɪstə(r)/ n (abbrev Mr) gospodin

mistletoe /'mɪsltəʊ/ n imela

mistook v irreg → mistake

mistress /'mɪstrɪs/ n 1 gospodarica, gazdarica 2 ljubavnica 3 poet ljubljena, gospa 4 GB učiteljica

mistrust /,mɪs'trʌst/ vt ne vjerovati, biti nepovjerljiv prema • n (of) nepovjerenje u

misunderstand /,mɪs,ʌndə'stænd/ vt irreg pogrešno razumjeti ~**ing** n nesporazum

misunderstood /,mɪs'ʌndə'stʊd/ v irreg → misunderstand

misuse /,mɪs'juːz/ vt pogrešno upotrijebiti/primijeniti; zloupotrijebiti • /,mɪs'juːs/ n zloupotreba

mitigate /'mɪtɪgeɪt/ vt ublažiti, olakšati **mitigating circumstances** olakotne okolnosti

mitten /'mɪtn/ n rukavica bez prstiju

mix /mɪks/ vt,vi 1 (up) (po)miješati (se) 2 (with) družiti se, slagati se 3 (up with) zamijeniti, pobrkati **4** (be/get **~ed up** in/with sth/sb) biti upleten u, uplesti se u, spetljati se s **5** miksati **~ed up** *adj* zbunjen, smeten, smušen **~up** *n* zbrka, pometnja **in ~ed company** u društvu žena **~ed doubles** *sport* mješoviti parovi • *n* mješavina, smjesa **~er** *n* miješalica, mikser **a good ~er** druželjubiva osoba **~ture** /'mɪkstʃə(r)/ *n* (of) mješavina, smjesa

moan /məʊn/ *n* jauk(anje), stenjanje; huka (vjetra) • *vi* **1** stenjati, jaukati; hukati **2** (about) jadati se, žaliti se na

moat /məʊt/ *n* jarak (oko zamka)

mob /mɒb/ *n* **1** svjetina, rulja, gomila **2** banda **3** (the ~) mafija • *vt* okružiti gomilom, navaliti, nahrupiti na

mobile /'məʊbaɪl/ *adj* **1** pokretan, pokretljiv **2** promjenljiv ~ **home** *US* kuća na kotačima

mobility /məʊ'bɪlətɪ/ *n* pokretnost

mobilize /'məʊbɪlaɪz/ *vt,vi* mobilizirati

moccasin /'mɒkəsɪn/ *n* mokasina

mock /mɒk/ *vt, vi* **1** (sb/at sb/sth) **1** rugati se, ismijavati, sprdati se (komu/čemu, iz koga/čega) **2** imitirati, oponašati • *adj* lažan, tobožnji, patvoren **~ery** /'mɒkərɪ/ *n* **1** izrugivanje, sprdnja **2** ismijavanje, oponašanje **3** *fig* lakrdija **make a mockery of** ismijati, pretvoriti u farsu **~ingbird** *n* američki drozd **~up** *n* maketa u naravnoj veličini

mode /məʊd/ *n* **1** način **2** tonalitet

model /'mɒdl/ *n* **1** uzorak, model, maketa **2** maneken(ka) **3** uzor **on the ~ of** po uzoru na • *adj* uzoran • *vt, vi* **1** (in) oblikovati, modelirati **2** raditi kao maneken(ka)/model   ~ **oneself/sth on sb/sth** slijediti čiji uzor, napraviti što po uzoru na

modem /'məʊdəm/ *n comp* modem

moderate (1) /'mɒdərət/ *adj* umjeren, (o)srednji

moderate (2) /'mɒdəreɪt/ *vt,vi* **1** smanjiti, ublažiti **2** obuzdati, smiriti (se) **moderation** /,mɒdə'reɪʃn/ *n* **1** umjerenost **2** (in) ublažavanje, umanjivanje **in moderation** umjereno

modern /'mɒdn/ *adj* moderan, nov, suvremen, današnji **~ize** /'mɒdənaɪz/

vt, vi modernizirati, osuvremeniti (se)

modest /'mɒdɪst/ *adj* (about) **1** skroman, čedan, jednostavan **2** (o)srednji, umjeren **~y** /'mɒdɪstɪ/ *n* skromnost

modicum /'mɒdɪkəm/ *n* (**a ~ of**) mrvica, truna, zrno, nešto malo

modify /'mɒdɪfaɪ/ *vt* **1** izmijeniti, preinačiti **2** ublažiti **3** *gram* odredivati smisao riječi **modification** /,mɒdɪfɪ'keɪʃn/ *n* izmjena, preinaka

module /'mɒdju:l/ *n* **1** sastavni dio; element (pokućstva/građevine) **2** modul

mog(gy) /'mɒgɪ/ *n GB coll* mačka, maca

mohair /'məʊheə(r)/ *n* moher

moist /mɔɪst/ *adj* vlažan, navlažen **~en** *vt,vi* navlažiti **~ure** /'mɔɪstʃə(r)/ *n* vlaga **moisturizer** *n* hidratantna krema

molar /'məʊlə(r)/ *n* kutnjak

molasses /mə'læsɪz/ *n* melasa, šećerni sirup

mold *US* → **mould**

mole (1) /məʊl/ *n* **1** krtica **2** špijun u vlastitim redovima,"krtica" **~hill** krtičnjak *make a mountain out of a ~hill* od buhe praviti slona

mole (2) /məʊl/ *n* madež

molest /mə'lest/ *vt* **1** dosađivati, dodijavati, uznemiravati **2** napastovati

mollify /'mɒlɪfaɪ/ *vt* ublažiti, smiriti, umiriti

molten /'məʊltən/ *adj* rastaljen

moment /'məʊmənt/ *n* **1** čas(ak), tren(utak) **2** *form* važnost, značenje **~ary** /'məʊməntrɪ/ *adj* trenutan **momentous** /mə'mentəs/ *adj* važan, značajan

momentum /mə'mentəm/ *n fig* **1** zamah **2** moment sile

monarch /'mɒnək/ *n* vladar, monarh **~y** /'mɒnəkɪ/ *n* monarhija

monastery /'mɒnəstrɪ/ *n* samostan **monastic** /mə'næstɪk/ *adj* **1** samostanski **2** redovnički

Monday /'mʌndɪ/ *n* ponedjeljak **on ~** u ponedjeljak **on ~s** ponedjeljkom

monetary /'mʌnɪtrɪ/ *adj* novčani, monetarni

money /'mʌnɪ/ *n* **1** novac **2** *fig*

bogatstvo **earn/make** ~ zaraditi novac ~**ed** *adj* imućan, bogat ~**-lender** lihvar, zelenaš ~ **order** poštanska uplatnica ~**-spinner** *GB coll* nešto što donosi veliku zaradu, nešto oko čega se vrti velika lova *coll*

mongol /'mɒŋgl/ *n* mongoloid

mongrel /'mʌŋgrəl/ *n* 1 pas mješanac, džukela 2 mješanac, križanac, hibrid

monitor /'mɒnɪtə(r)/ *n* 1 monitor, kontrolni uređaj 2 redar (u školi) 3 promatrač • *vt* pratiti, nadzirati, kontrolirati

monk /mʌŋk/ *n* redovnik

monkey /'mʌŋkɪ/ *n* 1 majmun 2 *coll* nestaško 3 *GB sl* 500 ž/$ ~ **nut** *GB* kikiriki ~ **wrench** francuski ključ ~ **business/tricks** psine, gluposti • *vi, vt* 1 (about/around) *coll* glupirati se 2 (with) petljati, prčkati po

monochrome /'mɒnəkrəum/ *adj* 1 jednobojan 2 *fig* dosadan, jednoličan ~ **television** crno-bijeli televizor

monopoly /mə'nɒpəlɪ/ *n* 1 (of) monopol, isključivo pravo (na što) 2 monopoli (igra) **monopolize** *vt* monopolizirati, imati monopol nad **monopolize the conversation** voditi glavnu riječ

monosyllable /'mɒnəsɪləbl/ *n* jednosložna riječ

monotonous /mə'nɒtənəs/ *adj* jednoličan, monoton; dosadan **monotony** /mə'nɒtənɪ/ *n* jednoličnost, monotonija

monster /'mɒnstə(r)/ *n* čudovište; nakaza **monstrosity** /mɒn'strɒsətɪ/ *n* 1 grozota 2 ružna građevina **monstrous** /'mɒnstrəs/ *adj* 1 čudovišan, grozan, užasan 2 divovski, golem 3 *coll* apsurdan, nevjerojatan

month /mʌnθ/ *n* mjesec, mjesec dana ~**ly** *adj* mjesečni ○ *adv* mjesečno ○ *n* mjesečnik

monument /'mɒnjumənt/ *n* (to) spomenik ~**al** /ˌmɒnju'mentl/ *adj* 1 spomenički 2 veličanstven, monumentalan 3 *coll* kolosalan, velik

moo /mu:/ *n* mukanje • *int* mu • *vi* mukati

mood /mu:d/ *n* 1 raspoloženje, ćud 2 *gram* način **in a good/bad** ~ u dobrom/lošem raspoloženju, dobre/loše volje **be in the** ~ **for** biti raspoložen, imati volju za ~**y** *adj* 1 ćudljiv 2 mrk, zlovoljan

moon /mu:n/ *n* Mjesec **once in a blue** ~ vrlo rijetko **be over the** ~ *coll* biti presretan ~**light** *n* mjesečina ○ *vi* raditi na crno/u fušu *coll* ~**lit** *adj* obasjan mjesečinom

moor (1) /muə(r)/ *n* *GB* pustopoljina, tresetište, vriština

moor (2) *vt, vi* usidriti (se), privezati (brod, čamac)

moose /mu:s/ *n* sjevernoamerički los

moot /mu:t/ *adj* a ~ **point/question** prijeporno/neriješeno/sporno pitanje • *vt* staviti na razmatranje, pokrenuti pitanje

mop /mɒp/ *n* 1 četka/otirač za pranje poda 2 raskuštrana kosa • *vt* (up) 1 obrisati, oprati (pod) 2 obrisati (znoj) 3 krpom pokupiti tekućinu; počistiti 4 *coll* dovršiti (posao) 5 potrošiti, iscrpsti (sredstva) ~**ping-up operations** *mil* operacije čišćenja

mope /məup/ *vi* biti potišten/pokunjen, prepustiti se tuzi ~ **around the house** vući se po kući

moral /'mɒrəl/ *adj* 1 moralan, ćudoredan 2 krepostan • *n* 1 pouka 2 (*pl*) moral, ćudorednost, ćudorede ~**e** /mɒ'rɑ:l/ *n* (+ *mil*) moral, samodisciplina ~**ity** /mə'rælətɪ/ *n* moralnost

moratorium /ˌmɒrə'tɔ:rɪəm/ *n* moratorij; odgoda plaćanja

morbid /'mɔ:bɪd/ *adj* nezdrav, morbidan

more /mɔ:(r)/ *adj, adv, n* više, još ~ **beautiful/easily** (than) ljepši/lakše (nego/od) **once** ~ još jednom **any** ~/**no** ~ više ~ **and** ~ sve više i više ~ **or less** otprilike, više ili manje **no** ~ ... **than** ništa više ... nego **what is** ~ štoviše ~**over** /mɔ:'rəuvə(r)/ *adv* osim toga, povrh toga; nadalje, uz to

morgue /mɔ:g/ *n* mrtvačnica

moribund /'mɔ:rɪbʌnd/ *adj* 1 na izdisaju, na samrti 2 *fig* mrtav

morning /'mɔ:nɪŋ/ *n* 1 jutro 2 prijepodne **this** ~ jutros **yesterday** ~ jučer ujutro **in the** ~ ujutro **from** ~ **till night** od jutra do mraka

moron /'mɔːrɒn/ *n* 1 slaboumnik, debil 2 *coll* budala, idiot

morose /mə'rəʊs/ *adj* mrzovoljan

morphine /'mɔːfiːn/ *n* morfij

Morse (code) /mɔːs/ *n* Morseova abeceda

morsel /'mɔːsl/ *n* 1 zalogaj 2 komadić, mrvica

mortal /'mɔːtl/ *adj* 1 smrtni 2 ljudski 3 smrtonosan 4 samrtan 5 doživotan • *n* smrtnik **~ity** /mɔː'tæləti/ *n* 1 smrtnost 2 mortalitet

mortar /'mɔːtə(r)/ *n* 1 žbuka 2 *mil* minobacač 3 mužar

mortgage /'mɔːgɪdʒ/ *n* hipoteka, zalog • *vt* založiti, opteretiti hipotekom

mortify /'mɔːtɪfaɪ/ *vt,vi* 1 poniziti, uvrijediti, posramiti, mučiti 2 *med* obamirati (meso)

mortuary /'mɔːtʃərɪ/ *n* mrtvačnica

mosaic /məʊ'zeɪɪk/ *n* mozaik

Moslem /'mɒzləm/ → **Muslim**

mosque /mɒsk/ *n* džamija

mosquito /mə'skiːtəʊ/ *n* komarac

moss /mɒs/ *n* mahovina **~y** *adj* obrastao mahovinom, poput mahovine

most /məʊst/ *adj, adv,* 1 najviše, naj- (za tvorbu superlativa); većina, najveći dio ~ **people** većina the ~ *expensive car* najskuplji auto *a* ~ *interesting book* vrlo zanimljiva knjiga **at (the)** ~/**at the very** ~ u najboljem slučaju **make the** ~ **of** iskoristiti što na najbolji način **~ly** *adv* (po)najviše, većinom, uglavnom

moth /mɒθ/ *n* 1 noćni leptir 2 (**clothes** ~) moljac **~ball** naftalinska kuglica **in ~balls** *fig* u naftalinu

mother /'mʌðə(r)/ *n* majka ~ **country** domovina **~hood** majčinstvo **~-in-law** punica; svekrva **~ly** *adv* majčinski **~-to-be** buduća majka ~ **tongue** materinski jezik • *vt* ponašati se majčinski prema komu, tetošiti

motif /məʊ'tiːf/ *n* 1 (glavni) motiv 2 uzorak

motion /'məʊʃn/ *n* 1 kretanje, gibanje, micanje 2 kretnja, pokret 3 prijedlog **put/set sth in** ~ pokrenuti što **go through the ~s** (of doing sth) *coll* učiniti što iz formalnosti/reda radi **~less** *adj* nepokretan, nepomičan ~

picture film • *vt,vi* (to) mahnuti komu, dati znak

motivate /'məʊtɪveɪt/ *vt* motivirati, potaknuti **motivation** /,məʊtɪ'veɪʃn/ *n* motivacija, pobuda **motive** /'məʊtɪv/ *n* 1 motiv, pobuda, povod 2 → **motif**

motley /'mɒtlɪ/ *adj* šaren, šarolik

motor /'məʊtə(r)/ *n* 1 motor, stroj 2 *GB arch* automobil • *adj* motorni; automobilski **~bike** motocikl, motor **~boat** motorni čamac **~cade** *n* povorka vozila **~cycle** motocikl **~ist** *n* vozač automobila ~ **vehicle** motorno vozilo **~way** auto-cesta • *vi GB* voziti se automobilom

mottled /'mɒtld/ *adj* išaran, pjegast

mould (1) /məʊld/ *n* 1 kalup, odljev, šablona 2 *fig* karakter, kov • *vt* 1 modelirati, formirati, oblikovati, ukalupiti (+ *fig*) 2 (to) pripiti se, priljubiti se (odjeća)

mould (2) *n* 1 plijesan 2 zemlja crnica, humus **~y** *adj* 1 pljesniv 2 ustajao 3 *fig* zastario **~er** *vi* (away) trunuti, propadati

moult /məʊlt/ *vt,vi* mitariti se; linjati se

mound /maʊnd/ *n* nasip, humak; brežuljak

mount (1) /maʊnt/ *vt,vi* 1 popeti se, penjati se; sjesti (na bicikl, konja), uzjahati; uzdići se 2 (up) (po)rasti, poveća(va)ti se 3 izvesti (napad) 4 montirati, nalijepiti, optočiti, učvrstiti, ugraditi; postaviti (izložbu, predstavu) 5 opasati **~ed police** konjička policija ~ **guard** (at/over) čuvati stražu • *n* 1 podloga, postolje, okvir 2 jahaća životinja

mount (2) *n* (u geogr. imenima) planina

mountain /'maʊntɪn/ *n* 1 planina 2 *fig* brdo, gomila, hrpa **~eer** /,maʊntɪ'nɪə(r)/ *n* planinar **~eering** *n* planinarenje **~eous** /'maʊntɪnəs/ *adj* 1 planinski, brdovit 2 golem ~ **lion** puma **~side** padina **~top** planinski vrh

mountebank /'maʊntɪbæŋk/ *n* varalica, šarlatan

mourn /mɔːn/ *vt,vi* (for/over) žaliti za, oplakivati, tugovati za **~er** *n* ožalošćeni **~ful** *adj* žalostan, tužan **~ing** *n* 1 žalost 2 crnina **be in ~ing** nositi crninu, biti u žalosti

mouse /maʊs/ *n* (*pl* **mice**) miš (+ *comp*) **~trap** mišolovka **mousy** *adj* 1 poput miša, mišji 2 mišje boje, sivkastosmeđ 3 *fig derog* plah, plašljiv, sramežljiv

mousse /muːs/ *n* pjena

moustache (**mustache** US) /mə'stɑːʃ/ *n* brk

mouth /maʊθ/ *n* 1 usta 2 ulaz, otvor 3 ušće **~ful** *n* 1 zalogaj 2 *coll* teško izgovorljiva riječ/fraza **by word of ~** usmenom predajom **down in the ~** potišten, snužden, tužan **a big ~** *fig* dugačak jezik **~organ** *coll* usna harmonika **~piece** 1 pisak (glazbala), usnik (lule) 2 *fig* koji govori u čije ime **~wash** 1 vodica za usta 2 *fig* cuga *coll* **~watering** *adj* koji izaziva zazubice • *vt,vi* /maʊð/ 1 otvarati usta 2 sipati riječi

move /muːv/ *n* 1 kretanje, micanje 2 pokret; potez 3 selidba 4 *fig* korak, mjera **on the ~** u pokretu **make a ~** **a.** krenuti, poći **b.** poduzeti korake **get a ~ on** *coll* požuriti se • *vt,vi* 1 kretati se, micati (se), pomaknuti (se), premjestiti 2 napredovati 3 preseliti se 4 dirnuti, ganuti 5 potaknuti, ponukati 6 (for) predložiti 7 povući potez 8 (on) poduzeti što 9 *comm* prodavati se **~ house** *GB* preseliti se **~ with the times** ići ukorak s vremenom **~ along** pomaknuti se naprijed **~ in** useliti se **~ off** otići, udaljiti se, odmaknuti se **~ on a.** napredovati, ići dalje, krenuti naprijed **b.** potjerati dalje **~ out** iseliti se **~ over** pomaknuti se, napraviti mjesta **~able** /'muːvəbl/ *adj* pomičan, pokretan, pokretljiv **~ables** *n pl* pokretna imovina, pokretnina **~ment** *n* 1 gibanje, kretanje 2 kretnja; pokret 3 razvoj, odvijanje 4 stavak 5 (**bowel ~ -ment**) stolica **~r** *n* predlagač **the prime ~r** glavni pokretač **movie** /'muːvɪ/ *n* US film **the movies** *n pl* US kino **moving** *adj* 1 dirljiv, ganutljiv 2 koji se pokreće, pokretljiv, pokretan

mow /məʊ/ *vt, vi irreg pp* (po)kositi **~ sb down** *fig* pokositi

mown *v irreg* → **mow**

Mr /'mɪstə(r)/ → **mister**

Mrs /'mɪsɪz/ *n* gospođa

Ms /mɪz/ *n* gospođa (oslovljavanje žene bez obzira na bračno stanje)

much /mʌtʃ/ *adj, adv, n* 1 mnogo 2 vrlo; uvelike; prilično, gotovo, skoro 3 velik dio **how ~ is ...?** koliko stoji/košta *coll* ...? **so ~** toliko **too ~** previše **as ~** (as) isto toliko (koliko) **~ as** koliko god, ma koliko (da) **~ the same** gotovo jednak, skoro isti **~ to my surprise** na moje veliko iznenađenje **this ~** ovoliko **make ~ of a.** pridavati preveliku važnost/pozornost **b.** dobro shvatiti/razumjeti

muck /mʌk/ *n* 1 blato; prljavština 2 (stajski) gnoj **make a ~ of sth** *GB coll* pokvariti, zabrljati **~y** *adj coll* 1 prljav, blatan 2 *GB* ružan, gadan (vrijeme) • *vt* gnojiti zemlju **~ about/around** *GB coll* **a.** glupirati se, budaliti **b.** motati se naokolo, besposličariti **~ in** *GB coll* uložiti zajedničke napore **~ out** očistiti (staju) od gnoja **~ up** *GB coll* **a.** zaprljati, zamazati **b.** zabrljati **~raking** *n fig* kopanje po prljavštini

mucus /'mjuːkəs/ *n* sluz, bale **mucous** /'mjuːkəs/ *adj* sluzav **mucous membrane** sluznica

mud /mʌd/ *n* blato **throw/fling/sling/ ~ at sb** *fig* blatiti koga, klevetati **~dy** *adj* 1 blatan 2 mutan 3 prljav (boja) 4 zbrkan, konfuzan **~guard** blatobran

muddle /'mʌdl/ *n* (**a ~**) nered, zbrka; smušenost **make a ~ of sth** pokvariti, zabrljati **~-headed** smušen, smeten • *vt* (up) 1 pomiješati, pobrkati 2 smesti, zbuniti 3 omamiti **~ up** pokvariti, zabrljati **~ through** nekako se provući

muff /mʌf/ *n* muf

muffin /'mʌfɪn/ *n* čajni kolačić

muffle /'mʌfl/ *vt* 1 prigušiti (zvuk) 2 (up) umotati, zamotati **~r** *n* 1 šal 2 US prigušivač

mug (1) /mʌg/ *n* 1 vrč, pehar; krigla *coll*; šalica za bijelu kavu 2 *GB coll* naivčina 3 *sl* lice, faca, njuška

mug (2) *vt,vi* **1** napasti, opljačkati, orobiti **2** (up) *GB coll* štrebati *coll*

muggy /'mʌgɪ/ *adj* sparan (vrijeme)

mulberry /'mʌlbrɪ/ *n* dud

mule (1) /mju:l/ *n* **1** mula, mazga **2** križanac **3** stroj za predenje

mule (2) *n* natikača

mull /mʌl/ *vt* (over) razmišljati, promisliti o ~**ed** *adj* kuhan (vino)

multi- /mʌltɪ/ *prefix* više-, multi-

multicoloured /'mʌltɪ,kʌləd/ *adj* šaren, višebojan

multilateral /,mʌltɪ'lætərəl/ *adj* mnogostran, višestran

multi-level *US* → **multistorey**

multiple /'mʌltɪpl/ *adj* mnogostruk, višestruk • *n* višekratnik

multiply /'mʌltɪplaɪ/ *vt,vi* **1** (by/together) pomnožiti **2** povećati **3** razmnožavati se **multiplication** /,mʌltɪplɪ'keɪʃn/ *n* množenje; razmnožavanje

multistorey *adj* višekatni

multitude /'mʌltɪtju:d/ *n* **1** mnoštvo **2** gomila, masa

mum (1) /mʌm/ *adj* keep ~ šutjeti, držati jezik za zubima • *int* tiho! pst! ~'s the word nikom ni riječi

mum(my) (2) *n* mama

mumble /'mʌmbl/ *vt,vi* (pro)mrmljati, mumljati

mummify /'mʌmɪfaɪ/ *vt* mumificirati, balzamirati **mummy** /'mʌmɪ/ *n* mumija

mumps /mʌmps/ *n med* mumps, zaušnjaci

munch /mʌntʃ/ *vt,vi* (away/at) žvakati; mljackati

mundane /mʌn'deɪn/ *adj* **1** svakodnevan, običan **2** ovozemaljski, svjetovni

municipal /mju:'nɪsɪpl/ *adj* gradski, općinski ~**ity** /mju:,nɪsɪ'pælətɪ/ *n* gradska općina; općina

munitions /mju:'nɪʃnz/ *n pl* vojna oprema

mural /'mjʊərəl/ *adj* zidni • *n* zidna slika, mural

murder /'mɜ:də(r)/ *n* ubojstvo, umorstvo **cry/scream/shout blue** ~ derati se iz petnih žila • *vt* **1** ubiti, umoriti **2** *coll* pokvariti, uništiti, izobličiti ~**er**

n ubojica ~**ous** *adj* ubilački; ubojit, smrtonosan

murky /'mɜ:kɪ/ *adj* taman, mračan

murmur /'mɜ:mə(r)/ *n* **1** mrmljanje; tihi šum **2** žubor(enje) **3** šum (srca) **4** gunđanje • *vt,vi* **1** mrmljati **2** žuboriti, romoniti **3** (at/against) gunđati, prigovarati

muscle /'mʌsl/ *n* **1** mišić **2** snaga not to move a ~ ni okom ne trepnuti ~**-bound** mišićav; nabildan *coll* ~**man 1** mišićav čovjek **2** tjelohranitelj; gorila *coll* **muscular** /'mʌskjʊlə(r)/ *adj* **1** mišićni **2** mišićav

muse (1) /mju:z/ *vi* (over/on/upon) utonuti u misli, zamisliti se nad

Muse (2) *n* muza

museum /mju:'zɪəm/ *n* muzej

mush /mʌʃ/ *n* kaša ~**y** *adj* **1** kašast **2** *coll* sladunjav

mushroom /'mʌʃrʊm/ *n* gljiva ~ **development** brzi/nagli razvoj • *vi fig* nicati kao gljive

music /'mju:zɪk/ *n* **1** glazba, muzika **2** note **face the** ~ suočiti se s neugodnostima/kritikama **set/put sth to** ~ uglazbiti ~ **centre** muzička linija ~ **hall** varijete ~**al** *adj* **1** glazbeni **2** muzikalan **3** melodičan ○ *n* mjuzikl ~**ian** /mju:'zɪʃn/ *n* glazbenik

musk /mʌsk/ *n* mošus

Muslim /'mʊzlɪm/ *n* musliman • *adj* muslimanski, islamski

mussel /'mʌsl/ *n* dagnja

must /mʌst/ *v modal* morati ~ **not** ne smjeti *they* ~ **have all gone home** mora da su svi otišli kući • *n fig* imperativ *the film is a* ~ ne smijete propustiti taj film

mustard /'mʌstəd/ *n* **1** gorušica **2** senf ~ **gas** iperit

muster /'mʌstə(r)/ *vt,vi* (up) **1** skupiti (se), okupiti (se) **2** prikupiti (snagu/hrabrost), pridobiti (podršku) • *n mil* smotra; zbor **2** okupljanje, skupljanje

musty /'mʌstɪ/ *adj* **1** pljesniv; ustajao **2** *fig* zastario

mute /mju:t/ *adj* nijem, bez glasa, tih • *n* nijema osoba • *vt* prigušiti (zvuk)

mutilate /'mju:tɪleɪt/ *vt* osakatiti, unakaziti (+ *fig*)

mutiny /'mju:tını/ *n* pobuna

mutt /mʌt/ *n coll* 1 budala 2 *US* pas mješanac, džukela

mutter /'mʌtə(r)/ *vt,vi* (at sb/to oneself) (pro)mrmljati, brundati, gunđati (na koga/za sebe) • *n* gunđanje, mrmljanje

mutton /'mʌtn/ *n* ovčetina

mutual /'mju:tʃʊəl/ *adj* 1 međusoban, obostran, uzajaman 2 zajednički

muzzle /'mʌzl/ *n* 1 gubica, njuška 2 brnjica 3 usta cijevi (puške, topa) • *vt* 1 staviti brnjicu na 2 *fig* ušutkati

my /maı/ *poss adj* moj, moja, moje *with ~ hands in ~ pockets* s rukama u džepovima **oh ~**! o moj bože! **~self** *reflex pron* 1 sebe, se, sebi, sobom 2 ja sam, osobno (**all**) **by ~self** sam, bez tuđe pomoći *I ~self wrote it/I*

wrote it ~self ja sam osobno to napisao

myopic /maı'ɒpık/ *adj* kratkovidan

myriad /'mırıəd/ *adj, n* bezbroj, mnoštvo

mystery /'mıstərı/ *n* 1 misterij, tajna, tajanstvenost, zagonetka 2 krimi-priča **~ play** misterij **mysterious** /mı'stıərıəs/ *adj* tajanstven, zagonetan

mystic /'mıstık/ *n* mistik **~(al)** *adj* mističan, tajanstven

mystify /'mıstıfaı/ *vt* smesti, zbuniti; mistificirati

mystique /mı'sti:k/ *n* tajna moć, tajna privlačnost, čar

myth /mıθ/ *n* 1 mit 2 bajka; izmišljotina **~ical** /'mıθıkl/ *adj* 1 mitski 2 izmišljen, nestvaran

mythology /mı'θɒlədʒı/ *n* mitologija

N

N, n /en/ 14. slovo engl. abecede, en

nab /næb/ *vt coll* uhvatiti, ščepati

nadir /'neɪdɪə(r)/ *n fig* samo dno, najniža točka

naff /næf/ *adj GB sl* blesav, bezvezan

nag (1) /næg/ *vi,vt* (at) prigovarati, gnjaviti, dosađivati • *n* dosadnjaković, gunđalo

nag (2) *n* ključe

nail /neɪl/ *n* 1 čavao **as hard as ~s** a. u odličnoj kondiciji b. nemilosrdan, tvrda srca 2 nokat **fight tooth and ~** boriti se noktima i zubima **~-biting** *adj* uzbudljiv, neizvjestan 3 *mod* za nokte • *vt* 1 zakovati, prikucati 2 *coll* ščepati 3 *coll* raskrinkati 4 **~ sb down** prisiliti (koga) da se izjasni

naive /naɪ'iːv/ *adj* naivan, bezazlen, lakovjeran **~ty/~té** *n* naivnost, bezazlenost

naked /'neɪkɪd/ *adj* 1 gol; ogoljen 2 jasan, neskriven, otvoren

name /neɪm/ *n* ime **first-/Christian/given ~** ime **family ~** prezime **call sb ~s** vrijeđati **~-day** imendan **not have a penny to one's ~** biti bez prebite pare **have a good/bad ~** biti na dobru/lošem glasu **in ~ only** samo na papiru **the ~ of the game** *sl* najbitnija stvar **~sake** imenjak **~less** *adj* 1 bezimen; anoniman 2 užasan, grozan • *vt* 1 (after/for) nazvati 2 navesti (čije) ime 3 nabrojiti 4 (as/for) imenovati, izabrati **~ly** *adv* konkretno, poimence

nanny /'næni/ *n* dadilja

nap /næp/ *vi* odspavati, prileći **catch sb ~ping** *coll* uloviti koga na spavanju • *n* kratak odmor

nape /neɪp/ *n* zatiljak

napkin /'næpkɪn/ *n* 1 ubrus, servijeta 2 *GB* pelena **sanitary ~** higijenski uložak

nappy /'næpi/ *n GB* pelena

narcotic /nɑː'kɒtɪk/ *n* 1 narkotik, droga 2 narkoman • *adj* uspavljujući

nark (1) /nɑːk/ *n GB sl* policijski doušnik

nark (2) *vt* uzrujati, ljutiti

narrate /nə'reɪt/ *vt* pripovijedati, pričati, prepričavati **~d by** *TV* tekst čitao **narrative** /'nærətɪv/ *n* pripovijetka ○ *adj* pripovjedački, pripovjedni **narrator** /nə'reɪtə(r)/ *n* pripovjedač

narrow /'nærəʊ/ *adj* 1 uzak **~gauge** *adj* uskotračan 2 (**~-minded**) uskogrudan, zadrt 3 tijesan, malen, za dlaku • *vt,vi* 1 suziti (se) 2 **~ down** skratiti, ograničiti **~ly** *adj* 1 za dlaku, jedva 2 pomno

nasal /'neɪzl/ *adj* nosni, nazalni • *n* nazal

nasty /'nɑːsti/ *adj* 1 neugodan, nezgodan; grub, zloban 2 težak, ozbiljan 3 odvratan, ružan 4 pokvaren

nation /'neɪʃn/ *n* nacija; narod **the United N~s** Ujedinjeni narodi **~wide** *adj* u cijeloj zemlji *adv* **~al** /'næʃnəl/ *adj* nacionalni; narodni **~ anthem** himna **~ government** vlada nacionalnog spasa **~ service** opća vojna obaveza ○ *n* državljanin **~alist** *n* nacionalist; borac za nacionalna prava ○ (**~alistic**) *adj* nacionalistički **~alism** *n* nacionalizam; borba za nacionalna prava **~ality** /,næʃə'næləti/ *n* 1 nacionalnost, državljanstvo 2 narod; narodnost **~alize** /'næʃnəlaɪz/ *vt* nacionalizirati

native /'neɪtɪv/ *adj* 1 rodni, domaći **~ language** materinski jezik **~ speaker** izvorni govornik *a ~ Dubliner* rođeni Dablinac 2 urođen 3 *derog* urođenički **go ~** *coll* sroditi se s okolinom • *n*

1 (of) koji je rodom iz, koji živi u 2 *derog* urođenik

Nativity /nəˈtɪvətɪ/ *n* (slika koja prikazuje) Kristovo rođenje ~ **scene/set** jaslice

natter /ˈnætə/ *vi* brbljati, čavrljati

natural /ˈnætʃrəl/ *adj* 1 prirodan, naravan 2 normalan, uobičajen 3 urođen 4 darovit, rođen (za što) 5 *arch euph* nezakonit ~**ism** *n* naturalizam ~**ize** *vt,vi* naturalizirati (se); prihvatiti (državljanstvo); poprimiti ~**ly** *adv* 1 prirodno 2 naravno

nature /ˈneɪtʃə(r)/ *n* priroda **by ~** po prirodi **naturism** *n* nudizam

naught /nɔːt/ *n arch* ništa

naughty /ˈnɔːtɪ/ *adj* 1 zločest, nestašan 2 *euph* škakljiv *fig*

nausea /ˈnɔːsɪə/ *n* mučnina ~**ting** *adj* odvratan, koji uzrokuje mučninu, koji tjera na povraćanje **nauseous** *adj* zgađen, koji osjeća mučninu

nautical /ˈnɔːtɪkl/ *adj* pomorski ~ **mile** morska milja

naval /ˈneɪvl/ *adj* mornarički

nave /neɪv/ *n* lađa (u crkvi)

navel /ˈneɪvl/ *n* pupak

navigate /ˈnævɪgeɪt/ *vt,vi* 1 kormilariti; pilotirati; upravljati 2 ploviti **navigator** *n* navigator **navigation** /ˌnævɪˈgeɪʃn/ *n* upravljanje; plovidba; navigacija **navigable** /ˈnævɪgəbl/ *adj* plovan

navvy /ˈnævɪ/ *n GB* radnik koji kopa kanale, gradi pruge i sl.

navy /ˈneɪvɪ/ *n* mornarica **merchant ~** trgovačka mornarica • *adj* tamnoplav

nay /neɪ/ *adv ne* • *n* glas protiv

Nazi /ˈnɑːtsɪ/ *n* nacist • *adj* nacistički ~**sm** *n* nacizam

Neanderthal /niːˈændətɑːl/ *n* 1 ~ **man** Neandertalac 2 *US coll* zadrta osoba, konzervativac

near /nɪə(r)/ *adj* 1 blizak 2 za dlaku izbjegnut • *adv* 1 blizu, nedaleko 2 gotovo ~**by** *adj* obližnji *adv* blizu ~**ly** *adv* gotovo

neat /niːt/ *adj* 1 uredan 2 čist 3 jednostavan 4 *US sl* super, odličan

nebulous /ˈnebjʊləs/ *adj* nejasan

necessary /ˈnesəsəɪ/ *adj* nužan **necessaries** *n pl* potrebne stvari **necessarily** *adv* nužno **necessity** /nɪˈsesətɪ/ *n* nužda, potreba **necessitate** /nɪˈsesɪteɪt/ *vt* učiniti nužnim

neck /nek/ *n* 1 vrat 2 vratina 3 grlo **up to one's ~** (in) do grla (u) ~ **and ~** izjednačen **stick one's ~ out** riskirati **by the ~** u boci 4 izrez, otvor V~ ~ V izrez ~**lace** /ˈneklɪs/ *n* lančić, ogrlica ~**line** izrez, otvor ~**tie** kravata

née /neɪ/ *adv* rođena, djevojačkog imena

need /niːd/ *n* potreba **be in ~ of** trebati **in ~** *euph* siromašan **if ~ be** bude li potrebno **a friend in ~ is a friend indeed** *prov* u nevolji se poznaje prijatelj • *v aux* trebati, morati **you ~n't** ne trebaš, ne moraš ~**ful** *n* **a.** *coll* sve što je potrebno **b.** *GB* novac ~**less** *adj* nepotreban ~**less to say** naravno, jasno ~**y** *adj* siromašan

needle /ˈniːdl/ *n* igla; iglica ~ **in a haystack** igla u plastu sijena ~**work** vez • *vt coll* zadirkivati, provocirati

negate /nɪˈgeɪt/ *vt* 1 uništiti 2 zanijekati, poreći

negative /ˈnegətɪv/ *adj* niječan; negativan (+ *fig*) • *n* 1 niječni odgovor 2 negativ • *vt coll* ne odobriti

neglect /nɪˈglekt/ *vt* zanemariti, zapustiti; ne učiniti • *n* zanemarivanje; zapuštenost ~**ful** *adj* nemaran, koji se ne brine

negligee /ˈneglɪʒeɪ/ *n* negliže

negligent /ˈneglɪdʒənt/ *adj* nemaran, koji se ne brine dovoljno

negligible /ˈneglɪdʒəbl/ *adj* zanemariv

negotiate /nɪˈgəʊʃɪeɪt/ *vi,vt* 1 pregovarati 2 postići pregovorima 3 *coll* postići, uspjeti, izvesti ~ *a river* prijeći rijeku **negotiator** *n* pregovarač **negotiation** /nɪˌgəʊsɪˈeɪʃn/ *n* 1 (~s) pregovori *pl* 2 nešto uspješno izvedeno

Negro /ˈniːgrəʊ/ *n derog* Crnac **Negress** /ˈniːgres/ Crnkinja

neigh /neɪ/ *vi* njištati

neighbour (-**bor** *US*) /ˈneɪbə(r)/ *n* susjed ~**hood** *n* susjedstvo, četvrt ~**ing** *adj* susjedni ~**ly** *adj* srdačan, dobrosusjedski

neither /ˈnaɪðə(r)/ *conj* ni ~..., **nor**...

ni..., ni... • *adv* ni *I don't know. -Me ~/~ do I.* Ja ne znam. -Ni ja.

neo- /'niːəʊ/ *prefix* neo-

neon /'niːɒn/ *n* 1 neon 2 *mod* neonski

nephew /'nevjuː, 'nefjuː/ *n* nećak

nerd /nɜːd/ *n coll* blesan, bezveznjaković

nerve /nɜːv/ *n* 1 živac 2 hrabrost, odvažnost 3 drskost, bezobrazluk • *vt,vi* (~ **oneself**) skupiti hrabrost **nervous** *adj* 1 koji ima tremu, koji se boji; napet 2 živčani **nervous breakdown** živčani slom, slom živaca **the nervous system** živčani sustav **nervy** *adj* 1 *GB sl* → **nervous** 1. 2 *US sl* bezobrazan

nest /nest/ *n* gnijezdo (+ *fig*) • **egg** novac spremljen za budućnost • *vi,vt* gnijezditi se; graditi gnijezdo

nestle /'nesl/ *vi,vt* smjestiti se (udobno), ležati

nestling /'neslɪŋ/ *n* ptić

net (1) /net/ *n* mreža (+ *fig*) • *vt* uloviti u mrežu/mrežom; prekriti/zaštititi mrežom ~**ting** *n* mreža ~**work** *n* mreža *fig*

net (2), **nett** *adj* netto • *vt* zaraditi

nettle /'netl/ *n* kopriva ~ **rash** koprivnjača • *vt* uzrujati

neurosis /njʊəˈrəʊsɪs/ *n* neuroza **neurotic** *adj* neurotičan

neuter /'njuːtə(r)/ *adj* 1 *gram* srednjeg roda 2 bespolan • *vt* sterilizirati (životinju)

neutral /'njuːtrəl/ *adj* nepristran; neutralan ~**ity** /njuːˈtrælɪti/ *n* neutralnost ~**ize** *vt* neutralizirati

neutron /'njuːtrɒn/ *n* neutron

never /'nevə(r)/ *adv* 1 nikad ~ **mind** nema veze, nije važno ~**theless** *adv* ipak, usprkos tome 2 uopće *he ~ showed up* nije se pojavio

new /njuː/ *adj* 1 nov ~**born** novorođen **brand** ~ nov novcat ~**comer** pridošlica ~**fangled** *adj* novotarije *n pl* ~**speak** *n* novogovor N~ **Year's Day** Nova godina 1. siječnja N~ **Year's Eve** Silvestrovo, Stara godina, 31. prosinca 2 mlad ~ **potatoes/peas** mladi krumpir/grašak ~ **Moon** mladi Mjesec ~**ly** *adv* nedavno

news /njuːz/ *n sg* vijesti *pl a piece of*

~/~ **item** vijest **break the** ~ priopćiti (ob. nešto neugodno) *that's* ~ *to me* nisam znao ~ **agency** novinska agencija ~**agent's** novinski kiosk ~**caster/reader** voditelj vijesti; spiker *coll* ~ **conference** konferencija za novinstvo ~**letter** bilten ~**paper a.** novine *pl* **b.** novinska kuća **c.** novinski papir ~**room** redakcija vijesti, desk

next /nekst/ *adj* idući, sljedeći *the ~ day* sutradan ~ **of kin** najbliža rodbina • *adv* 1 (odmah) zatim 2 idući put 3 ~ **to** odmah do, pokraj **the ~-to-last** predzadnji 4 ~ **to** skoro, gotovo ~**door** *adj* susjedni

nib /nɪb/ *n* pero, vršak nalivpera

nibble /'nɪbl/ *vt,vi* 1 (at/away/on) grickati; izgristi, progristi 2 (at) *fig* pokazati zanimanje (za)

nibs /nɪbz/ *n* **his** ~ *sl joc* njegovo veličanstvo

nice /naɪs/ *adj* 1 drag, srdačan, simpatičan, ljubazan 2 lijep, dobar ~**ty** *n* pojedinost **to a** ~**ty** točno, pomno

nick /nɪk/ *n* 1 urez, zarez 2 *GB sl* zatvor **the Old N~** Vrag **in the** ~ **of time** u zadnji tren • *vt* 1 zarezati 2 *GB sl* uhvatiti, ščepati 3 *GB coll* ukrasti, maznuti, zdipiti

nickel /'nɪkl/ *n* 1 *chem* nikl 2 *US* (novčić od) 5 centi • *vt* (~-**plate**) (po)niklati

nickname /'nɪkneɪm/ *n* nadimak • *vt* nadjenuti nadimak, prozvati

nicotine /'nɪkətiːn/ *n* nikotin

niece /niːs/ *n* nećakinja

niff /nɪf/ *n GB coll* smrad

nifty /'nɪfti/ *adj coll* zgodan, praktičan

niggard /'nɪɡəd/ *n* derog škrtac, cicija ~**ly** *adj* škrt

nigger /'nɪɡə(r)/ *n tab* derog *sl* crnčuga *tab* derog

niggle /'nɪɡl/ *vi* (about/over) cjepidlačiti, sitničariti; zanovijetati **niggling** *adj* 1 koji stalno zanovijeta 2 pipav, minuciozan

night /naɪt/ *n* 1 noć **by** ~ noću **good** ~! laku noć! 2 večer **last** ~ sinoć **first** ~ premijera **the other** ~ neku večer ~**cap** piće prije spavanja ~**dress** spavaćica ~**fall** sumrak ~**ingale** slavuj ~**mare** noćna mora ~ **owl** noćna ptica **~ly** adj, adv (koji se događa) svake večeri/noći **~s** noću **~school** večernja škola **~ shift** noćna smjena **~-time** noć **~ watchman** noćni čuvar

nihilism /'naɪɪlɪzəm/ n nihilizam

nil /nɪl/ n ništica, nula

nimble /'nɪmbl/ adj 1 brz, gibak, okretan 2 bistar, oštrouman

nine /naɪn/ num devet (9) **ninth** /naɪnθ/ num deveti

nineteen /ˌnaɪn'tiːn/ num devetnaest (19)

ninety /'naɪntɪ/ num devedeset (90)

ninny /'nɪnɪ/ n coll budala

nip /nɪp/ vt,vi 1 (at) uštipnuti; ugristi; ščepati 2 uništiti **~ in the bud** uništiti u začetku 3 (off) odrezati 4 (out) coll skoknuti

nipple /'nɪpl/ n 1 bradavica (grudi) 2 US dudica

nippy /'nɪpɪ/ adj 1 hladan 2 brz

nit /nɪt/ n gnjida **~picking** cjepidlačenje, sitničarenje **~wit** blesan

nix /nɪks/ adv US coll ne • vt odbiti; zabraniti

no /nəʊ/ adv ne **~ admittance** zabranjen ulaz **~-claim bonus** bonus (kod osiguranja) **~-go area** zabranjeno područje **~-man's-land** ničija zemlja **~-nonsense** adj praktičan; izravan; strog, poslovan **~ one** pron nitko **~-place** adv nigdje **~ smoking** zabranjeno pušenje **~ way** ni govora **~-win situation** bezizlazna situacija he's **~** expert nije on nikakav stručnjak

nob /nɒb/ n GB coll derog, joc bogataš

nobble /'nɒbl/ vt GB sl 1 onesposobiti 2 privući pozornost 3 nepošteno steći

noble /'nəʊbl/ adj 1 plemenit, otmjen 2 veličanstven, sjajan **~man** n plemić **~woman** plemkinja **nobility** /nəʊ'bɪlɪtɪ/ n 1 plemstvo 2 plemenitost, otmjenost **nobly** adv plemenito **nobly born** plemenita roda

nobody /'nəʊbədɪ/ pron nitko • n nitko i ništa

nocturnal /nɒk'tɜːnl/ adj noćni **nocturne** /'nɒktɜːn/ n nokturno

nod /nɒd/ vi,vt kimnuti (glavom)

~ding acquaintance (with) površno poznanstvo/poznavanje (s kim/čega) **~ off** vi zaspati • n kimanje glavom

node /nəʊd/ n čvor

nodule /'nɒdjuːl/ n kvržica

noggin /'nɒgɪn/ n 1 sl glava, mozak 2 kapljica (alkohola)

noise /nɔɪz/ n buka, galama, šum, neugodan zvuk make encouraging/ sympathetic etc. **~s** izraziti odobravanje/suosjećanje etc. • vt (about-/abroad/around) razglasiti **noisy** adj bučan

nomad /'nəʊmæd/ n nomad **~ic** /nəʊ'mædɪk/ adj nomadski

nom de plume /ˌnɒm də 'pluːm/ n umjetničko ime

nominal /'nɒmɪnl/ adj 1 nominalan; samo formalan, samo na papiru 2 neznatan, zanemariv 3 gram imenski

nominate /'nɒmɪneɪt/ n 1 nominirati, predložiti 2 imenovati **nomination** /ˌnɒmɪ'neɪʃn/ n nominacija; imenovanje **nominee** /ˌnɒmɪ'niː/ n kandidat

nominative /'nɒmɪnətɪv/ n gram nominativ

non- /ˌnɒn/ prefix ne- **~aggression** n nenapadanje **a ~ aggression pact** sporazum o nenapadanju **~aligned** adj nesvrstan **~alignment** n nesvrstanost **~commissioned officer** (NCO) mil dočasnik **~smoker** n 1 nepušač 2 GB vagon za nepušače **~starter** n GB coll bezizgledna zamisao **~violence** n nenasilje **~entity** /nɒ'nentətɪ/ n derog bezveznjaković, nula **~existent** adj nepostojeći **~fiction** n publicistika **~intervention**, **~interference** n pol nemiješanje **~profit-making** adj neprofitan **~proliferation** n ograničenje nuklearnog naoružanja **~resident** n stranac

nonchalant /'nɒnʃələnt/ adj nehajan, nemaran, ravnodušan, nonšalantan

noncommittal /ˌnɒnkə'mɪtl/ adj neodređen, suzdržan, koji se ne izjašnjava

nondescript /'nɒndɪskrɪpt/ adj neupadljiv, neuočljiv

none /nʌn/ pron 1 ništa 2 ni jedan 3 **~ but** samo 4 **~ other (than)** nitko drugi (doli) • *adv* 1 ništa 2 ~ **too** ne baš, ne osobito ~ **the less** *adv* ipak, unatoč tome

nonplussed /ˌnɒnˈplʌst/ *adj* zatečen

nonsense /ˈnɒnsns/ *n* 1 besmislica, besmisao 2 glupost, blesavoća **make (a)** ~ **of** pokvariti, upropastiti **no~** *adj* praktičan, izravan, strog, **nonsensical** /nɒnˈsensɪkl/ *adj* besmislen, glup, smiješan, apsurdan

noodle /ˈnuːdl/ *n* rezanac

nook /nʊk/ *n* kut, skrovište **search every** ~ **and cranny** pretražiti svaki kutak

noon /nuːn/ *n* podne

noose /nuːs/ *n* 1 omča 2 *fig* vješanje

nope /nəʊp/ *adv sl* ne

nor /nɔː(r)/ *conj* ni, niti

norm /nɔːm/ *n* norma **~al** /ˈnɔːml/ *adj* normalan, uobičajen **be back to ~al** ponovno raditi, vratiti se na staro **~ality** *n* /nɔːˈmælətɪ/ **~alcy** /ˈnɔːmlsɪ/ *n* normalnost, normalno stanje **~alize** *vt,vi* normalizirati (se) **~ally** /ˈnɔːməlɪ/ *adv* 1 normalno, uobičajeno 2 obično, inače **~ative** *adj* normativan

Norse /nɔːs/ *adj* (staro)norveški; vikinški

north (N~) /nɔːθ/ *n* sjever • *adj* sjeverni • *adv* sjeverno, na sjever, prema sjeveru **up** ~ *coll* na sjever(u) **~bound** *adj, adv* (koji se kreće) prema sjeveru **~east** sjeveroistok **~easterly**, **~eastern** *adj* sjeveroistočni **~erly**, **~ern** *adj* sjeverni **N~erner** *n* Sjevernjak (osoba) **~ernmost** *adj* najsjeverniji **~ward** *adj* koji se kreće prema sjeveru, sjeverni **~west** sjeverozapad

nose /nəʊz/ *n* nos (+ *fig*) **get up sb's ~** *coll* ljutiti se 1 oprezno/sporo se kretati 2 *coll fig* njuškati, zabadati nos (u) **~y** *adj* radoznao **~y parker** radoznalac

nosh /nɒʃ/ *vi GB sl* jesti • *n* klopa *coll*

nostril /ˈnɒstrəl/ *n* nosnica, nozdrva

not /nɒt/ *adv* ne ~ **at all a.** uopće ne **b.** (kao odgovor) nema na čemu

notable /ˈnəʊtəbl/ *adj* značajan, važan **notably** *adv* posebice, poglavito

notary /ˈnəʊtərɪ/ ~ **public** *n* bilježnik,

notar

notation /nəʊˈteɪʃn/ *n* notacija

notch /nɒtʃ/ *n* 1 urez, zarez 2 *coll* stupanj 3 *US* klanac • *vt* 1 urezati, zarezati 2 (~ **up**) *coll* zabilježiti (pobjedu)

note /nəʊt/ *n* 1 bilješka **~book** biljeznica **of** ~ važan; znamenit **take** ~ **of** obratiti pozornost **take** ~ voditi bilješke 2 pisamce, poruka 3 nota 4 ton (+ *fig*) 5 novčanica • *vt* uočiti, opaziti, obratiti/skrenuti pozornost (na), upamtiti, primiti na znanje **~d** *adj* znamenit, poznat

nothing /ˈnʌθɪŋ/ *pron* ništa **for ~ a.** besplatno **b.** ni za što ~ **doing** *sl* ništa od toga **be/have ~ to do with sth** nemati nikakve veze s čim **there's ~ to it** nije teško, nije nikakva posebna mudrost • *adv* uopće nije, nikako nije **~ness** *n* ništavilo

notice /ˈnəʊtɪs/ *n* 1 obavijest, oglas ~ **board** oglasna ploča 2 upozorenje **at short** ~ u zadnji čas **until further** ~ do daljnjega 3 obavijest o prestanku radnog odnosa/ugovora 4 pozornost **it has come to my** ~ saznao sam **pay no** ~ (**of**) ne obraćati pozornost (na) 5 ~**s** kritika • *vt,vi* opaziti, uočiti **~able** *adj* značajan, znatan, osjetan, primjetljiv

notify /ˈnəʊtɪfaɪ/ *vt* obavijestiti

notion /ˈnəʊʃn/ *n* zamisao, ideja, predodžba, pojam, stav, mišljenje **~al** *adj* 1 teoretski 2 nominalan, simboličan

notorious /nəʊˈtɔːrɪəs/ *adj* ozloglašen, zloglasan, poznat (po zlu) **notoriety** /ˌnəʊtəˈraɪətɪ/ *n* ozloglašenost

notwithstanding /ˌnɒtwɪθˈstændɪŋ/ *prep, adv* usprkos

nought /nɔːt/ *n* nula, ništica **~s and crosses** *GB* (igra) križić-kružić

noun /naʊn/ *n* imenica

nourish /ˈnʌrɪʃ/ *vt* 1 hraniti 2 *fig* gajiti (nadu/osjećaj) **~ing** *adj* hranjiv **~ment** *n* hrana

novel (1) /ˈnɒvl/ *n* roman ¶ **novela** = **short story** **~ist** romanopisac

novel (2) *adj* nov, originalan **~ty** *n* 1 novina, originalnost, nešto novo/nepoznato 2 *pl* sitnice, drangulije

November /nəʊ'vembə(r)/ n studeni
novice /'nɒvɪs/ n 1 početnik 2 novici-jat
now /naʊ/ adv, n, conj sad(a) **(every)** ~ **and then/again** svako toliko, povre-meno **from** ~ **on** odsad ~ **that** sad kad ~**adays** adv sad, danas, u današnje vrijeme N~... Onda/Dakle, ... is it, ~ ? A, je li?
nowhere /'nəʊweə(r)/ adv nigdje; nikamo ~ **near** ni blizu
noxious /'nɒkʃəs/ adj otrovan, štetan
nozzle /'nɒzl/ n rasprašivač
nth /enθ/ adj **for the ~ time** stoti/tisućiti/milijunti/iksti put **to the ~ degree** coll na kvadrat, jako
nuance /'nju:ɑ:ns/ n nijansa, fina razli-ka
nub /nʌb/ n bit, srž
nubile /'nju:baɪl/ adj form, joc mlada i privlačna, za udaju
nuclear /'nju:klɪə(r)/ adj nuklearni; atomski **nucleus** /'nju:klɪəs/ n jezgra (+ fig)
nude /nju:d/ adj 1 gol, nag 2 nudistički • n 1 akt 2 golotinja, nagost **in the ~** gol **nudism** n nudizam **nudist** 1 nu-dist 2 mod nudistički **nudity** obnaženost, golotinja
nudge /nʌdʒ/ vt gurnuti laktom, gurkati • n lagani udarac laktom
nugget /'nʌgɪt/ n grumen, gruda (zlata itd.)
nuisance /'nju:sns/ n gnjavaža, nezgo-da; gnjavator, dosadnjaković
nuke /nu:k/ n coll nuklearno oružje • vt napasti nuklearnim. oružjem
null /nʌl/ adj ~ **set** math prazan skup ~ **and void** nevaljan, poništen ~**ify** /'nʌlɪfaɪ/ vt form, leg poništiti ~**ity** n poništenje (braka)
numb /nʌm/ adj utrnuo, umrtvljen • vt utrnuti, umrtviti
number /'nʌmbə(r)/ n 1 (No., no.) broj **cardinal** ~ glavni b. **ordinal** ~ redni b. **a** ~ **of** nekoliko, više ~ **plate** GB registarska tablica **the sheer force/weight of** ~s brojčana nadmoć

N~ **Ten** → **Downing Street** 2 glazbeni broj, pjesma 3 coll haljina • vt, vi 1 brojiti, ubrojiti (se), odbrojiti 2 označiti brojevima
numeral /'nju:mərəl/ n brojka
numerical /nju:'merɪkl/ adj brojčani ~ **superiority** brojčana nadmoć
numerous /'nju:mərəs/ adj brojni
nun /nʌn/ n redovnica, časna sestra ~**nery** samostan
nuncio /'nʌnsɪəʊ/ n papin izaslanik, nuncij
nuptial /'nʌpʃl/ adj form bračni; vjenčani ~**s** n pl form vjenčanje
nurse /nɜ:s/ n 1 medicinska sestra **male** ~ medicinski tehničar 2 dadilja • vt 1 njegovati, brinuti se (za), liječi-ti 2 raditi kao med. sestra 3 dojiti 4 sisati 5 gajiti (osjećaje) ~**ry** n dječja soba ~**ry school** dječji vrtić ~**ry garden** rasadnik ~**ry rhyme** dječja pjesmica **mursing home** dom umirovljenika
nurture /'nɜ:tʃə(r)/ n lit odgoj • vt nje-govati, odgajati; razvijati; gajiti (os-jećaj)
nut /nʌt/ n 1 orah **hard/tough** ~ **to crack** tvrd orah 2 matica 3 (~case) coll luđak ~s adj lud ~**house** sl ludni-ca 4 ~s tab sl jaja tab sl 5 ~s **and bolts** osnovne stvari ~**shell** ljuska in a ~**shell** najkraće rečeno ~**ty** adj 1 s okusom oraha 2 lud, šašav **as ~ty as a fruit cake** potpuno lud
nutmeg /'nʌtmeg/ n muškatni oraščić
nutrient /'nju:trɪənt/ n hranjiva tvar **nutrition** /nju:'trɪʃn/ n hrana, pre-hrana, ishrana **nutritive** /'njutrɪtɪv/ adj 1 prehramben, hranidben 2 hra-njiv
nuzzle /'nʌzl/ vi, vt (up/against) dodiri-vati njuškom; ljubiti
nylon /'naɪlɒn/ n 1 najlon 2 mod naj-lonski
nymph /nɪmf/ n nimfa ~**et** n nimfeta, lolita ~**omania** nimfomanija ~**oma-niac** derog nimfomanka

O

O /əʊ/ 15. slovo engl. abecede; o

oak /əʊk/ n 1 hrast 2 hrastovina **~en** adj hrastov

oar /ɔː(r)/ n veslo **~sman/swoman** n veslač(ica)

oasis /əʊˈeɪsɪs/ n oaza

oat /əʊt/ 1 zob **feel one's ~s** coll pucati od energije **sow one's wild ~s** izludovati se u mladim danima **~meal** n zobena kaša

oath /əʊθ/ n 1 zakletva, prisega **swear/take an ~** položiti prisegu 2 kletva

obedient /əˈbiːdɪənt/ n poslušan **obedience** n poslušnost

obese /əʊˈbiːs/ adj gojazan **obesity** n gojaznost

obey /əˈbeɪ/ vt,vi poslušati, biti poslušan

obituary /əˈbɪtʃʊərɪ/ n osmrtnica; nekrolog

object /ˈɒbdʒɪkt/ n 1 predmet 2 svrha, cilj 3 objekt • vi,vt /əbˈdʒekt/ 1 (to) usprotiviti se 2 (against sb) that prigovoriti **~ion** n 1 prigovor 2 pogreška, nedostatak **~able** adj neugodan, neumjesan **~ive** adj objektivan ○ n 1 svrha 2 cilj 3 objektiv **~ivity** /ˌɒbdʒekˈtɪvətɪ/ n objektivnost

oblige /əˈblaɪdʒ/ vt 1 obvezati 2 **be ~d to** morati, biti natjeran 3 biti tako ljubazan 4 **be ~d** biti zahvalan **obliging** adj susretljiv **obligation** /ˌɒblɪˈɡeɪʃn/ n obaveza **be under an ~** biti dužnik **obligatory** /əˈblɪɡətrɪ/ adj obavezan

oblique /əˈbliːk/ n 1 kos 2 neizravan

obliterate /əˈblɪtəreɪt/ vt 1 izbrisati 2 istrijebiti

oblivion /əˈblɪvɪən/ n zaborav **oblivious** adj (of) nesvjestan

oblong /ˈɒblɒŋ/ adj četvrtast

obnoxious /əbˈnɒkʃəs/ adj 1 škodljiv, štetan 2 neugodan

obscene /əbˈsiːn/ adj bestidan, opscen **obscenity** n 1 opscenost 2 prostota

obscure /əbˈskjʊə(r)/ adj 1 taman, mračan 2 tajnovit, skrovit 3 nepoznat, opskuran • vt potamniti, zakriti **obscurity** n 1 tama 2 sjena, skrovitost **live in obscurity** živjeti u anonimnosti

obsequious /əbˈsiːkwɪəs/ adj (to/towards) pokoran, ulizivački

observe /əbˈzɜːv/ vt,vi 1 motriti, promatrati 2 primijetiti 3 poštovati, svetkovati **~r** n promatrač **observance** n svetkovanje **observant** adj 1 pronicljiv 2 koji se drži (propisa), koji poštuje/svetkuje **observation** /ˌɒbzəˈveɪʃn/ n 1 prismotra **observation post** mil promatračnica 2 pronicavost 3 zapažanje, primjedba, opservacija **observatory** /əbˈzɜːvətrɪ/ n opservatorij

obsess /əbˈses/ vt (+ pass) opsjedati, proganjati **~ion** n 1 opsjednutost 2 (about/with) opsesija, opsjednutost čime **~ive** adj opsesivan

obsolete /ˈɒbsəliːt/ adj zastario

obstacle /ˈɒbstəkl/ n (to) zapreka komu/čemu

obstetrics /əbˈstetrɪks/ n porodiljstvo **obstetrician** /ˌɒbstɪˈtrɪʃn/ n opstetričar

obstinate /ˈɒbstɪnət/ adj tvrdoglav, uporan

obstruct /əbˈstrʌkt/ vt 1 prepriječiti, zakrčiti 2 otežati **~ion** n 1 zapreka 2 zavlačenje, bacanje klipova pod noge

obtain /əbˈteɪn/ vt,vi 1 dobiti, postići 2 nabaviti

obtrusive /əbˈtruːsɪv/ adj nametljiv

obtuse /əbˈtjuːs/ adj tup (+ fig)

obvious /ˈɒbvɪəs/ adj očit, jasan

occasion /əˈkeɪʒn/ n 1 (for) prigoda, prilika, pravi čas **on this ~** ovom prigodom **rise to the ~** pokazati se 2 razlog, povod **~al** adj 1 povremen 2 prigodan **~ally** adv povremeno

occupy /ˈɒkjʊpaɪ/ vt 1 stanovati 2 okupirati 3 obuzeti 4 **be occupied with** baviti se čime 5 zauzimati **occupant** n 1 držalac, osoba u posjedu 2 stanar **occupation** /ˌɒkjuˈpeɪʃn/ n 1 uzimanje u posjed 2 okupacija 3 zanimanje **occupational** adj profesionalan

occur /əˈkɜː(r)/ vi 1 dogoditi se, zbiti se 2 (to) pasti (kome) na pamet 3 javljati se, nalaziti se **~rence** /əˈkʌrəns/ n događaj, pojava

ocean /ˈəʊʃn/ n ocean

o'clock /əˈklɒk/ part at five = u pet sati

October /ɒkˈtəʊbə(r)/ n listopad

octopus /ˈɒktəpəs/ n hobotnica

odd /ɒd/ adj 1 neparan 2 nesparen 3 viška • **man out a.** prekobrojan **b.** koji se ne uklapa 500 ~ **people** nešto više od 500 ljudi 4 povremen, neredovit 5 **the odd X** poneki X 6 čudan **~ity** n 1 osebujnost 2 neobična stvar, osobenjak • **~s** n pl 1 odnos oklada **the ~s are ten to one ~s -on** dobri izgledi 2 izgled, prilika za uspjeh, šansa **against all ~s** usprkos svemu **fight against the ~s** neravnopravno se boriti **the ~s are against you** nemaš izgleda 3 prednost (u igri) **be at ~s** (with/over/on) ne slagati se **~s and ends** sitnice

odious /ˈəʊdɪəs/ adj odvratan, mrzak

odour /ˈəʊdə(r)/ n 1 miris 2 smrad **body ~** smrad znoja

of /əv/ prep 1 od 2 → genitiv imenice (koga, čega) loss of appetite gubitak teka; a cup of coffee šalica kave; one of us jedan od nas 3 → posvojni pridjev love of God Božja ljubav; a friend of mine moj prijatelj 4 → pridjev man of great talent veoma talentiran čovjek 5 the city of Dublin grad Dublin; the island of Cres otok Cres

off /ɒf/ adv 1 uz glagole: **drive off** odvesti se **fall off** otpasti **kill off** pobiti **take off** skinuti → glagol **off**

colour a. loše **b.** prostački • adj 1 isključen 2 pokvaren 3 slobodan **a day off** slobodan dan 4 otkazan, prekinut (zaruke) 5 loš, slab **off season** podsezona **well off** dobrostojeći **you would be better off** bilo bi ti bolje • prep 1 sa 2 od **a long way off** daleko od 3 uz; od • vt sl ukokati sl

offal /ˈɒfl/ n iznutrice pl

off-beat adj coll nekonvencionalan

offence (**offense** US) /əˈfens/ n 1 (against) povreda (čega) 2 uvreda **give ~** (to) uvrijediti **take ~** (at) uvrijediti se (na) **No ~!** bez uvrede 3 ofenziva **offend** vi,vt 1 zgriješiti 2 uvrijediti 3 vrijeđati, smetati **offender** n prijestupnik, kriminalac **offensive** adj 1 uvredljiv 2 odvratan 3 ofenzivan, navalni • n ofenziva, napad

offer /ˈɒfə(r)/ vt,vi 1 ponuditi **~ sth** (**up**) (to God) prinijeti 2 (to) pružiti 3 pružati (se) • n ponuda **on ~** na prodaju **~ing** n 1 nuđanje 2 žrtva 3 dar

off-hand(ed) adj 1 improviziran 2 neljubazan; neformalan • adv na brzinu

office /ˈɒfɪs/ n 1 (+ pl) ured, uredske prostorije **~ block** poslovna zgrada 2 ministarstvo, ured vlade 3 visoka državna služba, položaj, funkcija **resign ~** dati ostavku na položaj **in ~** na vlasti **~ bearer** dužnosnik 4 dužnost 5 pl usluga, pomoć **~r** n 1 časnik 2 službenik **official** /əˈfɪʃl/ adj služben • n funkcionar, dužnosnik **officially** adv službeno

officiate /əˈfɪʃɪeɪt/ vi (as/at) 1 obnositi dužnost 2 služiti (misu), obaviti (vjenčanje)

officious /əˈfɪʃəs/ adj (previše) revan

offing /ˈɒfɪŋ/ n coll **in the ~** na vidiku

off-licence /ˈɒf laɪsns/ n trgovina alkoholnim pićima

off-peak /ˈɒf piːk/ adj izvansezonski, izvan špice

off-set /ˈɒfset/ vt nadoknaditi

off-shoot /ˈɒfʃuːt/ n 1 izdanak 2 fig ogranak

off-shore /ˌɒfˈʃɔː(r)/ adj 1 s kopna na more 2 priobalni

offspring /ˈɒfsprɪŋ/ n (pl ~) potomak,

potomstvo

off-white /ˌɒf 'waɪt/ adj prljavobijel

often /'ɒfn/ adv često as ~ as svaki puta ~ as not; more ~ than not vrlo često

off-the-record adj neslužben

ogle /'əʊgl/ vt proždirati pogledom

ogre /'əʊgə(r)/ n ljudožder, bauk ~ss n ljudožderka

oil /ɔɪl/ n 1 ulje burn the midnight ~ raditi dokasna 2 (~s) uljena boja, ulje 3 nafta strike ~ naći naftu ~cloth voštano platno ~skins pl nepromočiva odjeća ~y adj 1 uljast, mastan 2 fig slatkorječiv • vt nauljiti, podmazati

ointment /'ɔɪntmənt/ n mast

okay /ˌəʊ'keɪ/ adv, adj u redu • vt odobriti

old /əʊld/ adj star how ~ are you? koliko ti je godina? I am 40 years ~ imam 40 godina/40 mi je godina ~ age starost ~ age pensioner umirovljenik ~-fashioned adj staromodan ~ hat coll zastario ~ boy/girl nekadašnji učenik/-ca the ~ school (nečija) stara škola an ~ hand (at) iskusan (u)

olive /'ɒlɪv/ n maslina ~ branch maslinova grana • adj maslinast

Olympic /ə'lɪmpɪk/ adj the ~ Games n pl Olimpijada

omelette /'ɒmlɪt/ n omlet

omen /'əʊmen/ n znamen

ominous /'ɒmɪnəs/ adj koban, zloslutan

omit /ə'mɪt/ vt 1 ~ to do/doing sth propustiti 2 izostaviti, preskočiti **omission** /ə'mɪʃn/ n propust

omnipotent /ɒm'nɪpətənt/ adj svemoćan

omniscient /ɒm'nɪsɪənt/ adj sveznajući

on /ɒn/ adv be on biti upaljen, otvoren, uključen, važeći, u tijeku, u planu, na programu be on about sth coll a. mrmljati protiv b. trabunjati be on to sb/sth a. biti u vezi s b. biti na tragu (s ostalim gl. → glagol) • prep 1 (prostor) na, kod, pri 2 (vrijeme) po, nakon on Sunday u nedjelju on June 1st 1. lipnja on that day toga dana on

Xmas day na Božić 3 o 4 u 5 (smjer, cilj) prema, na, po 6 (stanje) be on fire gorjeti be on holiday biti na odmoru on business poslovno on sale na prodaju on foot pješke be on drugs drogirati se

once /wʌns/ adv 1 jedanput, jednom ~ a week jednom tjedno ~ more još jednom ~ and for all jednom zauvijek 2 kad, čim at ~ a. odmah b. u isto vrijeme all at ~ odjednom

oncoming /'ɒnkʌmɪŋ/ adj idući, sljedeći

one /wʌn/ num jedan • adj 1 jedini 2 neki 3 isti 4 jedan for ~ thing jedan je razlog it's all ~ to me svejedno mi je ~ and the same jedan te isti ~ and all svi redom ~-upmanship n nadmoć number ~ coll vlastita guzica coll tab ~-armed jednoruk ~ armed bandit coll jednoruki džek ~-horse adj a. jednopreg b. fig bijedan ~-off adj jedinstven ~-sided adj jednostran ~-time adj nekadašnji ~-way adj jednosmjeran • pron 1 There are two apples. Which ~ do you want? I want the red ~. Tu su dvije jabuke. Koju hoćeš? Crvenu. 2 (~ ... another/the other) jedan (drugi) 3 čovjek ~ never knows čovjek nikad ne zna

onerous /'ɒnərəs/ adj težak fig

oneself /wʌn'self/ reflex pron se, sam sebe

ongoing /'ɒngəʊɪŋ/ adj koji traje, stalni, tekući, nezaključeni

onion /'ʌnɪən/ n luk

onlooker /'ɒnlʊkə(r)/ n promatrač

only /'əʊnlɪ/ adv samo ~ too vrlo, posve if ~ da bar • adj jedini an ~ child jedinac, jedinica • conj (~ that) samo što

onset /'ɒnset/ n 1 navala 2 početak

onshore /'ɒnʃɔː(r)/ adj, adv prema obali

onslaught /'ɒnslɔːt/ n napad, navala

onto /'ɒntə/ prep na

onward /'ɒnwəd/ adj, adv prema naprijed, dalje

ooze /uːz/ n 1 mulj 2 iscjedak • vt, vi 1 cijediti se, curiti 2 propuštati 3 he ~d sweat iz njega se cijedio znoj

opal /'əʊpl/ n opal

opaque /əʊ'peɪk/ *adj* neproziran ~ *tights* guste hulahopke

open /'əʊpən/ *adj* 1 otvoren (~ *door*, ~ *sea*, ~ *car*, ~ *book*) **in the ~ air** vani ~ **air** *mod* na otvorenom 2 javan (~ *secret*) 3 slobodan (~ *position*) 4 neriješen (~ *question*) 5 otvoren, iskren, neprikriven, javan (~ *letter*) 6 izložen (~ *to attack*) 7 spreman, voljan **~-minded** *adj* bez predrasuda • *n* **the ~ vani come (out) in the ~** iznijeti/istupiti u javnost **~ly** *adv fig* otvoreno, bez uvijanja • *vt* vi otvoriti (se) ~ **fire** (at/on) otvoriti vatru na 2 ~ **with** započeti ~**er** *n* otvarač ~**ing** *n* 1 otvor, čistina 2 početak ~**ing speech** uvodni govor ~**ing ceremony** svečano otvorenje **the ~ing night** premijera 3 mogućnost zaposlenja, prilika za uspjeh

opera /'ɒprə/ *n* opera

operate /'ɒpəreɪt/ 1 *vt* rukovati, upravljati 2 *vi* raditi, funkcionirati 3 (**on sb/for sth**) operirati koga zbog čega **operating theatre** operacijska dvorana 4 *mil* djelovati **operation** *n* 1 djelovanje, rad **be in/bring sth into/come into operation** početi se primjenjivati 2 (*pl*) *mil, fig* djelovanje, akcija 3 (**on sb**) operacija nad kim **operational** *adj* 1 radni 2 **be operational** ući u upotrebu **operative** /'ɒpərətɪv/ *adj* 1 koji vrijedi, koji se primjenjuje 2 operativan ○ *n* radnik; operativac **operator** *n* 1 operater 2 *sl* pravi maher *sl* 3 centrala

opinion /ə'pɪnɪən/ *n* 1 mišljenje **in my ~** po mom mišljenju **public ~** javno mnijenje ~ **poll** ispitivanje javnog mnijenja 2 stručno mišljenje ~**ated** *adj* zadrt

opponent /ə'pəʊnənt/ *n* protivnik

opportune /'ɒpətjuːn/ *adj* 1 prikladan 2 pravovremen **opportunity** *n* prilika, šansa

oppose /ə'pəʊz/ *vt* 1 protiviti se 2 (**against/to**) suprotstaviti **as ~d to** za razliku od **opposite** /'ɒpəzɪt/ *adj* 1 (**to**) suprotan, drugi; nasuprot *adv* 2 oprečan 3 odgovarajući ○ *n* suprotnost **opposition** /,ɒpə'zɪʃn/ *n* 1 opreka, neslaganje **in opposition to** ne

slagati se s 2 oporba 3 otpor

oppress /ə'pres/ *vt* 1 tlačiti, ugnjetavati 2 *fig* mučiti **~or** *n* tiranin **~ion** *n* tiranija **~ive** *adj* 1 nepravedan 2 težak

opt /ɒpt/ *vi* 1 (**for**) odlučiti se za 2 (**out of**) odustati od, izdvojiti se iz

optic /'ɒptɪk/ *adj* 1 optički 2 očni **~al** *adj* optički **~ian** /ɒp'tɪʃn/ *n* optičar

optimism /'ɒptɪmɪzəm/ *n* optimizam

optimum /'ɒptɪməm/ *adj* optimalan

option /'ɒpʃn/ *n* 1 izbor **leave one's ~s open** ostaviti sebi otvoren izbor 2 mogućnost 3 *comm* opcija **~al** *adj* izborni, neobavezan

opulent / *adj form* bogat

or /ɔː(r)/ *conj* 1 ili ~ **else** ili, inače 2 to jest

oracle /'ɒrəkl/ *n* 1 proročište, proročanstvo 2 *fig* znalac

oral /'ɔːrəl/ *adj* 1 usni 2 usmeni 3 oralni

orange /'ɒrɪndʒ/ *n* 1 naranča 2 *mod* narančast

orator /'ɒrətə(r)/ *n* govornik ~**y** /'ɒrətrɪ/ *n* govorništvo

oratorio /,ɒrə'tɔːrɪəʊ/ *n* oratorij

orbit /'ɔːbɪt/ *n* orbita • *vt*, *vi* 1 kružiti oko/u orbiti 2 lansirati u orbitu

orchard /'ɔːtʃəd/ *n* voćnjak

orchestra /'ɔːkɪstrə/ *n* 1 orkestar 2 (~ **pit**) prostor za glazbenike ~ **stalls** *n pl* parket *sing* **~te** *vt* 1 orkestrirati 2 *fig* inscenirati

orchid /'ɔːkɪd/ *n* orhideja

ordain /ɔː'deɪn/ *vt* 1 zarediti 2 (**that**) dosuditi, odrediti

ordeal /ɔː'diːl/ *n* iskušenje, muka

order /'ɔːdə(r)/ *n* 1 redoslijed **in ~ of** poredani 2 red **in ~** u redu, uredan **in good/working ~** u dobrom stanju **out of ~** pokvaren 3 red, mir, disciplina **law and ~** poredak, red i mir 4 pravilo, propis **standing ~s** poslovnik ~ **of the day** dnevni red 5 naredba 6 narudžba **made to ~** izrađen po narudžbi ~-**form** narudžbenica 7 nalog za isplatu 8 red, orden 9 *pl* (svećenički, redovnički) red **take holy ~s** zarediti se 10 vrsta 11 stupanj 12 *mil* poredak **in ~ to** da bi • *vt* 1 naložiti, zapovjediti ~ **sb about**

naređivati (svojevoljno) 2 poslati 3 naručiti 4 organizirati ~ **ly** adj 1 uredan, metodičan 2 poslušan 3 mil dežuran n mil 1 posilni 2 bolničar

ordinal /'ɔ:dɪnl/ adj redni

ordinary /'ɔ:dɪnrɪ/ adj običan **out of the ~** neobičan

ordination /ˌɔ:dɪ'neɪʃn/ n zaređenje

ordnance /'ɔ:dnəns/ n mil 1 topništvo 2 komora **O~ Survey** britanski kartografski zavod

ore /ɔ:(r)/ n rudača

organ /'ɔ:gən/ n 1 organ 2 fig organ, tijelo 3 orgulje pl ~**ic** adj 1 organski 2 proizveden bez umjetnih gnojiva ~**ism** n organizam

organize /'ɔ:gənaɪz/ vt organizirati (se) **organization** n organizacija

orgasm /'ɔ:gæzəm/ n orgazam

orgy /'ɔ:dʒɪ/ n orgija

oriental /ˌɔ:rɪ'entl/ adj istočnjački, orijentalan • n Istočnjak

orientate /'ɔ:rɪənteɪt/ vt odrediti položaj ~ **oneself** orijentirati se

orifice /'ɒrɪfɪs/ n otvor

origin /'ɒrɪdʒɪn/ n 1 podrijetlo 2 izvor ~**al** /ə'rɪdʒənl/ adj 1 izvorni ~**al sin** istočni grijeh 2 originalan, nov, svjež 3 prvobitni • n original, izvornik ~**ally** adv 1 originalno, inovativno 2 u početku ~**ality** /əˌrɪdʒə'næləti/ n originalnost ~**ate** /ə'rɪdʒɪneɪt/ vi,vt 1 (from/in sth; from/with sb) potjecati od 2 biti začetnik

ornament /'ɔ:nəmənt/ n ukras • vt ukrasiti ~**al** /ˌɔ:nə'mentl/ adj ukrasni

ornate /ɔ:'neɪt/ adj kićen

orphan /'ɔ:fn/ n siroče • vt 1 učiniti siročetom 2 **be ~ed** ostati siroče ~**age** n sirotište

orthodox /'ɔ:θədɒks/ adj ortodoksan, pravovjeran **the O~ Church** Pravoslavna crkva ~**y** n pravovjerje

orthography /ɔ:'θɒɡrəfɪ/ n pravopis

orthopaedic /ˌɔ:θə'pi:dɪk/ ortopedski ~**s** n (+ sing) ortopedija

oscillate /'ɒsɪleɪt/ vi,vt 1 njihati (se) 2 titrati, oscilirati 3 fig kolebati se, oscilirati

ostensible /ɒ'stensəbl/ adj tobožnji **ostensibly** adv tobože, navodno, prividno **ostentation** /ˌɒsten'teɪʃn/ n

razmetanje **ostentatious** adj razmetljiv

ostracize /'ɒstrəsaɪz/ vt izopćiti **ostracism** /'ɒstrəsɪzəm/ n ostracizam, izopćenje

ostrich /'ɒstrɪtʃ/ n noj

other /'ʌðə(r)/ adj, pron 1 **the ~** drugi (od dva) **on the ~ hand** s druge strane 2 **the ~s** ostali **someday/ somewhere or ~** netko/jednog dana/ negdje ~ **things being equal** ako sve drugo ostane isto, da nije toga ~ **than** that osim toga **the ~ day** prije par dana, neki dan 3 **an~** → **another** 4 drukčiji

otherwise /'ʌðəwaɪz/ adv 1 drukčije **be ~ engaged** imati drugog posla 2 inače

otter /'ɒtə(r)/ n vidra

ouch /aʊtʃ/ int jao

ought to /ɔ:t/ modal (past **ought to have**) 1 morao bih, bi itd. 2 trebao bih, bi itd.

ounce /aʊns/ n unca **not an ~** nimalo, ni grama

our /'aʊə(r)/ adj naš (~ **house**) ~**s** pron naš (the house is ~) ~**selves** /aʊə-'selvz/ 1 reflex pron sebe, se, sebi, si 2 **we ~selves** mi sami

oust /aʊst/ vt (from) istisnuti, istjerati, zbaciti, svrgnuti

out /aʊt/ adv 1 (smjer) van 2 (mjesto) vani 3 do kraja **be ~ a.** izišao, na otvorenom, otkriven **b.** ugašen, nevažeći (s ostalim gl. →) ~ **and ~** potpun, pravi **be ~ for** biti željan **be ~ to do sth** težiti da ~ **of** prep **a.** izvan **b.** iz **c.** od **be ~ of patience** izgubiti strpljenje ~ **of work** nezaposlen **we are ~ of petrol** ponestalo nam je benzina ~ **of control** nekontroliran, pomahnitao

out- prefix 1 izvan 2 više, jače, bolje 3 nad-

outback /'aʊtbæk/ n unutrašnjost, zabit (u Australiji)

outbid vt irreg ~ **bid** (sb) ponuditi više od koga

outboard /'aʊtbɔ:d/ adj vanbrodski

outbreak /'aʊtbreɪk/ n provala, izljev, napad

outburst /'aʊtbɜ:st/ n izljev

outcast /'aʊtkɑːst/ n izopćenik

outcome /'aʊtkʌm/ n posljedica, ishod

outcrop /'aʊtkrɒp/ n fig pojava, izlazak na vidjelo

outcry /'aʊtkraɪ/ n 1 povik 2 povika

outdated /aʊt'deɪtɪd/ adj zastario

outdo /ˌaʊt'duː/ vt irreg → do nadmašiti

outdoor /'aʊtdɔː(r)/ adj na otvorenom, izvan kuće, za izlaske ~s adv vani

outer /'aʊtə(r)/ adj vanjski

outfit /'aʊtfɪt/ n 1 oprema, pribor 2 odjeća • vt opremiti, odjenuti ~ter n trgovac odijelima

outgoing /'aʊtgəʊɪŋ/ adj na odlasku, izlazni • ~s n pl izdaci

outgrow /ˌaʊt'grəʊ/ v irreg → grow prerasti (+ fig)

outhouse /'aʊthaʊs/ (pl → house) n pokrajnja zgrada

outing /'aʊtɪŋ/ n izlet

outlandish /aʊt'lændɪʃ/ adj neobičan, stran

outlaw /'aʊtlɔː/ n odmetnik • vt staviti izvan zakona, izopćiti

outlay /'aʊtleɪ/ n (on) novčani izdaci

outlet /'aʊtlet/ n 1 izlaz, ispust 2 fig odušak 3 prodajno mjesto

outline /'aʊtlaɪn/ n 1 obris 2 nacrt • vt skicirati

outlive /ˌaʊt'lɪv/ vt nadživjeti

outlook /'aʊtlʊk/ n 1 pogled 2 izgled, prognoza 3 nazor

outnumber /ˌaʊt'nʌmbə(r)/ vt brojčano nadmašiti

out-of-date /'aʊt əv deɪt/ adj zastario

outpatient /'aʊtpeɪʃnt/ n ambulantni pacijent

outpost /'aʊtpəʊst/ n 1 (isturena) utvrda 2 fig isturено mjesto

output /'aʊtpʊt/ n 1 proizvodnja 2 comp output, izlaz

outrage /'aʊtreɪdʒ/ n 1 strahota, nasilje 2 skandal • vt 1 povrijediti 2 skandalizirati ~ous /aʊt'reɪdʒəs/ adj šokantan, skandalozan, nečuven

outright /'aʊtraɪt/ adj 1 otvoren 2 čist, očit • adv 1 otvoreno 2 na licu mjesta

outrun /ˌaʊt'rʌn/ vt irreg → run prestići

outset /'aʊtset/ n početak

outshine /ˌaʊt'ʃaɪn/ v irreg →shine

nadmašiti, zasjeniti

outside /ˌaʊt'saɪd/ n vanjska strana, vanjština at the ~ najviše • adj /'aʊtsaɪd/ vanjski • adv izvana • prep 1 izvan 2 dalje od ~r /ˌaʊt'saɪdə(r)/ n stranac, autsajder

outsize /'aʊtsaɪz/ adj prevelik

outskirts /'aʊtskɜːts/ n pl periferija sing

outspoken /ˌaʊt'spəʊkən/ adj iskren, otvoren

outstanding /ˌaʊt'stændɪŋ/ adj 1 upadljiv 2 koji se ističe, izvanredan 3 nepodmiren, neobavljen

outstay /ˌaʊt'steɪ/ vt ostati dulje od ~ one's welcome ostati predugo

outward /'aʊtwəd/ adj 1 vanjski 2 na odlasku, na putu tamo • (~s) adv prema van ~ly adv izvana

outweigh /ˌaʊt'weɪ/ vt fig pretegnuti nad

outwit /ˌaʊt'wɪt/ vt nadmudriti

oval /'əʊvl/ n, adj oval(an)

ovation /əʊ'veɪʃn/ n ovacije pl

oven /'ʌvn/ n pećnica ~-proof adj vatrostalan

over /'əʊvə(r)/ adv (uz gl. →) 1 prošao, gotov, završen 2 previše 3 posvuda (all) ~ again još jednom ~ and ~ again stalno iznova • prep preko ~ my dead body preko mene mrtvoga (~ the weekend, ~ the frontier, wait ~ two hours), iznad, nad, (posvuda) po

over- prefix pre~

overall /ˌəʊvər'ɔːl/ adj ukupni • n pl kombinezon

overawe /ˌəʊvər'ɔː/ vt zastrašiti

overbalance /ˌəʊvə'bæləns/ vt, vi 1 izgubiti ravnotežu 2 prevagnuti nad

overbearing /ˌəʊvə'beərɪŋ/ adj zapovjednički

overboard /'əʊvəbɔːd/ adv preko ograde u more throw sb ~ fig riješiti se koga go ~ a. zapaliti se fig b. pretjerati

overcast /ˌəʊvə'kɑːst/ adj oblačan

overcharge /ˌəʊvə'tʃɑːdʒ/ vt, vi 1 previše naplatiti 2 preopteretiti

overcoat /'əʊvəkəʊt/ n ogrtač

overcome /ˌəʊvə'kʌm/ v irreg → come nadvladati, savladati

overdo /ˌəʊvə'duː/ v irreg → do 1 pretjerati 2 raskuhati, prepeći

overdose /'əʊvədəʊs/ n prevelika doza

overdraft /'əʊvədraːft/ n prekoračenje bankovnog računa; minus *coll*

overdraw /ˌəʊvə'drɔː/ *irreg* → **draw** 1 podići previše novca, otići u minus 2 pretjerati

overdue /ˌəʊvə'djuː/ adj 1 koji kasni 2 neplaćen/nevraćen navrijeme

overflow /ˌəʊvə'fləʊ/ vt, vi 1 prelijevati se, izlijevati se 2 ~ **with** biti prepun • n 1 poplava 2 višak

overgrown /ˌəʊvə'grəʊn/ adj 1 prevelik za svoje godine 2 (with) zarastao u **overgrowth** n prebrzi rast

overhead /ˌəʊvə'hed/ adv gore, na nebu • adj podignut, nadzemni ~ **charges/expenses** neproizvodni troškovi

overhear /ˌəʊvə'hɪə(r)/ v *irreg* → **hear** načuti, slučajno čuti

overlap /ˌəʊvə'læp/ vt, vi preklapati se (+ *fig*)

overleaf /ˌəʊvə'liːf/ adv na drugoj stranici

overload /ˌəʊvə'ləʊd/ vt 1 pretovariti 2 preopteretiti

overlook /ˌəʊvə'lʊk/ vt 1 gledati na, imati pogled na 2 previdjeti 3 prijeći preko 4 nadgledati

overnight /ˌəʊvə'naɪt/ adv 1 preko noći 2 večer prije **stay** ~ prespavati

overpass /'əʊvəpɑːs/ n nadvožnjak

overplay /ˌəʊvə'pleɪ/ vt ~ **one's hand** nepotrebno riskirati

overpower /ˌəʊvə'paʊə(r)/ vt svladati ~**ing** adj prejak, intenzivan, neizdrživ

overrate /ˌəʊvə'reɪt/ v precijeniti

override /ˌəʊvə'raɪd/ v *irreg* → **ride** prijeći preko, ne uzeti u obzir

overrule /ˌəʊvə'ruːl/ vt 1 odbaciti, ne prihvatiti 2 nadglasati

overseas /ˌəʊvə'siː(z)/ adj prekomorski, inozeman • adv u inozemstvu

oversee /ˌəʊvə'siː/ v *irreg* → **see** nadgledati ~**r** n nadglednik

overshadow /ˌəʊvə'ʃædəʊ/ vt zasjeniti

overshoot /ˌəʊvə'ʃuːt/ v *irreg* → **shoot** 1 premašiti (cilj) 2 *fig* zaletjeti se

oversight /'əʊvəsaɪt/ n 1 propust, previd 2 nadzor

oversleep /ˌəʊvə'sliːp/ v *irreg* → **sleep** zaspati, ne probuditi se navrijeme

overstate /ˌəʊvə'steɪt/ v preuveličati ~**ment** n pretjerivanje

overt /'əʊvɜːt/ adj otvoren

overtake /ˌəʊvə'teɪk/ vt *irreg* → **take** 1 prestići 2 zateći

overthrow /ˌəʊvə'θrəʊ/ v *irreg* → **throw** oboriti • n obaranje; pad

overtime /'əʊvətaɪm/ n prekovremeni rad • adv prekovremeno

overtone /'əʊvətəʊn/ n prizvuk

overture /'əʊvətjʊə(r)/ n uvertira (+ *fig*), prvi koraci

overweight /'əʊvəweɪt/ adj 1 pretežak 2 gojazan

overwhelm /ˌəʊvə'welm/ vt nadjačati, savladati ~**ing** adj 1 premoćan 2 prevelik

overwrought /ˌəʊvə'rɔːt/ adj 1 premoren 2 uzrujan

owe /əʊ/ vt, vi (sb sth/sth to sb/for sth) 1 dugovati komu što/za što, biti dužan 2 zahvaljivati za

owing /'əʊɪŋ/ adj neplaćen ~ **to** zahvaljujući, zbog

owl /aʊl/ n sova

own /əʊn/ adj, pron vlastiti, svoj **be on one's** ~ biti sam, samostalan **come into one's** ~ doći na svoje **get one's** ~ **back** osvetiti se • vt, vi 1 posjedovati 2 (~ to) priznati ~ **up** (to) priznati sve ~**er** n vlasnik ~**ership** n vlasništvo

ox /ɒks/ (pl **oxen**) n vol ~**blood** adj tamnocrven

Oxbridge /'ɒksbrɪdʒ/ n sveučilišta u Oxfordu i Cambridgeu

Oxford /'ɒksfəd/ n mod ~ **shoes** polucipele

oxygen /'ɒksɪdʒən/ n kisik ~ **mask** maska za kisik

oyster /'ɔɪstə(r)/ n oštriga

P

P, p /piː/ 1 16. slovo engl. abecede; pe
2 peni(ji)
pace /peɪs/ n 1 tempo keep ~ with
držati korak s 2 korak put sb
through his ~s staviti na probu •
vi,vt hodati, koračati
pacifist /ˈpæsɪfɪst/ n pacifist **pacify**
/ˈpæsɪfaɪ/ vt 1 umiriti 2 uspostaviti
mir
pack /pæk/ n 1 zavežljaj 2 naprtnjača 3
US paketić, kutija 4 čopor 5 fig hrpa
6 špil coll 7 tretman, pakung coll •
vi,vt 1 pakirati (se) send sb ~ing najuriti koga 2 nagurati se, ispuniti 3
ambalažirati ~ off otposlati ~age n
paket (+ fig) ~age tour/holiday
paket aranžman vt 1 pakirati 2 ambalažirati ~aging n ambalaža ~ed adj
prepun ~et n 1 paketić, kutija 2 sl
puno novca 3 (~ boat) poštanski
brod
pact /pækt/ n pakt
pad /pæd/ n 1 umetak, podstava,
uložak, jastučić 2 (note ~) bilježnica
3 sl stan • vt 1 podstaviti, obložiti 2
tapkati ~ding n podstava
paddle /ˈpædl/ n 1 veslo 2 lopatica •
vi,vt 1 veslati 2 brčkati se 3 plivati
kao pas
paddock /ˈpædək/ n obor, pašnjak
paddy /ˈpædɪ/ n rižište
padlock /ˈpædlɒk/ n lokot
padre /ˈpɑːdreɪ/ n vojni svećenik
pagan /ˈpeɪgən/ n neznabožac, poganin • adj poganski
page (1) /peɪdʒ/ n 1 stranica
page (2) n (~ boy) paž
page (3) vt 1 pozvati preko zvučnika 2
pozvati preko sono-uređaja ~r n
sono-uređaj
pageant /ˈpædʒənt/ n svečana povorka
~ry n raskošna svečanost
paid v irreg → pay

pail /peɪl/ n kantica
pain /peɪn/ n 1 bol 2 (~ in the neck)
gnjavator; gnjavaža on/under ~ of
pod prijetnjom 3 ~s pl dati take ~s
dati si truda be at ~s truditi se ~ed
adj (at) uvrijeđen ~ful adj bolan ~
killer n analgetik ~less adj bezbolan
~staking adj poman
paint /peɪnt/ n boja Wet ~! svježe obo-
jeno • vi,vt 1 bojati, ličiti 2 slikati 3
fig živo predočiti ~ the town red
proslaviti ~brush n kist ~er n 1 soboslikar 2 slikar ~ing n 1 slikanje 2
ličenje 3 slika ~work/~job n lak (automobila)
pair /peə(r)/ n (of) par (koga/čega) •
vi,vt 1 spariti (se) 2 staviti zajedno,
sastaviti
paisley /ˈpeɪzlɪ/ n kašmir (uzorak)
pajamas /pəˈdʒɑːməz/ US → **pyamas**
pal /pæl/ n prijatelj
palace /ˈpælɪs/ n palača ~ revolution
uklanjanje kralja/predsjednika
palate /ˈpælət/ n 1 nepce 2 fig ukus
pale (1) /peɪl/ adj blijed • vi problijedeti ~ (into insignificance) ~ the ~/be-
side blijedjeti pred ~face n bljedoliki
pale (2) n 1 kolac 2 → **paling go beyond the** ~ prijeći sve granice **paling** n kolje, ograda od kolja
palette /ˈpælɪt/ n paleta
pall (1) /pɔːl/ vi (on/upon) dosaditi
(komu)
pall (2) n 1 pokrov 2 plašt 3 lijes ~
bearer n nosač lijesa
pallet /ˈpælɪt/ n paleta
palliate /ˈpælɪeɪt/ vt 1 ublažiti 2 prikri-
vati, uljepšavati **palliative** /ˈpælɪətɪv/
adj palijativan
pallid /ˈpælɪd/ adj blijed (+ fig)
pallor /ˈpælə(r)/ n bljedoća
palm /pɑːm/ n 1 palma P~ Sunday
Cvjetnica 2 dlan • vt sakriti na dlanu;

maznuti *coll* ~ist *n* gatač iz dlana ~stry *n* gatanje iz dlana

palpable /'pælpəbl/ *adj* opipljiv

palpitate /'pælpɪteɪt/ *vi* 1 *med* nepravilno lupati 2 drhtati **palpitations** /,pælpɪ'teɪʃnz/ *n pl* tahikardija

palsy /'pɔːlzɪ/ *n* paraliza

paltry /'pɔːltrɪ/ *adj* bijedan

pamper /'pæmpə(r)/ *vt* razmaziti

pamphlet /'pæmflɪt/ *n* pamflet

pan (1) /pæn/ *n* 1 tiganj 2 **(sauce~)** posuda za kuhanje • *vi,vt* 1 (for) ispirati (zlato) 2 popljuvati *fig*

pan (2) *vi,vt* pratiti kamerom; kretati se

panache /pə'næʃ/ *n* stil

pancake /'pænkeɪk/ *n* palačinka

pancreas /'pæŋkrɪəs/ *n* gušterača

panda /'pændə/ *n* panda **P~ car** *GB* policijski automobil

pander /'pændə(r)/ *vt* ~ **to** podilaziti komu/čemu

pane /peɪn/ *n* staklo, okno

panegyric /,pænɪ'dʒɪrɪk/ *n* (on/upon) hvalospjev (komu/čemu)

panel /'pænl/ *n* 1 dio (vrata, zida); obloga; umetak 2 ploča 3 grupa, konzilij • *vt* (in/with) obložiti (zidove) ~**ling** *n* obloga

pang /pæŋ/ *n* 1 probadanje 2 *fig* bolni osjećaj

panic /'pænɪk/ *n* panika ~ **button** dugme za alarm • *vi,vt* uspaničiti (se); prestrašiti ~**ky** /'pænɪkɪ/ *adj* uspaničen ~**stricken** *adj* uspaničen

pannier /'pænɪə(r)/ *n* košara

panorama /,pænə'rɑːmə/ *n* panorama

pannpipes /'pæn paɪps/ *n pl* Panova svirala

pansy /'pænzɪ/ *n* 1 maćuhica 2 *derog sl* peder

pant /pænt/ *vi,vt* 1 dahtati 2 (out) protisnuti, propentati 3 (for) žudjeti • *n* dahtaj

panther /'pænθə(r)/ *n* 1 pantera 2 *US* → **cougar**

panties /'pæntɪz/ *n pl* gaćice

pantomime /'pæntəmaɪm/ *n* 1 dječji igrokaz 2 → **mime**

pantry /'pæntrɪ/ *n* ostava

pants /pænts/ *n pl* 1 → **panties** 2 *US* hlače **caught with one~s ~ down** uh-

vaćen na spavanju

panty hose *n US* hulahupke

pap /pæp/ *n* 1 kašica 2 smeće (knjiga, film)

papa *n* 1 /'pɑːpɑː/ *US* tata 2 /pə'pɑː/ *GB arch* tata

papacy /'peɪpəsɪ/ *n* 1 papinstvo 2 vladavina pape **papal** *adj* papinski

paper /'peɪpə(r)/ *n* 1 papir 2 novine *pl* 3 **(examination ~)** test 4 referat 5 tapeta 6 **~s** *pl* dokumenti on ~ crno na bijelo • *vt* 1 (in/with) staviti tapete 2 zataškati • *adj* papirnat (+ *fig*) ~**back** *n* (knjiga) u mekom uvezu ~ **clip** spajalica ~ **knife** nož za otvaranje pisama ~**weight** pritiskivač ~**work** administracija; papirologija *coll*

paprika /'pæprɪkə/ *n* crvena paprika

par /pɑː(r)/ *n* 1 **be on a ~ with** biti jednak 2 **below ~** ispod uobičajenog nivoa 3 (~ **value**) nominalna vrijednost **sell above** ~ prodati po većoj vrijednosti **at** ~ po nominalnoj vrijednosti

Para *n coll* → **paratrooper**

parable /'pærəbl/ *n* poučna priča; prispodoba

parachute /'pærəʃuːt/ *n* padobran • *vi,vt* iskočiti padobranom; dostaviti padobranom **parachutist** *n* padobranac

parade /pə'reɪd/ *n* 1 parada, mimohod, smotra 2 isticanje • *vi,vt* 1 stupati u povorci 2 okupiti za smotru; izvršiti smotru 3 *derog* paradirati; isticati

paradigm /'pærədaɪm/ *n* paradigma, primjer

paradise /'pærədaɪs/ *n* raj

paradox /'pærədɒks/ *n* paradoks ~**ically** *adv* paradoksalno

paraffin /'pærəfɪn/ *n* 1 petrolej 2 parafin

paragon /'pærəgən/ *n* uzor

paragraph /'pærəgrɑːf/ *n* odjeljak

parakeet /'pærəkiːt/ *n* papigica

parallel /'pærəlel/ *adj* (to/with) paralelan, usporedan s **run** ~ ići usporedo s • *n* paralela

paralyse /'pærəlaɪz/ *vt* 1 paralizirati **paralysis** /pə'ræləsɪs/ *n* paraliza (+ *fig*) **paralytic** /,pærə'lɪtɪk/ *n* paralitičar ○ *adj* paraliziran

paramedic /ˌpærə'medɪk/ *n US* hitna pomoć, član ekipe hitne pomoći

parameter /pə'ræmɪtə(r)/ *n* parametar

paramilitary /ˌpærə'mɪlɪtrɪ/ *adj* paravojni

paramount /'pærəmaʊnt/ *adj* najveći, prvenstveni

paranoia /ˌpærə'nɔɪə/ *n* paranoja **paranoid** /'pærənɔɪd/ *adj* paranoičan

paraphernalia /ˌpærəfə'neɪlɪə/ *n* 1 parafernalije *pl* 2 nepotrebna gnjavaža

paraphrase /'pærəfreɪz/ *vt* parafrazirati

parasite /'pærəsaɪt/ *n* parazit, nametnik (+ *fig*) **parasitic** *adj* 1 koji parazitira 2 uzrokovan nametnicima

parasol /'pærəsɒl/ *n* suncobran

paratrooper /'pærətru:pə(r)/ *n mil* padobranac **paratroops** /'pærətru:ps/ *n pl mil* padobranstvo

paratyphoid /ˌpærə'taɪfɔɪd/ *n* paratifus

parboil /'pa:bɔɪl/ *vt* napola skuhati

parcel /'pa:sl/ *n* 1 paket ~ **post** otprema paketa 2 *US, leg* parcela • *vt* ~ **out** razdijeliti ~ **up** upakirati

parch /pa:tʃ/ *vi,vt* isušiti

parchment /'pa:tʃmənt/ *n* pergamena

pardon /'pa:dn/ *n* 1 pomilovanje 2 oprost, oproštenje ~ **me/Beg your** ~ *int* a. oprosti(te) b. molim? c. ispričavam se • *vt* 1 (sb for sth) oprostiti komu što 2 pomilovati ~**able** *adj* razumljiv, oprostiv

pare /peə(r)/ *vt* 1 (down) podrezivati; potkresati *fig* 2 (away/off) oguliti

parent /'peərənt/ *n* roditelj **single** ~ samohrani roditelj ~**al** *adj* roditeljski ~**age** *n* porijeklo ~ **company** matična tvrtka

parenthesis /pə'renθəsɪs/ *n* (-**theses** *pl*) zagrada **parenthetic** *adj* koji pojašnjava

pariah /pə'raɪə/ *n* parija, izopćenik

parish /'pærɪʃ/ *n* 1 župa 2 *GB* mjesna zajednica 3 *coll* djelokrug ~**ioner** *n* župljanin ~ **priest** župnik

parity /'pærətɪ/ *n* jednakost **achieve** ~ **with** izjednačiti se s

park (1) /pa:k/ *n* park ~**way** *n US* drvored, aleja

park (2) *vi,vt* parkirati (se) **car** ~ parkiralište; garaža ~**ing** *n* mjesto za parkiranje ~**ing lot** *US* parkiralište

parlance /'pa:ləns/ *n* rječnik

parley /'pa:lɪ/ *vi* pregovarati • *n* pregovori *pl*

parliament /'pa:ləmənt/ *n* parlament ~**ary** *adj* parlamentaran

parlour (-**or** *US*) /'pa:lə(r)/ *n* salon **beauty** ~ kozmetički salon **ice-cream** ~ slastičarnica

parody /'pærədɪ/ *n* parodija • *vt* parodirati; izrugivati se iz

parole /pə'rəʊl/ *n* uvjetno puštanje iz zatvora • *vt* uvjetno pustiti

parquet /'pa:keɪ/ *n* ~ **floor** parket

parrot /'pærət/ *n* papiga (+ *fig*) ~ **fashion** papagajski • *vt* oponašati

parry /'pærɪ/ *vt* parirati; izbjeći; odbiti

parsimonious /ˌpa:sɪ'məʊnɪəs/ *adj* škrt

parsley /'pa:slɪ/ *n* peršin

parsnip /'pa:snɪp/ *n* pastrnjak

parson /'pa:sn/ *n* pastor ~**age** /'pa:snɪdʒ/ *n* pastorova kuća ~'s **nose** *coll* kokošja trtica; biškup *coll*

part /pa:t/ *n* 1 dio **the best/better** ~ of gotovo cijelo ~**time job** *adj* honorarni posao 2 udio, uloga **take** ~ sudjelovati **play a** ~ utjecati 3 strana **take sb's** ~ stati na čiju stranu 4 uloga **for my** ~ što se mene tiče **in** ~ dijelom **on sb's** ~ od strane koga ~ **and parcel** neizostavni dio • *vi,vt* 1 (from) rastati se s kim 2 rastaviti (se) 3 razmaknuti (se) 4 napraviti razdjeljak ~ **company** (with) rastati se s kim ~ **with** odijeliti se od ~**ing** *n* 1 rastanak 2 razdjeljak ○ *adj* oproštajni, na odlasku ~**ly** *adv* djelomično

partial /'pa:ʃl/ *adj* 1 djelomičan 2 pristran 3 (to) sklon čemu ~**ity** /ˌpa:ʃɪ'ælətɪ/ *n* 1 pristranost 2 (for) sklonost prema

participant /pa:'tɪsɪpənt/ *n* sudionik **participate** /pa:'tɪsɪpeɪt/ *vi* (in) sudjelovati u

participle /'pa:tɪsɪpl/ *n gram* particip, glagolski pridjev

particle /'pa:tɪkl/ *n* 1 čestica 2 *gram* riječca

particular /pə'tɪkjʊlə(r)/ *adj* 1 poseban

2 konkretan, određen 3 (about/over) osjetljiv, izbirljiv • *n* pojedinost in ~ osobito ~s *n pl* pojedinosti; (osobni) podaci ~ly *adv* posebno

partisan /,pɑ:tı'zæn/ *adj* pristran • *n* 1 partizan 2 vatreni pristaša (stranke i sl.)

partition /pɑ:'tıʃn/ *n* 1 pregrada 2 podjela • *vt* (into) podijeliti (na) ~ **off** pregraditi

partner /'pɑ:tnə(r)/ *n* partner, drug~ **in crime** suučesnik ~**ship** *n* 1 udruživanje 2 udruga; društvo, javno trgovačko društvo

partridge /'pɑ:trıdʒ/ *n* jarebica

party /'pɑ:tı:/ *n* 1 zabava; tulum *coll* **give/throw a** ~ napraviti tulum 2 grupa 3 ekipa, tim 4 stranka 5 strana • *vi* zabavljati se

pass /pɑ:s/ *vi,vt* 1 (by/through/across) proći, prolaziti (pored/kroz/preko) 2 prijeći, prelaziti 3 nadilaziti 4 (to) dodati (komu) 5 proći (ispit) 6 donijeti (odluku); izglasati (zakon) 7 *form* dogoditi se ~ **water** pomokriti se ~ **as/for** izdavati se (za koga/što) ~ **by/over** prijeći preko ~ **down/on** prenijeti na ~ **off a.** proći **b.** (as) predstavljati se kao ~ on poslati dalje ~ **out** onesvijestiti se ~ **over a.** prijeći preko **b.** zaobići ~ **up** propustiti • *n* 1 prolaz 2 iskaznica 3 prolazna ocjena 4 dovoljan (ocjena) 5 dodavanje (lopte) **make a** ~ **at** *sl* upucavati se (kome) ~**able** *adj* podnošljiv ~**ing** *n* kraj, smrt **in** ~**ing** usput ~**key** *n* otpirač

passage /'pæsıdʒ/ *n* 1 hodnik 2 prolaz 3 prelazak 4 tok, tijek 5 put; putna karta 6 odlomak

passenger /'pæsındʒə(r)/ *n* 1 putnik 2 *mod* putnički

passerby /,pɑ:sə 'baı/ *n* (**passersby** *pl*) prolaznik

passion /'pæʃn/ *n* 1 strast 2 bijes the P~ Muka Isusova ~**ate** *adj* strastven

passive /'pæsıv/ *adj* pasivan • *n* pasiv

Passover /'pɑ:səʊvə(r)/ *n* Pasha

passport /'pɑ:spɔ:t/ *n* putovnica

password /'pɑ:swɜ:d/ *n* lozinka

past /pɑ:st/ *adj* prošli ~ **master** (in/at/of) pravi majstor za • *prep* 1

iza 2 pored 3 preko ~ **hope** beznadežan ~ **it** *coll* nesposoban • *n* prošlost

pasta /'pæstə/ *n* tjestenina

paste /peıst/ *n* 1 glatka smjesa 2 škrobno ljepilo 3 pašteta 4 štras • *vt* zalijepiti ~**board** *n* 1 ljepenka 2 *mod fig* papirnat ~**up** *n* kolaž

pastel /'pæstl/ *n* 1 pastela 2 pastelna boja • *adj* pastelan

pasteurize /'pæstʃəraız/ *vt* pasterizirati

pastime /'pɑ:staım/ *n* zabava, razonoda

pastor /'pɑ:stə(r)/ *n* pastor ~**al** *adj* 1 svećenički 2 pastoralan

pastry /'peıstrı/ *n* 1 tijesto 2 kolač

pasture /'pɑ:stʃə(r)/ *n* pašnjak **out to** ~ na paši **put out to** ~ umiroviti • *vt,vi* napasati

pasty (1) /'pæstı/ *n* mesna pita

pasty (2) /'peıstı/ *adj* blijed

pat /pæt/ *n* 1 lagani udarac, pljesak 2 milovanje 3 kuglica • *vt* 1 tapšati 2 pogladiti, zagladiti ~ **sb on the back** čestitati komu • *adv* spremno, bez oklijevanja **know/have sth** ~ imati što u malom prstu • *adj* **too** ~ previše uvjerljiv/hitar

patch /pætʃ/ *n* 1 mrlja, šara 2 zakrpa 3 flaster; povez preko oka 4 period 5 nasad, parcela 6 teritorij 7 madež • *vt* zakrpati ~ **up a.** zabašuriti **b.** izgladiti ~**y** *adj* 1 nejednak; šaren 2 nepotpun

patella /pə'telə/ *n* meniskus

patent /'peıtnt/ *adj* 1 očit 2 zaštićen, patentiran ~ **leather** lakirana koža • *n* patent **take out a** ~ **on** patentirati • *vt* patentirati ~**ly** *adv* očito

paternal /pə'tɜ:nl/ *adj* očinski; s očeve strane **paternity** *n* očinstvo

path /pɑ:θ/ *n* 1 staza, put 2 putanja ~**finder** *n* 1 tragač 2 *fig* pionir ~**way** *n* staza; put *fig*

pathetic /pə'θetık/ *adj* jadan, bijedan

pathological /,pæθə'lɒdʒıkl/ *adj* patološki **pathology** /pə'θɒlədʒı/ *n* patologija **pathologist** /pə'θɒlədʒıst/ *n* patolog

patience /'peıʃns/ *n* strpljenje, strpljivost **patient** /'peıʃnt/ *adj* strpljiv o *n* pacijent, bolesnik

patriarch /'peɪtrɪɑ:k/ n patrijarh ~**al** adj patrijarhalan

patrimony /'pætrɪmənɪ/ n očevina

patriot /'pætrɪət/ n domoljub ~**ic** adj domoljubni ~**ism** n domoljublje

patrol /pə'trəʊl/ n patrola • vi,vt (sth) patrolirati čime

patron /'peɪtrən/ n 1 mecena 2 mušterija, klijent ~ **saint** svetac zaštitnik ~**ize** /'pætrənaɪz/ vt patronizirati, omalovažavati

patter /pætə(r)/ vi tapkati; lupkati; škrapati • n 1 lupkanje, tapkanje 2 brzi govor, blebetanje 3 žargon

pattern /'pætn/ n uzorak

paunch /pɔ:ntʃ/ n trbušina

pause /pɔ:z/ n stanka **give sb ~** nagnati koga da razmisli • vi zastati

pave /peɪv/ vt (with) poploçati ~ **the way for** fig utrti put çemu ~**ment** n ploçnik **paving** n 1 poploçena površina 2 graða za poploçavanje

paw /pɔ:/ n šapa • vi (at) 1 grepsti 2 fig grabiti, pipati

pawn (1) /pɔ:n/ vt založiti ~**broker** vlasnik zalagaonice ~**shop** zalagaonica

pawn (2) n pješak; pijun (+ fig)

pay /peɪ/ vi,vt irreg 1 (for sth/to sb) platiti što komu; isplatiti ~ **cash** platiti u gotovom ~ **by cheque** platiti çekom 2 isplatiti se 3 biti plaçen ~ **a visit** posjetiti ~ **attention** obratiti pozornost ~ **a compliment** uputiti kompliment ~ **through the nose** platiti previše ~ **back a.** vratiti novac **b.** vratiti (milo za drago) ~ **for** platiti, biti kažnjen za ~ **in**(to) uplatiti na ~ **off a.** vratiti sve **b.**isplatiti i otpustiti **c.** kupiti çiju šutnju ~**off** n mito ~ **out** platiti ~**out** n isplata ~ **over** (to) uplatiti na çije ime ~ **up** vratiti dug • n plaça ~**able** adj koji dospijeva ~**able to** na ime ~**check** US platna vreçica ~**day** dan isplate ~**master** blagajnik ~**ment** n isplata, plaça ~**ola** n mito ~ **phone** telefonska govornica ~**roll** n platni spisak ~**slip** odrezak plaçe

pea /pi:/ n grašak **as like as two ~s** (**in the pod**) sliçni kao jaje jajetu

peace /pi:s/ n 1 mir 2 mir, spokoj

breach of ~ remeçenje javnog reda i mira ~ **of mind** duševni mir **at** ~ **a.** miran, spokojan **b.** euphem mrtav **hold one's** ~ šutjeti **make one's** ~ **with** pomiriti se **s** ~**able** adj miroljubiv, miran ~**ful** adj miran ~**time** mirnodopsko vrijeme

peach /pi:tʃ/ n 1 breskva 2 coll divota

peacock /'pi:kɒk/ n paun **peahen** /'pi:hen/ n paunica

peak /pi:k/ n 1 vrh 2 vrhunac 3 štitnik (kape) • vi dostiçi vrhunac ~**ed** adj sa štitnikom

peal /pi:l/ n ~ **of bells** zvonjava ~ **of thunder** tutnjava groma ~ **of laughter** grohot • vi,vt (out) zvoniti

peanut /'pi:nʌt/ n kikiriki **for** ~**s** ni za što

pear /peə(r)/ n kruška ~~-**shaped** adj kruškast

pearl /pɜ:l/ n biser ~**y** adj biseran

peasant /'peznt/ n seljak (+ derog) ~**ry** n seljaštvo

peat /pi:t/ n treset

pebble /'pebl/ n oblutak; šljunak

peccadillo /,pekə'dɪləʊ/ n sitni grijeh

peck /pek/ vi,vt (at) 1 kljucati 2 jesti bez teka ~ **sb on the cheek** ovlaš poljubiti • n 1 kljucaj 2 poljubac ~**ing order** coll hijerarhija ~**ish** adj coll pomalo gladan

pecker /'pekə(r)/ n US sl pimpek tab **keep one's** ~ **up** GB ne klonuti duhom

pectoral /'pektərəl/ n grudni

peculiar /pɪ'kju:lɪə(r)/ adj 1 çudan, neobiçan 2 svojstven, osebujan 3 ekscentriçan ~**ity** n 1 svojstvenost, karakteristika 2 osebujnost ~**ly** adv 1 osobito 2 çudno 3 iskljuçivo

pedagogy /'pedəgɒdʒɪ/ n pedagogija

pedal /'pedl/ n pedala; papuçica • vi,vt 1 pritiskati pedalu 2 voziti (bicikl)

pedant /'pednt/ n cjepidlaka ~**ry** n cjepidlaçenje

peddle /'pedl/ vt 1 raspaçavati (drogu i sl.) 2 širiti (glasine) ~**r** n trgovac (drogom)

pedestrian /pɪ'destrɪən/ n pješak • adj 1 pješaçki ~ **precinct** pješaçka zona ~ **crossing** pješaçki prijelaz 2 fig prozaiçan, nezanimljiv

pediatrician /ˌpiːdɪəˈtrɪʃn/ n pedijatar
pediatrics /ˌpiːdɪˈætrɪks/ n pedijatrija
pedicure /ˈpedɪkjʊə(r)/ n pedikiranje
pedigree /ˈpedɪgriː/ n rodoslovlje, rodovnik • adj čistokrvan
pedlar /ˈpedlə(r)/ n pokućarac
pee /piː/ n coll piškiti
peek /piːk/ vi (at) viriti; gledati • n pogled **take a ~** naviriti se **~aboo** n (igra) sad me vidiš sad me ne vidiš
peel /piːl/ vt,vi guliti (se) • n kora
peep (1) /piːp/ vi 1 (at) navirivati se 2 pojavljivati se • n (at) virenje, pogled **take a ~** naviriti se; poluknuti coll **~hole** špijunka **~ing Tom** voajer
peep (2) n pijuk(anje), cijuk • vi pijukati, cijukati
peer (1) /pɪə(r)/ n 1 lord; član najvišeg britanskog plemstva 2 vršnjak **~less** adj bez premca
peer (2) vi zagledati se, motriti
peevish /ˈpiːvɪʃ/ adj čangrizav, zlovoljan
peg /peg/ n 1 klin, vješalica 2 (**clothes ~**) kvačica **off the ~** konfekcijski; standardni **square ~ in a round hole** čovjek na krivom mjestu • vt 1 pričvrstiti (klinom) 2 objesiti (rublje)
pekin(g)ese /ˌpiːkɪˈniːz/ n pekinezer
pelican /ˈpelɪkən/ n pelikan **~ crossing** prijelaz sa semaforom
pellet /ˈpelɪt/ n sačma
pelt (1) /pelt/ vt,vi 1 (with) gađati; obasuti (+ fig) 2 (down) liti kao iz kabla
pelt (2) n krzno, koža
pelvic /ˈpelvɪk/ adj zdjelični **pelvis** n zdjelica
pen (1) /pen/ n pero **fountain ~** nalivpero **ballpoint ~** kemijska olovka **felt-tip ~** flomaster **~knife** perorez • **~ name** pseudonim • vt napisati
pen (2) n obor • vt (up/in) zatvoriti (u obor/sobičak i sl.)
penal /ˈpiːnl/ adj 1 kazneni **~ servitude** robija 2 krivični kažnjiv **~lize** /ˈpiːnəlaɪz/ vt (for) 1 staviti u nepovoljan položaj 2 sport kazniti **~ty** /ˈpenltɪ/ n 1 (for) kazna; globa **~ty clause** penale **death ~ty** smrtna kazna **~ty kick** jedanaesterac **~ty area** kazneni prostor 2 neugodnost

penance /ˈpenəns/ n (for) pokora **do ~** vršiti pokoru
pence /pens/ n pl → **penny 20 ~** dvadeset penija
penchant /ˈpɑːnʃɑːn/ n (for) sklonost prema
pencil /ˈpensl/ n olovka **~ pusher** derog birokrat • vt **~ in** ubilježiti
pendant /ˈpendənt/ n privjesak
pending /ˈpendɪŋ/ prep form do • adj 1 neriješen, u tijeku 2 na pomolu
pendulum /ˈpendjʊləm/ n visak, njihalo
penetrate /ˈpenɪtreɪt/ vt,vi (into-/through) 1 probiti (se) kroz; prodrijeti 2 fig prozreti; razotkriti **penetrating** adj prodoran
penguin /ˈpeŋgwɪn/ n pingvin
penicillin /ˌpenɪˈsɪlɪn/ n penicilin
peninsula /pəˈnɪnsjʊlə/ n poluotok
penis /ˈpiːnɪs/ n penis
penitent /ˈpenɪtənt/ adj pokajnički • n pokajnik **penitence** n pokajanje **~ial** n pokornički **~iary** n zatvor
pennant /ˈpenənt/ n zastavica
penniless /ˈpenɪlɪs/ adj bez prebijene pare
penny /ˈpenɪ/ n (**pennies/pence** pl) peni; para fig **be two/ten a ~** biti na bacanje **in for a ~, in for a pound** što se započne mora se i dovršiti **~ dreadful** petparački roman **~-pincher** škrtac
pension (1) /ˈpenʃn/ n mirovina **~ scheme** uplaćivanje staža **~ fund** mirovinski fond • vt **~ off** umiroviti **~able age** dob za mirovinu (**old age**) **~er** n umirovljenik
pension (2) /ˈpɒnsɪɒn/ n pansion
pensive /ˈpensɪv/ adj zamišljen
Pentagon /ˈpentəgən/ n (**the ~**) Pentagon
Pentecost /ˈpentɪkɒst/ n Duhovi, Pedesetnica
penthouse /ˈpenthaʊs/ n stan u potkrovlju/na najvišem katu
pent-up /ˌpentˈʌp/ adj 1 zatvoren 2 fig zatomljen
penultimate /penˈʌltɪmət/ adj predzadnji
people /ˈpiːpl/ n 1 (+ pl) ljudi 2 narod, puk 3 narod • vt 1 nastavati 2 napuči-

ti

pep /pep/ *n* život *fig* ~ **talk** poticajni govor ~ **pill** stimulant

pepper /'pepə(r)/ *n* 1 papar 2 paprika • *vt* 1 (with) biti pun čega 2 popapriti ~**corn** zrno papra ~**corn rent** simbolična stanarina ~**mint** paprena metvica ~ **pot** paprenka ~**ry** *adj* 1 papren 2 prijeke ćudi

per /pɜ:/ *prep* po ~ **annum** godišnje ~ **capita** po glavi stanovnika **as** ~ prema **as** ~ **usual** *coll* po običaju ~ **cent**, ~**cent** *adv* posto ~**centage** *n* postotak

perambulator /pə'ræmbjʊleɪtə(r)/ *n form* dječja kolica

perceive /pə'si:v/ *vt* primijetiti; uvidjeti; shvatiti

perceptible /pə'septəbl/ *adj* primjetan **perception** *n* 1 opažanje, percepcija 2 oštroumnost **perceptive** *adj* oštrouman

perch /pɜ:tʃ/ *n* 1 prečka 2 uzvisina • *vi, vt* (on, upon) 1 spustiti se (ptice) 2 smjestiti (se)

percolate /'pɜ:kəleɪt/ *vi, vt* 1 probiti se (+ *fig*) 2 pripremati filter-kavu; kuhati se (filter-kava) **percolator** *n* aparat za filter-kavu

percussion /pə'kʌʃn/ *n* udaraljke *pl*

peremptory /pə'remptəri/ *adj* 1 zapovjednički 2 neotklonjiv

perennial /pə'reniəl/ *adj* 1 vječan 2 trajni (biljka) • *n* trajnica

perfect /'pɜ:fɪkt/ *adj* 1 savršen 2 potpun 3 *gram* svršen • /pə'fekt/ *vt* usavršiti • *gram* perfekt ~**ion** *n* 1 savršenstvo **to** ~**ion** savršeno 2 usavršavanje ~**ionist** *n* perfekcionist; pedant ~**ly** *adv* 1 savršeno 2 potpuno

perforate /'pɜ:fəreɪt/ *vt* 1 izbušiti 2 perforirati

perform /pə'fɔ:m/ *vt, vi* 1 izvesti; izvršiti; obaviti; učiniti 2 iskazati se ~**ance** *n* 1 izvedba 2 predstava 3 vršenje 4 rezultat 5 performansa ~**er** *n* izvođač; glumac; zabavljač

perfume /'pɜ:fju:m/ *n* 1 miomiris 2 parfem • *vt* (with) namirisati (čime)

perfunctory /pə'fʌŋktəri/ *adj* površan

perhaps /pə'hæps/ *adv* možda

peril /'perɪl/ *n* opasnost **at one's** ~ na vlastitu odgovornost ~**ous** *adj* opasan

perimeter /pə'rɪmɪtə(r)/ *n* 1 područje, prostor 2 opseg

period /'pɪərɪəd/ *n* 1 razdoblje ~ **costume** povijesne odore ~ **piece** antikvitet 2 (školski) sat 3 menstruacija 4 *US* točka ~**ic** *adj* periodičan, povremeni ~**ical** *n* časopis

peripheral /pe'rɪfərəl/ *n* periferan; marginalan

periscope /'perɪskəʊp/ *n* periskop

perish /'perɪʃ/ *vi, vt* poginuti ~ **the thought!** ne daj Bože! ~**able** *adj* lako pokvarljiv ~**ables** *n pl* lako pokvarljiva roba

periwinkle /'perɪwɪŋkl/ *n* 1 zimzelen 2 obalar (morski puž)

perjure /'pɜ:dʒə(r)/ *vt* ~ **oneself** krivo se zakleti **perjury** *n* krivokletstvo

perk (1) /pɜ:k/ *coll* → **perquisite**

perk (2) → **percolate** 2

perk (3) *vi, vt* ~ **up** živnuti ~**y** *adj* živahan

perm /pɜ:m/ *n* trajna (ondulacija); mini-val • *vt* dati trajnu

permanent /'pɜ:mənənt/ *adj* stalni ~ **wave** trajna ondulacija

permeable /'pɜ:mɪəbl/ *adj* propusan

permeate /'pɜ:mɪeɪt/ *vi, vt* (into-/through) prodrijeti (u/kroz); prožeti

permissible /pə'mɪsəbl/ *adj* dopušten **permission** *n* dopuštenje **permissive** *adj* popustljiv, liberalan

permit /'pɜ:mɪt/ *n* dopusnica, dozvola • *vt, vi* dopustiti **not be** ~**ted** ne smjeti

peroxyde /pə'rɒksaɪd/ *n* peroksid

perpendicular /,pɜ:pən'dɪkjʊlə(r)/ *adj* 1 uspravan 2 (to) okomit

perp /pɜ:p/ *n coll* počinitelj zločina

perpetrate /'pɜ:pɪtreɪt/ *vt* počiniti (zločin) **perpetrator** *n* počinitelj

perpetual /pə'petʃʊəl/ *adj* 1 neprestan 2 vječni **perpetuate** *vt* ovjekovječiti; održavati

perplex /pə'pleks/ *vt* zbuniti, smesti ~**ity** *n* smetenost

perquisite /'pɜ:kwɪzɪt/ *n form* beneficija

persecute /'pɜ:sɪkju:t/ *vt* proganjati **persecution** *n* progon

perseverance /,pɜ:sɪ'vɪərəns/ *n* upornost **persevere** *vi* (at/in/with) ustrajati

persist /pə'sɪst/ vi 1 (in/with) ustrajati, nastaviti, uporno nešto činiti 2 potrajati ~**ent** adj uporan; tvrdokoran

person /'pɜ:sn/ n (people coll/~s leg, form pl) 1 osoba 2 gram lice **in** ~ osobno ~ suffix ¶ koristi se kao spolno neutralni izraz u složenicama umjesto -man i -woman spokesperson, chairperson ~**able** adj pristao ~**al** adj 1 osobni 2 privatni ~**al assistant** tajnik ~**ality** n ličnost; poznata/javna ličnost ~**ally** adv 1 osobno 2 kao osoba 3 privatno ~**al property/estate** leg pokretna imovina ~**al stereo** walkman ~**ification** n utjelovljenje ~**ify** vt utjeloviti, personificirati ~**nel** n 1 osoblje, namještenici 2 kadrovska služba

perspective /pə'spektɪv/ n 1 perspektiva 2 perspektiva, gledanje 3 (of) pogled na

perspex /'pɜ:speks/ n GB TM pleksiglas

perspiration /ˌpɜ:spə'reɪʃn/ n znoj(enje) **perspire** /pə'spaɪə(r)/ vi znojiti se

persuade /pə'sweɪd/ vt 1 (into) nagovoriti (na što) 2 (out of) odgovoriti (od čega) 3 (of) form uvjeriti (u što) **persuasion** n 1 nagovaranje 2 form uvjerenje **persuasive** adj uvjerljiv

pert /pɜ:t/ adj 1 izazovan, drzak 2 sladak

pertain /pə'teɪn/ vt ~ **to** ticati se

pertinent /'pɜ:tɪnənt/ adj (to) relevantan, važan, koji se tiče

perturb /pə'tɜ:b/ vt form uznemiriti

peruse /pə'ru:z/ vt form pročitati; proučiti

pervade /pə'veɪd/ vt form prožeti **pervasive** /pə'veɪsɪv/ adj sveprisutan

perverse /pə'vɜ:s/ adj 1 nastran, izopačen 2 tvrdokoran ~**ly** adv kao za vraga **perversion** n nastranost, izopačenost **pervert** /pə'vɜ:t/ vt 1 izopačiti 2 zloupotrijebiti 3 iskriviti o /'pɜ:vɜ:t/ n perverznjak

pesky /'peskɪ/ adj nesnosan

pessimist /'pesɪmɪst/ n pesimist ~**ic** adj pesimističan **pessimism** n pesimizam

pest /pest/ n 1 štetočina 2 gnjavator; gnjavaža ~**er** vt (for/with) gnjaviti, salijetati ~**icide** /'pestɪsaɪd/ n pesticid ~**ilence** n pošast; kuga

pestle /'pestl/ n tučak

pet /pet/ n 1 kućni ljubimac 2 ljubimac 3 mod omiljen ~ **name** ime od milja • vt,vi maziti (se)

petal /'petl/ n latica

peter /'pi:tə/ vi ~ **out** zamrijeti, nestati

petit/petty bourgeois /ˌpetɪ 'buəʒwɑ:/ n, adj malograđanin; malograđanski

petite /pə'ti:t/ adj sitan

petition /pɪ'tɪʃn/ n 1 (for/against) peticija 2 molba • vi,vt (for/against) (za)tražiti

petrify /'petrɪfaɪ/ vt skameniti; užasavati

petrol /'petrəl/ n benzin ~ **station** benzinska stanica ~**eum** n nafta

petticoat /'petɪkəʊt/ n podsuknja; kombine

pettifogging /'petɪfɒgɪŋ/ n sitničarenje

petty /'petɪ/ adj 1 nevažan, neznatan 2 sitan fig, sitne duše 3 lakši (zločin) ~ **cash** blagajna ~ **larceny** sitna krađa ~ **officer** dočasnik (mornarica)

petulant /'petjʊlənt/ adj razmažen, ćudljiv

pew /pju:/ n klupa (u crkvi)

pewter /'pju:tə(r)/ n kositar

phantom /'fæntəm/ n 1 utvara, fantom 2 mod fantomski; lažni

pharaoh /'feərəʊ/ n faraon

pharisee /'færɪsi:/ n farizej

pharmaceutical /ˌfɑ:mə'sju:tɪkl/ adj farmaceutski **pharmacist** /'fɑ:məsɪst/ n 1 farmaceut 2 apotekar **pharmacy** /'fɑ:məsɪ/ n 1 apoteka 2 farmacija

phase /feɪz/ n 1 (in/of) faza (čega) 2 mijena • vt provesti u fazama ~ **in** postupno uvesti ~ **out** postupno ukinuti

pheasant /'feznt/ n fazan

phenomenal /fɪ'nɒmɪnl/ adj fenomenalan **phenomenon** n pojava; fenomen

phial /'faɪəl/ n bočica

Phi Betta Kappa n udruženje najboljih studenata; član tog udruženja

philanderer /fɪ'lændərə(r)/ n razvratnik

philantropist /fɪ'lænθrɒpɪst/ n filantrop philantropy n čovjekoljublje

philately /fɪ'lætəlɪ/ n filatelija

philistine /'fɪlɪstaɪn/ n filistar; malograđanin

philosopher /fɪ'lɒsəfə(r)/ n filozof philosophical /,fɪlə'sɒfɪkl/ adj filozofski philosophy n mudroslovlje; filozofija (+ fig)

philtre (-ter US) /'fɪltə(r)/ n napitak

phlegm /flem/ n 1 sluz 2 flegmatičnost ~atic /fleg'mætɪk/ adj flegmatičan, smiren

phobia /'fəʊbɪə/ n fobija, strah

phoenix /'fi:nɪks/ n feniks

phone /fəʊn/ n 1 telefon answer/pick up the ~ dići slušalicu 2 mod telefonski ~ book/directory telefonski imenik ~ box govornica ~-tapping prisluškivanje telefona • vt,vi telefonirati komu, nazvati koga, javiti (što/se) telefonski

phonetic /fə'netɪk/ adj fonetski ~s n fonetika

phoney /'fəʊnɪ/ adj coll lažan • n coll preserator coll

phosphorus /'fɒsfərəs/ n fosfor

photo /'fəʊtəʊ/ n fotografija; slika Photofit n TM fotorobot

photocopier /'fəʊtəʊ,kɒpɪə/ n fotokopirni stroj photocopy /'fəʊtəʊ,kɒpɪ/ vt fotokopirati n fotokopija

photogenic /,fəʊtəʊ'dʒɪnɪk/ adj fotogeničan

photograph /'fəʊtəgrɑ:f/ n fotografija take a ~ of slikati koga/što • vt slikati ~ well biti fotogeničan ~er /fə'tɒɡrəfə(r)/ n fotograf ~ic adj fotografski ~y /fə'tɒɡrəfɪ/ n fotografija (umijeće)

photostat /'fəʊtəstæt/ n fotokopija

photosynthesis /,fəʊtəʊ'sɪnθəsɪs/ n fotosinteza

phrase /freɪz/ n izraz; fraza • vt sročiti

physical /'fɪzɪkl/ adj 1 tjelesni ~ education/training tjelesni odgoj 2 fizikalan, prirodan 3 grub • n liječnički pregled ~ly adv 1 tjelesno 2 posve

physician /fɪ'zɪʃn/ n arch liječnik

physicist /'fɪzɪsɪst/ n fizičar physics n

fizika

physiognomy /,fɪzɪ'ɒnəmɪ/ n fizionomija

physiology /,fɪzɪ'ɒlədʒɪ/ n fiziologija

physiotherapy /,fɪzɪəʊ'θerəpɪ/ n fizioterapija

physique /fə'zi:k/ n vanjština

pianist /'pɪənɪst/ n klavirist piano /pɪ'ænəʊ/ n klavir grand piano koncertni klavir upright piano pijanino

pick /pɪk/ vt 1 izabrati 2 ubrati 3 kopati; čačkati 4 kljucati; glodati 5 čupati 6 prebirati po žicama ~ sb's brains iskoristiti čije znanje ~ sb's pocket ukrasti iz džepa ~pocket n džepar ~ a lock obiti bravu ~ a quarrel/fight izazvati svađu ~ at sth nevoljko/malo jesti ~ sth off ubrati ~ sb off ustrijeliti ~ on sb coll okomiti se na koga, imati pik na koga ~ out izabrati; izdvojiti; razabrati; prebirati ~ up a. dignuti; pokupiti; skupiti b. nastaviti c. dobiti; primiti d. uhititi e. popraviti se; povećati (brzinu) ~up n a. ručica gramofona b. (otvoreni) kamionet c. US ubrzanje ~me-up n 1 izbor take your ~ izaberi the ~ of najbolji 2 pijuk ~er n berač ~ings coll dobit, zarada ~y adj US izbirljiv

picket /'pɪkɪt/ n 1 kolac 2 straža; ophodnja 3 štrajkačka straža; štrajkači • vt,vi 1 iskolčati 2 postaviti stražu 3 okružiti štrajkačima

pickle /'pɪkl/ n 1 ocat; slana voda 2 ukiseljeno povrće; kiseli krastavac in a ~ coll u sosu fig • vt ukiseliti; usoliti ~d adj coll pijan

picnic /'pɪknɪk/ n piknik, izlet • vi ići na izlet/piknik

pictorial /pɪk'tɔ:rɪəl/ adj slikovni; ilustriran

picture /'pɪktʃə(r)/ n slika (+ fig); crtež put sb in the ~ upoutiti koga ~ book slikovnica ~ postcard razglednica ~s n pl GB coll 1 kino 2 filmska industrija • vt 1 zamisliti, predočiti sebi 2 naslikati; ncrtati ~sque adj slikovit

piddle /'pɪdl/ vi coll piškiti piddling adj malen, neznatan

pidgin /'pɪdʒɪn/ n pidžin jezik

pie /paɪ/ n pita as easy as ~ vrlo lako ~

in the sky neostvarljiv plan **~-eyed** *adj* pijan **have a finger in every ~** u svemu imati svoje prste

piebald /'paɪbɔːld/ *adj* crno-bijel (konj)

piece /piːs/ *n* 1 komad; dio **of a ~** isti a **~ of advice** jedan savjet a **~ of information** jedna obavijest **take to ~s** rastaviti na dijelove **fall to ~s** raspasti se **go to ~s** slomiti se *fig I'll give him a ~ of my mind* reći ću mu što mislim o njemu! 2 figura 3 (**~ of work**) djelo 4 novinski članak; TV prilog 5 novčić • *vt* **~ sth together** složiti, sastaviti cjelinu od dijelova **~meal** *adv* dio po dio

pier /pɪə(r)/ *n* molo; šetalište uz more

pierce /pɪəs/ *vt* probosti; probušiti; probiti; proparati; prodrijeti **piercing** *adj* prodoran, oštar

piety /'paɪətɪ/ *n form* pobožnost

piffle /'pɪfl/ *n coll* glupost

pig /pɪg/ *n* 1 svinja (+ *fig*) **~ in a poke** mačak u vreći **~s might fly** kad na vrbi rodi grožđe! **~headed** *adj derog* tvrdoglav **~let** *n* praščić **~sty** *n* svinjac **~tail** *n* repić, pletenica 2 *sl derog* murija, murjak • *vi* **~ out** *US* preždera(va)ti se **~gery** *n* a. svinjac b. svinjarija **~gy** *n* praščić ○ *adj* praseći **~gyback** *n, adv* (nošenje) na leđima **~gybank** *n* kasica-prasica

pigeon /'pɪdʒɪn/ *n* golub **~-chested** *adj* kokošjih prsa **~-hole** *n* pretinac, pregradak ○ *vt* a. klasificirati, svrstati b. pohraniti

pigment /'pɪgmənt/ *n* pigment

pike (1) /paɪk/ *n* štuka

pike (2) *n* koplje

pike (3) → **turnpike**

pilchard /'pɪltʃəd/ *n* sardela, srdjela

pile (1) /paɪl/ *n* 1 gomila, hrpa **make a/one's ~** obogatiti se 2 zgradurina • *vt,vi* 1 naslagati, staviti na hrpu, natrpati 2 nahrupiti **~ it on** pretjerivati **~ up** nagomilati se **~-up** *n* lančani sudar

pile (2) *n* stup, potporanj

piles /paɪlz/ *n pl coll* hemoroidi

pilfer /'pɪlfə(r)/ *vi,vt* krasti

pilgrim /'pɪlgrɪm/ *n* hodočasnik **the P~ Fathers** puritanci koji su osnovali koloniju Plymouth u Americi 1620. **~age** *n* hodočašće

pill /pɪl/ *n* 1 tableta 2 kontracepcijska pilula **be on the ~** uzimati kontracepcijske pilule **~box** a. kutija za lijekove b. bunker

pillage /'pɪlɪdʒ/ *vi,vt arch* harati, pljačkati

pillar /'pɪlə(r)/ *n* stup (+ *fig*) **~ box** poštanski sandučić

pillory /'pɪlərɪ/ *n* stup srama • *vt* 1 privezati za stup srama 2 *fig* ismijati, izvrgnuti ruglu

pillow /'pɪləʊ/ *n* jastuk **~case/~slip** jastučnica • *vt* nasloniti, poduprijeti jastukom

pilot /'paɪlət/ *n* pilot • *vt* pilotirati, upravljati; voditi, pokazati put • *adj* pokusni **~ light** žižak (na plinskom grijalu)

pimp /pɪmp/ *n* makro

pimpernel /'pɪmpənel/ *n bot* bedrinac

pimple /'pɪmpl/ *n* prištić

pin /pɪn/ *n* 1 pribadača 2 čavlić 3 igla **safety ~** sigurnosna igla; ziherica *coll* 4 *US* broš 5 kvačica 6 **~s** *coll* noge **~s and needles** *coll* trnci **on ~s** na iglama *fig* **~ball** fliper **~head** *sl* glupan **~point** *vt* odrediti; locirati ○ *adj* vrlo precizan; sitan **~prick** sitan ubod iglom; sitna neprilika **~stripe** sitna pruga • *vt* pričvrstiti pribadačama; pribosti; priklijestiti **~down** odrediti, odlučiti; identificirati **~on** prišiti *fig* **~up** *n* slika gole žene

pinafore /'pɪnəfɔː(r)/ *n* pregača

pincers /'pɪnsəz/ *n pl* kliješta **~ movement** *mil* dvojni obuhvat

pinch /pɪntʃ/ *vi,vt* 1 štipati, (u)štipnuti 2 (cipele) tiskati 3 *GB coll* ukrasti, maznuti 4 *coll* uhititi • *n* 1 uštip 2 koliko stane između dva prsta **with a ~ of salt** s rezervom 3 stiska, teškoća **at/in a ~** bude li nužno

pine (1) /paɪn/ *n* 1 (**~tree**) bor **~cone** češer 2 borovina **~y, piny** *adj* borov, poput bora

pine (2) *vi* (for) venuti; patiti, čeznuti (za)

pineapple /'paɪnæpl/ *n* 1 ananas 2 *sl* ručna bomba; kinder-jaje *sl*

pinion (1) /'pɪnɪən/ *vt form* sapeti, spu-

tati
pinion (2) *n* zupčanik
pinion (3) *n* krilo ptice; vršak krila
pink /pɪŋk/ *adj* 1 ružičast 2 *derog* koji simpatizira socijaliste **~o** *n coll derog* ljevičar • *n* 1 ružičasta boja **in the ~** odlična zdravlja 2 klinčić **~ie/~y** mali prst
pinnacle /ˈpɪnəkl/ *n* 1 vrhunac 2 *lit* tornjić
pint /paint/ *n* 1 pinta (cca 0.57 l) 2 *GB coll* krigla piva **~-size(d)** *adj* malen, sitan
pioneer /ˌpaɪəˈnɪə(r)/ *n* pionir, prvi naseljenik; prethodnica • *vt* prokrčiti put čemu
pious /ˈpaɪəs/ *adj form* pobožan
pip (1) /pɪp/ *n* sjemenka, koštica
pip (2) *n* tonski signal
pip (3) *n* 1 točka (na kocki, dominu) 2 *coll GB* zvjezdica (na epoleti)
pip (4) *vt* (**~ at the post**) *GB coll* pobijediti za dlaku
pipe /paɪp/ *n* 1 cijev 2 lula 3 gajde *pl* **~dream** neostvariv san **~line** plinovod, naftovod **in the ~line** u pripremi • *vt*,*vi* 1 provesti cijevima **~d TV** kabelska TV 2 piskutati; zviždati **~ down** *vi coll* smiriti se, stišati se **~ up** progovoriti; zapjevati **~r** *n* gajdaš **piping** *n* 1 cjevovod, cijevi 2 ukras, obrub (na haljini/torti) **piping hot** kipući
pipsqueak /ˈpɪpskwiːk/ *n derog* bezveznjaković
piquant /ˈpiːkənt/ *adj* pikantan (+ *fig*)
pique /piːk/ *vt* uvrijediti • *n* ljutnja
pirate /ˈpaɪərət/ *n* gusar • *vt* 1 gusariti 2 prodavati bez autorskih prava **piracy** /ˈpaɪərəsi/ *n* 1 gusarstvo 2 piratska prodaja
pirouette /ˌpɪruˈet/ *n* pirueta
Pisces /ˈpaɪsiːz/ *n astrol* Ribe
piss /pɪs/ *vi tab* 1 pišati *vulg* 2 (kiša) lijevati kao iz kabla **~ off**! *tab sl* goni se **~ sb off** ljutiti, ići na živce **~ed** *adj* 1 *GB* pijan 2 *US* ljutit • *n tab* pišalina *vulg* **have/take a ~** popišati se *vulg* **take the ~ (out of sb)** zafrkavati
pistil /ˈpɪstl/ *n* tučak
pistol /ˈpɪstl/ *n* pištolj
piston /ˈpɪstən/ *n* klip (motora)

pit (1) /pɪt/ *n* 1 rupa, jama 2 rudnik **~head** ulaz u rudnik **~man** rudar 3 stražnja sjedala parketa • *vt* izdubiti, izrovati **~ against** boriti se protiv
pit (2) *n US* koštica • *vt* izvaditi košticu
pitch (1) /pɪtʃ/ *vt*,*vi* 1 podići (šator) **~ camp** ulogoriti se 2 zadati određenu visinu (glasa, tona) **high-~ed** *adj* visok (glas) 3 pasti, srušiti (se) 4 (brod) propinjati se 5 baciti, hitnuti 6 biti strm • *n* 1 igralište, teren 2 visina (glasa, tona) 3 stupanj, razina 4 nagib **~er** *n* 1 vrč 2 bacač (u baseballu) **~fork** *n* vile *pl* ○ *vt* a. vilama bacati (sijeno) b. *fig* gurnuti
pitch (2) *n* bitumen, katran **~-black** *adj* crn kao katran/ugljen **~-dark** *adj* mračno kao u rogu **~-darkness** *n* mrkli mrak
pitfall /ˈpɪtfɔːl/ *n* zamka (+ *fig*)
pith /pɪθ/ *n* 1 srčika 2 *fig* srž, jezgra, bit **~y** *adj* jezgrovit
pitiful /ˈpɪtɪfl/ *adj* jadan, bijedan **pitiless** *adj* nemilosrdan
pittance /ˈpɪtns/ *n* crkavica
pituitary /pɪˈtjuːɪtəri/ *adj* **~ gland** hipofiza
pity /ˈpɪti/ *n* 1 samilost, sažaljenje **have/take ~** sažaliti se 2 šteta • *vt* žaliti
pivot /ˈpɪvət/ *n* stožer, ključna točka • *vi*,*vt* okretati se **~ on sth** ovisiti o čemu **~al** *adj* ključni
pixie, pixy /ˈpɪksi/ *n* vila, vilenjak
placard /ˈplækɑːd/ *n* transparent, plakat
placate /pləˈkeɪt/ *vt* smiriti
place /pleɪs/ *n* mjesto; kuća, stan; dužnost **in the first ~** u prvom redu, kao prvo **all over the ~** posvuda **in ~ of** umjesto **out of ~** neumjestan **take ~** dogoditi se, održati se **~-name** toponim • *vt* smjestiti, (po)staviti, zauzeti mjesto; uložiti **~ an order** naručiti **~ment** *n* namještenje, smještaj; plasman
placenta /pləˈsentə/ *n* (*pl* **~s**, **~e**) placenta
placid /ˈplæsɪd/ *adj* miran, smiren
plagiarize /ˈpleɪdʒəraɪz/ *vi*,*vt* plagirati **plagiarism** *n* plagijat
plague /pleɪg/ *n* 1 kuga (+ *fig*) 2

pošast, navala, najezda • *vt* mučiti, gnjaviti

plaice /pleɪs/ *n* (*pl* ~) riba iverak

plaid /plæd/ *n* karirano sukno

plain (1) /pleɪn/ *adj* 1 jednostavan, običan ~**-clothes** *adj* u civilu **it was ~ sailing** išlo je kao po loju 2 jednobojan, bez ukrasa 3 jasan, očevidan ~**-spoken** *adj* otvoren, izravan *euphem* neugledan, neprivlačan

plain (2) *n* (~s) ravnica, nizina

plaint /pleɪnt/ *n* 1 *leg* (op)tužba 2 *lit* tužaljka ~**iff** /ˈpleɪntɪf/ *n* tužitelj ~**ive** *adj* plačan, tugaljiv

plait /plæt/ *n* GB pletenica • *vt* (is)plesti

plan /plæn/ *n* 1 plan, osnova 2 tlocrt • *vt,vi* planirati; dizajnirati ~**ner** *n* planer ~**ning permission** građevinska dopusnica

plane (1) /pleɪn/ *n* 1 avion, zrakoplov **by ~** avionom 2 *geom* ravnina 3 razina • *adj* 1 ravan 2 dvodimenzionalan

plane (2) *n* blanja • *vt* (iz)blanjati

plane (3) *n* platana

planet /ˈplænɪt/ *n* planet ~**ary** *adj* planetaran

plank /plæŋk/ *n* 1 daska 2 *fig* načelo

plant /plɑːnt/ *n* 1 biljka 2 tvornica **power ~** elektrana 3 pogon, postrojenje • *vt* 1 (po)saditi, zasaditi; posijati (+ *fig*) ~**out** 2 *coll* podmetnuti, postaviti ~**er** *n* 1 plantažer 2 sadilica ~**ation** *n* 1 plantaža, nasad 2 *hist* naseljavanje

plaque /plɑːk/ *n* 1 spomen-ploča 2 zubne naslage *pl*

plasm /ˈplæzəm/ *n* (stanična) plazma (**blood**) ~**a** (krvna) plazma

plaster /ˈplɑːstə(r)/ *n* 1 žbuka 2 flaster 3 ~**of Paris** gips ~**cast** gips, longeta • *vt* 1 (o)žbukati, prekriti 2 slijepiti; zagladiti ~**ed** *adj* *sl* pijan

plastic /ˈplæstɪk/ *n* plastika ~**money** kreditne kartice • *adj* plastičan; koji se može modelirati ~**art** likovna umjetnost ~**surgery** plastična operacija ~**ine** /ˈplæstɪsiːn/ GB TM plastelin

plate /pleɪt/ *n* 1 tanjur 2 ploča, pločica 3 tablica 4 ilustracija 5 pozlata 6 srebrnina 7 (**dental** ~) umjetno zubalo •

vt pozlatiti ~**let** *n* krvna pločica, trombocit

plateau /ˈplætəʊ/ *n* (*pl* ~s, ~x) 1 visoravan 2 plato

platform /ˈplætfɔːm/ *n* 1 peron 2 platforma 3 govornica 4 program stranke ~**shoes** cipele debelih potplata

platinum /ˈplætɪnəm/ *n* platina

platitude /ˈplætɪtjuːd/ *n* opće mjesto, banalnost

platonic /pləˈtɒnɪk/ *adj* platonski

platoon /pləˈtuːn/ *n* vod

platter /ˈplætə(r)/ *n* 1 US veliki tanjur 2 *arch* plitica

plausible /ˈplɔːzəbl/ *adj* uvjerljiv, vjerojatan

play /pleɪ/ *n* 1 igra(nje); zabava **in ~** u šali **a ~ on words** igra riječima **bring into ~** upotrijebiti 2 kazališni komad, drama 3 *fig* sloboda, prostor ~**act** *vi* glumiti, izigravati ~**dough** US plastelin ~**ground** igralište ~**house** kazalište ~**room** igraonica ~**thing** igračka ~**wright** pisac kazališnih komada • *vt,vi* 1 igrati se 2 glumiti, igrati; odigrati, zaigrati; izigravati 3 svirati; puštati glazbu/ploče 4 izvesti ~**tricks on sb** varati ~**for time** pokušavati dobiti na vremenu ~**hard to get** *coll* dizati si cijenu hinjenom nezainteresiranošću ~**it by ear** postupati prema okolnostima, ne planirati unaprijed ~**(it) safe** ne riskirati ~**the game** biti pošten/častan ~**about/around** zabavljati se ~**along with sb** prihvatiti čiju igru ~**at sth** igrati se čega ~**back** ponovno preslušati/pregledati ~**down** umanjiti važnost ~**off** ne doigravanje ~**on** iskorištavati ~**up** naglasiti, istaknuti ~**up to sb** ulagivati se ~**with** poigravati se ~**with oneself** *euphem* masturbirati ~**er** *n* igrač; svirač ~**ful** *adj* razigran; nestašan, neozbiljan

plea /pliː/ *n* 1 *form* molba 2 *leg* iskaz optuženoga **he entered a ~ of "not guilty"** izjavio je da se ne osjeća krivim

plead /pliːd/ *vi,vt* *irreg* 1 (with) preklinjati (koga) 2 *leg* izjaviti, izjasniti se **how do you ~?** osjećate li se krivim?

pleasant /'pleznt/ *adj* ugodan **~ry** *n form* dosjetka

please /pli:z/ *vi,vt* 1 udovoljiti/ugoditi (komu), zadovoljiti (koga) 2 željeti, izvoljeti **if you ~** molim vas lijepo ~ **God** ako Bog da **~d** *adj* zadovoljan **(I'm) ~d to meet you** drago mi je (izričaj pri upoznavanju) **pleasing** *adj* 1 ugodan 2 zadovoljavajući • *int* molim (te/vas)

pleasure /'pleʒə(r)/ *n* 1 zadovoljstvo **take ~ in** uživati u **it was a ~** bilo mi je drago **at your ~** po vašoj želji **what's your ~?** izvolite? 2 zabava, razonoda

pleat /pli:t/ *n* nabor, plise • *vt* plisirati

plebeian /pli'bi:ən/ *n* plebejac • *adj* plebejski

plectrum /'plektrəm/ *n* trzalica

pled *v irreg* → **plead**

plegde /pledʒ/ *n* 1 (svečano) obećanje 2 zalog, znak • *vt* 1 obećati 2 obvezati se

plenary /'pli:nərɪ/ *adj form* 1 plenarni ~ **session** plenarna sjednica 2 neograničen, potpun

plenipotentiary /ˌplenɪpə'tenʃərɪ/ *adj* s punim ovlastima • *n* opunomoćeni poslanik

plenitude /'plenɪtju:d/ *n* 1 punoća 2 obilje

plenty /'plentɪ/ *n* (of) mnogo; obilje, izobilje **plentiful** *adj* obilan

pliable /'plaɪəbl/ *adj* 1 savitljiv 2 prilagodljiv

pliant /'plaɪənt/ *adj* povodljiv

pliers /'plaɪəz/ *n pl* kombinirke

plight /plaɪt/ *n* teške prilike, nedaće *pl*

plimsolls /'plɪmsɒlz/ *n pl* platnene tenisice

plinth /plɪnθ/ *n* podnožje stupa

plod /plɒd/ *vi* 1 klipsati, teško se kretati 2 (away/on) raditi, rintati

plonk /plɒŋk/ *vt coll* baciti • *n GB coll* loše vino

plot /plɒt/ *n* 1 radnja, fabula 2 (tajni) plan, zavjera 3 *US* tlocrt 4 parcela • *vt,vi* 1 kovati zavjeru/plan 2 grafički prikazati 3 označiti položaj, pratiti kretanje

plough (**plow** *US*) /plaʊ/ *n* 1 plug 2 **the P~** Veliki Medvjed • *vi,vt* 1 orati

2 *fig* probiti se (kroz što) ~ **sth back** ponovno uložiti **~man** *n* orač **~man's lunch** *GB* obrok od sira, kruha i salate

plow → **plough**

ploy /plɔɪ/ *n* taktika, trik

pluck /plʌk/ *vt,vi* 1 (out/from/off) čupati, iščupati 2 (o)čerupati (perje) 3 prebirati (po žicama) 4 ubrati ~ **at sth** vući, trzati ~ **up (one's) courage** skupiti hrabrost • *n coll* hrabrost **~y** *adj coll* hrabar, odlučan

plug /plʌg/ *n* 1 utikač 2 čep **~hole** *GB* odvod za vodu 3 *coll* dobra kritika; reklama **pull the ~** naglo prekinuti; ubiti se • *vt* začepiti ~ **in** ukopčati

plum /plʌm/ *n* 1 šljiva 2 *coll* dobro plaćen posao; nešto odlično • *adj* 1 tamnoljubičast 2 dobro plaćen **~my** *adj* 1 odličan 2 (glas) afektiran

plumage /'plu:mɪdʒ/ *n* perje

plumb /plʌm/ *vt* istraživati ~ **sth in** instalirati • *adv* ravno; potpuno • *adj* ravan, uspravan • *n* (~ **line**) visak **~er** *n* vodoinstalater **~ing** *n* vodovodne instalacije

plume /plu:m/ *n* pero; nešto u obliku pera **borrowed ~s** tuđe perje

plummet /'plʌmɪt/ *vi* naglo pasti, obrušiti se • *n* olovo, visak

plump /plʌmp/ *adj euphem* bucmast, debeljuškast • *vi,vt* ~ **down** *coll* pasti, svaliti se ~ **for** *GB* izabrati ~ **out/up** zaobliti (se)

plunder /'plʌndə(r)/ *vi,vt* (o)pljačkati • *n* plijen

plunge /plʌndʒ/ *vi,vt* 1 naglo pasti, srušiti se, zaletjeti se, uletjeti, baciti se, jurnuti; gurnuti, (za)rinuti, zabiti 2 propinjati se; ponirati • *n* 1 skok u vodu 2 nagli pokret **take the ~** poduzeti odlučujući korak **~r** *n* 1 guma za odčepljavanje vodovoda 2 klip

pluperfect /ˌplu:'pɜ:fɪkt/ *n gram* pluskvamperfekt

plural /'plʊərəl/ *n* množina **~ism** *n* pluralizam **~ity** /plʊə'rælətɪ/ *n US* najveći broj glasova

plus /plʌs/ *n* plus, više • *adj* 1 pozitivan 2 *coll* i više

plush (1) /plʌʃ/ *adj coll* skup, luksuzan, raskošan

plush (2) *n* pliš
Pluto /'plu:təʊ/ *n* Pluton
plutonium /plu:'təʊnɪəm/ *n* plutonij
ply /plaɪ/ *n* 1 sloj 2 nit **~wood** šperploča • *vi,vt* kružiti, (redovito) voziti
~ **sth** obasipati
pneumatic /nju:'mætɪk/ *adj* pneumat-
ski, zračni ~ **drill** GB pneumatska
bušilica
pneumonia /nju:'məʊnɪə/ *n* upala
pluća
poach (1) /pəʊtʃ/ *vt* poširati
poach (2) *vi,vt* 1 nedopušteno loviti
(na tuđem zemljištu) 2 *fig* prisvojiti,
ukrasti **~er** *n* krivolovac, zvjerokra-
dica
P. O. Box *n* poštanski pregradak
pocket /'pɒkɪt/ *n* 1 džep 2 *mod* džepni
3 izdvojena skupina, izolirano područje 4 rupa (u biljaru) **have sb in
one's** ~ imati vlast nad kim **pick sb's**
~ džepariti **~book** a. blok b. US lisnica ~ **money** džeparac • *vt* staviti u
džep
pockmark /'pɒk,mɑ:k/ *n* ožiljak (od
boginja) **~ed** *adj* kozičav
pod /pɒd/ *n* 1 mahuna 2 spremište za
gorivo • *vt* oguliti (iz mahune) **podgy**
/'pɒdʒɪ/ *adj coll* zdepast
podiatrist /pə'daɪətrɪst/ *n* US pediker
poem /'pəʊɪm/ *n* pjesma
poet /'pəʊɪt/ *n* pjesnik **~aster** *derog* sti-
hoklepac **~ess** pjesnikinja **~ic** *adj* 1
pjesnički 2 poetski **~ic licence** pjesnička sloboda **~ical** *adj* pjesnički, u
stihovima **~ry** /'pəʊɪtrɪ/ *n* pjesništvo,
poezija
po-faced GB *coll derog* kisela izraza
lica
poignant /'pɔɪnjənt/ *adj* bolan, tužan;
dubok
point /pɔɪnt/ *n* 1 šiljak, špica 2 rt 3 točka 4 bod, poen; jedinica, stupanj 5
mjesto; trenutak 6 smisao, svrha 7
pitanje 8 ~s GB skretnice **be on the ~
of doing sth** upravo se spremati što
učiniti **have a** ~ imati pravo **get the**
~ shvatiti **in** ~ **of fact** zapravo **make
one's** ~ izjasniti se, reći svoje **make
a** ~ **of sth** smatrati što važnim, osobito paziti na što **miss the** ~ ne shvatiti **press the** ~ inzistirati **that's not**

the ~ nije stvar u tome **that's beside
the** ~ nije o tome riječ **there's no** ~
nema smisla/svrhe **to the** ~ konkretan **boiling** ~ vrelište **freezing** ~
ledište **turning** ~ prekretnica ~ **of
view** stajalište, motrište **~blank** *adj,
adv* a. iz neposredne blizine b.
izravno, bez okolišanja ~ **duty**
služba prometnika na križanju • *vi,vt*
pokazati (prstom); uperiti, usmjeriti;
biti okrenut prema ~ **out** istaknuti;
pokazati ~ **to/towards** ukazivati **~ed**
adj 1 zašiljen 2 očevidan; značajan;
jasno istaknut; usmjeren protiv čega
~er *n* 1 kazaljka 2 *coll* smjernica 3
pas poenter **~less** *adj* besmislen
poise /pɔɪz/ *n* 1 držanje 2 ravnoteža 3
samouvjerenost, pribranost • *vt,vi* 1
održavati ravnotežu, balansirati 2
držati 3 **be ~d for/to** biti spreman
(na)
poison /'pɔɪzn/ *n* otrov ~ **gas** bojni
otrov **~pen letter** anonimno pismo
puno kleveta • *vt* otrovati, zatrovati
~ous *adj* otrovan
poke /pəʊk/ *vt,vi* 1 (iz)viriti, stršati 2
gurnuti; ubosti, zabosti ~ **one's nose
into sth** zabadati nos u što 3 poticati
(vatru) ~ **about/around** *coll* kopati
(po stvarima)
poker (1) /'pəʊkə/ *n* žarač
poker (2) *n* poker ~ **face** bezizražajno
lice
polar /'pəʊlə(r)/ *adj* 1 polarni 2 dijametralno suprotan **~ity** /pə'lærəti/ *n* 1
suprotnost 2 polaritet **~ize** *vi,vt* po-
larizirati
pole (1) /pəʊl/ *n* motka; stup ~ **vault**
skok s motkom **up the** ~ *sl* a. u
škripcu b. sulud **~ax(e)** mesarska
sjekira ○ *vt* srušiti; uništiti
pole (2) *n* pol **P~ Star** Sjevernjača
Pole *n* Poljak
polemic /pə'lemɪk/ *n form* polemika •
(**~al**) *adj* polemičan
police /pə'li:s/ *n* (+ *pl v*) policija, redarstvo • *vt* patrolirati; nadzirati
~man (~ **officer**) *n* policajac, redarstvenik **~woman** *n* policajka
policy (1) /'pɒləsɪ/ *n* politika; načelo
policy (2) *n* polica (osiguranja)
polio /'pəʊlɪəʊ/ *n* dječja paraliza

polish /'pɒlɪʃ/ vt (u)laštiti ~ **off** coll smazati ~ **up** usavršiti • n **1** laštilo **2** sjaj; dotjeranost; uglađenost
polite /pə'laɪt/ adj pristojan, uljudan
politic /'pɒlətɪk/ adj form razborit, mudar ~**al** adj politički ~**ian** /ˌpɒlɪ'tɪʃn/ n političar ~**ize** vt politizirati ~**s** n politika
polity /'pɒlətɪ/ n ustrojstvo političke jedinice
polka /'pɒlkə/ n polka ~ **dot** točkica
poll /pəʊl/ n **1** anketa **2** (~**s**) glasovanje, izbori **go to the** ~**s** izaći na izbore/glasališta ~ **tax** općinski porez • vt **1** anketirati **2** glasovati; dobiti stanovit broj glasova ~**ing station** glasačko mjesto, glasalište
pollen /'pɒlən/ n pelud
pollinate /'pɒlɪneɪt/ vt oprašiti
pollute /pə'luːt/ vt onečistiti, zagaditi **pollutant** n industrijski otpad **pollution** n zagađenost
polo /'pəʊləʊ/ n polo ~**-neck** adj uz vrat ~**-neck sweater** dolčevita coll
Polo n TM supermint TM
poly /'pɒlɪ/ n → **polytechnic**
poly- prefix poli-, više-
polyester /ˌpɒlɪ'estə(r)/ n poliester; sintetika coll
polysyllabic /ˌpɒlɪsɪ'læbɪk/ adj višesložan
polytechnic /ˌpɒlɪ'teknɪk/ n visoko politehničko učilište
pomegranate /'pɒmɪgrænɪt/ n šipak, nar
pommel /'pɒml/ n jabuka na sedlu
pom(my) /'pɒmɪ/ n Aus, NZ sl derog Englez
pomp /pɒmp/ n pompa ~**ous** adj derog pompozan, napuhan
ponce /pɒns/ n GB sl **1** makro **2** derog peder tab
pond /pɒnd/ n jezerce, ribnjak
ponder /'pɒndə(r)/ vi,vt promisliti, razmisliti
ponderous /'pɒndərəs/ adj form nezgrapan, težak
pong /pɒŋ/ n GB coll smrad
pontiff /'pɒntɪf/ n papa; visoki svećenik, (nad)biskup
pontifical /pɒn'tɪfɪkl/ adj papinski
pontoon /pɒn'tuːn/ n teglenica ~

bridge pontonski most
pony /'pəʊnɪ/ n poni, konj ~**tail** konjski rep
pooch /puːtʃ/ n coll pas
poodle /'puːdl/ n pudl, pudlica
pool (1) /puːl/ n **1** (**swimming** ~) bazen **2** lokva; mlaka; jezerce
pool (2) n **1** udruženje, grupa, pul **2** ukupni ulog **3** biljar **shoot** ~ igrati biljar **4** (**football**) ~**s** športska prognoza • vt udružiti
poop /puːp/ n krma
poor /pʊə(r)/ adj **1** siromašan **the** ~ sirotinja ~**house** n dom za sirotinju **2** loš, slab ~**-spirited** adj bojažljiv **3** jadan ~ **fellow/devil** jadnik
pop (1) /pɒp/ vi,vt **1** prasnuti, puknuti **2** skočiti, iskočiti ~**-eyed** adj razrogačenih očiju ~ **the question** coll zaprositi ~ **off** sl odapeti, riknuti sl • n **1** prasak **2** gazirano piće
pop (2) n, mod pop (glazba)
pop (3) /pɒp/ n US tata
popcorn /'pɒp,kɔːn/ n kokice pl
pope /pəʊp/ n (**P~**) Papa **popish** adj derog katolički
poplar /'pɒplə(r)/ n jablan
poppy /'pɒpɪ/ n mak
popsicle /'pɒpsɪkl/ n US TM voćni sladoled na štapiću
populace /'pɒpjʊləs/ n form svjetina, puk
popular /'pɒpjʊlə(r)/ adj omiljen; popularan; raširen; opći; pučki ~**ity** /ˌpɒpjʊ'lærətɪ/ n omiljenost, popularnost ~**ize** vt popularizirati; proširiti; pojednostaviti
populate /'pɒpjʊleɪt/ vt nastaniti, napučiti **population** /ˌpɒpjʊ'leɪʃn/ n stanovništvo **populist** /'pɒpjʊlɪst/ n populist **populous** /'pɒpjʊləs/ adj gusto naseljen/napučen
porcelain /'pɔːsəlɪn/ n porculan
porch /pɔːtʃ/ n **1** natkrovljeni ulaz **2** US veranda
porcupine /'pɔːkjʊpaɪn/ n dikobraz
pore (1) /pɔː(r)/ n pora
pore (2) vi ~ **over sth** proučavati
pork /pɔːk/ n svinjetina ~ **barrel** n US sl vladina pomoć nekom kraju iz političkih razloga ~**er** tovljeni praščić ~**y** adj coll debeo

porn /pɔ:n/ *n coll* pornografija • (~o) *adj* porno(grafski) **pornography** /pɔ:'nɒgrəfɪ/ *n* pornografija

porous /'pɔ:rəs/ *adj* porozan

porpoise /'pɔ:pəs/ *n* pliskavica

porridge /'pɒrɪdʒ/ *n* zobena kaša

port (1) /pɔ:t/ *n* 1 luka; lučki grad ~ of entry carinska luka ~ of call stanica 2 *fig* utočište

port (2) *n* lijeva strana broda

port (3) *n* porto

port (4) *vt* ~ arms! puške na pregled!

portable /'pɔ:təbl/ *adj* prenosiv

portend /pɔ:'tend/ *vt lit* navješćati **portent** /'pɔ:tent/ *n* nagovještaj

porter (1) /'pɔ:tə(r)/ *n* 1 nosač 2 vratar, portir

porter (2) *n arch* tamno pivo

portfolio /pɔ:t'fəʊlɪəʊ/ *n* (*pl* ~s) 1 fascikl, mapa 2 portfelj, dužnost ministra 3 dionice

porthole /'pɔ:t,həʊl/ *n* brodski prozor

portico /'pɔ:tɪkəʊ/ *n* trijem

portion /'pɔ:ʃn/ *n* 1 dio 2 porcija • *vt* ~ out podijeliti, razdijeliti

portly /'pɔ:tlɪ/ *adj euphem* krupan

portmanteau /pɔ:t'mæntəʊ/ *n* (*pl* ~s, ~x) kovčeg ~ word riječ stvorena kombinacijom dviju riječi

portrait /'pɔ:trɪt/ *n* portret

portray /pɔ:'treɪ/ *vt* prikazati, opisati; glumiti

pose /pəʊz/ *vi,vt* 1 pozirati; pretvarati se 2 predstavljati 3 postaviti (pitanje) • *n* poza; stav; držanje ~r 1 teško pitanje 2 (~ur) *n derog* pozer

posh /pɒʃ/ *adj coll* raskošan, otmjen, skup, bogataški

position /pə'zɪʃn/ *n* 1 položaj; mjesto; namještenje 2 stav • *vt* smjestiti, postaviti

positive /'pɒzɪtɪv/ *adj* 1 potpuno siguran 2 pozitivan 3 određen, konkretan, pravi • *n* pozitiv ~ly *adv* 1 sigurno, nedvojbeno 2 pozitivno 3 upravo

posse /'pɒsɪ/ *n* potjera

possess /pə'zes/ *vt form* 1 posjedovati 2 opsjedati, spopasti ~ed *adj* opsjednut ~ion *n* 1 vlasništvo, posjed 2 opsjednutost ~ive *adj* 1 posesivan 2 *gram* posvojni ~or *form* vlasnik

possible /'pɒsəbl/ *adj* moguć as soon as ~ što prije (moguće) **possibly** *adv* moguće; možda; ikako, nikako **possibility** /,pɒsə'bɪlətɪ/ *n* mogućnost

possum /'pɒsəm/ *n* (*pl* ~, ~s) oposum play ~ *coll* praviti se lud

post (1) /pəʊst/ *n* stup • *vt* plakatirati ~ no bills zabranjeno plakatiranje

post (2) *n GB* 1 pošta by ~ poštom by return of ~ odmah po primitku 2 poštanski ~box poštanski sandučić ~card a. dopisnica b. razglednica ~code poštanski broj ~man poštar ~mark poštanski žig P~master General ministar pošte i telekomunikacija ~ office poštanski ured, pošta • *vt* poslati poštom keep sb ~ed redovito izvještavati ~age *n* poštarina ~age stamp poštanska marka ~al *adj* poštanski

post (3) *n* 1 posao, namještenje 2 položaj; stražarsko mjesto; posada • *vt* rasporediti; imenovati; postaviti na dužnost

post- *prefix* post-, poslije-, po-

postdate /pəʊst'deɪt/ *vt* napisati kasniji datum (na)

poster /'pəʊstə(r)/ *n* poster, plakat ~ paint/colour tempera

posterior /pɒ'stɪərɪə(r)/ *adj* 1 kasniji 2 stražnji

posterity /pɒ'sterətɪ/ *n* budući naraštaji; potomci

postgraduate /,pəʊst'grædʒʊət/ *adj* postdiplomski

posthumous /'pɒstjʊməs/ *adj* posthumni

post-modernism *n* postmoderna

postmortem /,pəʊst'mɔ:təm/ *n* (~ examination) autopsija

postpone /pə'spəʊn/ *vt* odgoditi

postscript /'pəʊsskrɪpt/ *n* (P.S.) post scriptum; dodatak

postulate /'pɒstjʊleɪt/ *vt form* pretpostaviti, iznijeti hipotezu • *n* pretpostavka, hipoteza

posture /'pɒstʃə(r)/ *n* 1 držanje 2 položaj 3 stav

post-war /,pəʊst'wɔ:(r)/ *adj* poslijeratni

pot (1) /pɒt/ *n* 1 lonac; vrč; tegl 2 ulog 3 pogodak (u biljaru) 4 *sl* marihuana

take ~luck ići na sreću, prihvatiti što god ima ~ **plant** biljka lončanica **~shot** *coll* hitac bez ciljanja • *vi,vt* 1 (at) pucati (na) 2 posaditi 3 *GB* pogoditi kuglom u rupu **~ted** *adj* 1 u obliku paštete/namaza 2 *GB* skraćen, pojednostavljen **~ter** *n* lončar **~ter's wheel** lončarsko kolo **~tery** *n* 1 lončarija 2 pečena glina **~hole** *n* duboka jama/rupa

potable /'pəʊtəbl/ *adj form* pitak

potassium /pə'tæsɪəm/ *n* kalij

potato /pə'teɪtəʊ/ *n* (*pl* **~es**) krumpir **~ beetle** krumpirova zlatica

poteen /pɒ'ti:n/ *n Ir* ilegalno proizveden viski

potency /'pəʊtnsɪ/ *n* 1 jakost; snaga; djelovanje, učinak 2 potencija **potent** /'pəʊtnt/ *adj* 1 snažan, djelotvoran, 2 uvjerljiv **potential** /pə'tenʃl/ *adj* moguć, potencijalan o *n* mogućnost, potencijal

potion /'pəʊʃn/ *n* napitak

potty (1) /'pɒtɪ/ *adj GB coll* šašav; lud

potty (2) *n* kahlica

pouch /paʊtʃ/ *n* 1 kesa, vrećica, torbica 2 tobolac

pouf, pouffe /pu:f/ *n* tabure

poultry /'pəʊltrɪ/ *n* perad

pounce /paʊns/ *vi* (on) 1 skočiti, baciti se (na), zaskočiti 2 zgrabiti, uhvatiti se za

pound (1) /paʊnd/ *n* funta (novčana jedinica; mjera za težinu, cca 0.45 kg)

pound (2) *vt,vi* 1 lupati, udarati, tući 2 (z)drobiti 3 teško stupati

pour /pɔ:(r)/ *vt,vi* 1 lijevati, izliti, uliti, naliti; natočiti 2 teći, kuljati **~ing rain** gusta/jaka kiša **It never rains but it ~s** *prov* nesreća nikad ne dolazi sama

pout /paʊt/ *vi,vt* pućiti usne; duriti se

poverty /'pɒvətɪ/ *n* siromaštvo

powder /'paʊdə(r)/ *n* 1 prah 2 puder; talk ~ **room** *euphem* ženski WC 3 (gun~) barut **~ keg** bure baruta *fig* • *vt* naprašiti; napudrati **~ed** *adj* 1 u prahu 2 napudran **~y** *adj* prhak

power /'paʊə(r)/ *n* 1 vlast **in ~** na vlasti 2 ovlast ~ **of attorney** *leg* pravna punomoć 3 snaga; moć; sila **the ~s that be** *coll, joc* oni gore 4 energija;

struja ~ **cut** nestanak struje ~ **station/plant** elektrana 5 *math* potencija • *vt* pokretati • *adj* motorni **~boat** *n* gliser **~ful** *adj* snažan, moćan, jak **~less** *adj* nemoćan

powwow /'paʊwaʊ/ *n joc* sastanak, viječanje

pox /pɒks/ *n coll* sifilis

practicable /'præktɪkəbl/ *adj* izvediv

practical /'præktɪkl/ *adj* praktičan **~ly** *adv* praktično, gotovo

practice (**practise** US) /'præktɪs/ *n* 1 praksa, vježba, trening **put into ~** primijeniti, provesti 2 uobičajeni postupak, običaj • **practise** *vi,vt* 1 vježbati, trenirati 2 raditi (u struci) 3 vršiti, provoditi ~ **what you preach** postupaj prema onome što govoriš drugima **practising Catholic** praktični katolik

practitioner /præk'tɪʃənə(r)/ *n* stručnjak **general ~** liječnik opće prakse

pragmatic /præg'mætɪk/ *adj* pragmatičan

prairie /'preərɪ/ *n* prerija

praise /preɪz/ *vt* hvaliti; slaviti • *n* 1 *lit* hvala, slava 2 pohvala **~worthy** *adj* hvalevrijedan

pram /præm/ *n GB* dječja kolica

prance /pra:ns/ *vi* 1 propinjati se 2 poskakivati 3 hodati dignuta nosa

prank /præŋk/ *n* psina

prattle /'prætl/ *vi coll* blebetati, brbljati

prawn /prɔ:n/ *n* kozica

pray /preɪ/ *vi,vt* moliti (se) **~er** /preə(r)/ *n* 1 molitva 2 služba Božja **~ing mantis** *zoo* bogomoljka

preach /pri:tʃ/ *vi,vt* propovijedati, držati propovijed

preamble /pri:'æmbl/ *n* predgovor, uvodna izjava

prearrange /,pri:ə'reɪndʒ/ *vt* unaprijed ugovoriti

precarious /prɪ'keərɪəs/ *adj* nesiguran, nestabilan, opasan

precast /,pri:'ka:st/ *adj* (beton) u blokovima

precaution /prɪ'kɔ:ʃn/ *n* mjera opreza

precede /prɪ'si:d/ *vt form* prethoditi **preceding** *adj* prethodni **~nce** /'presɪdəns/ *n* (over) prednost, prioritet **~nt** /'presɪdənt/ *n* presedan

precept /'pri:sept/ n pravilo; uputa
precinct /'pri:sɪŋkt/ n 1 GB administrativna zona, dio grada 2 US gradska izborna jedinica 3 policijska postaja 4 ~s prostor ograđen zidovima 5 granica
precious /'preʃəs/ adj dragocjen ~ **metal** plemeniti metal ~ **stone** dragi kamen • adv coll vrlo • coll dragi, draga
precipice /'presɪpɪs/ n ponor
precipitate /prɪ'sɪpɪteɪt/ vt,vi form 1 ubrzati; strmoglaviti se 2 gurnuti 3 kondenzirati **precipitation** /prɪ,sɪpɪ-'teɪʃn/ n 1 oborine, padaline pl 2 form žurba, hitnja
precipitous /prɪ'sɪpɪtəs/ adj strm
precis /'preɪsi:/ n (pl ~ /'preɪsi:z/) sažetak
precise /prɪ'saɪs/ adj 1 točan, precizan **at that ~ moment** baš u tom trenutku 2 pedantan ~**ly** adv točno; upravo tako **precision** /prɪ'sɪʒn/ n točnost, preciznost ◦ adj precizan
preclude /prɪ'klu:d/ vt form spriječiti, onemogućiti, ne dopustiti
precocious /prɪ'kəʊʃəs/ adj prerano razvijen; starmal
precognition /,pri:kɒg'nɪʃn/ n predosjećaj
precondition /,pri:kən'dɪʃn/ n preduvjet
precook /pri:'kʌk/ vt unaprijed skuhati; djelomično skuhati
precursor /,pri:'kɜ:sə(r)/ n form preteča
predate /pri:'deɪt/ vt prethoditi, biti stariji od
predator /'predətə(r)/ n grabežljivac (+ fig) ~**y** adj grabežljiv
predecessor /'pri:dɪsesə(r)/ n prethodnik
predestine /,pri:'destɪn/ vt predodrediti
predetermine /,pri:dɪ'tɜ:mɪn/ vt form unaprijed odrediti/ugovoriti
predicament /prɪ'dɪkəmənt/ n neugodni uvjeti, škripac
predicate (1) /'predɪkət/ n predikat
predicate (2) /'predɪkeɪt/ vt form 1 (on) temeljiti se, zasnivati se (na) 2 tvrditi; pripisati

predict /prɪ'dɪkt/ vt proreći ~**able** adj predvidiv ~**ion** n proročanstvo
predominant /prɪ'dɒmɪnənt/ adj pretežit
preempt /,pri:'emt/ vt preduhitriti ~**ive** adj prvi ~**ive right** pravo prvokupa
preen /pri:n/ vi,vt 1 čistiti (se) (kljunom) 2 fig rediti se
prefab /'pri:fæb/ n coll montažna kućica • adj montažni ~**ricate** vt proizvoditi u dijelovima
preface /'prefɪs/ n uvod, predgovor
prefer /prɪ'fɜ:(r)/ vt (sth to sth) više voljeti (što od čega), radije htjeti ~**able** adj bolji ~**ence** n 1 izbor, nešto što je komu draže 2 prednost; povlastica ~**ential** adj povlašten
prefix /'pri:fɪks/ n gram prefiks
pregnancy /'pregnənsɪ/ n trudnoća **pregnant** adj 1 trudna 2 fig pun, bremenit
preheat /pri:'hi:t/ vt zagrijati
prehistoric /,pri:hɪ'stɒrɪk/ adj prapovijesni **prehistory** n prapovijest
prejudge /,pri:'dʒʌdʒ/ vt unaprijed stvoriti sud o komu/čemu
prejudice /'predʒudɪs/ n predrasuda • vt 1 **be ~d against** biti protiv **be ~d in favour** favorizirati 2 ugroziti ~**d** adj pun predrasuda
preliminary /prɪ'lɪmɪnərɪ/ adj preliminaran, pretkvalifikacijski
prelude /'prelju:d/ n uvod; preludij
premarital /,pri:'mærɪtl/ adj predbračni
premature /'premətjʊə(r)/ adj prerani; preuranjen
premeditated /,pri:'medɪteɪtɪd/ adj s predumišljajem
premier /'premɪə(r)/ n premijer • adj vrhunski
premiere /'premɪeə(r)/ n premijera • vt **be ~d** biti premijerno prikazan
premises /'premɪsəz/ n pl prostorije
premium /'pri:mɪəm/ n 1 novčani prinos (za osiguranje) 2 nagrada **at a ~ a.** iznad pariteta **b.** fig vrijedan zlata
premonition /,pri:mə'nɪʃn/ n slutnja, predosjećaj
preoccupation /,pri:ɒkjʊ'peɪʃn/ n 1 zaokupljenost 2 posao **preoccupy** vt zaokupiti

prep /prep/ *n* domaća zadaća ~**(aratory) school a.** *GB* privatna osnovna škola **b.** *US* privatna srednja škola ~**py** *n coll* bogati đak ○ *adj* šminkerski, snobovski

preparation /,prepə'reɪʃn/ *n* **1** priprema **2** pripravak **preparatory** /prɪ'pærətrɪ/ *adj* pripremni, uvodni **prepare** /prɪ'peə(r)/ *vt,vi* pripremiti (se) **prepared** *adj* **1** gotov, pripremljen **2** spreman

prepay /,pri:'peɪ/ *adj* unaprijed platiti; frankirati

preposition /,prepə'zɪʃn/ *n gram* prijedlog

preposterous /prɪ'pɒstərəs/ *adj* **1** besmislen **2** smiješan

prerequisite /,pri:'rekwɪzɪt/ *n form* preduvjet

presbitery /'prezbɪtrɪ/ *n* **1** prezbiterski sinod (u Prezbiterijanskoj crkvi) **2** župni dvor (katoličkog svećenika)

prescribe /prɪ'skraɪb/ *vt,vi* **1** prepisati **2** *form* propisati ~**d** *adj* propisan, određen **prescription** /prɪ'skrɪpʃn/ *n* recept **prescription charge** *GB* participacija **prescription drugs** lijekovi koji se dobivaju na recept

presence /'presns/ *n* **1** nazočnost **2** držanje ~ **of mind** pribranost **present** *adj* nazočan

present (1) /'preznt/ *n* dar **make sb a** ~ **of sth** pokloniti što komu ~ /prɪ'zent/ *vt* **1** (sth to sb/sb with sth) pokloniti što komu **2** predstavljati **3** podnijeti **4** davati, prikazivati ~ **oneself** javiti se; ukazati se ~**able** *adj* uredan, pristojan ~**ation** *n* **1** predstava **2** predaja **3** prezentacija **4** prikaz ~**ation copy** reklamni primjerak ~**er** *n* voditelj

present (2) *n* **1** sadašnjost **2** *gram* prezent **at** ~ trenutačno • *adj* sadašnji; ovaj ~**-day** *adj* današnji ~**ly** *adv* **1** uskoro **2** *US* trenutačno

preservation /,prezə'veɪʃn/ *n* očuvanje **preservative** /prɪ'zɜ:vətɪv/ *adj* konzervans **preserve** *vt* **1** sačuvati; očuvati **2** konzervirati ○ *n* **1** džem **2** rezervat

preset *vt irreg* → **set** unaprijed namjestiti

preshrunk /'pri:ʃrʌŋk/ *adj* koji se ne skuplja

preside /prɪ'zaɪd/ *vi* (at/over) predsjedavati ~**ncy** /'prezɪdənsɪ/ *n* **1** dužnost predsjednika **2** predsjedavanje ~**nt** /'prezɪdənt/ *n* predsjednik ~**ntial** *adj* predsjednički

press /pres/ *vt,vi* **1** pritisnuti, stisnuti, tiskati (se) **2** prešati, tiještiti **3** glačati **4** nagovarati **5** insistirati, navaljivati, tjerati ~ **charges** podići optužnicu ~ **home a.** iskoristiti do kraja **b.** navaliti ~**ed** *adj* (for) u stisci ~**gang** *vt* (into) *coll* natjerati ~**ing** *adj* hitan, neodložan ~**-up** *n* sklek • *n* **1** novinstvo, tisak ~ **agent** reklamni agent ~ **conference** tiskovna konferencija ~ **cutting** novinski isječak **2** tiskara **go to** ~ ići u tisak **3** naklada **4** tijesak, preša ~**ure** /'preʃə(r)/ *n* **1** pritisak (+ *fig*) **2** tlak ~**ure cooker** lonac na paru ~**urize** *vt* (into) natjerati

prestige /pre'sti:ʒ/ *n* prestiž, ugled **prestigious** *adj* prestižan

prestressed /,pri:'strest/ *adj* prenapregnut

presume /prɪ'zju:m/ *vt,vi* **1** pretpostaviti **2** usuditi se, drznuti se ~ **on/upon** okoristiti se **presumably** /prɪ'zju:məblɪ/ *adv* pretpostavljam/pretpostavlja se **presumption** /prɪ'zʌmpʃn/ *n* **1** pretpostavka **2** drskost **presumptuous** /prɪ'zʌmptʃʊəs/ *adj* drzak

presuppose /,pri:sə'pəʊz/ *vt* pretpostaviti

pretence (-**se** *US*) /prɪ'tens/ *n* pretvaranje **under false** ~**s** pod lažnim izgovorom **pretend** *vi,vt* **1** praviti se, hiniti **2** igrati se **pretend to** pretendirati na; uobražavati **pretender** *n* pretendent **pretension** /prɪ'tenʃn/ *n* pretenzija

pretext /'pri:tekst/ *n* izgovor, izlika

pretty /'prɪtɪ/ *adj* zgodan, sladak, lijep • *adv coll* prilično ~ **penny** *coll* prilično novca

pretzel /'pretsl/ *n* slanac, perec

prevail /prɪ'veɪl/ *vi* **1** (among/in) biti rasprostranjen **2** (against/over) pobijediti ~ **upon** nagovoriti

prevalent /'prevələnt/ *adj* koji prevladava, široko rasprostranjen

prevent /pri'vent/ *vt* (sth/sb from doing sth) spriječiti što/koga da učini što ~**ion** *n* prevencija, predobrana ~**ive** *adj* preventivan

preview /'pri:vju:/ *n* 1 privatna projekcija 2 najava

previous /'pri:vɪəs/ *adj* prethodni, prijašnji ~ **day** dan prije ~ **to** prije

prewar /ˌpri:'wɔ:(r)/ *adj* predratni

prey /preɪ/ *n* plijen, lovina **fall/be ~ to** pasti žrtvom; biti moren *fig* **beast of ~** grabežljivac **bird of ~** ptica grabljivica • *vt* ~ **on/upon** 1 loviti 2 moriti 3 iskorištavati

price /praɪs/ *n* cijena **not at any ~** ni po koju cijenu **high-~d** skup ~**less** *adj* neprocjenjiv

prick /prɪk/ *n* 1 ubod ~**s of conscience** grižnja savjesti 2 *tab* kurac *tab* 3 *tab* kreten *derog* • *vt, vi* ubosti (se), bockati; peći (+ *fig*) ~ **up one's ears** naćuliti uši

prickle /'prɪkl/ *n* bodljika • *vi, vi* bockati **prickly** *adj* 1 bodljikav, bockav 2 *fig* zeznut *coll*

pride /praɪd/ *n* 1 ponos **take ~ in sb/sth** ponositi se kime/čime 2 oholost • *v* ~ **oneself on/upon** ponositi se

priest /pri:st/ *n* svećenik ~**hood** *n* 1 svećenička služba 2 svećenstvo ~**ly** *adj* svećenički

prig /prɪg/ *n* cjepidlaka

prim /prɪm/ *adj* 1 ukočen 2 ćudoredan

prim(a)eval /praɪ'mi:vl/ *adj* drevan, iskonski

primary /'praɪmərɪ/ *adj* glavni, primaran; prvi ~ **school** osnovna škola • *n US* izbor kandidata **primarily** /'praɪmərəlɪ/ *adv* u prvom redu

primate /'praɪmeɪt/ *n* 1 *zoo* primat 2 primas

prime (1) /praɪm/ *n* napon, cvijet **in the ~ of life** u naponu snage **past one's ~** na zalasku • *adj* 1 glavni 2 vrhunski, najbolji ~ **cost** proizvodna cijena ~ **meridian** nulti meridijan ~ **minister** predsjednik vlade ~ **mover** pokretačka snaga ~ **rate** najniža kamatna stopa ~ **time** najgledaniji termin

prime (2) *vt* 1 obojiti temeljnom bojom 2 poučiti 3 nabiti 4 napuniti (vodom/benzinom)

primitive /'prɪmɪtɪv/ *adj* primitivan

primordial /praɪ'mɔ:dɪəl/ *adj form* prvobitan

primrose /'prɪmrəʊz/ *n* jaglac

primus /'praɪməs/ *n* (~ **stove**) primus, špiritno kuhalo

prince /prɪns/ *n* 1 kraljević, princ **P~ Charming** *coll* princ na bijelom konju 2 knez ~**ly** *adj fig* kraljevski ~**ss** *n* kraljevna, princeza

principal /'prɪnsəpl/ *adj* najvažniji, glavni • *n* 1 ravnatelj (škole) 2 *comm* glavnica ~**ity** *n* kneževina

principle /'prɪnsəpl/ *n* načelo **in ~** načelno **on ~** iz načela/principa *coll* ~**d** *adj* principijelan

print /prɪnt/ *n* 1 (tiskana) slova 2 otisak 3 primjerak (fotografije) 4 grafika 5 tkanina s uzorkom • *vi, vt* 1 tiskati 2 otisnuti 3 izraditi fotografiju 4 pisati tiskanim slovima ~**d matter** tiskanica ~**er** *n* 1 tiskar 2 *comp* pisač; printer *coll* ~**ing** *n* 1 tisak ~**ing error** tiskarska greška 2 izdanje ~**ing press/machine** tiskarski stroj

prior /'praɪə(r)/ *adj* 1 prethodni 2 važniji ~ **to** prije ~**ity** *n* (over) prednost (pred), prioritet **top ~ity** najvažnija stvar

prise /praɪz/ *vt* ~ **open** silom otvoriti

prison /'prɪzn/ *n* zatvor ~**er** *n* zatvorenik **be taken ~er** biti zarobljen **keep sb ~er** držati u zarobljeništvu ~**er of war** ratni zarobljenik

prissy /'prɪsɪ/ *adj coll* ukočen

pristine /'prɪsti:n/ *adj form* netaknut, kao nov

private /'praɪvɪt/ *adj* 1 privatan; osoban; intiman 2 u povjerenju 3 neslužben 4 miran, osamljen; povučen ~ **parts** *euphem* genitalije ~**ly** *adv* nasamo • *n* redov in ~ nasamo ~**s** *n pl* genitalije **privacy** /'prɪvəsɪ/ *n* 1 privatnost, mir 2 tajnovitost **privatize** /'praɪvɪˌtaɪz/ *vt* privatizirati

privilege /'prɪvəlɪdʒ/ *n* 1 povlastica 2 povlaštenost, nejednakost 3 čast ~**d** *adj* povlašten

privy /'prɪvɪ/ *adj* ~ **to** upućen u **P~**

Council *GB* Tajno vijeće **P~ Purse** *GB* apanaža • *n arch* dvorišni zahod

prize /praɪz/ *n* nagrada • *adj* 1 pobjednički 2 nagradni 3 *coll* najveći, pravi • *vt* 1 cijeniti, držati vrijednim 2 → **prise**

pro /prəʊ/ *n coll* profesionalac

probability /ˌprɒbə'bɪlətɪ/ *n* 1 vjerojatnost **in all** ~ najvjerojatnije 2 mogućnost **probable** /'prɒbəbl/ *adj* vjerojatan **probably** *adv* vjerojatno, najvjerojatnije

probation /prə'beɪʃn/ *n* 1 pokusni rok 2 uvjetna kazna ~**er** *n* 1 kandidat, iskušenik 2 stažist 3 uvjetno kažnjena osoba

probe /prəʊb/ *n* 1 sonda 2 (into) istraga (čega) • *vi,vt* (into) kopati po (+ *fig*); istraživati

problem /'prɒbləm/ *n* problem

procedure /prə'siːdʒə(r)/ *n* procedura

proceed /prə'siːd/ *vi* 1 (to/with) nastaviti se, ići dalje 2 prijeći na 3 kretati se, krenuti prema ~**ings** *n pl* 1 događaji 2 postupak 3 sudski postupak **start/take (legal)** ~**ings** pokrenuti **sudski postupak** 4 zapisnici ~**s** *n pl* utržak, zarada

process /'prəʊses/ *n* proces • *vt* 1 preradivati 2 obraditi 3 izraditi fotografiju ~**ion** *n* procesija; niz

proclaim /prə'kleɪm/ *vt* objaviti, proglasiti **proclamation** *n* proglas

procrastinate /prəʊ'kræstɪneɪt/ *vi form* otezati, oklijevati

procure /prə'kjʊə(r)/ *vt,vi* (for) nabaviti; dokopati se ~**ment** *n* nabava

prod /prɒd/ *vi,vt* 1 (at) gurkati, bockati 2 (into) potaknuti, podbosti

prodigal /'prɒdɪgl/ *adj* 1 rastrošan ~ **son** sin razmetni 2 bogat

prodigious /prə'dɪdʒəs/ *adj* fantastičan **prodigy** /'prɒdɪdʒɪ/ *n* čudo **child prodigy** čudo od djeteta

produce /prə'djuːs/ *vt,vi* 1 proizvoditi, davati 2 proizvoditi, izrađivati 3 stvoriti 4 izvući 5 predočiti 6 postaviti 7 producirati, financirati • /'prɒdjuːs/ *n* proizvod ~**r** *n* 1 proizvođač *n* producent

product /'prɒdʌkt/ *n* proizvod ~**ion** /prə'dʌkʃn/ *n* 1 proizvodnja 2 *mod* proizvodni 3 postava, predstava ~**ive** *adj* produktivan, plodan ~**ivity** /ˌprɒdʌk'tɪvətɪ/ *n* produktivnost, proizvodnost

profane /prə'feɪn/ *adj* 1 profan 2 prost 3 svjetovni **profanity** /prə'fænətɪ/ *n* prostota

profess /prə'fes/ *vt* 1 tvrditi 2 izjaviti, očitovati 3 ispovijedati ~**ed** *adj* 1 otvoren 2 lažan ~**ion** /prə'feʃn/ *n* 1 zanimanje, zvanje, struka 2 ispovijedanje ~**ional** *adj* 1 stručni 2 poslovan 3 profesionalan ○ *n* profesionalac ~**or** /prə'fesə(r)/ *n* 1 *GB* šef katedre, predstojnik odsjeka 2 *US* sveučilišni profesor

proficient /prə'fɪʃnt/ *adj* (at/in) vrstan **proficiency** *n* poznavanje

profile /'prəʊfaɪl/ *n* 1 profil **in** ~ iz profila 2 obris **high** ~ istaknut položaj **keep a low** ~ (on sth) ne isticati se, držati se po strani

profit /'prɒfɪt/ *n* 1 dobit, profit **make a** ~ zaraditi ~ **margin** zarada 2 korist • *vt* ~ **by/from** izvući korist iz, okoristiti se čime ~**ability** *n* rentabilnost ~**able** *adj* koji donosi dobit, isplativ ~**eer** *n* profiter

profound /prə'faʊnd/ *adj* dubok *fig*

profuse /prə'fjuːs/ *adj* 1 obilan, bogat 2 pretjeran **profusion** *n* obilje

progeny /'prɒdʒənɪ/ *n* potomstvo

prognosis /prɒg'nəʊsɪs/ *n* prognoza **prognosticate** /prɒg'nɒstɪkeɪt/ *vt form* predviđati

program /'prəʊgræm/ *n* 1 kompjuterski program 2 *US* → **programme** • *vt comp* programirati ~**ming language** programski jezik ~**me** *n* 1 program 2 TV emisija • *vt* programirati, podesiti ~(**m**)**er** *n* programer

progress /'prəʊgres/ *vi* napredovati • /prə'gres/ *n* 1 napredak **make** ~ napredovati 2 tok ~**ion** *n* napredovanje, progresija ~**ive** *adj* 1 rastući 2 napredan 3 progresivan

prohibit /prə'hɪbɪt/ *vt* (from) 1 zabraniti (što) 2 zapriječiti ~**ion** *n* 1 zabrana 2 prohibicija ~**ive** *adj* destimulirajući

project /'prɒdʒekt/ *n* projekt, plan • /prə'dʒekt/ *vt,vi* 1 projektirati 2 projicirati; davati *fig* 3 izbacivati 4 stršati ~**ile** /prə'dʒektaɪl/ *n* projektil ~**ion** *n* projekcija ~**or** *n* projektor

prole /prəul/ *n coll* proleter ~**tariat** /ˌprəuli'teəriət/ *n* proletarijat ~**tarian** *n* proleter

proliferate /prə'lɪfəreɪt/ *vi,vt* bujati, širiti se

prolific /prə'lɪfɪk/ *adj* plodan

prologue /'prəulɒg/ *n* uvod; predigra (+ *fig*)

prolong /prə'lɒŋ/ *vt* produžiti, prolongirati ~**ed** *adj* odulji

prom /prɒm/ *n coll* 1 *GB* promenada; promenadni koncert 2 *US* maturalna zabava

promenade /ˌprɒmə'na:d/ *n* promenada • *vt,vi* šetati

prominent /'prɒmɪnənt/ *adj* 1 ugledan 2 istaknut 3 značajan

promiscuous /prə'mɪskjuəs/ *adj* promiskuitetan **promiscuity** /ˌprɒmɪ'skju:əti/ *n* promiskuitet

promise /'prɒmɪs/ *n* obećanje **make a ~** dati obećanje **keep a ~** održati obećanje **break a ~** prekršiti obećanje **show ~** obećavati mnogo • *vt,vi* 1 obećati **the P~d Land** obećana zemlja 2 jamčiti 3 izgledati **promising** *adj* koji mnogo obećava/budi nadu **promissory note** zadužnica, vlastita mjenica

promontory /'prɒməntri/ *n* rt

promote /prə'məut/ *vt* 1 (na/u) promaknuti (na/u) 2 promicati, raditi na **promotion** *n* 1 promaknuće 2 promidžba

prompt (1) /prɒmpt/ *adj* hitan, pravovremen, bez odlaganja

prompt (2) *vt* 1 potaknuti 2 *theat* šaptati • *n* šaptanje ~**box** šaptaonica ~**er** *n* šaptač

promulgate /'prɒmlgeɪt/ *vt* proglasiti; objaviti

prone /prəun/ *adj* 1 ničice, potrbuške 2 ~ **to** sklon

prong /prɒŋ/ *n* šiljak, krak (vilice i sl.)

pronoun /'prəunaun/ *n gram* zamjenica

pronounce /prə'nauns/ *vt,vi* 1 proglasiti ~ (**up**)**on** izraziti svoje mišljenje ~ **oneself** izjasniti se ~ **for/against**

proglasiti nedužnim/krivim 2 izgovoriti ~**d** *adj* izrazit, jak ~**ment** *n* izjava

pronto /'prɒntəu/ *adj sl* smjesta

pronunciation /prəˌnʌnsi'eɪʃn/ *n* izgovor

proof /pru:f/ *n* 1 dokaz 2 ispit, kušnja 3 korektura; špalta *coll* ~**read** *vi,vt* korigirati ~**reader** *n* korektor 4 jakoća (alkoholnih pića) • *adj* (against) otporan na **bullet-~** neprobojan **water-~** nepromočiv • *vt* impregnirati

prop (1) /prɒp/ *n* 1 potporanj 2 oslonac (+ *fig*) • *vt* (up) podupreti, nasloniti o; držati

prop (2) *n coll theat* rekvizit

propaganda /ˌprɒpə'gændə/ *n derog* propaganda; agitprop

propagate /'prɒpəgeɪt/ *vt,vi form* 1 razmnožavati (se) 2 širiti (se)

propane /'prəupeɪn/ *n* propan

propel /prə'pel/ *vt* pokretati ~**ler** *n* propeler

propensity /prə'pensəti/ *n* prirodna sklonost

proper /'prɒpə(r)/ *adj* 1 prikladan, odgovarajući ~ **to** koji se tiče 2 pristojan 3 pošten, ispravan 4 čist *medicine* ~ 5 *coll* pravi, pošteni ~ **noun** *gram* vlastita imenica ~**ly** *adv* kako treba; pristojno; dobrano ~**ly speaking** u pravom smislu riječi

property /'prɒpəti/ *n* 1 imovina **man of ~** imućan čovjek **personal ~** pokretna imovina **real ~** nekretnine 2 imanje 3 vlasništvo 4 svojstvo 5 *theat* rekvizit ~**man/master** rekviziter

prophecy /'prɒfəsi/ *n* proročanstvo

prophesy /'prɒfɪsaɪ/ *vt,vi* proricati **prophet** *n* prorok **prophetic** *adj* proročanski

prophylactic /ˌprɒfɪ'læktɪk/ *n* 1 profilaksa 2 kondom • *adj* preventivni **prophylaxis** *n* profilaksa

propitious /prə'pɪʃəs/ *adj* (to sb/for sth) povoljan

proponent /prə'pəunənt/ *n* zagovornik

proportion /prə'pɔ:ʃn/ *n* 1 (of sth to sth) omjer (čega prema čemu) **in ~ to** u odnosu na **be out of ~** (to) biti nesrazmjeran 2 (*pl*) razmjer, sklad 3 ~**s**

pl veličina, razmjer 4 dio **~al**, **~ate** *adj* razmjeran

proposal /prə'pəʊzl/ *n* 1 prijedlog 2 prosidba **propose** *vt,vi* predložiti **propose a toast to sb/sb's health** nazdraviti komu **propose marriage** (za)prositi **proposition** /ˌprɒpə'zɪʃn/ *n* 1 tvrdnja; sud 2 pitanje, problem 3 prijedlog

proprietary /prə'praɪətrɪ/ *n* 1 patentiran, zaštićen 2 posjednički

proprietor /prə'praɪətə(r)/ *n* vlasnik

propriety /prə'praɪətɪ/ *n* 1 pristojnost, uljudnost 2 pravilnost

propulsion /prə'pʌlʃn/ *n* pogon

pro rata /ˌprəʊ 'rɑːtə/ *adv* razmjerno, ovisno o udjelu

prosaic /prə'zeɪɪk/ *adj* prozaičan, običan

proscribe /prə'skraɪb/ *vt* staviti izvan zakona; zabraniti

prose /prəʊz/ *n* 1 proza 2 *mod* prozni

prosecute /'prɒsɪkjuːt/ *vt* (sb for sth) krivično goniti **Public Prosecutor** javni tužitelj **prosecution** *n* 1 gonjenje 2 optužba, tužitelj

prospect /'prɒspekt/ *n* 1 panorama, pogled 2 (*pl*) izgled, perspektiva 3 mogućnost; mogući kupac • *vi* (for) tražiti (zlato i sl.) **~ive** *adj* potencijalni

prospectus /prə'spektəs/ *n* prospekt, brošura

prosper /'prɒspə(r)/ *vi* napredovati, prosperirati **~ity** /prɒ'sperətɪ/ *n* uspjeh, prosperitet **~ous** *adj* cvatući

prostitute /'prɒstɪtjuːt/ *n* prostitutka • *vt* (oneself) prostituirati se **prostitution** *n* prostitucija

prostrate /'prɒstreɪt/ *adj* 1 ničice 2 *fig* skrhan • /prɒ'streɪt/ *vt* 1 oboriti 2 (oneself) baciti se ničice 3 **be ~d with** biti savladan **prostration** *n* 1 iscrpljenost 2 ponizno klečanje

prosy /'prəʊzɪ/ *adj* suhoparan

protect /prə'tekt/ *vt* (from/against) štititi od **~ion** *n* 1 zaštita 2 protekcija **~ionism** *n* *comm* protekcionizam **~ive** *adj* 1 zaštitni 2 (towards) zaštitnički **~or** *n* zaštitnik

protégé /'prɒtɪʒeɪ/ *n* štićenik, proteže

protein /'prəʊtiːn/ *n* bjelančevina

protest /'prəʊtest/ *n* 1 prosvjed 2 *mod* prosvjedni • /prə'test/ *vt,vi* 1 izjaviti 2 (against) prosvjedovati **~er** *n* demonstrant

Protestant /'prɒtɪstənt/ *n* protestant **~ism** *n* protestantstvo

protocol /'prəʊtəkɒl/ *n* protokol

prototype /'prəʊtətaɪp/ *n* prototip

protozoa /ˌprəʊtə'zəʊə/ *n* *pl* praživotinje

protracted /prə'træktɪd/ *adj* duži, koji se oduljio, produljeni

protractor /prə'træktə(r)/ *n* kutomjer

protrude /prə'truːd/ *vi,vt* stršati **protrusion** /prə'truːʒn/ *n* izbočina, izbočenost

protuberant /prə'tjuːbərənt/ *adj* *form* ispupčen; izbuljen (oči) **protuberance** *n* ispupčenje

proud /praʊd/ *adj* 1 (of) ponosan (na) 2 ohol **~ flesh** divlje meso (ožiljak) **do sb ~** *coll* počastiti koga

prove /pruːv/ *vt,vi* *irreg* 1 (to sb) dokazati 2 **~ to be** pokazati se, ispostaviti se

provenance /'prɒvənəns/ *n* podrijetlo

proverb /'prɒvɜːb/ *n* poslovica **~ial** *adj* poslovičan

provide /prə'vaɪd/ *vt,vi* 1 (for) pobrinuti se, skrbiti 2 (sth for sb; sb with sth) opskrbiti koga čime, pružiti što komu, osigurati, nabaviti 3 predvidati, odrediti **~d** (that) *conj* ako

providence /'prɒvɪdəns/ *n* providnost **providential** /ˌprɒvɪ'denʃl/ *adj* sretan

province /'prɒvɪns/ *n* 1 pokrajina 2 (**~s** *pl*) provincija 3 djelokrug, polje **provincial** /prə'vɪnʃl/ *adj* 1 pokrajinski 2 *derog* provincijalan ○ *n* provincijalac

provision /prə'vɪʒn/ *n* 1 opskrba 2 priprava **make ~ for/against** osigurati se za/za slučaj 3 (*pl*) zalihe hrane 4 odredba • *vt* opskrbiti zalihama **~al** *adj* privremeni

proviso /prə'vaɪzəʊ/ *n* uvjet, klauzula **provisory** *adj* uvjetan

Provo /'prəʊvəʊ/ *n* *coll* član (militantnog krila) IRA-e

provocation /ˌprɒvə'keɪʃn/ *n* provokacija, izazivanje, izazov **provocative** /prə'vɒkətɪv/ *adj* izazovan

provoke /prə'vəʊk/ vt 1 izazivati 2 izazvati, prouzročiti 3 (sb into doing sth/to do sth) natjerati koga na što

provost /'prɒvəst/ n rektor ~ **marshal** načelnik vojne policije

prow /praʊ/ n pramac

prowess /'praʊɪs/ n vještina; srčanost

prowl /praʊl/ vi,vt vrebati, šunjati se • n **be on the ~** vrebati ~ **car** US (policijsko) patrolno vozilo ~**er** n napadač iz zasjede

proximity /prɒk'sɪmətɪ/ n form blizina

proxy /'prɒksɪ/ n 1 punomoć 2 opunomoćenik, službeni zastupatelj

prude /pru:d/ n pretjerano krepostan ~**ry** n pretjerana krepost **prudish** adj pretjerano krepostan

prudent /'pru:dnt/ adj razborit ~**ial** adj razborit **prudence** n razbor

prune (1) /pru:n/ n suha šljiva

prune (2) vt 1 podrezivati, kresati 2 fig čistiti **pruning shears** n pl vrtlarske škare

pry (1) /praɪ/ vi (into) gurati nos (u tuđe stvari), uhoditi ~ **about** njuškati

pry (2) vt (~ sth open) otvoriti, obiti ~ **a secret out of sb** izvući iz koga tajnu

psalm /sɑ:m/ n psalam

pseudo /'sju:dəʊ/ adj coll lažan, neiskren • n licemjer

pseudo- prefix pseudo-, nazovi- ~**nym** n pseudonim, lažno ime

pshaw /pʃə/ int fuj! pah! (prezir, negodovanje)

psyche /'saɪkɪ/ n 1 duša 2 psiha ~**delic** adj psihodeličan, halucinogen **psychiatry** /saɪ'kaɪətrɪ/ n psihijatrija **psychiatrist** n psihijatar **psychic** /'saɪkɪk/ n vidovnjak, medij ○ (**psychical**) adj 1 psihički 2 spiritistički **psychoanalysis** /,saɪkəʊə'næləsɪs/ n psihoanaliza **psychoanalist** n psihoanalitičar **psychology** /saɪ'kɒlədʒɪ/ n psihologija **psychologist** n psiholog **psychological** adj psihološki **psychopath** /'saɪkəpæθ/ n psihopat **psychosis** /saɪ'kəʊsɪs/ n psihoza **psychotherapy** /,saɪkəʊ'θerəpɪ/ n psihoterapija

pub /pʌb/ n GB pub (točionica alkohola); kafić ~ **crawl** n obilazak kafića,

pijanka

puberty /'pju:bətɪ/ n pubertet

pubic /'pju:bɪk/ adj stidni

public /'pʌblɪk/ adj javni; opće poznat ~**address system** razglas ~ **corporation** javno poduzeće ~ **enemy** narodni neprijatelj ~ **house** form → **pub** ~ **ownership** državno vlasništvo ~ **relations** n pl odnosi s javnošću ~ **school** a. GB privatna škola b. US državna škola ~ **utilities** n pl komunalne službe **go ~** com pustiti dionice u javnu prodaju **make sth ~** objaviti • n 1 the ~ javnost **in ~** javno 2 publika ~**an** n 1 vlasnik puba 2 bibl poreznik ~**ation** n 1 objavljivanje 2 publikacija ~**ist** /'pʌblɪsɪst/ n publicist ~**ity** /pʌb'lɪsətɪ/ n publicitet, reklama ~**ity agent** reklamni agent ~**ize** /'pʌblɪsaɪz/ vt dati publicitet, reklamirati **publish** /'pʌblɪʃ/ vt izdati, objaviti **publisher** n izdavač **publishing house** izdavačka kuća

puce /pju:s/ n ljubičastosmeđ

puck (1) /pʌk/ n vilenjak ~**ish** adj vilenjački

puck (2) n pak

pucker /'pʌkə(r)/ vt,vi nabrati (se) • n nabor

pudding /'pʊdɪŋ/ n 1 slatka krema **Christmas ~** božićni kolač **Yorkshire ~** lako tijesto 2 coll desert 3 kobasica **black ~** krvavica

puddle /'pʌdl/ n lokva

pudgy /'pʌdʒɪ/ adj bucmast

puerile /'pjʊəraɪl/ adj djetinjast

puerperal /pju:'ɜ:pərəl/ adj babinji

puff /pʌf/ n 1 puhanje, puckanje 2 jastučić (za puder) 3 puf coll (rukav i sl.) 4 napuhana hvala ~ **ball** (gljiva) puhara ~ **pastry** lisnato tijesto ~**y** adj 1 zadihan 2 natečen • vi,vt 1 puhati, puckati, dahtati ~**ed up** adj napuhan fig ~ **out** a. ugasiti b. naduti 2 fig napuhati (knjigu etc.)

pug /pʌg/ n mops ~**nosed** adj zatupasta nosa

pugilist /'pju:dʒɪlɪst/ n form šakač, boksač

pugnacious /pʌg'neɪʃəs/ adj borben, ratoboran

puke /pju:k/ vi,vt sl bljuvati • n bljuvotina

pull /pʊl/ *vt,vi* vući, povlačiti, natezati ~ **sth to pieces** a. rastrgati b. *fig* sasjeći ~ **one's weight** pošteno raditi ~ **at/on** potegnuti ~ **a fast one** *coll* prevariti ~ **sth down** srušiti ~ **in** a. ući u stanicu b. prići, dovesti se do ~ **sb in** privući ~ **sth off** uspjeti ~ **out** otisnuti se, krenuti prema ~ **out of sth** krenuti iz, povuci se ~ **(sb) out (of** sth) povući se ~**out** from povlačenje ~ **over** maknuti se u stranu ~**over** /ˈpʊləʊvə(r)/ *n* pulover ~ **round** oporaviti se ~ **through** izvući se, oporaviti se ~ **up** zaustaviti • *n* 1 potezanje 2 gutljaj, dim 3 privlačnost 4 ručka

pullet /ˈpʊlɪt/ *n* mlada kokoš

pulley /ˈpʊlɪ/ *n* kolotur

pulmonary /ˈpʌlmənərɪ/ *adj* dišni, dišnih organa

pulp /pʌlp/ *n* 1 meso 2 kaša(sta masa), celuloza ~**wood** celulozno drvo ~ **literature** roto-romani • *vt,vi* zgnječiti

pulpit (1) /ˈpʌlpɪt/ *n* propovjedaonica

pulse (1) /pʌls/ *n* bilo, puls **pulsate** *vi* pulsirati

pulse (2) *n* grahorice, mahunjače

pulverize /ˈpʌlvəraɪz/ *vt,vi* pretvoriti (se) u prah

pumice /ˈpʌmɪs/ *n* (~**stone**) plovućac

pummel /ˈpʌml/ *vt* udarati šakama

pump (1) /pʌmp/ *n* crpka • *vt,vi* 1 (out/up etc.) iscrpsti, crpsti; izvući *fig* 2 (in/up) napumpati, napuhati 3 pumpati ~ **up** pojačati

pump (2) *n* balerinka, niska cipela

pumpkin /ˈpʌmpkɪn/ *n* tikva

pun /pʌn/ *n* igra riječima ~**ster** *n* osoba sklona igri riječima

punch (1) /pʌntʃ/ *vt* udariti (šakom) • *n* 1 udarac **pull one's** ~**es** susprezati se ~**drunk** *adj* omamljen udarcima, grogi ~ **line** šlagvort *coll* ~**up** *n coll* šaketanje 2 *fig* energija

punch (2) *vt* 1 bušiti 2 štancati *coll* 3 (in/out) zabiti/izbiti • *n* šilo, perforator; punc, žig; sprava za zabijanje (čavala etc.)

punch (3) *n* punč

Punch *n* lutak **pleased as** ~ vrlo zadovoljan

punctual /ˈpʌŋktʃʊəl/ *adj* točan

punctuate /ˈpʌŋktʃʊeɪt/ *vt* 1 staviti interpunkciju 2 prekidati **punctuation** *n* interpunkcija

puncture /ˈpʌŋktʃə(r)/ *n* rupa, probušena guma • *vt,vi* probušiti (se)

pundit /ˈpʌndɪt/ *n* učen čovjek; mudrac (+ *derog*)

pungent /ˈpʌndʒənt/ *adj* prodoran, pikantan

punish /ˈpʌnɪʃ/ *vt* (with/by sth for sth) kazniti ~**able** *adj* kažnjiv ~**ment** *n* kazna **punitive** /ˈpjuːnɪtɪv/ *adj* kaznen

punk /pʌŋk/ *n* 1 trulo drvo, guba 2 punker 3 punk-glazba 4 propalica

punnet /ˈpʌnɪt/ *n* košarica

punt (1) /pʌnt/ *n* riječni čamac • *vt,vi* otiskivati (čamac) čakljom, voziti (se)

punt (2) *vt* udariti loptu (prije nego što padne na zemlju)

punt (3) *vi* kladiti se ~**er** *n* 1 kladitelj 2 mušterija

puny /ˈpjuːnɪ/ *adj* sitan, slabašan

pup /pʌp/ *n* 1 štene **sell sb a** ~ prodati komu rog za svijeću 2 *fig* umišljeni mladac ~**py** *n* štenac ~**py love** prva ljubav

pupil (1) /ˈpjuːpl/ *n* učenik

pupil (2) *n* zjenica

puppet /ˈpʌpɪt/ *n* 1 lutka; marioneta (+ *fig*) 2 *mod* lutkarski 3 *mod* marionetski

purchase /ˈpɜːtʃəs/ *n* 1 kupnja ~ **tax** porez na promet 2 uporište 3 vrijednost, prihod • *vt* kupiti; platiti *fig*

pure /pjʊə(r)/ *adj* čist **purify** /ˈpjʊərɪfaɪ/ *vt* očistiti **puritan** /ˈpjʊərɪtən/ *n* 1 (P~) puritanac 2 čistunac ○ *adj* puritanski **purity** *n* čistoća

purée /ˈpjʊəreɪ/ *n* pasirano (voće-/povrće) • *vt* pasirati

purgatory /ˈpɜːgətərɪ/ *n* čistilište

purge /pɜːdʒ/ *vt* 1 (of/from) očistiti (se) (od) 2 oprati (se) od krivnje 3 provesti čistku ~ *n* 1 čistka 2 čistilo

purl /pɜːl/ *n* krivi bod

purloin /pɜːˈlɔɪn/ *vt form* ukrasti

purple /ˈpɜːpl/ *adj* ljubičast **P~ Heart** odlikovanje za ranjenog vojnika

purport /ˈpɜːpət/ *n form* značenje,

smisao, svrha • *vt* **1** naizgled značiti
2 predstavljati se
purpose /'pɜ:pəs/ *n* **1** svrha, cilj, namjera **2** odlučnost, svrhovitost **on ~**
namjerno **to the ~** relevantan **to no ~**
uzalud **serve/answer one's ~** poslužiti svrsi **~ful** *adj* odlučan **~less** *adj*
besciljan
purr /pɜ:(r)/ *vi,vt* presti (mačka)
purse /pɜ:s/ *n* **1** novčarka (+ *fig*) **hold
the ~strings** kontrolirati troškove **2**
financije **3** novčana nagrada **4** *US*
torbica • *vt* (**up the lips**) napućiti
usne **~r** *n* brodski ekonom; administrator
pursuant /pə'sju:ənt/ *adj* **~ to** *form* u
skladu s
pursue /pə'sju:/ *vt* **1** proganjati (+ *fig*)
2 nastaviti **3** težiti **pursuit** /pə'sju:t/ *n*
(of) **1** potjera, potraga (za); lov (na)
in hot ~ za petama **2** zanimanje,
studij
purvey /pə'veɪ/ *vi,vt* (to, for) opskrblji-
vati (koga) **~or** *n* nabavljač
pus /pʌs/ *n* gnoj
push /puʃ/ *vi,vt* **1** gurati **2** reklamirati,
prodavati; gurati *fig* **3** prodavati
(drogu); dilati *sl* **4** pritisnuti **be ~ing
thirty** *coll* bližiti se tridesetoj **~bike**
bicikl **~chair** dječja kolica **~er** *n* **1**
laktaroš **2** *sl* preprodavač droge; diler
sl **~y** *adj* nametljiv, prodoran **~ sb
around** zapovijedati kome **~ off**
odgurnuti **~ over** gurnuti, srušiti **~
over** *sl* čas posla; lako žrtva **~ sth
through** progurati **~ sth up** povisiti
~up bra grudnjak s potpornjima • *n*
1 guranje, udarac **2** napor, napad **3**
odlučnost **when it comes to the ~**
kad dođe stani-pani
puss /pus/ *n* **1** mačka, maca **2** *coll* cura
~y *n* **1** (**~y-cat**) mica-maca **3** *sl* pička
~y-foot *vi coll* šunjati se; biti pretjerano oprezan
put (1) /put/ *vi,vt irreg* **1** staviti **2**
izreći, izraziti se **~ pressure on sb**
pritisnuti/natjerati koga **~ an end/a
stop to sth** prekinuti, ukinuti **~ sb to
death** ubiti, pogubiti **~ sb at ease**
učiniti da se tko osjeća opušteno **~ sb
to great inconvenience** prouzročiti
komu velike neugodnosti **~ sb in**

mind of sth/sb podsjetiti koga na
koga/što **~ sb out of his misery**
skratiti komu muke **~ sth/sb to test**
staviti na kušnju **~ sth/sb right** ispraviti koga/što **~ sth to sb; ~ it to
sb (that)** postaviti, predložiti, podnijeti **~ a price on** procijeniti **~ sth ac-
cross** (to sb) prenijeti **~ aside a.**
odložiti **b.** uštedjeti **c.** zanemariti **~
sth away a.** pospremiti **b.** uštedjeti **c.**
coll slistiti **d.** odreći se **~ sb away a.**
coll spremiti u ludnicu **b.** *coll* uspavati (psa i sl.) **~ sth back** vratiti **~ sth
down a.** sletjeti **b.** odložiti **c.** ugušiti
fig **d.** zapisati **~ sb down** ušutkati **~
sb down as** smatrati koga čime **~
down to** pripisati **~ sth forward a.**
iznijeti **b.** pomaknuti naprijed **~ sb
forward** predložiti **~ in** uskliknuti **~
in for sth** prijaviti se za a. **~ in** podnijeti **~ sth in/into** uložiti **~ off a.**
odložiti **b.** odbaciti **~ sb off** otresti se
~ sb off sth uništiti u komu volju za
~ sth on a. odjenuti, obuti **b.** hiniti **c.**
dodati **~ on weight** udebljati se **~ sb
on** *coll* varati **~ sth out** ugasiti **~ sb
out** uzrujati **~ sth through** provesti **~
sb through** to sb spojiti koga s kim
~ sb through sth podvrći koga čemu
I am hard ~ to it to teško mi je **~ sth
together** sastaviti **let's ~ our heads
together** posavjetujmo se **~ up** (at)
prenoćiti **~ up** (for sth) kandidirati se
~ sth up podići **~ up a fight** pružiti
otpor **~up job** prevara **~ sb up**
ponuditi smještaj komu **~ sb up to
sth** navesti koga na što **~ up with
sb/sth** podnositi
put (2) → **putt**
putative /'pju:tətɪv/ *adj* navodni
putrefy /'pju:trɪfaɪ/ *vt,vi* gnjiti, raspadati se **putrefaction** /,pju:trɪ'fækʃn/ *n*
gnjiljenje, raspadanje **putrid** *adj*
gnjio, truo (+ *fig* *adj*)
putsch /putʃ/ *n* puč
putt /pʌt/ *vi,vt golf* lako udariti loptu
~ing iron palica za lako udaranje
lopte
putty /'pʌtɪ/ *n* (staklarski) kit • *vt*
obložiti kitom
puzzle /'pʌzl/ *n* zagonetka **be in a ~**
biti zbunjen • *vt,vi* zbuniti, biti u ne-

doumici ~ **over sth** razbijati glavu (oko čega) ~ **sth out** razbijati glavu; doći do rješenja **~ment** n zbunjenost

pyjamas /pəˈdʒɑːməz/ n pl pidžama

pylon /ˈpaɪlɒn/ n stup (dalekovoda)

pyramid /ˈpɪrəmɪd/ n piramida

pyre /ˈpaɪə(r)/ n (pogrebna) lomača

pyrotechnics /ˌpaɪrəˈtɛknɪks/ n pl pirotehnika (+ fig)

python /ˈpaɪθn/ n piton

Q

Q, q /kju:/ 17. slovo engl. abecede; kve

quack (1) /kwæk/ *vi* gakati

quack (2) *n* šarlatan **~ery** šarlatanstvo

quadrangle /'kwɒdræŋgl/ *adj* četverokut **quadrangular** *adj* četverokutan

quadrant /'kwɒdrənt/ *n* kvadrant

quadraatic /kwɑ'drætɪk/ *adj* ~ **equation** kvadratna jednadžba

quadrophonic /,kwɒdrə'fɒnɪk/ *adj* kvadrofonski

quadruped /'kwɒdruped/ *n* četveronožna životinja

quadruple /'kwɒdru:pl/ *vt,vi* 1 pomnožiti sa četiri 2 učetverostručiti se • *adj* četverostruk

quadruplet /'kwɒdru:plet/ *n* četvorke

quaff /kwɒf/ *vt* (nadušak) ispiti, žedno piti

quagmire /'kwægmaɪə(r)/ *n* 1 vlažno/močvarno/blatno tlo 2 *fig* škripac; gabula *sl*

quail (1) /kweɪl/ *n* prepelica

quail (2) *vi* drhtati, strepiti

quaint /kweɪnt/ *adj* neobičan, starinski

quake /kweɪk/ *vi* tresti se, drhtati, drhtavati • *n coll* potres

Quaker /'kweɪkə(r)/ *n* Kveker

qualification /,kwɒlɪfɪ'keɪʃn/ *n* 1 kvalifikacija, sposobnost, preduvjet 2 svjedodžba, diploma 3 ograničenje; ograda *fig* **qualified** *adj* 1 kvalificiran, osposobljen 2 ograničen, nepotpun **qualifier** /'kwɒlɪfaɪə(r)/ *n* kvalifikator **qualify** /'kwɒlɪfaɪ/ *vi,vt* 1 kvalificirati (se), osposobiti (se) 2 ograničiti, izmijeniti, ublažiti

quality /'kwɒlətɪ/ *n* 1 kakvoća, kvaliteta 2 vrsnoća, odličnost 3 *mod* kvalitetan, vrstan 4 svojstvo, odlika

qualm /kwɑ:m/ *n* 1 dvojba, nedoumica 2 mučnina

quandary /'kwɒndərɪ/ *n* nedoumica

quantify /'kwɒntɪfaɪ/ *vt form* izmjeriti, odrediti

quantitative /'kwɒntɪtətɪv/ *adj* kvantitativan, količinski

quantity /'kwɒntətɪ/ *n* količina, kvantiteta, broj

quantum /'kwɒntəm/ *n* iznos ~ **leap** veliki korak naprijed

quarantine /'kwɒrənti:n/ *n* karantena • *vt* staviti u karantenu

quarrel /'kwɒrəl/ *n* 1 svađa, prepirka 2 zamjerka • *vi* 1 (about/over sth with sb) svađati se, prepirati se 2 ne slagati se **~some** *adj* svadljiv

quarry (1) /'kwɒrɪ/ *n* kamenolom • *vt* lomiti, kopati

quarry (2) *n* lovina, plijen

quart /kwɔ:t/ *n* mjerna jedinica za tekućinu (1.14 l) **put a ~ into a pint pot** *coll* pokušati što nemoguće/neizvedivo

quarter /'kwɔ:tə(r)/ *n* 1 četvrt(ina) **~final** četvrtzavršnica 2 četvrt sata, 15 minuta *a* ~ **past ten** 10:15 3 tri mjeseca, kvartal 4 *US* (novčić od) 25 centi 5 četvrt, dio grada 6 mjera za težinu (12.70 kg) 7 **~s** *mil* stan, prostorije **~master** *mil* ekonom 8 mjesto; smjer, strana • *vt* 1 podijeliti na četiri dijela; raščetvoriti 2 *mil* smjestiti, naći smještaj **~ly** *adj* tromjesečni, kvartalni *o n* tromjesečni časopis

quartet /kwɔ:'tet/ *n* kvartet

quash /kwɒʃ/ *vt form* 1 ne prihvatiti, ne odobriti, ukinuti 2 ugušiti (ustanak)

quasi- /'kweɪsaɪ/ *prefix* kvazi-

quatrain /'kwɒtreɪn/ *n* kvartina, strofa od 4 stiha

quaver /'kweɪvə(r)/ *vt,vi* 1 (za)drhtati 2 reći drhtavim glasom • *n* 1 podrhtavanje glasa 2 *GB mus* osminka

quay /ki:/ *n* molo

queasy /'kwi:zɪ/ *adj* koji osjeća mučninu *I feel* ~ mučno mi je

queen /kwi:n/ *n* **1** kraljica (+ *fig*) ~ **consort** (naslov) kraljeva supruga **the Q~'s English** najpravilniji engleski jezik **turn** ~'s **evidence** svjedočiti protiv suučesnika **2** matica **3** dama   (u kartama) **4** *sl* homoseksualac

queer /kwɪə(r)/ *adj* **1** *derog coll* homoseksualan **2** neobičan, čudan **feel** ~ osjećati se slabo **in** ~ **street** *GB sl* do grla u dugovima • *n derog coll* peder *derog vulg*

quell /kwel/ *vt* ugušiti, savladati; stišati, smiriti

quench /kwentʃ/ *vt* utažiti, ugasiti

querulous /'kwerʊləs/ *adj form* nezadovoljan, mrzovoljan, koji stalno gunđa/jada se

query /'kwɪərɪ/ *n* pitanje, dvojba • *vt* (is)pitati, izraziti sumnju (u što)

quest /kwest/ *n* potraga *in* ~ *of* u potrazi za • *vi* (for/after) tragati

question /'kwestʃən/ *n* **1** pitanje ~ **mark** upitnik ~ **master** voditelj kviza **2** dvojba, sumnja *in* ~ *o* kojem je riječ; dotični **(it is)** **out of the** ~ ne dolazi u obzir • *vt* **1** ispitati **2** dovesti u pitanje **~able** *adj* sumnjiv *it is* ~*able whether...* pitanje je je li... **~ing** *adj* upitan **~naire** /ˌkwestʃə'neə(r)/ *n* upitnik, anketni listić

queue /kju:/ *n GB* red **~–jump** *vi GB* preguravati se, ići preko reda • *vi* (~ up) čekati u redu

quibble /'kwɪbl/ *vi* (about/over sth, with sb) svađati se oko sitnica • *n* prigovor

quiche /ki:ʃ/ *n* francuska pita

quick (1) /kwɪk/ *adj* **1** brz; učinjen na brzinu **~–tempered** koji lako plane **~–witted** oštrouman **2** živ **~lime** živo vapno **~sand** živi pijesak **~silver** živa • *adv* brzo **~en** *vt,vi* ubrzati (se) **~ly** *adv* brzo; na brzinu

quick (2) *n* meso ispod nokta **cut sb to the** ~ dirnuti u živac *fig*

quid /kwɪd/ *n (pl* ~) *GB coll* funta

quiescent /kwaɪ'esnt/ *adj form* pasivan, nepokretan, uspavan

quiet /'kwaɪət/ *adj* **1** tih **2** miran • *n* tišina, mir **on the** ~ potajno **~en** *vt,vi* (down) umiriti (se) **~ly** *adv* tiho

quiff /kwɪf/ *n GB* kokotica *sl*

quill /kwɪl/ *n* **1** pero **2** bodlja

quilt /kwɪlt/ *n* poplun **~ed** *adj* vatiran

quince /kwɪns/ *n* dunja

quinine /kwɪ'ni:n/ *n* kinin

quintessence /kwɪn'tesns/ *n* bit, srž; utjelovljenje *fig*

quintet /kwɪn'tet/ *n* kvintet

quintuplet /'kwɪntjuːplet/ *n* petorke

quip /kwɪp/ *n* dosjetka

quirk /kwɜːk/ *n* **1** stjecaj okolnosti, igra slučaja **2** hir, mušica

quisling /'kwɪzlɪŋ/ *n derog* kvisling, petokolonaš

quit /kwɪt/ *vi,vt irreg* **1** prestati, prekinuti, napustiti, ostaviti **2** dati otkaz **~s** *adj* jedan-jedan; kvit

quite /kwaɪt/ *adv* **1** potpuno, sasvim **2** prilično, donekle **3** (kao odgovor) tako je, slažem se **4** *US* vrlo, jako **5** *US* odličan, sjajan *she's* ~ *a girl* prava je cura, cura i pol

quiver /'kwɪvə(r)/ *vi* (za)drhtati • *n* drhtaj

quiz /kwɪz/ *n* **1** kviz **2** *US* (kratki) test **~master** voditelj kviza • *vt* ispitivati **~zical** *adj* upitan

quorum /'kwɔːrəm/ *n* kvorum

quota /'kwəʊtə/ *n* kvota, norma

quote /kwəʊt/ *vi, vt* navesti, citirati ~ *a price* ponuditi cijenu • *n* navod *in* ~*s* pod navodnicima • *adv* citiram **quotation** *n* navod, citat **quotation mark** navodnik

quoth /kwəʊθ/ *v arch* reče

quotidian /kwəʊ'tɪdɪən/ *adj* svakodnevan

quotient /'kwəʊʃnt/ *n* kvocijent, količnik

R

R, r /ɑ:(r)/ *n* 18. slovo engl. abecede; er

rabbi /'ræbaɪ/ *n* rabin

rabbit /'ræbɪt/ *n* kunić

rabble /'ræbl/ *n* rulja, svjetina **~rous-ing** *adj* podstrekivački, demagoški

rabid /'ræbɪd/ *adj* 1 bijesan 2 *fig derog* zagrižen **rabies** /'reɪbiːz/ *n* bjesnilo

rac(c)oon /rə'kuːn/ *n* rakun

race (1) /reɪs/ *n* (u)trka • *vi,vt* 1 utrkivati se, natjecati se s kim 2 juriti **~course/~track** *US* trkalište **~horse** trkaći konj ~ **meeting** trke **~r** *n* trkač; trkaći konj/auto

race (2) *n* 1 rasa 2 pleme; narod 3 podrijetlo 4 pasmina **racial** /'reɪʃl/ *adj* rasni **racism** /'reɪsɪzəm/ *n* rasizam **racist** *n* rasist o *adj* rasistički

rack (1) /ræk/ *n* 1 polica; stalak; vješalica 2 kotač (mučilo) • *vt* (with/by) mučiti ~ **one's brains** razbijati si glavu

rack (2) *n* go to ~ **and ruin** potpuno propasti

racket, racquet (1) /'rækɪt/ *n* reket

racket (2) *coll* 1 buka, galama 2 ucjenjivanje; organizirani kriminal **~eer** *n* gangster, mafijaš

racy /'reɪsɪ/ *adj* uzbudljiv, pikantan (priča)

radar /'reɪdə(r)/ *n* radar

radiance /'reɪdɪəns/ *n* sjaj **radiant**/'reɪdɪənt/ *adj* sjajan, blistav **radiate** /'reɪdɪeɪt/ *vt,vi* 1 zračiti, isijavati (+ *fig*) 2 (from) širiti se **radiation** *n* zračenje **radiator** *n* 1 radijator 2 hladnjak (automobila)

radical /'rædɪkl/ *adj* korjenit, temeljit; radikalan • *n* radikal

radio /'reɪdɪəʊ/ *n* 1 radio 2 *mod* radijski, radio- ~ **set** radioprijemnik ~ **station** radiopostaja • *vi,vt* javiti radiom

radioactive /,reɪdɪəʊ'æktɪv/ *adj* radioaktivan

radish /'rædɪʃ/ *n* rotkvica

radius /'reɪdɪəs/ *n* (*pl* radii /'reɪdɪaɪ/) 1 polumjer, radijus 2 krug; doseg

raffle /'ræfl/ *n* lutrija

raft /rɑːft/ *n* 1 splav 2 (**life ~**) čamac za spasavanje • *vi,vt* splavariti **~er**, **~sman** *n* splavar

rafter /'rɑːftə(r)/ *n* rog krova, krovna greda

rag /ræg/ *n* 1 krpa 2 *pl* krpe, dronjci, prnje 3 *coll derog* (mjesne) novine **~-and-bone man** *GB* kramar ~ **doll** krpena lutka **~ged** /'rægɪd/ *adj* 1 odrpan 2 nedotjeran 3 čupav 4 neravan, hrapav; nazupčan (rub)

rage /reɪdʒ/ *n* 1 bijes 2 *coll* posljednji modni krik • *vi* 1 bjesnjeti, razbjesniti se 2 harati (bolest) **raging** *adj* silovit, snažan

raid /reɪd/ *n* 1 (iznenadni) upad, prepad, napad, pohod 2 racija **air ~** zračni napad • *vt,vi* 1 napasti, upasti, prodrijeti u; 2 izvršiti raciju 3 opljačkati; poharati **~er** *n* napadač; pljačkaš

rail (1) /reɪl/ *n* 1 ograda 2 prečka, vješalica 3 tračnica 4 željeznica **~ing(s)** *n* ograda, rešetka **~way/-~road** *US* a. željeznička pruga **b**. željeznica **~way line** željeznička pruga **~wayman** željezničar **~way station** kolodvor • *vt* 1 (in) ograditi 2 (off) odvojiti ogradom

rail (2) *vi* (against/at) grditi ~ **against fate** proklinjati sudbinu

rain /reɪn/ *n* kiša (+ *fig*) **in the ~** po/na kiši **it's ~ing** kiši, pada kiša **as right as** ~ zdrav kao dren (**come**) ~ **or shine** bez obzira na vrijeme **~bow** duga **take a ~ check on sth** *US coll* uzeti kasnije **~coat** kišni kaput, kabanica **~fall** kiša, oborine **~water**

kišnica ~y adj kišni, kišovit **for a ~y day** za crne dane • vi,vt 1 kišiti 2 liti (suze) 3 (sth on) obasuti, zasuti ~ **cats and dogs** padati kao iz kabla **it never ~s but it pours** nesreća nikada ne dolazi sama

raise /reiz/ vt 1 dignuti, podići 2 povisiti, povećati 3 promaknuti, unaprijediti 4 pobuditi (nadu) 5 prikupiti (novac) 6 novačiti 7 odgojiti 8 uzgajati 9 postaviti, potaknuti, pokrenuti (pitanje), uložiti (prosvjed), staviti (primjedbu) 10 izazvati (smijeh, strah), podići (prašinu, uzbunu) 11 podići, postaviti (spomenik) 12 skinuti (zabranu), prekinuti (opsadu) ~ **Cain/the devil/hell/the roof** coll dići strašnu galamu • n US povišica (plaće)

raisin /reizn/ n grožđica

rake (1) /reik/ n grablje • vt,vi 1 grabljati 2 prekapati ~ **in** coll zgrtati (novac) ~ **out** coll iskopati (podatak) ~ **up** coll **a.** kopati (po prošlosti), iskopati **b.** skucati (novac) ~**off** n coll derog dio zarade, postotak

rake (2) n razvratnik, bećar **rakish** adj 1 razuzdan 2 poletan, veseo, živahan

rally /ræli/ vt,vi 1 okupiti (se), skupiti (se), pridružiti se 2 pridobiti (podršku); pribrati (snagu) 3 oporaviti se ~ **round** coll skupiti se/sjatiti se oko; priskočiti u pomoć • n 1 miting, skup 2 reli

ram /ræm/ n 1 ovan 2 sprava za probijanje bedema 3 klip; čep • vt 1 zabušiti/zabiti se 2 (down) nabijati 3 (into) zabiti, nabiti, nagurati ~ **sth down sb's throat** nametati kome što

ramble /ræmbl/ vi 1 lunjati 2 (on/about) razbrbljati se o; udaljiti se od teme • n šetnja (u prirodi) ~**r** n 1 šetač, izletnik 2 (~**r rose**) ruža penjačica **rambling** adj nepovezan, nesuvisao, razvučen

rambunctious /ræm'bʌŋkʃəs/ adj raspojasan, bučan, glasan

ramp /ræmp/ n 1 nagib 2 izbočina; "ležeći" policajac coll

rampage /ræm'peidʒ/ n divljanje **be/go on the ~** divljati

rampant /ræmpənt/ adj 1 nezaus-tavljiv, raširen 2 bujan

rampart /ræmpaːt/ n 1 bedem, grudobran 2 fig branik

ramshackle /ræmʃækl/ adj raskliman, trošan

ran v irreg → **run**

ranch /raːntʃ/ n ranč, farma

rancid /rænsid/ adj užežen

rancour (-cor US) /ræŋkə(r)/ n form ogorčenost; pakost

random /rændəm/ n **at ~** nasumce • adj slučajan

randy /rændi/ adj GB coll pohotan, uspaljen

rang v irreg → **ring**

range /reindʒ/ n 1 raspon, niz 2 djelokrug, opseg, područje 3 domet, domašaj 4 streljana; poligon 5 (planinski) lanac 6 asortiman, izbor • vi,vt 1 kretati se, varirati 2 (over/through) lutati; prevaliti; prostirati se 3 (over) fig dotaknuti (mnoge teme), pokrivati (područje) 4 poredati, poslagati, svrstati 5 imati domet, nositi (oružje)

ranger /reindʒə(r)/ n 1 šumar 2 US pripadnik konjičke policije 3 US komandos

rank (1) /ræŋk/ n 1 niz, red, vrsta; stroj mil 2 čin, položaj **pull ~** pozvati se na čin/položaj **the ~ and file a.** obični vojnici **b.** obični članovi; obični ljudi **taxi ~** GB stajalište taksija • vi,vt 1 ubrajati se među, sloviti kao 2 poredati, poslagati, svrstati 3 US biti viši/stariji po činu od ~**ing** adj US najviši po činu

rank (2) adj 1 obrastao (biljka, tlo) 2 smrdljiv; odvratnog okusa 3 derog čisti, pravi (pravcati)

ransack /rænsæk/ vt 1 pretražiti, prekopati 2 opljačkati

ransom /rænsəm/ n otkupnina **hold sb to ~** oteti koga zbog otkupnine • vt otkupiti koga

rant /rænt/ vi (on) govoriti bombastično, grmjeti, rogoboriti

rap /ræp/ n 1 kucanje, udaranje 2 rap glazba **give sb a ~ on/over the knuckles** ukoriti koga **take the ~** (for sth) sl snositi krivnju, preuzeti odgovornost • vi,vt 1 kucati, lupati, udarati 2 izgrditi, ukoriti koga 3 *US sl* pričati, razgovarati

rape /reɪp/ *vt* silovati • *n* 1 silovanje 2 *form* oskvrnuće **rapist** *n* silovatelj

rapid /'ræpɪd/ *adj* brz, hitar; nagao **~fire** *adj* rafalni, brzometan (+ *fig*) **~s** *n pl* brzaci

rapport /ræ'pɔː(r)/ *n* odnos, veza

rapture /'ræptʃə(r)/ *n* oduševljenje, ushićenje, zanos **be in/go into ~s** oduševiti se

rare (1) /reə(r)/ *adj* 1 rijedak 2 čudan, neobičan **~ly** *adv* rijetko

rare (2) *adj* nedopečen, krvav (odrezak)

rascal /'rɑːskl/ *n* hulja

rash (1) /ræʃ/ *adj* brzoplet, nepromišljen

rash (2) *n* osip **come out in ~** dobiti osip, osuti se **a ~ of** *fig* niz

rasher /'ræʃə(r)/ *n* tanka kriška (slanine, šunke)

rasp /rɑːsp/ *n* rašpa **~ing** *adj* kreštav (glas)

raspberry /'rɑːzbrɪ/ *n* malina **blow/give sb a ~** *sl* izbeljiti se kome

rat /ræt/ *n* 1 štakor 2 *coll* hulja, izdajica **the ~ race** *coll* bespoštedna konkurencija **smell a ~** nanjušiti opasnost/prijevaru • *vi* (on) *coll* izdati; cinkati, otkucati *sl*

rate /reɪt/ *n* brzina; broj; cijena; mjera; stopa; tečaj; tarifa **birth ~** natalitet **death ~** mortalitet **~ of exchange** devizni tečaj **interest ~** kamatna stopa **at any ~** u svakom slučaju **first-~** prvorazredan • *vt,vi* 1 (at/among) (pro)cijeniti; smatrati, ubrajati 2 zavrijediti, zaslužiti 3 (at) *GB* procijeniti (oporezivanja) 4 kotirati **rating** *n* položaj, popularnost; rang, stupanj; ocjena; *TV* gledanost

rather /'rɑːðə(r)/ *adv* 1 prilično 2 radije, prije 3 točnije, odnosno 4 *GB coll* svakako **I would/I had/I'd ~ stay** radije bih ostao **~ cold day** prilično hladan dan **~ than** umjesto

ratify /'rætɪfaɪ/ *vt form* odobriti, potvrditi, ratificirati

ratio /'reɪʃɪəʊ/ *n* (of/to) omjer, odnos

ration /'ræʃn/ *n* obrok, porcija • *vt* 1 (sb to sth) ograničiti obroke, racionirati

2 (out) (po)dijeliti (obroke)

rational /'ræʃnəl/ *adj* razuman, racionalan **~e** /ˌræʃə'nɑːl/ *n* (for/of) *form* (osnovni) razlozi/načela **~ize** *vt* racionalno objasniti; racionalizirati

rattle /'rætl/ *vt,vi* 1 kloparati; štropotati, tandrkati; zveckati 2 *coll* uzdrmati **~ off** *coll* odverglati • *n* zvečka; čegrtaljka **~snake** čegrtuša

raucous /'rɔːkəs/ *adj* hrapav, promukao; bučan

raunchy /'rɔːntʃɪ/ *adj coll* pohotan, uspaljen; seksi *coll*

ravage /'rævɪdʒ/ *vt* poharati, pustošiti, razoriti, uništiti • *n* 1 pustošenje, uništavanje 2 *pl* pogubne posljedice **the ~s of time** zub vremena

rave /reɪv/ *vi* 1 buncati 2 bjesnjeti 3 (about) *coll* ludovati, šiziti (za kime/čime) • *n coll* hvalospjev **raving** *adj, adv* lud(o), mahnit(o)

raven /'reɪvn/ *n* gavran

ravenous /'rævənəs/ *adj* 1 vrlo gladan; proždrljiv 2 pohlepan

ravine /rə'viːn/ *n* klanac, gudura

ravishing /'rævɪʃɪŋ/ *adj* prekrasan; zanosan

raw /rɔː/ *adj* 1 sirov; neprerađen 2 neiskusan, nov 3 otvoren (rana); upaljen (koža); bolan 4 vlažan, hladan (vrijeme) 5 *coll* grub **~ materials** sirovine

ray /reɪ/ *n* 1 zraka; trak 2 *fig* tračak (nade)

raze /reɪz/ *vt* razoriti, sravniti

razor /'reɪzə(r)/ *n* britva **safety ~** aparat za brijanje **~ blade** britvica; žilet *coll*

re /riː/ *prep leg* u svezi

reach /riːtʃ/ *vt,vi* 1 doći do, dospjeti u, stići u 2 (out for) posegnuti (za čim); (is)pružiti (ruku) 3 dodati 4 nagnuti se 5 dohvatiti, dosegnuti 6 doprijeti, dosezati do, protezati/pružati se do 7 dostići (brzinu), postići (dogovor) • *n* dohvat, domet, domašaj, doseg **the upper ~es of the river** gornji tok rijeke **out of/beyond ~** nedostižan **within ~** nadohvat, nadomak

react /rɪ'ækt/ *vi* 1 (to) odgovoriti, reagirati na 2 (against) opirati se 3 (on) djelovati, utjecati **~ion** /rɪ'ækʃn/ *n* odgovor, reakcija ~**ionary** *n* reakcionar o *adj* reakcionaran

read /ri:d/ *vt,vi irreg* **1** (pro)čitati; očitati **2** glasiti **3** studirati **4** (pro)tumačiti ~ **out** pročitati naglas ~ **over/through** pročitati ~**able** *adj* **1** zanimljiv **2** čitak, čitljiv ~**er** *n* **1** čitatelj **2** korektor, lektor **3** *GB* docent **4** čitanka ~**ership** *n* **1** čitalačka publika **2** *GB* docentura ~**ing** *n* **1** čitanje **2** načitanost **3** tumačenje **4** štivo ~**ing room** čitaonica • *n* štivo

ready /'redi/ *adj* **1** (for sth/to do sth) gotov, spreman **2** voljan **3** brz **get/make** ~ spremiti (se) ~ **money/cash** gotov novac • *adv* unaprijed, već ~**made** konfekcijski; spreman, instant *fig* • *n* **at the** ~ u pripravnosti; "na gotovs" *coll* • *int* ~, **steady, go!** priprema, pozor, sad! **readily** *adv* **1** spremno, odmah **2** lako **readiness** *n* **1** (in/for) spremnost **2** voljnost **3** brzina

real /riəl/ *adj* **1** stvaran, istinski, zbiljski **2** pravi, čisti o *adv US coll* → **really for** ~ *US coll* ozbiljan, za ozbiljno ~ **estate/property** nekretnine ~**istic** /riə'listik/ *adj* realističan ~**ity** /ri'æləti/ *n* **1** stvarnost; postojanje **2** činjenica, istina, prava priroda čega ~**ly** *adv* stvarno, zaista, zbilja

realize /'riəlaiz/ *vt* **1** shvatiti, spoznati, uvidjeti **2** ostvariti (nade, ambicije) **3** prodati; ostvariti (dobit), zaraditi; unovčiti

realm /relm/ *n* kraljevstvo

realtor /'riəltə(r)/ *n US* prodavač nekretnina

reap /ri:p/ *vt,vi* žeti, požnjeti (+ *fig*)

rear (1) /riə(r)/ *n* **1** stražnji dio, pozadina **2** *mod* stražnji **3** stražnjica **at the** ~ **of** iza in the ~ **a.** otraga **b.** *mil* u pozadini **bring up the** ~ biti/stići posljednji ~**guard** *mil* zaštitnica ~**view mirror** retrovizor

rear (2) *vt,vi* **1** uzgajati; odgojiti **2** propeti se **3** (po)dići

rearrange /ri:ə'reindʒ/ *vt* preurediti, preinačiti

reason /'ri:zn/ *n* **1** razlog **2** razum, pamet **by** ~ **of** zbog **within** ~ u granicama razumnog **bring sb to** ~ urazu-

miti **listen to/hear** ~ poslušati savjet, dati si dokazati **it stands to** ~ logično je • *vi,vt* **1** razmišljati, razumno misliti **2** (that) zaključiti, smatrati **3** (with sb) raspravljati, uvjeravati ~**able** *adj* **1** razuman **2** prihvatljiv **3** umjeren (cijena) ~**ably** *adv* **1** razumno **2** prilično ~**ing** *n* argumentacija, logika

reassure /ri:ə'ʃʊə(r)/ *vt* (about) utješiti, umiriti; uvjeriti **reassurance** *n* uvjeravanje **reassuring** *adj* utješan

rebate /'ri:beit/ *n* popust, rabat

rebel /'rebl/ *n* **1** pobunjenik, odmetnik **2** *mod* pobunjenički • *vi* (against) (po)buniti se ~**lion** /ri'beliən/ *n* (po)buna

rebirth /ri:'bɜ:θ/ *n* preporod

rebound /ri'baʊnd/ *vi* **1** (from) odbiti se, odskočiti **2** ponovno porasti **3** (on/upon sb) *fig* vratiti se kome

rebuff /ri'bʌf/ *n form* (prezirno/hladno) odbijanje, ignoriranje • *vt* odbiti

rebuild /ri:'bild/ *vt irreg* (→ **build**) ponovno izgraditi, rekonstruirati

rebuke /ri'bju:k/ *vt* (for) ukoriti, zamjeriti, osuditi

rebut /ri'bʌt/ *vt* opovrgnuti, pobiti

recalcitrant /ri'kælsitrənt/ *adj* neposlušan, tvrdoglav

recall /ri'kɔ:l/ *vt* **1** sjetiti se koga/čega **2** (from/to) povući, opozvati, vratiti • *n* **1** opoziv **2** sjećanje **total** ~ savršeno pamćenje **beyond/past** ~ neopoziv

recant /ri'kænt/ *vt,vi* odreći se (uvjerenja)

recap /'ri:kæp/ *coll* → **recapitulate**

recapitulate /ri:kə'pitjuleit/ *vt,vi* ukratko ponoviti

recede /ri'si:d/ *vi* (from) **1** povući se, uzmaći **2** nestajati, gubiti se **3** ćelaviti

receipt /ri'si:t/ *n* **1** priznanica, račun **2** primitak **3** *pl* prihodi

receive *vt,vi* **1** primiti, dobiti **2** pretrpjeti, zadobiti **3** primiti/ dočekati koga **4** hvatati ~**r** *n* **1** slušalica **2** prijemnik **3** *GB* stečajni upravitelj

recent /'ri:snt/ *adj* nedavni, (naj)noviji, posljednji ~**ly** *adv* nedavno, u posljednje vrijeme

reception /rɪ'sepʃn/ *n* 1 doček 2 primanje, prijem 3 recepcija ~ **desk** recepcija ~**ist** *n* recepcionar

recess /rɪ'ses/ *n* 1 odmor, stanka 2 školski praznici 3 *pl fig* kutak **recession** /rɪ'seʃn/ *n* recesija

recipe /'resəpɪ/ *n* recept (+ *fig*)

reciprocal /rɪ'sɪprəkl/ *adj* uzajaman; recipročan

reckless /'reklɪs/ *adj* nepromišljen, neodgovoran, nesmotren

reckon /'rekən/ *vt* 1 (pro)računati, procijeniti 2 *coll* misliti 3 smatrati ~ **in** uračunati ~ **on** računati na ~ **with** a. obračunati/razračunati se s kim b. uzeti u obzir ~ **without** ne uzeti u obzir ~**ing** *n* procjena; računica

reclaim /rɪ'kleɪm/ *vt* (from) 1 tražiti povrat čega, vratiti 2 melorirati 3 reciklirati **reclamation** /ˌreklə'meɪʃən/ *n* 1 melioracija 2 recikliranje

recline /rɪ'klaɪn/ *vi,vt* nasloniti (se), leći

recognize /'rekəgnaɪz/ *vt* 1 prepoznati 2 priznati **recognition** /ˌrekəg'nɪʃn/ *n* 1 prepoznavanje 2 priznanje 3 spoznaja

recoil /rɪ'kɔɪl/ *vi* 1 (from) ustuknuti (pred); zgroziti se 2 trznuti (oružje) • *n* 1 uzmak 2 trzaj ~**less** *adj* bestrzajni

recollect /ˌrekə'lekt/ *vt* sjećati se, sjetiti se ~**ion** *n* 1 sjećanje 2 uspomena

recommend /ˌrekə'mend/ *vt* (for/as/to) 1 preporučiti 2 savjetovati, predložiti 3 ponuditi ~**ation** /ˌrekəmen'deɪʃn/ *n* 1 preporuka 2 vrlina

recompense /'rekəmpens/ *vt* (for) nadoknaditi; nagraditi • *n* naknada, odšteta; nagrada

reconcile /'rekənsaɪl/ *vt* (with) 1 uskladiti 2 pomiriti 3 izgladiti (svađu) ~ **oneself to sth/be** ~**d to sth** pomiriti se (s čime) **reconciliation** /ˌrekənˌsɪlɪ'eɪʃn/ *n* (between/with) 1 pomirenje 2 usklađenost

recondition /ˌriːkən'dɪʃn/ *vt* popraviti, izvršiti remont

reconnaisance /rɪ'kɒnɪsns/ *n* 1 izviđanje 2 *mod* izviđački **reconnoitre** /ˌrekə'nɔɪtə(r)/ *vt,vi* izvidati

reconsider /ˌriːkən'sɪdə/ *vt,vi* ponovno razmotriti

reconstruct /ˌriːkən'strʌkt/ *vt* obnoviti; rekonstruirati ~**ion** /ˌriːkən'strʌkʃn/ *n* obnova; rekonstrukcija

record /rɪ'kɔːd/ *vt,vi* 1 ubilježiti, zapisati 2 snimiti • /'rekɔːd/ *n* 1 zapis; zapisnik; *pl* arhiva; evidencija; registar 2 prošlost; dosje 3 rekord 4 *mod* rekordan 5 gramofonska ploča **off the** ~ *coll* neslužbeno, u povjerenju **on** ~ zabilježen, poznat **go on** ~ službeno izjaviti ~**er** *n* 1 blokflauta 2 (**tape** ~**er**) kazetofon, magnetofon ~ **player** gramofon

recoup /rɪ'kuːp/ *vt* nadoknaditi (trošak, gubitak)

recourse /rɪ'kɔːs/ *n* **have** ~ **to** obratiti se (za pomoć), pribjeći komu/čemu

recover /rɪ'kʌvə(r)/ *vi* 1 (po)vratiti, nadoknaditi; utjerati (dug) 2 (from) oporaviti se, osvijestiti se ~**y** *n* 1 povrat 2 oporavak

re-cover /riː'kʌvə(r)/ *vt* presvući, staviti nove navlake

recreate /ˌriːkri'eɪt/ *vt* obnoviti, oživiti

recreation /ˌrekri'eɪʃn/ *n* odmor, zabava, rekreacija ~ **ground** igralište

recrimination /rɪˌkrɪmɪ'neɪʃn/ *n* okrivljavanje, optuživanje

recruit /rɪ'kruːt/ *n* 1 novak, regrut 2 novi član • *vt,vi* 1 novačiti 2 zaposliti 3 vrbovati

rectangle /'rektæŋgl/ *n* pravokutnik **rectangular** /rek'tæŋgjulə(r)/ *adj* pravokutni

rectify /'rektɪfaɪ/ *vt* ispraviti

rector /'rektə(r)/ *n* 1 župnik 2 rektor ~**y** *n* župni dvor

recuperate /rɪ'kuːpəreɪt/ *vi,vt* ojačati, oporaviti se; (po)vratiti

recur /rɪ'kɜː(r)/ *vi* 1 (to) vratiti se; vraćati se u mislima 2 ponavljati se ~**rent** *adj* učestao

red /red/ *adj* 1 crven 2 crvenokos, rid 3 crn (vino) 4 *derog* komunistički, socijalistički; sovjetski • *n* 1 crvena boja, crvenilo 2 *derog* komunist **in the** ~ u minusu **paint the town** ~ lumpati **see** ~ razgnjeviti se ~**carpet treatment** svečani doček **R**~ **Cross** Crveni križ ~**currant** ribizl ~**haired** crvenokos, rid **catch sb** ~**handed** uhvatiti/zateći koga na djelu/u zločinu **~head** crvenokosi, crvenokosa **~hot a.** usijan b. *fig* gorljiv **~letter day** sretan/važan dan **~neck** *US coll* seljačina, primitivac **~ tape** *fig* birokracija, formalnosti **~den** *vi,vt* pocrvenjeti, zacrvenjeti se; obojiti crveno **~dish** *adj* crvenkast

redeem /rɪ'diːm/ *vt form* 1 izvršiti, ispuniti (obećanje) 2 iskupiti 3 spasiti 4 otkupiti, iskupiti 5 (from) izbaviti, osloboditi **~ing feature** pozitivna crta **redemption** /rɪ'dempʃn/ *n* otkupljenje

redeploy /ˌriː'dɪ'plɔɪ/ *vt mil* pregrupirati

redo /ˌriː'duː/ *vt irreg* (→ **do**) renovirati

redouble /rɪ'dʌbl/ *vt* udvostručiti

redress /rɪ'dres/ *vt* ispraviti; nadoknaditi • *n* naknada, zadovoljština

reduce /rɪ'djuːs/ *vt,vi* (from/to) 1 smanjiti, sniziti 2 svesti na; pretvoriti u 3 dovesti do/u, prisiliti na **reduction** /rɪ'dʌkʃn/ *n* (in/of) smanjenje, sniženje

redundant /rɪ'dʌndənt/ *adj* suvišan, nepotreban **~ labour** višak radne snage **be made ~** biti otpušten s posla **redundancy** /rɪ'dʌndənsɪ/ *n* 1 *GB* otpuštanje s posla 2 *gram* zalihost

reed /riːd/ *n* 1 trska; šaš 2 pisak **~y** *adj* 1 obrastao trskom/šašem 2 piskav

reef /riːf/ *n* greben

reefer /'riːfə(r)/ *n coll* 1 cigareta s marihuanom; džoint *sl* 2 hladnjača

reek /riːk/ *n* smrad, težak miris • *vi* (of/with) smrdjeti na (+ *fig*)

reel (1) /riːl/ *n* 1 navoj 2 smotak 3 rola (filma) • *vt* motati, namatati **~ off a.** odmotati **b.** *coll* sipati kao iz rukava

reel (2) *vi* 1 posrtati 2 vrtjeti se (u glavi)

ref /ref/ *coll* → **referee**

refectory /rɪ'fektərɪ/ *n* blagovaonica

refer /rɪ'fɜː(r)/ *vt,vi* **~ to** 1 misliti; spominjati, govoriti o, nazvati; ukazati na 2 konzultirati 3 odnositi se na 4 obratiti se 5 uputiti na 6 proslijediti **~ence** /'refrəns/ *n* (to) 1 spominjanje, aluzija na 2 konzultiranje, uputa, upućivanje (na bilješke)

3 preporuka **with/in ~ence to** u vezi s, gledе **for future ~ence** za ubuduće **make ~ence to** spomenuti; uputiti na; konzultirati, potražiti (u knjizi) **~ence book** priručnik **~ence library** priručna knjižnica

referee /ˌrefə'riː/ *n* 1 *sport* sudac 2 arbitar • *vt,vi sport* suditi

referendum /ˌrefə'rendəm/ *n* (*pl* **referenda, ~s**) *n* referendum

refill /ˌriː'fɪl/ *vt* ponovno napuniti • /'riː:fɪl/ *n* punjenje, patrona, uložak

refine /rɪ'faɪn/ *vt* 1 pročistiti, preraditi, rafinirati 2 (on/upon) poboljšati **~d** *adj* 1 profinjen, uglađen 2 usavršen, razrađen 3 rafiniran **~ment** *n* 1 (on) poboljšanje, preinaka 2 rafiniranje 3 profinjenost **~ry** /rɪ'faɪnərɪ/ *n* rafinerija

reflect /rɪ'flekt/ *vt,vi* 1 odbijati, odraziti 2 *fig* odražavati, pokazivati 3 (on/over) razmisliti o **~ on/upon sb/sth** štetiti **~ion** /rɪ'flekʃn/ *n* 1 odraz, refleksija 2 razmišljanje

reflex /'riː:fleks/ *n* refleks **conditioned ~** uvjetovani refleks

reflexive /rɪ'fleksɪv/ *adj gram* povratan

reform /rɪ'fɔːm/ *vt,vi* preustrojiti, preinačiti; popraviti (se) • *n* preustrojstvo, reforma **~atory** *n US* popravni dom

refrain (1) /rɪ'freɪn/ *vi* (from) uzdržati se (od)

refrain (2) *n* 1 pripjev 2 *fig derog* ista pjesma

refresh /rɪ'freʃ/ *vt* osvježiti, okrijepiti **~ments** *n pl* zakuska

refrigerate /rɪ'frɪdʒəreɪt/ *vt* zamrznuti (hranu) **refrigerator** *n* hladionik; frižider *coll*

refuel /ˌriː'fjuːəl/ *vt,vi* opskrbiti gorivom, uzeti gorivo

refuge /'refjuːdʒ/ *n* 1 utočište, sklonište 2 azil **take ~ in** naći utočište **~e** /ˌrefjuː'dʒiː/ *n* izbjeglica

refund /rɪ'fʌnd/ *n* naknada, povrat novca • *vt* nadoknaditi, platiti; vratiti (novac)

refurbish /ˌriː'fɜː.bɪʃ/ *vt* obnoviti (+ *fig*)

refuse (1) /rɪ'fjuːz/ *vt,vi* 1 odbiti, odbaciti 2 uskratiti **refusal** /rɪ'fjuːzl/

n odbijanje

refuse (2) /'refju:s/ *n* otpaci, smeće

refute /rɪ'fju:t/ *vt* opovrgnuti, pobiti (dokazom)

regain /rɪ'geɪn/ *vt* vratiti ~ **consciousness** osvijestiti se

regal /'ri:gl/ *adj* 1 kraljevski 2 *fig* divan, veličanstven

regard /rɪ'gɑ:d/ *n* 1 poštovanje 2 obzir 3 pažnja, pozornost 4 *pl* pozdravi **in this/that** ~ u tom pogledu **with/in** ~ **to** s obzirom na ~**less of** bez obzira na **hold sb in high** ~ visoko cijeniti koga *give my* ~*s to her* pozdravi je • *vt* 1 (as) smatrati; cijeniti 2 (with) gledati, promatrati ~**ing/as** ~**s** s obzirom na, što se tiče, glede

regenerate /rɪ'dʒenəreɪt/ *vt,vi* oživiti, obnoviti; ponovno izrasti

regime /reɪ'ʒi:m/ *n* režim

regiment /'redʒɪmənt/ *n mil* pukovnija

region /'ri:dʒən/ *n* područje, predio **in the** ~ **of** oko, otprilike

register /'redʒɪstə(r)/ *n* 1 popis, imenik, registar 2 raspon 3 *US* regulator • *vt,vi* 1 prijaviti (se), upisati (se), uknjižiti 2 zabilježiti, pokazivati 3 izražavati, odavati, pokazivati 4 izraziti 5 poslati preporučeno ~**ed** *adj* registriran ~**ed post** preporučeno pismo ~**ed trademark** zaštitni znak **registrar** /ˌredʒɪ'strɑ:(r)/ *n* 1 matičar 2 školski/sveučilišni tajnik **registration** /ˌredʒɪ'streɪʃn/ *n* upis, unos, registracija **registration** ~ **number** registarski broj **registry office** matični ured

regret /rɪ'gret/ *vt* 1 (za)žaliti 2 žaliti za čime ~**table** *adj* žalostan 1 *n* (at) žaljenje ~**ful** *adj* žalostan, tužan

regular /'regjʊlə(r)/ *adj* 1 pravilan 2 redovan; uobičajen; stalan 3 ispravan, točan 4 profesionalan, regularan 5 *coll* pravi 6 običan, normalan 7 *US* dobar, pošten • *n* 1 *coll* stalna mušterija, stalni gost 2 redovni vojnik **regulate** /'regjʊleɪt/ *vt* urediti; podesiti; regulirati **regulation** *n* 1 propis 2 podešavanje 3 *mod* propisan

rehabilitate /ˌri:ə'bɪlɪteɪt/ *vt* 1 rehabilitirati 2 obnoviti

rehearse /rɪ'hɜ:s/ *vt,vi* 1 vježbati,

imati probu/pokus 2 prepričavati; ponavljati **rehearsal** *n* pokus **dress rehearsal** generalni pokus

reign /reɪn/ *n* vladavina ~ **of terror** strahovlada • *vi* 1 (over) vladati (kime/čime) 2 zavladati

reimburse /ˌri:ɪm'bɜ:s/ *vt* (to/for) vratiti novac, nadoknaditi

rein /reɪn/ *n* uzda **give (free)** ~ **to sb/sth** dati odriješene ruke kome, dati oduška čemu **keep a tight** ~ **on sb/sth** držati čvrsto na uzdi • *vt* 1 (back/up) zauzdati, zaustaviti 2 (in) usporiti, zaustaviti (konja); obuzdati (+ *fig*)

reindeer /'reɪndɪə(r)/ *n* sob

reinforce /ˌri:ɪn'fɔ:s/ *vt* pojačati ~**d concrete** armirani beton ~**ment** *n* (po)jačanje (+ *mil*)

reinstate /ˌri:ɪn'steɪt/ *vt* (as/in) ponovno postaviti, vratiti (na dužnost)

reiterate /ri:'ɪtəreɪt/ *vt form* (još jednom) ponoviti

reject /rɪ'dʒekt/ *vt* odbiti, odbaciti ~**ion** /rɪ'dʒekʃn/ *n* odbijanje, odbacivanje • /'ri:dʒekt/ *n* roba s greškom; škart *coll*

rejoice /rɪ'dʒɔɪs/ *vi form* (at/over) radovati se, veseliti se

rekindle /ˌri:'kɪndl/ *vt,vi* 1 ponovno (se) zapaliti 2 *fig* oživiti (nade)

relapse /rɪ'læps/ *vi* (into) ponovno oboljeti; vratiti se na • *n* recidiv **have a** ~ ponovno oboljeti (nakon oporavka)

relate /rɪ'leɪt/ *vt,vi* 1 (to) ispričati, opisati 2 (to/with) povezati s ~ **to sb/sth** a. odnositi se na, ticati se koga/čega b. uspostaviti odnos s; imati razumijevanja za ~**d** *adj* (to) 1 u rodu 2 srodan, blizak **relating to** *prep* u vezi s, koji se odnosi na **relation** *n* 1 rođak(inja) 2 (of/to) veza 3 (between/with) odnos, veza **in/with relation to** u vezi s **relationship** *n* (between/to/with) 1 odnos, veza 2 srodnost **relative** /'relətɪv/ *n* rođak(inja) ○ *adj* 1 razmjeran, relativan 2 (to) koji se odnosi

relax /rɪ'læks/ *vt,vi* 1 opustiti (se) 2 olabaviti, omlitaviti 3 popustiti ~**ation** /ˌri:læk'seɪʃn/ *n* opuštanje, razonoda

relay /'ri:leɪ/ n 1 smjena 2 (~ **race**) štafetna utrka, štafeta 3 relej • /rɪ'leɪ/ vt irreg (→ **lay**) (to) prenijeti (poruku)

release /rɪ'li:s/ vt 1 (from) osloboditi, odriješiti, (is)pustiti, otpustiti; otkvačiti, odapeti 2 izdati • n 1 oslobođenje; odrješenje; puštanje; olakšanje 2 nova ploča/film 3 priopćenje 4 okidač, otponac, zapinjač, zavor

relent /rɪ'lent/ vi popustiti; smilovati se **~less** adj nesmiljen

relevant /'relǝvǝnt/ adj (to) značajan, važan, bitan, relevantan

reliable /rɪ'laɪǝbl/ adj pouzdan **reliance** /rɪ'laɪǝns/ n (on) pouzdanje, povjerenje; ovisnost, oslanjanje

relic /'relɪk/ n 1 (of) ostatak, trag, relikt 2 relikvija 3 ~s pl posmrtni ostaci

relief /rɪ'li:f/ n 1 olakšanje; ublaženje 2 fig promjena, osvježenje 3 (humanitarna) pomoć 4 (porezne) olakšice 5 US socijalna pomoć 6 smjena, zamjena 7 reljef 8 mod pomoćni; humanitarni **be/stand out in bold/ clear/sharp/strong ~ against** snažno odudarati od, jasno se isticati

relieve /rɪ'li:v/ vt 1 olakšati; ublažiti (bol) 2 smijeniti (stražu) **relieve sb of duty** razriješiti dužnosti **relieve oneself** euph izvršiti nuždu I was relieved laknulo mi je

religion /rɪ'lɪdʒǝn/ n vjera, religija **religious** /rɪ'lɪdʒǝs/ adj 1 vjerski 2 pobožan 3 strog, savjestan

relinquish /rɪ'lɪŋkwɪʃ/ vt odustati, odreći se

relish /'relɪʃ/ n 1 uživanje (u hrani/piću) 2 užitak 3 umak; ukiseljeno povrće; začin 4 okus • vt ~ (**doing**) **sth** uživati u čemu/radeći što ~ **the prospect of (doing) sth** radovati se čemu

relive /ˌri:'lɪv/ vt oživiti (sjećanja); ponovno proživjeti

relocate /ˌri:lǝʊ'keɪt/ vt,vi premjestiti (se), preseliti (se)

reluctant /rɪ'lʌktǝnt/ adj koji oklijeva; nesklon **~ly** adv nerado, nevoljko **reluctance** n nevoljkost, oklijevanje,

protivljenje

rely /rɪ'laɪ/ vi (on/upon) osloniti se na, pouzdati se u, računati na

remain /rɪ'meɪn/ vi (pre)ostati **~der** n ostatak, ostali **~ing** adj preostao **~s** n pl 1 ostaci 2 posmrtni ostaci

remake /ˌri:'meɪk/ n nova verzija

remand /rɪ'ma:nd/ vt vratiti u istražni zatvor ~ **in custody** zadržati u istražnom zatvoru (nakon suđenja) • n **on ~** u istražnom zatvoru

remark /rɪ'ma:k/ vt primijetiti, napomenuti • n 1 (about/on) primjedba, opaska **~able** adj 1 izvanredan, neobičan 2 (for) poznat po

remarry /ˌri:'mærɪ/ vt,vi ponovno (se) oženiti/udati

remedy /'remǝdɪ/ n lijek (+ fig) • vt popraviti, ispraviti, nadoknaditi

remember /rɪ'membǝ(r)/ vt,vi sjećati se; sjetiti se; pamtiti (koga/što) **remembrance** /rɪ'membrǝns/ n 1 sjećanje 2 (of) uspomena na

remind /rɪ'maɪnd/ vt podsjetiti, podsjećati **~er** n 1 podsjetnik 2 opomena

reminisce /ˌremɪ'nɪs/ vi (about) sjećati se **~nces** /ˌremɪ'nɪsnsɪz/ n pl sjećanja, uspomene **~nt** adj (of) koji podsjeća na

remission /rɪ'mɪʃn/ n 1 smanjenje zatvorske kazne 2 oprost (grijeha) 3 jenjavanje

remit /rɪ'mɪt/ vt,vi 1 oprostiti, oslobodoti, otpustiti 2 poslati (novac) 3 proslijediti, uputiti **~tance** n 1 novčana pošiljka 2 slanje/vraćanje novca

remnant /'remnǝnt/ n ostatak

remonstrate /'remǝnstreɪt/ vi (against/ with) negodovati (protiv čega/kod koga)

remorse /rɪ'mɔ:s/ n grižnja savjesti **~ful** adj pokajnički **~less** adj nemilosrdan, bezobziran, okrutan

remote /rɪ'mǝʊt/ adj 1 dalek, udaljen 2 zabačen 3 hladan, nepristupačan 4 slab, neznatan **have not the ~st idea/notion** (about sth) nemati pojma (o čemu) ~ **control** daljinsko upravljanje

remould (-**mold** US) /ˌri:'mǝʊld/ n protektirana/vulkanizirana guma

remove /rɪˈmuːv/ *vt,vi* 1 skinuti 2 premjestiti, preseliti (se) 3 pospremiti; odstraniti; ukloniti, maknuti 4 smijeniti • *n fig* korak, stupanj **cousin once ~d** rođak u prvom koljenu **removal** *n* uklanjanje; selidba **~r** *n* sredstvo za odstranjivanje

remuneration /rɪˌmjuːnəˈreɪʃn/ *n* (for) novčana naknada, plaća; nagrada

render /ˈrendə(r)/ *vt* 1 učiniti 2 izraziti (zahvalnost); pružiti (pomoć); (uz)-vratiti 3 podnijeti/položiti (račun) be **~ed speechless** zanijemiti **~ down** istopiti (mast) **~ up** predati (grad neprijatelju) **rendition** /renˈdɪʃn/, **~ing** *GB* n 1 izvedba 2 prijevod

renegade /ˈrenɪɡeɪd/ *n* odmetnik, otpadnik, prebjeg

renew /rɪˈnjuː/ *vt* 1 obnoviti; ponoviti; ponovno početi 2 produžiti 3 zamijeniti **~al** *n* 1 obnova 2 produženje

renounce /rɪˈnaʊns/ *vt* odreći se; odbaciti, odustati od

renovate /ˈrenəveɪt/ *vt* obnoviti, renovirati

renown /rɪˈnaʊn/ *n* slava, ime **~ed** *adj* (as/for) glasovit, poznat, slavan

rent /rent/ *n* 1 najam(nina), stanarina 2 renta • *vt,vi* 1 (from) unajmiti 2 (out/to) *US* iznajmiti **~al** *n* 1 najamnina 2 iznajmljivanje **video ~al** videoteka

renunciation /rɪ,nʌnsɪˈeɪʃn/ *n* odricanje/odustajanje od čega/koga

reorganize /riːˈɔːɡənaɪz/ *vt* preurediti, preinačiti, reorganizirati

rep (1) /rep/ *coll* → **representative**

rep (2) *coll* → **repertory**

repair /rɪˈpeə(r)/ *vt* 1 popraviti; zakrpati 2 ispraviti (nepravdu) • *n* popravak **in (a) good/bad (state of) ~** u dobrom/lošem stanju

reparation /ˌrepəˈreɪʃn/ *n* (to/for) nadoknada, odšteta; reparacija

repartee /ˌrepɑːˈtiː/ *n* (duhovit) odgovor, doskočica

repatriate /riːˈpætrɪeɪt/ *vt* (to) vratiti u domovinu

repay /rɪˈpeɪ/ *vt irreg* (→ **pay**) 1 isplatiti, otplatiti, vratiti novac 2 (by/for/with) nagraditi, odužiti se komu **~ment** *n* otplata; nagrada

repeal /rɪˈpiːl/ *vt* opozvati, ukinuti (zakon) • *n* opoziv, ukinuće

repeat /rɪˈpiːt/ *vt,vi* ponoviti (se) **~ oneself** ponavljati se • *n* 1 repriza 2 *mod* ponovljen **~edly** *adv* opetovano, uzastopce **~ing rifle/~er** *n* puška repetirka

repel /rɪˈpel/ *vt* 1 odbiti, potisnuti (napad) 2 izazivati odvratnost **~lent** *adj* odvratan o *n* sredstvo protiv kukaca

repent /rɪˈpent/ *vt,vi* (of) (po)kajati se (zbog čega); žaliti **~ance** *n* (for) (po)kajanje

repercussion /ˌriːpəˈkʌʃn/ *n* 1 odbijanje 2 odjek, odraz 3 *pl* (dalekosežne) posljedice, reperkusije

repertoire /ˈrepətwɑː(r)/ *n* repertoar

repertory /ˈrepətrɪ/ *n* repertoar **~ theatre** kazalište sa stalnom glumačkom postavom **in ~** na stalnom repertoaru

repetition /ˌrepɪˈtɪʃn/ *n* ponavljanje **repetitious** /ˌrepɪˈtɪʃəs/, **repetitive** /rɪˈpetətɪv/ *adj* koji se ponavlja, monoton

replace /rɪˈpleɪs/ *vt* 1 (with/by) zamijeniti; nadomjestiti 2 vratiti na mjesto **~ment** *n* (for) zamjena

replay /ˌriːˈpleɪ/ *vt,vi* ponovno odigrati/odsvirati • /ˈriːpleɪ/ *n* 1 ponovljena utakmica 2 snimka

replenish /rɪˈplenɪʃ/ *vt* (with) (ponovno) napuniti, nadopuniti

replete /rɪˈpliːt/ *adj* 1 (pre)sit 2 (with) prepun, krcat, dupkom pun

replica /ˈreplɪkə/ *n* kopija, replika, reprodukcija

reply /rɪˈplaɪ/ *vi,vt* (to) odgovoriti, uzvratiti • *n* odgovor

report /rɪˈpɔːt/ *n* 1 (of/on) izvješće, izvještaj 2 (+ *pl*) glasine, priče 3 (~ **card** *US*) školska svjedodžba 4 *form* prasak, pucanj • *vt,vi* 1 (on/to) izvijestiti, izvještavati, podnijeti izvješće 2 (for/to) (pri)javiti (se); tužiti **~age** /rɪˈpɔːtɪdʒ/ *n* izvješćivanje, reportaža **~ed speech** neupravni govor **~edly** *adv* navodno **~er** *n* izvjestitelj, novinar

repose /rɪˈpəʊz/ *n* mir, spokoj(nost); odmor, počinak, san • *vt,vi form* počivati; odmarati se; ležati

reprehensible /ˌreprɪ'hensəbl/ *adj* za osudu

represent /ˌreprɪ'zent/ *vt* 1 predstaviti; zastupati 2 objasniti, prikazati 3 označavati, simbolizirati 4 izraziti, iznijeti (pritužbe) ○ **oneself as/to be** izdavati se za **~ation** *n* 1 predstavljanje; zastupanje 2 izvođenje, predstava; prikaz **proportional ~ation** proporcionalna zastupljenost **~ations** *n pl* (about/to) pritužbe **~ative** *n* (of) predstavnik; zastupnik ○ *adj* 1 koji predstavlja/prikazuje/opisuje 2 tipičan, reprezentativan 3 predstavnički, zastupnički **House of R~atives** Zastupnički dom

repress /rɪ'pres/ *vt* potisnuti, svladati, ugušiti (pobunu) **~ion** *n* potiskivanje; represija

reprieve /rɪ'priːv/ *vt* odgoditi izvršenje smrtne kazne, pomilovati • *n* odgoda, pomilovanje

reprimand /'reprɪmɑːnd/ *vt* prekoriti, ukoriti • *n* ukor

reprint /ˌriː'prɪnt/ *vt,vi* ponovno tiskati • *n* pretisak

reprisal /rɪ'praɪzl/ *n* protumjera; odmazda, osveta

reproach /rɪ'prəʊtʃ/ *n* predbacivanje; prijekor **~ful** *adj* prijekoran • *vt* (for/with) predbacivati (komu što)

reproduce /ˌriːprə'djuːs/ *vt,vi* 1 razmnožavati (se) 2 ponovno proizvesti; reproducirati 3 regenerirati, ponovno izrasti **reproduction** /ˌriːprə'dʌkʃn/ *n* 1 razmnožavanje 2 kopija, reprodukcija **reproductive** *adj* 1 rasplodni 2 reprodukcijski; reproduktivan

reproof /rɪ'pruːf/ *n* prijekor, prigovor, zamjerka **reprove** /rɪ'pruːv/ *vt* (for) (iz)grditi, (u)koriti

reptile /'reptaɪl/ *n* gmaz

republic /rɪ'pʌblɪk/ *n* republika

repudiate /rɪ'pjuːdieɪt/ *vt form* 1 nijekati; odbiti 2 odreći se (koga)

repugnance /rɪ'pʌgnəns/ *n* (for/to) gnušanje **repugnant** *adj* gadan, odvratan

repulse /rɪ'pʌls/ *vt* odbiti (napad, ponudu) • *n* odbijanje **repulsion** /rɪ'pʌlʃn/ *n* 1 odbojnost 2 odbijanje **repulsive** *adj* odbojan

reputable /'repjʊtəbl/ *adj* ugledan, uvažen

reputation /ˌrepjʊ'teɪʃn/ *n* (for) ugled **have a ~ for** biti poznat po čemu

repute /rɪ'pjuːt/ *n* ugled **by ~** po čuvenju • *vt* **be ~d as/to be** biti poznat kao **~d** *adj* navodni **~dly** *adv* navodno

request /rɪ'kwest/ *n* 1 (for) zahtjev, (za)molba, traženje 2 glazbena želja • *vt* (za)tražiti, (za)moliti

require /rɪ'kwaɪə(r)/ *vt* 1 trebati, biti potreban 2 (~ sth of sb; ~ sb to do sth; ~ that) (za)tražiti, zahtijevati **~ment** *n* potrepština, potreba; zahtjev; uvjet

requisite /'rekwɪzɪt/ *adj* (for) nužan, potreban • *n* potrebna stvar, potrepština, pribor **requisition** /ˌrekwɪ'zɪʃn/ *n* zahtjev ○ *vt* (for) oduzeti, rekvirirati (u ratne svrhe)

requite /rɪ'kwaɪt/ *vt* 1 (with) *form* naplatiti; odužiti se za; uzvratiti (ljubav) 2 osvetiti

rerun /ˌriː'rʌn/ *vt irreg* → **run** reprizirati; ponoviti • *n* repriza; ponavljanje

rescind /rɪ'sɪnd/ *vt leg* poništiti (zakon), raskinuti (ugovor)

rescue /'reskjuː/ *vt* spasiti; osloboditi; pomoći • *n* spas; spašavanje; oslobođenje; akcija spašavanja **come/go to the ~** priskočiti u pomoć, spasiti **~ party** spasilačka ekipa **~r** *n* spasitelj

research /rɪ'sɜːtʃ/ *n* (in/into/on) (znanstveno) istraživanje • *vi,vt* istraživati, proučavati **~er** *n* istraživač, znanstvenik

resemble /rɪ'zembl/ *vt* (in) nalikovati, sličiti **resemblance** /ɪ'zembləns/ *n* (between/to) sličnost

resent /rɪ'zent/ *vt* biti ogorčen na, zamjeriti komu što **~ful** *adj* kivan, ogorčen, uvrijeđen **~ment** *n* (at/against/towards) negodovanje, ogorčenost, uvrijeđenost

reservation /ˌrezə'veɪʃn/ *n* 1 ograda, rezerva 2 rezervacija 3 rezervat 4 *US* prirodni rezervat **without ~** bezuvjetno, bezrezervno

reserve /rɪ'zɜːv/ *vt* (for) namijeniti;

odgoditi, odložiti; sačuvati; zadržati;
rezervirati **all rights** ~d sva prava
pridržana • *n* 1 zaliha, pričuva, rezerva 2 prirodni rezervat 3 *sport* rezerva, pričuvni igrač 4 (s)uzdržanost,
zatvorenost, hladnoća, rezerviranost
5 *mil* pričuva, rezerva 6 (~ **price**)
najniža cijena (na dražbi) **without** ~
bezrezervno, potpuno ~d *adj* uzdr-
žan

reservoir /'rezvwa:(r)/ *n* 1 spremište
2 akumulacijsko jezero ~s *pl* rezerve
fig

reset /ˌri:'set/ *vt irreg* → **set** 1 namjestiti 2 ponovno namjestiti/složiti/
umetnuti

resettle /ˌri:'setl/ *vi,vt* naseliti, preseliti

reshuffle /ˌri:'ʃʌfl/ *vi,vt* 1 još jednom
promiješati (karte) 2 izvršiti kad-
rovske promjene • *n* reorganizacija,
rekonstrukcija (vlade)

reside /rɪ'zaɪd/ *vi* živjeti ~ **in** pripadati
~**nce** /'rezɪdəns/ *n* 1 rezidencija 2 boravište **take up** ~**nce** nastaniti se ~**nt**
adj 1 nastanjen 2 kućni ○ *n* stanar
~**ntial** *adj* stambeni

residue /'rezɪdju:/ *n* 1 ostatak 2 talog

resign /rɪ'zaɪn/ *vi,vt* (from) dati ostavku, napustiti (položaj) ~ **oneself**
(to) pomiriti se s (čime/kime) ~**ation**
/ˌrezɪg'neɪʃn/ *n* 1 ostavka 2 rezignaci-
ja ~**ed** *adj* rezigniran, pomiren sa
sudbinom

resilient /rɪ'zɪlɪənt/ *adj* 1 elastičan 2
koji se lako oporavlja

resin /'rezɪn/ *n* smola

resist /rɪ'zɪst/ *vi,vt* pružati otpor,
odupirati se, braniti se, odolijevati,
boriti se protiv ~**ance** *n* 1 otpor **offer**
~**ance** pružiti otpor **take the line of
least** ~**ance** ići linijom manjeg otpora 2 otpornost ~**ant** *adj* (to) otporan
na **water-**~**ant** vodootporan

resolute /'rezəlu:t/ *adj* odlučan ~**ness**
n odlučnost **resolution** /ˌrezə'lu:ʃn/ *n*
1 *pol, tech* rezolucija **pass/carry/
adopt a** ~ prihvatiti rezoluciju **reject
a** ~ odbaciti rezoluciju 2 odluka 3
odlučnost 4 razrješenje

resolve /rɪ'zɒlv/ *vt,vi* 1 razriješiti 2
(on) donijeti odluku (o), odlučiti ~
into razložiti na • *n* 1 odluka 2 od-

lučnost

resort /rɪ'zɔ:t/ *n* 1 izletište **summer** ~
ljetovalište 2 posljednje sredstvo
have ~ **to** pribjeći čemu **as a/in the
last** ~ u krajnjem slučaju • *vt* ~ **to**
pribjeći, uteći se

resound /rɪ'zaʊnd/ *vi* odjekivati, odzvanjati ~**ing** *adj* 1 glasan 2 velik

resource /rɪ'sɔ:s/ *n* 1 izvor, sredstvo,
resurs, rezerva **natural** ~s prirodna
bogatstva 2 utočište 3 domišljatost
~**ful** *adj* domišljat, spretan

respect /rɪ'spekt/ *n* 1 (for) poštovanje
(prema) 2 obzir 3 ~s *pl* pozdrav **pay
one's** ~s **to** posjetiti **pay one's last**
~s **to** odati kome posljednju počast
in ~ **of a**. u pogledu, glede **b. za with**
~ **to** što se tiče • *vt* poštovati ~**ability**
n ugled, pristojnost ~**able** *adj*
ugledan, poštovan, pristojan ~**ful** *adj*
(to) pun poštovanja (prema) ~**ing**
prep glede ~**ive** *adj* svaki svoj *they
went to their respective homes* otišli
su svaki svom domu ~**ively** odnosno
*Dan and Bill have two and three kids
respectively* D. i B. imaju dvoje
odnosno troje djece

respiration /ˌrespə'reɪʃn/ *n* disanje **respiratory** /rɪ'spaɪərətrɪ/ *adj* dišni

respite /'respaɪt/ *n* 1 odmor **without** ~
bez prestanka 2 odgoda

resplendent /rɪ'splendənt/ *adj* blistav,
prekrasan

respond /rɪ'spɒnd/ *vi,vt* 1 (to) odgovoriti (na) 2 (by/with/to) reagirati
čime/na što, odgovoriti ~**ent** *n* 1 op-
tuženi 2 ispitanik

response /rɪ'spɒns/ *n* 1 odgovor 2
reakcija **responsive** *adj* 1 koji sluša
2 brz na odgovorima

responsibility /rɪˌspɒnsə'bɪlətɪ/ *n* odgovornost **take/claim** ~ **for** preuzeti
odgovornost za **responsible** *adj*
odgovoran (za) **make sb** ~ **for** staviti
komu u odgovornost

rest /rest/ *n* 1 odmor **lay sb at** ~
pokopati (+ *fig*) ~ **home** dom
umirovljenika ~ **room** *US* toalet 2
mirovanje **come to** ~ zaustaviti se 3
oslonac 4 stanka 5 ostatak • *vi,vt* 1
odmoriti se ~ **in peace** počivao u
miru 2 nasloniti 3 biti miran, imati

mira **let the matter ~** pustiti (na miru) **~ assured** budite uvjereni **~ on/upon** oslanjati se, stajati na **~ with sb** biti na komu **~less** adj nemiran

restaurant /'restrɒnt/ n restoran

restitution /ˌrestɪ'tjuːʃn/ n povrat

restock /riː'stɒk/ vi,vt (with) ponovno napuniti, nabaviti nove zalihe

restoration /ˌrestə'reɪʃn/ n 1 ponovna uspostava 2 obnavljanje **restore** vt 1 ponovno uspostaviti, vratiti 2 (to) ponovno dovesti (do) 3 obnoviti

restrain /ri'streɪn/ vt (from) obuzdati (se) **~ed** adj rezerviran **~t** n 1 samokontrola 2 kontrola, restrikcija **keep under ~t** držati pod nadzorom

restrict /ri'strɪkt/ vt ograničiti **~ed** adj 1 ograničen; dopušten samo (komu) 2 zabranjen, tajan **~ion** n ograničenje

result /ri'zʌlt/ vi (from) uslijediti, biti posljedica **~ in** prouzročiti • n posljedica, rezultat, ishod

resume /ri'zjuːm/ vi,vt 1 iznova početi, nastaviti (gdje se stalo) 2 ponovno zauzeti

résumé /'rezjuːmeɪ/ n 1 rezime 2 životopis

resurface /ˌriː'sɜːfɪs/ vt,vi 1 ponovno asfaltirati 2 ponovno izroniti na površinu

resurgence /ri'sɜːdʒəns/ n ponovno oživljavanje

resurrect /ˌrezə'rekt/ vt dići iz mrtvih, oživiti **~ion** n 1 ponovno oživljavanje 2 uskrsnuće

resuscitate /ri'sʌsɪteɪt/ vt reanimirati **resuscitation** n reanimacija

retail /'riːteɪl/ n 1 maloprodaja 2 mod maloprodajni **~ outlet** prodavaonica • adv u maloprodaji • vi,vt (at/for) prodavati se (po) **~er** n trgovac na malo

retain /ri'teɪn/ vt zadržati **~er** n 1 dugogodišnji sluga 2 honorar, predujam

retake /ˌriː'teɪk/ vi 1 ponovno zauzeti 2 ponovno snimiti 3 ponovno polagati (ispit)

retaliate /ri'tælieɪt/ vi (against) vratiti milo za drago, osvetiti se **retaliation** n odmazda **retaliatory** adj za

odmazdu

retard /ri'tɑːd/ vt usporiti **~ed** adj retardiran, zaostao

retch /retʃ/ vi pokušavati povraćati, rigati na suho

retention /ri'tenʃn/ n zadržavanje; pamćenje **retentive memory** dobro pamćenje

reticent /'retɪsnt/ adj rezerviran

retina /'retɪnə/ n mrežnica (oka)

retinue /'retɪnjuː/ n svita, pratnja

retire /ri'taɪə(r)/ vi,vt (from) 1 otići u mirovinu, umiroviti (se) 2 povući se **~d** adj u mirovini **~ment** n mirovina **~ment pension** mirovina

retort /ri'tɔːt/ vt odvratiti • n oštar/duhovit odgovor

retouch /ˌriː'tʌtʃ/ vt retuširati

retrace /ri'treɪs/ vt rekonstruirati

retract /ri'trækt/ vi,vt 1 povući, opozvati 2 uvući **~ion** n demanti, opoziv

retreat /ri'triːt/ n 1 povlačenje 2 utočište na osami 3 osama • vi povući se

retrench /ri'trentʃ/ vi smanjiti troškove

retrial /ˌriː'traɪəl/ n ponovno suđenje

retribution /ˌretri'bjuːʃn/ n kazna **retributive** /ri'trɪbjutɪv/ adj kaznen

retrieval /ri'triːvl/ n pronalaženje; nadoknađivanje; oduzimanje **retrieve** /ri'triːv/ vt 1 uzeti; pronaći; donijeti; izvući 2 spasiti, popraviti 3 aportirati

retrospect /'retrəspekt/ n in **~** gledano unazad **~ion** /ˌretrə'spekʃn/ n razmišljanje o prošlosti **~ive (exhibition)** n retrospektiva

return /ri'tɜːn/ vi,vt 1 vratiti (se) 2 uzvratiti 3 pol izabrati 4 leg donijeti odluku 5 donositi (dobit) 6 prijaviti (porez) • n 1 povratak **~ match** uzvratni susret **~ ticket** povratna karta 2 (pl) prihod 3 prijava **in ~** zauzvrat **in ~ for** u zamjenu za **many happy ~s!** sretan rođendan! **~able** adj povratni

reunion /ˌriː'juːnɪən/ n ponovni susret

reunite /ˌriːjuː'naɪt/ vi ujediniti se; ponovno se sastati

rev /rev/ vt coll (~ up) turirati

revalue /ˌriː'væljuː/ vt procijeniti

revamp /ˌriː'væmp/ vt coll renovirati

reveal /rɪ'viːl/ vt otkriti; objaviti

revel /'revl/ vi pijančevati, zabavljati se ~ler n sudionik veselice ~ry n veselica, pijanka

revelation /ˌrevə'leɪʃn/ n otkrivanje, objavljivanje

revenge /rɪ'vendʒ/ n osveta take ~ on osvetiti se • vt osvetiti ~ oneself on osvetiti se

revenue /'revənjuː/ n državni prihod

reverberate /rɪ'vɜːbəreɪt/ vi odzvanjati

reverence /'revərəns/ n štovanje hold in ~ štovati

Reverend /'revərənd/ n velečasni ~ Mother časna majka

reverent /'revərənt/ adj pun poštovanja ~ial adj pun poštovanja

reverie /'revərɪ/ n snatrenje, sanjarenje

reversal /rɪ'vɜːsl/ n 1 obrat, preokret 2 nevolja reverse adj obrnut ○ vi,vt 1 ići unatrag 2 preokrenuti 3 poništiti (presudu) reverse the charges nazvati na račun osobe koja prima poziv ○ n 1 do the reverse učiniti obratno 2 vožnja unatrag 3 udarac fig 4 revers reversion n 1 (to) povratak (na) 2 povrat revert vt ~ to vratiti se, vratiti se na staro; biti nasljedan

review /rɪ'vjuː/ n 1 pregled, revizija 2 kritika 3 smotra 4 (kazališna) revija • vt,vi 1 razmatrati 2 pisati kritiku be well ~ed dobiti dobre kritike 3 mil izvršiti smotru 4 US ponavljati gradivo

revile /rɪ'vaɪl/ vt kritizirati

revise /rɪ'vaɪz/ vt,vi 1 izmijeniti, preinačiti 2 ponavljati, pregledati 3 ponavljati revision /rɪ'vɪʒn/ n 1 revizija 2 ponavljanje

revival /rɪ'vaɪvl/ n 1 oživljavanje 2 ponovna postava revive vi,vt oživjeti; oživiti (koga)

revoke /rɪ'vəʊk/ vt poništiti revocation /ˌrevə'keɪʃn/ n poništenje

revolt /rɪ'vəʊlt/ n 1 pobuna 2 gađenje • vi,vt 1 pobuniti se 2 šokirati (se) ~ing adj odvratan

revolution /ˌrevə'luːʃn/ n revolucija, prevrat; obrtaj ~ary adj revolucionaran ○ n revolucionar, prevratnik revolutionize vt iz temelja izmijeniti revolve /rɪ'vɒlv/ vi,vt 1 (on) vrtjeti se

(oko) revolving doors okretna vrata 2 razmatrati revolve (a)round okretati se oko

revue /rɪ'vjuː/ n (kazališna) revija

revulsion /rɪ'vʌlʃn/ n gađenje

reward /rɪ'wɔːd/ n nagrada • vt (for/with) nagraditi (čime za što) ~ing adj zahvalan

rework /ˌriː'wɜːk/ vt razraditi

rhetoric /'retərɪk/ n 1 govorništvo 2 retorika; fraze ~al adj retorički

rheumatic /ruː'mætɪk/ adj reumatičan rheumatism n reuma

rhinestone /'raɪnstəʊn/ n lažni dijamant; štras coll

rhubarb /'ruːbɑːb/ n rabarbara

rhyme /raɪm/ n rima, srok no ~ or reason bez smisla • vi,vt rimovati (se) s

rhythm /'rɪðəm/ n ritam ~ic(al) adj ritmičan, u ritmu

rib /rɪb/ n rebro ~ cage grudni koš ~bed adj rebrast

ribald /'rɪbld/ adj prostački

ribbon /'rɪbən/ n 1 vrpca 2 dronjak

rice /raɪs/ n riža ~ paddy rižino polje

rich /rɪtʃ/ adj 1 bogat 2 dragocjen, obilan, izdašan, jak; težak (hrana); plodan ~es n pl bogatstvo

rick /rɪk/ n stog

rickets /'rɪkɪts/ n rahitis rickety adj klimav

ricochet /'rɪkəʃeɪ/ n odbijanje (metka) • vi (off) odbiti se (od)

rid /rɪd/ vt irreg osloboditi, riješiti get ~ of riješiti se ~dance n good ~dance dobro da smo ga se riješili

ridden v irreg ~ ring

-ridden /'rɪdn/ suffix 1 prepun worm-~ 2 vezan za bed-~ vezan za krevet

riddle (1) /'rɪdl/ n zagonetka

riddle (2) n rešeto • vt 1 prosijati 2 (with) izrešetati 3 be ~d with biti prepun (čega)

ride /raɪd/ n,vi,vt irreg 1 jahati (na čemu) 2 voziti (se) (čime/u čemu) 3 US putovati ~ high biti uspješan/na vrhu ~ down a. sustići b. srušiti ~ on ovisiti o ~ out prebroditi ~ up podići se • n 1 vožnja go for a ~ provozati se be in for a bumpy ~ očekivati teškoće have a rough ~ loše se provesti take sb for a ~ nasamariti 2

jahačka staza ~**r** *n* 1 jahač 2 dodatak
ridge /rɪdʒ/ *n* greben
ridicule /'rɪdɪkju:l/ *n* poruga • *vt* izrugivati se **ridiculous** /rɪ'dɪkjʊləs/ *adj* smiješan
rife /raɪf/ *adj* be ~ vladati, bjesnjeti *fig* **be ~ with** biti pun
riffraff /'rɪf ræf/ *n* ološ
rifle /'raɪfl/ *n* puška ~ **range** streljana • *vt* 1 žlijebiti 2 prekopati
rift /rɪft/ *n* pukotina; raskol *fig*
rig /rɪg/ *vt* 1 opremiti 2 namjestiti *fig* ~ **out** preodjenuti ~ **up** improvizirati • *n* 1 (~**ging**) snast 2 odjeća **drilling** ~ bušilica
right (1) /raɪt/ *adj* 1 desni 2 desničarski • *n* 1 desna strana 2 *pol* desnica • *adv* nadesno ~**-hand** *adj* desni ~**-handed** *adj* desnoruk ~**-hand man** desna ruka *fig* ~**ist** *n* desničar ~ **wing** desnica ~**-wing** *adj* desničarski
right (2) *adj* 1 ispravan 2 pravi 3 pravilan, točan ~ **triangle** pravokutni trokut be ~ imati pravo **put sth ~** popraviti, ispraviti **in one's ~ mind** pri zdravoj pameti • *n* 1 pravo, dobro 2 (to/of) pravo na **by ~ of** pravom **in one's own ~** svojom zaslugom **in the ~ u** pravu **of way** prednost 2 pravo prolaza • *adv* 1 točno, pravo, kako treba 2 baš 3 ravno 4 da, u redu ~ **and left** posvuda ~ **away** smjesta • *vt* ispraviti ~**ly** *adv* ispravno, točno, pravo ~**-minded** *adj* ispravnih načela
righteous /'raɪtʃəs/ *adj* pravedan
rigid /'rɪdʒɪd/ *adj* krut
rigorous /'rɪgərəs/ *adj* strog **rigour** *n* 1 rigoroznost, strogost 2 teškoća
rile /raɪl/ *vt coll* razljutiti; raspaliti *coll*
rim /rɪm/ *n* 1 rub 2 okvir • *vt* obrubiti
rind /raɪnd/ *n* kora
ring (1) /rɪŋ/ *n* 1 prsten (+ *fig*) 2 obruč (+ *fig*); krug 3 kolobar 4 ring, arena 5 grupa, kružok **run ~s round sb** nadmašiti koga • *vt* (with) 1 okružiti 2 prstenovati ~ **binder** *n* biljeznica sa spiralnim uvezom ~ **finger** prstenjak ~**leader** kolovođa ~**let** *n* uvojak ~ **road** obilaznica ~**worm** lišaj
ring (2) *vt*,*vi irreg* 1 pozvoniti, zvoniti 2 nazvati 3 odzvanjati ~ **a bell** zvučati poznato ~ **hollow** imati lažan

prizvuk ~ **true** zvučati istinito ~ **back** nazvati ponovno ~ **in a.** telefonom javiti **b.** zvonjavom najaviti ~ **off** prekinuti razgovor ~ **out** odjeknuti ~ **up** otkucati (iznos) • *n* 1 zvonjava 2 prizvuk 3 telefonski poziv **give sb a ~** nazvati koga **dead ~er** dvojnik, blizanac
rink /rɪŋk/ *n* skating ~ klizalište
rinse /rɪns/ *vt* isprati, isplahnuti ~ *n* 1 ispiranje 2 boja za kosu
riot /'raɪət/ *n* 1 neredi, demonstracije ~ **police** specijalni odredi policije 2 zabava ~ **of colour** obilje **run ~ a.** razulariti se **b.** bujati • *vi* sudjelovati u metežu/neredima **read the ~ act** narediti komu da se umiri ~**ous** *adj* divlji, razuzdan
rip /rɪp/ *vi*,*vt* 1 razderati (se) 2 *fig* sasjeći ~ **off** opljačkati ~**-off** *n* pljačka ~ **up** poderati ~ *n* poderotina
ripe /raɪp/ *adj* zreo **time is ~** kucnuo je čas ~**n** *vi*,*vt* sazrijeti
ripple /'rɪpl/ *vi*,*vt* 1 namreškati (se) 2 žuboriti • *n* 1 valić 2 *fig* val 3 nabor 4 žubor **a ~ of applause** slab pljesak
riptide /'rɪptaɪd/ *n* snažna plima
rise /raɪz/ *vi irreg* 1 podignuti se, dizati se, uzdići se 2 izlaziti (sunce) 3 (up) ustati 4 zaključiti (sjednicu) 5 ojačati 6 (up/against) pobuniti se ~ **above** nadvladati • *n* 1 (in) porast (čega) 2 uspon (+ *fig*) 3 povišica **give ~ to** prouzročiti **early ~r** *n* ranoranilac **rising** *n* ustanak o *adj* na usponu
risen *v irreg* → **rise**
risk /rɪsk/ *n* opasnost **at ~ u** opasnosti **take/run the ~** izlagati se opasnosti **at one's own ~** na vlastitu odgovornost **high-~** *adj* riskantan • *vt* izlagati opasnosti, riskirati, staviti na kocku ~**y** *adj* opasan, riskantan
rite /raɪt/ *n* obred **ritual** /'rɪtʃʊəl/ *adj* obredni o *n* obred
rival /'raɪvl/ *n* suparnik, konkurent • *vt* mjeriti se s ~**ry** *n* suparništvo
river /'rɪvə(r)/ *n* rijeka (+ *fig*) ~**bed** korito ~**side** obala rijeke
rivet /'rɪvɪt/ *n* zakovica • *vt* 1 pričvrstiti zakovicama **be ~ed to the spot** stajati kao ukopan 2 *fig* privući ~**ing** *adj*

zanimljiv,uzbudljiv, napet

rivulet /'rivjʊlit/ *n* potočić (+ *fig*)

roach /rəʊtʃ/ *n US coll* žohar

road /rəʊd/ *n* cesta ~ **accident** prometna nesreća **be on the ~ a.** putovati **b.** biti na putu **c.** biti na turneji ~**block** zapreka ~**house** gostionica (i sl.) uz glavnu cestu ~**man** cestar ~ **manager** organizator turneje ~ **roller** parni valjak ~**show** putujući zabavljači ~**side** rub ceste ~ **test** tehnički pregled ~**way** kolnik ~ **works** radovi na cesti

roam /rəʊm/ *vi,vt* lutati

roan /rəʊn/ *n, adj* šaren(ko) (konj)

roar /rɔ:(r)/ *vi,vt* urlikati, urlati ~**ing drunk** pijan kao čep ~**ing success** sjajan uspjeh

roast /rəʊst/ *vi,vt* peći • *n* pečenka • *adj* pečen; pržen

rob /rɒb/ *vt* **1** (sb of sth) ukrasti (komu što) **2** lišiti (koga/što čega) ~**ber** *n* pljačkaš ~**bery** *n* pljačka, grabež

robe /rəʊb/ *n* (*pl*) halja

robin /'rɒbin/ *n* crvendać

robust /rəʊ'bʌst/ *adj* **1** čvrst **2** oštar *fig*

rock (1) /rɒk/ *vi,vt* **1** ljuljati (se) **2** uzdrmati • *n* rock glazba ~**ing chair**; ~**er** *US n* stolica za ljuljanje **off one's** ~**er** *coll* lud ~**y** *adj* nesiguran

rock (2) *n* **1** stijena ~ **solid** čvrst kao stijena **2** kamen **3** *sl* dijamant **4** ~**s** *pl* stijenje **on the** ~**s a.** pred raspadom **b.** s ledom ~ **bottom 1** najniža točka **2** *mod* najniži, bagatelan (cijena) ~ **salt** kamena sol ~**y** *adj* kamenit

rocket /'rɒkit/ *n* raketa • *vi* naglo porasti; naglo se vinuti; prošišati

rod /rɒd/ *n* šipka, štap **fishing-~** štap za pecanje

rode *v irreg* → **ride**

rodent /'rəʊdnt/ *n* glodavac

roe /rəʊ/ *n* ikra ~ **deer** *n* jelen ~**buck** /'rəʊbʌk/ *n* jelen

roger /'rɒdʒə(r)/ *int* prijem

rogue /rəʊg/ *n* **1** hulja **2** vragolan ~**s'** **gallery** kartoteka kriminalaca • *adj* divlji, samotnjački ~**ry** *n* lopovština **roguish** *adj* nestašan

role /rəʊl/ *n* uloga ~ **model** model ponašanja, uzor

roll /rəʊl/ *vi,vt* **1** valjati (se), kotrljati

(se) **2** umotati/smotati (se) **3** (up) zasukati (rukave) **4** kolutati (očima) **5** baciti (kocku) **6** grmjeti **7** raditi, funkcionirati **8** *US sl* opljačkati (pijanca) ~ **in** stizati **be** ~**ing in it** zgrtati novac ~ **out a.** razvaljati **b.** razmotati • *n* **1** valjanje **2** smotuljak **3** pecivo **4** tutanj **5** popis imena **call the** ~ prozivati ~ **call** prozivka ~**ed gold** pozlata ~**er** *n* **1** valjak **2** uvijač **3** veliki val ~**er-skate** koturaljka ~**ing** *adj* **1** valovit, brežuljkast **2** postupan ~**ing pin** valjak za tijesto ~~**on** *adj* koji se nanosi kuglicom

roly-poly /'rəʊli 'pəʊli/ *n* kolač s pekmezom • *adj* bucmast

Roman Catholic *n, adj* rimokatolik, rimokatolički

romance /rəʊ'mæns/ *n* **1** romansa **2** romantika **3** ljubavni roman • *vi* (with) ljubovati s

Romance *adj* romanski

romantic /rəʊ'mæntik/ *adj* romantičan ~**ism** /rəʊ'mæntisizəm/ *n* romantizam

Romany /'rɒməni/ *n* **1** Rom **2** *mod* romski

romp /rɒmp/ *vi* ludovati • *n* **1** ludovanje **2** (film i sl.) zabava

roof /ru:f/ *n* krov ~ **of one's mouth** nepce • *vt* (with) staviti krov (od) ~ **in/over** staviti pod krov ~**ing** *n* materijal za krov ~ **rack** prtljažnik na krovu ~**top** *n* krov

rook /rʊk/ *n* **1** vrana **2** kula (šah) ~**ery** *n* kolonija vrana

rookie /'rʊki/ *n* neiskusan vojnik/policajac; guščer *coll*

room /ru:m/ *n* **1** soba **2** prostor, mjesto ~**mate** *n* cimer(ica) *coll* ~ **service** posluga u sobu ~**y** *adj* prostran

roost /ru:st/ *n* prečka za kokoši **rule the** ~ vladati ~**er** *n* pijetao

root /ru:t/ *n* **1** korijen (+ *fig*) **take ~** pustiti korijen ~ **and branch** u cijelosti • *vi,vt* **1** puštati korijen **2** rovati (+ *fig*) ~**ed** *adj* **1** ukorijenjen **2** ukopan

rope /rəʊp/ *n* **1** uže **2** niska **know the** ~**s** poznavati situaciju • *vt* **1** vezati **2** uhvatiti lasom ~ **off** odijeliti

rosary /'rəʊzəri/ *n* krunica

rose *v irreg* → **rise**

rose /rǝʊz/ *n* ruža ~ **hip** šipak ~**coloured glasses** ružičaste naočale *fig* ~ **window** rozeta **rosy** *adj* ružičast (+ *fig*)

rosé /ˈrǝʊzeɪ/ *n* ružica (vino)

rosemary /ˈrǝʊzmǝrɪ/ *n* ružmarin

roster /ˈrɒstǝ(r)/ *n* popis imena, raspored

rostrum /ˈrɒstrǝm/ *n* podij

rot /rɒt/ *vi, vt* trunuti (+ *fig*), gnjiliti • *n* 1 trulež 2 propadanje ~**ten** *adj* truo; pokvaren (+ *fig*); loš *fig*

rota /ˈrǝʊtǝ/ *n* raspored (rada)

rotary /ˈrǝʊtǝrɪ/ *adj* kružni

rotate /rǝʊˈteɪt/ *vi, vt* okretati (se), rotirati (se)

rote /rǝʊt/ *n* **learn by** ~ učiti napamet, bubati

rouge /ruːʒ/ *n* rumenilo • *vt* narumeniti

rough /rʌf/ *adj* 1 neravan, hrapav 2 grub (+ *fig*) 3 buran, uzburkan; oštar (vjetar) 4 naporan, neugodan **be ~ on** biti gadno *coll* 5 jednostavan ~ **diamond a.** nebrušen dijamant b. grubijan dobra srca • *vi* ~ **it** živjeti jednostavno/bez udobnosti ~ **up** oboriti se (na) • *adv* **sleep ~** spavati na otvorenom ~**age** *n* neprobavljive tvari ~**-and-tumble** *n* gužva, natezanje ~**en** *vt, vi* ogrubjeti; ogrubiti ~**ly** *adv* 1 grubo 2 ugrubo

round /raʊnd/ *adj* okrugao • *adv* 1 oko(lo), naokolo 2 posvuda, po cijelom **all year** ~ cijele godine **enough to go** ~ dovoljno za sve **the wrong way** ~ naopako ~ **about** oko **the other way** ~ obrnuto • *prep* oko; po; iza • *n* 1 krug; runda 2 metak 3 ~**s** *pl* posjet (pacijentima) • *vt* 1 skrenuti, zaći za, obići 2 zaobliti ~ **off** završiti ~ **up** skupiti ~**up** *n* a. skupljanje b. pregled c. racija ~**about** *n* kružni tok ○ *adj* obilazan ~**ed** *adj* zaobljen ~**ly** *adv* potpuno; oštro ~**sman** *n* dostavljač ~**table discussion** okrugli stol ~**the-clock** cjelodnevan, neprekidan ~**trip** *adj* povratni

rouse /raʊz/ *vt* (from/out of) razbuditi, probuditi, dići; potaknuti, raz-

dražiti **rousing** *adj* poticajan

rout /raʊt/ *n* povlačenje u neredu; poraz • *vt* natjerati u bijeg; poraziti, potući ~ **out** istjerati

route /ruːt/ *n* put; ruta

routine /ruːˈtiːn/ *n* 1 rutina 2 koraci • *adj* rutinski, redovni

rove /rǝʊv/ *vi, vt* lutati ~**r** *n* lutalica

row (1) /rǝʊ/ *n* red **in a ~** za redom ~ **houses** *US* kuće u nizu

row (2) /rǝʊ/ *vi, vt* veslati

row (3) /raʊ/ *n* 1 svađa, prepirka 2 raspra, kontroverzija 3 buka • *vi* svaditi se

rowdy /ˈraʊdɪ/ *adj coll* prost, grub

royal /ˈrɔɪǝl/ *adj* kraljevski (+ *fig*) • *n* član kraljevske obitelji ~**ty** *n* 1 kraljevska obitelj 2 tantijema, postotak

rub /rʌb/ *vi, vt* trljati (se) 2 izbrisati 3 dotaknuti 4 žuljati ~ **shoulders with** *coll* družiti se ~ **someone up the wrong way** zamjeriti se komu ~ **down** istrljati; ostrugati ~ **in** utrljati, utuviti ~ **off** izbrisati se ~ **off onto** prijeći na ~ **out** izbrisati • *n* problem

rubber /ˈrʌbǝ(r)/ *n* 1 guma 2 *GB* gumica (za brisanje) 3 *coll* kondom ~ **band** gumica ~**neck** *vi* izvijati vrat ~ **plant** fikus ~**stamp** *vt* službeno potvrditi ~ **tree** *n* kaučukovac ~**y** *adj* gumast

rubbish /ˈrʌbɪʃ/ *n* 1 smeće (+ *fig*) ~ **bin** kanta za smeće 2 *fig* glupost

rubble /ˈrʌbl/ *n* šuta; krš, ruševine

ruby /ˈruːbɪ/ *n* rubin

rucksack /ˈrʌksæk/ *n* ruksak, naprtnjača

ruction /ˈrʌkʃǝn/ *n* graja

rudder /ˈrʌdǝ(r)/ *n* kormilo

ruddy /ˈrʌdɪ/ *adj* rumen, rujan

rude /ruːd/ *adj* 1 nepristojan, prost 2 grub *fig*

rudimentary /ˌruːdɪˈmentrɪ/ *adj* 1 osnovan 2 primitivan **rudiments** *n pl* osnove

rueful /ˈruːfl/ *adj* tužan

ruffle /ˈrʌfl/ *vt* 1 razbarušiti 2 nakostriješiti 3 smesti, uzrujati • *n* nabor

rug /rʌg/ *n* 1 prostirka 2 pokrivač

rugged /ˈrʌgɪd/ *adj* 1 neravan, divlji 2 čvrst 3 markantan

ruin /ˈruːɪn/ *n* 1 propast **fall into ~**

propasti 2 ~s ruševina **lie in** ~s biti ruševina • *vt* upropastiti

rule /ru:l/ *n* 1 pravilo **as a** ~ u pravilu ~ **of thumb** praktično pravilo 2 vladavina ~ **of law** pravna država 3 ravnalo • *vi,vt* 1 vladati 2 presuditi ~ **out** isključiti ~**d** *adj* s crtama ~**r** *n* 1 vladar 2 ravnalo **ruling** *n* odluka, presuda **give a ruling** donijeti presudu ○ *adj* vladajući

rumble /ˈrʌmbl/ *vi,vt* 1 tutnjati **my stomach** ~s krulji mi u želucu 2 *coll* razotkriti • *n* tutnjava **rumblings** *n pl* mrmljanje, gunđanje

ruminant /ˈruːmɪnənt/ *n* preživač **ruminate** *vi* 1 preživati 2 *fig* razmatrati

rummage /ˈrʌmɪdʒ/ *vi* kopati, čeprkati

rummy /ˈrʌmɪ/ *n* remi

rumour /ˈruːmə(r)/ *n* glasina ~**ed** *adj* o kojem se govora/šapuće, navodni

rump /rʌmp/ *n* 1 sapi ~ **steak** ramstek 2 stražnjica 3 ostatak; batrljak *fig* 4 *mod* krnj

rumple /ˈrʌmpl/ *vt* zgužvati

run (1) /rʌn/ *vt,vi irreg* 1 trčati, pretrčati 2 održati se (trka) 3 ići, otići, proći 4 ići, voziti 5 teći; pustiti da teče 6 rastopiti se 7 upravljati 8 raditi, funkcionirati 9 pokrenuti 10 protezati se 11 vrijediti 12 davati se 13 objaviti 14 kandidirati se 15 krijumčariti ~ **errands for** biti čiji potrčko ~ **one's course** proći ~ **a bath** napuniti kadu **my nose is** ~**ning** curi mi iz nosa **the tap is** ~**ning** slavina je otvorena ~ **in the family** biti u krvi ~ **a temperature** imati visoku temperaturu ~ **dry** presušiti ~ **short** ponestajati ~ **across** naletjeti na ~ **away** pobjeći ~ **down** a. pregaziti b. zaustaviti se c. propadati ~ **into** a. naletjeti na b. susresti se s ~ **off** s lakoćom izvesti ~**off** *n* odlučujući susret/utrka ~ **on** a. potrajati b. pričati ~ **out** nestati time is ~**ning out** vrijeme istječe ~ **over** a.

zgaziti b. preliti se ~ **up** a. podići b. nabiti ~ **up against** naići na

run (2) *n* 1 trčanje, trka, staza 2 putovanje; linija 3 niz 4 prosjek ~**-of-the-mill** prosječan 5 tor **in the long** ~ dugoročno **on the** ~ u bijegu ~**away** *n* bjegunac ○ *adj* odbjegli, nekontroliran ~**down** *adj* rušěvan ~**ner** *n* 1 trkač, natjecatelj 2 krijumčar ~**ner-up** osvajač drugog mjesta ~**ning** *n* 1 trčanje 2 uprava ○ *adj* 1 tekući 2 neprekidan ~**ning commentary** komentar ~**ning costs** pogonski troškovi ○ *adv* zaredom ~**ny** *adj* 1 vodenast 2 koji curi ~s *n pl coll* proljev

rung *v irreg* → ring

rung /rʌŋ/ *n* prečka; stepenica *fig*

runway /ˈrʌnweɪ/ *n* pista

rupture /ˈrʌptʃə(r)/ *n* 1 prsnuće 2 prekid, raskid • *vi,vt* puknuti, prsnuti

rural /ˈrʊərəl/ *adj* seoski, ruralni

ruse /ru:z/ *n* lukavstvo

rush (1) /rʌʃ/ *vi,vt* 1 jurnuti, juriti 2 žuriti 3 hitno dovesti/učiniti 4 prenagliti se, prebrzo raditi 5 (into) nagoniti, požurivati 6 napasti na juriš ~ *n* 1 strka, jurnjava, navala 2 žurba ~ **job** hitan posao ~ **hour** prometna špica

rush (2) *n* rogoz

rust /rʌst/ *n* hrđa • *vi,vt* hrđati; izjesti ~**proof** *adj* nehrđajući ~**y** *adj* zahrđao (+ *fig*)

rustic /ˈrʌstɪk/ *adj* rustičan • *n* derog seljak

rustle /ˈrʌsl/ *vi,vt* 1 šuštati 2 krasti (stoku) ~ **up** *coll* smisliti/pronaći nešto • *n* šuštanje

rut (1) /rʌt/ *n* kolotečina (+ *fig*) • *vt* izbrazdati

rut (2) *n* tjeranje ~**ting** *adj* koji se tjera • *vt* tjerati se

ruthless /ˈruːθlɪs/ *adj* nemilosrdan

rye /raɪ/ *n* 1 raž 2 *mod* raženi 3 viski od raži

S

S, s /es/ 19. slovo engl. abecede; es

s (Saxon genitive) tvori posvojni oblik imenica u jednini i množini koja ne završava na -s *John's* Johnov *bear's* medvjeđi *children's* dječji (za imenice u množini dodaje se samo apostrof *boys' Smiths'*)

Sabbath /'sæbəθ/ n 1 nedjelja 2 šabes

sabbatical /sə'bætɪkl/ n studijska godina

sable /'seɪbl/ n 1 kuna 2 kunovina • *adj* 1 od kunovine 2 taman

sabotage /'sæbətɑːʒ/ n sabotaža • *vt* izvesti sabotažu; sabotirati **saboteur** /ˌsæbə'tɜː(r)/ n saboter

sabre (**-er** *US*) /'seɪbr/ n sablja ~-**rattlig** *fig* zveckanje oružjem

sachet /'sæʃeɪ/ n vrećica

sack (1) /sæk/ n 1 vreća 2 *coll* otkaz 3 *coll* krevet **hit the ~** *coll* ići u krpe • *vt* dati komu otkaz

sack (2) *vt* poharati

sacrament /'sækrəmənt/ n 1 otajstvo 2 (**the Holy**) **S~** pričest

sacred /'seɪkrɪd/ *adj* 1 vjerski 2 svet

sacrifice /'sækrɪfaɪs/ n 1 žrtva 2 odricanje • *vt,vi* žrtvovati **sacrificial** /ˌsækrɪ'fɪʃl/ *adj* žrtveni

sacrilege /'sækrɪlɪdʒ/ n svetogrđe **sacrilegious** *adj* svetogrdan

sacristy /'sækrɪstɪ/ n sakristija

sad /sæd/ *adj* žalostan, tužan **~ to say** nažalost **~den** *vt* rastužiti **~ly** *adv* 1 žalosno 2 nažalost **be ~ly mistaken** ljuto se varati

saddle /'sædl/ n sedlo **in the ~** *fig* za upravljačem • *vt* osedlati **~ sb with sb/sth** natovariti koga/što komu

sadism /'seɪdɪzəm/ n sadizam **sadist** n sadist **sadistic** *adj* sadistčan

safe /seɪf/ n sef • *adj* 1 (from) siguran/zaštićen (od) 2 neozlijeđen **~ return** sretan povratak **~ and sound**

živ i zdrav 3 siguran, pouzdan; neriskantan **be on the ~ side** osigurati se za svaki slučaj **play (it) ~** ne riskirati **it is ~ to say** može se slobodno reći **~-conduct** siguran prolaz; propusnica **~-deposit box** sef u trezoru banke **~guard** n zaštita, jamstvo sigurnosti *vt* (from/against) štititi, jamčiti sigurnost od **~keeping** n čuvanje **in my ~keeping** pohranjeni kod mene **~ty** n 1 sigurnost **road ~ty** sigurnost u prometu 2 *mod* sigurnosni **~ty catch** osigurač **~ty pin** sigurnosnica **~ty valve** a. sigurnosni ventil b. *fig* odušak

sag /sæg/ *vi* 1 objesiti se, visjeti 2 *fig* klonuti; opasti

sage (1) /seɪdʒ/ *adj* lit mudar • n mudrac

sage (2) n kadulja

Saggitarius /ˌsædʒɪ'teərɪəs/ n *astrol* Strijelac

said *v irreg* → **say**

sail /seɪl/ n jedro **in full ~** pod punim jedrima **set ~** otisnuti se • *vt,vi* 1 ploviti 2 upravljati 3 isploviti **~ing** n 1 plovidba 2 jedrenje 3 brod **~ing boat**, **~boat** jedrilica **~or** n mornar

saint /seɪnt/ n svetac **S~** (+ name) Sveti/Sveta **~ly** *adj* svetački **~'s day** blagdan sveca **All S~'s Day** Svi sveti

sake /seɪk/ n **for the ~ of** radi, za (čije) dobro **for my/your/etc sake** radi mene/tebe, mene/tebe radi **art for art's ~** larpurlartizam **for God's/Christ's/goodness ~** za ime Boga, za Boga miloga

salad /'sæləd/ n salata **~ days** mladi dani **~ dressing** začin za salatu

salami /sə'lɑːmɪ/ n salama

salary /'sælərɪ/ n plaća, osobni dohodak

sale /seɪl/ n 1 prodaja **make a ~** uspjeti

prodati **for** ~ prodaje se 2 rasprodaja **in** a ~/**on** ~ na rasprodaji 3 (~s) prodaja, promet, realizacija ~**sclerk** *US* prodavač ~**sman** *n* 1 prodavač 2 trgovački putnik ~**sperson** *n* prodavač, prodavačica ~**s representative** trgovački putnik ~**s slip** *US* račun ~**s tax** porez na promet

salient /'seɪlɪənt/ *adj* ključni

saliva /sə'laɪvə/ *n* slina ~**ry** /'sælɪvərɪ/ *adj* slinovni ~**te** /'sælɪveɪt/ *vi* sliniti (+ *fig*)

sallow /'sæləʊ/ *adj* nezdrav, žut

salmon /'sæmən/ *n* (*pl* ~, ~s) 1 losos 2 *mod* narančastoružičast

saloon /sə'lu:n/ *n* 1 (~ **car**) limuzina 2 salun

salt /sɔ:lt/ *n* sol • *vt* (po)soliti • *adj* slan ~**cellar**/~ **shaker** *US* soljenka ~**petre** /sɔ:lt'pi:tə(r)/ *n* salitra ~**water** *adj* morski ~**y** *adj* slan

salute /sə'lu:t/ *vi,vt* 1 mil pozdraviti 2 iskazati počast 3 pozdraviti • *n* 1 mil pozdrav 2 počasna salva

salvage /'sælvɪdʒ/ *n* 1 spašavanje tereta 2 spašeni teret • *vt* spasiti

salvation /sæl'veɪʃn/ *n* spas S~ **Army** Vojska spasa

salve /sælv/ *n* (ljekovita) mast • *vt* ~ **one's conscience** umiriti si savjest

same /seɪm/ *adj, pron* (onaj) isti **at the** ~ **time** istodobno **by the** ~ **token** isto tako **all the** ~ ipak • *adv* **the** ~ isto, na isti način ~ **as** baš kao i

sample /'sɑ:mpl/ *n* 1 uzorak 2 primjer • *vt* 1 kušati, degustirati 2 *fig* okusiti

sanctify /'sæŋktɪfaɪ/ *vt* 1 posvetiti 2 sankcionirati **sanctity** *n* svetost

sanctimonious /ˌsæŋktɪ'məʊnɪəs/ *adj* licemjeran

sanction /'sæŋkʃn/ *n* 1 odobrenje 2 sankcija, kaznena mjera • *vt* odobriti, prihvatiti

sanctuary /'sæŋktʃʊərɪ/ *n* 1 utočište 2 svetište

sand /sænd/ *n* pijesak • *vt* izgladiti, obrusiti ~**bank** prud ~**blast** čistiti pješčanim mlazom ~**er**, ~**ing machine** brusilica ~**paper** *n* brusni papir o *vt* brusiti ~**pit** pješčanik ~**stone** pješčenjak ~**storm** pješčana oluja ~**y** *adj* 1 pjeskovit 2 pješčan 3 boje pi-

jeska

sandal /'sændl/ *n* sandala

sandwich /'sænwɪdʒ/ *n* sendvič • *vt* (between) ugurati, stisnuti

sane /seɪn/ *adj* 1 duševno zdrav, pri zdravoj pameti 2 razuman **sanity** /'sænətɪ/ *n* duševno zdravlje; zdrav razum

sang *v irreg* → **sing**

sanitary /'sænɪtrɪ/ *adj* 1 sanitarni ~ **fittings** sanitarije 2 higijenski ~ **napkin/towel** higijenski uložak **sanitation** *n* 1 mjere za zaštitu zdravlja 2 odvoz smeća **sanitize** *vt fig* uljepšati

sank *v irreg* → **sink**

Santa Claus /'sæntə klɔ:z/ *n* Sveti Nikola, Djed Božićnjak

sap /sæp/ *n* 1 biljni sok 2 blesan • *vt* iscrpsti ~**ling** *n* mladica ~**py** *adj* blesav

sapphire /'sæfaɪə(r)/ *n* safir

sarcasm /'sɑ:kæzəm/ *n* sarkazam **sarcastic** *adj* sarkastičan

sardine /sɑ:'di:n/ *n* sardina

sardonic /sɑ:'dɒnɪk/ *adj* ciničan

sartorial /sɑ:'tɔ:rɪəl/ *adj* 1 *form* krojački 2 *iron* odjevni

sash (1) /sæʃ/ *n* 1 ešarpa, lenta 2 pojas

sash (2) *n* okvir (prozora) ~ **window** prozor na dizanje, engleski prozor

sassy /'sæsɪ/ *adj* drzak

sat *v irreg* → **sit**

Satan /'seɪtn/ *n* Sotona ~**ic** *adj* sotonski

satchel /'sætʃl/ *n* torba preko ramena

satellite /'sætəlaɪt/ *n* satelit

satin /'sætɪn/ *n* saten; satenski, poput satena

satire /'sætaɪə(r)/ *n* satira **satirical** /sə'tɪrɪkl/ *adj* satiričan

satisfaction /ˌsætɪs'fækʃn/ *n* 1 (at/with) zadovoljstvo 2 (of) zadovoljenje, zadovoljavanje, udovoljavanje (komu/čemu) **prove sth to one's** ~ potpuno koga uvjeriti 3 zadovoljština **satisfactory** *adj* zadovoljavajući **satisfy** /'sætɪsfaɪ/ *vt,vi* 1 zadovoljiti; udovoljiti 2 uvjeriti

satsuma /sæt'su:mə/ *n* mandarina

saturate/'sætʃəreɪt/ *vt* (with) 1 natopiti 2 zasititi ~**d** *adj* zasićen **saturation** *n* zasićenje, zasićenost

Saturday /'sætədɪ/ *n* subota

saturnine /'sætənaɪn/ adj sumoran, natmuren

sauce /sɔːs/ n 1 umak 2 bezobraština **saucy** adj 1 bezobrazan 2 pikantan fig

saucepan /'sɔːspən/ n posuda za kuhanje

saucer /'sɔːsə(r)/ n tanjurić **flying ~** leteći tanjur

sauerkraut /'sauəkraut/ n kiselo zelje

saunter /'sɔːntə(r)/ vi šetkati se

sausage /'sɒsɪdʒ/ n kobasica **garlic ~** češnjovka

saute /'səuteɪ/ vt propirjati

savage /'sævɪdʒ/ adj divlji; divljački, okrutan • n derog divljak • vt divlje napasti ~**ry** n divljaštvo

save /seɪv/ vt 1 (from) spasiti (od), izbaviti (iz) 2 štedjeti 3 čuvati, sačuvati 4 prištedjeti sebi 5 obraniti (gol) • n sport obrana ~**r** n štediša **saving grace** fig jedina dobra strana **savings** n pl ušteđevina **savings account** štedni račun **savings bank** štedionica

saviour (-**or** US) /'seɪvɪə(r)/ n spasitelj

savour (-**or** US) /'seɪvər/ vt (sth) uživati u čemu • **of** fig mirisati na • n slast ~**y** adj 1 ukusan, tečan 2 pikantan • n pikantno predjelo

savvy /'sævɪ/ n znanje, sposobnost

saw (1) v irreg → **see**

saw (2) /sɔː/ n pila • vt,vi irreg piliti ~**dust** piljevina ~**mill** pilana ~**n/ed-off shotgun** skraćena sačmarica

sawn v irreg → **saw**

say /seɪ/ vt irreg 1 (sth to sb) reći (što kome) **they ~** kaže se **he is said to be** za njega se priča da je 2 kazati, kazivati (**let's**) ~ recimo **having said that** no ipak **not to ~** da ne kažem ~ **for oneself/something** reći u svoju obranu/u korist čega ~ **no more!** sve je jasno ~ **no** (to) odbiti (što) **to ~ nothing of him** njega da i ne spominjem **when all is said and done** na kraju krajeva • n (in) udio u odlučivanju ~**ing** n izreka

scab /skæb/ n 1 krasta 2 fig štrajkolomac ~**by** adj krastav

scabbard /'skæbəd/ n korice pl (mača)

scabies /'skeɪbɪːz/ n svrab

scaffold /'skæfəuld/ n 1 skele pl 2 stratište ~**ing** n skele

scag /skæg/ n sl heroin

scald /skɔːld/ vt 1 ofuriti 2 zagrijati ~**ing** adj 1 vreo 2 fig oštar

scale (1) /skeɪl/ n 1 ljestvica (+ mus) **pay ~** raspon plaća 2 oznake na ravnalu 3 mjerilo **draw to ~** ucrtati po mjerilu ~ **model** maketa 4 razmjer pl **large-~** velik, opsežan **on a large ~** u velikim razmjerima **full-~ a.** u prirodnoj veličini **b.** potpun, totalni 5 (~**s**) vaga **tip the ~s** prevagnuti • vt (up/down) povećavati/smanjivati

scale (2) /skeɪl/ n 1 ljuska, krljušt 2 kamenac • vt ostrugati **scaly** adj 1 ljuskast 2 prekriven kamencem

scale (3) vt uzverati se uz

scallop /'skɒləp/ n jakovska kapica ~**ed** adj nazupčan(og ruba)

scalp /skælp/ n 1 skalp 2 tjeme • vt 1 skalpirati 2 preprodavati (ulaznice) ~**er** n US preprodavač; tapkaroš coll

scalpel /'skælpl/ n skalpel

scam /skæm/ n lukava prijevara

scamper /'skæmpə(r)/ vi odskakutati

scan /skæn/ vt 1 (for) pretraživati, tražiti što 2 preletjeti pogledom 3 tech skanirati • n 1 pregled (skanerom) 2 analiza ~**ner** n tech skaner

scandal /'skændl/ n sablazan, skandal, afera ~**ize** vt šokirati, sablazniti ~**monger** n klevetnik, ogovaratelj ~**ous** adj sramotan

scant /skænt/ adj jedva dovoljan, manjkav **pay ~ attention** jedva obratiti pozornost ~**y** adj oskudan

scapegoat /'skeɪpgəut/ n žrtveni jarac

scar /skɑː(r)/ n ožiljak (+ fig) • vt ostaviti ožiljke/ožiljak

scarce /skeəs/ adj rijedak, oskudan, nedovoljan **food is ~** hrane ima malo ~**ly** adv jedva, tek (što) **scarcity** n nedostatak

scare /skeə(r)/ vt preplašiti ~ **away** poplašiti, otjerati ~ **into** natjerati (na) ~ **the hell out of** preplašiti nasmrt **it ~d the shit out of me/I was ~d shitless** tab usrao sam se od straha tab • n panika **give sb a ~** prestrašiti koga ~**crow** strašilo ~**monger** n paničar **scary** adj strašan

scarf /skɑ:f/ n šal, marama

scarlet /'skɑ:lət/ adj grimizan ~ **fever** šarlah

scathing /'skeɪðɪŋ/ adj okrutan, bespoštedan

scatter /'skætə(r)/ vt,vi 1 raštrkati (se) 2 dati se u bijeg, natjerati u bijeg 3 razasuti, posijati ~**brain** n smušenjak ~**ed** adj rijedak

scavenge /'skævɪndʒ/ vi,vt 1 (on/for) lešinariti 2 iskoristiti ~**r** n strvinar, lešinar (+ fig)

scenario /sɪ'nɑːrɪəʊ/ n scenarij (+ fig)

scene /si:n/ n 1 prizor, scena 2 mjesto, poprište 3 pozornica fig ~**ry** n 1 krajolik, panorama 2 scenografija **scenic** adj živopisan

scent /sent/ n 1 miris 2 parfem 3 trag • vt,vi 1 nanjušiti 2 (with) namirisati

sceptic /'skeptɪk/ n skeptik ~**al** adj skeptičan ~**ism** n skepsa

schedule /'ʃedju:l, 'skedju:l US/ n 1 raspored, plan 2 red vožnje **ahead of/on/behind** ~ prije roka/na vrijeme/uz zakašnjenje • vt (for) dogovoriti ~**d flight** let po stalnom redu letenja

scheme /ski:m/ n plan, sistem, sustav • vi (for/against) kovati planove ~**r** n spletkar

schizophrenia /ˌskɪtsəʊ'fri:nɪə/ n shizofrenija **schizophrenic** adj shizofreničan o n shizofreničar

schmaltzy /'ʃmɔːltsɪ/ adj sladunjav

schmuck /ʃmʌk/ n kreten

scholar /'skɒlə(r)/ n 1 znanstvenik 2 (of) poznavalac čega, stručnjak za ~**ly** adj znanstvenički ~**ship** n 1 stipendija 2 učenost

school (1) /sku:l/ n škola **primary/ elementary** US ~ osnovna škola **secondary/high** US ~ srednja škola **private** ~ privatna škola **medical/law** ~ US medicinski/pravni fakultet ~**child/boy/girl** školarac, učenik osnovne škole ~**mate** školski drug ~**teacher** učitelj

school (2) jato (riba)

science /'saɪəns/ n 1 znanost 2 egzaktna/prirodna znanost **scientific** /ˌsaɪən'tɪfɪk/ adj znanstveni **scientist** n znanstvenik

scissors /'sɪzəz/ n pl škare

scoff /skɒf/ vi (at) izrugivati se (čemu)

scold /skəʊld/ vt izgrditi

scone /skɒn/ n okrugli kolačić

scoop /sku:p/ n 1 lopatica 2 žlica za sladoled 3 kugla (sladoleda) 4 ekskluzivna vijest • vt 1 grabiti 2 pokupiti

scoot /sku:t/ vi odjuriti, požuriti ~**er** n 1 romobil 2 motor, vespa

scope /skəʊp/ n 1 (of) domet, djelokrug, opseg, raspon 2 (for) prostor

scorch /skɔːtʃ/ vt 1 zapaliti, spržiti, oprljiti 2 juriti

score (1) /skɔː(r)/ n 1 rezultat 2 sport zgoditak, bod 3 partitura 4 (neizravnat) račun 5 (~ **mark**) urez, sjekotina **on that** ~ glede toga • vi,vt 1 postići (zgoditak i sl.) 2 dobiti (bod) 3 pratiti rezultat 4 napisati glazbu 5 zarezati 6 (with) povaliti (koga) coll 7 nabaviti drogu ~**board** n semafor

score (2) num arch dvadeset ~**s of people** deseci ljudi

scorn /skɔːn/ n (for) prezir prema ~**ful** adj preziran • vt prezreti

Scorpio /'skɔːpɪəʊ/ n astrol Škorpion

scorpion /'skɔːpɪən/ n štipavac, škorpion

scotch /skɒtʃ/ vt (sth) stati na kraj čemu

Scotch n škotski viski

scotch tape n TM selotejp

scot-free /skɒt'fri:/ adv nekažnjeno

scoundrel /'skaʊndrəl/ n hulja

scour /'skaʊə(r)/ vt 1 (for) pročešljati 2 ribati ~**er** n žica za čišćenje

scourge /skɜːdʒ/ n 1 pošast 2 bič fig • vt 1 bičevati 2 šibati, mučiti fig

scout /skaʊt/ n izviđač **talent** ~ lovac na talente • vi,vt tražiti, pretraživati

scowl /skaʊl/ n mrk pogled • vi (at) mrštiti se na koga

scraggy /'skrægɪ/ adj zakržljao

scram /skræm/ int briši! gubi se!

scramble /'skræmbl/ vi,vt 1 verati se 2 (for) boriti se, gurati se 3 pomiješati ~**d eggs** kajgana na mlijeku 4 elektronski ometati prisluškivanje 5 mil hitno uzletjeti • n 1 tarapana 2 motokros ~**r** n elektronski ometač prisluškivanja/gledanja

scrap (1) /skræp/ *n* 1 komadićak 2 ~s otpaci ∼ **metal** staro željezo • *vt* 1 otarasiti se 2 dati u staro željezo ∼**book** zbirka isječaka iz novina ∼ **heap** smetlište, otpad

scrap (2) *n* tučnjava • *vi* potući se

scrap (3) /skræp/ *vt,vi* 1 (sa)strugati; izgladiti 2 (on/against) vući, povući 3 oguliti, ogrepsti 4 izdupsti ∼ **a living/∼ by** životariti ∼ **through** provući se ∼ **up** skucati • *n* 1 ogrebotina 2 neprilika

scratch /skrætʃ/ *vt,vi* 1 ogrepsti, grepsti, izgrepsti 2 češati se 3 urezati 4 oguliti • *n* 1 ogrebotina 2 grebanje 3 češanje **from** ∼ ispočetka

scrawl /skrɔːl/ *vt* naškrabati • *n* 1 škrabotina 2 nečitljiv rukopis

scrawny /'skrɔːnɪ/ *adj* suhonjav

scream /skriːm/ *vi,vt* 1 kriknuti, vikati, vrištati, urlati, zavijati 2 *fig* zahtijevati • *n* vrisak, krik

screech /skriːtʃ/ *vi,vt* kričati, vrištati **come to a ∼ing halt** zaustaviti se uz škripu kočnica • *n* kričanje; škripa

screen /skriːn/ *n* 1 zaslon, paravan 2 fasada *fig* 3 ekran **adapt for the ∼** ekranizirati • *vt* 1 (from) štititi, zaklanjati 2 vršiti selekciju 3 prikazati ∼**ing** *n* 1 prikazivanje 2 selekcija 3 pregled ∼**play** scenarij

screw /skruː/ *n* 1 vijak **tighten the ∼s on** pritegnuti koga 2 *sl* zatvorski čuvar 3 *tab* komad za povaliti *sl* • *vt,vi* 1 pričvrstiti vijcima 2 pričvrstiti 3 zgužvati 4 *tab* povaliti ∼ **you!** jebi se! *tab* ∼ **up a. zeznuti b.** iskriviti (lice), stisnuti (oči) **c. be ∼ed up about** imati problema ∼**ball** *n* ludak ∼**driver** odvijač ∼ **top** navojni zatvarač ∼**y** *adj* čudan

scribble /'skrɪbl/ *vi,vt* (na)žvrljati • *n* 1 žvrljotina 2 nečitak rukopis ∼**r** *n derog* piskaralo

scribe /skraɪb/ *n* pisar, prepisivač

script /skrɪpt/ *n* 1 scenarij 2 pismo 3 rukopis 4 (∼s) pismeni test ∼**writer** scenarist

scripture, the Scripture(s) /'skrɪptʃə(r)/ *n* Sveto pismo

scroll /skrəʊl/ *n* svitak • *vt comp* pregledavati

scrooge /skruːdʒ/ *n* škrtac

scrotum /'skrəʊtəm/ *n* mošnje

scrounge /skraʊndʒ/ *vi,vt* žicati *coll*

scrub (1) /skrʌb/ *vi,vt* 1 ribati 2 zaboraviti, oprostiti se od ∼ **up** oprati ruke prije operacije • *n* ribanje ∼**ber** /'skrʌbə(r)/ *n* kurva, laka roba

scrub (2) *n* nisko raslinje

scruff /skrʌf/ *n* **the ∼ of the neck** šija

scruffy /'skrʌfɪ/ *adj* prljav

scrum(age) /skrʌm/ *n fig* otimanje, gužva

scrunch /skrʌntʃ/ *vt,vi* 1 zgužvati ∼ **dry** prstima osušiti kosu 2 škripati

scruple /'skruːpl/ *n* skrupula, obzir • *vi* imati skrupula **scrupulous** /'skruːpjʊləs/ *adj* 1 brižljiv 2 savjestan

scrutinize /'skruːtɪnaɪz/ *vt* pomno motriti **scrutiny** /'skruːtɪnɪ/ *n* oštro promatranje

scuba-diving /'skuːbə daɪvɪŋ/ *n* ronjenje

scuff /skʌf/ *vt,vi* oguliti (se) • (∼**mark**) oguljotina, ogrebotina

scuffle /'skʌfl/ *n* koškanje • *vi* koškati se

scull /skʌl/ *n sport* samac **double ∼** dvojac na pariće

scullery /'skʌlərɪ/ *n* stražnja kuhinja ∼ **maid** sudoperka

sculptor /'skʌlptə(r)/ *n* kipar **sculpture** *n* kip, kiparstvo **sculpt(ure)** *vt* oblikovati, isklesati

scum /skʌm/ *n* 1 pjena (koja nastaje pri kuhanju) 2 *fig* šljam, ološ

scurrilous /'skʌrɪləs/ *adj* otrovan *fig*

scurry /'skʌrɪ/ *vi* šmugnuti • *n* tapkanje

scurvy /'skɜːvɪ/ *n* skorbut

scuttle /'skʌtl/ *vt* hitro otapkati

scythe /saɪð/ *n* kosa (alat) • *vi* (down/through) pokositi (+ *fig*)

sea /siː/ *n* 1 more (+ *fig*) 2 *mod* morski **by ∼** brodom **be at ∼ a.** ploviti **b.** *fig* biti zbunjen ∼**bed** morsko dno ∼**board** primorje ∼**borne** pomorski ∼**food** plodovi mora ∼**gull** galeb ∼**horse** morski konjić **1000 m above ∼ level** 1000 m nadmorske visine ∼**man** mornar, pomorac ∼**manship** *n* mornarska vještina ∼**plane**

hidroavion **~shell** školjka **~shore** morska obala **~sick** koji pati od morske bolesti **~side** obala **~ urchin** ježinac **~weed** alge *pl* **~worthy** sposoban za plovidbu

seal (1) /si:l/ *n* (*pl* **~s/~**) tuljan **~skin** *n* tuljanova koža/krzno

seal (2) *n* 1 pečat 2 čep **set a ~ on sth** zapečatiti *fig* • *vt* 1 zapečatiti (+ *fig*) 2 (0/up/down) zalijepiti, zatvoriti **my lips are ~ed** ne smijem ništa reći **~ in** hermetički zatvoriti **~ off** blokirati **~er,** **~ant** *n* kit **~ling wax** pečatni vosak

seam /si:m/ *n* 1 šav **come apart at the ~s** pucati po šavu **burst at the ~s** *fig* eksplodirati *fig* 2 spoj, pukotina **~less** *adj* 1 bešavan 2 *fig* gladak **~stress** /'si:mstris/ *n* krojačica

sear /siə(r)/ *vt* ispržiti, ispeći (na naglo) **~ing** *adj* žestok

search /sɜ:tʃ/ *vi,vt* 1 (for) tražiti što 2 (through) prekapati (po čemu) 3 pretražiti • *n* potraga **in ~ of** u potrazi za **~ing** *adj* ispitivački **~light** reflektor **~ warrant** nalog za premetačinu

season (1) /'si:zn/ *n* 1 doba 2 sezona **out of ~** izvan sezone, u podsezoni **~al** *adj* sezonski

season (2) *vt* 1 začiniti **~ing** *n* začin 2 ostaviti da sazrije (drvo) **~ed** *adj fig* iskusan, prekaljen

seat /si:t/ *n* 1 sjedalo, mjesto (za sjedenje), stolac **take your ~** sjednite **have a ~** sjednite 2 mjesto (u parlamentu, odboru) 3 stražnji dio, stražnjica 4 sjedište **two~er** dvosjed • *vt* 1 posjesti **please be ~ed** molim vas, sjedite 2 imati mjesta **~ing** *adj* sjedenje **~ing capacity** broj sjedala **~ belt** sigurnosni pojas

secede /sɪ'si:d/ *vi* (from) odcijepiti se **secession** /sɪ'seʃn/ *n* odcjepljenje

secluded /sɪ'klu:dɪd/ *adj* samotan; usamljenički **seclusion** /sɪ'klu:ʒn/ *n* osamljeništvo

second (1) /'sekənd/ *num ord* drugi **~ary** *adj* sekundaran; manje važan **~ary education** srednje obrazovanje **~ly** *adv* u drugom redu, drugo **~s** *n pl coll* repete **~ best** ne najbolji **settle for ~ best** zadovoljiti se lošijim **~ to**

none najbolji **~ class** drugi razred **~ class** *adj* drugorazredan **~degree** *adj* drugog stupnja **~guess** *vt* pokušati predvidjeti **~hand** *adj, adv* iz druge ruke; rabljen **~ lieutenant** poručnik **be ~ nature** biti urođeno **~ rate** *adj* drugorazredan **~ sight** dovidost **on ~ thoughts** kad bolje razmislim

second (2) *n* sekunda

second (3) *n* sekundant

second (4) *vt* podržati

secrecy /'si:krəsɪ/ *n* tajnovitost

secret /'si:krɪt/ *adj* 1 tajan **keep sth ~ from** držati što u tajnosti pred 2 tajnovit • *n* tajna **~ive** *adj* tajnovit

secretary /'sekrətrɪ/ *n* tajnik, tajnica **~ of State** 1 *US* državni tajnik, ministar vanjskih poslova 2 *GB* ministar **secretarial** /ˌsekrə'teərɪəl/ *adj* tajnički

sect /sekt/ *n* sekta **~arian** *adj pol* sektaški

section /'sekʃn/ *n* 1 dio, odjel, dionica 2 kriška 3 presjek **cross~** poprečni p. 4 rez **~al** *adj* 1 u dijelovima 2 lokalni, sektaški 3 u presjeku

sector /'sektə(r)/ *n* sektor

secular /'sekjulə(r)/ *adj* svjetovni

secure /sɪ'kjuə(r)/ *adj* 1 (from/ against) siguran od 2 čvrsto zatvoren 3 osiguran 4 čvrst, zajamčen 5 miran, bezbrižan • *vt* 1 učvrstiti 2 (from/against) osigurati 3 postići 4 zajamčiti **security** /sɪ'kjuərətɪ/ *n* 1 sigurnost 2 osiguranje 3 zaštita 4 jamčevina 5 (*pl*) vrijednosni papiri **Security Council** Vijeće sigurnosti **security risk** potencijalni izdajnik

sedan /sɪ'dæn/ *n US* limuzina

sedate /sɪ'deɪt/ *adj* miran

sedative /'sedətɪv/ *n* sedativ, sredstvo za umirenje

sedition /sɪ'dɪʃən/ *n leg* pobuna (protiv ustavnog poretka)

seduce /sɪ'dju:s/ *vt* 1 zavesti 2 (into) navesti/namamiti na što **~r** *n* zavodnik **seduction** /sɪ'dʌkʃn/ *n* 1 zavođenje 2 čar **seductive** *adj* zavodljiv, zavodnički

see /si:/ *vi,vt irreg* 1 vidjeti 2 proći, proživjeti **~ better days** vidjeti boljih dana ~ **action** iskusiti borbu **3** uvidjeti, shvatiti ~ **reason** prihvatiti istinu **4** (sth as) gledati na, smatrati **do as one ~s** *fit* postupati po vlastitom nahođenju **5** zamisliti **6** (sb) posjetiti, otići kod, vidjeti se s kim **7** primiti **8** otpratiti **9** biti svjedokom *fig* ~ **eye to eye** (with) slagati se s ~ **red** pobjesniti ~ **the colour of sb's money** dobiti dokaz da će netko platiti ~ **the light a.** prosvijetliti se b. ugledati svjetlo dana *I am ~ing things* privida mi se ~ **about** dogovoriti se **We'll ~ about that** još ćemo vidjeti ~ **a lot/nothing of** viđati koga često/uopće ne viđati ~ **sb off** otpratiti ~ **through** prozreti ~ **sb through sth** izvući, provući se ~ **through** *adj* proziran ~ **to** pregledati ~ **to it** (that) pobrini se (da) ~**ing** *conj* (~ing that) budući da

seed /si:d/ *n* **1** sjeme; sjemenka **2** *mod* sjemenski **3** nositelj turnira

seedy /'si:dɪ/ *adj* zapušten, otrcan

seek /si:k/ *vi,vt irreg* **1** (after/for) tragati za, biti u potrazi za **2** nastojati

seem /si:m/ *vi* činiti se, doimati se **it ~s to me** čini mi se ~**ing** *adj* prividan ~**ingly** *adv* **1** kako se čini **2** naoko

seen *v irreg* → **see**

seep /si:p/ *vi* probijati (tekućina)

seesaw /'si:sɔ:/ *n* klackalica • *vi* kolebati se

seethe /si:ð/ *vi* kiptjeti, ključati (+ *fig*)

segment /'segmənt/ *n* **1** segment **2** kriška

segregate /'segrɪgeɪt/ *vt* segregirati, odijeliti ~**d** *adj* samo za bijelce/crnce i sl. **segregation** *n* segregacija

seismic /'saɪzmɪk/ *adj* seizmički, trusni **seismology** /saɪz'mɒlədʒɪ/ *n* seizmologija

seize /si:z/ *vt* **1** zaplijeniti **2** osvojiti **3** zgrabiti ~ **the opportunity** iskoristiti priliku **4** **be ~d with** biti obuzet čime ~ **on/upon** ohrabručke prihvatiti **seizure** /'si:ʒə(r)/ *n* **1** zapljena **2** napad

seldom /'seldəm/ *adv* rijetko

select /sɪ'lekt/ *vt* odabrati • *adj* probran, ekskluzivan ~**ion** *n* izbor ~**ive** *adj* **1** izbirljiv **2** selektivan ~**or** *n*

izbornik

self /self/ *n* svoje ja, svoja osobnost **one's old ~** onaj stari **one's true ~** prava priroda ~**ish** *adj* sebičan ~**less** *adj* nesebičan ~**same** *adj* isti taj

self- *prefix* samo-, auto- ~**absorbed** *adj* zaokupljen samim sobom ~**appointed** *adj* samozvani ~**assertive** *adj* prodoran ~**assured** *adj* samopouzdan ~**centered** *adj* samoživ ~**confessed** *adj* po vlastitom priznanju ~**confident** *adj* samopouzdan ~**congratulatory** *adj* samozadovoljan ~**conscious** *adj* **1** smeten, nelagodan **2** svjestan ~**contained** *adj* samodovoljan ~**defeating** *adj* kontraproduktivan ~**defence** *n* samoobrana ~**denial** *n* samoprijegor ~**determination** *n* samoodređenje ~**doubt** *n* nesigurnost ~**drive** *adj* bez vozača ~**educated** *adj* samouk ~**employed** *adj* privatnik ~**esteem** *n* samopoštovanje ~**explanatory** *adj* jasan ~**government** *n* samouprava ~**importance** *n* umišljenost ~**indulgence** *n* ugađanje samom sebi ~**interest** *n* vlastiti interes ~**made man** čovjek koji uspjeh duguje samo sebi ~**pity** *n* samosažaljenje ~**possessed** *adj* hladnokrvan, sabran ~**preservation** *n* samoočuvanje ~**raising flour** brašno s praškom za pecivo ~**reliant** *adj* koji se oslanja na vlastite snage ~**respect** *n* samopoštovanje, dostojanstvo ~**seeking** *adj* sebičan ~**service** *adj* sa samoposluživanjem ~**styled** *adj* samozvani ~**supporting** *adj* neovisan (financijski) ~**will** *n* samovolja

sell /sel/ *vi,vt irreg* **1** (sth to sb for sth) prodati **2** (at/for) stajati, prodavati se po **3** (0) prodavati se **4** trgovati **5** nasamariti ~**by date** datum upotrebljivosti ~ **sth/sb short** podcijeniti ~ **off** rasprodavati ~ **out a.** rasprodati **b.** *fig* prodati se ~**out** *n* **1** rasprodani koncert/utakmica i sl. **2** izdaja *fig*

sellotape /'seləteɪp/ *n* TM selotejp *coll* • *vt* zalijepiti selotejpom

selves /selvz/ *pl* → **self**

semaphore /'seməfɔ:(r)/ *n* željeznički

signal
semblance /'sembləns/ *n* privid
semen /'si:mən/ *n* sjeme, sperma
semester /si'mestə(r)/ *n* semestar
semi /'semi/ *n* 1 *GB* polusamostojeća kuća 2 *US* tegljač
semi- *prefix* polu- **~automatic** *adj* poluautomatski **~circle** *n* polukrug **~colon** *n* točka-zarez **~detached** *adj* naslonjen, prizidan **~final** *n* poluzavršnica
seminal /'seminl/ *adj* prekretni
seminar /'semina:(r)/ *n* seminar
seminary /'seminəri/ *n* sjemenište
semolina /,semə'li:nə/ *n* pšenična krupica; griz *coll*
senate /'senit/ *n* senat **senator** *n* senator
send /send/ *vt,vi irreg* poslati, odaslati **~ sb to school** dati koga na školovanje **~ sth flying** rasprišiti **~ sb reeling** izbaciti iz ravnoteže **~ sb to sleep** uspavati **~ forth buds** pupati **~ one's love** pozdraviti **~ word/a message** poručiti **~ sb packing** otprašiti koga **~ away/off** to poslati kamo **~ away for** naručiti **~ off** a. poslati b. izbaciti iz igre
senile /'si:nail/ *adj* senilan **senility** /si'niləti/ *n* senilnost
senior /'si:niə(r)/ *n, adj* 1 stariji 2 viši 3 student na zadnjoj godini 4 *US* maturant **~ citizen** umirovljenik **S~ Stariji**
sensation /sen'seiʃn/ *n* 1 osjet, osjećaj 2 senzacija **~al** *adj* senzacionalan
sense /sens/ *n* 1 razum, pamet 2 (of) osjet 3 (of) osjećaj za 4 (of) slutnja, osjećaj 5 značenje, smisao **no ~ in** nema smisla **what is the ~** ima li smisla **make ~ a.** nešto značiti, imati smisla **b.** biti mudro **make ~ out of** shvatiti **in a ~** u određenom smislu 6 *pl* pamet **be out of/take leave of one's ~s** poludjeti • *vt* osjetiti, naslutiti, otkriti **~less** *adj* bezuman **sensibility** /,sensə'biləti/ *n* tankoćutnost 2 (to) osjetljivost na **sensible** /'sensəbl/ *adj* razuman **sensitive** /'sensitiv/ *adj* 1 (0/to/about) osjetljiv (na) **sensory** /'sensəri/ *adj* osjetilan **sensual** /'senʃuəl/ *adj* puten, čulan **sensuous**

/'senʃuəs/ *adj* čulni
sent *v irreg* → **send**
sentence (1) /'sentəns/ *n* rečenica
sentence (2) *n* kazna **prison ~** zatvorska kazna **death ~** smrtna kazna **life ~** doživotni zatvor **pass/pronounce ~** (on sb) osuditi koga • *vt* (to) osuditi na
sentiment /'sentimənt/ *n* 1 sentimentalnost, osjećaji 2 osjećaj **strong public ~** uznemirenje javnosti **~al** *adj* sentimentalan
sentry /'sentri/ *n* stražar **~ box** stražarnica
separate /'sepəreit/ *vi,vt* 1 odijeliti, razdvojiti, dijeliti 2 (up/into) podijeliti na 3 (from) odijeliti 4 rastati se • /'seprət/ *adj* 1 različit **go one's ~ ways** raziči se 2 zaseban, poseban 3 odvojen **~ly** *adv* odvojeno • **~s** *n pl* kompleti (ženske odjeće) **separation** /,sepə'reiʃn/ *n* 1 (of) razdvajanje 2 (from) odvojenost 3 rastava **separatism** *n* /'sepərətizəm/ separatizam
septic /'septik/ *adj* zaražen, gnojan **~ tank** septička jama
September /sep'tembə(r)/ *n* rujan
sepulchral /si'pʌlkrəl/ *adj* grobni
sequel /'si:kwəl/ *n* nastavak
sequence /'si:kwəns/ *n* 1 (of) niz 2 slijed **in ~** po redu 3 sekvenca **~ of tenses** *gram* slaganje vremena
sequin /'si:kin/ *n* šljokica **~ed** *adj* posut šljokicama
serene /si'ri:n/ *adj* miran, vedar **serenity** /si'renəti/ *n* mirnoća, vedrina
serf /sɜ:f/ *n* kmet **~dom** *n* kmetstvo
sergeant /'sa:dʒənt/ *n* 1 *mil* narednik 2 policajac
serial /'siəriəl/ *n* serija • *adj* serijski **~killer** *n* višestruki ubojica **series** /'siəri:z/ *n* 1 niz, serija 2 biblioteka
serious /'siəriəs/ *adj* ozbiljan **be ~ about sth** misliti što ozbiljno, doista namjeravati
sermon /'sɜ:mən/ *n* (on) propovijed (+ *fig*) **~ize** *vi fig* propovati
serpent /'sɜ:pənt/ *n* guja (+ *fig*) **~ine** *adj* zavojit
servant /'sɜ:vənt/ *n* 1 sluga 2 službenik

serve /sɜ:v/ *vi,vt* **1** (in/on/under/as) vršiti službu, raditi (za) **2** poslužiti, služiti (što/koga/čime/kako) **3** (as) poslužiti kao **4** (for) poslužiti komu **5** odslužiti **6** *sport* servirati **~s you right** pravo ti budi • *n sport* servis

service /'sɜ:vɪs/ *n* **1** posluga, usluga **2** služba **railway ~** linija **secret ~** tajna služba **~s** vojna služba **active ~(s)** djelatna služba **3** usluga ~ **industry** uslužna djelatnost **be in ~** koristiti se **4** zasluga **do sb a great ~** učiniti kome veliku uslugu **5** služba Božja, obred **6** servis ~ **charge** napojnica **~man/~woman** *n* vojna osoba ~ **road** lokalna cesta ~ **station** automehaničarska radionica • *vt* servisirati • *adj* za zaposlene

serviette /ˌsɜ:vɪ'et/ *n* ubrus

serving /'sɜ:vɪŋ/ *n* porcija

servitude /'sɜ:vɪtju:d/ *n* ropstvo

sesame /'sesəmɪ/ *n* sezam

session /'seʃn/ *n* **1** zasjedanje **be in ~** zasjedati **2** sesija

set /set/ *vt,vi* **1** staviti ~ **down** spustiti ~ **eyes on sb** ugledati koga **2** smjestiti **3** ~ **free** osloboditi ~ **right** ispraviti ~ **fire to** zapaliti ~ **sb thinking** nagnati na razmišljanje **4** namjestiti ~ **the table** prostrijeti stol ~ **hair** napraviti frizuru **5** slagati (knjigu) **6** odrediti, postaviti, zadati ~ **sb to work** dati komu posao **7** umetnuti **8** stisnuti se, skrutnuti se, ukočiti se ~ **one's teeth** stisnuti zube ~ **one's heart on** žarko željeti **9** zalaziti, zaći ~ **about** baciti se na (posao/koga) ~ **apart from** razlikovati ~ **aside** staviti na stranu ~ **back** kočiti **~back** *n* zapreka, nedostatak ~ **down a.** iskrcati b. odrediti ~ **in** nastupiti ~ **off a.** otputiti se b. detonirati c. uzrokovati d. isticati ~ **on** nahuckati ~ **out a.** rasporediti b. započeti c. izložiti ~ **up a.** postaviti b. ustanoviti, uspostaviti c. opskrbiti d. smjestiti zamku **~up** *n* **a.** organizacija **b.** namještaljka ~ **up as a.** započeti posao **b.** postavljati se • *adj* **1** smješten **2** fiksan **3** obvezatan **be ~ on/upon** čvrsto odlučiti ~ **against** odlučno protiv **4** spreman, gotov **it is ~ to fall** najvjerojatnije će pasti **5** namješten **6** krut • *n* **1** set, komplet, servis, garnitura, zbirka, serija ~ **of circumstances** splet okolnosti ~ **of problems** zbir problema **2** aparat **TV ~** televizor **3** scena ~ **designer** scenograf **4** *film* lokacija **5** frizura **6** društvo **7** stvrdnjavanje, zgušnjavanje **8** držanje, položaj

setsquare /'set skweə(r)/ *n GB* trokut

settee /se'ti:/ *n* sofa

setting /'setɪŋ/ *n* **1** zalazak **2** okolica, pozadina **3** mjesto radnje **4** okvir

settle /'setl/ *vi,vt* **1** smjestiti ~ **back** zavaliti se **2** (on/over/upon) slegnuti se; sjatiti se; spustiti se na, zavladati čime **3** (down) smiriti se; posvetiti se **4** dogovoriti, uglaviti **5** urediti, srediti, izgladiti ~ **the dispute out of court** postići izvansudsku nagodbu **6** naseliti (se) **7** platiti, namiriti **8** slegnuti se ~ **for** zadovoljiti se ~ **into** naviknuti se ~ **on/upon** dogovoriti se, nagoditi se ~ **up** platiti **~d** *adj* ustaljen **~ment** *n* **1** dogovor, nagodba, razrješenje krize **2** naselje **3** naseljavanje **4** namirenje, isplata **~r** *n* doseljenik

seven /'sevn/ *num* sedam (7) **~teen** *num* sedamnaest (17) **~th** *num ord* sedmi **~th heaven** sedmo nebo **~ty** *num* sedamdeset (70)

sever /'sevə(r)/ *vt,vi* **1** presjeći, odsjeći **2** *fig* prekinuti (se) **~ance** *n* prekid **~ance pay** odšteta zbog gubitka posla

several /'sevrəl/ *pron* više, nekoliko

severe /sɪ'vɪə(r)/ *adj* **1** težak, ozbiljan **2** oštar **3** strog

sew /səʊ/ *vt,vi irreg* šivati, sašiti ~ **up 1** zašiti **2** *fig* srediti **~ing machine** šivaći stroj

sewage /'sju:ɪdʒ/ *n* otpad iz kanalizacije ~ **disposal system** kanalizacija

sewer /'sju:ə(r)/ *n* kanalizacija **~age** *n* kanalizacija

sex /seks/ *n* **1** spol **2** seks, spolno općenje **have ~** spolno općiti **3** *mod* spolni ~ **appeal** seksepil **~ism** *n* spolna diskriminacija **~ual** *adj* spolni, seksualni **~ual intercourse** spolni odnos **~uality** *n* spolnost **~y** *adj* 1 seksi 2 raspoložen za seks

shabby /ˈʃæbɪ/ *adj* 1 otrcan 2 nizak *fig*

shack (1) /ʃæk/ *n* koliba

shack (2) *vi* **~ up with** *coll* živjeti zajedno

shackle /ˈʃækl/ *n* **~s** *pl* lanci • *vt* okovati

shade /ʃeɪd/ *n* 1 hlad 2 sjenilo 3 sjenčanje 4 nijansa 5 **~s** *pl* tamne naočale **put in(to) ~** zasjeniti • *vt, vi* 1 (from) zasjeniti (od) 2 osjenčati 3 pretapati se **shady** *adj* 1 hladovit 2 sumnjiv

shadow /ˈʃædəʊ/ *n* sjena, sjenka **cast a/one's ~** bacati sjenu (+ *fig*) **be only a ~ of sb/sth** biti samo sjenka čega **not a ~ of doubt** ni najmanja sumnja **~ cabinet** *pol* vlada u sjeni **~y** *adj* 1 misteriozan 2 sjenovit

shaft /ʃɑːft/ *n* 1 držak (strelice, čekića i sl.) 2 osovina 3 rov, hodnik, cijev 4 zraka **get the ~** *sl* nadrapati • *vt sl* zaribati

shag (1) /ʃæg/ *n* duhan za motanje

shag (2) *vt tab* ševiti *tab*

shaggy /ˈʃægɪ/ *adj* kudrav, čupav

shah /ʃɑː/ *n* (iranski) šah

shake /ʃeɪk/ *vt, vi irreg* 1 (with) tresti (se) (od), protresti **~ oneself free** izmaći se **~ one's fist** prijetiti šakama **~ hands** rukovati se **~ one's head** odmahnuti glavom 2 (up) *fig* potresti 3 pokolebati **~sth/sb off** riješiti se koga/čega **~ out** istresti **~ up** prodrmati *fig* **~up** *n* reorganizacija • *n* 1 tresenje 2 *coll* frape 3 **~s** *pl* drhtavica **be no great ~s at/as** ne biti baš neki **~r** *n* posuda za miješanje **shaky** *adj* 1 potresen 2 nesiguran, klimav

shaken *v irreg* → **shake**

shall /ʃæl/ *v aux* 1 koristi se za tvorbu futura u 1. licu *sing* i *pl* (I, we) samo u vrlo formalnom jeziku → **will** 2 *leg* morati **~ not** ne smjeti

shallow /ˈʃæləʊ/ *adj* plitak (+ *fig*) **~s** *n pl* plićak

sham /ʃæm/ *n* prijevara, krivotvorina • *adj* lažan • *vi, vi* pretvarati se

shambles /ˈʃæmblz/ *n sing coll* zbrka, kaos, nered

shambolic /ʃæmˈbɒlɪk/ *adj coll* u pot-

punom kaosu

shame /ʃeɪm/ *n* 1 sram, stid **~ on you!** srami se! **have no ~** nemati srama 2 sramota 3 šteta • *vt* 1 osramotiti 2 posramiti **~faced** *adj* posramljen **~ful** *adj* sramotan **~less** *adj* besraman

shampoo /ʃæmˈpuː/ *n* šampon • *vt* šamponirati

shamrock /ˈʃæmrɒk/ *n* irska trolisna djetelina

shank /ʃæŋk/ *n* 1 os, ravni dio 2 koljenica (meso)

shan't /ʃɑːnt/ = **shall not**

shanty /ˈʃæntɪ/ *n* stračara **~ town** slam

shape /ʃeɪp/ *n* 1 oblik, obličje 2 kondicija, stanje **knock/lick into ~** dotjerati (u red) **take ~** poprimiti oblik, oblikovati se **~less** *adj* bezobličan • *vt* uobličiti, formirati **~ up a.** razvijati se **b.** poboljšati svoje ponašanje **~d** *adj* (like) u obliku (čega) **~ly** *adj* skladan

shard /ʃɑːd/ *n* krhotina

share /ʃeə(r)/ *n* 1 (in/of) dio (čega), udio (u čemu) **have no ~ in** ne sudjelovati u **go ~s** podijeliti troškove 2 (in) dionice (čega) • *vi, vt* (in/with/among/between) podijeliti, razdijeliti, dijeliti (na/s/među) **~ and ~ alike** pravedno podijeliti **~ holder** *n* dioničar

shark /ʃɑːk/ *n* (*pl* ~/~s)1 morski pas 2 *fig* (loan ~) zelenaš

sharp /ʃɑːp/ *adj* 1 oštar, zašiljen 2 nagao 3 oštar, jasan, izoštren 4 oštar, strog 5 *mus* povišen 6 šminkerski **~ end** *coll* zeznuti dio **~ practice** nepoštenje **~shooter** *n* snajperist • *adv* 1 točno **look ~** požuriti 2 *mus* previsoko **~en** *vt* zašiljiti, zaoštriti **~ener** *n* šiljilo

shatter /ˈʃætə(r)/ *vi, vt* 1 razbiti (se), razmrskati (se) 2 *fig* propasti 3 uzdrmati, potresti **~proof** *adj* otporan na udarce

shave /ʃeɪv/ *vt, vi* 1 brijati (se) 2 sastrugati; skinuti (+ *fig*) 3 okrznuti • *n* **have a ~** obrijati se **close ~ a.** izbrijavanje **b.** promašaj za dlaku **~n** *adj* izbrijan **~r** *n* brijaći aparat **shaving foam** pjena za brijanje

shawl /ʃɔ:l/ *n* šal

she /ʃi:/ *pron* ona

she- *prefix* označava ženku

sheaf /ʃi:f/ *n* svežanj

shear /ʃɪə(r)/ *vt,vi irreg* 1 strići (ovce) 2 lišiti

shears /ʃɪəz/ *n pl* škarc

sheath /ʃi:θ/ *n* 1 korice 2 kondom ~**ing** *n* oplata ~**e** /ʃi:ð/ *vt* 1 spremiti u korice 2 obložiti

shed (1) /ʃed/ *n* spremište, šupa

shed (2) *vt irreg* 1 gubiti, odbacivati (lišće, rogove i sl.) 2 ~ **tears** liti suzc ~ **light on** rasvijetliti (+ *fig*) ~ **blood** prolijevati krv

sheen /ʃi:n/ *n* sjaj

sheep /ʃi:p/ *n (pl* ~) ovca (+ *fig*) ~**dog** pas ovčar ~**ish** *adj* smeten

sheer /ʃɪə(r)/ *adj* 1 čisti 2 okomit 3 proziran

sheet /ʃi:t/ *n* 1 plahta 2 ploča (metala); list (papira); komad (tkanine); ploha ~ **iron** željezni lim ~**s of rain** pljusak

shelf /ʃelf/ *n* polica ~ **life** trajnost **off the** ~ standardni **on the** ~ odbačen; prestara za udaju

shell /ʃel/ *n* 1 ljuska, ljuštura (+ *fig*) ~**fish** *n* školjke i rakovi 2 granata, mina **be** ~**shocked** prolupati *sl* • *vt* 1 ljuštiti 2 (0/at) granatirati ~ **out** *coll* ispljunuti (novac)

shelter /ʃeltə(r)/ *n* sklonište; utočište; zaklon **bus** ~ nadstrešnica **take** ~ skloniti se • *vt,vi* 1 (from) štititi, zaklanjati 2 sklanjati se ~**ed** *adj* zaštićen; pod staklenim zvonom *fig*

shelve /ʃelv/ *vt* 1 spremiti na policu 2 odložiti

shepherd /ʃepəd/ *n* pastir • *vt* voditi, tjerati ~**ess** *n* pastirica ~'**s pie** pita od mesa i krumpira

sheriff /ʃerɪf/ *n* šerif

sherry /ʃerɪ/ *n* šeri ¶ = šeri brendi

shield /ʃi:ld/ *n* 1 štit 2 štitnik • *vt* (from) (za)štititi

shift /ʃɪft/ *vi,vt* 1 (po)maknuti 2 gnijezditi se 3 prebaciti 4 skrenuti 5 ukloniti ~ **gears** mijenjati brzine • *n* 1 pomak, promjena smjera, otklon 2 smjena 3 jednostavna haljina ~ **key** tipka za velika slova ~ **stick** mjenjač ~**less** *adj* lijen ~**y** *adj* prepreden

shilling /ʃɪlɪŋ/ *n* šiling ¶ nije u uporabi od 1971.

shimmer /ʃɪmə(r)/ *vi* ljeskati se • *n* ljeskanje

shin (1) /ʃɪn/ *n* goljenica ~**bone** cjevanica

shin (2) *vi* ~ **up** uzverati se ~ **down** kliznuti niz

shine /ʃaɪn/ *vi,vt irreg* 1 sijati (se), svijetliti, presijavati se; blistati (+ *fig*) 2 obasjati, uperiti (svjetlo) 3 laštiti • *n* sjaj **shiny** *adj* sjajan, blistav

shingle (1) /ʃɪŋgl/ *n* šljunak

shingle (2) *n* šindra

ship /ʃɪp/ *n* brod • 1 prevoziti brodom 2 slati, otpremiti ~**builder** brodograditelj(ska tvrtka) ~**ment** *n* 1 pošiljka 2 otprema ~**owner** *n* brodovlasnik ~**per** *n* prijevoznik, špediter ~**ping** *n* 1 promet brodova 2 brodovlje ~**wreck** *n* brodolom doživjeti brodolom ~**yard** *n* brodogradilište

shirk /ʃɜ:k/ *vi,vt* zabušavati

shirt /ʃɜ:t/ *n* košulja ~**front** *n* prednjica **in (one's)** ~**sleeves** samo u košulji

shit /ʃɪt/ *vi,vt tab* srati, posrati **se** ~ **oneself** usrati se (+ *fig*) • *n* 1 govno 2 sranje (+ *fig*) **I don't give a** ~ jebe mi se **no** ~ zezaš se ~**s** *n pl* sračka ~**ty** *adj* bezvezan ~**ty car** sranje od auta

shiver /ʃɪvə(r)/ *vi* (with) tresti se, drhtati (od) • *n* drhtaj ~**s** *pl* drhtavica **it gives me the** ~**s** od toga mc hvata jeza

shoal (1) /ʃəʊl/ *n* plićak, prud

shoal (2) *n* jato (riba/ljudi *fig*)

shock /ʃɒk/ *n* 1 prepast, šok 2 udarac ~ **treatment** terapija elektrošokovima ~ **troops** udarni odred ~ **wave** udarni val • *vt* 1 šokirati, užasnuti 2 udariti (struja) ~ **absorber** amortizer ~**ed** *adj* zaprepašten ~**ing** *adj* šokantan, sablažnjiv ~**ing pink** žarko ružičast ~**proof** otporan na udarce

shoe /ʃu:/ *n* 1 cipela 2 (**horse**~) potkova ~**lace/**~**string** *n* vezica ~**shine** čišćenje cipela **in sb's** ~**s** na nečijem mjestu **fill sb's** ~**s** zauzeti čije mjesto • *vt* potkivati

shone *v irreg* → **shine**

shoo /ʃu:/ *int* iš! • *vt* tjerati

shook *v irreg* → **shake**

shoot /ʃuːt/ *vt,vi irreg* **1** (at) pucati (na), (is)pucati; ispaliti (+ *fig*), dobaciti **2** pogoditi ~ **dead** ubiti ~ **down** srušiti **3** loviti **4** (pro)šišati ~**ing pain** prodorna bol **5** snimati **6** pupati **7** fiksati se • *n* izdanak ~**ing** *n* **1** pucnjava **2** atentat ~**ing star** zvijezda padalica ~**out** *n* obračun (pištoljima)

shop /ʃɒp/ *n* **1** prodavaonica **2** radionica **3** posao **set up** ~ početi posao **talk** ~ razgovarati o poslu • *vi,vt* kupovati ~ **assistant** prodavač ~**floor** radionica, proizvodna hala ~**keeper** *n* trgovac ~**lift** *vi* krasti po dućanima ~**per** *n* kupac ~**ping** *n* **1** kupovina **2** kupljene stvari ~**ping centre** trgovački centar

shore (1) /ʃɔː(r)/ *n* **1** obala **2** kopno

shore (2) *vt* (up) poduprijeti

shorn *v irreg* → **shear**

short /ʃɔːt/ *adj* **1** nizak **2** kratak **be** ~ **for** biti skraćeno od **at** ~ **notice** u zadnji tren, bez najave **in the** ~ **run** na kraći rok **3** otresit ~**tempered** *adj* razdražljiv **4** prhak **be** ~ **of** nemati dosta **be in** ~ **supply** manjkati **be** ~ **on** nemati baš puno • *adv* naglo run ~ ponestajati **cut sth** ~ naglo prekinuti **for** ~ skraćeno **in** ~ ukratko ~**age** *n* nedostatak, nestašica ~**bread** *n* čajni keks ~**change** *vt* **a.** uzvratiti premalo **b.** *coll* prevariti ~ **circuit** kratki spoj ~**circuit** *vi,vt* uzrokovati kratki spoj, pregorjeti ~**coming** *n* nedostatak ~ **cut** prečac ~**en** *vi,vt* skratiti ~**ening** *n* masnoća ~**fall** *n* manjak ~**hand** *n* stenografija ~**haul** *adj* na kratke pruge **be** ~**listed** *vt* biti u najužem izboru ~**lived** *adj* kratka vijeka ~**ly** *adj* uskoro ~**range** *adj* **a.** kratkoročni **b.** kratkog dometa ~**s** *n pl* kratke hlačice ~**sighted** *adj* kratkovidan (+ *fig*) ~ **story** novela ~**term** *adj* kratkoročni

shot (1) *v irreg* → **shoot**

shot (2) /ʃɒt/ *n* **1** pucanj **fire a** ~ opaliti ~**gun** *n* sačmarica, dvocijevka **2** *sport* udarac **3** strijelac **4** (at) pokušaj **5** sačma **6** fotografija; kadar **7** *coll* injekcija **8** gutljaj alkoholnog pića ~ **glass** čašica

should /ʃʊd/ *modal v* **1 I** ~ trebala bih *you shouldn't* ne bi smio *they* ~ *be here by now* trebali bi stići svaki čas *they* ~ *have been here by now* trebali su već stići **2** ~ *you leave, we would have to find somebody else* ako odeš, moramo naći nekog drugog

shoulder /ˈʃəʊldə(r)/ *n* rame ~ **blade** lopatica ~ **strap** naramenica ~ **to** ~ rame uz rame • *vt* **1** natovariti na rame **2** preuzeti na sebe **3** probiti se

shout /ʃaʊt/ *vi,vt* vikati, izvikivati, derati se ~ **at sb** izdirati se na koga ~ **from the rooftops** razglasiti ~ **down** nadvikati, nadglasati • *n* krik

shove /ʃʌv/ *vi,vt* **1** gurati (se) **2** zgurati ~ **aside** odgurnuti ~ **around** naređivati komu ~ **off** otisnuti se ~ **off!** gubi se! • *n* guranje **give a** ~ gurnuti

shovel /ˈʃʌvl/ *n* lopata • *vi,vt* zgrtati ~ **away** razgrtati

show /ʃəʊ/ *vt,vi irreg* **1** (sth to sb) pokazati (što komu); pokazivati (**just**) **go to** ~ (samo) pokazivati **2** vidjeti se **3** prikazivati se **4** izlagati **5** pojaviti se **6** (to) odvesti ~ **someone to the door** pokazati kome vrata **have nothing to** ~ **for** nemati se čime pohvaliti ~ **around** provesti po ~ **in** uvesti ~ **off** praviti se važan ~ **sth off** pohvaliti se čime ~**off** *n* preserant *coll vulg* ~ **out** ispratiti ~ **up** pojaviti se • *n* **1** predstava **run the** ~ *fig* biti glavni **2** emisija **3** izložba **4** izljev ~ **of strength** demonstracija sile **make a** ~ **of** hiniti što **5** izvedba, igra ~ **business** (~**biz** *coll*) industrija zabave, estrada ~**case** *n* **a.** vitrina **b.** *fig* prilika za izlaganje ~**down** *n* obračun ~ **jumping** preskakanje prepona ~**man** *n* predstavljač, zabavljač ~**piece** *n* uzoran primjerak ~**room** *n* izložbeni prostor ~**y** *adj* upadljiv, pun lažnog sjaja

shower /ˈʃaʊə(r)/ *n* **1** pljusak **2** tuš **3** tuširanje **have/take a** ~ otuširati se • *vi,vt* **1** pljuštati **2** prskati, zaliti **3** *fig* obasuti **4** tuširati se

shown *v irreg* → **show**

shrank *v irreg* → **shrink**

shrapnel /ˈʃræpnl/ *n* **a piece of** ~ šrapnel

shred /ʃred/ *vt* kosati, rezati, sjeći • *n* komadićak, mrva **there is not a ~ of** nema ni traga **tear to ~s** razderati na komadiće **~der** *n* 1 ribež 2 rezač dokumenata

shrew /ʃru:/ *n* goropadnica

shrewd /ʃru:d/ *adj* pametan, mudar, lukav

shriek /ʃri:k/ *vi,vt* kričati, vrištati

shrill /ʃrɪl/ *adj* 1 kreštav, prodoran 2 *fig* glasan

shrimp /ʃrɪmp/ *n* račić

shrine /ʃraɪn/ *n* hram

shrink /ʃrɪŋk/ *vi,vt irreg* 1 smanjiti (se), stisnuti (se) 2 povući se **~ from** prezati pred (čim) • *n coll* psihoanalitičar **~age** *n* smanjenje

shrivel /ʃrɪvl/ *vi,vt* navorati (se), smežurati (se), stisnuti (se)

shroud /ʃraʊd/ *n* 1 mrtvački pokrov 2 *fig* veo • *vt* **be ~ed in** biti zavijen u, biti skriven u

Shrove Tuesday /ʃrəʊv 'tju:zdi/ *n* fašnik, mesopust

shrub /ʃrʌb/ *n* grm **~bery** *n* grmlje, živica

shrug /ʃrʌg/ *vi,vt* slegnuti (ramenima) **~ off** prijeći preko • *n* slijeganje ramenima

shrunk *v irreg* → **shrink**

shrunken /ʃrʌŋkən/ *adj* smežuran, smanjen

shudder /ʃʌdə(r)/ *vi* (at) stresti se, zadrhtati • *n* drhtaj, potres

shuffle /ʃʌfl/ *vi,vt* 1 miješati (karte) 2 premetati 3 vući noge, vući se **~ off this mortal coil** *coll* otići na drugi svijet • *n* 1 miješanje (karata) 2 težak hod

shun /ʃʌn/ *vt* izbjegavati što, kloniti se čega

shunt /ʃʌnt/ *vt* 1 ranžirati, skrenuti na sporedni kolosijek 2 *fig* premjestiti (na manje važno mjesto) **~er** *n* skretničar

shush /ʃʊʃ/ *vt* ušutkati **~!** tiho!

shut /ʃʌt/ *vt,vi irreg* 1 zatvoriti 2 začepiti **~ away** izolirati **~ down** zatvoriti (se), prestati s radom **~down** *n* prekid rada **~ off** isključiti (se), zatvoriti (dovod) **~ off from** odsjeći od **~ out** ne pustiti unutra,

spriječiti što da uđe/prodre, isključiti **~ up a.** *coll* začepiti (gubicu) **b.** zatvoriti (se)

shutter /ʃʌtə(r)/ *n* 1 zatvarač fotoaparata **~ speed** ekspozicija 2 roleta, rebrenica

shuttle /ʃʌtl/ *n* 1 (**~ service**) česta redovna linija 2 čunak • *vt* prevesti

shuttlecock /ʃʌtlkɒk/ *n* loptica za badminton

shy /ʃaɪ/ *adj* stidljiv, plah **once bitten twice ~** tko se jednom opeče i na hladno puše **fight ~ of** izbjegavati • *vi* **~ at** poplašiti se koga/čega **~ away from** izbjegavati

Siamese /ˌsaɪə'mi:z/ *adj* sijamski **~ twins** sijamski blizanci

sibling /ˈsɪblɪŋ/ *n form* brat/sestra

sick /sɪk/ *adj* 1 bolestan **the ~** bolesnici **~ leave** bolovanje *I'm ~ and tired* dosta mi je, dozlogrdilo mi je 2 koji osjeća mučninu *she felt ~* bilo joj je mučno *it makes me ~ fig* gadi mi se 3 **be ~** *GB* povratiti • **~ up** *vt* povratiti **~en** *vt,vi* 1 izazivati mučninu *it ~ens me* smuči mi se od toga 2 razboljeti se **~ening** *adj* odvratan, grozan **~ly** *adj* 1 boležljiv, slab 2 koji izaziva mučninu **~ness** *n* 1 bolest 2 mučnina

side /saɪd/ *n* 1 strana **on every ~/on all ~s** sa svih strana **on the ~** sa strane **this ~ of** s ove strane **~ by ~** jedan uz drugoga **take ~s** (with) stati na čiju stranu **on the high** (etc.) **~** prilično visok (i sl.) **to be on the safe ~** za svaku sigurnost 2 slabina 3 polovica • *vi* (with) stati na čiju stranu • *adj* postranični, sa strane; sporedan **~n** *n pl* osobno naoružanje **~burns** *pl* zalisci **~car** prikolica motocikla **~dish/order** prilog jelu **~ effect** popratna pojava **~line a.** sporedno zanimanje **b.** *sport* aut-linija; *fig* aut **~long** *adj, adv* kos; iskosa **~on** neizravan **~saddle** žensko sedlo **~show** sporedna (cirkuska) predstava; *fig* igrarija, nešto nevažno **~splitting** *adj* urnebesno smiješan **~step** *vi,vt* izbjeći **~track** *vt* skrenuti o *n* digresija **~walk** *US* pločnik **~ways** *adv* postrance, ustranu

sidle /ˈsaɪdl/ *vi* plašljivo/stidljivo/oprezno prići

siege /siːdʒ/ n mil okruženje, opsada **lay ~ to** dovesti u okruženje **raise a ~** prekinuti opsadu

sieve /sɪv/ n 1 sito 2 cjediljka • vt prosijati; procijediti

sift /sɪft/ vt,vi 1 prosijati 2 (through) pomno pretražiti/provjeriti 3 (out, from) odvojiti

sigh /saɪ/ vi uzdahnuti, uzdisati • n uzdah

sight /saɪt/ n 1 vid; prizor; pogled **at/on ~** odmah **shoot at/on ~** pucati bez upozorenja **at the ~ of** ugledavši **by ~** iz viđenja **catch ~ of** ugledati **keep in ~** držati na oku **lose ~ of sb** izgubiti iz vida **at first ~** na prvi pogled **come into ~** pojaviti se **in ~** na vidiku 2 **~s** znamenitosti **~seeing** razgledavanje znamenitosti 3 **~s** ciljnik; optika **set one's ~s on sth** postaviti si za cilj • vt ugledati, opaziti

sign /saɪn/ n znak, oznaka, predznak, znamenje, upozorenje **there's no ~ of him** nema mu ni traga (ni glasa) **~post** putokaz **~ language** jezik gluhonijemih • vt,vi potpisati (se) **~ away** službeno se odreći **~ off** završiti emitiranje/pismo **~ on/up a.** zaposliti **b.** GB prijaviti se na burzu **~ on the dotted line** brzo i bezuvjetno potpisati **~ over** pripisati **~ to** dati znak **~atory** /ˈsaɪɡnətrɪ/ n potpisnik **signature** /ˈsɪɡnɒtʃə(r)/ n potpis

signal /ˈsɪɡnəl/ n signal, znak • vi,vt 1 dati znak, signalizirati 2 označiti • adj form znakovit

signet /ˈsɪɡnɪt/ n pečat **~ ring** prsten pečatnjak

significance /sɪɡˈnɪfɪkəns/ n značaj, značenje, smisao, važnost **significant** adj znatan, značajan, važan **signify** /ˈsɪɡnɪfaɪ/ vi,vi 1 značiti, označiti, predstavljati 2 dati znak 3 biti važan

silence /ˈsaɪləns/ n 1 tišina 2 šutnja • vt ušutkati (+ fig) **~r** n prigušivač **silent** /ˈsaɪlənt/ adj tih; bešuman, nečujan, nijem • **~ partner** US → **sleeping partner**

silhouette /ˌsɪluːˈet/ n silueta, obris • vt

be ~d (against) ocrtavati se (na)

silk /sɪlk/ n 1 svila **~-screen printing** svilotisak **~worm** svilac 2 mod svilen **~en** adj svilenkast **~y** adj svilenkast, gladak, nježan

sill /sɪl/ n prozorska daska

silly /ˈsɪlɪ/ adj blesav, glup, budalast, smiješan • n (~ **billy**) coll budala, glupan

silo /ˈsaɪləʊ/ n (pl **~s**) 1 silos 2 podzemni raketni spremnik

silt /sɪlt/ n mulj • **~ up** vt,vi začepiti (se) muljem

silver /ˈsɪlvə(r)/ n 1 srebro 2 (~**ware**) srebrnina 3 (~ **medal**) srebrna medalja • adj srebrn; srebrnast **~-tongued** adj slatkorječiv **~ wedding** srebrni pir • vt posrebriti **~y** adj srebrnast; zvonak (glas)

simian /ˈsɪmɪən/ adj tech majmunski

similar /ˈsɪmɪlə(r)/ adj (to) sličan **~ity** n (between/to) sličnost **~ly** adv 1 slično 2 jednako tako, na isti način

simile /ˈsɪmɪlɪ/ n poredba

simmer /ˈsɪmə(r)/ vi,vt 1 kuhati (se) na laganoj vatri 2 fig (with) ključati (od) **~ down!** smiri se! • n lagano kuhanje

simony /ˈsaɪmənɪ/ n simonija

simper /ˈsɪmpə(r)/ vi budalasto se smiješiti • n budalast smiješak

simple /ˈsɪmpl/ adj 1 jednostavan 2 običan 3 gram (rečenica) prost 4 naivan; budalast **~ fracture** unutarnji prijelom **~-minded** adj priprost; prostodušan **~ton** n budala **simplicity** /sɪmˈplɪsətɪ/ n jednostavnost; prostodušnost **simplify** /ˈsɪmplɪfaɪ/ vt pojednostaviti **simplistic** /sɪmˈplɪstɪk/ adj grubo pojednostavljen **simply** adv jednostavno; samo

simulate /ˈsɪmjʊleɪt/ vt simulirati **simulator** /ˈsɪmjuˌleɪtə(r)/ n simulator

simultaneous /ˌsɪmlˈteɪnɪəs/ adj istodoban; simultan

sin /sɪn/ n grijeh **original ~** istočni grijeh • vi (against) sagriješiti, zgriješiti **~ful** adj grešan **~ner** n grešnik

since /sɪns/ prep od • adv otada, odonda **ever ~** sve odonda **long ~** odavno • conj 1 otkad 2 budući da

sincere /sɪnˈsɪə(r)/ adj iskren **~ly** adv iskreno **Yours ~ly** (pozdravna for-

mula na kraju pisma) Sa štovanjem **sincerity** /sɪn'serəti/ n iskrenost
sine /saɪn/ n math sinus
sinew /'sɪnjuː/ n 1 tetiva 2 (pl) fig lit snaga, oslonac, temelj **~y** adj žilav; mišićav
sing /sɪŋ/ vi,vt irreg 1 pjevati 2 opjevati 3 zujati; zvoniti; zviždati ~ **out** viknuti, zavikati **~song** n 1 GB pjevanje, večer uz pjesmu 2 pjevuckanje (pri govoru) **~er** n pjevač(ica)
singe /sɪnʒ/ vt opržiti, osmuditi
single /'sɪŋgl/ adj 1 jedini, jedan; pojedini, pojedinačan; jednostruk 2 neoženjen, neudata 3 samohran 4 (soba) jednokrevetan 5 (krevet) za jednu osobu 6 (karta) jednosmjeran **in ~ file** u redu po jedan **~breasted** adj s jednostrukim kopčanjem **~handed** adj sam, bez tuđe pomoći **~minded** adj koji ima jedan cilj/namjeru **singly** adv sam • n 1 GB karta u jednom smjeru 2 sport pojedinačno natjecanje 3 singl-ploča; sinmglica coll 4 samac 5 coll porcija krumpirića • vt ~ **out** izdvojiti
singlet /'sɪŋglɪt/ n GB (muška) majica bez rukava; potkošulja
singular /'sɪŋgjʊlə(r)/ n jednina • adj form jedinstven, osobit, rijedak
sinister /'sɪnɪstə(r)/ adj zlokoban, zloslutan, mrk
sink /sɪŋk/ vi,vt irreg 1 (po)tonuti 2 potopiti (+ fig) 3 fig nestati; povući se; zaći; smanjiti se; spustiti se; pasti; izgubiti vrijednost; slabiti; pogoršati se 4 iskopati 5 zaboraviti, zanemariti 6 uložiti, investirati 7 (in, into) upiti se; urezati se (u pamćenje), biti shvaćen • n 1 sudoper 2 US umivaonik 3 fig leglo, jazbina **~er** n olovo (na udici)
sinuous /'sɪnjʊəs/ adj 1 vijugav 2 gibak
sinus /'saɪnəs/ n anat sinus
sip /sɪp/ vi,vt pijuckati • n gutljaj(čić)
siphon /'saɪfən/ n 1 slivnik 2 sifonboca • vt (off/out) isprazniti, ispumpati
sir /sɜː(r)/ n 1 gospodin 2 S~ (plemićki naslov) Sir
sire /'saɪə(r)/ n 1 otac čistokrvne živo-

tinje 2 arch veličanstvo • vt začeti
siren /'saɪərən/ n sirena
sis /sɪs/ n coll seka
sissy /'sɪsɪ/ coll derog mamina maza, slabić
sister /'sɪstə(r)/ n 1 sestra **~-in-law** šogorica, snaha 2 glavna medicinska sestra 3 časna sestra **~ly** adj sestrinski
sit /sɪt/ vi,vt irreg 1 sjediti; sjesti; posjesti 2 (o stvarima) nalaziti se, ležati, stajati 3 pristajati 4 zasjedati 5 (for) pozirati 6 (for) izaći na pismeni ispit ~ **back** a. nasloniti se b. opustiti se c. ništa ne poduzeti ~ **down** sjesti ~ **in** a. (for/as) zamijeniti b. mirno prosvjedovati ~ **on** sth odgađati odluku; ne objavljivati; ne odgovarati **~up** n trbušnjak coll **~ting duck/target** laka meta **~ting member** službeni član; zastupnik **~ting room** GB dnevna soba
site /saɪt/ n mjesto, lokacija **archaeological** ~ arheološko nalazište **building** ~ gradilište • vt smjestiti, locirati
situate /'sɪtjʊeɪt/ vt smjestiti; situirati **situation** /ˌsɪtjʊ'eɪʃn/ n 1 situacija 2 form namještenje, radno mjesto
six /sɪks/ num šest (6) **~th** num ord šesti **~th form** GB završni razred srednje škole **~teen** /sɪk'stiːn/ num šesnaest (16) **~teenth** num ord šesnaesti **~ty** /'sɪkstɪ/ num šezdeset (60) **~tieth** num ord šezdeseti
size /saɪz/ n 1 veličina 2 veličina, broj • vt ~ **up** procijeniti, odmjeriti **~able** adj znatan, povelik, popriličan
sizzle /'sɪzl/ vi cvrčati, pucketati **sizzling** adj vreo
skate /skeɪt/ n 1 (ice ~) sklizaljka 2 (roller ~) koturaljka • vi sklizati se ~ **over/round** sth preletjeti preko čega ~ **through** coll s lakoćom proći
skeet /skiːt/ n (~ shooting) gađanje glinenih golubova
skeleton /'skelɪtn/ n kostur (+ fig) ~ **in the cupboard/closet** neugodna tajna iz prošlosti ~ **key** otpirač • adj samo osnovni **skeletal** adj 1 poput kostura 2 u glavnim crtama
skeptic US → **sceptic**
sketch /sketʃ/ n 1 skica, studija 2 krat-

ki prikaz 3 skeč • *vi,vt* skicirati; iznijeti u glavnim crtama ~y *adj* površan, nepotpun

skew /skju:/ *vt* iskrenuti • *adj* iskrenut, nagnut

skewer /'skjuə(r)/ *n* ražnjić (štapić) • *vt* probosti, nabosti

ski /ski:/ *n* (*pl* ~**s**) skija ~ **jump** skijaški skokovi ~ **lift** žičara za skijaše • *vi* skijati se

skid /skɪd/ *vi* proklizati, zanijeti se • *n* 1 sklizanje (kotača) 2 potporanj **on the** ~**s** na klimavim nogama *fig* ~ **row** US *coll* okupljalište skitnica

skill /skɪl/ *n* 1 vještina 2 stručna sprema, kvalifikacija ~**ed** *adj* 1 vješt 2 stručan, kvalificiran

skim /skɪm/ *vt,vi* 1 (off) obrati (mlijeko) 2 (through/over) letimice pročitati 3 preletjeti, lagano dodirivati

skimp /skɪmp/ *vt,vi* (on) škrtariti ~y *adj* oskudan

skin /skɪn/ *n* 1 koža 2 kora; korica **by the** ~ **of one's teeth** za dlaku ~**deep** *adj* površan; prolazan ~**flint** škrtica ~**ful** *n coll* čašica *fig* ~ **graft** presađivanje kože ~**tight** *adj* pripijen ~**ny** *adj* mršav • *vt* 1 oderati kožu 2 oguliti 3 *coll* odrati, opelješiti *sl* ~**t** *adj* GB *coll* bez prebite pare; švorc *sl*

skip /skɪp/ *vi,vt* 1 skakutati, poskakivati; skočiti; preskočiti 2 GB preskakivati preko vijače/užeta 3 (off/out) *coll* pobjeći, zbrisati • *n* skok

skipper /'skɪpə(r)/ *n* kapetan (broda/ekipe)

skirmish /'skɜ:mɪʃ/ *n mil* manji okršaj, izolirani sukob

skirt /skɜ:t/ *n* 1 suknja 2 skut 3 granica, (ob)rub; štitnik • *vi,vt* (round/around) obilaziti ~**ing board** GB letvica uz donji rub zida

skit /skɪt/ *n* parodija, skeč

skitter /'skɪtə(r)/ *vi* trčkarati

skittish /'skɪtɪʃ/ *adj* živahan, nestašan, lakouman

skittle /'skɪtl/ *n* čunj ~**s** kuglanje

skivvy /'skɪvɪ/ *n* GB *derog* sluškinja • *vi coll* rintati

skulk /skʌlk/ *vi* skrivati se, šuljati se;

zabušavati

skull /skʌl/ *n* lubanja ~ **and crossbones** mrtvačka glava

skunk /skʌŋk/ *n* 1 tvor 2 *coll* podlac; svinja *fig*

sky /skaɪ/ *n* (*pl* **skies**) nebo **the** ~'**s the limit** *coll* bez ograničenja ~**high** *adv* do neba ~**lark** *n* ptica ševa ~**light** prozor na krovu ~**line** obzor, obrisi grada ~**rocket** *vi coll* naglo skočiti ~**scraper** *n* neboder ~**wards** *adv* nebu pod oblake

slab /slæb/ *n* 1 ploča 2 komad (kolača) 3 stol u mrtvačnici

slack /slæk/ *adj* 1 labav, opušten; slab, mlitav, trom 2 nemaran 3 slab (promet) ~ **season** mrtva sezona • *vi* 1 biti lijen/nemaran 2 ~ **off/up** smanjiti brzinu; opustiti se ~**s** *n pl* hlače ~**en** *vi,vt* olabaviti, smanjiti (se), opustiti (se)

slag /slæg/ *n* 1 šljaka, drozga 2 GB *sl* drolja • *vt* (off) GB *sl* 1 vrijeđati 2 zafrkavati

slain *v irreg* → **slay**

slam /slæm/ *vi,vt* 1 zalupiti (se) 2 baciti, tresnuti, udariti • *n* tresak, udarac

slander /'slɑ:ndə(r)/ *n* kleveta • *vt* (o)klevetati, uvrijediti

slang /slæŋ/ *n* slang, argo

slant /slɑ:nt/ *vi,vt* 1 nagnuti; biti nagnut/kos; koso ležati/padati 2 biti pristran • *n* 1 nagib 2 pristup, pogled

slap /slæp/ *n* pljuska • *vt* 1 pljusnuti 2 zapljuskivati ~**dash** *adj* nemaran, površan ~**stick** *n* jeftina komedija • *adv* ravno

slash /slæʃ/ *vi,vt* 1 (pre)rezati, razrezati, rasjeći 2 šibati, udarati 3 *fig* drastično smanjiti, skresati 4 žestoko napasti ~**ing** žestok • *n* 1 rez; posjekotina 2 kosa crtica (/)

slat /slæt/ *n* letvica

slate /sleɪt/ *n* 1 škriljevac 2 ploča 3 crijep 4 US *pol* stranačka lista • *vt* 1 pokriti (krov) 2 US izabrati; odrediti

slaughter /'slɔ:tə(r)/ *n* 1 pokolj, krvoproliće, masakr 2 klanje • *vt* 1 poubijati, pobiti, poklati 2 (za)klati ~**house** *n* klaonica

slave /sleɪv/ *n* rob (+ *fig*) ~**ry** *n* ropstvo

slaver /'slævə(r)/ vi sliniti

slay /sleɪ/ vt irreg lit, US umoriti, ubiti
~**er** n ubojica

sleazy /'sli:zɪ/ adj derog jeftin, prljav,
zapušten

sledge /sledʒ/ n saonice • vi,vt sanjkati se ~**hammer** n malj

sleek /sli:k/ adj gladak, sjajan;
ugladen • vt ugladiti

sleep /sli:p/ n spavanje, san **go to ~ a.**
zaspati **b.** (ruka, noga) utrnuti **put to
~ a.** uspavati **b.** euphem dati uspavati, eutanazirati ~**walker** n mjesečar •
vi,vt irreg 1 spavati 2 pružati smještaj (za) ~ **around** spavati sa svakim
~ **in** odspavati duže ~**er** n 1 spavač 2
GB željeznički prag 3 vlak s kolima
za spavanje ~**ing bag** vreća za spavanje ~**ing car** kola za spavanje ~**ing
policeman** izbočina na cesti (kojom
se usporava promet) ~**less** adj besan
~**y** adj pospan

sleet /sli:t/ n susnježica

sleeve /sli:v/ n 1 rukav **wear one's
heart on one's ~** otvoreno pokazivati osjećaje 2 GB omotnica

sleigh /sleɪ/ n konjske saonice

sleight /slaɪt/ n ~ **of hand** vještina,
spretnost

slender /'slendə(r)/ n 1 vitak 2 tanak 3
slab

slept v irreg → **sleep**

sleuth /slu:θ/ n coll detektiv

slew (1) v irreg → **slay**

slew (2) (**slue** US) /slu:/ vi,vt okrenuti
(se)

slice /slaɪs/ n 1 kriška, odrezak, komad; dio 2 lopatica (za tortu) 3 sport
rezana lopta • vt,vi 1 narezati,
razrezati, odrezati 2 porezati 3 rezati
loptu ~**d bread** kruh razrezan na
kriške

slick /slɪk/ adj 1 gladak, sklizak 2
vješt, spretan, okretan • n 1 **oil** ~ mrlja nafte 2 US ilustrirani časopis • vt
~ **down** zagladiti (kosu) ~**er** n 1 US
kišna kabanica 2 (**city** ~) ugla-
den/slatkorječiv prevarant

slide /slaɪd/ vi,vt irreg 1 kliziti, skliznuti,
poskliznuti se 2 šuljati se, iskrasti se,
sakriti (se) 3 spustiti se, pasti • n 1
sklizanje; pad fig; odron 2 tobogan 3

dijapozitiv **sliding rule** logaritamsko
računalo **sliding scale** klizna skala

slight (1) /slaɪt/ adj malen, neznatan,
slab, lagan, sitan **not in the ~est** ni
najmanje ~**ly** adv malo, pomalo, nešto

slight (2) vt omalovažavati • n (on/to)
omalovažavanje (koga, čega)

slim /slɪm/ adj 1 vitak 2 fig malen,
neznatan, slab • vi,vt 1 mršavjeti, biti
na dijeti 2 (down) smanjiti

slime /slaɪm/ n 1 sluz, sluzava tvar 2
glib, mulj **slimy** adj sluzav; ljigav (+
fig), udvoran

sling /slɪŋ/ vt irreg objesiti; prebaciti,
baciti, izbaciti ~**shot** US katapult • n 1
povez (za slomljenu ruku) 2 remenik 3
užad za dizanje 4 praćka

slink /slɪŋk/ vi irreg povući se pokun-
njeno; odšuljati se

slinky /'slɪŋkɪ/ adj coll pripijen,
gladak

slip (1) /slɪp/ vi,vt 1 poskliznuti se,
iskliznuti, sl kliznuti 2 iskrasti se;
kradomice dati 3 (by/through) prolaziti, proći ~ **through one's fingers**
izmaći se lUt **let sth** ~ **a.** propustiti **b.** izlanuti 4 (out) omaknuti se
5 brzo što učiniti 6 osloboditi se
čega, odvezati se 1 vt ~**ped my
mind/memory** zaboravio sam 7 pasti,
pokvariti se ~**on** (shoes) natikače
~**per** n papuča ~**pery** adj sklizav
~**shod** adj površan, nemaran • n 1
okliznuće, pad 2 (~**up**) pogreška ~
of the tongue lapsus 3 kombine 4
(**gym** ~) dres za tjelovježbu

slip (2) n 1 kartica; komadić papira 2
kalem 3 špalta

slit /slɪt/ n procijep, pukotina, prorez,
raspor • vt irreg prerezati, razrezati,
rasporiti

slither /'slɪðə(r)/ vi sklizati se; vijugati

sliver /'slɪvə(r)/ n oštar/tanak/sitan komad; krhotina

slob /slɒb/ n coll lijenčina, prljavac,
nemarna/neuredna osoba

slobber /'slɒbə(r)/ vi derog 1 sliniti,
balaviti 2 (over) raspekmeziti se

slog /slɒg/ vi coll rintati • n GB naporan posao

slogan /'sləʊgən/ *n* slogan, parola, krilatica

slop /slɒp/ *vt,vi* proliti (se) ~ **about/around** *coll* ljenčariti, povlačiti se okolo • *n* (~s) 1 ostaci hrane, prolivena/prljava tekućina 2 bezukusna hrana; splačine ~**py** *adj* 1 površan, nemaran 2 *coll* prljav, neuredan 3 *coll* sladunjav

slope /sləʊp/ *vi* spuštati se, biti nagnut/kos ~ **off** *coll* šmugnuti, zbrisati • *n* kosina, nagib

slosh /slɒʃ/ *vi,vt* 1 šljapkati 2 *GB* udariti ~**ed** *adj coll* pijan

slot /slɒt/ *n* 1 prorez, utor, otvor (za novčić/pismo) ~ **machine** automat 2 *TV, radio* termin • *vt* smjestiti

sloth /sləʊθ/ *n* 1 *zoo* ljenjivac 2 *lit, bibl* lijenost

slouch /slaʊtʃ/ *n* 1 pognuto/pogrbljeno držanje 2 lijenčina • *vi* nemarno hodati, gegati se, vući se

slough (1) /slaʊ/ *n* kaljuža, močvara

slough (2) /slʌf/ *vi,vt* (~ **off**) odbaciti kožu (zmija)

slovenly /'slʌvənlɪ/ *adj* neuredan, prljav

slow /sləʊ/ *adj* 1 spor, polagan ~ **motion** usporeni snimak 2 (sat) koji kasni 3 ~ **off the mark/on the uptake**) koji sporo kopča • *vi,vt* (down/up) usporiti • *adv* sporo ~**ly** *adv* sporo ~**worm** *n* sljepić

sludge /slʌdʒ/ *n* mulj, talog

slue *US* → **slew**

slug (1) /slʌg/ *n* puž golać

slug (2) *n* 1 komad metala 2 *US* metak 3 *coll* gutljaj alkohola

sluggard /'slʌgəd/ *n* lijenčina

sluggish /'slʌgɪʃ/ *n* 1 spor, trom 2 (poslovanje) slab, slaba prometa

sluice /slu:s/ *n* ustava ~ **valve** ispust • *vt,vi* 1 oprati/isprati mlazom vode 2 štrcati

slum /slʌm/ *n* siromašna četvrt

slumber /'slʌmbə(r)/ *vi lit* spavati • *n* san, spavanje

slump /slʌmp/ *vi* teško/naglo pasti • *n* 1 pad 2 kriza

slung *v irreg* → **sling**

slunk *v irreg* → **slink**

slur /slɜ:(r)/ *vt* nejasno izgovarati • *n* 1

nejasan govor 2 mrlja *fig* 3 uvreda; objeda

slurp /slɜ:p/ *vt,vi coll* srkati

slush /slʌʃ/ *n* 1 bljuzgavica 2 *coll* ljubić

slut /slʌt/ *n* 1 *derog* kurva 2 neuredna/šlampava žena

sly /slaɪ/ *adj* 1 tajnovit 2 podmukao, podao

smack /smæk/ *vt* 1 pljusnuti, lupiti 2 cmoknuti • *n* 1 udarac **have a ~ at sth** okušati se u čemu 2 glasan poljubac 3 *sl* heroin • *adv* ravno • *vi* ~ **of sth** mirisati na što *fig*

small /smɔ:l/ *adj* malen; sitan ~ **wonder** nije ni čudo ~ **arms** pješačko naoružanje ~ **fry** *coll* sitna riba *fig* ~ **change** sitniš ~ **intestine** tanko crijevo ~**pox** boginje

smarmy /'sma:mɪ/ *adj GB coll* ljigavo udvoran

smart (1) /sma:t/ *adj* 1 elegantan, dotjeran; monden, moderan 2 *US* pametan, oštrouman 3 bezobrazan 4 brz, snažan ~**arse/ass** *n vulg* pametnjaković *coll*

smart (2) *vt* 1 peći, bridjeti 2 biti povrijeđen

smash /smæʃ/ *vt,vi* 1 razbiti (se), razmrskati (se) 2 udariti • *n* 1 tresak 2 udarac 3 (~ **hit**) hit ~**ed** *adj coll* pijan ~**ing** *adj coll* super

smattering /'smætərɪŋ/ *n* 1 malen broj 2 ograničeno/površno znanje

smear /smɪə(r)/ *vt,vi* 1 razmazati, namazati, zamazati, zamrljati (se) 2 *fig* blatiti • *n* 1 mrlja 2 *med* bris 3 kleveta

smell /smel/ *n* 1 njuh 2 vonj; miris 3 zadah, smrad • *vt,vi* 1 (out) osjećati miris, namirisati, pomirisati; **I can ~ a rat** *coll* nešto mi je sumnjivo, nešto mi smrdi *coll* 2 (of) mirisati, imati miris (na/po) 3 smrditi ~**y** *adj* smrdljiv

smelt (1) *v irreg* → **smell**

smelt (2) *vt* taliti (rudu)

smile /smaɪl/ *n* osmijeh, smiješak • *vi,vt* (at/on/upon) smiješiti se, osmjehivati se

smirk /smɜ:k/ *n* glupav/samozadovoljan/zlurad osmijeh • *vi* ceriti se, kesiti se

smite /smaɪt/ *vi,vt irreg* 1 *lit, arch* udariti, uništiti 2 *fig* pogoditi, potresti; gristi (savjest) **smitten** *adj joc* zatreskan

smith /smɪθ/ *n* kovač **~y** *n* kovačnica

smithereens /ˌsmɪðə'ri:nz/ *n pl* krhotine, komadići

smitten *v irreg* → **smite**

smock /smɒk/ *n* radno odijelo, kuta

smoke /sməʊk/ *n* 1 dim **go up in ~** rasplinuti se *fig* **~stack** *n* (tvornički/brodski) dimnjak 2 *mod* dimni **~screen** dimna zavjesa 3 cigareta 4 *coll* grad • *vi,vt* 1 pušiti 2 dimiti (se); zadimiti (se) **~** sb dimom istjerati **~r** *n* a. pušač b. vagon za pušače **smoking** *n* pušenje **smoky** *adj* zadimljen; poput dima; zamagljen

smolder *US* → **smoulder**

smooth /smu:ð/ *adj* 1 gladak (+ *fig*); kao podmazan, bez problema 2 blaga okusa 3 ugladen, slatkorječiv, laskav • *vt* 1 (away/out/down) zagladiti, izravnati, izgladiti (+ *fig*) 2 utrljati

smote *v irreg* → **smite**

smother /'smʌðə(r)/ *vt* 1 ugušiti (+ *fig*); prigušiti 2 (with/in) prekriti, obasuti 3 zapretati (vatru)

smoulder /'sməʊldə(r)/ *vi* tinjati **~ing** *adj fig* pritajen

smudge /smʌdʒ/ *n* mrlja, packa • *vt,vi* zamrljati (se), zapackati (se)

smug /smʌg/ *adj* 1 samozadovoljan, samodopadan 2 uskogrudan

smuggle /'smʌgl/ *vt* krijumčariti; švercati *coll* **~r** *n* krijumčar; švercer *coll* **smuggling** *n* krijumčarenje; šverc *coll*

smut /smʌt/ *n* 1 mrlja 2 snijet 3 *coll* prostote, opscenosti **~ty** *adj* prljav; prost

snack /snæk/ *n* laki obrok; zalogaj **~ bar** zalogajnica • *vi US* prigristi, prezalogajiti

snaffle /'snæfl/ *vt GB coll* dignuti, zdipiti *sl*

snag /snæg/ *n coll* (neočekivana) teškoća; kvaka, mina *sl*

snail /sneɪl/ *n* puž

snake /sneɪk/ *n* zmija (+ *fig*) **~ in the grass** zmija u njedrima • *vi* vijugati

snap /snæp/ *vi,vt* 1 puknuti, slomiti (se), odlomiti (se) **~ one's fingers** pucnuti prstima 2 (at sth) zagristi (što) 3 (at sb) otresti se (na koga) 4 *coll* slikati • *n* 1 puckanje, zvuk pucanja, lom 2 (**~shot**) fotografija 3 *coll* energija, život • *adj* iznenadan, nagao, bez upozorenja **~pish** *adj* osoran **~py** *adj coll* moderan **make it ~py!** požuri! brže!

snare /sneə(r)/ *n* zamka, stupica (+ *fig*) • *vt* uloviti u stupicu

snarl (1) /sna:l/ *vi* (at) režati (na), zarežati (+ *fig*)

snarl (2) (**~up**) *n* zbrka; zastoj prometa

snatch /snætʃ/ *vi,vt* zgrabiti, ugrabiti **~ at sth** posegnuti za čim • *n* 1 zahvat, posezanje 2 dio; kratko vrijeme

snazzy /'snæzɪ/ *adj coll* moderan, atraktivan

sneak /sni:k/ *vi,vt irreg* (**~ up**) šuljati se, prišuljati se; prikrasti se, iskrasti se 2 *coll* ukrasti 3 *GB sl* tužiti (učitelju) **~er** *n US* tenisica **~ing** *adj* prikriven **~y** *adj* podmukao

sneer /snɪə(r)/ *n* podrugljiv smiješak/pogled/primjedba • *vi* podrugljivo se osmjehnuti/smijati; rugati se, izrugivati se

sneeze /sni:z/ *vi* kihnuti, kihati • *n* kihanje

snicker /'snɪkə(r)/ *US* → **snigger**

snide /snaɪd/ *adj* podrugljiv, podmukao, omalovažavajući

sniff /snɪf/ *vi,vt* 1 šmrcati, šmrkati 2 njuškati **~ out** nanjušiti 3 frknuti nosom **~ at sth** prezreti 4 udisati (ljepilo); snifati *sl*; šmrkati (kokain)

sniffle /'snɪfl/ *n* (**~s**) *coll* curenje iz nosa; začepljen nos

snigger /'snɪgə(r)/ *vi* (at) podrugljivo se smijuljiti, hihotati • *n* podrugljivo smijuljenje, hihot

snip /snɪp/ *n* rez **~s** *pl* škare za metal • *vt* rezati, strići

snipe (1) /snaɪp/ *vt,vi* (at) gadati snajperom • *n* 1 snajper 2 snajperist

snipe (2) *n* (*pl* ~, **~s**) šljuka

snippet /'snɪpɪt/ *n coll* komadić, djelić

snitch /snɪtʃ/ *vi,vt coll* 1 zdipiti 2 (on sb) cinkati (koga)

snivel /'snɪvl/ vi cviliti, cmizdriti, sliniti

snob /snɒb/ n derog snob **~berry** n snobizam **~bish** adj snobovski

snooker /'snu:kə(r)/ n biljar • vt coll dovesti u bezizlaznu situaciju

snoop /snu:p/ vi (about/around) derog njuškati, zabadati nos

snooty /'snu:tɪ/ adj coll arogantan, uobražen

snooze /snu:z/ vi coll drijemati

snore /snɔ:(r)/ vi hrkati • n hrkanje

snorkel /'snɔ:kl/ n disalica; cijev za dovod zraka • vi roniti

snort /snɔ:t/ vi,vt 1 frktati, frknuti 2 šmrkati

snot /snɒt/ n coll vulg šmrkalj **~ty** adj 1 vulg balav, šmrkav 2 sl uobražen

snout /snaʊt/ n njuška, rilo

snow /snəʊ/ n 1 snijeg **~ball** n gruda snijega o vi naglo rasti **~ball's chance in hell** nikakvi izgledi **~drift** snježni nanos **~flake** snježna pahuljica **~ gear** zimska oprema **~man** snjegović **~plough/~plow** ralica **~shoes** vi krplje **~white** adj snježnobijel **Snowhite** Snjeguljica 2 sl kokain • vi,vt 1 snježiti **it ~s** pada snijeg 2 US sl lagati i mazati **be ~ed in/up** biti zameten snijegom **be ~ed under** (with sth) biti zatrpan (čime) **~y** adj snježan; snježnobijel

snub (1) /snʌb/ vt ignorirati (koga)

snub (2) adj prćast (nos)

snuck v irreg → sneak

snuff /snʌf/ n burmut • vt,vi 1 (out) ugasiti (se) **~ it** GB coll umrijeti 2 njuškati

snuffle /'snʌfl/ vi šmrcati; govoriti kroz nos

snug /snʌg/ adj udoban, udobno smješten • n GB separe

snuggle /'snʌgl/ vi (up) coll udobno se smjestiti, ušuškati se

so /səʊ/ adv, adj tako; toliko **~ as to** kako bi **~ long!** do viđenja! **~-called** a. takozvani b. tobožnji • conj pa, tako da **~ what?** pa što? (i) što onda?

soak /səʊk/ vi,vt 1 (in/through) namočiti, smočiti, promočiti, natopiti 2 (up) upiti **~ed** adj mokar **~ing wet** skroz mokar

soap /səʊp/ n 1 sapun 2 (**~ opera**) TV sapunica, trakavica **coll** • vt nasapunati **~y** adj 1 sapunast, sapunjav 2 coll ljigavo udvoran

soar /sɔ:(r)/ vi 1 (visoko) letjeti, lebdjeti u zraku 2 uzletjeti, vinuti se; fig uzdizati se 3 skočiti fig

sob /sɒb/ vi,vt jecati • n jecaj

sober /'səʊbə(r)/ adj trijezan (+ fig) • vi,vt 1 (down) uozbiljiti se 2 **~ up** otrijezniti, rastrijezniti **sobriety** /sə'braɪətɪ/ n form trijeznost, trezvenost

soccer /'sɒkə(r)/ n GB nogomet

sociable /'səʊʃəbl/ adj društven, druželjubiv

social /'səʊʃl/ adj 1 društveni, socijalni 2 neslužben, prijateljski **~ly** adv 1 društveno, socijalno 2 neformalno, u društvu **~ism** n socijalizam **~ist** n socijalist o adj socijalistički **~ize** vi,vt 1 družiti se 2 socijalizirati **society** /sə'saɪətɪ/ n društvo

socio- /səʊsɪəʊ/ prvi dio složenice socio-, društveno- **~economic** adj društvenogospodarstveni

sociology /səʊsɪ'ɒlədʒɪ/ n sociologija

sock (1) /sɒk/ n čarapa **pull one's ~s up** coll popraviti se

sock (2) vt coll udariti, lupiti

socket /'sɒkɪt/ n 1 (očna) šupljina; čašica 2 utičnica

sod /sɒd/ n GB sl vulg derog kreten • vt,vi vulg **~ it!** dovraga **~ off!** goni se

soda /'səʊdə/ n 1 soda 2 US gazirano piće **~ fountain** US slastičarnica

sodden /'sɒdn/ adj 1 mokar, natopljen 2 gnjecav

sodium /'səʊdɪəm/ n natrij

sodomy /'sɒdəmɪ/ n form, leg protuprirodni blud; sodomija

sofa /'səʊfə/ n dvosjed, trosjed, sofa

soft /sɒft/ adj 1 mekan 2 tih, prigušen 3 blag; nježan; lagan; slab the **~ option** linija manjeg otpora **~-pedal** vt ublažiti **~-soap** vt smekšati fig **have a ~ spot for sb** biti slab na koga 4 bezalkoholan 5 (**~ in the head**) blesav **~en** vi,vt omekšati, smekšati (se); stišati se; ublažiti (se) **~en up** mil oslabiti **~ener** n omekšivač **~y/~ie** n coll a. osoba meka srca b. mekušac, slabić

soggy /ˈsɒgɪ/ adj vlažan, gnjecav

soil (1) /sɔɪl/ n tlo, zemlja **native ~** rodna gruda

soil (2) vt form zaprljati, (u)prljati (+ fig)

sojourn /ˈsɒdʒən/ n lit boravak • vi boraviti

solace /ˈsɒlɪs/ n utjeha

solar /ˈsəʊlə(r)/ adj sunčev, sunčan **S~ System** Sunčev sustav/sistem

solarium /səʊˈleərɪəm/ n svjetlarnik

sold v irreg → **sell**

solder /ˈsɒldə(r)/ n lem • vt (za)lemiti **~ing iron** lemilica

soldier /ˈsəʊldʒə(r)/ n vojnik **~ of fortune** plaćenik **~ly** adj vojnički **~y** n derog soldateska

sole (1) /səʊl/ n 1 taban 2 potplat

sole (2) n (riba) list

sole (3) adj jedini; isključivi **~ly** adv samo, isključivo

solemn /ˈsɒləm/ adj svečan; ozbiljan; uzvišen

solicit /səˈlɪsɪt/ vi,vt form 1 moliti, tražiti 2 prostituirati se **~ous** adj form 1 velikodušan 2 zabrinut, brižan

solicitor /səˈlɪsɪtə(r)/ n GB (niži) odvjetnik

solid /ˈsɒlɪd/ adj 1 čvrst, krut; solidan; pravi 2 homogen, jedinstven 3 pun, ispunjen 4 trodimenzionalan 5 neprekidan, neprekinut • n 1 kruta tvar 2 **~s** kruta hrana 3 geometrijsko tijelo **~arity** /ˌsɒlɪˈdærəti/ n solidarnost **~ify** /səˈlɪdɪfaɪ/ vt,vi 1 skrutnuti (se) 2 konsolidirati **~ity** n čvrstoća

soliloquy /səˈlɪləkwɪ/ n monolog

solitary /ˈsɒlɪtrɪ/ adj 1 samotan; osamljen; povučen **~ confinement** samica 2 jedan jedini **solitude** /ˈsɒlɪtjuːd/ n samoća

solo /ˈsəʊləʊ/ n (pl **~s**), adj, adv solo **~ist** n solist

solstice /ˈsɒlstɪs/ n suncostaj

soluble /ˈsɒljʊbl/ adj 1 topiv 2 form rješiv

solution /səˈluːʃn/ n 1 (to sth) rješenje (čega) 2 otopina

solve /sɒlv/ vt riješiti

solvent /ˈsɒlvənt/ adj solventan

sombre (**-ber** US) /ˈsɒmbə(r)/ adj ozbiljan; sumoran

some /sʌm/ adj 1 nekoliko; nešto; malo 2 neki, nekakav, jedan **~ day** jednog dana • pron neki, nešto • adv 1 oko 2 nešto **~ more** još malo **~body** pron netko **~how** adv nekako **~one** pron netko **~place** adv US negdje **~thing** pron nešto **have ~thing to do with** imati neke veze sa **~time** adv u neko doba, jednom o adj nekadašnji **~times** adv katkad **~way** adv US nekako **~what** adv 1 pomalo, donekle 2 prilično **~where** adv negdje

somersault /ˈsʌməsɔːlt/ n salto; kolut naprijed/natrag

son /sʌn/ n sin **~-in-law** zet **~-of-a-bitch** n tab pasji/kurvin sin; gad

song /sɒŋ/ n pjesma **burst into ~** zapjevati **~bird** ptica pjevica **~book** pjesmarica **make ~ and dance** coll dignuti galamu

sonic /ˈsɒnɪk/ adj zvučni

sonnet /ˈsɒnɪt/ n sonet

sonorous /səˈnɔːrəs/ adj zvučan, zvonak

soon /suːn/ adv uskoro, ubrzo **as ~ as possible** što prije **I'd just as ~ not** radije ne bih **too ~** prerano, prebrzo **not a moment too ~** u zadnji tren **~er** prije; radije **the ~er the better** što prije to bolje **no ~er... than** čim... kad **no ~er said than done** rečeno-učinjeno

soot /sʊt/ n čađa

soothe /suːð/ vt smiriti, umiriti; ublažiti

sop /sɒp/ vt **~ sth up** upiti **~ping** adj potpuno mokar

sophisticated /səˈfɪstɪkeɪtɪd/ adj profinjen, kultiviran, otmjen

sophomore /ˈsɒfəməː(r)/ n US student druge godine; učenik drugog razreda (srednje škole)

soporific /ˌsɒpəˈrɪfɪk/ adj uspavljujući

soppy /ˈsɒpɪ/ adj GB coll sladunjav

soprano /səˈprɑːnəʊ/ n sopran

sorcerer /ˈsɔːsərə(r)/ n čarobnjak **sorceress** čarobnica, vještica **sorcery** n čaranje

sordid /ˈsɔːdɪd/ adj 1 nečastan, podao

2 prljav (+ *fig*)

sore /sɔ:(r)/ *adj* **1** bolan ~ **throat** grlobolja **2** *US* ljutit, uvrijeđen

sorority /sə'rɒrətɪ/ *n US* udruženje studentica

sorrel /'sɒrəl/ *n* kiselica

sorrow /'sɒrəʊ/ *n* tuga

sorry /'sɒrɪ/ *adj* (for/about) tužan, žalostan, kojem je žao *I'm* ~ **a.** žao mi je **b.** moja sućut *she felt* ~ *for him* bilo joj ga je žao • *int* **1** oprosti(te) **2** molim?

sort /sɔ:t/ *n* vrsta **a** ~ **of** nekakav ~ **of** nekako • *vt, vi* razvrstati ~ **out a.** izdvojiti **b.** srediti; riješiti

sortie /'sɔ:ti:/ *n mil* **1** protunapad **2** borbeni let **3** *coll* izlet *fig*

sought *v irreg* → **seek** ~**after** *adj* tražen

soul /səʊl/ *n* duša (+ *fig*) ~**searching** *n* ispitivanje savjesti

sound (1) /saʊnd/ *n* **1** zvuk ~ **barrier** zvučni zid ~**proof** *adj* zvučno izoliran ~**track** glazba iz filma **2** glas • *vi, vt* **1** zvučati, zazvučati, začuti se, oglasiti (se), dati znak (čime) **2** činiti se **3** izmjeriti dubinu ~ **out** ispitati

sound (2) *adj* **1** zdrav **a** ~ **mind in a** ~ **body** u zdravlju tijelu zdrav duh **2** neoštećen **3** razborit, razuman; osnovan **4** poman, detaljan • *adv* ~ **asleep** u dubokučvrstu snu

sound (3) *n* tjesnac

soup /su:p/ *n* juha ~**kitchen** javna kuhinja • *vt* frizirati (motor)

sour /'saʊə(r)/ *adj* kiseo (+ *fig*) ~**(ed) cream** kiselo vrhnje • *vt, vi* ukiseliti (se)

source /sɔ:s/ *n* izvor (+ *fig*)

souse /saʊs/ *vt* **1** natopiti, smočiti **2** marinirati

south /saʊθ/ *n* jug **in the** ~ na jugu • *adj* južni • *adv* prema jugu, na jug ~**erly** *adj* južni ~**ern** *adj* južni **S~erner** Južnjak ~**paw** *coll* ljevak

souvenir /,su:və'nɪə(r)/ *n* suvenir

sovereign /'sɒvrɪn/ *n* **1** *form* vladar **2** *hist* zlatnik vrijednosti **1** funte • *adj* suveren, neovisan, samostalan ~**ty** *n* suverenost, neovisnost

soviet /'səʊvɪət/ *n* sovjet • *adj* sovjetski **the S~ Union** *hist* Sovjetski

Savez

sow (1) /səʊ/ *vi, vt irreg* posijati (+ *fig*)

sow (2) /saʊ/ *n* prasica, krmača

soy(a) /sɔɪ, /'sɔɪə/ *n* (~**bean**) soja

sozzled /'sɒzld/ *adj* pijan

spa /spa:/ *n* toplice *pl*

space /speɪs/ *n* **1** prostor; mjesto **2** svemir ~**craft/ship** svemirski brod ~**suit** skafander **3** razdoblje **4** razmak; prored ~ **bar** razmaknica **double spacing** dvostruki prored • *vt* razmaknuti ~**d out** *adj coll* pijan; drogiran; otkačen *sl* **spacious** /'speɪʃəs/ *adj* prostran

spade (1) /speɪd/ *n* lopata **call a** ~ **a** ~ reći bobu bob, a popu pop

spade (2) *n* pik **queen of** ~**s** pikova dama

spake *v irreg arch* → **speak**

spam /spæm/ *n TM* konzervirano meso, mesni doručak *TM*

span (1) *v irreg* → **spin**

span (2) /spæn/ *n* **1** raspon, razmak; vremensko razdoblje; trajanje **2** luk mosta • *vt* **1** premostiti **2** obuhvatiti

spangle /'spæŋgl/ *n* šljokica *coll*

spank /spæŋk/ *vt* isprašiti po turu, pljesnuti ~**ing** *n* batine

spanner /'spænə(r)/ *n GB* ključ za vijke **put/throw a** ~ **in(to) the works** pokvariti plan

spar (1) /spa:(r)/ *n* jarbol, stup, potporanj

spar (2) *vi* šakati se

spare /speə(r)/ *vt* (po)štedjeti, uštedjeti (trud) *have you got a moment to* ~? imate li trenutak slobodnog vremena? • *adj* **1** rezervni **2** slobodan **sparing** *adj* štedljiv

spark /spa:k/ *n* iskra (+ *fig*) ~**(ling) plug** svjećica • *vi, vt* **1** iskriti **2** potaknuti ~ **off** prouzročiti

sparkle /'spa:kl/ *vi* svjetlucati • *n* svjetlucanje ~**r** *n* prskalica **sparkling** *adj* **1** sjajan; iskričav *fig* **2** pjenušav

sparrow /'spærəʊ/ *n* vrabac

sparse /spa:s/ *adj* rijedak; oskudan

spasm /'spæzəm/ *n* grč ~**odic** *adj* **1** grčevit **2** neredovit

spastic /'spæstɪk/ *n* paraplegičar

spat *v irreg* → **spit**

spate /speɪt/ *n* **1** bujica, poplava **2**

navala, velik broj

spatial /'speɪʃl/ *adj form* prostoran

spatter /'spætə(r)/ *vt* (po)prskati, (po)škropiti

spatula /'spætjulə/ *n* lopatica, spatula

spawn /spɔːn/ *vi,vt* 1 mrijestiti se 2 *fig* stvoriti, roditi • *n* mrijest, ikra

spay /speɪ/ *vt* sterilizirati (ženku)

speak /spiːk/ *vi,vt irreg* (of/about/to/with) govoriti, progovoriti, razgovarati, reći; održati govor; pokazati ~ **one's mind** reći što se misli **~easy** *n* ilegalna točionica alkohola ~ **for sb** govoriti u čije ime **be spoken for** biti zauzet (osoba)/rezerviran (stvar) ~ **out** progovoriti; otvoreno reći ~ **up** govoriti glasnije; jasno reći **~er** *n* 1 govornik, osoba koja govori 2 *GB* predsjednik Donjeg doma 3 zvučnik

spear /spɪə(r)/ *n* 1 koplje 2 vlat • *vt* probosti, nabosti **~head** *n* vođa; predvodnica o *vt* predvoditi **~mint** *n* metvica

special /'speʃl/ *adj* poseban, osobit, specijalan ~ **school** škola za djecu s teškoćama u razvoju • *n* 1 posebna ponuda 2 izvanredna linija 3 poseban prilog **~ist** *n* specijalist **~ize** *vt,vi* (in) specijalizirati (se) (za što) **~(i)ty** /ˌspeʃɪ'æləti/ *n* 1 specijalnost 2 specijalitet **species** /'spiːʃiːz/ *n* (*pl* ~) vrsta

specific /spə'sɪfɪk/ *adj* određen, specifičan **~s** *n pl* konkretne pojedinosti **~ally** *adv* posebno, osobito; izričito; konkretno **~ation** *n* specifikacija

specify /'spesɪfaɪ/ *vt* odrediti, navesti, specificirati

specimen /'spesɪmɪn/ *n* 1 primjerak; uzorak 2 *coll* tip

speck /spek/ *n* točkica, mrlja, komadić, trunka

speckle /'spekl/ *n* šara, pjega

spectacle /'spektəkl/ *n* 1 spektakl 2 prizor 3 *fig* scena, predstava 4 **~s** naočale **spectacular** /spek'tækjulə(r)/ *adj* spektakularan

spectator /spek'teɪtə(r)/ *n* gledatelj

spectre (**-ter** *US*) /'spektə(r)/ *n form* duh, sablast

spectrum /'spektrəm/ *n* spektar (+ *fig*)

speculate /'spekjuleɪt/ *vi* 1 (about/on) nagadati, teoretizirati 2 špekulirati

speculation /ˌspekjʊ'leɪʃn/ *n* nagadanje; špekuliranje

sped *v irreg* → **speed**

speech /spiːtʃ/ *n* govor ~ **impediment** govorna mana **part of** ~ vrsta riječi ~ **therapy** govorne vježbe **give/make/deliver a** ~ (o)održati govor **~less** *adj* bez riječi; bez teksta *coll*

speed /spiːd/ *n* 1 brzina **pick up/gather** ~ ubrzati ~ **limit** ograničenje brzine **~boat** gliser 2 *sl* amfetamin; spid *sl* • *vi,vt* 1 (pro)juriti, hitati, žuriti se 2 voziti nedopuštenom brzinom **~ing** *n* prekoračenje dopuštene brzine ~ **up** ubrzati **~ometer** *n* brzinomjer **~y** *adj* brz

spell (1) /spel/ *vi,vt irreg* 1 sricati; pisati *how do you* **~**...? kako se piše...? 2 *coll* značiti ~ **out a.** izgovoriti slovo po slovo **b.** podrobno objasniti; nacrtati *coll* **~ing** *n* pisanje, način pisanja, pravopis

spell (2) *n* 1 razdoblje, (kratko) vrijeme 2 smjena 3 napadaj • *vt* US zamijeniti (na dužnosti)

spell (3) *n* 1 čarolija **cast a** ~ začarati **under a** ~ začaran **~bound** *adj* očaran

spelt *v irreg* → **spell**

spend /spend/ *vi,vt irreg* 1 trošiti, potrošiti, utrošiti **~thrift** *n* rasipnik 2 (vrijeme) provesti 3 *lit* istrošiti se, ostati bez snage **~ing money** džeparac

spent *v irreg* → **spend**

sperm /spɜːm/ *n* sperma ~ **whale** ulješura

spew /spjuː/ *vi,vt* 1 povraćati 2 *fig* šiknuti; rigati

sphere /sfɪə(r)/ *n* 1 kugla 2 sfera, djelokrug

sphinx /sfɪŋks/ *n* sfinga

spic /spɪk/ *n US derog tab* Portorikanac

spice /spaɪs/ *n* začin (+ *fig*) • *vt* ~ **up** (with) začiniti **spicy** *adj* pikantan (+ *fig*)

spick-and-span /'spɪkən'spæn/ *adj* tip-top

spider /'spaɪdə(r)/ *n* pauk **~web** *US* paučina

spigot /'spɪɡət/ *n* slavina

spike /spaɪk/ *n* 1 šiljak ~ **heels** visoke

tanke potpetice 2 bodlja 3 klas • vt 1 zašiljiti 2 dodati alkohola (u) **spiky** adj 1 bodljikav 2 uvredljiv

spill /spɪl/ vi,vt irreg 1 proliti (se) ~ **the beans** coll odati tajnu ~ **over** (into) proširiti se (na/u) • n 1 prolijevanje **oil** ~ izljevanje nafte 2 pad

spin /spɪn/ vi,vt irreg 1 vrtiti (se), okretati (se), okrenuti (se) my head is ~ning vrti mi se u glavi ~~dry centrifugirati 2 presti • n 1 okret(aj), vrtnja 2 kratka vožnja 3 nagli pad ~ning **wheel** n kolovrat ~~off n nusproizvod

spinach /'spɪnɪdʒ/ n špinat

spine /spaɪn/ n 1 kralježnica 2 bodljika ~~chilling adj jezovit **spinal** adj mekušast coll **spinal** adj hrptenični **spinal cord** leđna moždina **spiny** adj bodljikav

spindle /'spɪndl/ n 1 vreteno 2 osovina **spindly** adj štrkljast

spinster /'spɪnstə(r)/ n usidjelica

spiral /'spaɪərəl/ adj spiralan • n spirala • vi 1 vijugati 2 dizati se

spire /'spaɪə(r)/ n krović tornja

spirit /'spɪrɪt/ n 1 duh 2 stav, namjera 3 ~s raspoloženje 4 polet, energija 5 ~s alkoholna pića ~~level n libela ~~less adj bez poleta, potišten ~~ual adj duhovni; vjerski

spit (1) /spɪt/ vi,vt irreg 1 (at/on) pljunuti, ispljunuti 2 (out) osorno/ljutito reći ~ **it out!** coll govori! da čujemo! ~~fire n coll osoba koja lako plane ~~toon pljuvačnica • n pljuvačka; pljuvanje **the** ~ **of/the** ~~ting image of pljunuti, isti

spit (2) n 1 ražanj 2 rt

spite /spaɪt/ n pakost, zloba **in** ~ **of** unatoč • vt napakostiti ~~ful adj pakostan

spiv /spɪv/ n GB coll švercer

splash /splæʃ/ vi,vt 1 pljuštati, pljuskati; (po)prskati (se) 2 coll dati puno prostora ~ **out** coll spiskati (novac) • n 1 pljusak, pljuskanje; mrlja 2 senzacija 3 **a** ~ **of** GB malo

splatter /'splætə(r)/ vi,vt poprskati

splay /spleɪ/ vi,vt nakositi ~ **out** iskrenuti ~~footed adj širokih ravnih stopala

spleen /spliːn/ n 1 slezena 2 zlovolja; sjeta

splendid /'splendɪd/ adj sjajan, veličanstven

splendour (-dor US) /'splendə(r)/ n sjaj, divota

splice /splaɪs/ vt (to/onto/together) spojiti, zalijepiti

splint /splɪnt/ n udlaga

splinter /'splɪntə(r)/ n krhotina; špranja coll ~~proof adj pancirni ~ **group** disidenti

split /splɪt/ vi,vt irreg 1 (ras)cijepati, (raz)lomiti, (ras)parati, (ras)puknuti (se); (po)dijeliti (se) ~ **the difference** postići kompromis ~ **hairs** cjepidlačiti ~~level adj (stan/soba) na dva nivoa ~ **personality** podvojena ličnost ~ **second** djelić sekunde 2 ~ **up** prekinuti (s kim) 3 ~ (on sb) tužiti (koga) 4 sl otići • n 1 pukotina 2 fig raskol 3 podjela 4 banana split 5 **the** ~**s** sport špaga

splurge /splɜːdʒ/ vi,vt coll 1 privlačiti pozornost 2 spiskati (novac)

splutter /'splʌtə(r)/ vi,vt 1 zamuckivati 2 šištati, cvrčati

spoil /spɔɪl/ vt,vi irreg 1 pokvariti (se) 2 razmaziti (dijete); ugađati (kome) **be** ~ing **for sth** jedva čekati što be ~t **for choice** ne moći se odlučiti ~~sport coll osoba koja drugima kvari zabavu • ~**s** n pl form 1 privilegije 2 plijen

spoilt v irreg → spoil

spoke (1) v irreg → speak

spoke (2) /spəʊk/ n 1 žbica **put a** ~ **in sb's wheel** coll pokvariti kome planove 2 prečka ljestava

spoken v irreg → speak

spokesperson /'spəʊks,pɜːsən/ n 1 (spokesman) glasnogovornik 2 (spokeswoman) glasnogovornica

sponge /spʌndʒ/ n 1 spužva ~ **cake** biskvit 2 fig parazit • 1 vt,vi oprati/očistiti/upiti spužvom 2 vi,vt (off/on/from) živjeti na račun drugih **spongy** adj spužvast

sponsor /'spɒnsə(r)/ n 1 pokrovitelj, sponzor 2 kum(a) • vt sponzorirati, financirati ~~ship n pokroviteljstvo

spontaneous /spɒn'teɪnɪəs/ adj spontan **spontaneity** /ˌspɒntəˈniːətɪ/ n form spontanost

spoof /spuːf/ n coll (of/on) parodija • vt prevariti, nasamariti **~er** n varalica

spook /spuːk/ n coll 1 duh 2 špijun • vt US prestrašiti **~y** adj sablastan

spool /spuːl/ n navoj

spoon /spuːn/ n žlica **be born with a silver ~ in one's mouth** biti okružen bogatstvom od malih nogu **~feed** vt servirati na tanjuru fig **~ful** žlica • vt zagrabiti/izvaditi žlicom

spoor /spʊə(r)/ n trag (divlje životinje)

sporadic /spəˈrædɪk/ adj povremen, sporadičan

spore /spɔː(r)/ n spora

sporran /ˈspɒrən/ n kožna torbica (dio škotske nošnje)

sport /spɔːt/ n 1 (~s) šport; sport coll 2 ~s mod športski 3 coll fer/ ugodna/dobra osoba • vt nositi **~ing** adj športski, fer **~ive** adj veseo, živahan **~sman** n športaš **~manlike** adj športski, fer **~manship** n športsko/fer ponašanje

spot /spɒt/ n 1 točka **bright ~** svijetla točka **tender ~** slaba točka 2 mrlja 3 prištić **beauty ~** madež 4 mjesto **trouble ~s** krizna područja **in a ~** u škripcu **on the ~ a.** na mjestu, na licu mjesta **b.** smjesta **~ check** štihproba coll 5 TV, radio termin; spot • vt,vi opaziti **~ted** adj točkast; prošaran • adj koji se plaća/kupuje odmah • adv (~on) coll točno, na dlaku **~less** adj besprijekoran **~ter** n promatrač **~ter plane** mil izviđački zrakoplov **~ty** adj prištav; točkast

spotlight /ˈspɒtlaɪt/ n reflektor; svjetlost reflektora **in the ~** izvrgnut pogledu javnosti • vt skrenuti pozornost na što, istaknuti

spouse /spaʊz/ n leg, form suprug(a)

spout /spaʊt/ vi,vt (out) brizgati • n 1 otvor, grlo 2 mlaz

sprain /spreɪn/ vt uganuti • n uganuće

sprang v irreg → **spring**

sprawl /sprɔːl/ vi,vt protezati se, rastegnuti se; prostirati se; širiti se

spray (1) /spreɪ/ vi,vt prskati • n 1 kapljice 2 sprej

spray (2) n grančica

spread /spred/ vi,vt irreg 1 širiti (se), proširiti (se), raširiti (se) 2 prostirati se 3 namazati, mazati se • n 1 širenje; širina; raspon 2 veliki ilustrirani članak 3 namaz 4 coll gozba 5 US zemlja

spree /spriː/ n odavanje užitku **drinking ~** pijančevanje

sprig /sprɪg/ n grančica

sprightly /ˈspraɪtlɪ/ adj veseo, živahan

spring /sprɪŋ/ n 1 (~time) proljeće **~ onion** mladi luk 2 (~s) izvor **hot ~s** toplice 3 opruga 4 amortizer 5 elastičnost; živahnost 6 skok • vi,vi irreg 1 skočiti 2 (up) pojaviti se (niotkud) 3 neočekivano objaviti **~ from** potjecati **~ a leak** početi puštati vodu/curiti **~board** n odskočna daska (+ fig)

sprinkle /ˈsprɪŋkl/ vt,vi 1 poprskati, poškropiti; posipati 2 (kiša) sipiti **~r** n 1 vrtna prskalica 2 automatski požarni alarm

sprint /sprɪnt/ vi šprintati; trčati • n šprint

sprite /spraɪt/ n vila, vilenjak

sprocket /ˈsprɒkɪt/ n zubac **~ wheel** zupčanik

sprout /spraʊt/ vi,vt klijati • n 1 klica 2 (Brussels ~) prokulica

spruce (1) /spruːs/ n smreka; omorika

spruce (2) adj uredan; dotjeran, elegantan • vt,vi urediti (se)

sprung v irreg → **spring**

spry /spraɪ/ adj čio, vitalan

spud /spʌd/ n coll krumpir

spume /spjuːm/ n pjena

spun v irreg → **spin**

spunk /spʌŋk/ n 1 coll hrabrost 2 GB tab sl sperma

spur /spɜː(r)/ n 1 mamuza 2 poticaj **on the ~ of the moment** bez razmišljanja • vt 1 podbosti mamuzama 2 poticati; tjerati

spurious /ˈspjʊərɪəs/ adj form neistinit; neiskren; neprav

spurn /spɜːn/ vt prezreti, odbaciti

spurt /spɜːt/ vi,vt 1 šiknuti; izbacivati u mlazu 2 (for) napregnuti sve snage; povećati brzinu • n 1 mlaz 2 zamah fig

sputter /ˈspʌtə(r)/ vi,vt 1 frfljati 2

pucketati

spy /spaɪ/ *n* špijun • *vi,vt* 1 špijunirati 2 *lit* ugledati, opaziti

squab /skwɒb/ *n* mladi golub

squabble /'skwɒbl/ *vi* (about/over) svađati se, prepirati se • *n* prepirka

squad /skwɒd/ *n* 1 skupina, tim, ekipa 2 *mil* skupina vojnika; odred

squadron /'skwɒdrən/ *n* eskadra; eskadrila

squalid /'skwɒlɪd/ *adj* bijedan, prljav, neudoban

squall /skwɔːl/ *n* 1 olujni vjetar 2 *fig* svađa • *vi* derati se

squalor /'skwɒlə(r)/ *n* bijeda, prljavština, loši uvjeti

squander /'skwɒndə(r)/ *vt* (pro)tratiti

square /skweə(r)/ *n* 1 četverokut; kvadrat 2 trg 3 polje **back to ~ one** natrag na početak • *adj* 1 četvrtast 2 kvadratni 3 ravan; pod pravim kutem 4 **(fair and ~)** pošten **on the ~** pošteno **all ~** izjednačen • *vt,vi* 1 izravnati 2 podijeliti na četverokute 3 *math* kvadrirati 4 poklapati se; izjednačiti 5 *coll* podmititi **~ up** izravnati račune **~ up to sth** suočiti se s čime

squash (1) /skwɒʃ/ *vt,vi* 1 zgnječiti **~y** *adj* gnjecav 2 natrpati, stisnuti (se) 3 ušutkati • *n* 1 gužva, stiska 2 *sport* skvoš 3 sok

squash (2) *n US* buća; tikva

squat (1) /skwɒt/ *vi* 1 čučiti, čučnuti 2 bespravno stanovati/useliti se • *n* 1 čučanj 2 prazan stan **~ter** *n* bespravni stanar

squat (2) *adj* zdepast

squaw /skwɔː/ *n* Indijanka, skvo

squawk /skwɔːk/ *vi* 1 krieštati 2 *fig* jadati se • *n* krieštanje

squeak /skwiːk/ *vi* 1 cviliti, skvičati 2 škripiti 3 (through) provući se • *n* cvilež, škripa **~y** *adj* krieštav; škripav **~y clean** besprijekoran

squeal /skwiːl/ *vi* 1 vrištati 2 (on) *sl* cinkati • *n* vrisak

squeamish /'skwiːmɪʃ/ *adj* preosjetljiv

squeeze /skwiːz/ *vt,vi* stisnuti, istisnuti; (is)cijediti (+ *fig*); strpati, natrpati • *n* 1 stisak 2 stiska, gužva 3 nekoliko kapi 4 škripac **put the ~ on sb**

coll prišarafiti koga *sl*

squelch /skweltʃ/ *vi* šljapkati

squib /skwɪb/ *n* 1 žabica 2 satiričan članak

squid /skwɪd/ *n* (*pl* ~, ~s) lignja

squint /skwɪnt/ *vi* 1 žmirkati 2 škiljiti, zrikati • *n* razrokost

squire /'skwaɪə(r)/ *n* 1 vlastelin 2 štitonoša 3 *GB coll* gazda **~archy** *n* vlastela

squirm /skwɜːm/ *vi* previjati se, svijati se, grčiti se

squirrel /'skwɪrəl/ *n* vjeverica

squirt /skwɜːt/ *vt,vi* (po)prskati, štrcati • *n* štrcaj

stab /stæb/ *vt,vi* (at/in) probosti, ubosti, zabiti • *n* 1 ubod 2 *fig* bol, probadanje **have/make a ~ at sth** *coll* pokušati što

stable (1) /'steɪbl/ *adj* 1 čvrst, stabilan, stalan, uravnotežen 2 postojan **stability** /stə'bɪlətɪ/ *n* stabilnost; postojanost

stable (2) *n* 1 konjušnica, štala 2 ergela

stack /stæk/ *n* 1 hrpa, gomila 2 plast • *vt,vi* 1 (up) složiti na hrpu/u stog 2 *coll* namjestiti karte

stadium /'steɪdɪəm/ *n* (*pl* ~s, -dia) stadion

staff /stɑːf/ *n* 1 osoblje 2 *GB* namještenici *pl* 3 (*pl* **staves** /'steɪvz/) štap 4 jarbol 5 stožer

stag /stæg/ *n* 1 jelen 2 *GB* špekulant **~ party** momačka večer

stage /steɪdʒ/ *n* 1 pozornica (+ *fig*) 2 faza, razdoblje, stupanj 3 dionica 4 (**~coach**) poštanska kočija • *vt* 1 postaviti (predstavu) 2 organizirati, prirediti 3 *fig* inscenirati **~ fright** trema **~ manager** inspicijent

stagger /'stægə(r)/ *vi,vt* 1 teturati 2 preneraziti • *n* teturanje **~ing** *adj* nevjerojatan, slaman

stagnant /'stægnənt/ *adj* 1 stajaći, ustajao 2 koji stagnira **stagnate** /stæg'neɪt/ *vi* stagnirati

staid /steɪd/ *adj* ozbiljan, trezven

stain /steɪn/ *vt,vi* 1 (za)mrljati, zaprljati (se); okaljati (+ *fig*) 2 obojiti (tkaninu/drvo) • *n* 1 mrlja 2 *fig* ljaga 3 boja, močilo **~ed glass** vitraž **~less**

adj nehrđajući

stair /steə(r)/ *n* 1 stepenica, stuba 2 *lit* stepenište, stube **~case/way** stepenište, stubište **~s** *n pl* stepenice, stube

stake /steɪk/ *n* 1 kolac, stup 2 udio; interes 3 ulog **burn at the ~** spaliti na lomači **at ~** *fig* na kocki **~s** *n pl* 1 ulozi 2 konjske trke • *vt* 1 (on) kladiti se na što; staviti što na kocku 2 (up) poduprijeti kolcima 3 (off/out) iskolčati, ograditi **~** (out) **a claim** (to sth) polagati pravo na što **~ out** *US coll* tajno pratiti/promatrati

stale /steɪl/ *adj* 1 ustajao; pljesniv 2 otrcan (šala)

stalemate /'steɪlmeɪt/ *n* pat pozicija (+ *fig*) • *vt* dovesti u pat poziciju

stalk /stɔːk/ *n* 1 stabljika 2 stalak čaše • *vt,vi* 1 prišuljati se 2 uobraženo/uvrijeđeno/ponosno hodati

stall /stɔːl/ *n* 1 *GB* štand 2 WC/tuš kabina • *vt,vi* 1 zaustaviti (se) (motor) 2 *coll* odugovlačiti, otezati; izmotavati se 3 *coll* odgoditi; zadržati koga **~ for time** nastojati dobiti na vremenu

stallion /'stæliən/ *n* pastuh

stalwart /'stɔːlwət/ *adj* 1 snažan, jak 2 čvrst, odlučan

stamina /'stæmɪnə/ *n* izdržljivost

stammer /'stæmə(r)/ *vi,vt* zamuckivati, mucati • *n* mucanje

stamp /stæmp/ *vi,vt* 1 udarati nogom, toptati 2 zgaziti 3 (out) iskorijeniti; ugušiti; ugasiti (vatru) gaženjem 4 (on/with) udariti žig 5 staviti marku 6 (as) *fig* ožigosati **~ing ground** *coll* okupljalište, omiljeno mjesto • *n* 1 (poštanska) marka; biljeg 2 žig 3 *fig* trag **~ collector** filatelist

stampede /stæm'piːd/ *n* stampedo • *vi,vt* 1 izazvati stampedo; pobjeći glavom bez obzira 2 *fig* nagrnuti

stance /stæns/ *n* 1 *sport* položaj 2 (on) stajalište

stand /stænd/ *vi,vt irreg* 1 stajati 2 (up) ustati 3 (po)staviti, uspraviti 4 podnositi 5 nalaziti se 6 vrijediti **~ sb sth** častiti koga čime **~ by a.** podržati, pomoći kime b. biti pripravan **~by** *n* 1 rezerva 2 stanje pripravnosti

lista čekanja **~ down** odstupiti, povući se **~ for a.** značiti (kratica) **b.** dopustiti **c.** zagovarati **d.** *GB* kandidirati se **~ in for** zamjenjivati (koga) **~in** 1 zamkader, dubler 2 zamjena **~ out a.** isticati se; vidjeti se **b.** (against) protiviti se **~ sb up** *coll* ne doći na sastanak s kime **~ up for** stati u čiju obranu; podržati **~ up to sb** hrabro se oduprijeti komu **~ing** *adj* 1 stalan 2 stajaći ○ *n* 1 položaj; ugled 2 trajanje **~ing orders** poslovnik **of long ~ing** dugogodišnji **~offish** *adj* hladan, rezerviran **~point** gledište, stajalište **~still** mirovanje, zastoj; mrtva točka • *n* 1 štand 2 stalak; postolje 3 **~s** tribina 4 otpor 5 (on) stav 6 stajalište taksija **make a ~** usprotiviti se **take a/one's ~** zauzeti stav/stanovište

standard /'stændəd/ *n* 1 mjerilo, standard 2 *fig* norma, pravilo, zahtjev 3 zastava, stijeg • *adj* standardan; normalan, uobičajen **~ize** *vt* standardizirati, normirati, ujednačiti

stank *v irreg* → **stink**

staple (1) /'steɪpl/ *n* spajalica • *vt* pričvrstiti **~r** *n* spajalica, klamerica (sprava)

staple (2) *adj* glavni, osnovni • *n* glavni proizvod; osnovna namirnica

star /stɑː(r)/ *n* zvijezda (+ *fig*) **~dom** *n* filmska slava **~fish** morska zvijezda **~ry** *adj* zvjezdan; blistav **~ry-eyed** *adj coll* zanesen **the S~s and Stripes** *US* američka zastava **the S~ Spangled Banner a.** američka himna **b.** *US* američka zastava • *vt,vi* 1 (in) igrati glavnu ulogu 2 označiti zvjezdicom

starboard /'stɑːbəd/ *n* desna strana broda/zrakoplova

starch /stɑːtʃ/ *n* 1 škrob 2 štirka • *vt* štirkati **~y** *adj* uštirkan (+ *fig*)

stare /steə(r)/ *vi,vt* (at) buljiti • *n* (uporan) pogled

stark /stɑːk/ *adj* 1 ukočen 2 pust 3 gol (činjenica) 4 potpun • *adv* potpuno

starling /'stɑːlɪŋ/ *n* čvorak

start /stɑːt/ *vi,vt* (off/on/out/up) 1 (za)početi 2 krenuti, poći 3 pokrenuti (se); naviti (sat); upaliti (vatru) 4 lecnuti se, trgnuti se **5** osnovati, pokrenuti • *n* **1** početak **2** *sport* start **3** (on/over) prednost **4** trzaj **get off to a bad** ~ loše krenuti **~er** *n* **1** natjecatelj **2** starter **3** *GB coll* predjelo **~ing point** polazište

startle /'stɑ:tl/ *vt* iznenaditi, prenerazi-ti, uplašiti

starve /stɑ:v/ *vi,vt* **1** gladovati, skapavati od gladi **2** (out) izgladniti koga **be ~d of sth** biti lišen čega **starvation** *n* gladovanje, smrt od gladi

stash /stæʃ/ *vt coll* (away) sakriti, spremiti • *n* (tajna) zaliha

state /steɪt/ *n* **1** stanje **2** država **3** *mod* državni; svečan **4** položaj **5** raskoš, sjaj **in ~** svečano **~hood** *n* državnost **~ly** *adj* dostojanstven; veličanstven **~-of-the-art** *adj* najnoviji **~sman** *n* državnik • *vt* izjaviti, navesti, priopćiti **~ment** *n* **1** izjava, iskaz **2** izvješće, priopćenje **3** izvod

static /'stætɪk/ *adj* nepokretan, ustajao; statičan • *n radio, TV* smetnje

station /'steɪʃn/ *n* **1** postaja, stanica; kolodvor **2** (društveni) položaj ~ **wagon** *US* karavan • *vt* postaviti, razmjestiti, stacionirati **~ary** *adj* nepokretan, nepomičan

stationer /'steɪʃnə(r)/ *n* trgovac pisaćim priborom **~'s (shop)** papirnica **~y** *n* **1** pisaći pribor **2** papir za pisma, listovni papir

statistics /stə'tɪstɪks/ *n* statistika; statistički podaci

statue /'stætʃu:/ *n* kip

stature /'stætʃə(r)/ *n* **1** rast, stas **2** *fig* ugled, kalibar

status /'steɪtəs/ *n* stanje; položaj

statute /'stætʃu:t/ *n* statut **statutory** *adj* zakonski **statutory rape** *US* silovanje maloljetnice

staunch /stɔ:ntʃ/ *adj* pouzdan, vjeran • *vt* zaustaviti (krvarenje)

stave (1) /steɪv/ *n* crtovlje

stave (2) /steɪv/ *vt,vi* ~ **off** osloboditi, odgoditi, suzbiti, odvratiti

stay /steɪ/ *vi,vt* **1** ostati; zadržati se **2** (with/at) ostati u gostima; odsjesti ~ **put** *coll* ne micati se ~ **the night** prenoćiti ~ **up** ostati budan **~ing power** izdržljivost • *n* boravak

steadfast /'stedfɑ:st/ *adj form* **1** pouzdan **2** čvrst, postojan, uporan

steady /'stedɪ/ *adj* **1** čvrst, siguran **2** pravilan, ustaljen **3** stalan; pouzdan • *adv* **go ~** hodati *coll* • *vt,vi* učvrstiti; umiriti (se); ustaliti se

steak /steɪk/ *n* odrezak

steal /sti:l/ *vt,vi irreg* (u)krasti ~ **into** ušuljati se ~ **out** of iskrasti se **~th** /stelθ/ *n* **by ~th** krišom, potajno **~thy** *adj* nečujan, neprimjetan, potajan

steam /sti:m/ *n* **1** para **2** *fig* energija, snaga **~ engine** parni stroj **~er** *n* **1** parobrod **2** parni lonac **~roller** *n* parni valjak o *vt fig* pregaziti, prisiliti; prograti (zakonski prijedlog) **~ship** parobrod **~y** *adj* **1** pun pare **2** *coll* erotski • *vi,vt* **1** (away) isparavati se, pušiti se **2** kuhati na pari **3** (up) zamagliti se

steel /sti:l/ *n* **1** čelik **2** *lit* mač; bodež **cold** ~ hladno oružje **~works** čeličana **~y** *adj* čeličan (+ *fig*) • *vt* **1** očeličiti **2** otvrdnuti (srce); hrabriti koga **3** (oneself) smoći snage/hrabrosti

steep (1) /sti:p/ *adj* **1** strm **2** nagao

steep (2) /sti:p/ *vt,vi* (in) namakati (se), kiseliti **~ed in sth** ogrezao u

steeple /'sti:pl/ *n* šiljasti toranj, zvonik **~chase** trka sa zaprekama

steer /stɪə(r)/ *vt,vi* kormilariti, upravljati ~ **clear of** *coll* kloniti se koga/čega **~ing committee** upravljački odbor **~ing wheel** kormilo; upravljač

stellar /'stelə(r)/ *adj* zvjezdan

stem /stem/ *n* **1** deblo; stabljika; peteljka **2** stalak (čaše); usnik (lule) **3** osnova (riječi) • *vt,vi* **1** spriječiti, zaustaviti **2** (from) potjecati, proizlaziti

stench /stentʃ/ *n* smrad, zadah

stencil /'stensl/ *n* šablona; matrica • *vt* pisati/slikati pomoću šablone

stenographer /stə'nɒɡrəfə(r)/ *n US* stenograf

step /step/ *n* **1** korak (+ *fig*) **2** stepenica, stuba **3** pomak; stupanj; **take** ~s poduzeti korake/mjere **~ladder** (~s *GB*) sklopive ljestve • *vi,vt* koračati ~ **aside a.** stati u stranu **b.** *fig* povući se

~ down a. sići b. *fig* povući se **~ forward** istupiti **~ in** a. ući b. umiješati se, posredovati **~ off/out** izmjeriti koracima **~ on it!** daj gas! **~ out** a. produžiti korak b. *US* izaći, otići **~ up** povećati, pojačati, ubrzati **~ping-stone** a. kamen za prelaženje potoka b. *fig* stepenica (do uspjeha)

step- /step/ *prefix* **~brother** polubrat **~child** pastorak, pastorka **~daughter** pastorka **~father** očuh **~mother** maćeha **~sister** polusestra **~son** pastorak

stereo /'steriəu/ *adj* stereo

stereotype /'steriətaip/ *n* stereotip

sterile /'sterail/ *adj* 1 neplodan, nerodan; jalov (+ *fig*) 2 steriliziran

sterling /'stɜ:liŋ/ *n* (**pound ~**) britanska funta • *adj* 1 čist 2 *fig* istinski, pravi

stern (1) /stɜ:n/ *adj* strog

stern (2) *n* krma

stevedore /'sti:vədɔ:(r)/ *n US* lučki radnik

stew /stju:/ *vt,vi* pirjati • *n* gulaš **in a ~** *coll* a. uzrujan, zabrinut b. u neprilici; u sosu *coll*

steward /stjuəd/ *n* 1 stjuard, poslužitelj, konobar 2 organizator (konjskih trka) 3 opskrbnik 4 majordom, upravitelj imanja **~ess** *n* stjuardesa

stick /stik/ *n* 1 prut, suharak 2 štap 3 batina, šiba 4 palica 5 komad(ić) • *vt,vi irreg* 1 (za)bosti, nabosti (se), zataknuti 2 (za)lijepiti (se) 3 zaglaviti (se); zapeti 4 *coll* snositi 5 *GB coll* podnositi **~ about/around** *coll* biti u blizini **~ at nothing** ne prezati ni pred čim **~ out** a. stršiti; isplaziti (jezik); podmetnuti (nogu) b. *coll* isticati se c. izdržati do kraja **~ to** držati se čega **~ together** *coll* biti složni **~ up** *coll* opljačkati **~up** *n* oružana pljačka **~ up for** zauzeti se za **~ with** *coll* biti uz koga, držati se koga; nastaviti sa čime **~er** *n* naljepnica **~y** *adj* 1 ljepljiv 2 *coll* neugodan, škakljiv 3 (about) *coll* nesusretljiv

stickler /'stiklə(r)/ *n coll* **he is a ~ for punctuality** inzistira na točnosti

stiff /stif/ *adj* 1 ukočen; krut; tvrd; gust 2 usiljen, uštogljen 3 *coll* jak, žestok 4 oštar; težak **keep a ~ upper lip** stisnuti zube **~en** *vt,vi* ukočiti (se), ukrutiti (se) • *adv* **be frozen ~** smrznuti se do kostiju **scared ~** nasmrt preplašen • *n sl* leš

stifle /'staifl/ *vt,vi* (u)gušiti (se) **stifling** *adj* zagušljiv

stiletto /sti'letəu/ *n* bodež **~ heel** visoka peta

still (1) /stil/ *adv* 1 još uvijek 2 (pa) ipak 3 još (više) • *adj* 1 miran, nepomičan 2 tih • *vt form* umiriti, utišati • *n* 1 scena 2 *lit* mir, tišina **in the ~ of the night** u gluho doba noći **~born** mrtvorođen **~ life** (*pl* **~ lifes**) mrtva priroda

still (2) *n* kotao za pečenje rakije

stilt /stilt/ *n* 1 hodulja 2 potporanj **~ed** *adj* krut, neprirodan

stimulate /'stimjuleit/ *vt* (to sth/to do sth) poticati, podržavati, pobuditi **stimulus** /'stimjuləs/ *n* (*pl* **stimuli** /'stimjulai/) podražaj, poticaj

sting /stiŋ/ *vt,vi irreg* 1 (u)bosti (žalcem) 2 peći, boljeti • *n* 1 žalac 2 (oštra) bol; ubod

stingy /'stindʒi/ *adj* (with) škrt

stink /stiŋk/ *vi,vt irreg* 1 (of) smrdjeti (po) 2 *coll* biti grozan/odvratan • *n* smrad **~ing** *adj* smrdljiv

stint /stint/ *vt,vi* (sb of sth) štedjeti, škrtariti

stipulate /'stipjuleit/ *vt* predvidjeti, odrediti **stipulation** *n* odredba, uvjet

stir /stɜ:(r)/ *vt,vi* 1 promiješati 2 uskomešati, uznemiriti 3 micati se, pokrenuti se 4 (to) pobuditi, potaknuti (na) 5 dirnuti, ganuti 6 *coll* mućkati, spletkariti, širiti glasine **~ up** a. uzvitlati (prašinu), uzburkati, uzmutiti b. izazvati (nevolje); probuditi (sjećanja); podjarivati

stirrup /'stirəp/ *n* stremen

stitch /stitʃ/ *n* 1 šav 2 očica (kod pletenja) 3 bod 4 bol **a ~ in time saves nine** *prov.* bolje spriječiti nego liječiti • *vt,vi* (za)šiti

stoat /stəut/ *n* hermelin

stock /stok/ *n* 1 zaliha; roba 2 **~s** dionice 3 glavnica, kapital 4 temeljac (jelu) **5** popularnost **6** stoka **7** rod **8** usadnik; ručka in ~ na skladištu take ~ of procijeniti **~broker** burzovni mešetar ~ **exchange/market** burza **~holder** US dioničar **~pile** n zaliha o vt stvarati zalihe **~taking** inventura • vt **1** držati/imati (robu) u skladištu **2** (up/with) opskrbiti ~ **up** (on/with) opskrbiti se • adj uobičajen; otrcan ~ **phrase** izlizana fraza, kliše

stockings /ˈstɒkɪŋz/ n pl ženske čarape, najlonke

stocky /ˈstɒkɪ/ adj nabijen, zdepast

stodgy /ˈstɒdʒɪ/ adj coll teško probavljiv, težak (+ fig)

stoke /stəʊk/ vt,vi **1** (up/with) ložiti **2** fig podjarivati

stole, stolen v irreg → **steal**

stolid /ˈstɒlɪd/ adj flegmatičan; trom

stomach /ˈstʌmək/ n **1** želudac **2** trbuh **3** tek **4** sklonost, volja • vt fig podnijeti, probaviti

stone /stəʊn/ n **1** kamen **2** mjera za težinu (6,3 kg) **3** koštica **4** med kamenac **~d** adj sl drogiran; pijan ~ **deaf** gluh kao top **stony** adj **1** kamenit **2** fig hladan, tvrd, ukočen • vt **1** kamenovati **2** izvaditi košticu

stood v irreg → **stand**

stooge /stuːdʒ/ n **1** sporedni komičar, žrtva šale **2** coll nečija budala

stool /stuːl/ n **1** stolac (bez naslona) **2** med stolica

stoop /stuːp/ vi,vt **1** (down) pognuti se, sagnuti se **2** držati se pogrbljeno ~ **to sth** fig ponizti se

stop /stɒp/ vt,vi **1** (za)stati; zaustaviti (se) **2** prekinuti; prestati **3** (from) spriječiti; zadržati (koga) **4** (up) začepiti; zatvoriti **5** comm obustaviti isplatu ~ **at nothing** ne prezati ni pred čim ~ **by** navratiti, svratiti ~ **over** nakratko odsjesti, prekinuti putovanje • n **1** prekid, stanka **2** boravak **3** postaja, stanica, stajalište **4** (full ~) GB točka **bring sth to a ~/put a ~ to sth** okončati, zaustaviti **come to a ~** zaustaviti se **~page** /ˈstɒpɪdʒ/ n **1** obustava rada, štrajk **2** GB odbitak od plaće **3** zaustavljanje **~per** n čep **~watch** kronometar, štoperica

storage /ˈstɔːrɪdʒ/ n **1** skladištenje,

spremanje **2** skladište ~ **heater** termoakumulaciona peć

store /stɔː(r)/ vt **1** (up) spremati, gomilati (zalihe) **2** (away) uskladištiti; pohraniti **3** (with) opskrbiti • n **1** zaliha **2** skladište **3** US prodavaonica **4** riznica in ~ na skladištu; u pripremi **set great ~ by sth** pridavati čemu veliku važnost **~room** spremište, ostava **~s** n pl **1** vojne zalihe **2** robna kuća

storey (story US) /ˈstɔːrɪ/ n kat **a five- ~(ed) building** peterokatnica

stork /stɔːk/ n roda

storm /stɔːm/ n **1** oluja **2** fig bura, bujica, kiša ~ **in a teacup** GB coll bura u čaši vode **take by** ~ osvojiti na juriš (+ fig) ~ **trooper** jurišnik **~y** adj **1** olujan **2** fig buran • vt,vi **1** jurišati, osvojiti na juriš **2** (into) uletjeti, upasti **3** (at) bjesnjeti, galamiti, grmjeti na

story /ˈstɔːrɪ/ n **1** priča **2** sadržaj **3** opis, prikaz **to cut a long ~ short** ukratko rečeno

stout (1) /staʊt/ adj **1** krupan **2** čvrst, debeo, jak **3** odlučan, odvažan

stout (2) n tamno pivo

stove (1) /stəʊv/ n peć, štednjak

stove (2) v irreg → **stave**

stow /stəʊ/ vt (away) (na)tovariti, naslagati, spremiti **~away** n slijepi putnik

straddle /ˈstrædl/ vt,vi **1** opkoračiti **2** raskoračiti se

straight /streɪt/ adj **1** ravan **2** uspravan **3** (with) otvoren, pošten **4** ispravan **5** uzastopni **6** čist, nerazrijeđen **7** ozbiljan **8** sl heteroseksualan **put/get sth ~** dovesti što u red, urediti, pospremiti • adv **1** ravno **2** jasno, otvoreno **~away/~ off** odmah, smjesta **~ out** jasno, otvoreno, bez uvijanja ~ **up** GB coll najozbiljnije, stvarno **~en** vt,vi **1** (out) izravnati (se), ispraviti (se) **2** (raz)riješiti, raščistiti, srediti **3** (up) uspraviti se **~forward** adj **1** otvoren **2** jednostavan

strain (1) /streɪn/ vt,vi **1** naprezati (se) **2** (off/out) procijediti **3** pretjerati; prekoračiti **4** istegnuti (mišić) **~ed** adj **1** usiljen **2** napet, zategnut (odnos) **~er** *n* cjedilo • *n* **1** napetost; zategnutost **2** napor; opterećenje; pritisak, istegnuće, uganuće

strain (2) *n* **1** pasmina; rod, vrsta **2** ~s melodija **3** nasljedna osobina

strait /streɪt/ *n* (+ *pl*) tjesnac **in dire/desperate ~s** u teškom škripcu

straitjacket /'streɪt,dʒækɪt/ *n* luđačka košulja

strand (1) /strænd/ *n* **1** vlakno, pramen, nit **2** ~s *fig* niti

strand (2) *n poet* obala, žal • *vi,vt* nasukati (se) **be (left) ~ed** *fig* zaglaviti

strange /streɪndʒ/ *adj* **1** čudan, neobičan **2** nepoznat, stran **~r** *n* neznanac; stranac

strangle /'stræŋgl/ *vt* (za)daviti, gušiti **~hold 1** stisak oko vrata **2** (on) *fig* čvrsta kontrola (nad)

strap /stræp/ *n* pojas, remen • *vt* opasati/pričvrstiti/svezati remenom **~ping** *adj coll* kršan

stratagem /'strætədʒəm/ *n form* lukavština, varka

strategic /strə'tiːdʒɪk/ *adj* strateški **strategy** /'strætədʒɪ/ *n* strategija

stratum /'straːtəm/ *n* (*pl* **strata** /'straːta/) naslaga, sloj (+ *fig*)

straw /strɔː/ *n* **1** slama **2** slamka **the last ~/the ~ that breaks the camel's back** kap koja je prelila čašu **clutch at ~s** hvatati se za slamku **~ poll/vote** neslužbena predizborna anketa

strawberry /'strɔːbrɪ/ *n* jagoda

stray /streɪ/ *vi* (from) odlutati, zalutati, udaljiti se • *n* zalutala životinja, lutalica • *adj* povremen, rijedak **~ dog** pas lutalica **~ bullet** zalutali metak

streak /striːk/ *n* **1** pruga, trak **2** *fig* tračak **3** crta, karakteristika • *vi,vt* **1** juriti **2** isprugati

stream /striːm/ *n* **1** potok, rječica **2** tijek **3** *fig* bujica, mnoštvo, niz **4** (riječna) struja (+ *fig*) **~ of consciousness** struja/tok svijesti • *vi,vt* **1** (po)teći; lijevati **2** nadirati, nagrnuti **3** lepršati, vijoriti se **~er** *n* **1** duga papirna vrpca **2** uska zastavica **~line** *vt* modernizirati, poboljšati, pojednostaviti, učiniti ekonomičnim **~lined** *adj* aerodinamičan

street /striːt/ *n* ulica **man in the ~** običan/prosječan čovjek **~car** *US* tramvaj **~ cred(ibility)** *coll* popularnost (među mladima) **~ map** plan grada **~ walker** prostitutka **~wise** *coll* snalažljiv, koji poznaje zakon ulice

strength /streŋθ/ *n* **1** snaga; sila; jačina **2** brojno stanje **a show of ~** demonstracija sile **in ~** u velikom broju **go from ~ to ~** napredovati **on the ~ of** na temelju čega, potaknut čime **~en** *vt,vi* (p)ojačati (se), osnažiti

strenuous /'strenjʊəs/ *adj* **1** naporan **2** uporan

stress /stres/ *n* **1** napetost, napor; opterećenje, pritisak; stres **2** naglasak • *vt* istaknuti, naglasiti

stretch /stretʃ/ *vt,vi* **1** rastegnuti (se) **2** (out) ispružiti (se); protegnuti se **3** prostirati se **4** prekoračiti (ovlasti); pomaknuti (rok) **5** pretjerati • *n* **1** rastezanje, protezanje **2** rastezljivost **3** *mod* rastezljiv **4** (of) dionica (puta) **5** razdoblje **6** *sl* zatvorska kazna **at a ~** bez prekida **~er** *n* nosila *pl*

strew /struː/ *vt irreg* (on/over/with) posuti, razasuti

stricken /'strɪkən/ *adj* pogođen, obuzet

strict /strɪkt/ *adj* (with) strog; točan

stride /straɪd/ *vi irreg* **1** koračati, grabiti **2** (over/across) prekoračiti • *n* **1** dugačak/velik korak **2** *fig* napredak **get into one's ~** uhodati se **take sth in one's ~** svladati što s lakoćom

strident /'straɪdnt/ *adj* **1** kreštav, prodoran **2** *fig* glasan

strife /straɪf/ *n* razmirica, svađa; sukob

strike /straɪk/ *vt,vi irreg* **1** udariti; pogoditi; zadati (udarac) **2** (out) napasti **3** (into) utjerati (strah) **4** kresnuti **5** otkucati (sat) **6** štrajkati **7** naletjeti na **8** sklopiti (posao); napraviti (bilancu) **9** činiti se komu, dojmiti se **10** pasti na pamet **11** zauzeti (pozu) **be struck dumb** zanijemiti **~ down** oboriti **~ off** precrtati, prekrižiti **~ on/upon** pasti na pamet (ideja); smisliti (plan) **~ out/through** precrtati, prekrižiti **~ out** uputiti se **~ up a.** zapjevati, zasvirati **b.** (with) sklopiti (prijateljstvo) • *n* 1 štrajk 2 (zračni) napad **striking** *adj* izrazit, upadljiv

string /strɪŋ/ *n* 1 uzica 2 struna, žica 3 niska, ogrlica 4 niz 5 vlakno; tetiva **no ~s attached** bez posebnih uvjeta/obveza **~ beans** *US* mahune **the ~s** gudači instrumenti **~y** *adj* vlaknast; žilav • *vt,vi irreg* nanizati **~ sb along** *coll* vući za nos **~ along with sb** pridružiti se **be strung up** biti napet/napetih živaca

stringent /ˈstrɪndʒənt/ *adj* 1 oštar, strog 2 oskudan (o novcu)

strip /strɪp/ *vt,vi* 1 skinuti (se); oguliti, ogoliti; isprazniti 2 (down) rastaviti, razmontirati **~ sb of sth** oduzeti komu što • *n* uzak komad (papira), pojas (zemlje) **comic ~ (~ cartoon** *GB*) strip **~ lighting** neonska rasvjeta **~per** *n* 1 *coll* striptizeta 2 **(paint ~per)** razrjeđivač

stripe /straɪp/ *n* 1 pruga 2 oznaka čina

strive /straɪv/ *vi irreg* boriti se, težiti čemu, nastojati, truditi se, trsiti se

strode *v irreg → stride*

stroke /strəʊk/ *vt* gladiti, milovati, podragati • *n* 1 udarac 2 kap, udar; napadaj 3 potez (+ *fig*) 4 zamah; plivački stil 5 otkucaj (sata) 6 kosa crta, "kroz" **at a ~** jednim potezom/udarcem **on the ~ of one** točno u jedan sat

stroll /strəʊl/ *vi* šetati se • *n* šetnja

strong /strɒŋ/ *adj* jak, snažan; čvrst; oštar, strog **~hold** *n* uporište, utvrda

strove *v irreg → strive*

struck *v irreg → strike*

structure /ˈstrʌktʃə(r)/ *n* 1 građa, sastav, ustroj 2 građevina • *vt* strukturirati, ustrojiti

struggle /ˈstrʌgl/ *vi* (against/with) boriti se; otimati se, opirati se; nastojati, mučiti se • *n* 1 borba 2 napor

strum /strʌm/ *vi,vt* (on) drndati, nabijati (po gitari i sl.)

strung *v irreg → string*

strut (1) /strʌt/ *vi* šepiriti se

strut (2) *n* potporanj

stub /stʌb/ *n* 1 čik, opušak; ostatak olovke 2 odrezak (čeka) • *vt* **~ out** ugasiti (cigaretu)

stubble /ˈstʌbl/ *n* 1 strn; strnište 2 kratka oštra brada

stubborn /ˈstʌbən/ *adj* tvrdoglav

stuck *v irreg → stick*

stuck-up /ˌstʌkˈʌp/ *adj coll* uobražen

stud (1) /stʌd/ *n* 1 dugme ovratnika/manšete 2 zakovica **~ded with a.** optočen **b.** *fig* posut

stud (2) *n* 1 ergela 2 *tab coll* frajerčina

student /ˈstjuːdnt/ *n* 1 student 2 *US* učenik (srednjoškolac) 3 (of) proučavatelj

studio /ˈstjuːdɪəʊ/ *n* studio; atelje **~ flat** garsonijera

study /ˈstʌdɪ/ *n* 1 učenje; proučavanje 2 predmet proučavanja 3 istraživanje, analiza 4 studija; skica 5 radna soba • *vt,vi* 1 studirati 2 proučiti

stuff /stʌf/ *n coll* stvar(i), predmet(i), to • *vt* 1 (with/into) napuniti, natrpati, nagurati 2 preparirati 3 nadjenuti 4 **~ oneself with** prejesti se, preždrati se 5 (with) ključati koga čime **get ~ed** *GB sl* goni se **~y** *adj* 1 ustajao, zagušljiv 2 staromodan, konzervativan

stumble /ˈstʌmbl/ *vi* 1 (on/over) spotaknuti se (o) 2 posrtati 3 (at/over) zamuckivati, zastajkivati 4 (across/on/upon) nabasati **stumbling block** kamen spoticanja

stump /stʌmp/ *n* 1 panj 2 krnja, škrba; ostatak (olovke i sl.) 3 batrljak **stir your ~s** požuri! malo brže!

stun /stʌn/ *vt* 1 omamiti 2 zapanjiti **~ning** *adj* 1 prekrasan 2 zapanjujući

stung *v irreg → sting*

stunk *v irreg → stink*

stunt /stʌnt/ *n* akrobacija **pull a ~** izvesti vratolomiju **publicity ~** reklamni trik, reklama **~ man** kaskader

stunted /ˈstʌntɪd/ *adj* zakržljao

stupefy /ˈstjuːpɪfaɪ/ *vt form* 1 zapanjiti 2 omamiti

stupid /ˈstjuːpɪd/ *adj* glup **~ity** /stjuːˈpɪdətɪ/ *n* glupost

sturdy /ˈstɜːdɪ/ *adj* čvrst, jedar, krupan

stutter /ˈstʌtə(r)/ *vi,vt* (pro)mucati • *n* mucanje

sty /staɪ/ *n* svinjac

sty(e) /staɪ/ *n* ječmenac (na oku)

style /staɪl/ n 1 stil; način 2 vrsta, oblik 3 moda 4 naslov, titula • vt 1 dizajnirati, krojiti; frizirati 2 osloviti koga
stylish adj moderan, ukusan, elegantan stylist n 1 frizer 2 stilist
stymie /ˈstaɪmɪ/ vt coll onemogućiti
suave /swɑːv/ adj ugladen
sub /sʌb/ n coll 1 pričuvni igrač 2 podmornica 3 GB pretplata; članarina 4 GB akontacija 5 redaktor
subconscious /ˌsʌbˈkɒnʃəs/ adj podsvjestan • n the ~ podsvijest
subdue /səbˈdjuː/ vt 1 podjarmiti, pokoriti 2 svladati, obuzdati 3 prigušiti
subeditor /sʌbˈedɪtə(r)/ n redaktor
subject /ˈsʌbdʒɪkt/ n 1 tema 2 predmet razgovora 3 školski predmet 4 gram subjekt 5 podanik, građanin 6 (of/for) uzrok, povod ~ matter sadržaj, tema • adj (to) 1 podložan, podvrgnut; vezan (zakonom) 2 osjetljiv, sklon ~ to ovisno o; ako, pod uvjetom da • vt /səbˈdʒekt/ (to) 1 pokoriti 2 izložiti, izvrgnuti
sublet /ˌsʌbˈlet/ vt,vi dati u podnajam/podzakup
sublime /səˈblaɪm/ adj 1 uzvišen; dostojanstven 2 coll veličanstven 3 krajnji (neznanje)
submachine gun /ˌsʌbməˈʃiːnɡʌn/ n automat (oružje)
submarine /ˌsʌbməˈriːn/ adj podmorski, podvodni • n podmornica
submerge /səbˈmɜːdʒ/ vt,vi 1 uroniti, zaroniti 2 preplaviti, potopiti
submit /səbˈmɪt/ vt,vi (to) 1 podvrći (se) 2 predati se, popustiti, pomiriti se s 3 podastrijeti, podnijeti submission /səbˈmɪʃn/ n 1 podčinjenost 2 podnošenje 3 poslušnost 4 leg prijedlog, molba submissive adj pokoran, ponizan
subordinate /səˈbɔːdɪnət/ adj (to) podređen, sporedan, zavisan • n podređeni
subpoena /səˈpiːnə/ n leg sudski poziv • vt pozvati na sud
subscribe /səbˈskraɪb/ vi,vt 1 (to) pretplatiti se (na) 2 priložiti (novac) 3 (to) zagovarati ~r n pretplatnik subscription /səbˈskrɪpʃn/ n 1 pretplata;

članarina 2 dobrovoljni prilog
subsequent /ˈsʌbsɪkwənt/ adj kasniji, naknadni, slijedeći ~ to iza, nakon ~ly adv kasnije
subside /səbˈsaɪd/ vi 1 sleći se, uleknuti se 2 opadati, opasti; jenjati 3 fig splasnuti
subsidiary /səbˈsɪdɪərɪ/ adj (to) dopunski; pomoćni • n (of) podružnica
subsidize /ˈsʌbsɪdaɪz/ vt subvencionirati subsidy /ˈsʌbsədɪ/ n subvencija
subsist /səbˈsɪst/ vi (on) živjeti (od), preživljavati ~ence n preživljavanje; sredstva za život at ~ence level na egzistencijalnom minimumu
substance /ˈsʌbstəns/ n 1 tvar 2 form stvarnost 3 bit, suština; sadržaj 4 važnost 5 čvrstoća 6 form imetak
substantial /səbˈstænʃl/ adj 1 čvrst, jak 2 obilat (obrok) 3 bitan, znatan 4 postojeći, stvaran 5 form dobrostojeći   postići načelan dogovor substantially adv 1 prilično, znatno 2 uglavnom, većinom substantiate /səbˈstænʃɪeɪt/ vt potkrijepiti što, dokazati
substitute /ˈsʌbstɪtjuːt/ n (for) 1 nadomjestak; zamjena 2 pričuvni igrač • vt,vi (sth/sb for) nadomjestiti; zamijeniti substitution /ˌsʌbstɪˈtjuːʃn/ n zamjena
subterfuge /ˈsʌbtəfjuːdʒ/ n izlika; obmana
subtitle /ˈsʌbtaɪtl/ n podnaslov ~s n pl titlovi
subtle /ˈsʌtl/ adj 1 istančan, profinjen; blag 2 pronicav; lukav 3 vješt
subtract /səbˈtrækt/ vt (from) oduzimati ~ion /səbˈtrækʃn/ n oduzimanje
suburb /ˈsʌbɜːb/ n predgrađe ~an /səˈbɜːbən/ adj iz predgrađa, u predgrađu, prigradski ~ia n derog predgrađa; malograđanština
subversive /səbˈvɜːsɪv/ adj protudržavni, podrivački
subway /ˈsʌbweɪ/ n 1 pothodnik 2 US podzemna željeznica
succeed /səkˈsiːd/ vi,vt 1 (in doing sth) uspjeti 2 (to/as) naslijediti success /səkˈses/ n uspjeh successful adj uspješan succession /səkˈseʃn/ n 1 slijed 2 (of) niz, red 3 (to) naslijed-

stvo **successive** adj uzastopan **successor** n (to/as) nasljednik

succinct /sək'sıŋkt/ adj jasan, jezgrovit

succulent /'sʌkjʊlənt/ adj sočan

succumb /sə'kʌm/ vi (to) podleći čemu, popustiti pred čim

such /sʌtʃ/ adj, pron takav ~ **as** takav kakav, kao što je, kao na primjer ~ **and** ~ taj i taj ~ **a lovely day** tako lijep dan ~**like** adj takav, sličan o pron coll tome slično

suck /sʌk/ vt,vi 1 sisati 2 povući, progutati, uvući, upijati ~ **up to sb** GB coll ulizivati/uvlačiti se kome ~**er** n 1 prijanjaljka, sisaljka 2 izdanak, mladica 3 coll naivčina ~**le** vt,vi dojiti; sisati ~**ling** n odojak **suction** /'sʌkʃn/ n usisavanje

sudden /'sʌdn/ adj iznenadan, nagao, neočekivan **all of a** ~ iznenada ~**ly** adv iznenada, najednom

suds /sʌdz/ n pl pjena, sapunica

sue /s(j)u:/ vt,vi (for) tužiti

suede /sweɪd/ n antilop koža

suet /'su:ɪt/ n loj

suffer vi,vt 1 (from) patiti, trpjeti 2 (for) platiti (za što) 3 pretrpjeti, snositi 4 form podnositi ~**ing** n bol, patnja, stradanje

suffice /sə'faɪs/ vi,vt (for) biti dovoljan, dostajati, zadovoljiti ~ **it to say** dosta je ako se kaže **sufficient** /sə'fɪʃnt/ adj dovoljan, dostatan

suffix /'sʌfɪks/ n sufiks, dometak

suffocate /'sʌfəkeɪt/ vt,vi (za)daviti, (u)gušiti (se)

suffrage /'sʌfrɪdʒ/ n pravo glasa **universal** ~ opće pravo glasa

sugar /'ʃʊgə(r)/ n šećer ~ **beet/cane** šećerna repa/trska ~**y** adj 1 sladak 2 fig sladunjav • vt šećeriti

suggest /sə'dʒest/ vt 1 predložiti 2 ukazivati na što 3 pobuditi, dočarati ~**ion** /sə'dʒestʃən/ n 1 prijedlog, savjet, ideja 2 nagovještaj, prizvuk ~**ive** adj 1 dvosmislen (šala) 2 (of) koji podsjeća/ukazuje na

suicide /'s(j)u:ɪsaɪd/ n 1 samoubojstvo 2 samoubojica

suit /s(j)u:t/ n 1 odijelo; kostim 2 boja karata 3 parnica, tužba **follow** ~ **a.**

odgovarati na boju **b.** slijediti čiji primjer ~**case** kofer • vt 1 odgovarati, biti prikladan 2 pristajati ~ **yourself** kako hoćeš ~**able** adj (for/to) odgovarajući, pogodan, prikladan, primjeren ~**ably** adv prikladno, primjereno

suite /swi:t/ n 1 garnitura 2 apartman 3 pratnja, svita 4 suita

suitor /'s(j)u:tə(r)/ n 1 prosac 2 podnositelj tužbe

sulk /sʌlk/ vi duriti se ~**y** adj mrzovoljan

sullen /'sʌlən/ adj mrk, mrzovoljan

sulphur (**sulfur** US) /'sʌlfə(r)/ n sumpor

sultry /'sʌltri/ adj 1 sparan, zagušljiv 2 fig zavodljiv

sum /sʌm/ n 1 svota, iznos; zbroj 2 računski zadatak **in** ~ ukratko **do** ~**s** računati **lump** ~ okrugli iznos, paušalna svota ~ **total** ukupan iznos/zbroj • vt,vi ~ **up** 1 zbrojiti 2 sažeti 3 procijeniti

summary (1) /'sʌmərɪ/ n sažetak **summarize** vt sažeti

summary (2) adj leg prijek, skraćen **summarily** adv po kratkom postupku; bez suđenja

summer /'sʌmə(r)/ n ljeto

summit /'sʌmɪt/ n 1 vrh 2 form vrhunac 3 (~ **meeting**) sastanak na vrhu

summon /'sʌmən/ vt form 1 (službeno) pozvati 2 sazvati 3 (up) skupiti (snagu) ~**s** n pl sudski poziv o vt uručiti sudski poziv

sumptuous /'sʌmptʃʊəs/ adj raskošan, skupocjen

sun /sʌn/ n sunce ~**bathe** vi sunčati se ~**burn** n opeklina od sunca ~**dial** sunčani sat ~**down** n zalazak sunca ~**flower** suncokret ~**glasses** sunčane naočale ~**light** Sunčeva svjetlost ~**ny** adj 1 sunčan 2 vedar ~**rise** (~**up** coll) izlazak sunca, zora ~**set** zalazak sunca ~**shade** suncobran ~**shine a.** Sunčeva svjetlost **b.** fig radost ~**stroke** sunčanica ~**tan** preplanulost

sundae /'sʌndeɪ/ n voćni sladoled preliven sirupom

Sunday /'sʌndɪ/ n nedjelja ~ **best**

svečano odijelo ~ **school** nedjeljni vjeronauk

sundry /'sʌndrɪ/ *adj* razan, različit **sundries** *n pl* sitna roba, sitni izdaci, razno

sung *v irreg* → **sing**

sunk *v irreg* → **sink** ~**en** *adj* **1** potonuo **2** upao (obraz) **3** uleknut

super /'su:pə(r)/ *adj coll* sjajan, super

superannuation /ˌsu:pərˌænjʊ'eɪʃn/ *n form* (starosna) mirovina, penzija

superb /su:'pɜ:b/ *adj* izvanredan, odličan

supercilious /ˌsu:pə'sɪlɪəs/ *adj* umišljen

superficial /ˌsu:pə'fɪʃl/ *adj* površinski **2** površan, plitak

superfluous /su:'pɜ:fluəs/ *adj* nepotreban, suvišan

superhuman /ˌsu:pə'hju:mən/ *adj* nadljudski

superintend /ˌsu:pərɪn'tend/ *vt* nadgledati, nadzirati ~**ent** *n* **1** nadglednik, nadzornik, upravitelj **2** *GB* policijski inspektor

superior /su:'pɪərɪə(r)/ *adj* **1** pretpostavljen **2** (to) bolji; stariji/viši (po položaju) **3** jači, nadmoćniji • *n* pretpostavljeni, starješina ~**ity** /su:ˌpɪərɪ'ɒrəti/ *n* (in/over) nadmoć(nost), premoć

superlative /su:'pɜ:lətɪv/ *n gram* superlativ • *adj* izvanredan

supermarket /'su:pəmɑ:kɪt/ *n* samoposluživanje, supermarket

supernatural /ˌsu:pə'nætʃrəl/ *adj* nadnaravan

superpower /'su:pəˌpaʊə/ *n* velesila

supersonic /ˌsu:pə'sɒnɪk/ *adj* nadzvučan

superstition /ˌsu:pə'stɪʃn/ *n* praznovjerje **superstitious** /ˌsu:pə'stɪʃəs/ *adj* praznovjeran

supervise /'su:pəvaɪz/ *vt,vi* nadgledati **supervisor** *n* nadglednik

supper /'sʌpə(r)/ *n* večera

supplement /'sʌplɪmənt/ *n* **1** dodatak, dopuna **2** prilog • *vt* (by/with) dodati, (na)dopuniti ~**ary** *adj* dodatan, dopunski

supply /sə'plaɪ/ *vt* **1** dobavljati, nabavljati **2** dostavljati, isporučiti; op-

skrbiti • *n* **1** zaliha **2** dobava; isporuka; opskrba ~ **and demand** ponuda i potražnja **supplier** *n* dobavljač, opskrbljivač

support /sə'pɔ:t/ *vt* **1** (pod)nositi (teret); podupirati **2** uzdržavati **3** podržavati **4** bodriti, navijati za **5** potkrijepiti, potvrditi • *n* **1** potpora **2** nosač, potporanj **3** podrška **4** uzdržavanje, sredstva za život ~**er** *n* **1** pristaša, zagovornik **2** navijač

suppose /sə'pəʊz/ *vt* **1** pretpostaviti **2** držati, misliti **he was ~d to do it** on je to trebao učiniti • *conj* ~/**supposing (that)** što ako, recimo da, u slučaju da ~**d** *adj* navodni, tobožnji ~**ly** *adv* navodno, kako se misli **supposition** /ˌsʌpə'zɪʃn/ *n* pretpostavka

suppress /sə'pres/ *vt* **1** suzbiti, ugušiti; ukinuti **2** obuzdati

supreme /su:'pri:m/ *adj* **1** vrhovni **2** krajnji, najveći **3** izvanredan **supremacy** /su'preməsɪ/ *n* nadmoć

surcharge /'sɜ:tʃɑ:dʒ/ *n* nadoknada, doplata

sure /ʃʊə(r)/ *adj* (of/that) siguran, pouzdan, uvjeren **make ~ of sth/that a.** provjeriti, uvjeriti se u **b.** potruditi se da, ne zaboraviti da • *adv* **US** *coll* naravno, zaista **for ~** *coll* nedvojbeno, (za)sigurno ~**ly** *adv* **1** sigurno **2** dakako, jamačno, zacijelo; naravno

surety /'ʃʊərətɪ/ *n* **1** jamac **2** jamčevina, jamstvo

surf /sɜ:f/ *n* pjena valova • *vi* daskati (na valovima)

surface /'sɜ:fɪs/ *n* **1** površina **2** vanjština ~-**to-air missile** raketa zemlja-zrak ~ **mail** obična pošta • *vi,vt* **1** izroniti **2** obraditi

surfeit /'sɜ:fɪt/ *n* (of) prezasićenost (čime)

surge /sɜ:dʒ/ *n* (of) bujica, navala, provala; porast • *vi* **1** nadirati, nahrupiti **2** (up) obuzeti, prostrujati

surgeon /'sɜ:dʒən/ *n* kirurg **dental ~** stomatolog **surgery** /'sɜ:dʒrɪ/ *n* **1** kirurgija **2** kirurški zahvat, operacija **3** *GB* ordinacija **undergo surgery** podvrgnuti se operaciji

surly /'sɜ:lɪ/ *adj* mrzovoljan

surmise /sə'maɪz/ *vt,vi form* nagađati, pretpostaviti, slutiti

surmount /sə'maʊnt/ *vt* prebroditi, svladati

surname /'sɜ:neɪm/ *n* prezime

surpass /sə'pɑ:s/ *vt* nadmašiti

surplus /'sɜ:pləs/ *n* višak *army ~* vojni otpad

surprise /sə'praɪz/ *n* iznenađenje *take sb by ~* iznenaditi • *vt* iznenaditi **~d** *adj* (at/by) iznenađen, začuđen **surprising** *adj* iznenađujući, neočekivan

surrender /sə'rendə(r)/ *vt,vi* 1 (to) predati (se); izručiti 2 prepustiti, ustupiti 3 (oneself) prepustiti se (čemu) • *n* predaja

surreptitious /ˌsʌrəp'tɪʃəs/ *adj* kradomičan, potajan

surrogate /'sʌrəgeɪt/ *n* nadomjestak, zamjena, surogat

surround /sə'raʊnd/ *vt* 1 okružiti 2 opkoliti **~ing** *adj* okolni **~ings** *n pl* okolina

surveillance /sɜ:'veɪləns/ *n* prismotra, nadzor

survey /sə'veɪ/ *vt* 1 pregledati; razgledati; razmotriti 2 izmjeriti (zemljište) 3 anketirati • *n* 1 anketa 2 pregled; prikaz 3 geodetsko mjerenje **~or** *n* mjernik, geometar

survival /sə'vaɪvl/ *n* preživljavanje **survive** /sə'vaɪv/ *vt,vi* preživjeti; održati se **survivor** *n* (from/of) preživjeli

susceptible /sə'septəbl/ *adj* (to) podložan; osjetljiv na; sklon

suspect /sə'spekt/ *vt* 1 (na)slutiti 2 sumnjati (u što/na koga) 3 (of) sumnjičiti za • *n* /'sʌspekt/ osumnjičeni, sumnjivac • *adj* /'sʌspekt/ sumnjiv, dvojben

suspend /sə'sped/ *vt* 1 obustaviti; odgoditi 2 suspendirati **~ed sentence** uvjetna kazna **~ers** *n pl* 1 *GB* podvezice; halteri *coll* 2 *US* naramenice

suspense /sə'spens/ *n* napetost, neizvjesnost

suspension /sə'spenʃn/ *n* 1 obustava, odgoda; isključenje; suspenzija 2 ovjes **~ bridge** viseći most

suspicion /sə'spɪʃn/ *n* sumnja; sumnji-

čenje; slutnja **suspicious** /sə'spɪʃəs/ *adj* 1 sumnjiv 2 sumnjičav **be suspicious about/of** sumnjati na

suss /sʌs/ *vt GB coll ~* **sb/sth out** shvatiti; skužiti *sl*; prozreti

sustain /sə'steɪn/ *vt* 1 poduprijeti, podržati 2 održati 3 dati snage 3 pretrpjeti

swagger /'swægə(r)/ *vi* šepiriti se, paradirati

swallow (1) /'swɒləʊ/ *vt,vi* (up) (pro)gutati (+ *fig*) • *n* gutljaj

swallow (2) *n* lastavica

swam *v irreg* → **swim**

swamp /swɒmp/ *n* močvara • *vt* poplaviti **~ed with** *fig* preplavljen

swan /swɒn/ *n* labud

swap /swɒp/ *vt,vi* (for/with) *coll* mijenjati (se (s kime za što), trampiti • *n* izmjena, trampa

swarm /swɔ:m/ *n* 1 roj 2 *fig* gomila, mnoštvo • *vi* 1 rojiti se 2 nagrnuti, nahrupiti **~ with** vrvjeti od

swarthy /'swɔ:ðɪ/ *adj* garav

swastika /'swɒstɪkə/ *n* kukasti križ

swat /swɒt/ *vt* zgnječiti, ubiti (muhu)

sway /sweɪ/ *vi,vt* 1 ljuljati, njihati (se) 2 *fig* kolebati se 3 utjecati na • *n* 1 ljuljanje, njihanje 2 *lit* vlast

swear /sweə(r)/ *vi,vi irreg* 1 (at) kleti, psovati 2 prisegnuti; zakleti se **be sworn in** položiti (svečanu) prisegu **~word** psovka, prostota

sweat /swet/ *vi,vt* 1 znojiti se 2 *coll* preznojavati se • *n* 1 znoj; znojenje 2 težak posao **be in a ~** znojiti se **no ~!** *coll* nema frke! **~er** *n* pulover **~shirt** majica s dugim rukavima **~y** *adj* 1 znojan 2 vruć 3 naporan

sweep *vt,vi irreg* (away/off/up) 1 (po)mesti; čistiti 2 projuriti; nahrupiti 3 *fig* zahvatiti (oluja, panika) 4 prostirati se **~ing** *adj* 1 dalekosežan, sveobuhvatan, temeljit 2 općenit, uopćen 3 velik, značajan • *n* 1 metenje 2 zamah 3 dohvat, doseg 4 *coll* dimnjačar

sweet /swi:t/ *adj* 1 sladak (+ *fig*) 2 svjež; čist 3 (mio)mirisan • *n* bombon, slatkiš **~en** *vt,vi* zasladiti; postati sladak **~heart** zlato

swell /swel/ *vi,vt irreg* (up/with) nateći; nabreknuti, nabubriti; nabujati (rijeka) • *n* bibanje, valovitost • *adj US coll* sjajan ~ing *n* oteklina

sweltering /'sweltərɪŋ/ *adj* sparan

swept *v irreg* → **sweep**

swerve /swɜ:v/ *vi,vt* (naglo) skrenuti

swift /swɪft/ *adj* brz, hitar

swig /swɪg/ *vt,vi* (down/off) *coll* cugati, lokati • *n* gutljaj

swill /swɪl/ *vt,vi* 1 (out) isprati, isplahnuti 2 *coll* lokati • *n* napoj, splačine

swim /swɪm/ *vi,vt irreg* 1 plivati 2 preplivati • **my head is ~ming** vrti mi se u glavi • *n* plivanje **go for a ~** ići plivati ~**mer** *n* plivač ~**ming** *n* plivanje ~**ming costume/suit** kupaći kostim ~**ming trunks** kupaće gačice ~**ming pool** bazen

swindle /'swɪndl/ *vt,vi* prevariti • *n* prijevara

swine /swaɪn/ *n lit, fig* svinja

swing /swɪŋ/ *vi,vt irreg* 1 njihati, ljuljati (se); mahati, mlatarati 2 (into) skrenuti u 3 (round) zaći, zamaknuti; naglo se okrenuti • *n* 1 njihanje, ljuljanje; njihaj 2 ljuljačka 3 *fig* preokret, zaokret 4 snažan ritam **in full ~** u punom jeku/(za)mahu

swipe /swaɪp/ *n* 1 udarac, zamah 2 (verbalni) napad • *vi,vt* 1 (at) udariti, mlatnuti 2 *coll* ukrasti; maznuti *sl*

swirl /swɜ:l/ *vi,vt* kovitlati se, vrtjeti se; odnijeti, otpuhati • *n* vir, vrtlog

swish /swɪʃ/ *vt,vi* 1 fijuknuti; ošinuti, zamahnuti 2 šuštati (haljina) • *n* fijuk, zvižduk

switch /swɪtʃ/ *n* 1 prekidač 2 promjena 3 šiba, prut • *vt,vi* 1 promijeniti; skrenuti 2 prebaciti ~ **on** uključiti ~ **off** isključiti ~**board** a. kućna telefonska centrala b. razvodna ploča

swivel /'swɪvl/ *vt,vi* (round) okretati (se) (oko osi) ~ **chair** uredska stolica (na okretanju)

swollen *v irreg* → **swell**

swoon /swu:n/ *vi arch, fig* onesvijestiti se • *n* nesvijest

swoop /swu:p/ *vi* (down on) oboriti se, obrušiti se, navaliti • *n* 1 obrušavanje, nalet 2 racija

swop *v irreg* → **swap**

sword /sɔ:d/ *n* mač ~**fish** sabljarka

swore *v irreg* → **swear**

sworn *v irreg* → **swear** • *adj* zakleti ~

statement izjava pod prisegom

swot /swɒt/ *vt,vi* (up) *GB* bubati, štrebati • *n* štreber

swum *v irreg* → **swim**

swung *v irreg* → **swing**

sycamore /'sɪkəmɔ:(r)/ *n* 1 egipatska smokva 2 američka platana

sycophant /'sɪkəfænt/ *n form* ulizica, udvorica

syllable /'sɪləbl/ *n* slog

syllabus /'sɪləbəs/ *n* (*pl* ~es, -bi /'sɪləbaɪ/) nastavni plan i program

symbol /'sɪmbl/ *n* 1 simbol 2 oznaka, znak ~**ic** *adj* simboličan **be ~ic of** simbolizirati ~**ism** *n* simbolika ~**ize** *vt* simbolizirati

symmetrical /sɪ'metrɪkl/ *adj* simetričan **symmetry** /'sɪmətrɪ/ *n* 1 simetrija, razmjer 2 sklad **sympathy strike** štrajk podrške

sympathetic /ˌsɪmpə'θetɪk/ *adj* suosjećajan, samilostan; sklon **sympathy strike** štrajk podrške **sympathize** /'sɪmpəθaɪz/ *vi* (with) suosjećati; imati razumijevanja **sympathy** *n* 1 sućut, suosjećanje, samilost 2 razumijevanje, slaganje 3 solidarnost, podrška

symphony /'sɪmfənɪ/ *n* simfonija

symposium /sɪm'pəʊzɪəm/ *n* (*pl* ~s, -sia) simpozij

symptom /'sɪmptəm/ *n* simptom ~**atic** *adj* (of) simptomatičan; znak (čega)

synagogue /'sɪnəgɒg/ *n* sinagoga

synchronize /'sɪŋkrənaɪz/ *vt,vi* uskladiti, sinkronizirati

syndicate /'sɪndɪkeɪt/ *n* udruženje, konzorcij, trust

syndrome /'sɪndrəʊm/ *n* sindrom

synonym /'sɪnənɪm/ *n* sinonim, istoznačnica

synopsis /sɪ'nɒpsɪs/ *n* (*pl* synopses) kratak sadržaj, sažetak, sinopsis

syntax /'sɪntæks/ *n* sintaksa

synthesis /'sɪnθəsɪs/ *n* sinteza **synthesize** *vt* sintetizirati, umjetno proizvesti **synthetic** *adj* umjetan

syringe /sɪ'rɪndʒ/ *n* šprica (za injekcije)

syrup /'sɪrəp/ *n* sirup ~**y** *adj* derog sladunjav

system /'sɪstəm/ *n* 1 sustav, sistem 2 organizam ~**atic** *adj* sustavan

T

T, t /tiː/ 20. slovo engl. abecede; te

ta /taː/ *int GB coll* hvala

tab /tæb/ *n* 1 jezičac 2 etiketa 3 *coll* račun **pick up the ~** platiti račun **keep ~s/a ~ on** *coll* nadzirati

tabby /'tæbɪ/ *n* tigrasta/šarena mačka

tabernacle /'tæbənækl/ *n* 1 *bibl* šator zavjetni 2 bogomolja 3 svetohranište

table /'teɪbl/ *n* 1 stol **at ~** za stolom **turn the ~s** (on sb) naglo preuzeti vodstvo (nad kim) **~cloth** stolnjak **~land(s)** visoravan 2 *mod* stolni **~manners** ponašanje za stolom **~spoon** velika žlica 3 tablica **~ of contents** sadržaj 4 ploča • *vt* 1 *GB* dati na razmatranje 2 *US* skinuti s dnevnog reda

taboo /tə'buː/ *n, adj* tabu (+ *fig*) **~ subject** tabu/zabranjena tema

tabular /'tæbjʊlə(r)/ *adj* tabelarni **tabulate** /'tæbjuleɪt/ *vt* prikazati u obliku tablice

tacit /'tæsɪt/ *adj form* prešutan **~urn** /'tæsɪtɜːn/ *adj form* šutljiv

tack /tæk/ *n* 1 čavlić 2 široki/labavi bod 3 smjer plovidbe **change ~** *fig* promijeniti pristup • *vt,vi* 1 prikucati, zakucati 2 promijeniti smjer plovidbe 3 prišiti širokim bodom; priheftati *coll* **~ sth on** *coll* dodati, priljepiti

tackle /'tækl/ *vt,vi* 1 uhvatiti se u koštac s čim, prihvatiti se čega 2 *sport* baciti se na/napasti/oboriti protivnika • *n* 1 *sport* napad 2 oprema, pribor 3 kolotur

tacky /'tækɪ/ *adj* 1 ljepljiv 2 bijedan, otrcan

tact /tækt/ *n* takt **~ful** *adj* taktičan **~less** *adj* netaktičan

tactic /'tæktɪk/ *n* (~s) taktika **delaying ~** taktika odgađanja **~al** *adj mil* taktičan, taktički **~ian** *n* taktičar

tadpole /'tædpəʊl/ *n* punoglavac

taffeta /'tæfɪtə/ *n* taft

Taffy /'tæfɪ/ *n GB sl derog* Velšanin

tag (1) /tæg/ *n* 1 markica, naljepnica, etiketa 2 izreka • *vt,vi* označiti, obiljeziti, etiketirati (+ *fig*) **~ along** *coll* pridružiti se, prikrpati se kome **~ on** dodati

tag (2) /tæg/ *n* igra lovice

tail /teɪl/ *n* 1 rep (+ *fig*) **with one's ~ between one's legs** podvučena repa **~back** kolona vozila **~coat/~s** frak **~end** sam kraj **~piece** dodatak 2 **~s** pismo (novčića) 3 *coll* uhoda • *vt,vi coll* pratiti, slijediti **~ back** stvoriti kolonu **~ off** smanjiti se

tailor /'teɪlə(r)/ *n* krojač **~-made** *adj* a. skrojen po mjeri b. kao stvoren (za koga) • *vt* 1 krojiti/šivati (po mjeri) 2 *fig* prilagoditi

taint /teɪnt/ *vt* uprljati, okaljati *fig*; pokvariti; zaraziti **~** *n* mrlja *fig*, ljaga, trag

take /teɪk/ *vt,vi irreg* 1 uzeti, zauzeti, poduzeti, preuzeti, ponijeti, odnijeti, podnijeti, primiti, prihvatiti 2 biti potrebno 3 uspjeti; primiti se 4 zavoljeti **~ a seat/chair** sjesti **~ a walk** prošetati **~ a shower** istuširati se **~ a chance** riskirati **~ sb's advice** poslušati čiji savjet **~ advantage** (of sb/sth) iskoristiti (koga/što) **~ care** paziti, čuvati **~ an oath** prisegnuti **~ offence** uvrijediti se **~ pity** smilovati se **~ notes** voditi bilješke **~ a breath** udahnuti **~ sugar** (*in one's tea/coffee*) piti (čaj/kavu) sa šećerom **~ a bus** ići autobusom **~ sb's temperature** izmjeriti temperaturu **~ a photo** fotografirati **~ place** održati se **~ part** (in) sudjelovati (u) **~ pride in sb/sth** ponositi se (kime/čime) **~ heed** hajati **~ no notice** (of) ne obraćati pozornost (na) ~ **the trouble** potruditi se ~ **sb in one's arms** zagrliti (koga) ~ **hold of sth** zgrabiti što ~ **sb's word for it** povjerovati kome na riječ **what do you ~ me for?** za što me smatraš? **I ~ it...** koliko sam shvatio... **be ~n ill** razboljeti se ~ **it from me** vjeruj mi kad ti kažem ~ **sb unawares/by surprise** zateći/iznenaditi koga **I can't ~ it any longer** ne mogu to više podnijeti ~ **your time** ne žuri se ~ **after** sličiti ~ **apart** rastaviti ~ **away** odnijeti ~ **away (restaurant)** n restoran koji prodaje hranu za van ~ **back** povući (riječ) ~ **down a.** zabilježiti **b.** spustiti **c.** rastaviti ~ **in a.** primati **b.** suziti, ušiti **c.** obuhvatiti **d.** shvatiti, razumjeti **e.** slušati, gledati; vidjeti ~ **off a.** uzletjeti **b.** skinuti **c.** oduzeti **d.** oponašati ~ **on a.** primiti se čega; poprimiti **b.** zaposliti **c.** postati popularan **d.** boriti se (protiv) ~ **out a.** izvaditi; izvesti; skinuti ~ **it out on sb** iskaliti bijes na kome ~ **over** preuzeti (vlast/upravu) ~ **to sth/sb a.** odati se, posvetiti se (čemu) **b.** zavoljeti (koga/što) **c.** uteći se, pobjeći u ~ **up a.** dignuti **b.** početi se baviti čime **c.** zauzeti, ispuniti **d.** nastaviti **e.** (on) prihvatiti • n 1 prihod 2 *film* kadar ~**ings** n pl utržak

taken v *irreg* → **take**

talcum /'tælkəm/ n ~ **powder** talk

tale /teɪl/ n priča

talent /'tælənt/ n 1 dar, talent 2 *GB sl* zgodne cure, komadi pl ~**ed** adj darovit

talk /tɔːk/ vi,vt (to/with sb, about/of sth) pričati, govoriti, razgovarati ~ **big** hvaliti se **let's ~ business** prijedimo na stvar **now you're ~ing!** to volim čuti! **look who's ~ing!** tko mi se javlja! ~ **of the devil** mi o vuku, a vuk na vrata ~ **through one's hat** govoriti gluposti ~ **turkey** *US* otvoreno/ozbiljno razgovarati ~ **sb into sth** nagovoriti koga na što ~ **sb out of sth** odgovoriti koga od čega ~ **sth over** raspraviti što ~ **sb round** uvjeriti koga • n 1 razgovor **small ~** nevezan razgovor 2 predavanje 3

način govora, pričanje, brbljanje; naklapanje 4 ~**s** pl *pol* pregovori; razgovori ~**ative** adj razgovorljiv, brbljav

tall /tɔːl/ adj visok

tallow /'tæloʊ/ n loj (za svijeće)

tally /'tælɪ/ n 1 evidencija; rezultat 2 oznaka • vi slagati se, podudarati se

tambourine /ˌtæmbə'riːn/ n def

tame /teɪm/ adj 1 pitom, pripitomljen 2 *coll* dosadan • vt ukrotiti, pripitomiti

tamper /'tæmpə(r)/ vi ~ **with sth** namjerno pokvariti/izmijeniti/uništiti

tan /tæn/ vt,vi 1 štaviti 2 potamnjeti od sunca • n 1 žutosmeđa boja 2 brončana boja (kože)

tandem /'tændəm/ n bicikl za dvije osobe

tang /tæŋ/ n oštar okus/miris

tangent /'tændʒənt/ n *math* tangenta, dodirnica **go of at a** ~ naglo promijeniti temu, skakati s teme na temu ~**ial** /tæn'dʒenʃəl/ adj 1 dodirni 2 *fig* neizravan, sporedan

tangerine /ˌtændʒə'riːn/ n mandarina

tangible /'tændʒəbl/ adj opipljiv (+ *fig*)

tangle /'tæŋgl/ vt,vi (~ **up**) (za)petljati (se), (za)mrsiti (se), zaplesti se, zapeti ~ **with sb** *coll* svadati se s kim • n 1 splet **be in a** ~ biti zapetljan 2 zbrka, pomutnja 3 *coll* svada

tango /'tæŋgəʊ/ n tango • vi plesati tango **it takes two to** ~ za ples je potrebno dvoje, oboje su odgovorni

tank /tæŋk/ n 1 rezervoar 2 spremište 3 cisterna 4 bazen 5 tenk • vt ~ **up** napuniti, tankirati ~**ed up** *sl* pijan

tankard /'tæŋkəd/ n vrč

tanker /'tæŋkə(r)/ n 1 tanker 2 cisterna

tanner /'tænə(r)/ n kožar ~**y** n kožarnica

tannoy /'tænɔɪ/ n *TM* razglas

tantalize /'tæntəlaɪz/ vt izazivati, mučiti

tantamount /'tæntəmaʊnt/ adj (to) jednak, jednake vrijednosti, isti

tantrum /'tæntrəm/ n srdžba, ljutnja

tap (1) /tæp/ n 1 *GB* pipa, slavina 2 prisluškivanje, prislušni uređaj 3 čep **bačve on** ~ **a.** iz bačve, točen **b.** *fig* pri ruci • *vt* 1 točiti 2 načeti 3 prisluškivati (telefon) 4 iskoristiti, upotrijebiti

tap (2) *vi,vt* (on, at) lupkati; kuckati, kucnuti; potapšati • *n* lagani udarac; kuckanje; lupkanje **~-dancing** step (ples)

tape /teɪp/ *n* vrpca ~ **measure** (krojački) metar **~-worm** trakavica **red** ~ *fig* birokracija, nepotrebne formalnosti ~ **recorder** magnetofon, kasetofon ~ **deck** kasetofon • *vt* 1 snimiti (na vrpcu) 2 svezati vrpcom 3 zalijepiti selotejpom **have sb/sth ~d** *coll* shvatiti; pročitati *fig*

taper /ˈteɪpə(r)/ *vi,vt* (off) suziti se, stanjiti se; smanjiti se, stišati se • *n* tanka voštana svijeća

tapestry /ˈtæpɪstrɪ/ *n* tapiserija

tar /tɑː/ *n* katran • *vt* premazati katranom **~red with the same brush** koji ima iste nedostatke

tardy /ˈtɑːdɪ/ *adj form, lit* zakašnjeli; spor

tare /teə(r)/ *n econ* tara, težina ambalaže/vozila

target /ˈtɑːgɪt/ *n* 1 meta (+ *fig*) ~ **practice** *mil* vježbe gađanja 2 *fig* cilj

tariff /ˈtærɪf/ *n* 1 carina 2 *GB* cjenik

tarmac /ˈtɑːmæk/ *n* 1 asfalt 2 pista • *vt* asfaltirati

tarn /tɑːn/ *n* planinsko jezerce

tarnish /ˈtɑːnɪʃ/ *vi,vt* 1 izgubiti boju/sjaj; pomutiti, izblijediti 2 *fig* okaljati

tarpaulin /tɑːˈpɔːlɪn/ *n* cerada

tarry /ˈtærɪ/ *vi lit* zadržati se, zaostati

tart (1) /tɑːt/ *n* 1 pita 2 *coll derog* drolja • *vt* ~ **up** prenakititi, neukusno urediti

tart (2) *adj* kiseo, oštar, opor (+ *fig*)

tartan /ˈtɑːtn/ *n* tartan (škotska tkanina)

tartar /ˈtɑːtə(r)/ *n* (zubni) kamenac **~ic acid** vinska kiselina

task /tɑːsk/ *n* zadatak, zadaća **take sb to** ~ ukoriti ~ **force** 1 *mil* (borbeni) odred 2 radna skupina

tassel /ˈtæsl/ *n* ukrasne rese *pl*

taste /teɪst/ *n* 1 okus **have a** ~ okusiti; iskusiti ~ **bud** okusne bradavice 2 ukus **in bad/poor** ~ neukusan **to** ~

po ukusu • *vt* 1 kušati; okusiti 2 (of) imati okus (po) **~ful** *adj* ukusan **~less** *adj* bezukusan; neukusan **~r** *n* degustator **tasty** *adj* ukusan; sočan (+ *fig*)

ta-ta /ˌtə ˈtɑː/ *int coll* pa-pa

tattered /ˈtætəd/ *adj* poderan, pohaban **tatters** *n pl* dronjci **in tatters** *fig* uništen

tattle /ˈtætl/ *vi coll* brbljati, naklapati, tračati

tatoo (1) /təˈtuː/ *n* tetovaža • *vt* tetovirati

tatoo (2) *n* 1 vojna priredba 2 bubnjanje

tatty /ˈtætɪ/ *adj coll derog* neuredan, pohaban

taught *v irreg* → **teach**

taunt /tɔːnt/ *vt* (with/for) rugati, podbadati, ismijavati • *n* zajedljiva/podrugljiva primjedba

Taurus /ˈtɔːrəs/ *n astrol* Bik

taut /tɔːt/ *adj* napet **~en** *vt,vi* napeti (se)

tavern /ˈtævən/ *n arch, lit* krčma, gostionica

tawdry /ˈtɔːdrɪ/ *adj* napadan, neukusan, kičast

tawny /ˈtɔːnɪ/ *adj* smeđežut

tax /tæks/ *n* 1 porez **before/after** ~ bruto/neto **~-deductible** *adj* koji se odbija od poreza ~ **evasion** utaja poreza **~-collector**, **~man** poreznik **~-payer** porezni obveznik 2 teret, opterećenje • *vt* 1 ubirati porez, oporezovati 2 opterećivati, gnjaviti 3 ~ **sb with sth** optužiti, okriviti **~ation** /tækˈseɪʃn/ *n* porez(ovanje) **~ing** *adj* naporan, zahtjevan

taxi /ˈtæksɪ/ *n* taksi ~ **rank** stajalište taksija • *vi* rulati

taxidermy /ˈtæksɪdɜːmɪ/ *n* prepariranje životinja

tea /tiː/ *n* 1 čaj 2 popodnevna užina **high** ~ *GB* večera 3 *mod* čajni, za čaj **~-bag** filter vrećica ~ **party** čajanka **~-pot** čajnik ~ **towel** kuhinjska krpa **a storm in a ~-cup** bura u čaši vode, mnogo vike ni za što **not for all the** ~ **in China** *coll* ni za što na svijetu **it's not my cup of** ~ ne volim to, ne sviđa mi se

teach /tiːtʃ/ *vi,vt irreg* podučavati, učiti, naučiti (koga) **I'll ~ you!** naučit ću ja tebe! dat ću ja tebi! **~er** n učitelj, nastavnik, profesor **~in** rasprava, predavanje, seminar **~ing** n učenje, podučavanje, nastava, nastavnički posao **~ing hospital** klinika

team /ti:m/ n **1** momčad **2** ekipa, tim **3** zaprega; jaram • vi ~ **up with sb** zajedno raditi, udružiti se

teamster /'ti:mstə(r)/ n US vozač kamiona

tear (1) /tɪə(r)/ n suza **burst into ~s** briznuti u plač **shed ~s** liti suze **~s of joy** suze radosnice **in ~s** uplakan **~drop** suza ~ **gas** suzavac **~jerker** coll srcedrapateljni roman/film **~ful** adj **1** zaplakan **2** žalostan

tear (2) /teə(r)/ vt,vi irreg (po)trgati, rastrgati, istrgnuti, (is)parati, rasparati, (po)derati, razderati (se) ~ **one's hair** (out) čupati kosu fig ~ **apart** rastrgati; razdvojiti ~ **oneself away** (from) otrgnuti se, nevoljko se odvojiti/otići ~ **down** (s)rušiti ~ **up** razderati, raskinuti

tease /ti:z/ vi,vt **1** zadirkivati (koga); zafrkavati coll **2** šaliti se **3** dražiti, izazivati **4** US tapirati • n coll **1** zafrkant coll **2** osoba koja (samo) izaziva/draška **~r** n coll **1** teško pitanje **2** ↳ **tease**

teat /ti:t/ n **1** duda, dudica **2** sisa (životinje)

technical /'teknɪkl/ adj **1** tehnički **2** stručni **~ly** adv **1** tehnički **2** formalno **~ity** /ˌteknɪ'kælɪtɪ/ n tehnička/stručna/formalna pojedinost **technician** /tek'nɪʃn/ n tehničar **technique** /tek'ni:k/ n tehnika, metoda, postupak

teddy /'tedɪ/ n (**~bear**/beə(r)/) medvjedić

tedious /'ti:dɪəs/ adj dosadan, zamoran, nezanimljiv **tedium** /'ti:dɪəm/ n dosada, monotonija

tee /ti:/ n (golf) stalak za lopticu; startna točka

teem (1) /ti:m/ vi ~ **down/~ with rain** coll lijevati, padati kao iz kabla

teem (2) ~ **with** vrvjeti (čime)

teens /ti:nz/ n pl godine od 13. do 19. **in one's ~** mladi od 20 g. **teenage**

/'ti:neɪdʒ/ adj mlad, za mlade, mladih **teenager** n mladić/djevojka u dobi između 13 i 19 g., omladinac, tinejdžer

teeny weeny /'ti:nɪ'wi:nɪ/ adj majušan, sićušan

teeter /'ti:tə(r)/ vi (on) nesigurno hodati, njihati se; kolebati se ~ **on the brink/edge (of sth)** biti/nalaziti se na rubu (čega)

teeth n pl **tooth**

teethe /ti:ð/ vi dobivati zube **teething troubles a.** izbijanje prvih zubi **b.** fig početne teškoće

teetotaller /ti:'təʊtlə(r)/ n antialkoholičar

telecast /'telɪkɑ:st/ n TV prijenos/emisija • vt emitirati, prikazati/prenositi na TV

telecommunications /ˌtelɪkəˌmju:nɪ'keɪʃnz/ n pl telekomunikacije

telegram /'telɪɡræm/ n brzojav

telegraph /'telɪɡrɑ:f/ n telegraf ~ **pole** telegrafski stup • vt,vi brzojaviti

telepathy /tɪ'lepəθɪ/ n telepatija

telephone /'telɪfəʊn/ n telefon → **phone** • vt telefonirati (kome), nazvati (koga) telefonom

telephoto /ˌtelɪ'fəʊtəʊ/ adj ~ **lens** teleobjektiv

teleprompter /'telɪprɒmptə(r)/ n TM blesimetar sl

telescope /'telɪskəʊp/ n teleskop • vi,vt skratiti, zbiti, sabiti (se) **telescopic** adj **1** teleskopski ~ **sight** optika snajpera **2** sklopiv

televise /'telɪvaɪz/ vt prikazati/prenositi na televiziji **television** /'telɪvɪʒn/ n **1** televizija **2** televizijski **3** (**TV set**) televizor

telex /'teleks/ n teleks • vt,vi poslati teleks

tell /tel/ vt,vi irreg **1** ~ **sb sth,** ~ **sth** (to sb) reći, kazati **2** (is)pričati **3** zapovjediti, naložiti **4** (from, apart) razlikovati, razabrati **5** biti siguran, prepoznati, znati **6** form pokazati se, doći do izražaja **7** (on sb) tužiti, izdati **all told** sve u svemu ~ **me another** coll kako da ne! baš ti vjerujem! **there is no ~ing what...** tko zna što... **to ~ you the truth** iskreno govoreći ~ **sb off a.** ukoriti, izgrditi **b.** izdvojiti ~**tale** *adj* izdajnički • *n coll* izdajnik; tužibaba ~**er** *n* **1** blagajnik (u banci) **2** brojitelj glasova (u parlamentu) ~**ing** *adj* učinkovit; značajan

telly /'telɪ/ *n GB coll* → **television**

temerity /tɪ'merətɪ/ *n form* nepromišljenost; luda hrabrost

temp /temp/ *n coll* tajnica/tipkačica na zamjeni

temper (1) /'tempə(r)/ *n* (nagla) ćud, narav; raspoloženje **in a (bad) ~** ljutit, loše volje **lose one's ~/fly into a ~** planuti, razbjesniti se **bad-~ed** *adj* nagle ćudi, naprasit

temper (2) *vt* **1** kaliti, čeličiti **2** *form* ublažiti

tempera /'tempərə/ *n* boja za freske

temperament /'temprəmənt/ *n* temperament ~**al** *adj* **1** temperamentan; ćudljiv, promjenjiva raspoloženja **2** prouzročen temperamentom

temperance /'tempərəns/ *n* **1** *form* umjerenost, uzdržanost **2** apstinencija (od alkohola)

temperate /'tempərət/ *adj* **1** umjeren ~ **zone** umjereni klimatski pojas **2** suzdržan

temperature /'temprətʃə(r)/ *n* **1** temperatura **take sb's ~** izmjeriti temperaturu **2** vrućica; temperatura *coll* **run a ~** imati temperaturu

tempest /'tempɪst/ *n lit* oluja ~**uous** *adj* olujan; buran (+ *fig*)

temple (1) /'templ/ *n* hram, svetište

temple (2) *n* sljepoočnica

temporal /'tempərəl/ *adj* **1** *gram* vremenski **2** *form* zemaljski, svjetovni

temporary /'temprərɪ/ *adj* privremen

temporize /'tempəraɪz/ *vi form* odugovlačiti, otezati

tempt /tempt/ *vt* (into, to) iskušavati, stavljati na kušnju, dovesti u napast, mamiti ~ **fate/providence** izazivati sudbinu ~**ation** *n* iskušenje, napast

ten /ten/ *num* deset (10) ~ **to one** *coll* kladim se (da) ~**th** *num ord* deseti

tenable /'tenəbl/ *adj* **1** održiv, čvrst **2** (for) koji se daje na (određeni rok)

tenacious /tɪ'neɪʃəs/ *adj* ustrajan, uporan, žilav

tenant /'tenənt/ *n* **1** (pod)stanar **2** zaku-

pac **tenancy** *n* zakup

tend (1) /tend/ *vi* **1** (to, towards) naginjati, biti sklon, imati tendenciju, kretati se (k, prema) **2** ~ **to do sth** često/obično činiti **she ~s to get angry** zna se razljutiti ~**ency** /'tendənsɪ/ *n* **1** sklonost; tendencija; kretanje **2** *pol* struja unutar stranke ~**entious** /ten'denʃəs/ *adj form* derog tendenciozan

tend (2) *vt* **1** (to) *arch* njegovati, brinuti se za, čuvati, paziti **2** *US* posluživati (mušterije)

tender (1) /'tendə(r)/ *adj* **1** osjetljiv, bolan **2** mekan **3** nježan, pun ljubavi/suosjećanja, ljubazan **4** *lit* mlad ~**foot** *n coll* žutokljunac ~**hearted** *adj* meka srca

tender (2) *vi*,*vt* **1** ponuditi, dati **2** *form* podnijeti (ostavku) ~ *n* **1** predračun **2** ponuda **legal ~** zakonito sredstvo plaćanja

tendon /'tendən/ *n* tetiva

tendril /'tendrəl/ *n* **1** vitica (biljke penjačice) **2** *fig* uvojak kose

tenement /'tenəmənt/ *n* stambena zgrada (ob. u siromašnoj četvrti)

tenet /'tenɪt/ *n* načelo, doktrina

tenner /'tenə(r)/ *n GB coll* (novčanica od) 10 funti

tennis /'tenɪs/ *n* tenis

tenor /'tenə(r)/ *n* **1** tenor **2** pravac, tijek **3** smisao, sadržaj

tenpin /'tenpɪn/ *n* čunj ~ **bowling** *US* kuglanje

tense (1) /tens/ *adj* napet • *vt*,*vt* napeti, nategnuti

tense (2) *n gram* glagolsko vrijeme

tension /'tenʃn/ *n* **1** napetost **2** *pol* zategnutost **3** *tech* napon

tent /tent/ *n* šator

tentacle /'tentəkl/ *n* pipak, ticalo, krak

tentative /'tentətɪv/ *adj* **1** pokusni, provizoran **2** neodlučan, koji oklijeva

tenterhooks /'tentəhʊks/ *n* **on ~** na iglama

tenuous /'tenjʊəs/ *adj* slab, tanak

tenure /'tenjʊə(r)/ *n form* **1** pravo vlasništva **2** (~ **office**) mandat

tepee, teepee /'tiː.piː/ *n* indijanski šator

tepid /'tepɪd/ *adj* mlak (+ *fig*)

tercentenary /ˌtɜːsɛnˈtiːnərɪ/ n 300-godišnjica

term /tɜːm/ n 1 vremensko razdoblje; rok; termin 2 mandat, vrijeme službovanja 3 zatvorska kazna 4 tromjesečje, semestar 5 ~s pl uvjeti 6 izraz 7 math pribrojnik, član **in ~s of...**, **in ... ~s** s obzirom na, glede, što se tiče • **of abuse** uvreda, pogrda **in no uncertain ~s** jasno i glasno **come to ~s with sth** pomiriti se s čim **come to ~s with sb** nagoditi se s kim **be on good ~s with sb** biti u dobrim odnosima s kim **not be on speaking ~s with sb** ne razgovarati s kim **on equal ~s** ravnopravno • vt (as) nazvati, nazivati ~**inology** n terminologija

terminal /ˈtɜːmɪnl/ adj 1 neizlječiv 2 tromjesečni, semestralni • n terminal

terminate /ˈtɜːmɪneɪt/ vi,vt form okončati, prekinuti, zaustaviti se **termination** n 1 okončanje, završetak 2 euphem, tech abortus 3 gram dočetak

terminus /ˈtɜːmɪnəs/ n (pl ~es, termini) zadnja postaja, okretište

termite /ˈtɜːmaɪt/ n termit

terrace /ˈtɛrəs/ n 1 niz kuća 2 terasa 3 ~s GB tribina za stajanje ~**d house** kuća u nizu

terrain /tɛˈreɪn/ n predjel, teren

terrestrial /tɪˈrestrɪəl/ adj 1 zemaljski 2 kopneni

terrible /ˈterəbl/ adj užasan, grozan, strašan **terribly** adv užasno, strašno; jako

terrier /ˈterɪə(r)/ n terijer

terrific /təˈrɪfɪk/ adj coll sjajan, odličan; super coll

terrify /ˈterɪfaɪ/ vt prestrašiti, prestraviti **be terrified at/of** jako se bojati, groziti se, užasavati se

territorial /ˌterɪˈtɔːrɪəl/ adj form teritorijalni ~ **waters** teritorijalne vode **T~ Army** jedinice teritorijalne obrane • n pripadnik jedinica teritorijalne obrane **territory** n teritorij; predjel, prostor; područje

terror /ˈterə(r)/ n 1 strava, strah, užas **reign of ~** strahovlada ~**stricken/~struck** adj prestravljen 2 gnjavator, zločesto dijete 3 osoba koja ulijeva strah/terorizira okolicu ~**ism** terorizam ~**ist** terorist ~**ize** vt terorizirati, napadati, služiti se prijetnjama i zastrašivanjem

terry(cloth) /ˈterɪ/ n frotir

terse /tɜːs/ adj škrt na riječima, kratak, jezgrovit

tertiary /ˈtɜːʃrɪ/ adj form tercijaran ~ **education** visoko obrazovanje

tessellated /ˈtesəleɪtɪd/ adj popločan, mozaičkni

test /test/ n 1 test, provjera, ispit 2 pregled **blood ~** vađenje krvi 3 pokus, ispitivanje ~ **pilot** pokusni pilot ~ **tube** kušalica, epruveta ~**tube baby** dijete iz epruvete 4 kušnja **put to the ~** iskušati 5 mjerilo ~ **case** leg ogledni slučaj • vt ispitati; pregledati; iskušati

testament /ˈtestəmənt/ n 1 form (**last will and ~**) oporuka 2 svjedočanstvo 3 **Old/New T~** Stari/Novi zavjet

testate /ˈtesteɪt/ adj leg koji je ostavio oporuku **testator** n oporučitelj

testicle /ˈtestɪkl/ n testis

testify /ˈtestɪfaɪ/ vi,vt (against/for/to) svjedočiti

testimonial /ˌtestɪˈməʊnɪəl/ n 1 pismena preporuka 2 nagrada

testimony /ˈtestɪmənɪ/ n 1 svjedočenje, iskaz 2 svjedočanstvo, dokaz

testy /ˈtestɪ/ adj nabusit, naprasit, mrzovoljan, razdražljiv

tetchy /ˈtetʃɪ/ adj preosjetljiv, uvredljiv

tete-á-tete /ˌteɪt ɑː ˈteɪt/ n razgovor u četiri oka

tether /ˈteðə(r)/ n uzica, lanac **at the end of one's ~** na izmaku snage

Teutonic /tjuːˈtɒnɪk/ adj germanski

text /tekst/ n tekst, štivo; primjerak; biblijski citat ~**book** udžbenik ∘ adj **a.** savršen **b.** tipičan ~**book example** školski primjer ~**ual** /ˈtekstʃʊəl/ adj tekstualan, u tekstu, teksta

textile /ˈtekstaɪl/ n tekstil

texture /ˈteksɪʃə(r)/ n sastav, struktura, kakvoća

Thames /temz/ n Temza **set the ~ on fire** GB coll postići velik uspjeh

than /ðən/ conj, prep nego (tko/što), od (koga/čega)

thane /θeɪn/ n vlastelin; pripadnik

nižeg plemstva

thank /θæŋk/ vt (for) zahvaliti (za što, na čemu) ~ **you** hvala ~ **you very much** najljepša hvala ~ **God/goodness/heaven** hvala Bogu • ~**s** n pl zahvala, zahvalnost, hvala ~**s to** zahvaljujući (komu/čemu) ~**sgiving** n izraz zahvalnosti T~**sgiving Day** US Dan zahvalnosti (četvrti četvrtak u studenome) • ~**s** int hvala ~**s a lot** hvala lijepa ~**ful** adj zahvalan; zadovoljan ~**fully** adv nasreću ~**less** adj nezahvalan

that /ðæt/ adj (pl those) taj, onaj; tom, onom; tog, onog • pron to, ono ~ **is** to jest • conj da • relative pron koji, što • adv coll tako, toliko

thatch /θætʃ/ n slama (na krovu) • vt prekriti (krov) slamom

thaw /θɔ:/ vi,vt 1 rastopiti, otopiti, odmrznuti (se), kopnjeti 2 fig smekšati se • n 1 kopnjenje 2 pol poboljšanje odnosa

the /ðə/ def art određeni član, koristi se **a.** uz imenicu koja je već spomenuta ili određena kontekstom **b.** uz superlative pridjeva **c.** za supstantivizaciju pridjeva ~ **rich** bogataši **d.** u frazama • adv što..., to... ~ **sooner** ~ **better** što prije, to bolje

theatre (-ter US) /'θɪətə(r)/ n 1 kazalište 2 dvorana 3 US, Aus kino 4 fig pozornica, poprište ~**goer** n osoba koja često ide u kazalište **theatrical** /θɪ'ætrɪkl/ adj 1 kazališni 2 derog teatralan **theatricals** n pl kazališne predstave

thee /ði:/ pron arch tebi, tebe, tobom → **thou**

theft /θeft/ n krađa

their /ðeə(r)/ poss adj njihov, svoj • ~**s** pron njihovo, svoje

them /ðəm/ pron njih, njima ~**selves** pron sebe, se; sebi, si **(all) by** ~**selves** sami **in** ~**selves** sami po sebi

theme /θi:m/ n tema

then /ðen/ adv tada, onda **by** ~ dotad **from** ~ **on** otad **but** ~ **again** ali, ipak **now and** ~ povremeno • adj tadašnji, ondašnji

thence /ðens/ adv form otuda, odonuda

theology /θɪ'ɒlədʒɪ/ n teologija **theologian** /,θɪə'ləʊdʒən/ n teolog

theorem /'θɪərəm/ n teorem

theory /'θɪərɪ/ n teorija **theoretic(al)** /θɪə'retɪk, ɪkl/ adj teoretski **theorist, theoretician** n teoretičar **theorize** vi (about/on) teoretizirati, postaviti teoriju

therapy /'θerəpɪ/ n terapija **therapist 1** terapeut, specijalist **2** coll psihijatar **therapeutic** adj terapeutski

there /ðeə(r)/ adv tamo, ondje, tu ~ **he goes** eno ga **he's not all** ~ nisu mu sve na broju **get** ~ uspjeti **then and** ~ na licu mjesta, smjesta ~ **you are/go** izvoli(te) ~**abouts** tu negdje ~**after** form odonda, kasnije ~**by** time ~**in** form u tome ~**upon** tada, smjesta, odmah • pron ~ **is/are** ima, nalazi se, postoji, događa se ~ **int** eto, tako ~ **now** eto vidiš ~, ~ smiri se

therefore /'ðeəfɔ:(r)/ adv 1 stoga, zato, zbog toga 2 dakle

thermal /'θɜ:ml/ adj toplinski ~ **springs** toplice

thermodynamics /,θɜ:məʊdaɪ'næmɪks/ n termodinamika

thermometer /θə'mɒmɪtə(r)/ n toplomjer

thermonuclear /,θɜ:məʊ'nju:klɪə(r)/ adj termonuklearan

thermos /'θɜ:məs/ n TM (~ **flask**) termosica coll

thermostat /'θɜ:məstæt/ n termostat

thesaurus /θɪ'sɔ:rəs/ n rječnik sinonima

these pl → **this**

thesis /'θɪ:sɪs/ n (pl **theses**) 1 radnja, disertacija 2 teza

thespian /'θespɪən/ n form, joc glumac • adj glumački

they /ðeɪ/ pron oni, one, ona

thick /θɪk/ adj 1 debeo 2 gust 3 (with) pun čega, prekriven čime 4 izražen (naglasak) 5 nejasan, promukao (glas) 6 coll glup ~**set** adj nabijen ~**skinned** derog debelokožan **as** ~ **as thieves** coll prisni prijatelji **be** ~ **on the ground** coll biti brojan **the** ~ **end of** coll gotovo, skoro ~ **and fast** coll brzo i u velikom broju • n glavni dio, najčešći dio **through** ~ **and thin** u dobru i u zlu ~en *vi,vt* postati deblji, gušći etc.; zgusnuti, zadebljati ~ener *n* gustin *TM* ~ness *n* 1 debljina; gustoća 2 sloj ~et *n* guštik, šipražje

thief /θi:f/ *n* kradljivac, lopov **thieving** *n* krađa

thigh /θaɪ/ *n* bedro

thimble /'θɪmbl/ *n* naprstak

thin /θɪn/ *adj* 1 tanak 2 mršav 3 rijedak 4 *derog* proziran *fig*, slab, loš; vodenast ~-**skinned** osjetljiv, uvredljiv **disappear/vanish into** ~ **air** nestati; ispariti *fig* **have a** ~ **time** loše se provesti ~ **on top** *coll* proćelav • *vi,vt* 1 (down) razrijediti (se) 2 (out) prorijediti (se); oslabiti; dignuti se (magla) ~**ner** *n* razrjeđivač

thine /θaɪn/ *pron arch, bibl* tvoj

thing /θɪŋ/ *n* stvar, predmet, nešto **not a** ~ **ništa for one** ~ kao prvo **the** ~ **is** a. pitanje je b. stvar je u tome (da) **of all** ~s ni manje ni više (nego) **you're seeing** ~s priviđa ti se **poor** ~ jadničak, jadnica **have a** ~ **about sth** nešto posebno voljeti/mrziti **sure** ~ *coll* dobro, u redu, naravno

think /θɪŋk/ *vi,vt irreg* (about/of) 1 misliti, pomisliti; razmišljati, razmisliti 2 shvatiti, zamisliti; sjetiti se *I thought as much* to sam i mislio/očekivao ~ **twice** dobro promisliti ~ **highly/not much of sb** imati dobro/loše mišljenje o kome ~ **the world of sb** jako voljeti/cijeniti koga ~ **better of sth** predomisliti se ~ **sth out** promisliti o čemu, osmisliti što ~ **sth over** razmisliti o čemu ~ **sth up** izmisliti, smisliti • *n coll* **have a** ~ (about) razmisliti (o) ~ **tank** trust mozgova ~**ing** *n* razmišljanje *I've done some* ~*ing* razmislio sam **good** ~**ing!** dobra ideja! ○ *adj* koji misli, razmišlja; razuman, pametan

third /θɜ:d/ *num ord* treći ~ **degree** *coll* grubo policijsko ispitivanje ~ **party** *leg* treća osoba ~-**rate** *adj* trećerazredni

thirst /θɜ:st/ *n* žeđ (+ *fig*) • *vi* (**for/after sth**) žuditi za čime ~**y** *adj* 1 žedan 2 koji izaziva žeđ ~**y for** željan čega

thirteen /ˌθɜ:'ti:n/ *num* trinaest (13)

~**th** *num ord* trinaesti

thirty /'θɜ:tɪ/ *num* trideset (30) **thirtieth** /'θɜ:tɪɪθ/ *num ord* trideseti

this / ðɪs/ *pron* (*pl* **these**) ovaj, ova, ovo; taj, ta, to ~ **morning** jutros ~ **minute** odmah, smjesta **what's all** ~? što se događa, u čemu je stvar • *adv* ovako, ovoliko

thistle /'θɪsl/ *n* češljika, čičak

thither /'ðɪðə(r)/ *adv arch* tamo

thong /θɒŋ/ *n* bič; remen

thongs /θɒŋs/ *n pl US, Aus* japanke

thorax /'θɔ:ræks/ *n* prsni koš

thorn /θɔ:n/ *n* trn **a** ~ **in one's side** trn u oku ~**y** *adj* trnovit, bodljikav; *fig* težak

thorough /'θʌrə/ *adj* poman, temeljit, iscrpan, pedantan, potpun ~**going** *adj* poman, potpun

thoroughbred /'θʌrəbred/ *adj* čistokrvan, rasan

thoroughfare /'θʌrəfeə(r)/ *n* ulica, prometnica **No** ~ zabranjen prolaz

those *pl* → **that**

thou /ðaʊ/ *pron arch, bibl* ti

though /ðəʊ/ *conj* premda, makar, iako **as** ~ kao da • *adv* ali

thought /θɔ:t/ (2) *n* misao, zamisao, mišljenje; namjera **on second** ~**s** kad bolje promislim ~**ful** *adj* 1 zamišljen 2 pažljiv, brižan ~**less** *adj* nemaran, nepažljiv

thought (1) *v irreg* → **think**

housand /'θaʊznd/ *num* tisuća, tisuću (1000) ~**th** /'θaʊznθ/ *num ord* tisućiti

thrall /θrɔ:l/ *n lit* rob, kmet **in** ~ zarobljen *fig*

thrash /θræʃ/ *vt,vi* 1 mlatiti, tući, šibati 2 *coll* potući, poraziti 3 (~ **about**) bacati se, skakati, koprcati se 4 ~ **out** pretresti, raspraviti

thread /θred/ *n* 1 konac; nit (+ *fig*) ~**bare** *adj* izlizan, iznošen; *fig* otrcan 2 zavoj (na vijku, matici) • *vt* 1 uvesti konac u (iglu) 2 (onto) staviti film u projektor 3 nanizati ~ **one's way through** provući se, progurati se ~**ed** *adj* prošaran

threat /θret/ *n* prijetnja ~**en** *vt,vi* prijetiti; ugrožavati

three /θri:/ *num* tri (3) ~**cornered** *adj* a. trokutast b. trostran, između tri protivnika **~-D** (3-D) *adj* trodimenzionalan the **~** R's čitanje, pisanje i računanje **~some** *coll* troje ljudi, trojka

thresh /θreʃ/ *vi,vt* mlatiti (žito etc.) **~ing machine** vršilica

threshold /'θreʃhəʊld/ *n* prag (+ *fig*)

threw *v irreg* → **throwa**

thrice /θraɪs/ *adv arch* triput

thrift /θrɪft/ *n form* štedljivost **~y** *adj* štedljiv

thrill /θrɪl/ *n* uzbuđenje; jeza; drhtaj **~ing** *adj* uzbudljiv **~ed** oduševljen **~er** *n* triler

thrive /θraɪv/ *vi irreg* (on) bujati, uspijevati; napredovati, rasti

thriven *v irreg* → **thrive**

throat /θrəʊt/ *n* 1 grlo **sore ~** grlobolja 2 grkljan, vrat **force sth down sb's ~** natjerati koga da što prihvati **at each other's ~s** u svadi/prepirci **~y** *adj coll* grlen; promuklo

throb /θrɒb/ *vi* kucati, udarati, pulsirati

thrombosis /θrɒm'bəʊsɪs/ *n* tromboza

throne /θrəʊn/ *n* prijestolje **come to the ~ /ascend the ~** stupiti/popeti se na prijestolje

throng /θrɒŋ/ *n* mnoštvo, gomila • *vi,vt* gurati se, tiskati se, nahrupiti; preplaviti

throttle /'θrɒtl/ *vt* (za)daviti, (u)gušiti **~ down** smanjiti brzinu • *n* upusni priklopac

through /θru:/ *prep* 1 kroz **see ~** prozrijeti **see~** *adj* proziran **~ Sunday** US zaključno s nedjeljom 2 preko 3 zbog • *adv* do kraja, skroz **all ~** cijelo vrijeme **straight ~** bez zaustavljanja **get ~ a.** položiti b. *am I getting ~?* je li jasno? **put sb ~ to** spojiti s **wet ~** potpuno mokar **~ and ~** skroz-naskroz • *adj* 1 izravan, bez presjedanja; koji prolazi kroz 2 US gotov *I'm ~ with him* prekinula sam s njim **~out** *prep* kroz cijeli, za vrijeme cijelog, preko cijelog ○ *adv* posve; svuda; cijelo vrijeme

throve *v irreg* → **thrive**

throw /θrəʊ/ *vt,vi irreg* 1 baciti, bacati, dobaciti **~ a party** prirediti zabavu **~ open** otvoriti za javnost **~ about** razbacati; razbacivati se čime **~ sth**

away a. odbaciti **b.** baciti (u smeće) **~ sth off** riješiti se čega **~ out a.** izbaciti; odbaciti; baciti (u smeće) **b.** nabaciti se čime, dobaciti **~ sth together** nabacati **~ up a.** povratiti **b.** napustiti, dati otkaz • *n* bacanje, hitac; udaljenost, domet **within a stone's ~** vrlo blizu

thrown *v irreg* → **throw**

thru US *coll* → **through**

thrush (1) /θrʌʃ/ *n* drozd

thrush (2) *n* upala sluznice; kandidijaza

thrust /θrʌst/ *vt,vt irreg* gurnuti, gurati, rinuti; zabosti **~ upon** nametnuti • *n* 1 proboj, navala 2 *tech* potisak 3 bit, srž, ključna točka

thud /θʌd/ *n* tup udarac

thug /θʌg/ *n* razbojnik, nasilnik, huligan

thumb /θʌmb/ *n* palac **all ~s** *coll* nespretan **get the ~s down** biti odbijen; propasti **give the ~s up** odobriti **under sb's ~** pod čijom vlašću **~tack** čavlić • *vt,vi* 1 **~ a lift** auto-stopirati 2 **~ through** nabrzinu prolistati

thump /θʌmp/ *vt,vi* snažno udariti, lupiti, nabijati, bubnjati • *n* udarac **~ing** *adj coll* golem

thunder /θʌndə(r)/ *n* grmljavina **~bolt** grom (+ *fig*), munja **~clap** grom **~cloud** olujni oblak **~storm** oluja (s grmljavinom) **~struck** *adj* zapanjen, kao gromom pogođen **~ous** *adj* gromoglasan **~y** *adj* olujni, koji navješta grmljavinu

Thursday /'θɜːzdɪ/ *n* četvrtak

thus /ðʌs/ *adv form* tako, na taj način, time **~ far** dosad

thwart /θwɔːt/ *vt* spriječiti, pomrsiti

thy /ðaɪ/ *adj arch* tvoj **~self** *pron arch* sebe **→ yourself**

thyme /taɪm/ *n bot* majčina dušica

thyroid /'θaɪrɔɪd/ *n* (**~ gland**) štitna žljezda, štitnjača

tiara /tɪ'ɑːrə/ *n* tijara

tic /tɪk/ *n* tik

tick /tɪk/ *n* 1 kucanje, otkucaj (sata) **~tock** tik-tak 2 *coll* tren, časak 3 GB kvačica • *vi,vt* 1 kucati **~ away** otkucavati 2 označiti kvačicom *what makes him ~* što ga tjera, što voli **~**

sb off *coll* ukoriti koga; oprati koga *sl* **~ing-off** *n* bukvica ~ **over** sporo raditi **~er** *n sl* srce **~-tack toe** *US* križić-kružić

tick (2) *n* krpelj

tick (3) *n coll* (**on** ~) (na) kredit

ticket /'tɪkɪt/ *n* 1 (putna) karta; ulaznica **single** *GB*/**one-way** *US* ~ jednosmjerna karta **return** *GB*/**round-trip** *US* ~ povratna karta 2 ceduljica, oznaka 3 kazna za prometni prekršaj 4 *US pol* stranačka lista 5 ~ **of leave** *arch* uvjetno puštanje na slobodu • *vt* 1 označiti 2 *US* kazniti 3 namijeniti

tickle /'tɪkl/ *vt,vi* 1 škakljati 2 dražiti; zabaviti **be ~d pink** biti oduševljen • *n* škakljanje, svrbež **ticklish** *adj* škakljiv (+ *fig*)

tidbit /'tɪdbɪt/ *US* → **titbit**

tiddler /'tɪdlə(r)/ *n GB coll* 1 ribica 2 sitna riba *fig* 3 dijete

tiddly /'tɪdlɪ/ *adj GB coll* 1 sitan, zanemariv 2 pripit

tide /taɪd/ *n* 1 plima (+ *fig*); oseka 2 struja (+ *fig*) 3 *arch* doba godine/dana • *vt* ~ **sb over** pomoći, izdržati **tidal** *adj* plimni; u koji dopire plima i oseka

tidings /'taɪdɪŋz/ *n pl arch* vijesti

tidy /'taɪdɪ/ *adj* 1 uredan 2 *coll* znatan; *coll* oštrouman • *vt,vi* (~ **up**) pospremiti

tie /taɪ/ *n* 1 (**neck**~) kravata **bow** ~ leptir-kravata **~pin** igla za kravatu 2 veza 3 *fig* obaveza, teret 4 neriješen rezultat **~breaker** *sport* odlučujući krug/utakmica 5 *US* → **sleeper** • *vt,vi irreg* 1 vezati (se), zavezati, svezati ~ **sb down a.** vezati, ograničiti slobodu **b.** prisiliti na što ~ **in** (**with**) poklapati se (s) **be ~d up** biti zauzet 2 imati isti rezultat

tier /tɪə(r)/ *n* kat, red, sloj, razina

tiff /tɪf/ *n* svađa

tiger /'taɪgə(r)/ *n* tigar **tigress** tigrica

tight /taɪt/ *adj* 1 tijesan, pripijen, uzak 2 napet, čvrst, zbijen, neprobojan **in a** ~ **corner/spot** u škripcu **~fisted** *adj* škrt **~rope** žica **walk the ~rope** hodati po žici (+ *fig*) 3 (**~fisted**) *coll* škrt 4 *coll* pijan • *adv* čvrsto **~en** *vi,vt* učvrstiti, stegnuti, pritegnuti **~s** *n pl* 1 *GB* hulahopke 2 triko

tile /taɪl/ *n* 1 pločica 2 crijep **be on the ~s** zabavljati se, provoditi se

till (1) /tɪl/ *prep, conj* do, dok

till (2) *n* blagajna

till (3) *vt arch* obrađivati (zemlju)

tilt /tɪlt/ *vi,vt* 1 nagnuti (se) 2 (at) napadati ~ **at windmills** boriti se s vjetrenjačama

timber /'tɪmbə(r)/ *n* 1 *GB* drvo, drvena građa; šume 2 greda

timbre /'tæmbrə/ *n* boja glasa/zvuka

time /taɪm/ *vt* 1 tempirati **ill~d** u zao čas 2 mjeriti vrijeme • *n* 1 vrijeme; doba 2 put **every** ~ svaki put **two ~s as big** dvaput veći 3 ~**s** 3 **is** 9 3 puta 3 je 9 **have a good** ~ dobro se provesti **have an easy** ~ lagodno živjeti **at the same** ~ u isti čas, istodobno **by the** ~ dok **on** ~ na vrijeme **it is about** ~ krajnji je čas **all the** ~ stalno **one at a** ~ jedan za drugim **do** ~ (**in prison**) izdržavati zatvorsku kaznu **at one** ~ nekad **at the** ~ tada **at ~s** ponekad **before one's** ~ prije čijeg rođenja/dolaska **for a** ~ neko vrijeme **for the** ~ **being** zasada **from** ~ **out of mind** oduvijek **from** ~ **to** ~ od vremena do vremena **in no** ~ (**at all**) u tren oka **in** ~ **a.** s vremenom **b.** na vrijeme **c.** u ritmu **keep** ~ **a.** ići točno **b.** udarati ritam **take one's** ~ ne žuriti se ~ **after** ~ u više navrata ~ **bomb** tempirana bomba ~**-consuming** dugotrajan ~**less** *adj* vječan ~**ly** *adj* pravovremen ~**piece** *n* sat ~**r** *n* mjerač vremena, sat ~ **signal** signal točnog vremena ~**table** *n* raspored **timing** *n* sposobnost da se izabere pravi trenutak, osjećaj za pravo vrijeme

timid /'tɪmɪd/ *adj* strašljiv, plah

tin /tɪn/ *n* 1 kositar 2 limenka, konzerva 3 posuda za pečenje ~**ned** *adj* konzerviran ~**foil** *n* aluminijska folija ~ **hat** kaciga ~ **opener** otvarač za konzerve

tinder /'tɪndə(r)/ *n* ognjilo ~**dry** *adj* suh kao barut ~**box** *n fig* bure baruta

tinge /tɪndʒ/ *vt* **be ~ed with** biti prošaran; biti prožet • *n* nijansa

tingle /'tɪŋgl/ *vi* (**with**) gorjeti (od); bridjeti

tinker (1) /'tɪŋkə(r)/ n kotlokrpa

tinker (2) vi (with/about) čeprkati po, prtljati

tinkle /'tɪŋkl/ vi,vt zveckati

tinsel /'tɪnsl/ n srebrni ukrasi T~ Town coll Hollywood

tint /tɪnt/ n boja, ton • vt tonirati ~ed glass zatamnjena stakla

tiny /'taɪnɪ/ adj sićušan

tip (1) /tɪp/ n vršak, vrh • vt be ~ed with imati (kakav) vršak/vršak od ~ped cigar cigara s filterom

tip (2) vt,vi 1 prebaciti, izbaciti, iskrcati, izvrnuti 2 (over/up) prevrnuti (se) 3 nagnuti ~ the balance/scales prevagnuti

tip (3) n GB smetlište

tip (4) n napojnica • vt,vi dati napojnicu

tip (5) n savjet; mig • vt smatrati favoritom ~ off upozoriti ~-off n upozorenje, dojava

tipple /'tɪpl/ n coll kapljica ~r n ljubitelj kapljice

tipsy /'tɪpsɪ/ adj pripit

tiptoe /'tɪptəʊ/ n on ~ na prstima • vi hodati na prstima

tire (1) /'taɪə(r)/ vi,vt (of) umoriti se (od) she never ~s (of) nikad joj ne dosadi ~ out izmoriti ~d adj umoran, iscrpljen I am (sick) and ~d of sb/sth navrh mi je glave koga/čega ~less adj neumoran ~some adj 1 zamoran 2 odvratan

tire (2) US → tyre

tissue /'tɪʃuː/ n 1 tkivo 2 (~ paper) svileni papir 3 (paper ~) papirna maramica

tit /tɪt/ n coll tab sisa ~ty n coll cica

titbit /'tɪtbɪt/ n 1 oblizek 2 cveba fig

tit for tat n coll milo za drago

tithe /taɪð/ n desetina (crkvi)

titillate /'tɪtɪleɪt/ vt uzbuditi, nadražiti

title /'taɪtl/ n 1 naslov 2 titula 3 pravo ~deed isprava (o vlasništvu) ~holder nositelj titule ~ page naslovna strana ~d adj plemenit

titter /'tɪtə(r)/ vi hihotati se • n hihot

titular /'tɪtjʊlə(r)/ adj nominalni

to /tuː/ prep 1 (za tvorbu infinitiva) to sleep spavati 2 (za tvorbu dativa) talk to sb obraćati se komu give it to

John daj to Johnu kind to sb dobar prema komu 3 (smjer kretanja) do, prema, u 4 (vrijeme, količina) do made to measure načinjeno po mjeri • adv come to doći k sebi

toad /təʊd/ n žaba krastača ~stool n otrovna gljiva ~y n ulizica ○ vi (to) ulizivati se (komu)

toast (1) /təʊst/ n prepečenac • vt peći ~er n toster coll

toast (2) n 1 zdravica 2 slavljenik • vt ispiti zdravicu

tobacco /tə'bækəʊ/ n duhan ~nist n 1 prodavač duhanskih proizvoda 2 (prodavaonica) duhan coll

toboggan /tə'bɒgən/ n sanjke pl • vi sanjkati se

today /tə'deɪ/ adv danas • n danas ~'s današnji

toddle /'tɒdl/ vi gegati se ~r n dijete (koje je tek prohodalo)

toddy /'tɒdɪ/ n viski s vrućom vodom i šećerom

to-do /tə'duː/ n strka

toe /təʊ/ n (nožni) prst on one's ~s na oprezu ~ cap kapica (cipele) ~nail n nokat • vt ~ the line poštivati pravila

toffee /'tɒfɪ/ n karamela ~-nosed adj snobovski

together /tə'geðə(r)/ adv zajedno, skupa, istovremeno come ~ skupiti se put ~ sastaviti ~ness n bliskost, osjećaj jedinstva

toggle /'tɒgl/ n drvena kopča • vi comp seliti se

toil /tɔɪl/ n form težak rad, muka • vi 1 teško raditi, rintati 2 mučno se kretati

toilet /'tɔɪlɪt/ n 1 zahod 2 arch toaleta ~ paper/tissue n toaletni papir ~ roll n toaletni papir u roli ~-trained adj koji više ne treba pelene ~ water toaletna vodica ~ries n pl kozmetika

token /'təʊkən/ n 1 znak, obilježje, biljeg as a ~/in ~ of u znak (čega) 2 uspomena 3 poklon-bon 4 žeton • adj simboličan (+ derog) ~ism n derog lažno podilaženje manjinama

told v irreg → tell

tolerable /'tɒlərəbl/ adj kakav-takav, podnošljiv tolerance /'tɒlərəns/ n 1 (of/towards/for) tolerancija, snošljivost 2 prag izdržljivosti **tolerant** *adj* tolerantan, snošljiv **tolerate** /'tɒlə-reɪt/ *vt* tolerirati

toll (1) /təʊl/ *n* 1 namet (cestarina, mostarina, putarina i sl.) 2 *fig* danak **heavy death ~** velik broj mrtvih **~booth** naplatna kućica **~free** *adj*, *adv* besplatan; besplatno **~gate** rampa

toll (2) zvoniti, odbijati

tomato /tə'ma:təʊ/ *n* rajčica

tomb /tu:m/ *n* grob **~stone** nadgrobni kamen

tomboy /'tɒmbɔɪ/ *n* muškobanjasta djevojka

tomcat /'tɒmkæt/ *n* mačak

tome /təʊm/ *n* svezak; knjižurina

tomfoolery /,tɒm'fu:lərɪ/ *n* budalaština

toommy gun *n* automat

tommrorow /tə'mɒrəʊ/ *adv* sutra • *n* sutra **brighter ~** bolje sutra

tom-tom /'tɒmtɒm/ *n* tam-tam

ton /tʌn/ *n* tona (+ *fig*) **~nage** *n* 1 tonaža 2 trgovačka mornarica

tone /təʊn/ *n* zvuk; ton (+ *fig*), boja (zvuka) **~deaf** *adj* bez sluha **~less** *adj* bezbojan • *vt*, *vi* **~ down** ublažiti **~ up** očvrsnuti

tongs /tɒŋz/ *n pl* hvataljka

tongue /tʌŋ/ *n* jezik **have a sharp ~** biti jezičav **native ~** materinski jezik **set ~s wagging** izazvati tračeve **with one's ~ in cheek** s ironijskim odmakom **~-in-cheek** *adj* ironičan **~-tied** nijem *fig* **~ twister** teško izgovoriva riječ

tonic /'tɒnɪk/ *n* 1 okrepa; sredstvo za jačanje 2 (**~ water**) tonik

tonight /tə'naɪt/ *adv* noćas, večeras • *n* ova noć, ova večer

tonsil /'tɒnsl/ *n* krajnik; mandula *coll*

too /tu:/ *adv* 1 također 2 previše **only ~** itekako

took *v irreg* → **take**

tool /tu:l/ *n* 1 alat 2 oruđe (+ *fig*) 3 *tab* penis • *vt*, *vi* izraditi **~ up** opremiti potrebnim strojevima

toot /tu:t/ *vi*, *vt* trubiti

tooth /tu:θ/ *n* (**teeth** *pl*) 1 zub 2 zubac **~ and nail** zubima i noktima **have a sweet ~** voljeti slatko **be long in the ~** biti već postariji **~ache** zubobolja

~brush četkica za zube **~paste** pasta za zube **~pick** čačkalica **~some** *adj* slastan **~y** *adj* zubat, pun zuba

top (1) /tɒp/ *n* 1 vrh 2 najviši položaj 3 čep, poklopac 4 gornji dio, majica, košulja **at the ~ of one's voice** iz sveg grla **at ~ speed** najvećom brzinom **from ~ to toe** od glave do pete **get on ~ of** uništavati **off the ~ of one's head** otprilike, improvizirano **on ~ of** povrh **be on ~ of the world** biti presretan **over the ~** pretjeran **~ brass** *coll* glavešine *pl* **~coat** *n* a. završni sloj boje b. kaput **~ dog** glavni šef **~flight** *adj coll* najviši **~ hat** cilindar **~-heavy** preopterećen **~ knot** *n* punđa **~less** *adj* bez gornjeg dijela **~most** *adj* najviši **~notch** *adj coll* vrhunski **~ping** *n* preljev **~secret** *adj* strogo povjerljivi **~soil** površinski sloj tla • *adj* najviši, gornji • *vt* 1 prijeći, nadvisiti 2 prekriti **~ off** dovršiti **~ up** nadopuniti; nadoliti

top (2) zvrk **sleep like a ~** spavati kao top

topic /'tɒpɪk/ *n* tema **~al** *adj* aktualan

topple /'tɒpl/ *vi*, *vt* srušiti (se) (+ *fig*)

topsy-turvy /,tɒpsɪ 'tɜ:vɪ/ *adj*, *adv* u potpunom neredu

torch /tɔ:tʃ/ *n* 1 baterijska svjetiljka; baterija *coll* 2 baklja **carry a ~ for sb** biti zaljubljen u koga **~light** *n* svjetlost baklji **~light parade** baklja da

tore *v irreg* → **tear**

torment /'tɔ:ment/ *n* muka, agonija • *vt* mučiti

torn *v irreg* → **tear**

torpedo /tɔ:'pi:dəʊ/ *n* torpedo • *vt* torpedirati

torrent /'tɒrənt/ *n* bujica (+ *fig*) **~ial** *adj* neobuzdan *fig* o **~ rain** prolom oblaka

torrid /'tɒrɪd/ *adj* 1 žarki 2 *fig* divlji

tort /tɔ:t/ *n* prekršaj

tortoise /'tɔ:təs/ *n* kornjača **~shell** *n* kornjačevina

torture /'tɔ:tʃə(r)/ *n* mučenje • *vt* mučiti, baciti na muke

Tory /'tɔ:rɪ/ *n* član britanske Konzervativne stranke • *adj* torijevski, konzervativan

toss /tɒs/ *vi,vt* 1 (to sb) dobaciti komu 2 (~ **and turn**) prevrtati se 3 bacati ~ **up/a coin** bacati novčić 4 promiješati ~**ed salad** zelena/miješana salata 5 protresti

tot /tɒt/ *v* ~ **up** zbrojiti

total /'təʊtl/ *adj* 1 totalan, potpun 2 cjelokupni, konačan ~**ly** *adv* u potpunosti • *n* zbroj a ~ **of 100 people** ukupno 100 ljudi • *vt* (up) ukupno iznositi

totalitarian /,təʊtælɪ'teərɪən/ *adj* totalitaran

tote /təʊt/ *vt* 1 vući sa sobom 2 nositi (oružje) ~ **bag** vrećica

totter /'tɒtə(r)/ *vi* 1 klimati se, ljuljati se 2 teturati ~**y** *adj* klimav, teturav

touch /tʌtʃ/ *vi,vt* 1 dirati, doticati 2 dopirati do 3 doći blizu 4 dirnuti 5 ticati se ~ **bottom** doći do dna ~ **wood** pokucati u drvo ~ **down a.** sletjeti **b.** postići zgoditak ~-**down** *n* zgoditak ~ **off** izazvati, pokrenuti ~ (up)**on** dotaknuti se ~ **up** dotjerati • *n* 1 dodir, opip **to the** ~ na opip, pod rukom at the ~ **of a button** pritiskom na dugme **get in** ~ stupiti u vezu **lose** ~ **with** izgubiti kontakt **keep in** ~ ostati u vezi **be in** ~ čuti se **be out of** ~ **with** ne biti u toku **a woman's** ~ ženska ruka **lose one's** ~ izgubiti sposobnost 2 detalj **finishing** ~ završno dotjerivanje 3 **a** ~ **of flu** lagana gripa ~-**and-go** *adj* riskantan ~**ed** *adj* dirnut ~**ing** *adj* dirljiv ~**stone** *n* kamen kušač; odlučujući kriterij *fig* ~-**type** *vi* pisati naslijepo ~**y** *adj* osjetljiv

tough /tʌf/ *adj* 1 jak, čvrst, otporan 2 tvrd 3 nepopustljiv 4 težak, snažan 5 grub, opasan ~ **luck** šteta ~**en** *vi,vt* očvrsnuti, ojačati

tour /tʊə(r)/ *n* 1 (around) putovanje po ~ **operator** turistička agencija 2 obilazak 3 turneja • *vi* (round/around) putovati po ~**ism** *n* turizam ~**ist** *n* 1 turist 2 *mod* turistički ~**isty** *adj* *derog* namijenjen turistima

tour de force /,tʊə də 'fɔːs/ *n* izvanredno djelo

tournament /'tɔːnəmənt/ *n* turnir

tourniquet /'tʊənɪkeɪ/ *n* podveza žile

tousle /'taʊzl/ *vt* razbarušiti

tout (1) /taʊt/ *vi,vt* 1 mamiti kupce, vrbovati 2 reklamirati

tout (2) *n* preprodavač karata; tapkaroš *coll*

tow /təʊ/ *vt* vući, tegliti ~ **away** odvesti "paukom"~ **away zone** zona zabranjenog parkiranja • *n* **take in** ~ tegliti **with sb in** ~ skupa s kim

towards /tə'wɔːd(z)/ *adv* prema

towel /'taʊəl/ *n* ručnik, ubrus • *vt* istrljati ručnikom

tower /'taʊə(r)/ *n* kula, toranj • *vi* (**above/over**) nadvisivati ~ **block** neboder ~**ing** *adj* 1 visok 2 istaknut

town /taʊn/ *n* 1 grad(ić) 2 (**down~**) centar grada **go to** ~ (**on) a.** raspištoljiti se **b.** otići do kraja ~ **hall** gradska vijećnica ~ **house** kuća u gradu ~ **planning** urbanizam ~**ship** *n* 1 *US, Canada* grad sa samoupravom 2 *South Africa* crnačko naselje

toxic /'tɒksɪk/ *adj* otrovan, toksičan

toy /tɔɪ/ *n* igračka • *adj* mali, -igračka ~ **dog** psetance • *vt* ~ **with** poigravati se s

trace /treɪs/ *vt* 1 (to/back to) slijediti trag (do), pronaći (u), pratiti 2 precrtati • *n* **trag in** ~**s** u tragovima ~ **element** oligoelement ~**r** *n* svjetleći metak **tracing paper** paus-papir

track /træk/ *vt,vi* ići čijim tragom, slijediti trag ~-**down** pronaći • *n* 1 trag **cover one's** ~ zamesti svoj trag **keep** ~ **of** biti u toku 2 staza 3 pruga 4 putanja **stop in one's** ~**s** stati kao ukopan 5 (*pl*) gusjenice (tenka) 6 snimka ~ **event** atletska utrka ~ **record** reputacija ~**suit** *n* trenirka ~**er** *n* tragač

tract (1) /trækt/ *n* traktat

tract (2) *n* 1 pojas (zemljišta) 2 trakt, sustav

traction /'trækʃn/ *n* 1 vuča 2 trenje **lose** ~ izgubiti uporište, okretati se u prazno 3 *med* ekstenzija

tractor /'træktə(r)/ *n* traktor

trade /treɪd/ *n* 1 trgovina 2 posao, privreda 3 zanat, profesija 4 poslovanje ~-**off** *n* ustupak ~ **gap** trgovinski deficit ~**mark** *n* tvornički znak; zaštitni znak (+ *fig*) ~ **price** cijena na veliko **~r** *n* trgovac **~sman** *n* 1 trgovac 2 dostavljač **~(s)** **union** sindikat • *vi,vt* 1 (with sb/in sth) trgovati 2 (for) zamijeniti **~ sth in** dati što staro za novo

tradition /trə'dıʃn/ *n* tradicija **~al** *adj* tradicionalan

traffic /'træfik/ *n* 1 promet **~ circle →** **roundabout ~ jam** krkljanac **~ light/signal** semafor 2 promet, trgovina • *vt* **~ in** trgovati (drogom i sl.)

tragedy /'trædʒədı/ *n* tragedija (+ *fig*) **tragic** /'trædʒık/ *adj* tragičan (+ *fig*)

trail /treıl/ *n,vt* 1 (along/behind) vući (za sobom) 2 slijediti trag 3 vući se **~ off** utihnuti • *n* 1 trag 2 staza 3 oblak, trag **~er** *n* 1 prikolica 2 najava za novi film; foršpan *coll* 3 *US* → **caravan**

train (1) /treın/ *n* 1 vlak 2 povorka 3 povlaka **~ of thought** tijek misli

train (2) /treın/ *vt* 1 podučavati 2 dresirati 3 trenirati 4 naciljati **~ee** *n* naučnik, početnik **~er** *n* 1 trener 2 tenisica **~ing** *n* 1 poduka 2 trening

trait /treıt/ *n* obilježje

traitor /'treıtə(r)/ *n* izdajnik

trajectory /trə'dʒektərı/ *n* putanja

tram /træm/ *n* tramvaj **~lines** *n* tračnice

tramp /træmp/ *vi,vt* gaziti • *n* 1 skitnica 2 *US* kurva 3 šetnja 4 topot **~ steamer** brod slobodne plovidbe

trample /'træmpl/ *vi,vt* zgaziti, pogaziti

trance /tra:ns/ *n* trans

tranquilizer /'træŋkwılaızə/ *n* sredstvo za umirenje; sedativ

transaction /træn'zækʃn/ *n* transakcija

transcend /træn'send/ *vt* nadići **~ental** *adj* transcendentalan

transcribe /træn'skraıb/ *vt* 1 prepisati 2 transkribirati

transcript /'trænskrıpt/ *n* prijepis **~ion** *n* transkripcija

transfer /'trænsfз:/ *vi,vt* 1 (from/to) preseliti (se), prijeći 2 prenijeti • *n* 1 preseljenje, premještaj 2 transfer **~ passenger** putnik koji nastavlja putovanje 3 prijelazna karta 4 doznaka, uplata, prijenos **~able** *adj* preno-

siv **~ence** *n* prijenos

transfigure /træns'fıgə(r)/ *vt* preobraziti

transfix /træns'fıks/ *vt* (with) 1 probosti 2 **be ~ed** stajati kao ukopan

transform /træns'fɔ:m/ *vt* transformirati, pretvarati, izmijeniti **~ation** *n* pretvorba **~er** *n* transformator

transfusion /træns'fju:ʒn/ *n* transfuzija

transgress /trænz'gres/ *vt,vi* 1 prijeći 2 zgriješiti

transient /'trænzıənt/ *adj* prolazan

transistor /træn'zıstə(r)/ *n* tranzistor

transit /'trænsıt/ *n* 1 transport 2 tranzit 3 *mod* tranzitni **~ion** /træn'zıʃn/ *n* prijelaz **~itive** *adj gram* prijelazan **~ory** *adj* prolazan

translate /trænz'leıt/ *vi,vt* (from/into) prevoditi **translation** *n* prijevod; prevođenje **translator** *n* prevoditelj

translucent /trænz'lu:snt/ *adj* proziran; mutan

transmission /trænz'mıʃn/ *n* prijenos

transmit /trænz'mıt/ *n* 1 (to) slati, emitirati 2 prenositi, širiti **~ter** *n* prijenosnik

transom /'trænsəm/ *n* 1 dovratak 2 *US* okno nad vratima

transparency *n* 1 prozirnost 2 dijapozitiv **transparent** *adj* 1 proziran 2 jasan; očit

transpire /træn'spaıə(r)/ *vi* 1 ispostaviti se 2 *coll* dogoditi se

transplant /træns'pla:nt/ *vt* presaditi, transplantirati • *n* /'trænspla:nt/ 1 transplantacija 2 transplantat

transport /'trænspɔ:t/ *n* prijevoz, transport **~er** *n* transporter /træn'spɔ:t/ *vt* prevoziti **~ation** /,trænspɔ:'teıʃn/ *n US* transport

transverse /'trænzvз:s/ *adj* poprečan

transvestite /trænz'vestaıt/ *n* transvestit

trap /træp/ *n* 1 klopka, zamka **set a ~** postaviti zamku 2 *coll* gubica 3 dvokolica (kočija) • *vt* 1 zarobiti, uhvatiti u klopku 2 (into) navesti na 3 loviti (zamkama) **~door** *n* vrata u podu **~per** *n* traper, lovac **~shooting** *n* gađanje glinenih golubova

trash /træʃ/ *n* smeće (+ *fig*) **~can** *US*

kanta za smeće ~y *adj* bezvrijedan

trauma /'trɔ:mə/ *n* trauma; ozljeda ~**tic** *adj* traumatski ~**tize** *vt* izazvati traumu

travel /'trævl/ *vi,vt* 1 putovati; proputovati; prijeći ~ **light** putovati bez mnogo prtljage 2 raditi kao trgovački putnik • *n* putovanje, put ~ **agency** putnička agencija ~**led** *adj* (koji je) iskusan putnik ~**ler** *n* 1 putnik 2 (~**ling salesman**) trgovački putnik ~**ling** *adj* 1 putujući 2 putni ~**logue** *n* putopis ~**sick** *adj* kojem je mučno od putovanja

travesty /'trævəstɪ/ *n* travestija, farsa

trawl /trɔ:l/ *vi,vt* loviti kočama • *n* 1 koča 2 (~ **line**) parangal ~**er** *n* kočarica

tray /treɪ/ *n* pladanj

treacherous /'tretʃərəs/ *adj* izdajnički **treachery** *n* izdaja

treacle /'tri:kl/ *n* melasa **treacly** *adj* 1 ljepljiv 2 *fig* sladunjav

tread /tred/ *vi,vt irreg* 1 gaziti, nagaziti 2 koračati 3 krčiti ~ **warily** oprezno postupati ~ **on sb's corns/toes** nagaziti komu na žulj • *n* 1 korak 2 profil (gume) 3 stepenica ~**mill** *n* žrvanj *fig*

treason /'tri:zn/ *n* izdaja **high** ~ veleizdaja ~**able** *adj* izdajnički

treasure /'treʒə(r)/ *n* blago **art** ~**s** vrijedne umjetnine ~ **trove** nađeno blago; riznica *fig* • *vt* čuvati kao najveću vrijednost ~**r** *n* rizničar the **Treasury** *n* ministarstvo financija

treat /tri:t/ *vi,vt* 1 postupati s kim, tretirati koga ~ **as** smatrati 2 obraditi, tretirati 3 (for) liječiti zbog 4 (to) počastiti čime • *n* (ugodno) iznenađenje **it is my** ~ ja častim ~**ment** *n* 1 tretman, postupanje (prema kome) 2 postupak, liječenje

treatise /'tri:tɪz/ *n* traktat

treaty /'tri:tɪ/ *n* sporazum, ugovor

treble (1) /'trebl/ *adv* triput veći/više • *vi,vt* triput se povećati

treble (2) *n* 1 sopran 2 sopranski registar ~ **clef** violinski ključ

tree /tri:/ *n* stablo

trefoil /'trefɔɪl/ *n* trolist

trek /trek/ *vi* prohodati • *n* hodanje

trellis /'trelɪs/ *n* rešetka

tremble /'trembl/ *vi* (with/at/for) drhtati od/pred, tresti se • *n* drhtaj

tremendous /trɪ'mendəs/ *adj* 1 ogroman, golem 2 fantastičan

tremor /'tremə(r)/ *n* 1 potres 2 drhtaj

tremulous /'tremjʊləs/ *adj* drhtav

trench /trentʃ/ *n* rov ~ **coat** kišni kaput

trenchant /'trentʃənt/ *adj* oštar, bridak

trend /trend/ *n* trend ~**setter** *coll* onaj koji uvodi modne novosti ~y *adj* u trendu *n* onaj koji je u trendu

trepidation /,trepɪ'deɪʃn/ *n* uzrujanost

trespass /'trespəs/ *vi* 1 (on) *leg* narušavati posjed 2 (against) ogriješiti se o, zgriješiti • *n* 1 *leg* smetanje posjeda 2 grijeh

trestle /'tresl/ *n* postolje; nogari *pl*

trial /'traɪəl/ *n* 1 suđenje **be/go on ~ for** ići na sud zbog **he stands** ~ **for** sudi mu se zbog 2 pokus 3 *mod* pokusni 4 iskušenje ~ **and error** metoda pokušaja i pogrešaka ~ **run** pokusna vožnja

triangle /'traɪæŋgl/ *n* trokut **triangular** *adj* trokutast

tribal /'traɪbl/ *adj* plemenski **tribe** *n* pleme **tribesman** *n* član plemena

tribulation /,trɪbjʊ'leɪʃn/ *n* muka

tribunal /traɪ'bju:nl/ *n* pravobranilaštvo, sud

tributary /'trɪbjʊtrɪ/ *n* pritok

tribute /'trɪbju:t/ *n* 1 čast, štovanje **pay** ~ **to** iskazati čast, čestitati **it is a** ~ **to sb/sth** za to se može zahvaliti komu/čemu 2 danak

trice /traɪs/ *n* **in a** ~ u tren oka

trick /trɪk/ *n* 1 trik, opsjena 2 podvala, varka 3 šala 4 štos *coll* **know all the** ~**s of the trade** biti premazan svim mastima 5 navika 6 *sl* mušterija (prostitutke) **do the** ~ *coll* djelovati **never miss a** ~ imati oči stalno otvorene • *vt* prevariti, nasamariti ~**ery** *n* podvale, smicalice *pl* ~ **or treat** (riječi kojima maškare traže nagrade večer uoči Svisvetih) ~**ster** *n* varalica ~**y** *adj* 1 zapetljan, škakljiv, neugodan 2 lukav, pun smicalica

trickle /'trɪkl/ *vi* curkati, cijediti se • *n* potočić *fig* tricycle /'traɪsɪkl/ n tricikl

trident /'traɪdnt/ n trozubac

tried v irreg → try

triennial /traɪ'enɪəl/ adj trogodišnji

trifle /'traɪfl/ n 1 voćni kolač s kremom 2 trica a ~ pomalo • vt ~ with poigravati se trifling adj bijedan

trigger /'trɪgə(r)/ n okidač ~-happy adj brz na okidaču • vt (off) uzrokovati

trill /trɪl/ n ćurlik

trilogy /'trɪlədʒɪ/ n trilogija

trim /trɪm/ vt 1 podšišati; potkresati (+ fig) 2 (with) ukrasiti, optočiti 3 praćati (jedra) • n 1 šišanje 2 stanje, spremnost in good ~ raspoložen 3 ukras • adj uredan; pristao ~ming n dodatak, prilog

trinity /'trɪnətɪ/ n trojstvo the Holy T~ Sveto Trojstvo

trinket /'trɪŋkɪt/ n tričarija, sitan nakit

trip /trɪp/ vi,vt 1 (over) spotaknuti se 2 (up) navesti na pogrešku 3 posakivati 4 aktivirati ~wire mine potezna mina 5 sl biti na tripu ~ the lights fantastic plesati • n 1 put business ~ službeni put 2 sl trip be on a power ~ uživati u osjećaju moći 3 put

tripe /traɪp/ n tripice, fileki pl

triple /'trɪpl/ vi,vt potrostručiti • adj trostruk ~ jump troskok ~ts n pl trojke

triplicate /'trɪplɪkət/ n in ~ u tri primjerka

tripod /'traɪpɒd/ n tronožac

trite /traɪt/ adj otrcan, plitak

triumph /'traɪʌmf/ n trijumf, pobjeda, slavlje • vi (over) nadvladati, pobijediti ~ant adj trijumfalan, pobjednički, pobjedonosan

trivia /'trɪvɪə/ n pl sitnice, beznačajni podaci ~l adj trivijalan, svakodnevni, beznačajan

trod, trodden v irreg → tread

trolley /'trɒlɪ/ n kolica

trombone /trɒm'bəʊn/ n trombon

troop /truːp/ n 1 skupina 2 vod ~s pl vojnici ~ carrier vozilo za prijevoz trupa ~er n 1 konjanik 2 US policajac • vi marširati • adj vojni ~ movement pokreti vojske

trophy /'trəʊfɪ/ n trofej

tropic /'trɒpɪk/ adj obratnica ~al adj tropski ~s n pl tropi

trot /trɒt/ n kas the ~s coll trčkavica, proljev • vi,vt kasati, ići kasom; kaskati ~ter n svinjska nogica

trouble /'trʌbl/ n 1 problem 2 nevolja, opasnost run into ~ naletjeti na poteškoću get into ~ uvaliti se u neprilike 3 trud 4 (pl) pol nemiri • vt,vi 1 zabrinjavati, brinuti 2 (for) (za)gnjaviti 3 truditi se 4 mučiti ~maker buntovnik; gnjavator ~shooter stručnjak za otklanjanje kvarova ~some adj koji gnjavi ~ spot krizno područje

trough /trɒf/ n 1 korito 2 polje niskog tlaka

trounce /traʊns/ vt poraziti hametice

trousers /'traʊzəs/ n pl hlače

trout /traʊt/ (~/~s pl) pastrva

trowel /'traʊəl/ n zidarska lopatica

truancy /'truːənsɪ/ n bježanje s nastave; markiranje truant /'truːənt/ n markirant play truant markirati

truce /truːs/ n primirje

truck /trʌk/ n US kamion • vt prevoziti kamionom ~er n vozač kamiona

truculent /'trʌkjʊlənt/ adj čangrizav

trudge /trʌdʒ/ vi vući se

true /truː/ adj 1 istinit come ~ obistiniti se it is ~ istina je 2 istinski, pravi, stvarni 3 (to) vjeran ~blue adj coll pouzdan, odan, pravi ~-life story priča iz stvarnog života truly adv uistinu, zaista

truffle /'trʌfl/ n 1 tartuf 2 pralina

truism /'truːɪzəm/ n očita istina

trump /trʌmp/ n (~ card) adut • vt adutirati ~ up izmisliti, namjestiti

trumpet /'trʌmpɪt/ n truba • vi,vt 1 trubiti 2 udarati na sva zvona ~er n trubač

truncheon /'trʌntʃən/ n pendrek

trundle /'trʌndl/ vi,vt drndati, vući

trunk /trʌŋk/ n 1 deblo 2 škrinja; kovčeg 3 surla 4 trup 5 ~s pl kupaće gaće 6 US → boot ~ call n međugradski poziv ~ road magistralna cesta

truss /trʌs/ vt (up) vezati

trust /trʌst/ n 1 povjerenje put one's ~ in sb/sth uzdati se u koga/što, osloniti se na **take sth on** ~ povjerovati na riječ 2 zaklada 3 skrbništvo, briga 4 trust • *vt* 1 vjerovati komu **tried and ~ed** provjeren 2 pouzdati se u ~ **you to do it** i opet si to učinio 3 vjerovati **in** uzdati se u ~ **to** oslanjati se na ~**ee** *n* 1 izvršitelj oporuke, skrbnik 2 upravitelj ~**ful, ~ing** *adj* pun povjerenja ~ **fund** zaklada ~**worthy** *adj* pouzdan ~**y** *adj* vjeran

truth /truːθ/ *n* 1 istina **to tell the ~** istinu govoreći **in ~** ustvari 2 istinitost 3 iskrenost ~**ful** *adj* 1 istinit 2 istinoljubiv

try /traɪ/ *vi,vt* 1 pokušati, nastojati ~ **one's best/hardest** truditi se iz petnih žila ~ **and come** *coll* pokušaj doći ~ **one's hand at** okušati se u 2 probati, iskušati 3 (sb for sth) suditi komu zbog čega 4 ~ **this for size!** što kažeš na ovo ~ **on** isprobati • *n* pokušaj ~**ing** *adj* težak, iscrpljujući ~**out** *n* probno natjecanje

tsar → **czar**

tse tse fly /ˈtsetsɪ/ *n* muha ce-ce

T-shirt /ˈtiː ʃɜːt/ *n* majica (s kratkim rukavima)

tub /tʌb/ *n* 1 bačva, kaca 2 posuda 3 *coll* kada

tubby /ˈtʌbɪ/ *adj* zdepast

tube /tjuːb/ *n* 1 cijev **test ~** kušalica 2 tuba **the ~** *GB coll* podzemna željeznica 4 *coll* televizija **tubing** *n* cijevi *pl* **tubular** /ˈtjuːbjʊlə(r)/ *adj* cjevast

tuber /ˈtjuːbə(r)/ *n* gomolj

tuberculosis /tjuːˌbɜːkjʊˈləʊsɪs/ *n* tuberkuloza, sušica

tuck /tʌk/ *vt* 1 (in/up) podvrnuti 2 (into) ugurati 3 tutnuti, gurnuti ~ **away** sakriti ~ **in** *coll* navaliti na jelo ~ **up** ušuškati u postelju • *n* porub, ušitak

Tuesday /ˈtjuːzdɪ/ *n* utorak **on ~** u utorak

tuft /tʌft/ *n* busen; čuperak

tug /tʌg/ *vi,vt* (at) vući za, izvući • *n* 1 **give a (sharp) ~** (naglo) povući 2 (~**boat**) remorker ~**-of-war** povlačenje konopca; povuci-potegni *fig*

tuition /tjuːˈɪʃn/ *n* 1 poduka 2 nastava

tulip /ˈtjuːlɪp/ *n* tulipan

tumble /ˈtʌmbl/ *vi,vt* 1 strovaliti se, smandrljati se ~ **down** srušiti se; propasti *fig* ~ **off** poiskakati s 2 oboriti; posrušiti; ispremetati; razbarušiti • *n* pad ~**down** *adj* ruševan ~**-dryer** sušilo za rublje ~**r** *n* čaša

tummy /ˈtʌmɪ/ *n coll* trbuh; tibica *coll*

tumour (-or *US*) /ˈtjuːmə(r)/ *n* tumor, izraslina

tumult /ˈtjuːmʌlt/ *n* strka, galama ~**uous** *adj* bučan

tuna /ˈtjuːnə/ *n* (~/~s *pl*) tunj ~ (**fish**) tunjevina

tune /tjuːn/ *n* 1 melodija **sing out of ~** krivo pjevati **in ~ with** u skladu s **out of ~ with** u raskoraku s **to the ~ of** *coll* u iznosu od **change the ~** pjevati drugu pjesmu • *vt* 1 ugoditi 2 podesiti, namjestiti 3 (in to) prebaciti (na kanal) **stay ~d** ostanite na programu ~**less** *adj* monoton ~**r** *n* radio-prijemnik

tunic /ˈtjuːnɪk/ *n* 1 tunika 2 dolama

tunnel /ˈtʌnl/ *n* 1 tunel ~ **vision** *fig* ograničenost • *vt,vi* prokopati tunel

turbine /ˈtɜːbaɪn/ *n* turbina

turbo /ˌtɜːbəʊ/ *n* turbo(-pogon)

turbulence /ˈtɜːbjʊləns/ *n* 1 turbulencija 2 *pol* previranje **turbulent** *adj* nemiran

turd /tɜːd/ *n tab* govno (+ *fig*)

tureen /tjʊˈriːn/ *n* zdjela za juhu

turf /tɜːf/ *n* 1 tratina **the ~** konjske trke 2 *sl* teritorij (bande)

turkey /ˈtɜːkɪ/ *n* 1 puran 2 puretina 3 *US sl* bezveznjaković 4 *US sl* propala stvar

turmoil /ˈtɜːmɔɪl/ *n* previranje, nemir, kaos

turn (1) /tɜːn/ *vi,vt* 1 okretati, okrenuti (se) 2 (over/inside out/upside down) preokrenuti, okrenuti (se) na drugu stranu/naglavce 3 skrenuti ~ **back** vratiti (koga) ~ **round** okrenuti se ~ **the corner a.** skrenuti za ugao b. *fig* proći najgore 4 (on/towards) uperiti na/prema ~ **one's back on** okrenuti leđa kome 5 ~ **pale** problijedeti ~ **grey** posijedjeti ~ **traitor** premetnuti se u izdajnika ~ **politician** postati političarem ~ **from sth into** pretvoriti se iz čega u što **6** proći ~ **40** navršiti 40 godina **7** ukiseliti ~ **sb's brain** učiniti ludim ~ **a blind eye on** zažmiriti na ~ **a deaf ear to** oglušiti se na **make heads** ~ izazvati senzaciju ~ **the tables on sb** okrenuti batinu, preokrenuti situaciju ~ **tail** podvući rep ~ **against** okrenuti se protiv ~ **down** a. stišati b. odbiti ~ **in** a. predati b. zaraditi c. *coll* otići u postelju ~ **off** a. isključiti, zatvoriti b. skrenuti c. zgaditi se komu ~**off** *n* a. sporedna cesta b. razočaranje ~ **on** a. uključiti, otvoriti b. ovisiti o c. uzbuđivati d. navaliti na ~ **out** a. isključiti b. izbaciti c. doći d. povaditi sve iz, izvrnuti e. pokazati se, ispasti (na kraju) ~ **over** a. razmotriti b. imati promet ~ **over to** predati u ruke ~ to obratiti se ~ **up** a. pojačati b. pojaviti se c. iskrsnuti d. iskopati e. potkratiti ~**ed-up** *adj* a. podvrnut b. prćast

turn (2) *n* **1** okret **give sth a** ~ okrenuti što **2** skretanje, zavoj **make a** ~ skrenuti **3** red, prilika **ask everybody in** ~ pitati sve redom **take** ~s redati se **4** prijelaz **take a** ~ **for the worse** poći na gore **do sb a good/bad** ~ učiniti komu uslugu/naškoditi komu **at every** ~ na svakom koraku ~**about** *n* preokret ~**coat** *n* prebjeg ~**ing** *n* skretanje ~**ing point** prekretnica ~**key** *adj* po sistemu ključ ~ **out** *n* a. broj prisutnih b. odaziv glasača ~**over** *n* promet, prodaja

turnip /'tɜːnɪp/ *n* bijela repa
turnpike /'tɜːn,paɪk/ *n* (~ **road**) *US* autoput (na kojem se plaća cestarina)
turnstile /'tɜːn,staɪl/ *n* križna rampa
turntable /'tɜːn,teɪbl/ *n* gramofon, okretna ploča gramofona
turpentine /'tɜːpəntaɪn/ *n* terpentin
turps /tɜːps/ *coll* → **turpentine**
turquoise /'tɜːkwɔɪz/ *n* **1** tirkiz **2** *mod* tirkizan; od tirkiza
turret /'tʌrɪt/ *n* **1** kula **2** kupola (tenka)
turtle /'tɜːtl/ *n* kornjača ~**neck** *n US* dolčevita

turtledove /'tɜːtl,dʌv/ *n* grlica
tusk /tʌsk/ *n* kljova
tussle /'tʌsl/ *vi* (with) *coll* pokefati se s *coll* • *n* koškanje
tussock /'tʌsək/ *n* busen trave
tutor /'tjuːtə(r)/ *n* **1** (privatni) učitelj **2** mentor • *vt* **1** biti mentor **2** (in) podučavati koga čemu ~**ial** *n* konzultacija
tut-tut /,tʌt 'tʌt/ *vi* puckati jezikom
tutu /'tuːtuː/ *n* baletna suknjica
tuxedo /tʌk'siːdəʊ/ *n US* smoking
TV dinner *n* gotova večera iz dubokog smrzavanja
twang /twæŋ/ *n* **1** brujanje **2** unjkanje **3** okus, prizvuk
twat /twɒt/ *n tab* pizda *tab* (+ *fig*)
tweak /twiːk/ *vt* **1** zavrnuti (nos, uho) **2** poboljšati
tweet /twiːt/ *vi* cvrkutati ~**er** *n* zvučnik visokotonac
tweezers /'twiːzəz/ *n pl* pinceta
twelfth /twelfθ/ *num ord* dvanaesti **T~~day** Tri kralja
twelve /twelv/ *num* dvanaest
twenty /'twentɪ/ *num* dvadeset ~~ **vision** savršen vid
twice /twaɪs/ *adv* dvaput ~ **the amount/as much** dvaput toliko
twiddle /'twɪdl/ *vi,vt* petljati po, vrtjeti ~ **one's thumbs** okretati palčeve (+ *fig*)
twig /twɪg/ *n* grančica
twilight /'twaɪlaɪt/ *n* sumrak **twilit** *adj* u sumraku
twin /twɪn/ *n* **1** blizanac **2** dvojnik • *adj* tijesno povezan ~**towns** zbratimljeni gradovi, gradovi prijatelji ~ **bed** poseban krevet (u dvokrevetnoj sobi) ~ **set** vesta i pulover
twine /twaɪn/ *n* jaki konac • *vi,vt* obaviti se; usukati
twinge /twɪndʒ/ *n* probadanje **a** ~ **of conscience** grižnja savjesti
twinkle /'twɪŋkl/ *vi* treperenje, sjaj • *vi* svjetlucati, treperiti **twinkling** *n* tren
twirl /twɜːl/ *vi,vt* vrtjeti (se) • *n* okret
twist /twɪst/ *vi,vt* **1** uvrtati (se), okrenuti ~ **off** skinuti **2** izobličiti se **3** (round) uviti, isplesti **4** biti pun zavoja ~**ing** *adj* zavojit **5** iskrenuti; izvrnuti *fig* ~ **sb round one's little fin-**

ger motati koga oko malog prsta ~ **someone's arm** *fig* pritegnuti koga • *n* 1 okret, uvrtanje 2 zavoj 3 preokret ~ **of fate** igra sudbine 4 smotak ~**ed** *adj* izopačen

twit /twit/ *n* budala

twitch /twitʃ/ *n* trzaj • *vi,vt* trzati (se)

twitter /'twitə(r)/ *n* cvrkutati • *n* 1 cvrkut 2 usplahirenost

two /tu:/ *num* dva, dvije, dvoje, dvoja **divide in** ~ raspoloviti **the** ~ **of them** obadva, obadvije, obadvoje **put** ~ **and** ~ **together** zbrojiti dva i dva **that makes** ~ **of us** *coll* ja također ~**bit** *adj* sitan ~**edged** *adj* dvosjekli ~**faced** *adj* dvoličan ~**piece** *adj* dvodijelan ~**ply** *adj* dvoslojan ~**some** *n* par ~**time** *vt* varati ~**tone** *adj* dvobojan ~**way** *adj* dvosmjeran ~**way mirror** lažno ogledalo

tycoon /tai'ku:n/ *n* magnat

tying → **tie**

type /taip/ *n* 1 tip 2 vrsta 3 slova *pl* • *vi,vt* 1 tipkati 2 identificirati ~**cast** *vt* *irreg* (→ **cast**) davati stalno iste uloge ~**face** *n* vrsta slova ~**script** *n* prijepis ~**setter** *n* slovoslagar ~**writer** *n* pisaći stroj **typing** *n* strojopis **typist** *n* tipkač **typo** *n* tiskarska pogreška

typhoid /'taifɔid/ *n* (~ **fever**) trbušni tifus

typhoon /tai'fu:n/ *n* tajfun

typhus /'taifəs/ *n* pjegavi tifus

typical /'tipikl/ *adj* tipičan **typify** /'tipifai/ *vt* 1 biti tipičan za 2 utjelovljavati 3 klasificirati

typographer /tai'pɒgrəfə(r)/ *n* 1 tiskar 2 slagar **typographic** /,taipə'græfik/ *adj* tiskarski

tyrannical /ti'rænikl/ *adj* tiranski **tyranny** /'tirəni/ *n* tiranija **tyrant** *n* tiranin

tyre /'taiə(r)/ *n* guma

U

U, u /juː/ 21. slovo engl. abecede; u

ubiquitous /juːˈbɪkwɪtəs/ adj form koji se svugdje nalazi/pojavljuje, sveprisutan

udder /ˈʌdə(r)/ n vime

ugh /ɜː/ int fuj

ugly /ˈʌɡlɪ/ adj ružan; gadan; neugodan; prijeteći ~ **customer** coll opasan tip

ulcer /ˈʌlsə(r)/ n čir **stomach ~** čir na želucu

ulterior /ʌlˈtɪərɪə(r)/ adj daljnji; skriven ~ **motive** skrivena namjera

ultimate /ˈʌltɪmət/ adj 1 krajnji, zadnji, posljednji 2 temeljni, osnovni, glavni • n vrhunac **~ly** adv na koncu, na kraju

ultimatum /ˌʌltɪˈmeɪtəm/ n (pl **~tums**, **~ta**) ultimatum

ultra- /ˌʌltrə/ prefix ultra-, nad-

ultrasonic /ˌʌltrəˈsɒnɪk/ adj nadzvučni **ultrasound** n ultrazvuk

ultraviolet /ˌʌltrəˈvaɪələt/ adj ultraljubičast

um /əm/ int hm

umbilical /ʌmˈbɪlɪkl/ adj ~ **cord** pupčana vrpca

umbrella /ʌmˈbrelə/ n 1 kišobran 2 fig zaštita, okrilje

umpire /ˈʌmpaɪə(r)/ n sport sudac • vi, vt suditi

umpteen /ˈʌmptiːn/ adj coll iks, nebrojeno

un- /ʌn/ prefix 1 ne- 2 od- (ot-) 3 raz- (ras-) 4 protu-

unabated /ˌʌnəˈbeɪtɪd/ adj form nesmanjen

unadvised /ˌʌnədˈvaɪzd/ adj form nepromišljen

unanimous /juːˈnænɪməs/ adj jednoglasan **~ly** adv jednoglasno **unanimity** n form jednoglasnost

unawares /ˌʌnəˈweəz/ adv neočeki-
vano, nenajavljeno **catch/take sb ~** zateći, iznenaditi

unbending /ˌʌnˈbendɪŋ/ adj nepopustljiv

uncalled-for /ʌnˈkɔːld fɔː(r)/ adj nezaslužen, nepotreban, koji nije na mjestu

uncanny /ʌnˈkænɪ/ adj neobičan, čudnovat

unceremonious /ˌʌnˌserɪˈməʊnɪəs/ adj 1 nepristojan 2 neformalan, neusiljen

uncertain /ʌnˈsɜːtn/ adj nesiguran **in no ~ terms** vrlo jasno, jasno i glasno

uncle /ˈʌŋkl/ n ujak; stric; tetak U~ **Sam** personifikacija SAD-a

uncomfortable /ʌnˈkʌmftəbl/ adj 1 neudoban 2 neugodan

uncommitted /ˌʌnkəˈmɪtɪd/ adj neutralan, neopredijeljen

uncommonly /ʌnˈkɒmənlɪ/ adv form vrlo, neobično, izuzetno

uncompromising /ʌnˈkɒmprəmaɪzɪŋ/ adj beskompromisan

unconditional /ˌʌnkənˈdɪʃənl/ adj bezuvjetan

unconscious /ʌnˈkɒnʃəs/ adj 1 u nesvijesti, onesviješten 2 nesvjestan 3 nenamjeran

unconsidered /ˌʌnkənˈsɪdəd/ adj nepromišljen

uncork /ˌʌnˈkɔːk/ vt odčepiti

uncountable /ʌnˈkaʊntəbl/ adj gram nebrojiv

uncouth /ʌnˈkuːθ/ adj neotesan, nepristojan

uncover /ʌnˈkʌvə(r)/ vt otkriti

uncut /ˌʌnˈkʌt/ adj 1 neskraćen, integralan (film, knjiga) 2 nebrušen (dragi kamen)

undeceive /ˌʌndɪˈsiːv/ vt form reći istinu, otvoriti kome oči, razuvjeriti koga

under /ˈʌndə(r)/ prep pod, ispod • adv

ispod **down ~** u Australiji ili N. Zelandu

under- /'ʌndə(r)/ *prefix* pod-

underachieve /,ʌndərə'tʃi:v/ *vi euph* podbaciti **~r** *n euph* loš učenik

underage /,ʌndər'eɪdʒ/ *adj* maloljetan

undercarriage /'ʌndəkærɪdʒ/ *n* stajni trap (letjelice)

undercharge /,ʌndə'tʃɑ:dʒ/ *vt,vi* premalo naplatiti

undercoat /'ʌndəkəʊt/ *n* prvi sloj boje, podloga

undercover /,ʌndə'kʌvə(r)/ *adj* tajni

undercurrent /'ʌndəkʌrənt/ *n* 1 struja (vode) 2 skrivene misli/osjećaji

undercut /,ʌndə'kʌt/ *vt irreg* prodavati po nižoj cijeni

underdeveloped /,ʌndədɪ'veləpt/ *adj* **~ country** nerazvijena zemlja

underdog /'ʌndədɒg/ *n* slabija strana; podčinjeni

underestimate /,ʌndər'estɪmeɪt/ *vi,vt* podcijeniti

undergo /,ʌndə'gəʊ/ *vt irreg* proći, doživjeti, biti podvrgnut

undergraduate /,ʌndə'grædʒʊət/ *n* (dodiplomni) student

underground /'ʌndəgraʊnd/ *adv* 1 pod zemljom 2 u tajnosti; u ilegali • *adj* 1 podzemni 2 tajni; ilegalni 3 alternativni, avangardan • *n* 1 *GB* podzemna željeznica 2 ilegala 3 podzemlje

undergrowth /'ʌndəgrəʊθ/ *n* grmlje, nisko raslinje

underhand /'ʌndəhænd/ *adj* nepošten, prikriven

underlie /,ʌndə'laɪ/ *vt irreg* nalaziti se u pozadini/iza čega

underline /,ʌndə'laɪn/ *vt* 1 podcrtati 2 naglasiti, istaknuti

underling /'ʌndəlɪŋ/ *n* podređeni

undermentioned /,ʌndə'menʃnd/ *adj GB form* niženavedeni

undermine /,ʌndə'maɪn/ *vt* podrovati, podrivati; potkopati; minirati *sl*

underneath /,ʌndə'ni:θ/ *prep, adv* ispod • *n coll* dno

undernourished /,ʌndə'nʌrɪʃt/ *adj* pothranjen

underpants /'ʌndəpænts/ *n pl* muške gaće

underpass /'ʌndəpɑ:s/ *n* podvožnjak

underpay /,ʌndə'peɪ/ *vt* nedovoljno platiti

underpin /,ʌndə'pɪn/ *vt* poduprijeti, podupirati

underprivileged /,ʌndə'prɪvəlɪdʒd/ *adj euph* siromašan

underrate /,ʌndə'reɪt/ *vt* podcijeniti

undersecretary /,ʌndə'sekrətrɪ/ *n* (državni) podtajnik; dominstar

undersell /,ʌndə'sel/ *vt* 1 prodavati po nižoj cijeni 2 nedovoljno istaknuti čije dobre strane

undersexed /,ʌndə'sekst/ *adj* koji ima slab spolni nagon

undershirt /'ʌndəʃɜ:t/ *n US* pancirka

underside /'ʌndəsaɪd/ *n* podnožje; donja strana

undersigned /,ʌndə'saɪnd/ *adj form* niže potpisani

understaffed /,ʌndə'stɑ:ft/ *adj* koji nema dovoljno radnika

understand /,ʌndə'stænd/ *vi,vt irreg* 1 razumjeti, shvatiti 2 (about) razumjeti se u što 3 čuti, biti obaviješten **give sb to ~** dati (kome) do znanja 4 podrazumijevati **~able** /,ʌndə'stændəbl/ *adj* razumljiv **~ing** *n* 1 razumijevanje 2 znanje 3 sporazum, nagodba ○ *adj* pun razumijevanja, uviđavan

understate /,ʌndə'steɪt/ *vt* ublažiti, umanjiti **~d** *adj* neupadljiv **understatement** /'ʌndə'steɪtmənt/ *n* eufemizam, ublaženi izraz

understudy /'ʌndəstʌdɪ/ *n* zamjenik glumca • *vt* biti zamjena glumcu

undertake /,ʌndə'teɪk/ *vt irreg form* 1 poduzeti 2 prihvatiti se (čega) 3 preuzeti obavezu **undertaking** *n* 1 pothvat 2 obećanje

undertaker /'ʌndəteɪkə(r)/ *n* pogrebnik

under-the-counter /,ʌndə ðə 'kaʊntə(r)/ *adj coll* tajni, ilegalan; kupljen/prodan ispod pulta *sl*

undertone /'ʌndətəʊn/ *n* 1 prizvuk 2 tih glas

undertow /'ʌndətəʊ/ *n* podmorska struja

undervalue /,ʌndə'vælju:/ *vt* podcijeniti

underwater /'ʌndəwɔ:tə(r)/ *adj* podvodni • *adv* pod vodom

underwear /ˈʌndəweə(r)/ *n* rublje

underweight /ˌʌndəweɪt/ *adj* lakši/mršaviji nego što bi trebalo

underworld /ˈʌndəwɜːld/ *n* 1 *myth* drugi svijet 2 podzemlje *fig*

underwrite /ˌʌndəˈraɪt/ *vt* potpisati policu osiguranja

undies /ˈʌndiz/ *n pl coll* rublje

undo /ʌnˈduː/ *vt irreg* 1 odvezati, otkopčati, odmotati 2 uništiti **~ing** *n* kraj, propast **~ne** *adj* otkopčan, odvezan

undreamed /ʌnˈdriːmd/ *adj* ~**-of** nezamisliv

undress /ʌnˈdres/ *vt* razodjenuti get **~ed** razodjenuti se; skinuti se *coll*

undue /ˌʌnˈdjuː/ *adj form* pretjeran, nepotreban, neprimjeren **unduly** *adv* pretjerano

undulate /ˈʌndjʊleɪt/ *vi* biti valovit **undulating** *adj* valovit, brežuljkast

undying /ˌʌnˈdaɪŋ/ *adj* vječan

unearned /ˌʌnˈɜːnd/ *adj* 1 nezaslužen 2 koji nije stečen radom

unearth /ʌnˈɜːθ/ *vt* 1 iskopati 2 *fig* otkriti, iščačkati **~ly** *adv* 1 natprirodan; strašan 2 *coll* nemoguć; nerazuman

uneasy /ʌnˈiːzɪ/ *adj* 1 nemiran, tjeskoban, napet 2 nestabilan

unemployed /ˌʌnɪmˈplɔɪd/ *adj* nezaposlen **unemployment** /ˌʌnɪmˈplɔɪmənt/ *n* nezaposlenost

unending /ʌnˈendɪŋ/ *adj* neprekidan, kojem nema kraja

unequal /ˌʌnˈiːkwəl/ *adj* (to) 1 nejednak 2 neravnopravan 3 nesposoban

unequalled /ˌʌnˈiːkwld/ *adj* bez premca, jedinstven, nenadmašan

unequivocal /ˌʌnɪˈkwɪvəkl/ *adj* jasan, nedvojben

uneven /ʌnˈiːvən/ *adj* 1 nejednak, neujednačen 2 nepravilan 3 neravnopravan

unexampled /ˌʌnɪgˈzɑːmpld/ *adj form* besprimjeran, izuzetan

unfailing /ʌnˈfeɪlɪŋ/ *adj* stalan, pouzdan, uvijek prisutan

unfair /ˌʌnˈfeə(r)/ *adj* nepošten, nepravedan

unfaltering /ʌnˈfɔːltərɪŋ/ *adj* nepo-

grešiv

unfavourable /ʌnˈfeɪvərbl/ *adj* nepovoljan, negativan

unfeeling /ʌnˈfiːlɪŋ/ *adj* bezosjećajan, okrutan

unfit /ˌʌnˈfɪt/ *adj* 1 nepripremljen, koji nije u dobroj fizičkoj kondiciji 2 (for) neprikladan, neprimjeren, nesposoban

unfold /ʌnˈfəʊld/ *vi, vt* 1 razviti (se) 2 ispričati (što)

unforeseen /ˌʌnfɔːˈsiːn/ *adj* nepredviđen

unfortunate /ʌnˈfɔːtʃʊnət/ *adj* 1 nesretan 2 zlosretan; žalostan • *n* nesretnik **~ly** *adv* nažalost, na nesreću

unfounded /ˌʌnˈfaʊndɪd/ *adj* neutemeljen, neosnovan

unhappy /ʌnˈhæpɪ/ *adj* nesretan, nezadovoljan

unhealthy /ʌnˈhelθɪ/ *adj* nezdrav

unheard /ʌnˈhɜːd/ *adj* ~**-of** nečuven

unhoped /ʌnˈhəʊpt/ *adj* ~**-for** neočekivan, neslućen

unicorn /ˈjuːnɪkɔːn/ *n myth* jednorog

unification /ˌjuːnɪfɪˈkeɪʃən/ *n* ujedinjenje

uniform /ˈjuːnɪfɔːm/ *n* 1 uniforma, odora 2 kuta • *adj* jednak, jednolik, jednoličan **~ed** *adj* uniformiran **unify** /ˈjuːnɪfaɪ/ *vt* 1 ujediniti, sjediniti 2 učiniti jednakim

unilateral /ˌjuːnɪˈlætrəl/ *adj* jednostran

uninhibited /ˌʌnɪnˈhɪbɪtɪd/ *adj* nesputan, bez kompleksa/inhibicija

union /ˈjuːnɪən/ *n* 1 savez 2 udruga **trade ~** sindikat 3 jedinstvo 4 *lit, form* brak **~ize** *vt, vi* udružiti se u sindikat

unique /juːˈniːk/ *adj* 1 jedinstven 2 *coll* izuzetan, bez premca

unison /ˈjuːnɪsn/ *n* jednoglasje **in ~** jednoglasno

unit /ˈjuːnɪt/ *n* jedinica **kitchen ~** kuhinjski element **visual display ~** (VDU) monitor

unite /juːˈnaɪt/ *vi,vt* ujediniti (se), sjediniti (se), združiti (se), udružiti (se) **~d** *adj* ujedinjen, sjedinjen, udružen **the U~ Kingdom (of Great Britain and Northern Ireland)** Ujedinjeno Kraljevstvo (Velike Britanije i

Sjeverne Irske) **the U~ States (of America)** Sjedinjene (Američke) Države **the U~ Nations** Ujedinjeni narodi

unity /'ju:nəti/ *n* **1** jedinstvo, jedinstvenost; cjelina **2** sloga, složnost

universal /ˌju:nɪ'vɜ:sl/ *adj* (sve)opći, univerzalan **~ly** *adv* opće-, od svih; posvuda **universe** /'ju:nɪvɜ:s/ *n* svemir; svijet

university /ˌju:nɪ'vɜ:səti/ *n* **1** sveučilište **2** *mod* sveučilišni

unkempt /ˌʌn'kempt/ *adj* neuredan

unkind /ʌn'kaɪnd/ *adj* neljubazan, nepažljiv, neugodan

unknown /ˌʌn'nəʊn/ *adj* nepoznat ~ **quantity** *n math* nepoznanica

unlawful /ʌn'lɔ:fʊl/ *adj* protuzakonit, nezakonit

unlearn /ˌʌn'lɜ:n/ *vt* odučiti se od, zaboraviti

unleash /ʌn'li:ʃ/ *vt* pustiti (s lanca) ~ **one's fury** dati oduška bijesu

unleavened /ˌʌn'levnd/ *adj* beskvasan

unless /ən'les/ *conj* ako ne, osim ako

unlike /ˌʌn'laɪk/ *prep* različit od *it's ~ her* nije joj slično **~ly** *adj* nevjerojatan, neuvjerljiv

unlisted /ʌn'lɪstɪd/ *adj* **1** *US* koji nije naveden u telefonskom imeniku **2** *comm* koji nije na službenom popisu dionica

unlock /ʌn'lɒk/ *vt* otključati

unlucky /ʌn'lʌki/ *adj* nesretan, loše sreće; koji donosi nesreću

unmarried /ʌn'mærɪd/ *adj* neoženjen, neudan ~ **mother** samohrana majka

unmask /ʌn'mɑ:sk/ *vt* raskrinkati

unmistakable /ˌʌnmɪ'steɪkəbl/ *adj* jasan, nedvojben, očit

unmitigated /ʌn'mɪtɪgeɪtɪd/ *adj* potpun, pravi, neublažen

unnerve /ʌn'nɜ:v/ *vt* obeshrabriti, pokolebati, poljuljati (samo)pouzdanje

unpack /ʌn'pæk/ *vi, vt* raspakirati (se)

unparalleled /ʌn'pærəleld/ *adj form* bez premca, nenadmašan

unpleasant /ʌn'pleznt/ *adj* neugodan

unprecedented /ʌn'presidentɪd/ *adj* bez presedana; nečuven, nezapamćen

unprintable /ˌʌn'prɪntəbl/ *adj* koji nije za objavljivanje; nepristojan

unprovoked /ˌʌnprə'vəʊkt/ *adj* ničim izazvan

unquestionable /ˌʌn'kwestʃənəbl/ *adj* nedvojben, neosporan, neupitan

unquote /ʌn'kwəʊt/ *adv* kraj navoda/citata

unravel /ʌn'rævl/ *vt, vi* rasplesti (se)

unrelenting /ˌʌnrɪ'lentɪŋ/ *adj* nesmanjen

unrequited /ˌʌnrɪ'kwaɪtɪd/ *adj* neuzvraćen

unreserved /ˌʌnrɪ'zɜ:vd/ *adj* **1** potpun, neograničen, bezrezervni **2** nerezerviran, slobodan

unrest /ʌn'rest/ *n* nemiri *pl*

unrivalled /ʌn'raɪvld/ *adj* nedostižan, bez premca

unruly /ʌn'ru:li/ *adj* neposlušan, nepokoran

unsaid /ˌʌn'sed/ *adj* neizrečen

unscramble /ˌʌn'skræmbl/ *vt* dekodirati

unscrew /ʌn'skru:/ *vt* odviti, skinuti vijke; odčepiti

unseemly /ʌn'si:mli/ *adj* nedoličan

unsettle /ʌn'setl/ *vt* uznemiriti

unshakeable, unshakable /ʌn'ʃeɪkbl/ *adj* nepoljuljan, čvrst

unsightly /ʌn'saɪtli/ *adj* ružan

unsound /ʌn'saʊnd/ *adj* **1** nezdrav **2** neutemeljen, neosnovan **3** neprihvatljiv **of ~ mind** *leg* neuračunljiv

unspeakable /ʌn'spi:kəbl/ *adj* neizreciv; strašan, užasan

untie /ʌn'taɪ/ *vt* odvezati

until /ən'tɪl/ *prep, conj* do, dok

untimely /ʌn'taɪmli/ *adj* **1** preran **2** neprikladan

unto /'ʌntu:/ *prep arch* to

untold /ˌʌn'təʊld/ *adj* **1** neizreciv, neizmjeran **2** neizrečen, neispričan

untoward /ˌʌntə'wɔ:d/ *adj* neočekivan, nepredviđen; nepovoljan, nepogodan

unusual /ʌn'ju:ʒl/ *adj* neuobičajen, neobičan, drukčiji **~ly** *adv* **1** neuobičajeno, neobično; izuzetno, jako

unveil /ʌn'veɪl/ *vt* **1** otkriti **2** prikazati javnosti

unvoiced /ʌn'vɔɪst/ *adj* neizrečen

unwaged /ʌn'weɪdʒd/ *adj euph GB*

nezaposlen, bez stalnih primanja

unwarranted /ʌn'wɒrəntɪd/ *adj* neželjen, nepoželjan

unwell /ʌn'wel/ *adj euph* bolestan

unwind /ˌʌn'waɪnd/ *vt,vi* **1** odmotati, razmotati **2** *coll* opustiti se

up /ʌp/ *adv, prep* gore, prema gore, naviše, uz **be ~ against sth** suočiti se s čime **~s and downs** usponi i padovi, sreća i nesreća **~ the republic!** živjela republika! **what's ~?** što se zbiva? što ima nova? **what are you ~ to?** što smjeraš? **be/feel ~ to sth** biti/osjećati se sposoban za što **it's ~ to you** o tebi ovisi **~-and-coming** poduzetan, koji obećava **~bringing** *n* odgoj **~country** *adv* u unutrašnjosti **~date** *vt* osuvremeniti, upotpuniti **~heaval** *n* **a.** erupcija **b.** preokret, pobuna **~hill** *adv* uzbrdo **~hold** *vt* **a.** podržati, braniti **b.** potvrditi **~keep** *n* održavanje (čega); uzdržavanje (koga) **~land** *n* brdoviti kraj; visoravan **~lift** *vt* uzdignuti **~most/~permost** *adj* najviši, glavni **~pish/~pity** *adj* umišljen, napuhan, uobražen **~right** *adj* **a.** uspravan **b.** častan, ispravan **~rising** *n* ustanak, pobuna **~roar** metež, zbrka **~roarious** bučan **~root** *vt* **a.** iščupati **b.** *fig* iskorijeniti **~shot** *n* ishod **~side-down** *adv* naopako, naglavce; u neredu **~stage** *adv* u/prema dnu pozornice ∘ *vt* odvratiti pozornost od čega **~stairs** *adv* na (gornjem) katu, gore **~standing** *adj* **a.** uspravan **b.** zdrav, čio **c.** častan, odgovoran **~start** *n* skorojević **~stream** *adv* uzvodno **~surge** *n* izljev **~tight** *adj* **a.** napet **b.** otresit, neljubazan **c.** zadrt **~to-date** *adj* moderan, suvremen **~-to-the-minute** najnoviji **~town** *adv* US u/prema predgrađu, izvan gradskog središta **~turn** *n* promjena nabolje **~ward(s)** *adv* prema gore **~wind** *adv* uz vjetar • *vt, vi* povisiti, dignuti (se), skočiti

upon /ə'pɒn/ *prep form* → **on** *once ~ a time* jednom davno ∘ *conj* odmah nakon, netom

upbraid /ʌp'breɪd/ *vt* grditi, kuditi

upholster /ˌʌp'həʊlstə(r)/ *vt* tapecirati,

podstaviti

upper /'ʌpə(r)/ *adj* gornji, viši **~ class** viši stalež, viša klasa **the U~ House** Gornji dom

upset /ˌʌp'set/ *vi,vt irreg* **1** prevrnuti **2** uznemiriti, uzrujati **3** pomutiti • /'ʌpset/ *n* pomutnja, poremećaj

uranium /jʊ'reɪnɪəm/ *n chem* uran

Uranus /'jʊərənəs/ *n* Uran

urban /'ɜ:bən/ *adj* gradski

urbane /ɜ:'beɪn/ *adj* uglađen, profinjen, uljudan

urchin /'ɜ:tʃɪn/ *n* **1** *arch, joc* deran **2 sea ~** morski jež

urge /ɜ:dʒ/ *vt* (po)tjerati, natjerati, zdušno nagovarati, tražiti, zahtijevati, predlagati, isticati važnost čega • *n* poriv **urgent** /'ɜ:dʒənt/ *adj* **1** hitan **2** *form* uporan, ustrajan **urgency** /'ɜ:dʒənsɪ/ *n* hitnost, hitnja, nužda, važnost

urine /'jʊərɪn/ *n* mokraća **uric** /'jʊərɪk/ *adj* mokraćni **urinal** /'jʊərɪnl/ *n* **1** pisoar **2** javni zahod **3** bolnička guska **urinary** *adj* mokraćni **urinate** *vi* (po)mokriti (se)

urn /ɜ:n/ *n* urna

us /əs, ʌs/ *pron* **1** nas; nam(a) **2** *GB coll* mi, meni

use (1) /ju:z/ *vt* **1** upotrebljavati, rabiti; koristiti (se čime), služiti se čime *I could ~* dobro bi mi došlo **2** iskoristiti **3** (~ **up**) potrošiti **4** *form* ponijeti se prema kome **~d** *adj* rabljen • /n korisnik **~r-friendly** *adj* prilagođen prosječnom korisniku, kojim se lako služiti bez stručnog znanja • /ju:s/ *n* upotreba, uporaba; korist **come into ~** početi se upotrebljavati **go/fall out of ~** prestati se upotrebljavati **put to good ~ / make good ~ of** korisno upotrijebiti, iskoristiti **have no ~ for** ne voljeti **it's no ~** nema svrhe **lose the ~ of one's legs** ne moći više hodati **give sb the ~ of sth** dati kome što na korištenje **~ful** *adj* koristan **~less** beskoristan; koji nema svrhe; *coll* loš

use (2) / *vi* **~d to, didn't ~ to** označava svršenu prošlu radnju *I ~d to like him* nekoć mi se sviđao *he ~d to smoke 30 cigarettes a day* nekad je pušio 30 cigareta na dan

used /ju:st/ *adj* ~ **to** naviknut **get** ~ **to** naviknuti se

usher /'ʌʃə(r)/ *n* 1 (~**ette** *nf*) razvođač publike (kino i sl.) 2 vratar • *vt* 1 odvesti, uvesti, ispratiti 2 ~ **sth in** najaviti, objaviti

usual /'ju:ʒl/ *adj* uobičajen, običan **as** ~ kao (i) obično ~**ly** *adv* obično, najčešće

usurer /'ju:ʒərə(r)/ *n* lihvar, zelenaš **usury** *n* lihvarstvo **usurious** *adj* lihvarski, zelenaški

usurp /ju:'zɜ:p/ *vt* bespravno zauzeti, uzurpirati, prisvojiti

utensil /ju:'tensl/ *n* pribor, sprava, po-

suda

utility /ju:'tɪlətɪ/ *n form* 1 korisnost, korist, probitak 2 *pl* javne, komunalne službe ~ **room** ostava

utilize /'ju:tɪlaɪz/ *vt form* iskoristiti, upotrijebiti

utmost /'ʌtməʊst/ *adj* krajnji, najveći

utopian /ju:'təʊpɪən/ *adj* utopijski

utter (1) /'ʌtə(r)/ *adj* potpun ~**ly** *adv* potpuno, posve, sasvim

utter (2) *vt lit* izgovoriti, izreći, izustiti, oglasiti se ~**ance** *n* izricaj, izjava, izgovor

U-turn *n* 1 polukružno zaokretanje 2 *fig* zaokret za 180°

uvula /'ju:vjʊlə/ *n anat* resica

V

V, v /vi:/ *n* 22. slovo engl. abecede; ve

vacancy /'veɪkənsɪ/ *n* 1 praznina 2 prazno/slobodno mjesto; slobodna soba; nepopunjeno radno mjesto **vacant** /'veɪkənt/ *adj* prazan, slobodan, nepopunjen **situations ~** namještenja - potražnja **vacate** /və'keɪt/ *vt* isprazniti, napustiti **vacation** /və'keɪʃn/ *n* praznici *pl*, godišnji odmor ○ *vi* provoditi praznike/g. odmor

vaccinate /'væksɪneɪt/ *vt* (against) cijepiti **vaccine** /'væksi:n/ *n* cjepivo

vacilate /'væsɪleɪt/ *vi* (between) kolebati se (između), biti neodlučan

vacuous /'vækjʊəs/ *adj* prazan, isprazan; tup **vacuity** /və'kju:ətɪ/ *n* 1 praznina, ispraznost 2 glupost, tupost

vacuum /'vækjʊəm/ *n* 1 vakuum 2 *fig* praznina **~ cleaner** usisavač **~-packed** *adj* vakuumiziran • *vt* usisati, očistiti usisavačem

vagabond /'vægəbɒnd/ *n* skitnica, vagabund

vagary /'veɪgərɪ/ *n* hir

vagina /və'dʒaɪnə/ *n* rodnica, vagina

vagrancy /'veɪgrənsɪ/ *n* skitnja **vagrant** /'veɪgrənt/ *n* leg osoba bez stalnog prebivališta, skitnica

vague /veɪg/ *adj* mutan, nejasan, maglovit, neodređen; mračan *fig*

vain /veɪn/ *adj* 1 tašt, umišljen 2 uzaludan **in ~** uzalud 3 *arch, bibl, lit* (is)prazan **~glory** *n lit* taština, oholost

vale /veɪl/ *n* dol, dolina

valediction /,vælɪ'dɪkʃn/ *n form* oproštaj **valedictory** /,vælɪ'dɪktərɪ/ *adj form* oproštajni

valency /'veɪlənsɪ/ *GB*, **valence** /'veɪlənsɪ/ *US n chem* valencija

valentine /'væləntaɪn/ *n* 1 čestitka za Valentinovo 2 osoba kojoj se šalje čestitka/s kojom se izlazi za V.

valet /'vælɪt/ *n* 1 (osobni) sluga 2 **~ing service** služba za pranje i održavanje automobila

valiant /'væljənt/ *adj form, lit* junački, odvažan

valid /'vælɪd/ *adj* 1 vrijedan 2 koji vrijedi, valjan **~ate** *vt* proglasiti valjanim, ozakoniti

valise /və'li:z/ *n* putni kovčeg

valley /'vælɪ/ *n* dolina

valour (**-lor** *US*) /'vælə(r)/ *n* junaštvo, odvažnost

value /'vælju:/ *n* 1 vrijednost **~-added tax** (VAT) porez na promet **~ judgment** vrijednosni sud 2 isplativost *it's good ~* razmjerno je jeftino • *vt* 1 procijeniti (vrijednost) 2 cijeniti, smatrati vrijednim **~er** *n* procjenjivač **valuable** /'væljʊəbl/ *adj* vrijedan, dragocjen • *n* dragocjenost **valuation** /,væljʊ'eɪʃn/ *n* procjena, proračun

valve /vælv/ *n* 1 ventil 2 zasun, vratnica

vamp /væmp/ *n* vamp

vampire /'væmpaɪə(r)/ *n* vampir

van (1) /væn/ *n* kombi, kamionet

van (2) → **vanguard**

vandal /'vændl/ *n* razbijač **~ism** uništavanje javne imovine

vane /veɪn/ *n* krilo (vjetrenjače, propelera i sl.)

vanguard /'vængɑ:d/ *n* prethodnica, čelo (+ *fig*)

vanilla /və'nɪlə/ *n* 1 vanilija 2 *mod* s okusom/od vanilije

vanish /'vænɪʃ/ *vi* 1 nestati 2 izumrijeti

vanity /'vænətɪ/ *n* 1 taština, oholost, umišljenost 2 *lit, bibl* prolaznost, ispraznost

vanquish /'væŋkwɪʃ/ *vt* pobijediti, potući, poraziti

vantagepoint /'vɑ:ntɪdʒpɔɪnt/ *n* 1 povoljan položaj 2 stajalište

vapid /'væpɪd/ *adj* bezivotan, dosadan

vapour /'veɪpə(r)/ *n* 1 para 2 *fig* tlapnja 3 ~s nesvjestica **vaporize** *vi,vt* pretvoriti (se) u paru, isparavati se

variable /'veərɪəbl/ *adj* 1 promjenjiv 2 neujednačen • *n math* varijabla

variance /'veərɪəns/ *n* nesklad

variant /'veərɪənt/ *adj* različit, drukčiji • *n* varijanta

varied /'veərɪd/ *adj* raznolik

variety /və'raɪətɪ/ *n* 1 raznolikost, raznovrsnost 2 vrsta 3 varijetet

various /'veərɪəs/ *adj* razni, mnogobrojni, mnogi

varnish /'vɑːnɪʃ/ *n* lak **nail** ~ lak za nokte • *vt* lakirati

vary /'veərɪ/ *vi* 1 razlikovati se 2 kretati se (od... do), varirati

vascular /'væskjʊlə(r)/ *adj* krvožilni, vaskularan

vase /vɑːz/ *n* vaza

vasectomy /və'sektəmɪ/ *n* vazektomija

vassal /'væsl/ *n* vazal

vast /vɑːst/ *adj* golem **~ly** *adv* uvelike

vaudeville /'vɔːdəvɪl/ *n* vodvilj

vault /vɔːlt/ *n* 1 trezor 2 grobnica 3 svod **~ed** *adj* nadsvođen **~ing horse** *sport* konj • *vi* (over) preskočiti **pole ~** skok s motkom

vaunt /vɔːnt/ *vt* hvaliti (se)

veal /viːl/ *n* teletina

vector /'vektə(r)/ *n* vektor

veer /vɪə(r)/ *vi* skrenuti (s/na)

veg /vedʒ/ → **vegetable**

vegetable /'vedʒtəbl/ *n* 1 povrće 2 *fig* biljka • *adj* biljni

vegetarian /,vedʒɪ'teərɪən/ *adj* vegetarijanski • *n* vegetarijanac

vegetate /'vedʒɪteɪt/ *vi* vegetirati (+ *fig*)

vegetation /,vedʒɪ'teɪʃn/ *n* vegetacija

vehement /'viːəmənt/ *adj* žestok, jak, gorljiv, snažan

vehicle /'viːɪkl/ *n* 1 vozilo 2 sredstvo

veil /veɪl/ *n* veo (+ *fig*) **take the ~** zarediti se • *vt* prekriti velom (+ *fig*) **~ed** *adj* skriven, prikriven

vein /veɪn/ *n* 1 vena 2 žila (+ *fig*) 3 ton, raspoloženje

velar /'viːlə(r)/ *adj* stražnjonepčan, ve-

larni

velcro /'velkrəʊ/ *n TM* "čičak" (tkanina za pričvršćivanje)

veld, veldt /velt/ *n* južnoafrička stepa

vellum /'veləm/ *n* pergament od kože; *fig* vrsta pisaćeg papira

velocity /vɪ'lɒsətɪ/ *n phys* brzina

velour /və'lʊə(r)/ *n* velur

velvet /'velvɪt/ *n* baršun **~y** *adj* 1 baršunast 2 (vino) pitak, blag

venal /'viːnl/ *adj form* potkupljiv, nepošten

vend /vend/ *vt leg* 1 prodati 2 nuditi na prodaju **~ing machine** automat za prodaju (cigareta etc.) **~or** *n* prodavač

vendetta /ven'detə/ *n* krvna osveta

veneer /və'nɪə(r)/ *n* 1 furnir 2 *fig* krinka • *vt* furnirati

venerable /'venərəbl/ *adj* 1 častan 2 veličanstven, dostojanstven 3 velečasni **venerate** /'venəreɪt/ *vt form* štovati

venereal /və'nɪərɪəl/ *adj med* venerični, spolni

venetian /və'niːʃn/ *adj* ~ **blinds** rebrenice

vengeance /'vendʒəns/ *n* 1 osveta **take ~** (on sb) osvetiti se (kome) 2 **with a ~** *coll* svom snagom, još jače **vengeful** *adj lit* osvetoljubiv

venial /'viːnɪəl/ *adj form* 1 nevažan, oprostiv 2 lakši (grijeh)

venison /'venɪzn/ *n* srnetina, meso divljači

venom /'venəm/ *n* (zmijski) otrov (+ *fig*) **~ous** *adj* otrovan (+ *fig*)

venous /'viːnəs/ *adj med* venski

vent /vent/ *vt* (on sb) iskaliti (što, na kome), dati oduška (čemu) • *n* 1 oduška, ispuh **give ~ to sth** iskaliti što, dati oduška čemu 2 *zoo* crijevni otvor 3 prorez **~ilate** *vt* (pro)zračiti, (pro)vjetriti **~ilator** *n* 1 ventilator 2 *med* respirator

ventricle /'ventrɪkl/ *n* 1 *med* klijetka 2 *zoo* šupljina

ventriloquism /ven'trɪləkwɪzəm/ *n* trbuhozborstvo

venture /'ventʃə(r)/ *n* pothvat **joint ~** zajedničko ulaganje • *vi,vt* 1 odvažiti se, usuditi se **if I may ~ an opinion**

smijem li primijetiti **2** staviti na kocku **nothing ~, nothing gain** *prov* tko ne riskira, ne profitira

venue /'venju:/ *n* mjesto zbivanja (dvorana, stadion), ugovoreno mjesto

Venus /'vi:nəs/ *n* Venera

veracity /və'ræsəti/ *n* istinitost, vjerodostojnost

veranda /və'rændə/ *n* veranda

verb /vɜ:b/ *n* glagol **~al** /'vɜ:bl/ *adj* **1** govorni, usmeni, verbalan **2** glagolski **~alize** /'vɜ:bəlaiz/ *vt,vi* izraziti riječima, pretočiti u riječi **~ally** *adv* usmeno **~atim** /vɜ:'beitim/ *adj, adv* od riječi do riječi **~ose** /vɜ:'bəus/ *adj form* preopširan

verdict /'vɜ:dikt/ *n* **1** presuda **2** mišljenje

verge /vɜ:dʒ/ *n* rub **on the ~ of** na rubu • *vi* (on, upon) biti na rubu

verify /'verifai/ *vt* potvrditi, provjeriti

verily /'verəli/ *adv bibl* uistinu

verisimilitude /,verisi'militju:d/ *n form* vjerodostojnost, istinitost

veritable /'veritəbl/ *adj form* pravi

vermilion /və'miliən/ *n mod* cinober

vermin /'vɜ:min/ *n* (+ *pl*) **1** štetočina **2** gamad **3** *fig* paraziti

vernacular /və'nækjulə(r)/ *n* govoreni/pučki jezik

versatile /'vɜ:sətail/ *adj* **1** svestran **2** za mnogostruku namjenu

verse /vɜ:s/ *n* **1** stih **2** strofa, kitica **3** *bibl* redak **~ed** *adj* (in) upućen, iskusan **versification** /,vɜ:sifi'keiʃn/ *n* versifikacija, metar

version /'vɜ:ʃn/ *n* **1** verzija **2** izdanje **3** prijevod **the Authorized V~** prijevod Biblije na engleski iz 1611.

versus /'vɜ:səs/ (vs, v) *prep leg, sport* protiv

vertebra /'vɜ:tibrə/ *n* kralježak

vertical /'vɜ:tikl/ *adj* okomit, vertikalan

vertigo /'vɜ:tigəu/ *n* vrtoglavica **vertiginous** /vɜ:'tidʒinəs/ *adj form* vrtoglav; koji osjeća vrtoglavicu

verve /vɜ:v/ *n* zanos, žar

very /'veri/ *adv* **1** vrlo **2** naj- **the ~ best** najbolji **3 not ~** ne baš • *adj* baš/upravo taj; pravi; sam **the ~ thought**

(of) sama pomisao (na) **V~ light** svjetleća raketa

vespers /'vespəz/ *n* večernja služba Božja

vessel /'vesl/ *n* **1** plovilo, brod **2** posuda **3** (krvna) žila

vest /vest/ *n* **1** maja, potkošulja **2** *US* prsluk **3** pancirna košulja; pancirka *coll* • *vt* **be ~ed in/with** biti u rukama; imati ovlast **have a ~ed interest in sth** imati vlastiti interes u čemu

vestibule /'vestibju:l/ *n* **1** *form* predvorje **2** *US* hodnik koji povezuje dva vagona

vestige /'vestidʒ/ *n* **1** ostatak **2** *fig* trunka, zrnce

vestment /'vestmənt/ *n* halja, ruho

vestry /'vestri/ *n* sakristija; kapelica

vet (1) /vet/ *n coll* veterinar

vet (2) *vt* *GB coll* pomno pregledati/ispitati/provjeriti

vet (3) *n coll* veteran

veteran /'vetərən/ *n* **1** veteran **2** *mod* veteranski; prekaljen **V~s Day** *US, Can* 11. studenoga

veterinary /'vetrinri/ *adj* veterinarski **~ surgeon/veterinarian** veterinar **~ science** veterina

veto /'vi:təu/ *n* veto • *vt* staviti veto na

vex /veks/ *vt arch* **1** razljutiti, uzrujati **2** gnjaviti, mučiti, dosađivati **~ed question** sporno/prijeporno pitanje, problem **~ation** *n arch* **1** ljutnja, srdžba **2** nevolja, jad

via /'vaiə/ *prep* preko, putem

viable /'vaiəbl/ *adj* **1** koji se može održati na životu **2** *fig* izvediv, moguć, održiv **viability** /,vaiə'biləti/ *n* sposobnost da se održi na životu

viaduct /'vaiədʌkt/ *n* vijadukt

vibes /vaibz/ *n pl coll* vibracije, atmosfera, fluid

vibrant /'vaibrənt/ *adj* **1** živ, snažan, jak **2** sonoran

vibraphone /'vaibrəfəun/ *n* metalofon

vibrate /vai'breit/ *vi, vt* **1** titrati, drhtati **2** odzvanjati **vibration** /vai'breiʃn/ *n* titranje, titraj, podrhtavanje, vibracija

vicar /'vikə(r)/ *n* **1** (u Anglikanskoj c.) vikar **2** (u Katoličkoj c.) namjesnik, predstavnik **~age** *n* vikarijat

vicarious /vɪˈkeərɪəs/ *adj* 1 neizravan, posredan 2 za drugog/druge

vice (1) /vaɪs/ *n* porok, opačina, mana **vicious** /ˈvɪʃəs/ *adj* opak, okrutan, pokvaren, zao, opasan **vicious circle** začarani krug *fig*

vice (2), (**vise** *US*) *n* škripac **~like grip** čelični stisak

vice versa /ˌvaɪsɪ ˈvɜ:sə/ *adv* obrnuto, obratno

vice- *prefix* pod-, (-pot), vice-

viceroy /ˈvaɪsrɔɪ/ *n* potkralj

vicinity /vɪˈsɪnɪtɪ/ *n* blizina, susjedstvo **in the ~** (of) blizu

victim /ˈvɪktɪm/ *n* žrtva **~ize** *vt* (sb) 1 učiniti (koga) žrtvom 2 nepravedno postupiti (prema kome), oštetiti (koga)

victor /ˈvɪktə(r)/ *n lit, form* pobjednik **~ious** *adj* pobjednički **~y** *n* pobjeda

Victorian /vɪkˈtɔ:rɪən/ *adj* viktorijanski

victual /ˈvɪtl/ *vt form* opskrbiti živežnim namirnicama **~s** *n pl* živežne namirnice

video /ˈvɪdɪəʊ/ *adj* 1 vizualan 2 video • *n coll* 1 videosnimka 2 videokaseta 3 videorekorder • *vt* (**~tape**) snimiti na video

vie /vaɪ/ *v irreg* natjecati se

view /vju:/ *n* 1 pogled, vidokrug, vidik **in full ~ of X** tako da ga je X mogao jasno vidjeti **bird's eye ~** ptičja perspektiva **~finder** tražilo 2 gledište, stajalište, motrište, mišljenje **in my ~** po mom mišljenju **fall in with sb's ~s** prihvatiti čije mišljenje, složiti se s kim **world~** svjetonazor **in ~ of** uzevši u obzir **on ~** izložen **with a ~ to** da bi, kako bi **~point** stajalište • *vt* smatrati, gledati (na), razgledati **~ing figures** gledanost **~er** *n* 1 gledatelj 2 gledalo za dijapozitive

vigil /ˈvɪdʒɪl/ *n* bdjenje **~ance** /ˈvɪdʒɪləns/ *n* oprez **~ant** /ˈvɪdʒɪlənt/ *adj* oprezan, na oprezu **~ante** /ˌvɪdʒɪˈlæntɪ/ *n* samozvani čuvar javnog reda i mira, čovjek koji je uzeo pravdu u svoje ruke

vigour (-**gor** *US*) /ˈvɪgə(r)/ *n* energija, snaga, krepkost, živost **vigorous** *adj* energičan, žustar, odlučan, silovit

vile /vaɪl/ *adj* 1 opak, zao 2 sramotan, odvratan 3 *coll* grozan, užasan **vilify** /ˈvɪlɪfaɪ/ *vt form* (o)klevetati, ocrniti, sramotiti **vilification** *n* kleveta, objeda, pogrda, ocrnjivanje

villa /ˈvɪlə/ *n* vila

village /ˈvɪlɪdʒ/ *n* selo **~r** seljanin

villain /ˈvɪlən/ *n* hulja, nitkov, negativac, zločinac

villein /ˈvɪleɪn/ *n hist* kmet; slobodnjak

vinaigrette /ˌvɪnɪˈgret/ *n* začin za salatu (ulje, ocat, sol, papar)

vindicate /ˈvɪndɪkeɪt/ *vt* 1 osloboditi optužbe 2 opravdati

vindictive /vɪnˈdɪktɪv/ *adj* osvetoljubiv

vine /vaɪn/ *n* 1 (**grape~**) loza 2 biljka penjačica **~yard** *n* vinograd

vinegar /ˈvɪnɪgə(r)/ *n* ocat **~y** *adj* 1 kiseo 2 *fig* oštar, opor

vino /ˈvi:nəʊ/ *n coll* vino **~us** *adj form, joc* 1 boje vina 2 pijan

vintage /ˈvɪntɪdʒ/ *n* berba • *adj* **~ car** klasični automobil, old-timer

vintner /ˈvɪntnə(r)/ *n* vinar

vinyl /ˈvaɪnɪl/ *n* vinil

viola /vɪˈəʊlə/ *n* viola

violate /ˈvaɪəleɪt/ *vt* 1 prekršiti; povrijediti (zračni prostor); narušiti 2 oskvrnuti 3 obeščastiti, silovati **violation** *n* kršenje; povreda (zračnog prostora)

violence /ˈvaɪələns/ *n* 1 nasilje 2 silina, golema snaga, žestina **violent** /ˈvaɪələnt/ *adj* nasilan, agresivan, žestok, silovit, neobuzdan

violet /ˈvaɪələt/ *n* 1 ljubičica 2 ljubičasta boja • *adj* ljubičast

violin /ˌvaɪəˈlɪn/ *n* violina

viper /ˈvaɪpə(r)/ *n* zmija otrovnica (+ *fig*)

virago /vɪˈrɑ:gəʊ/ *n form derog* rospija, vještica, jezičava baba

viral /ˈvaɪərəl/ *adj* virusni

virgin /ˈvɜ:dʒɪn/ *n* djevica **the Blessed V~ Mary** Blažena Djevica Marija **the V~ Queen** Elizabeta I. **~ forest** prašuma • *adj* netaknut **~al** *adj* djevičanski **~ity** *n* djevičanstvo

Virgo /ˈvɜ:gəʊ/ *n astrol* Djevica

virile /ˈvɪraɪl/ *adj* 1 muževan 2 snažan **virility** /vɪˈrɪlətɪ/ *n* muževnost

virtual /'vɜ:tʃʊəl/ adj praktički, zbiljski, pravi, stvarni **~ly** adv gotovo, skoro, praktično

virtue /'vɜ:tʃu:/ n 1 form vrlina, krepost 2 dobra strana, odlika **by/in ~ of** preko, putem, zbog, na temelju **virtuous** /'vɜ:tʃʊəs/ adj form krepostan

virtuosity /,vɜ:tʃʊ'ɒsɪtɪ/ n virtuoznost **virtuoso** /,vɜ:tʃʊ'əʊzəʊ/ n virtuozo

virulent /'vɪrʊlənt/ adj 1 med virulentan, otrovan, opasan po život 2 form otrovan, pakostan

virus /'vaɪərəs/ n virus

visa /'vi:zə/ n viza **entry/exit ~** ulazna/izlazna v.

visage /'vɪzɪdʒ/ n lit lice

vis-L-vis /,vi:zɑ:'vi:/ prep form s obzirom na, u odnosu na

viscount /'vaɪkaʊnt/ n vikont

vise US → **vice** (2)

visible /'vɪzəbl/ adj 1 vidljiv, jasan, očit 2 koji se često viđa u javnosti **visibility** /,vɪzə'bɪlɪtɪ/ n vidljivost **visibly** adv vidljivo, vidno, očito **vision** /'vɪʒn/ n 1 vid 2 vizija 3 dalekovidnost 4 priviđenje **visionary** /'vɪʒənrɪ/ n vizionar   adj 1 vizionarski 2 zamišljen, nestvaran

visit /'vɪzɪt/ vt, vi 1 posjetiti, biti u posjetu, doći u posjet **~ing hours** vrijeme posjeta 2 pregledati, izvršiti inspekciju **~ sth on sb** bibl kazniti • n posjet **pay a ~ to** posjetiti **~ation** n 1 form obilazak, inspekcija 2 form kazna (Božja) 3 coll dug, zamoran posjet **~or** n posjetitelj, gost, turist **~'s book** knjiga gostiju

visor /'vaɪzə(r)/ n 1 hist vizir 2 obod, štitnik

vista /'vɪstə/ n vidik, pogled; niz

visual /'vɪʒʊəl/ adj vidni, vizualan **~ize** vt predočiti, dočarati, stvoriti sliku

vital /'vaɪtl/ adj 1 najvažniji, ključni, osnovni **~ statistics a.** GB coll joc obujam grudi, struka i bokova **b.** službeni podaci o čijem životu 2 važan za život **~ organ** vitalni organ **~s** vitalni organi 3 form pun života, energičan **~ity** /vaɪ'tælɪtɪ/ n 1 životna snaga, vitalnost 2 otpornost, izdržljivost **~ly** adv izuzetno, silno

vitamin /'vɪtəmɪn/ n vitamin

vitiate /'vɪʃɪeɪt/ vt form iskvariti, oslabiti

vitreous /'vɪtrɪəs/ adj tech, med staklen, staklast

vitriol /'vɪtrɪəl/ n 1 chem vitriol 2 fig zajedljivost, jetkost

vituperation /vɪ,tju:pə'reɪʃn/ n form psovanje, kletve

viva /'vaɪvə/ n GB coll (**~ voce**) usmeni ispit

vivacious /vɪ'veɪʃəs/ adj pun života, živahan

vivid /'vɪvɪd/ adj živ, živopisan, žarki **~ imagination** bujna mašta

vixen /'vɪksn/ n lisica (ženka)

viz. /vɪz/ adv a to je, a to su, konkretno ¶ obično se čita: namely

vizier /vɪ'zɪə(r)/ n vezir

V-neck n V-izrez

vocabulary /və'kæbjʊlərɪ/ n rječnik, vokabular, fond riječi

vocal /'vəʊkl/ adj 1 govorni **~ cords** glasnice 2 vokalni 3 coll glasan, koji se čuje • **~s** n pl pjevač(ica) **~ist** pjevač(ica)

vocation /vəʊ'keɪʃn/ n 1 poziv 2 sposobnost, dar **~al** adj profesionalni, stručni **~al guidance** profesionalna orijentacija

vocative /'vɒkətɪv/ n gram vokativ

vociferate /və'sɪfəreɪt/ vi form vikati, galamiti **vociferous** /və'sɪfərəs/ adj form glasan

vodka /'vɒdkə/ n votka

vogue /vəʊg/ n moda **all the ~** vrlo moderan, po zadnjoj modi • adj moderan, trenutačno popularan

voice /vɔɪs/ n 1 glas (+ fig) **at the top of one's ~** na sav glas **~-over** TV, film glas izvan kadra 2 gram stanje • vt izraziti, izreći, izgovoriti **~d** adj phon zvučni **~less** bezvučni

void /vɔɪd/ adj 1 prazan **~ of sth** koji nema čega 2 koji nije pravovaljan • n praznina (+ fig), prazan prostor

volatile /'vɒlətaɪl/ adj 1 hlapljiv 2 promjenjiv, nepostojan 3 nagao, eksplozivan fig

volcano /vɒl'keɪnəʊ/ n (pl **~oes/~os**) vulkan **volcanic** /vɒl'kænɪk/ adj 1 vulkanski 2 fig neobuzdan, vatren

volition /vəˈlɪʃn/ n form volja; voljni čin

volley /ˈvɒlɪ/ n 1 rafal 2 sport volej ~**ball** n odbojka

volt /vəʊlt/ n volt ~**age** n napon

volte-face /ˌvɒlt ˈfɑːs/ n form nagla promjena stava

voluble /ˈvɒljʊbl/ adj form 1 brbljav, koji previše priča 2 (pre)opširan

volume /ˈvɒljuːm/ n 1 zapremnina 2 količina, broj 3 glasnoća, jačina zvuka **turn down/up the** ~ stišati/poglasniti 4 svezak 5 knjiga **voluminous** /vəˈljuːmɪnəs/ adj form 1 golem, bogat, prostran 2 derog (pre)opsežan; plodan (pisac)

voluntary /ˈvɒlɒntrɪ/ adj 1 dobrovoljan, dragovoljan 2 voljni

volunteer /ˌvɒlɒnˈtɪə(r)/ n dobrovoljac, dragovoljac

voluptuary /vəˈlʌptʃʊərɪ/ n lit, derog pohotljivac, razbludnik **voluptuous** /vəˈlʌptʃʊəs/ adj 1 senzualan, puten, čulan 2 derog razvratan, razbludan

vomit /ˈvɒmɪt/ vi,vt 1 povratiti, povraćati 2 fig rigati, bljuvati • n povraćena tvar

voracious /vəˈreɪʃəs/ adj 1 proždrljiv, lakom, pohlepan 2 fig gladan

vortex /ˈvɔːteks/ n (pl ~es, **vortices**) 1 vir 2 fig vihor

vote /vəʊt/ n 1 glasovanje; glas

give/cast a/one's ~ **for/against** glasovati za/protiv ~ **of confidence** glasovanje o povjerenju ~ **of thanks** javna zahvala 2 glasački listić 3 pravo glasa • vi,vt glasovati, izglasati ~ **sb/sth down** glasovanjem otkloniti ~ **sth through** izglasati ~**r** n glasač

votive /ˈvəʊtɪv/ adj zavjetni

vouch /vaʊtʃ/ vi ~ **for sb** jamčiti za koga ~**er** n 1 GB bon 2 vaučer ~**safe** vt form, lit udostojiti se

vow /vaʊ/ n 1 prisega 2 zavjet • vt 1 prisegnuti 2 zavjetovati se

vowel /ˈvaʊəl/ n samoglasnik, vokal

vox pop /vɒks/ GB coll anketa

voyage /ˈvɔɪɪdʒ/ n putovanje, put • vi, vt form putovati ~**r** n putnik

voyeur /vwaˈjɜː(r)/ n voajer

vs. versus

V-sign n 1 dva prsta u znak pobjede 2 dvojka sl (vulgarna gesta)

vulcanize /ˈvʌlkənaɪz/ vt vulkanizirati

vulgar /ˈvʌlgə(r)/ adj neukusan, nepristojan, prost, prostački, vulgaran ~ **fraction** math razlomak ~**ity** /vʌlˈgærətɪ/ n neukus, prostota, vulgarnost

vulnerable /ˈvʌlnərəbl/ adj ranjiv, osjetljiv, nezaštićen **vulnerability** n ranjivost, osjetljivost, nezaštićenost

vulture /ˈvʌltʃə(r)/ n 1 lešinar, strvinar 2 fig zelenaš, profiter

W

W, w /ˈdʌblju:/ 23. slovo engl. abecede; dvostruko ve

wacky /ˈwæki/ adj US coll šašav

wad /wɒd/ n svežanj; kuglica

waddle /ˈwɒdl/ vi gegati se

wade /weid/ vi,vt (across) pregaziti (rijeku)

wafer /ˈweifə(r)/ n 1 oblata 2 hostija

waffle /ˈwɒfl/ n vafl

waft /wɒft/ vt,vi donijeti, dolebdjeti

wag (1) /wæg/ vt,vi mahati (repom)
tongues are ~ging priča se

wag (2) n coll šaljivčina

wage (1) /weidʒ/ n (+ pl) tjedna plaća, nadnica

wage (2) vt ~ (a) **war against/on** voditi rat protiv

wager /ˈweidʒə(r)/ n form oklada •
vt,vi kladiti se

wag(g)on /ˈwægən/ n 1 (zaprežna) kola 2 GB teretni vagon **~-lit** n spavaća kola **on the ~** coll koji je prestao piti

wail /weil/ vi jadikovati; derati se; zavijati • n dernjava; huka

waist /weist/ n 1 struk 2 pojas **~coat** GB prsluk **~line** struk

wait /weit/ vi,vt 1 (for) (pri)čekati 2 (at/on US) posluživati **I can't ~** jedva čekam ~ **on sb hand and foot** dvoriti koga **~er** n konobar **~ress** n konobarica **~ing room** čekaonica • n čekanje **lie in ~ for** vrebati

waive /weiv/ vt form odreći se (prava)

wake (1) /weik/ vi,vt irreg (up) (pro)buditi (se); trgnuti (se) **~n** vi,vi (up) probuditi (se)

wake (2) n brazda (iza broda) **in the ~ of** nakon, iza

wake (3) n karmine pl

walk /wɔ:k/ vi,vt 1 hodati, ići, pješačiti, šetati; ići korakom 2 otpratiti 3 izvesti u šetnju ~ **off/away with** coll

a. odnijeti, ukrasti, pobjeći s b. lako osvojiti/pobijediti ~ **out** a. demonstrativno izaći b. stupiti u štrajk **c.** (on sb/sth) napustiti, ostaviti (na cjedilu) **~out** n 1 demonstrativni izlazak 2 štrajk **~-up** n US coll zgrada bez lifta ~ **over** coll lako pobijediti **~ing papers** US coll otkaz • n 1 hod(anje); korak 2 šetnja 3 staza it's a ten minutes' ~/ten-minute ~ to je deset minuta hoda **from all ~s/every ~ of life** iz svih slojeva društva

wall /wɔ:l/ n 1 zid 2 stijenka ~**-to-~** adj a. preko cijelog poda b. coll neprestan **off-the-~** adj US coll luckast **be/go up the ~** coll razbjesnjeti se **~ed** adj opasan zidinama • vt ~ **off** odvojiti/pregraditi zidom ~ **up** zazidati **~paper** tapeta

wallet /ˈwɒlit/ n 1 lisnica 2 US ženska torbica

wallop /ˈwɒləp/ n coll udarac • vt coll 1 odalamiti 2 (at) poraziti (u čemu) **~ing** adj coll golem

wallow /ˈwɒləʊ/ vi (in) valjati se (u blatu)

wally /ˈwɒli/ n GB coll kreten

walnut /ˈwɔ:lnʌt/ n orah

walrus /ˈwɔ:lrəs/ n morž

waltz /wɔ:ls/ n valcer • vi,vt plesati valcer

wan /wɒn/ adj lit blijed, slab

wand /wɒnd/ n (**magic ~**) čarobni štapić

wander /ˈwɒndə(r)/ vi,vt 1 (about) lutati 2 (away/off) odlutati, zalutati 3 (through/over) putovati 4 (from) udaljiti se fig **~er** n lutalica

wane /wein/ vi 1 slabiti, nestajati 2 padati (Mjesec) • n on the ~ u opadanju

wank /wæŋk/ vi GB tab sl drkati tab sl **~er** n GB tab sl seronja tab

wanna /ˈwɒnə/ coll ~ 1 want to 2

want a

want /wɒnt/ *vt,vi* 1 željeti, htjeti 2 trebati, tražiti 3 nemati, nedostajati, oskudijevati čime • *n* 1 nedostatak, nestašica 2 (nužna) potreba; želja

wanton /'wɒntən/ *adj* 1 bezrazložan, samovoljan 2 *form* raskalašen

war /wɔ:(r)/ *n* rat **be at ~ with** u ratu/zaraćen (s/protiv) **declare ~ on** objaviti rat (komu/čemu) **go to ~ against** krenuti u rat, zaratiti **make/wage ~ on/against** voditi rat, ratovati (protiv) **~fare** rat(ovanje) **~head** bojna glava (rakete) **~lord** *derog* ratni vođa **~monger** ratni huškač **~ring** *adj* zaraćen **~rior** *n* ratnik **~time** *n* **a.** ratno vrijeme **b.** *mod* ratni **~torn** *adj* ratom poharan

ward /wɔ:d/ *n* 1 (bolnički/zatvorski) odjel 2 štićenik • *vt* (off) izbjeći, odagnati **~en** *n* nadzornik, nadstojnik **traffic ~en** prometnik

wardrobe /'wɔ:drəʊb/ *n* 1 ormar za odjeću 2 odjeća, garderoba

warehouse /'weəhaʊs/ *n* skladište

wares /weəz/ *n pl* roba (na prodaju)

warm /wɔ:m/ *adj* 1 topao (+ *fig*) 2 svjež (trag/miris) **I'm ~** toplo mi je **~th** *n* toplina • *vt,vi* grijati (se) **~ over** *US* podgrijati **~ up a.** *GB* podgrijati **b.** zagrijati (se)

warn /wɔ:n/ *vt,vi* 1 (of/against) upozoriti (na), opomenuti 2 obavijestiti, podsjetiti **~ sb off** odvratiti **~ing** *n* upozorenje, opomena

warp /wɔ:p/ *vi,vt* 1 svijati (se) 2 *fig* iskriviti (se) • *n* 1 iskrivljenje 2 osnova (tkanja)

warrant /'wɒrənt/ *n* sudski nalog **search ~** nalog za pretres **~ officer** časnički namjesnik **~y** *n* jamstvo • *vt* 1 opravdavati 2 jamčiti

warren /'wɒrən/ *n* 1 kunićnjak 2 *fig* labirint

wart /wɔ:t/ *n* bradavica **~hog** bradavičasta svinja

wary /'weəri/ *adj* oprezan

was *v irreg* → **be**

wash /wɒʃ/ *vt,vi* 1 (o)prati (se), isprati; (o)čistiti; umiti 2 (against/over) oplakivati, preplaviti 3 natapati; podlokati **~ away** otplaviti **~**

away/off/out oprati, očistiti, obrisati **~ down a.** temeljito oprati (mlazom) **b.** (with) zaliti **~ up a.** *GB* prati posuđe **b.** *US* oprati se, umiti se • *n* 1 pranje; umivanje 2 praonica 3 brazda broda 4 *US* → **washing** 5 napoj; splačine *pl* **~basin/~bowl** *US* umivaonik **~ed-out** *adj* 1 ispran 2 blijed **~ed-up** *adj coll* propao **~er** *n* 1 brtva, brtveni prsten 2 perač, pralja 3 *US* stroj za pranje rublja **~ing** *n* 1 pranje; umivanje 2 rublje za pranje, oprano rublje **~ing machine** stroj za pranje rublja, perilica **~ing-up** *n GB coll* pranje posuđa **~room** *US* (javni) WC

wasp /wɒsp/ *n* osa

wastage /'weɪstɪdʒ/ *n* trošenje, gubitak, šteta

waste /weɪst/ *n* 1 gubitak, trošenje; traćenje 2 otpad 3 *lit* pustoš • *vt* 1 (on) tratiti, rasipati 2 *US sl* likvidirati **~ away** mršaviti, slabiti • *adj* 1 beskoristan 2 pust, neobrađen **lay ~** opustošiti, poharati **~land** pustoš, pustopoljina **~ paper** stari papir **~paper basket** *GB* koš za smeće

watch /wɒtʃ/ *vi,vt* 1 gledati, motriti, promatrati 2 (pri)paziti na 3 stražariti **~ it!** *coll* pazi! oprezno! **~ out for** čuvati se, paziti na **~ over** (pri)čuvati, (pri)paziti na • *n* 1 ručni sat 2 straža; stražar(i) 3 noćna straža **keep ~** stražariti **on ~** na straži **be on the ~ for** čuvati se, paziti se **~dog a.** pas čuvar **b.** *fig* nadzorni organ **~ful** *adj* (for) budan, oprezan, pažljiv **~man** stražar; (noćni) čuvar **~tower** promatračnica **~word** parola, deviza

water /'wɔ:tə(r)/ *n* voda **by ~** brodom/čamcem, vodenim putem **still ~s run deep** *prov* tiha voda brege dere **fish in troubled ~s** *fig* loviti u mutnom **hold ~** izdržati probu **in deep ~** u neprilikama • *vt,vi* 1 zalijevati, škropiti 2 suziti (oči), curiti (sline) 3 napojiti (se) 4 navodnjavati **~ down** razvodniti (+ *fig*) **it makes my mouth ~** od toga mi rastu zazubice **~cress** potočarka **~fall** slap, vodopad **~front** luka, dokovi **~ heater** bojler **~(ing) hole** pojilište (+

fig) ~ **lily** lokvanj, lopoč ~**logged** natopljen vodom, pun vode ~ **main** glavna vodovodna cijev ~**mark** vodeni žig ~**melon** lubenica ~**mill** vodenica ~**proof** nepromočiv ~**shed** a. razvođe b. *fig* prekretnica ~ **supply** vodovod; opskrba vodom ~**tight** a. nepropustan b. *fig* pouzdan ~**works** vodovod ~**y** *adj* voden(kast), vodnjikav, razvodnjen

wave /'weɪv/ *vt,vi* (at/to/in) 1 mahati, mahnuti 2 lepršati ~ **goodbye to** *fig* oprostiti se od, otpisati • *n* 1 val (+ *fig*) 2 mahanje, domahivanje ~**length** valna dužina (+ *fig*) **wavy** *adj* valovit

waver /'weɪvǝ(r)/ *vi* 1 oklijevati, (po)kolebati se 2 posrtati, teturati 3 svjetlucati, treperiti

wax (1) /wæks/ *n* vosak • *vt* navoštiti ~**(ed) paper** *US* voštani/masni papir

wax (2) *vi* 1 rasti (Mjesec) 2 *arch* postati

way /weɪ/ *n* 1 put; cesta; staza 2 način; postupak; mogućnost 3 običaj, navika **this** ~ ovuda **on the/one's** ~ **to** na putu do **we must be on our** ~ moramo krenuti **lose one's** ~ izgubiti se **lead the** ~ prednjačiti a **long** ~ **from** daleko od **all the** ~ **from** čak od **in a** ~ na neki način **by** ~ **of** preko, putem **be/get/stand in the** ~ smetati, ispriječiti se na putu **get/move out of one's** ~ maknuti se (kome) s puta **go out of the/one's** ~ **to do sth** dati sebi truda **give** ~ **(to)** a. popustiti b. *GB* dati prednost (u prometu) **make** ~ **(for)** napraviti mjesta (za) **under** ~ a. na putu b. u tijeku **by the** ~ usput rečeno, inače, **nego no** ~ nipošto ~ **in** n ulaz ~ **out** n izlaz (+ *fig*) **one** ~ **or another** u svakom slučaju **have/get one's own** ~ imati/učiniti po svome • *adv* daleko ~ **back in 1968** davne 1968. godine

waylay /,weɪ'leɪ/ *vt irreg* postaviti zasjedu, napasti, presresti; zaustaviti

wayward /'weɪwǝd/ *adj* svojeglav

we /wi:/ *pers pron* mi

weak /wi:k/ *adj* 1 slab; krhak, nejak; popustljiv 2 razvodnjen ~**en** *vt,vi* 1 (o)slabiti 2 popustiti ~**ling** *n* slabić

~**ness** *n* 1 slabost 2 slaba strana, nedostatak

wealth /welθ/ *n* bogatstvo **a/the** ~ **of** *form* mnoštvo, obilje ~**y** *adj* bogat

wean /wi:n/ *vt* odbiti od sise ~ **sb from sth** odučiti koga od čega **be** ~**ed on sth** odrasti uz što/pod utjecajem čega

weapon /'wepǝn/ *n* oružje ~**ry** *n* naoružanje

wear /weǝ(r)/ *vt,vi irreg* 1 nositi (odjeću) 2 iznositi (se), pohabati (se) 3 držati se ~ **away** izblijedjeti, izbrisati se, istrošiti se ~ **down** a. smanjiti (se), stanjiti (se), istrošiti (se) b. slomiti, iscrpsti ~ **off** proći ~ **on** odužiti se, otegnuti se ~ **out** a. pohabati se; istrošiti se b. iscrpsti, izmoriti **worn-out** *adj* 1 iznošen 2 iscrpljen ~**ing** *adj* zamoran, naporan • *n* 1 nošenje 2 habanje, trošenje 3 izdržljivost, trajnost 4 (u složenicama) odjeća **foot**~ obuća **under**~ donje rublje ~ **and tear** svakodnevno trošenje

weary /'wɪǝrɪ/ *adj* (of) 1 iscrpljen, izmučen, umoran 2 *coll* naporan • *vi,vt* (of/with) *form* umoriti se, umarati

weasel /'wi:zl/ *n* lasica

weather /'weðǝ(r)/ *n* vrijeme **under the** ~ *coll* boležljiv ~ **forecast** vremenska prognoza ~**man** *coll* meteorolog ~ **vane** vjetrokaz • *vt,vi* 1 prebroditi 2 izložiti vremenu (kiši, vjetru, suncu)

weave /wi:v/ *vi,vt irreg* 1 tkati 2 *fig* skovati 3 (is)plesti 4 (*pt* weaved) vijugati ~**r** *n* tkalac, tkalja • *n* tkanje, način tkanja

web /web/ *n* 1 paučina 2 *fig* mreža, splet 3 plivaća kožica

wed /wed/ *vt,vi irreg* oženiti (se), vjenčati (se) **the newly**~**s** mladenci ~**ding** *n* vjenčanje, svadba ~**ding dress** vjenčanica ~**ding ring** vjenčani prsten ~**lock** *leg* brak

wedge /wedʒ/ *n* 1 klin 2 komad, kriška • *vt* 1 zaglaviti klinom 2 stijesniti, zgurati, uklijestiti

Wednesday /'wenzdɪ/ *n* srijeda **on** ~ u srijedu

wee (1) /wi:/ *adj coll* majušan, sićušan

the ~ hours *US* sitni sati
wee(-wee) (2) *vi* piškiti
weed /wi:d/ *n* 1 korov 2 *GB coll derog* slabić 3 *sl* marihuana **run to ~s** obrasti korovom **~-killer** herbicid • *vt,vi* 1 plijeviti 2 (sb/sth out) odijeliti, pročistiti, prorijediti, riješiti se
week /wi:k/ *n* tjedan **~day** radni dan **~end** vikend **~ly** *adj* tjedni o *adv* tjedno o *n* tjednik
weep /wi:p/ *vi,vt irreg* (over/for) *lit* 1 plakati 2 curiti **~ing willow** žalosna vrba
weigh /wei/ *vt,vi* 1 težiti 2 vagati 3 (against) odvagnuti, odmjeriti, procijeniti, usporediti 4 (with sb) imati velik utjecaj na, biti od velike važnosti za ~ **anchor** dignuti sidro, otploviti ~ **down a.** opteretiti, pritisnuti, saviti **b.** (with) potištiti, utući ~ **on** mučiti, opterećivati ~ **out** odvagnuti (teret) ~ **up** *fig* odvagnuti, procijeniti, prosuditi **weight** /weit/ *n* 1 težina 2 uteg 3 teret (+ *fig*) 4 mjera za težinu 5 važnost, značenje **lose weight** smršaviti **put on weight** udebljati se
weight lifting/training dizanje utega o *vt* staviti uteg, opteretiti; ponderirati
weir /wiə(r)/ *n* 1 brana 2 vrša
weird /wiəd/ *adj* 1 sablastan, nadnaravan, tajanstven 2 *coll* čudan, neobičan; otkačen *coll* **~o** *coll* ekscentrik; otkačenjak *coll*
welcome /'welkəm/ *adj* dobrodošao **your're** ~ nema na čemu, molim • *n* dobrodošlica, srdačan doček • *vt* 1 zaželjeti dobrodošlicu, srdačno dočekati 2 pozdraviti (prijedlog), prihvatiti
weld /weld/ *vt,vi* 1 variti 2 *fig* spojiti, povezati **~er** *n* varilac, zavarivač • *n* var, zavareno mjesto
welfare /'welfeə(r)/ *n* 1 dobro(bit) 2 socijalna skrb 3 *US* socijalna pomoć ~ **state** socijalna država, država blagostanja ~ **officer/worker** socijalni radnik
well /wel/ (1) *adv* 1 dobro, povoljno; pristojno 2 potpuno, sasvim, temeljito 3 prilično, dosta, dobrano 4 pravilno, u redu **he's doing ~ a.** dobro mu

ide, napreduje **b.** dobro mu je, oporavlja se **as ~ a.** isto tako, jednako **b.** osim toga, uz to, također **as ~ as** isto tako ... kao ~ **done!** bravo! • *adj* 1 zdrav 2 zadovoljan, povoljan, dobar 3 poželjan, preporučljiv, prikladan, zgodan • *int* dakle, dobro, no ~, ~! vidi, vidi! • *prefix* **~-behaved** pristojan, dolična ponašanja **~-being** *n* dobro(bit); ugoda **~-done** dobro pečen **~-heeled** *coll* bogat, potkožen **~-known** poznat **~-meaning** dobronamjeran, dobrohotan **~-meant** dobronamjeran **~-off** bogat **~-read** načitan **~-to-do** *coll* bogat, imućan
well (2) *n* 1 bunar; izvor 2 (naftna) bušotina 3 okno • *vi* ~ **out** (from/of) izvirati, istjecati, briznuti ~ **up** navrijeti; nakupiti se
wellingtons (wellies *coll*) /'weliŋtənz/ *n pl* gumene čizme
went *v irreg* → **go**
wept *v irreg* → **weep**
were *v irreg* → **be**
werewolf /'wiəwulf/ *n* vukodlak
west /west/ *n* zapad **the W~ a.** Zapad, zapadne zemlje **b.** američki zapad **to the ~ of** zapadno od • *adj* zapadni • *adv* zapadno, prema zapadu ~ **of** zapadno od **~erly** *adj* zapadni **~ern** *adj* zapadni o *n* kaubojski film, vestern **~erner** zapadnjak **~ernize** *vt* pozapadnjačiti **~ward** *adj* na zapad, prema zapadu **~ward(s)** *adv* prema zapadu
wet /wet/ *adj* 1 mokar, vlažan 2 kišovit 3 *GB coll* slab, popustljiv **get ~ through** pokisnuti do gole kože **~ blanket** *coll* osoba koja kvari raspoloženje ~ **suit** ronilačko odijelo • *n* 1 **the ~** kiša; mokro tlo 2 vlaga • *vt irreg* navlažiti, smočiti ~ **the bed** pomokriti se u krevet
whack /wæk/ *vt coll* odalamiti, zviznuti • *n* 1 udarac 2 *GB* komad, dio
whale /weil/ *n* kit **~bone** kitova us **~r** *n* kitolovac **whaling** *n* lov na kitove
wharf /wɔ:f/ *n* obala, kej, pristanište
what /wɒt/ *adj* kakav, koji ~ **time is it** koliko je sati – *a good idea* baš dobra ideja ~ *a mess* kakav nered • *pron* što

~ for a. zbog čega **b.** za što, čemu **~'s more** štoviše **~(so)ever** *adj* **1** koji god, bilo koji **2** (u neg. reč.) baš nikakav/nikoji ○ *pron* **1** ma što, bilo što, što god **2** *US coll* svejedno

wheat /wiːt/ *n* pšenica

wheedle /'wiːdl/ *vt* **~ sth out of sb** izmoljakati, iskamčiti

wheel /wiːl/ *n* **1** kotač; kolo **2** upravljač; kormilo **3** *mil* okret **4** *pl sl* auto **~barrow** tačke **~chair** invalidska kolica • *vt,vi* **1** (pre)voziti, gurati (na kotačima) **2** (about/around) naglo se okrenuti **3** kružiti (ptice) **~ and deal** *coll* mućkati, mutiti **~er-dealer** maher

wheeze /wiːz/ *vi* dahtati • *n* dahtanje, soptanje

when /wen/ *adv, conj, pron* kada **~ever** *adv, conj* kad god, bilo kada, uvijek kada

where /weə(r)/ *adv, conj* **1** gdje, kamo, kuda **2** tamo gdje **~ from** odakle? **~abouts** *n* boravište **~as** *conj* **1** dok **2** *leg* budući da **~by** *adv form* **1** čime, kako **2** po kojem, prema čemu **wherever/~soever** *adv* bilo gdje/kamo/kuda, gdjegod **the ~withal** *n* nužna sredstva

whet /wet/ *vt form* **1** je brusiti **2** *fig* pobuditi **~stone** *n* brus

whether /'weðə(r)/ *conj* je li **1 2** bez obzira je li, bilo da

which /wɪtʃ/ *adj, pron* **1** koji, koja, koje **2** što **after ~** nakon čega **~(so)ever** *adj, pron* koji god, bilo koji

whiff /wɪf/ *n* dašak, miris

while /waɪl/ *n* (kratko) vrijeme, časak **a little ~ ago** malo prije **for a ~** načas **in a ~** uskoro **once in a ~** katkad **it is worth ~** isplati se, vrijedi truda **make sth worth one's ~** naplatiti komu trud • *conj* **1** dok, za vrijeme **2** iako **3** dok naprotiv • *vt* **~ away** provesti, protratiti

whim /wɪm/ *n* hir, mušica

whimper /'wɪmpə(r)/ *vi,vt* cmizdriti, cviljeti

whimsical /'wɪmzɪkl/ *adj* hirovit, mušičav; čudnovat

whine /waɪn/ *vi* **1** cviljeti; zavijati **2**

jadikovati, kukati

whinny /'wɪnɪ/ *vi* njištati • *n* njisak, njištanje

whip /wɪp/ *n* bič • *vt,vi* **1** bičevati, šibati **2** tući **~ped cream** tučeno vrhnje **3** *coll* potući **4** *GB coll* ukrasti **~ out** potegnuti (nož) **~ up a.** potaknuti, pobuditi **b.** smućkani

whirl /wɜːl/ *vi,vt* okretati (se), (za)vrtjeti (se), kovitlati se • *n* **1** kovitlac **2** živost **~pool** vir, vrtlog **~wind** pijavica, zračni vrtlog

whirr(r) /wɜː(r)/ *vi* brujati, zujati; lepetati

whisk /wɪsk/ *n* **1** zamah (repom) **2** peruška; metlica **3** pjenjača • *vt* **1** mahnuti (repom), otjerati, otresti **2** pospremiti, skloniti **3** (away/off) odvesti, prebaciti **4** tući (jaja)

whisker /'wɪskə(r)/ *n* **1** *pl* zalisci **2** (mačji) brk **by a ~** *GB coll* za dlaku

whisky (-skey *US, Ir)* /'wɪskɪ/ *n* viski

whisper /'wɪspə(r)/ *vi,vt* **1** (to) šap(u)tati **2** šuštati • *n* **1** šapat **2** šuštanje **in a ~** šaptom

whistle /'wɪsl/ *n* **1** zviždaljka **2** zviždanje; zvižduk • *vi,vt* **1** zvižd(uk)ati **2** fijukati **3** prosvirati (metak)

white /waɪt/ *adj* **1** bijel **2** blijed **3** sijed **~-collar worker** činovnik **~ elephant** beskorisna stvar, skupa za održavanje **W~hall** *fig* britanska vlada **~ heat** bijelo usijanje **~ lie** nedužna laž **~ spirit** *GB* razrjeđivač **~wash** *n* **a.** vapno **b.** *fig* uljepšavanje, zataškavanje ○ *vt* **a.** objeliti, okrečiti **b.** *fig* uljepšati

Whitsun /'wɪtsn/ *n* Duhovi

whittle /'wɪtl/ *vt* (away/down) **1** rezbariti, rezuckati **2** *fig* smanjiti

whiz(z) /wɪz/ *vi* zujati, fijukati • *n* **1** zujanje, fijuk **2** *coll* stručnjak **~ kid** *coll* mladi genijalac, lumen

who /huː/ *pron* **1** tko **2** koji **~dun(n)it** /ˌhuːˈdʌnɪt/ *n coll* krimić **~(so)ever** *pron* bilo tko, tko god, bilo koji

whole /həʊl/ *adj* cijeli, čitav, sav; potpun **~-hearted** iskren, bezrezervan **a ~ lot of** *US coll* mnogo **the ~ lot** sve **~meal bread** kruh od cjelovitog brašna **~sale** n veleprodaja ○ adj veleprodajni ○ adv na veliko **~saler** trgovac na veliko **~some** adj a. zdrav (hrana) b. moralno koristan/poželjan

wholly adv u cijelosti, potpuno • n 1 cjelina, sve 2 (jedno) cijelo **as a ~** u cjelini **on the ~** uglavnom, sve u svemu

whom /hu:m/ pron koga, komu

whooping cough /'hu:pɪŋ/ n hripavac

whopping /'wɒpɪŋ/ adj coll vrlo velik • adv vrlo

whore /hɔ:(r)/ n kurva

whose /hu:z/ pron čiji

why /waɪ/ adv, conj zašto; zbog čega • int pa, no, dakle • n **the ~(s) and (the) wherefore(s)** razlozi, uzroci

wick /wɪk/ n stijenj

wicked /'wɪkɪd/ adj 1 zao, opak, pokvaren 2 zločest

wicker /'wɪkə(r)/ adj pleter od pruća **~work** pleter; košaračka roba

wicket /'wɪkɪt/ n vrata (u kriketu)

wide /waɪd/ adj širok • adv široko **~-awake** a. potpuno budan b. oprezan **~ly** adv 1 nadaleko, naširoko 2 vrlo, u velikoj mjeri **~n** vt,vi proširiti (se) **~ open** širom otvoren **~spread** raširen

widow /'wɪdəʊ/ n udovica **~ed** adj obudovljen **~er** n udovac

width /wɪtθ/ n širina

wield /wi:ld/ vt imati, upotrijebiti, vršiti (moć, utjecaj)

wife /waɪf/ n (pl **wives**) supruga; žena coll

wig /wɪg/ n vlasulja

wiggle /'wɪgl/ vt,vi micati; migoljiti se; vrpoljiti se

wild /waɪld/ adj 1 divlji 2 pust 3 plašljiv 4 olujan 5 snažan, žestok 6 bijesan, lud 7 neobuzdan 8 nepromišljen 9 slučajan **~erness** /'wɪldənɪs/ n divljina; pustoš **like ~fire** munjevitom brzinom **~-goose chase** uzaludna potraga, uzaludan trud/pothvat **~life** priroda, flora i fauna • adv divlje

wilful (**willful** US) /'wɪlfl/ adj 1 tvrdoglav, uporan 2 namjeran

will (1) /wɪl/ v aux (za tvorbu futura) he ~ do it on će tø učiniti that ~ be

the postman bit će da je to poštar

will (2) n 1 volja 2 (čvrsta) odluka 3 želja 4 oporuka ill ~ mržnja, neprijateljstvo **when there's a ~, there's a way** prov sve se može kad se hoće **~ing** adj 1 voljan; spreman 2 dobrovoljan, dragovoljan **~ingly** adv drage volje, rado **~ingness** n spremnost, želja **~power** snaga volje **~y-nilly** adv hoćeš-nećeš • vt 1 htjeti, željeti 2 (sth to sb/ sb sth) ostaviti oporukom

willies /'wɪlɪz/ n pl coll trnci, žmarci

willow /'wɪləʊ/ n vrba **~y** adj vitak

willy, willie /'wɪlɪ/ n GB coll pimpek, pišo

wilt /wɪlt/ vi 1 (u)venuti 2 klonuti

wily /'waɪlɪ/ adj podmukao, prepreden

wimp /wɪmp/ n coll mlakonja, kržljavac

win /wɪn/ vt,vi irreg 1 pobijediti, dobi(va)ti 2 osvojiti 3 (pri)dobiti, steći, zaraditi **~ hands down** lako pobijediti **~ the day/field** pobijediti **~ sb/sth back** ponovo osvojiti/steći/zadobiti **~ner** n pobjednik, dobitnik **~ning** adj 1 pobjednički 2 privlačan **~ning post** sport cilj **~nings** n pl dobitak na klađenju • n pobjeda, uspjeh; dobitak

wince /wɪns/ vi (at) trgnuti se • n trzaj **without a ~** ne trepnuvši

winch /wɪntʃ/ n vitlo; dizalica • vt dići vitlom/dizalicom

wind (1) /wɪnd/ n 1 vjetar 2 dah 3 miris, njuh 4 nadutost 5 coll prazne riječi 6 (**the ~**) duhačka glazbala **break ~** pustiti vjetar **get ~ of** coll načuti, nanjušiti • vt 1 (**be ~ed**) ostati bez daha 2 nanjušiti **~cheater/~breaker** US vjetrovka **~fall** f ig neočekivana dobit **~mill** vjetrenjača **~pipe** dušnik **~screen/~shield** US vjetrobran **~swept** a. vjetrovit b. raskuštran **~y** adj vjetrovit

wind (2) /waɪnd/ vt,vi irreg 1 okretati, vrtjeti 2 (up) naviti (sat); izvući/dizati vitlom 3 omotati, namotati 4 krivudati **~ down** opustiti se **~ up** a. zaključiti b. zatvoriti (tvrtku) c. završiti, naći se 4 GB coll zezati, zafrkavati **~ing** adj krivudav, vijugav, zavojit

windlass /'wɪndləs/ n vitlo

window /'wındəu/ n 1 prozor 2 izlog ~ **dressing a.** uređenje izloga b. *fig* uljepšavanje; lakirovka *coll* **~pane** okno go **~shopping** razgledavati izloge **~sill** prozorska daska

wine /waın/ n vino • vt ~ **and dine sb** ugostiti jelom i pilom

wing /wıŋ/ n 1 krilo (+ *fig, sport*) 2 *GB* blatobran **on the ~** u letu **take ~** poletjeti **take ~s** nestati **~ed** *adj* krilat **~er** n *sport* krilo in **the ~** *fig* u prikrajku

wink /wıŋk/ *vi,vt* 1 namignuti 2 treptati 3 svjetlucati 4 *GB* dati žmigavac 5 (at sth) zažmiriti na • n mig, namigivanje **~ers** n *pl GB* žmigavci

winter /'wıntə(r)/ n 1 zima 2 *mod* zimski **~time** zima ~ **wheat** ozima pšenica **wintry/~y** *adj* 1 zimski 2 *fig* hladan • *vi* prezimiti, zimovati

wipe /waıp/ *vt,vi* (o)brisati, (o)čistiti ~ **away** obrisati (suze) ~ **off a.** obrisati (crtež) b. riješiti se (duga) ~ **out a.** isprati b. skinuti (ljagu) c. razoriti, istrijebiti

wire /'waıə(r)/ n 1 žica; struna 2 *US* brzojav **live ~ a.** žica pod naponom b. *coll* energična osoba **~less** n *GB arch* radio ○ *adj* bežični **~tapping** prisluškivanje telefonskih razgovora **wiring** n električni vodovi *pl* **wiry** *adj fig* žilav, snažan • *vt* 1 (up) uvesti struju 2 svezati žicom 3 *US* brzojaviti 4 postaviti prislušne aparate, ozvučiti

wise (1) /waız/ mudar, pametan, razborit **get ~ to** *coll* prozreti, shvatiti **~crack** *coll* duhovita primjedba ~ **guy** *coll derog* pametnjaković • *vt,vi* ~ **up** *US coll* opametiti (se), shvatiti

wise (2) *suffix* **tax/money/sales~** što se tiče/glede poreza/novca/prodaje

wish /wıʃ/ *vt,vi* 1 željeti 2 zaželjeti ~ **sb well** zaželjeti sreću ~ **for** željeti, čeznuti za *I ~ I were rich* da sam barem bogat • n želja **best ~es** srdačan pozdrav **make a ~** zaželjeti što **~ful thinking** samozavaravanje, puste želje, iluzije

wishy-washy /'wıʃı wɒʃı/ *adj* 1 razvodnjen 2 blijed (boja) 3 *fig* mlak

wisp /wısp/ n 1 rukovet 2 čuperak 3 pramen (dima, pare)

wistful /'wıstfl/ *adj* čeznutljiv, sjetan, zamišljen

wit /wıt/ n 1 pamet, razbor, razumijevanje 2 dosjetljivost, duhovitost 3 veliki duh, čovjek velikog duha **be at one's ~s end** biti izvan sebe **have/keep one's ~s about one** biti trezven **live by/on one's ~s** snalaziti se **~ticism** n dosjetka **~ty** *adj* duhovit

witch /wıtʃ/ n vještica **~craft** čarobnjaštvo **~hunt** *fig* lov na vještice

with /wıð/ *prep* s, sa; kod; od; protiv; usprkos **write ~ a pencil** pisati olovkom **tremble ~ fear** tresti se od straha ~ *John away* a. nema, imat ćemo više mjesta ~ **it** *sl* moderan, u tijeku **~/at that** odmah potom, nato, zatim

withdraw /wıð'drɔ:/ *vt,vi irreg* (→ **draw**) (from) povući (se); ispisati (učenika); podići (novac) **~al** /wıð'drɔ:əl/ n povlačenje **~n** *adj* povučen (osoba)

wither /'wıðə(r)/ *vt,vi* 1 (up) osušiti 2 (away) uvenuti, osušiti se, usahnuti **give sb a ~ing glance** ošinuti pogledom

withhold /wıð'həuld/ *vt irreg* (→ **hold**) (from) 1 zadržati, spriječiti 2 prešutjeti, ne odati; ne objaviti 3 odbiti, uskratiti

within /wı'ðın/ *adv, prep* unutar ~ **two hours** u roku od dva sata ~ **20 metres of the house** ni 20 m od kuće ~ **reach** nadohvat **from ~** iznutra

without /wı'ðaut/ *adv, prep* 1 bez 2 *arch* izvan, vani ~ **doubt** nesumnjivo, zacijelo *he left ~ telling me* otišao je a da mi nije rekao

withstand /wıð'stænd/ *vt irreg* (→ **stand**) izdržati, odoljeti

witness /'wıtnıs/ n 1 svjedok 2 svjedočanstvo, svjedočenje **bear ~ to sb/sth** svjedočiti o **call to ~** pozvati za svjedoka • *vt,vi* 1 vidjeti, biti očevidac/svjedok, biti nazočan 2 (to sth/to doing sth) posvjedočiti, potvrditi 3 potpisati kao svjedok 4 odavati, pokazivati

wizard /'wızəd/ n 1 čarobnjak 2 stručnjak, genij(alac)

wobble /'wɒbl/ *vi,vt* **1** klimati (se); teturati **2** drhtati (glas)

woe /wəʊ/ *n* **1** bol, jad, tuga **2** *pl* nevolje, brige

wog /wɒg/ *n GB derog sl* crnac, azijat

woke, woken *v irreg* → **wake**

wolf /wʊlf/ *n* (*pl* **wolves**) vuk **a ~ in sheep's clothing** vuk u janjećoj koži **cry ~** dizati lažnu uzbunu **keep the ~ from the door** životariti **~hound** vučjak • *vt* (down) halapljivo gutati

woman /'wʊmən/ *n* (*pl* **women** /'wɪmɪn/) **1** žena **2** spremačica **~doctor** liječnica **~ driver** vozačica **women's lib** pokret za ženska prava **~hood** *n* **1** žene, ženski rod **2** zrelost, ženskost **~ize** *vi* juriti za ženama **~izer** *n* ženskar **~kind** *n* ženski rod **~ly** *adj* ženski, ženstven **womenfolk** *coll* žene

womb /wu:m/ *n* maternica; majčina utroba

won *v irreg* → **win**

wonder /'wʌndə(r)/ *vi,vt* **1** (about/if/ whether/what etc.) pitati se, zanimati se, htjeti/voljeti znati, biti znatiželjan **2** (at/that) čuditi se; diviti se; biti iznenaden *I ~ who did it* da mi je znati tko je to učinio *I ~ if I can/could have some more tea* da li bih mogao dobiti još malo čaja • *n* **1** čudo **2** čuđenje, divljenje **do/work ~s** činiti čuda **~ful** *adj* čudesan, (pre)divan, prekrasan; izvrstan, sjajan

won't /wəʊnt/ = **will not**

woo /wu:/ *vt* snubiti; udvarati se

wood /wʊd/ *n* **1** drvo, građa **2** (+ *pl*) šuma **out of the ~** *fig* izvan opasnosti **~cutter** drvosječa **~ed** *adj* šumovit **~en** *adj* **1** drven **2** *fig* drven, ukočen **~pecker** djetlić, žuna **the ~wind** drvena duhačka glazbala **~work a.** *GB* stolarstvo, tesarstvo **b.** drvena građa; drvenarija **~worm** crvotočina **~y** *adj* **a.** drvenast **b.** šumovit

woof /wu:f/ *n coll* lavež • *int* vau

wool /wʊl/ *n* vuna **dyed in the ~** *fig* zadrt **put the ~ over one's eyes** mazati oči **~gathering** rastresenost **~len/~en** *US adj* vunen **~ly** *adj* **1** vunast, mekan **2** nejasan, smušen

wop /wɒp/ *n tab derog sl* Talijan; dignuti

sl

word /wɜ:d/ *n* **1** riječ **2** vijesti, glas **in a ~** jednom riječju **in other ~s** drugim riječima **break/keep one's ~** prekršiti/održati riječ **eat one's ~** priznati grešku; povući riječ **have a ~ with** porazgovarati **send ~** javiti, obavijestiti **take sb's ~ for it** vjerovati kome na riječ **~ for ~** od riječi do riječi **~ing** *n* tekst, formulacija **~less** *adj* bez riječi, nijem, zanijemio **be ~-perfect** znati napamet svaku riječ **~y** *adj* rječit, opširan, rastegnut • *vt* izraziti riječima, formulirati, sročiti

wore *v irreg* → **wear**

work /wɜ:k/ *n* **1** rad; posao **2** trud **3** djelo **4** ručni rad **5** *pl* tvornica; mehanizam (sata) **the ~s** *coll* sve, komplet **at ~** na poslu; na djelu **be at ~ on** raditi na **in ~** zaposlen **out of ~** nezaposlen **go/set to ~** započeti rad, primiti se posla **have one's ~ cut out** imati pune ruke posla **public ~s** javni radovi **~ of art** umjetničko djelo **~aday** *adj* svakidašnji, običan **~aholic** *n* radoholičar **~bench** radni stol **~book** vježbenica **~day** *US* radni dan **~force** radna snaga **~man** radnik **~manship** vještina, izradba **~shop 1** radionica **2** seminar • *vi,vt* **a.** raditi **b.** djelovati; funkcionirati **3** uspjeti; upaliti *coll* **4** siliti/tjerati na rad; pokretati **5** rukovati, upravljati **6** *coll* izvesti, srediti **7** ši(va)ti; vesti **8** mijesiti **9** vreti, kipjeti **~ off** odraditi (dug) **~ on a.** djelovati/utjecati na **b.** raditi na (čemu), truditi se oko (čega) **~ out a.** izračunati, riješiti **b.** dokučiti, shvatiti **c.** uspjeti **d.** funkcionirati, ispasti, pokazati se **e.** izraditi, razraditi, razviti **f.** (at) izaći, iznositi (cijena) **g.** vježbati **~ up a.** izazvati, pobuditi, uzrujati **b.** postupno napredovati/postići, poboljšati **c.** obraditi, proraditi, proučiti **d.** oblikovati, prerađti **~able** *adj* upotrebljiv; izvediv **~er** *n* radnik **~ing** *adj* radni **~ing capital** obrtna sredstva **~ing class** radnička klasa **~ing-class** *adj* radnički **~ing day** radni dan **~ing hours** radno vrijeme

world /wɜːld/ n 1 svijet 2 mod svjetski **all over the ~** po cijelom svijetu, širom svijeta **on top of the ~** presretan **what in the ~** što zaboga **think the ~ of** visoko cijeniti **~-famous** svjetski poznat **~ly** adj svjetovni, ovozemaljski **~wide** adj svjetski, općepoznat ◦ adv širom svijeta

worm /wɜːm/ n 1 glista 2 crv (+ fig) **~-eaten a.** crvotočan **b.** coll ofucan • vt 1 (oneself/one's way in/ into/through) provući se, uvući se, gmizati, puzati; uvlačiti se 2 (sth out of sb) izmamiti, izvući (tajnu) 3 dati (životinji) sredstvo protiv glista

worn v irreg → **wear**

worry /ˈwʌrɪ/ vt,vi 1 brinuti; mučiti, opsjedati; smetati 2 (about/ over/that) brinuti se, uzrujavati se 3 gristi, (ras)trgati, **worried** adj (about) zabrinut, uzrujan **worried sick** strašno zabrinut • n briga, zabrinutost

worse /wɜːs/ adj comp (→ **bad**) gori, lošiji **they were none the ~ for it** nije im naškodilo **the ~ for wear** istrošen, otrcan; iscrpljen **~ luck** coll nažalost, na nesreću • adv 1 gore, lošije 2 jače, više **none the ~** ništa manje **be ~ off** lošije proći/stajati • n **a change for the ~** promjena nagore **~n** vi,vt pogoršati (se)

worship /ˈwɜːʃɪp/ n 1 obožavanje, bogoštovlje 2 fig obožavanje, divljenje 3 Božja služba; molitva 4 obred **place of ~** bogomolja, crkva, hram • vt,vi 1 obožavati (+ fig) 2 moliti se Bogu, ići na misu **~per/~er** US n vjernik; obožavatelj

worst /wɜːst/ adj sup (→ **bad**) najgori, najlošiji • adv najgore, najlošije • n ono najgore **at (the) ~** u najgorem slučaju **if the ~ comes to the ~** u najgorem slučaju **get the ~ of it** proći najgore, izvući kraći kraj

worsted /ˈwʊstɪd/ n tkanina od češljane vune, kamgarn

worth /wɜːθ/ adj vrijedan **it's ~ 50 pounds** vrijedi 50 funti **it's not ~ waiting for him** ne isplati se čekati ga **it's not ~ it** ne isplati se, nije vrijedno truda **be ~ one's while** isplatiti se,

biti vrijedno truda • n vrijednost **~less** adj bezvrijedan; beznačajan **~while** adj vrijedan, koji se isplati **~y** /ˈwɜːðɪ/ adj 1 dostojan 2 (of) vrijedan (čega) ◦ n form važna/ugledna ličnost

wotcher /ˈwɒtʃə(r)/ int GB sl bok! zdravo!

would /wʊd/ v irreg 1 u neupravnom govoru zamjenjuje **will** (1) 2 (za tvorbu kondicionala) *If he paid me, I ~ do it* kad bi mi platio, učinio bih to *If he had paid me, I ~ have done it* da mi je platio, bio bih to učinio *W~ you like some tea?* Želite li čaja?

would-be adj 1 derog navodni, nazovi- 2 potencijalan; nadobudan

wound v irreg → **wind**

wound /wuːnd/ n rana, ozljeda • vt raniti **seriously/badly ~ed** teško ranjen **the ~ed** n ranjenici pl

wove, woven v irreg → **weave**

wrangle /ˈræŋgl/ vi natezati se, svađati se, prepirati se

wrap /ræp/ vt,vi 1 (up/in) oviti, omotati, umotati (+ fig) 2 (around/round) omotati, zamotati; ogrnuti 3 (up) toplo se obući, umotati se 4 (up) coll završiti, zaključiti (posao) **~ped up in** fig zadubljen u **~per** n omot, ovitak **~ping(s)** n omot • n US (ženski) ogrtač **keep sth under ~s** coll čuvati/držati u tajnosti

wrath /rɒθ/ n form, lit gnjev

wreak /riːk/ vt lit (on) izvršiti (osvetu) nad ~ **havoc** (po)harati, (o)pustošiti

wreath /riːθ/ n vijenac **~e** /riːð/ vt,vi lit 1 omotati, okružiti, obaviti, prekriti; ovjenčati 2 (into) isplesti

wreck /rek/ n 1 brodolom 2 olupina (broda) 3 fig propast 4 ruševina; olupina 5 coll krntija 6 propao čovjek **~age** /ˈrekɪdʒ/ n ostaci, krhotine • vt **be ~ed** 1 doživjeti brodolom 2 uništiti; pokvariti, upropastiti, osujetiti

wren /ren/ n palčić, kraljić

wrench /rentʃ/ vt 1 (from/off) istrgnuti, oteti 2 iščašiti, uganuti 3 fig izokrenuti • n 1 trzaj 2 uganuće 3 ključ (za matice)

wrestle /ˈresl/ vi (with) 1 hrvati se 2 fig

mučiti se s **~r** *n* hrvač **wrestling** *n* hrvanje

wretch /retʃ/ *n* jadnik, bijednik, nesretnik **~ed** /ʹretʃɪd/ *adj* **1** bijedan, jadan, nesretan **2** grozan, ružan (vrijeme); očajan **3** proklet **4** nevaljao

wriggle /ʹrɪgl/ *vi,vt* koprcati se; vrpoljiti se; migoljiti (se) **~ out of sth** *coll* izvući se, izmigoljiti se

wring /rɪŋ/ *vt irreg* **1** zavrnuti **2** stisnuti (ruku) **3** (sth out; sth out of/from sth) (is)cijediti, izažimati **4** *fig* izvući, iznuditi (priznanje) **~ sb's neck** zavrnuti kome vratom **~ one's hands** kršiti ruke

wrinkle /ʹrɪŋkl/ *n* bora; nabor • *vi,vt* **1** naborati (se) **2** namrštiti

wrist /rɪst/ *n* ručni zglob, zglavak **~watch** ručni sat

writ /rɪt/ *n* (sudbeni) nalog **Holy W~** Sveto pismo

write /raɪt/ *vi,vt irreg* pisati; napisati **~ down** pribilježiti, zapisati **~ off** a. otpisati, prekrižiti b. poništiti (dug) **~off** *n* otpisan/poništen dug **~ out** a. napisati (u cijelosti); načisto prepisati b. ispisati, napisati **~r** *n* književnik, pisac **writing** *n* **1** rukopis

2 književno djelo, članak, tekst **3** pisanje **4** *mod* pisaći **in writing** napismeno

writhe /raɪð/ *vi* svijati se, grčiti se (od boli)

written *v irreg* → **write**

wrong /rɒŋ/ *adj* netočan, pogrešan, kriv, nepravedan **you're ~** nemaš pravo **something is ~ with** nešto nije u redu s **what's ~ (with)** što je, što nije u redu • *adv* netočno, pogrešno, krivo **get it/sb ~** pogrešno shvatiti **go ~** a. pogriješiti b. poći nizbrdo; pokvariti se c. poći krivim putem • *n* nepravda, krivnja; zabluda; zlo **be in the ~** biti u krivu, imati krivo **do ~** činiti krivo/nažao, griješiti • *vt* činiti krivo, nanijeti nepravdu **~doer** krivac, počinitelj **~doing** nedjelo, prijestup **~ful** *adj* **1** nepravedan **2** nezakonit

wrote *v irreg* → **write**

wrought /rɔːt/ *adj lit* izrađen, oblikovan, izazvan **~ iron** kovano željezo **~up** *adj* uzrujan, nervozan, napet

wrung *v irreg* → **wring**

wry /raɪ/ *adj fig* kiseo, ciničan, ironičan

X

X, x /eks/ 24. slovo engl. abecede; iks
xenophobia /ˌzenəˈfəʊbɪə/ *n* ksenofobija
xerox /ˈzɪərɒks/ *vt TM* fotokopirati • *n* fotokopija

Xmas /ˈkrɪsməs/ *n coll* Christmas
X-ray /ˈeks reɪ/ *n* 1 rendgenska zraka 2 rendgenska snimka • *vt* učiniti rendgensku snimku
xylophone /ˈzaɪləfəʊn/ *n* ksilofon

Y

Y, y /waɪ/ 25. slovo engl. abecede; ip-silon

yacht /jɒt/ *n* 1 jahta 2 športska jedrili-ca **~ing** *n* jedrenje, jedriličarstvo

yak /jæk/ *n* jak

yam /jæm/ *n* 1 bot jam 2 *US* slatki krumpir

yank /jæŋk/ *vi,vt* *coll* naglo povući, trznuti, istrgnuti • *n* trzaj

Yank /jæŋk/ *n* GB *coll* Amer

Yankee /ˈjæŋkɪ/ *n* *coll* 1 Amerikanac 2 *US* Sjevernjak, Jenki

yap /jæp/ *vi* lajati (+ *fig*)

yard (1) /jaːd/ *n* dvorište

yard (2) *n* 1 jard (0.9144 m) **~stick** mjerilo 2 križ jarbola

Yard /jaːd/ *n* **the ~** Scotland Yard

yarn /jaːn/ *n* preda **spin a ~** ispričati (dugačku/nevjerojatnu/pretjeranu) priču, razvezati priču, nabajati

yaw /jɔː/ *vi* skrenuti s pravca

yawn /jɔːn/ *vi* 1 zijevnuti, zijevati 2 zinuti, razjapiti se • *n* zijev(anje)

ye (1) /jiː/ *pron* *arch* vi

ye (2) → **the**

yea /jeɪ/ *adv* *arch*, *coll* da • *n* glas "za"

yeah /jeə/ *adv* *coll* da

year /jɜː(r)/ *n* godina **~ after ~** iz go-dine u godinu **~ in ~ out** svake go-dine **~book** godišnjak **since the ~ dot** *coll* odavno **~long** *adj* (jed-no)godišnji **~ly** *adj* godišnji • *adv* godišnje

yearn /jɜːn/ *vi* (for) *lit* žudjeti, čeznuti **~ing** *n* žudnja

yeast /jiːst/ *n* kvasac, kvas

yell /jel/ *vi,vt* ~ (at) vikati, derati se ~ **out** kriknuti • *n* krik, vrisak

yellow /ˈjeləʊ/ *adj* 1 žut **the Y~ Pages** *TM* poslovni telefonski imenik 2 *sl* kukavica • *vi,vt* požutjeti, požutiti

yelp /jelp/ *vi* (za)cviliti

yen (1) /jen/ *n* želja, žudnja

yen (2) *n* jen

yeoman /ˈjəʊmən/ *n* GB 1 *hist* slobod-njak, maloposjednik **~ service** velika pomoć, podrška, usluga 2 kraljevski stražar

yer *coll* → **your**

yes /jes/ *adv* da, jest • *n* 1 potvrdni odgovor 2 glas "za"

yesterday /ˈjestədɪ/ *adv*, *n* jučer **the day before ~** prekjučer **~'s** jučerašnji **I wasn't born ~** nisam od jučer

yet /jet/ *adv* još, dosad **as ~** dosad • *conj* ali, ipak

yeti /ˈjetɪ/ *n* jeti

yew /juː/ *n* tisa

Yiddish /ˈjɪdɪʃ/ *n* jidiš

yield /jiːld/ *vt,vi* 1 dati, davati, donijeti 2 *lit* predati (se), povući se 3 popusti-ti 4 dati prednost (u prometu) • *n* urod, prihod **~ing** *adj* mekan, gibak; popustljiv

yippee /ˈjɪpɪ/ *int* jupi!

yob /jɒb/, **yobbo** /ˈjɒbəʊ/ *n* GB neote-sanac, klipan

yodel /ˈjəʊdl/ *vi,vt* jodlati

yoga /ˈjəʊɡə/ *n* joga

yoghurt, yogurt, yoghourt /ˈjɒɡət/ *n* jogurt

yoke /jəʊk/ *n* 1 jaram (+ *fig*); par volo-va 2 *fig, lit* spona • *vt* 1 upregnuti 2 vezati, sjediniti, udružiti

yokel /ˈjəʊkl/ *n* *joc, derog* seljo

yolk /jəʊk/ *n* žumanjak

yonder /ˈjɒndə(r)/ *adv* *arch* onamo

you /juː/ *pron* ti, tebe, tebi, tobom; vi, vama, vas

young /jʌŋ/ *adj* mlad **the night is still ~** večer/noć je tek počela **the ~** mladi **~ster** *n* mladić • *n* 1 **the ~** mladi, mladež 2 mladunčad

your /jɔː(r)/ *adj poss* tvoj, vaš, svoj **~s** *pron poss* tvoj, vaš, svoj **~self** (*pl* **~selves**) *pron reflex* sebe (se), sebi

(si) **all by ~self** sam
youth /ju:θ/ *n* 1 mladost 2 mladić **the ~** mladi, mladež **~ful** *adj* mladenački, mlad
yowl /jaʊl/ *vi* zavijati, tuliti
yo-yo /ˈjəʊjəʊ/ *n* 1 jojo 2 blesan, čov-

jek kojeg se može vući za nos
yuck /jʌk/ *int coll* bljak, fuj **~y** *adj coll* odvratan
yule /ju:l/ *n arch* Božić **~ log** badnjak (drvo; kolač) **~tide** *lit* Božić
yuppie /ˈjʊpɪ/ *n* mladi poslovni čovjek

Z

Z, z /zed / 26. slovo engl. abecede; ze

zany /ˈzeɪnɪ/ adj šašav

zap /zæp/ n coll živahnost, energija • vt,vi 1 (po)juriti, projuriti 2 napasti; uništiti

zeal /ziːl/ n form žar, oduševljenje ~**ous** adj gorljiv, oduševljen, revan

zealot /ˈzelət/ n derog fanatik

zebra /ˈziːbrə/ n zebra ~ **crossing** zebra

zenith /ˈzenɪθ/ n zenit, vrhunac

zeppelin /ˈzepəlɪn/ n cepelin

zero /ˈzɪərəʊ/ n nula, ništica ~ **hour** mil vrijeme početka operacije • vi ~ **in on sth** 1 naciljati 2 upraviti pozornost

zest /zest/ n 1 uzbuđenje, užitak 2 polet, žar 3 korica (limuna/naranče)

zigzag /ˈzɪgzæg/ n mod cik-cak, vijugav • vi vijugati, kretati se u cik-cak

zillion /ˈzɪlɪən/ n coll (~s) tisuće, milijarde, iks

zinc /zɪŋk/ n cink

Zionism /ˈzaɪənɪzəm/ n cionizam **Zionist** cionist

zip code /ˈzɪp kəʊd/ n US poštanski broj

zip /zɪp/ n 1 (~ **fastener, zipper**) patentni zatvarač 2 zvižduk (metka) 3 živahnost, energija • vt ~ **up** zatvoriti patentni zatvarač

zither /ˈzɪðə(r)/ n citra

zit /zɪt/ n US prištić

zodiac /ˈzəʊdɪæk/ n zodijak

zombi(e) /ˈzɒmbɪ/ n zombi

zone /zəʊn/ n područje, zona, pojas • vt podijeliti u područja

zonked /zɒŋkt/ adj (~ **out**) sl 1 pijan; drogiran 2 iscrpljen, premoren

zoo /zuː/ n (~**logical gardens**) zoološki vrt ~**logist** zoolog ~**logy** zoologija

zoom /zuːm/ vi 1 coll prozujati, proletjeti 2 coll skočiti, naglo se povećati 3 ~ **in/out** (on) zumirati ~ **lens** zum coll

English abbreviations
Engleske kratice

A	1 *GB* major road 2 amp(ere) 3 atomic (A-bomb)
A1	*coll* first class; excellent
AA	1 *GB* Automobile Association 2 Alcoholics Anonymous (udruženje liječenih alkoholičara) 3 anti-aircraft
AAA	Automobile Association of America
ABC	American Broadcasting Company
a/c	account
AC	alternating current
A.D.	anno Domini
ADC	aide-de-camp
AI	1 artificial intelligence 2 artificial insemination
AIDS	Acquired Immune Deficiency Syndrome
a.k.a.	also known as
A-level	advanced level
a.m.	ante meridiem, in the morning
AM	amplitude modulation
AP	Associated Press
APC	armoured personnel carrier
arr	arrival
asap	as soon as possible
ASCII	American Standard Code for Information Interchange
att.	1 attention 2 attorney
Att. Gen.	Attorney General
av	average
Ave.	Avenue
AWACS	aiborne warning and control system
AWOL	absent without leave
b.	born
B.A.	1 Bachelor of Arts 2 British Airways
b and b	bed and breakfast
B.B.C.	British Broadcasting Corporation
B.C.	before Christ
Blvd.	Boulevard
B.O.	1 body odour 2 box office
BR	British Rail
Bros	Brothers
BSc	Bachelor of Science
C	Celsius, centigrade
c.	1 century 2 cent 3 circa 4 carat
CAD/CAM	computer-aided design and manufacture

CD	1 compact disc 2 Civil Defence 3 Corps Diplomatique
CD-ROM	compact disc read-only memory
C.E.T.	Central European Time
cf	compare
C.I.A.	Central Intelligence Agency
CID	Criminal Investigations Department
C-in-C	Commander-in-Chief
CNN	Cable News Network
Co	1 company 2 county
c/o	care of
CO	Commanding Officer
COD	cash on delivery, *US* collect on delivery
C of E	Church of England
Col.	Colonel
Con	Conservative Party
contd	continued
Corp	corporation
CPA	certified public accountant
CSE	Certificate of Secondary Education
cu	cubic
cv, CV	curriculum vitae
cwt	hundredweight
d	1 date 2 day 3 degree 4 penny 5 died
DA	District Attorney
DC	1 direct current 2 District of Columbia
Dec.	December
Dem	Democrat(ic)
dep	departure
dept	department
DIY	do-it-yourself
DJ	1 disc jockey 2 dinner jacket
DM	Deutsche Mark
DNA	deoxyribonucleic acid
D.O.A.	dead on arrival
D.P.	displaced person
D Phil	→PhD
Dr	1 Doctor 2 (u imenu ulice) Drive
DST	daylight-saving time
DTs	delirium tremens
dz.	dozen
E	east(ern)
ECG	1 electrocardiogram 2 electrocardiograph
ECU	European Currency Unit

ed.	1 editor 2 edited by
EDT	Eastern Daylight Time
EEC	European Economic Community
EEG	1 electroencephalogram 2 electroencephalograph
EFTA	European Free Trade Association
e.g.	exempli gratia, for example
EKG	*US* →ECG
ELT	English language teaching
ENT	ear, nose and throat
EST	1 *US* Eastern Standard Time 2 electric-shock treatment
ETA	estimated time of arrival
et al.	et alii, and others
etc.	et cetera, and so on
ETD	estimated time of departure
EU	European Union
ext.	1 extension 2 extra
F	Fahrenheit
FA	Football Association
FBI	Federal Bureau of Investigation
FC	football club
Feb.	February
FM	1 field marshal 2 frequency modulation
FO	Foreign Office
f.o.b.	free on board (franko brod)
Fr	1 Father 2 franc
Fri.	Friday
ft	foot, feet
FY	fiscal year
fyi	for your information
G	1 gravity 2 *US sl* grand, $ 1,000
GATT	General Agreement on Tariffs and Trade
GB	Great Britain
GBH	grievous bodily harm
GCE	General Certificate of Education
GCSE	General Certificate of Secondary Education
GDP	Gross Domestic Product
GHQ	general headquarters
GI	1 government issue 2 *sl* američki vojnik
gld	guilder
GMT	Greenwich mean time
GNP	Gross National Product
GOP	Grand Old Party (Republikanska stranka u SAD)
Gov	governor

govt	government
GP	general practitioner (liječnik opće prakse)
GPO	General Post Office
GS	**1** general secretary **2** general staff
gtd	guaranteed

h	hour
ha	hectare
HC	House of Commons
hcf	highest common factor
HE	His/Her Excellency
HF	high frequency
hi-fi	high fidelity
HIV	human immunodeficiency virus
HL	House of Lords
HM	His/Her Majesty
HMS	**1** His/Her Majesty's service **2** His/Her Majesty's ship
HO	**1** head office **2** Home Office
hon	honorary
Hon	honourable
HP	**1** horsepower **2** hire purchase
HQ	headquarters
hr	hour
HR	House of Representatives
HRH	His/Her Royal Highness
hrs	hours
ht	height
HV	high voltage
hwy	highway

I	island(s), isle(s)
IBRD	International Bank for Reconstruction and Development
ICBM	intercontinental ballistic missile
ICU	intensive care unit
ie	id est, that is
IMF	International Monetary Fund
in	inch
Inc	incorporated
Interpol	International Police Organization
IOU	I owe you (pismena obveza vraćanja duga)
IPA	International Phonetic Alphabet
IQ	intelligence quotient
IRA	Irish Republican Army
IT	information technology
ital	italics

ITV	Independent Television
Jan	January
Jnr, Jr	junior
Jul	July
Jun	June
junc(t)	junction
KKK	Ku Klux Klan
KO	knockout
Kt	Knight
L	1 lake 2 learner driver 3 large (size)
l	1 litre 2 line
LA	Los Angeles
LAN	local area network
lb	pound (mjera za težinu)
l/c	letter of credit
LC	Library of Congress
LCD	1 lowest common denominator 2 liquid crystal display
Lib	Liberal Party
lit	literature; literary
ll	lines
LP	long-playing (record)
Lsd	pounds, shillings and pence
LSD	lysergic acid diethylamide
LSE	London School of Economics
Ltd	limited
m	1 metre 2 mile 3 million 4 masculine
M	1 medium (size) 2 motorway
MA	Master of Arts
Mar	March
MASH	mobile army surgical hospital
max	maximum
MC	1 master of ceremonies 2 Medical Corps 3 member of Congress
MCP	male chauvinist pig
MD	1 Doctor of Medicine 2 medical department
Messrs	messieurs
MIA	missing in action
MI5	britanska vojna kontraobavještajna služba
MI6	britanska vojna obavještajna služba
misc	miscellaneous
Miss	gospođica
Mon	Monday

MOT	Ministry of Transport; **MOT test** tehnički pregled vozila
MP	**1** Member of Parliament **2** military police(man)
mpg	miles per galon
mph	miles per hour
Mr	mister
Mrs	gospođa
MS	manuscript
MSc	Master of Science
Msgr	monsignor
MSS	manuscripts
Mt	Mount
N	north(ern)
NASA	National Aeronautics and Space Administration
NATO	North Atlantic Treaty Organization
NBA	National Basketball Association
NBC	National Broadcasting Company
NBS	National Bureau of Standards
NCO	noncommissioned officer (dočasnik)
NE	northeast(ern)
NFL	National Football League
NHS	National Health Service
no.	number
nos.	numbers
NW	northwest(ern)
NY	New York
NYC	New York City
NZ	New Zealand
OAP	old age pensioner
ob.	obiit, died
Oct	October
OECD	Organization for Economic Cooperation and Development
O-level	ordinary level
ono	or near(est) offer (okvirna cijena, cijena po dogovoru)
OPEC	Organization of Petroleum Exporting Countries
OR	operating room
OSCE	Organization for Security and Cooperation in Europe
Oxon	Oxford University
oz	ounce(s)
p	**1** page **2** penny, pence **3** population
PA	**1** personal assistant **2** public address (sys-tem)
PAYE	**1** pay as you earn **2** pay as you enter
pc	percent

PC	1 personal computer 2 police constable 3 political correctness
PD	1 police department 2 postal district
PE	physical education
PEN	(International Association of) Poets, Playwrights, Editors Essayists and Novelists
PG	parental guidance
PhD	Doctor of Philosophy
PI	public information
plc	public limited company
pm	post meridiem, in the afternoon
PM	prime minister
PO	1 post office 2 postal order
POE	1 port of embarkation 2 port of entry
pop	population
POW	prisoner of war
pp	pages
PR	public relations
pro	professional
PRO	public relations officer
prof	professor
pt	1 part 2 pint 3 point 4 port
pta	peseta
PTA	Parent-Teacher Association
PTO	please turn over
PVC	polyvinyl chloride
q	question
QE2	Queen Elizabeth the Second (brod)
QM	quartermaster
qr	quarter
qt	quart
R	river
RA	1 rear admiral 2 Royal Academy 3 Royal Artillery
RAF	Royal Air Force
RAM	random access memory
R 'n' B	rhythm and blues
R and D	research and development
R 'n' R	rock and roll
RC	Roman Catholic
Rd	Road
REM	rapid eye movement
rep	representative
Rep	Republican
Rev	Reverend

RIP	rest in peace
RN	1 Royal Navy 2 registered nurse
RNA	ribonucleic acid
ROM	read-only memory
RPG	rocket propelled grenade
rpm	revolutions per minute
RS	recording secretary
RSVP	please reply
S	1 south(ern) 2 small (size)
sae	stamped addressed envelope
SAS	Special Air Service
Sat	Saturday
SC	1 Security Council 2 Supreme Court
SDP	Social Democratic Party
SE	southeast(ern)
SEATO	Southeast Asia Treaty Organization
sec	second
Sept	September
SF	science fiction
shipt	shipment
SI	Systeme International, međunarodni sustav mjernih jedinica
Snr	Senior
SOB	son of a bitch
SOS	save our souls
Sq	Square
Sr	senior
SS	1 saints 2 steamship
St	1 Saint 2 Street
STD	subscriber trunk dialling
Sun	Sunday
SW	southwest(ern)
t	1 tonne 2 ton
TB	tuberculosis
td	touchdown
TEFL	teaching English as a foreign language
temp	1 temperature 2 temporary
TESOL	teaching English to speakers of other for-eign languages
Thur(s)	Thursday
TKO	technical knockout
TM	trademark
TNT	trinitrotoluene
tsp	teaspoon(ful)
TUC	Trades Union Congress

Tue(s)	Tuesday
U	1 upper class 2 *film* universal
UCCA	Universities Central Council on Admissions
UCLA	University of California at Los Angeles
UDA	Ulster Defence Association
UFO	unidentified flying object
UHF	ultra-high frequency
UK	United Kingdom
UN	United Nations
UNESCO	United Nations Educational, Scientific and Cultural Organization
UNICEF	United Nations International Children's Fund
UPI	United Press International
US(A)	United States (of America)
USS	United States Ship
v.	1 *GB* versus, against 2 verse
V	volt(s)
VAT	value added tax
VC	Victoria Cross
VCR	video-cassette recorder
VD	venereal disease
VDU	visual display unit
vet	1 veteran 2 veterinarian
VHF	very high frequency
VIP	very important person
viz	namely
VLF	very low frequency
vol	volume
VP	vice president
vs.	*US* versus, against
W	1 west(ern) 2 watt(s) 3 women's (size)
WASP	White Anglo-Saxon Protestant
WC	water closet
Wed(s)	Wednesday
WHO	World Health Organization
wkly	weekly
WPC	Woman Police Constable
wt	weight
XL	extra large (size)
y	1 yard 2 year

Y	1 yen **2** *US coll* → YMCA, YWCA
yd	yard
YHA	Youth Hostels Association
YTS	Youth Training Scheme
YMCA	Young Men's Christian Association
YWCA	Young Women's Christian Association
yr	year
ZPG	zero population growth

OSNOVE ENGLESKE GRAMATIKE

Nepravilni glagoli
Tvorba riječi

BASIC ENGLISH GRAMMAR

Irregular verbs
Word formation

Nouns - Imenice

Tvorba množine

Pravilne imenice tvore množinu dodavanjem nastavka **-s** koji se izgovara /s/ iza bezvučnoga glasa, a /z/ iza zvučnoga:

pot	lonac	*pots* /pɒts/
leg	noga	*legs* /legz/

Imenice koje završavaju glasom /s/, /z/, /ʃ/, /ʒ/, /tʃ/ ili /dʒ/ dobivaju nastavak **-(e)s**, koji se izgovara /ɪz/:

bus	autobus	*buses* /ˈbʌsɪz/
nose	nos	*noses* /ˈnəʊzɪz/
beach	žal	*beaches* /ˈbiːtʃɪz/
wish	želja	*wishes* /ˈwɪʃɪz/
edge	rub	*edges* /ˈedʒɪz/
prize	nagrada	*prizes* /ˈpraɪzɪz/

Imenice koje imaju dočetak suglasnik **+y** tvore množinu s pomoću nastavka **-s**, a **y** se mijenja u **ie**:

country	zemlja	*countries* /ˈkʌntrɪz/

Iznimka su vlastita imena:

Kennedy	*The Kennedys*

Imenice koje imaju dočetak samoglasnik **+y** tvore množinu na pravilan način:

boy	dječak	*boys* /bɔɪz/

Imenice koje završavaju na **-f** i **-fe** mijenjaju te dočetke u **-ves**.

half	polovica	*halves*
wife	supruga	*wives*

Od ovog pravila postoje brojne iznimke koje su navedene u Rječniku.

Neke imenice tvore množinu s pomoću nastavka **-en**:

ox	vol	*oxen*
child	dijete	*children*

Neke imenice ne tvore množinu s pomoću nastavaka, nego mijenjanjem osnovnog samoglasnika:

man	muškarac	*men* (i sve složenice)
woman	žena	*women* (+ složenice)

foot	stopalo	*feet*
tooth	zub	*teeth*
goose	guska	*geese*
mouse	miš	*mice*
louse	uš	*lice*

Postoje imenice koje u množini ne mijenjaju oblik:

fish, sheep, deer, trout, salmon, swine, plaice, mackerel, grouse; aircraft

Neke imenice imaju latinski plural:

phenomenon	pojava	*phenomena*
criterion	kriterij	*criteria*
datum	podatak	*data*
medium	sredstvo	*media*
crisis	kriza	*crises*
analysis	raščlamba	*analyses*
cactus	kaktus	*cacti* ili *cactuses*
fungus	gljiva	*fungi* ili *funguses*
formula	formula	*formulae* ili *formulas*

Postoje imenice koje u hrvatskom jeziku imaju množinu, a u engleskom su nebrojive (uncountable), pa se upotrebljavaju samo u jednini:

savjet	*advice*
nekoliko savjeta	*several pieces of advice*
informacija	*information*
nekoliko informacija	*some information, several pieces of information*

Imenica *news*, premda ima nastavak -**s**, gramatički je jednina i uza se uvijek ima glagol u jednini:

That is good news. To je dobra vijest.
The news is on at six o'clock. Vijesti su na programu u šest sati.

Neke imenice u množini mijenjaju osnovno značenje. Takvi su slučajevi navedeni u Rječniku.

Padeži

U engleskom jeziku imenice se ne mijenjaju po padežima kao u hrvatskome.

Antun voli pse.
Anthony likes dogs.

U hrvatskom jeziku možemo i zamijeniti poredak riječi, a da se ne promijeni smisao, nego samo stil:

Pse voli Antun.

Oblik *pse* (akuzativ) kazuje nam da je riječ o objektu, a ne subjektu. Oblik *Antun* (nominativ) kazuje nam da je riječ o subjektu.

Kad bismo isto učinili s engleskom rečenicom, bitno bismo izmijenili njezino značenje:

Dogs like Anthony značilo bi: Psi vole Antuna, jer u engleskom jeziku subjekt u pravilu stoji na prvom mjestu u rečenici, a objekt na trećem.

Dakle, u hrvatskom jeziku odnose među riječima i njihovu funkciju u rečenici određuju padežni oblici (pse, psi, Antun, Antuna), a u engleskom mjesto riječi u rečenici (subjekt - predikat - objekt).

Engleske imenice ipak poznaju poseban padežni oblik koji odgovara hrvatskom genitivu ili pak posvojnome pridjevu. Taj se oblik naziva Genitive Case ili Saxon Genitive.

Saxon Genitive tvori se dodavanjem nastavka -'s na imenicu:

mother	majka	*mother's*	majčin
the world	svijet	*the world's future*	budućnost svijeta

Imenice u množini koje završavaju na **-s** tvore Saxon Genitive samo dodavanjem apostrofa:

ladies	dame	*ladies' room*	ženski WC

Vlastita imena koja završavaju na -s, mogu se u genitivu pisati na dva načina:

James	*James'* ili *James's*
Yeats	*Yeats'* ili *Yeats's*

Imenice u množini koje ne završavaju nastavkom -s tvore Saxon Genitive na pravilan način:

children	djeca	*children's room*	dječja soba

Saxon Genitive u pravilu se rabi za osobe, gradove i zemlje. U ostalim slučajevima upotrebljavamo tzv. Norman Genitive (izričaj s prijedlogom *of*). Usporedi:

John's leg
My sister's leg   ali: *the leg of the table*

Croatia's future
Zagreb's future   ali: *the future of the film industry*

Saxon Genitive može izražavati i vrijeme:

ten minutes' walk	dvije minute hoda
an hour's drive	dva sata vožnje

Upotrebljava se i za neke lokale

hairdresser's	frizerski salon
butcher's	mesnica

Brojni izričaji u kojima se pojavljuje imenica u genitivu navedeni su u Rječniku.

Rod imenice

U engleskom jeziku imenice poznaju samo prirodni, a ne i gramatički rod. To znači da su ženskog roda imenice koje označavaju ženske osobe (*woman, girl, mother, sister, aunt, nun, lady, queen...*), a muškog roda imenice koje označavaju muške osobe (*man, boy, father, uncle, gentleman, king...*).

Imenice koje mogu označavati osobe oba spola (*teacher, president, nurse, driver...*) mogu biti muškog ili ženskog roda, ovisno o kontekstu.

Imenice koje označavaju predmete ili pojave u pravilu se smatraju srednjim rodom (zamjenjuje ih zamjenica *it*).

Zemlje, automobili i brodovi mogu se smatrati srednjim rodom, ali i - afektivno - ženskim. Tako se može reći:

Croatia and its history	ili
Croatia and her history	Hrvatska i njezina povijest

She can do 130 miles per hour   Može postići brzinu od 200 km/h

Životinje su u načelu srednji rod (*it*), osim ako im je spol poznat (konji, kućni ljubimci i sl.).

Pronouns – Zamjenice

Personal pronouns - Osobne zamjenice

Subject - nominativ

	Jednina	Množina
1. lice	I	we
2. lice	you	you
3. lice	he, she, it	they

¶ *You* je zamjenica za drugo lice jednine i množine. Nekadašnji oblik za jedninu (*thou*) očuvao se u dijalektima i starijim tekstovima. Neki dijalekti također poznaju posebne oblike (*yous, ye*) ili izričaje (*you people; you guys* US coll) za 2. lice množine.

¶ Engleski jezik ne poznaje posebni oblik za Vi iz štovanja. *You* se nikad ne piše velikim početnim slovom (osim, dakako, na početku rečenice).

¶ *I* se uvijek piše velikim slovom.

¶ zamjenice *he* i *she* rabe se za osobe muškog odnosno ženskog roda, a *it* za predmete, pojave i životinje (vidi napomene uz rod imenica).

Object – Kosi padež

me	us
you	you
her, him, it	them

Possessive adjectives and pronouns – Posvojne zamjenice i pridjevi

Ispred imenice stoje posvojni pridjevi:

my book	our book
your book	your book
his/her/its book	their book

Posvojna zamjenica *its* piše se bez apostrofa.

Dalje od imenice ili bez imenice stoje posvojne zamjenice:

the book is mine	the book is ours
the book is yours	the book is yours
the book is his/hers/its	the book is theirs

Whose book is this? - It's mine.

Adjectives – Pridjevi

U engleskom jeziku pridjevi ne mijenjaju rod, broj ni padež.
Kao i u hrvatskom jeziku, engleski pridjevi poznaju tri stupnja: pozitiv (*positive*), komparativ (*comparative*) i superlativ (*superlative*).

Komparativ se tvori dodavanjem nastavka **-er** na osnovu pridjeva. Superlativ se tvori dodavanjem nastavka **-est**. Superlativ iziskuje određeni član **the**:

long   longer   the longest
Jednosložni pridjevi na **-e** dobivaju nastavak **-r** odnosno **-st**:
fine   finer   the finest

Kod jednosložnih pridjeva koji završavaju suglasnikom taj se suglasnik udvostručuje:

big   bigger   the biggest

Pridjevi koji završavaju na **-y** mijenjaju taj dočetak u **i**:

angry   angrier   the angriest

Višesložni pridjevi, kao i neki dvosložni, komparativ i superlativ ne tvore s pomoću nastavaka, nego dodavanjem riječi **more** odnosno **the most** ispred pridjeva:

expensive   more expensive   the most expensive

Nepravilnu komparaciju imaju neki vrlo česti pridjevi:

good	better	the best
bad, ill, evil	worse	the worst
much, many	more	the most
little	less	the least

Adverbs – Prilozi

Kao i u hrvatskom, pridjevi u engleskom jeziku označavaju mjesto, vrijeme, način, uzrok, stupanj.

Radi uštede prostora, u Rječniku nisu posebno navedeni svi prilozi načina koji se tvore dodavanjem nastavka **-ly** pridjevu:

slow	slowly
bad	badly

Napomene:

Pridjevi koji završavaju na suglasnik + **le**, gube dočetno **e**:

simple	simply
idle	idly

Dočetno **-e** ne gubi se prije nastavka **-ly** u ostalim slučajevima:

fortunate   fortunately

U pridjeva koji završavaju na **-y**, dočetak se mijenja u **i** prije nastavka **-ly**:

happy	happily
lucky	luckily

Pridjevi koji završavaju na **-ful**, pravilno tvore prilog dodavanjem nastavka **-ly**:

beautiful	beautifully
successful	successfully

¶ Dvostruko l (-lly) kod pisanja imaju samo prilozi izvedeni iz pridjeva koji završavaju na l.

Pridjevu *good* odgovara prilog *well*.

Prilozi se komparaju jednako kao i pridjevi, ali superlativ priloga nema uza se određeni član the.

Verbs – Glagoli

U engleskom jeziku u funkciji pomoćnoga glagola (glagola s pomoću kojeg se tvore složena vremena, niječni oblici, pitanja) mogu stajati glagoli **be** (biti), **have** (imati) i **do** (činiti). Budući da i sami pokazuju neke nepravilnosti, navodimo najprije njihove paradigme u jednostavnim vremenima. U zagradama su navedeni kraći, razgovorni oblici.

to be

Present Simple

Izjavni oblik	Niječni oblik
I am (I'm)	I am not (aren't)
you are (you're)	you are not (aren't)
he/she/it is (he's, she's,it's)	he/she/it is not (isn't)
we are (we're)	we are not (aren't)
you are (you're)	you are not (aren't)
they are (they're)	they are not (aren't)

Upitni oblik	Niječno-upitni oblik
am I?	am I not? (aren't I?)
are you?	are you not? (aren't you?)
is he/she/it?	is he/she/it not? (isn't he/she/it?)
are we?	are we not? (aren't we?)
are you?	are you not? (aren't you?)
are they?	are they not? (aren't they?)

Past Simple

Izjavni oblik	Niječni oblik
I was	I was not (wasn't)
you were	you were not (weren't)
he/she/itwas	he/she/it was not (wasn't)
we were	we were not (weren't)
you were	you were not (weren't)
they were	they were not (weren't)

Upitni oblik	Niječno-upitni oblik
was I?	was I not? (wasn't I?)
were you?	were you not? (weren't you?)
was he/she/it?	was he/she/it not? (wasn't he/she/it?)
were we?	were we not? (weren't we?)
were you?	were you not? (weren't you?)
were they?	were they not? (weren't they?)

to have

Present Simple

Izjavni oblik	Niječni oblik
I have (I've)	I have not (haven't)
you have (you've)	you have not (haven't)
he/she/it has (he's, she's, it's)	he/she/it has not (hasn't)
we have (we've)	we have not (haven't)
you have (you've)	you have not (haven't)
they have (they've)	they have not (haven't)

Upitni oblik	Niječno-upitni oblik
have I?	have I not? (haven't I?)
have you?	have you not? (haven't you?)
has he/she/it?	has he/she/it not? (hasn't he/she/it?)
have we?	have we not? (haven't we?)
have you?	have you not? (haven't you?)
have they?	have they not? (haven't they?)

Past Simple

Izjavni oblik		Niječni oblik	
I	(I'd)	I	
you	(you'd)	you	
he/she/it	(he'd)	he/she/it	
we	had (we'd)	we	had not (hadn't)
you	(you'd)	you	
they	(they'd)	they	

Upitni oblik		Niječno-upitni oblik		
	I?	had I not?		I?)
	you?	had you not?		you?)
	he/she/it?	had he/she/it not?	(hadn't	he/she/it?)
had	we	had we not?		we?)
	you?	had you not?		you?)
	they?	had they not?		they?)

to do

Present Simple

Izjavni oblik   Niječni oblik

I do   I do not (don't)
you do   you do not (don't)
he/she/it does   he/she/it does not (doesn't)
we do   we do not (don't)
you do   you do not (don't)
they do   they do not (don't)

Upitni oblik   Niječno-upitni oblik

do I?   do I not? (don't I?)
do you?   do you not? (don't you?)
does he/she/it?   does he/she/it not? (doesn't he/she/it?)
do we?   do we not? (don't we?)
do you?   do you not? (don't you?)
do they?   do they not? (don't they?)

Past Simple

Izjavni oblik   Niječni oblik

I   I
you   you
he/she/it   he/she/it
we   did   we   did not (didn't)
you   you
they   they

Upitni oblik   Niječno-upitni oblik

    I?   did I not?   I?)
    you?   did you not?   you?)
did he/she/it?   did he/she/it   (didn't   he/she/it?)
    we?   did we not?   we?)
    you?   did you not?   you?)
    they?   did they not?   they?)

Tvorba vremena

Jednostavna vremena

Present Simple

Tvori se od tzv. golog infinitiva (infinitiv bez riječce **to**). Nastavak, **-s**, poznaje jedino treće lice jednine:

I look	we look
you look	you look
he/she/it looks	they look

Za tvorbu upitnog, niječnog i niječno upitnog oblika rabi se Present Simple pomoćnoga glagola **to do**(→) i infinitivna osnova bez nastavka:

do I look?
does he/she/it look?

I do not (don't) look
he/she/it does not (doesn't) look

do I not look? (don't I look?)
does he/she/it not look? (doesn't he/she/it look?)

Past Simple

Za tvorbu ovog vremena na osnovu se kod pravilnih glagola dodaje nastavak **-ed** u svim licima:

I looked	we looked
you looked	you looked
he/she/it looked	he/she/it looked

Nepravilni glagoli rabe poseban oblik, naveden u tablici nepravilnih glagola (Irregular Verbs). Primjerice, glagol *leave*:

I left
he/she/it left

Upitni, niječni i niječno upitni oblici rabe Past Simple pomoćnoga glagola **to do** (→) i osnovu bez nastavka:

did I look?
did he/she/it look?

I did not (didn't) look
he/she/it did not (didn't) look

did I not look? (didn't I look?)
did he/she/it not look? (didn't he/she/it look?)

I didn't leave
did I leave?
did I not leave?

Složena vremena

Present Perfect

Kod pravilnih glagola ovo se vrijeme tvori od osnove na koju se dodaje nastavak **-ed** i pomoćnoga glagola **to have** (→) u prezentu:

I have (I've) looked   we have (we've) looked
you have (you've) looked   you have (you've) looked
he/she/it has (he's, she's, it's) looked   they have (they've) looked

Nepravilni glagoli rabe poseban oblik, naveden u tablici (→ Irregular Verbs). Primjerice, glagol *leave*:

I have left   I have not left   have I left?   have I not left?

Niječni se oblik tvori dodavanjem riječce **not** poslije pomoćnoga glagola:

I have not (haven't) looked
he/she/it has not (hasn't) looked

Upitni se oblik tvori s pomoću inverzije. Pomoćni glagol dolazi na prvo mjesto, pa subjekt, pa glagol (s nastavkom!):

have I looked?
has he/she/it looked?

I u niječno upitnom obliku glagol zadržava nastavak:

have I not looked? (haven't I looked?)
has he/she/it not looked? (hasn't he/she/it looked?)

Past Perfect

Ovo se vrijeme tvori jednako kao i Present Perfect, ali umjesto prezenta pomoćnoga glagola **to have** (→) rabi njegov Past Simple:

I had (I'd) looked   we had (we'd) looked
you had (you'd) looked   you had (you'd) looked
he/she/it had (he'd, she'd) looked   they had (they'd) looked

I had not (hadn't) looked
had I looked?   had I not (hadn't I) looked?

Present Progressive (Continuous)

Ovo složeno vrijeme tvori se prezentom pomoćnoga glagola **to be** (→) i glagolskom osnovom s nastavkom **-ing**:

I am (I'm) looking	we are (we're) looking
you are (you're) looking	you are (you're) looking
he/she/it is (he's, she's, it's) looking	they are (they're) looking

Upitni oblik dobiva se jednostavnom inverzijom. Glagol zadržava nastavak **-ing**:

am I looking?
are you looking?
is he/she/it looking?

Niječni oblik dodaje riječcu **not** pomoćnom glagolu:

I am not looking
you are not (aren't) looking
he/she/it is not (isn't) looking

Niječno upitni oblik:

am I not looking? (aren't I looking?)
are you not looking? (aren't you looking?)
is he/she/it not looking? (isn't he/she/it looking?)

Past Progressive (Continuous)

Ovo se vrijeme tvori na isti način kao i Present Progressive (→), ali umjesto prezenta pomoćnoga glagola **to be** rabimo njegov Past Simple (→ to be):

I was looking	was I looking?
I was not (wasn't) looking	was I not looking? (wasn't I looking?)
you were looking	were you looking?
you were not (weren't) looking	were you not looking? (weren't you looking?)

Future Tense

Buduće se vrijeme tvori s pomoću glagola **will (shall)** i infinitivne osnove bez nastavka:

I will (shall) look	we will (shall) look
you will look	you will look
he/she/it will look	he/she/it will look

Oblik **will** u prvom licu jednine i množine futura uglavnom je istisnuo stariji oblik **shall**. Shall u futuru još rabe (većinom stariji) govornici britanske varijante engleskog jezika i nekih dijalekata. Shall se još često čuje u pitanjima.

I/we will not (won't) look; I/we shall not (shan't) look *GB, arch*
you/he/she/it/they will not (won't) look

will (shall) I look?	will I not look? (Won't I look?)
shall I not look?	(Shan't I look?) GB
will you look?	will you not look? (won't you look?)

Conditional

Kondicional je glagolski oblik koji se tvori s pomoću glagola **would** (**should**) i infinitivne osnove bez nastavka:

I would (should) look	we would (should) look
you would look	you would look
he/she/it would look	they would look

Would je u prvom licu jednine i množine kondicionala gotovo potpuno istisnuo **should**, koji rabe još samo govornici (uglavnom stariji) britanskog engleskog i nekih dijalekata. U suvremenom engleskom, **should** se (u svim licima) rabi u značenju *trebati*.

Imperativ

Zapovjedni način tvori se od golog infinitiva (infinitiv bez riječce **to**) za drugo lice jednine i množine:

look!

U prvom i trećem licu rabi se riječ **let**. Zamjenica je u kosom padežu:

let me look	let us (let's) look
let him/her/it look	let them look

Niječni oblik:

do not (don't) look!
don't let me look
don't let us look (let's not look)
don't let him/her/it/them look

Modals – Modalni glagoli

Glagoli **can, could, will, would, shall, should, may, might, must, ought, need, dare** nazivaju se modalnim glagolima jer mijenjaju značenje glavnoga glagola uz koji se nalaze. U upotrebi je i stariji naziv *defektivni glagoli* jer svi oni (osim **need** i **dare**) nemaju pravi infinitiv ni sve glagolske oblike.
Glavni glagol dolazi u rečenici poslije modala, u obliku golog infinitiva (infinitiv bez riječce **to**):

I can look	we may look
you must look	you should look
he/she/it could look	they might look

Iznimka je **ought**, uz koji dolazi puni infinitiv glagola:

you ought to look

Niječni oblici:

cannot (can't)	may not (mayn't)
could not (couldn't)	might not (mightn't)
must not (mustn't)	will not (won't)
would not (wouldn't)	shall not (shan't)
should not (shouldn't)	ought not (oughtn't)
need not (needn't)	dare not (daren't)

Upitni oblici tvore se inverzijom:

can I look?	can I not look? (can't I look?)
must she look?	must she not look? (mustn't she look?)

¶ **Need** i **dare** mogu se upotrebljavati kao modali, ali i kao pravilni glagoli:

I need look	need I look?	I need not (needn't) look
I need to look	do I need to look?	I do not (don't) need to look

Numbers – Brojevi

Cardinal	Glavni	Ordinal	Redni
1 one	jedan	1st first	prvi
2 two	dva	2nd second	drugi
3 three	tri	3rd third	treći
4 four	četiri	4th fourth	četvrti
5 five	pet	5th fifth	peti
6 six	šest	6th sixth	šesti
7 seven	sedam	7th seventh	sedmi
8 eight	osam	8th eighth	osmi
9 nine	devet	9th ninth	deveti
10 ten	deset	10th tenth	deseti
11 eleven	jedanaest	11th eleventh	jedanaesti
12 twelve	dvanaest	12th twelfth	dvanaesti
13 thirteen	trinaest	13th thirteenth	trinaesti
14 fourteen	četrnaest	14th fourteenth	četrnaesti
15 fifteen	petnaest	15th fifteenth	petnaesti
16 sixteen	šesnaest	16th sixteenth	šesnaesti
17 seventeen	sedamnaest	17th seventeenth	sedamnaesti
18 eighteen	osamnaest	18th eighteenth	osamnaesti
19 nineteen	devetnaest	19th nineteenth	devetnaesti

20 twenty	dvadeset	20th twentieth	dvadeseti
21 twenty-one	dvadeset i jedan	21st twenty-first	dvadeset i prvi
22 twenty-two	dvadeset i dva	22nd twenty-second	dvadeset i drugi
23 twenty-three	dvadeset i tri	23rd twenty-third	dvadeset i treći

30 thirty	trideset	30th thirtieth	trideseti
40 forty	četrdeset	40th fortieth	četrdeseti
50 fifty	pedeset	50th fiftieth	pedeseti
60 sixty	šezdeset	60th sixtieth	šezdeseti
70 seventy	sedamdeset	70th seventieth	sedamdeseti
80 eighty	osamdeset	80th eightieth	osamdeseti
90 ninety	devedeset	90th ninetieth	devedeseti

100 one/a hundred	sto, stotina	100th one/a hundredth	stoti
200 two hundred	dvjesto, dvjesta, dvije stotine	200th two hundredth	dvjestoti

1 000 one/a thousand	tisuća	1 000th one/a thousandth	tisućiti
10 000 ten thousand	deset tisuća	10 000th ten thousandth	deset tisućiti
100 000 one/a hundred	sto tisuća	100 000th one/a hundred thousandth	sto tisućiti
1 000 000 one/a million	milijun	1 000 000th one/a millionth	milijunti

1 000 000 000	one/a thousand million; one/a billion *US*	milijarda
1 000 000 000 000	one/a billion; one/a trillion *US*	bilijun

Collective numbers

6	a half dozen, half a dozen	pola tuceta
12	a/one dozen	tucet
20	a/one score	dvadeset komada
144	a/one gross	gros, veliki tucet

Irregular verbs – Nepravilni glagoli

* označava da se oblik rabi samo iznimno

¶ Izvedeni glagoli imaju isti nepravilni oblik kao i osnovni
e.g. *become*   *became*   *become* → *come*
      understand *understood* *understood* → *stand*
      upset   *upset*   *upset* → *set*

Infinitive	Past Tense	Past Participle
abide	abided /ə'baɪdɪd/,	abided, *abode
/ə'baɪd/	*abode /ə'bəʊd/	
arise	arose	arisen
/ə'raɪz/	/ə'rəʊz/	/ə'rɪzn/
awake	awoke	awoken
/ə'weɪk/	/ə'wəʊk/	/ə'wəʊkən/
be	was /wɒz; wəz/,	been
/bɪ; biː/	were /wə(r); wɜː(r)/	/biːn; US bɪn/
bear	bore	borne
/beə(r)/	/bɔː(r)/	/bɔːn/
beat	beat	beaten
/biːt/		/biːtn/
begin	began	begun
/bɪ'gɪn/	/bɪ'gæn/	/bɪ'gʌn/
beseech	besought /bɪ'sɔːt/,	besought, beseeched
/bɪ'siːtʃ/	beseeched /bɪ'siːtʃt/	
bet	bet,	bet, betted
/bet/	betted /'betɪd/	
bid	bade /beɪd/,	bidden, *bid
/bɪd/	*bid	
bind	bound	bound
/baɪnd/	/baʊnd/	
bite	bit	bitten
/baɪt/	/bɪt/	/bɪtn/
bleed	bled	bled
/bliːd/	/bled/	
bless	blessed	blessed,
/bles/	/blest/	*blest
blow	blew	blown /bləʊn/,
/bləʊ/	/bluː/	*blowed /bləʊd/
break	broke	broken
/breɪk/	/brəʊk/	/'brəʊkən/
breed	bred	bred
/briːd/	/bred/	
bring	brought	brought
/brɪŋ/	/brɔːt/	
build	built	built
/bɪld/	/bɪlt/	

burn /bɜ:n/	burnt /bɜ:nt/, burned /bɜ:nd/	burnt, burned
burst /bɜ:st/	burst	burst
bust /bʌst/	bust /bʌst/, busted /bʌstɪd/	bust, busted
buy /baɪ/	bought /bɔ:t/	bought
cast /kɑ:st; US kæst/	cast	cast
catch /kætʃ/	caught /kɔ:t/	caught
chide /tʃaɪd/	chided /ˈtʃaɪdɪd/, chid /tʃɪd/	chided, chid, chidden /ˈtʃɪdn/
choose /tʃu:z/	chose /tʃəʊz/	chosen /ˈtʃəʊzn/
cleave /kli:v/	cleaved /kli:vd/, clove/kləʊv/, cleft /kleft/	cleaved, cloven /ˈkləʊvn/, cleft
cling /klɪŋ/	clung /klʌŋ/	clung
come /kʌm/	came /keɪm/	come /kʌm/
cost /kɒst/	cost	cost
creep /kri:p/	crept /krept/	crept
crow /krəʊ/	crowed /krəʊd/, arch crew /kru:/	crowed
cut /kʌt/	cut	cut
deal /di:l/	dealt /delt/	dealt
dig /dɪg/	dug /dʌg/	dug
dive /daɪv/	dived /daɪvd/, US dove /dəʊv/	dived
do /du:/	did /dɪd/	done /dʌn/
draw /drɔ:/	drew /dru:/	drawn /drɔ:n/
dream /dri:m/	dreamt /dremt/, dreamed /dri:md/	dreamt, dreamed
drink /drɪŋk/	drank /dræŋk/	drunk /drʌŋk/
drive /draɪv/	drove /drəʊv/	driven /ˈdrɪvn/
dwell /dwel/	dwelt /dwelt/	dwelt

eat	ate	eaten
/iːt/	/et; US eɪt/	/ˈiːtn/
fall	fell	fallen
/fɔːl/	/fel/	/ˈfɔːlən/
feed	fed	fed
/fiːd/	/fed/	
feel	felt	felt
/fiːl/	/felt/	
fight	fought	fought
/faɪt/	/fɔːt/	
find	found	found
/faɪnd/	/faʊnd/	
flee	fled	fled
/fliː/	/fled/	
fling	flung	flung
/flɪŋ/	/flʌŋ/	
fly	flew	flown
/flaɪ/	/fluː/	/fləʊn/
forecast	forecast,	forecast,
ˈfɔːkɑːst;	forecasted	forecasted
US -kæst/	/ˈfɔːkɑːstɪd/	
forget	forgot	forgotten
/fəˈget/	/fəˈgɒt/	/fəˈgɒtn/
forsake	forsook	forsaken
/fəˈseɪk/	/fəˈsʊk/	/fəˈseɪkən/
freeze	froze	frozen
/friːz/	/frəʊz/	/ˈfrəʊzn/
get	got	got,
/get/	/gɒt/	US gotten /ˈgɒtn/
gird	girded /ˈgɜːdɪd/,	girded, girt
/gɜːd/	girt /gɜːt/	
give	gave	given
/gɪv/	/geɪv/	/ˈgɪvn/
go	went	gone
/gəʊ/	/went/	/gɒn; US gɔːn/
grin	ground	ground
/graɪnd/	/graʊnd/	
hang	hung /hʌŋ/,	hung, *hanged
/hæŋ/	*hanged /hæŋd/,	
have	had	had
/hæv; həv/	/hæd/	
hear	heard	heard
/hɪə(r)/	/hɜːd/	
heave	heaved /hiːvd,/,	heaved, hove
/hiːv/	hove /həʊv/	
hew	hewed	hewed,
/hjuː/	/hjuːd/	hewn /hjuːn/

hide	hid	hidden
/haɪd/	/hɪd/	/'hɪdn/
hit	hit	hit
/hɪt/		
hold	held	held
/həʊld/	/held/	
hurt	hurt	hurt
/hɜːt/		
input	input,	input, inputted
/'ɪnpʊt/	inputted /'ɪnpʊtɪd/	
keep	kept	kept
/kiːp/	/kept/	
kneel	knelt /nelt/,	knelt,
/niːl/	US kneeled /niːld/	US kneeled
knit	knitted /'nɪtɪd/,	knitted,
/nɪt/	*knit	*knit
know	knew	known
/nəʊ/	/njuː; US nuː/	/nəʊn/
lay	laid	laid
/leɪ/	/leɪd/	
lead	led	led
/liːd/	/led/	
lean	leant /lent/,	leant, leaned
/liːn/	leaned /liːnd/	
leap	leapt /lept/,	leapt, leaped
/liːp/	leaped /liːpt/	
learn	learnt /lɜːnt/,	learnt,
/lɜːn/	learned /lɜːnd/	learned
leave	left	left
/liːv/	/left/	
lend	lent	lent
/lend/	/lent/	
let	let	let
/let/		
lie (2)	lay	lain
/laɪ/	/leɪ/	/leɪn/
light	lit /lɪt/,	lit, *lighted
/laɪt/	*lighted /'laɪtɪd/	
lose	lost	lost
/luːz/	/lɒst/	
make	made	made
/meɪk/	/meɪd/	
mean	meant	meant
/miːn/	/ment/	
meet	met	met
/miːt/	/met/	
mow	mowed	mown /məʊn/,
/məʊ/	/məʊd/	mowed

output /ˈaʊtpʊt/	output, outputted /ˈaʊtpʊtɪd/	output, outputted
pay /peɪ/	paid /peɪd/	paid
plead /pliːd/	pleaded /ˈpliːdɪd/, US pled /pled/	pleaded, US pled
prove /pruːv/	proved /pruːvd/	proved, US proven /ˈpruːvn/
put /pʊt/	put	put
quit /kwɪt/	quit, quitted /ˈkwɪtɪd/	quit, quitted
read /riːd/	read /red/	read /red/
rid /rɪd/	rid	rid
ride /raɪd/	rode /rəʊd/	ridden /ˈrɪdn/
ring /rɪŋ/	rang /ræŋ/	rung /rʌŋ/
rise /raɪz/	rose /rəʊz/	risen /ˈrɪzn/
run /rʌn/	ran /ræn/	run /rʌn/
saw /sɔː/	sawed /sɔːd/	sawn /sɔːn/, US sawed
say /seɪ/	said /sed/	said
see /siː/	saw /sɔː/	seen /siːn/
seek /siːk/	sought /sɔːt/	sought
sell /sel/	sold /səʊld/	sold
send /send/	sent /sent/	sent
set /set/	set	set
sew /səʊ/	sewed /səʊd/	sewn /səʊn/, sewed
shake /ʃeɪk/	shook /ʃʊk/	shaken /ˈʃeɪkən/
shear /ʃɪə(r)/	sheared /ʃɪəd/	shorn /ʃɔːn/, sheared
shed /ʃed/	shed	shed

shine /ʃaɪn/	shone /ʃɒn; US ʃoʊn/, *shined /ʃaɪnd/	shone, *shined
shit /ʃɪt/	shit, shitted /ʃɪtɪd/, shat /ʃæt/	shit, shitted shat
shoe /ʃuː/	shod /ʃɒd/	shod
shoot /ʃuːt/	shot /ʃɒt/	shot
show /ʃoʊ/	showed /ʃoʊd/	shown /ʃoʊn/, showed
shrink /ʃrɪŋk/	shrank /ʃræŋk/, shrunk /ʃrʌŋk/	shrunk
shut /ʃʌt/	shut	shut
sing /sɪŋ/	sang /sæŋ/	sung /sʌŋ/
sink /sɪŋk/	sank /sæŋk/	sunk /sʌŋk/
sit /sɪt/	sat /sæt/	sat
slay /sleɪ/	slew /sluː/	slain /sleɪn/
sleep /sliːp/	slept /slept/	slept
slide /slaɪd/	slid /slɪd/	slid
sling /slɪŋ/	slung /slʌŋ/	slung
slink /slɪŋk/	slunk /slʌŋk/	slunk
slit /slɪt/	slit	slit
smell /smel/	smelt /smelt/, smelled /smeld/	smelt, smelled
smite /smaɪt/	smote /smoʊt/	smitten /'smɪtɪn/
sow /soʊ/	sowed /soʊd/	sown /soʊn/, sowed
speak /spiːk/	spoke /spoʊk/	spoken /'spoʊkən/
speed /spiːd/	sped /sped/, *speeded /'spiːdɪd/	sped, *speeded
spell /spel/	spelt /spelt/, spelled /speld/	spelt, spelled
spend /spend/	spent /spent/	spent
spill /spɪl/	spilt /spɪlt/, spilled /spɪld/	spilt, spilled
spin /spɪn/	spun /spʌn/, *arch* span /spæn/	spun

spit /spɪt/	spat /spæt/, US spit	spat, US spit
split /splɪt/	split	split
spoil /spɔɪl/	spoilt /spɔɪlt/, spoiled /spɔɪld/	spoilt, spoiled
spread /spred/	spread	spread
spring /sprɪŋ/	sprang /spræŋ/	sprung /sprʌŋ/
stand /stænd/	stood /stʊd/	stood
stave /steɪv/	staved /steɪvd/, *stove /stəʊv/	staved, *stove
steal /sti:l/	stole /stəʊl/	stolen /ˈstəʊlən/
stick /stɪk/	stuck /stʌk/	stuck
sting /stɪŋ/	stung /stʌŋ/	stung
stink /stɪŋk/	stank /stæŋk/, stunk /stʌŋk/	stunk
strew /stru:/	strewed /stru:d/	strewn /stru:n/, strewed
stride /straɪd/	strode /strəʊd/	stridden /ˈstrɪdn/
strike /straɪk/	struck /strʌk/	struck
string /strɪŋ/	strung /strʌŋ/	strung
strive /straɪv/	strove /strəʊv/	striven /ˈstrɪvn/
swear /sweə(r)/	swore /swɔ:(r)/	sworn /swɔ:n/
sweep /swi:p/	swept /swept/	swept
swell /swel/	swelled /sweld/	swollen /ˈswəʊlən/, swelled
swim /swɪm/	swam /swæm/	swum /swʌm/
swing /swɪŋ/	swung /swʌŋ/	swung
take /teɪk/	took /tʊk/	taken /ˈteɪkən/
teach /ti:tʃ/	taught /tɔ:t/	taught
tear /teə(r)/	tore /tɔ:(r)/	torn /tɔ:n/

tell	told	told
/tel/	/təʊld/	
think	thought	thought
/θɪŋk/	/θɔ:t/	.
thrive,	thrived /θraɪvd/,	thrived,
/θraɪv/	throve /θrəʊv/	*arch* thriven
		/ˈθrɪvn/
throw	threw	thrown
/θrəʊ/	/θru:/	/θrəʊn/
thrust /θrʌst/	thrust	thrust
/θrʌst/		
tread	trod	trodden /ˈtrɒdn/,
/tred/	/trɒd/	trod
wake	woke /wəʊk/,	woken /ˈwəʊkən/,
/weɪk/	*arch* waked /weɪkt/	*arch* waked
wear	wore	worn
/weə(r)/	/wɔ:(r)/	/wɔ:n/
weave	wove /wəʊv/,	woven /ˈwəʊvn/,
/wi:v/	*weaved /wi:vd/	*weaved
wed	wedded /ˈwedɪd/,	wedded, wed
/wed/	wed	
weep	wept	wept
/wi:p/	/wept/	
wet	wet,	wet, wetted
/wet/	wetted /ˈwetɪd/	
win	won	won
/wɪn/	/wʌn/	
wind (3)	wound	wound
/waɪnd/	/waʊnd/	
work	worked /wɜ:kt/,	worked, *wrought
/wɜ:k/	*wrought /rɔ:t/	
wring	wrung	wrung
/rɪŋ/	/rʌŋ/	
write	wrote	written
/raɪt/	/rəʊt/	/ˈrɪtn/

Word formation – Tvorba riječi

Adjective formation
Tvorba pridjeva

Noun + ending
Imenica + nastavak

-able	comfort - comfortable	udoban
	reason - reasonable	razuman

-al	coast - coastal	obalni
	crime - criminal	zločinački
-ful	beauty - beautiful	lijep
	colour - colourful	živopisan
-ic, -ical	geography - geographical	zemljopisni
	period - periodic	periodičan
	poetry - poetic	pjesnički
	satire - satirical	satirički
-ish	child - childish	djetinjast
	fool - foolish	budalast
-less	hope - hopeless	beznadan
	pain - painless	bezbolan
-ous	danger - dangerous	opasan
	space - spaceous	prostran
-y	dirt - dirty	prljav
	luck - lucky	sretan

Verb + ending
Glagol + nastavak

-able	cure - curable	izlječiv
	pay - payable	plativ
-ative	decorate - decorative	ukrasni
	talk - talkative	razgovorljiv
-ed	excite - excited	uzbuđen
	interest - interested	zainteresiran
-ing	excite - exciting	uzbudljiv
	interest - interesting	zanimljiv

Adjectiv + ending
Pridjev + nastavak

-ish	big - biggish	ovelik
	blue - bluish	plavičast
-most	southern - southernmost	najjužniji
	top - topmost	najviši

Adverbe formation
Tvorba priloga

Adjective + ending
Pridjev + nastavak

-ly	busy - busily	marljivo
	quick - quickly	brzo
	true - truly	istinski
	unbelievable - unbelievably	nevjerojatno

Noun formation
Tvorba imenica

Verb + ending
Glagol + nastavak

-al	deny - denial	poricanje
	refuse - refusal	odbijanje
-ance, -ence	appear - appearance	pojava
	perform - performance	izvedba
	exist - existence	postojanje
-ation, -ion, -tion	combine - combination	spajanje, spoj
	elect - electio	izbor
	object - objection	prigovor
-ee	employ - employee	namještenik
	escape - escapee	bjegunac
-er	dance - dancer	plesač(ica)
	dry - drier	sušilo
	work - worker	radnik, radnica
-ing	dance - dancing	ples(anje)
	meet - meeting	sastanak
	run - running	trčanje
-ment	develop - development	razvoj
	enjoy - enjoyment	užitak
	treat - treatment	postupanje
-or	act - actor	glumac
	invent - inventor	izumitelj
	visit - visitor	posjetitelj

Adjective + ending
Pridjev + nastavak

-ity, -ty	regular - regularity	pravilnost
	certain - certainty	izvjesnost
-ness	great - greatness	veličina
	happy - happiness	sreća
	kind - kindness	ljubaznost
	meaningless - meaninglessness	besmislenost

Noun + ending
Imenica + nastavak

-ist	biology - biologist	biolog
	guitar - guitarist	gitarist
	linguistics - linguist	jezikoslovac, lingvist
	novel - novelist	romanopisac

Verb formation
Tvorba glagola

Adjective + ending
Pridjev + nastavak

-en	dark - darken	zamračiti
	tight - tighten	stegnuti
-ify	intense - intensify	pojačati
	simple - simplify	pojednostaviti
-ize, -ise	legal - legalize, legalise	ozakoniti
	modern - modernize, modernise	modernizirati

Noun + ending
Imenica + nastavak

| -ize, -ise | hospital - hospitalize, hospitalise | smjestiti u bolnicu |
| | television - televise | prenositi na televiziji |

**HRVATSKO – ENGLESKI
RJEČNIK**

**CROATIAN – ENGLISH
DICTIONARY**

A

A, a 1st letter of Cro. alphabet; a • *conj* and, but
abdicirati *v* (0) abdicate
abeced|a *nf* alphabet **~ni** *adj* alphabetic(al)
abnormalan (*α*) *adj* abnormal
abolicija *nf* 1 abolition 2 amnesty
abonent *nm* subscriber
abortus *nm* abortion **napraviti ~** have an a.
Adam *nm* Adam **~ova jabučica** Adam's apple
adapt|acija *nf* 1 adaptation 2 adjustment **~irati** *v* 1 (koga/što/se) adapt, modify, adjust (sth/sb/oneself) 2 redo (stan)
adekvatan (*α*) *adj* adequate
administra|cija *nf* 1 administration 2 office 3 *fig* clerical/paper work **~tivan** (*α*) *adj* administrative, clerical **~tor** *nm* administrator, manager
admiral *nm* admiral **~ski** *adj* admiral's **~ski brod** flag ship
adres|a *nf* address **nova ~a** forwarding a. **popis ~a** mailing list **ići na čiju ~u** *fig* be aimed at sb **obratiti se na krivu/pravu ~u** *fig* go to/get the wrong/right person **~ar** *nm* address book **~irati** *v* (što na koga) address sth to sb
adut *nm* trump(card) **glavni ~** 1 ace card 2 *fig* main asset
advokat → **odvjetnik**
aerodinami|ka *nf* aerodynamics **~čan** (*α*) *adj* streamlined **~čnost** *nf* good aerodynamic design
aerodrom *nm* airport
afekt *nm* fit of passion/rage **~irati** *v* (0) put on airs **~iran** *adj* affected, blasé
afera *nf* scandal
afinitet *nm* affinity **imati ~a za** be interested in, show inclination to

afirm|acija *nf* recognition **~irati** *v* (se) prove one's worth, earn recognition
ag|a *nm* agha
agen|cija *nf* agency **~t** *nm* agent
agit|acija *nf* agitation, canvassing (for) **~ator** *nm* agitator, canvasser **~irati** *v* (0/za koga/za što) agitate, canvass
agonija *nf* agony, (last) throes
agrar|an (*α*) *adj* agrarian **~na reforma** land reform
agregat *nm* power generator **~no** *adj* **stanje** physical condition, state
agres|ija *nf* (na) aggression (against) **izvršiti ~iju** invade, attack **~ivan** *adj* (*α*) aggressive **~or** *nm* aggressor, invader
agronom *nm* agronomist **~ija** *nf* agronomy
Ahil *nm* Achilles **~ova peta** Achilles' heel (+ *fig*)
ajme *intr* my goodness
ajvar *nm* hot paprika sauce
akadem|ija *nf* 1 academy 2 commemoration, gala **umjetnička ~ija** a. of arts **~ija znanosti i umjetnosti** a. of arts and sciences **pedagoška ~ija** teacher(s') training college **vojna ~ija** military a. **~ik** (*Npl* **~ici**) *nm* academician **~ski** *adj* academic **~ski građanin** university student/graduate
akcent *nm* accent, stress (+ *fig*)
akcept|irati *v* (što) *com* accept, honor **~ni** *adj* **nalog** acceptance order
akcija *nf* 1 action 2 campaign 3 → **dionica**
aklimatizirati *v* (koga/se na što) acclimatize (sb/oneself to), get acclimatized
ako *conj* if
akontacija *nf* advance (payment)
akord *nm* chord
akrediti|v *nm* 1 *com* letter of credit 2

credentials *pl* ~**ran** *adj* accredited

akroba|cija *nf* acrobatics ~**t** *nm* acrobat ~**tski** *adj* acrobatic

akt *nm* 1 act 2 document 3 nude ~**ovka** *nf coll* briefcase, attache case

aktiva *nf* assets

aktiv|an (*a*) *adj* 1 active 2 on active service 3 engaged in ~**irati** 1 (koga/što) activate; (bombu) detonate, set off 2 (se) become active, engage in ~**ist** *nm* activist ~ **nost** *nf* activity

aktual|an (*a*) *adj* current, topical, relevant ¶ actual ~**nost** *nf* relevance

akumula|tor *nm* accumulator *GB*, battery *US* ~**cijsko** *adj* **jezero** storage lake

akusti|čan (*œ*) *adj* acoustic; (glazba) unplugged ~**ka** *nf* (*Dsg* ~ci) acoustics

akutan (*a*) *adj* acute

akvarel *nm* 1 (tehnika) water colours 2 (slika) water colour

akvarij *nm* aquarium

akviziter *nm* salesman

alarm *nm* alarm ~**antan** (*a*) *adj* alarming ~**irati** *v* (koga/što) alert

alat *nm* tool(s)

album *nm* album

alegori|čan (*a*) *adj* allegoric(al) ~**ja** *nf* allegory

aleja *nf* avenue; lane

alga *nf* seaweed, alga

ali *conj* but; however

alimentacija *nf* alimony

alka *nf* 1 ring **Sinjska** ~ jousting tournament in Sinj ~**r** *nm* lancer from Sinj 2 (na vratima) knocker

alkemija *nf* alchemy (+ *fig*)

alko|hol *nm* alcohol ~**holni** *adj* alcoholic ~**holičar** *nm* alcoholic ~**test** *nm* alcoholic ~**holni** breath test, breathalyser

alp|inist *nm* alpinist, mountaineer ~**ski** *adj* alpine, mountain

alternativa *nf* alternative ~**n** (*a*) *adj* alternative

alu|dirati *v* (na što) allude to, hint at ~**zija** *nf* allusion, hint

aluminij *nm* aluminium; aluminum *US*

alva → **halva**

amandman *nm* amendment

amater *nm* amateur ~**ski** *adj* 1 amateur

2 *derog* amateurish

ambalaža *nf* packaging

ambasada, ambasador → **veleposlanstvo**

ambici|ja *nf* ambition ~**ozan** *adj* (*a*) ambitious

ambijent *nm* surroundings, environment, ambiance, atmosphere

ambulant|a *nf* clinic **pacijent** ~**e** outpatient

amen *nm* amen

amnesti|ja *nf* amnesty ~**rati** *v* (koga) give/extend ~ to

amonijak *nm* ammonia

amortiz|acija *nf* 1 (zajma) amortization 2 depreciation ~**irati** *v* (dug) amortize ~**acijski** *adj* **fond** sinking fund

ampula *nf* vial, ampoule

amput|acija *nf* amputation ~**irati** *v* (što) amputate (+ *fig*)

analfabet *nm* 1 illiterate person 2 *fig* ignoramus

analgetik *nm* analgesic, painkiller

analiz|a *nf* analysis ~**irati** *v* (koga/što) analyse

analog|ija *nf* analogy **po** ~**iji** by analogy ~**an** *adj* (*a*) 1 (čemu) analogous with 2 analog(ue)

ananas *nm* pineapple

anarhija *nf* anarchy

anatomija *nf* anatomy

anđe|o *nm* (*Gsg* ~la) angel ~**o čuvar** guardian angel ~**oski** *adj* angelic(al); celestial *fig*

anegdota *nf* anecdote

anemi|ja *nf* an(a)emia ~**čan** *adj* (*a*) an(a)emic (+ *fig*); lifeless *fig*

anestezija *nf* an(a)estesia

angaž|irati *v* 1 (koga za što) engage sb for/in sth, employ in, commission sb to do sth 2 (se u čemu) become involved 3 (se za koga) intercede for, speak in sb's favour, do sb a favour ~**man** *nm* 1 involvement 2 contract

angina *nf* tonsilitis

animir|ati *v* (koga za što) animate, rouse sb's interest ~~**dama** *nf coll* bar girl ~**ani** *adj* **film** animated film

anket|a *nf* opinion poll/survey **provoditi** ~**u**/~**irati** *v* (koga o čemu) conduct an opinion poll ~**ni** *adj* **listić**

questionnaire

anomalija *nf* anomaly

anoniman *adj* (*a*) anonymous

anorganski *adj* inorganic

ansambl *nm* combo, band, ensemble

antena *nf* antenna *US*, aerial *GB* **satelitska ~** (satellite) dish

anti|čki *adj* of classical antiquity, classical **~ka** *nf* classical antiquity

antifašizam *nm* anti-Fascism

antikvarijat *nm* 1 antique shop 2 secondhand bookshop

antipati|čan *adj* (*a*) unpleasant, offensive **~čan mi je** I can't stand him, I don't like him **~ja** *nf* animosity, dislike, antipathy

antiteza *nf* (čemu) antithesis of

antilop *nm coll* suede **od ~a** suede

antilopa *nf* antelope

antologij|a *nf* anthology **~ski** *adj* unforgettable, historic

antracit *nm* anthracite **boje ~a/~ni** *adj* charcoal

anuitet *nm* annuity

anulirati *v* (što) annul, cancel

apanaža *nf* 1 civil list 2 allowance

aparat *nm* 1 device 2 appliance 3 *fig* apparatus **~ura** *nf* equipment, machinery

apartman *nm* suite, apartment

apati|čan *adj* (*a*) apathetic **~ja** *nf* apathy

apciha *int* atishoo

apel *nm* (za) an appeal/plea (for) **~irati** *v* (na koga) make an appeal to sb, entreat sb

apetit *nm* appetite

aplauz *nm* applause

apoen *nm* **u ~ima od** in denominations of

apokalipsa *nf* apocalypse

apokrifan *adj* (*a*) apocryphal

apostol *nm* apostle **~ski** *adj* apostolic

apostrof *nm* apostrophe

apoteka *nf* chemist's, pharmacy; drugstore *US* **~r** *nm* pharmacist, chemist **~rska mjera** apothecaries' weight

apsolut|an *adj* (*a*) absolute **~izam** *nm* absolutism **~no** *adv* absolutely, completely

apsolv|ent *nm* student who has completed his course of studies, student who has to pass his final exams **~irati** *v* (što) finish, complete

apsorbirati *v* (što) absorb

apstin|ent *nm* abstainer, tee-totaller **~irati** *v* (0, od) abstain (from)

apstra|hirati *v* (što) abstract **~kcija** *nf* abstraction, abstract idea **~ktan** *adj* (*a*) abstract

apsurd *nm* absurdity **~an** *adj* (*a*) absurd

arak *nm* sheet (of paper)

aranž|irati *v* (što) arrange, set up **~man** *nm* arrangement **paket ~man** package tour

arbitraža *nf* arbitration

arena *nf* arena

argument *nm* argument, point, reason **~acija** *nf* argumentation **~iran** *adj* well-argumented, reasonable **~irati** *v* (što) make (out) a case (for/against)

arhaičan *adj* (*a*) archaic

arheolo|g *nm* archeologist **~gija** *nf* archeology **~ški** *adj* archeological **~ško nalazište** archeological site

archipelag *nm* archipelago

arhitekt *nm* architect **~ura** *nf* architecture **~onski** *adj* architectural

arhiv *nm* archives, records office

arija *nf* air, tune

aristokracija *nf* aristocracy

aritmeti|čki *adj* arithmetical **~ka** *nf* arithmetic

arkanđe|o *nm* (*Gsg* ~la) archangel

armija *nf* army

armirani *adj* **~ beton** reinforced concrete, ferro-concrete

arogantan *adj* (*a*) arrogant

aroma *nf* aroma, flavour **~tičan** *adj* (*a*) aromatic, fragrant

arsen *nf* arsenic

arsenal *nm* arsenal (+ *fig*)

arterija *nf* artery

arteški *adj* **~ bunar** artesian well

artikl *nm* article, item

artikul|acija *nf* articulation **~iran** *adj* articulate, well-spoken

artiljerija *nf* → **topništvo**

artist *nm* artiste

as *nm* 1 ace **~ u rukavu** ace in the hole, ace up one's sleeve 2 ace, champion

asfalt *nm* 1 asphalt 2 tarmac **~iran** *adj* tarmac **~irati** *v* (što) tarmac

asimetričan *adj* (a) asymmetric(al)

asimil|acija *nf* assimilation **~irati** (što) assimilate

asistent *nm* 1 assistant 2 (na fakultetu) assistant lecturer

asket *nm* ascetic

asoci|jacija *nf* association **~rati** *v* 1 (što s čime) associate with 2 (koga na što) remind sb of sth

asocijalan *adj* (a) asocial

aspekt *nm* aspect

astma *nf* asthma **~tičan** *adj* (a) asthmatic

astronom *nm* astronomer **~ija** *nf* astronomy **~ski** *adj* astronomical

ataše *nm* attache **~ za tisak** press a. **vojni/kulturni ~** military/cultural a.

ateist *nm* atheist

atelje *nm* studio

atentat *nm* assassination **izvršiti ~ na koga** assassinate sb **~or** *nm* assassin

atest *nm* certificate, attest

atlas *nm* atlas

atlet *nm* athlete, sportsman **~ičar** *nm* (track and field) athlete **~ika** *nf* athletics **dvoranska ~ika** indoor a. **laka ~ika** track and field events **teška ~ika** boxing, wrestling, weightlifting **~ski** *adj* athletic

atmosfer|a *nf* atmosphere **~ske** *adj* **smetnje** *nf pl* atmospherics

atom *nm* atom **~ski** *adj* atomic, nuclear

atrak|cija *nf* attraction, sight **~tivan** *adj* (a) attractive, handsome

atribu|t *nm* attribute **~cija** *nf* attribution

audici|ja *nf* audition **ići na ~u za (ulogu)** audition for (the role of), be auditioned for

audijenci|ja *nf* audience **biti u ~i kod** have an a. with **tražiti ~u** seek an a. **dobiti ~u** be granted an a., be received

aula *nf* hall

aureola *nf* halo

auspuh *nm* *coll* exhaust (pipe); tail pipe *US*

Austro-Ugarska *nf* Austria-Hungary **austrougarski** *adj* Austro-Hun-garian

aut *nm* *sport* out

autentič|an *adj* (a) authentic, genuine **~nost** *nf* authenticity **dokazati ~nost čega** authenticate

auto *nm* *coll* car **~bus** *nm* 1 bus 2 (na međugradskim linijama) coach 3 (na kat) doubledecker **ići ~busom** go by bus, take a/the bus to **~busni** *adj* **kolodvor** *nm* bus/coach station **~busna stanica** bus stop **~cesta** *nf*/**~put** *nm* motorway *GB*; express-way; (s naplatom cestarine) turnpike, (besplatna) freeway *US* **~mobil** *nm* car, automobile **~mobilistički** *adj* car racing **~mobilska** *adj* **industrija** car/automobile industry **~limar** (car) body mechanic **~limarska radioni-ca** *nf* body shop **~mehaničar** (garage/car) mechanic **~mehani-čarska radionica** garage, repair shop, service station **~prijevoznik** *nm* haulier *GB*, hauler *US*, (za selidbe) removals **~stopirati** *v* (0) hitchhike **~stoper** *nm* hitchhiker

auto- *prefix* auto-, self-

autobiografija *nf* autobiography

autogen *adj* **~o zavarivanje** autoge-nous welding

autogol *nm* *sport* own goal

autogram *nm* autograph

autohton *adj* native, indigenous

automat *nm* 1 vending machine, dis-penser, (za igre na sreću) gambling machine 2 *fig* automaton 3 subma-chine gun **~izirati** *v* (što) automate, automatize **~ski** *adj* automatic, un-conscious **~ski** *adv* 1 automatically, mechanically 2 routinely

autonom|ija *nf* autonomy, home rule **~an** *adj* (a) autonomous **~ni živčani sustav** autonomic nervous system **~aštvo** *nn* home rule movement **~aš** *nm* advocate of home rule

autoportret *nm* self-portrait

autopsija *nf* post mortem, autopsy

autor *nm* author **~izirati** *v* (što) autho-rize, approve, sign **~ski** *adj* authorial **~sko pravo** copyright **odstupiti ~ska prava** sell c. **prihodi od ~skih prava** royalties **~stvo** *nn* authorship

autorit|et *nm* 1 (za) authority (on), ex-

pert (in, for) **2** authority, power
imati ~eta have/wield a. **~aran** *adj*
(*a*) authoritarian **~ativan** *adj* (*a*) authoritative

avangard|a *nf* **1** avant-guarde, under-
ground **2** *pol* vanguard **~ni** *adj* avant-
garde

avantura *nf* adventure **ljubavna ~**
(love) affair, (kratka) one-night stand
→ **pustolovina**

avenija *nf* avenue, boulevard

averzija *nf* aversion, dislike

avijacij|a *nf* aviation **poljoprivredna
~a** agricultural a. **podrška ~e** *mil* air
support/cover → **zrakoplovstvo**

avion *nm* airplane; plane *coll* **~ski** *adv*
by air(mail) → **zrakoplov**

a vista *adj, adv com* at sight **~ mjenica** sight bill

avizo *nm* letter of advice

azbest *nm* asbestos

Azija *nf* Asia **Mala ~** A. Minor
Jugoistočna ~ South-East A.

azil *nm* asylum **zatražiti politički ~**
seek political a. **~ant** *nm* political
refugee, asylum seeker

azur *nm* azure **~an** *adj* (*a*) azure, sky-
blue

ažur|an *adj* (*a*) up-to-date, prompt
~irati bring up to date, update

B

B, b (be) 2nd letter of Cro. alphabet **nije rekao ni a ni be** he didn't say a word

bab|a *nf* **1** old woman **2** grandmother **3** *derog* old bat **4** *derog* sissy **trla ~a lan da joj prođe dan** *prov* idle talk **~aroga** *nf* bogey(man) **~lji** *adj* old women's **~lje ljeto** Indian summer

babica *nf* midwife

babilonsk|i *adj* **kula ~a** the tower of Babel

babinje *nf pl* puerperium

bac|ač *nm* thrower **~ač plamena** *mil* flame thrower **raketni ~ač** rocket launcher **~anje** *nn* throw **slobodno ~anje** free throw **imati čega na ~anje** have plenty of sth **~ati** *v impf* → **baciti ~ati klipove pod noge** put a spoke in sb's wheel **~iti** *v* **1** (što) throw, cast, fling; (odbaciti) throw away, discard, dump **~iti pismo** post/mail a letter **~iti bombu** drop a bomb **~iti na tržište** launch **2** (se) throw/fling oneself **~iti se na** pounce on **~iti se na posao** get to work

bacil *nm* baccilus; germ, bug *coll*

bačv|a *nf* barrel, cask, keg

badem *nm* almond

Badnj|ak *nm* Christmas Eve **~a** *adj* **večer** Christmas Eve

bagatela *nf coll* dirt cheap *adj*, *adv*

bager *nm* dredge(r), excavator

bagra *nf derog* gang, rabble

bagrem *nm* locust(tree)

bahat *adj* arrogant

bajka (*Gsg* ~ci) *nf* **1** fairy-tale **2** *fig* fable, a pack of lies

bajuneta *nf mil* bayonet

baka *nf* grandmother, granny, grandma

bakalar *nm* cod(fish)

bakandža *nf* hob-nailed/heavy boot

bak|ar *nm* (*Gsg* ~ra) copper **~ren** *adj* copper; (kosa) auburn **~renjak** *nm* (*Npl* ~renjaci) copper **~ropis** *nm* etching **~rorez** *nm* copperplate

baklja *nf* torch

bakterija *nf* bacterium; germ *coll*

bal *nm* ball, dance **kad je ~ nek je ~** *coll* in for a penny in for a pound

bala *nf* bale, pack; (tkanine) bolt

balada *nf* ballad

balast *nm* ballast (+ *fig*); liability *fig*

bal|av *adj* **1** snotty **2** *fig* young, green **~avac** *nm* (*Gsg* ~avca, *Vsg* ~avče, *Npl* ~ci) brat **~avica** *nf* chit **~e** *nf pl* snot

balčak *nm* hilt

baldahin *nm* canopy **krevet s ~om** four-poster bed

balega *nf* dung **~r** *nm* dung-beetle

bale|rina *nf* ballet-dancer **~rinke** *nf pl* pumps **~t** *nm* ballet **~tan** *nm* (male) ballet-dancer **~tna** *adj* **suknjica** tutu

balkon *nm* balcony; (kazalište) dress circle

balon *nm* **1** balloon, hot-air b. **2** *coll* (alkotest) breathalyser **~er/~ac** (*Gsg* ~ca) raincoat

balvan *nm* (large) log

balzamirati *v* (koga, što) embalm

bambus *nm* bamboo

ban *nm* (u Hrvatskoj) governor, ban

banal|an *adj* (*α*) banal, commonplace **~nost** *nf* **1** banality **2** platitude

banan|a *nf* banana **kora ~e** b. skin

bančiti *v* (0) go on a binge

band|a *nf* gang, band **~it** *nm* bandit

bank|a *nf* (*Dsg* ~ci) bank **Narodna ~a** National B. **trgovačka ~a** merchant b. **kreditna ~a** credit b. **~ar** *nm* banker **~arski** *adj* banker's **~arstvo** *nn* banking **~ovni** *adj* bank-, banking **~ovni račun** bank account **~ovni ulog** bank deposit **~ovna doznaka** bank transfer

bankrot *nm* bankruptcy **~irati** *v* (0) go bankrupt

ban|uti *v* (0) (*pres* ~em) burst in

bapsk|i *adj derog* old-women's **~e priče** old wives' tale

bar (1), **barem** *adv* at least **da ~** if only, I wish

bar (2) *nm* bar, night-club

bar|a *nf* pond, pool, marsh **~uština** *nf* swamp, bog

bara|ka *nf* (*Dsg* ~ci) hut

baražn|i *adj* **~a vatra** barrage

barbar|in *nm* barbarian **~stvo** *nm* barbarism

barem → **bar** (1)

barijera *nf* barrier

barikada *nf* barricade, road block

barka *nf* boat

barok *nm* the baroque **~ni** *adj* baroque

barometar *nm* barometer (+ *fig*)

baršun *nm* velvet **~ast** *adj* velvet, velvety

barun *nm* baron **~ica** *nf* baroness

barut *nm* powder **bačva ~a** *fig* powder keg **~ni** *adj* powder **~ni naboj/~no punjenje** p. charge

bas *nm* **1** bass voice, basso **2** (**~ gitara**) bass (guitar) **~ist** *nm* bass player

basn|a *nf* fable **~oslovan** *adj* (*a*) fabulous

bastion *nm* (**posljednji**) ~ *fig* (the last) bastion/stronghold

baš *adv* just, precisely, exactly; absolutely **~ ništa** nothing at all, absolutely nothing **baš sam htio ući** I was about to enter **~ tamo** right there

baština *nf* inheritance, heritage (+ *fig*) **~ica** *nf* heiress **~ik** *nm* (*Npl* ~ici) heir **~iti** (*što*) inherit

bat *nm* mallet

bat|ak *nm* (*Gsg* ~ka) leg (of chicken); drumstick *coll*

bataljun *nm* → **bojna**

baterija *nf* **1** battery **2** *coll* flashlight, torchlight **3** *mil* → **bitnica**

batin|a *nf* club **~e** *pl* beating; licking *coll*

batrlj|ak *nm* (*Gsg* ~ka, *Npl* ~ci) stump

bauk *nm* bogey(man); bugbear

bauljati *v* (0) stagger, wobble

baviti *v* (se čime) **1** engage in, be active in **2** be busy (doing sth/with sth) **3** be concerned with, deal with **4** study, pursue

baza *nf* **1** base, basis, foundation **2** *mil* base **3** *chem* base, alkali

bazen *nm* **1** swimming pool **2** basin

bazga *nf* elder

baždariti *v* (što) gauge, calibrate

bdje|ti *v* (0) (*pres* bdim, bdijem) **1** keep vigil, sit/stay up, keep awake **2** (nad) *fig* watch over **~nje** *nn* vigil; (uz mrtvaca) wake

beba *nf* **1** baby **2** (lutka) doll

Beč *nm* Vienna **bečki** *adj* Viennese

bećar *nm* *coll* rake **~ac** *nm* (*Gsg* ~ca) humorous Slavonian folk song

beda|k *nm* (*Npl* ~ki) *coll* fool **~st** *adj* foolish, silly

bedem *nm* (defensive) wall, rampart

bedr|o *nn* thigh **~ena** *adj* **kost** femur **~enica** *nf* anthrax

bedž *nm* *coll* badge, button

bek|nuti (0/što) (*pres* ~nem) *fig* **ni ~nuti** not say a word

beletristika *nf* fiction

beneficij|a *nf* benefit, perquisite; perk *coll*

benzin *nm* petrol *GB*, gas(oline) *US* **bezolovni ~** unleaded p. **~ski** *adj* petrol/gasoline **~ska stanica/crpka** filling/petrol/gasoline station

berba *nf* **1** picking, harvesting, gathering **2** (vina) vintage

beretka *nf* beret

bermude *nf pl coll* (Bermuda) shorts

bernardin|ac *nm* (*Gsg* ~ca) St. Bernard

prefix (ispred bezvučnih suglasnika) → **bez-** **~an** *adj* sleepless **~carinski** *adj* duty-free **~ciljan** *adj* (*a*) aimless **~cjenje** *nn* **u ~cjenje** for a song/pittance **~kamatan** *adj* (*a*) interest-free **~karakteran** *adj* (*a*) **1** weak, unprincipled **2** rotten *coll* **~kičmenjak** *nm* (*Vsg* ~kičmenjače, *Npl* ~kičmenjaci) *fig* weakling, wimp **~kompromisan** *adj* (*a*) uncompromising, unyielding **~konačan** *adj* (*a*) endless, infinite **~koris|tan** *adj* (**~korisna** *f*) useless **~kraj** *nm* infinity **u ~kraj** endlessly, interminably **~krajan** *adj* (*a*) **1** endless, interminable **2** *fig* abysmal **~kralježnjak** *nm* (*Npl* ~kralježnjaci) invertebrate **~krupulozan** *adj* (α) unscroupulous, ruthless **~krvan** *adj* (α) anemic **~kućnik** *nm* (*Vsg* ~kućniče, *Npl* ~kućnici) homeless (person) **~mislen** *adj* absurd, senseless, pointless **~mislica** *nf* absurdity, nonsense; bull *coll* **~mrtan** *adj* (α) immortal **učiniti** (koga/što) **~mrtnim** immortalize **~mrtnik** *nm* (*Npl* ~mrtnici) immortal **~mrtnost** *nf* immortality **~parica** *nf* lack of money, poverty **~platan** *adj* (α) free (of charge), complimentary **~platno** *adv* free (of charge) **~pomoćan** *adj* (α) helpless **~poslen** *adj* idle **~posličar** *nm* loafer **~pravan** *adj* (α) illegal **~predmetan** *adj* (α) pointless, irrelevant **~prijekoran** *adj* (α) immaculate, impeccable **~puće** *nn* wilderness **~raman** *adj* (α) shameless, impudent **~težinski** *adj* weightless **~težinsko stanje** zero gravity **~tidan** *adj* (α) shameless, impudent **~trzajni** *adj* recoilless **~vijest** *nf* do **~vijesti** *fig* to death **~bešćutan** *adj* (α) callous **bešuman** *adj* (α) noiseless, silent

beton *nm* concrete **prednapregnuti ~** pre-stressed c. **~irati** *v* (što) lay c. **~ski** *adj* concrete

bez *prep* without, lacking **biti ~** lack **~ mirisa** fragrance-free

bez- *prefix* -less, -free; without **~akonje** *nn* anarchy **~alkoholan** *adj* (α) non-alcoholic, soft **~azlen** *adj* harmless, innocent **~bojan** *adj* (α) **1** colourless, (glas) toneless **2** drab **~bolan** *adj* (α) painless **~božan** *adj* (α) ungodly **~božnik** *nm* (*Vsg* ~božniče, *Npl* ~božnici) atheist **~brižan** *adj* (α) carefree **~broj** *nm* myriad, legion **~brojan** *adj* (α) countless, innumerable **~dan** *nm* abyss **~dušan** *adj* (α) heartless, callous **~glav** *adj* helter-skelter, headlong **~graničan** *adj* (α) boundless, limitless **~grešan** *adj* (α) free from sin **~grešno začeće** immaculate conception **~imen** *adj* nameless, unknown, anonymous **~izlazan** *adj* (α) hopeless, dire **~izražajan** *adj* (α) expressionless, blank, vacant **~ličan** *adj* (α) impersonal, nondescript **~načajan** *adj* (α) insignificant, trivial, minor **~nadan** *adj* (α) hopeless, desperate **~nađe** *nn* despair **~obrazan** *adj* (α) impudent, cheeky **~obziran** *adj* (α) ruthless **~okusan** *adj* (α) tasteless, bland **~opasan** *adj* (α) harmless, safe **~osjećajan** *adj* (α) unfeeling, insensitive **~razložan** *adj* (α) **1** groundless, unfounded **2** unprovoked, uncalled for **~rezervan** *adj* (α) unquestioned, full, absolute **~ub** *adj* tootless **~ukusan** *adj* (α) insipid, tasteless **~uman** *adj* (α) insane, mindless, mad **~uvjetan** *adj* (α) **1** unconditional, absolute **2** *leg* non-suspended **~vezan** *adj* (α) dumb, ridiculous **~veznjak** *nm* (*Vsg* ~veznjače, *Npl* ~veznjaci) *coll* nerd, jerk **~vlađe** *nn* anarchy **~voljan** *adj* (α) listless, lethargic **~vrijedan** *adj* (α) worthless, useless

bež *nm* beige

bežični *adj* wireless; (telefon) cordless

bežívotan *adj* (α) lifeless

bibati *v* (se) billow

Biblija *nf* the Bible

biblioteka *nf* library **~r** *nm* librarian **~rstvo** *nn* Library science

bicikl *nm* bicycle; bike *coll*; push-bike *coll GB* **voziti se ~om** ride a b.; cycle **~istički** *adj* cycling **~izam** *nm* (*Gsg* ~izma) cycling

bič *nm* whip **~evati** *v* (koga) whip, flog

biće *nn* being, creature **ljudsko ~** human b.

bifte|k *nm* (*Npl* ~ci) beefsteak

bigamija *nf* bigamy

bijed|a *nf* **1** misery, wretchedness, poverty **2** *fig* meanness, misery **~an** *adj* (α) **1** miserable, pathetic **2** paltry **3** poor, destitute **~nik** (*Vsg* ~niče, *Npl* ~nici) *nm* poor devil, wretch

bijeg *nm* escape, flight **biti u ~u** be on the run **natjerati u ~** put to flight

bijel *adj* (*comp* bjelji) white **~a kava** cafe au lait **u po ~a dana** in broad daylight **~ac** *nm* (*Gsg* ~ca, *Vsg* ~če) **1** white (man), Caucasian **2** white horse **~iti** *v* (što) **1** bleach **2** whitewash

bijes *m* rage, fury **~an** *adj* (*a*) **1** (na koga) furious with; mad at **2** rabid, mad

bik *nm* **1** bull **2** *astrol* Taurus **borba s ~ovima** bullfight

bilanca *nf* balance, (izvještaj) balance sheet **trgovinska ~** b. of trade, visible b. **platna ~** b. of payments

bilo *nm* **1** *geogr* ridge **2** pulse

bilten *nm* bulletin, newsletter

biljar *nm* pool; snooker **~ski** *adj* **štap** cue

bilj|e *nn* plants **ljekovito ~e** medicinal herbs, herbal remedies **~ka** *nf* (*Gsg* ~ci) plant **~ni** *adj* vegetable **~ožder** *nm* herbivore

bilje|g *nm* (*Npl* ~zi) tax stamp

bilje|ška *nf* (*Gsg* ~ŝci) **1** note **2** footnote **hvatati ~ške** take notes, jot down **~žiti** *v* (što) **1** take notes, jot down **2** (u što) register, enter **3** record **~žnica** *nf* notebook **javni ~žnik** *nm* (*Npl* ~žnici) notary (public)

binaran *adj* (*a*) binary

biografija *nf* **1** biography **2** curriculum vitae, resume

biolo|g *nm* (*Npl* ~zi) biologist **~gija** *nf* biology **~ški** *adj* biological

bira|č *nm* voter, constituent, elector **~čko** *adj* tijelo electorate **~lište** *nn* polling station **~n** *adj* choice, exquisite **~ti** *v* (koga, što) **1** choose, pick **2** *pol* elect

birokra|cija *nf* bureaucracy, red tape **~t** *nm* bureaucrat

bisage *nf pl* saddle bags

biser *nm* **1** pearl **2** *fig* pearl, gem **~ni** *adj* pearl **~nica** *nf* pearl shell

biskup *nm* bishop **~ija** *nf* diocese, bishopric **~ski** *adj* ured chancery

biskvit *nm* sponge cake

bist|ar *adj* (*a*) **1** clear **2** *fig* clever, bright **~riti** *v* **1** (što) clarify **2** (se) clear up

bit *nf* essence **u ~i** essentially, in fact **~an** *adj* (*a*) essential, crucial

bitanga *nf* rogue

biti *v* (0) *irreg* **be ne ~ ni za što** be good for nothing **što ti je?** what is the matter with you? **bilo kada**

whenever **što je bilo, bilo je; bilo pa prošlo** let bygones be bygones

bitnica *nf mil* battery

bi|tka *nf* (*Dsg* ~tci/ci) battle **voditi ~tku** fight a b.

bivol *nm* buffalo

bivš|i *adj* former, ex- • *nm coll* ex (husband) **~a** ex (wife)

bizaran *adj* (*a*) bizarre

bizon *nm* bison

bižuterija *nf* costume jewellery

bjegun|ac *nm* (*Npl* ~če, *Gsg* ~ca) fugitive, run-away

bjelančevina *nf* protein

bjelanj|ak *nm* (*Gsg* ~ka, *Npl* ~ci) (egg-)white

bjel|ina *nf* **1** whiteness **2** (u tekstu) blank **~kast** *adj* off-white **~kinja** *nf* white woman **~očnica** *nf* white of the eye **~ogorica** *nf* deciduous forrest/trees **~okost** *nf* ivory

bjes|nilo *nm* **1** rage **2** rabies **~noća** *nf* rabies **~njeti** *v* **1** (0/na koga/zbog čega) rage (against), be furious with, rave **2** *fig* rage **~omučan** *adj* (*a*) raving

bjež|ati *v* (0) (*pres* ~im) **1** run away, flee, be on the run **2** (od čega/pred čim) run from, flee (from) **~ati glavom bez obzira** run like hell

blag *adj* (*comp* blaži) mild (+ *fig*), gentle, soft **najblaže rečeno** to say the least, to put it mildly **~o** *adv* tebi! lucky you! **postupati ~o** (s kim) treat leniently

blagajn|a *nf* **1** cashier's, till, check-out **2** teller's counter **3** box-office **4** treasury **državna ~a** national treasury **~ik** *nm* (*Npl* ~ici) **1** cashier **2** treasurer, purser, paymaster

blagdan *nm* holiday **državni ~** public/national h.

blago *nn* treasure (+ *fig*), riches; (stoka) cattle **~dat** *nf* boon, blessing; amenity **~glagoljiv** *adj* eloquent, glib **~naklon** *adj* benevolent **~naklonost** *nf* benevolence, grace, favour **~slov** *nm* blessing, benediction **dati ~slov** *fig* approve; okay **coll ~sloviti** *v* (koga, što) **1** bless, give one's blessing **2** consecrate **~stanje** *nn* prosperity, welfare **B~vijest** *nf*

Annunciation

blagova|onica *nf* 1 dining-room 2 mess **~ti** *v* (što) eat, dine

blam|aža *nf coll* disgrace **~irati** (koga/se) disgrace (sb/oneself)

bla|tan *adj* (*a*) muddy **~iti** *v* (koga/što) *fig* defame, slander **~čenje** *nn* smear campaign **~tnjav** *adj* muddy **~to** *nn* 1 mud; mire (+ *fig*) 2 *fig* gutter živo **~to** quicksand **~tobran** *nm* (bicikla) mudguard; wing *GB*, fender *US*

blažen *adj* 1 blissful 2 blessed **proglasiti ~im** beatify

blebe|tati *v* (0) (*pres* **~ćem**) chatter **~tav** *adj* chattering **~talo** *nn/***~tuša** *nf* chatterbox, big mouth

blef *nm* bluff **~irati** *v* (0) bluff

blej|ati *v* (0) (*pres* **~im**) 1 (ovca) bleat 2 gape

blesa|n *nm* moron, stupid **~v** *adj* stupid

blijed *adj* (*comp* bljeđi) 1 pale 2 *fig* colourless, lifeless 3 faint **~ kao smrt/krpa** deathly pale **~i osmijeh** bleak smile

blindiran *adj* bullet-proof

bliskost *nf* closeness, intimacy, familiarity

blista|ti *v* (0/se) glitter, sparkle, glow **~v** *adj* glowing, radiant, bright; brilliant (+ *fig*)

blitva *nf* Swiss chard

bli|zak *adj* (**~ska** *f*) close, intimate **~ski prijatelj** bosom friend **~z** *adj* (*comp* bliži) close **~zina** *nf* nearness, closeness, proximity **u ~zini** close by, nearby, not far (from), in the vicinity (of) **gledati iz ~zine** get a close look **iz neposredne ~zine** at close range, at point blank **~zu** *adv* near, close by **ne ići ~zu** keep one's distance *prep* almost, just under, close to

blizan|ac *nm* (*Gsg* **~ca**) twin (brother) **~ka** twin (sister) **jednojajčani ~ci** identical twins **~ci** *astrol* Gemini

bliž|iti *v* (se) approach, come closer **~nji** *nm* neighbour, fellow human being

blok *nm* 1 block 2 notepad, sketchpad 3 *pol* bloc 4 *med* block **~ada** *nf* 1 blockade 2 freeze **~irati** (koga/što) 1 block, obstruct 2 seal (off) 3 freeze

blud *nm* fornication, lechery, lust **~an** *adj* (*a*) lewd **~nica** *nf* harlot, whore **~nik** *nm* (*Vsg* **~niče**, *Npl* **~ici**) lecher

blud|iti *v* (0) wander, roam **~nja** *nf* delusion **zavesti u ~nju** deceive, mislead

bluza *nf* blouse

bljed|ilo *nn* pallor **~olik** *adj* pale-faced **~unjav** *adj* pale, sickly

bljes|ak *nm* (*Gsg* **~ka**) flash **~kalica** *nf* flash (bulb) **~nuti** *v* (0) (*pres* **~nem**) flash, flare

blještav *adj* dazzling

bljutav *adj* insipid, tasteless

blju|vati *v* (0/što) (*pres* **~jem**) vomit; throw up, puke *coll* **~votina** *nf* 1 vomit 2 *fig* rubbish

bljuzga(vica) *nf* slush

bob (1) *nm* broad bean(s) **ne vrijedi ni pišljiva ~a** it is not worth a dime/penny **reći ~u ~ a popu pop** call a spade a spade

bob (2) *nm sport* bob-sled/-sleigh

bobica *nf* 1 berry 2 (grožđa) grape

boc|a *nf* bottle **puniti** *v* (što) **u ~e** bottle

boc|nuti *v* (koga, što) 1 prick, sting, prod 2 *fig* tease **~kati** *v impf*

bočic|a *nf* 1 *dem* **~ boca** 2 vial 3 feeding/nursing bottle **hraniti na ~u** bottle-feed

bočni *adj* side-, sideways

bod (1) *nm* stitch

bod (2) *nm* point **dobiti ~** score a p. **s tri ~a razlike** by three points **~ovati** *v* (što) (*pres* **~ujem**) rate

bod|ar *adj* (*a*) fresh, alert **~riti** *v* (koga) 1 cheer 2 encourage

bodež *nm* dagger

bodlj|a *nf* prick, spike, barb **~ika** *nf* prick, thorn **~ikav** *adj* prickly, spiky, spiked **~ikava žica** barbed wire

bog (**Bog**) *nm* (*Vsg* Bože) god, God **~ i batina** big boss, bigshot **B~a mi** I swear to God **kako ~ zapovijeda** properly **za B~a (miloga)** for Christ's sake **ni za B~a** not on your life **hvala B~u!** thank God **ne daj Bože** God forbid **ništa pod milim B~om** nothing at all • *int* Hi! Hello!; Bye! **~inja** *nf* goddess **~obojazan** *adj* (*a*) God-fearing **~ohulan** *adj* (*a*) blasphemous **~omoljac** nm (Gsg ~omoljca, Vsg ~omoljče) derog bigot **~omoljka** nf (Dsg ~omoljci) **1** derog bigoted woman **2** praying mantis **Bogorodica** nf Mother of God **~oslovni** adj theological **~oslužje** nn liturgy, service

bogalj nm cripple

bogat adj **1** rich, wealthy **2** fig (čime) rich (in) **3** lavish **~aš** nm rich man **~iti** v (se) (na čemu/na čiji račun) get rich on, make money on, profit from **~o** adv fig lavishly, elaborately **~o se** oženiti/udati marry money **~stvo** nn **1** riches, wealth, fortune **2** richness, abundance **prirodna ~stva** natural resources **~un** nm derog filthy rich

boginje nf pl **velike/crne ~** small-pox **male ~** chicken pox

boj nm battle **~evi** adj mil live **~eva glava** warhead **~ište** nn battlefield, front, theatre **~ni** nf front **~na nf battalion **~ni** adj combat, war- **~ni otrov** poison gas **~nik** nm (Vsg ~niče, Npl ~nici) Major **~ovnik** nm (Vsg ~ovniče, Npl ~ovnici) fighter, soldier

boj|a nf **1** colour; (ton) hue, tint **2** paint; (za kosu) dye; (industrijska) dye-stuff **TV u ~i** colour TV **~ice** nf pl colours **drvene ~ice** crayons **~iti** v (što) **1** colour **2** paint **3** dye

boja|ti v (se) (pres bojim) **1** (koga/čega) be afraid of **2** (za koga/što) fear for **~zan** nf (Gsg ~zni) fear, apprehension, anxiety **~žljiv** adj timid

bojkot nm boycott **~irati** v (koga/što) boycott

bojler nm water heater

bok (1) nm **1** hip **2** side, flank **uz ~** by/at one's side **stati komu uz ~** fig be equal with

bok (2) int coll hi!

boks nm boxing **~ač** nm boxer, prize-fighter **~ati** v (0) box **~er** nm **1** (pas) boxer **2** knuckle duster **~erice** nf pl coll boxer shorts

bol nm/f **1** pain (+ fig) **2** (zub, glava, leđa, uho, trbuh) ache **3** fig anguish **nanijeti/zadati ~** hurt, cause/implict pain **imati ~ove** be in pain, hurt **~an**

adj (a) painful (+ fig), sore, aching **~na točka** sore spot/subject **~esnički** adj invalid, sick- **~esnik** nm (Vsg ~če, Npl ~ci) sick man/person, patient **~esno** adv mobidly **~esno uredan** compulsively clean **~est** nf sickness, illness, disease **dječje ~esti** childhood diseases; teething troubles fig **~estan** adj (~esna f) **1** sick, ill **2** fig morbid, sick **teško ~estan** seriously ill **smrtno ~estan** terminally ill **~ežljiv** adj sickly **~nica** nf hospital **primiti u ~nicu** hospitalize, admit to h. **otpusiti iz ~nice** discharge from h. **~ničar** nm male nurse, orderly **~ničarka** nf nurse **~nički** adj hospital **~ovanje** nn sick leave **~ovati** v (0/od čega) be ill (with); suffer from

boljje comp adv better → **dobro brže** quickly **~i** comp adj → **dobar**

boljeti v (što koga) hurt (+ fig), ache **boli** it hurts **boli me** I am in pain **boli me glava** I have a headache **boli me grlo** I have a sore throat **boli me za to** vulg fig I don't give a damn

bomba nf bomb **ručna ~** hand grenade **~rdirati** v (što) bomb, bombard, shell **~rder** nm bomber **~š** nm bomber

bombon nm sweet GB, candy US **čokoladni ~** chocolate **~ijera** nf **1** sweet shop, candy store **2** a box of chocolates

bon nm voucher **~ za topli obrok** luncheon v.

bonitet nm credit rating

bonton nm (good) manners; etiquette

bonus nf bonus

bor nm **1** pine(tree) **2** Christmas tree **~ovina** nf pine, pinewood

bora nf wrinkle, line **~ti** v (se) wrinkle, crease

bor|ac nm (Gsg ~ca, Vsg ~če, Npl ~ci) **1** fighter **2** (za) champion, advocate of **~ba** nf **1** struggle, fight (+ fig) **2** campaign **~ben** adj aggressive, fighting; combat mil **~ilački** adj sportovi martial arts **~ilište** nn arena, ring **~iti** v (se s kim/čim, protiv koga/čega) fight (against/0), struggle

borav|ak nm (Gsg ~ka) stay; residence

dozvola ~**ka** residence permit **dnevni** ~**ak** living room ~**išna** *adj* **taksa** accommodation fee ~**ište** *nn* abode, current address ~**iti** *v* (0) stay

borovica *nf* juniper

borovnica *nf* blueberry

bosiljak *nf* (*Gsg* ~**ka**) basil

bos(onog) *adj* barefoot

bosti *v* (koga/što/čime) (*pres* ~**dem**) 1 prick 2 stab 3 sting, bite

botaničar *nm* botanist ~**čki** *adj* vrt botanical gardens ~**ka** *nf* (*Dsg* ~**ci**) botany

božanski *adj* divine ~**anstven** *adj* heavenly ~**anstvo** *nn* deity ~**ica** *nf* goddess ~**ji** *adj* divine **za ime** ~**je** for God's sake

Božić *nm* Christmas **b**~**ni** *adj* Christmas **b**~**na** **pjesma** C. carol **b**~**na čestitka** C. card **b**~**nica** *nf* C. bonus

braco *nm* little brother, kid brother

bračni *adj* marriage, marital ~ **par** married couple ~ **drug** spouse

braća *nf pl* → **brat**

brada *nf* 1 chin 2 beard **pustiti** ~**u** grow a b. **uhvatiti Boga za** ~**u** be on top of the world **govoriti u** ~**u** mumble ~**at** *adj* bearded

bradavica *nf* 1 wart 2 (na grudima) nipple

brak *nm* marriage, matrimony **ući u/sklopiti** ~ marry, get married **divlji** ~ common law marriage ~**orazvodni** *adj* divorce

brana *nf* dam ~**ik** *nm* (*Npl* ~**ici**) 1 rampart 2 (auto) bumper **stajati na** ~**iku** defend ~**itelj** *nm* 1 defender 2 *leg* counsel for the defence ~**itelj po službenoj dužnosti** court-appointed defender ~**iti** *v* 1 (koga/što od/protiv) defend (from), protect (from) 2 (koga/što) stand up for 3 (što komu) forbid 4 (se) defend oneself, fight back

brašno *nn* flour, meal

brat *nm* (*pl* braća) brother **topli** ~ *coll* derog faggot *sl* derog ~**ić** *nm* cousin ~**imiti** *v* (se) fraternize ~**oubilački** *adj* fratricidal, ~**ovština** *nf* brotherhood, guild ~**ski** *adj* brotherly, fraternal ~**stvo** *nn* brotherhood, frater-

nity

bravla *nf* lock **obiti** ~**u** pick a l. ~**ar** *nm* locksmith

bravo *int* well done!

brazda *nf* 1 (izorana) furrow 2 groove 3 (broda) wake

brazgotina *nf* scar

brbljalti *v* (0) chat ~**v** *adj* chatty, voluble ~**vost** *nf* volubility

brčići *nm pl* clipped moustache *sg*

brčkati *v* 1 (što) dabble 2 (se) paddle

brdlo *nm* 1 mountain, hill 2 *fig* pile ~**ovit** *adj* hilly ~**ski** *adj* mountain, highland

breme *nn* burden (+ *fig*), load

breslkva *nf* (*Gpl* ~**aka**/~**kvi**) peach

breza *nf* birch

brežuljlak *nm* (*Gsg* ~**ka**, *Npl* ~**ci**) hill, hillock, knoll

brid *nm* edge ~**ak** *adj* (britka *f*) 1 sharp, cutting 2 *fig* poignant ~**jeti** *v* (0/od) (*pres* ~**im**) smart with

brilga *nf* (*Dsg* ~**zi**) 1 worry, trouble 2 care 3 concern, business **nije me** ~**ga/baš me** ~**ga** I don't give a damn **voditi** ~**gu o** take care of (budi) **bez** ~**ge** don't worry **zadavati** ~**gu** cause anxiety **biti u** ~**zi** worry

brigadla *nf* brigade ~**ir** *nm mil* brigadier

brijalč *nm* barber ~**čnica** *nf* barber's (shop) ~**nje** *nn* shaving, shave **za** ~**nje** shaving **aparat za** ~**nje** razor, shaver ~**ti** *v* 1 (koga/što) shave 2 (0) *fig* cut 3 (se) shave (oneself), get a shave

brijeg *nm* (*Npl* bregovi) hill

brijest *nm* elm

briljant *nm* (*Gpl* ~**ata**) brilliant ~**tan** *adj* (**a**) 1 diamond 2 *fig* brilliant ~**tin** *nm* brilliantine, grease

brinluti *v* (*pres* ~**em**) 1 (se za koga/što) take care of, care for, look after ~**uti se sam za sebe** fend for oneself 2 (se zbog koga/čega) be concerned about 3 (se) worry, fret 4 (koga) worry, cause anxiety

brisalč *nm* wiper ~**ti** 1 wipe (off/away) ~**ti prašinu** dust 2 dry 3 erase, delete, strike out

britvla *nf* razor ~**ica** *nf* razor blade

briznuti *v* (0) spurt ~ **u plač** burst into

tears

briž|an *adj* (*a*) 1 solicitous, attentive 2 anxious **~ljiv** *adj* careful, meticulous

brk *nm* (*Npl* ~ovi, brci) moustache; (mačji) whisker **u ~** *fig* in/to the face **~at** *adj* with a moustache

brklja *nf* barrier

brlo|g *nm* (*Npl* ~zi) den, lair (+ *fig*)

brnjica *nf* muzzle

brod *nm* 1 ship, vessel, boat 2 (crkve) nave **~ar, ~ovlasnik** *nm* (*Npl* ~ovlasnici) shipowner, shipping company, ship line **~ogradilište** *nn* shipyard **~ogradnja** *nf* 1 shipbuilding (industry) 2 naval architecture **~olom** *nm* shipwreck **~olomac** *nm* (*Gsg* ~olomca) shipwrecked man **~ovlje** *nn* fleet **~ski** *adj* ship-, ship's

broj *nm* 1 number 2 (novina) copy, issue 3 (veličina) size 4 count, toll **poštanski ~** postal code *GB*; zip code *US* **~ač** *nm* counter **~an** *adj* (*a*) numerous **~ati** *v* (0/koga/što) count **~čani** *adj* numerical **imati ~čanu nadmoć** outnumber **~idba** *nf* statistics **~ilo** *nf* counter, meter **~ka** *nf* (*Dsg* ~ci) figure; digit

bron|ca *nf* bronze **~čan** *adj* bronze

broš *nm* brooch

broš|ura *nf* brochure, booklet **~iran** *adj* paperback

bršljan *nm* ivy

brtv|a *nf* gasket **~iti** *v* (što) 1 seal 2 insulate

brucoš *nm* coll freshman, fresher

bruj|ati *v* (0) (*pres* ~im) drone; hum (+ *fig*)

bru|s *nm* whetstone **~silica** *nf* grinder **~siti** *v* (što) grind, whet, sharpen; (dijamante) cut; polish (+ *fig*) **~sni** *adj* grinding **~sni papir** emery paper **~šen** *adj* ground; cut; polished

brusnica *nf* cranberry

brutalan *adj* (Ž) brutal

bruto *adj, adv* gross **imati ~ prihod** gross

brvn|ara *nf* log cabin **~o** *nn* plank (bridge)

brz *adj* (*comp* brži) 1 fast, quick 2 *form* rapid 3 prompt **~aci** *nm pl* the rapids **~ati** *v* (0) hurry **~ina** *nf* speed; velocity; promptness; (auto) gear **na ~inu** *a*. in a hurry *b*. off-handedly **ići ~inom od 60 km/h** do 60 kms an hour **puna ~ina** full/top speed **ubaciti u ~inu** shift into gear **~inomjer** *nm* speedometer **~o** (*comp* brže) *adv* 1 fast, quickly 2 soon **~ojav** *nm* telegram, cable **~ojaviti** *v* (komu/što) (send a) cable **~oplet** *adj* rash

bub|a *nm* 1 bug 2 *coll* (Volkswagen) beetle **~a mara** ladybird **staviti komu ~u u uho** make sb think

bub|anj *nm* (*Gsg* ~nja) 1 drum 2 cylinder **~njati** *v* (0) drum **~njar** *nm* drummer **~njić** *nm* ear-drum

bubati *v* (što) swot, bone up

bubn|uti *v* (*pres* ~em) 1 (koga/što) punch, hit 2 (što) blurt out

bubre|g *nm* (*Npl* ~zi) kidney **upala ~ga** nephritis **živjeti kao ~g u loju** live in clover, live a life of ease **~žni** *adj* kidney; renal *med*

bubriti *v* (0) swell, become distended

bubuljica *nf* pimple, spot

bucmast *adj* chubby, plump

buča|n *adj* (*a*) noisy, loud, roaring **~ti** *v* (0) make (a lot of) noise

budal|a *nf* fool **ispasti ~a/napraviti ~u od sebe** make a f. of oneself **praviti koga ~om** make a fool of sb, fool sb **~ast** *adj* foolish, silly **~aština** *nf* nonsense

bud|an *adj* (*a*) 1 awake 2 *fig* alert **~ilica** *nf* alarm clock **~iti** *v* 1 (koga) wake up, try to wake up 2 (što) *fig* arouse, stir up 3 (se) wake up **~no** *adv* **paziti** keep an eye on **~nost** *nf* vigilance

buduć|i *adj* future, -to-be, prospective **• ~i da** *conj* since, as **~nost** *nf* 1 future (+ *fig*) 2 *fig* prospects

budžet *nm* → proračun

buđenje *nn* 1 awakening (+ *fig*) 2 (telefonsko) wake-up call

buha *nf* flea **leglo ~** *fig* fleabag **pun ~** flea-bitten **~ra** *n sl* (zatvor) joint *sl*

buj|an *adj* (*a*) lush, rich, lavish, exuberant **~nih oblina** buxom **~ati** *v* (0) 1 grow 2 rise 3 *fig* swell, expand, develop **~ica** *nf* torrent

bu|ka *nf* (*Dsg* ~ci) noise, din **mnogo ~ke nizašto** much ado about nothing **~kač** *nm* malcontent, rabble-rouser

buket *nm* bunch
bukn|uti *v* (0) (*pres* ~em) **1** (požar) burst into flames; flare up (+ *fig*) **2** *fig* flare (up) **3** *fig* break out
buk|va *nf* beech ~ov *adj* beech ~ovina *nf* beech(wood) ~vica *nf fig* rebuke očitati ~vicu kome lecture sb
bula *nf* bull
buldozer (buldožer *coll*) *nm* bulldozer
bulevar *nm* boulevard ~ski *adj* tisak gutter press
bulj|iti *v* (0/u koga/što) stare at, gape at ~ook *adj* goggle-eyed
bumbar *nm* bumble-bee
bun|a *nf* rebellion ~iti *v* **1** (koga) incite to rebellion/mutiny, stir up sedition **2** (se) rebel **3** (se) complain, protest, resist
bunar *nm* well
bun|cati *v* (0/što) **1** rave, be delirious **2** *fig* talk nonsense ~ilo *nn* delirium, fever ~ovan *adj* (α) drowsy, half-asleep
buncek *nm cul* pork hock
bunda *nf* fur coat
bunker *nm* bunker, pillbox
bunt *nm* rebellion, discontent ~ovan (æ), ~ovnički *adj* rebellious ~ovnik *nm* (*Vsg* ~ovniče, *Npl* ~ovnici) rebel;

troublemaker
bur|a *nf* **1** bora, north-easter(n wind) **2** *fig* gale, storm, tumult izazvati ~u (čega) raise/cause a storm of ~an *adj* (α) tempestuous, violent, wild (+ *fig*) ~na prošlost a chequered career/past
burad *nn pl* → **bure**
bure *nn* → **bačva**
burek *nm cul* meat-pie
burz|a *nf* exchange, market ~a vrijednosnih papira stock-exchange/market robna ~a commodity e. crna ~a black market ~a rada employment office, Jobcentre biti na ~i *coll* be on the dole ~ovni *adj* mešetar stock-broker
burž|oaski *adj* bourgeois ~oazija *nf* bourgeoisie, middle class ~uj *nm* bourgeois
busen *nm* (a piece of) turf
buš|ilica *nf* drill; drilling/boring machine; borer; punch ~iti *v* (što) **1** drill **2** pierce, perforate ~otina *nf* **1** bore (hole) **2** (naftna) oil-well
but *nm* leg
butelja *nf* 0.7-litre (wine) bottle
butik *nm* (*Npl* ~ci) boutique
buzdovan *nm* mace

C

C, c (ce) 3rd letter of Cro. alphabet

cakli|na *nf* enamel **~ti** *v* (se) glimmer

car *nm* emperor **ruski ~** tsar, czar **~ica** *nf* empress, tsarina **~evati** *v* (0) (*pres* ~ujem) reign **~ski** *adj* imperial **~ski rez** Caesarian section **~stvo** *nn* empire **životinjsko ~stvo** the animal kingdom **~stvo snova** the Land of nod

carin|a *nf* customs, duty; tariff **~arnica** *nf* c. office, the customs **~ik** *nm* (*Npl* ~ici) c. officer **~initi** *v* (što) 1 clear through the customs 2 collect customs duty on **~ski** *adj* customs

cedulja *nf coll* slip, note

ceh *nm* 1 guild 2 *coll* bill

celer *nm* celery

celibat *nm* celibacy

celofan *nm* cellophane

celuloza *nf* 1 cellulose 2 pulp 3 fibre, bulk

celzij *nm* 5 stupnjeva **~a** 5 degrees Celsius/centigrade

cement *nm* cement **~irati** *v* (što) cement

cent|ar *nm* (*Gsg* ~ra, *Npl* ~ri) centre **~ar grada** downtown *US* **~rala** *nf* headquarters, head office **električna ~rala** power station/plant **telefonska ~rala** telephone exchange; (tvrtke) switchboard **~ralan** *adj* (ā) central **~ralno grijanje** central heating

centrifuga *nf* spin-drier **~lan** *adj* (ā) centrifugal

cenzur|a *nf* censorship **~irati** *v* (koga/što) censor

cerada *nf* tarpaulin, tarp *coll*

cer|ekati *v* (se) snigger, titter **~iti** *v* (se) smirk, leer

ceremonij|a *nf* ceremony, rite; pageant **~l** *nm* ceremonial **~lan** *adj* (ā) ceremonious, ceremonial

cest|a *nf* road **~arina** *nf* toll **~ovni** *adj* road

čiča *nf* **~ zima** bitter cold

čičati *v* (0) squeal

ciferšlus *nm coll* zip (fastener); zipper *US*

Ciganin *nm*, **Ciganka** *nf*, **ciganski** *adj* Gypsy, Gipsy

cigar|a *nf* cigar **~eta** *nf* cigarette

cigla *nf* brick

cijediti *v* 1 (što) drain, filter 2 (što) squeeze 3 (se) ooze, drip

cijel *adj* whole, entire **~o** *nn* integer, whole number **dva ~a pet** two point five

cije|na *nf* price **biti na ~ni** be valued highly **ispod ~ne/u pola ~ne** cheaply, at half-price, **ni po koju ~nu** under no circumstances **po svaku ~nu** at all costs **po ~nu života** risking one's own life **~niti** *v* (koga, što) respect, think highly of **~njeni** *adj* (u naslovu pisma) Dear

cijepati *v* 1 (što) chop (drvo), split (atome) 2 (se) rip, tear

cijepiti *v* 1 (što) graft 2 (koga) vaccinate, inoculate 3 (se) be inoculated

cijev *nf* pipe, tube; hose **puščana ~** barrel **mokraćna ~** urethra

cijukati *v* (0) squeak

cik *nm* **u ~ zore** at daybreak

cik-cak *adj, adv* zig-zag **ići u ~** zig-zag

cikla *nf* beetroot

ciklama *nf* cyclamen

ciklon *nm* 1 cyclone, tornado 2 cyclone **~a** *nf* low-pressure area, low

ciklus *nm* cycle

cilindar *nm* 1 top hat 2 cylinder

cilj *nm* 1 target 2 *fig* objective, goal, target, purpose 3 (winning) post **pogoditi ~** hit the t. **postići ~** attain one's goal/aim **~ati** *v* (0/na koga/na što) take aim; aim at (+ *fig*) **~nik** *nm*

(*Npl* ~nici) sight

cimer *nm coll* roommate

cimet *nm* cinnamon

cini|čan *adj* (*a*) cynical ~**k** *nm* (*Vsg* ~če, *Npl* ~ci) cynic

cin|k *nm* zinc ~**čan** *adj* zinc

cipela *nf* shoe; (visoka) boot

cirkul|acija *nf* circulation ~**ar** *nm* circular (letter) ~**ar(na pila)** chain saw ~**irati** *v* (0) circulate

cirkus *nm* circus (+ *fig*); fuss *fig*

cista *nf* cyst

cisterna *nf* 1 cistern, tank 2 tanker

cit|at *nm* quotation, quote ~**irati** *v* (koga/što) quote

civil *nm* civilian **policajac u** ~**u** plainclothes policeman ~**ni** *adj* civil, civilian ~**izacija** *nf* civilization ~**ilizirati** *v* 1 (koga/što) civilize 2 (se) become civilized

cjedi|lo *nn* 1 (čaj) strainer 2 (povrće) colander **ostaviti na** ~**u** leave in the lurch

cjel|ina *nf* whole, entirety ~**odnevan** *adj* (*a*) round-the-clock ~**okupan** *adj* (*a*) overall, total, entire ~**ovit** *adj* complete, integral ~**ovitost** *nf* integrity

cjen|ik *nm* price-list ~**kati** *v* (se) haggle

cjepanica *nf* log

cjepidla|čiti *v* (0) split hairs ~**ka** *nm/f* (*Dsg* ~ci) hair-splitter

cjepivo *nn* vaccine ~ **protiv bjesnoće** rabies shot *coll*

cjevanica *nf* shin

cjevovod *nm* pipeline

cmizdriti *v* (0) whine

cmoknuti *v* (koga/se) smack ~ **jezikom** click one's tongue

cof *nm coll* bobble, pom-pom

crijep *nm* roof-tile

crijev|o *nn* intestine, gut **debelo/tanko** ~**o** large/small i. **slijepo** ~**o** appendix ~**ni** *adj* intestinal

crk|avati *v* (0) (od) *coll* be dying (with/of) ~**avati od gladi** *coll* be starving ~**avati od smijeha** *coll* die laughing ~**nuti** *v* (0) (*pres* ~nem) 1 (osoba) croak *coll* ~**nuti od gladi** starve 2 (stvar) go dead ~**otina** *nf* 1 carrion 2 *fig* listless person

crkv|a *nf* church **ići u** ~**u** go to church ~**eni** *adj* ecclesiastic, church

crn *adj* (*comp* ~ji) black ~**e misli** gloomy thoughts ~**i dani** rainy day ~**o vino** red wine ~**ac** *nm* (*Gsg* ~ca) 1 Black, negro 2 African American ~**čiti** *v* (0) slave (away) ~**kinja** *nf* black woman ~**ica** *nf* rich soil ~**ina** *nf fig* mourning ~**o** *adv* black, in black; gloomily *fig* ○ *n* black **nositi** ~**o** dress in black, wear black ~**o na bijelo** in writing ~**ogorica** *nf* conifers ~**o-bijel** *adj* black and white ~**omanjast** *adj* dark (haired)

crp|sti *v* (što) (*pres* ~em) 1 pump, draw 2 *fig* derive, gain (strength) ~**ka** *nf* (*Gpl* ~aka/~ki) pump **benzinska** ~**ka** filling station, petrol station *GB*; gas station *US*

crt|a *nf* 1 line 2 feature, trait ~**e lica** features **u glavnim** ~**ama** in general terms **opisati u glavnim** ~**ama** draw an outline ~**ač** *nm* drawer, draughtsman ~**aći** *adj* drawing ~**anje** *nn* drawing ~**ati** *v* (0/koga/što) draw ~**ež** *nm* drawing ~**ica** *nf* 1 hyphen 2 sketch ~**ovlje** *nn mus* stave; staff *US*

crv *nm* worm **raditi kao** ~ slave away ~**ljiv** *adj* maggoty, maggot-ridden ~**točan** *adj* (*a*) worm-eaten

crve|n *adj* red ~**nilo** *nn* 1 redness; (face) ruddiness, high colour 2 lipstick; rouge, blusher ~**njeti** *v* (se) blush ~**nkast** *adj* reddish ~**no** *adv* red, in red ○ red

cugati *v* (0/što) *coll* drink, swig

cupkati *v* (0) hop

cur|a *nf coll* 1 girl, lass 2 girlfriend ~**ica** *nf* little girl

curi|ti *v* (0) flow, run, leak ~ **mi iz nosa** my nose is running

cva|sti *v* (0) (*pres* ~tem) flower, bloom, blossom ~**t** *nm* bloom

cvije|će *nn* flowers *pl* ~**t** flower, blossom **u** ~**tu mladosti** in the prime of life

cviljeti *v* (0) (*pres* cvilim) squeal, whine, whimper

cvjećar *nm* florist ~**nica** *nf* flower shop

cvjetača *nf* cauliflower

cvjet|ni *adj* floral ~**ati** *v* (0) 1 bloom,

blossom (+ *fig*) **2** *fig* flourish **~njak** *nm* (*Npl* ~njaci) flower garden **C~nica** *nf* Palm Sunday
cvoko|tati *v* (0) (*pres* ~ćem) **cvokoće zubima** his teeth are chattering **~tati od zime** shiver with cold

cvrč|ak *nm* (*Gsg* ~ka, *Npl* ~ci) cricket **~ati** *v* (0) **1** chirp **2** (mast) sizzle
cvikeraš *nm* derog four-eyes
cvrku|t *nm* chirping **~tati** *v* (0) (*pres* ~ćem) chirp (+ *fig*)
cvrljiti *v* (se) sizzle

Č

Č, č 4th letter of Cro. alphabet

ča *pron dial* what

čačka|lica *nf* toothpick ~**ti** *v* 1 (što) pick 2 (po čemu) tinker with

čađa *nf* soot ~**v** *adj* sooty

čaga *nf sl* dance ~**ti** *v* (0) *sl* dance

čahura *nf* 1 chrysalis; cocoon (+ *fig*) 2 pod 3 *mil* cartridge 4 (zglob) capsule

čaj *nm* tea ~ **od metvice** mint tea/infusion ~**ni** *adj* **kolačić** biscuit ~**nik** *nm* (*Npl* ~nici) tea-pot

čak *adv* even, as ... as

čam|ac *nm* (*Gsg* ~ca) boat ~**ac za spašavanje** life b.

čamiti *v* (0) languish

čangrizav *adj* cantankerous, morose

čaplja *nf* heron

čar *nm* charm; attraction ~**olija** *nf fig* magic ~**ati** *v* (0) practice witchcraft, charm, cast spells ~**oban** *adj* (*a*) 1 magic (+ *fig*) ~**obni štapić** m. wand 2 fascinating, charming, enchanting ~**obnica** *nf* sorceress, witch, enchantress ~**obnjak** *nm* (*Vsg* ~obnjače, *Npl* ~obnjaci) wizard, sorcerer (+ *fig*) ~**olija** *nf* magic, witchcraft

čarapa *nf* 1 stocking 2 sock **odjel ~** hosiery

čarka *nf mil* skirmish

čas *nm* moment, instant **došao si u pravi/krivi ~** your timing is good/bad **kucnuo je moj ~** my time has come **istog ~a** right away **to je ~ posla** *coll* it won't take a minute • *adv* ~ ... ~ ... alternately ... and ... ~**ak** *nm* (*Gsg* ~ka) moment

čas|ni *adj* honourable ~**na riječ** a. word of honour **b.** *coll* cross my heart ~**na sestra** nun, sister ~**nik** *nm* (*Vsg* ~niče, *Npl* ~nici) officer ~**no** *adv* honourably ~**t** *nf* honour **služiti na ~t komu** do sb credit **svaka ti ~t** well done, good for you ~**t mi je** I

have the honour ~**titi** *v* 1 (koga, što) honour, respect 2 (koga čime) treat sb to sth, buy sb sth **ja ~tim** it's on me 3 (se) feast ~**tohlepan** *adj* (*a*) ambitious

časopis *nm* magazine, periodical, journal

čaš|a *nf* glass ~**ica** 1 dem 2 *coll* a drink

čav|ao *nm* (*Gsg* ~la, *Npl* ~li) nail **zabiti ~ao u** drive a n. into **pričvrstiti ~lima** nail ~**lić** *nm* drawing pin *GB*, thumb-tack *US*

čavka *nf* jackdaw

čavrljati *v* (0) chat

čedan *adj* (*a*) chaste, modest, virtuous

čedo *nn* baby, infant ~**morstvo** *nn* infanticide

čega *Gsg* → **što**

čegrt|aljka *nf* (*Dsg* ~aljci) rattle ~**uša** *nf* rattle-snake

ček *nm* cheque *GB*, check *US* **barirani** ~ crossed c. ~**ovna** *adj* **knjižica** cheque book

čeka|onica *nf* 1 waiting room 2 lobby, departure lounge ~**ti** *v* (0/koga/što) wait (for) ~**j malo** wait a minute **jedva ~m** I can't wait

čekić *nm* hammer **udarati ~em** hammer

čekinja *nf* bristle ~**v** *adj* bristly; (brada) stubbly

čeli|čan *adj* (*a*) 1 steel (+ *fig*) 2 *fig* iron; robust ~**čni lim** s. plate ~**čiti** *v* (koga/što/se) steel, harden ~**čana** *nf* steel works ~**k** *nm* steel

čel|ni *adj* frontal ~**nik** *nm* (*Npl* ~nici) leader ~**o** *nn* 1 forehead 2 *fig* (stola) head **biti na ~u** head; lead (utrka) **izbiti na ~o** take the lead

čeljad *nn* pl people, folks ~**e** *nn* arch man, creature

čeljust *nf* 1 (gornja/donja ~)

(upper/lower) jaw **2** *pl* jaws

čempres *nm* cypress

čemu *Dsg* → **što**

čep *nm* plug, stopper, cork **~ić** *nm* suppository

čepiti *v* (0) *coll* kick one's heels

čeprkati *v* (što, po čemu) **1** pick **2** rummage **~ po čijoj prošlosti** rake up sb's past

čerupati *v* (koga, što) pluck, fleece (+ *fig*)

čest *adj* (*comp* češći) frequent, common **~o** *adv* often, frequently **~o zalaziti nekamo** frequent a place

čestica *nf* **1** particle **2** plot (of land)

čestit *adj* **1** honest **2** *fig* good, sound, proper **~ Božić** Merry Christmas **~ati** *v* (komu na čemu) congratulate sb on sth **~ati komu rođendan/Božić** wish sb a happy birthday/merry Christmas **~amo!** congratulations! **~ka** *nf* (*Dsg* ~ci) **1** (Christmas, birthday) card **2** congratulation

češ|alj *nm* (*Gsg* ~lja, *Npl* ~ljevi) comb **~ljaonica** hairdresser's **~ljati** *v* (koga/što/se) comb (sb's/one's hair)

češati *v* (koga/što/se) scratch

češer *nm* cone

češći *comp* → **čest**

češnjak *nm* garlic **češanj ~a** a clove of g.

četa *nf mil* company → **satnija**

četk|a *nf* brush **~ica za zube** tooth brush **~ati** *v* (koga/što/se) brush

četinar *nm* conifer

četiri *num* four (4)

četni|k *nm* (*Npl* ~ci) Chetnik

četrdeset *num* forty (40) **~i** *num ord* fortieth

četver|ac *nm* (*Gsg* ~ca) *sport* four; quadruple scull **~o** *num* four (persons etc.) **~okut** *nm* quadrangle **~onožac** *nm* (*Gsg* ~onošca) quadruped, four-legged animal

četvor|ica *num* four ¶ used only for men/males **~ni** *adj* square **~ka** *nf* **1** number four **2** foursome, group of four

četvrt *nf* **1** quarter **~ sata** a q. of an hour **2** (grad) quarter, neighbourhood, area **~ast** *adj* square **~i** *num*

ord fourth **~ina** *nf* quarter **~ak** *nm* (*Gsg* ~ka) Thursday **Veliki ~ak** Maundy T. **~završnica** *nf* quarterfinals

čezn|uti *v* (za kim/za čim) yearn for **~ljiv** *adj* yearning, wistful

čežnja *nf* yearning, longing

čič|ak *nm* (*Gsg* ~ka, *Npl* ~ci) bur

čigra *nf* top

čiji *interr + rel pron* whose

čik *nm* cigarette butt; fag-end *coll* **~pauza** *coll* five-minute break

čim *conj* as soon as **~ prije** as soon as possible

čime *Isg* → **što**

čimbeni|k *nm* (*Npl* ~ci) factor, element

čimpanza *nf* chimpanzee; chimp *coll*

čin *nm* **1** act, action, deed **svršeni ~** fait accompli, accomplished fact **2** act **3** rank, position **~iti** *v* **1** (što) do, act, perform **2** (se) seem, appear **~i mi se** it seems to me

činovni|k *nm* (*Vsg* ~če, *Npl* ~ci) clerk **~čki** *adj* clerical

činjeni|ca *nf* fact **~čni** *adj* factual, based on fact

čio *adj* hale and hearty

čip|ka *nf* (*Dsg* ~ci) lace **~kast** *adj* lace **obrubljen ~kom** lace-trimmed

čips(i) *nm pl* crisps GB, chips US

čir *nm* boil, ulcer **~ na želucu** (gastric/stomach) ulcer

čist *adj* **1** (neuprljan) clean **2** (neokaljan; bez primjesa) pure **3** (piće) neat **4** (pošten; bez ispravaka) fair **5** (profit) net **~ kao sunce** spotless **~o zlato** solid gold **to nisu ~a posla** there's something fishy **~ač** *nm* cleaner **~ač mina** *mil* minesweeper **~ačica** *nf* cleaning woman/lady **~ilište** *nn* purgatory **~ina** *nf* clearing **~ionica** (kemijska) *nf* dry-cleaner's **~iti** *v* (što/se) clean, clear, remove, cleanse **~ka** *nf* purge **~oća** *nf* cleanliness **~okrvan** *adj* (α) purebred, thoroughbred **~unac** *nm* (*Gsg* ~unca, *Vsg* ~unče) obsessively clean (person); *fig* bigot; (moralni) bigot

čišćenje *nn* cleaning, cleansing **sredstvo za ~ 1** cleaning agent **2** *med* purgative, laxative **etničko ~** ethnic cleansing **mlijeko za** ~ cleanser

čit|ač *nm tech* reader, scanner ~**atelj** *nm* reader ~**ateljstvo** *nf* reading public ~**anka** *nf* (*Dsg* ~nci) textbook ~**aonica** *nf* reading room ~**ati** *v* (što/koga *fig*) read ~**ko** *adv* 1 legibly 2 articulately ~**ljiv** *adj* readable, legible

čitav *adj* whole, entire, complete ~ **dan** all day long

čizma *nf* boot

član *nm* 1 member 2 *gram* article ~**arina** *nf* membership fee, subscription ~**ska** *adj* **iskaznica** membership card ~**stvo** *nn* membership

član|ak *nm* (*Gsg* ~ka, *Npl* ~ci) 1 *leg* article 2 (newspaper) article **uvodni** ~**ak** editorial, leading a. 3 ankle

čmar *nm* anus

čobanin *nm* shepherd

čokolad|a *nf* chocolate ~**ni** *adj* **bonbon** chocolate

čokot *nm* vine

čopor *nm* 1 pack (+ *fig*) 2 (lavova) pride

čovječan *adj* (*a*) humane ~**anstvo** *nn* humanity, humankind

čovje|k *nm* (*Npl* ljudi) 1 man 2 one ~**k ne zna što bi mislio** one doesn't know what to think ~**koljubiv** *adj* philanthropic ~**komrzac** *nm* (*Gsg* ~komrsca) misanthrope ~**čuljak** *nm* (*Gsg* ~čuljka, *Vsg* ~čuljče, *Npl* ~čuljci) little man, dwarf

črčkati *v* (0/što) scribble; doodle

čuč|anj *nm* (*Gsg* ~nja, *Npl* ~njevi) 1 squat(ting position) 2 knee-bend ~**ati** *v* (0) squat ~**nuti** *v* (0) squat down ~**avac** *nm* (*Gsg* ~avca) squat toilet

čud|ak *nm* (*Npl* ~aci) eccentric, queer fellow; weirdo *coll* ~**an** *adj* (*a*) strange, odd, queer ~**esan** *adj* (*a*) wonderful; miraculous ~**iti** *v* (koga) 1 amaze, make sb wonder ~**i me** *coll* I am surprised 2 ~**iti** *v* (se

komu/čemu) wonder at ~**novati** *adj* **kljunaš** platypus ~**o** *nn* miracle, wonder ~**o od djeteta** child prodigy **nije** ~ (da) it is no wonder; small wonder (that) **pravo je** ~**o** it is a miracle **naći se u** ~**u** be at a loss ~**otvorac** *nm* (*Gsg* ~otvorca, *Vsg* ~otvorče) miracle-worker ~**otvoran** *adj* (*a*) miraculous ~**ovište** *nn* monster ~**ovišan** *adj* (*a*) monstrous

čuđenje *nn* wonder, astonishment **pogledati s** ~**m** look in astonishment

čujan *adj* (*a*) audible

čul|an *adj* (*a*) sensual ~**o** sense

čun *nm* canoe

čunj *nm* (nine)pin

čup|ati *v* 1 (koga/što) pluck, pull out ~**ati kosu** *fig* tear one's hair, be distraught 2 (se) *fig* scuffle, fight ~**av** *adj* shaggy, dishevelled ~**avac** *nm* (*Gsg* ~avca, *Vsg* ~avče) 1 mophead 2 thick shaggy carpet/rug ~**erak** *nm* (*Gsg* ~erka, *Npl* ~erci) tuft ~**kati** *v* (što) pluck/pick at

ču|ti *v* 1 (koga/što) hear 2 (se) hear from each other, be in touch, speak ~**ven** *adj* famous, noted; (vino) fine

čutura *nf* flask, canteen

čuva|r *nm* 1 (security) guard, watchman 2 caretaker 3 guardian, protector ~**ti** *v* 1 (što) keep, preserve 2 (koga/što) guard, watch over, protect ~**j (se)!** watch out! 3 ~**ti** (se) take care of oneself, look after oneself 4 ~**j** (se) beware, watch out for, stay away from

čvar|ak *nm* (*Gsg* ~ka, *Npl* ~ci) crackling

čvor *nm* 1 knot 2 (~ište) *fig* junction, hub

čvor|ak *nm* (*Gsg* ~ka, *Npl* ~ci) starling

čvrst *adj* (*comp* čvršći) 1) firm, solid, strong, hard (+ *fig*) 2) uncompromising **politika** ~**e ruke** hard-line politics 2 tight 3 fixed, steady ~**oća** *nf* firmness

Ć

Ć, ć 5th letter of Cro. alphabet

ća *adv dial* away, off **idem ~** I'm off

ćaća *nm coll* Pa, dad

ćaknut *adj coll* daft

ćaskati *v* (0) chatter

će (*III sg + pl*), **ću** (*I sg*), **ćeš** (*II sg*), **ćemo** (*I pl*), **ćete** (*II pl*) *v* → **htjeti**

ćela *nf* bald head/spot **~v** *adj* bald **~vac** *nm* (*Gsg* ~vca, *Vsg* ~vče) bald man/guy; baldie *coll derog* **~viti** *v* (0) grow bald

ćelija *nf* (prison) cell

ćevap *nm* kebab **~čić** *nm* grilled minced meat finger

ćirilica *nf* (the) Cyrillic (alphabet/script)

ćorav *adj derog* 1 blind in one eye 2 *coll* short-sighted, weak-sighted **okani se ~a posla** it's no use, forget it

ćud *nf* temper, disposition **blage ~i** good-natured **to mi je po ~i** it's to my liking **koliko ljudi toliko ~i** it takes all sorts to make this world **~ljiv** *adj* 1 fickle 2 wayward

ćudore|dan *adj* (α) moral **~đe** *nn* morality

ćuk *nm* little-owl

ćup *nm* jar, crock

ćurlikati *v* (0) trill

ćuš|ka *nf* (*Dsg* ~ci) slap **opaliti ~ku** slap **~kati** *v impf* **~nuti** *v* (koga) slap

ćutjeti *v* (što) feel

D

D, d (de) 6th letter of Cro. alphabet

da *conj* **1** to, in order to, so that • **~ ne bi** so as not to **2** that *znam* **~ si ovdje** I know (that) you are here **~ vidim** let me see **3** if **~ sam znao, došao bih** if I had known I would have come **4** if only **~ mi je 100 $** if only I had $ 100 **~ se nisi usudio** don't you dare • *adv* yes

dab|ar *nm* (*Gsg* ~ra, *Npl* ~rovi) beaver

dadilja *nf* nurse, nanny

dagnja *nf* mussel

dah *nm* breath **ostati bez ~a** be out of breath **b** *fig* be breathless/astounded **doći do ~a** recover one's breath **~nuti** *v* (0) breathe **~tati** *v* (0) pant, gasp, breathe hard

dakako *adv* of course, certainly, indeed

dakle *conj* then, therefore, hence, consequently • *adv coll* well

daktilograf *nm* typist **~ija** *nf* typing

dalek *adj* (*comp* dalji) far (off), distant **~o** *adv* a long way (off/away), far (away) **~ometan** *adj* (α) long-range **~osežan** *adj* (α) far-reaching **~ovidan** *adj* (α) **1** far-sighted **2** *fig* visionary **~ozor** *nm* field-glasses, binoculars **~ovod** *nm* transmission line

dalj|e *adv comp* farther, further **~i** *adj comp* farther, further **~ina** *nf* distance **iz ~ine** from afar **~inski** *adj* **upravljač** remote control **~nji** *adj* further, additional **do ~njega** until further notice

dama *nf* **1** lady **2** (igra) draughts *pl* GB; checkers *pl* US

dan *nm* day **slobodan ~** day off **Sudnji ~** doomsday **svaki drugi ~** every other day **~ za ~om** day after day **neki ~** the other day **za koji ~** one of these days, soon **~as** *adv* **1** today **do ~as** to date **2** (u današnje vrijeme) nowadays **~ašnji** *adj* today's, present-day, modern **~ašnjica** *nf* today, the present **~onoćno** *adv* day and night

dan|ak *nm* (*Gsg* ~ka) tribute

dangub|a *nf* loafer **~iti** *v* (0) idle away, loaf

danju *adv* by day, during the day

dapače *conj* indeed

dar *nm* **1** present, gift **2** talent **~ežljiv** *adj* generous **~ežljivost** *nf* generosity **~ivati** *v impf* **~ovati** *v* (komu što) (*pres* ~ujem) give sth to sb/sb sth **~ovit** *adj* gifted, talented

da|ska *nf* board, plank; surfboard; (zahodska) toilet seat **odskočna ~ska** spring-board **~skanje** *nn* surfing **~šćan** *adj* made of planks **~ščara** *nf* wooden shack **~ščica** *nf* board

daš|ak *nm* (*Gsg* ~ka) breath

dati *v* **1** (što kome) give sth to sb/sb sth, donate, bestow upon **~ na znanje** inform, let know **~ ploda** yield fruit/result **~ povoda** give rise to, serve as a pretext **~ sve od sebe** do one's best/utmost, spare no effort **~ u najam** rent, let **~ život za** sacrifice one's life for **2** (dopustiti) let **3** (što učiniti) have sth done **4** (se komu) **ne da mi se to učiniti** I don't feel like doing it **ne ~ se** resist

dat|irati *v* (0) (iz) date from/back to **~um** *nm* date

datote|ka *nf* (*Dsg* ~ci) *comp* file

dava|telj *nm* donor **~telj krvi** blood donor **~ti** *v impf* (*pres* dajem) → **dati ~ti se** (film) be on

daviti *v* **1** (koga) strangle; pester *fig* **2** (se) (čime) choke on/suffocate; be drowning

davn|i *adj* ancient **~ina** *nf* old times, time long gone **od ~ina** from time immemorial **~o** *adv* a long time ago, long ago

debata *nf* debate

deb|elo *adj* (~ela *f*, ~lji *comp*) **1** fat, thick **2** (osoba) fat, overweight ~**elo crijevo** large intestine ~**elokožac** *nm* (*Gsg* ~elokošca, *Vsg* ~elokošče, *Npl* ~elokošci) thick-skinned/insensitive person ~**ljko** *nm* fatty, fatso ~**eljuškast** *adj* plump ~**ljati** *v* (se) put on weight ~**ljina** *nf* (osoba) obesity; thickness

deblo *nn* (tree)trunk, bole

decimal|an *adj* (a) decimal ~**ni zarez** d. point

dečko *nm* **1** lad, boy **2** boyfriend **3** (karta) jack, knave

defekt *nm* **1** defect **2** breakdown

deficit *nm* deficit **biti u ~u** show a d.

defini|cija *nf* definition ~**rati** *v* (koga/što) define ~**tivan** *adj* (a) conclusive, final ~**tivno** *adv* definitely

deformacija *nf* deformation, disfigurement

degener|acija *nf* degeneration ~**ik** *nm* (*Vsg* ~iče, *Npl* ~ici) **1** degenerate **2** *fig coll* moron ~**irati** *v* (0) degenerate, decline

degustacija *nf* tasting

deka *nf* blanket

dekada *nf* decade

dekadentan *adj* (a) decadent

dekan *nm* dean ~**at** *nm* dean's office

deklar|acija *nf* declaration ~**irati** *v* **1** (što) declare **2** (se kao) declare oneself to be

deklinacija *nf* declension

dekolt|e *nm* neckline; cleavage *coll* ~**iran** *adj* low-cut

dekoncentriran *adj* distracted

dekor *nm* **1** decor **2** setting

dekret *nm* decree, order

delega|cija *nf* delegation ~**t** *nm* delegate

delikat|an *adj* (a) delicate; sensitive ~**esa** *nf* delicacy

delinkvent *nm* delinquent

deložacija *nf* eviction

demanti *nm* denial; disclaimer ~**rati** *v* **1** (što) deny **2** (koga) prove wrong

deminutiv *nm* diminutive

demokra|cija *nf* democracy ~**t** *nm* democrat ~**tski** *adj* democratic

demonstr|acija *nf* **1** demonstration **2** ~**acije** *pl* demonstration; demo *coll* ~**ant** *nm* demonstrator ~**ativan** *adj* demonstrative, ostentatious ~**irati** *v* (0) demonstrate

demontirati *v* (što) dismantle; (bombu) defuse

depilator *nm* hair-remover

deponij *nm* tip *GB*, dump *US* ~**rati** *v* (što) deposit

deportirati *v* (koga) deport

depr|esija *nf* depression ~**imiran** *adj* depressed

deran *nm* urchin

derati (1) (*pres* derem) *v* **1** (što/koga/kožu komu) flay, skin **2** (što) rend, tear apart

derati (2) *v* (se) shout, scream

deratizacija *nf* rat poisoning

derište *nn* brat

derivat *nf* derivative **naftni ~i** petroleum products

desant *nm mil* landing operation

desert *nm* sweet; dessert *US;* pudding *GB*

deset *num* ten (10) ~**ak** *nm* a dozen **na ~ke** dozens/scores ~**nik** *nm* (*Vsg* ~niče, *Npl* ~nici) corporal ~**ero** *num* ten people ~**i** *num ord* tenth ~**ica** *nf* (number) ten ~**ina** *nf* **1** tenth **2** *mil* squad **na ~ine** dozens, in their dozens ~**ljeće** *nn* decade ~**orica** *nf* ten men

desiti se → dogoditi se

desn|i (1) *adj* right, righthand ~**a ruka** *fig* right-hand man ~**ica** *nf* **1** right hand **2** *pol* the right ~**ičar** *nm* rightwinger ~**ičarski** *adj* right-wing, rightist

desni (2) *nf pl* gums

destil|acija *nf* distillation ~**irati** *v* (što) distil

dešnja|k *nm* (*Npl* ~ci) right-handed person

detalj *nm* detail ~**an** *adj* (a) detailed

detektiv *nm* detective **privatni ~** private investigator; p. eye *coll* ~**ski** *adj* detective

deterdžent, detergent *nm coll* soap/washing powder **~ za pranje posuđa** washing-up liquid

deva *nf* camel

devalvacija *nf* devaluation

devedeset *num* ninety (90) **~i** *num ord* ninetieth

devet *num* nine (9) **~ero** *num* nine people **~i** *num ord* ninth **~ica** *nf* (number) nine **~naest** *num* nineteen **~nica** *nf* novena

deviz|a *nf* 1 motto 2 *pl* foreign currency/exchange **~e** *pl coll* hard currency

dezert|er *nm* deserter **~irati** *v* (0) desert

dezinf|ekcija *nf* disinfection **sredstvo za ~ekciju** disinfectant **~icirati** *v* (koga/što) disinfect

dežur|ati *v* (0) be on duty/on call **~ni** *adj* **časnik** duty officer **~stvo** *nn* duty

dići *v* → **dignuti**

dignuti *v* (*pres* dignem) 1 (koga/što) lift, raise; (sidro) weigh; (zastavu) hoist **~ prašinu** stir up interest **~ galamu/poviku** raise hell **~ nos** put on airs 2 (se) rise, raise oneself, stand up; (iz kreveta) get up 3 (se kome) *sl tab* get a hard on

dijabetes *nm* diabetes

dijafragma *nf* diaphragm

dijagnoza *nf* diagnosis

dijagonal|a *nf* diagonal **~n** *adj* (a) diagonal

dijalekt *nm* dialect

dijalo|g *nm* (*Npl* ~zi) dialogue; conversation

dijamant *nm* diamond **~an** *adj* (a) diamond

dijametralno *adv* diametrically

dijapozitiv *nm* slide

dije|liti *v* 1 (što čime) divide sth by sth 2 (koga/što) separate, divide 3 (što komu) distribute to/among, deal, hand out 4 (što s kim) share, have sth in common with 5 (se) come apart, separate 6 (se na što) fall into, be divided into **~ljenje** *nn* division

dijet|a *nf* diet **biti na ~i** diet **~alan** *adj* (a) low-calorie

dijete *nn* (*Gsg* djeteta, *Npl* djeca) child **vanbračno ~** child born out of the wedlock **čudo od djeteta** child prodigy

di|ka *nf* (*Dsg* ~ci) glory, pride

dikobraz *nm* porcupine

dikt|at *nm* 1 dictation **pisati po ~atu** take dictation 2 dictates *pl* **~ator** *nm* dictator **~atura** *nf* dictatorship **~irati** *v* (komu/što) dictate

diletant *nm* derog amateur

diljem *adv* throughout, across

dim *nm* smoke **~iti** *v* (0/se/što) smoke **~njačar** *nm* chimneysweep **~njak** *nm* (*Npl* ~njaci) chimney; funnel; smokestack

dimenzija *nf* dimension

dina *nf* dune

dinami|čan *adj* (æ) dynamic **~ka** *nf* (*Dsg* ~ci) dynamics; trends

dinamit *nm* dynamite

dinamo *nm* dynamo

dinja *nf* melon

dio *nm* (*Gsg* dijela, *Npl* dijelovi) 1 part, portion, section 2 share **rezervni ~** spare part **sastavni ~** constituent (part) **~ba** *nf* division, partition **~nica** *nf* 1 (ceste) section 2 share 3 *mus* part **~ničar** *nm* shareholder *GB*; stockholder *US* **~nički** *adj* **~ničko društvo** joint-stock company

dioptrij|a *nf* diopter **naočale s ~om** prescription glasses

diplom|a *nf* degree (in) **~irati** *v* (što) graduate from, have a degree in **~irani profesor** B.A. **~ski** *adj* ispit graduation/final exam

diploma|cija *nf* diplomacy **~t** *nm* diplomat **~tski** *adj* diplomatic

dir|ati *v impf* → **dirnuti** **~ati u srce** touch, move **~ljiv** *adj* touching, moving

direk|cija *nf* management, administration **~tan** *adj* (a) direct, straight **~tor** *nm* director; manager; executive **generalni ~tor** general manager **~tor škole** principal, headmaster

dirigent *nm* conductor

dir|nuti *v* (koga/što) (*pres* ~nem) 1 touch 2 *fig* touch, affect **~ati** *v impf*

disa|nje *nn* breathing, respiration **~ti** *v* (0) (*pres* dišem) breathe

disciplin|a *nf* discipline **~iran** *adj* disciplined **~ski** *adj* disciplinary

disertacija *nf* **doktorska ~** doctoral thesis/dissertation

disk *nm* 1 disk (+ *comput*), disc 2 *sport* discus **bacanje ~a** discus throw **~eta** nf comput floppy disk

disko(teka) nf disco(theque)

diskre|cija nf discretion, secrecy **~tan** adj (a) discreet; (nenametljiv) delicate

diskreditirati v 1 (koga) discredit, destroy sb's reputation 2 (se) lose face, compromise

diskriminacij|a nf dicrimination **provoditi ~u** discriminate against

disku|sija nf discussion **~tirati** v (o čemu) discuss sth

diskvalificirati v (koga/što) disqualify

dispanzer nm out-patient unit, health care centre

distributer nm authorized dealer, distributor

dišni adj respiratory

div nm giant **~ovski** adj gigantic, jumbo

div|an adj (a) wonderful, brilliant, great **~iti** v (se komu/čemu) admire sb/sth **~no** adv great, brilliant **~no smo se proveli** we had a great time **~ota** nf marvel, beauty

diverz|ant nm mil 1 commando 2 saboteur **~ija** nf sabotage

dividenda nf dividend

divizija nf mil division

divlj|ač nf game **~ački** adj savage, barbarous **~ak** nm (Vsg **~**ače, Npl **~**aci) savage **~akuša** nf hoyden **~aštvo** nn savagery, brutality **~ati** v (0) rage **~i** adj wild **~i brak** common-law marriage **~ina** nf wilderness

diza|lica nf 1 crane 2 (auto)jack **~lo** nm lift GB; elevator US **~ti** v impf → **dignuti ~nje utega** sport weight-lifting

dje|ca nn pl children **~čak** nm (Vsg **~**čače, Npl **~**čaci) boy **~čji** adj infant, baby, children('s); infantile (+ derog) **~čja kolica** pram GB; baby buggy US **~čji vrtić** nm kindergarten, nursery **~čurlija** nf brats **~tinjarija** nf tomfoolery **~tinjast** adj childish **~tinjstvo** nn childhood, infancy

djed nm grandfather, grandpa

djelat|an adj (a) active **~nik** nm (Npl **~**nici) worker, employee **~nost** nf activity

djel|o nn 1 action, act, deed **krivično ~o** criminal offense **provesti u ~o** implement, realize **uhvatiti koga na ~u** catch sb red-handed 2 work **~okrug** nm field, domain **~otvoran** adj (a) efficient, efficacious, effective **~ovanje** nn action, effect, operation **~ovati** v (pres **~**ujem) 1 (0) act, operate, perform 2 (0) have effect, work 3 (na koga) affect/influence sb

djelomice, djelomično adv partly

djetelina nf clover **četverolisna ~** four-leaf clover

djeveruša nf bridesmaid

djevi|ca nf 1 virgin 2 astrol Virgo **~čanski** adj virginal, untouched **~čanstvo** nn virginity

djevoj|ački adj 1 girlish 2 girl-, girls' **~ačko prezime** maiden name **~čica** nf (little) girl **~ka** nf (Dsg **~**ci) 1 girl 2 girlfriend

dla|ka nf (Gsg **~**ci) 1 hair 2 (životinje) fur **na ~ku na a T za ~ku** by a hair's breadth **nemati ~ke na jeziku** not mince words

dlan nm palm

dlijeto nn chisel

dnevn|i adj daily, everyday **~i red** agenda **~i boravak** living-room **~i list** daily (paper) **~ica** nf per diem allowance **~ik** nm (Npl **~**ici) 1 diary **voditi ~ik** keep a diary 2 daily paper 3 TV evening news **~o** adv every day, daily

dno nn bottom

do prep 1 (mjesto) beside, near, by 2 (vrijeme) up to, until, till **od ... ~** from ... to **od riječi ~ riječi** word by word **~ viđenja** (good)bye

do- prefix 1 (glagoli kretanja) **doja-hati** come on horseback **dotrčati** come running **dostići** reach 2 **dopisati** add (write in addition) 3 (imenice dužnosti) deputy, vice-

dob nf age **u ~i od pet godina** at the age of five

doba nn time, times, age **godišnje ~** season **~ dana** time of day **moderno ~** modern age **u isto ~** at the same time **u svako ~** at any time

dobaci|ti v (komu što) 1 throw at/to 2 make/pass a (rude) remark, comment

~vati *v impf*

dob|ar *adj* (æ) (*comp* bolji) **1** good; kind **2** right ○ *nm* (ocjena) C **~ro** *nn* **1** good, well-being **2** farm, estate ○ *adv* well **~ro došli** welcome *nije mi ~ro* I feel sick **~robit** *nf* welfare, benefit **~ročinitelj** *nm* benefactor **~roćudan** *adj* (a) good-natured; benign **~rodošlica** *nf* welcome **~rodušan** *adj* (a) kind-hearted **~ronamjeran** *adj* (a) well-meaning, friendly **~rota** *nf* goodness, kindness **~rotvor** *nm* benefactor **~rotvoran** *adj* (a) charitable **~rotvorna organizacija** charity

dobav|iti *v* (što) supply, procure, purchase **~ljač** *nm* supplier **~ljati** *v impf*

dobi|t *nf* profit **~tak** *nm* (*Gsg* ~tka, *Npl* ~ci) **1** gain, profit **2** (igra na sreću) winnings *pl* **biti na ~tku** profit **~ti** *v* (koga/što) (*pres* ~jem) get, receive, obtain, gain; (utakmicu) win; (bolest) catch, contract **~tnik** *nm* (*Vsg* ~tniče, *Npl* ~tnici) winner **~vati** *v impf*

dobrovolj|jac *nm* (*Gsg* ~ca, *Vsg* ~če, *Npl* ~ci) volunteer **~ački** *adj mil* volunteer **~ni** *adj* voluntary **~no** *adv* voluntarily, of one's own free will **~no se javiti** volunteer

docent *nm* (senior) lecturer; assistant lecturer *US*

dočarati *v* (što) conjure up

dočasni|k *nm* (*Npl* ~ci) non-commissioned officer

doček *nm* welcome, reception **~ Nove godine** New Year's party

dočepati *v* (se koga/čega) get hold of sb/sth, seize, grab

doč|uti *v* (što) (*pres* ~ujem) hear (a rumour) **~ula sam** it has reached my ears

doći *v* (0) (*pres* dođem) come (to), arrive (0/in/at) **~ do zaključka** come to/arrive at/reach a conclusion *došlo je do nesreće* there was an accident **~ k sebi** recover, come to (0) **~ po koga/što** pick sth/sb up **dobro ~** come in handy

doda|tak *nm* (*Gsg* ~tka, *Npl* ~ci) addition, appendix **~tan** *adj* (a) additional **~ti** *v* **1** (što) add **2** (komu što) pass

sb sth/sth to sb, hand **~vati** *v impf* (*pres* ~jem)

dodijeliti *v* (komu što) (zadaću) assign, allot; (sredstva) earmark, allocate; (stipendiju) grant

dodir *nm* touch, contact **~nuti** *v* **1** (koga/što) touch **2** (se čega) touch upon **~ivati** *v* (*pres* ~ujem) **1** *impf* **2** (se) touch, be in contact

doduše *adv* on je ~ *bogat ali nema sreće* he might be rich but he's not happy

doga *nf* Great Dane

događa|j *nm* event, occurence **~ti** *v impf* → događiti

doglavni|k *nm* (*Npl* ~ci) second in command, lieutenant

dogled|an *adj* (a) **~no vrijeme/~na budućnost** foreseeable future

dogoditi *v* (se) happen, occur, take place

dogor|jeti *v* (0) (*pres* ~im) burn out

dogov|or *nm* **1** agreement, deal **2** appointment **~oriti** *v* **1** (se o čemu) agree upon, come to an agreement (on) **2** (što) arrange, set up; schedule **~arati** *v impf*

dograd|iti *v* build an extension/annexe **~nja** *nf* extension, annexe

dogurati *v* (0) *fig daleko* ~ go far, come up in the world ~ *do* make it to, end up as

doho|dak *nm* (*Gsg* ~tka) income; (osobni) salary

dohvat *nm* na ~ **ruke** within (one's) reach **~iti** *v* (koga/što) get hold of, grab

doigravanje *nn sport* playoff

doimati *v impf* → dojmiti

doista *adv* really, indeed

dojad|iti *v* (komu što) **~lo mi je** I am fed up with; I am tired/sick of

doj|am *nm* (*Gsg* ~ma, *Npl* ~movi) impression **imati ~am** be under the i. **~miti** *v* (se koga) impress

dojav|a *nf* tip-off *coll* **~iti** *v* (što komu) inform, report, notify **~ljivati** *v impf*

doj|enče *nn* (*Npl* ~enčad) infant, baby **~enje** *nn* nursing **~iti** *v* (0/koga) nurse **~ka** *nf* (*Dsg* ~ci) breast

dojučerašnji *adj* former, recent

dojuriti *v* (0) come running

dok (1) *conj* while ~ **ne dođe** until she arrives

dok (2) *nm* dock

dokad *adv* (for) how long

dokaz *nm* proof, evidence ~**ati** *v* 1 (komu što) prove sth to sb/sb sth 2 (se) prove/show one's worth ~**ivati** *v impf* ~**ni** *adj* **materijal** evidence

dokle *adv* how far, how long ~ **god** as long as

dokolica *nf* leisure

dokoljenka *nf* knee-high stocking

dokopati *v* (se čega) get hold of, come by

dokrajla *adv* to the end ~**čiti** *v* (koga/što) finish off

doktor *nm* 1 ~ **liječnik** 2 doctor ~ **društvenih znanosti** PhD ~**at** *nm* doctorate, doctor's degree, PhD ~**irati** *v* (0/iz čega) take one's doctor's degree (in)

doktrina *nf* doctrine

dokučiti *v* (što) 1 reach 2 *fig* grasp

dokument *nm* document ~**aran** *adj* (α) documentary ~**arni film**; ~**arac** *nm* (Gsg ~arca) *coll* documentary

dol *nm* dell, vale ~**ina** *nf* valley

dola|zak *nm* (Gsg ~ska, Npl ~sci) arrival ~**ziti** *v impf* → **doći ne** ~**zi u obzir** it is out of the question

dolčevit(k)a *nf coll* polo neck

doličan *adj* (α) proper

dolijati *v* (0) get caught

dolijevati *v* (0) pour (on), add

dolik|ovati *v* (kome/se kome) (*pres* ~**ujem**) befit

dolje *adv* 1 down, below 2 downwards

dom *nm* 1 home 2 (institucije) house, hall, centre 3 *pol* house, chamber za**stupnički** ~ house of representatives **županijski** ~ house of counties ~**a** *adv* home ~**aći** *adj* 1 home-made 2 domestic 3 inland, domestic, internal ~**aćica** *nf* 1 housewife, home-maker 2 hostess ~**aćin** *nm* host ~**aćinstvo** *nn* 1 household 2 domestic science ~**ar** *nm* janitor

domah|nuti *v* (komu) wave to sb, beckon sb ~**ivati** *v impf*

domamiti *v* (koga) lure

domašaj *nm* 1 range 2 reach

domino *nm* (igra) dominoes

domi|sliti *v* (se) 1 guess 2 (čemu) come up with sth ~**šljat** *adj* clever, ingenious

domjen|ak *nm* (Gsg ~ka Npl ~ci) party

domobran *nm* Home Guardsman

domoći *v* (se čega) (*pres* domognem) lay one's hands on, get hold of

domoro|dac *nm* (Gsg ~ca, Npl ~ci) native

domov|ina *nf* homeland ~**nica** *nf* citizenship certificate ~**inski** *adj* **rat** war of independence

donde *adv* as far as that

donedavno *adv* until recently

donekle *adv* to some/a certain extent, up to a point

donijeti *v* (što komu) (*pres* donesem) bring ~ **korist** yield profit ~ **plod** bear fruit ~ **odluku** reach/make a decision ~ **presudu** reach a verdict ~ **zakon** pass a law

donosit|i *v impf* → **donijeti** ~**elj** *nm* bearer

donji *adj* lower

dopa|sti *v* (*pres* ~**dnem**) 1 (komu/koga) fall to one's share 2 (se komu) *dopao mi se* I like him ~**dati** *v impf* ~**dljiv** *adj* likeable, pretty

dopirati *v impf* → **doprijeti**

dopis *nm* (business/official) letter, memo ~**ati** *v* (što) (*pres* dopišem) add ~**ivanje** *nn* correspondence ~**ivati** *v* 1 (što) *impf* 2 (se s kim) write to sb regularly ~**nica** *nf* postcard ~**nik** *nm* (Npl ~nici) correspondent

dopla|titi *v* (za što) pay extra for ~**tak** *nm* (Gsg ~tka) bonus **dječji** ~**tak** child benefit ~**ćivati** *v impf*

doprem|a *nf* delivery ~**iti** *v* (što) deliver

dop|rijeti *v* (do koga/čega) (*pres* doprem) (manage to) reach sb/ (up to) sth

doprin|os *nm* 1 contribution 2 tax ~**ijeti** *v* (čemu) (*pres* ~**esem**) *coll* contribute to

dopun|a *nf* supplement, addition, annex ~**iti** *v* 1 (koga) elaborate 2 (što) replenish; supplement

dopu|snica *nf* permit ~**st** *nm* leave (of

absence) ~stiti *v* (što komu) let sb do sth, allow sth/sb to do sth, permit sth ~štati *v impf* ~štenje *nn* permission

doput|ovati *v* (0) (*pres* ~ujem) come, arrive

dorastao *adj* (dorasla *f*) 1 (čemu) up to sth 2 (komu) sb's equal

doruč|ak *nm* (*Gsg* ~ka) breakfast ~kovati *v* (*pres* ~kujem) 1 (0) have breakfast 2 (što) breakfast on sth, have sth for b.

dosad(a) *adv* till now, hitherto ~ nepoznat as yet unknown ~ašnji *adj* outgoing, departing

dosa|da *nf* boredom ~dan *adj* (*a*) boring ~diti *v* (komu čime) bore sb with ~dno mi je I am bored ~divati *v* 1 (komu čime) *impf* 2 (se) be bored

dose|gnuti *v* (što) reach ~g *nm* (*Npl* ~zi) 1 reach, range 2 achievement

dose|liti *v* (se) move to sth/in ~ljenik *nm* (*Npl* ~ljenici) settler, immigrant

dosje *nm* dossier, file record

dosjet|iti *v* (se) 1 guess 2 call to mind 3 (čemu) come up with sth ~ka *nf* (*Dsg* ~ci) witticism

doskočiti *v* 1 (komu) outwit, thwart 2 (čemu) find a way around sth

doslov|an *adj* (*a*) literal

dosluh *nm* u ~u s in collusion with

dosljedan *adj* (*a*) consistent

dosp|ijeće *nn* maturity ~jeti (0) (*pres* ~ijem) be due, mature ~ijevati *v impf*

dosta *adv* 1 enough ~ mi je svega I've had enough 2 (prilično) quite

dostav|a *nf* delivery ~iti *v* deliver ~ljati *v impf* ~ljač *nm* courier; delivery man ~nica *nf* delivery bill

dosti|ći (*pres* ~gnem) 1 (koga/što) catch up with 2 (što) reach, attain 3 (0) suffice ~gnuće *nn* achievement ~zati *v impf* (*pres* ~žem)

dostojan *adj* (*a*) (koga/čega) worthy of ~stven *adj* dignified ~stvenik *nm* (*Npl* ~stvenici) dignitary ~stveno *adv* with dignity ~stvo *nn* dignity

dostupan *adj* (*a*) accessible; available

došapnuti *v* (komu što) whisper (into sb's ear)

Došašće *nn* Advent

došlja|k *nm* (*Vsg* ~če, *Npl* ~ci) newcomer

došuljati *v* (se) steal into/up to

dotada *adv* up to that time, until then nikad ~ never before

dotaknuti → dodirnuti

dotica|lj → dodir ~ti *v* → dodirivati

dotični *adj* in question, concerned

dotjer|an *adj* 1 smart, well-groomed 2 elaborate ~ati *v* 1 (koga/što) drive 2 (koga/se) dress up; preen oneself 3 (što) elaborate, touch up

dotle *adv* so far

dotrajati *v* (0) wear out

dotu|ći *v* (koga) (*pres* ~čem) *fig* finish off

doušni|k *nm* (*Vsg* ~če, *Npl* ~ci) informer

dovabiti *v* (koga) lure

dovesti (1) *v* (*pres* dovedem) 1 (koga/što komu/kamo) bring sb/sth to ~ do ludila drive crazy ~ u napast lead into temptation ~ sa sobom bring along ~ u red put sth in order, fix ~ u nepriliku put in an awkward position 2 (do čega) lead to sth

dovesti (2) *v* (*pres* dovezem) 1 (koga/što) bring, carry, convey 2 (se) arrive by car

dovikivati *v* (što komu) call out, shout

dovlačiti *v impf* → dovući

dovod *nm* supply ~iti *v* (komu što/koga) supply sb with sb/sth

dovolj|an *adj* (*a*) sufficient • *nm* (ocjena) D, pass ~no *adv* sufficiently, enough *nije* ~no jak he is not strong enough

dovrš|iti *v* (što) end, finish, complete, bring to an end ~avati *v impf*

dovući *v* (koga/što/se) drag

doza *nf* dose prevelika ~ overdose

dozivati *v impf* → dozvati

dozlogrdi|ti *v* (komu) ~lo mi je I am fed up (with it)

dozna|čiti *v* (komu/što) remit, transfer, make payable to ~ka *nf* (*Dsg* ~ci) 1 cash remittance 2 bank transfer

doznati *v* (što) learn, find out

dozvati *v* (koga/što) summon, call

dozvola *nf* permit, licence vozačka ~ driving *GB*/driver's *US* licence radna ~ work permit građevinska ~

planning permission

doživljeti v (što) (pres ~im) 1 live to see 2 experience, undergo ~jeti **duboku starost** live to an old age ~ljaj nm experience

doživot|an adj (a) life-long ~ni predsjednik president for life ~ni zatvor life sentence

drag adj (comp draži) dear ~i kamen precious stone ~e volje with pleasure **milo za ~o** tit for tat ~a nf dear, honey, sweetheart ~i nm dear ~o adv ~o mi je a. I am glad b. (kod upoznavanja) glad/pleased to meet you, how do you do ~ocjen adj precious, valuable ~ocjenost nf (predmet) valuable ~ovolja|c nm (Gsg ~ovoljca) volunteer ~ulj nm jewel (+ fig) ~uljar nm jeweller

dram|a nf 1 drama (+ fig) 2 play ~atičan adj (a) dramatic ~atičar nm playwright ~atizirati v (0/što) dramatize ~ski adj dramatic

drangulij|a nf coll trinket ~e pl odds and ends

drastičan adj (a) drastic

draškati v (koga) tickle

draž nm charm ~estan adj (a) charming, lovely ~ica nf anat clitoris

dražb|a nf auction **dati na ~u** put up for a.

draži → drag

dražiti v (koga/što) tease

dre|čati v (0) scream ~čav adj (colour) loud ~ka nf (Dsg ~ci) screaming, noise ~knuti v (što/na koga) shout (at sb)

drek nm tab shit, crap

dren → drijen

dres nm coll 1 jersey 2 (gimnastički) leotard

dresirati v (koga) coll train

drevan adj (a) ancient

drhtati v (0) (od) shake (all over), tremble, shiver (with)

drijemati v (0) drowse, doze

drijen nm dogwood **zdrav kao ~** fit as a fiddle

drkati v (0) tab wank, jerk off

drlja|ča nf harrow ~ti v (0/što) 1 harrow 2 fig scrawl

drmati v (što/koga/se) shake

drobi|lica nf ~lica za cement cement mill ~ti v 1 (koga/što) crush 2 (što) fig talk nonsense, blather

drog|a nf drug ~irati v (se) take/do drugs, be on drugs ~iran adj drugged; high, stoned coll

drolja nf slut, whore

dronj|ak nm (Gsg ~ka, Npl ~ci) rag

drpati v (koga/se s kim) tab coll grope sb, neck with sb, snog

drsko adv brazenly ~st nf impudence; the cheek coll

dru|g nm comrade, mate **bračni ~g/~žica** spouse ~garica nf comrade

drugdje adv elsewhere **negdje ~** somewhere/some place else

drug|i num ord second • adj 1 (the) other (of two); another (više od dva) svaki ~i dan every other day **s ~e strane** on the other hand 2 different **biti u ~om stanju** be pregnant ~orazredan adj (a) second-class; second-rate, inferior

drukčije adv otherwise ~i adj different

društv|en adj 1 social ~eno vlasništvo a. social ownership b. public property ~ene znanosti humanities, arts 2 sociable, outgoing ~o nn 1 society 2 association 3 company **osiguravajuće ~o** insurance company ~o s ograničenim jamstvom limited liability company (Ltd.); incorporated company (Inc.) US **praviti komu ~o** keep sb c.

druž|ba nf society ~eljubiv adj gregarious ~ina nf bunch, gang ~iti v (se) mingle with

drv|o nn 1 tree 2 wood ~o za ogrjev firewood 3 timber ~arnica nf woodshed **Božićno ~ce** Christmas tree ~eće nn trees ~en adj wooden (+ fig) ~ni adj timber ~odjelac nm (Gsg ~odjelca, Vsg ~odjelče) carpenter ~ored nm tree-lined avenue ~osječa nm woodcutter, lumberjack

drzak adj (drska f) impudent, impertinent, fresh

dr|žak nm (Gsg ~ška, Npl ~šci) handle ~žanje nn attitude, carriage, behaviour ~žati v 1 (koga/što) hold 2 (koga/što) keep 3 (se) act, behave

~žati se po strani keep aloof **4** (što) deliver **5** (što) think, hold **~žati do koga** respect sb **6** (se čega) stick to, follow

država nf state **~ljanin** nm citizen **strani ~ljanin** foreign national, alien **~ljanstvo** nn citizenship **~ni** adj **1** state-owned, state **2** national **~žavni udar** coup d'etat **~nik** nm (Npl **~nici**) statesman **~nost** nf statehood

dublna nf depth iz **~ine srca** from the bottom of one's heart **~inski** adj in-depth **~ok** adj (comp **dublji**) deep; profound (osjećaj) **~oki tanjur** soup plate **~oko** adv deep, deeply

dućan nm coll shop GB; store US

dud nm mulberry **~ov svilac** silkworm

dudla nf (varalica) dummy, comforter; (na bočici) teat GB; nipple US **hraniti na ~u** bottle feed

dug (1), **~ačak** (a) adj (comp dulji/duži) long, lengthy **~o** adv long, for a long time **raspravljati na ~o i na široko** discuss at length/interminably **~ogodišnji** adj of long standing, old **~onog** adj long-legged **~onja** nm lanky (guy) **~oprugaš** nm long-distance runner **~oročni** adj long-term **~otrajan** adj (a) protracted **~oljast** adj oblong

dug (2) debt **~ovati** v (komu što) (pres **~ujem**) owe sth to sb

duga nf rainbow

duh nm **1** ghost, spirit **opsjednut ~ovima** haunted **2** fig spirit **klonuti ~om** lose heart **klonuo ~om** dispirited **Duh Sveti** Holy Spirit, Holy Ghost **Duhovi** nm pl Pentecost **~ovit** adj witty **~ovitost** nf wit **~ovni** adj spiritual

duhački adj wind

duhan nm **1** tobacco **2** coll tobacconist's **~ski** adj tobacco

dukat nm ducat, golden coin

dulji adj → **dug** (1) **~na** nf length; longitude

dunja nf quince

dupe nn tab arse

dupin nm dolphin

dupkom adv **~ pun** chock-full

duplja nf hole **očna ~** eye socket

dupsti v (što) (pres **dubem**) hollow out

dur nm major **F-dur** F major

duriti (se) sulk

dušla nf soul **mirne ~e** safely, without any qualms **~om i tijelom** wholeheartedly **~o!** baby! honey! **~evan** adj (a) mental **Dušni dan** All Souls' Day

dušik nm chem nitrogen

dušnik nm windpipe, trachea

duž prep along

dužlan adj (a) (komu) indebted to **~no poštovanje** due respect **biti kome ~an** owe sb, be in sb's debt **~nik** nm (Vsg **~niče**, Npl **~nici**) debtor

duži → **dug** **~na** nf length

dužnlost nf duty; obligation, responsibility; office **~ik** nf (Npl **~nici**) official

dva num (dvije, dva) two (2) **~ po ~** in twos, two by two **~deset** num twenty (20) **~deseti** num ord twentieth **~desetorica** nf twenty men **~naest** num twelve (12) **u pet do ~naest** fig at the eleventh hour **~naesterac** nm (Gsg **~naesterca**), med duodenum **~naesti** num ord twelfth **~put** adv twice

dvjesto num two hundred (200)

dvo- prefix two-, double- **~boj** nm duel **~broj** nm double issue **~cijevka** nf **1** double-barrelled gun **2** sl tab AC/DC **~djelan** adj (a) two-part; (kostim) two-piece **~dnevan** adj (a) two-day **~godišnji** adj two-year (old) **~mjesečni** adj bimonthly **~jac** nm (Gsg **~jca**) sport pair **~jac bez kormilara** coxless pair **~jac na parade** double scull **~jac** adj double **~jci** nm pl twins **~je** num two people (of different sex) **njih ~je** these two **~jica** num two men **~jezičan** adj (a) bilingual **~jni** adj double; dual **~jnik** nm (Vsg **~jniče**, Npl **~jnici**) double **~krevetna** adj **soba** double room **~ličan** adj (a) two-faced, hypocritical **~ličnost** nf duplicity, hypocrisy **~motorac** nm (Gsg **~ca**) twin engine plane **~papkar** nm cloven-hoofed animal **~pek** nm rusk **~sjekli** adj double-edged to **je ~sjekli mač** it cuts both ways **~smislen** adj ambiguous **~smislenost** nf **1**

ambiguity **2** double entendre **~sobni** *adj* two-room **~spolac** *nm* (*Gsg* ~spolca) hermaphrodite **~struk** *adj* twofold, double **~taktni** *adj* two-stroke **~točka** *nf* colon **~trećinska** *adj* **većina** two-thirds majority **~umiti** *v* (se) be in two minds **~žilni** *adj* two-wire

dvoj|ba *nf* doubt **~ben** *adj* doubtful, uncertain **~iti** *v* (0) doubt

dvor *nm* court **~anin** *nm* courtier **~ska** *adj* **dama** lady in waiting **~ska luda** court jester

dvorana *nf* hall **plesna ~** ballroom

dvor|ac *nm* (*Gsg*~ca) castle

dvor|iti *v* (koga) serve, wait on **~kinja** *nf* charlady, charwoman

dvoriš|ni *adj* courtyard **~ni prozor** rear window **~na soba** back room **~te** *nn* courtyard, yard

Dž

Dž, dž 7th letter of Cro. alphabet
džamija *nf* mosque
džem *nm* jam
džemper *nm* jumper, sweater
džep *nm* pocket **poznavati koga/što kao svoj ~** know like the back of one's hand **imati dubok ~** be loaded **~ar** *nm* pick-pocket **~arac** *nm* (*Gsg ~arca*) pocket-money, spending money, allowance **~ni** *adj* pocket
džin *nm* gin
džip *nm* jeep
džokej *nm* jockey
džumbus *nm coll* hulabaloo; mess
džungla *nf* jungle

Đ

Đ, đ 8th letter of Cro. alphabet
đa|čki *adj* ~**čki dom** *nm* dormitory ~**k**
nm (*Vsg* ~če, *Npl* ~ci) **1** schoolboy;
pupil (+ *fig*) **2** *fig* disciple
đakon *nm* deacon

đav|ao *nm* (*Gsg* ~la, *Npl* ~oli) → **vrag**
đipati *v* (0) jump up and down, caper
đon *nm coll* sole ~**iti** *v* (cipele) sole
đumbir *nm* ginger
đurđica *nf* lily of the valley

E

E, e 1 9th letter of Cro. alphabet 2 *int*
   well 3 **e da bi** in order to, so as to
ebanovina *nf* ebony
efekat *nm* effect; impact **~an** *adj* (*a*) effective; impressive; striking **~ivan**
   adj (*a*) actual
efikasan *adj* (*a*) efficient, productive
egocentričan *adj* (*a*) egocentric
egzaktan *adj* (*a*) exact; precise
egzistencijal|an *adj* (*a*) **~ni mini-
   mum** substistence level **ispod ~nog
   minimuma** below the poverty line
egzotičan *adj* (*a*) exotic
ekcem *nm med* rash, eczema
ekipa *nm* team, crew **glumačka ~** cast
ekolo|gija *nf* ecology, environmental
   protection **~g** *nm* (*Npl* ~zi) environ-
   mentalist
ekonom *nm* estate manager **~ičan** *adj*
   (*a*) economical, cost-effective **~ija** *nf*
   1 (znanost) economics 2 (gospodarstvo) economy **~ika** *nf* applied
   economics **~ist** *nm* economist
   diplomirani ~ist business school
   graduate **~ski** *adj* economic **~ski
   fakultet** business school
ekran *nm* screen **mali ~** *fig* TV, the
   small screen **veliki ~** *fig* silver screen
   ~izirati *v* (što) film, make a screen
   version
eks *adv coll* **na ~!** bottoms up! down
   the hatch!
ekscelencij|a *nf* Excellency **Vaša ~o**
   Your E.
ekscentričan *adj* (*a*) eccentric
eksces *nm* outrage, incident; excesses
   pl
ekshumirati *v* (koga/što) exhume, dis-
   inter
ekskluzivan *adj* (*a*) exclusive, prestigious
ekskomunicirati *v* (koga) excommunicate

ekskurzija *nf* excursion, trip
ekspanzija *nf* expansion **~van** *adj* (*a*)
   expansive
ekspedicija *nf* expedition
ekspeditiv|an *adj* prompt, expeditious
   ~nost *nf* expedition
eksperiment *nm* experiment **~alan**
   adj (*a*) experimental, trial **~irati** *v*
   (0) experiment
ekspert *nm* expert **~iza** *nf* expert anal-
   ysis/opinion
eksploat|acija *nf* exploitation **~irati** *v*
   (koga/što) exploit
eksplo|dirati *v* (0) explode, go off
   ~zija *nf* explosion **~ziv** *nm* explosive
   ~zivan *adj* (*a*) explosive
ekspon|at *nm* exhibit **~irati** *v* 1
   (koga/što čemu) expose to 2 (se) *fig*
   expose oneself, go out on a limb
ekspres *adv* express
ekstaz|a *nf* ecstasy **u ~i** ecstatic, en-
   raptured
extra *adj* special; extra
ekstravagantan *adj* (*a*) extravagant,
   outlandish
ekstrem *nm* extreme **~an** *adj* (*a*) extreme; extremist **~ist** *nm* extremist
ekvator *nm* equator
ekvinocij *nm* equinox
elaborat *nm* report, (feasibility) study
elan *nm* zest **pun ~a** enthusiastic
elastičan *adj* (*a*) elastic, flexible (+
   fig)
elegan|cija *nf* style, elegance **~tan** *adj*
   (*a*) elegant, stylish, smart
elektr|ana *nf* power plant/station
   ~icitet *nm* electricity **~ičan** *adj* (*a*)
   (proizvodnja, uporaba) electric; (koji
   se tiče e.) electrical **~ična energija**
   electricity, power **~ičar** *nm* electrician **~ificirati** *v* (što) 1 introduce
   electricity 2 (željeznica) electrify
   ~ika *nf* electric power **~izirati** *v*

(koga, što) electrify (+ *fig*) **~oda** *nf* electrode **~omagnetski** *adj* electromagnetic **~omotor** *nm* electric motor **~otehničar** electrical engineer **~otehnika** *nf* electrical engineering

elektron *nm* electron **~ika** *nf* 1 electronics 2 electronic engineering **~ski** *adj* electronic

element *nm* element **~aran** *adj* (*a*) elementary **~arna nepogoda** natural disaster

eliminirati *v* (koga/što) eliminate

elisa *nf* propeller

elita *nf* elite **~n** *adj* (*a*) 1 elite 2 *mil* crack

emajl *nm* enamel **~iran** *adj* (*a*) enamelled, glazed

emancipacija *nf* emancipation; (ženska) women's lib *coll*

embargo *nm* embargo **nametnuti/ uvesti ~** impose an e. **ukinuti ~** lift an e.

emigra|cija *nf* emigration **~nt** *nm* 1 emigrant 2 (politički) emigré

emi|sija *nf* 1 *phys* emission 2 *TV, radio* programme, show, broadcast **~tirati** *v* (što) 1 emit 2 broadcast, go on the air

emoci|ja *nf* emotion **~onalan** *adj* (*a*) emotional

empirijski *adj* empirical

enciklopedija *nf* encyclopaedia

energ|etika *nf* power, power supply **~ičan** *adj* (*a*) energetic, vigorous **~ičnost** *nf* 1 energy 2 forcefulness **~ija** *nf* energy **pun ~ije** bristling with e.

Englez *nm* **praviti se ~** play possum

enklava *nf* enclave

eno *int* there **~ ga!** there he is

entuzijaz|am (*Gsg* **~ma**) enthusiasm **pun ~ma** keen

ep *nm* epic **~ika** *nf* epic poetry **~ski** *adj* epic

epidemija *nf* epidemic **izbila je ~ gripe** there is an outbreak of flu

epilep|sija *nf* epilepsy **~tični** *adj* **napad** epileptic fit, seizure **~tičar** *nm* epileptic

epilog *nm* epilogue

epizod|a *nf* episode, instalment **~na uloga** supporting part

epoha *nf* epoch, age **~lan** *adj* (*a*) epoch-making

epoleta *nf* epaulette

epruvet|a *nf* test-tube **dijete iz ~e** test-tube baby

era *nf* era, age

erekcija *nf* erection; hard-on *tab sl*

ergela *nf* stud-farm

erker *nm* bay window

erotičan *adj* (*a*) erotic

erozija *nf* erosion

erupcija *nf* eruption

esej *nm* essay

eskadr|a *nf* fleet; squadron **~ila** *nf* squadron

eskontn|i *adj* **~a stopa** discount rate

estet|ika *nf* aesthetics **~ski** *adj* aesthetic, tasteful

estrada *nf* show business; showbiz *coll*

etapa *nf* stage; lap, leg *sport*

etaž|a *adj* storey, floor **~no** *adj* **vlasništvo** condominium ownership

eter *nm* ether **biti u ~u** *TV, radio* be on the air **~ičan** *adj* (*a*) ethereal **~ično ulje** essential oil

eti|čki *adj* ethical **~ka** *nf* ethics

etiket|a *nf* 1 manners *pl* 2 label (+ *fig*) **~irati** *v* (koga/što) label

etnički *adj* ethnic

eto *int* there

Euharistija *nf* Eucharist

eunuh *nm* eunuch

evaku|acija *nf* evacuation **~irati** *v* (koga/što) evacuate

evanđe|lje *nn* Gospel **~lje po Ivanu G.** according to St John **~lski/~oski** *adj* evangelical

evangelički *adj* evangelical

eventual|an *adj* (*a*) possible **~no** *adv* perhaps ¶ eventually = na kraju

eviden|cija *nf* records, files **voditi ~ciju** keep records/files **biti u policijskoj ~ciji** have a (permanent) record ¶ evidence = dokazi **~tan** *adj* (*a*) evident **~tirati** *v* (koga, što) register, record

evo *int* here

evocirati *v* (što) evoke

evolu|cija *nf* evolution **~irati** *v* (0) evolve

F

F, f (ef) 10th letter of Cro. alphabet

fabula *nf* plot, story(line)

faca *nf coll* **1** face **2** bloke *GB*, guy *US*

fagot *nm* basoon ¶ faggot = svežanj pruća

fah *nm coll* trade

fajront *nm coll* closing time

fak|at *nm* → **činjenica** ~**tičan** *adj* (α) → **činjenični**

faks (1) *nm coll* college, faculty; school *US*

faks (2) *nm coll* fax **poslati ~om** fax

faktor *nm* factor; element

faktur|a *nf* invoice ~**irati** *v* (što komu) invoice

fakultet *nm* **1** (određeni) faculty, college; school *US* **2** (uopće, visoko obrazovanje) university ~**sko** *adj* **obrazovanje** university (degree)

fali|ti *v* (komu što) *coll* **nedostajati malo mi je ~lo da ga udarim** I almost hit him **samo mi još to ~** that's all I need now

falsifi|cirati *v* (što) falsify; forge; counterfeit ~**kat** *nm* forgery ~**kator** *nm* forger

familijaran *adj* (α) intimate, informal

fanati|čan *adj* (α) fanatical ~**k** *nm* (*Vsg* ~**če**, *Npl* ~**ci**) fanatic

fanfara *nf* fanfare, flourish

fanta|stičan *adj* (α) fantastic (+ *fig*) ~**zija** *nf* **1** imagination, fancy **2** fantasy **3** *coll* **kolač je ~zija** the cake is wonderful ~**zirati** *v* (0) dream, fantasize

far *nm* headlight

farm|a *nf* farm ~**er** *nm* farmer

farmac|eut *nm* pharmacist, pharmaceutical chemist ~**ija** *nf* pharmacy

farsa *nf* farce, mockery

fasada *nf* facade, front (+ *fig*)

fascikl *nm* folder, file

fascin|irati *v* (koga) fascinate ~**antan**

adj (α) fascinating

faši|st *nm* fascist ~**stički** *adj* fascist ~**zam** *nm* (*Gsg* ~**zma**) fascism

fašnik *nm coll* → **poklade**

fatalan *adj* (α) fatal

fatamorgana *nf* mirage

favorit *nm* favourite

faza *nf* stage, phase

fazan *nm* pheasant

federa|cija *nf* federation ~**lni** *adj* federal ~**tivni** *adj* federative

feferon *nm* chilli pepper

fekalije *nf pl* faeces

feljton *nm* → **podlistak**

fen *nm coll* hair-drier **sušiti ~om** blow-dry

feniks *nm* phoenix

fenomen *nm* phenomenon ~**alan** *adj* (α) *coll* great, brilliant

fer *adj coll* fair

ferment *nm* ferment ~**acija** *nf* ferment, fermentation ~**irati** *v* (0) ferment

festival *nm* festival

fetiš *nm* fetish ~**izam** *nm* (*Gsg* ~**izma**) fetishism

feud *nm* fief ¶ = feud ~**alac** *nm* feudal lord ~**alizam** *nm* (*Gsg* ~**alizma**) feudalism, feudal system

fićuk *nm coll* whistle ~**ati** *v* (0) whistle

fig|a *nf coll* fig **dobit ćeš frišku ~u** you won't get anything **držati ~e** (komu) keep one's fingers crossed (for sb)

figur|a *nf* **1** figure **plesna ~a** dance step **2** (u igri) piece **šahovska ~a** chess-man ~**ativan** *adj* (α) figurative ~**ica** *nf dem* figurine ~**irati** *v* (0) (kao) play the role of

fijasko *nm* fiasco, flop **doživjeti ~** (predstava) flop

fijuk *nm* (wind) whistle; whiz ~**ati** *v* (0) whistle

fik|cija *nf* fiction ~**tivan** *adj* (α) fictitious

fiks *nm sl* shot, fix **~ati** *v* (se čime) shoot up sth, mainline **~er** *nm* drug addict; junkie *sl*

fiks|an *(a)* fixed **~irati** *v* 1 (što) fix 2 (koga) stare at sb

fikus *nm* rubber-plant

filatelija *nf* stamp collecting, philately

filharmonija *nf* philharmonic

filigran *nm* filigree

filijala *nf* → **podružnica**

filistar *nm* Philistine

film (1) *nm* 1 film 2 (kino) film *GB*; movie *US*; motion picture; picture, flick *coll* **crtani ~** cartoon **igrani ~** feature film **nijemi ~** silent movie **snimati ~** film *GB*; shoot *US* **~aš** *nm* film maker **~ski** *adj* film **~ska verzija** screen version **~ski poljubac** French kiss

film (2) *nm* film, (thin) layer

filolog *nm* philologist **klasična ~ija** classical studies

filozof *nm* 1 philosopher 2 *coll derog* smartarse *vulg* **~ija** *nf* philosophy **~irati** *v* (0) 1 philosophize 2 *coll* complicate **~ski** *adj* philosophical (+ *fig*) **~ski fakultet** Faculty of Arts, F. of Philosophy

filt|ar, filter *nm* (*Gsg* ~ra) filter **~rirati** *v* (što) filter

fin *adj* fine; delicate; (hrana) delicious; (osoba) refined; well-mannered **~oća** *nf* fineness, delicacy, good manners

final|an *adj* (a) → **konačan ~ni proizvod** end/finished product **~e** *nm* 1 *sport* finals *pl* 2 *mus* finale

financi|je *nf pl* finances; funds **ministarstvo ~ja** Ministry of Finance; Treasury Department *US*; Department of the Exchequer *GB* **~jaš** *nm* financier **~jer** (čega) *nm* sponsor **~jski** *adj* financial **~jska godina** fiscal year **~jska sredstva** *pl* finances, funds **~rati** *v* (koga/što) finance, provide funds

finesa *nf* nicety

firma *nf coll* 1 (tvrtka) firm 2 (potvrda) confirmation **~ti** *v* (koga/se) confirm/be confirmed

fiskalan *adj* (a) fiscal

fitilj *nm coll* fuse

fizi|čar *nm* physicist **~čki** *adj* physical; bodily → **tjelesni ~čki radnik** manual worker, handyman **~ka** *nf* physics **~kalni** *adj* physical

fiziolog *nm* physiologist **~ija** *nf* physiology

fizionomija *nf* physiognomy, features

fizioterapija *nf* physical therapy

flanel *nm* flannel

flaster *nm coll* 1 adhesive tape 2 plaster *GB*; bandage *US*; Band-Aid *TM*

flaš|a *nf coll* bottle **~irati** *v* (što) bottle

flauta *nf* flute

flegmatičan *adj* (a) indifferent, cool, phlegmatic

flert *nm coll* flirtation **on voli ~ovati** he is a flirt

fliper *nm coll* pinball (machine)

flomaster *nm coll* felt-tip pen

floskula *nm* platitude

flota *nf* fleet

fluor *nm* fluorine **~escentan** *adj* (a) fluorescent; day-glo *coll*

fobija *nf* phobia

fokus *nm* focus **izoštriti ~, ~irati** *v* (što) bring into focus

folirati *v* (0/kome) *sl* give/feed sb a line

folija *nf* foil **prozirna ~** cling film

folklor *nm* folklore **~ni** *adj* folk

fond *nm* fund **stočni ~** livestock **~ riječi** vocabulary

fon|etika *nf* phonetics **~etski** *adj* phonetic ○ *adv* phonetically **~ologija** *nf* phonology

for|a *nf sl* 1 joke, trick **pasti na ~u, popušiti ~u** fall for it **u čemu je ~a?** what's the point? **to je dobra ~a** it's cool **nije ~a** it's not fair **na koju ~u ...** how the hell ... 2 *sport* **dati kome ~e** give sb the advantage

form|a *nf* 1 form, shape **biti u (dobroj) ~i** be fit/in good shape 2 formality, convention, appearance **~acija** *nf mil* formation, force **~alan** *adj* (a) formal **~alnost** *nf* formality **~at** *nm* form, size **~atirati** *v* (što) *comp* format **~irati** *v* 1 (što) mould, shape 2 (se) take shape

formul|a *nf* formula **~acija** *nf* wording **~ar** *nm* form **ispuniti ~ar** fill in *GB*/out *US* a f. **~irati** *v* (što) formulate, word

forsirati *v* 1 (koga/se) push sb/oneself hard 2 (što) insist on sth

forum *nm* 1 forum 2 institution, body

fosfor *nm* phosphorus

fosil *nm* fossil

fotelja *nf* 1 armchair 2 *coll derog* good position, cushy job

foto|aparat *nm* camera **~geničan** *adj* (α) photogenic **~graf** photographer; pixer *coll* **~grafija** *nf* 1 photography 2 photo(graph), snapshot **~grafirati** *v* (koga/što) photograph, take sb's picture/picture of sb/sth **~grafski** *adj* photographic **~grafsko pamćenje** photographic memory, total recall **~kopirati** *v* (što) photocopy; xerox *TM coll* **~kopija** *nf* photocopy **~kopirni** *adj* **stroj** photocopier **~montaža** *nf* trick photograph **~reportaža** *nf* picture report **fotoreporter** *nm* press photographer **~robot** *nm* identikit picture, Photofit *TM*, composite **~slog** *nm* photosetting

fra *nm* father, friar

fragment *nm* fragment

frajer *nm* coll 1 guy, bloke, dude 2 boyfriend

frak *nm* tailcoat, tails *pl*

frakcija *nf* faction

francu|z *nm* coll (kruh) baguette, French stick **~ski** *adj* **ključ** spanner *GB*; (monkey) wrench *US*

franko *adv* free **~ brod** free on board **~ skladište** ex warehouse

franjev|ac *nm* (Gsg ~ca, Vsg ~če) Franciscan (friar)

frape *nm* milk shake

fras *nm* coll fit

frat|ar *nm* (Gsg ~ra, Npl ~ri) friar

fraza *nf* 1 phrase 2 (*pl*) *derog* cliches, empty words, rhetoric

frcati *v* (0) (iskre) fly; (suze) roll down

fregat|a *nf* frigate **kapetan ~e** commander

frekvencija *nf* frequency

frenetičan *adj* (α) frenzied; (pljesak) ecstatic

freska *nf* fresco

frfljati *v* (0) mumble

frigati *v* (što) *coll* 1 fry 2 *euphem* screw

frigidan *adj* (α) frigid

friz|er *nm* hairdresser **~erski salon** hairdresser's **~irati** *v* 1 (koga/što) dress/style/do one's hair 2 (što) *fig* misrepresent 3 (motor) soup up **~ura** *nf* hairdo, hairstyle **ići na ~uru** have one's hair done, get a hairdo

frižider *nm* coll fridge *coll*

fr|ka *nf* (Dsg ~ci) *sl* trouble; (a spot of) bother *GB coll* **nema ~ke** no problem, no sweat **bilo ga je ~ka** he was afraid

frk|nuti *v* (0) 1 (~nuti nosom) snort (derisively) 2 (mačka) spit **~tati** *v* → *impf* frknuti

fronta *nf* front **~lan** *adj* (α) frontal; (sudar) head-on

frotir *nm* terrycloth

frula *nf* pipe

frustr|acija *nf* frustration **~iran** *adj* frustrated

fućkati *v coll* 1 (0/što) whistle **~ na što** *coll* not give a damn about sth 2 (se komu za koga/što) *coll* not give a damn abouth sb/sth

fuj *int* phew, ugh, yuck

fundus *nm* holdings *pl*

funkci|ja *nf* function; office **~onalan** *adj* (α) functional **~onirati** *v* (0) function, work **ne ~onirati** be out of order

funta *nf* pound; (novac) quid *GB sl*

furati *v coll* 1 (s kim) go out with 2 (što) wear; carry 3 (se na što) be into sth

furnir *nm* veneer

fusnota *nf coll* footnote

fuš *nm* gray economy **raditi u ~u** moonlight **~ati** (što) bungle

futrola *nf coll* 1 case 2 holster

fuzija *nf* 1 *phys* fusion 2 *econ* merger

G

G, g (ge) 11th letter of Cro. alphabet
ga *pron* Gsg, Asg him
gacati *v* (0) (kroz vodu) wade
gaće|e *nf pl* underpants, pants **~ice** *nf* knickers, panties **kupaće ~e** swimming trunks **muške ~e** briefs, jocks *coll*
gad *nm* scoundrel; bastard *tab* **~an** *adj* (*a*) nasty, ugly, bad **~iti** *v* (se komu) be disgusted with **~iš mi se** you make me sick **~ljiv** *adj* squeamish **~no** *adv* badly **~ost** *nf* filth, smut **~ura** *nf* bitch
gađati *v* (koga/što) 1 shoot/fire (at) 2 target
gaj *nm* grove
gajde *nf pl* bagpipes
gajiti *v* (što) raise, grow **~ nadu** cherish/harbour hope
gakati *v* (0) quack
gala *nf* gala
galaktika *nf* galaxy
galam|a *nf* noise, racket **~iti** *v* (0) make noise, raise hell
galantan *adj* (*a*) courteous, gallant
galanterija *nf* haberdashery **kožna ~** leather goods
galeb *nm* seagull
galerija *nf* gallery
galij|a *nf* galley **~ot** *nm* galley-slave
galop *nm* gallop, canter **~irajući** *adj* galloping (+ *fig*)
galvanizirati *v* (što) *tech* electroplate
gamad *nn pl* vermin (+ *fig*)
ganut|i *v* (koga) move, affect **~ljiv** *adj* moving
garan|cija *nf* 1 *com* guarantee; insurance; collateral; security 2 warranty **proizvod ima ~ciju od 12 mjeseci** the product comes with a 12-month warranty 3 guarantee, assurance **~tirati** *v* (što) guarantee, warrant **~tni** *adj* **~tno pismo** letter of indemnity

nity
garaža *nf* garage
gard|a *nf* the Guard **Zbor narodne ~e** (Croatian) National Guard **~ist** *nm* guardsman
garderoba *nf* 1 wardrobe; clothes 2 left luggage office 3 cloak-room
garnitura *nf* set
garnizon *nm* garrison
garsonijera *nf* studio (flat)
gas *nm* accelerator pedal; gas *coll* **dati ~** step on it
gas|iti *v* 1 (što) (cigaretu/vatru) put out, extinguish 2 (što) (svjetlo, TV) switch off, turn off 3 (što) (žeđu) quench 4 (što) (vapno) slake 5 (se) fade 6 (se) (automobil) stall 7 (se) be abolished **~nuti** *v* (0) go out
gat *nm* pier
gata|ti *v* (komu) tell sb's fortune **~ti iz dlana** read sb's palm **~ra** *nf* fortune-teller
gavran *nm* raven
gaz *nm* 1 ford 2 (broda) draught **~iti** *v* (što/koga) tread on, trample
gaza *n* gauze
gazda *nm* 1 boss, master 2 landlord **~rica** *nf* landlady
gaziran *adj* (piće) carbonated
gdje *adv, conj* where
gegati *v* (se) waddle
geler *nm coll* (a piece of) shrapnel
gem *nm* 1 (tenis) game 2 (~išt) white wine with mineral water
gen *nm* gene **~etika** *nf* (*Dsg* ~etici) genetics **~etski** *adj* genetic
generacija *nf* 1 generation 2 year, class
general *nm* general **~ bojnik** major general
general|izirati *v* (što) generalize **~ni** *adj* general
generalka *nf coll* 1 dress rehearsal 2

overhaul **3** spring-clean(ing)

genij *nm* genius **~alan** *adj* (ā) ingenious, brilliant **~alan čovjek** a man of genius **~alno** *adv coll* great

genitalije *nf pl* genitals

geode|t *nm* surveyor **~zija** *nf* geodesy

geografija *nf* → zemljopis

geometar *nm* surveyor

geometrija *nf* geometry

gepard *nm* cheetah

geril|la *nf* guerilla **~ac** *nm* (*Gsg* ~ca, *Vsg* ~če) guerilla, **~ski** *adj* guerilla **~ski rat** g. warfare

geslo *nn* slogan, motto

gest|a *nf* gesture **lijepa ~a** nice gesture **~ikulirati** *v* (0) gesticulate

geto *nm* ghetto

gi|bak *adj* (gipka *f*) supple, flexible **~banj** *nm* (*Gsg* ~bnja) spring **~banje** *nn* motion, movement **~bati** *v* **1** (što) move **2** (se) move, be in motion **~pkost** *nf* flexibility, suppleness

gimnasti|čar *nm sport* gymnast **~čka** *adj* **dvorana** gym(nasium) **~ka** *nf* (*Dsg* ~ci) gymnastics

gimnazija *nf* secondary school, grammar school *GB*; high school *US*

ginekolog *nm* gynaecologist **~ija** *nf* gynaecology

gips *nm* **1** gypsum, plaster of Paris **2** *coll* plaster cast

gitar|a *nf* guitar **svirati ~u** play the g.

gizd|av *adj* **1** proud, vain **2** dandified **~elin** *nm* dandy, fop

glača|llo *nn* iron **~ti 1** iron, press **2** smooth **3** rub; buff, polish

glad *nm* hunger; famine **umirati od ~i** be starving **štrajk glađu** hunger strike **~an** (ā) *adj* hungry **~ovati** *v* (0) (*pres* ~ujem) **1** starve, famish **2** fast

gla|dak *adj* (glatka *f*) smooth **~diti** *v* (koga/što) smooth **~tko** *adv* smoothly **~tko odbiti** flatly refuse

glagol *nm* verb **~ski** *adj* verbal

glagolj|ica *nf* Glagolitic script/alphabet **~aš** *nm* Glagolitic priest

glas *nm* **1** voice; sound **na sav ~/iz sveg ~a** at the top of one's voice/lungs **ne dati/pustiti ~a od sebe** remain silent, not utter a sound **2** vote (opće) **pravo ~a** (universal) suffrage **dati svoj ~ za** cast one's vote for **3** news **4** repute, fame **doći na ~** make a reputation **biti na ~u** be renowned **uživati dobar ~** have a good reputation **loš ~** bad reputation **~ač** *nm* voter **~ački** *adj* electoral **~ački listić** ballot paper **~ačka kutija** ballot box **~alište** *nn* polling station **izaći na ~ališta** go to the polls **~an** *adj* (ā) loud **~ati v** (se) make sounds **~ilo** *nn* newspaper; organ **~ina** *nf* rumour **pronose/čuju se ~ine** it is rumoured **~iti v 1** (kako) go/run as follows, say **2** (na koga) be made out to; be addressed to **~nica** *nf* vocal cord **~nik** *nm* (*Vsg* ~niče, *Npl* ~nici) messenger, herald **~no** *adv* aloud, loud(ly) **~nogovornik** *nm* (*Vsg* ~nogovorniče, *Npl* ~nogovornici) spokesman, spokesperson **~ovanje** *nn* voting, vote **javno/tajno ~ovanje** open/secret ballot **~ovati v** vote, cast one's vote **~ovit** *adj* famous **~ovir** *nm* piano

glav|a *nf* head **od ~e do pete** from head to toe/foot **klimati ~om** nod **usijana ~a** hothead **ne znam gdje mi je ~a** I am all mixed up **bez ~e i repa** all mixed up, higgledy-piggledy **razbijati ~u** rack one's brains **ne ide mi u ~u** I fail to understand, it escapes me **~om bez obzira** helter skelter **dajem ~u** I bet **izgubiti ~u a.** lose one's nerve **b.** get killed **ni za živu ~u** not on your life **nositi ~u u torbi** live dangerously **utuviti kome u ~u** get it through to sb **raditi komu o ~i** plot against somebody **igrati se ~om** risk one's life **~a obitelji** head of the family **~a države** head of state **potrošnja po ~i stanovnika** per capita consumption **~ar** *nm* head **~ešina** *nf* big boss **~ica** *nf* **1** *dem* small head **bistra ~ica** *nf* smart boy/girl **2** (salate, kupusa) head **~ić** *nm* glans **~injati** *v* (0) totter **~obolja** *nf* headache

glavni *adj* main, chief, major; head **~ zgoditak** *nm* first prize, jackpot **~ grad** capital

glavnica *nf* capital

glavnina *nf* **1** *mil* main forces **2** the

major/main part of, most of, the bulk of

glazb|a *nf* music ~**alo** *nn* musical instrument ~**eni** *adj* musical ~**enik** *nm* (*Npl* ~**enici**) musician

glazura *nf* 1 enamel 2 (na kolaču) icing

gle! *int* look!

gled|alište *nn* hall, stand ~**atelj** *nm* viewer, spectator ~**ateljstvo** audience; *nn* viewers, spectators, *pl* ~**ati** *v* 1 (koga/što) look at 2 (koga/što) watch, view ~**ati komu kroz prste** overlook sb's faults ~**ati prijekim okom** look askance at ~**ati s visoka** look down upon 3 (na) face, have a view of 4 (na) regard ~**ište** *nn* point of view, viewpoint

glež|anj *nm* (*Gsg* ~**nja**) ankle ~**njerica** *nf* chelsea boot, ankle boot

glib *nm* mire

glin|a *nf* clay ~**eno** *adj* posuđe earthenware

gliser *nm coll* speed-boat

glista *nf* 1 earthworm 2 worm

globa *nf* fine

globus *nm* globe

gloda|lica *nf* milling machine ~**ti** *v* (što) gnaw at ~**vac** *nm* (*Gsg* ~**vca**) rodent

glog *nm* hawthorn

glomazan *adj* (*a*) bulky

gložiti *v* (se) (oko čega) squabble (over), bicker

gluh *adj* deaf, hard of hearing ~ **kao top** deaf as a doorpost **u** ~**o doba noći** in the dead of night ~**oća** *nf* deafness ~**onijem** *adj* deaf-mute, deaf-and-dumb

glum|a 1 *nf* acting 2 play-acting, pretence ~**ac** *nm* (*Gsg* ~**ca**) actor ~**ački** *adj* actors', thespian ~**ačka družina** company, troupe ~**atati** *v* (0) overact ~**ica** *nf* actress ~**iti** *v* 1 (0) act 2 (koga) play (the part of) 3 (što) act, play-act

glup *adj* stupid; dumb *coll* ~**ača** *nf* stupid woman/girl ~**an** *nm* blockhead, nitwit ~**ost** *nf* 1 stupidity 2 blunder, stupid thing to do **govoriti** ~**osti** talk nonsense ~**ost!** nonsense! rubbish!

gljiva *nf* mushroom ~**ica** *nf* fungus ~**ični** *adj* fungal ~**ična kožna bolest** ringworm

gmaz *nm* reptile

gmiza|ti *v* (0) crawl, creep ~**vac** (*Gsg* ~**vca**) reptile

gnijezd|o *nn* nest **saviti** ~**o** build one's nest **topničko** ~**o** artillery emplacement **mitraljesko** ~**o** machinegun nest ~**iti** *v* (se) 1 nest 2 shift uncomfortably

gnoj *nm* 1 pus *med* 2 manure ~**an** *adj* (*a*) festering, purulent ~**iti** *v* 1 (što) manure 2 (se) fester ~**ivo** *nn* manure, fertilizer

gnusan *adj* (*a*) loathsome, foul

gnuša|ti *v* (se koga/čega) loathe ~**m se nasilja** I loathe violence

gnjav|ator *nm coll* bothersome/obnoxious person; pain in the neck ~**aža** *nf* botheration, nuisance ~**iti** *v* 1 (koga/što) bother, annoy 2 (se čime) bother with

gnjecav *adj* mushy, soggy

gnječiti *v* (koga/što) press, squeeze, crush

gnjev *nm* anger, wrath **iskaliti** ~ vent one's anger ~**an** *adj* (*a*) furious, irate

gnjida *nf* 1 nit 2 *fig* louse

gnji|lost, ~**loća** *nf* rot, rottenness ~**o** *adj* (~**la** *f*) rotten, decayed ~**ljeti** *v* (0) rot, decay

god *part* **dokle god** as long as **gdje** ~ wherever **tko** ~ whoever **kad** ~ whenever

godi|na *nf* year **prijestupna** ~**na** leap year **iz** ~**ne u** ~**nu** year after year **imam pet** ~**na** I am five (years old) **biti u** ~**nama** be well advanced in years **dobra** ~**na** good vintage, vintage year ~**šnjak** *nm* (*Npl* ~**šnjaci**) year book ~**šnje** *adv* yearly, annually ~**šnji** *adj* yearly, annual ~**šnji odmor** holiday *GB*; vacation *US*, annual leave ~**šnjica** *nf* anniversary ~**šte** *nn* year

goditi *v* (komu) please **to mi godi** that feels good

gojazan *adj* (*a*) obese, overweight

gol (1) *adj* nude, naked, bare ~ **golcat** stark naked ~**e činjenice** bare/plain facts ~**a istina** plain truth ~**im ruka-**

ma with one's bare hands **~obrad** *adj* beardless **~oglav** *adj* without a hat, uncovered **~oruk** *adj* unarmed **~otinja** *nf* nudity

gol (2) *nm coll* goal **~man** *nm* goalkeeper, goalie **dati** ~ score

golem *adj* huge, enormous; vast

golub *nm* 1 pigeon ~ **pismonoša** carrier/homing pigeon 2 *fig* dove **~ica** *nf* dove **~inji** *adj* dove, dove-like

goljenica *nf* shin-bone

gomila *nf* 1 (stvari) heap, pile 2 (ljudi) crowd, mob **~ti** *v* 1 (što) stockpile, hoard 2 (se) gather 3 (vojsku) build up

gomolj *nm* tuber

goni|č *nm* driver **~č robova** slave-driver **~č stoke** drover **~ti** *v* (koga) 1 drive, herd 2 pursue **krivično ~ti** prosecute ~ **se** get out of here! get lost!

gor|a *nf* mountain **~je** *nn* m. range **~ovit** *adj* mountainous **~ski** *adj* mountain **~štak** *nm* (*Vsg* **~štače**, *Npl* **~štaci**) highlander; hillbilly *US derog*

gor|ak *adj* (α) bitter (+ *fig*) **~čina** *nf* bitterness

gore (1) *adv* 1 above 2 up, upwards 3 at the top **~dolje** up and down

gor|e (2) *adv comp* → **zlo, loše ~i** *adj comp* → **zao, loš** worse **iz zla u ~e** from bad to worse

gorila *nf* gorilla

gorivo *nn* fuel **napuniti rezervoar ~m** fill the car up

gor|jeti *v* (0) (*pres* **~im**) **~ući** *adj fig* burning

gorljiv *adj* ardent

gornji *adj* upper, top, higher

goropad|an *adj* (α) bad-tempered, aggressive

gorostas *nm* giant

Gosp|a *nf* Our Lady **Velika ~a** Assumption (Day) **~od** *nm* the Lord **~odnji** *adj* of Our Lord **g~oda** *nf pl* 1 gentlemen 2 gentry (+ *derog*) **~odin** *nm* 1 (uz prezime) Mister (Mr) 2 (obraćanje) sir 3 gentleman **g~odski** *adj* 1 gentlemanly 2 stately, grand **g~oda** *nf* 1 Missis (Mrs) 2 Ms 3 madam, lady **g~odica** *nf* 1 Miss 2 young lady

gospodar *nm* master, lord **dobar ~** good husbandman **~ica** *nf* mistress **~iti** *v* 1 (kime/čime) rule over 2 (0) manage **~ski** *adj* economic **~stvenik** *nm* (*Npl* **~stvenici**) businessman **~stvo** *nn* 1 economy 2 farm

gost *nm* 1 guest **biti ~ (kod koga) u ~ima** be visiting (sb) 2 customer **~ionica** *nf* inn; restaurant **~ioničar** *nm* innkeeper **~iti** *v* (se) feast **~olju-biv** *adj* hospitable **~oprimstvo** *nn* hospitality **~ovanje** *nn* guest performance; tour

gošća *nf* (lady) guest

gotov *adj* 1 done, finished **dovesti koga pred ~ čin** leave sb no choice, present sb with a fait accompli 2 ready ~ **novac** cash **~an** *nm* lazybones **~ina** *nf* cash **~o** *adv* almost **~o nikad** hardly ever **~o je** it is (all) over; it is done

govedina *nf* beef **~o** *nn* ox, cow **~a** *pl* cattle

govn|o *nn tab* shit **biti u ~ima (do grla)** be in the shit, be up shit creek **on je obično ~o** he's a piece of shit

govor *nm* speech **ni ~a** (it is) out of the question **~iti** *v* 1 speak **~iti engleski** speak English **~iti sebi u bradu** mutter to oneself 2 (o čemu) speak/talk about sth 3 (komu što) tell sth to sb 4 (komu) address, talk to **~iti komu "ti"** be on first name terms with sb **~kati** *v* (se) **~ka se** rumour has it, it is rumoured, there are rumours **~ni** *adj* spoken **~na mana** speech impediment **~nica** *nf* 1 woman-speaker 2 platform, rostrum **telefonska ~nica** phone booth/box **~nik** *nm* (*Vsg* **~niče**, *Npl* **~nici**) speaker

gozba *nf* feast

grab *nm* hornbeam

grab|lež *nf* robbery **~iti** *v* (što) 1 clutch, grasp at 2 take away, grab 3 ladle, scoop, dip **~iti vodu** draw water 4 (trčati) lope **~ljiv** *adj* 1 rapacious, greedy 2 predatory **~ežljivac** *nm* (*Gsg* **~ežljivca**, *Vsg* **~ežljivci**) predator, beast of prey **~ežljivost** *nf* rapacity **~ljivica** *nf* bird of prey

grablje *nf pl* rake *sg*

graciozan *adj* (a) graceful ¶ gracious = milostiv

grad (1) *nm* city; town **glavni ~** capital **~ić** *nm* small town **~onačelnik** *nm* (*Vsg* ~onačelniče, *Npl* ~onačelnici) mayor **~ski** *adj* 1 urban 2 municipal, city, town

grad (2) *nm* hail

gradilište *nn* building site **~telj** *nm* builder **~teljstvo** *nn* building trade **~ti** *v* (što) build (+ *fig*), construct, erect

gradivo *nn* material, subject matter

grad|a *nf* 1 building material 2 matter, substance 3 (tjelesna) build **~evina** *nf* building   **~evinar** *nm* builder, building contractor **~evinski, ~evni** *adj* construction **~evinarstvo** *nn* civil engineering

građan|in *nm* 1 citizen 2 resident 3 town-dweller **~ski** *adj* 1 civil; civic 2 bourgeois

grafi|čki *adj* graphic **~ka** *nf* 1 graphic 2 print **~kon** *nm* graph, chart

grah *nm* beans *pl* **zrno ~a** bean

graja *nf* uproar, clamour

grak|nuti *v* (0) (*pres* ~nem) 1 croak, crow 2 *fig* yell, cry out **~tati** *v impf*

gram *nm* gram(me) **ni ~a** not an ounce/pinch

gramati|čar *nm* grammarian **~čki** *adj* grammatical **~ka** *nf* (*Dsg* ~ci) grammar

gramofon *nm* record player

gramziv *adj* greedy, covetous

gra|na *nf* branch (+ *fig*), bough **pasti na niske ~ne** be down on one's luck, fall upon bad times **~nati** *v* (se) branch out, ramify **~nčica** *nf* twig **maslinova ~nčica** olive branch **~nje** *nn* branches

granat|a *nf* shell ¶ grenade = ručna bomba **~irati** *v* (što) shell

grani|ca *nf* 1 boundary; border; frontier 2 limit, borderline **prijeći ~cu** *fig* exceed the limit, go over the line, get out of hand **~čiti** *v* (s kim/čim) border on (+ *fig*) **~čni** *adj* 1 border 2 borderline

granu|ti *v* **sunce je ~lo** the sun rose

granit *nm* granite

graš|ak *nm* (*Gsg* ~ka) peas **zrno ~ka**

pea **~ka** *nf* **znoja** bead of sweat

grb *nm* coat of arms **~oslovlje** *nn* heraldry

grba *nf* hump **~ča** *nf* **biti kome na ~či** be a burden to sb **~v** *adj* 1 hunchbacked 2 bumpy **~vac** *nm* (*Gsg* ~vca, *Vsg* ~vče) hunchback

grcati *v* (0) **sob ~u dugovima** be up to the neck in debts

grč *nm* cramp; spasm **~evit** *adj* 1 spasmodic, convulsive 2 *fig* frantic **~iti** *v* (što/se) convulse, contort

grd|an *adj* (a) monstrous **~iti** *v* (koga) scold **~no** *adv* **se prevariti** be very much mistaken **~oba** *nf* 1 ugliness 2 monster **~osija** *nf* behemoth

grebati *v impf* → grepsti

greben *nm* reef

gred|a *nf* beam, rafter; transom **~ica** *nf* bed

grejp *nm* *coll* grapefruit ¶ grape = zrno grožđa

grepsti *v* 1 (koga/što/se) scratch 2 (se za što) try to get hold of, suck one's way to

greš|an, grješan *adj* sinful **~nica** *nf* sinful woman, sinner **~nik** *nm* (*Vsg* ~niče, *Npl* ~nici) sinner

greš|ka *nf* (*Gpl* ~aka) mistake, error, fault

grgljati *v* (što/0) gargle

grickati *v* (što) nibble (at)

grija|č *nm* heater **~lica** *nf* heater **električna ~lica** electric h. **~nje** *nn* heating **~ti** *v* 1 (što) warm 2 (se) warm oneself **~ti se na suncu** bask in the sunshine

grije|h *nm* sin **laki ~h** venial sin **smrtni ~h** mortal sin **~šiti** *v* 1 (0) sin 2 (0) err, make mistakes 3 (0/u čemu) be mistaken **~šiš** you're making a mistake; you're wrong

grimas|a *nf* grimace, face **praviti ~e** pull faces

gripa *nf* flu; influenza *form*

gri|sti *v* (*pres* ~zem) 1 (koga/što) bite **~ze ga savjest** he suffers pangs of conscience 2 (se) bite each other 3 (se) *fig* fret, torment oneself **~žnja** *nf* **savjesti** remorse

griva *nf* mane

griz *nm* *coll* semolina

grkljan *nm* larynx

gr|lat *adj fig* loud **~en** *adj* throaty, guttural **~ić** *nm* (boce) neck **~ić mater-nice** cervix **~o** *nm* throat **boli me ~o** I have a sore throat **usko ~o** *fig* bottleneck **100 ~a stoke** a hundred head of cattle

grlica *nf* turtledove

grliti *v* (koga/što/se) embrace, hold (sb/sth/each other), hug

grm *nm* bush, shrub **~lje** *nn pl* shrubbery, undergrowth

grm|jeti *v* (0) thunder, roar (+ *fig*) **~ljavina** *nf* thunder

grob *nm* grave, tomb **biti jednom no-gom u ~u** have one foot in the grave **~ar** *nm* grave-digger, sexton **~lje** *nn* graveyard, cemetery **crkveno ~lje** churchyard **~ni** *adj* sepulchral **~ni kamen** tombstone **~nica** *nf* crypt, vault

grof *nm* count; earl *GB* **~ica** *nf* countess **~ovija** *nf* county

grohot *nm* loud laughter, gale of laughter **~om se smijati** roar with laughter

groktati *v* (0) grunt

grom *nm* thunder(bolt), thunderclap **kao ~ iz vedra neba** as a bolt from the blue **~ki** *adj* booming **~obran** *nm* lightning conductor/rod **~oglasan** *adj* (a) booming

gromada *nf* huge black, boulder

groteska *nf* grotesque **~n** *adj* (a) grotesque

groz|a *nf* horror, terror, dread **~an** *adj* (a) horrible, dreadful; awful *fig* **~iti** *v* (se) **1** (čega) be terrified of, shudder at **2** (komu) threaten **~no** *adv coll fig* awfully **~ota** *nf* atrocity, horror, outrage

gro|zd *nm* **1** (grožđa, banane) bunch **2** cluster (+ *fig*) **~žđe** *nn pl* grapes **~ždica** *nf* raisin, currant, sultana

grozni|ca *nf* **1** fever; (high) temperature *coll* **imati ~cu** run a fever **zlat-na ~ca** gold rush **2** (na usni) cold sore **~čav** *adj* feverish

grub *adj* **1** rude, brusque **2** rough, coarse **~ijan** *nm* brute

gruda *nf* lump **~ snijega** snowball **rodna ~** native soil **~ti** *v* (se) throw

snowballs, have a snowball fight

grud|i *nf pl* breast(s), bosom **~njak** *nm* (*Npl* ~njaci) brassiere; bra **~obran** *nm* parapet, breastwork

grumen *nm* lump; (zlata) nugget

grunt *nm coll* → **zemljište**

grunuti *v* (0) boom, thunder

grup|a *nf* group; party **radna ~a** working group, task force **~irati** *v* (koga/što/se) group (into)

grušalti *v* (se) coagulate, clot **~nje** *nn* coagulation, clotting

gruvati *v impf* → **grunuti**

guba *nf* leprosy • *adj sl* cool, awesome **~v** *adj* leprous **~vac** *nm* (*Gsg* ~vca, *Vsg* ~vče) leper

gubic|a *nf* **1** snout, muzzle **2** *fig* nose, face; mug *sl* **začepi ~u** *vulg* shut your face **razbiti komu ~u** punch sb in the nose

gubi|tak *nm* (*Gsg* ~tka, *Npl* ~ci) loss **pretrpjeti teške ~tke** sustain heavy casualties/losses **~ti** *v* **1** (što) lose **~ti boju** fade **2** (se) disappear, fade out **~ se!** get lost! **~taš** *nm* loss-making/money-losing company

gucnuti *v* (što) sip **voli ~** he is fond of a tipple

gudač *nm* string player **~čki** *adj* string **~čki instrumenti** stringed instruments, the strings **~lo** *nn* bow

gudura *nf* gorge

guja *nf* viper

guk|ati *v* (0) coo **~nuti** *v* (0) **1** coo **2** *fig* say something **~ni golube** *coll* out with it

gulaš *nm* stew, goulash

guli|ti *v* **1** (što) peel **~ti komu kožu a** flay sb **b** *fig* fleece **2** (se) peel **~koža** *nm* robber, shark *fig*

gum|a *nf* **1** rubber **2** tire *US*, tyre *GB* **~ast** *adj* rubbery **~en** *adj* rubber **~ica** *nf* **1** rubber *GB*; eraser *US* **2** condom *GB*; rubber *US*

gunđa|ti *v* (0) **1** mumble, grumble **2** *fig* gripe, bitch (about)

gungula *nf* tumult

gunj *nm* blanket

gur|ati *vb* **1** (koga/što) push, shove **2** (se) elbow/push one's way through **~kati** *v* (koga/se) nudge (sb/each other) **~nuti** *v* (koga/što) push, thrust

gurman *nm* gourmet
gusar *nm* pirate, buccaneer ~**ski** *adj* pirate
gusjenica *nf* caterpillar
gusj|i *adj* goose
guska *nf* 1 goose 2 bed urinal
gust *adj* (*comp* gušći) thick; dense **bilo je** ~**o** *adv* it was rough ~**iš** *nm* thicket
guš|a *nf med* goitre ~**iti** *v* 1 (koga) strangle 2 (što) stifle 3 (se) choke
gušći *comp* → gust
gušt *nm coll* thrill; kick *coll* **iz** ~**a** for kicks ~ **mi je** I get a kick out of it

došao mi je ~ I felt like it
gušter *nm* 1 lizard 2 *mil sl* rookie
gušterača *nf* pancreas
gut|ati *v* (što) swallow ~**ati svaku riječ** listen with rapt attention ~**ati pogledom** ogle ~**ljaj** *nm* gulp, sip
guverner *nm* governor
guz|a *nf coll* bottom, butt, bum ~**ica** *nf tab* arse *GB*, ass *US*
gužva *nf* 1 crowd **velika je** ~ the place is packed 2 a lot of work 3 trouble ~**ti** *v* 1 (što/se) crumple, crease 2 (se) be jostled in the crowd

H

H, h (ha) 12th letter of Cro. alphabet
habati v (se) wear
haj|ati v (0) (pres ~em) heed, care
hajde int come on! **~mo!** come on! let's go!
hajdu|k nm (Vsg ~če, Npl ~ci) brig-and; bandit (+ fig)
haj|ka nf (Dsg ~ci) hunt, chase, pur-suit; hue and cry fig
halabu|ka nf (Dsg ~ci) racket, hulla-baloo, hubbub
halapljiv adj voracious, greedy
halo int hallo, hello, hullo
halter nm coll suspender belt; garter belt
halucin|acija nf hallucination **~irati** v (0) hallucinate
halva nf halva(h) **prodaje se/ide kao ~** it sells like hot cakes
halj|a nf robe **~etak** nm (Gsg ~etka, Npl ~eci) jacket **~ina** nf dress, gown **kućna ~ina** dressing-gown
hametice adv **~ potući** rout
hangar nm hangar
hansaplast nm TM → **flaster**
harambaša nm brigand chief
harati v (0) (čime) go on a rampage; (bolest) rage, be rife/rampant
harfa nf harp
haringa nf herring **dimljena ~** kipper
harmoni|ja nf harmony **~ka** nf (Dsg ~ci) accordion **usna ~ka** mouth or-gan, harmonica **~ka-vrata** folding door
haubica nm howitzer
hazard|er nm gambler **~ni ~dna** adj **igra** nf game of chance
heftati v (što) coll baste, tack
hegemonija nf hegemony
hektar nm hectare
heli|kopter nm helicopter; chopper coll **~drom** nm heliport
hemofili|ja nf haemophilia **~čar** nm haemophiliac

hemoroidi nm pl haemorrhoids; piles coll
hendikepiran adj handicapped
here|tik nm (Vsg ~tiče, Npl ~tici) heretic **~za** nf heresy
hermelin nm ermine
hermeti|čan adj (a) hermetic (+ fig), air-tight
heroj nm hero
heterogen adj heterogenous
hibridan adj (a) hybrid
hidrauličan adj (a) hydraulic
hidro|avion nm hydroplane **~elek-trana** nf hydroelectric plant **~genska** adj **bomba** nf hydrogen bomb; H-bomb coll **~gliser** nm hydrofoil
higijen|a nf hygiene **~ski** adj hygienic **~ski uložak** sanitary napkin/towel
hihotati v (0/se) giggle
hijena nf hyena
hijerarhija nf hierarchy
hiljada → **tisuća**
himb|a nf deceit **~en** adj deceitful, false
himna nf 1 (**državna ~**) national an-them 2 (**crkvena ~**) hymn
hiniti v (što) feign, dissemble **~ bolest** malinger
hip nm instant **u ~u** in a jiffy
hiper- prefix hyper-, over-
hipno|tizirati v (koga) hypnotize, mes-merise **~za** nf hypnosis, hypnotism
hipodrom nm race course, racetrack
hipofiza nf pituitary gland
hipohondar nm hypochondriac
hipote|ka nf (Dsg ~ci) mortgage **dići ~ku na kuću** mortgage a house
hipoteza nf hypothesis
hir nm caprice; whim **modni ~** fad **~ovit** adj capricious, wayward
histeri|čan adj (a) hysterical **~čni na-padaj** hysterics pl **~ja** nf hysteria

hit *nm coll* hit **filmski ~** blockbuster **~ knjiga** bestseller

hi|tac *nm* (*Gsg ~ca, Npl ~ci*) shot **ispaliti ~ac** fire a shot **~tnuti** *v* (*što*) (*pres ~nem*) throw

hit|an *adj* (*a*) urgent **~na služba** casualty/emergency ward **~na pomoć** ambulance **~ar** *adj* (*a*) quick, swift **~ati** *v* (0) hurry, rush **~ar** *adj* (*a*) quick, swift

hlače *nf pl* (a pair of) trousers; pants *US*

hlad *nm* shade **~ovina** *nf* shade

hlad|an *adj* (*a*) cold, cool (+ *fig*) **~no oružje** cold steel **~iti** *v* (koga/što/se) cool **~no** *adv* coldly, cooly **~no mi je** I am cold **~noća** *nf* coldness **~nokrvan** *adj* (*a*) cool, calm ostati **~nokrvan** keep one's cool **~nokrvno umorstvo** murder in cold blood **~njača** *nf* 1 cold storage 2 refrigerated truck; reefer *coll* **~njak** *nm* (*Npl ~njaci*) refrigerator **~etina** *nf* jelly

hlapiti *v* (0) 1 evaporate (+ *fig*) 2 go flat 3 *fig* fade, vanish

hljeb *nm* loaf (of bread)

hmelj *nm* hop(s)

hobotnica *nf* octopus

hoću (I sing), **hoćeš** (II sing), **hoće** (III sing+pl), **hoćemo** (I pl), **hoćete** (II pl) *v → htjeti*

hod *nm* 1 walk 2 (način) gait 3 *mot* action **brzim ~om** at a brisk pace **rješavati probleme u ~u** solve things as one goes along **sat ~a** an hour's walk **~ati** *v* (0) 1 walk **~ati na prstima** tiptoe **~ati ruku pod ruku** w. arm in arm **~ati u snu** sleepwalk 2 (s kim) go (steady) with sb, go out with sb, date sb **~nik** *nm* (*Npl ~nici*) corridor; (house) hallway **~ulje** *nf pl* stilts

hodoča|snik *nm* (*Vsg ~sniče, Npl ~snici*) pilgrim **~šće** *nn* pilgrimage **~stiti** *v* (0) go on a pilgrimage

hokej *nm* ice hockey **~ na travi** (field) hockey

homogen *adj* homogenous

homoseksual|ac *nm* (*Gsg ~ca, Vsg ~če, Npl ~ci*) homosexual; gay *coll* **~an** *adj* (*a*) homosexual; gay *coll*

horizont *nm* horizon

honorar *nm* fee; payment **~ni** *adj rad* free-lance job/work

hormon *nm* hormone

horoskop *nm* horoscope **~ski znak** sign (of the zodiac) *što si po ~u?* what is your sign?

ho-ruk! *int* heaveho!

hostija *nf* host, wafer

hotel *nm* hotel **luksuzan ~** five-star hotel

hotimi|ce *adv* intentionally, on purpose **~čan** *adj* (*a*) intentional, deliberate

hrab|ar *adj* (*a*) brave, courageous **~riti** *v* (koga) encourage, cheer **~rost** *nf* courage **izgubiti ~rost** lose one's nerve; chicken out *coll*

hra|kati *v* (0) expectorate, hawk **~čak** *nm* (*Gsg ~čka, Npl ~čci*) phlegm; gob *coll*

hram *nm* temple, shrine

hram|lati *v* (0) (*pres ~ljem*) limp

hra|na *nf* food **stočna ~na** fodder, animal food **stan i ~na** board and lodging **~narina** *nf* sick-pay **~nitelj** *nm* breadwinner, provider **~niti** *v* 1 (koga) feed 2 (se čime) feed on, eat **~njiv** *adj* nourishing, nutritious

hrapav *adj* rough, hoarse

hrast *nm* oak **~ovina** *nf* oak(wood)

hr|bat *nm* (*Gsg ~pta*) 1 back 2 (mountain) ridge

hrč|ak *nm* (*Gsg ~ka, Npl ~ci*) hamster

hrđa *nf* rust **~ti** *v* (0) rust **~v** *adj* rusty

hren *nf* horse radish **~ovka** *nf* (*Dsg ~ovci*) frankfurter

hrid(ina) *nf* cliff, rock

hripa|ti *v* (0) wheeze **~vac** *nm* (*Gsg ~vca*) *med* whooping cough

hrkati *v* (0) (*pres hrčem*) snore

hrliti *v* (0) rush

hrom *adj* lame, limping

hrop|tati *v* (0) breathe with difficulty, wheeze **~ac** *nm* (*Gsg ~ca*) death rattle

hrpa *nf* heap, pile **staviti na ~u** heap, pile

hrskav *adj* crisp, crunchy **~ica** *nf* cartilage *med*; gristle

hrt *nm* greyhound **afganistanski ~** Afghan hound **ruski ~** borzoi

hrva|č *nm* wrestler **~nje** *nn* wrestling

~ti *v* (se) wrestle; grapple

hrvatstvo *nn* Croatianness, Croatian national identity/feeling

hrzati *v* (0) neigh

htjeti *v irreg* (koga/što) **1** want **2** be willing ~ **dobro** mean well **baš** ~ insist on **kako hoćeš** as you like it **radi što hoćeš** suit yourself **baš sam htio ustati, kad** ... I was about to get up, when ... **htio bih** I would like **hoćeš-nećeš, htio-ne htio** willy-nilly

hu|ka *nf* (*Dsg* ~ci) (waves) roar; (wind) howling, moaning; (owl) hoot ~**čati** *v* (0) roar, moan, hoot ~**knuti** *v* (0) **1** exhale (sharply); blow **2** hoot (once)

hulahupke *nf pl coll* tights

huliti *v* (0/koga/što) blaspheme

hulja *nf* rascal, scoundrel

hum|ak *nm* (*Gsg* ~ka, *Npl* ~ci) knoll, mound

human *adj* humane ~**itaran** *adj* (α) humanitarian ~**itarna pomoć** h. aid, relief ~**ost** *nf* humanity, humane treatment

humor *nm* humour **crni** ~ black h.

smisao za ~ sense of h. ~**ističan** *adj* (α) funny, humorous

hunjavica *nf* head cold; the sniffles *coll*

huška|č *nm* instigator **ratni** ~**č** warmonger ~**ti** *v* (koga) **1** (na što) incite to sth, stir up sth **2** (protiv koga) set sb against sb; (psa) sic

hval|a *nf* **1** thanks *pl* ~**a lijepa** thank you, many thanks, thanks a lot, thank you very much **Bogu** ~**a** thank God **2** praise ~**evrijedan** *adj* (α) praiseworthy ~**isati** *v* (se čime) boast/brag about ~**isavac** *nm* (*Gsg* ~isavca, *Vsg* ~isavče, *Npl* ~isavci) boaster, braggart ~**iti** *v* **1** (koga/što) praise **2** (se čime) pride oneself on, boast ~**ospjev** *nm* eulogy

hvastati *v* (se) brag

hvat *nm* fathom

hvata|ljka *nf* (*Dsg* ~ljci) grip; tongs *pl* ~**ti** **1** (koga/što) grasp at **2** (koga/što) try to catch, hunt, chase **3** (se) clutch at, grab hold of **4** (se) ~ **se mrak** it's getting dark

I

I, i 13th letter of Cro. alphabet
i *conj* 1 and 2 as well, too **i ... i ...** both ... and ...
iako *conj* although
ičiji *adj* anybody's
ići *v* (0) (*pres* idem) go, move ~ **pješice** walk, go on foot ~ **autom** go by car, drive ~ **za čim** strive for **ne ide mi u glavu** it's beyond me ~ **na živce** (komu) annoy sb **ide mi od ruke** I am good at it
ideal *nm* ideal ~**an** *adj* (a) ideal ~**ist** *nm* idealist ~**istički** *adj* idealistic ~**izam** *nm* (Gsg ~izma) idealism
ideja *nf* idea, notion
identi|čan *adj* (a) identical ~**ficirati** *v* (koga/što) identify ~**tet** *nm* identity
ideolog *nm* ideologist ~**ija** *nf* ideology
idil|a *nf* idyll ~**ičan** *adj* (a) idyllic, arcadian
idiot *nm* idiot
idol *nm* idol ~**opoklonstvo** *nn* idolatry
idući *adj* next, following, further
igdje *adv* anywhere
igl|a *nf* needle **biti na** ~**ama** be jittery, be on pins and needles ~**ica** *nf* 1 small needle 2 spine
ignorirati *v* (koga/što) ignore, take no notice of, not heed
igr|a *nf* 1 play 2 game **hazardna** ~**a** gamble ~**a riječima** pun, a play on words **biti u** ~**i** be in the game **u** ~**i su milijuni** millions are at stake ~**ač** *nm* player ~**ačka** *nf* toy ~**ačnica** *nf* gambling-house, casino ~**aća** *adj* **karta** (playing) card ~**alište** *nn* playground **športsko** ~**alište** ground, field; (za golf) putting green **nogometno** ~**alište** pitch **tenisko** ~**alište** court ~**arija** *nf* child's play, kids' stuff ~**ati** *v* 1 (se) play ~**ati se sa životom** risk one's life 2 (koga/što) play ~**ani film** feature film 3 (0) be

on ~**okaz** *nm* play
ikad(a) *adv* ever **bolje** ~ **nego nikad** better late than never
ikakav *adj* (a) of any kind, any
ikako *adv* in any way **ako** ~ **možeš** if you possibly can
ikoji *adj* 1 anyone, anybody 2 whichever
ikona *nf* icon
ikra *nf* roe, spawn
ikserice *nf pl coll* knock knees
ilegal|a *nf pol* underground ~**ac** *nm* (Gsg ~ca, Vsg ~če) member of the Underground ~**an** *adj* (a) illegal
ili *conj* or **ili ... ili ...** either ... or
ilovača *nf* clay
ilustr|acija *nf* illustration ~**iran** *adj* picture-, illustrated ~**irati** *v* (što) illustrate
iluz|ija *nf* illusion ~**oran** *adj* (a) illusory
imalo *adv* even a little bit, in any way, at all
imanje *nn* (landed) property, estate; farm
imati *v* (koga/što) have, possess **ima li još maslaca?** is there any butter left? ~**ti na pameti** bear in mind **ima dva dana kako se nismo vidjeli** I haven't seen him for two days
ime *nn* (Gsg ~na) name **vlastito** ~ first name **u** ~ **a.** in the name of **b.** on behalf of **u to** ~ to this purpose ~**nica** *nf* gram noun ~**nik** *nm* (Npl ~nici) register **telefonski** ~**nik** directory ~**novanje** *nn* appointment ~**novati** *v* (*pres* ~nujem) 1 (koga) name, specify 2 (koga čime) appoint, name ~**njak** *nm* (Vsg ~njače, Npl ~njaci) namesake
imit|acija *nf* imitation ~**irati** *v* (koga/što) imitate
imov|ina *nf* belongings *pl*, possessions

pl, property **pokretna ~ina** movables **pl nepokretna ~ina** real estate, realty **~inski** adj property **~ni** adj financial

imperativ nm imperative

imperijali|stički adj imperialist **~zam** nm (Gsg ~zma) imperialism

imponirati v (komu čime) impress sb with sth

impoten|cija nf impotence **~tan** adj (a) impotent

impozantan adj (a) impressive, formidable

impresi|ja nf impression **~onizam** nm sg (Gsg ~onizma) impressionism **~van** adj (a) impressive

improviz|acija nf improvisation; make-shift solution **~iran** adj make-shift, impromptu **~irati** v (0/što) improvise, ad-lib

impuls nm impulse

imućan adj (a) well off, well-to-do

imun adj (na) immune to **~itet** nm immunity

inače adv 1 else, otherwise 2 by the way

inačica nf variant

inat nm 1 obstinacy 2 spite **~iti** v (se) stand one's ground, not budge an inch

incident nm incident

indeks nm 1 index 2 student record book

indicij|a nf indication **~e** pl leg circumstantial evidence

indiferentan adj (a) indifferent, unconcerned

indigo nm indigo **~ papir** carbon paper

indirektan adj (a) indirect

indiskre|cija nf indiscretion **~tan** adj (a) indiscreet

individualan adj (a) individual, personal

industrij|a nf industry **~alac** nm (Gsg ~alca) industrialist **~ski** adj industrial

infekcija nf infection

inflacija nf inflation

inform|acija nf information **jedna ~acija** a piece of information **~atika** nf (Dsg ~atici) information/computer

science **~ativan** adj informative **~ativna emisija** news programme **~irati** v (koga) inform, notify, brief

infuzij|a nf infusion **primati ~u** be on IV/on a drip

inicijativ|a nf initiative **pokrenuti ~u** launch the i. **preuzeti ~u** take the i.

injekcija nf injection; shot coll

inkuba|cija nf incubation **~tor** nm incubator

inkvizi|cija nf the Inquisition **~tor** nm inquisitor

inozem|an adj (a) foreign **ministarstvo ~nih poslova** 1 ministry of foreign affairs 2 GB the Foreign Office 3 US the State Department **~stvo** nn foreign countries, overseas **biti u ~stvu** be abroad

inscenirati v (što) 1 stage 2 fig stage-manage, engineer

insekt → kukac

insert nm film clip

inspek|cija nf inspection **~tor** nm inspector

inspicijent nm stage manager

inspir|acija nf inspiration **~irati** v (koga na što) inspire

instal|acija nf installation **~acije** pl fittings **električne ~acije** wiring **~ater** nm electrician; (vodovoda) plumber **~irati** v (što) install, fit

instinkt nm instinct **~ivan** adj (a) instinctive

institu|cija nf institution **~t** nm institute

instruk|cija nf 1 instruction 2 tuition **davati ~cije** give private lessons **~tor** nm instructor; tutor

instrument nm instrument

integr|alan adj (a) integral **~itet** nm integrity

intelekt nm intellect **~ualac** nm (Gsg ~ualca) intellectual; egghead coll; white-collar **~ualan** adj (a) intellectual

inteligen|cija nf 1 intelligence 2 (klasa) intelligentsia **~tan** adj (a) intelligent

intendant nm 1 mil quartermaster 2 manager

intenzi|van adj (a) intense **~tet** nm intensity, force

interes nm interest ~**antan** adj (a) interesting ~**ent** nm interested party, prospective buyer ~**irati** v 1 (koga) interest sb, be of interest to sb 2 (se) be interested in, take an interest in ~**ni** adj of interest

internacionalan adj (a) international

internat nm boarding school

intern|i adj internal ~**a medicina** internal medicine

interpretacija nf interpretation

interpunkcija nf punctuation

interven|cija nf intervention ~**irati** v (0) intervene

intervju nm interview ~**irati** v (koga) interview

intim|an adj (a) intimate ~**no rublje** underwear, lingerie ~**ni prijatelj** close friend ~**ni odnos** intercourse

intonacija nf intonation

intrig|a nf intrigue, plot ~**irati** v 1 (0) plot 2 (koga) arouse sb's interest

intuicija nf intuition

invalid nm disabled person, invalid ~**ska** adj mirovina disability pension

invazija nf invasion

invent|ar nm 1 inventory 2 equipment; fixture (+ fig) ~**ura** nf stock-taking

investi|cija nf investment ~**rati** v (što u što) invest in ~**tor** nm investor

inzistirati (0/na čemu) insist (on sth)

inženjer nm engineer ~**ac** nm (Gsg ~ca) mil engineer

inje nn hoar-frost

ipak adv however, yet, nevertheless

iracionalan adj (a) irrational

irelevantan adj (a) irrelevant

iritirati v 1 (koga) irritate, annoy 2 (što) irritate, chafe

ironi|čan adj (a) ironic(al) ~**ja** nf irony

iscijediti v (koga/što) squeeze dry, drain

iscijeliti|ti v (koga/što) heal, cure ~**elj** nm healer

iscijep|ati v (što) chop (up) ~**kati** v (što) 1 chop finely 2 cut up, divide in small pieces

iscrp|an adj (a) exhaustive, detailed ~**ljen** adj 1 exhausted 2 (rudnik) worked out ~**ljenost** nf exhaustion, fatigue ~**ljivati** v impf (pres ~ljujem)

~**iti** v (koga/što) exhaust

iscuriti v (0) trickle/leak/ooze out

ise|liti v 1 (0/se) move out 2 (koga) evict ~**ljavati** v impf (pres ~ljujem) ~**ljenik** nm (Vsg ~ljeniče, Npl ~ljenici) emigrant **politički ~ljenik** emigré

isfućkati v (koga/što) hiss, boo

ishlapiti v 1 evaporate 2 (piće) go flat 3 fig grow senile

ishod nm outcome, result

ishrana nf deit, nutrition

isisati v (što) (pres isišem) suck out

isje|ckati v (što) cut to pieces, chop finely ~**čak** nm (Gsg ~čka, Npl ~čci) section ~**čak iz novina** press clipping ~**ći** v (što) (pres isiječem) cut up

iskak(iv)ati v impf (pres iskakujem) → **iskočiti**

iskaliti v 1 (što na kome/čemu) vent 2 (se na kome/čemu) take it out on sb/sth

iskapati v impf → **iskopati**

iskašlj|ati v (što/se) (pres ~em) cough up

iskaz nm statement; evidence ~**ati** v (pres iskažem) 1 (što) display 2 (se) give a good account of oneself, prove one's worth ~**ivati** v impf ~**nica** nf osoba ~**nica** identity card **članska ~nica** membership card

iskesiti v 1 ~ **zube** snarl 2 (se) grin

iskititi v (što) fig embellish

isklesa|ti v (što) (pres isklešem) carve sth in stone **kao ~n** chiselled

iskliznuti v (0) (pres iskliznem) slide, slip ~ **s tračnica** be derailed

isključ|eno adv out of the question ~**enje** nn (iz škole) expulsion ~**iti** v 1 (koga) exclude; sport send off GB 2 (koga/što) rule out 3 (što) switch/turn off; disconnect 4 (se) fig switch off ~**iv** adj 1 exclusive 2 inflexible, intolerant ~**ivo** adv exclusively, solely

iskočiti v (0) jump out of/off; (padobranom) bale out GB, bail out US ~ **iz vlastite kože** go crazy, go up the wall

iskonski adj primeval

iskonstruiran adj fabricated

iskop|ati v (koga/što) dig out, excavate; unearth (+ fig) ~**avati** v impf

~ina *nf* excavated object, fossil

iskopčati *v* (što) disconnect, unplug

iskoprcati *v* (se) (manage to) disentangle/extricate oneself

iskorijeniti *v* (što) eradicate

iskori|stiti *v* (koga/što) make use of, put to use, profit by; take advantage of, exploit **~stiti priliku** take the opportunity **~štavati** *v impf* exploit

iskovati *v* (što) *(pres* iskujem) 1 (novac) mint 2 (predmet; prijateljstvo) forge 3 (riječ) coin

iskra *nf* spark

iskra|sti *v* (se) *(pres* ~dem) steal/sneak out **~dati** *v impf*

iskrca|ti *v* (koga/što) put ashore, disembark 2 (što) unload 3 (se) disembark, land **~vanje** *nn* 1 disembarkation; unloading 2 *mil* invasion, landing

iskrčiti *v* (što) clear (land)

iskren *adj* sincere, open, frank **~ost** *nf* sincerity

iskre|nuti *v* (što) *(pres* ~nem) 1 reverse, invert 2 (zglob) sprain 3 turn upside down **~tati** *v impf (pres* ~ćem)

iskriv|iti *v* 1 (što) twist, bend (out od shape); distort 2 (se) bend **~ljavati** *v impf*

iskrižati *v* (što) cross out

iskrs|nuti *v* (0) *(pres* ~nem) crop up **~avati** *v impf*

iskrvariti *v* (0) bleed to death

iskuhati *v* (što) boil

iskup|iti *v* (se) redeem oneself; make up for sth **~ljenje** *nn* redemption

iskus|an *adj* (*a*) experienced, skilled **~tvo** *nn* experience

iskuš|ati *v* (koga) 1 try out 2 test, put to the test **~avati** *v impf* **~enje** *nn* temptation **pasti/doći u ~enje** fall into temptation, be tempted

iskvar|en *adj* corrupt, depraved **~iti** *v* (koga) corrupt, ruin

Islam *nm* Islam **i~ski** *adj* Islamic

ismija|ti *v* (koga/što); (se iz koga/čega) *(pres* ismijem) scoff at, ridicule **~vati** *v impf*

ispad *nm* excess, outrage, scene, incident

ispaliti *v* (što na koga/što) **~ metak**

fire a shot on/at

ispariti *v* (0) 1 evaporate 2 *fig* vanish into thin air

ispa|sti *v* (0) *(pres* ~dnem) 1 fall out 2 *sport* be eliminated **~lo mi je iz ruke** I dropped it **~sti budala** make a fool of oneself **~dati** *v impf*

ispaša *nf* pasture

ispaštati *v* (što) expiate, atone for, pay for

ispavati *v* (se) get enough sleep

ispe|ći *v* (što) *(pres* ispečem) (kruh, glinu) bake; (meso) roast, grill; (rakiju) distill **~ zanat** learn one's trade **ispeci pa reci** look before you jump

ispetljati *v* (se) disentangle/extricate oneself

ispijen *adj* (lice) haggard, gaunt

ispipati *v* (što) 1 feel all over 2 *fig* find out, detect, put out feelers *coll*

ispirati *v impf* → **isprati**

ispis *nm* (kompjutorski) printout **~ati** *v* *(pres* ispišem) 1 (što) write out 2 (se) leave 3 (koga) remove, eliminate **~ivati** *v impf (pres* ~ujem)

ispit *nm* exam(ination), test **prijamni ~** entrance exam **pismeni/usmeni ~** written/oral e. **vozački ~** driving t. **polagati ~** sit for/take an exam/a test **položiti ~** pass the e./t. **pasti na ~u** fail the e./t. **~ati** *v* (koga) 1 question, interrogate 2 (koga/što) investigate, examine, test **~ivati** *v (pres* ~ujem) 1 *impf* 2 keep asking questions **~ivač** *nm* examiner **~ivanje** *nn* 1 investigation 2 interrogation 3 test, study, analysis **~ujući** *adj* inquiring, probing

ispi|ti *v* (što) *(pres* ~jem) drink up **~ti do dna** empty **~ti komu krv** *fig* bother, harass **~jati** *v impf*

ispjevati *v* (što) compose

isplakati *v (pres* isplačem) 1 (što) cry 2 (se) cry one's eyes out, have a good cry

isplat|a *nf* payment **dan ~e** pay day **~iti** *v* 1 (koga/komu što) pay (out) 2 (se) pay **ne ~i mi se** it is not worth my while

isplaziti *v* (što) **~ jezik** stick one's tongue out

isplesti *v* (što) *(pres* ispletem) knit;

(hair) plait

isplivati *v* (0) **1** swim out, rise to the surface **2** *fig* get out of the trouble

isploviti *v* (0) leave harbour, set sail

isplju|nuti *v* (što) spit out ~**vak** *nm* (*Gsg* ~vka, *Npl* ~ vci) spittle; sputum *med*

ispočetka *adv* **1** at first **2** all over again

ispod *prep* below, under, beneath, underneath

isporu|čiti *v* (komu što) deliver ~**ka** *nf* (*Dsg* ~ci) delivery

isposl|ovati *v* (*pres* ~ujem) (komu što) procure

ispov|ijed *nf* confession ~**jediti** *v* **1** (koga/što/se) confess **2** (koga) hear sb's confession ~**ijedati** proclaim one's faith ~**jednik** *nm* (*Vsg* ~jedniče *Npl* ~jednici) confessor

isprašiti *v* (što) dust ~ **komu leđa/tur** thrash sb, give sb a licking

isprati *v* (*pres* isperem) **1** (što) wash out; rinse; (ranu) bathe **2** (se) wash away; (mrlja) come out in the wash

ispratiti *v* (koga) see sb off ~ **pogledom** gaze after

isprav|ak *nm* document; deed ~**e** *pl* papers

isprav|ak *nm* (*Gsg* ~ka, *Npl* ~ci) correction, amendment ~**an** *adj* (α) correct; in (good) order ~**iti** *v* **1** (koga/što/se) correct sb/sth/oneself **2** (što) amend, set right ~**iti nepravdu** redress the wrong ~**ljati** *v impf* ~**ljač** *nm tech* rectifier

isprazniti *v* **1** (što) empty; vacate; unload **2** (se) empty

isprebijati *v* (koga) beat up

ispred *prep* **1** in front of **2** ahead of

isprekida|n *adj* **1** broken **2** intermittent

ispremiješati *v* (što) stir, mix, mix up

ispremještati *v* (koga/što) shift/move from one place to another

ispresijecati *v* (što) intersect, (criss)cross

ispri|čati *v* **1** (što) tell, relate **2** (koga) excuse **3** (se) excuse oneself; apologize ~**čnica** *nf* note ~**ka** *nf* (*Dsg* ~ci) excuse, apology

ispriječiti *v* (se) stand in the way,

block the way

isprositi *v* (koga) ask one's hand in marriage

isprsiti *v* (se) **1** swagger **2** *fig coll* pay the bill

ispružiti *v* **1** (što) extend, stretch out **2** (se) stretch oneself **3** (se) *coll* lie down, have a nap

isprva *adv* at first

ispržiti *v* (što) grill, roast, broil; fry

ispucati *v* **1** (0) be chapped/cracked, split **2** (se) let off steam

ispu|niti *v* **1** (što) (obećanje) fulfil, keep; (dužnost) perform; (obrazac) fill in/out; (želju) meet, make one's wish come true; (nadu) realize **2** (koga čime) fill sb with sth ~**njavati** *v impf* ~**njenje** *nn* realization, coming to life

ispupč|en *adj* bulging, prominent; convex ~**enost** *nf* convexity ~**iti** *v* (se) bulge

ispu|stiti *v* (što) **1** omit, leave out **2** let out, emit ~**stiti vjetar** break wind ~**stiti dušu** give up the ghost ~**stiti iz ruke** let go, drop ~**štati** *v impf*

istaknuti *v* (što) (*pres* istaknem) emphasize, stress ~ *adj* prominent, distinguished

istančan *adj* **1** (ukus) refined, sophisticated **2** (njuh) keen

iste|ći *v* (0) (*pres* ~čem) **1** flow out **2** (rok) expire ~**k** *nm* expiration, expiry

iste|gnuti *v* (što) (*pres* ~gnem) **1** sprain **2** stretch out ~**zati** *v impf* (*pres* ~žem)

iste|sati *v* (što) (*pres* ~šem) carve out (in wood)

ist|i *adj* the same ~**i otac** (the spitting) image of his father ~**o** *adv* the same, likewise, equally ~**o tako** likewise, as well ~**odoban** *adj* (α) simultaneous ~**odobno** *adv* at the same time ~**oimen** *adj* of the same name ~**okračan** *adj* (α) isosceles ~**omišljenik** *nm* (*Npl* ~omišljenici) supporter ~**smjeran** *adj* (α) parallel ~**osmjerna struja** direct current ~**vjetan** *adj* (α) identical

isticati *v impf* (*pres* ističem) → **istaknuti**

istin|a *nf* truth govoriti ~**u** tell the

truth **nije** ~a it is not true **~i za volju** the truth is **~u govoreći** to tell the truth **~it** *adj* true **~oljubiv** *adj* truthful **~ski** *adj* real, true

istis|nuti *v* 1 (što) (*pres* ~nem) squeeze out 2 (koga) oust **~nina** *nf* displacement **~kivati** *v impf*

istjecati *v impf* (*pres* istječem) → **istjeći**

istjer|ati *v* (koga) drive/turn out **~ati vraga iz koga** exorcize sb **~ivati** *v impf*

isto|čni *adj* 1 eastern; (vjetar) easterly 2 Oriental 3 (grijeh) original **~čno** *adv* (od) (to the) east of; eastwards **~čnjak** *nm* (*Npl* ~čnjaci) 1 Oriental 2 easterly wind **~k** *nm* the East; the Orient **Bliski ~** the Near/Middle East **Daleki ~** the Far East

istopiti *v* (što) melt down, render

istovar *nm* unloading **~iti** *v* (što) unload **~ivati** *v impf*

istra|ga *nf* (*Dsg* ~zi) investigation; inquest; probe **voditi ~gu o** investigate sth, conduct an investigation into **~žitelj** *nm* investigator **~žiti** *v* (što) 1 investigate; probe 2 explore; study **~živati** *v impf* **~živač** *nm* 1 explorer 2 researcher 3 (nafte) prospector **~živanje** *nn* study, research **~žni** *adj* **~žni postupak** investigation **~žni sudac** investigating judge **~žni zatvor** detention pending trial **biti u ~žnom zatvoru** be on remand

istrč|ati *v* (*pres* ~im) 1 (0) run out, come out running **~ati pred rudo** jump the gun 2 (se) have a good run 3 (se) *fig* be rash

istrebljivati *v impf* (*pres* istrebljujem) → **istrijebiti**

istresti *v* (*pres* istresem) 1 (što) shake out; empty, dump 2 (se na koga) snap at

istrgnuti *v* (*pres* istrgnem) 1 (što) pluck out, tear out; wrench 2 (se) wrest oneself free

istrijebiti *v* (koga/što) exterminate

istrljati *v* (što) rub (down)

istrošiti *v* 1 (što) use up 2 (se) wear out

istu|ći *v* (koga) (*pres* ~čem) beat up, lick

istup *nm* address to the public, statement **~ati** *v impf* **~iti** *v* 1 (0) come/step forward 2 (0) speak 3 (iz čega) quit, resign, leave

isu|kati *v* (što) (*pres* ~čem) draw

Isus *nm* Jesus **~ Krist** Jesus Christ **~ovac** *nm* (*Gsg* ~ovca, *Vsg* ~če) Jesuit

isušiti *v* 1 (što) drain off, reclaim 2 (se) dry up, wither

išamarati *v* (koga) box sb's ears, slap sb's face

išara|n *adj* 1 mottled, speckled, dappled 2 scribbled all over **~ti** *v* (koga/što) 1 dapple 2 scribble all over

iščašiti *v* (što) sprain, dislocate

iščeprkati *v* (što) unearth, dig up (+ *fig*)

iščešljati *v* (što) comb out

iščetkati *v* (što) brush

iščez|nuti *v* (0) (*pres* ~nem) vanish **~avati** *v impf*

iščupati *v* (što) pluck/pull/tear out; uproot

išijas *nm* sciatica

išta *pron* (*Gsg* ičega) anything

itko *pron* (*Gsg* ikoga) anyone, anybody

iver *nm* 1 chip 2 *anat* patella 3 (fish) sole **~ica** *nf* chipboard

iz *prep* 1 from 2 out of

iza *prep* 1 behind 2 after **~ toga** afterwards

izabra|nik *nm* (*Vsg* ~niče, *Npl* ~nici) **~nik srca** sweetheart, one's beloved **~ti** *v* (koga/što za koga/što) (*pres* izaberem) 1 choose, select 2 *pol* elect sb sth

izaslan|ik *nm* (*Vsg* ~iče, *Npl* ~ici) envoy **~stvo** *nn* delegation; mission

izaz|ivač *nm* challenger **~ivački** *adj* provocative, challenging **~ivati** *v impf* **~vati** *v* (što ~ovem) 1 (koga) challenge, provoke, defy **~vati na dvoboj** challenge sb to a duel 2 (što) cause; invite **~ov** *nm* challenge **~ovan** *adj* (*a*) 1 defiant 2 provocative, alluring

izbaci|ti *v* (koga/što) throw out; (iz škole) expel; (iz stana) evict **~vač** *nm* bouncer, chucker-out *coll*

izbavit|i *v* 1 (koga) deliver, liberate, rescue; redeem 2 (se) free oneself **~elj** *nm* redeemer

izbezum|iti *v* 1 (koga) drive sb crazy 2 (se) lose one's mind, go crazy *fig* **~ljen** *adj* frantic

izbijati *v impf* → **izbiti** *izbijaju mu zubi* he is teething

izbijeliti *v* (što) bleach

izbirljiv *adj* fastidious; choosy *coll*

izbi|ti *v* (što) (*pres* ~jem) 1 knock out **~j si to iz glave** forget it 2 (voda, biljka) gush, spout; spring forth, sprout, bud 3 (znoj) exude 4 (zubi) grow 5 (bolest) break out, erupt

izbivati *v* (0) be absent/away

izbje|ći *v* (*pres* ~gnem) 1 (koga/što) manage to avoid, escape 2 flee **~gavati** *v impf* shun **~gavati odgovor** evade the answer **~gavati posao** shirk **~glica** *nm* refugee

izblebe|tati *v* (se/što) (*pres* ~ćem) spill the beans, blab

izbliza *adv* 1 at close quarters 2 closely

izblju|vati *v* (što/se) (*pres* ~jem) vomit, throw/sick up

izboč|en *adj* bulging, protruding **~ina** *nf* bulge **~iti** *v* (se) bulge out, protrude

izbor *nm* choice, selection; assortment, range **~i** *pl pol* election(s) **izići na ~e** turn up to vote, go to the polls **~ni** *adj* electoral **~ni okrug** constituency **~ni sustav** electoral system **~no mjesto** polling station **~nik** *nm* (*Vsg* ~niče, *Npl* ~nici) *sport* selector

izbo|sti *v* (koga/što) (*pres* ~dem) stab

izbrazda|n *adj* furrowed, lined **~ti** *v* (što) line, plough

izbrijati *v* (što) shave clean/closely

izbri|sati *v* (*pres* ~šem) 1 (što) erase, wipe off, rub off; remove 2 (se) be erased

izbrojiti *v* (koga/što) count

izbuljiti *v* (što) ~ **oči** stare, goggle at

izbušiti *v* (što) punch, pierce, perforate

izdahn|uti *v* (0) (*pres* ~em) 1 exhale 2 die, pass away

izdaj|a *nf* treachery, treason, betrayal **~ica** *nm/f* traitor **~nički** *adj* treacherous, treasonable **~stvo** *nn* treason

izdaleka *adv* from a distance, from afar **ni ~** not by far

izdan|ak *nm* (*Gsg* ~ka, *Npl* ~ci) 1 sprout, shoot 2 *fig* offshoot

izda|nje *nn* 1 edition 2 issue **~tak** *nm* (*Gsg* ~tka, *Npl* ~ci) expense, expenditure **~ti** *v* 1 (što) publish (knjigu); issue, release **~ti nalog** decree, order 2 (koga/što) betray; tell, leak (tajnu) **~vač** *nm* publisher **~vački** *adj* publishing **~vačko poduzeće** publishing house, publishers **~vati** *v impf*

izder|ati *v* (se) (*pres* ~em) shout/snap at

izdi|ći *v* (se) (*pres* ~gnem) rise above

izdisaj *nm* 1 exhalation 2 one's last breath

izdrž|ati *v* (*pres* ~im) endure, bear, stand, hold out, resist **~ati kaznu** serve the sentence **~ljiv** *adj* hardy, tough **~ljivost** *nf* stamina

izdu|psti *v* (što) (*pres* ~bem) hollow out, carve, chisel out

izdv|ojiti *v* 1 (što/koga od čega) separate, sort out; isolate 2 (što za što/koga) earmark, set aside, allocate (sredstva) 3 (što) single out 4 (se) detach oneself; stand aloof **~ajati** *v impf*

izgara|nje *nn* combustion **motor s unutarnjim ~njem** internal-combustion engine **~ti** *v* (0) burn **~ti na poslu** work hard **~ti za čim** crave for

izgaziti *v* (koga/što) trample down

izgin|uti *v* (0) (*pres* ~em) perish

izglačati *v* (što) iron (out), press

izgladiti *v* (što) 1 plane, file 2 *fig* iron out, smooth over

izglad|njeti *v* (0) (*pres* ~nim) famish, starve

izglasati *v* (što) vote for sth/sb ~ **zakon** pass the law

izgled *nm* 1 looks, appearance; air 2 prospects, promise **~ati** *v* (0) look, appear, seem

izgnan|ik *nm* (*Vsg* ~iče, *Npl* ~ici) exile **~stvo** *nn* exile

izgnjaviti *v* (koga) bore to death

izgnječiti *v* (što/koga) knead, squash

izgnjiliti *v* (0) rot away, decay

izgon *nm* expulsion, banishment **~iti** *v* (koga) ~ **na pašu** put out to grass

izgor|jeti v (0) (pres ~im) burn down ~jeti do temelja burn to the ground ~jeti na suncu get sun-burned

izgov|or nm 1 pronunciation 2 excuse, subterfuge ~ovoriti v 1 (što) pronounce; utter 2 (se čime) plead sth ~arati v impf

izgraditi v (što) build, construct, erect

izgrditi v (koga) chide, reprove

izgred nm breach of the peace; outrage, excess

izgre|psti v (koga/što) (pres ~bem) scratch

izgri|sti v (pres ~zem) 1 (koga/što) bite 2 (što) corrode; eat away 3 (se) fig eat one's heart out

izgub|iti v 1 (koga/što) lose ~iti boju fade ~iti svijest faint ~iti iz vida lose sight of ~iti strpljenje lose patience, lose one's temper 2 (se) get lost 3 (se) disappear, vanish; fade away ~ljen adj 1 lost, missing 2 confused

izgurati v (koga/što) shove out, push out; oust fig

izgužvati v (što) rumple, crumple

izići v (pres iziđem) 1 come out (of), emerge (from); leave, get out (of), step out (of) 2 be published 3 (come) rise ~ na vidjelo come to light ~ pobjednikom come out a winner ~ na kraj s kim cope with ~ u susret fig comply with; cooperate ~ (van) s kim go out with, have a date with

izigrati v (koga/što) deceive, double-cross

izisk|ivati v (što) (pres ~ujem) call for

izjadati v (se) tell one's woes; cry on sb's shoulder

izjaloviti v (se) fail, come to nothing

izjasniti v (se) declare oneself

izjav|a nf statement ~iti v (što) state ~ljivati v impf

izjedati v impf 1 (što) corrode; erode 2 (koga) worry 3 (se) fret

izjednačiti v 1 (koga s kim) equate 2 (što) standardize ~ rezultat equalize

izjesti v pf → izjedati

izjuriti v (0) rush/dash out

izlaga|č nm exhibitor; participant ~nje nn presentation ~ti v (pres izlažem) 1 (što) exhibit, display 2 (što čemu)

expose sth to sth 3 (što/o čemu) expound 4 (se) expose oneself

izlaj|ati v (što/se) (pres ~em) fig blab

izlan|uti v (što) (pres ~em) blab, blur out

izla|z nm exit; way out (+ fig) nema ~za there's no way out ~zak nm (Gsg ~ska, Npl ~sci) going out, date ~ziti v impf → izići ~zni adj outgoing ~ženje nn publication

izle|ći v (što/se) (pres ~gnem) hatch

izlet nm trip, excursion, outing ~nik nm (Npl ~nici) , holidaymaker, tourist

izliječiti v 1 (koga/što) cure 2 (se) get well, be cured

izlijepiti v (što) paste, stick up

izlijevati v impf → izliti

izli|ka nf (Dsg ~ci) excuse, pretext

izlišan adj (ā) superfluous, unnecessary, redundant

izliza|n adj (ā) threadbare, worn ~ti v (se) (pres izližem) wear out

izlo|g nm (Npl ~zi) shop window razgledavanje ~ga window shopping ~žak nm (Gsg ~ška, Npl ~sci) exhibit ~žba nf exhibition; show, display ~žben adj show, exhibition, display ~žen adj 1 displayed, on display 2 exposed to 3 open/subject to ~žiti v 1 (koga/što) display, exhibit, show; expose to (suncu); expound (misli) 2 (se) expose oneself to, invite

izluč|ina nf secretion ~iti v 1 (što) secrete 2 (koga) eliminate ~ivati v impf ~ni adj eliminating

izluditi v (koga) drive crazy

izlječiv adj curable

izljev nm 1 discharge 2 outburst ~ krvi h(a)emorrhage

izmak nm biti na ~u run out on je na ~ku snaga his strength is failing/ebbing ~nuti v (pres ~nem) 1 (0) escape 2 (što) snatch away 3 (komu/čemu) manage to escape 4 (se) dodge, duck

izmamiti v 1 (koga) draw out 2 (što) elicit ~ suze move to tears

između prep between (dvoje); among (više od dvoje) ~ ostalog among other things

izmi|cati v (pres ~čem) 1 impf → iz-

maknuti 2 (čemu) shirk from, evade, elude **~če mi tlo pod nogama** I am losing ground

izmijeniti v 1 (koga/što/se) change, alter, modify 2 (što) exchange

izmiješati v (što) 1 mix, blend 2 confuse 3 (karte) shuffle

izmiriti v 1 (koga s kim) reconcile, conciliate 2 (se s kim) make peace with, make it up with **~ se sa sudbinom** resign oneself to one's faith

izmi|sliti v (što) make up, invent; fabricate **~šljati** v impf **~šljen** adj fictitious **~šljotina** nf fabrication

izmjen|a nf change, alteration; exchange **~jivati** v impf alternate; intermittent **~ična struja** alternating current **~njivati** v 1 impf → **izmijeniti** 2 (se) take turns

izmjeriti v (koga/što/se) measure, gauge, size up

izmlatiti v (koga) thrash

izmoliti v (što) (molitvu) say

izmor|en adj exhausted **~iti** v 1 (koga) exhaust, tire out 2 (se) be exhausted, get tired

izmotavati v (se) hedge

izmožden adj emaciated, haggard

izmrcvariti v (koga) 1 mangle 2 wear out 3 torture

izmrviti v (što) crumble

izmuč|en adj exhausted; tortured, agonized, pained **~iti** v 1 (koga) exhaust, wear out; torture, torment 2 (se) work too hard

izmu|sti v (koga/što) (pres ~zem) 1 milk 2 fig bleed, fleece

iznad prep above; over **~ svega** above all

iznajm|iti v (što komu) let, lease, hire (out); charter (zrakoplov, brod) **~lji-vati** v impf **~ljuje se** to let

iznaka|ziti v (koga/što) disfigure **~žen** adj disfigured, misshapen

iznemo|ći v (0) (pres ~gnem) be exhausted, lose one's strength **~glost** nf exhaustion **raditi što do ~glosti** do sth till one drops

iznena|da adv suddenly, all of a sudden **~dan** adj (α) sudden, unexpected **~diti** v 1 (koga čime) surprise, take sb by surprise, astonish 2 be sur-

prised **~đenje** nn 1 (pojava koja iznenađuje) surprise 2 (osjećaj) astonishment **~đivati** v impf **~đujući** adj amazing

iznevjeriti v (koga) betray, fail

iznijeti v (što) (pres iznesem) 1 carry/take out **~ živu glavu** save one's skin **~ na vidjelo** bring to light, divulge 2 put forward, present

iznikn|uti v (0) (pres ~em) crop up (+ fig)

iznim|an adj (α) exceptional; extraordinary, outstanding **~ka** nf (Dsg ~ci) exception

iznos nm amount **~iti** v 1 impf → **iznijeti** 2 amount to, total

iznošen adj worn-out

iznova adv anew, afresh; again

iznuditi v (što od koga) extort

iznutr|a adv from within; on the inside **~ice** n pl offal

izobilje nn abundance, plenty; affluence

izobličiti v 1 (što) distort 2 (se) distort, become distorted **~avati** v impf **~en** adj distorted

izobrazba nf training

izol|acija nf 1 tech insulation 2 isolation **~ator** nm insulator **~irati** v 1 (koga/što) isolate 2 (što) insulate; (zvučno) soundproof

izopač|en adj debased, perverted, sick **~iti** v 1 (što) distort 2 (koga) debase, corrupt 3 (se) go wrong

izopćiti v (koga iz čega) banish from, excommunicate from **~ iz društva** put beyond the pale

izosta|ti v (0) (pres ~nem) 1 be absent, fail to appear 2 be overdue/late **~ti s predavanja** miss/skip/cut coll classes **~jati** v impf **~nak** nm (Gsg ~nka, Npl ~nci) absence, failure to appear/attend

izoštr|iti v (što) sharpen 2 (na što) focus on **~avati** v impf

izrabljiva|ti v impf (pres izrabljujem) exploit, take advantage of **~č** nm exploiter **~čki** adj exploiting

izračunati v (što) calculate; work/figure out

izra|dba nf 1 manufacturing, making 2 quality, workmanship **~diti** v (što) manufacture, make ~đivati v impf

izras|lina nf growth ~ti v (0) (pres ~tem) 1 grow pustiti da ~te grow ~ti u koga/što grow up to be sb/sth 2 sprout

izravan adj (a) direct, straight

izravnati v (što) straighten, level ~ račun settle the account

izra|z nm 1 expression, word, term 2 expression, face ~zit adj pronounced, characteristic ~ziti v (što/se) express (sth/oneself) ~zito adv markedly, distinctly ~žaj nm expression ~žajan adj (a) expressive, vivid ~žavati v impf

izre|ći v (što) (pres ~knem) utter, say; state ~ći presudu pass the sentence ~ka nf (Dsg ~ci) saying; proverb

izrešetati v (koga/čime) riddle with

izre|z nm neckline; cut haljina s ~zom low-cut dress ~zak nm (Gsg ~ska, Npl ~sci) (newspaper) cutting; clipping ~zati v (što) (pres ~žem) cut up/out ~zivati v impf

izribati v (što) 1 give a (good) scrub 2 shred 3 grate

izri|cati v impf → **izreći** ~čan adj (a) gram declarative ~čit adj explicit, express ~čito adv explicitly

izrigati v (što/se) vomit

izrod nm degenerate, freak, monster ~iti v (se u što) degenerate into

izroniti v (0) emerge, surface

izručiti v (koga/što) 1 hand over; extradite 2 deliver

izrug|ivati v (se iz koga/čega) (pres ~ujem) mock sb/sth, ridicule, poke fun at

izubijati v (se) be bruised all over

izuč|iti v (što) learn, train as ~avati v (što) study ~en adj trained, skilled

izum|rijeti v (0) (pres ~rem) become extinct, die out ~irati v impf

izumit|elj nm inventor ~i v (što) invent

izustiti v (što) utter

izu|ti v (pres ~jem) 1 (cipele) take off 2 (se) take off one's shoes ~vati v impf

izuz|etak nm (Gsg ~etka, Npl ~eci) exception ~etak od pravila e. to the rule ~etan adj (a) exceptional, outstanding ~ti v (koga/što od čega)

(pres ~mem) exempt from ~imati v impf

izva|dak nm (Gsg ~tka, Npl ~ci) excerpt, extract ~dak iz računa bank statement ~diti v (koga/što iz čega/odakle) take out, pull out, draw out ~diti zub pull out/extract a tooth; have one's tooth pulled out ~diti korijen math extract a root

izva|gati v (koga/što/se) (pres ~žem) weigh

izvaliti v 1 (što) blurt out 2 (se) sprawl out

izvan prep outside, out of ~ upotrebe out of use ~ sebe beside oneself ~ zemlje abroad ~a adv from the outside; externally ~redan adj (a) 1 extraordinary, outstanding 2 occasional, irregular ~redni profesor senior lecturer; associate professor US ~redno stanje state of emergency ~redno adv exceptionally ~školski adj extracurricular

izve|dba nf 1 performance 2 implementation, realization 3 construction ~denica nf derivative ~div adj feasible ~sti v (pres ~dem) 1 (što) carry out, accomplish, perform; pull off coll 2 (što iz čega) derive sth from sth ~sti zaključak draw a conclusion, deduce 3 drive the car out ~sti koga van take sb out (on a date)

izve|sti (2) (što) (pres ~zem) export

izvi|djeti v (0) (pres ~dim) scout, reconnoitre ~dnica nf recon(naissance) party ~dnički adj reconnaissance ~dač nm (boy) scout ~đanje nn reconnaissance ~đati v impf

izvijestiti v (koga/što o čemu) report to sb on sth; brief sb on sth

izvir|ati v (0) (pres ~em) 1 spring 2 arise from

izviri|ti v (0) 1 peep out 2 protrude, stick out ~vati v impf

izviždati v (koga) hiss, boo; give sb the bird sl

izvjesni adj certain

izvje|stitelj nm reporter, correspondent ~šće nn, ~štaj nm report ~štavati v impf → **izvijestiti**

izvještačen adj affected ~ost nf pretence, airs and graces

izvjetriti v 1 (se) evaporate 2 (što) air
izvježbati v 1 (koga) train 2 (što/se) become practised in
izvlačiti v impf → **izvući**
izvod nm ~ **iz matične knjige rođenih** birth certificate ~ **s računa** bank statement ~**iti** v impf → **izvesti**
izvojevati v (što) win
izvoli|jevati v (što) put on airs, be spoiled ~**te**? can I help you? ~**te**! here you are; please, help yourself ~**te** **ući** come in, please
izvor nm source, spring, well ~**an** adj (a) original ~**nik** nm (Npl ~nici) original ~**ski** adj spring
izvoz nm export ~**ni** adj export ~**nik** nm (Npl ~nici) exporter
izvrg|nuti v (pres ~nem) 1 (koga čemu) subject to, expose to ~**nuti ruglu** ridicule 2 (se čemu) run the risk of, expose oneself to 3 (se u što) turn into ~**avati** v impf
izvrn|uti v (pres ~em) 1 (što) tip over, overturn 2 (se) turn over; capsize

izvrs|no adv brilliantly ~**tan** adj (~na f) excellent, first-rate
izvrš|iti v (što) carry out, put into effect, implement, perform, execute ~**iti svoju dužnost** do one's duty ~**iti svoje obveze** meet one's obligations ~**iti pritisak** exert pressure ~**iti samoubojstvo** commit suicide ~**iti zločin** perpetrate a crime ~**avati** v impf ~**ni** adj executive ~**na vlast** the executive ~**itelj** nm executor
izvući v (se) izvučem) 1 (koga/što/se iz/odakle) pull out (of); drag out (of) ~ **ždrijeb** draw lots ~ **batine** get a licking ~ **kraći kraj** get the wrong end of the stick ~ **korist** derive profit, profit from ~ **iz neprilike** help out of the trouble 2 (se) get away scotfree coll, get away with it; extricate oneself; (bolesnik) pull through
iživ|jeti v (se) (pres ~im) indulge in, let oneself go ~**ljavati** v (se na komu/čemu) torture/abuse sb/sth, take it out on sb

J

J, j 14th letter of Cro. alphabet

ja *pron* mene, me, *Dsg* meni, mi, *Asg* mene, me, *Isg* mnome, *Lsg* meni) I **svoje ~** self **nemati svoje ~** have no integrity **od mene** from me **daj m(en)i** give it to me **vidio me** he saw me **dođi sa mnom** come with me

jablan *nm* poplar

jabučica *nf* small apple **Adamova ~** Adam's apple **očna ~** eyeball

jabu|ka *nf* (*Dsg* ~ci) apple **~ka ne pada daleko od stabla** the chip off the old block

jač|ati *v* 1 (0) grow stronger 2 (što) fortify, strengthen **~i** *comp* → **jak tko ~i taj kvači** dog eat dog

jad *nm* 1 sorrow, grief 2 distress, misfortune, misery 3 care, trouble, worry **na jedvite ~e** with great difficulty **~an** *adj* (*a*) 1 unfortunate, sorry 2 wretched, poor 3 lame, flimsy **~an ja** poor me **~ati** *v* (se) complain, bemoan **~ikovati** *v* (0) (*pres* ~ikujem) lament **~ikovka** *nf* lament **~nik** *nm* (*Vsg* ~niče, *Npl* ~nici) miserable sod, poor devil

Jadran *nm* the Adriatic **~sko more** the A. Sea

jaganj|ac *nm* (*Gsg* ~ca, *Vsg* ~če) lamb **J~ac Božji** Lamb of God

jaglac *nm* primrose

jagm|a *nf* (za čim) rush/scramble for **~iti** *v* (se) scramble for

jagod|a *nf* strawberry **šumska ~a** wild s. **~ica** *nf* 1 (prsta) fingertip 2 cheekbone

jahač *nm* horseman, rider **~čki** *adj* riding **~čka vještina** horsemanship **~ći** *adj* riding **~nje** *nn* horse(back) riding **~ti** *v* (*pres* jašem) 1 (što) ride 2 (0) ride, go on horseback **~ti na čemu** *fig coll* insist on

jahta *nf* yacht

jaj|e *nn* egg; ovum **~e** *nn* 1 egg **pečeno/meko kuhano/tvrdo kuhano ~e** fried/soft-boiled/hard-boiled egg **pokvareno ~e** rotten egg **sličan kao ~e ~etu** the spitting image of **kao po ~ima** gingerly 2 **~a** *pl tab* bollocks, balls **~nik** *nm* (*Npl* ~nici) ovary **~ovod** *nm* Fallopian tube **~olik** *adj* egg-shaped

jak *adj* 1 strong, powerful; (vino) heady; (zima) severe; (konkurencija) fierce; (kiša) heavy **~a strana** forte **~o** *adv* very **~ost** *nf* strength

jal *nm* envy, jealousy **~an** *adj* (*a*) (na koga) envious (of)

jalov *adj* 1 barren 2 *fig* futile

jam|a *nf* pit, hole **~ica** *nf* dimple

jam|ac *nm* (*Gsg* ~ca) guarantor **~čevina** *nf* 1 security, insurance, guarantee, collateral 2 bail **~čiti** *v* 1 (što) guarantee, safeguard 2 (za koga) vouch for **~stvo** *nn* guarantee, security, insurance, pledge

jamačno *adv* undoubtedly

jantar *nm* amber

janje *nn* lamb **~ći** *adj* lamb **~tina** *nf* lamb

jao! *int* ouch

japanke *nf pl* flip-flops *GB*; thongs *US*

jar|ac *nm* (*Gsg* ~ca, *Vsg* ~če) 1 billygoat, he-goat 2 *astrol* Capricorn **~e** *nn* kid **~eći** *adj* kidn

jar|ak *nm* (*Gsg* ~ka, *Npl* ~ci) ditch

jar|am *nm* (*Gsg* ~ma) yoke (+ *fig*)

jarebica *nf* partridge

jarbol *nm* mast **~ za zastavu** flag-pole, flagstaff

jarki *adj* bright, dazzling, glaring

jaružalo *nn* excavator; dredge(r)

ja|san *adj* (*a*) 1 clear; bright; distinct; transparent 2 (očit) evident, obvious; explicit, plain **~no** *adv* 1 clearly 2 of course **~no i glasno** loud and clear

jasen *nm* ash(tree)

jasl|e *nf pl* manger **~ice** *nf* 1 crib, manger 2 (ustanova) creche, nursery 3 Nativity scene

jasmin *nm* jasmine

jasto|g *nm* (*Npl* ~zi) lobster

jastreb *nm* hawk

jastu|čić *nm* cushion; pad **~čnica** *nf* pillow-case **~k** *nm* (*Npl* ~ci) pillow

jato *nn* 1 (ptice) flock 2 (ribe) school, shoal

jau|k *nm* (*Npl* ~ci) wail, cry, moan **~kati** *v* (0) (*pres* ~čem) moan, wail **~knuti** *v* (0) (*pres* ~knem) cry out (in pain)

java *nf* reality

jav|an *adj* (a) public **~na kuća** brothel; whorehouse *vulg* **~na sablazan** scandal **~na tajna** open secret **~ni život** public life **~no mnijenje** public opinion **~no** *adv* publicly, openly, in public **~nost** *nf* the public

jav|iti *v* 1 (što) report 2 (komu što) let sb know about sth, inform, notify 3 (se komu) report; answer; get in touch (with sb) 4 (se) emerge **~ljati** *v impf*

javor *nm* maple

jaz *nm fig* gap; abyss

jazav|ac *nm* (*Gsg* ~ca, *Vsg* ~če) badger **~čar** *nm* dachshund

jazbina *nm* den, lair

je *v* → **biti**

jeca|j *nm* sob, moan **~ti** *v* (0) sob

ječ|am *nm* (*Gsg* ~ma) barley

ječmen|ac *nm* (*Gsg* ~ca) sty(e)

jeb|ati *v* (koga/se) (*pres* ~em) *tab* fuck *tab* **~i se** *tab* fuck you **~em ti mater** *tab* fuck you

jedaći *adj* ~ **pribor** cutlery

jedak *adj* (jetka *f*) acrid, caustic (+ *fig*)

jed|an (a) 1 *num* one (1) **~an jedini** single, the only one **ni ~an** not a single one **~an te isti** the very same, selfsame **~an po ~an** one by one **~an drugoga** one another, each other **i ~an i drugi** both **~an za drugim** one after the other/another **još ~an** another one **~nom riječju** in a word 2 *pron* certain, a(n) **~anaest** *num* eleven (11) **~anaesterac** *nm* (*Gsg*

~anaesterca) penalty kick **~anput** *adv* once **~inac** *nm* (*Gsg* ~inca) only child/son **~ini** *adj* the only, sole **~inica** *nf* 1 unit 2 only child/daughter 3 (ocjena) fail **~inka** *nf* individual **~ino** *adv* only, solely **~instven** *adj* 1 united 2 unique **~instvo** *nn* unity **~nadžba** *nf* equation **~nak** *adj* 1 equal 2 same, identical 3 equivalent **~nako** *adv* equally **~nako tako** likewise **~nakost** *nf* equality **~nina** *nf gram* singular **~no** *adv coll* some **~nobojan** *adj* (a) monochrome **~nodnevan** *adj* (a) one-day, daylong **~nodušan**, **~noglasan** *adj* (a) unanimous **~nogodišnji** *adj* one-year **~nokatan** *adj* (a) two-storey **~nokratan** *adj* (a) single **~noličan** *adj* (a) 1 uniform 2 monotonous **~nom** *adv* once **~nook** *adj* one-eyed **~norog** *nm* (*Npl* ~norozi) unicorn **~nosmjeran** *adj* (a) one-way **~nostavan** *adj* simple, plain, unsophisticated **~nostran** *adj* 1 one-sided, unilateral 2 (pristran) biased **~nostruk** *adj* single

jedar *adj* (a) healthy, buxom

jednja|k *nm* (*Npl* ~ci) oesophagus; gullet

jedr|enjak *nm* (*Npl* ~enjaci) sailing ship **~enje** *nn* sailing; yachting; boating **~ilica** *nf* 1 sailing-boat 2 glider, sailplane **~iličar** *nm* yachtsman **~iličarstvo** *nn* 1 yachting, sailing 2 gliding **~iti** *v* (0) 1 sail 2 glide **~o** *nn* sail **razapeti ~a** set sail **spustiti ~a** strike/lower sail

jedva *adv* hardly, scarcely, barely ~ **jedvice** with great difficulty

jeftin *adj* cheap, inexpensive; good value *coll* **vrlo** ~ dirt cheap

jegulja *nf* eel

jek *nm* height **u punom ~u** in full swing

jeka *nf* echo

jel|a *nf* fir **~ovina** *nf* fir, deal

jelen *nm* stag, deer **~gljiva** *nf* truffle

jelo *nn* 1 food, fare 2 dish **glavno ~** main dish, entree 3 meal **~vnik** *nm* (*Npl* ~vnici) menu, bill of fare

jenjati *v* (0) subside, die down, abate

jer *conj* because, as, for

jesam, jesi, jest, jesu *v* → biti

jesen *nf* autumn; fall *US* ~**ski** *adj* autumn(al); fall *US*

jest *adv* indeed, yes

jesti *v* (što) (*pres* jedem) eat ~**v** *adj* edible

jetr|a *nf* liver ~**en** *adj* liver; hepatic *med*

je|za *nf* horror, dread; shudder **hvata me** ~**za** I shiver (with fear) ~**ziv** *adj* horrible, ghastly ~**žiti** *v* (se) shiver **koža mi se** ~**ži** my flesh creeps

jezero *nn* lake

jezgr|a *nf* core, nucleus, pith ~**ovit** *adj* pithy, concise

jezi|čac *nm* (*Gsg* ~čca) needle, indicator ~**čan** *adj* linguistic ~**čav** *adj* sharp-tongued ~**čina** *nf fig* big mouth ~**čni** *adj* language, linguistic ~**k** *nm* (*Npl* ~ci) 1 tongue **imati dug** ~**k** be a big mouth **razvezao mi se** ~**k** my t. loosened ~**k za zube!** keep your mouth shut 2 language **književni** ~**k** standard l. **materinski** ~**k** mother-tongue, native language **moj je materinski** ~**k**... I am a native speaker of .. ~**koslovac** *nm* (*Gsg* ~koslovca) linguist ~**koslovlje** *nn* linguistics

jezuit *nm* Jesuit

jež *nm* hedgehog **morski** ~ sea-urchin ~**evi** *pl* (zapreke za tenkove) hedgehogs

jod *nm* iodine

jogun|ast *adj* wilful, skittish ~**iti** *v* (se) 1 balk, flinch 2 refuse obstinately

jogurt *nm* yog(h)urt

joj *int* ow, ouch

joj → ona

jorgovan *nm* lilac

još *adv* still ~ **nije došao** he hasn't come yet ~ **jedan** another one ~ **jednom** once more/again ~ **jedanput** toliko twice as much ~ **ne** not yet ~ **nešto?** anything else? ~ **nikada** never before ~ **neviđen** unprecedented ~ **jučer** only yesterday ~ **u 19. st.** as early as the 19th c. ~ **bolji** better still, even better ~ **dva dana** another two days, two more days ~ **malo a.** just a bit more **b.** soon

ju → ona

jubilej *nm* jubilee

jučer *adv* yesterday ~**ašnji** yesterday's

jug *nm* south ~**o** *nn* southerly wind ~**istočan** *adj* (*a*) south-east; south-eastern ~**istočnjak** *nm* south-easterly (wind) ~**oistok** *nm* south-east

juha *nf* soup

jun|ac *nm* (*Gsg* ~ca) bullock ~**e** *nn* young cow ~**ica** *nf* heifer ~**etina** *nf* baby-beef

juna|čiti *v* (se) boast ~**čina** *nm* 1 hero 2 *derog* braggart ~**čki** *adj* brave, heroic ~**k** *nm* (*Vsg* ~če, *Npl* ~ci) hero, brave man ~**kinja** *nf* heroine ~**štvo** *nn* 1 courage, heroism 2 exploit

jurisdikcija *nf* jurisdiction, competence

juriš *nm* charge **zauzeti na** ~ take by storm, storm ~**ati** *v* (0/na koga/što) charge at, storm ~**ni** *adj* assault

jur|iti *v* (0) run, dash, race ~**iti za kim/čim** chase, be after ~**njava** *nf* rush ~**njava automobilima** car chase

jut|arnji *adj* morning ~**ro** *nn* morning ~**ros** *adv* this morning

juž|ni *adj* south, southern ~**ni vjetar** southerly wind ~**njak** *nm* (*Vsg* ~njače, *Npl* ~njaci) southerner

K

K, k (ka) 15th letter of Cro. alphabet

k(a) *prep* to, towards

kabanica *nf* overcoat **kišna ~** mackintosh, raincoat

kab|ao *nm* (*Gsg* ~la) bucket, pail **(kiša) pada kao iz ~la** it is pouring with rain

kab|el *nm* (*Npl* ~lovi/~eli) cable **~elski** *adj* cable

kabina *nf* cabin; cubicle; booth

kabriolet *nm* convertible, soft top

kaciga *nf* helmet

kačkati *v* (0/što) crochet

kad(a) *adv, conj* when **kako ~** as the case may be **~god** whenever

kada *nf* bathtub

kadar (1) *adj* (*a*) capable (of), able (to)

kad|ar (2) *nm* 1 *film* frame 2 *coll* personnel

kadionica *nf* censer

kafić *nm coll* café

kaj *pron* dial what

kaja|nje *nn* remorse, repentance **~ti** *v* (se) (*pres* kajem) repent

kajgana *nf* scrambled eggs

kaka|o *nm* (*Gsg* ~a) cocoa

kakav *adj* (*a*) what kind of **bilo ~** any there is **~ takav** passable

kako *adv* how, in what way/manner **bilo ~ bilo** at any rate, anyway **~ kada** it depends **~ gdje** it varies from place to place **~ ... tako ...** as ... so ... **~tako** so-so **i te ~** very, all too **•** *conj* 1 as soon as 2 as, like **~ došlo tako prošlo** easy come easy go **~ bi** *conj* in order to, so as to

kaktus *nm* cactus

kakvoća *nm* quality

kal *nm* dirt, mud

kalendar *nm* calendar

kalež *nm* cup; chalice

kalfa *nm* journeyman

kalibar *nm* (+ *fig*) calibre *GB*, caliber

US

kalij *nm* potassium

kaliti *v* 1 (što) temper 2 (koga/se) harden

kalori|čan *adj* high-calorie **~ja** *nf* calorie

kalorifer *nm* fan heater

kalup *nm* 1 mould, cast, die 2 *fig* pattern; model

kaljača *nf* galosh

kalj|av *adj* muddy **~uža** *nf* mire

kamat|a *nf* interest **~ni** *adj* interest **~na stopa** interest rate

kamen *nm* stone; rock **temeljni ~** cornerstone **~ smutnje** stumbling-block **nadgrobni ~** tombstone **pao mi je ~ sa srca** that's a weight off my mind **~ac** *nm* (*Gsg* ~ca) 1 scale 2 *med* stone, calculus **zubni ~ac** tartar **bubrežni ~ac** kidney stones **žučni ~ac** gallstones **~i** *adj* stone **~i ugljen** pit-coal **~ica** *nf* 1 oyster 2 stone **~it** *adj* stony, rocky **~olom** *nm* quarry **~ovati** *v* (koga) (*pres* ~ujem) stone (to death)

kamer|a *nf* camera **~man** *nm* cameraman

kamin *nm* fireplace

kamion *nm* lorry *GB*; truck *US* **~ s prikolicom** articulated l./t.

kamo *adv* where (to) **~ sreće** if only

kamp *nm* camping site **~ kućica/prikolica** *nf* caravan *GB*; trailer *US* **~irati** *v* (0) camp

kampanja *nf* campaign

kana *nf* henna

kanal *nm* 1 (umjetni) canal 2 channel **odvodni ~** sewer; gutter **~izacija** *nf* sewerage, sewers

kanarin|ac *nm* (*Gsg* ~ca) canary

kancelar *nm* chancellor **~ija** *nf* ured

kandid|at *nm* candidate, applicant **~irati** *v* 1 (koga) nominate 2 (se) ap-

ply 3 (se) *pol* run *US*; stand *GB*
kandža *nf* (ptice) talon; claw
kanistar *nm* jerrycan
kaniti *v* (što) *coll* intend
kanoni|k *nm* (*Vsg* ~če, *Npl* ~ci) canon
kantina *nf* canteen, cafeteria
kanjon *nm* canyon, gorge
kao *adv* as; like ~ **da** as if/though
kaos *nm* chaos
kap *nf* 1 drop 2 stroke; apoplexy **udarila ga je** ~ he had a stroke ~**aljka** *nf* (*Dsg* ~aljci) dropper ~**ati** *v* (0) drip, drop ~**avac** *nm* (*Gsg* ~avca) gonorrhea ~**lja** *nf* drop ~**ljica** *nf* droplet ~**ljice za nos** nose drops ~**nuti** *v* (0) (*pres* ~nem) drop
kapa *nf* cap, bonnet, hat
kapacitet *nm* capacity; volume
kap|ak *nm* (*Gsg* ~ka, *Npl* ~ci) 1 (očni ~ak) (eye)lid 2 shutter
kapar *nm* caper
kapel|a *nf* chapel ~**an** *nm* curate ~**ica** *nf* chapel, small church
kapetan *nm* captain; master; skipper
kapilara *nf* capillary
kapital *nm* capital ~**ist** *nm* capitalist
kapitul|acija *nf* capitulation, surrender ~**irati** *v* (0) surrender, capitulate
kapsula *nf* 1 case 2 percussion cap 3 capsule
kapuljača *nf* hood
kaput *nm* coat, overcoat ~**ić** *nm* jacket
karakter *nm* character, nature ~**an** *adj* (α) firm, principled ~**ističan** *adj* (α) (za) characteristic (of), typical, peculiar ~**istika** *nf* (*Dsg* ~istici) trait, feature, characteristic ~**izirati** *v* (koga/što) characterize
karamela *nf* toffee *GB*; taffy *US*
karanfil *nm* carnation
karantena *nf* quarantine
karati *v* (koga) 1 *arch* scold 2 *vulg tab* screw *vulg*
karaula *nf* watchtower
karavana *nf* caravan
karcinom *nm* carcinoma
kardinal *nm* cardinal
karfiol *nm* → **cvjetača**
karijer|a *nf* career ~**ist** *nm* careerist, high flier
karijes *nm* tooth decay
kari|ka *nf* (*Dsg* ~ci) link

karik|atura *nf* caricature; cartoon ~**irati** *v* (koga/što) caricature
kar|iran *adj* check, chequered ~**o** *nm* diamonds *pl*
karneval *nm* carnival
karoserija *nf* (car) body
kart|a *nf* 1 card 2 ticket **povratna** ~**a** return/round-trip t. **zemljopisna** ~**a** map **pomorska** ~**a** chart **auto**~ road map ~**ati** *v* (0/se) play cards ~**ica** *nf* card ~**on** *nm* cardboard **žuti** ~**on** *sport* yellow card ~**onski** *adj* cardboard ~**oteka** *nf* (*Dsg* ~oteci) files
kas *nm* trot ~**(k)ati** *v* (0) trot, canter
kas|an *adj* (α) 1 late 2 overdue ~**no** *adv* late ~**nije** *adv* later ~**niji** *adj* later, subsequent, further ~**niti** *v* (0) be late
kaset|a *nf* cassette, tape ~**ofon** *nm* cassette player, tape recorder/deck ~**na** *adj* **bomba** cluster bomb
kaskader *nm* stunt man
kas|kati *v* (0) amble ~ **za** tag behind
kastrirati *v* (koga) castrate; (mačka) neuter
kaša *nf* mash **zobena** ~ oatmeal; porridge ~**st** *adj* mushy, pulpy
kašal|j *nm* (*Gsg* ~lja) cough **to nije mačji** ~**alj** it's no trifling matter ~**ljati** *v* (0) (*pres* ~ljem) cough
kat *nm* floor, storey **prvi** ~ first floor; second floor *US* **kuća na dva** ~**a** two-storey/two-storied house
katalo|g *nm* (*Npl* ~zi) catalogue
katast|ar *nm* (*Gsg* ~ra) land register
katastrofa *nf* disaster, catastrophe ~**lan** *adj* (α) disastrous, catastrophic
katedra *nf* chair
katedrala *nf* cathedral
kategori|čan *adj* (α) categorical ~**ja** *nf* category
katekiz|am *nm* (*Gsg* ~ma) catechism **kateheta** *nm* catechist
katkad(a) *adv* sometimes, from time to time
katoli|cizam *nm* (*Gsg* ~cizma) Catholicism ~**čki** *adj* Catholic ~**k** *nm* (*Npl* ~ci) Catholic
katran *nm* tar
kaucija *nf* 1 bail 2 refundable charge for returnable bottles
kauč *nm* couch, sofa

kaučuk *nm* rubber

kava *nf* coffee ~**na** *nm* coffee house

kavalir *nm* gentleman

kavez *nm* cage

kazališ|ni *adj* theatrical, theatre ~**na predstava** play ~**ni glumac** stage actor ~**te** *nn* theatre

kaza|lo *nn* index ~**ljka** *nf (Dsg* ~ljci*)* 1 pointer, indicator 2 (sata) hand

kazati *v (pres* kažem*)* (što komu) say ~ **kome** tell sb, say to sb **kaže se/kažu** people say **kako se na engleskom kaže** ... how do you say ... in English? **kazivati** *v* (što) narrate, tell

kazeta *coll* → **kaseta**

kazn|a *nf* punishment **novčana** ~**a** fine **smrtna** ~**a** death sentence; capital punishment **osuditi na** ~**u zatvora** sentence to prison ~**eni udarac** penal ~**eni udarac** penalty kick ~**ionica** *nf* penitentiary ~**iti** *v* (koga čime) punish ~**iv** *adj* punishable

kažiprst *nm* index finger

kažnj|avati *v impf* → **kazniti biti** ~**avan** have a police record ~**enik** *nm (Vsg* ~eniče, *Npl* ~enici*)* convict ~**iv** *adj* punishable

kć|i *(Asg* ~er*)*, ~**erka** *(Dsg* ~erci*)* *nf* daughter

keks *nm* biscuit; cookie *US*

kelj *nm* kale, savoy

kenjati *v (0) tab* crap, have/take a crap

kemi|čar *nm* chemist ~**ja** *nf* chemistry **anorganska** ~**ja** inorganic c. ~**jski** *adj* chemical ~**ijska čistionica** dry cleaner's ~**kalije** *nf pl* chemicals

kerami|ka *nf (Dsg* ~ci*)* ceramics, pottery ~**čki** *adj* ceramic

kesiti *v* 1 (se) grin 2 ~ **zube** bare one's teeth

keste|n *nm* chestnut **divlji** ~**n** horse c. **pitomi** ~**n** sweet c. ~**njast** *adj* chestnut ~**nje** *nm* chestnuts **vaditi za koga** ~**nje iz vatre** do the dirty work for sb

kič *nm* kitsch, trash ~**ast** *adj* gaudy

kićen *adj* ornate; florid

kid|ati *v* 1 (što) tear/rend apart 2 (0) *impf* ~**nuti** *v (0) (pres* ~nem*)* run off, beat it

kih|nuti *v (0) (pres* ~nem*)* sneeze ~**ati** *v impf (pres* kišem*)*

kikić *nm sl* toddler, tot, kid

kikiriki *nm* peanut

kiks *nm sl* blunder, bloomer

kila (1) *nf med* hernia ~**v** *adj* 1 herniated 2 *fig coll* bungling

kila (2) *nf coll* kilo(gramme)

kilomet|ar *nm* kilometre **na** ~**re** *fig* for miles ~**raža** *nf* mileage

kim|nuti *v (pres* ~nem*)* (~ **glavom**) nod (one's head) ~**ati** *v impf*

kino *nn* cinema; (movie) theater *US*; the movies *coll* ~**teka** *nf (Dsg* ~teci*)* 1 motion picture archive 2 repertory cinema

kiosk *nm* kiosk; news-stand

kip *nm* statue, sculpture ~**ar** *nm* sculptor ~**arstvo** *nn* sculpture ~**ić** *nm dim* statuette

kip|jeti *v* (0) *(pres* ~im*)* boil; seethe (+ *fig*)

kirur|g *nm (Npl* ~zi*)* surgeon ~**gija** *nf* surgery ~**ški** *adj* surgical ~**ški zahvat** surgery*f*

kise|lina *nf* acid ~**liti** *v* 1 (što) pickle 2 (što) add acid; acidify 3 (se) turn sour ~**o** *adj* (~la *f*) 1 acid 2 (okus) sour 3 *fig* sulky ~**li krastavac** gherkin ~**li kupus** sauerkraut ~**la voda** *coll* mineral water

kisik *nm* oxygen

kist *nm* (paint) brush

kiš|a *nf* rain ~**ica** *nf* drizzle **pada** ~**a** it is raining ~**a lijeva** it is pouring with rain ~**an** *adj* (a) rainy ~**ni kaput** raincoat ~**iti** *v* (0) rain ~**nica** *nf* rainwater ~**obran** *nm* umbrella ~**ovit** *adj* rainy

kit (1) *nm* whale ~**olovac** *nm (Gsg* ~olovca, *Vsg* ~olovče*)* whaler

kit (2) *nm* putty

kit|a *nf* bunch, bouquet ~**ica** *nf* 1 small bouquet 2 stanza

kit|iti *v* (koga/što/se) decorate, adorn, trim ~**ničarka** *nf* milliner ~**njast** *adj* bushy

klackalica *nf* seesaw

klada *nf* block, log

kladi|onica *nf* betting shop; bookmaker's ~**oničar** *nm* bookmaker; bookie *coll* ~**ti** *v* (se) bet

kladivo *nn sport* hammer

klan|ac *nm (Gsg* ~ca*)* gorge

klanjati v (se) (muškarac) (make a) bow; (žena) curtsey

kla|nje nn slaughter(ing) **stoka za ~nje** beef cattle **~onica** nf abbatoir, slaughterhouse **~ti** v (pres koljem) (koga/se) slaughter/butcher sb/each other

klapa nf 1 (Dalmatian) choir 2 set, bunch 3 film clapperboard

klarinet nm clarinet

klas nm ear **~je** nn ears (of grain)

klas|a nf class **~ificirati** v (koga/što) classify **~ni** adj class

klasi|čan adj (a) classic(al) **~k** nm (Npl ~ci) classic **~ka** nf (Dsg ~ci) classical literature/music; classics

klat|iti v (se) 1 swing 2 loaf, roam **~no** nn pendulum

klaun nm clown

klavi|jatura nf keyboard **~r** nm (grand) piano **~rist** nm piano player **~rski** adj piano

kle|čati v (0) (pres ~čim) kneel **~knuti** v (0) (pres ~knem) kneel down

klempav adj **~e uši** (pas) floppy ears; (osoba) jug ears

klep|etati v (0) (pres ~ećem) 1 rattle 2 fig chatter **~etuša** nf chatter-box **~nuti** v (koga po čemu) (pres ~nem) whack/hit sb over sth

kler nm clergy

klesa|r nm stone-mason, stone-cutter **~ti** v (što) (pres klešem) carve, chisel

klet|i v (pres kunem) 1 (koga/što) swear at sb, curse sb/sth 2 (0) curse, swear 3 (se čime) swear by **~va** nf curse

klevet|a nf slander; libel **~ati** v (koga) (pres klevećem) slander, defame; libel **~nik** nm (Vsg ~niče, Npl ~nici) slanderer

klic|a nf 1 germ (+ fig) 2 sprout, shoot **~onoša** nm carrier

kli|cati v (pres ~čem) 1 (0/komu) cheer 2 (što) shout

klijati v (0) germinate; sprout

klijent nm client

kliješta nn pl 1 pincers pl 2 pliers pl 3 (rak) claws pl

klijet nf vineyard shed

klika nf clique

klikn|uti v (0/što) (pres ~nem) ex-

claim, cry out

klima nf climate **~tski uređaj** coll air-conditioner **~tizacija** nf air-conditioning **~tski** adj climatic

klimakterij nm menopause

klim|ati v 1 (što) jolt, shake **~ati glavom** nod one's head 2 (se) be loose; totter **~nuti** v (što/o) (pres ~nem) nod **~av** adj shaky, wobbly; rickety

klin nm wedge, pin **~ac** nm (Gsg ~ca) 1 dim 2 kid, little boy

klini|čki adj clinical **~ka** nf (Dsg ~ci) clinic(al hospital)

klip nm 1 corn-cob 2 piston **bacati komu ~ove pod noge** put a spoke in sb's wheel

klipan nm oaf, lummox

klipsati v (pres klipšem) (0) trudge along

klistir nm enema **~irati** v (koga) 1 administer an enema 2 fig bother

klisura nf cliff

kliše(j) nm fig cliche, hackneyed phrase

kliz|ač nm (ice) skater **~alište** nn skating rink **~aljka** nf (Dsg ~aljci) ice-skate **~ati** v (se) (pres kližem) skate **~av** adj slippery **~iti** v (0) slide; glide **~nuti** v (0) (pres ~nem) slip

klobu|čar nm hat-maker, hatter **~k** nm (Npl ~ci) hat

klokan nm kangaroo

kloniti v (se koga/čega) avoid, shun, stay away from

klonu|lost nf exhaustion; low spirits **~ti** v (0) (pres klonuti) collapse; sink, flag **~ti duhom** lose heart

klopa nf sl grub coll; nosh GB sl; chow sl

klop|ka nf (Dsg ~ci) trap

klor nm chlorine

klošar nm bum, tramp; dosser GB sl; (žena) bag lady

klozet nm lavatory; bathroom US euphem

klu|b nm club **~pski** adj club

klupa nf bench (crkvena) pew (školska) desk **optuženička ~** (prisoner's) dock

klupko nn ball, skein

kljast adj lame, crippled

kljova *nf* tusk
kljucati *v* (koga/što) peck (at)
ključ *nm* 1 key (+ *fig*) 2 clef *mus* 3 (alat) spanner *GB*; wrench *US* ~anica *nf* key-hole ~ni *adj* key, crucial ~na kost collar-bone
ključati *v* (0) boil, seethe
ključati *v* (koga čime) stuff; cram
kljun *nm* beak, bill čudnovati ~aš *nm* platypus
kljuse *nn* nag, jade
kljuvati *v* (što) peck
kmečati *v* (0) (*pres* ~im) whimper
kmet *nm* serf ~stvo *nn* serfdom
knejginja *nf* princess ~z *nm* prince ~ževina *nf* principality
knjilga *nf* (*Dsg* ~zi) book matična ~ga register ~govodstvo *nn* book-keeping, accountancy dvojno ~govodstvo double entry book-keeping ~govođa *nm* book-keeper, accountant ~ški *adj* bookish; literary ~ški moljac bookworm ~žara *nf* book-shop; bookstore *US* ~ževni *adj* literary ~ževnik *nm* (*Vsg* ~ževniče, *Npl* ~ževnici) writer, author ~ževnost *nn* literature ~žica *nf* booklet, brochure štedna ~žica savings book radna ~žica employment record ~žiti *v* (što) enter, log in ~žnica *nf* library ~žničar *nm* librarian
koalicija *nf* coalition
kob *nf* fate, destiny, fortune zla ~ misfortune ~an *adj* (*a*) fatal
ko|bac *nm* (*Gsg* ~pca) sparrow-hawk
kobasica *nf* sausage
kobil|a *nf* mare ~ica *nf* keel
kock|a *nf* 1 cube ~a šećera sugarcube 2 gambling ~e dice bacati ~e roll the d. baciti ~u cast/draw lots staviti na ~u risk, gamble 3 ~e (dječje) blocks, bricks ~anje *nn* gambling ~ar *nm* gambler ~arnica *nf* gambling-house ~ast *adj* 1 cubical 2 coll chequered ~ati *v* (se) play dice, gamble
koča *nf* dragnet
kočija *nf* coach, carriage ~š *nm* coachman
koč|iti *v* 1 (0) brake 2 (što) hinder, check 3 (se) stiffen, go rigid/stiff ~nica *nf* brake ručna ~nica handbrake

kod (1) *prep* at, by; with; beside, near, in, on ~ kuće at home ~ nas here, in this country ~ mene at my place
kod (2) *nm* code ~irati *v* (što) 1 code 2 scramble
kodeks *nm* 1 code 2 codex
kofein *nm* caffeine bez ~a decaffeinated
koincidencija *nf* coincidence
kojekak|av *adj* (*a*) (of) dubious ~o *adv* carelessly
koji *rel pron* 1 which 2 who 3 that • *interrog pron* who, what ~put sometimes, from time to time ~god whichever, any bilo ~ any kako ~ it varies za ~ trenutak in a minute
kokain *nm* cocaine; coke *coll*
koket|a *nf* flirt ~irati *v* (s kim) flirt
kokice *nf pl* popcorn
kokoda|kati *v* (0) (*pres* ~čem) cackle
kokos *nm* coconut
kokoš *nf* hen ~injac *nm* (*Gsg* ~injca) henhouse ~ji *adj* chicken
kokot *nm* 1 cock; rooster *US* 2 hammer napeti ~ cock the gun
koks *nm* coke
koktel *nm* cocktail
kol|a *nn pl* 1 cart; van; waggon 2 car(riage) 3 car mrtvačka ~a hearse ~a za spavanje sleeping car; sleeper *US* ~ni *adj* ulaz driveway ~nik *nm* road ~odvor *nm* railway station autobusni ~odvor bus/coach station ~osijek *nm* (*Npl* ~osijeci) track, rails izbaciti koga iz ~osijeka *fig* throw sb off uski ~osijek narrow gauge ~otečina *nf* wheeltrack; rut (+ *fig*)
kolabirati *v* (0) collapse
kol|ac *nm* (*Gsg* ~ca) pole, staff, stake nabiti na ~ac impale
kolač *nm* cake; pastry
kola|ti *v* (0) circulate; run
koleb|ati *v* (se) hesitate, falter, waver ~ljiv *adj* 1 fluctuating 2 hesitant, wavering
koleg|a *nm* colleague; workmate; schoolmate ~ij *nm* course ~ijalan *adj* (*a*) friendly, ready to help
kolera *nf* cholera
koliba *nf* hut
kolica *nn pl* barrow; pushcart; trolley dječja ~ pram; pushchair, buggy *GB*

baby carriage; stroller *US* **invalid-ska** ~ wheel-chair

količina *nf* quantity, amount

kolijev|ka *nf* (*Dsg* ~ci) cradle, cot

kolik|i *interrog pron* how big/large/wide/long/etc ~o *adv* how much/many; how long ~o ti je godi-na? how old are you? ~o je sati? what time is it? ~o hoćeš as much as you like

kolni|k *nm* (*Npl* ~ci) roadway; carriageway *GB* ~čki *adj* trak lane

kolo *nn* folk dance, reel voditi ~ lead the dance ~vođa *nm fig* ringleader

kolokvij *nm* preliminary exam; prelim *coll*

kolona *nf* column

kolonija *nf* colony ~jalan *adj* (*a*) colonial ~st *nm* settler, colonist

kolosije|k *nm* (*Npl* ~ci) (railway) track

kolotur *nm* pulley

kolovoz *nm* August

kolporter *nm* newsvendor

koludrica *nf* nun

kolut *nm* 1 ring, hoop 2 (užeta) coil; (vrpce) spool ~ naprijed forward roll ~ati *v* očima roll one's eyes

koljač *nm* 1 cut-throat, butcher 2 (zub) fang

koljen|o *nn* 1 knee na ~ima down on one's knees 2 rođak u prvom/dru-gom ~u cousin once/twice removed s ~a na ~o from father to son

komad *nm* 1 piece 2 portion, part 3 (kazališni) play 4 *sl* bird *GB*; chick *US*; (muškarac) hunk ~ati *v* (koga/što) (cut up)/carve

komarac *nm* (*Gsg* ~ca) mosquito

kombajn *nm* combine harvester

kombi *nm* van

kombin|acija *nf* combination ~at *nm* combine; plant ~e *nm coll* slip ~ezon *nm* overalls *pl* ~irati *v* (što) combine ~irke *nf pl* pliers

komedija *nf* comedy

koment|ar *nm* commentary ~ator *nm* commentator ~irati *v* (koga/što) comment on, remark on

komercijalan (*a*) *adj* commercial

komešati *v* (se) stir, move

komet *nm* comet

komfor *nm* amenities *pl* ~an *adj* (*a*) with all modern conveniences

komiča|n *adj* (*a*) comic(al), humor-ous, funny ~r *nm* comedian

komisij|a *nf* commission ~ska *adj* prodaja sale on c.

komitet *nm* committee

komor|a *nf* chamber gospodarska ~a ch. of commerce ~ni *adj* chamber

kompas *nm* compass

kompjutor *nm coll* → računalo

kompleks *nm* 1 complex, hang-up 2 complex ~an *adj* (*a*) complex

komplet *nm* 1 set 2 (odjeća) ensemble

kompli|cirati *v* (što) complicate ~kacija *nf* complication

kompliment *nm* compliment udijeliti ~ pay a c.

kompo|nirati *v* (što) compose ~zicija *nf* 1 composition 2 train ~zitor *nm* composer ¶ compositor = slovosla-gar

kompot *nm* stewed fruit

kompromis *nm* compromise

kompromitirati *v* 1 (koga) compro-mise, discredit 2 (se) c./d. oneself

komuna *nf* commune ~lan *adj* (*a*) communal, municipal ~lije *nf pl* util-ities

komuni|cirati *v* (s kim) communicate ~kacija *nf* communication ~kativan *adj* (*a*) communicative, outgoing

komuni|st *nm* communist ~zam *nm* (*Gsg* ~zma) communism

kon|ac (1) *nm* (*Gsg* ~ca) 1 thread 2 (kirurški) suture

kon|ac (2) *nm* end, conclusion na ~cu finally na ~cu ~ca after all ~ačan *adj* (*a*) final, conclusive ~ačno *adv* finally, at long last

koncentr|acija *nf* concentration ~acij-–ski *adj* logor c. camp ~ičan *adj* (*a*) concentric ~irati *v* (što/se) concen-trate, focus

koncep|t *nm* draft (version) ~cija *nf* concept(ion), basic idea

koncert *nm* 1 (izvedba) concert; gig *coll* 2 (djelo) concerto

koncesija *nf* 1 concession 2 *econ* li-cence; franchise

kondukter *nm* conductor; ticket col-lector

konfederacija *nf* confederation

konfekcij|a *nf* ready-made clothes **industrija** ~**e** garment industry
konferencija *nf* conference
konfiscirati *v* (što) confiscate, seize
kongres *nm* congress
konjunktura *nf* market conditions **povoljna** ~ boom **loša** ~ slump
konkret|an *adj* (α) 1 concrete 2 substantial ~**no** *adv* 1 exactly 2 namely
konkur|encija *nf* competition **oštra** ~**encija** fierce/keen c. ~**ent** *nm* competitor ~**entan** *adj* (α) competitive ~**irati** *v* 1 (za što) apply for 2 (komu) compete with, be sb's rival
konoba *nf* 1 cellar 2 tavern ~**r** *nm* waiter ~**rica** *nf* waitress
konop, konop|ac *nm* (Gsg ~ca) cord, line, rope ~**lja** *nf* hemp
konspiracija *nf* conspiracy, plot ~**tivan** *adj* (α) secret
konstatacija *nf* statement
konstitu|cija *nf* constitution, build ~**cionalan** *adj* (α) constitutional ~**tivan** *adj* (α) constituent
konstruk|cija *nf* structure; framework ~**tor** *nm* builder, designer ~**tivan** *adj* (α) constructive
kontakt *nm* contact ~**-emisija/program** phone-in *GB*/call-in *US* (show)
kontekst *nm* context
kontinent *nm* continent ~**alan** *adj* (α) continental
kontingent *nm* 1 quota 2 *mil* contingent
kontinuitet *nm* continuity
kontra- *prefix* counter-
kontraadmiral *nm* rear admiral
kontrabas *nm* double-bass
kontracepcij|a *nf* birth control, contraception **sredstvo za** ~**u** contraceptive
kontradik|cija *nf* contradiction ~**toran** *adj* (α) contradictory
kontrapunkt *nm* counterpoint
kontrast *nm* contrast ~**an** *adj* (α) contrasting
kontrol|a *nf* 1 control; supervision 2 check ~**iran** *adj* 1 controlled 2 under control ~**irati** *v* (koga/što/se) control ~**ni** *adj* control ~**na točka** checkpoint ~**ni toranj** control tower o *nm*

sch written exam, test ~**lor** *nm* inspector, controller
konvenci|ja *nf* convention ~**onalan** *adj* (α) conventional
konvertibilan *adj* (α) convertible; (valuta) hard
konvoj *nm* convoy
konzerv|a *nf* tin; can *US* ~**irati** *v* (što) 1 conserve, preserve 2 can
konzervativ|ac *nm* (Gsg ~ca, Vsg ~če) conservative ~**an** *adj* (α) conservative
konzervatorij *nm* music academy
konzul *nm* consul **generalni** ~ consul-general ~**at** *nm* consulate
konzumirati *v* (što) 1 consume, use 2 (brak) consummate
konj *nm* 1 horse ~ **za vuču** draught-horse 2 (šah) knight 3 *sport* vaulting-horse **biti na** ~**u** be sitting pretty ~**anik** *nm* (Vsg ~aniče, Npl ~anici) horseman, rider; trooper **morski** ~ sea-horse ~**ica** *nf* cavalry ~**ički** *adj* cavalry; equestrian *US* ~**okradica** *nm* horse-thief ~**ski** *adj* horse(-) ~**ska snaga** horsepower ~**ušar** *nm* groom ~**ušnica** *nf* horse-stable
konjak *nm* cognac, brandy
kooperacija *nf* cooperation, collaboration
koordin|acija *nf* 1 coordination 2 c. committee ~**irati** *v* (što/koga) coordinate ~**ata** *nf* grid refererence; coordinate *math*
kopa|č *nm* digger ~**ti** *v* (0/što) dig; burrow
kopačka *nf* football boot
kopča *nf* buckle; clasp
kopij|a *nf* 1 copy 2 fake ~**rati** *v* (koga/što) copy; imitate, ape
kopile *nn* bastard
kopit|ar *nm* hoofed animal, ungulate ~**ati** *v* (se) kick ~**o** *nn* hoof
kopkati *v* (koga) perturb, intrigue
koplje *nn* 1 spear, lance, pike 2 *sport* javelin **bacanje** ~**a** javelin throw **oko toga se lome** ~**a** *fig* it is highly controversial **na pola** ~**a** at half-mast
kopn|en *adj* land ~**ena vojska** army, ground troops ~**o** *nn* land, mainland
kop|njeti *v* (0) (*pres* ~**nim**) (snijeg) thaw, melt (away)

koprcati v (se) wriggle, squirm

koprena nf veil

kopriv|a nf (stinging) nettle **neće grom u ~e** the devil looks after his own

koprodukcija nf coproduction

kor nm choir

kor|a nf 1 (drva) bark; (sira) rind; (kruha) crust; (voća) peel 2 crust **~ice** nf pl (knjige) cover; (mača) sheath, scabbard

kora|čati v (0) pace, walk **~čnica** nf march **~k** nm (Npl ~ci) step (+ fig); pace **poduzeti ~ke** take steps **~k po ~k** step by step **~kom** adv at walking pace **držati ~k s** keep step with; keep abreast of **fig na svakom ~ku** at every turn **~knuti** v (0) (pres ~knem) take a step

korbač nm horse-whip

korekt|an adj (α) fair **~ura** nf correction; proof-reading **~or** nm proofreader

koreograf nm coreographer

korespondencija nf correspondence

koridor nm corridor

korigirati v (što/koga) correct

korijen m root **drugi/kvadratni ~** square r. **uhvatiti ~** take/strike r. **~ski** adj etymological

koris|nik nm (Npl ~nici) user **~t** nf benefit, advantage, good, profit, good use **biti od ~ti** be of use **izvući ~t** derive profit, benefit **~tan** adj (α) useful **~titi** v 1 (komu/čemu) be of use to 2 (što se za što) be used, serve as 3 (što) use, put to use 4 (se čime) use, make use of **~toljubiv** adj greedy **~toljublje** nn greed

koriti v (koga) reproach; scold

korito nn 1 trough 2 river-bed

korizm|a nf Lent **~eni** adj Lenten

korjenit adj radical, thorough

kormil|ar nm 1 helmsman 2 sport coxwain **bez ~ara** coxless **~ariti** v (0/čime) steer **~o** nn helm, rudder **preuzeti ~o** take the helm

korner nm sport corner kick

kornjača nf tortoise; turtle

korota nf mourning

korov nm weed(s)

korpus nm 1 mil corps 2 corpus

koru|mpiran adj corrupt, crooked **~pcija** nf corruption

korvet|a nf corvette **kapetan ~e** lieutenant commander

kos (1) nm blackbird

kos (2) adj oblique, slanting, inclined, tilted, lopsided **~a crta** slant **~i toranj** the Leaning Tower **~ina** nf slope, gradient

kosa (1) nf hair **~ mi se diže** my hair stands on end

kos|a (2) nf scythe **~ilica** nf (lawn) mower **~iti** v (što) (travu) mow; reap

kosinus nm math cosine

kosit|ar nm (Gsg ~ra) tin **~ren** adj tin

kositi v (se s čim) run counter to

kosn|uti v (koga/se koga) (pres ~em) move, touch, distress

kost nf bone **riblja ~** fishbone **slonova ~** ivory **biti ~ i koža** be skin and bones **~ur** nm skeleton

kostim nm 1 suit 2 costume **~irani** adj **ples** fancy dress ball; masked ball

kostrijet nf hair-cloth

kostriješiti v (se) bristle

koš nm basket **~ za smeće** litter bin; waste basket **baciti u ~** discard, dump **prsni ~** chest, rib cage **~ara** nf basket, hamper **~arica** nf small basket **dati komu ~aricu** fig give sb the boot **~arka** nf (Dsg ~arci) basketball **~arkaš** nm basketball player

koš|čat adj bony, raw-/big-boned **~tan** adj bone **~tica** nf kernel, stone, pip, seed **~tunjav** adj gaunt, bony **~tunjavo voće** stone fruit

košnica nf bee-hive

koštac nm **uhvatiti se u ~ s** come/get to grips with

košta|ti v coll cost **koliko to ~?** how much does it cost?

košulj|a nf shirt **luđačka ~a** strait jacket **~ica** nf (metka) jacket

kot nf hind, roe, doe

kota nf hill

ko|tac nm (Gsg ~ca) pigsty

kotač nm wheel

kot|ao nm (Gsg ~la, Npl ~lovi) 1 kettle; cauldron (+ fig) 2 boiler **~lovnica** nf boiler room **~lovina** nf roast meat

kotar nm district

kotirati v (0) rank, rate; be quoted (on the exchange) **visoko ~ be** in demand, be highly valued

kotiti v (se) litter, breed

kotlina nf basin, valley

kotrljati v (što/se) roll

kotura|ljke nf pl roller-skates; inline skates, Rollerblades *TM* **~ti** v (se) skate

kotva nf 1 armature 2 anchor

kov nm cast **staroga ~a** of the old school **~ač** nm (black)smith **~ačnica** nf smithy, forge **~ani novac** coins **~ano željezo** wrought iron **~anica** nf coin **~ati** v (pres kujem) (što) 1 forge 2 (novac) mint 3 fig plot **~ati koga u zvijezde** extol **~ina** nf metal **~nica** nf mint

kovče|g nm (Npl ~zi) suitcase; trunk **mrtvački ~g** coffin

kovrča nf curl **~v** adj curly

koz|a nf (she-/nanny-)goat **~ji** adj goat **~ja bradica** goatee **vodene ~ice** chicken-pox **~ičav** adj pock-marked

kozmeti|čar nm beautician **~čki** adj salon beauty parlour **~čki tretman** facial **~ka** nf (Dsg ~ci) cosmetics pl

kozm|ički adj cosmic **~opolit** nm cosmopolitan

kož|a nf 1 skin 2 (materijal) leather **~ica** nf 1 (nokta) cuticle 2 membrane, film **~nat** adj leather **~ni** adj skin; leather

krabulja nf mask

kra|dljivac nm (Gsg ~dljivca, Vsg ~dljivče) thief **~dom** adv furtively, clandestinely **~đa** nf theft; larceny leg

krafna nf coll doughnut

krah nm complete failure, crash; bankruptcy econ

kraj nm 1 end **biti pri ~u** (čega/s čim) **a.** be nearly finished **b.** be running out **na ~u snaga** at the end of one's tether **ići/bližiti se ~u** draw to a close **privesti ~u** bring to an end, conclude **na ~u** in/at the end **do ~a** to the end **s ~a na ~a** throughout **izaći na ~ s kim/čim** cope with **na ~u ~eva** after all, when all is said and done **nije mi ni na ~u pameti** I wouldn't dream of it **sastavljati ~ s ~em** make ends

meet 2 area, region 3 (kopno) mainland • prep beside, next to, side by side with, alongside, near **~obraz, ~olik** nm landscape, scenery

krajni|k nm (Npl ~ci) tonsil

kraj|nost nf extreme **~nji** adj extreme, utmost **~nje je vrijeme** it is high time

krak nm 1 arm 2 tentacle 3 leg **~at** adj long-legged

kralj nm king **Sveta tri ~a a.** three wise men, Magi **b.** (blagdan) Epiphany **~evati** v (0) (pres ~ujem) reign **~ević** nm prince **~evina** nf kingdom **~evna** nf princess **~evski** adj 1 royal 2 regal **~evstvo** nm kingdom **~ica** nf queen

kralješ|nica, kralježnica nf backbone, spine **~ak** nm (Gsg ~ka, Npl ~ci) vertebra **~njak** nm (Npl ~njaci) vertebrate

kras|an adj (α) beautiful, lovely, splendid **~iti** v (koga/što) adorn **~i ga pamet** he is very smart **~opis** nm calligraphy

krasta nf scab **~ča** nf toad **~vac** nm (Gsg ~vca) cucumber **kiseli ~vac** gherkin, pickle

krasti v (pres kradem) (što) steal

kraš nm karst

krat|ak adj (α) short, brief **~ke hlače** shorts **~ko oružje** sidearms pl **~ica** nf abbreviation **~iti** v (što) 1 shorten, cut (short) 2 crop 3 abridge **~iti vrijeme** while away the time **~kometražni** adj film short **~koročan** adj (α) short-term **~kotrajan** adj (α) 1 short-lived 2 temporary **~kovidan** adj (α) short-/near-sighted **~kovidnost** nf short/near-sightedness, myopia

krav|a nf cow **~lji** adj sir cottage cheese

kravata nf tie

krcat adj loaded, laden, crammed, packed

krčiti v (što) clear **~ put** fig pave the way, blaze the trail

krčma nf inn; pub **~r** nm inn-keeper; publican, landlord **praviti račun bez ~a** count one's chickens before they are hatched

krdo *nn* herd

kre|acija *nf* (modna) creation, design ~**ativan** *adj* (*a*) creative ~**ator** *nm* (fashion) designer ~**irati** *v* (što) design

kreda *nf* chalk

kredenc *nm* kitchen cupboard/cabinet

kredit *nm* credit ~**irati** *v* (koga) finance, grant a loan to

kreketati *v* (0) croak

krema *nf* cream

krem|atorij *nm* crematorium ~**irati** *v* (koga) cremate

kremen *nm* flint(stone)

kre|nuti *v* (*pres* ~nem) (0) start, set out/forth ~**tati** *v* (*pres* ~ćem) 1 *impf* 2 (se) move, be on the move *vlak kreće u 5* the train leaves at 5 3 (se) *cijene se kreću* prices range ~**tnja** *nf* movement, gesture

krepak *adj* (*a*) robust, strong, vigorous

kreten *nm* cretin, idiot, creep *sl*

kreveljiti *v* (se) grimace, pull/make faces

krevet *nm* bed *ići u* ~ go to bed, turn in ~**nina** *nf* bedclothes

krezub *adj* toothless

krh|ak *adj* (*a*) brittle, fragile; (osoba) frail ~**otina** *nf* fragment, chip, sliver ~**otine granata** shrapnel

kričav *adj* loud

krigla *nf coll* beer mug

krijes *nm* bonfire ~**nica** *nf* glow-worm, firefly

kriješt|ati *v* (0) (*pres* ~im) screech

krijumčar *nm* smuggler ~**iti** *v* (što) smuggle

kri|k *nm* (*Npl* ~ci) cry, scream **posljednji modni** ~**k** the latest fashion ~**knuti** *v* (0) (*pres* ~knem) cry out, scream

kril|at *adj* winged ~**atica** *nf* catchword ~**o** *nn* 1 wing **plućno** ~**o** lung 2 lap *sjediti kome u* ~*u* sit on sb's lap

kriminal *nm* crime ~**ac** *nm* (*Gsg* ~ca, *Vsg* ~če) criminal ~**an** *adj* (*a*) 1 criminal 2 *coll* horrible ~**istički** *adj roman* (krimić *coll*) crime story; whodunit *coll*

krinka *nf* mask, disguise

Krist *nm* Christ **prije** ~**a** before Christ, BC **poslije** ~**a** AD, in the year of our Lord

kristal *nm* crystal ~**an** *adj* (*a*) crystal(line) ~**no** *adv* **jasno** crystal clear

kriška *nf* slice, piece

krišom *adv* surreptitiously

kriterij *nm* criterion

kriti|čan *adj* (*a*) 1 (stanje) critical, serious 2 (osoba) fault-finding, hard to please 3 (odlučujući) crucial ~**čar** *nm* critic, reviewer ~**čki** *adj* critical ~**ka** *nf* (*Dsg* ~ci) 1 criticism 2 review, critique ~**zirati** *v* (koga/što) criticize

kriv *adj* 1 false ~**a prisega** perjury 2 wrong 3 guilty **biti** ~ **za što** be g. of **ni** ~ **ni dužan** completely innocent **tko ti je** ~ you have only yourself to blame **on je** ~ **it** is his fault ~**ac** *nm* (*Gsg* ~ca) culprit ~**da** *nf* injustice ~**ični** *adj* criminal, penal ~**ina** *nf* curve, bend ~**iti** *v* 1 (koga za što) blame sth on sb/sb for sth 2 (se) contort ~**nja** *nf* guilt, fault, blame guilt, crime, sin ~**o** *adv* 1 wrong, incorrectly ~**o razumjeti** misunderstand *pro*ći ~**o** go wrong **imati** ~**o** be in the wrong 2 falsely, wrongly **učiniti komu** ~**o** do sb wrong ~**o mi je** I am not happy ~**onog** *adj* bandy-legged, knock-kneed ~**otvoren** *adj* forged, counterfeit ~**otvorina** *nf* forgery, fake ~**otvoritelj** *nm* forger ~**otvoriti** *v* (što) forge, falsify, fabricate ~**o**-**vjerac** *nm* (*Gsg* ~ovjerca) heretic ~**udati** *v* (0) (pres ~udam) meander, zigzag ~**udav** *adj* zigzag, meandering ~**ulja** *nf* curve

kriza *nf* crisis ~**no** *adj* **područje** trouble spot

krizma *nf coll* confirmation

križ *nm* cross (+ *fig*) **raspeti na** ~ crucify ~**a** *nn pl* small of the back ~**alj**-**ka** *nf* (*Dsg* ~aljci) cross-word (puzzle) ~**anac** *nm* (*Gsg* ~anca) 1 mongrel, cross-breed, half-breed 2 hybrid ~**ar** *nm* crusader ~**arski pohod/rat** crusade (+ *fig*) ~**ati** *v* 1 (što) cross out 2 (koga/što s kim/čim) cross-breed 3 (se) cross/bless oneself 4 (se) intersect ~**ni** *adj* **put** 1 Way of the Cross 2 *fig* terrible ordeal

krkljan|ac *nm* (*Gsg* ~ca) traffic jam; gridlock *US*

krletka *nf* birdcage

krma *nf* stern

krmelj *nm* sleep (in one's eyes) *coll*

krmača *nf* sow

krntija *nf* jalopy; banger *GB*

krnj *adj* incomplete; mutilated; chipped; rump *pol* ~iti ugled kome discredit sb

kročiti *v* (0) pace; tread; set foot in

kroj *nm* cut, design ~ač *nm* tailor ~ačica *nf* dress-maker ~iti *v* (što) cut (out) ~iti pravdu mete out justice ~iti sudbinu shape the destiny

krokodil *nm* crocodile

krom *nm* chromium ~irati *v* (što) plate with c. ~iran *adj* chrome-plated

kroničan *adj* (α) 1 chronic 2 *fig* inveterate

kroni|čar *nm* chronicler ~ka *nf* (*Dsg* ~ci) chronicle; diary

kronolo|gija *nf* chronology ~ški *adj* chronological

krošnja *nf* treetop

krot|ak *adj* (α) tame, meek ~itelj *nm* tamer ~iti *v* (koga/što) tame

krov *nm* roof slamnati ~ thatched r. ~ište *nn* roof truss ~ni *adj* prozor dormer ; skylight ~na greda rafter

kroz *prep* 1 (prostor, uzrok, sredstvo) through ~a smijeh laughingly 2 (vrijeme *coll*) ~ nekoliko dana within the next few days ~ cijeli život throughout one's life

krpa *nf* cloth; rag kuhinjska ~ dish cloth, tea towel ~ti *v* (što) mend, patch; (čarape) darn

krpelj *nm* tick

krs|ni *adj* baptismal ~ kum godfather ~ni list certificate of baptism; birth certificate ~no ime Christian name ~tionica *nm* baptismal font ~titi *v* (koga) 1 baptize, christen 2 name, nickname ~titke *nf pl* christening

krstari|ca *nf* cruiser ~ti *v* (0) cruise

krš *nm* 1 rocks, crags 2 mess, jumble ~an *adj* (α) strapping ~evit *adj* rocky, craggy, rugged

kršćan|in *nm* Christian ~ski *adj* Christian ~stvo *nn* Christianity,

Christendom

krš|enje *nn* violation, breach ~iti *v* (što) violate

krštenje *nn* baptism vatreno ~ baptism of fire

krti|ca *nf* mole ~čnjak *nm* (*Npl* ~čnjaci) molehill

kru|g *nm* (*Npl* ~govi) 1 circle 2 *fig* cycle 3 range, reach 4 class, set, circle(s) 5 field, scope 6 *sport* lap ~žiti *v* (0) circle, circulate, go round ~že glasine it is rumoured, there are rumours ~žni *adj* circular ~žnica *nf* circle

kruh *nm* 1 bread crni ~ brown b. stari ~ stale bread 2 *fig* b., livelihood, living

kruli|ti *v* (0) rumble ~ mi u želucu my stomach rumbles

krumpir *nm* potato ~-pire *coll* mashed potatoes; mash *coll* ~ov *adj* potato ~ova zlatica Colorado beetle; potato bug *US*

krun|a *nf* crown ~ica *nf* rosary (beads) ~ski *adj* crown

krup|an *adj* (α) 1 big, large 2 major

krupica *nf* semolina

kruška *nf* pear

krušn|i *adj* ~a peć baking oven

krut *adj* 1 hard, stiff 2 *fig* strict, unbending 3 *fig* harsh, cruel, severe

krv *nf* blood piti komu ~ suck sb's b. ~ nije voda b. is thicker than water ide mi ~ I am bleeding ~arenje *nm* bleeding; h(a)emorrhage *med* ~ariti *v* (0) bleed ~av *adj* bloody ~avica *nf* black pudding ~avo *adv* zaslužiti earn by hard work ~ni *adj* blood ~ni neprijatelj mortal enemy ~na osveta vendetta ~nički *adj* murderous ~nik (*Vsg* ~niče, *Npl* ~nici) executioner ~oločan *adj* (α) bloodthirsty ~oproliće *nn* bloodshed, carnage ~otok *nm* bloodstream, circulation

krzmati *v* (0) hesitate

krzn|ar *nm* furrier ~en *adj* fur ~o *nn* fur, coat; pelt

kržljav *adj* puny, stunted ~ac *nm* (*Gsg* ~ca, *Vsg* ~če) derog runt

kub *nm* *math* cube ~ik *nm* (*Npl* ~ici) *coll* cubic metre

kuc|ati *v* (0) 1 knock 2 (srce) beat 3

(sat) tick 4 (se) clink glasses **~nuti** *v* (0) give a knock/tap **~nuo je čas** the time has come (žila) **~avica** *nf* artery

kučine *nf pl* tow, oakum

kuć|a *nf* house **javna ~a** brothel ¶ public house = krčma **kod ~e** at home **ići ~i** go home **ostati u ~i** stay in/indoors **~anica** *nf* housewife; homemaker **~anski** *adj* domestic, household **~anski aparati** household appliances **~anstvo** *nn* household **~edomaćin** *nm* host **~epazitelj** *nm* caretaker, janitor **~erak** *nm* (*Gsg* ~erka, *Npl* ~erci) hovel **~evlasnik** *nm* (*Npl* ~evlasnici) landlord **~ica** *nf* cottage **puževa ~ica** shell **~ište** *nn* case, casing **~ni** *adj* domestic, indoor, home, family **~ni (broj)** extension (number) **~ni pritvor** house arrest **~ni ogrtač** dressing gown **~na pomoćnica** maid

kuda *adv* which way

kudikamo *adv* by far

kudjelja *nf* hemp, tow

kudrav *adj* shaggy

kuga *nf* plague

kugl|a *nf* 1 ball, sphere, globe 2 bullet, shot 3 *sport* shot **bacanje ~e** shotput 3 bowl **~ana** *nf* skittle/bowling *US* alley **~anje** *nn* skittles, bowling **~ati** *v* (se) play skittles, bowl **~ica** *nf* pellet, globule; (sladoleda) scoop **~ični** *adj* **ležaj** ball-bearing

kuh|ača *nf* wooden spoon **~alo** *nn* cooker **~anje** *nn* cooking, cookery **~ar** *nm* cook **~arica** *nf* 1 cook 2 cook(ery) book **~ati** *v* 1 (0/što) cook; boil; (čaj) make, brew 2 (0) *fig* seethe 3 (se) cook, boil; (na laganoj vatri) simmer 4 (se) be hot **~inja** *nf* 1 kitchen 2 cuisine, cooking **~injski** *adj* kitchen **~injska sol** table salt

kuja *nf* bitch

kuk *nm* hip

kuka *nf* hook **~st** *adj* barbed, hooked **~sti križ** swastika

kuk|ac *nm* (*Gsg* ~ca) bug *US coll*, insect

kuka|ti *v* (0) lament **~van** *adj* (α) wretched, miserable, sad **~vica** *nf* 1 (osoba) coward 2 (ptica) cuckoo **~vički** *adj* cowardly **~vština** *nf* cowardice

kukolj *nm* weed

kukuljica *nf* 1 hood, hood 2 cocoon, chrysalis

kukuri|kati *v* (0) (*pres* ~čem) crow **~ku** *int* cock-a-doodle-doo

kukuruz *nm* maize; corn *US* **klip ~a** corncob **~ni** *adj* maize, corn **~no brašno** corn meal **~ovina** *nf* maize stalks, corn straw

kula *nf* 1 tower 2 (šah) rook, castle

kulisa *nf* scenery **iza ~** *fig* behind the scenes

kulmin|acija *nf* culmination, peak **~irati** *v* (0) culminate, come to a head

kuloar *nf* lobby **po ~ima se priča** it is rumoured in the corridors

kult *nm* cult **~iviran** *adj* sophisticated, refined **~ura** *nf* 1 culture 2 crop **~uran** *adj* 1 cultural 2 (osoba) cultured, civilized

kuljati *v* (0) gush (out)

kum *nm* godfather; sponsor **vjenčani ~** best man **~a** *nf* godmother **~če** *nn* godchild/son/daughter **~iti** *v* (koga) beseech, entreat **~ovati** *v* (*pres* ~ujem) (čemu) *fig* be behind sth

kuna *nf* 1 marten 2 (novac) (the) kuna

kunda|k *nm* (*Npl* ~ci) rifle butt/stock

kunić *nm* rabbit

kunjati *v* (0) drowse

kup (1) *nm* heap, stack, pile

kup (2) *nm* *sport* cup

kup|ac *nm* (*Gsg* ~ca) 1 buyer 2 customer **~iti** (1) *v* (što) buy, purchase **~nja** *nf* 1 purchase, buying 2 shopping **~ovati** *v impf* (*pres* ~ujem) **~oprodajni** *adj* **ugovor** sales contract **~ovni** *adj* purchasing **~ovna moć** purchasing power

kup|ač *nm* bather **~ći** *adj* **kostim** bathing suit, swim suit **~aće gaće** *nf pl* bathing trunks **~alište** *nn* 1 public baths 2 seaside resort 3 beach **~anje** *nn* 1 swim(ming), bathing 2 (u kadi) bath **~ati** *v* 1 (se) bathe, take a swim 2 take/have a bath **~elj**, **~ka** *nf* bath **parna ~elj** Turkish bath

kupe *nm* compartment

kupina *nf* 1 blackberry 2 (grm) bramble

kupi|ti (2) *v* (koga/što) collect, gather
kupola *nf* 1 dome 2 (tenka) turret
kupus *nm* cabbage
kur|ac *nm* (*Gsg* ~ca) *tab* cock, dick, prick **idi u ~ac!** *tab* fuck off
kurton *nm sl* rubber, johnny
kurv|a *nf tab* whore, tart **~ati** *v* (se) whore **~iš** *nm* lecher
kurziv *nm* italics *pl*
kustos *nm* curator
kuš|ati *v* 1 (što) taste 2 (što) try 3 (koga) put to test; tempt **~nja** *nf* test, trial; temptation; ordeal **~alica** *nf* test-tube
kuštrav *adj* dishevelled
kut *nm* 1 corner 2 angle **pravi/ tupi/oštri ~** right/obtuse/acute a. **~ak** *nm* (*Gsg* ~ka, *Npl* kuci) nook **~omjer** *nm* protractor **~njak** *nm* (*Npl* ~njaci) molar
kutija *nf* box, case, container **glasačka ~** ballot box
kuverta *nf coll* envelope
kutlača *nf* ladle
kužan *adj* 1 contagious 2 pestilential, poisoned
kužiti *v* (što/o) *sl* get, dig (it)
kvačica *nf* 1 clip, peg, catch **~ za rublje** clothes peg, clothespin 2 (znak) tick
kvačilo *nn* clutch

kvadrat *nm* 1 square 2 *coll* square metre **~ura** *nf* floor area **~ura kruga** squaring the circle
kvaka *nf* 1 (door) handle, (door) knob 2 *fig* snag, hitch, catch
kvalifi|ciran *adj* qualified, skilled **~cirati** *v* (se) qualify **~kacija** *nf* qualification
kvaliteta *nf* quality
kvar *nm* 1 breakdown, defect, fault 2 damage **~iti** *v* 1 (koga) corrupt 2 (što) damage, ruin, spoil 3 (se) break down; go bad, spoil, rot; (zubi) decay
kvartal *nm* quarter
kvarcati *v* (se) be on/use a sunbed
kvartet *nm* quartet
kvas|(ac) *nm* (*Gsg* ~ca) yeast
kvazi *prefix* quasi
kvislin|g *nm* (*Npl* ~zi) Quisling
kvit *adv coll* even, quits
kviz *nm* quiz show
kvo|cati *v* (0) cluck **~čka** *nf* broodhen
kvorum *nm* quorum
kvota *nf* quota
kvrcn|uti *v* (*pres* ~em) 1 (0) snap 2 (koga/što) flip
kvr|ga *nf* gnarl, knot; lump, bump, swelling **~gav** *adj* gnarled, knotty **~žica** *nf* nodule, lump

L

L, l (el) 16th letter of Cro. alphabet

labav *adj* loose

labilan *adj* (α) unstable

labirl|nt *nm* (*Gpl* ~nata) labyrinth, maze

laboratorij *nm* lab(oratory)

labu|d *nm* swan ~đi *adj* pjev swan song

laćati *v impf* → **latiti se**

ladanj|e *nf na* ~**u** in the country

ladica *nf* drawer

lađa *nf* ship, boat, vessel, craft

lagan *adj* 1 light 2 (jednostavan) easy 3 slow 4 gentle, soft ~**a povreda** slight/minor injury

lagati *v* (0) (*pres* lažem) lie, tell lies

lagodan *adj* (α) easy ~ **život** a life of ease

lahor *nm* gentle breeze

lai|čki *adj* lay ~**k** *nm* (*Npl* ~ci) layman

lajati *v* (0) (*pres* ~em) bark ~**av** *adj* big-mouthed

lajtmotiv *nm* leit-m̄otiv

lak (1) *adj* → **lagan** ~**a atletika** track-and-field ~**a kategorija** lightweight ~**a pobjeda** easy victory ~**a žena** loose woman ~**o naoružanje** light armaments ~**u noć!** good night ~**o** *adv* easily; lightly ~**o pokvarljiv** perishable ~**o razumljiv** easy to understand ~**oća** *nf* ease, facility; lightness ~**omislen**, ~**ouman** *adj* (α) reckless, careless; frivolous ~**ovjeran** *adj* (α) gullible

lak (2) *nm* lacquer; varnish ~ **za kosu** hair spray ~ **za nokte** nail polish/varnish ~**(irana) koža** patent leather ~**irati** *v* (što) varnish; (auto) paint

lak|at *nm* (*Gsg* ~ta) elbow ~**tariti** *v* (se) elbow one's way; play rough ~**taš** *nm* derog pushy guy

lakmus *nm* ~ **papir** litmus paper

laknuti *v* (komu) be relieved

lakom *adj* (na što) greedy for, avid for, keen on; ravenous ~**ica** *nf* greedy person; glutton ~**iti** *v* (se) covet sth ~**ost** *nf* greed, covetousness; gluttony

lakrdija *nf* farce ~**š** *nm* comedian, buffoon

lakš|e *adv comp* → **lako** ~**e ozlijeđen** slightly injured ~**i** *adj* 1 *comp* → **lak** 2 minor

lalo|ka *nf* (*Dsg* ~ci) jowl

lamp|a → **svjetiljka** ~**ion** *nm* Chinese lantern

lan *nm* flax ~**en** *adj* flaxen; (tkanina) linen **sjeme** ~**a** linseed

lan|ac *nm* (*Gsg* ~ca, *Npl* ~ci) chain (+ *fig*) **planinski** ~**ac** mountain range ~**čan** *adj* chain ~**čić** *nm* small chain; chain (necklace)

lane *nn* fawn

lani *adv* last year

lansir|ati *v* (što) launch ~**na** *adj* rampa launching pad

lanjski *adj* last year's **briga me za to kao za** ~ **snijeg** I couldn't care less

lasica *nf* weasel

laska *nf*, ~**nje** *nn* flattery; cajolery ~**ti** *v* (komu) flatter sb ~**v** *adj* flattering ~**vac** *nm* (*Gsg* ~vca, *Vsg* ~vče) sycophant

lasta(vica) *nf* swallow **jedna** ~ **ne čini proljeće** *prov* one swallow does not make a summer

lašti|lo *nn* polish ~**ti** *v* (što) polish; (cipele) shine

latica *nf* petal

latin|ica *nf* Latin alphabet/script ~**ski** *adj* Latin

latiti *v* (se čega) take up (oružje); tackle sth, get down to

lav *nm* lion; Leo *astrol* ~**ica** *nf* lioness ~**lji**, ~**ovski** *adj* lion's

lavanda *nf* lavender

lavor *nm* wash-basin

la|ž *nf* lie **nedužna ~ž** white lie **~žac** *nm* (*Gsg* ~šca, *Vsg* ~šče) liar **~žan** *adj* (*α*) false **~žljiv** *adj* lying, false **~žljivac** *nm* (*Gsg* ~žljivca, *Vsg* ~žljivče, *Npl* ~žljivci) liar

lebd|jeti *v* (0) (*pres* ~im) float, hover **~dilica** *nf* hovercraft

lecn|uti *v* (se) (*pres* ~em) start, wince

leća *nf* **1** lentil **2** lens **kontaktna ~** contact lens

leći (1) *v* (0) (*pres* legnem) lie down; go to bed

leći (2) *v* (što) (*pres* ležem) lay (eggs)

led *nm* ice **hladan kao ~** ice-cold **probiti ~** break the ice (**piće**) **s ~om** on the rocks **~en** *adj* **1** icy, frozen **2** iced **~eni brijeg** iceberg **~eno doba** Ice Age **~enjak** *nm* (*Npl* ~enjaci) glacier **~ište** *nn* freezing point **~iti** *v* (što/se) freeze **~olomac** *nm* (*Gsg* ~olomca) icebreaker **~omat** *nm* ice machine

led|a *nn pl* back **natovariti što komu na ~a** saddle sb with sth **Bogu za ~ima** God-forsaken place **~ni** *adj* back; dorsal **~na moždina** spinal cord **~no plivanje** backstroke

legal|an *adj* (*α*) legal **~izirati** *v* (što) legalize

legenda *nf* **1** legend **2** key **~ran** *adj* (*α*) legendary, fabled

legij|a *nf* legion **~onar** *nm* (rimski) legionary; legionnaire

legitim|an *adj* (*α*) legitimate **~nost** *nf* legitimacy

leglo *nn* **1** litter **2** *fig* den

legura *nf* alloy

lekcij|a *nf* lesson **očitati komu ~u** lecture sb

lektira *nf* reading (matter)

lektor *nm* proofreader, editor **~irati** *v* (što) proofread, edit

lelujati *v* (se) sway

lemilo *nn,* **~lica** *nf* soldering iron **~ti** *v* (što) solder

lenta *nf* sash

leopard *nm* leopard

lepet *nm* flutter

lepeza *nf* fan

lepršati *v* (0) flutter **~v** *adj* **1** fluttering **2** *fig* light, effortless

leptir *nm* butterfly **noćni ~** moth **~ kravata** bow tie

leš *nm* corpse, dead body **~ina** *nf* carcass **~inar** *nm* vulture (+ *fig*)

let *nm* flight **~ač** *nm* flier, airman **~eći** *adj* flying **~enje** *nn* flying **~imice** *adv* in passing, perfunctorily **~imičan** *adj* (*α*) perfunctory, cursory **~imičan pogled** glance **~jeti** *v* (*pres* ~im) **1** fly **2** *fig* rush

le|tak *nm* (*Gsg* ~tka, *Npl* ~ci) leaflet

letva *nf* lath

lezbijka *nf* lesbian, homosexual (woman)

lež|aj *nm* **1** bed **2** berth, **3** bearing **kuglični ~aj** ball-bearing **~aljka** *nf* (*Dsg* ~aljci) deck-chair **~ati** *v* (0) **1** lie **2** be located/situated **~ati u zatvoru** be in prison, do time **ne ~i mi to** I am not good at it, that's not my cup of tea

ležeran *adj* (*α*) *coll* easygoing, laid back

li *part* **1** (za tvorbu pitanja) **jesam li**? am I? **nije li čudno**? isn't it strange? **sjećate li se**? do you remember? **2** (pogodba) **pokušaš li** if you try to enter **3** (namjera) **ne bi li** in order to, in an attempt to **4** (usklično) **lijepe li žene**! what a beautiful woman!

libela *nf* spirit level

liberal *nm* liberal **~an** *adj* (*α*) liberal

libiti *v* (se) be reluctant, hang back

li|ce *nn* **1** face **2** expression **namršteno ~ce** frown face **kiselo ~ce** long face **crte ~ca** features **reći što komu u ~ce** tell sb sth to his face **~cem u ~ce** face to face **3** *gram* person **4** character **5** obverse (novčić); right side (tkanina); exterior **na ~cu mjesta** on the spot, at the scene **~cemjer** *nm* hypocrite **~cemjeran** *adj* (*α*) hypocritical **~cemjerje** *nn* hypocrisy **~čan** *adj* (*α*) facial **~čne kosti** cheekbones

licencija *nf* license *US*, licence *GB*

licit|acija *nm* auction **~irati** *v* (0/što) bid (for)

lič|in|ka *nf* (*Gsg* ~aka/~ki) larva

ličiti *v* (što) paint, decorate

lift *nm* *coll* lift; elevator *US*

liga *nf* league; division *sport*

lignja *nf* squid

lihva *nf* usury **~r** *nm* usurer, moneylender

liječ|enje *nn* medical treatment **pod-vrgnuti se ~enju** undergo treatment **~iti** *v* 1 (koga zbog čega) treat sb for sth 2 (koga/što) treat, cure, heal **vrijeme ~i rane** time is a great healer 3 (se) undergo treatment, be treated for **~nica** *nf* lady doctor **~nički** *adj* medical **~nik** *nm* (*Vsg* ~niče, *Npl* ~nici) doctor, physician **~nik opće prakse** general practitioner, GP **kućni ~nik** family doctor

lijegati *v impf* → leći

lijek *nm* medicine, drug; remedy **~ u slobodnoj prodaji** (bez recepta) over-the-counter m. **toga nema ni za ~** it is not to be had for love or money

lijen *adj* lazy **~čina** *nm* lazy-bones, idler

lijep *adj* beautiful; handsome, lovely, good-looking; pretty, nice, fair

lijepiti *v* 1 (što) glue, paste, stick 2 stick to; be sticky

lijes *nm* coffin; casket *US*

lijev|ak *nm* (*Gsg* ~ka, *Npl* ~ci) funnel **~anje** *nn* 1 pouring 2 casting, founding **~ati** *v* 1 (što) pour **~a kao iz kabla** it is pouring (with rain), it is raining cats and dogs 2 (što) cast **~ano željezo** cast iron

lijev|i *adj* left(hand) **ustati na ~u nogu** get up on the wrong side of the bed **s ~a** from the left **~o** *adv* left, on the left, to the left

lik *nm* 1 figure, shape 2 image 3 character **~ovna** *adj* **umjetnost** visual arts *pl*

liker *nm* liqueur

lik|ovati *v* (0) (*pres* ~ujem) triumph (over)

likvid|acija *nf* liquidation **~an** *adj* (α) solvent **~irati** *v* (koga/što) liquidate; (tvrtku) wind up

lim *nm* sheet metal, sheeting, plate **~ar** *nm* 1 tinsmith 2 plumber **~en** *adj* tin **~ena glazba** brass band **~enka** *nf* (*Dsg* ~enci) tin; can *US*

limf|a *nf* lymph **~ni** *adj* lymphatic **~na žlijezda** lymph gland

limun *nm* lemon **~ada** *nf* 1 lemonade 2 *fig* soap opera, mush

limuzina *nf* sedan *US*, saloon *GB* **velika ~** limousine; limo *coll*

lingvisti|ka *nf* (*Dsg* ~ci) linguistics

linij|a *nf* 1 → **crta ~a manjeg otpora** line of least resistance 2 line, service **~ski** *adj* **brod** liner

linoleum *nm* lino(leum)

linjati *v* (se) moult

lipa *nf* lime-tree, linden

lip|anj *nm* (*Gsg* ~nja) June

lipican|ac *nm* (*Gsg* ~ca) Lipizaner (horse)

lip|sati *v* (0) (*pres* ~šem) die; collapse with fatigue

liptati *v* (0) gush

lira *nf* 1 lyre 2 (novac) lira

lir|ika *nf* (*Dsg* ~ici) lyric poetry **~ski** *adj* lyric(al)

li|sac *nm* (*Gsg* ~sca, *Vsg* ~šče) fox (+ *fig*) **~sica** *nf* fox; (ženka) vixen **~sice** *nf pl* handcuffs **staviti ~sice komu** handcuff sb **~sičji** *adj* fox

lis|nat *adj* leafy **~nato tijesto** puff pastry **~nica** *nf* wallet **~t** *nm* 1 leaf **naše gore ~t** our fellow-countryman 2 (riba) plaice 3 (knjiga) leaf; (papir) sheet 4 newspaper 5 calf **~ta** *nf* list **~tati** *v* 1 (0) leaf 2 (što) leaf through **~tić** *nm* 1 small leaf 2 leaflet 3 foil

listopad *nm* October

lišaj *nm* lichen (+ *med*)

lišce *nn* tiny face

lišće *nn* foliage, leaves *pl*

liš|en *adj* deprived, robbed **~en slobode** under arrest **~iti** *v* 1 (koga čega) deprive, rob; free **~iti čina** degrade **~iti nasljedstva** disinherit **~iti slobode** place under arrest, imprison **~iti života** kill 2 (se čega) deprive oneself of, go without **~avati** *v impf*

litanije *nm pl* litany

literatura *nf* literature

liti *v* → **lijevati ~ suze** shed tears

litica *nf* cliff, crag

litr|a *nf* litre **~ena** *adj* **boca** (one-)litre bottle

liturgija *nf* liturgy

livada *nf* meadow

liza|lica *nf* lollypop **~ti** *v* (što) (*pres* ližem) lick

logi|čan *adj* (α) logical **~ka** *nf* (*Dsg* ~ci) logic

logor *nm* camp **koncentracijski ~** concentration camp **~aš** *nm* camp inmate, prisoner

loj *nm* 1 tallow 2 (jestiv) suet **kao po ~u** like clockwork **živjeti kao bubreg u ~u** live in clover **~anica** *nf* tallow-candle

lojal|an *adj* (a) loyal **~nost** *nf* loyalty

lokal *nm coll* 1 premises 2 bar **~izirati** *v* (koga/što) localize **~ni** *adj* local

lokati *v* 1 (0) *fig* booze 2 (što) guzzle down

lokomotiva *nf* locomotive, engine

lokot *nm* padlock

lok|va *nf* (*Gpl* ~ava/~vi) pool, puddle

lom *nm* 1 break, breaking 2 *med* fracture 3 *phys* refraction 4 split **~an** *adj* fragile **~iti** *v* 1 (što) break (up), split **~iti ruke** wring one's hands 2 (se) break up/against; waver, be in two minds *fig* **~ljiv** *adj* brittle

lomač|a *nf* 1 pyre 2 stake **spaliti na ~i** burn at the stake

lon|ac *nm* (*Gsg* ~ca, *Npl* ~ci) pot; saucepan **~čanica** *nf* pot plant **~čar** *nm* potter **~čarska** *adj* roba pottery, earthenware **~čić** *nm* jar

lopat|a *nf* 1 shovel, spade 2 paddle **~ica** *nf* 1 trowel 2 shoulder-blade (jelen) **~ar** *nm* fallow-deer

lopov *nm* 1 thief 2 scoundrel **~ština** *nf* thievery, robbery, double-dealing

lopt|a *nf* ball **igrati se ~om** play ball **~ast** *adj* round **~ati** *v* (se) play ball

los *nm* moose, elk

losion *nm* lotion

losos *nm* salmon

loš *adj* 1 bad, poor, inferior 2 bad, evil **~a vremena** hard times **u ~em stanju** in bad repair **~e** *adv* badly, poorly

lov *nm* hunt; chase **ići u ~** go hunting/shooting **~ac** *nm* (*Gsg* ~ca, *Vsg* ~če) 1 hunter, huntsman 2 fighter(plane) **~ački** *adj* pas hound **~ačka priča** *fig* tall story **~ačka puška** sporting/hunting rifle **~ina** *nf* 1 game 2 catch, haul **~ište** *nn* hunting/shooting-ground **~iti** *v* 1 (koga/što) chase, try to catch 2 (0/što) hunt **~iti ribe** fish **~iti u mutnom** fish in troubled waters **~očuvar**

nm game-keeper **~ostaja** *nf* close(d) season

lova *nf sl* bread, dough *US*; lolly *GB*

lovor *nm* laurel; bay **~ov** *adj* **vijenac** laurel wreath **~ike** *nf pl* laurels

loza *nf* 1 vine 2 lineage, stock, birth, descent

lozinka *nf* password

loža *nf* 1 box 2 lodge

lož|ač *nm* stoker **~ionica** *nf* boiler-room **~iti** *v* (što/0) 1 fire 2 heat **~ulje** fuel oil

lubanja *nf* skull

lubenica *nf* watermelon

luckast *adj* silly, daft **biti ~** have bats in the belfry

luč *nm* torch

lučiti *v* 1 (što od čega) distinguish between two things 2 (što od čega) separate sth from sth 3 (što) secrete

lučk|i *adj* port, harbour **~i kapetan** harbour-master **~i radnik** dock worker **~a kapetanija** port authorities *pl*

lu|d *adj* 1 insane, deranged 2 crazy, mad 3 frantic, raving, wild 4 absurd, preposterous 5 reckless **praviti se ~d** play the fool **~da kuća** madhouse, bedlam **~da** *nf* fool **dvorska ~da** court jester **~dilo** *nn* madness, insanity, frenzy **do ~dila** to distraction **~dnica** *nf* 1 mental hospital 2 madhouse **~dost** *nm* 1 madness, lunacy 2 absurdity, act of folly **~dovati** *v* (*pres* ~ujem) rave **~dovati za kim** be crazy about **~dački** *adj* manic, lunatic **~dačka košulja** strait-jacket **~dak** *nm* (*Npl* ~đaci) madman, lunatic

lug (1) *nm* lye

lug (2) *nm* grove **~ar** *nm* 1 game-keeper 2 forester

luk (1) *nm* onion **bijeli ~** garlic **mladi ~** spring onion; scallion *US* **~ovica** *nf* bulb

luk (2) *nm* 1 arch, vault 2 *tech* arc 3 curve **zaobići u širokom ~u** give sb/sth a wide berth, steer clear of 4 bow

luk|a *nf* (*Dsg* ~ci) harbour, port; haven (+ *fig*) **~obran** *nm* jetty

lukav *adj* cunning, sly, artful **~ac** *nm* (*Gsg* ~ca, *Vsg* ~če) cunning guy, sly old fox **~ost** *nf* cunning **~ština** *nf* ruse, trick

luksus *nm* luxury **~an** *adj* (*a*) luxurious, de luxe, luxury

lula *nf* pipe

lumen *nm coll* whizz kid

lumpati *v* (0) go on a spree, go on a pub-crawl

lunapark *nm* amusement park

lunjati *v* (0) loaf

lup|a *nf* banging, pounding, thuds **~ati** *v* 1 (koga/što) beat, batter, strike, smite, hit 2 (0) bang, thud **~ati nogama** stamp (one's feet) **~ati vratima** slam/bang the door **~ati šakama po** stolu slam one's fists on the table **~etati** *v* (što) *coll* babble, chatter, prattle; talk nonsense **~iti, ~nuti** *v pf*

lupež *nm* knave, villain

luster *nm coll* chandelier

luta|lica *nm* wanderer, rover **vitez ~lica** knight errant **~ti** *v* (0) wander, roam, rove

lut|ka *nf* (*Gpl* ~taka) doll; puppet **krojačka ~ka** dummy **~ka u izlogu** manequin **kazalište ~aka** puppet theatre

lutrij|a *nf* lottery (+ *fig*) **dobiti na ~i** win the l.

luž|ina *nf* alcali **~nat** *adj* alkaline

LJ

Lj, lj 17th letter of Cro. alphabet

ljag|a *nf* blemish, stain; dishonor **bez ~e** spotless, blameless, immaculate

lječilište *nn* sanatorium, health resort

ljekarn|a *nf* pharmacy, chemist's *GB*; drugstore *US* **~ik** *nm* (*Npl* ~ici) pharmacist; apothecary

ljekovit *adj* medicinal, curative

ljenč|ariti *v* (0) laze (about/around) idle, do nothing

ljep|ak *nm* (*Gsg* ~ka) glue **~ak za muhe** fly-paper **pasti na ~ak** walk into a trap **dobiti koga na ~ak** trick sb **~enka** *nf* cardboard **~ilo** *nn* glue, adhesive **~ljiv** *adj* sticky; (ruke) clammy

ljep|ota *nf* beauty **~otan** *nm* handsome man; hunk *coll* **~otica** *nf* beauty **~ši** *adj comp* → **lijep** **~uškast** *adj* pretty

ljeskati *v* (se) shimmer, glitter

ljestv|e *nf pl* ladder **~ica** *nf* scale

lješnja|k *nm* (*Gsg* ~ci) hazelnut

ljet|i *adv* in/during the summer **~ni** *adj* summer **~nikovac** *nm* (*Gsg* ~nikovca) summer residence, villa **~o** *nn* 1 summer **bablje ~o** Indian summer 2 *arch* year **~opis** *nm* chronicle, annals *pl* **~opisac** *nm* (~opisca) chronicler, historian **~os** *adv* last summer **~ovalište** *nn* summer resort **~ovanje** *nn* summer holidays; vacation *US* **ići na ~ovanje** go on holiday **~ovati** *v* (0) (*pres* ~ujem) be on holiday spend one's holidays; vacation *US*

ljetina *nf* crops *pl*, harvest

ljeva|č *nm* founder **~onica** *nf* foundry

ljev|ak *nm* (*Npl* ~aci) left-handed man **~ica** *nf* 1 left hand 2 *pol* left (wing) **~ičar** *nm* leftist **~oruk** *adj* left-handed

ljigav *adj* slimy **~ac** *nm* (*Gsg* ~ca, *Vsg* ~če, *Npl* ~ci) slimy character

ljiljan *nm* lily

ljub|ak *adj* (ljupka *f*) charming, delightful, sweet **~akati** *v* (0/se) flirt; smooch *coll* **~av** *nf* love; affection, fondness **stara ~av** old flame **~av na prvi pogled** (0/se) love at first sight **meni za ~av** for my sake **voditi ~av s kim** make love to sb **iz ~avi** for love **brak iz ~avi** love match **~avni** *adj* love **~avni odnos** love affair **~avnica** *nf* mistress; lover **~avnik** *nm* (*Vsg* ~vniče, *Npl* ~vnici) lover **~azan** *adj* (*α*) kind, friendly **budite tako ~azni pa otvorite prozor** would you be so kind as to open the window? **~aznost** *nf* kindness, amiability **~ić** *nm coll* love story **~imac** *nm* (*Gsg* ~imca, *Vsg* ~imče) favourite, darling **kućni ~imac** pet **~itelj** *nm* lover, devotee, buff, fan, aficionado **~iti** *v* 1 (koga/što/se) kiss sb/sth/each other 2 love, cherish **~ljen** *adj* beloved **~omora** *nf* jealousy **~omoran** *adj* (*α*) jealous (of)

ljubi|(či)ca *nf* violet **~čast** *adj* purple **svijetlo~čast** lilac

ljud|i *pl irreg* → **čovjek** people; men; folks **~ožder** *nm* cannibal; (životinja) man-eater **~ski** *adj* human **~ski rod** mankind, human race **~stvo** *nn mil* crew; men; manpower

ljulja|čka *nf* (*Dsg* ~čci) swing **~ti** *v* 1 (koga/što) swing, rock 2 (se) swing, sway, roll

ljupko *adv* gracefully **~st** *nf* charm, grace

lju|ska *nf* (*Dsg* ~sci) 1 shell, husk 2 (ribe) scale **~skav** *adj* scaly, flaky **~štiti** *v* 1 (što) peel; hull, shell; (ribu) scale 2 (se) peel, scale, flake, come off in flakes **~štura** *nf* shell

ljut *adj* 1 angry, mad, cross **~ kao ris** mad as hell 2 hot **~a zima** bitter cold, severe winter **~a rana** grievous wound ~it *adj* angry ~iti *v* **1** (koga) make angry, anger, irritate **2** (se na koga) be angry with ~nja *nf* anger ~o *adv* sorely, badly ~o se varaš you are gravely mistaken **ljutič** *nm* buttercup

M

M, m (em) 18th letter of Cro. alphabet
ma *conj* ~ **i** (**ako**)... even (if)... ~ **tko** whoever ~ **što** whatever
maca *nf coll* kitty, pussycat
mač *nm* sword **trgnuti** ~ draw the s. **~evanje** *nn* fencing **~evatelj** *nm* fencer **~evati** *v* (se) fence
mač|ak *nm* (*Gsg* ~ka) tomcat; tom *coll* ~**ak u vreći** a pig in a poke ~**e/~ić** *nn* kitten ~**ji** *adj* cat's; feline ~**ka** *nf* (*Dsg* ~ki, *Gpl* ~aka/~ki) **1** cat **2** *sl* bird *GB*; broad, chick *US* **3** (riba) dogfish **igrati se** ~**ke i miša** play cat and mouse (with) **kad** ~**ka ode, miševi kolo vode** when the cat's away the mice will play
maćeh|a *nf* stepmother ~**inski** *adv* heartlessly
mada *conj* although, (even) though
madež *nm* mole
madrac *nm* mattress
mađioničar *nm* magician, conjurer
maestral *nm* sea breeze
mafija *nf* mafia (+ *fig*), the mob ~**š** *nm* gangster, mobster
magar|ac *nm* (*Gsg* ~ca, *Vsg* ~če, *Npl* ~ci) donkey, ass (+ *fig*); jackass *fig* **s konja na** ~**ca** from bad to worse ~**e** *nn* ass ~**eći** *adj* donkey's ~**eće uši** dog-ears
magija *nf* magic ~**čan** *adj* (*a*) magic
magist|ar *nm* (*Gsg* ~ra, *Npl* ~ri) **1** (*nf* ~rica) Master of Arts, M. of Science ¶ titule **MA**, **MSc** pišu se iza imena i prezimena ~**erij** *nm* Master's degree ~**rirati** *v* (0) earn/receive/take/obtain a Master's degree **2** (*nf* ~ra) pharma- '~**ist**
magistrala *nf* main road
magl|a *nf* fog ~**ica** *nf* mist, haze ~**ovit** *adj* **1** foggy **2** misty, hazy **3** *fig* vague
magnet *nm* magnet (+ *fig*) ~**ičan** *adj* magnetic (+ *fig*) ~**ski** *adj* magnetic

magnetofon *nm* (reel-to-reel) tape recorder
mah (1) *nm* **dati** ~**a** (čemu) give impetus (to) **u isti** ~ at the same time **na** ~**ove** at intervals **u prvi** ~ at first ~**ati** *v impf* (*pres* mašem) ~**nuti** *v pf* (0, kome/čime) wave (one's hand) ~**ati krilima** flap one's wings ~**ati repom** wag one's tail ~**om** *adv* chiefly, mainly, mostly
mah (2) *nm* Mach
mahagonij *nm* mahogany
mahnit *adj* frantic, frenzied ~**ost** *nf* frenzy ~**ati** *v* (0) rave
mahovin|a *nf* moss **obrastao** ~**om** moss-grown, mossy
mahun|a *nf* pod ~**e** French beans, green beans ~**ast** *adj* leguminous
maj|ka *nf* (*Dsg* ~ci/~ki) mother **časna** ~**ka** Mother Superior ~**čin** *adj* mother's ~**činski** *adj* motherly ~**činstvo** *nn* motherhood
majmun *nm* monkey **čovjekoliki** ~ ape ~**ski** *adj* apish ~**irati** *v* (se) *coll* monkey about/around, fool around
majoneza *nf* mayonnaise
major → **bojnik**
majstor *nm* **1** master craftsman **2** (slikar) (old) master **3** *coll* past master, expert **4** *coll* mechanic/-plumber/repairman etc. ~**ski** *adj coll* masterly
majušan *adj* (*a*) tiny, diminutive
mak *nm* (*Npl* ~ovi) poppy **tjerati** ~ **na konac** split hairs **biti manji od** ~**ova zrna** feel/look small
makar *conj* **1** although, (even) though **2** at least
maketa *nf* scale model
makija *nf* maquis
maknu|ti *v* **1** (što/koga) remove, move **nije (ni) prstom** ~**o** he didn't lift his finger **2** (se) move, shift

makro *nm coll* pimp

makro- *prefix* macro-

maksim|alan *adj* (*a*) maximal; utmost; extreme **~um** *nm* maximum

malaksati *v* (0) lose strength, become exhausted

malari|ja *nf* malaria **~čan** *adj* (*a*) malarial

malčice *adv coll* a bit, a little

mal|en *adj* (*comp* manji) small, little **od ~ena** since childhood **~enkost** *nf* trifle **~i** *adj* little **~i prst** little finger GB, pinkie US ○ *nm* kid, boy **brodski ~i** cabin boy **~a** *nf* kid, girl **trgovina na ~o** retail sale

malign *adj* (*a*) malignant

malin|a *nf* raspberry **~ovac** *nm* (*Gsg* ~ovca) r. juice

mališan *nm* small boy/child, toddler

malo *adv* (*a*) little, (*a*) few, some; a (little) bit **~ pomalo** little by little **čekaj ~** wait a minute **~tko** few (people) **~prije** a little while ago **ni ~** not a bit, not in the least **~brojan** *adj* (*a*) small in number, few **~dušan** *adj* (*a*) low-spirited **~građanin** *nm derog* (petit/petty) bourgeois, snob **~građanski** *adj* middle-class, snobbish **~kalibarski** *adj* small-calibre **~ljetan** *adj* (*a*) underage **~ljetnik** *nm* (*Vsg* ~ljetniče, *Npl* ~ljetnici) minor **~posjednik** *nm* (*Vsg* ~posjedniče, *Npl* ~posjednici) smallholder **~prodaja** *nf* retail **~uman** *adj* (*a*) feeble-minded

malteški *adj* Maltese

maltretirati *v* (koga) *coll* harass

malverzacija *nf* embezzlement, fraud

malj *nm* mallet, sledge hammer

malj|e *nf pl* down, hair **~av** *adj* hairy

mam|a *nf coll* mum, mummy GB; mom, mommy US, ma ¶ često se piše velikim početnim slovom **~in sin** mother's boy, sissy

mam|ac *nm* (*Gsg* ~ca) bait, decoy, lure (+ *fig*) **~iti** *v* (koga/što) lure

mamur|an *adj* (*a*) **biti ~an** have a hangover

mamut *nm* mammoth **~ski** *adj* mammoth

mana (1) *nf* fault, flaw, defect

mana (2) *nf* manna

mandarin(k)a *nf* mandarin, tangerine, satsuma

mandat *nm* mandate; term of office

maneken *nm* (~ka *nf*) (fashion) model

manev|ar *nm* (*Gsg* ~ra, *Npl* ~ri) manoeuvre (+ *fig*) **~rirati** *v* (0) manoeuvre **~arski prostor** room for manoeuvre, elbowroom

manifest *nm* manifesto **~acija** *nf* 1 manifestation 2 event **~irati** *v* (što/se) manifest

manija|k *nm* (*Vsg* ~če, *Npl* ~ci) maniac

manipulirati *v* (0, kime/čime) 1 manipulate 2 handle

maniriz|am *nm* (*Gsg* ~ma) mannerism

mansarda *nf* penthouse, loft

manualan *adj* (*a*) manual

manj|ak *nm* (*Gsg* ~ka) 1 *econ* deficit 2 deficiency 3 shortage, lack **~e** *adv* less; fewer **ni ~e ni više** (nego) no less (than) **~i** *adj comp* smaller; minor **~ina** *nf* minority **nacionalna/etnička ~ina** national/ethnic minority, minority group **~kati** *v* (0, komu/čemu) be short of, lack **~kav** *adj* deficient, imperfect, incomplete

mapa *nf* portfolio

mar *nm* diligence, effort

maraton *nm* marathon (+ *fig*) **~ac** *nm* (*Gsg* ~ca, *Vsg* ~če, *Npl* ~ci) marathon runner **~ski** *adj* marathon

marelica *nf* apricot

margarin *nm* margarine; marge *coll*

margina *nf* margin **~lan** *adj* (*a*) marginal, fringe

marinirati *v* (što) marinate

marionet|a *nf* puppet (+ *fig*) **~ski** *adj fig* puppet

mariti *v* (0, za koga/što) care

mark|a *nf* (*Gpl* maraka) 1 (poštanska) (postage) stamp 2 (njemačka) (German) mark 3 (model) brand, make 4 (oznaka) mark; label **~ica** *nf* tag **~irati** *v* 1 (što) label, mark 2 (0) *sl* play truant, cut classes; play hookey US **~antan** *adj* (*a*) striking

marki|z *nm* (*Vsg* ~že) marquis **~za** *nf* marchioness

marljiv *adj* diligent, hardworking, industrious

marš *nm* march **~irati** *v* (0) march

maršal *nm* marshal

marva *nf* cattle, livestock

marža *nf econ* margin

mas|a *nf* mass **~ovan** *adj* (*a*) mass **~ivan** *adj* (*a*) massive

masakr *nm* massacre; slaughter **~irati** *v* (koga) massacre; slaughter, butcher

mas|aža *nf* massage **~irati** *v* (koga) massage **~er** *nm* masseur **~erka** *nf* masseuse

masiv *nm* massif

mask|a *nf* mask (+*fig*) **~enbal** *nm* fancy-dress party/ball **~irati** *v* 1 (koga/što) mask 2 (se) disguise oneself (as) **~irna** *adj* uniforma camouflage

maskara *nf* mascara

maskota *nf* mascot

mas|lac *nm* butter **~o** *nn* rendered butter **to je njegovo ~o** it's his doing

maslač|ak *nm* (*Gsg* ~ka, *Npl* ~ci) dandelion

maslin|a *nf* olive **~ast** *adj* olive green **~ik** *nm* (*Npl* ~ici) olive grove **M~ska gora** Mount Olivet

masnica *nf* bruise

mas|noća *nf* fat, grease **~t** *nf* 1 lard; fat, grease 2 ointment, cream **premazan svim ~tima** crafty, wily **~tan** *adj* (~na *f*) fatty; greasy

mason *nm* Mason, Freemason **~stvo** *nn* (free)masonry

mastilo → **tinta**

mašice *nf pl* tongs

mašiti *v* (se čega) reach for

mašt|a *nf* imagination; fancy; fantasy **plod** (čije) **~e** a figment of one's imagination **~ati** *v* (0, o komu/čemu) fantasize **~arija** *nf* fancy; fantasy **~ovit** *adj* imaginative

mat (1) *adj* matte

mat (2) *nm* checkmate **~irati** *v* (koga) checkmate (+*fig*)

matemati|ka *nf* mathematics; maths *GB coll*; math *US coll* **~čar** *nm* mathematician **~čki** *adj* mathematical

mater → **mati**

materija *nf* 1 matter 2 (tema) subject matter **~l** *nm* 1 material 2 (tkanina) fabric **~lizam** *nm* (*Gsg* ~lizma) materialism

mater|inski *adj* motherly **~inski jezik** mother tongue, native language **~instvo** *nn* motherhood, maternity **~nica** *nf* womb; uterus *med*

mati *nf* (*Gsg* matere, *Dsg* materi, *Asg* mater) mother **~ca** *nf* 1 (pčela) queen bee 2 mother country

matič|ar *nm* registrar **~na knjiga** (**rođenih/umrlih/vjenčanih**) register (of births/deaths/marriages) **~ni ured** registrar's/registry office

matrica *nf* 1 stencil 2 matrix

matrijarhat *nm* matriarchy

matur|a *nf* graduation (from secondary/high school) **~alni ispit** final/school leaving examination **~alna večer** prom night *US* **~irati** *v* (0) complete secondary schooling *GB*, graduate from high school *US*

mauzolej *nm* mausoleum

maz|a *nf* (**mamina ~a**) *coll* pet, mother's boy/girl **~iti** *v* 1 (koga/što) fondle, pet, stroke 2 (se) pet, neck

maz|ati *v* (*pres* mažem) 1 (što) smear; soil 2 spread 3 (se) *coll* make up one's face, put make-up on **lagati i ~ati** *sl* snow **~ati** (**kome**) **oči** throw dust in sb's eyes **~arija** *nf coll* daub **~ivo** *nn* grease

mazga *nf* mule

maznuti *v sl* 1 (koga) bash, clout, wallop 2 (što) nick, pinch

mazohi|st *nm* masochist **~zam** *nm* (*Gsg* ~zma) masochism

mažuran *nm* marjoram

me *pron* me

meč *nm* match

mećava *nf* snowstorm, blizzard

med *nm* honey **~en** *adj* sweet (as honey) **~eni mjesec** honeymoon **~ovina** *nf* mead

medalj|a *nf* medal **~on** *nm* medallion

medicin|a *nf* medicine **~ar** *nm coll* medic **~ski** *adj* medical

medij *nm* 1 (okružje, sredstvo, osoba) medium 2 **~i** *pl* (TV etc.) the media

mediokritet *nm derog* mediocrity

medit|acija *nf* meditation **~irati** *v* (0) meditate

Mediteran *nm* the Mediterranean (Sea)

medo *nm* teddy (bear)

meduza *nf* jellyfish

medvje|d *nm* bear **Veliki M~** the Great Bear; the Big Dipper *US*, the Plough *GB* **Mali M~** the Little Bear; the Little Dipper *US* **~dski/ ~đi** *adj* bear's **~da usluga** disservice

međa *nf* border, boundary **~š** *nm fig* milestone, landmark

među *prep* between; among **~ inim/ostalim** among other things

među- *prefix* inter- **~gradski** *adj* 1 (vlak) inter-city 2 (tel. poziv) long-distance **~državni** *adj* interstate **~igra** *nf* interlude **~narodni** *adj* international **~soban** *adj* (α) mutual **~tim** *adv* however, on the other hand, but **~vrijeme** *nn* interval **u ~vremenu** meanwhile, in the meantime

mehani|čar *nm* mechanic **~čki** *adj* mechanical **~ka** *nf* (*Gsg* ~ci) mechanics **~zam** *nm* (*Gsg* ~zma, *Npl* ~zmi) mechanism

mek|(an) *adj* (*comp* ~ši) soft, tender **~a srca** tenderhearted **~šati ~** (koga/što) soften **~ušac** *nm* (*Gsg* ~ušca, *Npl* ~ušci) 1 mollusc 2 *fig* wimp, weed

melankoli|ja *nf* melancholy **~čan** *adj* (α) melancholic, melancholy

melasa *nf* molasses *pl*

melior|acija *nf* (land) reclamation **~irati** *v* (što) reclaim

melodi|ja *nf* tune, melody, air **~čan** *adj* (α) melodious, melodic

melodram|a *nf* melodrama **~ski, ~atičan** *adj* (α) melodramatic

membrana *nf* membrane

memoari *nm pl* memoirs

memorandum *nm* 1 memorandum 2 letterhead

memorija *nf* memory

meni (1) *pron Dsg* (to) me

meni (2) *nm coll* menu

menopauza *nf* menopause, change of life

menstruacija *nf* period

mental|ni *adj* mental **~itet** *nm* mentality

mentol *nm* menthol, mint

mentor *nm* mentor; tutor

meridijan *nm* meridian

mes|ar *nm* butcher (+ *fig*) **~nat** *adj* fleshy; meaty **~ni** *adj* meat **~ni doručak** *TM* spam **~na industrija** meat-processing industry **~nica** butcher's (shop) **~o** *nn* meat; flesh ¶ meat je meso kao hrana, flesh na tijelu čovjeka ili životinje **mljeveno ~o** minced meat **topovsko ~o** *fig* cannon fodder **~ojed/~ožder** *nm* carnivore

mesija *nm* Messiah

mesti *v* (*pres* metem) (što) sweep

mešetar *nm* (burzovni ~) (stock) broker **~iti** *v* (0) (act as a) broker

meta *nf* target (+ *fig*) **laka ~** *fig* sitting duck

metafizi|ka *nf* (*Dsg* ~ci) metaphysics **~čki** *adj* metaphysical

metafor|a *nf* metaphor **~ičan** *adj* (α) metaphorical, figurative

me|tak *nm* (*Gsg* ~tka, *Npl* ~ci) bullet

metal *nm* metal **~ni** *adj* metal, metallic **~urgija** *nf* metalurgy

metan *nm* methane

met|ar *nm* 1 metre **kvadratni ~ar** square m. 2 (sprava) tape measure **~rički** *adj* metric

metati *v impf* (*pres* mećem) → **metnuti**

meteor *nm* meteor **~ski** *adj* meteoric (+ *fig*)

meteorolo|g *nm* (*Npl* ~zi) meteorologist **~gija** *nf* meteorology **~ški** *adj* meteorological **~ški izvještaj** weather report

metež *nm* disarray, mayhem; disorder, uproar

metil *nm* methyl **~ni alkohol** methyl alcohol

metilj *nm* fluke

metla *nf* broom, brush

metnuti *v* (što) put, place

metod|a *nf* method **~ičan** *adj* (α) methodical **~ologija** *nf* methodology

metropola *nf* metropolis; capital

metvica *nf* mint

mezanin *nm* mezzanine

mezim|ac *nm* (*Gsg* ~ca, *Vsg* ~če, *Npl* ~ci) favourite; blue-eyed boy *derog*

mi (1) *pron* we

mi (2) *pron Dsg* (to) me

micati *v impf* (*pres* mičem) **1** (koga/što, čime) move **2** (se) move, stir **ne miči se** keep still; stay put *coll*

mig *nm* (*Npl* ~ovi) **1** wink **2** *fig* hint **dati** (komu) ~ give/drop a hint

migoljiti *v* (se) wriggle

migracija *nf* migration

migrena *nf* migraine

mijaukati *v* (*pres* mijaučem) (0) mew, miaow

mijeh *nm* (*Npl* mjehovi) **1** (za vatru/orgulje) bellows **2** (za gajde) bag **3** (za vino) wineskin

mije|na *nf* change **mjesečeve ~ne** the phases of the moon **~njati** *v* (koga/što/se) change

mijesiti *v* (što) knead

miješa|ti *v* **1** (što) mix; blend; combine; mingle; (karte) shuffle **2** (što) stir **3** (se, u što) meddle (in/with), interfere (in/with) **ne ~j se** stay out of it **~lica** *nf* mixer

mikro- *prefix* micro- **~b** *nm* microbe **~fon** *nm* microphone; mike *coll* **~skop** *nm* microscope **~skopski** *adj* microscopic (+ *fig*)

mikser *nm* **1** (električni) mixer, blender, liquidizer **2** *TV, film* mixer **3** cocktail shaker

mili- *prefix* milli-

milijarda *nf* billion

milijun *nm* million **~aš** *nm* millionaire

milina *nf* delight, pleasure

milit|antan *adj* (*a*) militant

milodar *nm* alms *pl*, largesse

milom *adv* of one's own free will, willingly **~ ili silom** by hook or by crook → **mio**

milosnica *nf arch* mistress

milosr|dan *adj* (*a*) charitable; merciful; compassionate **~đe** *nn* charity; compassion; sympathy

milost *nf* (*Gsg* ~i/milošću) **1** mercy **na** (čiju) ~ **i nemilost** at the mercy of (sb) **u čijoj ~i** in sb's favour **2** (Božja ~) grace **Vaša M~i** Your Grace **~inja** *nf* alms *pl*, charity, handout **~iv** *adj* merciful; gracious

milovati *v* (koga/što/se) caress, stroke

milozvučan *adj* (*a*) sweet(-sounding)

milja *nf* mile **morska ~** nautical/sea

mile

miljeni|k *nm* (*Vsg* ~če, *Npl* ~ci) favourite

miljeti *v* (*pres* milim) (0) crawl; (kukac) creep

mimi|ka *nf* (*Dsg* ~ci) mimicking; mime **~krija** *nf* mimicry

mimo *adv* past, by; beside **~hod** *nm* march-past; parade **~ići** *v* (*pres* ~iđem) **~ilaziti** *v impf* **1** (koga/što) pass sb by **2** (se) miss one another

mimoza *nf* **1** mimosa **2** *fig* shrinking/wilting violet

min|a *nf* **1** mine **čišćenje ~a** mine clearing/disposal/sweeping **polagati ~e** lay mines **2** (iz minobacača) mortar shell **tromblonska ~a** rifle-launched grenade **3** (kem. olovke) refill **4** (obične olovke) lead **~irati** *v* (što) **1** mine **2** *fig* undermine **~obacač** *nm* mortar **~olovac** *nm* (*Gsg* ~olovca, *Npl* ~olovci) mine sweeper **~opolagač** *nm* mine layer **~ski detektor** mine detector **~sko polje** minefield

mineral *nm* mineral **~na voda** mineral/spring water

mini *adj* mini **~ca** *nf coll* mini (skirt)

minijatura *nf* miniature

minim|alan *adj* (*a*) minimal **~alni osobni dohodak** minimum wage **~um** *nm* minimum

minist|ar *nm* (*Gsg* ~ra, *Npl* ~ri) (**~rica** *nf*) minister; secretary **~ar inozemnih/vanjskih poslova** Foreign Minister; Foreign Secretary *GB*; Secretary of State *US* **~ar unutarnjih poslova** Interior Minister; Interior Secretary *US*; Home Secretary *GB* **~arski** *adj* ministerial **~arstvo** *nn* ministry; department; office *GB* **~arstvo inozemnih/vanjskih poslova** Foreign Ministry/M. of Foreign Affairs; Foreign Office *GB*; State Department, Department of State *US* **~arstvo unutarnjih poslova** M. of Internal Affairs; Home Office *GB*; Interior Department *US*

ministr|ant *nm* altar boy

minuciozan *adj* (*a*) meticulous

minu|li *adj* past **~li rad** years in service **~ti** *v* (0) **1** elapse, pass by **2** expire, run out **3** abate

minus *adj, prep, nm* minus **biti u ~u** *coll* be in the red **ući u ~** run into debt

minut|a *nf* minute **za ~u** in a minute

mi|o *adj* (**~la** *f*) **1** dear **2** sweet, charming, lovable **~lo za drago** tit for tat **do ~le volje** to one's heart's content **~omiris** *nm lit* fragrance, sweet smell

mir *nm* **1** peace **2** calm, quiet **javni red i ~** law and order **iz čista ~a** for no reason, out of the blue **~an** *adj* (*a*) peaceful; calm, quiet; still **~iti** *v* **1** (koga) make peace (with); reconcile **2** (se s čime) resign; come to terms with **3** (se s kime) make up (with) **~no** *int mil* attention **~nodopski** *adj* peacetime **~oljubiv** *adj* peacable; friendly **~otvorac** *nm* peacemaker **~ovati** *v* (0) be still **~ovni** *adj* peace **~ovne snage UN-a** UN peacekeeping force

miraz *nm* dowry

miri|s *nm* **1** smell, scent **2** (ugodan) fragrance, perfume, aroma **3** (neugodan) odour **~sati** *v* (*pres* **~šem**) **1** (što/koga) smell, sniff (at) **2** (po čemu) smell of **3** (0) smell nice **~san** *adj* (*a*) fragrant

mirovin|a *nf* **1** (novac) pension **2** (stanje) retirement **biti u ~i** be retired **otići u ~u** retire **~sko** *adj* **osiguranje** pension scheme/plan

mirta *nf* myrtle

mis|a *nf* Mass **služiti ~u** celebrate Mass **svečana ~a** high (solemn) mass

mi|sao *nf* (*Gsg* **~sli**, *Isg* **~sli/~šlju**, *Npl* **~sli**) thought; idea **slijed ~sli** train of thought **~saon** *adj* reflective **~sliti** *v* (0, što) **1** (o, na) think (of, about); reflect **2** (smatrati) think, believe, hold, consider **3** (podrazumijevati) mean **~slilac/~slitelj** *nm* thinker **~slen** *adj* abstract

misi|ja *nf* mission **~onar** *nm* missionary

mist|erij *nm* mystery **~eriozan** *adj* (*a*) mysterious **~ičan** *adj* (*a*) mystical **~ificirati** *v* (koga/što) mystify **~ik** *nm* (*Vsg* **~iče**, *Npl* **~ici**) mystic **~ika**

nf (*Dsg* **~ici**) mysticism

miš *nm* (*Npl* **~evi**) mouse **slijepi ~** bat **tresla se brda, rodio se ~** a storm in a teacup **siromašan kao crkveni ~** very poor **pokisnuti kao ~** get soaked/wet through **~ji** *adj* mouse **~olovka** *nf* mouse-trap **~omor** *nm* rat poison **~ić** *nm* muscle **~ićav** *adj* muscular, brawny

mišljen|je *nn* opinion **po mom ~u** in my opinion

mit *nm* (*Npl* **~ovi**) myth **~ologija** *nf* mythology **~ološki** *adj* mythological **~ski** *adj* mythical

mitariti *v* (se) moult

mitin|g *nm* (*Npl* **~zi**) rally

mit|iti *v* (koga) bribe **~o** *nn* bribe; bribery

mitnica *nf hist* toll-house

mitra *nf* mitre

mitralj|ez *nm coll* machine-gun **~esko** *adj* **gnijezdo** machine-gun nest **~irati** *v* (koga/što) machine-gun

mjed *nm* brass **~en** *adj* brass, brazen

mjehur *nm* (mokraćni **~**) bladder **žučni ~** gall bladder **~ić** *nm* bubble

mjenica *nf* bill of exchange

mjenjač *nm* gear lever/stick *GB*; gear shift, shift stick *US*

mjenjačnica *nf* exchange office/counter

mjer|a *nf* measure (*+fig*); measurement **poduzeti ~e** take measures **ovo je prevršilo (svaku) ~u** this is too much, this has gone too far **u tolikoj ~i** to such an extent **~e opreza** precautions **po ~i** made-to-measure **uzeti (kome) ~u (za odjeću)** take sb's measurements **~ač** *nm* gauge **~ica** *nf* cup, measure **~ilo** *nn* scale, standard, criterion **~iti** *v* (koga/što) measure **ne može se ~iti** (s) it can't/doesn't compare (with) **~nik** *nm* (*Vsg* **~niče**, *Npl* **~nici**) surveyor **~odavan** *adj* (*a*) competent; relevant

Mjese|c (1) *nm* (*Vsg* **~če**) Moon **mladi ~c** new moon **m~čar** *nm* sleepwalker **m~čariti** *v* (0) sleepwalk **m~čina** *nf* moonlight

mjese|c (2) *nm* month **~čni** monthly **~čnica** *nf* period **~čnik** *nm* (*Npl* **~čnici**) monthly (magazine)

mje|sto nn 1 place; spot **opće ~sto** commonplace, platitude **na licu ~sta** on the spot, there and then **~sto zločina** scene of the crime 2 (small) town **~sni** adj local **~stimice** adv locally, in places **~stimičan** adj (α) local; scattered; sporadic **~štanin** nm local, resident

mješan|ac nm (Vsg ~če, Npl ~ci) 1 mulatto derog 2 (pas) mongrel

mješavina nf mixture, blend

mješina nf 1 (wine)skin 2 fig (trbušina) paunch

mješovit adj mixed **trgovina ~om robom** grocer's (shop)

mlačan adj (α) lukewarm

mlad adj (comp mlađi) young; new **~i krumpiri** new potatoes **~a** nf bride **~alački** adj youthful **~enci** nm pl newlyweds **~enka** nf bride **~ež** nf the young, youth **~ica** nf shoot **~ić** nm young man, youth **~o** nn young **dobiti ~e** fig coll have kittens **~olik** adj youthful **~ost** nf youth **~oženja** nm (bride)groom **~unče** nn young

mlađak nm new moon

mlak adj lukewarm, tepid (+ fig) **~onja** nm wimp

mlaka nf pool, puddle

mlat nm flail **~arati** v (0) (čime) wave, swing **~ilo** nn flail **~iti** v 1 (koga/što) beat, strike, hit 2 (žito) thresh **~titi praznu slamu** fig talk nonsense 3 (se) fight

mla|z nm (Npl ~zovi) jet **~zni** adj jet, jet-propelled **~zni pogon** jet propulsion **~žnjak** nm (Npl ~žnjaci) jet (aircraft/plane)

Mleci nm pl hist Venice

mliječni adj milk, milky; dairy **~čni proizvodi** dairy products **M~čna Staza** Milky Way **~čni zub** milk/baby tooth **~ko** nn milk

mlin nm (flour)mill, watermill **~ac** (za kavu) nm (Gsg ~ca, Npl ~ci) coffee grinder **~ar** nm miller **~arski** adj mill

mlitav adj sluggish, flabby

mlohav adj slack, limp, loose

mljackati v (0) smack (one's lips)

mljekar nm milkman **~a** nf dairy **~ica** nf milkmaid, dairymaid **~ski** adj

dairy

mlje|ti v (što) (pres meljem) grind **~veno meso** minced meat

mnijenje nn opinion **javno ~** public opinion

mnog|i adj many; numerous; plentiful **~o** adv a lot of; many; much **~o-** prefix poly-, multi- **~oboštvo** nn polytheism **~obrojan** adj (α) numerous **~ostran** adj many-sided **~ostruk** adj manifold

mnoštvo nn 1 (ljudi) multitude, crowd 2 (mnogo) plenty, a lot of

množ|enik nm (Npl ~enici) factor **~enje** nn multiplication **tablica ~enja** multiplication table **~ina** nf 1 gram plural 2 plenty, abundance **~itelj** nm factor **~iti** v (što/se) multiply

mobil|an adj (α) mobile **~izacija** nf conscription GB, draft US; mobilization **~izirati** v 1 (koga) conscript GB, draft US 2 (koga/što) mobilize

mobitel nm mobile phone, car phone

močiti v (što/se) soak

močvara nf swamp, marsh, bog **~n** adj (α) swampy, marshy

moć nf 1 power 2 (sposobnost) ability **~an** adj (α) powerful **~i** v (što) (pres Isg mogu, IIIsg može, IIIpl mogu) be able (to), can, be capable of **~nik** nm (Vsg ~niče, Npl ~nici) lord; big shot coll

mod|a nf fashion, vogue **~eran** adj (α) 1 fashionable 2 (suvremen) modern, contemporary

mod|ar adj (α) 1 deep blue 2 (lice, koža) livid **~ra galica** blue vitriol

model nm model **~irati** v (što) model

modificirati v (što) modify

modrica nf bruise; (na oku) black eye

mogranj nm pomegranate

mogu v I sg, III pl → **moći**

moguć adj possible **~e** adv possibly **~nost** nf possibility

moj prep poss my; mine

mok|ar adj (α) wet **potpuno ~ar** wet through; soaking wet **udaren je ~rom krpom (po glavi)** he has bats in the belfry

mokasinke nf pl 1 moccasins 2 loafers

mokr|aća nf urine **~aćni** adj 1 med

urinary 2 *chem* uric **~aćna cijev** urethra **~aćovod** *nm* ureter **~iti** *v* (0) urinate, pass water

mol (1) *nm* minor key **f-~** F minor

mol (2) *nm* pier, jetty, dock, quay

mol (3) *nm* whiting

mol|ba *nf* 1 plea; request 2 application 3 petition **~ećiv** *adj* pleading, suppliant **~itelj** *nm* applicant; petitioner; supplicant **~iti** *v* (koga/što) 1 (tražiti) ask, request **~im a.** please b. (odgovor na "hvala") you're welcome 2 beg, plead 3 (preklinjati) implore, entreat, beseech 4 (se) pray, say one's prayers **~itva** *nf* prayer **~itveni** *adj* prayer **~itvenik** *nm* (*Npl* ~itvenici) prayer book

molekula *nf* molecule **~ran** *adj* (*a*) molecular

molj|ac *nm* (*Gsg* ~ca, *Npl* ~ci) moth

moljakati *v* (koga/što) *derog* pester, annoy with requests

mom|ak *nm* (*Gsg* ~ka, *Vsg* ~če, *Npl* ~ci) 1 young fellow, boy, youth 2 bachelor **~ački** *adj* batchelor **~čad** *nn* team **~čadski** *adj* team

moment *nm* moment **~alan** *adj* (*a*) instant(aneous)

monar|h *nm* (*Npl* ~si) monarch **~hija** *nf* monarchy **~hist** *nm* monarchist

monden *adj* jet-set, posh

moneta *nf* currency, money **~rni** *adj* monetary

mono- *prefix* mono- **~gamija** *nf* monogamy **~grafija** *nf* monograph **~gram** *nm* monogram **~kl** *nm* monocle **~lit** *nm* monolith **~log** *nm* (*Npl* ~lozi) monologue **~pol** *nm* monopoly **~polizirati** *v* (što) monopolize **~ton** *adj* monotonous **~tonija** *nf* monotopy

monstru|m *nm* monster **~ozan** *adj* (*a*) monstruous

monsun *nm* monsoon

mont|er *nm* fitter **~irati** *v* (što) 1 instal, fit; assemble 2 *TV, film* edit 3 *fig* rig; stage **~aža** *nf* 1 fitting, installation 2 *TV, film* montage, editing 3 (prostorija) cutting room **~ažer** *adj* editor **~ažni** *adj* prefabricated

monumentalan *adj* (*a*) monumental

mora *nf* nightmare

moral *nm* 1 (ćudoređe) moral 2 (duh) morale **podignuti (kome) ~** boost sb's morale **~an** *adj* (*a*) moral **~nost** *nf* morality

morati *v* (što) have to, must, be obliged to

morbidan *adj* (*a*) morbid

mor|e *nn* sea **~eplovac** *nm* (*Gsg* ~eplovca, *Vsg* ~eplovče, *Npl* ~eplovci) seafarer **~nar** *nm* sailor, seaman, mariner **~narica** *nf* navy **trgovačka ~narica** merchant navy; merchant marine *US* **~narički** *adj* naval **~narski** *adj* sailor's **~ski** *adj* sea, nautical

morfij *nm* morphine

morfologija *nf* morphology

moriti *v* (koga) 1 (ubijati) murder 2 (mučiti) torment

mortalitet *nm* mortality (rate)

morž *nm* walrus

most *nm* (*Npl* ~ovi) bridge **~iti** *v* (što) bridge **~obran** *nm* bridgehead

mošnice *nf pl,* **mošnja** *nf* scrotum

mošt *nm* must

mošus *nm* musk

motati *v* 1 (koga/što) twist, wind **~ (koga) oko prsta** twist sb around one's little finger 2 (što, u papir) wrap 3 (cigaretu) roll 4 (se) hang around, stick around

motel *nm* motel

moti|ka *nf* (*Dsg* ~ci) hoe

motiv *nm* 1 motive 2 (u umjetnosti) motif **~acija** *nf* motivation **~irati** *v* (koga/što) motivate

motk|a *nf* pole **skok s ~om** pole vault

motocikl *nm* motorcycle, motorbike

motor *nm* 1 *phys* motor 2 (automobila etc.) engine 3 *coll* motorbike **~ički** *adj* motor **~ika** *nf* motor functions **~ist** *nm* motorcyclist; biker *coll* **~istički** *adj* motorcycle **~ni** *adj* motor

motriti *v* (koga/što) watch, observe, look at

mozai|k *nm* (*Npl* ~ci) mosaic

mo|zak *nm* (*Gsg* ~zga, *Npl* ~zgovi) brain **~zgati** *v* (0) rack one's brains, ponder **~ždani/~zgovni** *adj* brain, cerebral **~ždina** *nf* marrow **leđna ~ždina** spinal cord

možda *adv* perhaps, maybe

može v 1 *III sg →* **moći** 2 *coll* alright	*adj* (*a*) grumpy **~žnja** *nf* hatred
mra|čan *adj* (*a*) dark, obscure, murky, gloomy **~čiti** v (se) get/grow dark, darken **~čnjak** *nm* (*Npl* ~čnjaci) weirdo **~k** *nm* dark(ness)	**mrz|al** *adj* (*a*) chilly, freezing, frosty **~nuti** v (0) freeze
	muca|ti v (0) stutter, stammer **~vac** *nm* (*Gsg* ~vca, *Npl* ~vci) stutterer, stammerer
mramor *nm* marble **~ni** *adj* marble	
mrav *nm* ant **~injak** *nm* (*Npl* ~injaci) anthill **~lja kiselina** formic acid **~ojed** *nm* anteater	**muč|an** *adj* (*a*) painful, unpleasant **~enik** *nm* (*Vsg* ~eniče, *Npl* ~enici) martyr **~eništvo** *nn* martyrdom **~enje** *nn* torture, torment **~ilište** *nn* torture chamber **~itelj** *nm* torturer **~iti** v 1 (koga) torture, torment 2 (koga) harass; hassle *fig* 3 (se) suffer **~nina** *nf* nausea, sickness **~no mi je** I feel sick
mraz *nm* (*Npl* ~ovi/~evi) frost	
mrcina *nf* 1 carrion 2 *fig* swine, scumbag	
mrcvariti v (koga/što) mutilate, maim; torture, maltreat, harass	
mrčiti v (što) stain, smudge	
mrdati v (se/0, čime) move **mrdnuti** v *pf*	**mučki** *adj* treacherous, underhand(ed) *adv* treacherously, underhandedly
mrena *nf* cataract	**muć|ak** *nm* (*Gsg* ~ka, *Npl* ~ci) bad/addled egg **pokvaren je kao ~ak** he's rotten to the core
mreškati v (se) ripple	
mrež|a *nf* net; *fig* network **TV~a** TV network **paukova ~a** cobweb **~aste** *adj* **čarape** fishnet stockings **~nica** *nf* retina	**mućka** *nf coll* set-up, trick **~ti** v 1 (što) shake 2 (0/što) *coll* wheel and deal
	muda *nn pl* testicles **imati ~** have guts; have balls *vulg*
mrgod|an *adj* (*a*) sullen, grumpy **~iti** v (se) frown	**mud|ar** *adj* (*a*) wise, sage **~rac** *nm* wise man, sage **~rijaš** *nm derog* wise guy, smartarse **~rolija** *nf* scheme, trick **~roslovlje** *nn* philosophy **~rost** *nn* wisdom
mrijest *nf* roe, spawn **~iti** v (se) spawn	
mrk *adj* dark; gloomy; sullen **~li mrak** pitch darkness	
mrkva *nf* carrot	
mrlja *nf* stain, smear, blemish (+ *fig*), smudge	**muh|a** *nf* fly **ubiti dvije ~e jednim udarcem** kill two birds with one stone **kao ~a bez glave** helter-skelter **~olovka** *nf* (*Dsg* ~olovci) flypaper
mrmljati v (0, što) mutter; mumble, grumble	
mrmor *nm* murmur **~iti** v (0) murmur	**muhara** *nf* toadstool
mrsiti (1) v (što/se) 1 tangle 2 ruffle	**muk** *nm* hush, silence
mrsiti (2) v (0) eat meat	**muka** *nf* (*Dsg* muci) 1 torture, torment; suffering 2 *bibl* Passion
mrsko *adv →* **mrzak**	
mršav *adj* thin, skinny	**mukao** *adj* (mukla *f*) (zvuk) hollow, dull
mrštiti v (se) frown	
mrt|av *adj* (*a*) dead **~vac** *nm* dead man **~vački** *adj* deadly **~vačnica** *nf* morgue **~vilo** *nn* stupor **~vorođenče** *nn* stillborn baby **~vozornik** (*Vsg* ~vozorniče, *Npl* ~vozornici) *nm* coroner	**mukati** v (*pres* mučem) (0) moo
	mukotrpan *adj* (*a*) hard, arduous
	mul|a *nf* mule **~ac** *nm* (*Gsg* ~ca, *Npl* ~ci) 1 bastard (+ *fig*) 2 brat, rascal
	mulat *nm* mulatto
mrv|a *nf* 1 crumb 2 *fig* a (tiny) bit **~ica** *nf* crumb **~iti** v (što/se) crumble **~ljiv** *adj* crumbly	**mulj** *nm* silt, slough, mud **~ati** v (što, 0) 1 (grožđe) press 2 *sl* hedge, play for time **~evit** *adj* muddy
	mumi|ja *nf* mummy **~ficirati** v (koga/što) mummify
mr|zak *adj* (~ska *f*) hateful, odious, abominable **~ziti** v (koga/što/se) hate (sb/sth/one another), detest, abhor **~zovolja** *nf* bad/ill temper **~zovoljan**	**mumi(j)ati** v (0, što) mumble
	municija *nf* ammunition
	munj|a *nf* (flash of) lightning

mur|ija *nf sl* cops *pl* ~**jak** *nm sl* cop;
copper *GB*
murva *nf* mulberry
musav *adj* dirty, scruffy
muskulatura *nf* muscles, muscular
system
musliman *nm* Muslim (Moslem) ~**ski**
adj Muslim
musti *v* (*pres* muzem) (koga/što) milk
(+ *fig*)
muši|ca *nf* 1 fly; gnat 2 (prednji
ciljnik) *coll* sight 3 (hir) whim ~**čav**
adj capricious, fickle
mušk|arac *nm* (*Gsg* ~arca, *Vsg* ~arče,
Npl ~arci) man, male ~**arčina** *nm*
he-man ~**i** *adj* manly ~**i rod** *gram*
masculine gender ~**o** *nn* male
~**obanja** *nf* tomboy ~**ost** *nn* man-
hood
mušketir *nm* musketeer
mušterija *nf coll* customer
mut|acija *nf* mutation ~**irati** *v* (0) *on*
~*ira* his voice is breaking

mut|an *adj* (*ā*) 1 turbid, muddy, thick;
dull; vague *fig* 2 *sl* suspicious, dodgy
loviti u ~**nome** fish in troubled waters ~**iti** *v* (što) 1 make muddy 2 stir,
beat 3 *sl* wheel and deal ~**ivoda** *nm*,
nf troublemaker
mutav *adj* 1 *tab*, *derog* dumb 2 *coll*
tongue-tied; quiet
muza *nf* muse
muz|ara *nf* milch cow (+ *fig*) ~**ilica** *nf*
milking machine
muzej *nm* museum
muzi|ka *nf* (*Dsg* ~ci) music ~**kalan**
adj (*ā*) musical ~**čki** *adj* musical
muž *nm* (*Npl* ~evi) 1 husband 2 *arch*
man; gentleman ~**ev** *adj* husband's
~**evan** *adj* (*ā*) masculine, manly, virile ~**evnost** *nf* masculinity, manli-
ness, virility ~**ić** *nm* hubby
mužja|k *nm* (*Npl* ~ci) male ~**čki** *adj*
male
mužnja *nf* milking

N

N, n (en) 19th letter of Cro. alphabet

na *prep* on; at; in ~ *engleskom* in English *prevesti* ~ *engleski* translate into E. ~ *dan/sat* per day/hour ~ *poslu* at work ~ *primjer* for example ~ *sastanku* at/the meeting ~ *silu* by force ~ *trgu* in the square ~ *tržištu* on the market ~ *tržnici* in the market ~ *ulici* in *GB*/on *US* the street

na- *prefix* izražava **1** dovršenost radnje: *napisati* write down **2** izvršenje do pune mjere: *najesti se* eat one's fill **3** djelomično izvršenje radnje: *nagristi* bite into **4** smjer: *naići* come across

nabac|ati *v* (što) pile up, jumble up ~**iti 1** (što) throw **2** (se čime) fling, hurl ~**ivati** *v impf*

nabadati *v impf* → **nabosti**

nabasati *v* (0, na koga/što) run into, come across

nabav|a *nf* purchase; acquisition ~**iti** *v* (što) acquire, obtain, get; buy, purchase ~**ljač** *nm* supplier ~**ljati** *v impf* ~**ni** *adj* purchasing

nabij|ati *v* **1** (koga/što) ram, cram, stuff **2** (oružje) load, charge **3** (se) bruise oneself ~**oj** *nm* charge ~**ojnjača** *nf* cartridge belt

nabolje *adv* poći/ići ~ get better, improve

nabor *nm* fold, pleat

nabo|sti *v* (*pres* ~dem) (koga/što/se) prick (oneself)

nabožan *adj* religious

nabrajati *v impf* → **nabrojiti**

nab|rati *v* (*pres* ~erem) **1** (što) pleat ~**rati obrve** knit one's brows **2** (što/čega) pick

nabrek|lina *nf* swelling, bulge ~**nuti** *v* (0) swell

nabrojiti *v* (što/koga) list, name, enumerate

nabrusiti *v* **1** (što) sharpen **2** (se) *coll* get worked up/angry

nabrzinu *adv* quickly, in haste *posao obavljen* ~ rush job

nabubati *v* (što) *coll* swot up

nabubriti *v* (0) swell

nabujati *v* (0) (rijeka) rise

nabusit *adj* rude, snappish

naceriti *v* (se) snigger, titter

nacij|a *nf* nation ~**onalan** *adj* (α) national ~**onalist** *nm* nationalist ~**onalistički** *adj* nationalist ~**onalizacija** *nf* nationalization ~**onalizam** *nm* (*Gsg* ~onalizma) nationalism ~**onalizirati** *v* (što) nationalize ~**onalnost** *nf* nationality

nacijepati *v* (što) chop (up)

naciljati *v* (koga/što) take aim (at)

naci|zam *nm* (*Gsg* ~zma) Nazism ~**st** *nm* Nazi ~**stički** *adj* Nazi

nacrt *nm* **1** plan **2** (zakona) draft (bill) ~**ati** *v* **1** (koga/što) draw **2** (se) *sl* show up

načas *adv* for a moment

načekati *v* (se) wait (for) a long time

načel|an *adj* (α) **1** principled **2** general ~**ni dogovor** agreement in principle ~**o** *nn* principle **u ~u a.** (u glavnim crtama) in principle **b.** (iz principa) on principle

načelni|k *nm* (*Vsg* ~če, *Npl* ~ci) head, chief ~**k Glavnog stožera** chief of staff

nač|eti *v* (*pres* ~nem) (što) (bocu, bačvu; temu) broach

načičkati *v* (što čime) stud (with)

način *nm* manner, way, fashion **na taj** ~ in this way

načiniti *v* (što) make → **učiniti**

načitan *adj* well-read, literate

načrčkati v (što) scribble, scrawl

načuditi v (se) ne mogu se (dovoljno) ~ I'm amazed/astonished, I can't get over it

načuti v (što) hear rumours (about/of)

naći v (pres nađem) 1 (koga/što/se) find (oneself/each other) 2 (se s kim) meet (sb)

naćuliti v (što) ~ uši prick up one's ears (+ fig)

nad adv above, over

nad- prefix super-, supra-, over-, out-

nada nf hope ~ti v (se, čemu) hope

nadahnu|će nn inspiration ~ti v (koga/što) inspire ~to adv with inspiration

nadaleko adv far ~ i naširoko far and wide, everywhere

nadalje adv further(more), moreover, in addition i ~ still

nadaren → darovit

nadasve adv above all

nadbiskup nm archbishop ~ija nf archdiocese

nadčovjek nm (Npl nadljudi) superman

nadesno adv (to the) right ~! int mil right turn

nadglasati v (koga/što) 1 be louder (than) 2 outvote

nadgled|ati v (koga/što) oversee, supervise ~nik nm (Npl ~nici) overseer, supervisor

nadgradnja nf superstructure (+ fig)

nadgrobni adj ~ kamen/spomenik tombstone, gravestone

nadignuti v 1 (koga/što) raise, lift; (poduprijeti) prop up 2 (se) rise; (parket) warp

nadilaziti v (koga/što) surpass, exceed

nadim|ak nm (Gsg ~ka, Npl ~ci) nickname

nadimati v 1 (koga/što) blow up, inflate 2 (se) swell; (grudi) heave

nadir|ati v (pres ~em) (0) advance

nadjačati v (koga/što) overpower; get/gain the upper hand

nadje|nuti v 1 (što čime) stuff (with) 2 (komu što) give (name) to sb ~nuti nadimak nickname ~v nm stuffing; dressing US

nadlaktica nf upper arm

nadlanica nf the back of one's hand

nadle|štvo nn competent authorities ~žan adj (a) competent ~žnost nf competence; jurisdiction potpadati pod (čiju) ~žnost fall within the competence/jurisdiction (of)

nadlijetati v (koga/što) fly over, overfly

nadljudski adj superhuman

nadmašiti v (koga/što) surpass, excel, outdo ~ samoga sebe excel oneself

nadme|tati v (pres ~ćem) (se) 1 compete, contest 2 (na dražbi) bid

nadmoć nf superiority (over) **broj-čana** ~ numerical s. ~an adj (a) superior

nadmorsk|i adj ~a visina height above sea level 200 m ~e visine 200 m above sea level

nadmudriti v (koga) outwit, outsmart

nadnaravan adj (a) supernatural

nadnev|ak nm (Gsg ~ka, Npl ~ci) date

nadni|ca nf wage ~čar nm wage labourer

nadobud|an adj (a) eager, ambitious ~na osoba eager beaver coll

nado|ći v (pres ~đem) (0) rise

nadodati v (što) add

nadohvat adv ~ ruke within reach, at hand

nadoknad|a nf compensation ~iti v (što) compensate (for), make up for

nadolje adv down(ward)

nadomak adv at hand

nadomjestak nm substitute, surrogate

nadoplat|iti v (što) pay extra ~a nf additional payment

nadove|zati v (pres ~žem) (se) add

nadrapati v (0) coll be in trouble, get into trouble

nadraž|aj nm irritation ~iti v (koga/što) irritate, chafe

nadreali|zam nm (Gsg ~zma) surrealism ~st nm surrealist ~stički adj surrealist(ic)

nadređeni adj superior

nadri- prefix pseudo-, quasi- ~liječnik nm quack doctor

nadrljati v 1 (što) scribble, scrawl 2 (0) coll get into trouble

nadrobiti v (što) 1 crumble 2 sl talk nonsense/drivel

nadstojni|k *nm* (*Vsg* ~če, *Npl* ~ci) caretaker; janitor *US*; warden

nadstrešnica *nf* eaves *pl*; porch; shelter

nadugačko *adv* (~ **i naširoko**) in great detail, at (great) length

nadušak *adv* **ispiti** ~ drink at a gulp, toss off, drain

nadut *adj* **1** flatulent **2** *fig* arrogant, puffed up ~**i** *v* → **napuhati** ~**ost** *nf* flatulence

nadvi|kati *v* (*pres* ~čem) (koga/što) be louder (than)

nadvisiti *v* (koga/što) be taller/higher than; tower over/above

nadviti *v* (se) **1** lean over **2** *fig* loom (over)

nadvožnja|k *nm* (*Npl* ~ci) flyover *GB*, overpass *US*

nadvratni|k *nm* (*Npl* ~ci) lintel

nadzemaljski *adj* supernatural, unearthly

nadz|irati *v* (koga/što) **1** control **2** supervise, oversee **3** monitor, observe ~**or** *nm* control; supervision; surveillance ~**orni** *adj* supervising, supervisory, control ~**ornik** *nm* (*Vsg* ~orniče, *Npl* ~ornici) supervisor; superintendent; overseer; controller

nadzvučni *adj* supersonic

nadživjeti *v* (koga/što) outlive

naelektrizirati *v* (koga/što) electrify

naft|a *nf* oil, petroleum ~**alin** *nm* naphthalene; mothballs *pl* ~**ni** *adj* petroleum, oil ~**ni derivati** petroleum-based products ~**ni izvor** oil well ~**ovod** *nm* oil pipeline

nagađati *v* (što) guess, speculate, conjecture

naganjati *v* (koga/što) chase, run after

nagl|ao *adj* (*f* ~la) **1** sudden, abrupt, headlong **2** (nepromišljen) rash **3** (osoba) short-tempered; hotheaded

nagaziti *v* (na koga/što) step on, tread on

nagi|b *nm* slope, slant, incline; gradient ~**njati** *v* (0/čemu) incline (to/towards), tend to, be partial to

naglas *adv* aloud

naglas|ak *nm* (*Gsg* ~ka, *Npl* ~ci) **1** accent **2** stress, emphasis ~**iti** *v* (što) **1** accentuate **2** stress, emphasize, point out

naglavce *adv* **1** upside down **2** head-first; headlong

nagl|iti *v* (0) be rash, rush (into) ~**o** *adv* **1** (odjednom) suddenly, abruptly **2** (nepromišljeno) rashly, headlong

nagluh *adj* hearing-impaired, hard of hearing

nagnati *v* (koga/što) drive, force ~ **u bijeg** put to flight

nagnut *adj* tilted, sloping, slanting, lop-sided; leaning, bent ~**i** *v* (*pres* ~em) **1** (što) tilt, slope, slant **2** (se) lean, bend

nagod|ba *nf* settlement, deal, compromise ~**iti** *v* (se) make/strike a deal, reach a settlement, compromise

nagomilati *v* (što/se) pile/heap up, accumulate, build up

nagon *nm* instinct ~**ski** *adj* instinctive

nagore *adv* **ići/poći** ~ get worse

nagovarati *v* *impf* (koga, na što) try to persuade; urge

nagovijest *nf* indication, omen ~**iti** *v* (što/komu) **1** announce, give a hint **2** (predskazati) portend, herald

nagovor *nm* persuasion ~**iti** *v* (koga, na što) persuade, talk sb into sth

nagrabusiti *v* (0) *coll* get into trouble

nagrad|a *nf* prize, award; *fig* reward **Nobelova** ~**a** Nobel prize **dodijeliti** ~**u** award a prize **dobiti** ~**u** win a p. **svečana dodjela** ~**a** award-winning ceremony ~**iti** *v* (koga/što) reward; award a prize (to) ~**ni** *adj* prize

nagrditi *v* (što/koga) make ugly, deface, blemish

nagri|sti *v* (*pres* ~zem) (što) corrode, eat away/into

nagrnuti *v* (0) crowd/rush/pour into

nagurati *v* **1** (koga/što) stuff/cram/pack into **2** (se) crowd into

nahlad|a *nf* cold ~**iti** *v* (se) catch (a) cold

nahoče *nn* (*Npl* ~ad) foundling

nahodati *v* (se) walked off one's feet/legs, walk one's legs off

nahođenj|e *nn* **prema vlastitom** ~**u** at one's (own) discretion **postupiti prema** ~**ma** ~**u** use one's discretion

nahraniti *v* (koga) feed

nahrupiti *v* (0) rush/pour into

nahuškati v (koga) set on, incite (against)

naići v (pres naiđem) **1** (0) come along, happen to be passing by **2** (0, na što) come across, stumble (up)on, encounter **3** (0, na koga) run into, meet **nailaziti** v impf

naigrati v (se) play to one's heart's content

naime adv that is (to say), I mean, in other words (¶ namely = konkretno, poimence)

naiskap adv ispiti ~ (drink up) at one go

naiv|ac nm (Gsg ~ca) **1** (~čina nm) naive person; sucker, dupe sl **2** (umjetnik) naive artist ~**an** adj (α) naive, gullible

naizgled adv seemingly, apparently

naizmjen|ice adv by turns, alternately ~**ičan** adj (α) alternate, done by turns

naizust adv **1** by heart, from memory **2** all in one breath

naj- prefix ~**veći** adj the biggest ~**bolji** adj the best ~**skuplji** the most expensive ~**brže** adv fastest (¶ uz priloge ne stoji određeni član the)

naj|am nm (Gsg ~ma, Npl ~movi) hire, lease, rent, charter ~**amni** adj **rad(nik)** wage labour(er) ~**amnina** nf rent ~**miti** v → **unajmiti, iznajmiti** ~**modavac** nm (Gsg ~modavca) leg lessor ~**moprimac** nm (Gsg ~moprimca) leg lessee

najav|a nf **1** announcement **2** TV, radio headline ~**iti** v **1** (koga/što) announce **2** (se komu) make an appointment (with)

najbolj|e adv best ~**i** adj the best

najebati v (0) vulg get screwed/fucked up, get in the shit

najedanput adv all at once, suddenly

najednom adv at once, suddenly

naje|sti v (se) (pres ~dem) eat one's fill, stuff oneself; be full

najezda nf invasion

naježi|ti v (se) get goose pimples/bumps ~**o sam se** (od užasa) it made my flesh creep, it sent shivers down my spine

najgore adv worse ~**i** adj the worse

najlon nm **1** nylon **2** (~**vrećica**) coll plastic bag ~**ke** nf pl coll tights; stockings

najmanj|e adv (at) least **ni** ~**e** not in the least ~**i** adj **1** the smallest **2** fig the least

najposlije adv at last, finally, eventually

najprije adv (at) first

najvećma adv mostly, for the most part

najviše adv most; no more than, at the most

najzad adv finally, at last

nakap|ati v (što) fill by dropping ~**nica** nf reservoir

nakašljati v (se) clear one's throat

nakaza nf monster, freak

nakit nm jewel(le)ry ~**iti** v (koga/što) decorate, adorn

naklada nf **1** (izdanje) edition **2** (novina) circulation **3** number of copies

naklapa|ti v (0) prattle ~**nja** nf pl rumours, gossip

naklon nm bow; (ženski) curts(e)y ~**iti** v (se) bow; curtsey ~**ost** nf favour

naknad|a nf compensation **u** ~**u za** in compensation/recompense/ return for

naknadan adj (α) additional; subsequent

nakon adv after, following

nakostriješiti v (se) bristle (up); fig bristle (with anger); (kosa) stand up/on end

nakot nm brood, litter ~**iti** v **1** (koga) produce/have young **2** (se) breed

nakovanj nm anvil

nakratko adv briefly, for a short time, for a while

nakrcati v (što/koga) load

nakresa|n adj sl pie-eyed, sloshed, plastered

nakriv|iti v (što/se) slant, tilt

nakupac nm wholesale buyer

nakupi|na nf accumulation ~**ti** v (što/se) accumulate

nalagati v impf → **naložiti; lagati**

nalaz nm finding(s), report, results pl ~**ište** nn **1** (nafte) oil field **2** (zlata) mine **3** (arheološko) site ~**iti** v impf find ~**nik** (Vsg ~niče, Npl ~nici) finder ~**ni ured** lost and found office

US, lost property office *GB*

nalet *nm* 1 (napad) onslaught 2 (vjetra) gust **~jeti** *v* 1 (0, na što) stumble (up)on sth; hit 2 (0, na koga) run into sb

naličje *nn* 1 the reverse, the back (of sth) 2 *fig* the seamy side (of sth)

nalijepiti *v* 1 (što) stick, paste 2 (se) stick

nalijevati *v impf* → **naliti**

nalijevo *adv* (to the) left **~!** *int mil* left turn

naliti *v* 1 (što) pour 2 (se) *sl* get pissed/sloshed/plastered

nalivpero *nn* fountain pen

nalo|g *nm* order; (sudski) writ **uhidbeni ~g** warrant for sb's arrest **~g za pretraživanje** search warrant **po (čijem) ~u** by order of **~godavac** *nm* 1 mandator, principal 2 boss, superior **~žiti** (1) *v* (što komu) order, give/issue an order

nalo|kati *v* (se) (*pres* **~čem**) *coll* get sloshed/pie-eyed

naložiti (1) *v* (što, komu) order, give an order

naložiti (2) *v* (što) **~ vatru** kindle/light a fire

nalupati *v* 1 (koga) beat (up), thrash 2 (se) stuff oneself

naljepnica *nf* sticker

naljutiti *v* (koga) anger, annoy

namagarčiti *v* (koga) swindle, cheat, fool

namakati *v impf* → **namočiti**

namaknuti *v* (što) procure, secure; (sredstva) raise

namamiti *v* (koga) lure, allure

namatati *v impf* → **namotati**

nama|z *nm* 1 (sirni i sl.) spread 2 (boje) coat **~zati** *v* (*pres* **~žem**) 1 (što/koga čime) (kremu) apply, put; (maslacem) butter; (mašću) grease 2 (se) put on make up; (kremom) apply cream to one's face

name|t *nm* tax; tribute; toll **~tati** *v* (*pres* **~ćem**) *impf* **~tati se** be pushy **~će mi se pomisao** it strikes me **~će se pitanje** the question arises **~će se odgovor** the obvious answer is... **~ljiv** *adj* pushy, forward **~tnuti** *v* 1 (što) impose, force sth on sb 2 (se)

assert oneself **~tnik** (*Npl* **~tnici**) *nm* parasite

namig|nuti *v* (0, komu) wink (at) **~uša** *nf* flirt

namije|niti *v* (što) intend for, design for *ovo je* **~njeno tebi** this is for you

namiri|sati *v* (*pres* **~šem**) 1 (što/koga/se) perfume, scent 2 (što/koga) smell, sniff

namir|iti *v* (što) **~iti dug** settle the debt **~iti potrebe** satisfy the needs **~iti zahtjeve** meet the demands **~nice** *nf pl* provisions, groceries, victuals

namjen|a *nf* purpose **~ski** *adj* special-purpose, earmarked

namjer|a *nf* intention, aim, purpose **u ~i da** in order to, so as to **~an** *adj* (*a*) intentional, deliberate **~avati** *v* (što) intend **~no** *adv* deliberately, on purpose, intentionally **~iti** *v* (se) run into, meet **putnik ~nik** *nm* (*Vsg* **~niče**, *Npl* **~nici**) chance traveller

namjesni|čki *adj* gubernatorial **~k** *nm* (*Vsg* **~če**, *Npl* **~ci**) 1 governor 2 (kraljevski) regent

namje|stiti *v* 1 (što) place, fix, set; (krevet) make; (stan) furnish; (izbore) rig 2 (komu) frame sb, set sb up **~štaj** *nm* furniture **~štaljka** *nf* set-up **~štenik** *nm* (*Npl* **~štenici**) employee

namlatiti *v* 1 (koga) beat up 2 (što) **~ novca** *coll* make a load of money

namnožiti *v* (se) breed, multiply

namočiti *v* (što) soak

namotati *v* (što) wind, reel

namreškati *v* (što/se) ripple

namrgoditi *v* (se) frown, scowl

namrijeti *v* (što komu) bequeath

namrštiti *v* (se/što) frown **~ čelo** knit one's brow

namučiti *v* 1 (koga) tire sb out, make sb work hard 2 (se) be exhausted, work hard, go through a great deal of trouble with sth/sb

nanijeti *v* (što) 1 (snijeg etc.) drift 2 (bol/štetu komu) inflict sth (up)on sb

nanizati *v* (što) 1 (na konac) thread 2 (nabrojiti) list

naniže *adv* down(ward)

nanos *nm* drift **~iti** *v impf* → **nanijeti**

nanjušiti *v* (koga/što) smell out (+ *fig*)

naobla|čiti *v* (se) become cloudy/overcast **~ka** *nf* cloud **umjerena ~ka** moderate cloud

naobrazba *nf* education, schooling

naoča|le *nf pl* glasses, spectacles **sunčane ~le** sunglasses, shades **~le za šport** goggles **nositi ~le** wear g./s. **~rka** *f* cobra

naočit *adj* handsome, dashing, striking

naočnjaci *nm pl* blinkers *GB*, blinders *US*

naodmet *adv* **nije ~** there's no harm in sth, it wouldn't hurt

naoko *adv* seemingly

naokolo *adv* (all) around, round

naopako *adv* upside down; inside out; back to front **poći ~** go wrong

naoruža|nje *nn* weaponry; armament **~ti** *v* (koga/se) arm (oneself) **~n do zuba** armed to the teeth

naoštriti *v* (što) sharpen

napa|d *nm* attack; assault; (snažan) onslaught; (kratak) raid **fizički ~d** *leg* assault (and battery) **zračni ~d** air raid **izvršiti/početi ~d** carry out/launch/mount an attack **odbiti ~d** repel an attack **~dač** *nm* attacker, assailant; aggressor **~dački** *adj* aggressive **~daj** *nm med* fit (+ *fig*), seizure, attack **~d je najbolja obrana** good offence the best defence **~dan** *adj* (*a*) glaring; gaudy, garish **~dati** *v impf* **~st** *nf* **1** (iskušenje) temptation **dovesti u ~st** tempt **2** (gnjavator) nuisance, gadfly **~stan** *adj* (~sna *f*) **1** tempting **2** pushy, forward **~sti** *v* (*pres* ~dnem) (koga/što) attack; (fizički) assault; (žestoko) assail **~stovati** *v* **1** tempt **2** harass

napajati *v* **1** (koga) water **2** (što) (strujom) feed, supply

napakostiti *v* (0, komu) spite

napamet *adv* by heart, by memory

napatiti *v* (se) suffer much, go through hell

nap|et *adj* tense, tight, taut; (film) gripping, full of suspense **~eti** *v* **1** (što) tighten, tense **2** (se) tense (up) **~etost** *nf* **1** tension, strain **2** (iščekivanje) suspense **~injati** *v impf*

napipati *v* (što/koga) feel, grope

napi|sati *v* (*pres* ~šem) (što) write (down), put down

napi|tak *nm* (*Gsg* ~tka *Npl* ~ci) potion, drink **~ti** *v* (se) **1** have a drink **2** get drunk

napjev *nm* tune, air

napla|ćivati *v impf* **~ta** *nf* (re)payment; collection; charge; reimbursement **~titi** *v* (što komu) charge sb for sth; collect **~tna** *adj* **kućica** toll booth/box

naplav|ina *nf* alluvium **~iti** *v* (što) wash ashore **~ni** *adj* alluvial

napoj *nm* slop(s)

napojiti *v* (koga) (stoku) water; (osobu) give sb a drink/to drink **nahraniti i ~** wine and dine

napojnica *nf* tip

napokon *adv* at last, finally

napola *adv* by half **~ učinjen** half done **podijeliti račun ~** go halves

napomen|a *nf* remark, comment, observation; note **~uti** *v* (što) comment/remark (up)on; mention

napon *nm* (električni ~) voltage **u ~u snage** in the prime of life, in one's prime, in the pink

napor *nm* effort, exertion **uložiti ~** make an effort **~an** *adj* (*a*) hard, strenuous, arduous

napose *adv* **1** especially, particularly **2** separately

naposljetku *adv* eventually, finally

naprama *adv* **3 ~ 1** (3:1) 3 to 1

naprasit *adj* quick-tempered

naprav|a *nf* device, gadget **~iti** *v* **1** (što) make, do **2** (se) form **~iti se lud** play dumb

naprečac *adv* offhand, rashly

napre|dak *nm* (*Gsg* ~tka, *Npl* ~ci) progress, headway, improvement, advance(s) **postići ~dak** make progress/headway/advances, improve **postići značajan ~dak** make/achieve a breakthrough **~dan** *adj* (*a*) progressive; advanced, developed **~dovati** *v* (0) progress, improve, get along; (dijete/biljka) thrive **~dovati na poslu** get up the promotion ladder

napre|gnuti *v* (se) strain **~zanje** *nn* strain, exertion **~zati** *v impf* (*pres* ~žem)

napreskok *adv* at random, unsystematically

napretek *adv* in abundance, more than enough, plenty

napričati *v* 1 (se) have a long talk/chat 2 (što) **svašta (komu)** ~ give sb a load of bull

naprijed *adv* (kretanje) forward, onward(s), ahead; (sprijeda) in front ~! *int* come in *sat mi ide* ~ my watch is fast/gaining

naprotiv *adv* on the contrary

naprs|lina *nf* crack **~nuti** *v* (0) crack

naprs|tak *nm* (*Gsg* ~ka, *Npl* ~ci) thimble

naprt|iti *v* 1 (koga čime) saddle/load sb with sth 2 (se čime) shoulder, put sth on one's back **~njača** *nf* knapsack

napucati *v* 1 (koga) shoot 2 (što) (loptu) kick 3 (koga) *sl* dump sb

napuč|enost *nf* population, number of inhabitants **~iti** *v* (što) populate, people

napućiti *v* (što) ~ **usne** pout

napu|hati *v* (*pres* ~šem) 1 (što) inflate, blow up 2 (se) inflate **~havati** *impf* **~han** *adj* 1 inflated, blown up; bloated 2 (umišljen) big-headed, puffed-up 3 (od vjetrova) flatulent 4 (preuveličan) blown up (out of all proportion) **~hnuti** *v* → **napuhati**

napuk|lina *nf* crack **~nuti** *v* (0) crack

napumpati *v* 1 (što) pump (up), (zrakom) blow up 2 (koga) *sl vulg* knock up

napuniti *v* (što) 1 fill (up), top up 2 (oružje) load ~ **u boce** bottle ~ 20 **godina** turn/reach 20

napustiti *v* 1 (koga) leave; abandon, desert, walk out on sb 2 (što) leave, walk out (of sth) ~ **položaje** *mil* retreat, withdraw

napušiti *v* (se) *sl* get stoned

napu|tak *nm* (*Gsg* ~tka, *Npl* ~ci) instruction(s); advice **~titi** *v* (koga) advise

nara|cija *nf* narration **~tivan** *adj* (*α*) narrative **~tor** *nm* narrator

naradi|ti *v* (se) work hard *danas sam se* ~o I've had a long day

naram|ak *nm* (*Gsg* ~ka, *Npl* ~ci) armful **nositi u ~ku** carry in one's arms

naramenic|a *nf* 1 strap **~e** *pl* (za hlače) braces *GB*, suspenders *US* 2 epaulet(te)

naranča *nf* orange **~da** *nf* orange, orangeade **~st** *adj* orange

nara|sti *v* (0) 1 grow 2 *fig* grow, increase, rise **~štaj** *nm* generation

narav *nf* nature; temper; temperament, disposition; character **~an** *adj* (*α*) natural **~no** *adv* of course, certainly, naturally, sure

naravnati *v* (što) 1 flatten, straighten 2 adjust, set

naravoučenije *nn* moral (of the story)

narci|sa *nf* (cvijet) daffodil, narcissus **~zam** *nm* narcissism

nared|ba *nf* command, order; ordinance **~iti** *v* (što) order, command **~nik** *nm* (*Vsg* ~niče, *Npl* ~nici) sergeant

nare|zak *nm* (*Gsg* ~ska, *Npl* ~sci) slice **hladni ~sci** cold cuts **~zati** *v* (što) cut, slice (up)

naribati *v* (što) grate

nari|caljka *nf* dirge, lament, keen **~cati** *v* (*pres* ~čem) (0) lament, keen, wail

narječje *nn* dialect

nark|oman *nm* drug addict **~omanija** *nf* drug addiction **~otik** *nm* narcotic(s), drug(s) **~oza** *nf* narcosis, an(a)esthesia **~ić** *nm sl* junkie

naročit *adj* special, particular **~o** *adv* especially, particularly, in particular

narod *nm* (the) people; folk; nation **Ujedinjeni n~i** the United Nations **~ni** *adj* people's, popular, folk; national **~na poslovica/izreka** proverb, saying **~nost** *nf* nationality **~ski** *adj* popular **~njak** *nm* (*Npl* ~njaci) 1 populist; nationalist 2 *coll* folk song/singer

narogušiti *v* (se) bristle (with anger)

naru|čiti *v* (što) order; commission **biti kao ~čeno** be very convenient, fit the bill **~čitelj** *nm econ* consignee, ordering party **~džba** *nf* order **~džbenica** *nf* order form

naruč|je *nn* (**~aj** *nm*) embrace **nositi u ~ju** carry in one's arms **uzeti u ~je** take in one's arms

narugati *v* (se komu) make fun of sb,

ridicule, deride

naruku *adv* ići ~ be favourable/convenient, play into sb's hands

narukvica *nf* bracelet

narušiti *v* (što) 1 (zdravlje) impair, ruin, damage 2 (mir) break

nas *pron* us kod ~ a. at our place b. in this country

nasad *nm* plantation **cvjetni ~i** flower beds **~iti** *v* (što) 1 (naglaviti) fit 2 (kvočku) set 3 (se) *coll* make a mistake

nasamariti *v* (koga) fool, take for a ride

nasamo *adv* alone, in private

nasanjkati *v* (koga) *coll* take for a ride

nase|liti *v* (što/se) settle **~ljavati** *v impf* inhabit **~lje** *nn* 1 settlement 2 town quarter; residential area **stambeno ~lje** housing estate **~ljen** *adj* 1 settled 2 inhabited, populated **~ljenost** *nf* population

nasi|lan *adj* (a) violent **~lnički** *adj* violent **~lnik** *nm* (*Npl* ~lnici) bully, tyrant **~lu** *adv* by force **~lje** *nn* violence

nasip *nm* embankment, dike, levee **~ati** *v impf* → **nasuti**

nasje|sti *v* (*pres* ~dnem) (0, na što) fall for sth

nasla|da *nf* (great) pleasure, relish **~đivati** *v* (se čime) revel in sth

nasla|ga *nf* (*Dsg* ~zi) layer, sediment, deposit **~gati** *v* (*pres* ~žem) (što) pile up, stack up

naslanjati *v* (se) lean against, rest on/against

naslije|diti *v* 1 (što) inherit 2 (koga) succeed **~đe** *nn* heritage; legacy; (predmet) heirloom

naslijepo *adv* blindly, without looking

naslo|n *nm* back; rest **~niti** *v* (što/se) lean/rest against/on **~njač** *nm* armchair

naslov *nm* 1 title 2 (novinski) headline 3 address **~iti** *v* (što) 1 entitle 2 address **~na** *adj* **stranica** front/cover page **~na uloga** title role

naslutiti *v* (što) feel, have a hunch/premonition **dati ~i** give a hint

naslje|dan *adj* (a) hereditary **~dnica** *nf* heiress **~dnik** *nm* (*Vsg* ~dniče,

Npl ~dnici) heir; successor **~dstvo** *nn* inheritance; succession **lišiti ~dstva** disinherit

nasmija|ti *v* 1 (koga) make sb laugh 2 (se, komu/čemu) laugh (at sb/sth) **~vati** *v impf*

nasmrt *adv* ~ (koga) **uplašiti** scare sb to death, scare the hell out of sb

nasrditi *v* (se, na koga) get angry (with sb)

nasr|nuti *v* (0,na koga) lunge (at sb); thrust (at sb) **~taj** *nm* lunge, assault **~tati** *v impf* **~tljiv** *adj* aggressive; pestilent

nastajati *v impf* → **nastati**

nasta|mba *nf* house, building, dwelling **~niti** *v* (se) settle, set up home, take up residence

nasta|nak *nm* (*Gsg* ~nka) emergence, beginning **~ti** *v* (*pres* ~nem) (0) emerge, arise, come about

nastav|a *nf* 1 classes *pl* 2 teaching, tuition **~ni** *adj* teaching, school **~ni plan i program** curriculum, syllabus **~nički** *adj* teacher's **~nički zbor** teaching staff **~nik** *nm* (*Vsg* ~niče, *Npl* ~nici) teacher

nastav|ak *nm* (*Gsg* ~ka, *Npl* ~ci) 1 continuation; resumption 2 *gram* ending 3 (knjige, filma) sequel 4 (serije) part, instal(l)ment **~iti** *v* 1 (što) continue, carry on, keep on, go on; resume 2 (se) continue, go on **~ljati** *v impf* **~lja se** to be continued

nastavati *v* (što) inhabit

nastoj|ati *v* (*pres* ~im) (0,oko čega) endeavour, try; make an effort **~anja** *nf pl* efforts

nastradati *v* (0) get hurt; suffer; have an accident

nastran *adj* perverted, perverse **~a osoba** pervert **~ost** *nf* perversity

nastrijeliti *v* (koga) shoot, wound

nastrojen *adj* inclined, disposed **slobodoumno ~** liberal-minded

nastup *nm* 1 (predstava) performance, show 2 (držanje) manner; approach, attitude **~ati** *v impf* (0, u čemu) take part in, appear **u filmu ~a** the film features **~iti** *v* (0) 1 appear 2 (početi) begin, set in **~io je oprezno** his approach was cautious **~ni** *adj* inaugural

nasukati v (*pres* nasučem) (se) run aground, be stranded

nasumce adv at random, randomly

nasuprot prep opposite (to), across the road from, facing ~ **tomu** on the other hand, conversely

nasušni adj necessary

nasuti v (*pres* naspem) (što) ~ **šljunkom** gravel ~ **pijeskom** cover/fill with sand

naš pron poss our; ours u ~*oj zemlji* in this country **Lijepa ~a a.** Croatian national anthem **b.** fig Croatia

našali|ti v (se) make/crack a joke ~*o sam se s njime* I played a joke on him

naširoko adv in great detail, at length

naškoditi v (0,komu) do harm (to sb), harm, injure

natalitet nm birthrate

nataložiti v (se) settle, form (a) sediment

natapati v (što) **1** soak, steep **2** (zemlju) water

natašte adv on an empty stomach

nateći v (0) swell

nate|gnuti v (što) stretch, tighten ~**zati** v impf

natikača nf slip-on, mule

natje|canje nn competition, contest ~**catelj** nm competitor, contestant ~**cateljski** adj competitive ~**cati** v (se) (*pres* ~čem) **1** compete, take part in a competition/contest **2** (za posao) apply for ~**čaj** nm competition *raspisuje se* ~*čaj za* applications are invited for

natjera|ti v (koga/što) force, make, drive ~**vati** v **1** impf **2** (koga) chase, run after

natkriliti v (koga/što) tower over

natkriti v (koga/što, čime) roof (with sth), cover

natmuren adj gloomy, sullen, dark

natočiti v (što) pour

natopiti v pf → **natapati**

natovariti v (što) load, burden

natpis nm inscription, writing **nadgrobni** ~ epitaph

natpolovič|an adj (a) ~**na većina** absolute majority

natprirodan adj (a) supernatural

natprosječan adj (a) above-average

natrag adv back; backward(s)

natraške adv backward(s)

natrčati v (0, na koga/što) run into sb/sth, collide with sb/sth

natrij nm sodium ~**ev klorid** sodium chloride

natrljati v (koga/što) rub

natrpati v (što) fill, cram, pack, stuff

natru|ha nf (Gsg ~si) dash, tinge, trace

natucati (1) v (što) ~ *francuski* speak a little French

natu|cati (2) v (što) (zdrobiti) pound, crush ~**čen** adj bruised ~**či** v (*pres* ~čem) **1** (koga) beat (up) **2** (što) bruise, hurt

natukn|ica nf **1** (u rječniku) entry, headword **2** prompt, cue ~**uti** v (što) mention; hint at

natur|a nf platiti u ~**i** pay in kind ~**alizirati** v (se) become naturalized ~**alizam** nm (Gsg ~alizma) naturalism

nau|čiti v **1** (što) learn **2** (koga) teach ~**čnik** nm (Vsg ~čniče, Npl ~čnici) apprentice, trainee ~**kovanje** nn apprenticeship

nauditi v (0, komu) harm sb, do harm to sb

nauljiti v (što) oil

naumiti v (što) set one's mind on sth, be up to sth

naušnica nf earring

nauštrb adv at the expense of, to the detriment of

nauznak adv supine, on one's back

nava|la nf **1** onslaught, attack, charge **2** (gužva) rush ~**liti** v (0, na koga/što) attack, charge; rush ~**li!** go for it, go get it ~**li na klopu!** tuck in ~**lni** adj **igrač** forward ~**ljivati** v **1** impf **2** pester

navečer adv in the evening **danas** ~ tonight, this evening **sutra** ~ tomorrow night/evening

nave|sti v (*pres* ~dem) **1** (što/koga) mention, name **2** (što) quote, cite **3** (koga na što) cause, make

naviga|cija nf navigation ~**cijski** adj navigational ~**tor** nm navigator

naviljač nm fan, supporter **izgredi** ~**jača** hooliganism ~**jati** v **1** (0, za koga) support sb; root for sb *US*; (povicima) cheer (on) **2** (što) wind up ~ti *v pf* ~nuti *v pf*

navijestiti *v* (što) **1** announce **2** (predskazati) herald, portend, forebode

navik|a *nf* habit iz ~e out of h. moć ~e force of h. **nemam ~u** (što činiti) I'm not in the habit of (doing sth) ~avati *v impf* ~nuti *v* **1** (se, na što) get used to sth, become/grow accustomed to sth **2** (koga, na što) get sb into the habit of, accustom (to)

navl|irati *v* (0) gush (out), spout (out), well (out/up) ~rijeti *v pf* ~rle su mu suze na oči tears welled (up) in his eyes

naviše *adv* upward

navla|čiti *v* (koga/što) drag, pull ~ka *nf* (*Dsg* ~ci) cover

navlas *adv* completely ~ **jednak** identical ~**tito** *adv* particularly

navlaš *adv* intentionally

navlažiti *v* (što/se) damp(en), moisten

navod *nm* **1** (citat) quotation **2** (tvrdnja) allegation ~**iti** *v impf* ~**nici** *nm pl* quotation marks, inverted commas pod ~**nicima** in quotes ~**ni** *adj* alleged ~**no** *adv* allegedly, reportedly; supposedly

navodnjava|nje *nn* irrigation ~**ti** *v* (što) irrigate

navoj *nm* (vijka) thread

navrat (1) *adv* ~**nanos** helter-skelter, in a rush

navrat (2) *nm* time, occasion

navratiti *v* (0) drop in/by, call on, pop in

navrh *adv* ~ **brda** at the top of the hill ~ **glave mi je** I'm fed up with him/it

navršiti *v* **1** (što) ~ 25 *godina* reach/turn 25 **2** (se) *sutra će se navršiti točno 5 godina od...* it will be exactly 5 years tomorrow since...

navrtka *nf* → **matica**

navući *v* (*pres* navučem) (što) pull on/over ~ **na sebe** bring upon oneself, incur

nazad *adv* back, backward(s) ~**ak** *nm* (*Gsg* nazatka, *Npl* nazaci) setback; regression; step backwards ~**an** *adj* (α) backward ~**njak** *nm* (*Npl* ~njaci) reactionary ~**ovati** *v* (0) regress, deteriorate

nazalni *adj* nasal

nazdravi|ti *v* (0, komu/čemu) toast, drink/propose a toast (to), drink sb's health ~**mo nevjesti** here's to the bride

nazirati *v* **1** (što/koga) discern (the shape of sth/sb) **2** (se) be seen, be outlined

naz|iv *nm* name; term, expression **stručni** ~**iv** technical term ~**ivati** *v impf* ~**ivlje** *nn* terminology, nomenclature ~**ivnik** *nm* (*Npl* ~ivnici) denominator **najmanji zajednički** ~**ivnik** lowest common denominator (LCD) ~**ovi-** *prefix* pseudo-, would-be ~**vati** *v* (*pres* ~ovem) **1** (koga/što) call, name; term **2** (koga) (telefonom) phone, call/ring (up), give sb a call/ring

nazna|čiti *v* (što) designate; indicate; mark ~**ka** *nf* (*Dsg* ~ci) **1** designation; mark **2** note, remark

nazoč|an *adj* (α) present ~**nost** *nf* presence; attendance

nazor *nm* opinion, view; conviction

nazu|ti *v* (*pres* ~jem) (što) put on, slip on (one's shoes/slippers) ~**vci** *nm pl* **1** overshoes, galoshes **2** leg-warmers

nažalost *adv* unfortunately, regrettably

nažao *adv* učiniti (komu što) ~ hurt/harm sb, do sb harm

nažderati *v* (se) *derog, coll* pig out, stuff oneself, gorge oneself (on sth)

nažuljati *v* (koga) chafe, rub sore

ne *adv* no; not ~ *trči* don't run

ne- *prefix* un-, in-, non-, dis-

neandertalac *nm* **1** Neanderthal man **2** *fig* neanderthal, caveman

nebitan *adj* (α) unimportant

neb|o *nn* **1** sky **2** (raj, + *fig*) heaven **sedmo** ~**o** seventh heaven ~**u pod oblake** sky-high **s** ~**a pa u rebra** out of the blue ~**eski** *adj* heavenly, celestial ~**eski plav** sky-blue ~**eska tijela** heavenly bodies ~**eski svod** heaven(s), firmament ~**oder** *nm* high-rise; skyscraper, tower block

nebriga *nf* negligence

nečastivi *nm* Satan, devil

nečiji *pron* someone's, somebody's

nečist *adj* unclean, dirty, impure, foul; polluted • *nf* excrement

nečitljiv *adj* illegible

nečuven *adj* unheard-of; outrageous

neća|k *nm* (*Vsg* ~če, *Npl* ~ci) nephew ~**kinja** *nf* niece

neću *v aux* (I) will not

nedaća *nf* trouble, misfortune, adversity

nedaleko *adv* not far (away/off), near, close

nedavno *adv* recently, lately, a while ago, the other day

nedjelo *nn* crime, misdeed

nedjelj|a *nf* Sunday u ~u on S. ~om on Sunday(s) Cvjetna ~a Palm S.

nedogled *nm* u ~ endlessly

nedonošče *nn* premature baby

nedosta|jati *v* (komu što/tko) ~je mi (tko) I miss (him/her) ~je mi (što) I lack, I'm short of ~tak *nm* (*Gsg* ~tka, *Npl* ~ci) 1 shortage, lack 2 (mana) shortcoming, drawback, fault, defect ~tan *adj* (α) insufficient

nedoumica *nf* dilemma

nedovoljan *adj* (α) insufficient • *nm* (ocjena) fail, F

nedugo *adv* not for long ~ zatim shortly after

nedužan *adj* (α) innocent, guiltless, blameless

nedvojben *adj* doubtless; unmistakable; indisputable

neg|acija *nf* negation ~ativ *nm* negative ~**ativan** *adj* (α) negative ~**irati** *v* (što) deny

negdje *adv* 1 somewhere; someplace *US* 2 (vremenski) sometime

nego *adv* than • *conj* but ~ što! of course; you bet *coll*

negodovati *v* (0) 1 express one's dissatisfaction/indignation 2 protest

nehaj *nm* indifference, carelessness, negligence ~**an** *adj* (α) indifferent, careless, negligent

nehat *nm* ubojstvo iz ~a manslaughter

nehoti|ce *adv* unintentionally, accidentally ~**čan** *adj* (α) unintentional, accidental

neimaština *nf* poverty, privation

neiskren *adj* insincere, false

neizbježan *adj* (α) inevitable, unavoidable

neizmjeran *adj* (α) immense, infinite

neizvjesnost *nf* suspense

neka *adv* ~ dođe let him come; he should come; he may/can come

nekad(a) *adv* long ago, a long time ago; before ~ašnji *adj* former, onetime

nekakav *adj* some; a sort/kind of

nekako *adv* somehow, in a/some way

nekamo *adv* somewhere; someplace *US*

neki *pron* a certain, some

nekolicina *nf* a few, several

nekoliko *adv* a few, several, some, a number of

nekretnina *nf* real estate, real property

nekrolog *nm* obituary

nekrst *nm* non-Christian; heathen

nektar *nm* nectar

nekud(a) *adv* somewhere

nekulturan *adj* (α) uncultured; ill-mannered

nelagodan *adj* (α) uncomfortable, uneasy

neman *nf* monster

nemar *nm* neglect, indolence ~**an** *adj* (α) negligent, indolent

nema|ti *v* (koga/što) not have, have no, lack ~ there is/are no ~ ga he is not here/in, he's gone ~ mi olovke my pen is missing

nemilice *adv* relentlessly

nemilost *nf* disfavour biti u (čijoj) ~i be in disfavour (with sb), be in sb's bad books pasti u ~ fall into disfavour, fall from grace

nemir *nm* restlessness ~i *pl* unrest, disturbance ~**an** *adj* (α) 1 restless, fidgety 2 (more) choppy, rough 3 (doba, vremena) troubled, turbulent

nemoć *nf* 1 weakness, feebleness 2 incapacity 3 impotence ~**an** *adj* (α) 1 weak, feeble 2 incapable, powerless 3 impotent

nemoguć *adj* impossible, unfeasible

nemoj *v imper* don't! ~**mo** don't let's, let's not

nemoral *nm* immorality ~**an** *adj* (α) immoral

nemrs *nm* abstinence from meat

nenadmašan *adj* (α) unequalled, unexampled, unmatched, unparalleled

neo- *prefix* neo-

neobičan *adj* (α) unusual, extraordinary, strange

neodoljiv *adj* irresistible

neosporan *adj* (α) unquestionable, indisputable, undeniable

neotesan *adj* (α) crude, boorish ~**ac** *nm* (*Npl* ~**ci**) boor

neovis|an *adj* (α) independent ~**nost** *nf* independence

neozbiljan *adj* (α) frivolous, silly

nepar *nm* odd number ~**an** *adj* (α) odd

nep|ce *nn* palate ~**čani** *adj* palatal

nepismen *adj* illiterate

neplodan *adj* (α) barren, arid; sterile, infertile

nepobitan *adj* (α) irrefutable

nepogoda *nf* storm, bad weather **elementarna** ~ natural disaster

neposred|an *adj* (α) 1 direct 2 (vremenski) immediate **u** ~**noj blizini** in the immediate vicinity of

nepošten *adj* dishonest, unfair; underhand

nepovrat *nm* otići **u** ~ be lost, be gone forever, go down the drain

nepoznanica *nf* math, fig unknown quantity

nepravda *nf* injustice, wrong

nepregledan *adj* (α) 1 immense, vast, infinite 2 badly laid out, confusing ~ **zavoj** blind turning

neprekidan *adj* (α) continuous, steady; incessant, continual

neprijatelj *nm* enemy; foe *lit*; adversary, opponent ~**ski** *adj* enemy; hostile, unfriendly ~**stvo** *nn* enmity; hostility; animosity, antagonism

nepril|ika *nf* (*Dsg* ~**ci**) trouble, difficulty; awkward/embarrassing/difficult situation; mess

neprocjenjiv *adj* invaluable, priceless

nepun *adj* not full **prije** ~**ih godinu dana** less than a year ago

nepušač *nm* nonsmoker

nerad *nm* idleness ~**nik** *nm* (*Vsg* ~**niče**, *Npl* ~**nici**) idler

nerc *nm coll* mink

nered *nm* mess, disarray ~**i** *pl* riot, disorder, disturbance, violence

nerotkinja *nf* infertile woman

nervozan *adj* (α) irritable, edgy

nesanica *nf* insomnia

neseser *nm coll* dressing case

nesilica *nf* battery hen, laying hen

neslan *adj* saltless; insipid ~**a šala** practical joke

nesporazum *nm* 1 misunderstanding 2 disagreement, difference of opinion

nesre|ća *nf* 1 unhappiness 2 bad luck, misfortune **na** ~**ću** unfortunately 3 accident **prometna** ~ traffic accident, car crash ~**tan** *adj* (α) 1 unhappy, miserable 2 unlucky, unfortunate ~**tan slučaj** accident ~**tnik** *nm* (*Vsg* ~**tniče**, *Npl* ~**tnici**) poor fellow/guy

nesta|jati *v* (0) disappear, vanish ~**je nam** (čega) we're running short/out of sth ~**nak** *nm* (*Gsg* ~**nka**) disappearance ~**šica** *nf* shortage, lack ~**ti** *v pf* ~**lo je struje** there's been a power cut/failure ~**ni!** get lost! ~**le osobe** missing persons ~**li u borbi** missing in action, MIAs

nestašan *adj* (α) playful, frisky, mischievous

nesti *v* (što) lay (eggs)

nesumnjiv *adj* doubtless, unquestionable, unmistakable, certain

nesv|ijest *nf* faint, loss of consciousness **pasti u** ~**ijest** faint, lose consciousness, pass out **biti u** ~**ijesti** be unconscious ~**jesno** *adv* unconsciously; mechanically ~**jestica** *nf* fainting spell

nešto *pron* something • *adv* some

netko *pron* someone, somebody

neto *adj* net(t)

netočan *adj* (α) incorrect, inaccurate, wrong

netopir *nm* bat

netremice *adv* fixedly, without a blink

neugledan *adj* (α) plain, nondescript

neugodan *adj* (α) 1 unpleasant, disagreeable 2 embarrassing, awkward

neuk *adj* uneducated, illiterate

neukus *nm* bad taste ~**an** *adj* (α) 1 (hrana) tasteless 2 (postupak etc.) in bad/poor taste 3 (kičast) gaudy

neuljudan *adj* (α) rude, impolite, ill-mannered

neumoljiv *adj* relentless, merciless

neurolog *nm* neurologist **~ija** *nf* neurology

neuro|za *nf* neurosis **~tičan** *adj* (*a*) neurotic

neuspje|h *nm* (*Npl* ~si) failure **~šan** *adj* (*a*) unsuccessful, failed **~šna o-soba** failure

neurokirur|g *nm* (*Npl* ~zi) brain surgeon

neutral|an *adj* (*a*) neutral **~izirati** *v* (koga/što) neutralize **~nost** *nn* neutrality

neuvijen *adj* blunt, straightforward

nevera *nf* storm

nevezan *adj* 1 untied, free, loose 2 unconnected **~i razgovor** informal conversation, small talk, chat

nevidljiv *adj* invisible

neviđen *adj* unseen; unprecedented

nevin *adj* innocent **~a je** she's a virgin **~ost** *nf* 1 innocence 2 virginity

nevjer|ica *nf* disbelief **~nik** *nm* (*Npl* ~nici) infidel **~ojatan** *adj* (*a*) incredible, amazing

nevjesta *nf* bride

nevolja *nf* trouble; misery, affliction, distress

nevoljko *adj* unwillingly

nevrijeme *nn* bad weather; storm

nezadovolj|an *adj* (*a*) discontent(ed), dissatisfied (with) **~stvo** *nn* discontent, dissatisfaction

nezakonit *adj* illegal, unlawful, illicit

nezapamćen *adj* unprecedented

nezaposlenost *nf* unemployment

nezavisnost *nf* independence

nezgoda *nf* accident, bad luck, misfortune **~n** *adj* (*a*) inconvenient, awkward

nezna|lica *nm/f* ignorant **~nac** *nm* (*Gsg* ~nca, *Npl* ~nci) stranger **~nje** *nn* ignorance

neznatan *adj* (*a*) negligible, minor, insignificant

neženja *nm* bachelor, single/unmarried man

ni *conj* neither, nor (¶ uz negacije: either, or) **~ ja** me neither **~...**, **~** neither..., nor... **~ jedan ~ drugi** neither of them both **čak ~** not even **~ govora!** no way

ni|cati *v* (*pres* ~čem) (0) germinate, sprout, spring (up)

ničij|i *pron* nobody's, no one's **~a zemlja** no-man's-land

nigdje *adv* nowhere

nijansa *nf* shade, nuance

nije *v aux* (he/she/it) is not, has not

niječan *adj* (*a*) negative

nijedan *adj* (*a*) 1 (od troje ili više) none (of) 2 (od dvoje) neither (of) **~put** *adv* not once, never, not a single time

nije|kati *v* (*pres* ~čem) (što) deny, negate

nijem *adj* mute

nikad(a) *adv* never

nikak|av *adj* (*a*) no **on nije ~av stručnjak** he's no expert **hrana je bila ~va** the food was lousy

nikako *adv* 1 in no way 2 (nipošto) by no means, not at all

nikamo *adv* nowhere

nikoji *pron* no, none

niknuti *v pf* → **nicati**

nikotin *nm* nicotine

nikud(a) *adv* nowhere

nimalo *adv* not a bit, not at all, not in the least

nimfa *nf* nymph

niotkuda *adv* from nowhere; out of thin air

nipošto *adv* by no means, not at all; under no circumstances **~!** not on your life, no way

nisam *v aux* I am not, I have not → **biti**

nisko *adv* low **~ pasti** stoop low **~gradnja** *nf* civil engineering

nišan *nm* → **ciljnik**

ništ|a *pron* nothing (¶ uz negaciju anything), not a thing **~arija** *nf/m* bum, good-for-nothing **~avan** *adj* (*a*) 1 worthless, insignificant 2 *leg* invalid, null and void **~avilo** *nn* nothingness **~ica** *nf* zero

nit *nf* 1 thread (+ *fig*) 2 (žarulje) filament

niti *conj* → **ni**

nitko *pron* nobody, no one **~ i ništa** nobody

nitkov *nm* scoundrel, villain

niv|elirati *v* (što) level **~o** *nm* level

niz (1) *nm* series, sequence, succession, string, line ~ **godina** for many years **kuće u ~u** terraced houses *GB*, row houses *US* ~**ati** *v* (*pres* nižem) (što) **1** arrange in a line/sequence etc. **2** (na konac) string **3** (nabrojiti) list

niz (2) *adv* along, down ~**brdica** *nf* downward slope, declivity ~**brdo** *adv* downhill ~**vodno** *adv* downstream

nizak *adj* (*f* niska, *comp* niži) **1** low **2** (osoba) short **3** (podao) low, base **niži** (po položaju) junior, low-level, low-ranking

nizin|a *nf* plain, lowland(s) ~**ski** *adj* lowland

no *conj* but, however ~? and then? well?

nobelovac *nm* Nobel Prize winner

noć *nf* night ~**as** *adv* **1** last night **2** *coll* tonight ~**ašnji** *adj* **1** last night's **2** *coll* tonight's ~**enje** *nn* accommodation (for the night), (a night's) lodging, bed ~**enje i doručak** bed and breakfast ~**iti** *v* (0) spend the night ~**ni** *adj* night, nighttime, nocturnal ~**na posuda** chamber pot ~**u** *adv* at night ~**obdija** *nm* night watchman

nog|a *nf* (*Dsg* nozi) **1** (cijela) leg **2** (stopalo) foot **na ratnoj nozi** on the warpath **od malih ~u** since childhood **ustati na lijevu ~u** get up on the wrong side of the bed **dati (kome) ~u** *sl* ditch/dump sb, give sb the elbow **dobiti ~u** *sl* be/get ditched **popiti s ~u** have a quick drink, knock back **dobiti ~e** disappear, be stolen ~**avica** *nf* trouser leg ~**irati** *v* (koga) sack ~**omet** *nm* soccer, football ~**ometaš** *nm* soccer player, footballer ~**ostup** *nm* pavement *GB*, sidewalk *US*

noj *nm* ostrich

nok|at *nm* (*Gsg* ~ta, *Npl* ~ti) nail

nokaut *nm* knock-out

nomad *nm* nomad

nomin|alan *adj* (*a*) nominal ~**irati** *v* (koga/što) nominate

non-stop *adv* nonstop; 24-hour-a-day, round-the-clock

norm|a *nf* **1** norm, standard **2** quota **is-puniti/premašiti ~u** fulfil/exceed

the quota ~**irati** *v* (što) **1** standardize, set the norm **2** set the (production) quota

normal|an *adj* (*a*) normal ~**izacija** *nf* normalization ~**izirati** *v* (što) normalize ~**no** *adv* **1** (uobičajeno) normally **2** (naravno) naturally

nos *nm* nose ~**at** *adj* large-nosed ~**ni** *adj* nasal ~**nica** *nf* nostril ~**orog** *nm* (*Npl* ~orozi) rhinoceros; rhino *coll* **gurati/zabadati** ~ (u što) poke one's nose (into), pry

nos|ač *nm* **1** porter **2** carrier ~**ač zrakoplova** aircraft carrier ~**eća** *adj* pregnant ~**ila** *nn pl* stretcher ~**iljka** *nf* litter, sedan chair ~**iti** *v* **1** (što/koga) carry **2** (što) (na sebi) wear **3** (se, s kim/čim) cope with, handle ~**i se!** get lost, bugger off *vulg* ~**iv** *adj* portable ~**ivi zid** weight-bearing wall ~**ivost** *nf* capacity, tonnage **brod** ~**ivosti 5.000 tona** a 5,000-ton ship

nostalgi|ja *nf* **1** nostalgia **2** homesickness ~**čan** *adj* (*a*) **1** nostalgic **2** homesick

nošnja *nf* costume, dress **narodna** ~ national costume/dress

not|a *nf* note ~**ar** *nm* notary ~**es** *nm* memo pad

notoran *adj* (*a*) notorious

nov *adj* new; fresh; latest

nov|ac *nm* (*Gsg* ~ca) money ~**čani** *adj* monetary ~**čanica** *nf* note *GB*, bill *US* ~**čarka** *nf*, ~**čanik** *nm* (*Npl* ~čanici) purse *GB*, wallet ~**čić** *nm* coin

nova|čenje *nn* conscription *GB*, draft *US* ~**k** *nm* (*Npl* ~ci) conscript *GB*, draftee *US*; rookie *sl* ~**čiti** *v* (koga) conscript *GB*, draft *US*

novela *nf* short story (¶ novel = roman)

novina *nf* novelty, innovation

novin|ar *nm* journalist, reporter ~**arski** *adj* journalist ~**arstvo** *nn* journalism ~**e** *nf pl* newspaper; paper *coll* ~**ski** *adj* newspaper ~**ska agencija** news agency ~**stvo** *nn* the press **konferencija za ~stvo** press/news conference

novo- *prefix* neo-; newly, recently

~**imenovani** newly/recently appointed

novopečeni *adj* new, fresh; fledgling

novorođenče *nn* newborn baby

novotarija *nf derog* newfangled thing

nozdrva *nf* nostril

nož *nm* knife; cutter ~**ice** *nf pl* scissors

nožni *adj* foot ~ **prst** toe

nudi|st *nm* nudist ~**stički** *adj* nudist ~**zam** *nm* (*Gsg* ~zma) nudism

nuditi *v* (što) offer

nuklearn|i *adj* nuclear ~**a centrala** nuclear power plant

nul|a *nf* zero, nil, nought; nothing; (tenis) love ~**ti** *adj* zero

nuž|an *adj* (*a*) necessary, indispensable, imperative ~**da** *nf* need, necessity **u** ~**di** in an emergency ~**nik** *nm* (*Npl* ~nici) toilet; bathroom, restroom *US*

NJ

Nj, nj (1) 20th letter of Cro. alphabet

nj (2) → **njega** (2)

njakati *v* (0) bray

njed|ra *nn pl* (*G* ~ara) *lit* bosom

nje|ga (1) *nf* (*Dsg* ~zi) care **~govati** *v* (koga/što) **1** care for, look after, nurse **2** *fig* cultivate, foster

njega (2) *pron* him

njegov *pron poss* his

njemu *pron* (to) him

njezin *pron poss* her (¶ bez imenice: hers)

njež|an *adj* (α) gentle, tender, soft, delicate **~nost** *nf* tenderness, affection

njih *pron* them

njihalo *nn* pendulum

njiha|ljka *nf* swing **~ti** *v* (*pres* njišem) (koga/što/se) swing, rock, sway

njihov *pron poss* their (¶ bez imenice: theirs)

njima *pron* (to) them

njištati *v* (0) neigh

njiva *nf* field

njoj *pron* (to) her

nju *pron* her

nju|h *nm* (sense of) smell **~šiti** *v* (0/koga/što) smell, sniff **~ška** *nf* snout, muzzle **~škalo** *nn* snooper, busybody, nosey parker **~škati** *v* **1** (0/koga/što) sniff **2** (0/što) pry, snoop (around), nose

O

O, o (1) 21st letter of Cro. alphabet

o (2) *prep* about; on; against ~ *svom trošku* at one's own expense

oaza *nf* oasis

o- (ob-, oba-; op-) *prefix* **1** *o-baviti* envelop, wrap around *o-kružiti* surround *op-kopati* dig a ditch around **2** svršena radnja *o-brati* pick, finish picking *o-piti se* get drunk

oba *num* (G ~ju, D/L/I ~ma/oboma) both (of them), (each of) the two ¶ za dvije osobe/stvari muškoga ili srednjega roda (→ *obje, oboje, obojica*)

obad *nm* gadfly, horsefly

obal|a *nf* (mora) coast, shore; coastline; (jezera) bank, shore; (rijeke) bank ~**ni** *adj* coastal

obamr|ijeti *v* (0) (*pres* ~em) **1** become paralyzed/comatose **2** become numb

obl|ao *adj* (~la *f*) round(ed)

obarač *nm* trigger

obasjati *v* (koga/što) cast/shed/throw light on, illuminate

obas|uti *v* (koga) (*pres* ~pem) shower with; deluge/overwhelm with ~**uti koga pažnjom** lavish attention on sb ~**ipati** *v impf*

obaveza → **obveza**

obavijest *nf* notice; information; notification ~**iti** *v* (koga) inform, notify, let sb know

obav|iti (1) *v* (što) do, get sth done; carry out, perform, execute; finish ~**ljati** *v impf*

obav|iti (2) *v* (što) wind/coil round, wrap in; envelop/shroud in ~**jati** *v impf*

obavještajac *nm* (Gsg ~jca, Npl ~jci) intelligence agent/officer ~**jna** *adj* **služba** intelligence (service) ~**vati** *v impf* → **obavijestiti**

obaz|irati *v* (se) **1** (na koga/što) pay attention to, take notice of **2** (za kim/čim) look back/round ~**irati se na** disregard, ignore ~**riv** *adj* **1** considerate **2** cautious, circumspect

obdukcija *nf* autopsy, post-mortem (examination)

obeća|nje *nn* promise **održati/ispuniti** ~**nje** keep/fulfil one's p. **dati** ~**nje** make a p. ~**ti** *v* (komu što) promise ~**vati** *v* **1** (komu što) *impf* **2** (0) show great promise ~**vati brda i doline** promise the moon/the earth

obescijeniti *v* (što) depreciate

obeshrabriti *v* **1** (koga) discourage, dishearten **2** (se) lose heart

obespraviti *v* (koga) deprive sb of their rights

obeščastiti *v* (koga) **1** dishonour, disgrace **2** rape, violate

obeštetiti *v* (koga) compensate, indemnify, recompense, reimburse

obezobraziti *v* (se) become impudent/impertinent/cheeky

obič|aj *nm* custom; convention; practice; habit; way ~**aj je da** it is customary/usual to ~**ajno** *adv* common law ~**an** *adj* (α) common, usual; ordinary, normal; commonplace ~**avati** *v* be in the habit of doing sth ~**avao sam ići** I used to go ~**no** *adv* usually, generally **kao i** ~**no** as usual

obi|ći *v* (koga/što) (*pres* ~đem) **1** visit **2** inspect; tour

obijes|t *nf* wantonness ~**tan** *adj* (~na *f*) wanton; prankish

obi|lan *adj* (α) abundant; ample, rich ~**lje** *nn* abundance, plenty, profusion ~**lovati** *v* (čime) (*pres* ~lujem) abound in

obila|zak *nm* (Npl ~sci) tour; rounds *pl*; inspection ~**ziti** *v impf* → **obići** ~**znica** *nf* ring road *GB*; beltway *US*

obilježiti *v* (koga/što) **1** mark; characterize 2 celebrate **~je** *nn* characteristic, feature, mark, trait **~avati** *v impf*

obistiniti *v* (se) come/prove true, be realized

obitelj *nf* family **~ski** *adj* family

obi|ti *v* (što) (*pres* **~jem**) break into; burgle, burglarize; force (open); rob **~ti bravu** force/pick a lock

obja|sniti *v* (komu što) explain, clarify; comment **~šnjenje** *nn* explanation **~šnjiv** *adj* explicable **~šnjavati** *v impf*

objav|a *nf* 1 proclamation; promulgation 2 announcement; notice **~iti** *v* (što) 1 annouce, make known 2 proclaim, promulgate 3 issue, release, make public 4 (knjigu) publish; (vijest) broadcast; (rat) declare **~ljivati** *v impf*

oblje *num* (*G* **~iju**, *D/L/I* **~jema**) both (of them/the women) (¶ za dvije osobe/stvari ženskoga roda)

objed *nm* lunch, luncheon, dinner; meal

objeda *nf* false accusation; imputation; slander

objekt *nm* 1 object; thing 2 building, structure; facility; installation **~ivan** *adj* (*a*) objective, impartial, unbiased **~ivnost** *nf* objectivity, impartiality

objektiv *nm* lens

objelodaniti *v* (što) publish; make public/known; disclose; reveal

objeručke *adv fig* eagerly; with open arms

objesiti *v* 1 (što) hang (up), put up, suspend; dangle 2 (koga) hang 3 (se) hang oneself 4 (se) (odjeća) droop, sag **~ nos** *fig* sulk

obla|čan *adj* (*a*) cloudy, overcast **~čiti** (1) *v* (se) get cloudy **on vedri i ~či** *fig* he calls the shots *coll* **~k** *nm* (*Npl* **~ci**) cloud **prolom ~ka** downpour **nebu pod ~ke** sky-high, high into the sky

oblačiti (2) *v* 1 (koga) dress 2 (se) dress, get dressed

oblast *nf* 1 region 2 field, sphere

obli|k *nm* (*Npl* **~ci**) form, shape **~kovati** *v* (*pres* **~kujem**) 1 (koga/ što) form, shape, mould, fashion; design

2 (se) take form/shape

oblin|a *nf* roundness **ženske ~e** curves *pl*, figure

obli|ti *v* (*pres* **~jem**) **~o ga je hladan znoj** he broke out in a cold sweat **~ven** *adj* (čime) drenched/dripping with sth

obli|zati *v* (*pres* **~žem**) 1 (što) lick (up), lick sth clean 2 (se) lick/smack one's lips

obližnji *adj* nearby, neighbouring, adjacent

oblo|g *nm* (*Npl* **~zi**) compress **~žiti** *v* (što) cover, coat, line, panel

oblu|tak *nm* (*Gsg* **~tka**, *Npl* **~ci**) pebble

obljetnica *nf* anniversary

obljuba *nf* sexual intercourse

obma|na *nf* delusion; deception; fraud; hoax **~nuti** *v* (*pres* **~nem**) (koga) delude, deceive, beguile **~njivati** *v impf*

obnašati *v* (što) **~ dužnost** hold an office, discharge a duty

obnažiti *v* (što) bare, expose

obn|ova *nf* 1 renewal; renovation, restoration 2 reconstruction 3 resumption 4 revival, rebirth **~ova sudskog postupka** retrial, reopening of a case **~oviti** *v* (što) 1 renew, restore, renovate 2 rebuild, reconstruct 3 re-establish, reintroduce 4 resume 5 refresh; refurbish; revive **~avljati** *v impf*

obod *nm* brim

obogatiti *v* 1 (koga/što) enrich, make rich 2 (se) become/get rich

oboje *num* (*Gsg* **~ga/~jega**, *Dsg* **~ma/~me/~jem**, *Npl* **~ji**, *Gpl* **~jih**, *Dpl* **~jima**) both (of them) (¶ za osobe/stvari od kojih je jedna muškoga, a druga ženskoga roda)

obojen *adj* coloured **~eni metali** nonferrous metals **~iti** *v* (koga/što) colour, paint; dye; stain

obojica *num* both (of them/the men) (¶ za dvije muške osobe)

obo|ljeti *v* (0/od čega) (*pres* **~lim**) fall/get ill/sick, be taken ill

obor *nm* pen, enclosure; (za konje) paddock; (za ovce) fold

oborine *nf pl* precipitation; rainfall

oboriti v 1 (koga/što) knock/pull/run down, topple; (vladu) overthrow; (avion) shoot/bring down, down; (tvrdnju) refute; (stablo) cut down, fell; (rekord) break ~ **pogled** drop/lower one's eyes ~ **s nogu a.** (bolest) strike down **b.** fig floor, knock out 2 (se na) attack, swoop down on

oboružati v 1 (koga/što) arm, supply/provide with arms 2 (se) arm oneself

obostran adj mutual, reciprocal; joint; bilateral

obožava|telj nm admirer; fan ~**ti** v (koga/što) adore, admire; worship, idolize

obračun nm 1 statement (of accounts) 2 settlement, settling of accounts 3 showdown; fight; shoot-out ~**ati** v 1 (što) settle (up), settle/square accounts 2 (se) settle accounts, get even

obraćeni|k nm (Npl ~ci) convert, proselyte

obrad|a nf 1 (podataka) processing; editing; analysis; treatment 2 (industrijska) processing 3 (zemlje) cultivation, tillage ~**iti** v (što) 1 analyze; deal with 2 elaborate 3 process; treat 4 (zemlju) cultivate, till 5 (koga) fig work on ~**iv** adj arable

obrad|ovati v (pres ~ujem) 1 (koga) make happy 2 (se) rejoice

obra|mbeni adj 1 defensive; defence 2 protective ~**na** nf 1 defence (+ leg, sport) 2 protection **nužna** ~**na** self-defence ~**niti** v (koga/što) 1 (manage to) defend 2 protect; shield 3 (gol) save 4 (se) defend oneself

obrast|i v (čime) (pres ~em) overgrow; be overgrown/covered with

obrat nm 1 turn; turn of events; turning point 2 reversal; turnabout; change, shift ~**an** adj (ä) 1 reverse, converse, inverse 2 contrary, opposite

ob|rati v (što) (pres ~erem) 1 (voće) pick, finish picking 2 (mlijeko) skim

obrat|iti v 1 (koga) convert; win over, bring around, sway 2 (se) be converted 3 (se kome) turn to; consult, con-

tact, see, address ~**iti pozornost** pay attention to ~**nica** nf tropic ~**no** adv 1 conversely, reversely, in reverse (order) 2 on the contrary 3 the other way round; vice versa

obraz nm 1 cheek; face 2 fig honour, reputation **imati** ~**a reći** have the cheek to say **nemati** ~**a** be shameless/impudent/cheeky

obra|zac nm (Gsg ~sca, Npl ~sci) 1 form; blank 2 pattern; model; formula

obrazina nf mask

obrazl|oženje nn explanation; justification ~**ožiti** v (što) explain; justify ~**agati** v impf

obraz|ovan adj educated; trained ~**ovanje** nn education; schooling; training **osnovno** ~**ovanje** primary/elementary e. **srednje(školsko)** ~**ovanje** secondary(-school) e. **visoko(školsko)** ~**ovanje** university e. **više** ~**anje** two-year college-level e. ~**ovanje uz rad** on-the-job/in-service training ~**ovati** v (pres ~ujem) 1 (koga) educate; train 2 (što) form, set up 3 (se) get/receive an/one's education ~**ni** adj educational; teaching

obred nm rite ~**ni** adj ritual

obre|zati v (pres ~žem) 1 (što) clip, cut, trim 2 (koga) circumcise

obrij|ati v (pres ~em) 1 (koga/što) shave; shave off 2 (se) shave, have/get a shave

obris nm outline, contour

obri|sati v (koga/što) (pres ~šem) 1 wipe (off/clean), dry, mop (up) 2 erase, rub out 3 (prašinu) dust 4 (se) come/rub off

obrn|ut adj 1 → **obratan** 2 upside down; bottom up; inside out ~**uti** v (pres ~em) 1 (što) turn, reverse; invert 2 (se) turn around; change ~**uto** adv **razmjeran** in inverse proportion/relation to

obro|k nm (Npl ~ci) 1 meal 2 instalment

obron|ak nm (Gsg ~ka, Npl ~ci) slope

obr|t nm 1 craft, handicraft(s), trade; small business 2 (kapitala) turnover; (novca) circulation **otvoriti** ~**t** open a business, start one's own business

~taj nm turn, revolution **~tati** v (što) (pres **~ćem**) 1 turn, revolve, rotate 2 (sredstva) turn over **~tna** adj **sredstva** working capital **~tnik** nm (Vsg ~niče, Npl ~tnici) artisan, craftsman; tradesman; small business owner

obrub nm hem; rim; edge **~iti** v (što) hem; trim

obruč nm 1 hoop, ring 2 mil circle, encirclement

obrušiti v (se) dive; swoop down on

obrva nf (eye)brow

obučiti v (koga) train, instruct, teach, coach

obu|ća nf footwear; shoes **~ći** v (pres ~čem) 1 (što) put on 2 (koga) dress, clothe 3 (se) get dressed, put one's clothes on

obuhvat|iti v 1 (što) include, encompass, comprise, cover 2 (koga) embrace, put one's arms around **~ćati** v impf

obuj|am nm (Gsg ~ma) volume; capacity; circumference **~miti** v (koga/što) embrace, enfold, encircle, clasp

obu|ka nf (Dsg ~ci) training, instruction; classes **strojeva ~ka** mil drill

obustav|a nf 1 cessation; suspension; discontinuance 2 (novca) deduction **~a rada** strike, industrial action **~a vatre** cease-fire **~iti** v (što) halt, stop, discontinue, suspend, cut off **~ljati** v impf

obu|ti v (koga/što/se) (pres ~jem) put/pull on (one's) shoes **~vati** v impf

obuzdati v 1 (koga/što) curb, check, restrain 2 (se) refrain from; keep one's temper

obuz|eti v (koga/što) (pres ~mem) overcome, seize, grip, take hold of

obve|za nf 1 obligation, duty 2 commitment 3 responsibility; liability **vojna ~za** military service **~zan, ~zatan** adj (a) 1 (koji se mora učiniti) obligatory, compulsory; binding; required 2 (koji mora što učiniti) obliged, bound **~zatno** adv **ga kupi** make sure that you buy it **~zati** v (pres ~žem) 1 (koga) oblige, put/place under an obligation, bind 2

(se) commit oneself, make a commitment/pledge **~znica** nf obligation, bond, debenture **državne ~znice** government **porezni ~znik** nm (Npl ~znici) taxpayer **vojni ~znik** nm conscript; draftee US **~zivati** v impf

obzir nm regard, consideration; respect **bez ~a na** without regard to/for, regardless/irrespective of s **~om na** with/in regard to, in respect of, in view of, regarding, concerning **uzeti u ~** take into consideration/account, consider, make allowance(s) for **~an** adj (a) considerate; tactful; careful

obznaniti v (što) proclaim, announce, make known/public

obzor nm horizon

ocariniti v (što) charge customs duty on

oc|at nm (Gsg ~ta) vinegar

ocean nm ocean

oc|ijeniti v (koga/što) 1 evaluate, estimate, assess; appraise; rate 2 (učenika) mark GB; grade US 3 review **~jena** nf 1 evaluation, estimate, assessment; appraisal; rating; (sud) judg(e)ment 2 (školska) mark GB; grade US 3 review

ocrniti v (koga/što) blacken, vilify

ocrta|ti v (koga/što) outline, delineate; sketch, portray **~vati** v (se) impf be outlined against, loom, stand out against

oča|j nm despair, desperation, dismay **~an** adj (a) 1 desperate, despondent; wretched 2 coll awful, dreadul **~avati** v (0) despair, give up (hope) **~nički** adj desperate **~nik** nm (Npl ~nici) desperate/wretched man/person

oča|ti v (koga/što) charm, fascinate **~vajući** adj charming, fascinating

oček|ivanje nn expectation, anticipation **iznad ~ivanja** beyond expectation **~ivati** v (koga/što) (pres ~ujem) expect, anticipate; await, wait for

Očenaš nm the Lord's Prayer, Our Father

očerupati v 1 (što) pluck 2 (koga) sl fleece

očev adj father's; paternal

očevi|d nm (on-the-spot) investigation **~dac** nm (Gsg ~ca) eyewitness **~dan** adj (a) (self-)evident, obvious, manifest

oči nf pl (→ **oko**) eyes **~ u ~** face to face **bježi/gubi mi se s ~ju** get out of my sight **gledati drugim ~ma** see sth differently **gutati/proždirati ~ma** ogle sb **pogledati činjenicama u ~** face (the) facts **upadati u ~** stand out **zamazati kome ~** throw dust in sb's eyes **~ca** nf 1 (na čarapi) ladder GB; run US 2 (pletenje) stitch **~gledan** adj (a) obvious, evident, clear, manifest **~jukati** v (0) (s kim) flirt

očins|ki adj fatherly; paternal **~tvo** nn fatherhood, paternity

očistiti v (što) clean (up), cleanse; clear; purify; purge

očit adj obvious, (self-)evident; clear, plain, patent, manifest

očita|ti v (što) read (off) **~ti kome bukvicu** give/read sb a lecture/lesson

očit|ovati v (se) (pres ~ujem) 1 manifest itself, be evident, show 2 (o čemu) take a stand on sth

oč|ni adj eye; ocular, ophthalmic med **~ni kapak** eyelid **~ni liječnik** oculist, ophthalmologist **~ni živac** optic nerve **~na jabučica** eyeball **~na šupljina** eye socket, orbit **~njak** nm (Npl ~njaci) eyetooth, canine tooth; fang

oču|h nm (Npl ~si) stepfather

očuvati v 1 (što) preserve; sustain; save, keep safe 2 (se) be preserved, survive

očvrsn|uti v (0) (pres ~em) grow strong/sturdy

oćelav|jeti v (0) (pres ~im) grow bald, lose one's hair

od prep 1 of 2 from 3 (vremenski) since 4 (komparativ) than 5 (pasiv) by ~ ... **do** from ... to (+ vremenski from ... until/till) ~ **jučer** since yesterday ~ **sada** from now on ~ **sutra** from/as of tomorrow **jedan ~ deset** one in ten, one out of ten ~ **straha** out of/from fear **drhtati ~ straha** tremble with fear **zaštititi ~ napada**

protect against attack **sok ~ naranče** orange juice

od- (oda-; ot-) prefix 1 **od-letjeti** fly off/away **od-sjeći** cut off 2 **od-zdraviti** return the greeting 3 svršena radnja **od-svirati** play, finish playing

oda nf ode

odab|ir nm selection **~rati** v (koga/što) (pres ~erem) choose, select, pick out **~ran** adj chosen, selected **~irati** v impf

odagnati v (što) drive away, dispel

odahn|uti v (0) (pres ~em) be/feel relieved, heave a sigh of relief

odakle adv from where ~ **si?** where are you from? ~ **znaš?** how do you know?

odalamiti v (koga) whack coll; clobber sl

odan adj (komu/čemu) devoted, dedicated; faithful; loyal **~ost** nf devotion, dedication; loyalty

odande adv from there, from that place/direction

odap|eti v (pres ~nem) 1 (što) shoot, fire 2 (0) sl kick the bucket **~injati** v impf

od|ar nm (Gsg ~ra) bier **ležati na svečanom ~ru** lie in state

oda|slati v (što) (pres ~šaljem) 1 send, dispatch 2 send off; send out; transmit **~šiljač** nm (radio) transmitter **~šiljati** v impf

odati v 1 (koga/što) betray; inform against/on sb; disclose, divulge, reveal; show ~ **počast** pay/do homage to 2 (se) betray oneself, give oneself away ~ **se piću** take to drink

odatle adv 1 from there, from that place/direction, thence 2 hence; therefore

odavde adv from here, from this place

odavno adv for a long time, long ago, a long time ago

odaz|iv nm response **slab/velik ~iv birača** a light/heavy poll/turnout **~vati** v (se) (pres ~ovem) 1 (kome) answer; call back 2 (na što) respond to; accept (an invitation) **~ivati** v (se) impf

odbaci|ti v (što) 1 (stvar) throw away/off; discard 2 (tvrdnju) deny, dismiss, reject, renounce **3** (napad) repel, repulse **4** (koga) *coll* give sb a lift/ride, drop sb off

odbi|ti *v* (koga/što) (*pres* ~jem) **1** refuse, reject, rebuff, decline, turn down **2** (oduzeti) subtract **3** deduct **4** (napad) repel, repulse **5** (udarac) parry, ward off **6** (od sise) wean **7** (se) bounce off **~tak** *nm* (*Gsg* ~tka, *Npl* ~ci) deduction **~jati** *v impf*

odbljes|ak *nm* (*Gsg* ~ka, *Npl* ~ci) reflection, flash

odbojan *adj* (*a*) repulsive **~nik** *nm* (*Npl* ~nici) bumper

odbojka *nf* (*Dsg* ~ci) volleyball

odbor *nm* committee; board; council **biti u ~u** be/serve on a committee **nadzorni ~** supervisory/watchdog committee **upravni ~** management committee; board of directors

odbroj|iti *v* (što) count; count down **dani su mu ~eni** his days are numbered

odbrusiti *v* (0) (kome) *coll* retort, snap back at sb

odcijepiti *v* (se) break away, secede **~jepljenje** *nn* secession

oder|ati *v* (koga/što) (*pres* ~em) **1** flay, skin; tear off **2** *coll* fleece, rip off, rook

odfurati *v* (koga/što) *sl* whisk (away/off)

odgađati *v impf* → **odgoditi**

odgod|a *nf* postponement, delay; deferment **~iti** *v* (što) postpone, put off, delay; defer

odgoj|iti *v* (koga/što) bring up; breed; cultivate; raise, rear **~oj** *nm* **1** upbringing, education **2** (uljudnost) (good) manners; breeding **tjelesni ~oj** physical education/training; gym *coll* (**dobro**) **~ojen** *adj* well-bred, well-mannered **~ajati** *v impf*

odgone|tka *nf* (*Dsg* ~ci/~tki) solution, answer (to a riddle) **~tnuti** *v* (što) (*pres* ~tnem) solve (a riddle), decipher; figure/puzzle out

odgov|arati *v impf* **1** (komu/čemu/za što) correspond/answer to; be adequate, be right for; fit; suit; match **~arati potrebama** meet the needs **2** (za koga/što) be responsible/account-able for, answer for **3** (komu) (drsko) answer sb back **~or** *nm* answer, reply, response **~oran** *adj* (*a*) responsible, accountable, answerable **~oriti** *v* **1** (0/komu) answer, reply, respond **2** (koga od čega) dissuade from, talk sb out of **~ornost** *nf* responsibility, accountability; liability **na vlastitu ~ornost** at one's own risk, at one's peril **pozvati na ~ornost** bring/call to account **preuzeti ~ornost** *a.* assume/take responsibility **b.** (za napad) claim responsibility for

odgri|sti *v* (što) (*pres* ~zem) bite off

odgurn|uti *v* (koga/što) (*pres* ~em) push/shove away, give a push

odigrati *v* **1** (što) play, finish playing **2** (se) take place, occur, happen

odijeliti *v* (koga/što/se) separate; partition; segregate

odije|lo *nm* clothes, dress; (muško) suit **~vati** *v* **1** (koga) dress, clothe **2** (se) dress, put on one's clothes

odio → **odjel**

odista *adv* really, indeed, in fact

odjav|iti *v* **1** (što) cancel **2** (program) sign off **3** (se) check out (of a hotel) **~ljivati** *v impf*

odjeb|ati *v* (*pres* ~em) *tab* ~i! fuck off! piss off! sod off!

odjeća *nf* clothes, clothing; garment(s) **muška ~** men's wear **ženska ~** women's/ladies' wear

odjedanput, **odjednom** *adv* **1** at a time, at one go **2** suddenly, all of a sudden

odje|k *nm* (*Npl* ~ci) **1** echo, reverberation **2** *fig* response **~knuti** *v* (0) (*pres* ~knem) **1** echo, reverberate; ring with **2** *fig* resound, have repercussions **~knuo je hitac** a shot rang out **~kivati** *v impf*

odje|l *nm* **1** department, division, section **2** (bolnički) ward, department **~ljak** *nm* (*Gpl* ~ljka, *Npl* ~ljci) **1** (u vlaku) compartment **2** (u tekstu) passage **3** pigeonhole **~ljenje** *nn* *mil* squad, section

odje|nuti *v* (*pres* ~nem) **1** (koga) clothe, dress; attire **2** (se) put on one's clothes, dress **~ven** *adj* dressed **~vni** *adj* **predmet** an article of clothing

odjuriti v (0) run/rush/speed/dash away/off

odla|ganje nn 1 postponement, delay 2 (otpada) (waste) disposal **~gati** v (što) (pres ~žem) 1 postpone, put off, delay 2 lay/put aside; lay/put down; take off; dispose

odlanuti v (komu) be/feel relieved, feel relief

odla|zak nm (Gsg ~ska, Npl ~sci) departure, leaving **~ziti** v (0) be leaving, be going away, be about to depart

odletjeti v (0) (pres ~im) 1 fly away/off; take wing 2 (avionom) fly (to) **~jeti u zrak** blow up

odlič|an adj (a) 1 excellent; exquisite 2 (ocjena) A; top mark GB grade US **~je** nn medal, decoration, order **~nik** nm (Npl ~nici) distinguished/prominent person/figure

odlijepiti v 1 (što) unglue, unstick, take/get off 2 (se) come off, come unstuck 3 (se) fig tear oneself away

odli|ka nf (Dsg ~ci) distinction, distinctive feature/trait; characteristic **~kaš** nm top/A student **~kovanje** nn medal, decoration, order, award **~kovati** v (pres ~kujem) 1 (koga/što) award, decorate 2 (se) be characterized/distinguished/marked by; stand out, excel

odlom|ak nm (Gsg ~ka, Npl ~ci) 1 fragment, bit, piece 2 (teksta) passage; paragraph; section

odložiti v pf → **odlagati**

odlu|čan adj (a) 1 determined, resolute; firm 2 (čas) decisive, critical **~čiti** v 1 (što) decide; determine; resolve; decree 2 (se) decide; make up one's mind **~čivanje** nn decision-making **~čnost** nf determination, resolution **~čujući** adj decisive, crucial **~ka** nf (Dsg ~ci) decision donijeti **~ku** make/take/reach a decision **~čivati** v impf

odlutati v (0) wander (off), stray

odljev nm 1 drain 2 (novca) outflow, outgo 3 (kovine) casting

odma|gati v (komu/čemu) (pres ~žem) hinder

odmagliti v (0) coll run away; make off

odmah adv immediately, instantly, at once, right away **~ do** right next to, close to

odmahn|uti v (0) (pres ~em) 1 (kome) wave back (to sb) 2 (čime) **~uti glavom** shake one's head 3 fig wave sth aside, shrug sth off

odmakn|uti v (pres ~em) 1 (što) move away 2 (kome) leave sb behind 3 (0) be well under way 4 (se) move away, move/get/stand back

odmaralište nn holiday GB vacation US seaside/tourist resort

odmazd|a nf retaliation, reprisal

odmetn|ik nm (Vsg ~iče, Npl ~ici) outlaw; renegade; rebel **~uti** v (se) (pres ~em) become an outlaw

odmicati v impf (→ **odmaknuti**)

odmjer|iti v 1 (koga/što) measure (off/out); determine/judge the length of 2 (komu što) allot **~iti pogledom** give sth/sb the once-over coll **~iti koga od glave do pete** look sb up and down **~en** adj level-headed **~avati** v impf

odmoći v pf → **odmagati** (komu) do sb a disservice

odmor nm 1 rest; repose 2 break; recess 3 holiday(s) GB; vacation US **na mjestu ~** mil at ease **~an, ~en** adj (a) rested, refreshed, fresh **~ište** nn 1 resting place; rest area 2 (na stubištu) landing **~iti** v (se) rest; take a rest/break

odmota|ti v 1 (što) unwrap, unfold; unwind; unfurl; untwist 2 (se) become unwrapped/undone; unwind, uncoil **~vati** v impf

odmrzn|uti v (što/se) (pres ~em) melt, thaw (out); defrost

odnedavno adv lately, of late, recently

odnekle, odnekud(a) adv from somewhere, from some place/direction

odn|ijeti v (koga/što) (pres ~esem) take (away), carry (off) **~ijeti pobjedu win**

odnos nm 1 relation; relationship 2 connection, reference 3 proportion; ratio **u ~u na** in relation/regard/reference to **biti u dobrim ~ima** be on good terms with **u radnom ~u** employed **spolni ~** sexual intercourse **~iti** *v* 1 (što) *impf* → **odnijeti** 2 (se na koga/što) refer to, relate to, concern; apply to; affect 3 (se prema komu/čemu) treat **~iti se neprijateljski** be hostile **~no** *adv* 1 respectively *Ivan i Petar imaju 25 ~no 30 godina* I. and P. are 25 and 30 respectively 2 *coll* or, in other words, that is; or rather

odobr|avanje *nn* 1 approval, approbation, endorsement 2 acclamation, applause, cheering **~iti** *v* (što) 1 approve, authorize, endorse, sanction; okay *coll* 2 grant 3 ratify 4 cheer **~enje** *nn* 1 approval, endorsement 2 clearance, permission, permit; okay, go-ahead *coll* **~avati** *v impf*

odobrovoljiti *v* 1 (koga) cheer sb up 2 (se) get into a good mood

odoj|ak *nm* (*Gsg* ~ka, *Npl* ~ci) sucking pig

odoka *adv* approximately, roughly

odo|ljeti *v* (kome/čemu) (*pres* ~lim) resist, withstand **~lijevati** *v impf*

odonda *adv* ever since, since then, from that time

odonud(a) *adv* from there, from that place/direction

odora *nf* 1 garb, robe(s) 2 *mil* uniform

odostrag(a) *adv* 1 from the back, from behind 2 at the back

odovud(a) *adv* from here, from this place/direction

odozdo *adv* from below, from beneath, from the bottom

odozgo *adv* from above, from the top

odras|tao *adj* (~la *f*) grown-up, adult **~ti** *v* (0) (*pres* ~tem) grow up

odra|z *nm* 1 reflection 2 repercussion, backlash 3 *sport* takeoff **~ziti** *v* 1 (što) reflect, mirror 2 (se) reflect, be reflected, affect; take off *sport* **~žavati** *v impf*

odre|ći *v* (se) (*pres* ~čem/~knem) 1 (čega) renounce; abandon 2 (koga) disown; give up **~ći se prijestolja** abdicate

odred *nm* detachment, unit, squad

odreda *adv* without exception, uniformly

odred|ba *nf* (*Gpl* ~aba/~bi) 1 provision, term 2 decree, regulation

odredište *nn* destination

odre|diti *v* 1 (što) determine, fix, set 2 (što) decree; decide; stipulate 3 (lijek) prescribe 4 (koga) designate, appoint 5 (što za što) appropriate, earmark 6 (se) take a stand **~đen** *adj* 1 definite, specific, particular 2 explicit, unambiguous **~đivati** *v impf*

odre|zak *nm* (*Gsg* ~ska, *Npl* ~sci) 1 (iz novina) cutting, clipping 2 (meso) chop, cutlet, steak 3 (ček) coupon; stub **~zati** *v* (što) (*pres* ~žem) 1 cut off; chop/hack/slice off; sever 2 amputate

odri|canje *nn* 1 (self-)sacrifice, self-denial 2 renunciation **~cati** *v* (se) (*pres* ~čem) *impf* → **odreći se**

odrije|šiti *v* (što) untie, undo, unfasten **~iti od grijeha** absolve from sins **dati ~ene ruke** give sb a free hand **~iti kesu** loosen the purse strings

odrješit *adj* energetic, resolute

odron *nm* landslide

odrpan *adj* ragged, tattered

odrubiti *v* (što) cut off **~ glavu** behead/decapitate sb

održa|va(nje *nn* 1 maintenance, upkeep 2 survival **~ati** *v* 1 (koga/ što) keep, hold; maintain; preserve **~ati obećanje** keep a promise **~ati predavanje** give/deliver a lecture 2 (se) hold out, survive 3 (se) (događaj) be held, take place **~iv** *adj* viable; (tvrdnja) tenable

odsad(a) *adv* from now on, henceforth

odseliti *v* (se) move (away), move house, change one's address

odsjaj *nm* reflection; flash

odsječ|ak *nm* (*Gsg* ~ka, *Npl* ~ci) segment; section

ods|jeći *v* (koga/što) (*pres* ~iječem) 1 cut off, sever 2 amputate 3 say curtly **noge su mi se ~jekle** I was petrified/transfixed

odsjediti *v* (0) 1 sit through 2 *coll* do/serve time (in prison)

odsje|k *nm* (*Npl* ~ci) section; department, division; part

odsje|sti *v* (0) (*pres* ~dnem) stay (at a hotel)

odsk|akati *v impf* (*pres* ~ačem) stand out ~**očiti** *v* (0) **1** leap, jump **2** rebound, bounce back/off **3** recoil, spring back ~**očna** *adj* daska springboard (+*fig*) ~**ok** *nm* (*Npl* ~oci) **1** rebound **2** *sport* takeoff ~**akivati** *v impf*

odslušati *v* (koga/što) hear out ~ **predmet** complete a course

odslužiti *v* (što) serve out; serve one's term ~ **vojsku** complete one's military service

odspavati *v* (0) take a nap

odstraniti *v* (koga/što) remove, eliminate

odstrel *nm* cull

odstup|anje *nn* **1** departure **2** deviation **3** *mil* retreat, withdrawal **4** (ostavka) resignation **5** (zemlje) cession ~**iti** *v* (0) **1** depart **2** deviate **3** retreat, withdraw **4** resign, step down **5** cede; give up, surrender **ne ~iti ni za pedalj** not budge an inch ~**nica** *nf mil* retreat

odsudan *adj* (ā) crucial, decisive

odsut|nost *nf* absence ~**an** *adj* (ā) absent ~**an duhom** absent-minded

odsvirati *v* (što) play

odšetati *v* (0) walk away

odškrin|uti *v* (što) (*pres* ~em) open slightly, open sth a crack **ostaviti vrata ~uta** leave the door ajar

odštet|a *nf* damages *pl*, indemnity, compensation; (ratna) reparations *pl* ~**ni** *adj* **zahtjev** indemnity/compensation claim

odudarati *v* (0) stand out; clash/jar withr

odugovlačiti *v* (što/s čim) delay, stall

oduljiti *v* **1** (što) drag/draw out, prolong **2** (se) drag on, drag/draw out

odum|rijeti *v* (0) (*pres* ~rem) **1** die away/off/out **2** (vrsta) become extinct **3** atrophy ~**irati** *v impf*

odup|rijeti *v* (se) (*pres* ~rem) **1** (čemu) resist, oppose, stand up to **2** (o što) push against ~**irati** *v* (se) *impf*

oduran *adj* (ā) disgusting

odusta|ti *v* (od čega) (*pres* ~nem) give up; abandon

oduš|ak *nm* (*Gsg* ~ka, *Npl* ~ci) outlet, vent, relief **dati ~ka** give vent to

oduševljiti *v* **1** (koga) excite, thrill **2** (se) be thrilled ~**ljen** *adj* enthusiastic, thrilled ~**ljenje** *n* enthusiasm; elation, delight ~**ljavati** *v impf*

oduvijek *adv* from/since time immemorial, from time out of mind

oduz|eti *v* (*pres* ~mem) **1** (što komu) deprive of, strip of; withdraw **2** (što komu) take away, remove, seize **3** (što od čega) deduct; subtract **4** (se) be/become paralysed/numb ~**imanje** *nn* subtraction; deduction ~**imati** *v impf*

odužiti *v* (se) (komu) repay, reimburse, pay back; give in return (+*fig*)

odva|gati *v* (koga/što) (*pres* ~žem) **1** weigh out **2** *fig* weigh (up)

odvajati *v impf* → **odvojiti**

odvaliti *v* **1** (što) break/push off ~ **pljusku** slap sb's face ~ **posao** *coll* be through, knock off **2** (se) come/break/fall off

odvaž|an *adj* (ā) bold, daring ~**iti** *v* (se) dare, venture ~**nost** *nf* boldness, daring; nerve, spunk

odve|sti (1) *v* (koga/što) (*pres* ~dem) take (away); lead

odve|sti (2) *v* (*pres* ~zem) **1** (koga/što) drive away/to, give a ride/lift; transport; remove, move **2** (se) drive away/off, ride off

odve|zati *v* (koga/što) (*pres* ~žem) untie, undo, unbind, unfasten

odvij|ač *nm* screwdriver ~**jati** *v* **1** (što) *impf* → **odviti 2** (se) take place; develop, proceed, be in progress ~**ti** *v* (što/se) (*pres* ~jem) **1** unwind; unfold; unfurl **2** unscrew

odvikn|uti *v* (*pres* ~em) **1** (koga od čega) break sb's habit **2** (se) break a/one's habit; kick a habit *sl*

odvjetni|čki *adj* lawyer's ~**čka komora** the Bar Association ~**čki ispit** bar examination ~**k** *nm* (*Vsg* ~če, *Npl* ~ci) lawyer; barrister, solicitor *GB*; attorney *US*; counsel

odvlačiti *v* (koga/što) drag/draw/haul away ~ **pozornost** divert sb's attention, distract

odvod *nm* **1** drain **2** conduit ~**iti** *v impf*

→ **odvesti** ~**ni** *adj* drain(ing), drainage

odvoj|ak *nm* (*Gsg* ~ka, *Npl* ~ci) branch road; (pruga) branch line ~**en** *adj* 1 separate(d); disconnected 2 isolated ~**iti** *v* 1 (koga/što od koga/čega) separate, detach; disconnect, dissociate 2 (sredstva) allocate, earmark 3 (se) separate; break away, secede 4 (se) come off, become loose 5 (se) branch off

odvoziti *v impf* → **odvesti** (2)

odvrat|iti *v* 1 (0) answer 2 (koga od čega) dissuade 3 (što) divert; ward off ~**iti pogled** avert one's eyes ~**an** *adj* (α) disgusting, repulsive, sickening ~**nost** *nf* disgust, repulsion

odvu|ći *v* (koga/što) (*pres* ~čem) drag/haul away; (vozilo) tow away

odzv|anjati *v impf* (0) reverberate ~**oniti** *v* (0) ring off ~**onilo mu je** he is finished, he is done for

ofenziva *nf* offensive

oficir → **časnik**

ofucan *adj* shabby

og|anj *nm* (*Gsg* ~nja) fire; flame

ogavan *adj* (α) disgusting, loathsome

oglad|njeti *v* (0) (*pres* ~nim) be/become hungry

ogla|s *nm* 1 advertisement; advert, ad *coll* 2 notice 3 announcement 4 bill, poster ~**siti** *v* 1 (što) advertise; announce; put up a notice 2 (se) utter a sound ~**sna** *adj* **ploča** notice board *GB*; bulletin board *US* **mali** ~**snik** *nm* (*Npl* ~snici) classified ads *pl* ~**šavati** *v impf*

ogled|alo *nm* mirror ~**an** *adj* (α) specimen ~**ni primjerak** sample, specimen copy ~**ati** *v* (se) 1 look around; turn around 2 (s kime) compete

oglu|ha *nf leg* default ~**šiti** *v* 1 (0) become deaf 2 (se na što) turn a deaf ear to; ignore 3 (se) *leg* default, fail to appear in court

ognjište *nn* 1 fireplace, hearth 2 *fig* home

ogoliti *v* (koga/što/se) lay bare (+ *fig*), denude

ogorč|en *adj* bitter, embittered; indignant ~**enje** *nn* bitterness; indignation, resentment ~**iti** *v* (koga) exas-

perate, gall

ogovara|nje *nn* gossip, backbiting ~**ti** *v* (koga) backbite; bad-mouth *US sl*

ograd|a *nf* 1 fence, railings *pl*; (stuba) banister(s) 2 enclosure 3 *fig* reservation ~**iti** *v* 1 (što) fence around/in/off, enclose, rail in/off 2 (se) dissociate/distance oneself from

ogran|ak *nm* (*Gsg* ~ka, *Npl* ~ci) 1 branch 2 (društva) (local) branch; lodge; chapter *US* (puta) side-road; (pruge) branch line ~**ičiti** *v* 1 (koga/što) limit, restrict; confine 2 (se) confine oneself ~**ičen** *adj fig* narrow(-minded) ~**ičenje** *nn* limitation, restriction ~**ičenje brzine** speed limit ~**ičavati** *v impf*

ogre|botina *nf* scratch ~**psti** *v* (*pres* ~bem) 1 (koga/što) scratch 2 (se) get scratched 3 (se za što) *sl* bum, cadge; wheedle

ogriješiti *v* (se) 1 commit a sin, transgress 2 (o koga/što) sin/offend against ~ **se** **o zakon** violate/break the law

ogrjev *nm* firewood; fuel

ogrlica *nf* 1 necklace 2 (pseća) collar

ogrn|uti *v* (se) (*pres* ~em) wrap oneself, slip/throw sth on

ogroman *adj* (α) *coll* huge, enormous, immense, vast

ogrozd *nm* gooseberry

ogrtač *nm* overcoat **kišni** ~ raincoat **kućni** ~ dressing gown, housecoat

ogrub|jeti *v* (0) (*pres* ~im) become rough/coarse

oguglati *v* (0) become dull(ed)/jaded/hardened/inured/indifferent

oguliti *v* 1 (što) (koru) peel (off) 2 (što) (kožu) flay, skin 3 (koga) *sl* fleece *coll*; rip off *sl* 4 (se/što) scrape

ohladiti *v* 1 (što) cool, chill 2 (se) go/grow cold 3 (se) *fig* cool down, chill out *sl*; calm down; grow indifferent

ohol *adj* haughty, proud

ohrabriti *v* (koga/što) encourage

ojačati *v* 1 (koga/što) strengthen, reinforce 2 (0) strengthen, grow strong(er)

okaljati *v* (što) 1 soil 2 *fig* blemish, smear, tarnish

okamina *nf* fossil

okarakterizirati *v* (koga/što) characterize; describe, portray

oki|dač *nm* **1** (na oružju) trigger **2** (na aparatu) release **~nuti** *v* (što) (*pres* ~nem) pull the trigger, fire **~dati** *v impf*

okititi *v* (koga/što) decorate

oklad|a *nf* bet, wager **dobiti ~u** win a bet **~iti** *v* (se) bet, wager

okleve|tati *v* (koga) (*pres* ~ćem) slander, calumniate; defame; (u tisku) libel

oklijeva|nje *nn* hesitation; reluctance; vacillation **~ti** *v* (0) hesitate

oklop *nm* **1** armour; (armour) plate **2** mail **3** (kornjače) shell **~ni** *adj* armoured **~njača** *nf* battleship

ok|no *nn* (*Gpl* ~ana/~na) **1** window; windowpane **2** (rudnik) shaft, pit

ok|o (1) *nn* (→ *pl* oči) **1** eye **2** (mreža) mesh **oštro ~o** keen/sharp sight **baciti ~o na** cast an eye on **biti kome trn u ~u** be a thorn in one's side **držati na ~u** keep an/one's eye on **ne sklopiti ~a not** sleep a wink **zapeti za ~o** catch sb's eye **golim ~om** with the naked/unaided eye **u četiri ~a** privately, in confidence

oko (2) *prep* around, round

oko (3) *adv* about, approximately ~ *40 ljudi* about/some 40 people

okoli|ca *nf* surroundings *pl*; environs *pl*; neighbourhood **~na** *nf* environment **~š** *nm* **1** landscape, scenery **2** environment

okolišati *v* (0) beat about the bush, be evasive

okolni *adj* surrounding; neighbouring; roundabout

okolnost *nf* circumstance; situation **olakotne ~i** extenuating/mitigating circumstances **otežavajuće/otegotne ~i** aggravating circumstances **stjecajem ~i** by coincidence

okolo *prep* around, round ~ **naokolo** round and round

okomi|ca *nf* vertical/perpendicular line **~t** *adj* **1** (na što) vertical, perpendicular (to sth) **2** sheer **~to** *adv* (u križaljkama) down

okomiti *v* (se) (na koga) attack, lash out at

okončati *v* (što) finish, terminate, end, bring to an end

okopa|ti *v* (što) hoe **~vati** *v impf*

okor|io *adj* (~jela *f*) hardened, incorrigible, inveterate

okoristiti *v* (se) (kime/čime) profit from/by; take advantage of

okosnica *nf* skeleton; framework; backbone

okotiti *v* (koga/se) have (young), give birth to

okov|i *nm pl* shackles **~ati** *v* (*pres* okujem) **1** (koga) chain; shackle **2** (što) reinforce with metal; stud

okre|nuti *v* (što/koga) (*pres* ~nem) **1** turn **2** (naglavce) turn upside down; (izvrnuti) turn inside out **3 biti ~nut prema** be directed at/towards, look towards, face **4** (tel. broj) dial **5** (se) turn around **~t** *nm* turn; turning **~taj** *nm* revolution **~tan** *adj* (*a*) nimble **~tati** *v* (što/koga/se) (*pres* ~ćem) turn (around), rotate, revolve, spin **~tište** *nm* terminus

okre|pa *nf* refreshment **~ijepiti** *v* **1** (koga) refresh, invigorate **2** (se) refresh oneself

okrilje *nn* shelter, protection **pod ~m** under the auspices/aegis of **pod ~m tame** under cover of darkness

okriv|iti *v* (koga) **1** blame, put the blame on **2** accuse, charge, indict **~ljenik** *nm* (*Npl* ~ljenici) the accused, defendant

okrnjiti *v* **1** (što) chip (off), notch **2** (ugled) damage, harm

okršaj *nm* skirmish (+ *fig*), exchange of fire, (short) engagement

okru|g *nm* (*Npl* ~zi) district **~gao** *adj* (~gla *f*) round; circular **~glica** *nf* dumpling

okruniti *v* (koga) crown

okrut|an *adj* (*a*) cruel, brutal, ruthless **~nost** *nf* cruelty, brutality

okruž|enje *nn* environment **u ~enju** under siege, surrounded **~iti** *v* **1** (koga/što) surround **2** (se) surround oneself with **~ni** *adj* district **~nica** *nf* circular (letter)

okrvavljen *adj* bloodstained

okrzn|uti v (koga/što) (*pres* ~em) graze; scratch

oku|ka nf (*Dsg* ~ci) bend, turn, curve

oku|lar nm eyepiece ~**ist** nm oculist, eye specialist

okup nm **na** ~**u** assembled, together, present **držati se na** ~**u** stick together

okup|acija nf occupation ~**acijski** adj occupation, occupying ~**ator** nm occupying force(s) ~**irati** v (koga/što) occupy

okupati v 1 (koga) give a bath to; bath *GB* 2 (se) have/take a bath; (na otvorenom) bathe; go for/have a swim

okup|iti v (koga/se) bring/come together, gather, rally, assemble ~**lja- lište** nn haunt; hangout sl ~**ljati** v impf

okus nm taste ~**iti** v (što) taste; have a taste of

okušati v (se) (u čemu) try one's hand at

okvir nm 1 frame 2 fig framework, scope, context 3 (za metke) clip **u** ~**u** under; as part of ~**ni** adj framework, general, broad

olako adv lightly

olak|otan adj (a) extenuating, mitigating ~**šanje** nn relief ~**šati** v (što) 1 alleviate; lighten; ease; relieve 2 facilitate, make easy/easier 3 (se) coll relieve oneself ~**šica** nf exemption, relief; benefit

oličenje nn personification; embodiment

olimpijada nf the Olympic Games

ološ nm scum

olov|ka nf (*Dsg* ~ci, *Gpl* ~aka/~ki) pencil **kemijska** ~**ka** ballpoint pen; Biro *TM*

olovo nn lead

oltar nm altar

oluja nf storm; tempest

olu|k nm (*Npl* ~ci) gutter, drainpipe

olupina nf wreck (+ fig)

omakn|uti v (se) (*pres* ~em) slip, lose one's footing

omalovažavati v (koga/što) belittle

omamiti v (koga) daze; (udarcem) stun; (pićem) intoxicate

omča nf noose

omediti v (što) limit, demarcate, mark off

omekš|ati v (što/koga/se) soften ~**ivač** nm softener

ome|sti v (koga/što) (*pres* ~tem) hinder, frustrate, thwart ~**tati** v impf (radiovalove) jam

omiljen adj favourite; popular

omjer nm 1 proportion, ratio 2 (zemljovid) scale

omladin|a nf youth, young people/generation ~**ski** adj youth

omlet nm omelet(te)

omogućiti v (što) 1 (učiniti mogućim) enable, make possible 2 (osigurati) ensure, provide

omot nm 1 wrapping; cover (knjige) dust jacket; (gram. ploče) sleeve 2 parcel ~**ati** v (što) wrap up, envelop ~**nica** nf envelope

omražen adj hateful

omršav|ljeti v (0) (*pres* ~im) lose weight, grow slim/thin

on pron he **to je** ~ that's him ~**a** pron she **to je ona** that's her

onaj (ona, ono) pron that, that one, the one

onak|av adj (a) such, that kind of ~**o** adv in that way/manner, like that **i**~**o** anyway

onda adv 1 then; at that time 2 after that **pa što** ~ so what ~**šnji** adj the then, of that time

ondje adv (over) there, in that place

onemoćati v (0) lose strength

onemogućiti v 1 (koga) thwart 2 (što) make/render impossible

onesposobiti v (koga/što) incapacitate, disable; put out of action

onesvijestiti v 1 (koga) knock out, knock sb senseless 2 (se) faint, lose consciousness

ono (1) pron it

ono (2) pron → **onaj**

onolik|i adj so big/large/tall, such a big ~**o** adv so much/many ~**o koliko** as much/many as

onuda adv that way, there

opadati v impf → **opasti**

opak adj wicked, evil

opaliti (1) v 1 (0) (osoba) fire; (oružje)

go off 2 (koga) punch, sock; (nogom) kick

opaliti (2) *v* (koga/što) burn, parch, singe; tan

opametiti *v* (se) come to one's senses; wise up *US coll*

opa|sač *nm* belt ~**sati** *v* (koga/što) (*pres* ~**šem**) 1 belt 2 *fig* enclose 3 (se) put a belt on

opas|an *adj* (*a*) dangerous, risky, hazardous ~**nost** *nf* danger, peril, hazard **u slučaju** ~**nosti** in an emergency **izložiti se** ~**nosti** take a risk

opas|ka *nf* (*Dsg* ~ci) remark, observation; comment

opa|sti *v* (0) (*pres* ~**dnem**) 1 fall (off) 2 decrease, drop; abate, subside

opat *nm* abbot ~**ica** *nf* 1 abbess 2 *coll* nun ~**ija** *nf* abbey

opaziti *v* (koga/što) notice

opć|enito *adv* generally, in general ~**i** *adj* general, common, broad; universal; public

općin|a *nf* 1 municipality, borough; district 2 local authorities/government 3 (zgrada) town hall ~**ski** *adj* municipal

općiti *v* (s kim) communicate **spolno** ~ have sexual intercourse with

ope|ći *v* (*pres* ~**čem**) 1 (koga/što) burn 2 (se) get burned; burn one's fingers *fig*

ope|ka *nf* (*Dsg* ~ci) brick

opeklina, opekotina *nf* burn

oper|acija *nf* surgery; operation (+ *mil*) ~**acijski** *adj* operating ~**acijska dvorana** operating theatre ~**ativan** *adj* operational; operative ~**ativni zahvat** surgery ~**irati** *v* 1 (koga/što) operate on 2 (čime) operate, handle, manipulate

opet *adv* again; once more, one more time ~**ovano** *adj* repeatedly; again ~**ovati** *v* (što) (*pres* ~**ujem**) repeat, reiterate

ophodnja *nf mil* patrol

opijati *v* (se) drink heavily

opip *nm* touch ~**ati** *v* (koga/što) feel, touch ~**ljiv** *adj* palpable, tangible

opir|ati *v* (se) (komu/čemu) (*pres* ~**em**) resist, oppose, withstand

opi|s *nm* 1 description 2 account ~**sati**

v (koga/što) (*pres* ~**šem**) 1 describe 2 (krug) circumscribe ~**sivati** *v impf*

opi|ti *v* (se) (*pres* ~**jem**) get drunk

opkoliti *v* (koga/što) surround; besiege

oplata *nf* (drvena) panelling

oplod|iti *v* (što/koga) 1 fertilize 2 make pregnant ~**nja** *nf* fertilization **umjetna** ~**nja** artificial insemination

oploviti *v* (što) sail round, circumnavigate

opljačkati *v* (koga/što) 1 rob 2 loot, plunder, sack

opna *nf* membrane

opoj|an *adj* (*a*) intoxicating ~**no sredstvo** narcotic, intoxicant

opom|ena *nf* 1 warning; caution 2 reprimand ~**enuti** *v* (koga) (*pres* ~**enem**) 1 warn 2 caution; admonish 3 reprimand ~**injati** *v impf*

oponašati *v* (koga/što) 1 immitate; mimic 2 copy

opor *adj* acrid, tart; harsh, unpleasant

oporav|ak *nm* (*Gsg* ~**ka**) recovery, recuperation ~**iti** *v* (se) recover, recuperate ~**ljati** *v* (se) *impf*

oporb|a *nf* opposition ~**en** *adj* opposition

oporez|iv *adj* taxable, liable/subject to taxation ~**ovati** *v* (koga/što) (*pres* ~**ujem**) tax, impose a tax on

oporu|ka *nf* (*Dsg* ~ci) (last) will, testament

opovrgn|uti *v* (što) (*pres* ~**em**) deny

opozicija → **oporba; opreka**

opoz|iv *nm* 1 recall 2 revocation; repeal; cancellation ~**vati** *v* (*pres* ~**ovem**) 1 (koga) recall 2 (što) revoke, repeal, rescind; cancel

op|rati *v* (*pres* ~**erem**) 1 (koga/što) wash 2 (se) wash (oneself)

opravda|n *adj* justified; legitimate, valid ~**nje** *nn* justification; excuse ~**ti** *v* (koga/što) 1 justify, vindicate, warrant 2 excuse

opre|čan *adj* (*a*) contrary, opposite ~**ka** *nf* (*Dsg* ~ci) contrast, opposition

opred|ijeliti *v* (se) opt (for), decide (on) ~**jeljenje** *nn* commitment

oprem|a *nf* equipment; outfit; gear; kit ~**iti** *v* (koga/što) equip, fit out

oprez *nm* caution **biti na** ~**u** be on

one's guard **mjere** ~a precautions ~an *adj* (α) cautious; careful

opr|ost *nm* 1 pardon; amnesty *pol* 2 (od grijeha) absolution ~**ostiti** *v* 1 (komu što) forgive ~**ostite!** excuse me, I'm sorry 2 (se s kim) say goodbye to, take (one's) leave of ~**oštaj** *nm* leave-taking, parting ~**oštajni** *adj* farewell ~**aštati** *v impf*

opru|ga *nf* (*Dsg* ~zi) spring

opsada *nf* siege

opse|g *nm* 1 perimeter 2 *fig* extent, scope ~**žan** *adj* (α) extensive, large-scale; comprehensive

opsjed|ati *v* (što/koga) besiege, beleaguer (+ *fig*) ~**nut** *adj* 1 besieged, under siege 2 *fig* obsessed ~**nutost** *nf* obsession

opskrb|a *nf* supply; provision ~**iti** *v* 1 (koga/što) supply; provide 2 (se) stock up on/with sth

opst|anak *nm* (*Gsg* ~anka) survival ~**ati** *v* (0) (*pres* ~anem) survive ~**ojnost** *nf* survival, endurance; existence

opšir|an *adj* (α) extensive; detailed ~**no** *adv* in detail

optere|titi *v* (što/koga) burden; load, weight ~**ćivati** *v impf*

opti|čar *nm* optician ~**čki** *adj* optical ~**čki nišan** telescopic sight ~**ka** *nf* (*Dsg* ~ci) optics

optim|alan *adj* (α) optimum, optimal ~**ist** *nm* optimist ~**istički** *adj* optimistic (about)

optjecaj *nm* circulation

optuž|ba *nf* accusation, charge, indictment **podići** ~**bu** bring a charge, press charges ~**enik** *nm* (*Npl* ~enici) the accused, defendant ~**iti** *v* (koga za što) 1 accuse of, charge with 2 blame ~**nica** *nf* indictment

opunomoć|enik *nm* (*Npl* ~enici) authorized person, attorney ~**iti** *v* (koga/što) authorize, empower, give power of attorney

opu|stiti *v* (što/se) relax ~**šten** *adj* relaxed, easygoing, laid-back

opust|jeti *v* (0) (*pres* ~im) become deserted/desolate

opustošiti *v* (što) devastate, ravage, lay waste

opuš|ak *nm* (*Gsg* ~ka, *Npl* ~ci) cigarette end/butt; fag-end *GB coll*

or|ač *nm* ploughman ~**anica** *nf* arable land ~**ati** *v* (što/0) (*pres* ~em) plough; plow *US*

ora|h *nm* (*Npl* ~si) walnut **tvrd** ~**h** *fig* hard/tough nut to crack

oran *adj* (α) eager

or|ao *nm* (*Gsg* ~la, *Npl* ~lovi) eagle ~**lovski** *adj* **nos** aquiline nose

oraspoložiti *v* (koga) put sb in a good mood

ordinacija *nf* surgery; doctor's office, consulting room

organ *nm* 1 organ 2 *fig* body **državni** ~**i** authorities, government bodies ~**i zakona/reda** law-enforcement officers, police ~**izacija** *nf* organization ~**izam** *nm* (*Gsg* ~izma) 1 organism 2 body, constitution, system ~**izator** *nm* organizer; sponsor ~**izirati** *v* (što) organize; arrange; sponsor; stage ~**ski** *adj* organic

orgazam *nm* orgasm **doživjeti** ~ have an orgasm; come *sl*

orgija *nf* orgy

orgulje *nf pl* organ

orhideja *nf* orchid

original *nm* 1 original 2 master copy ~**an** *adj* (α) original; genuine

orijent|acija *nf* orientation; direction, course **izgubiti** ~**aciju** lose one's bearings ~**ir** *nm* landmark ~**irati** *v* (se) orientate/orient *US* oneself, find/get one's bearings

oriti *v* (se) resound

orkest|ar *nm* (*Gsg* ~ra) orchestra; band

orma *nf* harness, gear

ormar *nm* 1 (za odjeću) wardrobe; (ugrađeni) closet *US* 2 (s policama) cupboard 3 (s ladicama) chest of drawers 4 (za knjige) bookcase ~**ić** *nm* 1 cabinet 2 locker 3 (kuhinjski) kitchen unit 4 (noćni) bedside table

oronu|o *adj* (~la *f*) 1 dilapidated 2 (osoba) decrepit

ortoped *nm* orthop(a)edic surgeon ~**ija** *nf* orthop(a)edics ~**ski** *adj* orthop(a)edic

oruđe *nn* tools, implements, instruments *pl*

oružjan *adj* armed **~ane snage** armed forces **~je** *nn* arms, weapons *pl* **hladno ~je** cold steel **vatreno ~je** firearms **~ni** *adj* **list** gun licence

os *nf* (*Gsg/Npl/Gpl* **~i**) axis

os|a *nf* wasp **~injak** *nm* (*Npl* **~injaci**), **~inje** *adj* **gnijezdo** 1 wasp nest 2 *fig* hornet's nest

osakatiti *v* (koga/što) mutilate, maim, cripple

os|am *num* eight (8) **~mi** *num ord* the eighth **~amdeset** *num* eighty (80) **~amdeseti** *num ord* eightieth **~amnaest** *num* eighteen (18)

osam|a *nf* isolation, seclusion **~ljen** *adj* lonely, lonesome

osamosta|liti *v* (se) become independent, gain independence **~ljenje** *nn* independence

osebujan *adj* (a) peculiar

osedlati *v* (konja) saddle

oseka *nf* low tide, ebb

osigur|ač *nm* fuse **~an** *adj* 1 insured, covered 2 secured **~anik** *nm* (*Npl* **~nici**) insured person/party, policy holder **~anje** *nn* 1 insurance; assurance 2 security; protection **imovinsko/životno ~anje** property/life insurance **socijalno ~anje** social/welfare *US* security; National Insurance *GB* **~ati** *v* 1 (koga/što) insure, cover 2 (se) ensure, make sure/certain; safeguard; secure 3 (sredstva) earmark 4 (se) insure oneself, take out a policy **~avajuće** *adj* **društvo** insurance company **~nina** *nf* insurance money, premium **~avati** *v impf*

osijed|ljeti *v* (0) (*pres* **~im**) become/grow grey

osim *prep* except (for) **~ toga** besides, in addition

osip *nm* rash

osipati *v* (se) *fig* (članstvo) shrink

osje|ćaj *nm* feeling **~ćajan** *adj* (a) sensitive **~ćati** *v* (koga/što/se) feel **~t** *nm* feeling, sensation **~tan** *adj* (a) marked, noticeable **~tilo** *nn* 1 sense 2 sensor **~titi** *v* (što) feel **~tljiv** *adj* sensitive; delicate

oskud|an *adj* (a) meagre, poor **~ica** *nf* 1 poverty 2 (čega) shortage, lack **~ijevati** *v* (čime/u čemu) lack

oskvrn|uti *v* (što) (*pres* **~em**) desecrate, profane, violate

oslabiti *v* (0) become weak, lose strength; decline, subside

oslanjati *v* (se) *impf* → **osloniti se**

oslić *nm* hake

oslijep|iti *v* (koga) blind **~jeti** *v* (0) (*pres* **~im**) go blind, lose sight

osloboditi *v* 1 (koga/što) free, set free, liberate; release 2 (se) free oneself 3 (se čega/koga) get rid of **~ optužbe** acquit sb

oslon|ac *nm* (*Gsg* **~ca**, *Npl* **~ci**) 1 support (+ *fig*) 2 footing, foothold **~iti** *v* (se) (na koga/što) 1 lean on/against 2 *fig* depend on, rely on, count on

osloviti *v* (koga) address **~ljavati** *v impf*

oslu|hnuti *v* (0/što) (*pres* **~hnem**) listen attentively **~škivati** *v impf* listen for

osm|ijeh *nm* smile **~jehnuti** *v* (se) (*pres* **~jehnem**) smile **~jehivati** *v* (se) *impf*

osmjeliti *v* (se) dare, venture

osmrtnica *nf* obituary (notice)

osn|ivač *nm* founder **~ovati** *v* (što) (*pres* **~ujem**) found, establish, set up, start, launch **~ova** *nf* base, foundation; basis; grounds; groundwork **~ovan** *adj* justified **~ovano** *adv* with reason **~ovica** *nf* base, basis **~ovni** *adj* basic, fundamental **~ovna škola** primary/elementary *US* school **~ivati** *v impf*

osob|a *nf* person, individual **~an** *adj* (a) personal, individual; private **~no vozilo** passenger car **~ina** *nf* characteristic, feature **~it** *adj* special, outstanding **~lje** *nn* personnel, staff **~no** *adv* personally, in person

osoran *adj* (a) arrogant, rude

osovina *nf* 1 axis 2 shaft **~ kotača** axle

ospice *nf pl* measles

ospor|iti *v* (koga/što) dispute, contest, challenge **~avati** *v impf*

osposob|iti *v* 1 (što) fix, put sth in working order, make operational 2 (koga) train, make fit **~ljavati** *v impf*

osramotiti *v* 1 (koga) disgrace 2 (se) disgrace oneself

osrednji *adj* 1 medium; moderate; average 2 mediocre

ostajati *v impf* → **ostati**

ostali *adj* other, remaining • *nm pl* the others, the rest

ostan|ak *nm* (*Gsg* ~ka, *Npl* ~ci) stay

ostar|jeti *v* (0) (*pres* ~im) get/grow old, age

osta|tak *nm* (*Gsg* ~tka, *Npl* ~ci) 1 rest, remnant 2 (iznosa) balance **posmrtni** ~**ci** (mortal) remains ~**ci jela** leftovers ~**ti** *v* (0) (*pres* ~nem) 1 stay; remain 2 stay behind 3 be left ~**ti bez** run out of ~**ti kod/pri/uz** stick to; stand by

ostavina *nf* inheritance

ostav|iti *v* (koga/što) 1 leave; abandon; leave behind 2 (nasljedstvo) bequeath 3 (se čega) give up, quit, stop ~**ka** *nf* (*Dsg* ~ci) resignation **podnijeti** ~**ku** resign, tender one's resignation ~**ština** *nf* heritage, inheritance; legacy ~**ljati** *v impf*

ostriga *nf* oyster

ostru|ga *nf* (*Dsg* ~zi) spur

ostvar|enje *nn* realization; fulfilment; implementation; achievement ~**iti** *v* 1 (što) realize, carry out, fulfil, implement ~**iti dohodak** earn an income, generate revenue ~**iti dobit** make a profit 2 (se) come true, come to fruition, materialize ~**iv** *adj* feasible

osu|da *nf* condemnation ~**diti** *v* 1 (koga/što) condemn 2 (koga) sentence, convict ~**đen na propast** doomed (to failure) ~**đenik** *nm* (*Npl* ~đenici) convict ~**đivati** *v impf*

osujetiti *v* (što) frustrate, foil, thwart

osumnjič|enik *nm* (*Npl* ~enici) suspect ~**iti** *v* (koga) suspect

osušiti *v* 1 (što) dry; (meso) smoke 2 (se) dry up/out

osvaja|č *nm* 1 conqueror, invader 2 (medalje) winner 3 (žena) lady-killer ~**nje** *nn* conquest ~**ti** *v impf* → **osvojiti**

osvan|uti *v* (0) (*pres* ~em) 1 dawn 2 appear

osve|ta *nf* revenge ~**titi** *v* 1 (koga/što) avenge, revenge 2 (se komu za što) avenge/revenge oneself on sb for sth

~**tljiv**, ~**toljubiv** *adj* vindictive ~**tnik** *nm* (*Npl* ~tnici) avenger ~**ćivati** *v impf*

osvije|stiti *v* (se) 1 come round/to, regain consciousness 2 *fig* come to one's senses

osvijetliti *v* 1 (koga/što) light up, illuminate 2 (film) expose

osvit *nm* dawn, daybreak

osvjedoč|iti *v* (se) be convinced; see for oneself

osvjet|lati *v* (što) polish, shine ~**ljavati** *v impf* → **osvijetliti** ~**ljenje** *nn* lighting

osvjež|avajući *adj* refreshing ~**iti** *v* 1 (koga/što) refresh, freshen up; (znanje) brush up 2 (se) refresh oneself, freshen up

osvoj|iti *v* 1 (što) conquer, capture; win (+ *sport*) 2 (koga) charm

osvr|nuti *v* (se) (*pres* ~nem) 1 look/turn back/(a)round 2 (na što) *fig* comment on ~**t** *nm* review

ošamariti *v* (koga) slap sb's face

ošin|uti *v* (koga/što) (*pres* ~em) strike; whip, lash ~**uti pogledom** give sb a withering look **kao gromom** ~**ut** thunderstruck

ošišati *v* 1 (koga) cut sb's hair 2 (se) have a haircut

ošit *nf* diaphragm

ošt|ar *adj* (*a*) 1 (nož) sharp 2 *fig* harsh, severe 3 (mjere) tough ~**ar kut** acute angle ~**rica** *nf* cutting edge ~**riti** *v* (što) sharpen ~**rokondža** *nf* shrew, vixen ~**rouman** *adj* (*a*) shrewd

ošte|ćenje *nn* damage; injury ~**titi** *v* (koga/što) damage, injure

otac *nm* (*Gsg* oca, *Npl* očevi, *Gpl* očeva/~a, *Dpl* očevima) father

otada *adv* from/since then, from/since that time, after that

ot|eći (1) *v* (0) (*pres* ~ječem) flow away/out, run out

ote|ći (2) *v* (0) (*pres* ~čem) swell

otegn|uti *v* (*pres* ~em) 1 (što) drag out, prolong ~**uti papke** *coll* kick the bucket 2 (se) drag on

otegotan → **otežavajući**

oteklina *nf* swelling

ot|eti *v* (*pres* ~mem) 1 (koga/što) grab; (osobu) kidnap, abduct; (vozilo) hijack 2 (se) break free/loose; escape (+ *fig*)

ote|zati *v* (*pres* ~žem) 1 (s čim) delay; stall 2 (u govoru) drawl

oteža|vajući *adj* aggravating ~ti *v* (što) 1 make sth (more) difficult 2 obstruct ~vati *v impf*

otići *v* (0) (*pres* odem/otiđem) go (away), leave, depart *odoh ja*! I'm off, I'm out of here ~ po koga/što (go and) get, fetch

otima|č robber ~čina *nf* robbery; plunder; extortion ~ti *v* 1 (koga/što) *impf* → oteti 2 (se) struggle

otirač *nm* doormat

otis|ak *nm* (*Gsg* ~ka, *Npl* ~ci) imprint, mark ~ci prstiju fingerprints ~nuti *v* (*pres* ~nem) 1 (što) print, imprint 2 (se) push off; (brod) set sail

otjecati *v impf* → oteći (1)

otjerati *v* (koga) drive away, chase away

otkač|en *adj sl* weird; offbeat ~enjak *nm* (*Npl* ~enjaci) *sl* weirdo, wacko ~iti *v* 1 (što/se) → otkvačiti 2 (se) *sl* freak out, get high/stoned; flip (out)

otkada, otkako *adv* since, since when

otka|z *nm* 1 notice 2 cancellation dati ~z *a.* hand in one's notice, quit *b.* (kome) dismiss; fire, sack *coll* ~zati *v* (*pres* ~žem) 1 (što) cancel, call off 2 (kome) give notice 3 (0) fail, break down ~zni *adj* rok notice period

otkin|uti *v* (*pres* ~em) 1 (što) break/tear off 2 (se) break/come off

otkloniti *v* (što) 1 eliminate, prevent 2 refuse

otključati *v* (što) unlock

otkočiti *v* (oružje) slip/flip off the safety catch; (vozilo) release the brake

otkopati *v* (što) dig up/out, unearth, excavate

otkopčati *v* (što) unbutton; unfasten; unbuckle; (gumb) undo

otkri|će *nn* 1 discovery; find 2 invention ~ti *v* (*pres* ~jem) 1 (koga/što) discover; find 2 (što) invent 3 (što) reveal; disclose 4 (koga/što) uncover 5 (se) uncover oneself 6 (se) give oneself away

otkuca|j *nm* stroke; (sata) tick; (srca)

heartbeat ~ti *v* (što) 1 (sat) strike 2 type (out/up) 3 (koga) *sl* squeal on sb *sl*; tell on sb *coll*

otkup *nm* 1 purchase 2 redemption 3 ransom ~iti *v* 1 (što) buy (up), purchase; buy back, redeem 2 (koga) ransom ~nina *n* ransom

otkvačiti *v* 1 (što) unhook, unhitch, release 2 (se) come off/loose

otmi|ca *nf* 1 (osobe) kidnapping, abduction 2 (vozila) hijacking ~čar *nm* 1 kidnapper 2 hijacker

otmjen *adj* elegant, stylish; classy *coll*

oto|čje *nn* archipelago ~čni *adj* island ~k *nm* (*Npl* ~ci) island; isle

otopiti *v* (što/se) 1 melt, thaw 2 dissolve

otpa|d *nm* waste ~dak *nm* (*pl* ~ci) refuse, waste(s), rubbish ~dni *adj* waste ~dnik *nm* (*Npl* ~dnici) 1 outcast, dropout; renegade 2 apostate

otpa|sti *v* (0) (*pres* ~dnem) 1 fall off, come off 2 (natjecanje) drop out 3 be out of the question 4 (na što) ~sti na što account for, go for ~dati *v impf*

otpirač *nm* skeleton key

otpi|ti *v* (što) (*pres* ~jem) drink off a little, take a sip

otpla|titi *v* (što) pay off; repay ~ta *nf* 1 payment 2 instalment na ~tu on hire purchase *GB*; on the installment plan *US* ~ćivati *v impf* (*pres* ~ćujem) pay by instalments

otpon|ac *nm* (*Gsg* ~ca, *Npl* ~ci) release; trigger

otpor *nm* 1 resistance 2 opposition pružati ~ put up/offer r. ~an *adj* (*a*) 1 resistant 2 tough 3 immune ~nik *nm* (*Npl* ~nici) resistor ~nost *nf* resistance

otprašiti *v* (koga) *coll* send sb packing

otpratiti *v* (koga) see sb off ~ do kuće see/walk sb home

otpravni|k *nm* (*Vsg* ~če, *Npl* ~ci) ~k poslova charge d'affaires ~k vlakova train dispatcher

otprem|a *nf* dispatching ~iti *v* (koga/što) dispatch, forward, ship ~nica *nf* dispatch note

otprije *adv* from before

otprilike *adv* about, roughly, approximately

otpu|snica *nf* discharge certificate ~**st!** *mil* dismissed! ~**stiti** *v* 1 (koga) dismiss; fire, sack *coll* 2 (koga) discharge, release 3 (što) loosen ~**štati** *v impf*

otput|ovati *v* (0) (*pres* ~ujem) leave, depart, go on a trip/journey

otraga *adv* behind, at/in the back, in the rear

otrcan *adj* 1 shabby, 2 *fig* trite

otrč|ati *v* (0) (*pres* ~im) run away/off

otres|it *adj* curt ~**ti** *v* (*pres* ~em) 1 (što) shake off/down 2 (se) get rid of ~**ti se na koga** snap at sb

otrgn|uti *v* (*pres* ~em) 1 (što) tear off/away 2 (se) break free

otrijezniti *v* (se) 1 sober up, become sober 2 *fig* sober down

otr|ov *nm* poison ~**ovan** *adj* (a) poisonous; venomous; toxic ~**ovanje** *nn* poisoning; intoxication ~**ovati** *v* (*pres* ~ujem) 1 (koga/što) poison 2 (se) poison oneself ~**ovnica** *nf* poisonous/venomous snake

otuda *adv* 1 from there, from that place/direction 2 hence

otuđ|en *adj* estranged, alienated ~**enje** *nn* 1 estrangement, alienation 2 misappropriation, theft ~**iti** *v* 1 (što) misapropriate, steal 2 (se) become estranged/alienated

otup|iti *v* (što) blunt ~**jeti** *v* (0) (*pres* ~im) 1 become blunt/dull 2 *fig* become jaded/numb

otv|arač *nm* opener ~**or** *nm* opening, aperture; orifice; hole ~**oren** *adj* 1 open 2 overt 3 frank ~**orenje** *nn* opening; inauguration ~**oriti** *v* (što) 1 open (up) 2 inaugurate 3 *coll* (radio) turn on, switch on 4 (se) open (up) ~**arati** *v impf*

ova → **ovaj**

ovacije *nf pl* ovation, cheering

ovaj (ova, ovo) *pron* this; this one

ovak|av *adj* (a) such, such as this, like this, (of) this kind ~**o** *adv* (in) this way, like this, thus

ovamo *adv* (over) here

ov|an *nm* (*Gsg* ~na, *Npl* ~novi) 1 ram 2 *astrol* Aries 3 *hist* battering ram ~**ca** *nf* sheep; ewe ~**čar** *nm* 1 shepherd 2 (pas) sheepdog **njemački** ~**čar** Alsatian *GB*; German shepherd *US* ~**čarstvo** *nn* sheep farming ~**četina** *nf* mutton

ovdašnji *adj* local

ovdje *adv* here, in this place

oveći, ovelik *adj* rather/fairly large

ovime *adv* hereby

ovis|an *adj* (a) 1 dependent on 2 addicted to; hooked on *coll* ~**iti** *v* (o kome/čemu) depend on ~**i o tebi** it's up to you ~**nik** *nm* (*Npl* ~nici) (drug) addict

ovjekovječ|iti *v* (koga/što) (*pres* ~ujem) immortalize

ovjeriti *v* (što) verify, authenticate; certify, attest

ovladati *v* (čime) master; gain control

ovlast *nf* authority, authorization; power of attorney ~**iti** *v* (koga/što) authorize, empower

ovlaš *adv* lightly

ovo → **ovaj**

ovogodišnji *adj* this year's, of this year

ovoj *nm* bandage ~**nica** *nf* membrane; shell, casing

ovratni|k *nm* (*Npl* ~ci) collar

ovrh|a *nf* seizure ~**ovoditelj** *nm* distraining officer; bailiff *GB*

ovuda *adv* this way, in this direction

ozakoniti *v* (što) legalize

ozar|en *adj* beaming (with joy) ~**iti** *v* (se) beam (with joy)

ozbilj|an *adj* (a) serious; grave ~**no** *adv* seriously **misliti** ~**no** be serious, mean it **shvaćati** ~**no** take seriously

ozdraviti *v* (0) get better

ozlijediti *v* 1 (koga) injure, wound 2 (se) hurt oneself; get hurt/injured

ozloglašen *adj* disreputable, infamous; notorious

ozlovoljiti *v* (koga) put in a bad mood, annoy

ozljed|a *nf* injury **pretrpjeti** ~**e** suffer/sustain injuries

ozna|čiti *v* (što) mark ~**ka** *nf* (*Dsg* ~ci) mark, sign ~**ke** *pl mil* insignia, markings

oznojiti *v* (se) sweat, perspire **dobro se** ~ work up a good sweat

ozon *nm* ozone ~**ski** *adj* **omotač** ozone layer

ozračiti *v* (koga/što) expose to radiation; irradiate

ozračje *nn* atmosphere

ozvuč|enje *nn* sound system; public-address system **~iti** *v* (što) bug, wire, tap

ožalo|stiti *v* 1 (koga) sadden, make sad 2 (se) become sad **~šćena** *adj* **obitelj** bereaved family

ožed|njeti *v* (0) (*pres* ~nim) become thirsty

oženiti *v* 1 (koga) marry 2 (se) get married, marry

ožigo|sati *v* (koga/što) (*pres* ~šem) *fig* brand, stigmatize

ožilj|ak *nm* (*Gsg* ~ka, *Npl* ~ci) scar

oživ|iti *v* (koga/što) 1 revive, resuscitate, restore to life 2 *fig* liven up **~jeti** *v* (0) (*pres* ~im) 1 come to life, revive, recover 2 *fig* liven up **~ljavati** *v impf* **~otvoriti** *v* (što) realize, bring to fruition, breathe life into, make viable

ožuj|ak *nm* (*Gsg* ~ka) March

P

P, p (pe) 22nd letter of Cro. alphabet

pa *conj* 1 and 2 so ~ **ipak** yet, still, nevertheless ~ **makar** even if, even though ~ **što onda** so what

pabirčiti *v* (što) glean

pacijent *nm* patient

pač|e (1) *nn* (*Gsg* ~eta, *Npl* ~ad) duckling **ružno** ~**e** ugly d.

pače (2) *adv* furthermore

pačetvorina *nf* rectangle

pad *nm* 1 fall (+ *fig*); decrease *fig* 2 (ispit) failure 3 slope ~**ati** *v* *iter* → **pasti** ~a **kiša** it is raining ~**avine** *nf pl* precipitation ~**avica** *nf* epilepsy ~**avičar** *nm* epileptic ~**ina** *nf* slope, hillside ~**obran** *nm* parachute ~**obranac** *nm* (*Gsg* ~obranca, *Vsg* ~obrancē) 1 parachutist 2 *fig* gatecrasher

pahulj|(ic)a *nf* 1 flake 2 down ~**ast** *adj* downy, soft

pak *conj* **on je** ~ **htio** ... he, on the other hand, wanted

pak|ao *nm* (*Gsg* ~la) hell ~**len** *adj* ~ infernal (+ *fig*) ~**eni stroj** explosive device ~**enski** *adv* as hell

pak|et *nm* parcel, package, packet ~**irati** *v* (što/se) pack (sth/oneself)

pakos|t *nf* malice ~**tan** *adj* (~na *f*) malicious ~**titi** *v* (komu) spite sb

pakt *nm* treaty **sklopiti** ~ make/conclude a t.

pal|ac *nf* (*Gsg* ~ca) 1 (ruka) thumb 2 (noga) big toe 3 inch ~**čić** *nm* wren

palača *nf* palace; mansion

palačinka *nf* 1 crepe 2 pancake

palenta *nf* maize porridge

paleta *nf* 1 palette 2 *fig* range

pal|ež *nm* arson ~**ikuća** *nm/f* arsonist ~**iti** *v* (što) 1 burn, set fire to, set sth ablaze/on fire 2 light 3 turn/switch on 4 parch **to kod mene ne** ~**i** *coll* I don't fall for that

palica *nf* sport bat; (policijska) baton

palma *nf* palm(tree)

palub|a *nf* deck

palj|ba *nf* fire, firing **obustaviti/ otvoriti** ~**bu** (na) cease/open fire on/at ~**evina** *nf* burning ~**enje** *nn* ignition

pam|ćenje *nn* memory ~**titi** *v* (koga/što) remember **od** ~**tivijeka** from time immemorial

pamet *nf* intelligence, brains **palo mi je na** ~ it has occured to me, I have an idea **ni na kraj** ~**i mi nije** I wouldn't dream of **naučiti koga** ~**i** teach sb a lesson ~**an** *adj* (*a*) intelligent, smart ~**njaković** *nm* derog smart aleck; smarty, smart arse *coll*

pamflet *nm* pamphlet, political tract

pamu|k *nm* cotton ~**čan** *adj* (*a*) cotton

pancir košulja *nf*, **pancirka** *nf* coll flak jacket

pandan *nf* counterpart

pandur *nm* 1 *hist* policeman 2 *sl* cop *coll*

pandža *nf* claw

pani|ka *nf* (*Dsg* ~ci) panic ~**čan** *adj* (*a*) panic-stricken, terrified ~**čar** *nm* scaremonger

pano *nm* (*Gsg* ~a) billboard

pansion *nm* 1 board and lodging 2 (ustanova) boarding house

pantera *nf* panther

pantomima *nf* 1 pantomime, dumb show 2 (igra) charade

panj *nm* tree stump; chopping block

papa *nm* the Pope

papa test *nm* smear test, Pap smear/test

pap|ak *nm* (*Gsg* ~ka, *Npl* ~ci) 1 hoof 2 *fig* nerd **otegnuti** ~**ke** kick the bucket

pap|ar *nm* (*Gsg* ~ra) pepper ~**ren** *adj* hot ~**rena cijena** exorbitant price ~**rena šala** dirty joke ~**riti** *v* (što) (season with) pepper

paperje nn down

papig|a nf parrot ~**ica** nf budgerigar; budgie coll

papir nm paper **vrijednosni ~i** pl securities ~**nat** adj paper ~**nica** nf stationery shop

paprat nf fern

papri|ka nf (Dsg ~ci) **1** (povrće) pepper **2** (začin) paprika **ljuta** ~**ka** chilli ~**kaš** nm hot stew

papuč|a nf slipper ~**ar** nm henpecked husband ~**ica** nf pedal

par nm **1** (čega) a pair of **2** couple **3** (nekoliko) a couple of **4** equivalent, match

par|a (1) nf vapour, steam **punom** ~**om** (**naprijed**) full steam ahead ~**ni** adj steam(-driven) ~**ni kotao** boiler

par|a (2) nf cent, dime US, penny GB ~**e** pl coll money **biti pun** ~**a** be loaded coll **ne vrijedi ni** ~**e** it's not worth a damn **bez prebite** ~**e** flat broke; skint GB sl

parada nf parade, pageant

paradoks nm paradox ~**alan** adj (α) paradoxical

paraf nm initial ~**irati** v (što) initial

parafin nm parrafin wax

parafraz|a nf paraphrase ~**irati** v (koga/što) paraphrase

paragraf nm paragraph; clause, section

paralel|a nf parallel ~**an** adj (α) (s) parallel (to/with) ~**no** adv fig simultaneously

paraliz|a nf paralysis (+ fig) ~**irati** v (koga) paralyse

paran adj (α) (broj) even

paranoja nf paranoia

parati v (što) **1** tear/rip (apart) **2** fig streak across

paravan nm screen (+ fig); front fig

parazit nm **1** parasite (+ fig) **2** fig freeloader

parcela nf plot

pardon int excuse me, beg your pardon

parf|em nm perfume, fragrance ~**imerija** nf pharmacy, drugstore

parirati v (komu/čemu) **1** counter, parry (+ fig) **2** fence

paritet nm parity

pariti (1) v (koga s kim/se) couple, mate

pariti (2) v (što) steam ~ **oči** feast one's eyes on

park nm park, common **vozni** ~ fleet, car pool

parket nm **1** parquet (floor) **2** (kazalište) orchestra stalls

parki|rati v (se/što) park **nepropisno** ~**rati** park illegally ~**ralište** nn car park GB; parking lot US ~**ng** nm coll parking place

parlamen|t nm (Gpl ~ata) parliament ~**taran** adj (α) parliamentary

parni|ca nf lawsuit **dobiti/izgubiti** ~**cu** win/lose the l. **podići** ~**cu** file a suit; sue ~**čiti** v (se) litigate

parobrod nm steamship

parodi|ja nf parody, travesty fig ~**rati** v (što) parody

parola nf slogan

particip|acija nf prescription charge ~**irati** v (0) participate in, share

partija nf **1** party **2** game

partitura nf score

partizan nm partisan

partner nm partner

pas (1) nm (Gsg psa, Npl psi) dog ~ **čuvar** guard dog ~ **lutalica** stray **morski** ~ shark

pas (2) nm **1** → **pojas 2** → **struk oko** ~**a** round the waist

pasati v (komu) (pres pašem) coll **1** **paše mi kravata** this tie suits me **2** **paše mi ovo vino** I enjoy this wine

pasirati v (što) puree

pasiv|a nf com liabilities ~**an** adj (α) passive ~**nost** nf passivity

pask|a nf supervision, control **držati pod** ~**om** control, keep under close scrutiny

pasmina nf breed

pasta nf paste, cream

pastela nm crayon ~**n** adj (α) pastel

pasteriza|irati v (što) pasteurize ~**n** adj pasteurized

pasti (1) v (0) (pres padnem) **1** fall (down/off) **2** fig fall, collapse **3** fall, decrease; (na ispitu) fail **pala je odluka** the decision was reached ~ **u nesvijest** faint ~ **u zaborav** fall into oblivion ~ **mrtav** die; drop dead ~ **kome na pamet** occur to sb **pao mi je kamen sa srca** I was relieved

pasti (2) v (0/što) (*pres* pasem) graze ~**r** n 1 shepherd 2 priest ~**rski** adj 1 shepherd('s) 2 pastoral

pastor|ak nm (Gsg ~ka, Npl ~ci) stepson ~**ka** nf (Dsg ~ci) stepdaughter

pastrva nf trout

pastu|h nm (Npl ~si) stud (+ fig)

pasus nm paragraph

paš|a nf grazing **odvesti na** ~**u graze** ~**njak** nm (Npl ~njaci) grazing land, pasture

pašteta nm cul paté

pat nm (~ **pozicija**) stalemate (+ fig)

pat|ak nm (Gsg ~ka, Npl ~ci) drake

patent nm 1 patent 2 gadget ~**-zatvarač** zip fastener ~**irati** v (0/što) patent ~**iran** adj patent ~**ni** adj ured Patent Office

patetičan adj (α) melodramatic

patina nf patina (+ fig); verdigris

pat|iti v 1 (od čega) suffer from, have ~**iti od pretjerane čistoće** be compulsively clean, be a stickler for cleanliness 2 (0) suffer, be in agony ~**nički** adj agonized, suffering ~**nik** nm (Vsg ~niče, Npl ~nici) sufferer

patka nf duck **novinska** ~ canard

patlidžan nm aubergine GB; eggplant US

patolo|gija nf pathology ~**ški** adj pathological (+ fig)

patrijar|h nm (Npl ~si) patriarch ~**halan** adj (α) patriarchal

patriot nm patriot ~**ski** adj patriotic

patr|ljak nm (Gsg ~ka, Npl ~ci) stump

patrol|a nf patrol ~**ni** adj patrol

patrona nf coll cartridge

patul|jak nm (Gsg ~ka, Vsg ~če, Npl ~ci) dwarf, midget ~**ast** adj dwarf, miniature

patvori|na nf falsification, sham ~**ti** v (što) 1 falsify 2 adulterate

pau|k nm (Npl ~ci) 1 spider 2 coll tow truck ~**kova mreža** fig spider's web ~**čina** nf cobwebs

paun nm peacock ~**ica** nf peahen

paušal|an adj (α) 1 ~**ni iznos** lump sum ~**na cijena** flat rate 2 fig offhand

pauz|a nf 1 pause 2 break ~**a za ručak** lunch b. ~**irati** v (0) take a break ~**irati godinu dana** take a year off

paviljon nm 1 pavillion 2 marquee

pazikuća nm/f caretaker GB; janitor US

paziti v 1 (0/na koga/na što) watch out (for), be careful, pay attention 2 (koga/što) look after, mind 3 (se) look after oneself, take good care of oneself; be on guard **pazi!** int watch out!

pazuho nn armpit **pod** ~**m** under the arm

paž|ljiv adj 1 careful, meticulous 2 attentive 3 kind, considerate ~**nja** nf coll 1 attention **obratiti** ~**nju** pay a. (to) **skrenuti (komu)** ~**nju na što** call sb's a. to 2 kindness, courtesy

pčel|a nf (honey)bee ~**ar** nm beekeeper ~**arstvo** nn beekeeping ~**injak** nm (Npl ~injaci) bee house, apiary; beehive (+ fig) ~**inji** adj **vosak** beeswax

pecati v (što) angle (+ fig), fish

pecivo nn roll, bun **prašak za** ~ baking powder

pec|nuti v (koga) 1 sting 2 fig tease ~**kati** v impf

pečat nm seal, stamp **udariti** ~ affix a s. ~**iti** v (što) seal, stamp ~**ni** adj **vosak** sealing wax

peče|n adj 1 (meso) roast 2 (kruh, posuđe) baked ~**nje** nn roast meat

peć nf 1 stove, furnace ~ **na drva** wood s. **visoka** ~ blast f. 2 oven ~**nica** nf oven ~**i** v (pres pečem) 1 (što) (kruh, grnčariju) bake, (meso) roast, (alkohol) make 2 (0) burn, scorch 3 (se) roast 4 (0/koga) burn, sting **peče me savjest** I have a guilty conscience **peku me oči** my eyes smart

pećina nf cave

pedago|g nm education counsellor, supervisor ~**gija** nf pedagogy, teaching ~**ška akademija** teachers' training college

pedala nf pedal

pedalj nm 1 (mjera) hand 2 fig inch

pedant|an adj (α) thorough, meticulous; pedantic derog ~**erija** nf perfectionism

peder *nm coll derog* gay, homosexual; poof(ter) *GB sl*; faggot *US sl*

pedeset *num* fifty (50) **~i** *num ord* fiftieth

pedijat|ar *nm* p(a)ediatrician **~rija** *nf* p(a)ediatrics

pediker *nm* chiropodist; podiatrist *US*

pehar *nm* cup (+ *sport*), goblet

pekar *nm* baker **~a ~nica** *nf* bakery

pekmez *nm* jam

pelene *nf pl* nappy *GB*; diaper *US*

pelerina *nf* cape

pelin *nm* wormwood **~kovac** *nm* (*Gsg* ~kovca) absinthe

pelir *nm* (~ papir) flimsy

pelud *nm* pollen **~na** *adj* **groznica/hunjavica** hay fever

pendre|k *nm* (*Npl* ~ci) truncheon

penetrirati *v* (što) penetrate; infiltrate

pentagon *nm* pentagon **P~** the Pentagon

penzi|ja → **mirovina ~oner** → **umirovljenik**

penjač *nm* climber **~čica** *nf* (biljka) climber, vine **~ti** *v* (se) (na što) climb sth; (po čemu) climb (all) over

pepe|o *nm* (*Gsg* ~la) ashes *pl* **P~lnica** *nf* Ash Wednesday **~ljara** *nf* ashtray **~ljast** *adj* 1 (lice) ashen 2 (kosa) ash blond **P~ljuga** *nf* Cinderella

per|ač *nm* washer, cleaner **~ačica** *nf* washerwoman **~ilica za rublje/posuđe** washing machine/dishwasher

perad *nf pl* poultry **~ar** *nm* poultry-man, chicken farmer **~arstvo** *nm* chicken farming

peraja *nf* 1 (riba) fin 2 (sisavac; umjetna) flipper

percepcija *nf* perception

perce *nn dim* tiny feather, down **lak kao ~** light as a feather

perčin *nm* queue

perfidan *adj* (a) perfidious, trecherous

perforacija *nf* perforation

pergamen|t *nm* (*Gpl* ~ata) parchment

perifer|an *adj* (a) 1 peripheral; marginal (+ *fig*) 2 minor **~ija** *nf* outskirts

peri|ka *nf* (*Dsg* ~ci) → **vlasulja**

perina *nf* eiderdown, quilt, duvet

period *nm* → **razdoblje**

periskop *nm* periscope

perivoj *nm* park, gardens

perj|e *nn* feathers *pl*, plumage **~anica** *nf* feathered headdress

pernica *nf* pencil box

per|o *nn* 1 (ptičje) feather, quill 2 quill 3 *arch* pen 4 *fig* writer **čovjek od ~a** man of letters **~olak** *adj* featherweight

peron *nm* platform

personificirati *v* (koga/što) personify

perspektiv|a *nf* 1 prospect(s), future 2 perspective **iz moje ~e** from my point of view, from where I stand 3 (umjetnost) perspective **u ~i** foreshortened **~an** *adj* (a) promising

peršin *nm* parsley

perušati *v* (koga/što) 1 pluck 2 *fig* fleece

peruš|ka *nf* (*Dsg* ~ci) feather duster

perverz|an *adj* (a) perverted, sick; kinky *coll* **~ija** *nf* (sexual) perversion **~njak** *nm* (*Vsg* ~njače, *Npl* ~njaci) *coll* pervert

pesimist *nm* pessimist **~ičan** *adj* (a) pessimistic

pest *nf* fist

pet *num* five (5) **ni ~ ni šest** without further ado **~ica** *nf coll* 1 (ocjena) A 2 the/number five **~ero** *num* five **~ero-** *prefix* five- **~i** *num ord* fifth **~ina** *nf* fifth (of) **~o-** *prefix* five- **~okolonaš** *nm* fifth columnist **~okraka** five-point star **~orica** *nf* five (men) **~parački** *adj* roman dime novel

pet|a *nf* heel **biti za ~ama** (komu) be at sb's heels; dog sb **visoke/niske ~e** high/low heels **cipele s visokom ~om** high-heeled shoes **~ni** *adj* iz **~nih žila** for all one's worth

pet|ak *nm* (*Gsg* ~ka) Friday **Veliki ~ak** Good Friday

peteljk|a *nf* (*Dsg* ~ci) stem

peticija *nf* petition, appeal

petlj|a *nf* 1 loop, noose **imati ~u** have guts 2 cloverleaf, spaghetti junction **~ati** *v* 1 (0) complicate, muddle 2 (0) mess about; (oko čega) tinker with 3 (se u što) meddle in, interfere with

petnaest *num* fifteen (15) **~i** *num ord* fifteenth

petrolej *nm* paraffin, oil **~ka** *nf* (*Dsg* ~ci) *coll* oil lamp

petsto *num* five hundred (500)

pič|ka *nf* (*Gpl* ~aka/~ki) *tab* cunt, pussy

piće *nn* 1 drink, beverage **bezalkoholno** ~e soft d., non-alcoholic b. **žestoka** ~a spirits 2 a drink **idemo na** ~e let's go for a d.

pidžama *nf* pajamas, pyjamas *pl*

pijan *adj* 1 drunk, intoxicated **mrtav** ~/~ **kao majka/zemlja** drunk as a lord, dead drunk; sozzled *coll* 2 (od) *fig* d./i. with ~**ac** *nm* (*Gsg* ~ca, *Vsg* ~če) drunkard, drunk ~**čevati** *v* (0) go on a drinking spree, go boozing

pijanino *nm* upright piano

pijavica *nf* 1 leech (+ *fig*) 2 (vjetar) whirlwind

pijes|ak *nm* (*Gsg* ~ka) sand **bacati kome** ~**ak u oči** try to cloud the issue **živi** ~**ak** quicksand **gurati glavu u** ~**ak** bury one's head in the sand

pije|tao *nm* (*Gsg* ~tla), ~**vac** *nm* (*Gsg* ~vca) rooster *US*; cock

pijetet *nm* respect

pijuckati *v* (što) sip (at)

piju|k *nm* (*Npl* ~ci) pickaxe

pijukati *v* (0) peep, cheep

pik *nm* 1 **imati** ~ **na nekoga** have it in for sb 2 spade ~**ova** *adj* **dama** queen of spades

pikantan *adj* (a) 1 spicy, savoury 2 *fig* saucy, juicy

pikirati *v* (0) 1 nosedive 2 aim at

pil|a *nf* saw ~**ana** *nf* sawmill ~**iti** *v* 1 (što) saw (at) 2 (koga) *coll* bore

pil|e *nn* (*Gsg* ~eta, *Npl* ~ići) chicken ~**etina** *nf* chicken (meat)

pilot *nm* pilot, flier ~**irati** *v* (0/avionom) fly (a plane)

pilula *nf* pill ~ **za spavanje** sleeping p.

piljevina *nf* sawdust

piljiti *v* (0) (u koga/što) stare (at), gape (at)

pimpek *nm* *coll* willy

pinceta *nf* (a pair of) tweezers

pingvin *nm* penguin

pionir *nm* pioneer

pip|a *nf* tap *GB*, faucet *US* **voda iz** ~**e** tap water **zatvoriti** ~**u** *fig* stop the flow ~**ac** *nm* (*Gsg* ~ca) tap

pip|ak *nm* (*Gsg* ~ka, *Npl* ~ci) feeler, tentacle

pipa|ti *v* (koga/što) touch, feel, grope ~**v** *adj* awkward, tedious, slow

pir *nm* feast **zlatni** ~ golden wedding

piramida *nf* pyramid

pirat *nm* pirate ~**sko** *adj* **izdanje** bootleg (record)

pire *nm* (*Gsg* ~a) puree ~ **od krumpira** mashed potatoes **kesten**-~ pureed chestnuts

piriti *v* 1 (0) **vjetar piri** there is a light breeze 2 (vatru) blow (up)

pirjati *v* (što) stew

pis|ac *nm* (*Gsg* ~ca, *Vsg* pišče) writer, author ~**aći** *adj* writing ~**aći stroj** typewriter ~**aći pribor** stationery ~**anje** *nn* writing ~**ar** *nm* clerk ~**ati** *v* (*pres* pišem) 1 (0) write 2 (što/komu) write 3 spell ~**karalo** *nn* hack (writer) ~**karati** *v* (0/što) scribble ~**men** *adj* 1 literate 2 articulate 3 written ~**meno** *adv* in writing ~**menost** *nf* 1 literacy 2 literature ~**mo** *nn* 1 letter **Sveto** ~**mo** the Holy Scriptures 2 literature, writing ~**monoša** *nm* postman *GB*, mailman *US*

pis|ak *nm* (*Gsg* ~ka) 1 screech, whistle 2 mouthpiece ~**kav** *adj* shrill ~**nuti** *v* **da nisi ni** ~**nuo!** keep your mouth shut!

pisanica *nf* Easter egg

pisoar *nm* urinal

pista *nf* 1 runway 2 (trkalište) racetrack 3 (modna) catwalk 4 (skijanje) ski-run, piste

piš|ati *v* (0) *vulg* piss ~**kiti** *v* (0) pee, piddle

piškota *nf* sponge finger

pišljiv *adj* rotten (+ *fig*), measly

pišta|l|jka *nf* (*Dsg* ~ljci) whistle ~**ti** *v* (0) 1 whistle 2 screech

pištolj *nm* pistol

pita *nf* pie

pitak *adj* (a) 1 (voda) drinking 2 *fig* smooth

pita|nje *nn* 1 question **biti u** ~**nju** be at stake, be uncertain **odgovoriti na** ~**nje** answer a q. **postaviti** ~**nje** ask a q. **dovoditi u** ~**nje** question 2 matter, affair, issue ~**ti** *v* 1 (koga/što) ask sb 2 (za koga) inquire after/about sb 3 (za što) ask for 4 (se) ask oneself, wonder

piti *v* (0/što) (*pres* pijem) 1 drink 2 *euph* have a drinking problem ~ **u čije zdravlje** d. sb's health **ne zna se tko pije tko plaća** this is a total chaos ~ **krv** *fig* torture, plague

pitom *adj* 1 tame, domesticated 2 quiet, pleasant ~**i brežuljci** rolling hills

pitom|ac *nm* (*Gsg* ~ca, *Vsg* ~če) 1 pupil 2 cadet

piton *nm* python

piv|o *nn* beer, (englesko) ale, (svijetlo) lager, (tamno) stout ~**nica** *nf* pub ~**ovara** *nf* brewery ~**ski** *adj* **kvasac** brewer's yeast

pizda *nf tab* cunt, pussy

pjeg|a *nf* spot; freckle ~**av** *adj* (životinja) spotted; (lice) freckled, freckly; (konj) piebald ~**avac** *nm* (*Gsg* ~avca) typhus ~**ica** *nf* freckle

pjen|a *nf* foam, froth; (pivo) head; mousse ~**ast** *adj* foamy, frothy ~**iti/~ušati** *v* (se) foam, froth ~**ušac** *nm* (*Gsg* ~ušca) sparkling wine, champagne ~**ušav** *adj* fizzy, sparkling

pjeskovit *adj* sandy

pjesm|a *nf* 1 song; track 2 poem **uvijek ista** ~**a** the same old tune ~**arica** *nf* songbook ~**ica** *nf* ditty

pjesni|k *nm* (*Vsg* ~če, *Npl* ~ci) poet ~**čki** *adj* poetic ~**čka sloboda** p. license ~**štvo** *nn* poetry

pješ|ačiti *v* (0) go on foot, walk ~**ački** *adj* 1 pedestrian 2 *mil* infantry ~**aštvo** *nn mil* infantry ~**ak** *nm* (*Vsg* ~ače, *Npl* ~aci) 1 pedestrian 2 infantryman 3 (šah) pawn ~**ice/~ke** *adv* on foot

pješčan *adj* sandy ~**i prud** sandbank ~**i sat** hourglass ~**ik** *nm* (*Npl* ~ici) sandstone

pjev *nm* song **labuđi** ~ swan-song ~**ač** *nm* singer ~**anje** *nn* singing ~**ati** *v* (0/što) sing ~**ica** *nf* (ptica ~ica) songbird ~**ušiti** *v* (0/što) hum, croon

plač *nm* crying, weeping ~**an** *adj* (*a*) tearful ~**ljiv** *adj* weepy, tearful ~**ljivac** *nm* (*Gsg* ~ljivca, *Vsg* ~ljivče) *derog* cry-baby

plać|a *nf* salary, pay, wages ~**anje** *nn* payment ~**ati** *v* (0/što/za što/komu) pay (+ *fig*) ~**en** *adj* paid, hired ~**eni ubojica** hired gun, hit man ~**enik** *nm*

(*Npl* ~enici) mercenary

plad|anj *nm* (*Gsg* ~nja) platter, tray

plafon *nm* ceiling

plagijat *nm* plagiarism ~**or** *nm* plagiarist

plah *adj* shy, timid

plahovit *adj* wild, hot-tempered

plahta *nf* (bed)sheet

plakat *nm* poster, bill

plakati *v* (0) (*pres* plačem) cry, weep

plam|en *nm* flame, fire **u** ~**enu** in flames, on fire • *adj* fiery, blazing ~**enac** *nm* (*Gsg* ~enca) 1 (ptica) flamingo 2 pennant ~**enik** *nm* (*Npl* ~enici) burner, (električni) ring ~**sati**, ~**tjeti** *v* (čime/od čega) (*pres* ~tim) burn, blaze (with) (+ *fig*)

plan *nm* 1 plan, schedule **nastavni** ~ curriculum 2 (grada) map 3 layout 4 (projekt) blueprint ~**irati** *v* (što) plan ~**ski** *adj* planned

pland|ovati *v* (0) (*pres* ~ujem) *fig* do nothing

planet *nm* planet

planin|a *nf* mountain ~**ar** *nm* mountaineer, climber, hiker ~**ariti** *v* (0) go mountaineering ~**arenje** *nn* mountaineering ~**ski** *adj* mountain; (predio) mountainous ~**ski vijenac** mountain range

plantaža *nf* plantation

plan|uti *v* (0) (*pres* ~em) 1 burst into flames, catch fire 2 *fig* explode, fly into rage/passion

plas|irati *v* 1 (što) (novac) invest; (robu) sell, market 2 (se) ~**irati se na drugo mjesto** come/finish/be placed second ~**irati se u finale** enter the finals ~**man** *nm* 1 sales 2 capital investment 3 rank, position

plast *nm* haystack

plastelin *nm* plasticine

plasti|čan *adj* (*a*) 1 plastic ~**čna operacija/kirurgija** p. surgery ~**čna masa** plastic ~**čna vrećica** polythene/plastic bag 2 *fig* vivid ~**čnost** *nf fig* vividness ~**ka** *nf* (*Dsg* ~ci) plastic

plaš|iti *v* 1 (koga čime) frighten, scare (with) 2 (se čega) be afraid of, fear sth ~**ljiv** *adj* timid, easily frightened

plašt *nm* 1 cloak, cape 2 *fig* cover,

guise
platana *nf* plane
platež|an *adj* (α) **~no sredstvo** legal tender **~na moć/sposobnost** solvency
platforma *nf* platform **naftna ~** oil rig
platina *nm* platinum **~st** *adj* platinum
p!at|iša *nm* payer **~iti** *v* 1 (komu što) pay (to) sb (for) sth **~iti mjenicu** honour a bill **~iti u naturi/naravi** p. in kind **~iti komu piće** buy/stand sb a drink 2 (za) *fig* pay for **~it će mi on to** I'll pay him back/out for that **~ni** *adj* **promet** financial transactions **zavod za ~ni promet** clearing house **~ni popis** payroll **~ni nalog** money order
platn|o *nn* 1 (tkanina) linen 2 (slikarsko) canvas **filmsko ~o** (silver) screen **~en** *adj* linen
plav *adj* 1 blue 2 blond, fair **~etnilo** *nn* azure **~okos** *adj* blond, fair(-haired) **~uša** *nf* blonde
plaziti *v* (0) crawl, creep
plaža *nf* beach
pleć|a *nf* shoulders **~at** *adj* broad-shouldered **~ka** *nf* (*Dsg* ~ci) shoulder
pleksiglas *nm* TM perspex; plexiglass *US*
pleme *nn* tribe, clan **~nski** *adj* tribal
plemenit *adj* 1 noble, highborn 2 thoroughbred 3 noble, magnanimous 4 (kovina) precious **~ost** *nf* nobleness, nobility
plem|ić *nm* nobleman **~kinja** *nf* noblewoman **~stvo** *nn* nobility, aristocracy
plenar|an *adj* (α) plenary **~no zasjedanje** p. session
ples *nm* 1 dance 2 dance, ball 3 (~anje) dancing **~ač** *nm* dancer **~ati** *v* (0) (*pres* plešem) dance **~ati kako drugi svira** d. to sb's tune **~ni** *adj* dancing, ball
ple|sti *v* 1 (što) (wool) knit; (hair) braid, twist 2 (se) meddle, poke one's nose in **~te mu se jezik** his speech is blurred **~taći** *adj* knitting **~ten** *adj* knit(ted) **~teni stolac** wicker chair **~tenica** *nf* plait **~tenina** *nf* knitwear
plijen *nm* 1 prey, kill **postati ~om** fall

prey to 2 plunder, booty, spoils, loot **~iti** *vt* 1 (čime) *fig* captivate (with) **~ pažnju** capture attention 2 confiscate
plijesan *nf* mould; mildew
plijeviti *v* (što) weed (out)
plima *nf* high tide **~ dolazi** the t. sets in **~ i oseka** the tides, the ebb and flow
plin *nm* gas **~ara** *nf* gas-works **~omjer** *nm* gasmeter **~ovit** *adj* gassy, gasseous **~ovod** *nm* (gas) pipeline **~ski** *adj* gas **~ska peć** gas fire
pliš *nm* velvet **~an** *adj* 1 velvet, plush 2 (igračka) cuddly
plitak *adj* (α) 1 shallow 2 *fig* superficial
plitica *nf* plate, platter
pliva|č *nm* swimmer **~ti** *v* (0) 1 swim 2 float, keep afloat
ploč|a *nf* 1 slab, tablet 2 board **školska ~a** blackboard 3 (gramofonska ~a) record **nadgrobna ~a** gravestone **~ica** *nf* 1 tile 2 plate
ploćn|ik *nm* (*Npl* ~ici) pavement *GB*; sidewalk *US*
plod *nm* 1 fruit (+ *fig*) 2 produce 3 *fig* result, product **donijeti ~a** yield fruit **uroditi ~om** *fig* bear fruit **~an** *adj* (α) fertile; fruitful, productive; (pisac) prolific **~nost** *nf* fertility **~onosan** *adj* fertile, productive, profitable
ploha *nf* surface; facet
plomb|a *nf coll* 1 filling 2 seal **~irati** *v* (zub) fill
plosnat *adj* flat
ploška *nf* (*Dsg* ~ci) slice
plošni *adj* surface, flat, superficial
plot *nm* fence **ograditi ~om** fence in
plotun *nm mil* salvo, volley
plov|an *adj* (α) navigable **~idba** *nf* navigation; (sea) voyage **brod duge ~idbe** ocean-going ship **~iti** *v* (0) navigate, sail
pluć|a *nn pl* lungs **upala ~a** pneumonia **~ni** *adj* pulmonary, lung **~no krilo** lung
plug *nm* plough *GB*, plow *US*
plus *nm* 1 plus 2 *fig* asset, plus **biti u ~u** *coll* be in the black
pluta|ča *nf* buoy **~ti** *v* (0) float
plut|o *nn* cork **~en** *adj* cork

Pluton *nm* Pluto
pljačka *nf* robbery **~š** *nm* robber, looter **~ti** *v* (koga/što) rob, plunder, loot
pljen|idba *nf* leg execution, seizure, confiscation
pljes|ak *nm* (*Gsg* ~ka) applause **~kati** *v* 1 (0) applaud, clap (one's) hands 2 (koga) (po leđima) slap sb on the back **~nuti** *v* 1 (0) (rukama) clap hands 2 (se) (po čemu) slap (one's forehead etc)
pljesniv *adj* mouldy, musty **~iti** *v* (0/se) mould, grow mouldy
pljev|a *nf* chaff **ima ih kao ~e** there are loads of them
pljos|ka *nf* (*Dsg* ~ci) hipflask, canteen
pljoštimice *adv* flat, with the flat of (the sword etc)
pljuckati *v* (što) spit
pljunuti *v* (0, na koga/što) spit (out), spit at • *adj* the spitting image of
pljus|ak *nm* (*Gsg* ~ka) (heavy) shower, downpour
pljus|ka *nf* (*Dsg* ~ci) box on the ears, slap **~kati** *v impf* **~nuti** *v* (*pres* ~nem) 1 (koga) slap 2 (0) fall with a splash 3 (0) *coll* (na ispitu) fail; flunk *US*
pljuštati *v* (0) 1 (kiša) pour (down) 2 *fig* pour in
pljuva|čka *nf* (*Dsg* ~čci) spit, saliva **~čnica** *nf* spitoon **~ti** *v* (*pres* pljujem) 1 (0) spit 2 (koga) *fig* criticise ruthlessly, disparage
pneumatsk|i *adj* pneumatic **~a bušilica** pneumatic drill *GB*; jackhammer *US* **~e kočnice** air-brakes
po *prep* (komu/čemu) 1 (mjesto) about, around, all over; down, on, in, over **doći ~ koga** during, in; after, on **~ cijeli dan** all day long 3 (sredstvo) through, after, by, as regards 4 by, in 5 according to; **~ Ustavu** under the Constitution
po- *prefix* (+ pridjev) rather ..., -ish **podebeo** rather thick, thickish
po- *prefix* (+ glagol) radnja je u potpunosti izvršena nad svakim od objekata (**poubijati** kill every one)
pobacati *vt* (što) throw (everything) away

poba|citi *v* (0) have a miscarriage; have an abortion **~čaj** *nm* (spontani) miscarriage; abortion
pobijati *v* (koga/što) refute, contest, dispute, challenge
pobijediti *v* 1 (koga/što) conquer, defeat, beat 2 (0) (u/na čemu) be victorious, carry victory, win sth
pobi|ti *v* (*pres* ~jem) 1 (koga) kill (to the last man), slaughter 2 (što) refute
pobje|ći *v* (0) (*pres* ~gnem) escape, run away, flee
pobjed|a *nf* victory **odnijeti ~u** win/carry the day **~nički** *adj* victorious, triumphant **~nik** *nm* (*Vsg* ~niče, *Npl* ~nici) victor; (natjecanje) winner **~onosan** *adj* (α) triumphant
pobjeđivati *v iter →* pobijediti
pobjes|njeti *v* (0) (*pres* ~nim) go mad (with anger)
pobliže *adv* in detail; closely
pobljuvati *v* (se/što) vomit, throw up, puke, sick up
pobočn|ik *nm* (*Vsg* ~iče, *Npl* ~ici) aide(-de-camp)
pobojati *v* (se za što) be afraid for, fear for
pobolijevati *v* (0/od) be ailing
poboljša|nje *nn* improvement **~ti** *v* (što/se) ameliorate, improve, amend, reform **situacija se ~la** the situation improved **stanje joj se ~va** she is on the mend
poborn|ik *nm* (*Vsg* ~iče, *Npl* ~ici) champion, advocate, proponent
pobož|an *adj* (α) pious, religious, devout **~no** *adv* devoutly; raptly *fig* **~nost** *nf* piety; devotion
pobrati *v* (što) (*pres* poberem) 1 pick, gather 2 pick up
pobratim *nm* blood-brother
pobrinuti *v* (se za koga/što) take care of, see to
pobrkati *v* 1 (što) confuse, mix up 2 (se) get all mixed up
pobu|da *nf* motive **~diti** *v* (što) arouse, inspire, stimulate, incite **~đivati** *v impf* (*pres* ~đujem)
pobu|na *nf* revolt, riot; mutiny **~niti** *v* 1 (se) protest, revolt, rise up 2 (koga) stir up revolt among **~njenički** *adj* rebel **~njenik** *nm* (*Vsg* ~njeniče, *Npl*

~njenici) insurgent, rebel

pocijepati *v* 1 (što) tear (apart), rip 2 (se) get/be torn/ripped

pocinčan *adj* galvanized

pocrkati *v* (0) *coll* die off

pocr|niti *v* (što) blacken ~**njeti** *v* (0) (*pres* ~nim) 1 become/turn black 2 (get a) tan

pocrve|niti *v* (što) paint red ~**njeti** *v* (0) (*pres* ~nim) blush, go red in the face

počas|ni *adj* honorary ~**t** *nf* homage, respects **iskazati** (**kome**) ~**t** pay homage to ~**titi** *v* (koga čime) buy sb sth; treat sb to sth

počelo *nn* element

počeš|ati *v* (koga/što/se) (*pres* ~em) scratch

počešljati *v* (koga/što/se) comb; do one's hair

poče|tak *nm* (Gsg ~tka, Npl ~ci) beginning, start, opening, outset, starting point **od** (**samog**) ~**tka** from the (very) beginning **od** ~**tka do kraja** from first to last, throughout the ... **na** ~**tku** **a.** first of all **b.** at the beginning ~**tak 20. st.** early 20th c. **za** ~**tak** to begin with ~**ti** *v* (što) (*pres* počnem) 1 begin, start 2 take the lead/initiative ~**tni** *adj* initial; preliminary ~**tnica** *nf* 1 *primer* 2 beginner ~**tnički** *adj* beginners'

počinit|elj *nm* perpetrator ~**i** *v* (što) (ubojstvo) commit; (zločin) perpetrate

počinjati *v impf* → **početi**

počistiti *v* (što) clean up

počiva|ti *v* (0) rest; sleep; lie, rest ~**o u miru** rest in peace ~**ti u** *fig* lie in, rest with

počupati *v* 1 (što) pluck (off), pull out 2 (se s kime) (have a) scrap (with)

poći *v* (0) (*pres* pođem) 1 (kamo) set off, set out, depart, start on 2 (čime) take ~ **krivim putem** take the wrong path, go astray ~ **duljim putem** take the long way ~ **za nekog** marry sb **pošlo mi je za rukom** I managed to do it

pod (1) *prep* (koga/što; kim/čim) under, below, beneath, underneath; by

pod (2) *nm* floor

pod- *prefix* + glagol 1 radnja je usmjerena/odvija se prema dolje, ispod (**pod**+**vući** underline) 2 radnja je izvršena samo djelomično (**pod**+**napiti se** get tipsy)

podalje *adv* further down/on **držati se** ~ stand aloof

podan|ik *nm* (Vsg ~iče, Npl ~ici) subject

podao *adj* (podla f) mean, treacherous

podastrijeti *v* (što komu) submit

poda|tak *nm* (Gsg ~tka, Npl ~ci) fact ~**ci** *pl* data, information **obrada** ~**taka d.** processing

podat|an *adj* (α) soft, pliable, flexible ~**i** *v* (se komu) yield to

podaviti *v* (koga/se) suffocate, strangle, drown

podbaciti *v* (0) fail, fall short (of expectations)

podbadati *v impf* 1 (konja) spur 2 (koga na što) incite sb to, urge sb to, egg sb on

podbočiti *v* 1 (glavu) prop one's head on one's hands 2 (se) stand with arms akimbo

podbosti *v pf* → **podbadati**

podbra|dak *nm* (Gsg ~tka, Npl ~ci) double chin

podbrusiti *v* ~ **pete** take to one's heels

podbuh|ao *adj* (~la f) swollen, bloated, puffy

podcijeniti *v* (koga/što) underestimate, underrate ~**jenjivati** *v impf*

podcrtati *v* (što) underline, underscore (+ *fig*)

podčiniti → **podrediti, pokoriti**

podebljati *v* (što) make thicker; print in bold

podera|ti *v* (što) tear (to shreds), rent ~**n** *adj* torn, ragged

podgrijati *v* (što) warm up, reheat

podičiti *v* (se čime) take pride in, pride oneself on

podi|ći *v* (*pres* ~gnem) 1 (koga/što) pick up, lift; (+ *fig*) build, erect; (novac) draw; (cijenu) raise, increase; (ovratnik) turn up; (zastavu) hoist; collect 2 (se) rise (up), get up; rise up in arms; go up, soar (+ *fig*)

podije|liti *v* 1 (što čime) divide (sth by

sth) **2** (što komu) distribute, dispense; administer; share among; assign, allot **3** (se) split

podilazi|ti v (komu) curry favour with **jeza me ~** it gives me the creeps

podivlja|ti v (0) **1** go wild **2** fig go mad

podizati v impf → **podići**

podjariti v (koga) incense, fire

podjarmiti v (koga) subjugate, conquer

podjednak adj roughly equal, more or less the same

podjela nf division; distribution; partition

podjetinjiti v (0) go senile

podl|ac nm mean guy, scoundrel ~**ost** nf meanness; a mean thing to do

podlaktica nf forearm

podlegn|uti v (čemu) (pres ~**em**) succumb to, yield to, sink under

podlis|tak nm (Gsg ~tka, Npl ~ci) column

podlo|ga nf (Dsg ~zi) **1** base, foundation, ground **2** support **3** background **na crnoj ~zi** against a black background ~**žak** nm (Gsg ~ška) coaster, beermat ~**žan** adj **1** (čemu) subject to, liable to **2** (komu) dependent on, subordinate to ~**žiti** v **1** (koga) subjugate **2** (što) support, prop (up); (odjeću) pad, line ~**žnost** nf submissiveness

podljev nm med haematoma

podma|zati v (pres ~**žem**) **1** (što) grease, lubricate, oil **kao ~zano** fig smoothly **2** (koga) fig grease sb's palm

podmetati v impf → **podmetnuti**

podmetnuti v **1** (što pod što) put sth under sth, prop up from below **2** (što komu) foist sth on sb; frame coll **~ nogu komu** trip sb up

podmićivati v impf → **podmititi**

podmiriti v (što) settle, pay, square, balance **~ potrebe** meet the needs

podmit|iti v (koga, čime) bribe, buy/pay off ~**ljiv** adj corrupt, venal

podmla|dak nm (Gsg ~tka) new generation; progeny; (organizacije) Junior ....

podmor|nica nf submarine ~**ski** adj submarine

podmuk|ao adj (~la f) perfidious, false, treacherous, insidious

podnaslov nm subtitle

podne mn noon, midday **u ~** at noon **prije ~** in the morning, a. m. **poslije ~** in the afternoon, p. m. ~**vni** adj midday ~**vnica** nf meridian

podneblje nn climate

podnijeti v **1** (koga/što) bear, endure, put up with, suffer, stand **2** (što) report; file, submit **~ tužbu** file/bring a suit

podno prep (čega) at the foot of

podnositelj n applicant; plaintiff

podnositi v impf → **podnijeti**

podnošljiv adj bearable, tolerable, passable

podnožje nn foot, base

podoban adj (α) **1** suitable **2** (politički ~) derog loyal to the regime

podočnjaci nm pl dark rings/smudges around/under the eyes

podojiti v (koga) **1** milk **2** (dijete) nurse

podoknica nf serenade

podrazumijevati v **1** (što) presume, assume, imply **2** (što pod čim) mean sth by sth **3** (se) go without saying

podraž|aj nm stimulus ~**iti** v (koga) stimulate, arouse

podre|diti v (što čemu) subordinate ~**đen** adj subordinate to, inferior, junior ~**đenost** nf inferior rank, inferiority ~**đivati** v impf

podre|zati v (što) (pres ~**žem**) (granu) prune; clip, trim

podrhtavati v (0) (od) tremble, quiver (with)

podrignuti v (0/se) belch, burp

podrijetlo nn origin, descent

podroban adj (α) detailed, full

podrš|ka nf (Dsg ~ci) support, backing **pružiti ~ku** (give) support (to)

područ|je nn territory; area; field fig; domain ~**ni** adj district, regional

podrug|ivati v se (komu/čemu) mock, sneer at ~**ljiv** adj mocking, scornful

podrum nm cellar; basement ~**arstvo** nn wine production

podružni adj branch, subsidiary ~**ca** nf branch office

podrža|ti v (koga/što) support, back

~vati *v impf*

podsje|ćati *v* (koga na koga/što) remind sb of (sb/sth else) **~titi** *v* **1** (koga na što/da učini što) remind sb (to do sth) **2** (se) remember **~tnik** *nm* (*Npl* ~tnici) memo, memo pad, reminder

podsm|ijeh *nm* sneers *pl* **izložen ~ije-hu** sneered at **~jehnuti** *v* (se komu/čemu) sneer at **~jehivati** *v impf* **~ješljiv** *adj* scornful

podstanar *nm* subtenant, lodger

podstav|a lining **~iti** *v* (što/čime) line with **~ljati** *v impf* **~ljen** *adj* (čime) lined with

podsuknja *nf* slip, petticoat

podsv|ijest *nf* subconsciousness **u ~ijesti** at the back of one's mind **~jestan** *adj* (α) subconscious

poduč|avati *v* (koga/što; koga u čemu) teach **~iti** *v pf* teach sb sth, show sb how to do sth

podudarnost *nf* coincidence

podu|ka *nf* (*Dsg* ~ci) tuition

podup|irati *v* (koga, što) **1** hold up, prop/shore up; underpin (+ *fig*) **2** *fig* assist, support, favour **3** *fig* second **~rijeti** *v pf*

poduz|eće *nn* company, firm, enterprise **~etan** *adj* (α) enterprising, active **~eti** *v* (što) do **~ti mjere** take action/measures **~etnički** *adj* entrepreneurial **~etnik** *nm* (*Vsg* ~etniče, *Npl* ~etnici) entrepreneur; contractor **(slobodno) ~etništvo** *nn* (free) enterprise **~etnost** *nf* enterprising spirit, daring **~imati** *v impf*

podval|a *nf* fraud, swindle **~iti** *v* (kome) swindle

podvezica *nf* garter

podvi|g *nm* (*Npl* ~zi) exploit; accomplishment

podvi(nu)ti *v* (što pod što) fold (back); hem in; tuck in/up; double **~ rep** turn tail

podvlačiti *v impf* → **podvući**

podvod|ač *nm* pimp, ponce **~iti** *v* (0) pimp

podvodan *adj* (α) underwater

podvojen *adj* **1** split **2** divided **~ost** *nf* **mišljenja** dissension

podvolj|ak *nm* (*Gsg* ~ka, *Npl* ~ci)

double chin

podvor|ba *nf* service **~iti** *v* (koga čime) serve, attend to, wait on **~nik** *nm* (*Vsg* ~niče, *Npl* ~nici) caretaker *GB*; janitor *US*

podvostručiti *v* (što/se) double

podvožnja|k *nm* (*Npl* ~ci) underpass

podvrg|nuti *v* (*pres* ~nem) **1** (koga čemu) subject to **2** (se) undergo, go through **~avati** *v impf*

podvrn|uti *v* (što) (*pres* ~em) roll up; tuck in

podvu|ći *v* (*pres* ~čem) **1** (što) underline (+ *fig*) **2** **~ći noge** tuck one's legs under **3** (se) slip under

podzem|an *adj* (α) underground (+ *fig*) **~lje** *nn* underground (+ *fig*); underworld

poe|tičan *adj* poetic **~tika** *nf* poetics **~zija** *nf* poetry

pogača *nf* round bread

pogađati *v impf* **1** (što) try to guess **2** (koga) *fig* hit hard **3** (se) haggle

poganin *nm* pagan, heathen

pogasiti *v* **1** (što) extinguish, switch off **2** (se) go out

pogaziti *v* (koga, što) run over **~ svoju riječ** break one's word

pogibati *v impf* → **poginuti**

pogibelj *nf* danger, peril **~an** *adj* (α) dangerous

pogibija *nf* death

pogin|uti *v* (0) (*pres* ~em) die; perish; be killed

pogladiti *v* (koga, što) stroke, caress

poglav|ar *nm* superior, head **~arstvo** *nf* administration, authorities, government **~ica** *nm* chieftain

poglavit *adj* main, chief **~o** *adv* mainly, chiefly, in the first place

poglavlje *nn* chapter

pogled *nm* **1** look; glance **na prvi ~** at first sight **2** view, sight **~ na** view of **u ~u** (koga/čega) with regard to, as regards **u svakom ~u** in every respect **~ati** *v* **1** (koga/što) look at **mrko ~** frown upon **2** (se) exchange looks **~avati** *v* **1** (koga/što) keep glancing at **2** (se) be exchanging glances

pognojiti *v* (što) manure, fertilize

pogn|ut *adj* bent down, bowed down

~ute glave (with one's) head bowed **~uti** v (*pres* ~em) 1 (što) (leđa) bend; (glavu) bow down 2 (se) bend down, stoop

pogo|dak nm (*Gsg* ~tka, *Npl* ~ci) hit **pun ~dak** bull's eye; bingo *int* **~dan** *adj* (a) adequate, suitable, propitious **~dnost** *nf* convenience, amenity; favourable condition **~dba** *nf* deal, bargain **sklopiti ~dbu** make/close a deal **~dben** *adj gram* conditional **~diti** v 1 (koga/što) hit, strike; affect, touch fig 2 (što) guess 3 (se) strike a deal, reach an agreement **~dovati** v (komu/čemu) (*pres* ~ujem) favour, be favourable to

pogon nm 1 (tvornica) plant 2 drive **na parni ~** steam-powered **prednji ~** front-wheel drive **pustiti u ~** put into operation

pogorša|ti v 1 (što) aggravate, make worse 2 (se) (odnosi, zdravlje) deteriorate; (vrijeme) change for the worse **~vati se** v *impf*

pogostiti v 1 (koga) entertain; wine and dine *coll* 2 (se čime) feast on

pogotovo *adv* especially, in particular

pogovor nm epilogue **bez ~a** without demur

pograbiti v 1 (koga, što) grab, seize, snatch 2 (se) grapple

pograničļan *adj* (a) border **~no područje** b. area **~ni sukob** b. incident

pogrb|iti v (se) stoop, bend one's back **~ljeno** *adj* držanje stoop **~ljenost** *nf* stoop

pogrda *nf* insult, abuse **~n** *adj* (a) abusive, insulting

pogreb nm funeral, burial **~ni** *adj* 1 funeral **~na kola** hearse **~no poduzeće** undertaker *GB*, funeral parlor *US* 2 *fig* funereal **~nik** nm (*Vsg* ~niče, *Npl* ~nici) undertaker

pogreš|an *adj* (a) wrong, incorrect, inaccurate **~iv** *adj* fallible **~ka** *nf* (*Dsg* ~ci) error, mistake; flaw, defect **bez ~ke** faultless **~no** *adv* erroneously, wrongly

pogriješiti v (0) make a mistake

pogub|an *adj* (a) lethal; dangerous **~iti** v 1 (koga) execute, put to death 2 (što) lose **~ljenje** nn execution

pogušiti v 1 (koga) strangle 2 (se) suffocate

pohaba|n *adj* worn (out), shabby **~ti** v (se) wear out

pohađati v (što) attend

poharati v (što) devastate, lay waste; plunder

pohitati v (0) rush **~ komu u pomoć** r. to sb's rescue

pohlepa *nf* greed **~n** *adj* (a) greedy, avid

pohod nm 1 *mil* campaign 2 visit **~iti** v (koga) visit

pohot|a *nf* lust **~an, ~ljiv** *adj* lecherous, lewd, lustful

pohran|a *nf* deposit; safe-keeping; custody **~iti** v (što, kod koga) deposit, leave in sb's safekeeping **~iti u banci** put into bank for safe-keeping

pohrliti v (0) rush, run

pohval|a *nf* praise; acknowledgement, citation **dobiti ~u** be commended **~an** *adj* (a) commendable **~no** *adv* **se izraziti o komu** praise sb, speak highly of **~iti** v 1 (koga, što) praise, compliment 2 (se, čime) boast (of)

pohvatati v (koga, što) catch, seize, capture **~ sve konce** have the situation under control

poigra|ti v (se) 1 (s čim) play with sth for a while 2 (s kime) trifle with **~vati** v *impf*

poima|nje nn 1 idea, conception 2 view **~ti** v (što) conceive

poimence *adv* by name **~ navesti** specify

poispadati v (0) 1 (from the game) drop 2 (hair) fall

poistovje|titi v 1 (što s čime) equate 2 (se s kime) identify oneself with sb **~ćivati** v *impf*

poj nm 1 chant 2 (ptičji) song

pojača|lo nn amplifier **~nje** nn *mil* reinforcements, backup **~ti** v 1 (što) fortify; strengthen; reinforce; (zvuk) amplify; turn up 2 (se) gather strength; grow; rise; increase **~avati** v *impf*

poj|am nm (*Gsg* ~ma, *Npl* ~movi) notion, concept **nemati ~ma** have no idea **~miti** v (što) understand, grasp **~mljiv** *adj* conceivable **~movni** *adj* notional

pojas *nm* 1 belt ~ **za spašavanje** life-belt 2 waist 3 *fig* area, belt; zone

pojav|a *nf* 1 phenomenon 2 appearance, emergence 3 figure, appearance, looks **on je prava ~a** he is a fine figure of a man **~iti** *v* (se) appear, emerge; show up; (disease) break out **~ljivati** *v* (se) appear

pojedin|ac *nm* (*Gsg* ~ca, *Vsg* ~če, *Npl* ~ci) individual, person **~ačan** *adj* (α) individual **~ačno** *adv* one by one, individually **~i** *adj* particular **~ost** *nf* detail

pojednostavniti *v* (što) simplify

pojefti|niti *v* 1 (0) become cheaper 2 (što) reduce the price **~njenje** *nn* price reduction, sale

poje|sti *v* (*pres* ~dem) 1 (što) eat up 2 (se) *fig* **~sti se živ/od muke** eat one's heart out, suffer

poji|lište *nn* watering-hole

pojuriti *v* (0) break into a run, bolt ~ **za kim** race/chase after sb

pokaj|anje *nn* repentance **čin** ~anja act of contrition **~ati** *v* 1 (se za što) repent sth 2 (se zbog čega) regret sth **~nik** *nm* (*Vsg* ~niče, *Npl* ~nici) repentant person, penitent **~nički** *adj* penitent, contrite

pokal *nm sport* cup

pokapati *v impf* → **pokopati**

pokarati *v* 1 (koga) rebuke 2 (koga/se) *vulg* hump

pokaz *nm coll* (bus) pass **~an** *adj* (α) demonstrative **~atelj** *nm* indicator; index **~ati** *v* (*pres* pokažem) 1 (komu/što) point out, indicate, show; demonstrate **~at ću ja tebi** I'll show you 2 (se kime/čime) prove (to be), turn out (to be) 3 (se) appear, emerge **~ati primjer** set an example **~ati zube** *fig* show one's teeth **~ati prstom** (na) point one's finger at (+ *fig*) **~ivač** *nm* indicator

pokidati *v* (što) tear up

pokis|ao *adj* (~la *f*) 1 wet **~ao do kože** w. through, drenched 2 blue, down **kao ~la kokoš** down in the dumps **~nuti** *v* (0) get caught in the rain, get drenched in the rain

poklad|e *nf pl* carnival **~nica** *nf* doughnut

poklanjati *v impf* → **pokloniti**

poklapati *v* (se s čim) 1 dovetail (with), tally with 2 coincide

poklati *v* 1 (koga) slaughter, massacre 2 (se) *fig* have a vicious fight

pokleknuti *v* (0) 1 genuflect 2 (pred kim/čim) *fig* knuckle under, give in to

poklič *nm* cry

poklisar *nm* envoy, ambassador

poklon *nm* 1 present, gift **dati na ~** give (away) 2 (muškarac) bow; (žena) curtsey **~ik** *nm* (*Vsg* ~iče, *Npl* ~ik) follower, devotee, fan **~iti** *v* 1 (što komu) give sb sth as a present 2 (komu/čemu što) devote **~iti komu život** spare sb/sb's life 3 (se) bow, curtsey

poklop|ac *nm* lid, top **biti svakom loncu ~ac** have a finger in every pie **~iti** *v* 1 (što) put a lid on, close, cover, stop 2 (se) coincide

pokoj *nm* rest, peace ~ **mu vječni** may he rest in peace **~ni** *adj* the late **~nik** *nm* (*Npl* ~nici) the deceased

pokolebati *v* 1 (koga u nakani) discourage sb from doing sth; weaken sb's resolve 2 (se) waver

pokolj *nm* massacre, slaughter, carnage

pokoljenje *nn* generation

pokop *nm* funeral, burial **~ati** *v* 1 (koga/što) bury 2 (koga) *fig* pull to pieces **~avati** *v impf*

pokor|a *nf* 1 penance, atonement 2 (stvar) trouble; (osoba) trial **~an** *adj* (α) obedient, humble **~iti** *v* 1 (koga/što) conquer, subjugate 2 (se komu/čemu) submit to, obey sb/sth **~nik** *nm* (*Vsg* ~niče, *Npl* ~nici) penitent **~nost** *nf* obedience **držati u ~nosti** subjugate

poko|siti *v* 1 (što) mow, cut 2 (koga) *fig* mow down; knock down

pokraj *prep* (koga/čega) beside, by, next to, alongside; (kretanje) along, past **~nji** *adj* side

pokrajin|a *nf* province, region **~ski** *adj* regional, provincial

pokra|sti *v* (*pres* ~dem) 1 (koga) rob 2 (što) steal

pokre|nuti v 1 (što) move, shift; set in motion, start, initiate (+ *fig*) ~**nuti pitanje** raise the question/issue ~**nuti parnicu** file a suit ~**nuti krivični postupak** bring criminal charges 2 (se) move, rouse oneself ~**ni se!** get a move on! ~**t** *nm* 1 movement, motion 2 *pol* movement 3 *mil* advance **u** ~**tu** in motion; on the move ~**tač** *nm* founder **glavni** ~**tač** *fig* prime mover ~**tan** *adj* (*a*) moving, mobile, moveable ~**tna imovina** personal property/estate ~**tati** v (*pres* ~**ćem**) 1 (što/se) iter → **pokrenuti** 2 (što) propel **para** ~**će motor** the engine runs on steam/is steam-driven ~**tljiv** *adj* mobile; able to walk ~**tnine** *nf* movables

pokri|će *nn* backing, cover **ček bez** ~**ća** check that bounced ~**ti** v 1 (koga/što) cover 2 (se) cover (oneself) ~**ti se ušima** *coll* eat humble pie ~**vač** *nm* cover(let), blanket ~**vati** v (koga/što) *mil* cover

pokrov *nm* shroud

pokrovitelj *nm* patron; sponsor ~**stvo** patronage, sponsorship ~**ski** *adj* patronizing

pokrpati v (što) patch up

pokr|stiti v 1 (koga) convert to Christianity 2 (se) be converted to C.

pokucati v (0) knock ~ **na vrata** knock at the door ~ **o drvo** knock on/touch wood

pokućar|ac *nm* (*Gsg* ~ca, *Vsg* ~če) door to door salesman

pokućstvo *nn* furniture

pokud|a *nf* censure, criticism, rebuke ~**iti** v (koga) censure

pokunj|iti v (se) 1 be ashamed 2 lose heart, become dispirited ~**en** *adj* downcast, depressed ~**enost** *nf* low spirits

pokupiti v 1 (koga/što) pick (up) 2 (se) *coll* leave

pokup|ovati v (što) (*pres* ~**ujem**) buy (up)

pokus *nm* 1 experiment, test 2 rehearsal ~**ni** *adj* trial, experimental, test; (životinja) laboratory ~**ni kunić** *fig* guinea pig

pokušaj *nm* attempt, try ~**j umorstva**

attempted murder ~**ti** v (što) attempt, try ~**o ga je ubiti** he tried to kill him ~**vati** v *impf*

pokvar|en *adj* 1 (stroj) broken, out of order 2 (hrana) gone bad, rotten 3 (osoba) corrupt, bad ~**enost** *nf* depravity, corruption ~**enjak** *nm* bad guy **stari** ~**enjak** dirty old man ~**iti** v 1 (što) spoil, ruin, destroy; break ~**iti želudac** get food poisoning ~**iti komu planove** upset sb's plans 2 (se) break down; (hrana) go bad

pol *nm* pole

pola *adv* half **na** ~ **puta** halfway (across/down) **na** ~ half(-) **po** ~ in half ~ **sata** half an hour ~ **pet** half (past) four

polagan *adj* slow; gradual

pola|gati (*pres* ~**žem**) v *impf* → **položiti** ~**gati nadu** (u koga/što) pin one's hopes on ~**gati pravo na što** lay claim on

polako *adv* (*comp* **polakše**) slowly ~! take it easy!

polakomiti v (se za kim/čim) covet

polarn|i *adj* polar ~**a svjetlost** aurora borealis, the northern lights

pola|zak *nm* (*Gsg* ~**ska**, *Npl* ~**sci**) departure ~**zište** *nn* *fig* starting point; standpoint ~**ziti** v (0) start, depart, leave ~**znik** *nm* (*Vsg* ~**zniče**, *Npl* ~**znici**) (course) participant, student

poledica *nf* black ice

poleđina *nf* back

polemi|čan *adj* (*a*) controversial ~**ka** *nf* (*Dsg* ~**ci**) debate, controversy ~**zirati** v (s kim) argue

polet *nm* enthusiasm, zeal ~**an** *adj* (*a*) enthusiastic, vigorous, lively

polet|jeti v (0) (*pres* ~**im**) (zrakoplov) take off, be(come) airborne; (ptica) fly away

polica (1) *nf* shelf

polica (2) *nf* insurance policy

polic|ajac *nm* (*Gsg* ~**ajca**, *Vsg* ~**ajče**, *Npl* ~**ajci**) police officer ~**ija** *nf* the police ~**ijski** *adj* police ~**ijski sat** curfew ~**ijska postaja** p. station

poligon *nm* *mil* army range; testing ground

polijetati v *impf* → **poletjeti**

polijevati v (koga/što/se čime) pour

sth over sb/sth/oneself

poliklini|ka *nf* (*Dsg* ~ci) health care centre

polip *nm* 1 polyp 2 *med* adenoid

polirati *v* (što) polish

poli|ti *v* (koga/što/se čime) (*pres* ~jem) splash sth over sb/sth/oneself

politi|čki *adj* political ~**čar** *nm* politician ~**ka** *nf* (*Dsg* ~ci) 1 politics 2 policy ~**kant** *nm derog* demagogue ~**zirati** *v* 1 (0) discuss politics 2 (što) turn sth into a political issue, politicize

poli|zati *v* (što) (*pres* ~žem) lick (up)

polnoćka *nf* midnight mass

polomiti *v* (koga/što/se) break

polovan *adj* (*a*) secod-hand, used

polovi|ca *nf* half **bolja** ~**ca** *iron* one's better half ~**čan** *adj* (*a*) incomplete ~**čne mjere** half(way) measures

polož|aj *nm* 1 position, location 2 state, condition, status, rank 3 function, capacity ~**iti** *v* (što) 1 put/set down, place, lay (down) 2 (ispit) pass 3 (novac) deposit 4 (oružje) lay down 5 (zakletvu) take

poltron *nm* sycophant

polu- *prefix* half-, semi-, hemi- ~**brat** *nm* half-brother ~**cilindar** *nm* (*Gsg* ~cilindra) bowler hat ~**dragi** *adj* semiprecious ~**finale** *nn* semifinals ~**godište** *nn* semester ~**kat** *nm* mezzanine ~**krug** *nm* semicircle ~**krvan** *adj* (*a*) half-breed ~**kugla** *nf* hemisphere ~**mjer** *nm* radius ~**mjesec** *nm* half-moon, crescent ~**otok** *nm* (*Npl* ~otoci) peninsula ~**proizvod** *nm* semi-finished product ~**san** *nm* doze biti u ~**snu** be half-asleep ~**sestra** *nf* half-sister ~**vodič** *nm tech* semiconductor ~**vrijeme** *nn* half time

polučiti *v* (što) obtain, achieve

poludjeti *v* (0) (*pres* ~im) go crazy

polu|ga *nf* (*Dsg* ~zi) 1 lever 2 (zlato) ingot

polut|ka *nf* (*Dsg* ~ci) hemisphere

polj|ana *nf* meadow, field ~**e** *nn* field (+ *fig*) **bojno** ~**e** battle-field ~**odjelac** *nm* (*Gsg* ~odjelca, *Vsg* ~odjelče) farmer ~**odjelstvo** *nn* agriculture, farming ~**oprivreda** *nf* agriculture ~**oprivredni** *adj* agricultural ~**ski**

adj cvijet wild flower ~**ski miš** field mouse ~**ski krevet** camp bed; cot *US* ~**ska kuhinja** field kitchen ~**ski put** dirt road

poljepšati *v* (koga/što) make sb/sth (more) beautiful, make sth look better

polju|bac *nm* (*Gsg* ~pca) kiss ~**biti** *v* 1 (koga/što) kiss 2 (se) kiss each other

poljuljati *v* (što) shake, weaken, undermine

pomaga|č *nm* assistant, helper ~**lo** *nn* aid ~**ti** *v impf* → **pomoći**

pomahnitati *v* (0) go wild, run amok

pomajka *nf* (*Dsg* ~ci) step-mother

pomakn|uti *v* (koga/što/se) (*pres* ~em) move, shift

pomalo *adv* slightly **malo-**~ little by little, inch by inch, step by step

pomaljati *v* (se) appear, emerge

pomam|a *nf* 1 rage, frenzy 2 craze ~**an** (*a*) frantic, wild ~**iti** *v* (se) 1 go wild 2 (za kim/čim) be crazy about

pomanjkanje *nn* 1 lack, shortage 2 deficiency

poma|st *nf* ointment **posljednja** ~**st** Extreme Unction ~**zanje** *nn* anointment ~**zanik** *nm* (*Vsg* ~zniče) (~ Božji) (the Lord's) anointed ~**zati** *v* (koga) (*pres* ~žem) anoint

pome|sti (1) (*pres* ~tem) *v* (koga/što) foil, prevent ~**tnja** *nf* confusion, disturbance, commotion

pome|sti (2) *v* (što) sweep ~**tač** *nm* sweeper

pome|tati (1) *v* (što) (*pres* ~ćem) put (up)

pometati (2) *v impf* → **pomesti** (2)

pomi|cati *v impf* → **pomaknuti** ~**čan** *adj* movable, mobile

pomiješati *v* 1 (što) mix 2 (se) mingle

pomilova|nje *nn* amnesty, pardon ~**ti** *v* (koga) pardon

pomir|ba *nf* reconciliation ~**iti** *v* (se) make up, reconcile ~**iti se s čim** become reconciled to ~**ljiv** *adj* conciliatory

pomi|sao *nf* (*Gsg* ~sli) thought, idea ~**sao na** thought of ~**sliti** *v* (na koga/što) think of ~**šljati** *v* (na što) be thinking of, contemplate

pomladiti *v* 1 (koga/što) rejuvenate,

revive, give a new lease of/on life **2** (se) become young again

pomno *adv* carefully; closely

pomnožiti *v* (što sa čim) multiply by

pomnja *nf* care, attention

pomoć *nf* help; aid; assistance; support; advice **hitna ~ a.** (vozilo) ambulance **b.** (služba) emergency (room/ward) **socijalna ~** welfare; the dole *coll* **pružiti ~** (offer) help **priskočiti u ~** come/rush to sb's aid **biti od ~i** be of assistance **u~!** help! **~i ~** (komu pomognem) help; aid; assist, be of assistance, lend/give a hand **~ni** *adj* auxiliary; subsidiary **~nik** *nm* (*Npl* ~nici) assistant **kućna ~nica** *nf* maid **~u** *adv* (čega) by means of

pomodan *adj* (*a*) fashionable, trendy

pomokriti *v* (se) urinate **~ se u krevet** wet one's bed

pomol *nm* **biti na ~u** loom **~iti** *v* **1** (se) appear **2** (što) expose, show **~iti nos** peep; show up

pomoliti *v* (se) pray, say a prayer

pomor *nm* mass death

pomor|ac *nm* (*Gsg* ~ca, *Vsg* ~če, *Npl* ~ci) seaman, mariner **~ski** *adj* sea, maritime **~stvo** *nn* maritime affairs

pomp|a *nf* pomp **~ezan, ~ozan** *adj* (*a*) pompous

pomrač|en *adj* (um) deranged **~iti** *v* (što) darken, obscure; (sunce) eclipse

pomrčina *nf* eclipse

pomr|ijeti *v* (0) (*pres* ~em) die (off)

pomrsiti *v* (što) **~ komu račune** put a spoke in sb's wheels

pomučiti *v* (se) make an effort, try hard, work hard

pomućivati *v impf* → **pomutiti ~en** *adj* (um) deranged

pomu|sti *v* (koga) (*pres* ~zem) milk

pomut|iti *v* (što) **1** cloud, dim **2** *fig* confuse, trouble, dim **~iti** (komu) **pamet** drive sb insane **~iti** (komu) **planove** thwart sb's plans **~nja** *nf* confusion, bewilderment

ponada|ti *v* (se) begin to hope (in vain)

ponajbolji *adj* one of the best, among the best

ponajprije *adv* first of all

ponajviše *adv* mostly, chiefly

ponaosob *adv* one by one, individually *razgovarao je sa svakim ~* he spoke to each man (in private)

ponaša|nje *nn* behaviour **lijepo ~nje** good manners **~ti** *v* (se) behave **pazi kako se ~š** behave (yourself)

ponavlja|č *nm* pupil who has to repeat a year in school **~nje** *nn* repetition; revision **~ti** *v impf* **1** (što/se) repeat sth/oneself **~ti razred/godinu** repeat a year **2** (što) (gradivo) revise; review US

ponedjelj|ak (*Gsg* ~ka) *nm* Monday **u ~ak** on Monday **~kom** on Mondays

ponegdje *adv* in places, here and there

ponekad *adv* from time to time, on and off, sometimes

poneki *pron* some of • *adj* certain

ponesta|ti *v* (komu čega) run out of; run short of **~je nam benzina** we're running out of petrol **~jati** *v impf*

ponešto *pron* a little (something), a bit

ponijeti *v* (*pres* ponesem) **1** (što) take/carry/bring (along) **~ što sa sobom** take with **2** (koga) carry away, charm **3** (se) act **~ se prema komu lijepo/ružno** treat sb well/badly

poniknuti *v* (*pres* ~em) **1** (0) sprout **2 ~uti glavom** lower one's head

ponir|ati *v* (0) (*pres* ~em) dive, plummet

poništ|iti *v* (što) (ček) cancel; (dozvolu) revoke; (sudsku odluku) reverse; (ugovor) void, declare null and void; (brak) annul **~avati** *v impf*

poniž|an *adj* (*a*) humble, abject **~ziti** *v* **1** (koga) humiliate, humble **2** (se) demean oneself **~znost** *nf* humility, submissiveness **~žavati** *v impf* **~ženje** *nn* humiliation

ponoć *nf* midnight **u ~** at m.

ponor *nm* abyss, precipice **~nica** *nf* underground stream

ponos *nm* pride **~an** *adj* (*a*) proud **~iti** *v* (se kime/čime) be proud of

ponov|ni *adj* second, another **~no** *adv* again **~iti** *v* **1** (što) repeat, say once again; revise, review **2** (što za kim) repeat sth after sb **3** (se) *fig* buy new clothes

ponton *nm* pontoon **~ski** *adj* most p. bridge

ponud|a *nf* 1 offer **zahvaliti se na ~i** decline an o. 2 *comm* tender, bid **dati ~u za** bid/tender for **~a i potražnja** supply and demand **~iti** *v* 1 (komu što) offer **~ brak komu** propose to sb 2 (se) offer one's help 3 (se čime) help oneself to sth

ponukati *v* (koga na što) 1 encourage 2 make/induce sb do sth

ponjušiti *v* (koga/što) sniff (at)

poočim *nm* step-father

poodavna *adv* a long time ago

pooštr|iti *v* (što) **~iti kazne** increase fines, impose stiffer fines **~iti mjere protiv** take stronger measures; crack/clamp down on **~avati** *v iter*

popadati *v* (0) fall down, collapse

pop|eti *v* (se na što) (*pres* **~nem**) climb (sth) **~eo mi se navrh glave** I am sick and tired of him

popijev|ka *nf* (*Dsg* **~ci**) song, ditty

popipati *v* (koga/što/se) feel

popis *nm* 1 list 2 register **~ stanovništva** census **~ati** *v* (koga/što) (*pres* **popišem**) make a list, take inventory/stock **~ivač** census-taker **~ivati** *v iter*

popišati *v* (se) *vulg* piss, take a piss, go for a piss; have a slash *GB coll*

popiti *v* (što) drink up **~ nadušak** drain the glass (in a gulp)

popizditi *v* (0) *tab sl* get pissed off

poplaćati *v* (što) pay, settle

poplav|a *nf* flood (+ *fig*), floods **~iti** *v* (što) flood **~ljivati** *v impf* flood, overflow

popločati *v* (što) pave; tile

poplun *nm* quilt, duvet

poplju|vati *v* (koga/što) (*pres* **~jem**) *fig* (osobu) criticize; (knjigu i sl.) slate

popodne *nn* afternoon • *adv* in the afternoon

popola *adv* fifty-fifty; in half

popovati *v* (komu) *fig* lecture, sermonize, preach

popra|titi *v* (što čime) **~titi suzama/pljeskom/zvižducima** cry/applaud/jeer at sth **~titi bilješkama** annotate, gloss **~ćen** *adj* accompanied **~tan** *adj* accompanying **~tna pojava** side-effect **~tno pismo** covering letter

poprav|ak *nm* (*Gsg* **~ka**, *Npl* **~ci**) repair **~ilište** *nn* community home *GB*; reformatory *US* **~iti** *v* 1 (što) repair, fix, mend **~iti kravatu** straighten one's tie **~iti frizuru** touch up one's hair(do) 2 (se) reform, mend one's ways **~ljati** *v impf*

popreč|an *adj* (α) transversal, lateral **~ni presjek** cross section **~no** *adv* across, diagonally

popričati *v* (s kim) have a chat with

poprijeko *adv* diagonally, across **gledati koga ~** frown at sb **uzduž i ~** everywhere, all over the place

popriličan *adj* (α) of considerable size/importance

poprim|iti *v* (što) assume, adopt, acquire **~ati** *v impf*

poprište *v* scene; site; battlefield

poprsje *nn* bust

poprska|ti *v* (što/koga čime) sprinkle/spray sth all over sth/sb, sprinkle/spray sth/sb with **~n krvlju** blood-spattered

popucati *v* (0) snap, split

popudbina *nf* 1 travelling expenses 2 provisions (for travel)

popular|an *adj* (α) 1 popular 2 (cijene) affordable **~nost** *nf* fame, popularity

popuniti *v* 1 (što) fill in/out **~ prazninu** fill in the gap 2 (se) gain weight

popust *nm* reduction, discount, price cut **~iti** *v* 1 (komu) give in to, yield 2 (što) slacken, loosen 3 (0) become loose, give in, slacken 4 (0) (kiša) slacken, let up **~ljiv** *adj* (over)indulgent; lenient

popušiti *v* 1 (što) smoke 2 (što) *fig coll* screw up **~ foru** *coll* fall for the trick, buy it 3 (komu) *tab* give sb head, suck sb off

popuštati *v impf* → **popustiti**

poput *prep* (koga/čega) like

pora *nf* pore

poraba *nf* use

poradi *prep* **1** on account of **2** with the aim of, for the purpose of

porađati *v impf* **1** (koga) assist in childbirth ~ **bebu** deliver a baby **2** (se) give birth to a baby

porast *nm* (čega) increase/growth in/of **u** ~**u** on the rise; on the increase ~**i** *v* (0) (*pres* ~**em**) increase, go up, rise

poratni *adj* post-war

poravnati *v* **1** (što) (zemlju) level; (račune) settle; (margine) justify, align **2** (se) come abreast

poraz *nm* defeat **pretrpjeti** ~ be defeated ~**an** *adj* (α) disastrous, crushing ~**iti** *v* (koga) defeat, overpower

porazbijati *v* (što) break/smash up

porazgovarati *v* (s kim/se) have a chat, have a word

poražavati *v impf* → **poraziti**

porculan *nm* china, porcelain ~**ski** *adj* china ~**ski servis** china

poreći *v* (što) (*pres* ~**knem**) deny

pored *prep* (koga/čega) → **pokraj, uz**

pore|dak *nm* (*Gsg* ~**tka**) **1** order, sequence, arrangement **2** system, law and order ~**dati** *v* (koga/što/se) line up

pored|ba *nf* comparison; simile ~**ben** *adj* comparative

poreme|ćaj *nm* disorder, collapse, breakdown (**umno**) ~**ćen** *adj* (mentally) deranged, unbalanced ~**titi** *v* (što) derange, disturb, throw into confusion ~**titi ravnotežu** disturb the balance

porez *nm* tax; taxation ~**ni** *adj* tax ~**nik** *nm* (*Vsg* ~**niče**, *Npl* ~**nici**) tax collector

pore|zati *v* (*pres* ~**žem**) **1** (koga/što) cut **2** (se) cut oneself, get cut

poribiti *v* (što) stock with fish

poricati *v impf* → **poreći**

porijek|lo *nn* origin(s), descent **nepoznatog** ~**a** of unknown origin **irskog** ~**a** of Irish descent **vući** ~**o od** have one's origins in, trace one's origins (back) to

poriluk *nm* leek

porin|uti *v* (što) (*pres* ~**em**) (brod) launch

poriv *nm* drive, impetus, impulse, urge

porječje *nn* river basin

porječkati *v* (se) have words, squabble

porn|ić *nm sl* blue film; skin flick *sl* ~**ografija** *nf* pornography; porn *coll* ~**ografski** *adj* pornographic; porn(o) *coll*

porobiti *v* (koga/što) enslave

poročan *adj* (α) sinful, immoral, bad

poro|dica *nf* family ~**diljski** *adj* do-pust maternity leave ~**diti** → **roditi** ~**đaj** *nm* childbirth; delivery ~**đajni** *adj* **bolovi** labour pains, contractions

poro|k *nm* (*Npl* ~**ci**) vice, bad habit

porot|a *nf* jury ~**nik** *nm* (*Vsg* ~**niče**, *Npl* ~**nici**) juror

porozan *adj* (α) porous

port|a *nf* **1** doorway, entrance **2** porter's lodge; gatehouse; reception desk ~**afon** *nf* entryphone, intercom ~**ir** *nm* doorkeeper, doorman; porter *GB*; receptionist ~**irnica** → **porta** (2)

portfelj *nm* → **lisnica**

portret *nm* portrait ~**irati** *v* **1** (koga) make/paint sb's portrait **2** (što/koga) *fig* portray ~**ist** *nm* portrait painter, portraitist

porub *nm* hem, border, selvage ~**iti** *v* (što) hem, border, edge

poručiti *v* **1** (što) send a message, send word, advise **2** (po koga) send for

poručni|k *nm* (*Vsg* ~**če**, *Npl* ~**ci**) Lieutenant

poru|ga *nf* (*Dsg* ~**zi**) derision, mockery, ridicule, scoff

poru|ka *nf* (*Dsg* ~**ci**) message

porume|njeti *v* (0) (*pres* ~**nim**) blush, flush

porušiti *v* (što) pull/knock/tear down

poruž|njeti *v* (0) (*pres* ~**nim**) become ugly, lose one's beauty

posada *nf* crew

posaditi *v* **1** (biljku) plant **2** (koga) *coll* seat, sit, set, place

posakrivati *v* (koga/što/se) hide

pos|ao *nm* (*Gsg* ~**la**, *Npl* ~**lovi**) **1** work; labour **2** job **3** business; affairs, dealings *pl* **4** deal, transaction **fizički** ~**ao** manual work/labour **umni** ~**ao** intellectual work **ići na** ~**ao** go to work **imati** ~**ao** have a job

imati ~la be busy, have work to do
imati ~la s kim have dealings with
imati pametnijeg ~la have other fish to fry *coll* **sklopiti ~ao** make a deal **latiti se ~la** get down to work **gledati svoj ~ao/svoja posla** mind one's own business **pričati o ~lu** talk business/shop **sitni ~lovi** errands **vanjski/unutarnji ~lovi** foreign/internal affairs

posavjet|ovati *v* (*pres* ~ujem) **1** (koga) advise, counsel **2** (se s kim) consult (with)

poseban *adj* (a) special, extra, particular; separate

posegn|uti *v* (*pres* ~em) **1** (za čim) reach out for, grab/snatch at **2** (čime na koga) draw sth on sb

poseniliti *v* (0) become senile, be in one's dotage

posesivan *adj* (a) possessive

posezati *v impf* → **posegnuti**

posezona *nf* off-peak season, off-season, low season

posij|ati *v* (što) (*pres* ~em) sow

posij|e *nf pl* bran

posijed|jeti *v* (0) (*pres* ~im) go grey

posin|ak *nm* (*Gsg* ~ka, *Npl* ~ci) foster/adopted son

posipati *v* (koga/što čime) sprinkle, strew (with) **~ se pepelom** be in/wear sackcloth and ashes

posj|eći *v* (*pres* ~iječem) **1** (koga/što) cut **2** (stablo) cut down, fell **3** (se) cut oneself

posjećivati *v impf* → **posjetiti**

posjed *nm* property, estate; possession **~nik** *nm* (*Npl* ~nici) owner, proprietor **~ovati** *v* (što) (*pres* ~ujem) own, possess

posjedati *v* (0) sit down, take seats, be seated

posjekotina *nf* cut, laceration

posje|sti *v* (*pres* ~dnem) (koga) seat, sit

posje|t *nm* visit, call, attendance **~titelj** *nm* visitor, caller, guest **~titi** *v* (koga/što) visit, pay a visit/call to, call (up)on, come round **~tnica** *nf* (visiting) card; business card **~ćivati** *v impf*

poska|kati *v* (0) (*pres* ~čem) jump,

leap, spring **~kivati** *v impf*

poskidati *v* (što) take off, get/take down

poskočiti → **poskakati**

posko|k *nm* (*Npl* ~ci) viper

poskup|iti *v* (što) increase/raise/hike (up) *coll* the price of **~jeti** *v* (0) become more expensive, go up **~ljenje** *nn* price increase/rise

posla|gati *v* (što) (*pres* ~žem) arrange, put in order, file, stack

poslanica *nf* epistle **papina ~** (papal) bull **predsjednička ~** presidential address

posla|nik → **izaslanik**; zastupnik **~nje** *nn* mission

poslastica *nf* **1** delicacy, dainty; goody *coll* **2** titbit *GB*; tidbit *US* (+ *fig*)

poslati *v* (koga/što) (*pres* pošaljem) send (away/off); dispatch, forward **~ po** send for

poslije *adv* afterwards, later (on), then
• *prep* (koga/čega) after **~ podne** in the afternoon **~podne** *nn* afternoon **~podnevni** *adj* afternoon **~diplomski** *adj* postgraduate *GB*; graduate *US* **~ratni** *adj* postwar

poslo|davac *nm* (*Gsg* ~davca, *Npl* ~davci) employer **~van** *adj* (a) business; businesslike **~vna zgrada** office block/building **~vanje** *nn* business, transaction, dealing, operation **~vati** *v* (0) (*pres* poslujem) conduct/do/transact business, operate; run a business, be in business **~vnica** *nf* office; branch (office) **~vnik** *nm* (*Npl* ~nici) rules of procedure, standing orders, rule book **~vođa** *nm* foreman

poslovica *nf* proverb

poslu|ga *nf* (*Dsg* ~zi) service; servants, attendants *pl*

posluš|an *adj* (a) obedient, compliant **~ati** *v* (koga/što) **1** listen to; hear out; lend an ear to **2** obey; take/follow sb's advice **~nik** *nm* (*Npl* ~nici) *derog* minion

poslužitelj *nm* attendant **~ti** *v* **1** (što) serve **2** (koga) wait on sb **3** (koga čime) serve sb (with) sth, serve sth to sb **4** (čemu) serve (as/for/to do sth) **5**

(se čime) help oneself to sth ~**vati** *v impf*

posljedi|ca *nf* consequence, effect, result **snositi** ~**ce** take the consequences; face the music *coll* **uzrok i ~ca** cause and effect ~**čan** *adj* (*a*) consequent

posljednj|i *adj* 1 last; final 2 latest u ~**e vrijeme** recently, in recent times, lately, of late

posmrtn|i *adj* posthumous ~**i govor/~o slovo** funeral oration ~**i ostaci** (mortal) remains ~**a maska** death mask

posoliti *v* (što) salt, add salt to

pospan *adj* sleepy, drowsy ~**ac** *nm* (*Gsg* ~ca, *Npl* ~ci), ~**ko** *nm coll* sleepyhead

pospješiti *v* (što) hasten, accelerate, speed up, step up

posprdan *adj* (*a*) mocking, derisive, jeering, scoffing; scornful

posprem|iti *v* (što) 1 tidy up, put in order 2 clear away, put away **veliko ~anje** *nn* spring-clean(ing)

posramiti *v* 1 (koga) make sb feel ashamed; shame, embarrass, put sb to shame 2 (se) be ashamed/embarrassed; blush

posra|n *adj vulg fig* shitty; lousy ~**nac** *nm* (*Gsg* ~nca, *Npl* ~nci) shitpants ~**ti** *v* (se) (*pres* **poserem**) *vulg* shit, take a shit; shit oneself

posrebren *adj* silver-plated

posreć|iti *v* (se) ~**lo mi se** I was/got lucky

posred *prep* (čega) in the middle of

posred|an *adj* (*a*) indirect ~**nik** *nm* (*Npl* ~nici) 1 intermediary; go-between 2 (u sukobu) mediator 3 (u trgovini) middleman, agent ~**ovati** *v* (*pres* ~ujem) 1 (0) mediate sth/between sb; act as an intermediary 2 (u čemu) intervene (in sth) 3 (kod koga) use one's influence with sb ~**stvom** *adv* through, by means of

posrijedi *adv* **što je** ~? what's the matter? what is it about? ~ **je nesporazum** this is a misunderstanding

posr|nuti *v* (0) (*pres* ~nem) 1 stumble, trip over 2 *fig* lapse ~**tati** *v impf* 1 → **posrnuti** 2 stagger, totter

pos|t *nm* fast, fasting ~**ni** *adj* **dan** fast day, day of fast

postaja *nf* station **autobusna** ~ bus stop **željeznička** ~ railway/train station

postajati *v impf* → **postati**

postan|ak *nm* (*Gsg* ~ka, *Npl* ~ci) origin, genesis, beginning; formation

postar|ati (1) *v* (se) grow old, age ~**iji** *adj* elderly

postarati (2) *v* (se) → **pobrinuti se**

posta|ti *v* (*pres* ~nem) 1 (što) become, get, grow, turn 2 (0) originate, arise, develop, come into existence

postava *nf* 1 (glumačka) cast 2 *sport* lineup

postav|iti *v* 1 (što) place, put, set, position; stand; raise, erect 2 (koga) appoint, install (as) ~**iti izložbu** mount/put on/stage an exhibition ~**iti pitanje** ask/pose a question ~**iti temelje** lay the foundation ~**iti stražu** post the guard ~**iti zahtjev** put in/submit a request ~**iti jednadžbu** formulate/state an equation ~**ka** *nf* (*Gsg* ~ci) 1 postulate; proposition 2 tenet ~**ljati** *v impf*

postdiplomski → **posljediplomski**

postelj|a *nf* bed **prikovan/privezan za** ~**u** bedridden **na samrtnoj** ~**i** on one's deathbed ~**ica** *nf* placenta ~**ina** *nf* bedclothes, bed linen, bedding

posti|ći *v* (što) (*pres* ~**gnem**) achieve, accomplish, attain, gain, obtain ~**ći sporazum** reach (an) agreement ~**ći uspjeh** achieve success, make the grade ~**ći zgoditak** score a goal ~**ći brzinu** reach a speed ~**gnuće** *nn* achievement, accomplishment; success ~**zati** *v impf*

postiti *v* (0) fast

posto *adv* per cent, percent ~**tak** *nm* (*Gsg* ~tka, *Npl* ~ci) percentage (point)

postojan *adj* 1 steady, stable, constant 2 steadfast 3 adamant, firm, persevering 4 (boja) fast

postoj|ati *v* (0) (*pres* ~**im**) exist, be ~**e** there are ~**i** there is ~**bina** *nf* 1 native country, homeland 2 home, habitat ~**eći** *adj* existing

postolar *nm* shoemaker; cobbler

postolje nn 1 pedestal, base 2 stand

postrance adv 1 sideways 2 aside, apart **držati se ~** keep oneself apart, keep in the background, keep a low profile

postrijeljati v (koga) shoot/mow down, kill them all

postrojlba nf mil formation **~iti** v (koga/se) line up, draw sb up in ranks

postrojenje nn installation, plant

postuplak nm (Gsg ~ka, Npl ~ci) 1 procedure 2 behaviour, manner; treatment 3 action **povesti sudski ~ak** start/take/institute/initiate legal proceedings, take legal action **smaknuti po kratkom ~ku** execute summarily **~iti** v 1 (0) act 2 (s kim/s čim) treat, deal with; handle **~ati** v impf

postuplan adj (a) gradual; progressive **~no** adv gradually, by degrees, step by step

posuda nf container; vessel;, receptacle form **noćna ~** chamber pot

posuldba nf (Gpl ~daba/~dbi) loan **~diti** v (što) 1 (komu) lend; loan US 2 (od koga) borrow **~đenica** nf loanword, borrowing **~đivati** v impf

posuđe nn dishes pl; tableware

posumnjati v (u koga/što) suspect, become suspicious of, doubt

posustalti v (0) (pres ~nem) fall behind

posušiti v (koga/što/se) dry (up)

posuti v pf → **posipati**

posvaditi, posvađati v (koga) cause sb to quarrel 2 (se) quarrel, fall out, have a fight/row

posve adv completely, entirely, utterly, wholly

posvelta nf 1 consecration 2 dedication, inscription **~titi** v 1 (što/koga) consecrate 2 (što komu/čemu) dedicate, devote 3 (se) dedicate/devote oneself to

posvijetliti v 1 (što) light (sb's way); shine (a torch) on 2 (0) become light/brighter (in colour)

posvjedočiti v (što) witness, bear witness to, testify

posvojliti v (koga) adopt **~ni** adj gram possessive

posvuda adv everywhere, all about/around, all over

pošalica nf joke, jest

pošast nf plague (+ fig)

pošašaviti v (0) coll go crazy/mad/nuts; go bonkers/crackers GB coll

pošiljlatelj nm sender **~ka** nf (Dsg ~ci) parcel, package; shipment

pošiziti v (0) coll 1 go berserk, freak out, flip (one's lid) 2 (za kim/za čim) go mad about

poškakljati v (koga) tickle

poškropiti v (koga/što čime) sprinkle (with water)

pošpricati v (koga/što) spray, sprinkle, squirt

pošlta nf 1 post GB; mail US 2 (ured) post office **~om** adv by post/mail **poslati ~om** post GB; mail US; send by post/mail **~anski** adj postal **~anski broj** postcode GB; zip code US **~anska marka** postage stamp **~anski pretinac** post office box (P.O. Box) **~anski sandučić** letterbox, pillar box, postbox GB; mailbox US **~anska uplatnica** postal order **~ar** nm postman GB; mailman, mail carrier US **~arina** nf postage

poštapalica nf mannerism in speech

poštedla nf exemption (from work); restricted duty **~jeti** v (koga) 1 spare, exempt 2 save (from)

poštlen adj 1 honest; fair 2 decent **~eno** adv 1 honestly; fair 2 decently 3 very much, thoroughly; properly coll **~enjačina** nf, **~enjak** nm (Npl ~enjaci) coll honest person **~enje** nn honesty **~enja mi!** upon my honour! **~ovanje** nn respect, esteem, regard **~ovatelj** nm admirer, devotee, worshipper **~ovati** v (pres ~ujem) 1 (koga/što) respect, esteem, hold in (high) esteem 2 (što) honour, observe, comply with **~ivati** v impf

pošto conj when, after • adv coll how much **~ poto** at all costs, whatever the cost

pošumliti v (što) afforest **~ljavanje**, **~ljivanje** nn afforestation

potajlan adj (a) secrete; clandestine

~ice, ~no adv secretly

potakn|uti v (koga/što) (pres ~em) encourage, inspire, prompt, stimulate, urge

potamaniti v (koga/što) exterminate, kill off

potam|niti v (što) darken, dim, obscure ~njeti v (0) (pres ~nim) become/get/grow dark, darken, dim

potanko adv in detail, minutely ~ **obrazložiti** elaborate ~st nf detail ~sti pl details, particulars **ulaziti u ~sti** go into detail

potapš|ati v (koga/što) (pres ~em) pat, tap

pote|ći v (0) (pres ~čem/~knem) 1 begin to flow 2 → **potjecati**

potegn|uti v (koga/što) (pres ~em) 1 pull 2 pull out, draw (out) ~uti **pištolj** draw/pull a gun (on sb) 3 ~uti iz **boce** take a pull/swig ~uti dim take a drag/puff **dobro ~uti a.** put in a lot of hard work **b.** take a good/long swig **povuci-potegni** tug-of-war

poten|cija nf 1 potency; virility 2 math power **dići na drugu ~ciju** raise to the second power ~cijal nm potential; capability; resources pl ~cijalan adj (a) potential; possible; would-be ~cijalni **kupac** prospective buyer ~cirati v (što) 1 intensify 2 math raise to a power 3 coll accentuate, emphasize ~tan adj (a) potent; powerful

poteškoća → **teškoća**

potez nm 1 move (+ fig) **genijalan ~** brilliant move, a stroke of genius 2 line 3 stretch, section, route ~ati v impf → **potegnuti**

pothodni|k nm (Npl ~ci) underpass; subway GB

pothranjen adj undernourished ~ost nf undernourishment

pothvat nm enterprise, undertaking, venture; feat

potica|j nm initiative, impetus, stimulus, encouragement ~jni adj **odbor** steering committee ~ti v impf → **potaknuti**

potilj|ak nm (Gsg ~ka, Npl ~ci) the back of one's head

potis|ak nm thrust (Gsg ~ka, Npl ~ci)

~nuti v (što/koga) (pres ~nem) 1 press, push 2 hold back, curb, suppress 3 supersede 4 force to retreat, roll back, drive off

potišten adj depressed, dejected, in low spirits; down in the dumps coll

potje|cati v (0) (pres ~čem) 1 (od koga/čega) come/descend/originate from 2 (iz čega) result/originate/stem from, be caused by

potjer|a nf 1 pursuit, chase, manhunt 2 pursuers pl; posse US ~ati v 1 (koga/što) chase (away), drive (away) 2 (koga) urge, press, hurry up 3 (koga) dismiss, sack; send packing 4 (0/što) sprout ~nica → **tjeralica**

potka|zati v (koga) (pres ~žem) denounce, inform against/on ~zivač nm informer

potkivač nm blacksmith, farrier ~ti v impf → **potkovati**

potkoljenica nf shin

potkontinent nm subcontinent

potkopati v (što) 1 dig under sth 2 fig undermine, subvert

potkova nf horseshoe ~n adj 1 shod 2 fig well trained/versed, experienced, seasoned ~ti v (konja) shoe

potkož|an adj (a) subcutaneous ~iti v (se) fig feather one's nest, line one's pockets ~njak nf (Npl ~njaci) boil

potkradati (1) v (koga/što) pilfer, steal (from)

potkrada|ti (2) v (se) sneak/slip/steal/creep in ~ju se pogreške mistakes creep in

potkraj prep (čega) towards/at the end of ~ **dana** later in the day ~ **ljeta** in late summer

potkra|sti v (se) pf → **potkradati se** ~la mi se pogreška I didn't notice a mistake

potkratiti v (što) 1 shorten; cut down 2 (kosu) bob, crop, trim

potkrijepiti v (što) substantiate

potkrovlje nn attic, loft

potkup|iti v (koga) buy sb off, bribe ~ljiv adj bribable, corrupt; venal form; bent GB sl

potlač|en adj oppressed, downtrodden ~enost nf oppression ~iti v (koga) oppress; subjugate

potleušica *nf* hovel, shanty, shack

potmu|o *adj* (*f* ~la) muffled, dull

poto|čić *nm* small stream, brook; rill *poet* **~čnica** *nf* forget-me-not **~k** *nm* (*Npl* ~ci) brook, stream; creek *US*

potom *adv* afterwards, later, subsequently, then **o tom** ~ *coll* **a.** leave that for later **b.** we'll see

potom|ak *nm* (*Gsg* ~ka, *Npl* ~ci) descendant; issue *leg* **~stvo** *nn* posterity, offspring, progeny

poton|uti *v* (0) (*pres* ~em) sink, go down; founder *form* **kao da su mu sve lađe ~ule** as though all his hopes were dashed

potonji *adj* **1** later, subsequent **2** (ovaj ~) the latter

potop *nm* flood, deluge **opći** ~ the Flood **~iti** *v* (što) **1** (brod) sink **2** flood, overflow

potpa|la *nf* drvo za **~lu** kindling **~liti** *v* (što) **1** light **2** set ablaze, set fire to, set on fire **3** inflame **~ljivač** *nm* arsonist

potpa|sti *v* (pod što/koga) (*pres* ~dnem) come/fall under, be subject to

potpetica *nf* (shoe) heel

potpiriti *v* (vatru) fan, stir, kindle **2** (što) *fig* stir up, inflame, kindle

potpis *nm* signature **~ati** *v* **1** (što) sign **2** (se) sign (one's name) **~nik** *nm* (*Npl* ~nici) signatory **država ~nica** signatory state

potpitanje *nn* secondary question

potplat *nm* sole

potpla|ćen *adj* bribed, corrupt; bent *GB sl* **~titi** *v* (koga) buy sb off, bribe; grease sb's palm *coll*

potpomagač *nm* accomplice; abettor *leg* **~agati** *v* (koga/što) (*pres* ~ažem) **1** support, assist, aid, back **2** subsidize, sponsor **~oći** *v pf*

potpora *nf* **1** support, backing **2** subsidy, subvention **~nj** *nm* support, buttress, prop, pillar

potporučni|k *nm* (*Vsg* ~če, *Npl* ~ci) Second Lieutenant (2nd Lt)

potprašiti *v* ~ **pete** take to one's heels ~ **kome pete** put sb to flight

potpredsjedni|k *nm* (*Vsg* ~če, *Npl* ~ci) vice-president **~k vlade** deputy prime minister

potpukovni|k *nm* (*Vsg* ~če, *Npl* ~ci) Lieutenant Colonel

potpun *adj* complete, entire, full, total, utter **u ~osti** in full, in one's entirety

potra|ga *nf* (*Dsg* ~zi) search; quest *lit* **u ~zi za** in search/pursuit/quest of

potraj|ati *v* (0) (*pres* ~em) **1** last; take time **2** drag on/out; go on

potraž|iti *v* (koga/što) **1** look for, seek, try to find **2** ask for **3** (riječ) look up **~ivanje** *nn* claim, credit, demand **~ivanja i dugovanja** credits and debits **~ivati** *v* (što) claim, demand **~nja** *nf* demand **ponuda i ~nja** supply and demand

potrbuš|ke *adv* face down(wards), prostrate, on one's stomach **~nica** *nf* peritoneum

potrč|ati *v* (0) (*pres* ~im) run, break into a run, start running

potre|ba *nf* need; necessity **u slučaju ~be** if necessary, if need be **~ban** *adj* (α) necessary, required, needed **prijeko ~ban** indispensable **~bit** *adj* → **potreban 2** needy **~pština** *nf* necessity, requirement, requisite

potres *nm* **1** earthquake, quake **coll 2** *fig* shock **3** (društveni) upheaval ~ **mozga** concussion **~an** *adj* (α) moving, touching, affecting **~en** *adj* shaken, shocked, agitated **~ti** *v* **1** (koga) shake, agitate, affect **2** (što) shake

potrgati *v* (što) **1** break, pull apart, pull to pieces, tear (up) **2** pluck (off/out)

potroš|ač *nm* **1** consumer **2** buyer, customer **~ački** *adj* consumer **~ačko društvo** consumer society **~ak** *nm* (*Gsg* ~ka, *Npl* ~ci) consumption, expenditure **~iti** *v* (što) **1** spend **2** consume, expend, use up, run out of **~ni** *adj* consumer **~nja** *nf* **1** consumption **2** spending **roba široke ~nje** consumer goods

potrpati *v* (što) cram, pack, stuff (in/into)

potruditi *v* (se) make an effort, try hard, exert oneself ~ **se da** make sure/certain that, see to it that

potucati *v* (se) roam, wander; bum around *sl*

potu|ći *v* (*pres* ~čem) 1 (koga/što) beat, defeat; thrash *coll*; rout 2 (koga) kill (off); annihilate 3 (se) come to blows, get into a fight

potužiti *v* (se) (na što/koga) complain (about/of)

potvr|da *nf* 1 confirmation; acknowledgment 2 receipt; certificate 3 approval, sanction; ratification 4 (krizma) Confirmation ~**dan** *adj* (α) affirmative, positive ~**diti** *v* (što) 1 confirm; acknowledge 2 certify; attest 3 approve, endorse, sanction; ratify ~**divati** *v impf*

poubijati *v* (koga) kill (off); slaughter

pouč|ak *nm* (*Gsg* ~ka, *Npl* ~ci) theorem ~**an** *adj* (α) instructive, informative, edifying, useful ~**iti** *v* (koga/što/čemu) 1 teach, instruct (in) 2 advise

pougljeniti *v* (0) char, become charred

pou|ka *nf* (*Dsg* ~ci) moral **izvući** ~**ku** learn one's lesson

poumir|ati *v* (0) (*pres* ~em) die (off/out)

pouzda|n *adj* reliable, trustworthy, sure ~**no** *adv* confidently; certainly, for sure ~**nost** *nf*, ~**nje** *nn* confidence, reliance, trust ~**ti** *v* (se) (u koga/što) rely on, have confidence in, put one's trust in

pouzećem *adv* cash/collect *US* on delivery (COD) **poslati** ~ send sth COD

povaliti *v* 1 (koga/što) fell, topple, knock/throw down 2 (žito) flatten, lay flat 3 (se) sprawl out, throw oneself down 4 (koga) *vulg sl* ball, bed, lay, have it off with sb

povampiriti *v* (se) *fig derog* resurrect, reawake

povečerje *nn* lights-out; taps *US mil*

povećalo *nn* magnifying glass **pod** ~**alom javnosti** under public scrutiny ~**anje** *nn* increase, growth; augmentation *form* ~**ati** *v* (što) 1 increase; augment *form*; expand ~**ati plaću** raise sb's pay 2 (fotografiju) enlarge, blow up 3 magnify 4 (se) increase, grow ~**i** *adj* rather big/large, biggish

povelja *nf* charter

poven|uti *v* (0) (*pres* ~em) wither, fade

poveseliti *v* (se) be glad/happy, rejoice

pove|sti (1) *v* (*pres* ~zem) 1 (koga/što) drive; give sb a lift/ride, drop 2 (se) get a lift, take a ride

pove|sti (2) *v* (*pres* ~dem) 1 (koga) take 2 (što) begin, start, initiate 3 (0) *sport* take the lead, go into the lead, be ahead

pov|esti (3) *v* (se) (za kim) (*pres* ~dem) follow sb's lead ~**oditi se** *v impf*

pove|z *nm* 1 bandage 2 (preko očiju) blindfold ~**zati** *v* (što) (*pres* ~žem) 1 tie (together/up) 2 bandage (up), bind (up) 3 connect, link, tie up 4 catch on (to) 5 (s kim) get in touch with, make contact with, link up with

povijati *v impf* → **poviti**

povijes|t *nf* history **ući u** ~**t** go down in/make history ~**t bolesti** medical/case history ~**ni** *adj* historical; (važan) historic

povijuša *nf* creeper

povi|k *nm* (*Npl* ~ci) cry, shout, exclamation ~**ka** *nf* (*Dsg* ~ci) outcry ~**kati** *v* (0/što) (*pres* ~čem) cry out, shout

povi|siti *v* (što) raise; heighten; elevate ~**šenje** *nn* rise; increase ~**šica** *nf* (plaće) (pay) rise *GB*; raise *US*

povi|ti *v* (*pres* ~jem) 1 (što) bend; weigh down 2 (ranu) bandage (up), bind (up) 3 (dijete) swaddle 4 (se) bend (down), stoop (down)

povjer|enik *nm* (*Npl* ~enici) commissioner; representative ~**enstvo** *nn* 1 commission 2 agency, branch ~**enje** *nn* confidence, trust **izglasati** ~**enje komu** give a vote of confidence in sb ~**iti** *v* 1 (koga/što kome) entrust sb/sth to sb, entrust sb with sth 2 (što) confide sth to sb 3 (se) confide in sb ~**ljiv** *adj* 1 confidential 2 reliable, trustworthy ~**ljivo** *adv* confidentially **strogo** ~**ljivo** strictly confidential, classified ~**ovati** *v* (*pres* ~ujem) 1 (komu/(u) što) believe 2 ((u) što) swallow *coll*; buy *sl*

povjesničar, povjesni|k *nm* (*Npl* ~ci) historian; chronicler

povješati *v* (koga/što) hang (up)

povjetar|ac *nm* (*Gsg* ~ca, *Npl* ~ci) breeze

povlač|enje *nn* retreat, withdrawal, pullout ~**iti** *v* 1 *impf* → **povući** 2 (koga/što) drag (along) 3 (se) hang around; drift

povlađ|ivati *v* (komu) (*pres* ~ujem) humour sb; agree with sb

povla|ka *nf* (*Dsg* ~ci) dash

povla|stica *nf* privilege; benefit, concession ~**šten** *adj* privileged

povod *nm* motive, reason **dati** ~**a čemu/za što** lead/cause sb to **bez** ~**a** without any reason ~**ca** *nm* (*Gsg* ~ca, *Npl* ~ci) bridle ~**iti** *v* (se) (za kim) follow sb's lead, imitate ~**ljiv** *adj* impressionable, easily led/influenced ~**om** *adv* 1 in connection with, in/with reference to, regarding 2 on the occasion of

povod|anj *nm* (*Gsg* ~nja) flood, deluge, inundation

povoj *nm* 1 bandage 2 swaddling clothes **u** ~**ima** *fig* in its infancy

povolj|an *adj* (~a) 1 favourable, propitious; auspicious form 2 suitable; convenient ~**na cijena** reasonable price ~**an vjetar** fair wind

povor|ka *nf* (*Dsg* ~ci) procession ~**ka automobila** motorcade

povraća|nje *nn* vomiting **ide mi na** ~**nje** I feel sick ~**ti** *v* *impf* → **povratiti**

povra|t *nm* return ~**tak** *nm* (*Gsg* ~tka, *Npl* ~ci) 1 return **u** ~**tku** on the way back 2 reversion form; recurrence; relapse ~**tan** *adj* (~a) 1 return ~**tna karta** return ticket *GB*; round-trip ticket *US* 2 recurring, recurrent 3 *gram* reflexive ~**titi** *v* (što) 1 vomit, disgorge; throw up *coll*; sick up *GB coll*; puke *sl* 2 *coll* return, give back; get back, recover, regain, recoup; restore ~**tnik** *nm* (*Npl* ~tnici) repatriate, returnee

povrće *nn* vegetable(s)

povreda *nf* 1 injury 2 violation, breach

povremen *adj* periodic(al), occasional; intermittent, sporadic

povrh *prep* (čega) 1 above, over 2 besides; in addition to ~ **svega** on top of it all ~ **toga** in addition, besides, moreover

povrijediti *v* 1 (koga/što) injure, hurt, (do sb) harm 2 (što) violate

površ|an *adj* (~a) 1 superficial 2 negligent ~**ina** *nf* 1 surface 2 area, floor space ~**inski** *adj* surface

povrt|larstvo *nn* 1 vegetable growing 2 (na veliko) market gardening *GB*; truck farming *US* ~**njak** *nm* (*Npl* ~njaci) vegetable/kitchen garden

povučen *adj* 1 (osoba) withdrawn, introvert 2 (mjesto) secluded; solitary

povu|ći *v* (koga/što) (*pres* ~čem) 1 pull, drag, draw; tug at 2 withdraw; pull out; recall 3 (rečeno) take back 4 (dim) inhale, draw on a cigarette; take a drag *sl*; (iz boce) take a swig 5 (se) withdraw, retreat; retire

poz|a *nf* pose; attitude *form* **zauzeti** ~**u** strike a pose/an attitude

pozabaviti *v* (se) (s kim/čim) take care of; tackle, discuss, deal with, address sth

pozadin|a *nf* 1 background; back; rear **držati se u** ~**i** remain in the background 2 *mil* rear

pozajm|iti *v* (što) 1 (od koga) borrow, take out a loan 2 (komu) lend; loan *US* ~**ljivati** *v* *impf*

pozamanterija *nf* haberdashery; notions *pl US*

pozatvarati *v* 1 (što) shut, close (down) 2 (koga) lock up, imprison

pozdrav *nm* 1 greeting; salutation *form*; salute *mil* 2 regards, respects *pl* ~**iti** *v* (koga) 1 greet; salute *mil, form* 2 give/send one's regards/ respects/love to sb 3 (koga/što) welcome 4 (se) (s kim) say hello to; say goodbye to **možeš se** ~**titi s time** *coll* you can kiss it goodbye, you can forget about it ~**ni** *adj* **govor** welcoming speech

pozele|njeti *v* (0) (*pres* ~nim) become/go/turn green ~**njeti od bijesa** be livid (with rage) *coll*

pozer *nm* *derog* poseur; poser *coll*

pozicij|a *nf* 1 position *fig* standpoint ~**sko** *adj* **svjetlo** *nn* sidelight *GB*;

parking light *US*

pozirati *v* 1 (komu) pose/sit for (sb/one's portrait) 2 (0) pose

pozitiv *nm* 1 *gram* positive 2 positive (photograph) **~an** *adj* (*a*) 1 positive 2 affirmative **~na bilanca** favourable trade balance

poziv *nm* 1 call 2 invitation 3 *leg* summons, subpoena **uručiti sudski ~** serve a summons/subpoena on sb 4 (u vojsku) call-up *GB*; draft *US* 5 vocation, profession **~ati** *v impf* 1 → **pozvati** 2 (se) (na što) quote; refer to **~ni** *adj* **broj** (dialling) code, prefix *GB*; area code *US*; international/country access code **~nica** *nf* invitation (card)

pozlat|a *nf* gilt **~iti** *v* (što) gild, plate with gold

pozliti *v* (komu) feel/get sick

pozna|nik *nm* (*Npl* ~nici) acquaintance **~nstvo** *nn* acquaintance **~t** *adj* 1 known 2 familiar **zvuči ~to** it sounds familiar, it rings a bell 3 famous, well-known 4 (po zlu) notorious **~ti** *v* (koga/što) (*pres* ~jem) 1 know 2 be acquainted/familiar with 3 recognize 4 (se) know each other **~vatelj** *nm* connoisseur (of); expert (at/in/on); pundit **~vati** *v impf*

pozor *nm* attention **priprema, ~, sad!** ready, steady, go! on your mark(s), get set, go! **~no** *adv* attentively **~nost** *nf* attention **obratiti ~nost komu/čemu** pay attention to **privući/pobuditi čiju ~nost** attract/draw/catch one's attention

pozornica *nf* stage

pozorni|k *nm* (*Npl* ~ci) policeman; police constable *GB*; patrolman *US*; beat cop *sl*

pozva|n *adj* 1 called; invited 2 competent, qualified **~ti** *v* (koga/što) (*pres* pozovem) 1 call 2 invite 3 call in, send for 4 summon *form* 5 (na sud) summons, subpoena 6 (u vojsku) conscript; call up *GB*; draft *US* 7 (se) → **pozivati se ~ti na odgovornost** call sb to account, bring sb to book

pozvoniti *v* (0) ring (the bell)

požaliti *v* (što) be sorry for, regret

požar *nm* fire; conflagration *form* **rat-**

---

ni ~ the flames of war

požder|ati *v* (*pres* ~em) 1 (koga/što) *derog* devour; gobble up, wolf down **coll** 2 (se) *fig* eat one's heart out

požel|jan *adj* (*a*) desirable **~ni neženja** eligible bachelor **~eti** *v* (koga/što) wish (for), want; long (for) **~eti komu što** wish sb sth

poženiti *v* 1 (koga) marry off 2 (se) get married

pož|eti *v* (što) (*pres* ~anjem/~njem) reap (+ *fig*), harvest

pož|vljeti *v* (0) (*pres* ~im) live

požrtvov|an *adj* (*a*) self-sacrificing **~nost** *nf* self-sacrifice

požuda *nf* lust **~an** *adj* (*a*) lustful

požuriti *v* 1 (0/se) hurry (up); make haste, hasten *form*; get a move on **coll** 2 (koga) hurry (up)

požut|jeti *v* (0) (*pres* ~im) become/go/turn yellow

pra- *prefix* 1 pre-, proto- 2 great- 3 original, primeval, primordial

pra|baka, prababa *nf* great-grandmother **~čovjek** *nm* (*Npl* ~ljudi) prehistoric man

praćakati *v* (se) flounder (about), splash about; squirm, wriggle

prać|ka *nf* (*Gpl* ~aka/~ki) catapult *GB*; slingshot *US*

prad|avni *adj* prehistoric, ancient **~jed** *nm* (*Npl* ~djedovi) 1 great-grandfather 2 *fig* forefather, ancestor **~jedovski** *adj* ancestral **~omovina** *nf* original homeland

prag *nm* (*Npl* ~ovi) threshold (+ *fig*) **kućni ~** doorstep **željenički ~** railway sleeper *GB*; railroad tie *US* **prijeći/prekoračiti kome ~** cross sb's threshold, set foot in sb's house

pragmatičan *adj* (*a*) pragmatic

prah *nm* 1 powder 2 dust **cvijetni ~** pollen **mlijeko u ~u** powdered milk **pretvoriti/smrviti/samljeti u ~** reduce/crush/grind to powder/dust, pulverize

pra|izvedba *nf* premiere, first/opening night, first performance **~jezik** *nm* (*Npl* ~jezici) protolanguage

prak|sa *nf* practice **provesti u ~si** put sth into practice 2 practical training; practical experience/skills **~tici-**

rati v (što) 1 practise 2 usually do, be in the habit of doing sth ~**tičan** adj (a) practical ~**tičar** nm 1 practical person 2 practitioner ~**tički**, ~**tično** adv 1 practically, in practice 2 coll practically, virtually; for all practical purposes ~**tikant** nm trainee

pralja nf washerwoman

pram|ac nm (Gsg ~ca, Npl ~ci) bow(s); prow lit

pramen nm 1 (kose) lock, tuft; strand 2 (magle) patch; (dima) wisp

pra|nje nn washing u ~**nju** in the wash ~**nje mozga** brainwashing ~**onica** nf 1 laundry 2 (automatska) launderette GB; laundromat US 3 (automobila) car wash

prao|tac nm (Gsg ~ca) forefather, ancestor

prapor|ac nm (Gsg ~ca) bell (on a horse)

prapra- prefix great-great-

pras|ac nm (Gsg ~ca, Npl ~ci) pig (+ fig), hog ~**ica** nf sow kasica ~**ica** coll piggybank ~**iti** v (se) farrow

pras|ak nm (Gsg ~ka, Npl ~ci) explosion, detonation; bang; burst ~**kati** v (0) explode, go off ~**kav** adj explosive ~**kavi glasovi** plosives ~**kozorje** nn dawn (+ fig), daybreak u ~**kozorje** at the crack of dawn, at (the) break of dawn ~**nuti** v (0) (pres ~nem) explode, go off; burst ~**nuti u smijeh** burst into laughter

pra|stanovnik nm (Npl ~stanovnici) aboriginal/native inhabitant ~**star** adj ancient, primeval; age-old

praš|ak nm (Gsg ~ka, Npl ~ci) powder ~**ak za pranje rublja** washing powder ~**ina** nf dust brisati ~**inu** dust dići/dizati ~**inu** kick up/raise a dust about ~**iti** v 1 (što) dust 2 (0) raise dust 3 (se) gather dust **raditi da se sve** ~**i** work like hell 4 (0) coll speed; bomb (along) coll; belt (along) GB sl 5 (po kome) coll shoot at; bang away at coll ~**nica** nf anther ~**nik** nm (Npl ~nici) stamen ~**njav** adj dusty

praštati v (komu što) forgive; pardon

prašuma nf virgin/primeval forest; (tropska) rain forest

prateći adj 1 accompanying 2 ancil-

liary, auxiliary, supporting 3 mil escort

prati v (pres perem) 1 (koga/što) wash ~ **rublje** do the washing, do the laundry ~ **ruke (od čega)** wash one's hands (of sth) (+ fig) ~ **suđe** wash up, do the washing-up GB; wash the dishes US ~ **novac** launder money 2 (se) wash (oneself)

prat|ilac nm (Gsg ~ioca, Npl ~ioci) 1 escort; guide 2 companion 3 follower 4 mus accompanist ~**ilica**/~**ilja** nf 1 lady companion 2 (djevojke) chaperon 3 runner-up (in the Miss World contest) ~**iti** v (koga/što) 1 follow ~**iti u stopu** watch closely, shadow; tail coll ~**ila nas je nesreća** we were dogged by bad luck 2 see; see off ~**iti doma** see/walk sb home 3 escort 4 accompany (+ mus) ~**nja** nf 1 accompaniment (+ mus) 2 escort; convoy 3 retinue, suite

praunu|k nm (Npl ~ci) great-grandson ~**ka** nf (Dsg ~ci) great-granddaughter

prav|ac nm (Gsg ~ca, Npl ~ci) 1 direction 2 straight line 3 fig course, line, orientation 4 style, trend; school (of thought)

prav|da nf justice dijeliti/krojiti ~**du** administer/dispense/mete out justice ~**da je zadovoljena** justice has been done ~**dati** v 1 (koga/što) justify, defend 2 (se) argue, quarrel ~**edan** adj (a) 1 just 2 righteous lit; equitable, fair 3 innocent ~**ednik** nm (Npl ~ednici) just/righteous person **spavati snom** ~**ednika** sleep the sleep of the just ~**edno** adv justly ~**ednost** nf justice, righteousness

pravi adj 1 right 2 real, true; actual 3 genuine, authentic 4 proper 5 regular 6 ~**i pravcati** real, veritable, downright, out-and-out

pravi|ca nf 1 justice; righteousness 2 ~**ce** pl hist privileges, rights ~**čan** adj (a) 1 just; righteous lit; equitable; even-handed

pravil|an adj (a) 1 regular 2 correct, right ~**nik** nm (Npl ~nici) rulebook; statute; regulations pl ~**nost** nf regularity ~**o** nn 1 rule; principle 2 regulation **u** ~**u** as a rule ~**o trojno** *math* rule of three **iznimka potvrđuje** ~**o** the exception proves the rule

praviti *v* (što) 1 make 2 produce, manufacture 3 form 4 create; cause ~ **gluposti** play the fool, fool around 5 (se) pretend (to be), make believe, act; fake *coll* ~ **se lud** play dumb ~ **se važan** show off, put on airs

prav|ni *adj legal; juridical form* ~**na država** rule of law ~**ni fakultet** the Faculty of Law, law school ~**ni lijek** legal remedy/redress ~**na osoba** legal person/entity, corporate body ~**nik** *nm* (Npl ~nici) lawyer; attorney *US*; jurist *form*

prav|o (1) *adv* 1 straight; directly 2 right **imati** ~**o** be right; have (got) a point ~ **mu bilo/budi** serves him right ~**o da kažem** to tell (you) the truth

prav|o (2) *nn* 1 law; jurisprudence *form* **krivično** ~**o** criminal law 2 right **u** ~**u si** you are right **nisi u** ~**u** you are wrong **dati kome za** ~**o** concede that sb is right, agree with sb **imati** ~**o na** have a right to, be entitled to **nemati** ~**a** have no right/business **s** ~**om** rightly ~**o glasa** right to vote, franchise **građanska/ljudska** ~**a** civil/human rights 3 claim **polagati** ~**o na** lay claim to ~**obranitelj** *nm* lawyer, legal officer; attorney *US* **pučki** ~**obranitelj** ombudsman

pravocrtan *adj* (α) rectilinear

pravodob|an *adj* (α) timely ~**no** *adv* in (good) time, in due course

pravokut|an *adj* (α) rectangular ~**nik** *nm* (Npl ~nici) rectangle

pravomoćan *adj* (α) effective, valid

pravopis *nm* spelling, orthography ~**ni** *adj* orthographic ~**na pogrèška** spelling mistake

pravorije|k *nm* (Npl ~ci) court ruling, verdict, adjudication

pravoslav|ac *nm* (Gsg ~ca, Npl ~ci) member of the Orthodox Church ~**an** *adj* (α) Orthodox

pravosu|dni *adj* judicial ~**đe** *nn* 1 justice 2 judicature; judiciary

pravovaljan *adj* valid ~**ost** *nf* validity

pravovjeran *adj* (α) orthodox

pravovremen → **pravodoban**

praz|an *adj* 1 empty ~**nih ruku** empty-handed 2 vacant ~**an pogled** vacant look 3 (gol) bare 4 blank ~**na stranica** blank page ~**na kaseta** blank tape

prazni|k *nm* (Npl ~ci) holiday; vacation *US* **državni** ~**k** national holiday **ljetni** ~**ci** summer holiday(s) *GB*/vacation *US* ~**k za oko** sight for sore eyes ~**čki** *adj* festive

prazn|ina *nf* 1 emptiness 2 void 3 blank space 4 gap ~**iti** *v* 1 (što) empty; clear out; vacate *form* 2 (se) empty; (baterija) discharge ~**o** *adv* **gledati** look/stare vacantly ~**oglav** *adj* empty-headed ~**ovjeran** *adj* (α) superstitious ~**ovjerje** *nn* superstition

praživotinj|a *nf* 1 prehistoric animal 2 ~**e** *pl* protozoa

prčkati *v* (0) (po čemu) 1 rummage (about) through, root about among 2 tamper with

prčvarnica *nf derog* (low) dive *coll*; joint *sl*

prćast *adj* (nos) snub, turned-up

prćiti *v* (usta) pout

prd|ac *nm* (Gsg ~ca, Npl ~ci) *tab* fart ~**jeti**, ~**iti** *v impf* (0) *tab* fart ~**nuti** *v pf* (pres ~nem) *tab* fart, let/blow a fart ~**onja** *nm tab derog* fart

prebaciti *v* 1 (što preko čega) throw over 2 (što na koga/što) shift ~ **krivicu/odgovornost na druge** shift the blame/responsibility onto others; pass the buck ~ **na drugi program** switch (it) over to another channel 3 (koga preko čega) take across 4 (koga/što) transport; transfer; give sb a lift/ride, drop sb off ~ **normu** exceed one's work norm/quota 5 (0) overshoot 6 (se) get across, go over to 7 (se) switch (over) to

prebir|ati *v* (pres ~em) 1 (što) sort; clean ~**ati po gitari** pluck the guitar ~**ati krunicu** count one's beads 2 (po čemu) sort through

prebi|ti *v* (pres ~jem) 1 (koga) beat up 2 (što) break (in two) 3 (dugove) clear, offset **bez** ~**te**/~**jene pare** flat/stony broke *coll*; skint *GB coll*

prebivališt|e *nn* 1 residence; dwelling

form **bez stalnog ~a** of no fixed abode/address **2** habitat

prebje|ći *v* (0) (*pres* ~gnem) defect; escape **~g** *nm* (*Npl* ~zi) defector

prebo|ljeti *v* (što/koga) (*pres* ~lim) get over

prebrati *v pf* → **prebirati** (1)

prebroditi *v* (što) *fig* get over, overcome, surmount

prebrojiti *v* (što/koga) count

precijeniti *v* (koga/što) overestimate, overrate

preciz|an *adj* (*a*) precise; accurate **~na mehanika** precision mechanics **~irati** *v* (što) specify, be specific, stipulate **~no** *adv* with precision **~nost** *nf* precision; accuracy

precrtati *v* (što) **1** copy, trace **2** cross off/out

preča *nf sport* horizontal/high bar

prečac *nm* short cut **ići ~em** take a short cut **na ~** hastily, rashly; suddenly

preč|i *adj comp* → **prijek imati ~eg posla** have other fish to fry

prečica *nf* → **prečac**

prečka *nf* **1** rung **2** *sport* crossbar

preču|ti *v* (što) (*pres* ~jem) not hear, not catch, miss

pred *prep* (kim/čim, koga/što) **1** in front of; before **doći ~ koga** come to meet sb **2** *coll* before **3** *coll* ahead of

preda|h *nm* (*Npl* ~si) break; breathing space; breather *coll* **bez ~ha** without a break **~hnuti** *v* (0) (*pres* ~hnem) **1** take a breath **2** have/take a break/breather

predaja *nf* **1** delivery **2** surrender, capitulation **3 usmena ~** oral tradition

pre|dak *nm* (*Gsg* ~tka, *Npl* ~ci) ancestor

predan *adj* dedicated **~o** *adv* with dedication

preda|ti *v* (koga/što komu) **1** deliver **~ti pismo na poštu** post *GB*/mail *US* a letter **~ti molbu** put in/send in/submit an application **2** present; hand (in) **3** hand over **4** surrender, give up **5** (se) give oneself up, turn oneself in; surrender; give up **6** (se komu/čemu) devote oneself to, give oneself over to **~vač** *nm* lecturer;

teacher, instructor **~vanje** *nn* lecture; talk; class **održati kome ~vanje** give sb a lecture (on), lecture sb about sth/for doing sth **~vaonica** *nf* lecture hall/room, classroom **~vati** *v* (*pres* ~jem) **1** *impf* → **predati 2** (kome o čemu/što kome) lecture (on sth), teach

predbaciti *v* (komu što) reproach sb/oneself for sth, criticize; throw sth (back) in sb's face *coll*

predbiljež|ba *nf* reservation, booking **~iti** *v* **1** (koga za što) put sb down for, put sb on the list for **2** (se za što) subscribe (to sth); book (in advance), reserve, make a booking/reservation

predgovor *nm* preface, foreword

predgrađe *nn* suburb **iz ~a** suburban

predgrupa *nf* supporting band

predigra *nf* **1** prelude (+ *fig*) **2** *sport* preliminary match **3** (u seksu) foreplay

predikat *nm* predicate

pred|io *nm* (*Gsg* ~jela, *Npl* ~jeli) **1** region, area **2** landscape **u ~jelu srca** in the region of the heart

predionica *nf* spinning mill, cotton mill

predivan *adj* (*a*) wonderful, splendid, marvellous

predivo *nn* yarn

predjelo *nn* hors d'oeuvre, appetizer; starter *GB coll*

predlaga|č *nm* proposer **~ti** *v impf* → **predložiti**

predlo|žak *nm* (*Gsg* ~ška, *Npl* ~šci) model, pattern, sample **~žiti** *v* **1** (što komu) propose, suggest **2** (koga) propose/nominate sb for/as

predmet *nm* **1** object; thing; item **oštar/tup ~** sharp/blunt instrument **2** subject; topic; matter **držati se ~a** keep to the point **~ podsmijeha** the object of ridicule, laughing stock **3** (školski) subject **4** *leg* case

prednost *nf* **1** advantage; head start (+ *sport*) **~i i mane** advantages and disadvantages, merits and demerits **2** priority, precedence; privilege **dati ~** (komu/čemu) **a.** give priority to **b.** prefer **dame imaju ~!** ladies first! **imati ~ a.** be at an advantage, have an advantage over **b**. have priority over **c**. (u prometu) have (the) right of way **dati ~** (u prometu) give way; yield *US*

prednj|ačiti *v* **1** (0) be ahead of, lead **2** (u čemu) excel, distinguish oneself; lead the field/way in **~ak** *nm* (*Npl* ~aci) front tooth **~i** *adj* front **~e noge** front legs, forelegs

predočiti *v* **1** (što sebi) imagine, picture, visualize **2** (što kome) illustrate; explain **3** (što) show, present, produce

predodređen *adj* (za što) **1** predestined **2** predetermined

predodžb|a *nf* (*Gpl* ~aba/~bi) conception, idea, notion; image, picture **kri-va ~ba** misconception

predomi|sliti *v* (se) change one's mind **~šljati** *v impf* (se) keep changing one's mind; vacillate, hesitate, waver

predosje|ćaj *nm* premonition, foreboding, hunch; presentiment *form* **~titi** *v* (što) have a premonition of

predračun *nm* estimate

predradnja *nf* preliminary/preparatory work

predrasuda *nf* prejudice

predratni → prijeratni

predsezona *nf* off-peak season, off-season, low season

predsjed|anje *nn* chairmanship **pod ~anjem** under the chairmanship of, chaired by **~atelj** *nm* chairman, chair, president **~ati** *v* (čime) chair, preside (at/over) **~nički** *adj* presidential **~nik** *nm* (*Vsg* ~niče, *Npl* ~nici) president; chairman **~ništvo** *nn* presidency; chairmanship

predsoblje *nn* **1** hall **2** antechamber, anteroom

predstav|a *nf* **1** performance, play; show **2 → predodžba ~iti** *v* **1** (sebi/komu što) imagine, picture; describe, portray, illustrate **2** (koga komu) introduce; present *form* **3** (što) present, show; represent **4** (se) introduce oneself **~ljati** *v* **1** *impf* → **predstaviti 2** (koga/što) represent **3** (što) play, perform, act **to ne ~lja problem** it presents no problem

predstav|ka *nf* (*Dsg* ~ci, *Gpl* ~aka/~ki) petition

predstavni|čki *adj* representative **~k** *nm* (*Npl* ~ci) **1** representative, delegate, deputy **~k za tisak** spokesman **2** agent **3** example **~štvo** *nn* **1** representation **2** branch (office); agency **3** **diplomatsko ~štvo** diplomatic mission

predstojni|k *nm* (*Npl* ~ci) head, chief, director

predstraža *nf* advance guard

predugo *adv* too long, overlong

predugovor *nm* preliminary agreement

preduhitriti *v* (koga/što) forestall; preempt

preduj|am *nm* (*Gsg* ~ma) advance

predumišljaj *nm* premeditation **ubojstvo s ~em** premediatated murder

preduvjet *nm* prerequisite (of/for/to), precondition (of/for)

predvečer *adv* at dusk **~je** *nn* evening **u ~je rata** on the eve of the war

predvid|jeti *v* (što) (*pres* ~im) **1** predict **2** foresee, envisage; envision *US*; anticipate **~iv** *adj* foreseeable

predvodi|ti *v* **1** (koga/što) lead, head **2** (0) lead the way **~nik** *nm* (*Npl* ~nici) leader

predvorje *nn* (entrance) hall, vestibule, lobby, foyer

predzadnji *adj* the last but one, next to last, penultimate

predziđe *nn* bulwark

predzna|k *nm* (*Npl* ~ci) **1** sign, omen, forerunner **2** *math* sign

predznanje *nn* previous/background knowledge **s ~m** well prepared

pređa *nf* yarn

preferirati *v* (koga/što) prefer

prefik|s *nm* (*Gpl* ~asa/~sa) prefix

preformulirati *v* (što) reword, rephrase

prefrigan *adj coll* crafty, cunning, sly, wily

pregača *nf* apron

prega|lac *nm* (*Gsg* ~oca, *Npl* ~oci) hard-working person

pregazi|ti *v* (koga/što) **1** (rijeku) wade across, ford **2** (vozilom) run down/over **3** (nogama) trample down **4** (vojska) overrun **5** *fig* rout **~lo ga**

vrijeme he is behind the times

pregib *nm* 1 bend 2 joint ~ati *v* (što) bend; flex

pregled *nm* 1 examination; inspection **carinski** ~ customs inspection **liječnički** ~ medical/physical (examination); checkup *coll* 2 revision 3 review, survey, overview, summary ~ **vijesti** news bulletin/roundup ~**an** *adj* (*a*) clearly laid-out ~**ati** *v* (koga/što) 1 examine, inspect, check, go through 2 (tekst) revise 3 overlook 4 ~**ati novine** scan the newspaper

pregnuće *nn* exertion, effort, endeavour

pregor|jeti *v* (0) (*pres* ~im) 1 burn 2 (jelo) burn, be burnt 3 (osigurač) blow; (žarulja) burn out

pregov|arač *nm* negotiator ~**arački** *adj* negotiating ~**arački stol** negotiating table ~**arati** *v* (0/s kim/o čemu) negotiate ~**ori** *nm pl* negotiations, talks

pregra|da *nf* 1 partition 2 (na brodu/u avionu) bulkhead ~**dak** *nm* (*Gsg* ~tka, *Npl* ~ci) 1 compartment 2 (u štali) stall, box ~**diti** *v* (što) 1 partition (off) 2 reconstruct, rearrange, convert

pregrij|ati *v* (što/se) (*pres* ~em) overheat

pregri|sti *v* (što) (*pres* ~zem) bite/gnaw through

pregrm|jeti *v* (što) (*pres* ~im) overcome, weather, come/go through ~**jeti najgore** be past the worst

pregršt *nf* handful, armful

pregrupirati *v* (koga/što) regroup

pregurati *v* (što) overcome, ride out; tough it out *coll*

prehla|da *nf* cold ~**diti** *v* (se) catch (a) cold ~**đen** *adj* **on je** ~**đen** he has (got) a cold

prehra|mbeni *adj* food ~**mbena industrija** food processing industry ~**na** *nf* 1 feeding; nutrition 2 diet; food ~**niti** *v* 1 (koga) feed, provide for, support, maintain 2 (se) subsist, live, provide for/support oneself

preimenovati *v* (što) rename

preina|čiti *v* (što) alter, modify, re-

model ~**ka** *nf* (*Dsg* ~ci) alteration, modification

preispitati *v* (što) 1 re-examine 2 reconsider, review

prejak *adj* too strong

preje|sti *v* (se) (*pres* ~dem) eat too much; stuff oneself *coll*

prejudicirati *v* (što) prejudge

prekaljen *adj* seasoned

prekasno *adv* too late

preki|d *nm* interruption, break ~**d trudnoće** abortion ~**d vatre** ceasefire **na** ~**de** on and off, intermittently ~**dač** *nm* switch; circuit breaker ~**nuti** *v* (*pres* ~nem) 1 (što) break, interrupt; cut off, sever; snap 2 (što) discontinue, suspend; cut short 3 (što/s čim) stop; cease 4 (odnos) break off 5 (koga) interrupt; disturb 6 (se) break; snap

prekip|jeti *v* (0) (*pres* ~im) boil over ~**jelo mu je** he blew up

prekjučer *adv* the day before yesterday

preklani *adv* the year before last

preklapa|ti *v impf* → **preklopiti**

preklinj|ati *v* (koga) (*pres* ~em) beg, implore; entreat *form*; beseech *lit*

preklopiti *v* 1 (što) fold (up) 2 (se s čim) overlap, coincide

preko *prep* (čega) 1 across 2 over; beyond, above 3 more than, over 4 during ~ **cijele godine** throughout the year, all (the) year round ~ **noći** overnight 5 through; by; via, by way of ~ **telefona/radija** *coll* over the phone/the radio ~ **mjere** excessively, too much ~ **volje** unwillingly, reluctantly ~ **reda** out of turn **ići** ~ **reda** jump the queue **prijeći** ~ **čega** pass over; disregard **prijeći** ~ **svega** forget everything, forgive sb

prekobrojan *adj* (*a*) extra, excess, surplus

prekomjer|an *adj* (*a*) excessive ~**ni rad** overwork

preko|morski *adj* overseas ~**oceanski** *adj* overseas ~**oceanski brod** ocean liner

prekopati *v* (što) 1 dig up 2 *coll* rummage through, root among, search

prekopirati *v* (što) copy; trace

prekoračiti *v* 1 (koga/što) step over 2 (što) *fig* overstep, exceed

prekoriti *v* (koga) reproach, reprimand, rebuke, scold; chide *lit*

prekosutra *adv* the day after tomorrow

prekovremen|i *adj* ~**i rad** overtime (work) ~**o** *adv* overtime

prekrasan *adj* (a) beautiful, wonderful, marvellous

prekrcati *v* (što) transfer

prekretnica *nf* milestone, watershed; turning point, crossroads, critical juncture

prekri|ti *v* (koga/što) (*pres* ~jem) cover (up) ~**vač** *nm* bedspread

prekriž|iti *v* 1 (što) cross ~**iti ruke** cross/fold one's arms 2 (koga/što) cross out/off 3 (se) cross/bless oneself, make the sign of the cross ~**je** *nn* crossroads, crossing

prekrstiti *v* 1 (koga) convert 2 (koga/što) *coll* rename, give a new name to sb/sth

prekrš|aj *nm* 1 violation, breach 2 offence 3 *sport* foul ~**itelj** *nm* offender, violator ~**iti** *v* (što) break, breach, violate

preksinoć *adv* the night before last

preksutra *adv* the day after tomorrow

prekup *nm* repurchase ~**ac** *nm* (*Gsg* ~ca, *Npl* ~ci) middleman

prekvalifikacija *nf* retraining

prela|zak *nm* (*Gsg* ~ska, *Npl* ~sci) 1 crossing 2 *fig* transition

prelet *nm* overflight ~**jeti** *v* (što/preko čega) 1 overfly, fly over 2 skim through/over, glance at/down/over/through

prelež|ati *v* (bolest) (*pres* ~im) stay in bed

prelijeva|ti *v* (se) 1 *impf* → preliti se 2 (boje) change colours

preliminaran *adj* (a) preliminary; preparatory

prelistati *v* (što) leaf through, thumb through, browse through

preli|ti *v* (što) (*pres* ~jem) 1 overflow 2 pour 3 decant 4 (se) flood; overflow, brim over, spill over **kap koja je** ~**la čašu** the last/final straw

prelomiti *v* (što) 1 break (in two/half)

2 fold in two 3 (se) break up, snap 4 (se) (svjetlost) refract

prelja *nf* spinner

preljev *nm* 1 icing, topping 2 (boje) nuance, hue

preljub *nm* adultery ~**nica** *nf* adulteress ~**nički** *adj* adulterous ~**nik** *nm* (*Npl* ~nici) adulterer

prema *prep* (komu/čemu) 1 towards, in the direction of 2 opposite (to), across from 3 according to, in line with; pursuant to; under 4 **tri ~ pet** three to five 5 compared to, in comparison with **ljubav ~ djetetu** love for one's child **grub ~ komu** rude to sb ~ **tome** consequently, accordingly, therefore

prem|ac *nm* (*Gsg* ~ca) **bez** ~**ca** matchless, peerless, unrivalled, second to none, beyond compare **nema mu** ~**ca** he has no equal

premalo *adv* too little/few, not enough, insufficiently ~ **plaćen** underpaid

premašiti *v* (što) 1 shoot/throw over 2 exceed, surpass

prema|z *nm* coat (of paint) ~**zati** *v* (što) (*pres* ~žem) paint, coat with paint; spread ~**zan svim mastima** crafty, cunning, sly, wily

premda *conj* (even) though, although; albeit *form*

preme|tačina *nf* search **nalog za** ~**tačinu** search warrant **izvršiti** ~**tačinu** conduct a search, search/ransack (a house) ~**tati** *v impf* (*pres* ~ćem) (što) rummage (through); search, ransack ~**tnuti** *v pf* **preko glave** go through a lot

premija *nf* 1 premium 2 (first) prize, award

premijer *nm* premier, prime minister

premijera → **praizvedba**

premin|uli *adj* the deceased, the defunct, the departed ~**uti** *v* (0) (*pres* ~em) pass away, die

premisa *nf* premise

premjeriti *v* (što) measure; (zemljište) survey

premje|stiti *v* 1 (koga/što) move (from one place to another), transfer, shift, relocate 2 (se) move (to another place), transfer; change places, swap round ~**štaj** *nm* transfer ~**štati** *v impf*

premlatiti *v* (koga) beat up, beat black and blue ~ **na mrtvo ime** beat the (living) daylights out of sb

premoć *nf* superiority ~**an** *adj* (ȁ) superior

premoren *adj* exhausted, fatigued ~**ost** *nf* exhaustion, fatigue; overwork

premostiti *v* (što) bridge, span ~ **jaz** bridge a/the gap ~ **razlike** overcome differences

premotati *v* 1 (što) rewrap 2 (ranu) rebandage 3 (vrpcu) rewind 4 (dijete) change the baby's nappy 5 (vunu) coil

premr|lijeti *v* (0) (*pres* ~em) be terrified/petrified ~**ijeti od straha** be paralysed with fear

premudar *adj* (ȁ) very wise, sagacious; omniscient

prenag|ao *adj* (*f* ~la) rash, impulsive, hasty, abrupt ~**liti** *v* (0/se) be rash, act rashly/impulsively

prenapučen *adj* overpopulated

prenatovaren *adj* overloaded

prenatrpan *adj* overcrowded; packed/crammed/stuffed full

pren|avljanje *nn* affectation ~**avljati** *v* (se) show off, put on airs, give oneself airs; affect, pretend to be

prenema|gati *v* (se) (*pres* ~žem) → **prenavljati se**

preneraziti *v* 1 (koga) astound, dumbfound 2 (se) be astounded/dumbfounded/dumbstruck

pren|esen *adj* 1 carried, transported 2 figurative, metaphorical ~**ijeti** *v* (*pres* ~esem) 1 (koga/što) carry, move, transfer; convey *form* 2 (bolest/emisiju) transmit 3 (poruku) relay; convey 4 (vijest) broadcast 3 (vlasništvo na koga) convey, transfer, make sth over to ~**ositi** *v impf*

prenoći|šte *nn* place to spend the night, room for the night ~**ti** *v* (0) spend the night, stay the night, stay overnight

prenosi|telj *nm* ~**telj bolesti** carrier (of a disease) ~**v** *adj* 1 transferable 2 portable 3 (bolest) contagious, infectious

pren|uti *v* (*pres* ~em) 1 (koga) rouse (from sleep); startle 2 (se) wake up suddenly; start

preoblačiti *v impf* → **preobući**

preobli|čiti, preoblik|ovati *v* (koga/ što) (*pres* ~kujem) reshape, refashion, transform transformation

preobratiti *v* (koga/se) convert (to)

preobra|zba *nf* transformation, metamorphosis ~**ziti** *v* (koga/se) transform, change ~**žaj** *nm* 1 transformation; metamorphosis 2 reformation ~**ženje** *nn eccl* transfiguration

preobu|ći *v* (se) (*pres* ~čem se) 1 change (one's clothes) 2 (u koga) disguise oneself as

preobu|ti *v* (se) (*pres* ~jem) change one's shoes/boots

preodgojiti *v* (koga) re-educate; reform, reorient

preokre|nuti *v* (*pres* ~nem) 1 (što) turn over; turn upside down; turn inside out; invert 2 (se) overturn, turn over 3 (se) *fig* change ~**t** *nm* 1 change, turn of events 2 (društveni) upheaval

preokupiran *adj* preoccupied (with)

preosta|li *adj* remaining; leftover ~**ti** *v* (0) (*pres* ~nem) remain, be left (over)

preot|eti *v* (koga/što) (*pres* ~mem) 1 take back; regain control of 2 grab/snatch from; wrench/wrest from

prepad *nm* surprise attack **na** ~ by surprise **pljačkaški** ~ hold-up; stick-up *coll*

prepakirati *v* (što) repack, repackage

preparat *nm* 1 preparation 2 (mikroskopski) specimen

prepariran|je *nn* taxidermy ~**ti** *v* (životinju) stuff

prepa|sti *v* (*pres* ~dnem) 1 (koga) scare, give sb a scare, startle 2 (se) be frightened/startled

prepatiti *v* (što) suffer, endure

prepe|čen *adj* overdone ~**čenac** *nm* (*Gsg* ~čenca, *Npl* ~čenci) toast ~**ći** *v* (što) (*pres* ~čem) 1 cook/roast too long, burn 2 roast again; (kruh) toast 3 (rakiju) distil again

prepelica *nf* quail

prepiliti v (što) saw (through)

prepir|ati v (se) (pres ~em) quarrel, argue, squabble, bicker **~ka** nf (Dsg ~ci, Gpl ~aka/~ki) quarrel, argument, squabble

prepi|sati v (pres ~šem) 1 (što) copy; transcribe 2 (lijek) prescribe 3 (što na koga) convey, make sth over to sb 4 (u školi) crib sth off/from sb conf ~sivati v impf (u školi) cheat **~ska** nf (Dsg ~sci, Gpl ~saka/~ski) correspondence

prepjev nm rendition of a poem, verse translation **~ati** v (pjesmu) render a poem (into another language)

preplan|uo adj (f ~ula) (sun)tanned **~uti** v (0) (pres ~em) tan, get a tan

preplašiti v 1 (koga) frighten, scare, give sb a scare; startle 2 (se) be/become frightened/scared/startled

preplatiti v (koga/što) overpay, pay too much; be overcharged

preplaviti v (što) (+ fig) overflow; flood, inundate

preple|sti v (pres ~tem) 1 (što) interweave, interlace, intertwine 2 (se) be interwoven/interlaced, intertwine

preplivati v (što) swim (across)

prepoloviti v 1 (što) cut/divide/split into halves, cut in half, halve 2 (se) be halved, be reduced by half

prepona nf 1 groin 2 sport hurdle **utrka s ~ma** hurdle race **~š** nm hurdler

preporod nm rebirth, regeneration; revival; renaissance **~iti** v 1 (koga/što) regenerate, revive 2 (se) regenerate, feel regenerated, be born again

preporu|čiti v 1 (koga/što) recommend 2 (komu što) recommend, advise **~čeno pismo** registered letter **~čeno** adv by registered post GB/mail US **~čljiv** adj advisable **~ka** nf (Dsg ~ci) 1 recommendation; suggestion 2 reference

prepotentan adj (a) arrogant, haughty, snooty; stuck-up coll

prepoznat|i v (koga/što) 1 recognize; know by 2 identify **~ljiv** adj recognizable

geoprav|iti v (što) 1 alter; modify; change **~iti odijelo** alter a suit 2 falsify **~ka** nf (Dsg ~ci) alteration,

modification, change

prepreden adj crafty, cunning, sly, wily

prepre|ka nf (Dsg ~ci) obstacle (+ fig)

prepričati v (što) retell; tell

preprije čiti v (što) block, bar, obstruct

preproda|ja nf resale **~ti** v (što) resell **~vač** nm 1 middleman 2 (ulaznica) (ticket) tout GB; scalper US

prepržiti v (što) 1 fry too much; toast 2 fry again

prepucavati v (se) coll squabble, wrangle (over)

prepun adj 1 too full, overfull 2 (over)crowded, packed; jam-packed coll 3 crammed/stuffed full 4 (čaša) brimful **~iti** v (što) overfill, fill sth too full

prepustiti v 1 (što komu) leave sth to sb; give up, cede, yield 2 ~ koga samom sebi leave sb to himself/herself, leave sb to his/her own devices 3 (se komu/čemu) give oneself up to

preračunati v 1 (što u što) convert (into) 2 (se) miscalculate, make a miscalculation

prera|da nf 1 processing, manufacture **~da nafte** oil refinement 2 adaptation **~diti** v (što) 1 process, manufacture 2 alter, modify; remodel, remake, reshape 3 adapt, rewrite **~devina** nf product **~divački** adj manufacturing **~divati** v impf

preran adj too early, premature, untimely

prerast|i v (pres ~em) 1 (koga/što) outgrow; grow out of 2 (u što) grow/develop/turn into 3 (što) exceed, surpass

prere|zati v (što) (pres ~žem) cut (through); cut in two **~zati si žile** slash one's wrist(s)

prerija nf prairie

prer|ovati v (što) (pres ~ujem) 1 dig up/through, burrow 2 rummage through, root among

preruš|iti v 1 (koga) disguise 2 (se u koga) disguise oneself as **~en** adj in disguise

presaditi v (što) transplant

presahn|uti v (0) (pres ~em) dry up, go/run dry

presavi|ti *v* (što) (*pres* ~jem) bend; fold

presedan *nm* precedent **bez ~a** without precedent, unprecedented **stvoriti ~** create/establish/set a precedent (for sth)

preseliti *v* 1 (koga/što) move; relocate, transplant; resettle 2 (se) move, move house

preseravati *v* (se) *tab sl* show off; shoot a line

presijavati *v* (se) glimmer

pres|ijecati *v impf* 1 (što) cross, traverse; intersect 2 (se) intersect **~jeći** *v* (*pres* ~iječem) 1 (što) cut (through); cut in two; sever **~jeći komu put** block sb's way **~jeći kroz šumu** cut across/through the woods 2 (koga) cut in on sb **~jeklo me u križima** the pain shot up my back, I felt a shooting pain in my back

presjedati *v impf* → **presjesti**

presjed|jeti *v* (što) (*pres* ~im) sit through

presje|k *nm* (*Npl* ~ci) 1 section **nacrtati u ~ku** draw sth in section **poprečni ~k** cross-section 2 summary

presje|sti *v* (0) (*pres* ~dnem) change (trains, etc.), transfer

presk|očiti *v* (koga/što) 1 jump/leap/hop over/across 2 *fig* skip, leave out, pass over **~akati** *v impf*

preslica *nf* distaff

preslikati *v* 1 (što) copy; trace 2 (se) *fig* reflect on

presložiti *v* (što) rearrange

preslušalnje *nn* hearing; interrogation **~ti** *v* 1 (koga) interrogate, cross-examine; grill *coll* 2 (što) listen to/through

presnimiti *v* (što) make/do a copy of sth

presoliti *v* (što) salt too much, put too much salt in

prespavati *v* 1 (0) spend the night, stay overnight 2 (što) sleep through; sleep off; oversleep (and miss)

prespojiti *v* (koga) put through

presre|sti *v* (koga/što) (*pres* ~tnem) intercept; waylay **~tač** *nm* interceptor

presretan *adj* (α) very happy, overjoyed, delighted, over the moon

prest|ajati (1) *v* (što) (*pres* ~ojim) stand through

prestajati (2) *v impf* → **prestati**

presta|nak *nm* (*Gsg* ~nka, *Npl* ~nci) end, cessation **bez ~nka** constantly, ceaselessly **~ti** *v* (*pres* ~nem) 1 (0) stop, be over, cease, leave off 2 (što/s čim) stop, quit, cease; cut *sl* **~ti pušiti** give up/quit smoking

pre|sti *v* (*pres* ~dem) 1 (što) spin 2 (0) (mačka) purr

presti|ći, presti|gnuti *v* (koga/što) (*pres* ~gnem) 1 overtake, pass 2 forestall

prestiž *nm* prestige **~an** *adj* (α) prestigious

prestolonasljedni|k *nm* (*Vsg* ~če, *Npl* ~ci) crown prince, heir to the throne

prestrašiti *v* 1 (koga) frighten, scare, give sb a fright/scare 2 (se) be frightened/scared

prestraviti *v* 1 (koga) horrify, terrify 2 (se) be horrified

prestrojiti *v* (se) 1 (vojska) re-form 2 (auto) change/shift lanes

prestrukturirati *v* (što) restructure

prestupiti *v* (0) 1 violate, break (the law); trespass (on) **~ preko praga** cross a threshold 2 (0) *sport* step over the line; (tenis) foot-fault

presud|a *nf* judgment, sentence, verdict, ruling **~an** *adj* (α) crucial; decisive **~iti** *v* (što) pass judgment (on); bring in/deliver/reach a verdict **sam sebi ~iti** take one's own life

presušiti *v* (0) dry up, go/run dry

presv|lačiti *v impf* **~laka** *nf* (*Dsg* ~laci) cover(ing); upholstery **~ući** *v* 1 (se) change (one's clothes), get changed 2 (koga/što) change 3 (zmija) shed (the skin)

preša *nf* press

prešu|tjeti *v* (što) (*pres* ~tim) say nothing (about sth), keep (sth) secret

preteča *nf* predecessor, precursor, forerunner

prete|ći *v* (*pres* ~knem) 1 (koga/što) (vozilom) overtake 2 (nadmašiti) outdo, surpass 3 (stići prije) get (swh) before sb

pretegnuti *v* (0) overbalance; outweigh

preten|ciozan *adj* (*a*) pretentious ~**dent** *nm* (na) pretender (to) ~**dirati** *v* (na što) pretend (to) ~**zija** *nf* pretension

prete|zati *v impf* (*pres* ~žem) → **pretegnuti** ~**žan** (*a*), ~**žit** *adj* predominant, prevailing ~**žito**, ~**žno** *adv* predominantly, mostly, chiefly

prethod|an *adj* (*a*) preceding, previous, prior ~**iti** *v* (0/čemu) precede ~**nica** *nf mil* advance guard/party ~**nik** *nm* (*Vsg* ~niče, *Npl* ~nici) predecessor; precursor, forerunner ~**no** *adv* in advance, prior to

preti|lost *nf* obesity ~**o** *adj* (*f* ~la) obese

pretis|ak *nm* (*Gsg* ~ka, *Npl* ~ci) reprint

pretje|cati *v impf* (*pres* ~čem) (koga/što) overtake

pretjer|an *adj* excessive; exaggerated ~**ano** *adv* to excess, too ~**ati** *v* (0, u čemu) exaggerate; overdo; go too far ~**ivati** *v impf*

pretkljetk|a *nf* (*Gpl* ~i) atrium

pretkraj *adv* (čega) by the end of

pretočiti *v* (što/se u što) pour (into)

pretopiti *v* 1 (što) remould, recast 2 (se) blend (into), assimilate (into)

pretovar *nm* (re)loading ~**iti** *v* (što) 1 (re)load 2 overload

pretplat|a *nf* subscription ~**iti** *v* (se) (na što) subscribe (to) ~**nički** *adj* subscriber(s') ~**nik** *nm* (*Vsg* ~niče, *Npl* ~nici) subscriber

pretposljednji *adj* the last but one, penultimate

pretpostav|iti *v* 1 (što) suppose, assume, presume; guess coll 2 (što čemu) favour, prefer ~**ka** *nf* (*Gsg* ~ci) assumption, presumption; hypothesis ~**ljeni** *nm* (one's) superior

pretpovijes|ni *adj* prehistoric(al) ~**t** *nf* prehistory

pretpremijera *nf* preview, prevue

pretprošl|i *adj* ~**i tjedan** two weeks ago ~**e godine** two years ago

pretra|ga *nf* 1 search 2 *med* test ~**žiti** *v* (što/koga) 1 search (around/through) 2 (tjelesno) frisk coll

pretrčati (0) *v* run (across/over)

pretres *nm* search ~**ti** *v* (što) search

pretrgnuti *v* 1 (što/se) break, snap 2 (se) *fig* break one's back

pretrpati *v* (što/koga/se) cram, stuff

pretrp|ljeti *v* (što) (*pres* ~im) suffer, sustain, experience, be through

pretu|ći *v* (*pres* ~čem) (koga) beat up

pretv|arač *nm* transformer ~**arati** *v* 1 (što/se) transform, turn into, convert 2 (se) feign, act, pretend ~**orba** *nf* 1 transformation, metamorphosis 2 *econ* transfer of ownership; privatization ~**oriti** *v* (što/koga/se) transform, turn (into), change (into)

preudati *v* (se) remarry

preuranjen *adj* premature

preure|diti *v* (što) redo, redecorate, do up ~**divati** *v impf*

preustrojiti *v* (što) restructure

preuveliča|n *adj* blown up, exaggerated ~**ti** *v* (što) blow up, exaggerate ~**vati** *v impf*

preuzet|an *adj* (*a*) presumptuous ~**nost** *nf* presumption

preuzeti *v* (koga/što) take over ~ **odgovornost** claim responsibility

preuzvišenost *nf* eminence

preva|ga *nf* (*Dsg* ~zi) dominance ~**gnuti** *v* (0) outweigh

prevaliti *v* 1 (što/se) overturn 2 (udaljenost) cover 3 (godine) turn, be over

prevar|ant *nm coll* swindler ~**iti** *v* 1 (koga) cheat, deceive; trick, swindle 2 (se) make a mistake

preventiva *nf* prevention ~**n** *adj* (*a*) prevent(at)ive

preves|lati *v* 1 (što) row across 2 (koga) *sl* take for a ride

preve|sti (1) *v* (*pres* ~zem) transport; (avionom) fly, (brodom) ship; take/drive across

preve|sti (2) *v* (*pres* ~dem) translate, (usmeno) interpret

previd *nm* oversight, omission ~**jeti** *v* (što) overlook, omit

previr|anje *nn* turmoil, ferment ~**ati** *v* (0) (*pres* ~em) ferment (+ *fig*)

previše *adv* too much/many

previti *v* (što/koga) dress (sb's wound)

prevla|dati *v* 1 (što) overcome 2 (0) prevail, win ~**ast** *nf* (nad) predominance, the upper hand, power (over sb)

prevla|ka *nf* (*Dsg* ~ci) isthmus, strip

prevo|dilac *nm* (*Gsg* ~dioca, *Gpl* ~dilaca), ~**ditelj** *nm* translator; interpreter ~**diti** *v* (što) translate, (usmeno) interpret ~**đenje** *nn* translation

prevrat *nm* revolution ~**nički** *adj* revolutionary ~**nik** *nm* (*Vsg* ~niče, *Npl* ~nici) revolutionary

prevr|nuti *v* 1 (što) overturn, turn over 2 (se) turn/fall over; (brod) capsize ~**tati** *v impf* ~**tljiv** *adj* fickle, inconstant

prevršiti *v* (što) overstep, exceed ~ **svaku mjeru** overstep the mark, go too far

prevući *v* 1 (što) pull across/over 2 (što čime) coat (with)

prezadovoljan *adj* (*a*) delighted, thrilled

prezalogajiti *v* (što) snack, have a bite

prezasi|ćen *adj* satiated, surfeited; fed up ~**ćenost** *nf* surfeit, satiety ~**titi** *v* 1 (što/koga) satiate, surfeit 2 (se) become satiated/surfeited; get fed up

prezati *v* (0) shy away from, flinch **ne** ~ **ni pred čim** stick/stop at nothing

prezent *nm gram* present (tense) ~**acija** *nf* presentation ~**irati** *v* (što) present

prezervativ *nm* condom, sheath, prophylactic *US* (¶ preservative = konzervans)

prezidati *v* (što) partition off

prezime *nm* surname, family name

prezim|iti *v* (0) 1 spend the winter 2 (životinje) hibernate 3 (ptice) winter ~**ljavanje** *nn* 1 winterization 2 hibernation

prez|ir *nm* → **prijezir** ~**iran** *adj* scornful, contemptuous, disdainful ~**irati** *v* (koga/što) despise, look down on, scorn, disdain ~**rijeti** *v impf*

preznojiti *v* (se) get in a sweat

prezre|o *adj* (*f* ~la) overripe

prežaliti *v* (što/koga) get over (sth/sb)

prežde|rati *v* (se) pig out, gorge oneself with/on ~**vati** *v* (se) *impf*

preživa|č *nm* ruminant ~**ti** *v* (0) ruminate

preživ|io *adj* (*f* ~jela) 1 surviving 2 outmoded, obsolete ~**jeti** *v* (što) survive ~**ljavati** *v impf* jedva ~**ljavati** live from hand to mouth

prežvakati *v* (što) chew

prgav *adj* quick-tempered

prhak *adj* (*a*) crisp

prhnuti *v* (0) (ptica) fly off

prhut *nm* dandruff

pri *adv* at, by, near ~ **novcu sam** I'm loaded ~ **ruci** at hand, handy **nije** ~ **sebi** he's not himself **nije** ~ **zdravoj pameti** he's taken leave of his senses

pri- *prefix* izražava 1 spajanje: **pričvrstiti** attach 2 blizinu: **približiti se** approach 3 dodavanje: **pribrojiti** add 4 ublažavanje: **priglup** simple

prianjati *v* (0, uz što) cling, adhere (to)

pribadača *nf* pin

pribiti *v* (što) nail, pin

pribje|ći *v* (*pres* ~gnem) (0, čemu) resort to, turn to ~**žište** *nn* sanctuary, refuge

približ|an *adj* (*a*) approximate ~**avanje** *nn pol* rapprochement ~**iti** *v* 1 (što/koga) bring closer/nearer 2 (se) come closer/nearer, approach

pribojavati *v* (se) fear, be concerned/worried about

pribor *nm* set, kit, equipment, gear **uredski** ~ stationary

pribra|n *adj* (osoba) calm, composed; concentrated ~**nost** *nf* presence of mind, calm ~**ti** *v* (se) pull oneself together, get a grip on oneself

pribrojati *v* (što) (*pres* ~im) add

priča *nf* story, tale, narrative ~**lica** *nf/m* chatterbox, prattler ~**ti** *v* 1 (što) talk, tell ~**ti priču** tell a story/tale 2 (0, o čemu) talk (about/of) ~ **se** (**da**) the story goes, the rumour has it (that)

pričekati *v* (koga/što) wait for (sb/sth)

prićes|ni *adj* Communion, Eucharistic ~**nik** *nm* (*Vsg* ~niče, *Npl* ~nici) communicant (Sveta) ~**t** *nf* (Holy) Communion, the Eucharist ~**titi** *v* 1 (koga) give C. 2 (se) take/receive C.

priči|niti *v* 1 (što) do, cause, inflict 2 (se) ~**nilo mi se** (**da**) it seemed to me, I thought (that) ~njati *v impf*

pričuv|a *nf* reserve(s) ~ati *v* (što/koga) keep, look after, take care of ~ni *adj* reserve ~nik *nm* (*Npl* ~nici) reservist

pričvrstiti *v* (što) fasten, clip

prići *v* (0, komu/čemu) (*pres* priđem) approach, come up to

prida|vati *v* (što komu/čemu) (*pres* ~jem) ascribe (to), attach (to)

pridjev *nm* adjective ~ski *adj* adjectival

pridobi|ti *v* (koga/što) (*pres* ~jem) win sb over, persuade

pridodati *v* (što čemu) add (to)

pridon|ijeti *v* (0, čemu) (*pres* ~esem) contribute (to)

pridošlica *nm/f* newcomer, new arrival

pridrijemati *v* (0) nap, take/have a nap

pridružiti *v* (koga/što/se) join

pridrž|ati *v* (*pres* ~im) 1 (koga/što) hold ~ati pravo reserve the right 2 (se) hold onto ~avati *v* (se) 1 *impf* 2 (zakona, propisa) abide by, comply with

prignuti *v* (što/se) bend over/down

prignječiti *v* (koga/što) squeeze, crush, press

prigod|a *nf* 1 occasion ~om (čega) on the occasion of svečana ~a special occasion 2 opportunity, chance ~an *adj* suited for the occasion ~na marka commemorative stamp

prigorje *nn* foothill(s)

prigov|arati *v* (0, komu/što) complain, criticize, find fault with, nag ~or *nm* objection, complaint ~oriti *v* (komu/čemu) make a complaint, object (to sth)

prigrabiti *v* (što/se) seize, snatch

prigradski *adj* suburban

prigri|sti *v* (što) (*pres* ~zem) snack, have a bite

prigrliti *v* (koga/što) embrace (+*fig*)

prigusti|ti *v* (0, komu) ~lo mu je he's in trouble

priguš|en *adj* subdued, muffled ~iti *v* (što) subdue, muffle ~ivač *nm* silencer

prihod *nm* income, revenue; takings, proceeds

prihva|ćati *v impf* ~t *nm* admission, reception ~tilište *nn* shelter, welfare centre ~titi *v* 1 (što) accept, take 2 (koga) admit, receive 3 (se čega) take sth up, tackle, grapple with ~tljiv *adj* acceptable

prijam *nm* admission; reception, welcome ~ni *adj* ispit entrance exam(ination) ~nica *nf* receipt ~nik *nm* (*Npl* ~nici) receiver

prijašnji *adj* previous; onetime, former

prijatelj *nm* friend; mate, pal, chum, buddy *coll* ~ se u nuždi poznaje a f. in need is a f. indeed ~evati *v* (0, s kim) (*pres* ~ujem) be friends with sb; hang out with sb *coll* ~ski *adj* friendly, amiable, amicable ~stvo *nn* friendship

prijati *v* (0, komu) to be to one's liking/taste, suit one

prijatan *adv* → ugodan

prijav|a *nf* 1 registration 2 (pritužba) complaint 3 (na natječaj) application 4 (policiji) report ~ak *nm* (*Gsg* ~ka, *Npl* ~ci) *mil* report ~iti *v* (koga/što/se) 1 register 2 file a complaint 3 apply, enter 4 report ~ljivati *v impf* ~nica *nf* registration/application form

prije *prep* (koga/čega) before ~ godinu/tjedan dana a year/week ago • *adv* earlier, before(hand), in advance malo ~ a while ago

priječiti *v* (što komu) obstruct, impede, hinder ~ put be in the way

prijeći *v* (što) (*pres* prijeđem) 1 cross, cover 2 (količinski) exceed 3 (0, preko čega) *fig* overlook

prijedlo|g *nm* (*Npl* ~zi) 1 suggestion, proposal; motion 2 *gram* preposition

prijek *adj* 1 short 2 urgent ~e ćudi short/quick tempered ~i sud court-martial dati koga na ~i sud court-martial sb

prijeko *adv* 1 (vrlo) urgently 2 (s druge strane) over there

prijekor *nm* reproach, rebuke ~an *adj* (α) reproachful

prijelaz *nm* 1 crossing; transfer 2 change, transition ~an *adj* (α) 1 transitional; provisional 2 *gram* transitive 3 (zarazan) contagious

prijelom *nm* fracture

prijem *nm* → **prijam**

prijenos *nm* 1 *TV, radio* transmission, coverage 2 *leg* conveyance

prijepis *nm* transcript; copy

prijepodne *nn* morning ~**vni** *adj* morning

prijepor *nm* controversy, discussion ~**an** *adj* (ā) controversial

prijepotopni *adj* antediluvian

prijesan *adj* (ā) 1 raw 2 undercooked

prijesto|lnica *nf* metropolis, capital (city) ~**lje** *nn* throne **stupiti na ~lje** ascend the throne

prijestup *nm* 1 transgression, offence 2 *sport* foot fault ~**na** *adj* **godina** leap year ~**nik** *nm* (*Vsg* ~niče, *Npl* ~nici) offender; transgressor

prijet|iti *v* (0, komu/čime) threaten (sb with sth), menace ~**nja** *nf* threat, menace **pod ~njom** (čega) under threat of, on/under pain of

prijetvoran *adj* (ā) dissembling, false

prijevara *nf* scam, swindle, set-up, trick, deceit

prijevod *nm* translation

prijevoj *nm* 1 *geogr* saddle 2 *gram* ablaut, vowel gradation

prijevoz *nm* transport(ation), haulage, conveyance

prijezir *nm* scorn, contempt, disdain ~**a vrijedan** contemptible, despicable

prika|z *nm* review, survey ~**za** *nf* apparition, spectre ~**zanje** *nn* mystery, miracle ~**zati** *v* (*pres* ~žem) 1 (što) show, present 2 (se) appear ~**zivati** *v* (se) (*pres* ~zujem) 1 *impf* 2 (film) be on, be showing

prikladan *adj* (ā) suitable, appropriate

priklati *v* (koga/što) (*pres* prikoljem) slaughter, cut sb's throat

priklije|štiti *v* (koga/što) *fig* corner, nail

prikloniti *v* 1 (koga) win sb over, persuade 2 (se) incline (to/towards)

priklopiti *v* (što) add, put in

priključ|ak *nm* (*Gsg* ~ka, *Npl* ~ci) connection, link, hookup ~**iti** *v* 1 (što) connect, link, attach, hook up 2 (se) join

prikolica *nf* 1 trailer 2 (kamp-kućica) caravan *GB*; trailer *US* 3 (motocikla) sidecar

prikopčati *v* (što) buckle; hook up; clasp

prik|ovati *v* (koga/što) (*pres* ~ujem) nail, chain **stajao je kao ~ovan** he stood rooted to the spot

prikraćivati *v impf* → **prikratiti**

prikradati *v* (se) → **prikrasti**

prikraj|ak *nm* (*Gsg* ~ka, *Npl* ~ci) **iz ~ka** from the corner **u ~ku** in the wings

prikra|sti *v* (se) (*pres* ~dem) sneak up (on sb)

prikratiti *v* (što) shorten, cut short ~ **muke** put (sb) out of their misery

prikri|ti *v* conceal, cover (up), hide ~**vati** *v impf* ~**ven** *adj* secret, veiled

prikrpati *v coll* 1 (što komu) pin (the blame) on sb 2 (se) tag along

prikucati *v* (što) pin, nail

prikučiti *v* 1 (što) bring closer 2 (se) come closer

prikupiti *v* (što) gather, collect; (no-vac) raise

prikvačiti *v* (što/se) hook, clip (on/to-gether)

prilagati *v impf* → **priložiti**

prilago|dba *nf* adaptation, adjustment ~**diti** *v* (koga/što/se) adapt ~**dljiv** *adj* adaptable ~**đen** *adj* adapted ~**đivati** *v impf*

prilaz *nm* access, approach ~**iti** *v impf* (0, komu/čemu) approach, come closer/nearer

prile|ći *v* (0) (*pres* ~gnem) 1 lie down for a while, take a nap 2 fit ~**žnica** *nf* mistress

priličan *adj* (ā) considerable ~**no** *adv* considerably, fairly, rather, quite

priličiti *v* (0, komu/čemu) befit, be proper/suitable for

prilijepiti *v* (što/se) stick, glue, paste (on) ~ **se za koga** cling to sb like a leech

prili|ka *nf* (*Dsg* ~ci) 1 opportunity, chance 2 (prigoda) occasion 3 ~**ke** *pl* circumstances, conditions, situation ~**kom** during **drugom ~kom** some other time **po ~ci** roughly **po svoj ~ci** in all likelihood **slika i ~ka** spitting image **na svoju sliku i ~ku** in one's own image **tom ~kom** then

prilo|g *nm* (*Npl* ~zi) **1** (jelu) side dish/order **2** (dar) donation, contribution **3** *gram* adverb **u ~gu** (u pismu) enclosed **čemu/komu ~g** in favour of sth/sb **~ški** *adj* adverbial **~žiti** *v* (što) **1** (darovati) donate **2** (u pismu) enclose **~žni** *adj* adverbial

priljep|ak *nm* (*Gsg* ~ka, *Npl* ~ci) limpet (+fig) **~čiv** *adj* (bolest) contagious

priljev *nm* influx

priljubiti *v* **1** (što) join, attach **2** (se) cling (to), snuggle up (to)

primać|i (1) *adj* **~a soba** reception room

primaći (2) *v* → **primaknuti**

primaknuti *v* **1** (koga/što) bring/ move/draw closer/nearer **2** (se) come closer/nearer, approach

prim|alac (*Gsg* ~aoca, *Npl* ~aoci), **~atelj** *nm* recipient; addressee; consignee **~alja** *nf* midwife **~anja** *nn pl* income, salary **~anje** *nn* reception **~ati** *v impf* **~itak** *nm* (*Gsg* ~itka, *Npl* ~ici) receipt **~iti** *v* **1** (koga/što) receive, accept, admit, get, take (on) **biti ~ljen u** (punopravno) **članstvo** be admitted to (full) membership **~iti** (što) **k znanju/na znanje** take notice of sth **dobro je to ~ila** she took it well **2** (se) (biljka) take root **~iti se posla** get (down) to work

primam|iti *v* (koga/što) lure, attract **~ljiv** *adj* attractive, tempting **~ljivati** *v impf* **~ljivost** *nf* attraction, allure

primaran *adj* (α) primary

primas *nm* primate

primat *nm* priority

primicati *v impf* → **primaknuti**

primijeniti *v* (što) apply, use

primijetiti *v* (koga/što) notice, observe

primiri|sati *v* (što) (*pres* ~šem) smell, sniff

primir|iti *v* (se) calm/quieten down; (pojava) abate **~je** *nn* truce, armistice, (prekid vatre) cease-fire

primis|ao *nf* (*Gsg* ~li) ulterior motives *pl*

primitiv|ac *nm* (*Gsg* ~ca, *Npl* ~ci) caveman, brute, boor **~an** *adj* (α) **1** primitive **2** (osoba) narrow-minded

~izam *nm* (*Gsg* ~izma) narrow-mindedness, bigotry

primjećivati *v impf* → **primijetiti**

primjed|ba *nf* (*Gpl* ~aba/~bi) remark, observation, comment

primje|na *nf* application, use **~njiv** *adj* applicable, useful **~njivost** *nf* applicability

primjer *nm* example, instance; (slučaj) case; (uzor) model **na ~** for example/instance **kao na ~** such as **~ak** *nm* (*Gsg* ~ka, *Npl* ~ci) copy, sample **~an** *adj* (α) exemplary **~en** *adj* (za) appropriate, suitable (for/to), proper **~enost** *nf* suitability **~ice** *adv* for example/instance

primjesa *nf* dash, tinge, trace

primjetan *adj* (α) noticeable, conspicuous

primopredaja *nf* takeover

primor|ac *nm* (*nf* ~ka) person from the coast **~je** *nn* coastal/maritime region **~ski** *adj* coastal, maritime

primorati *v* (koga/se) force, make, compell

princ *nm* prince **~ na bijelom konju** Prince Charming **~eza** *nf* princess

princip *nm* principle **iz ~a** on p. **u ~u** in p. **~ijelan** *adj* (α) (high-) principled **~ijelnost** *nf* principle(s)

prin|ijeti *v* (*pres* ~esem) (što) contribute, give, offer **~os** *nm* crops

prinova *nf* something new **~ u obitelji** addition to the family

prinuda *nf* → **prisila**

priobalni *adj* coastal, maritime

prionuti *v* (0) **1** (na što) apply oneself (to), get down to **2** (za što) (uz što) cling to

priopć|avati *v impf* **~enje** *nn* statement **~enje za tisak** press release **izdati ~enje** issue/release/give a statement **~iti** *v* (što, komu) state, give a statement, say, inform; (objaviti, najaviti) announce

prior *nm* prior **~a** *nf* prioress **~itet** *nm* priority **~itetan** *adj* (α) top-priority

pripa|dan *adj* (α) belonging, pertinent (to) **~dati** *v* (0, komu/čemu) belong (to); be part of **~dnik** *nm* (*Vsg* ~dniče, *Npl* ~dnici) member **~dnost** *nf* membership, association, belonging, being part of **~sti** *v* (0,

komu/čemu be granted/given/allotted to sb

pripaziti *v* (koga/što/se) take care of, look after; watch/look out

pripe|ći *v* (0) (*pres* ~čem) scorch ~**ka** *nf* scorcher, sizzler

pripi|jen *adj* tight, clinging ~**ti** *v* (se) ~jem) cling

pripi|sati *v* (što) (*pres* ~šem) ascribe, attribute (to) ~**sati krivnju** (komu) lay/put the blame (on)

pripit *adj* tipsy, merry

pripitomiti *v* (se/koga/što) tame, domesticate

pripjev *nm* refrain, chorus

pripoj|iti *v* (što/se) annex, join, unite ~**enje** *nn* annexation

pripomo|ć *nf* assistance, support, aid, relief ~**ći** *v* (*pres* ~gnem) (0, komu) help out, assist

pripov|ijest, ~**ijetka** *nf* narrative, story ~**ijedati** *v impf* (što) narrate, tell a story ~**jedač** *nm* narrator ~**jedni** *adj* narrative

priprav|a *nf* preparation ~**ak** *nm* (*Gsg* ~ka, *Npl* ~ci) preparation ~**an** *adj* (*a*) prepared, willing, ready ~**iti** *v* (što/se) prepare ~**ljati** *v impf* ~**nik** *nm* (*Vsg* ~niče, *Npl* ~nici) trainee, junior ~**nost** *nf* readiness, preparedness **stanje** ~**nosti** red alert

priprem|a *nf* preparation, arrangement(s) (for) ~**an** *adj* (*a*) prepared, ready ~**ati** *v impf* ~**iti** *v* (koga/što/se) prepare, arrange, get ready, make

priprijetiti *v* (0/komu) threaten

priprost *adj* common, crude; simple

pripucati *v* (0/na koga) open fire (on)

pripustiti *v* (koga/što) let in, admit

priračunati *v* (što) add (up)

prira|slica *nf med* adhesion ~**st** *nm*, ~**štaj** *nm* rise, growth, increase

prire|dba *nf* show, performance, event ~**diti** *v* (što) arrange, prepare, organize ~**đivati** *v impf*

pripep|ak *nm* (*Gsg* ~ka, *Npl* ~ci) hanger-on

prirez *nm* surtax; municipal tax

prirod|a *nf* nature ~**an** *adj* (*a*) natural ~**opis** *nm* natural science ~**oslovlje** *nn* natural science/history

prirođen *adj* innate, inborn

prirok *nm gram* predicate

priruč|an *adj* (*a*) handy ~**nik** *nm* (*Npl* ~nici) manual, handbook

pris|an *adj* (*a*) close, intimate ~**nost** *nf* intimacy, closeness

priseb|an *adj* (*a*) calm, composed ~**nost** *nf* presence of mind

prise|ga *nf* (*Dsg* ~zi) oath **pod** ~**gom** under/on oath ~**gnuti** *v* (0) swear (an oath); be sworn in

prisil|a *nf* coercion ~**iti** *v* (koga/se) force, coerce, make, compel ~**an** *adj* coercive ~**ni rad** hard labour

prisje|sti *v* (0/komu) ~**lo mi je** I'm fed up

prisjetiti *v* (se) recall, recollect

priskočiti *v* (0/komu) come to sb's aid, help

priskrbiti *v* (što) procure, obtain; provide

prisloniti *v* (što/se) lean (against)

prislonjenica *nf* proclitic

prisluš|kivač *nm* tap, bug ~**kivati** *v* (koga/što) (*pres* ~kujem) **1** eavesdrop (on sb) **2** (telefon) listen in (on/to), (wire)tap, bug ~**ni** *adj* **uređaj** bugging device

prismotra *nf* surveillance

prispje|će *nn* arrival ~**jeti** *v* (*pres* ~jem) (0) arrive

prispodob|a *nf* comparison; simile; metaphor ~**iti** *v* (koga/što/se) compare

prista|jati *v* (0) **1** *impf* → ~**ti 2** (komu, uz što) suit, fit, match ~**lica**, ~**ša** *nm/f* supporter ~**nak** *nm* (*Gsg* ~nka, *Npl* ~nci) consent, assent ~**nište** *nn* pier ~**o** *adj* (*f* ~la) handsome, good-looking ~**ti** *v* (0) **1** dock (at) **2** (na što) agree (to), assent, consent, say yes

pristaviti *v* (što) ~ **čaj** put the kettle on

pristi|ći *v* (*pres* ~gnem) (0) arrive

pristoj|an *adj* (*a*) **1** decent, proper **2** (uljudan) polite, good-mannered ~**nost** *nf* **1** decency **2** politeness, good manners

pristojba *nf* due, fee

pristran *adj* biased, partial ~**ost** *nf* bias, partiality

pristup *nm* access, approach **zabranjen** ~ **a.** no admittance **b.** (na privatni posjed) no trespassing ~**ačan**

adj (*a*) accessible; (osoba) affable ~**iti** *v* (0) **1** approach, step forward **2** (učlaniti se) join, enter ~**ni** *adj* inaugural ~**nica** *nf* application form ~**nina** *nf* membership fee

prisu|stvovati (0, čemu) (*pres* ~**stvujem**) be present (at) ~**tan** *adj* (*a*) present ~**tnost** *nf* presence

prisv|ajati *v impf* ~**ojiti** *v* (koga/što) usurp, arrogate, seize, take possession of

prišapnuti *v* (komu/što) **1** whisper (into sb's ear) **2** give a hint/tip

prišarafiti (koga) *sl* put/tighten the screws on sb

priši|ti *v* (što) (*pres* ~**jem**) **1** sew sth on **2** (komu) *fig* pin (the blame) on sb

prišt *nm* pimple, spot ~**av** *adj* pimply, spotty ~**ić** *nm* *euphem* spot

prišted|jeti *v* (što) (*pres* ~**im**) save, put by

prišuljati *v* (se) sneak up (on sb)

pritajiti *v* (se) lie low

prite|ći *v* (*pres* ~**knem**) (komu) ~**ći upomoć** come to sb's aid, give sb a helping hand

prite|gnuti *v* **1** (što) tighten **2** (koga) → **prišarafiti** ~**zati** *v impf* (*pres* ~**žem**)

pritis|ak *nm* (*Gsg* ~**ka**, *Npl* ~**ci**) pressure ~**kati** *v impf* ~**nuti** *v* (koga/što) press, exert pressure (+*fig*), pressurize

pritje|caj *nm* influx, inflow ~**cati** *v* (*pres* ~**čem**) (0) **1** flow into **2** → **pritjecati**

pritjerati *v* (koga) ~ **uza zid** corner (sb)

pritok *nm*, ~**a** *nf* tributary

pritrč|ati *v* (0, komu/čemu) (*pres* ~**im**) run up to, come running

prituž|ba *nf* (*Gpl* ~**aba/**~**bi**) complaint

pritvor *nm* custody, detention **u** ~**u** in custody/detention, on remand **u kućnom** ~**u** under house arrest ~**en** *adj* **1** → **u** ~**u 2** (vrata) ajar ~**iti** *v* **1** (koga) take into custody, detain **2** (što) leave (the door) ajar

priučiti *v* **1** (koga) train in the basics, give basic training to **2** (se) get used to

priupitati *v* (koga/što) ask, inquire

priuštiti *v* (komu/što) afford **ne mogu sebi to** ~ I can't afford it

privat|an *adj* (*a*) private; personal ~**izacija** *nf* privatization ~**nik** *nm* (*Vsg* ~**niče**, *Npl* ~**nici**) private owner, small business owner, entrepreneur ~**nost** *nf* privacy

prive|sti *v* (*pres* ~**dem**) (koga/što) **1** arrest **2** bring, lead, take ~**sti kraju** bring to an end/a close ~**sti pameti** bring sb to his/her senses

prive|zati *v* (*pres* ~**žem**) tie (up)

privi|dan *adj* (*a*) apparent, seeming ~**djeti** *v pf*, ~**đati** *v impf* (se) ~**đa mi se** I'm seeing things ~**đenje** *nn* apparition ~**mađa** ~**đenja** I'm hallucinating, I'm seeing things

priviknuti *v* (se) get used/accustomed to

privilegij *nm* privilege

privi(nu)ti *v* **1** (koga) embrace, clasp in one's arms **2** (se) snuggle up to

privi|tak *nm* (*Gsg* ~**tka**, *Npl* ~**ci**) **1** (ugovora) annex(e) **2** (pisma) enclosure

privjes|ak *nm* (*Gsg* ~**ka**, *Npl* ~**ci**) **1** (lančić s ~**kom**) pendant **2** (za ključeve) key ring

privlač|an *adj* (*a*) attractive, appealing, charming, tempting ~**iti** *v* (koga/što/se) attract, allure, appeal to, charm, draw, tempt ~**nost** *nf* attraction, allure, appeal, charm, magnetism

privoditi *v impf* → **privesti**

privo|la *nf* assent, consent ~**ljeti** *v* (*pres* ~**lim**) **1** (koga) persuade **2** (0, na što) agree, give one's consent

privr|eda *nf* economy ~**edni** *adj* economic ~**eđivati** *v impf* ~**ijediti** (što) earn, make

privržen *adj* (komu) devoted (to) ~**ost** *nf* devotion

privu|ći *v* (što/koga/se) (*pres* ~**čem**) **1** draw, bring/move closer **2** attract

prizdrav|iti *v* (0) get well, recover ~**ljati** *v impf*

prizem|an *adj* (*a*) **1** (stan) ground-floor *GB*, first-floor *US*; (zgrada) single-story **2** *fig* cheap, low, vulgar ~**lje** *nn* ground floor *GB*; first floor *US* ~**ljenje** *nn* landing ~**ljiti** *v* **1**

(što/se) land 2 (koga) *fig* talk sense into sb 3 (se) *fig* come to one's senses ~**nica** *nf* single-story house; bungalow *GB* ~**no** *adv* on the g./f. floor

priz|iv *nm* leg appeal **uložiti** ~**iv** lodge an appeal ~**ivati** *v impf* (koga/što) ~**ivati duhove** take part in a spiritualist seance ~**ivni sud** court of appeal ~**vati** *v pf*

prizma *nf* prism

prizna|nica *nf* receipt, confirmation ~**nje** *nn* 1 acknowledgment, recognition 2 admission, confession **odati komu** ~**nje** (za što) give sb the credit (for sth) ~**ti** *v* 1 (što/koga) acknowledge, recognize 2 (što) admit, confess ~**vati** *v impf*

prizor *nm* scene; sight

priželjk|ivati *v* (što/koga) (*pres* ~ujem) wish for, hope for

prkos *nm* spite, defiance ~**an** *adj* (*a*) spiteful, defiant ~**iti** *v* (0, komu/čemu) spite, defy

prlja|ti *v* 1 (što/koga) dirty, soil 2 (se) get dirty ~**v** *adj* dirty (+*fig*), (jako) filthy, scruffy ~**vac** *nm* (*Gsg* ~vca, *Npl* ~vci) (*nf* ~vica), ~**vko** *nm* dirty/filthy/scruffy person ~**vština** *nf* dirt, filth

prnj|e *nf pl* rags, tatters ~**av** *adj* ragged, tattered

pro- (1) *prefix* pro-

pro- (2) *prefix* izražava 1 kretanje kroz što: **probiti** pierce 2 kretanje pokraj čega: **projuriti** whizz by 3 početak radnje: **progovoriti** start speaking

prob|a *nf* 1 test 2 rehearsal **generalna** ~ dress r. 3 (kod krojača) fitting ~**ati** *v* (što) try, test; rehearse → **kušati** ~**ni** *adj* trial, pilot, test

probav|a *nf* digestion ~**iti** *v* (što) digest (+*fig*) ~**ljiv** *adj* digestible ~**ni** *adj* digestive

probd|jeti *v* (što) (*pres* ~im) ~ **noć** stay up all night

probi|jati *v impf* ~**tačan** *adj* (*a*) profitable, lucrative ~**tak** *nm* (*Gsg* ~tka, *Npl* ~ci) profit, benefit ~**ti** *v* (*pres* ~jem) 1 (što) pierce ~**ti led** break the ice 2 (se) make one's way through 3 (se) *fig* make it, make the grade, get ahead

probisvijet *nm/f* good-for-nothing

problem *nm* problem ~**atičan** *adj* (*a*) problematic(al), problem ~**ski** *adj* problem

problijed|jeti *v* (0) (*pres* ~im) go/grow pale

probo|j *nm* breakthrough ~**jan** *adj* (*a*) 1 piercing 2 (osoba) pushy ~**sti** *v* (*pres* ~dem) (koga/što/se) pierce ~**sti nožem** stab

prob|rati *v* (koga/što) (*pres* ~erem) pick, select, choose

probuditi *v* (koga/se) wake up

probušiti *v* (što/se) pierce, puncture, perforate

procedura *nf* procedure

proces *nm* process; (suđenje) trial

procesija *nf* procession

procijediti *v* (što) 1 strain 2 (reći) say through/between one's teeth

proc|jeniti *v* (koga/što) assess, appraise, estimate, evaluate ~**jena** *nf* assessment, appraisal, estimate, evaluation ~**jenitelj** *nm* assessor ~**jenjivač** *nm* assessor, appraiser ~**jenjivati** *v impf*

procjep *nm* crack, cleft, split

procv|asti *v* (0) (*pres* ~atem) bloom, come into flower, blossom; flourish *fig* ~**at** *nm* flourishing ~**jetati** *v* (0) bloom, blossom

proče|lnik *nm* (*Vsg* ~lniče, *Npl* ~lnici) head ~**lje** *nn* front, facade

proče šljati *v* (što) comb through

proči|stač *nm* filter ~**stiti** *v* (što/koga/se) filter, clear, purify ~**ščavati** *v impf* ~**ščenje** *nn* catharsis

pročitati *v* 1 (što) read (through) 2 (koga, čije namjere) *coll* suss out, get wise to

proču|ti *v* (se) (*pres* ~jem) widely known; earn fame

proćelav *adj* balding

pro|ći *v* (*pres* ~đem) 1 (0) pass **bilo pa** ~**šlo** it's history **dobro smo** ~**šli** we did well **dobro je** ~**šlo** it went well 2 (što) go through sth

proda|ja *nf* sale **na** ~**ju** for sale ~**jni** *adj* sales ~**ti** *v* 1 (što/koga) sell 2 (se) *fig* sell out ~**vač** *nm* seller, salesman, vendor, dealer ~**vaonica** *nf* shop *GB*, store *US* ~**vati** *v impf*

proder|ati *v* (se) (*pres* ~em) yell out

prodika *nf* sermon, lecture

prodiskutirati *v* (što) discuss sth

prod|or *nm* advance, breakthrough, push ~**oran** *adj* (*a*) 1 penetrating, piercing 2 (osoba) pushy ~**ornost** *nf* pushiness ~**rijeti** *v* (0) (*pres* ~rem) penetrate, break through, make one's way through

prodrijemati *v* (0) nap, snooze

prodrmati *v* (što/koga/se) shake, jolt

produbiti *v* (što) deepen; (*fig*) intensify; (izdubiti) hollow out

produ|cent *nm* producer ~**cirati** *v* 1 (što) produce 2 (se) show off ~**kcija** *nf* production ~**kt** *nm* product ~**ktivan** *adj* (*a*) productive ~**ktivnost** *nf* productivity

produhovl|jen *adj* spiritual; refined

produ|ljiti *v* (se) lengthen, extend ~**žetak** *nm* (*Gsg* ~žetka, *Npl* ~žeci) extension ~**žiti** (što/se) lengthen, extend ~**žni** *adj* **kabel** extension cable

profan *adj* profane ~**irati** *v* (koga/što) profane

profes|ija *nf* profession ~**ionalac** *nm* (*Gsg* ~ionalca) professional; pro *coll* ~**ionalan** *adj* (*a*) professional ~**ionalizam** *nm* (*Gsg* ~ionalizma) professionalism ~**or** *nm* 1 (sveučilišni) professor *US*, lecturer *GB* 2 (nastavnik) teacher 3 (diplomirani) B. A. ~**ura** *nf* professorship

profil *nm* profile ~**irati** *v* (što) profile

profinjen *adj* refined, sophisticated ~**ost** *nf* refinement, sophistication

profit *nm* profit ~**er** *nm* profiteer ~**erstvo** *nn* profiteering ~**irati** (0) profit; benefit ~**ni** *adj* profit

profućkati *v* (što) *sl* squander, waste

proglas *nm* proclamation, declaration ~**iti** *v* 1 (što) proclaim, declare 2 (koga čim/za što) appoint ~**iti pobjednikom** announce the winner ~**iti krivim** find sb guilty

progleda|ti *v* (0) be able to see ~**la sam** my eyes were open

progna|nik *nm* (*Vsg* ~niče, *Npl* ~nici) displaced person ~**ti** *v* (koga) displace, expell, exile, ban ~**nstvo** *nn* exile

progno|stičar *nm* prognosticator

~**stički** *adj* prognostic ~**za** *nf* prognosis; forecast **vremenska** ~**za** weather forecast ~**zer** *nm* forecaster ~**zirati** *v* (što) forecast, prognosticate

progon *nm* 1 persecution, pursuit, chase 2 (izgon) expulsion, displacement ~**itelj** *nm* persecutor ~**iti** *v* (koga) persecute, pursue, chase, hunt ~**stvo** *nn* exile

progor|jeti *v* (0) (što) (*pres* ~im) burn through

progovoriti *v* (0) start speaking, speak, break the silence

program *nm* 1 program(me) 2 (kompjutorski) program 3 *TV, radio* station, channel (¶ programme = emisija) ~**er** *nm* programmer ~**irati** *v* (što) program(me) ~**ski** *adj* program(me)

progres *nm* progress ~**ija** *nf math* progression ~**ivan** *adj* (*a*) progressive

progri|sti *v* (što) (*pres* ~zem) bite through, corrode

progunđati *v* (što) mutter, mumble

progurati *v* 1 (što) push through 2 (se) push/elbow one's way

progutati *v* (što) swallow, gulp

prohibicija *nf* prohibition

prohladan *adj* (*a*) cool

prohod|an *adj* (*a*) passable, negotiable ~**ati** *v* 1 (0) start walking, learn to walk; be back on one's feet 2 (što) walk

prohtje|ti *v* (se) ~**lo mi se** I felt a sudden wish/craving (for sth)

prohujati *v* (0) pass by, blow over

proigrati *v* (što) gamble away ~ **priliku** miss a/the chance/opportunity

proiste|ći *v* (0, iz čega) (*pres* ~čem/~knem) result from, derive from

proiz|aći *v* (0, iz čega) (*pres* ~ađem) result from, arise from, follow ~**laziti** *v* impf

proizv|esti *v* (*pres* ~edem) (što) produce, make, manufacture, turn out ~**od** *nm* product, produce ~**odni** *adj* production ~**odnost** *nf* productivity ~**odnja** *nf* production, manufacture ~**ođač** *nm* producer, manufacturer, maker

proizvolj|an *adj* (*a*) arbitrary; random ~**nost** *nf* arbitrariness; random choice

proj|ekcija *nf* projection, showing ~**ektor** *nm* projector ~**icirati** *v* (što) project, show

projek|t *nm* (*Gpl* ~ata) project ~**tant** *nm* planner, designer, architect ~**tirati** *v* (što) plan, design

projektil *nm* projectile, missile

projuriti *v* (0) run/rush/dash/drive through/by/past

prokartati *v* (što) gamble away

proka|zati *v* (*pres* ~žem) (koga/što) denounce, inform against ~**zivač** *nm* informer

proki|snuti *v* (0) leak ~**šnjavati** *v impf*

proklam|acija *nf* proclamation ~**irati** *v* (što) proclaim

prokl|et *adj* 1 damned, accursed 2 (u govoru) damn(ed), goddamn(ed), bloody, bleeding, blasted ~**eti** *v* (koga/što) (*pres* prokunem) damn, curse ~**etnik** *nm* (*Vsg* ~niče, *Npl* ~nici) damned soul ~**etstvo** *nn* damnation, curse ~**injati** *v imf* (*pres* ~injem) curse

proklijati *v* (0) sprout

proklitika *nf* → **prislonjenica**

proključati *v* (0) boil, come to the boil

prokljuviti *v* (što) *coll* figure out, suss out

proknjižiti *v* (što) enter (in the accounts)

prokockati *v* (što) gamble away

prokomentirati *v* (što) comment (up)on, make a comment on/about, remark (up)on, pass remarks on/about

prokop *nm* ditch, passage ~**ati** *v* (što) dig (through)

prokrčiti *v* (što) clear ~ **put** *fig* pave the way for sth/sb

prokrijumčariti *v* (što) smuggle

prokrvariti *v* (0) start bleeding

prokuhati *v* (što) boil

prokulica *nf* brussels sprout

prokuljati *v* (0) gush, spout, spurt, pour (out)

prokušati *v* (što) try, test

prokužiti *v* (što/koga) *sl* suss out, get wise to

prolamati *v* (se) *impf* → **prolomiti**

prolaz *nm* 1 passage **zabranjen** ~ no thoroughfare, no way through 2 (između sjedala) aisle 3 (nadsvođeni) arcade 4 (na ispitu) pass ~**an** *adj* (α) 1 passing, transitory, transient 2 → **prohodan** ~**na ocjena** pass ~**iti** *v impf* pass (through) ~**nik** *nm* (*Vsg* ~niče, *Npl* ~nici) passer-by ~**nost** *nf* transience, transitoriness

prolet|arijat *nm* proletariat ~**er** *nm* proletarian ~**erski** *adj* proletarian

prol|etjeti *v* (0) (*pres* ~etim) fly through/past/by ~**ijetati** *v impf*

proli|jevati *v impf* ~**ti** *v* (što/se) (*pres* ~jem) spill ~**ti suze** shed tears ~**ti krv** spill blood

prolistati *v* 1 (0) come into leaf 2 (što) leaf through

prolo|g *nm* (*Npl* ~zi) prologue

prolom *nm* clearing, gap, breach ~ **oblaka** cloudburst ~**iti** *v* (se) ring out

prolongirati *v* (što) prolong, put off, delay

proljeće *nn* spring(time) ~**tni** *adj* spring(time) ~**tos** *adv* last spring

proljev *nm* diarrhoea; the runs *pl coll*

promakn|uće *nn* promotion ~**uti** *v* 1 (koga) promote 2 (0, komu) ~**ulo mi je** it escaped my attention, I missed it

promaš|aj *nm* miss; failure, flop *fig* ~**iti** *v* (što) miss

promatra|č *nm* observer, monitor ~**čka** *adj* **misija** monitoring mission ~**čnica** *nf* observation post ~**ti** *v* observe, monitor; watch

promeškoljiti *v* (se) fidget, stir

promet *nm* 1 traffic, transport(ation), conveyance **ministarstvo** ~**a** department/ministry of transport(ation) 2 (poslovanje) turnover 3 transactions 4 (optjecaj) circulation ~**alo** *pl nn* vehicle ~**an** *adj* (α) busy ~**ni** *adj* traffic ~**na nesreća** traffic accident, car crash ~**nica** *nf* road ~**nik** *nm* (*Vsg* ~niče, *Npl* ~nici) traffic police officer ~**ovati** *v* (0) (*pres* ~ujem) run

prometnuti *v* (se, u što) change/turn into

promi|catelj *nm* promoter ~**cati** *v* (*pres* ~čem) (što) promote ~**džba** *nf* promotion

promijeniti *v* (koga/što/se) change

promiješati *v* (što) stir

promil *nm* per mil(l)
prominentan *adj* (*a*) prominent
promiskuitet *nm* promiscuity ~**an** *adj* (*a*) promiscuous
promi|sliti *v* (0, o čemu) think over, consider, reflect ~**šljati** *v impf* ~**šljen** *adj* 1 sensible, prudent, discreet 2 (namjeran) deliberate, intentional
promje|na *nf* change ~**njiv** *adj* changeable, changing ~**njivost** *nf* changeability
promjer *nm* 1 diameter 2 (kalibar) calibre, gauge
promo|cija *nf* promotion ~**tor** *nm* promotor
promočiti *v* (0) soak through
promoliti *v* 1 (što) show 2 (0/se) appear, show oneself
promotriti *v* (koga/što) watch, observe, examine, consider
promozgati *v* (0) consider, think over, reflect upon
promrmljati *v* (što) mutter, mumble
promrsiti *v* (što) say (sth) between/through one's teeth
promrz|lina *nf* frostbite ~**nuti** *v* (0) freeze
promucati *v* (što) stutter, stammer
promućkati *v* (što) shake
promuk|ao *adj* (~**la** *f*) hoarse, husky ~**lost** *nf* hoarse/husky voice ~**nuti** *v* (0) lose one's voice
promumljati *v* (što) mumble
prona|ći *v* (*pres* ~**đem**) (što/koga) 1 find, locate 2 (izumiti) invent, discover ~**lazač** *nm* inventor, discoverer ~**lazak** *nm* (*Gsg* ~laska, *Npl* ~lasci) invention, discovery ~**laziti** *v impf*
pronevjer|a *nf* embezzlement, fraud ~**itelj** *nm* embezzler ~**iti** *v* (što) embezzle
proni|cljiv *adj* 1 (pogled) piercing 2 keen, sharp, intuitive ~**knuti** *v* (0, u što) 1 see through (sb/sth) 2 (dokučiti) fathom
pron|ijeti *v* (*pres* ~**esem**) 1 (što) carry, spread 2 (se) spread ~**ositi** *v impf*
pronjuškati *v* (što) snuff out
propadati *v* (0) decline, decay; sink
propag|anda *nf* 1 (politička) propaganda 2 (ekonomska) advertising ~**andni** *adj* 1 propaganda 2 *econ* ad-

vertising, commercial ~**ator** *nm* propagator ~**irati** *v* (što) propagate
propa|lica *nm/f* good-for-nothing; tramp *GB*, bum *US* ~**o** *adj* (*f* ~la) failed; wasted; ruined; decrepit ~**st** *nf* ruin, destruction ~**sti** *v* (*pres* ~dnem) be ruined/destroyed, fail, go to the dogs; (plan) fall through; (na ispitu) flunk
proparati *v* 1 (što) slit, tear, rip 2 (se) tear, rip 3 (se) (zvuk) ring out
propeler *nm* propeller
propentati *v* (što) mutter, stutter
prop|eti *v* (se) (*pres* ~nem) rear
propi|s *nm* regulation, rule ~**san** *adj* (*a*) in line with the regulations ~**sati** *v* (što) (*pres* ~šem) prescribe; stipulate
propi|šati *v* (što) *vulg* ~ **krv** piss blood
propi|ti *v* (*pres* ~jem) 1 (što) squander (on drink) 2 (se) take to drink
propješačiti *v* (0/što) walk
propjevati *v* (0) start singing
propla|kati *v* (0) (*pres* ~čem) start crying
proplan|ak *nm* (*Gsg* ~ka, *Npl* ~ci) clearing, glade
proplivati *v* (0) start swimming, learn to swim
proporci|ja *nf* proportion ~**onalan** *adj* (*a*) proportional, proportionate ~**onalni izborni sustav** proportional representation **obrnuto** ~**onalan** inversely proportionate
propov|ijed *nf* sermon, homily ~**ijedati** *v* (što) preach ~**jedaonica** *nf* pulpit ~**jednik** *nm* (*Vsg* ~jedniče, *Npl* ~jednici) preacher
propozicija *nf* 1 proposition 2 rule
propuh *nm* draught *GB*, draft *US* **na** ~**u** in a draught
propupati *v* (0) come into bud
propu|snost *nf* pass, permit ~**snost** *nf* permeability, porosity ~**st** *nm* omission, oversight ~**stan** *ad* (*f* ~sna) permeable, porous ~**stiti** *v* 1 (koga/što) allow to enter/pass through 2 (što) omit, fail to notice 3 (priliku) miss, let slip ~**štati** *v impf* (0) leak
propušiti *v* (0) start smoking
proput|ovati *v* (što) (*pres* ~ujem) travel around

proračun *nm* budget; estimate, calculation ~**at** *adj* calculated; (osoba) calculating ~**ati** *v* (što) estimate, calculate ~**ski** *adj* budgetary

prora|da *nf* studying, going through ~**diti** *v* 1 (što) study, go through 2 (0) start working/operating/functioning ~**đivati** *v impf*

prore|ći *v* (*pres* ~knem) (što, komu) prophesy, predict, foretell ~**ći** (komu) **sudbinu** tell (sb's) fortune

prored *nm* spacing

prorešetati *v* (koga) 1 riddle with bullets 2 *coll* examine thoroughly

prore|z *nm* (na odjeći) slit; (za novac) slot ~**zati** *v* (*pres* ~žem) (što) cut through, slit

proricati *v impf* → **proreći**

pror|ijediti *v* (što/se) thin (out) ~**jeđivati** *v impf*

proro|čanski *adj* prophetic(al) ~**čanstvo** *nn* prophecy, augury ~**čište** *nn* oracle ~**k** *nm* (*Vsg* ~če, *Npl* ~ci) prophet, oracle

pror|ovati *v* (što) (*pres* ~ujem) tunnel

pro|sac *nm* (*Gsg* ~sca, *Vsg* ~šče, *Npl* ~sci) suitor ~**sidba** *nf* (*Gpl* ~sidaba/~sidbi) suit ~**siti** *v* 1 (koga) propose (to), ask sb to marry one 2 (0/što) beg 3 → **moliti** ~**sjačiti** *v* (0/što) beg ~**sjački** *adj* beggar's ~**sjački štap** *fig* poverty ~**sjak** *nm* (*Vsg* ~sjače, *Npl* ~sjaci) beggar

prosij|ati *v* (što) (*pres* ~em) sieve, sift (out)

prosik|tati *v* (što) (*pres* ~ćem) hiss (out)

prosin|ac *nm* (*Gsg* ~ca) December ~**ački** *adj* December

prosipati *v impf* → **prosuti**

prosje|čan *adj* (*a*) average; mediocre ~**čnost** *nf* mean, mediocrity ~**k** *nm* (*Npl* ~ci) average, mean

prosjediti *v* (što) sit through

proslav|a *nf* celebration ~**iti** *v* 1 (što) celebrate 2 (koga) make famous 3 (se) become famous, achieve fame

proslijediti *v* 1 (0) continue, go on 2 (što) send, pass on

proslov *nm* prologue

proso *nm* millet

prospavati *v* (što) sleep through

prospek|t *nm* (*Gpl* ~ata) brochure, leaflet, prospectus

prosperi|rati *v* (0) prosper, thrive, do well ~**tet** *nm* prosperity

prost *adj* common, vulgar, crude, indecent ~**ački** *adj* → **prost** ~**ak** *nm* (*Vsg* ~ače, *Npl* ~aci) boor, lout ~**odušan** *adj* (*a*) naive, sincere, frank ~**ota** *nf* obscenity, dirty/four-letter word ~**ote** *pl* bad language

prostata *nf med* prostate (gland)

prostir|ač *nm* mat; rug ~**ati** *v* (*pres* ~em) 1 (što) spread ~**ati stol** lay the table 2 (se) spread, extend, stretch ~**ka** *nf* (*Dsg* ~ci) mat

prostitu|cija *nf* prostitution ~**irati** (se) prostitute ~**tka** *nf* prostitute

prost|or *nm* space, room **kazneni** ~**or** penalty area/box **poslovni** ~**or** business premises, offices *pl* **zrační** ~**or** airspace **zrakoprazni** ~**or** vacuum ~**orni** *adj* (*a*) **metar** cubic metre ~**orija** *nf* room ~**ran** *adj* spacious, roomy; vast, ample ~**ranstvo** *nn* expanse(s)

prostrijel|ni *adj* ~**na rana** gunshot wound ~**iti** *v* (koga/što) shoot (through)

prostr|lijeti (*pres* ~em) *v pf* → **prostirati**

prosu|dba *nf* opinion, inference, judgment ~**diti** *v* (što) form an opinion, judge, decide ~**đivati** *v impf*

prosušiti *v* (što/se) dry

pros|uti *v* (*pres* ~pem) (što/se) spill, scatter, strew

prosv|ijećen *adj* enlightened ~**ijećenost** *nf* enlightenment ~**ijetliti** *v* 1 (koga/što) enlighten 2 (0) light (up) ~**ječivati** *v impf* ~**jeta** *nf* education ~**jetitelj** *nm* enlightener ~**jetiteljski** *adj* enlightening ~**jetiteljstvo** *nn* the Enlightenment ~**jetni** *adj* education(al), school

prosvirati *v* 1 (0) start playing 2 (što) ~ **komu glavu** put a bullet through sb's head

prosvjed *nm* protest **uložiti/uputiti** ~ file/lodge a protest ~**ni** *adj* protest ~**ovati** *v* (*pres* ~ujem) (0, protiv koga/čega) protest (against)

prosvrdlati *v* (što) drill/bore through

prošap(u)|tati *v* (što) (*pres* ~ćem) whisper

prošarati *v* (što) streak

prošek *nm* sherry

prošе|tati *v* (*pres* ~tam/~ćem) **1** (koga) walk **2** (se) take a walk, go for a walk

proširiti *v* (što/se) spread

prošišati *v* (0) whizz by/past

prošli *adj* past, gone ~e **godine/subote** last year/Saturday ~i **puta** last time ~ost *nf* past, history

prošnja *nf* → **prosidba**

proštenje *nn* feast, fete

protegnuti *v* (što/se) stretch

protein *nm* protein

protekcija *nf* favouritism

protest *nm* protest ~ant *nm* Protestant ~antizam *nm* (*Gsg* ~antizma) Protestantism ~antski *adj* Protestant ~irati *v* (0, protiv koga/čega) protest (against) ~ni *adj* protest

prote|tika *nf* (*Dsg* ~tici) prosthetics ~za *nf* prosthesis **zubna** ~za dentures *pl*

protež|e *nm/f* protege(e) ~irati *v* (koga) favour

protisnuti *v* (što) **1** press, squeeze, crush **2** (reći) say through/between one's teeth

protiv *prep*, *adv* against **razlozi za i** ~ pros and cons ~an *adj* (α) contrary ~nički *adj* opposition ~nik *nm* (*Vsg* ~niče, *Npl* ~nici) opponent, rival, adversary ~ništvo *nn* opposition, rivalry ~no *adv* contrary to

protjerati *v* (koga) chase/drive away; (iz doma) expel, displace; (izgnati) banish, exile; (stranca) deport

protkati *v* (što, čime) streak with

protokol *nm* protocol

prototip *nm* prototype

protratiti *v* (što) waste, squander

protrč|ati *v* (*pres* ~im) (0) run through/past/by

protres|ti *v* (što/koga/se) (*pres* ~em) shake

protrnuti *v* (0) shudder

protu- *prefix* anti-, counter-, un-

protuha *nf/m* tramp *GB*; bum *US*

protumačiti *v* (što, komu) explain (sth to sb)

protuotrov *nm* antidote

protuprirod|an *adj* (α) unnatural ~ni **blud** *leg* sodomy

protureformacija *nf* Counter-Reformation

proturječ|an *adj* (α) contradictory ~iti *v* (0, komu/čemu) contradict ~je *nn* contradiction

protuslov|an *adj* (α) contradictory ~iti *v* (0, komu) contradict

protuteža *nf* counterbalance

protutnj|ati *v* (0) (*pres* ~im) rumble (through)

protuvrijednost *nf* equivalent value

protuzakonit *adj* illegal, unlawful, against the law

prouč|avatelj *nm* researcher ~avanje *nn* research (into), study ~avati *v* (što) *impf* study, research, examine ~iti *v* *pf*

prouzročiti *v* (što) cause

prova *nf* prow

proval|a *nf* **1** outbreak, outburst ~a **smijeha** a gale of laughter **2** *mil* invasion, incursion **3** (u kuću) *leg* breaking and entering, break-in ~ija *nf* abyss, chasm ~iti *v* **1** (0, u što) break in(to) **2** (0, iz čega) burst, gush **3** (se) fall in; burst open **4** (što) ~iti **šifru** break/crack the code ~nik *nm* (*Vsg* ~niče, *Npl* ~nici) burglar

prove|dba *nf* implementation, enforcement ~sti *v* (*pres* ~dem) **1** (što) implement, enforce, carry out, realize **2** (što) (vrijeme/praznike/ etc.) spend **3** (koga) take, lead, guide (through) **4** (se) (dobro se ~sti) have a good time

provenijencija *nf* provenance

proventilirati *v* (što) air

proveseliti *v* (se) have a good time, enjoy oneself

providnost *nf* providence

provincij|a *nf* **1** province **2** (izvan gl. grada) the provinces *pl* ~al *nm* provincial ~alac *nm* (*Gsg* ~alca, *Npl* ~alci) provincial ~alan *adj* (α) provincial ~alizam *nm* (*Gsg* ~alizma) provincialism ~ski *adj* provincial

proviriti *v* (0) peep; protrude

provizija *nf* commission

provizoran *adj* (α) provisional, temporary

provjer|a *nf* check, inspection ~**iti** *v* (koga/što) check, inspect, make sure, verify

provjetriti *v* (što) air

provlačiti *v impf* 1 (što/se) → **provući** 2 (se) run through

provo|cirati *v* (koga/što) provoke ~**kacija** *nf* provocation ~**kativan** *adj* (α) provocative ~**kator** *nm* agent provocateur

provod *nm* good time, entertainment ~**iti** *v impf* → **provesti**

provrtljeti *v* (što) (pres ~im) drill/bore through

provu|ći *v* (pres ~čem) 1 (što) drag/pull through 2 (se) sneak through; (na ispitu) scrape through

proz|a *nf* prose ~**aičan** *adj* (α) prosaic ~**ni** *adj* prose

prozboriti *v* (što) utter

proze|bao *adj* (f ~bla) frozen ~**psti** *v* (pres ~bem) (0) freeze, be chilled

prozir|an *adj* (α) see-through, transparent, clear ~**nost** *nf* transparency

proziv|ati *v impf* → **prozvati** ~**ka** *nf* (Dsg ~ci) roll call

prozor *nm* window; (na krovu) skylight; (brodski) porthole ~**ski** *adj* window

prozrač|an *adj* (α) thin, light, transparent ~**iti** *v* (što/se) air

prozrijeti *v* (koga/što) see through sb/sth

prozujati *v* (0) whizz by/past

proz|vati *v(pres ~ovem)* (koga) 1 call the roll 2 (nazvati) (nick)name, dub 3 *pol* criticize, denounce

prožd|irati *v* (što) (pres ~irem) devour, guzzle, gorge ~**irati pogledom** leer, eye, ogle ~**rijeti** *v* (što) devour, gobble (up), gulp (down) ~**rljiv** *adj* gluttonous, greedy ~**rljivac** *nm* (Gsg ~rljivca) glutton, pig ~**rljivost** *nf* gluttony

prož|eti *v* (pres ~mem) (koga/što) imbue (with), permeate (through/ into) ~**imati** *v impf*

proživ|ljeti *v* (što) 1 go/be through, experience 2 (dio života) spend ~**lja-vati** *v impf*

prožva|kati *v* (što) (pres ~čem) chew

prpošan *adj* (α) pert

prs|a *nn pl* chest → **grudi** ~**iti** *v* (se) brag ~**na** *adj* kost breastbone, sternum ~**ni** koš thorax ~**no plivanje** breaststroke

prska|lica *nf* sparkler ~**ti** *v* (što/koga/se) spray, splash, shower

prslu|k *nm* (Npl ~ci) waistcoat GB; vest US

prsnuti *v* (0) burst, gush

prst *nm* (Gpl ~iju) (ruke) finger; (nožni) toe; (palac) thumb **progledati (komu) kroz ~e** turn a blind eye **imati što u malom ~u** have sth at one's fingertips **ne vidi se ~ pred nosom** it's pitch dark **otisak ~a** fingerprint **nije (ni) ~om maknuo** he didn't lift/raise a finger ~**e k sebi!** hands off **sam kao ~** all alone ~**en** ring ~**enast** *adj* ring-shaped ~**enovati** *v* (pres ~enujem) (koga) (pticu) ring ~**enjak** *nm* (Npl ~enjaci) ring finger

pršić *nm* powder

pršljen *nm* vertebra

prštat|i *v* (0) (pres ~im) spurt, jet, squirt

pršut *nm* prosciutto

prtlja|ga *nf* luggage GB; baggage US ~**žni** *adj* luggage, baggage ~**žnik** *nm* (Npl ~žnici) boot GB; trunk US

prtljati *v* (0) fumble, bungle, botch; (brbljati) flounder

pruće *n pl* → **prut**

pru|ga *nf* (Dsg ~zi) 1 (željeznička) railway (railroad US) track(s)/line 2 (linija) route 3 (uzorak) stripe ~**gast** *adj* striped

prut *nm* stick, twig

pruž|ati *v* 1 (što) extend, offer, give 2 (se) extend, stretch, spread ~**iti** *v pf*

prv|ak *nm* (Npl ~aci) 1 champion 2 (čelnik) leader ~**aš** *nm* first-former GB/grader US ~**enstven** *adj* chief, principal, primary ~**enstveno** *adv* primarily, in the first place ~**enstvo** *nn* 1 championship 2 priority ~**i** *num ord* first ~**i susjed** next-door neighbour ~**ijenac** *nm* (Gsg ~ijenca) 1 firstborn 2 first work/etc.

prvo- *prefix* first- ~**bitan** *adj* (α) original, primary, prim(a)eval ~**klasan**,

~razredan *adj* (*a*) first-class, first-rate **~ligaš** *nm* major-league team/player **~rođenče** *nn* firstborn (child) **~stolnica** *nf* cathedral **~ško-lac** *nm* first-former *GB* **~tisak** *nm* (*Gsg* ~ska) incunabula

pržiti *v* (što/se) fry; grill **sunce ~** it's sizzling hot

psal|am *nm* (*Gsg* ~ma) psalm

ps|eći *adj* dog's, dog **~etarnica** *nf* kennels **~eto** *nn* dog **~ić** *nm* doggy, doggie

pseudonim *nm* pseudonym, pen name, alias

psih|a *nf* psyche **~ički** *adj* psychic(al), mental **~ijatar** *nm* (*Gsg* ~ijatra) psychiatrist, therapist; shrink *coll* **~ijatrija** *nf* psychiatry **~ijatrij-ski** *adj* psychiatric **~o-** *prefix* psycho- **~oanalitičar** *nm* (psycho)ana-lyst **~oanaliza** *nf* psychoanalysis **~ofizički** *adj* psychophysical **~olog** *nm* (*Npl* ~lozi) psychologist **~ologija** *nf* psychology **~ološki** *adj* psycho-logical **~opat** *nm* psychopath **~opatija** *nf* psychopathy **~osomat-ski** *adj* psychosomatic **~za** *nf* psy-chosis

psi|kati *v* (0) (*pres* ~čem) hiss

psina *nf* prank, practical joke

psov|ati *v* (koga/što/0) (*pres* psujem) swear (at) **~ka** *nf* swearword

ps(ss)t *int* s(ss)h, hush

pšeni|ca *nf* wheat **~čni** *adj* wheat

pti|ca *nf* bird **~ca selica** b. of passage **noćna ~ca** *fig* night owl **kao ~ca na grani** free as a bird **svaka ~ca svome jatu leti** birds of a feather (flock together) **~čar** *nm* gundog; bird dog *US* **~čica** *nf* birdie **~čji** *adj* bird's, bird **~čja perspektiva** bird's-eye view **~čurina** *nf* big bird **~ć** *nm* baby bird, chick

pubertet *nm* puberty **~ski** *adj* adoles-cent

publi|cirati *v* (što) publish **~cist** *nm* writer **~citet** *nm* publicity **~ka** *nf* public; audience; spectators *pl* **~kacija** *nf* publication

puc|anj *nm* shot **~ati** *v* (0) 1 shoot (at), fire (shots) at 2 (na što) *coll* have one's eyes on **~kati**, **~ketati** *v* (0)

crackle, pop **~ketati prstima** snap one's fingers **~njava** *nf* shooting

puce *nn* button

puč *nm* coup (d'état), putsch

puč|anin *nm* commoner **~anstvo** *nn* the people **~ki** *adj* popular, national **~ki jezik** vernacular **~ka škola** pri-mary school

pućkati *v* (što) (lulu) puff (at one's pipe)

pud|er *nm* powder **~rijera** *nf* compact

puding *nm* pudding, custard

pudl *nm*, **~ica** *nf* poodle

puh *nm* dormouse

puh|ači *nm pl* the wind **~ački** *adj* in-strument wind instrument **~aljka** *nf* blowpipe **~ati** *v* (0) blow **~nuti** *v* (0) blow, start blowing

puk *nm* (common) people

puki *adj* mere, sheer

puk|nuti *v* (0) crack; snap; break **~oti-na** *nf* crack, chink, split

pukovni|ja *nf* regiment **~k** *nm* (*Vsg* če, *Npl* ~ci) colonel

pulover *nm* pullover

puls *nm* pulse **~irati** *v* (0) pulse, throb, pulsate

pult *nm* counter

puma *nf* puma, cougar, mountain lion

pump|a *nf* pump **~ati** *v* (što) pump **~erice** *nf pl* plus fours

pun *adj* full, filled; (pištolj) loaded **~ašan** *adj* (*a*) plump **~ina** *nf* ful(l)ness **~iti** *v* (što/se) fill **~o** *adv* a lot; many; much **~oglavac** *nm* (*Gsg* ~oglavca) tadpole **~okrvan** *adj* (*a*) full-blooded; (konj) thoroughbred **~oljetan** *adj* (*a*) of age, major **~ol-jetnost** *nf* majority **~omastan** *adj* (*a*) unskimmed **~omoć** *nf* power of at-torney; authorization **~opravan** *adj* (*a*) full **~ovažan** *adj* (*a*) valid

punč *nm* punch

punđa *nf* bun

punkcija *nf* biopsy

punjenje *nn* filling; refill

pup *nm* bud **~ati** *v* (0) come into bud **~oljak** *nm* (*Gsg* ~oljka, *Npl* ~oljci) bud

pup|ak *nm* (*Gsg* ~ka, *Npl* ~kovi) navel; belly button *coll* **~čana** *adj* **vrpca**, **~kovina** *nf* umbilical cord

pura *nf* turkey hen **~n** *nm* turkey

purgatorij *nm* Purgatory

puritan|ac *nm* (*Gsg* ~ca) Puritan **~izam** *nm* (*Gsg* ~izma) Puritanism

purpur *nm* purple

pusa *nf coll* kiss

puslica *nf* meringue

pust (1) *nm* felt **~en** *adj* felt

pust (2) *adj* deserted, desolate; empty **~ara** *nf* wilderness **~inja** *nf* desert **~injak** *nm* (*Vsg* ~injače, *Npl* ~injaci) hermit **~injski** *adj* desert **~opoljina** *nf* wasteland **~oš** *nf* deserted area; desolation **~ošiti** *v* (što) devastate, ravage

pustiti *v* (koga/što) **1** let **2** (na slobo-du) let go/loose; set free, release **3** (na ispitu) pass sb **4** (bradu etc.) grow

pustolov *nm* adventurer **~an** *adj* (*a*) adventurous **~ina** *nf* adventure

puš|ač *nm* smoker **~iti** *v* (0/što/se) smoke

puš|čani *adj* gun-, rifle- **~ka** *nf* (*Dsg* ~ci, *Gsg* ~aka) rifle, gun **lovačka ~ka** shotgun **~kar** *nm* gunsmith **~karanje** *nm* sporadic gunfire, skir-mish **~karnica** *nf* **1** embrasure **2** gunshop **~komet** *nm* range (of a gun) **na ~komet** (with)in range

puštati *v impf* → pustiti

put (1) *nm* (*Npl* ~evi/ovi) **1** way **2** road; path, trail, track **preko ~a** op-posite, across the road (from) **3** (putovanje) journey, trip, travel **poslovni ~** business trip **sretan ~**! have a safe journey **~anja** *nf* orbit **~eljak** *nm* (*Gsg* ~eljka, *Npl* ~eljci), **~ić** *nm* (foot)path **~ni** *adj* travelling **~na torba** suitcase **~nički** *adj* **vlak** passenger train **~nički ček** traveller's cheque **~nik** *nm* (*Vsg* ~niče, *Npl* ~nici) traveller, passenger; (na posao) commuter **trgovački ~nik** sales representative **~okaz** *nm* sign-post **~opis** *nm* travelogue **~opisni** *adj* travel **~ovanje** *nn* travel, travel-ling, journey, voyage, passage, tour **~ovati** *v* (0) (*pres* ~ujem) travel; (na posao) commute **~ovnica** *nf* passport **~ujući** *adj* travelling, itinerant

put (2) *nf* **1** complexion **2** flesh *fig* **~en** *adj* carnal, sensual **~enost** *nf* sensu-ality

put (3) *prep* towards, to

put(a) *adv* time **ovaj/idući ~** this/next time **dva ~** twice **pet ~** five times **sedam ~ osam** (7x8) seven times eight

putar (1) *nm coll* → maslac

putar (2) *nm* roadman, road mender

pu|zati (*pres* ~žem), **~ziti** *v* (0) crawl, creep **~zavica** *nf* creeper

puž *nm* snail; (golać) slug **~eva** *adj* **kućica** snail shell **~evim korakom** at a snail's pace

R

R, r (er) 23rd letter of Cro. alphabet

rabarbara *nf* rhubarb

rabat *nm com* rebate, discount

rabin *nm* rabbi

rab|iti *v* (što) use **~ljen** *adj* second-hand, used

racija *nf* (police) raid

racional|an *adj* (ā) 1 rational 2 economic **~izirati** *v* (što) 1 rationalize 2 streamline, make economic

račić *nm* shrimp

račun *nm* 1 bill; check *US* 2 account **tekući ~** current account **žiro~** drawing account **izravnati ~** settle an a. (+ *fig*) 3 calculation; calculus *math* **na moj ~** at my expense **voditi ~a** (o komu/čemu) take into consideration/account **~alo** *nn* computer **~aljka** *nf* (*Dsg* ~aljci) abacus, slide rule **~ati** *v* 1 (komu što) charge sb for sth 2 (0) calculate 3 (što/da) think, reckon, figure **~ati na koga/što** count on **~ica** *nf fig* motivation **~ovodstvo** *nn* 1 accountancy 2 accountancy department **~ovođa** *nm* accountant **~ski** *adj* arithmetic

račvati *v* (se) bifurcate, branch off, fork

rad *nm* (*Npl* ~ovi) 1 work 2 activity 3 labo(u)r 4 paper, thesis **ručni ~** embroidery **fizički ~** manual labour **~in** *adj* hard-working **~inost** *nf* industry; diligence **kućna ~inost** cottage industry **~ionica** *nf* workshop **~iti** *v* 1 (što) do; (izrađivati) make 2 (0) be employed, work 3 act **~iti na crno** moonlight *coll* **o čemu se ~i?** what is it about? **~ni** *adj* work(ing) **~ni staž** years of service **~na soba** study **~na snaga** labour, workforce, manpower **~nik** *nm* (*Vsg*~niče, *Npl*~nici) worker; employee **~nički** *adj* workers', labour **~nja** *nf* 1 shop, (small) busi-

ness 2 action, plot 3 thesis; essay

radi *prep* 1 in order to, to 2 for the sake of, for sb's sake

radijacija *nf* radiation

radijator *nm* radiator

radije *adv* rather, sooner

radikalan *adj* (ā) radical

radio *nm* radio **~amater** *nm* amateur radio operator; ham *coll* **~aparat** *nm* (radio) set, tuner **~stanica** *nf* (radio) station

radio|aktivan *adj* radioactive **~aktivnost** *nf* radioactivity **~terapija** *nf* radiotherapy, X-ray therapy

radius *nm* 1 radius 2 range

rado *adv* gladly, willingly **suza ~snica** *nf* tear of joy **~st** *nf* joy, delight, happiness **~stan** *adj* (~sna *f*) glad, joyful **~vati** *v* (*pres* radujem) 1 (se) rejoyce, take delight in **unaprijed se ~vati** look forward to (doing sth) 2 (koga) please **~znalost** *nf* curiosity **~znao** *adj* (~znala *f*) curious; nosy **~znalac** *nm* (*Gsg* ~znalca, *Vsg* ~znalče) curious person; nosey parker *coll*

rađati *v impf* → **roditi**

rafal *nm* volley, burst

rafin|erija *nf* refinery **~iran** *adj* 1 refined 2 sophisticated 3 cunning **~irati** *v* (što) refine

raga *nm* jade, nag

rahao *adj* (rahla *f*) soft, fluffy

rahiti|čan *adj* (ā) rickety **~s** *nm* rickets

raj *nm* paradise, heaven **~ski** *adj* celestial, heavenly

rajčica *nf* tomato

rak *nm* (*Npl* ~ovi) 1 crayfish, crab; crawfish *US* 2 *astrol, med* cancer

raketa *nf* rocket **~ni** *adj* rocket

rakija *nf* brandy, spirit

ral *nm* about half an acre

ralica *nf* snowplough

ralje *nf pl* jaws

rame *nn* (*Gsg* ramèna, *Npl* raména) shoulder **slegnuti ~nima** shrug (one's shoulders) **~ uz ~** s. to s. **širokih ~na** broad-shouldered

ran *adj* early **~ije** *adv* earlier; previously **~iti** *v* (0) get up early **tko ~o ~i dvije sreće grabi** *prov* early bird catches the worm **~o** *adv* early **~oranilac** (*Gsg* ~oranioca) early bird *coll*

ra|na *nf* wound; injury **laka ~na** minor i., flesh w. **teška ~na** serious i., bad w. **~niti** *v* (koga) wound, injure, hurt **biti ~njen** be wounded, sustain i. **~njavati** *v impf* **~njenik** *nm* (*Vsg* ~njeniče, *Npl* ~njenici) wounded/injured man/person **~njenici** *pl* the wounded **~njiv** *adj* vulnerable

ran|ac *nm* (*Gsg* ~ca) knapsack

rang *nm* rank, status

ranžirni *adj* **~ kolodvor** marshalling yard

ras|a *nf* 1 race 2 breed **~ist** *nm* racist **~an** *adj* (*a*) (konj) thoroughbred; (pas) purebred **~ni** *adj* racial

rasadni|k *nm* (*Npl* ~ci) nursery (garden); hotbed (+ *fig*)

rasc|ijepati *v* (što) chop up **~ijepiti** *v* (što) split, cleave **~jep** *nm* cleft; split (+ *fig*); schism *fig* **~cjepkati** *v* (što) *fig* fragment

rascvjetati *v* (se) bloom, blossom

rasedlati *v* (koga) unsaddle

rase|liti *v* (koga) displace; resettle **~ljen** *adj* displaced

rashladiti *v* (što) cool, chill, refrigerate

rashod *nm* expenses *pl*, expenditure

rasip|an *adj* (*a*) extravagant; spendthrift; lavish; prodigal **~ati** *v* (što) 1 squander, fritter away 2 scatter, strew **~nik** *nm* (*Npl* ~nici) spendthrift **~nost** *nf* dissipation, extravagance

rasje|ći *v* (što) (*pres* ~čem) cut (up); slash open

raskalašen *adj* debauched, lewd, wanton

raski|d *nm* separation, severance **~nuti** *v* 1 (što) break (off), sever, tear apart 2 (s kim) break (off) with

rasklapati *v impf* → **rasklopiti**

rasklima|n *adj* rickety, shaky, wobbly **~ti** *v* 1 (što) (make) loose, loosen 2 (se) become loose

rasklopiti *v* (što) 1 unfold, open 2 take apart, dismantle

raskol *nm* split; schism; rift

raskolačiti *v* **~ oči** stare, gape

raskomadati *v* (koga/što) dismember, tear to pieces

raskomotiti *v* (se) make oneself comfortable, make oneself at home

raskopati *v* (što) dig up; ransack

raskopčati *v* (što) unbutton, undo

raskorak *nm fig* discrepancy **u ~u** (s) out of step with, at variance with

raskoš *nm/f* luxury, splendour, magnificence **~an** *adj* (*a*) luxurious, sumptuous; luxuriant

raskraviti *v* (se) thaw; mellow

raskrčiti *v* (što) clear (land)

raskrinkati *v* (koga) unmask, expose

raskrižje *nn* cross-roads, crossing, intersection

raskrstiti *v* (s kim/čim) break off (with sb); give up (sth)

raskrvariti *v* 1 (što) cause to bleed 2 (se) start bleeding

raskuštran *adj* dishevelled

raskužiti *v* (što) disinfect

raskvasiti *v* 1 (što) soak 2 (se) become sodden/soggy; lose shape

raslinje *nn* vegetation

rasol *nm* brine

raspačavati *v* (što) distribute, disseminate; (drogu) push, peddle

raspad *nm* disintegration, breakdown, breakup **~ati** *v* (se) 1 fall to pieces, disintegrate 2 decay, rot, decompose

raspaliti *v* 1 (koga) incense 2 (se) blaze up; become incensed, flare up *fig* 3 (koga) whack

rasparati *v* (što) rip (up)

raspa|sti *v* (se) (*pres* ~dnem se) → **raspadati se**

rasp|elo *nn* crucifix, cross **~eti** *v* (*pres* ~nem) 1 (koga) crucify 2 (što) unfurl **~injati** *v impf* **~injati na muke** torment

raspetljati *v* (što) unravel

raspiri|ti *v* (što) stir up (+ *fig*); foment *fig* **~vati** *v impf*

raspisati *v* (što) **~ natječaj** advertise

for, invite tenders **~ tjeralicu** issue
an arrest warrant **~ izbore** call elec-
tions

raspit|ati v 1 (se) make enquiries, en-
quire **~ivati** v impf

rasplakati v 1 (se) burst into tears 2
(koga) make sb cry

rasplamsati v (se) blaze up, flare up

raspl|esti v (što/se) disentangle (+ fig)
~esti kosu let one's hair down **~et**
nm denouement **~itati** v impf (pres
~ićem)

raspli|nuti v (se) evaporate; fade away
(+ fig) **~njač** nm carburettor GB, carburetor US

rasplod nm breeding **~ni** adj breeding
~na kobila brood mare **~ni konj**
stud-horse

raspod|ijeliti v (što komu) distribute,
divide **~jela** nf distribution

raspojasan adj riotous, unbridled

raspola|gati v (čime) (pres **~žem**)
have at one's disposal; control, do as
one wishes

raspoloviti v (što) halve, break/split in
two

raspolož|en adj **dobro ~en** in a good
mood **loše ~en** in a bad mood **~en
sam za to/da to učinim** I feel like
it/doing it **~enje** nn mood, frame of
mind **~iv** v (koga/se) liven up, cheer
up **~iv** adj available

raspon nm span, scope, range

raspor nm slit **~ak** nm (Npl **~ci**) fly

raspore|d nm 1 schedule; timetable 2
arrangement 3 (vojske) deployment
~diti v 1 (što) arrange, organize 2
(koga) assign; (vojsku) deploy **~đi-
vati** v (pres **~đujem**) impf

rasporiti v (koga/što) rip up, slit

raspoznati v (koga/što) 1 make out 2
distingusih, tell apart

raspra nf argument, dispute **~va** nf debate, discussion **sudska ~va** trial
~viti v (što) discuss **~vljati** v impf

raspredati v (što) discuss in detail

raspričati v (se) ramble (on about)

rasproda|ja nf (clearance) sale **~n** adj
sold out **~ti** v (što/se) sell out

rasprostirati v (se) extend, stretch

rasprostranjen adj frequent, common, widespred **~ost** nf spread

rasprostrijeti v 1 (što) spread out 2
(se) coll fall flat

rasprs|nuti v (se) explode, burst, blow
up **~kavajuća** adj **bomba** fragmen-
tation bomb **~kavati** v impf

raspršiti v (koga/što/se) disperse

raspu|knuti v (pres **~knem**) (se) crack,
split, burst

raspu|stiti v 1 (koga/što) disband;
(parlament) dissolve 2 (se) let oneself go; grow undisciplined **~štati** v
impf **~šten** adj 1 dissolved 2 dis-
banded 3 unruly, wild **~štenica** nf
derog divorcee

rasrditi v 1 (koga) make angry 2 (se)
get angry

rast nm 1 growth; increase 2 stature,
height **~i** v (0) (pres **~em**) grow, rise,
develop; increase, intensify

rastaliti v (što) melt; (rudača) smelt

rasta|nak nm (Gsg **~nka**, Npl **~nci**)
farewell, leave-taking; parting **~ti** v
(pres **~nem**) (se) 1 (s kim/čim) part
(with), take leave (of) 2 separate
~viti v (koga/što od koga/čega) separate, part; disconnect; dismantle
~vljati v impf **~jati** v impf

rastapati v impf → **rastopiti**

raste|gnuti v (što/se) stretch **~zanje**
nn expansion, distension, dilation
~zati v impf (pres **~žem**) **~gljiv** adj
tensile; flexible fig

rastere|titi v (koga) take the load off
(sb), relieve (of) **~ćivati** v impf

rastjerati v (što/se) scatter, disperse

rastopi|ti v 1 (što) dissolve, melt,
thaw; (mast) render 2 (se) melt, thaw
3 fig be in seventh heaven

rastresen adj absent-minded, distracted **~ost** nf absent-mindedness

rastrgati, rastrgnuti v (koga/što) tear
(to pieces), mutilate

rastrijezniti v (koga/se) sober up

rastrojen adj (mentally) deranged
duševna ~ost nf mental derangement

rastrubiti v (što) trumpet, shout from
the housetops, broadcast

rastumačiti v (što komu) explain, expound

rastužiti v 1 (koga) sadden, distress 2
(se) sadden, become sad

rasu|lo nn disintegration, chaos **~ti** v

(što/se) scatter **~ti** *adj* **teret** bulk cargo

rasvijetliti *v* (što) *fig* shed light upon, clarify

rasvjeta *nf* light(ing)

raščešljati *v* (što) comb (out)

raščistiti *v* 1 (što) *fig* sort out **~ račune** settle the score 2 (se) clear (up)

rašča|mba *nf* analysis **~niti** *v* (što) analyse

raščupa|n *adj* dishevelled **~ti** *v* (koga/što) dishevel, ruffle

raširiti *v* (što/se) spread (out); broaden, dilate; circulate

rašlj|ar *nm* diviner **~ast** *adj* forked **~e** *nf pl* 1 fork 2 divining rod

raštrkati *v* (se) scatter

rat *nm* (*Npl* ~ovi) war; warfare **Prvi svjetski ~** World War I/One, the 1st World War **voditi ~** (protiv) make/wage war (upon/against) **navijestiti ~** declare war **~ište** *nn* battlefield, theatre **~ni** *adj* war(time) **~no stanje** state of war **~na mornarica** navy **~ni zarobljenik** prisoner of war; POW **~nički** *adj* warlike **~nik** *nm* (*Vsg* ~niče, *Npl* ~nici) warrior, fighter **~oboran** *adj* (*a*) bellicose, belligerent, aggressive **~ovati** *v* (*pres* ~ujem) (protiv koga) wage war

rata *nf* instalment

ratar *nm* farmer **~stvo** *nn* farming

ratificirati *v* (što) ratify

rav|an *adj* (*a*) 1 level, flat, even; straight; erect 2 (komu) a match for sb **nema mu ~na** he has no equal • *nf* plain **~nalo** *nn* ruler **~natelj** *nm* director; (škole) headmaster; principal; (dirigent) conductor *US* **~nati** *v* 1 (što) straighten (up) 2 (čime/kime) rule, manage, run; (orkestrom) conduct 3 (se) follow, conform to **~nica** *nf* plain **~nina** *nf* plane **u ~nini** (s) flush/level with **~no** *adv* 1 straight, direct 2 exactly **~nodnevica** *nf* equinox **~nodušan** *adj* (*a*) indifferent, unconcerned **~nomjeran** *adj* (*a*) even, steady **~nopravan** (komu) *adj* (*a*) equal (to/with) **~nopravnost** *nf* equality, equal rights **~noteža** *nf* balance

razab|rati *v* (*pres* ~erem) (što) 1 discern 2 understand **~irati** *v impf*

raz|ni *adj* different, diverse, various, varied; miscellaneous **točka ~no** other business **~nobojan** *adj* multicoloured; motley **~noličan** *adj* (*a*) heterogeneous, varied **~nolik** *adj* varied **~nolikost** *nf* variety **~norodan** *adj* (*a*) heterogenous **~novrstan** *adj* (~novrsna *f*) heterogenous

razap|eti *v* (*pres* ~nem) 1 (koga) crucify 2 (što) spread; (jedra) set; (šator) pitch

razara|č *nm* destroyer **~ti** *v impf* → **razoriti**

razas|uti *v* (*pres* ~pem) (što) scatter

razaznati *v* (koga/što) discern, make out

razbac|ati *v* (koga/što) throw all around **~ivati** *v impf* **~ivati se novcem** squander one's money

razbarušiti *v* (koga/što) tousle, ruffle

razbaštiniti *v* (koga) disinherit

razbibri|ga *nf* (*Dsg* ~zi) pastime, hobby

razbij|ač *nm* hoodloom, thug, vandal **~jati** *v impf* **~jati glavu** rack one's brains **~ti** *v* 1 (što/se) break, shatter, smash 2 (koga) beat sb to pulp

razbjesniti *v* 1 (koga) infuriate, make sb angry 2 (se) get angry

razbježati *v* (se) scatter

razblažiti *v* (što) dilute

razblud|an *adj* (*a*) 1 voluptuous 2 lecherous

razboj *nm* 1 loom 2 *sport* parallel bars

razboj|nik *nm* (*Vsg* ~niče, *Npl* ~nici) 1 robber 2 bandit, miscreant **~stvo** *nn* robbery

razboljeti *v* (se) fall ill

razbor *nm* reason, sense **~it** *adj* prudent, sensible **~itost** *nf* prudence, (common) sense

razbuditi *v* (koga/se) awaken

razdani|ti *v* (se) dawn **čim se ~** at first light

razder|ati *v* (*pres* ~em) (koga/što) tear to pieces

razdi|jeliti *v* (što) 1 distribute 2 separate 3 divide, partition **~oba** *nf* distribution, allocation; division, partition

razdirati *v* 1 *impf* → **razderati** 2 rack

razdjelj|ak *nm* (*Gsg* ~ka, *Npl* ~ci) part

razdoblje *nn* period; era, times

razdor *nm* **1** rupture **2** split, rift (+ *fig*) **sijati** ~/**sjeme** ~a sow (the seeds of) dissension

razdragan *adj* (*a*) overjoyed

razdražen *adj* irritated, exasperated ~**enost** *nf* temper ~**iti** *v* (koga) irritate, provoke ~**ljiv** *adj* irascible, short-tempered

razdrmati *v* (koga) shake up

razdružiti *v* (se) separate, divide, dissociate

razdv|ojiti *v* (koga/što) separate, keep apart; disengage; detach ~**ajati** *v impf*

razgaliti *v* (se) **1** bare one's breast **2** let it all hang out *coll*

razglabati *v* (što) discuss in detail

razgla|s *nm* public addres system, PA (system) ~**siti** *v* **1** (što) spread the rumour, make sth public **2** (se) spread, leak ~**šavati** *v impf*

razgled|ati *v* (što) inspect, scrutinize ~**ati znamenitosti** see the sights, go sightseeing ~**avati** *v impf* ~**nica** *nf* picture postcard

razgoliti *v* **1** (koga) strip; expose (+ *fig*) **2** (se) lay bare, expose **3** (se) strip

razgorjeti *v* (se) blaze up

razgoropaditi *v* (se) become violent

razgov|arati *v* (0/o komu/čemu/s kim) talk (to sb about sb/sth); discuss (sb/sth with sb) ~**or** *nm* conversation; talk; discussion ~**oran** *adj* (*a*) colloquial ~**orljiv** *adj* talkative, garroulous

razgovijetan *adj* (*a*) articulate, clear

razgrab|iti *v* (što) grab **roba je bila** ~**ljena** the goods sold like hot cakes

razgra|diti *v* (što/se) erode, disintegrate, decompose ~**đivati** *v impf*

razgranat|i *v* (se) branch out; ramify; expand *fig* ~**ost** *nf* ramification

razgraničiti *v* delimitate; distinguish *fig* ~**avati** *v impf* **crta** ~**enja** line of demarcation/confrontation

razgr|nuti *v* (što) **1** expose **2** draw open, open ~**tati** *v impf*

razi|ći *v* (se) part; break up ~**lazak** *nm* (*Gsg* ~laska) parting; separation; breakup ~**laziti** *v* (se) **1** *impf* **2** (u mišljenju) dissent **mišljenja se** ~**laze** opinions differ

razina *nf* level

razjapiti *v* (što) open wide

razjar|en *adj* furious ~**iti** *v* (koga/se) → **razbjesniti**

razja|sniti *v* (što komu) explain; clarify ~**šnjavati** *v impf*

razjediniti *v* (koga/se) disunite, cause strife

razlagati *v impf* → **razložiti**

razlaz *nm* *fig* rift

razle|ći *v* (se) (*pres* ~nem) resound, reverberate

razletjeti *v* (se) **1** scatter **2** blow up

razli|čak *nm* (*Gsg* ~ka, *Npl* ~ci) cornflower

razli|čit *adj* **1** different **2** various ~**čitost** *nf* difference; diversity ~**ka** *nf* (*Dsg* ~ci) **1** difference; distinction **2** balance **bez** ~**ke** indiscriminately *u čemu je* ~**ka** *između...?* what is the difference between...? **za** ~**ku od** as opposed to **praviti** ~**ku a.** make/draw a distinction **b.** treat differently; discriminate against ~**kovati** *v* (*pres* ~kujem) **1** (koga/ što/koga od koga) tell two persons/things apart, tell sb from sb, distinguish **2** (se) differ; vary

razlijegati *v impf* → **razleći**

razli|ti *v* (što/se) spill; (rijeka) flood ~**jevati** *v impf*

razlo|g *nm* (*Npl* ~zi) reason, ground; occasion ~**žan** *adj* (*a*) reasonable ~**žiti** *v* (što) analyse; expound

razlom|ak *nm* (*Gsg* ~ka, *Npl* ~ci) fraction ~**iti** *v* (što) break

razlučiti *v* **1** (što) discern **2** (što od čega) distinguish; separate

razljutiti *v* **1** (koga) make angry **2** (se) get angry

razma|k *nm* (*Npl* ~ci) **1** distance **2** interval **u** ~**cima** at intervals **3** (u pisanju) space ~**knica** *nf* space bar ~**knuti** *v* **1** (što/koga) push apart, move aside **2** (se) come apart, move away ~**knutih zuba** gap-toothed

razma|hati *v* (*pres* ~šem) (se) **1** spread quickly, gather momentum **2** wave about

razmatati v impf → **razmotati**

razmatrati v impf → **razmotriti**

razmazati v (pres ~žem) spread/smear all over

razma|ziti v (koga) spoil, pamper ~žen adj spoilt

razmeđe nn boundary; divide

razmekšati v (što/se) soften; mellow; (meso) tenderize

razme|tati v (se) (pres ~ćem) show off, brag, boast ~tljiv adj big-mouthed ~tljivac nm (Gsg ~tljivca, Vsg ~tljivče) big-mouth, braggart ~tnuti v (što) annul

razmicati v impf → **razmaknuti**

razmijeniti v (što) exchange; (novac) change

razmimoi|ći v (pres ~đem) (se) go separate ways; disagree fig ~laziti v impf

razmirica nf disagreement; quarrel

razmi|sliti v (0/o komu/čemu) consider, think (sth/sb) over ~šljati v impf reflect, meditate, ponder

razmjer nm proportion; scale ~an adj (a) proportionate ~no adv proportionately; comparatively

razmjestiti v (koga/što) arrange; (vojsku) deploy

razmnožavati v (se) multiply; breed

razmotati v (što) unwrap

razmotriti v (što) take into consideration, consider

razmrsiti v (što) disentangle (+ fig)

razmutiti v (što) beat, whip

razn|ijeti v (pres ~esem) (koga/što) blow to pieces

raznos|ač nm messenger, delivery-man ~iti v (što) deliver; spread

raznježiti v (se) be moved, go soft

razočara|nost nf disappointment ~ti v 1 (se) be disappointed 2 (koga) disappoint

razod|jenuti v (koga/se) undress, strip ~ijevati v impf

razonoda nf pastime, hobby

razor|an adj (a) destructive, devastating ~iti v (što) destroy, ruin, wreck

razoruža|ti v (koga) disarm ~nje nn disarmament

razotkri|ti v (pres ~jem) 1 (koga/što) uncover; unmask, expose fig 2 (se)

expose oneself, come out in the open

razra|diti v (što) work out (the details), elaborate ~đivati v impf

razred nm 1 class 2 classroom, schoolroom; (đaci) class 3 form; grade US ~nik nm (Vsg ~niče, Npl ~nici) form-master, class-master

razre|z nm slit ~zati v (pres ~žem) 1 cut; slice; slash; (meso) carve 2 (porez) assess

razr|ijediti v (što) dilute, water down; rarefy ~jeđivati v impf

razr|iješiti v 1 (što) disentangle; solve 2 (čega) (grijeha) absolve from ; (dužnosti) exempt/release from; suspend ~ješavati v impf

razrogačiti v (što) ~ oči stare, gape

razrok adj wall-eyed

razr|ovati v (pres ~ujem) (što) dig up

razrušiti v (što) pull/knock down

razudb|a nf post mortem, autopsy izvršiti ~u autopsy

razular|en adj unruly ~iti v (se) become unruly

razum nm intellect, reason zdrav ~ common sense ~an adj (a) reasonable, sensible ~jeti v (što/koga) (pres ~ijem) understand pogrešno ~jeti v misunderstand ~ljiv adj 1 understandable 2 intelligible

razuvjer|iti v 1 (koga od čega) dissuade 2 (se) convince oneself to the contrary ~avati v impf

razuzdan adj → **razularen**

razveden adj 1 divorced 2 (obala) indented

razvedr|iti v 1 (se) clear (nebo); cheer up 2 (koga) cheer up; brighten ~avati v impf

razvese|liti v 1 (koga) cheer up; amuse 2 (se) cheer up

razve|sti v (se) (pres ~dem) get a divorce, get divorced

razve|zati v (pres ~žem) 1 (što) untie 2 (se) come undone ~zao mu se jezik he became talkative 3 (0) prattle on

razvi|jač nm developer ~jati v impf ~ti v 1 (što) develop; (zastavu) unfurl; (trupe) deploy 2 (se) develop

razvikan adj famed, touted, hyped

razvlačiti v impf → **razvući**

razvod nm divorce

razvodniti v (što) water down
razvođe nn watershed
razvoj nm development
razvojač|iti v (koga) demilitarize ~enje nn demilitarization
razvrat nm debauchery ~an adj (a) lecherous ~nik nm (Vsg ~niče, Npl ~nici) debauchee, fornicator, lecher
razvrgnuti v (što) 1 dissolve 2 divorce 3 cancel, break off
razvrstati v (koga/što) sort, classify
razvu|čen adj drawn out; long-winded ~ći v (pres ~čem) 1 (tijesto) roll out 2 spread out; drag out
raž nf rye ~en adj rye
ražalostiti v 1 (koga) sadden, distress 2 (se) become sad
rož|anj nm (Gsg ~nja, Npl ~njevi) barbecue ~njići nm pl shish kebab **štapić za** ~njiće skewer
ražestiti v 1 (koga) enrage 2 (se) lose one's temper
reagirati v (na što) respond, react (to)
reak|cija nf 1 chem pol reaction 2 response 3 backlash ~cionar nm reactionary ~tor nm reactor
real|an adj (a) 1 real, existing 2 realistic ~ist nm realist ~izacija nf 1 realization 2 implementation ~izirati v (što) realize, carry out ~nost nf reality
rebr|ast adj ribbed ~asti samt corduroy ~o nn rib
recenzija nf review
recepcija nf (hotela) reception (desk)
recept nm 1 recipe 2 (liječnički) prescription
recesija nf recession
recidiv nm relapse
recipro|citet nm reciprocity ~čan adj (a) reciprocal
rečenica nf sentence; clause
reći v (pres rečem, reknem) (što komu) say sth to sb, tell sb sth **hoću** ~ I mean **tako** ~ so to speak **recimo** (da) say
red nm (Npl ~ovi) 1 row, file, line; rank mil 2 queue **stati u** ~ queue up; line up US **vozni** ~/~ **vožnje** timetable; schedule US **dnevni** ~ agenda 3 order **u** ~**u** OK, all right 4 (stupanj) order, rank 5 (stalež) order 6 succes-

sion; shift, turn **na meni je** ~ it is my turn **po** ~**u**, ~**om** in turn ~**ak** nm (Gsg retka, Npl reci) line ~**ar** nm (u školi) monitor; bouncer ~**arstveni** adj **sat** curfew ~**arstvenik** nm (Vsg ~arstveniče, Npl ~stvenici) police officer; (police) constable GB ~**arstvo** nn police ~**atelj** nm director ~**ni** adj ordinal ~**om** adv one after the other, by turns **svi** ~**om** all and sundry ~**oslijed** nm order, sequence
redakcija nf editorial office; desk, newsroom; editorial staff
redov|an adj (a) regular, ordinary, usual ~**ni profesor** full professor ~**it** adj regular ~**nica** nf nun ~**nik** nm (Vsg ~niče, Npl ~nici) monk
refer|ada nf service ~**at** nm paper ~**endum** nm referendum ~**ent** nm officer in charge
refleks nm reflex
reforma nf reform ~**cija** nf the Reformation ~**tor** nm reformer
refren nf refrain, chorus
regal nm shelves
regij|a nf region, area ~**onalan** adj (a) regional
regist|ar nm (Gsg ~ra) register, file ~**arski** adj **broj** registration number GB; license plate number US ~**racija** nf 1 registration 2 coll number/license plate ~**rirati** v (što) register, enter, record
regul|acija nf regulation, adjustment ~**aran** adj (a) regular ~**ator** nm regulator ~**irati** v (što) regulate, adjust, control
rehabilitacija nf rehabilitation
reket nm racket
reklam|a nf 1 advertisement 2 TV commercial 3 advertising, publicity ~**acija** nf complaint, claim ~**irati** v (što) 1 advertise, promote 2 complain ~**ni** adj advertising, publicity
rekonstru|irati v (što) reconstruct ~**kcija** nf reconstruction
rekonvalescent nm convalescent
rekord nm record **srušiti** ~ break the r. ~**an** adj (a) 1 record(-breaking) 2 (žetva) bumper ~**er** nm record-holder
rekreacija nf recreation
rektor nm rector, vice-chancellor

počasni ~ chancellor
rela|cija *nf* 1 relation 2 section **~tivan** *adj* (α) relative, comparative
religi|ja *nf* religion **~ozan** *adj* (α) religious, devout
relikvija *nf* relic
reljef *nm* relief
remek-djelo *nn* masterpiece
remen *nm* 1 strap 2 belt
remetiti *v* (što) disturb
rendgen *nm* X-ray(s) **napraviti ~** (have an) X-ray **~ski** *adj* X-ray
renesansa *nf* Renaissance
renome *nm* reputation
renovirati *v* (što) renovate, refurbish
rentabilan *adj* (α) profitable
rep *nm* (*Npl* ~ovi) 1 tail 2 queue **stajati u ~u** queue (up); line (up) *US* **~atica** *nf* comet
repa *nf* turnip **šećerna ~** sugar-beet
repertoar *nm* repertoire, repertory
repli|ka *nf* (*Dsg* ~ci) 1 retort 2 replica 3 *pol* response **~cirati** *v* (komu) *pol* respond (to)
report|aža *nf* report, story, feature **~er** *nm* reporter
reprezenta|cija *nf* 1 national team 2 expense account, entertainment funds **~tivan** *adj* (α) grand
reprodukcija *nf* reproduction, copy
republi|čki *adj* republic **~ka** *nf* (*Dsg* ~ci) republic **~kanac** *nm* (*Gsg* ~kanca, *Vsg* ~kanče) republican
reputacija *nf* reputation
resa *nf* tassel
resi|ti *v* (koga) adorn *Ivu rese ljepota i pamet* Iva is endowed with both beauty and brains
resko → rezak
restauracija *nf* 1 restoration 2 restaurant
restoran *nm* restaurant
rešet|ka *nm* grate, grid, lattice, trellis *iza* **~aka** *fig* behind bars **~o** *nn* sieve **kroz sito i ~o** through thick and thin
retorički *adj* rhetorical
retro- *prefix* retro- **~vizor** *nm* rearview mirror
retuširati *v* (što) retouch
reuma *nf* rheumatism
rev|an *adj* (α) eager, zealous **~nost** *nf* zeal

revanš *nm* revenge; return match; returned favour **~irati** *v* (se komu za što) 1 return sb a favour 2 get even with
revati *v* (0) bray
revija *nm* review **modna ~** fashion show
reviz|ija *nf* 1 revision 2 *comm* auditing **~or** *nm* auditor
revoluci|ja *nf* revolution **~onar** *nm* revolutionary **~onaran** *adj* (α) revolutionary
revolver *nm* (hand)gun **~aš** *nm* gunfighter, gunslinger
rez *nm* cut **~ač** *nm* cutter **~ak** *adj* (reska *f*) 1 tart, sour 2 cutting **~anac** *nm* (*Gsg* ~anca) noodle **~ti** *v* (što) (*pres* režem) cut; slice; (meso) carve; engrave **~bar** *nm* engraver, carver **~barija** *nf* carving, engraving
rezerv|a *nf* reserve **~at** *nm* 1 reserve, preserve 2 (za Indijance) reservation **~iran** *adj* 1 *fig* reserved 2 booked **~iranost** *nf* reserve **~irati** *v* (što) book **~ni** *adj* spare **~oar** *nm* reservoir; tank
rezidencija *nf* residence, mansion **~lan** *adj* (α) residential
rezolucija *nf* resolution
rezultat *nm* result **dati ~a** yield results **~irati** *v* (čime) result in; (iz čega) result from
rež|anj *nm* (*Gsg* ~nja, *Npl* ~žnjevi) lobe
rež|ati *v* (0) (*pres* ~im) growl
reži|ja *nf* *theat* production; *film* direction **~e** *nf pl* overheads
režim *nm* regime
rib|a *nf* fish **biti kao ~a u vodi** be in one's element **~ar** *nm* fisherman **~ariti** *v* (0) fish **~arnica** *nf* fishmarket; fishmonger's *GB* **~arstvo** *nf* fishing **~lji** *adj* fish **~njak** *nm* (*Npl* ~njaci) fishpond **~olov** *nm* fishery **~olovac** *nm* (*Gsg* ~olovca, *Vsg* ~olovče) fisherman; angler **~ič** *nm* angler
rib|ati *v* (što) 1 grate 2 scrub **~ež** *nm* grater
ribiz(l) *nm* redcurrant
ricinus *nm*, **~ovo ulje** *nn* castor oil
riđ *adj* red; (konj) bay **~okos** *adj* red-haired

rigati *v* (što) vomit; puke *sl*; spew *fig*

riječ *nf* 1 word 2 term, expression **dati ~** give one's word **držati koga za ~** take sb at his w. **moliti za ~** ask permission to speak; ask for the floor **doći do ~i** get a word in edgeways, get a chance to say sth **upasti u ~** interrupt **voditi glavnu ~ a.** monopolize the conversation **b.** *fig* rule the roost **~ je o tome** the point in question is **u knjizi je ~ o** the book deals with **od ~i do ~i** word for word

riječn|i *adj* river **~a riba** freshwater fish

rije|dak *adj* (~tka *f*) (*comp* rjeđi) 1 infrequent 2 rare, unusual 3 thin, rare **~tko** *adv* seldom, rarely **~tkost** *nf* 1 (stvar) rarity, curiosity 2 infrequency

rije|ka *nf* (*Dsg* ~ci) river

riješiti *v* 1 (što) solve; resolve, settle; deal with 2 (se koga/čega) get rid of

ri|kati *v* (0) (*pres* ~čem) roar **~knuti** *v* (0) 1 *pf* 2 *sl* die; peg out, conk out *coll*

rilo *nn* trunk

rim|a *nf* rhyme **~ovati** *v* (se) (*pres* ~ujem) rhyme

rimokatoli|čki *adj* Roman Catholic **~k** *nm* (*Npl* ~ci) Roman Catholic

ris *nm* lynx **bijesan kao ~** furious

risati *v* (0/što) (*pres* rišem) draw

risk|antan *adj* (α) risky **~irati** *v* (0/što) risk

rit *nf coll vulg* butt, arse

rit|am *nm* (*Gsg* ~ma) rhythm, beat

rit|ati *v* (se) kick **~nuti** *v* (koga) kick

rizi|k *nm* (*Npl* ~ci) risk

riznica *nf* 1 treasury 2 *fig* treasure trove

riža *nf* rice

rječ|it *adj* eloquent; well-spoken **~itost** *nf* eloquence **~kati** *v* (se) squabble **~nik** *nm* (*Npl* ~nici) 1 (knjiga) dictionary 2 vocabulary **bogat ~nik** large v.

rješavati *v impf* → **riješiti**

rob *nm* (~inja *nf*) slave **~iti** *v* (0/što/koga) rob, plunder **~lje** *nn* slaves *pl* **trgovac ~ljem** slave-trader **~ovati** *v* (*pres* ~ujem) 1 (čemu) be a slave to, be addicted to 2 (0) slave **~ovlasnik** *nm* (*Npl* ~ovlasnici)

slave-owner **~ovlasništvo** *nn* slavery

rob|a *nf* 1 goods *pl*, merchandise; commodity 2 *coll* clothes **~a široke potrošnje** consumer goods **mješovita ~a** groceries **burza ~a** a commodity exchange **~na** *adj* **kuća** department store

robot *nm* robot

ročište *nn* hearing

rod *nm* 1 sex, gender 2 *gram* gender 3 stock, family; tribe **otmjena ~a** of noble birth 4 kin, relative 5 genus, species **ljudski ~** mankind **~ vojske** branch of service **~bina** *nf* relations, kin **~ilište** *nn* lying-in/maternity hospital **~ilja** *nf* pregnant woman **~itelj** *nm* parent **~iteljski** *adj* parental **~iteljski sastanak** parent-teacher meeting **~iti** *v* 1 (koga) give birth to 2 (0) yield, bear fruit 3 (se) be born **~ni** *adj* native **~nica** *nf* vagina **~om iz Zagreba** a native of Zagreb **~oskvrnuće** *nn* incest **~ovnik** *nm* (*Npl* ~ovnici) pedigree

roda *nf* stork

rođ|ak *nm* (*Vsg* ~če, *Npl* ~ci) relative **~akinja** *nf* relative **~en** *adj* born **~en sam u Zagrebu** I was born in Z. **~ena** née, maiden name **~ena majka** one's own mother **~endan** *nm* birthday **~enje** *nn* 1 birth 2 nativity

rog *nm* horn; (jelena) antler **mračno je kao u ~u** it is pitch-dark **nabiti komu ~ove** cuckold, cheat on **~onja** *nm fig* cuckold

rogač *nm* carob

rogoboriti *v* (0) grumble, gripe

rogoz *nm* rush

roj *nm* swarm **~iti** *v* (se) swarm

rok *nm* term, period, date **krajni ~** deadline **vojni ~** military duty; national service *GB* **u ~u od** within, not later than **~ovnik** *nm* diary; filofax *TM*

rok|tati *v* (0) (*pres* ~ćem) grunt

roleta *nf* blind

roman *nm* novel **~izirati** *v* (što) fictionalize **~opisac** *nm* (*Gsg* ~opisca) novelist

romanički *adj* Romanesque

romanski *adj* Romance (¶ Roman ↔ rimski)

romb *nm* rhomb

romobil *nm* scooter

roni|lac *nm* (*Gsg* ~oca) diver **~lački** *adj* diving **~ti** *v* 1 (0) dive 2 **~ti suze** shed tears

ropotarnica *nf* at tic

rops|ki *adj* servile **~tvo** *nn* slavery, bondage

ros|a *nf* dew **~ulja** *nf* drizzle

roštilj *nm* grill; barbecue *US*

rotirati *v* (koga/što) rotate

rotkv|ica *nf* radish

rov *nm* trench; (u rudniku) gallery, pit **~ati** *v* (0) (*pres* rujem) dig, burrow, root; rummage *fig*

rovariti *v* (0/protiv koga) plot

rožn|at *adj* horn **naočale s ~atim okvirom** horn-rimmed glasses **~ica** *nf* cornea

rt *nm* cape, headland

rub *nm* 1 edge (+ *fig*); (šume) fringe; (čaše) brim; (tanjura) rim; (stranice) margin; (grada) outskirts *pl* 2 border 3 *fig* verge

ru|bac *nm* (*Gsg* ~pca) scarf

rub|alj *nm* (*Gsg* ~lja) rouble

rubin *nm* ruby

rublje *nn* linen; underwear **žensko ~** lingerie **prljavo ~** *fig* dirty linen

rubri|ka *nf* (*Dsg* ~ci) column, section

ruč|ak *nm* (*Gsg* ~ka) lunch, dinner **~ati** *v* (0) (have) lunch

ruč|e *nf pl sport* parallel bars **~ica** *nf* 1 *dim* small hand 2 handle **~ka** *nf* handle **~ni** *adj* manual **~ni sat** wristwatch **~ni rad a.** hand-made item **b.** embroidery **~nik** *nm* (*Npl* ~nici) towel

rud|a *nf* ore **~ar** *nm* miner **~arski** *adj* mining **~arstvo** *nn* mining **~ni** *adj* mineral **~nik** *nm* (*Npl* ~nici) mine, pit

rudo *nn* shaft **trčati pred ~** jump the gun

rug|alica *nf* satire, lampoon **ptica-~alica** mocking-bird **~ati** *v* (se komu/čemu) deride sb/sth, mock, scoff at, make fun of **~lo** *nn* disgrace **predmet ~la** laughing-stock **~oba** *nf* 1 monstrosity 2 monster; eyesore

ruho *nn* clothes *pl*, attire

ruj|an *nm* (*Gsg* ~na) September • *adj* red

ru|ka *nf* (*Dsg* ~ci) 1 (šaka) hand 2 (od zapešća do ramena) arm **pružiti kome ~ku** give sb one's hand **pružiti si ~ke** join hands **ostati praznih ~ku** be left empty-handed **desna ~ka** *fig* right hand **~ku na srce** frankly **pri ~ci** available, at hand **na svoju ~ku** on one's own (authority) **ide mu od ~ke** he's good at **u najmanju ~ku** at least **~ke uvis!** hands up! **~kom rađen** hand made **u neku ~ku** to a certain extent **ići komu na ~ku** be of help to sb **pošlo mi je za ~kom** I made it **iz prve ~ke** first-hand **dići ~ku na koga** raise one's hand against sb **dići ~ku na sebe** commit suicide **~kav** *nm* sleeve **zasukati ~kave** *fig* roll up one's sleeves, get to work **~kavac** *nm* (*Gsg* ~kavca) backwater **~kavica** *nf* glove **~komet** *nm* handball **~kopis** *nm* 1 hand-writing 2 manuscript **~kotvorina** *nf* handicraft **~kovati** *v* (*pres* ~kujem) 1 (čime) operate 2 (se) shake hands **~kovoditelj** *nm* manager **~kovoditi** *v* (čime) manage, run **~kovodstvo** *nn* leadership; management

rulati *v* (0) taxi

ruleta *nf* roulette

rulja *nf* mob, rabble; crowd

rum *nm* rum

rume|n *adj* red, (lice od uzbuđenja) flushed; (lice od zdravlja) ruddy **~nilo** *nf* rouge **~njeti** *v* (se) blush

runda *nf coll* round

runo *nn* fleece

runolist *nm* edelweiss

rup|a *nf* 1 hole 2 *fig* dump **zadnja ~a na svirali** the fifth wheel on the coach

rupčić *nm* handkerchief

ruš|evan *adj* (*a*) dilapidated **~evina** *nf* ruin; rubble **~iti** *v* 1 (što) pull down 2 (koga/što) overthrow 3 (koga) (na ispitu) fail 4 (se) be falling down

ruta *nf* route

rutav *adj* hairy

rutin|a *nf* routine **~ski** *adj* routine

ruž *nm* lipstick

ruža *nf* rose

ružan *adj* (*a*) 1 ugly 2 foul, bad

ružičast *adj* pink
ružmarin *nm* rosemary

rzati *v* (0) (*pres* ~žem) neigh, whinny

S

S, s (es) 24th letter of Cro. alphabet

s(a) *prep* **1** (kim/čim) with, along/together with **2** (koga/čega) from s **moje strane** on my part **sa zapada** from the west **pet metara sa sedam** five metres by seven **pasti sa stabla** fall off a tree

sabi|ti *v* (*pres* ~jem) **1** (što) compress **2** (koga/se) crowd, squeeze, drive together

sablas|t *nf* ghost, specter, apparition ~**tan** *adj* (*f* ~na) ghostly, spectral, unearthly, eerie

sabla|zan *nf* scandal, shock ~**zniti** *v* **1** (koga) shock **2** (se) be scandalized/shocked ~**žnjiv** *adj* **1** shocking **2** easily shocked

sablja *nf* sabre; sword ~**rka** *nf* (*Dsg* ~rci) swordfish

sabor *nm* **1** parliament **2** assembly **3** (crkveni) synod **4** convention, congress ~**nica** *nf* parliament building/chamber ~**ski** *adj* parliament(ary) ~**ski zastupnik** member of Parliament

sabot|aža *nf* sabotage ~**er** *nm* saboteur ~**irati** *v* (što) sabotage

sabra|n *adj* → **pribran** ~**na djela** collected writings, complete works ~**ti** → **pribrati**

sačekati → **pričekati, dočekati**

sačm|a *nf* shot; buckshot **zrno** ~**e** pellet ~**arica** *nf* shotgun

sačuva|ti *v* (koga/što) preserve; conserve; keep; maintain **Bože** ~**j!** God forbid!

saće *nn* honeycomb

sad(a) *adv* now, at present ~ **kad** now that ~**ašnji** *adj* present, current, present-day ~**ašnjica** *nf* the present, present time

sadi|st *nm* sadist ~**stički** *adj* sadistic ~**zam** *nm* (*Gsg* ~zma) sadism

sad|iti *v* (što) plant ~**nica** *nf* seedling, nursery plant

sadra *nf* plaster of Paris

sadrža|j *nm* **1** content; subject matter **2** contents **3** table of contents ~**jan** *adj* (*a*) substantial, meaningful ~**vati** *v* (što) **1** contain, hold **2** comprise; include

safir *nm* sapphire

sag *nm* carpet, rug

sagledati *v* (što) **1** perceive, realize **2** examine, look into/at

sagn|uti *v* (*pres* ~em) **1** (što) bend, bow **2** (se) stoop (down); duck

sagnji|ti *v* (0) (*pres* ~jem) rot, decay, putrefy

sagorjeti → **izgorjeti**

sagraditi → **izgraditi**

saj|am *nm* fair **stočni** ~**am** cattle fair ~**meni** *adj* **dan** market day ~**mište** *nn* fairground

sako *nm* jacket

sakralan *adj* (*a*) sacral; church, holy

sakrament *nm* sacrament

sakristija *nf* sacristy

sakri|ti *v* (*pres* ~jem) **1** (koga/što) hide; conceal **2** (se) hide, go into hiding

saksofon *nm* saxophone; **sax** *coll*

salama *nf* salami

salata *nf* salad **zelena** ~ **a.** lettuce **b.** green salad

saldo *nm* balance

salije|tati *v* (koga) (*pres* ~ćem) importune, pester

saliven *adj* **stoji kao** ~**o** it fits like a glove

salo *nn* fat; lard

salon *nm* reception/drawing room **frizerski** ~ hairdresser's (shop) **izložbeni** ~ showroom **kozmetički** ~ beauty parlour/salon ~ **zabavnih igara** amusement arcade ~**ske** *adj*

cipele (**~ke** *coll*) court shoes, pumps **~ski političar** armchair politician

salto *nm* somersault **napraviti ~** turn a somersault

salva *nf* salvo (+ *fig*)

salveta *nf coll* → **ubrus**

sam *adj* **1** alone; on one's own **2** oneself **3** single-handed, unaided **4** pure; nothing but **5** the very **~ ~cat** all alone **~ od sebe** by itself **~ po sebi** in itself **to se razumije ~o po sebi** it goes without saying **~ac** *nm* (*Gsg* **~ca**, *Npl* **~ci**) bachelor; single man **lokal za ~ce** singles bar **~ački stan** bachelor flat **~ica** *nf* solitary confinement

samilos|t *nf* compassion, pity **~tan** *adj* (*f* **~na**) compassionate

samit *nm* summit (meeting)

sam|ljeti *v* (*pres* **~eljem**) **1** (što) grind, mill **2** (meso) mince **3** (koga) *fig* crush, make mincemeat of

samo (1) *adv* **1** only; just; not more than **2** merely, solely **ne ~ … nego i** not only … but also

samo- (2) *prefix* self-, auto-

samo|bitan *adj* (*a*) authentic **~bitnost** *nf* identity **~ča** *nf* solitude, loneliness **~dopadan** → **samozadovoljan** **~držac** *nm* (*Gsg* **~dršca**, *Npl* **~dršci**) autocrat, absolutist **~glasnik** *nm* (*Npl* **~glasnici**) vowel **~hrana** *adj* **majka** single mother **~inicijativno** *adv* on one's own initiative **~ljubiv** *adj* self-ish **~obrana** *nf* self-defence **~posluživanje** *nn* supermarket **~pouzdanje** *nn* self-confidence, self-reliance **~prijegor** *nm* self-denial, self-abnegation **~stalan** *adj* (*a*) independent; autonomous **~stalnost** *nf* independence; autonomy **~stan** *nm* **1** monastery **2** (ženski) convent, nunnery **~stojeća** *adj* **kuća** detached house **~stojnost** *nf* independence **~strijel** *nm* crossbow **~svijest** *nf* self-confidence, self-possession **~svojan** *adj* (*a*) characteristic, special, specific **~tan** *adj* (*a*) lonely, solitary; desolate **~tnik** *nm* (*Npl* **~tnici**) lonely man, loner **~tnjak** *nm* (*Npl* **~tnjaci**) lone wolf/ranger **~ubojica** *nm* suicide **~ubojstvo** *nn* suicide

~uk *adj* self-educated, self-taught **~uprava** *nf* self-government, self-rule **~uvjeren** *adj* self-assured, self-confident **~vlada** *nf* autocracy, absolutism **~volja** *nf* arbitrariness, self-will, tyranny **~zadovoljan** *adj* (*a*) self-satisfied, smug, complacent **~zatajan** *adj* (*a*) self-effacing **~zvani** *adj* self-styled **~živ** *adj* self-ish, self-centred, self-seeking

samrt *nf* **na ~i** on one's deathbed, dying **~ni** *adj* death, mortal **~ni hropac** death rattle

samt *nm* corduroy **~erice** *nf pl coll* corduroys; cords *coll*

san *nm* (*Gsg* **sna**, *Npl* **snovi/sni**) **1** dream **2** sleep, slumber **zimski ~** hibernation **hvata me ~** I *feel sleepy*

sanacija *nf* rehabilitation, reorganization, reconstruction

sanatorij *nm* sanatorium

sandala *nf* sandal

sandolina *nf* flat-bottomed canoe

sandu|čić *nm dim* small trunk **poštanski ~čić** letterbox; mailbox *US* **~k** *nm* (*Npl* **~ci**) trunk, chest, box **mrtvački ~k** coffin

sanirati *v* (što) rehabilitate, reorganize, reconstruct, repair

sanitarni *adj* sanitary

sanitet *nm* medical corps **~ski** *adj* medical **~sko vozilo** ambulance

sankcij|a *nf* sanction **~onirati** *v* (što) sanction

sanj|ar *nf* dreamer, daydreamer **~arenje**, **~arija** *nf* daydreaming, reverie **~ariti** *v* (0) daydream **~ati** *v* (koga/što/0/o čemu) dream (about/of) **~iv** *adj* drowsy, sleepy, somnolent

sanjk|ati *v* (se) sledge, toboggan; sled *US* **~e** *nf pl* sledge, toboggan; sled *US* **motorne ~e** snowmobile

saonice *nf pl* **1** → **sanjke 2** (konjske) sleigh

saopćenje → **priopćenje**

sapi *nm pl* croup, crupper

sapun *nm* soap **~ati** *v* **1** (koga/što) soap; lather **2** (se) soap oneself **~ica** *nf* **1** (soap)suds; lather **2** *sl* soap opera; soap *coll*

sardina *nf* (tinned) sardine

sarka|stičan adj (α) sarcastic ~**zam** nm (Gsg ~zma) sarcasm

sarkofa|g nm (Npl ~zi) sarcophagus

sarma nf cul stuffed cabbage

sasjeći → isjeći, posjeći

saslušа|nje nn hearing; interrogation ~**ti** v 1 (koga) interrogate 2 (koga/što) hear, listen (to); (do kraja) hear out

sasta|jalište nn meeting place/point ~**nak** nm (Gsg ~nka, Npl ~nci) 1 meeting 2 appointment 3 date za-kazati ~**nak** call/convene a meeting; make an appointment ~**ti** v (se) (pres ~nem) meet ~**jati** v impf

sastav nm composition; structure; make-up ~**ak** nm (Gsg ~ka, Npl ~ci) composition, essay ~**iti** v (što) 1 assemble, put together 2 join, unite 3 write; draft, draw up; compose; compile ~**ljač** nm constructor; composer; compiler ~**ni** adj component, constituent, integral ~**ljati** v impf

sastoj|ak nm (Gsg ~ka, Npl ~ci) ingredient; component, constituent element ~**ati** v (se) (pres ~im) consist of, be composed of, be made up of, comprise

sasvim → posve, potpuno

saši|ti v (što) (pres ~jem) sew (up); make (a dress)

sat nm 1 (zidni) clock; (ručni) (wrist)watch; timepiece; (sunčani) sundial; (pješčani) hourglass 2 (vrijeme) hour 3 (školski) class, lesson, period **blok** ~ double period **ras-pored** ~**i** timetable, schedule **sitni** ~ small hours **koliko je** ~**i**? what's the time? what time is it? ~ **ide naprijed** the clock/watch gains/is fast ~ **ide natrag** the clock/watch loses/is slow **znati koliko je** ~**i** fig know the score

satelit nm satellite ~**ska** adj **antena** satellite dish

satir|a nf satire ~**ičan** adj (α) satirical ~**ičar** nm satirist

satnica nf 1 timetable, schedule 2 hourly wage

satni|k nm mil (Vsg ~če, Npl ~ci) captain

saučešće nn → sućut

sav (sva, sve) adj (Npl svi, sve, sva) 1 all, entire, whole 2 all over; through

savez nm alliance; union; association; league; federation ~**ni** adj federal ~**nički** adj allied ~**nik** nm (Npl ~nici) ally ~**ništvo** nn alliance

savijača nf strudel ~**ti** v (što) (pres ~jem) 1 bend; fold 2 roll, curl 3 twine, twist 4 (se) bend; (od bola) writhe; warp ~**ti gnijezdo** build/ make a nest ~**tljiv** adj flexible, elastic, pliable ~**jati** v impf

savjes|t nf conscience **nečista** ~**t** bad/guilty conscience **grižnja** ~**ti** remorse, pangs/pricks of conscience ~**tan** adj (f ~na) conscientious, scrupulous; thorough

savjet nm 1 (a piece of) advice; counsel lit; guidance 2 (vijeće) council **član** ~**a** councillor ~**nik** nm (Npl ~nici) adviser; counsellor ~**odavan** adj (α) advisory ~**ovanje** nn 1 consultation 2 conference, symposium ~**ovati** v (pres ~ujem) 1 (koga/komu) advise, counsel; recommend, suggest 2 (se) confer, consult

savlad|ati v 1 (koga/što) defeat; overpower; conquer, subdue 2 (prepreku) overcome, surmount 3 (osjećaje, vještinu) master 4 (zavoj) negotiate 5 (se) restrain oneself ~**iv** adj surmountable

savršen adj perfect ~**stvo** nf perfection

sazdati v (što) build, construct; make, create

saziv nm convocation **u sadašnjem** ~**u parlamenta** in the present parliament

sazna|nje nn (→ spoznaja) idea; fact; insight, knowledge ~**ti** v (što) find out, learn, come to know

sazr|eo adj (f ~ela) ripe; mature ~**ijeti** v (0) (pres ~im) grow ripe, ripen; mature

saz|vati v (što) (pres ~ovem) call, convene, convoke, summon

sazviježđe → zviježđe

saža|lijevati v impf (koga) pity ~**liti** v (se nad kim) have/take pity on, show compassion ~**ljenje** nn pity, compassion, commiseration; sympathy ~**ljiv**

adj compassionate; pitiful

saž|et *adj* condensed **~etak** *nm* (*Gsg* ~etka, *Npl* ~eci) summary, abstract **~eti** *v* (što) (*pres* ~mem) condense, reduce, sum up **~eto** *adv* concisely **~imati** *v impf*

scen|a *nf* 1 stage 2 scene (+ *fig*) **~arij** *nm* scenario (+ *fig*), screenplay; script **~arist** *nm* screenwriter, scriptwriter **~ograf** *nm* set designer **~ografija** *nf* set design, setting **~ski** *adj* stage

se(be) *pron* 1 oneself 2 each other, one another **spava mi se** I am sleepy **ne da mi se** I don't feel like **obuci se** get dressed **priča se** people say, rumour has it, it is rumoured **doći k sebi** come to, recover

sebič|an *adj* (*a*) selfish **~nost** *nf* selfishness **~njak** *nm* (*Npl* ~njaci) selfish person

secesija *nf* 1 secession 2 Art Nouveau

secirati *v* (što) dissect

sed|am *num* seven (7) **~amdeset** *num* seventy (70) **~amnaest** *num* seventeen (17) **~mi** *num ord* seventh **~mica** *nf* number/figure seven **~mina** *nf* a/one seventh **~morica** *nf* seven men/boys

sedativ *nm* sedative, tranquilizer

sedef *nm* mother-of-pearl, nacre

sed|lati *v* (koga/što) saddle **~o** *nn* saddle

sef *nm* safe, safe deposit box, strongbox

sekretar → **tajnik**

seksual|an *adj* (*a*) sexual **~nost** *nf* sexuality

sekta *nf* sect **~ški** *adj* sectarian **~štvo** *nn* sectarianism

sektor *nm* sector

sekunda *nf* second

sekundaran *adj* (*a*) secondary

selek|cija *nf* selection **~tivan** *adj* (*a*) selective **~tor** *nm* selector

selendra *nf* one-horse town, backwater, hicksville; backwoods *pl*

seli|ca *nf* migratory bird, migrant **~dba** *nf* 1 removal, moving 2 migration **~ti** *v* (koga/što/se) move; migrate

selo *nn* 1 village 2 the country *to je za*

mene špansko ~ it's Greek/double Dutch to me

selja|čina *nm derog* peasant; hick, hillbilly, redneck *US coll* **~čki** *adj* peasant, country, rustic **~k** *nm* (*Npl* ~ci) peasant, farmer, countryman **~nka** *nf* country/peasant woman/girl **~nin** *nm*, **~nka** *nf* villager **~štvo** *nn* peasantry

semafor *nm* 1 traffic lights 2 *sport* scoreboard

semanti|ka *nf* (*Dsg* ~ci) semantics

semest|ar *nm* (*Gsg* ~ra, *Npl* ~ri) semester, term

seminar *nm* seminar, workshop **~ski rad** seminar/term paper

senat *nm* senate **~or** *nm* senator **~ski** *adj* senatorial

sendvič *nm* sandwich

senf *nm* mustard

senzaci|ja *nf* sensation **~onalan** *adj* (*a*) sensational **~onalistički** *adj* sensationalist

senzibil|an *adj* (*a*) sensitive **~nost** *nf* sensibility

seoba *nf* migration

seoski *adj* village, country, rural, rustic

separatizam *nm* (*Gsg* ~atizma) separatism **~e** *nm* (*Gsg* ~a, *Npl* ~i) booth, separate seating **~irati** *v* (koga/ što/se) separate; isolate

serij|a *nf* 1 series; batch 2 *TV* serial **~ski** *adj* serial **~ska proizvodnja** assembly-line production

servi|rati *v* (što) serve **~s** *nm* 1 service (+ *sport*) 2 repair shop, service station, garage **čajni ~s** tea service/set **~sirati** *v* (što) service

sest|ra *nf* (*Gpl* ~ara) sister **časna ~ra** nun, sister **medicinska ~ra** nurse **~rična** *nf* cousin **~rinski** *adj* sisterly, sister

sezam *nm* sesame

se|zati *v* (0) (*pres* ~žem) stretch, extend; reach

sezon|a *nf* season **~ski** *adj* season, seasonal **~ski radnik** seasonal/migrant worker

sfera *nf* sphere; field

sfinga *nf* sphinx

shema *nf* scheme, sketch, plan, out-

line, model ~tizirati v (što) schema-
tize ~tski adj schematic
shizofreni|čar nm schizophrenic;
schizo coll ~ja nf schizophrenia
shod|an adj (a) → primjeren ~no
čemu according to, in accordance/
line with
shva|ćanje nn 1 understanding, com-
prehension, grasp 2 opinion, view,
idea ~titi v (koga/što) understand, realize, grasp, see krivo ~titi misunderstand ~tljiv adj understandable,
comprehensible ~ćati v impf
si|ći v (0) (pres ~đem) come down, get
down/off, climb down, descend,
alight ~ći s uma lose one's mind
sićušan adj (a) tiny, minute; itsy-bit-
sy, teeny-weeny coll
sida nf AIDS, Aids
sidr|ište nn anchorage ~o nn anchor
siga nf stalactite, stalagmite **ledena ~**
icicle
signal nm signal; sign, warning
~izirati v (što/0) signal
sigur|an adj (a) 1 safe, secure 2 cer-
tain, confident, sure 3 firm, steady 4
reliable, dependable ~nosni adj safety ~nost nf 1 safety, security 2 cer-
tainty, confidence **za svaku ~nost** to
be on the safe side
si|jati (1) v (što) (pres ~em) 1 sow 2
fig disseminate, spread ~ati razdor
sow/stir up dissension
si|jati (2) v (što) (pres ~em) sift
sije|čanj nm (Gsg ~nja) January
sijed adj grey ~jeti v (0) (pres ~im)
grey, become/grow/turn grey
sijeno nn hay
sijeva|ti v (0) lighten, flash ~ there's
lightening ~ti očima glare
sik|tati v (0) (pres ~ćem) hiss
si|la nf 1 force 2 power; might 3 coll
many, plenty, multitude **na ~u** by
force **viša ~a** act of God; force ma-
jeure ~an adj (a) 1 mighty; intense 2
enormous, immense 3 a lot of; heaps
of coll ~ina nf force; power; might
~iti v (koga) force, coerce, compel;
press, urge ~nik nm (Npl ~nici)
tyrant, despot, oppressor ~no adv 1
powerfully 2 violently 3 enormously,
immensely, vastly 4 awfully,

tremendously ~om adv by force
milom ili ~om by hook or by crook
~om otvoriti force open
sila|zak nm (Gsg ~ska, Npl ~sci) de-
scent ~zan adj (a) descending;
downward; falling ~ziti → sići
silicij nm silicon
silos nm silo
silova|nje nn rape ~telj nm rapist ~ti v
(koga) 1 rape; violate lit 2 fig force
silovit adj violent; strong
silueta nf silhouette
simbol nm symbol; mark, sign ~ičan
adj (a) symbolic(al) ~ika nf (Dsg
~ici) symbolism ~izirati v (što) sym-
bolize
simetrija nf symmetry
simfonija nf symphony
simpati|čan adj (a) likable, nice,
friendly, pleasant ~ja nf 1 liking,
fancy; affinity 2 sweetheart, heart-
throb ~zer nm sympathizer ~zirati v
1 (koga) like, fancy, take a liking to
2 (što) sympathize (with)
simpozij nm symposium
simptom nm symptom ~atičan adj (a)
symptomatic
simulirati v 1 (0/što) simulate; fake,
feign, pretend 2 (bolest) malinger
sin nm son **mamin ~** mother's/mam-
ma's US boy **kakav otac takav ~**
like father, like son
sinagoga nf sinagogue
sindika|list nm trade unionist ~lizam
nm (Gsg ~lizma) trade unionism,
trade union movement ~t nm (trade)
union; labor union US
sindrom nm syndrome
sinkronizirati v (što) 1 (uskladiti) synchronize 2 film dub 3 TV voice over
sinoć adv last night, yesterday
evening ~nji adj last night('s)
sinonim nm synonym
sinopsis nm synopsis
sintak|sa nf syntax ~tički adj syntac-
tic
sinte|tičan adj synthetic ~tika nf (Dsg
~tici) synthetics ~tizirati v (što) synthesize ~za nf synthesis
sinus nm 1 med sinus 2 math sine
sin|uti v (0) (pres ~em) shine; flash
~ulo mi je it dawned (up)on me, it

struck me

sinjli *adj* ashen, leaden, grey-blue

sipa *nf* cuttlefish

sipati *v* (što) pour ~ **kao iz rukava** pour sth out, reel off

sipiti *v* (0) drizzle

sir *nm* cheese

sirena *nf* 1 siren; horn, hooter 2 (morska) siren, mermaid

siro|če *nn* (*Npl* ~čad) orphan ~**mah** *nm* (*Npl* ~masi) poor man, pauper ~**mašan** *adj* (α) poor, needy ~**mašt-vo** *nn* poverty, privation ~**ti** *adj* poor; miserable, wretched ~**tinjski** *adj* poor people's ○ *adv* in poverty, poorly, miserably ~**tinjska četvrt** slum ~**tište** *nn* orphanage

sirov *adj* raw; uncooked; crude; unprocessed ~**ina** *nf* 1 raw material 2 *sl* boor

sirup *nm* syrup

sis|a *nf* breast; tit *coll* **odbiti od ~e** wean sb ~**aljka** *nf* (*Dsg* ~aljci) 1 suction pump 2 sucker ~**ati** *v* (što/0) (*pres* sišem) suck, suckle ~**avac** *nm* (*Gsg* ~avca, *Npl* ~avci) mammal

sistem *nm* (→ **sustav**) system ~**atičan** *adj* (α) systematic ~**atizirati** *v* (što) systematize ~**atski** *adj* systematic ~**atski pregled** physical

sit *adj* 1 full, satiated, replete 2 (koga/čega) *fig* fed up with, sick and tired of **najesti se do ~a** eat one's fill

sit|an *adj* (α) 1 tiny, minute, diminutive, small 2 petty, trifling, trivial 3 fine ~**an novac** small change ~**na duša** petty-minded person ~**na roba** sundries ~**nica** *nf* 1 trifle; detail 2 ~**nice** *pl* sundries, bits and pieces, odds and ends ~**ničav** *adj* hairsplitting, petty, pedantic ~**niš** *nm* small/loose change ~**nozor** *nm* microscope

sito *nn* sieve **kroz ~ i rešeto** through thick and thin

situ|acija *nf* situation ~**iran** *adj* situated **dobro ~iran** well-off, well-to-do ~**irati** *v* (koga/što/se) situate, place; find a position

siv *adj* grey ~**ilo** *nn* 1 greyness 2 monotony, tedium, drabness ~**kast** *adj* greyish

sja|hati *v* (0) (*pres* ~šem) dismount, get off

sjaj *nm* 1 radiance, brilliance, brightness, shine; glare, glow, glitter 2 splendour, lustre ~**jan** *adj* (α) 1 shining, radiant, brilliant; glowing 2 splendid, superb; great *coll* ~**ti** *v* (0/se) 1 shine, radiate; glow, glare, glitter 2 beam ~**jiti** *v* *impf*

sjatiti *v* (se) flock together

sjebati *v* (koga/što) *tab sl* fuck up, screw up

sje|cište *nn* intersection, junction ~**ckati** *v* (što) chop up, cut; (meso) hash ~**ča** *nf* felling, cutting down ~**čivo** *nn* blade, cutting edge

sjeća|nje *nf* memory, remembrance, recollection ~**ti** *v* (se) *impf* → **sjetiti se**

sjeći *v* (*pres* siječem) 1 (što) cut, chop, hew; hack 2 (se) intersect

sjedalo *nn* seat

sjedina *nf* grey hair

sjedi|niti *v* (što/se) unite; join; fuse; merge

sjedi|šte *nn* seat; headquarters, head office, building ~**ti** *v* (0) 1 sit, be seated 2 *coll* sit about/around ~**ti na dvije stolice** have a foot in both camps ~**ti na ušima** be deaf, not listen

sjedelj|ka *nf* (*Dsg* ~ci) get-together

sjednica *nf* session, meeting

sjedokos *adj* grey-haired

sjekira *nf* axe; hatchet

sjekutić *nm* incisor

sjeme *nn* 1 seed 2 semen **posijati ~ razdora** sow the seeds of dissension ~**nište** *nn* seminary ~**nka** *nf* (*Dsg* ~nci) seed

sjen|a *nf* 1 shadow 2 (hlad) shade **baciti ~u na** cast a shadow on **baciti u ~u** put in(to) the shade **pratiti koga kao ~a** shadow sb ~**čati** *v* (što) shade; hatch

sjenica (1) *nf* (ptica) titmouse

sjenica (2) *nf* bower, arbour

sjeni|k *nm* (*Npl* ~ci) hayloft

sjenovit *adj* shady

sje|sti *v* (0) (*pres* ~dnem) 1 sit (down), take a seat 2 fit into place **novac nije ~o na račun** the money has not been credited to/has not hit *coll* my account ~sti u auto get into the car ~sti na avion take a plane

sjeta *nf* melancholy, sadness, low spirits ~n *adj* (*a*) melancholy, wistful

sjetiti *v* (se) 1 remember, recall, recollect 2 think of, occur to one, be struck by an idea, hit (up)on an idea

sjetva *nf* sowing; sowing time

sjever *nm* the north ~ac *nm* (*Gsg* ~ca) north/northerly wind ~ni *adj* north, northern, northerly ~ni medvjed polar bear ~ni pol the North Pole ~njača *nf* the Pole/North Star ~njak *nm* (*Npl* ~njaci) northerner ~oistočni *adj* northeastern, northeast, northeasterly ~oistok *nm* northeast ~ozapad *nm* northwest ~ozapadni *adj* northwestern, northwest, northwesterly

skafander *nm* spacesuit

skaj *nm coll* leatherette

skak|ač *nm* 1 jumper 2 diver 3 (šah) knight ~aonica *nf* 1 ski jump 2 divingboard ~ati *v impf* (*pres* skačem) → skočiti ~avac *nm* (*Gsg* ~avca, *Npl* ~avci) 1 grasshopper; locust 2 *sl* flick-knife, switchblade ~utati *v* (0) (*pres* ~ućem) hop, skip

skala *nf* scale

skameniti *v* (se) be petrified (+ *fig*)

skandal *nm* scandal ~ozan *adj* (*a*) scandalous, shocking

skandirati *v* (0) chant, cheer

skapa|ti *v* (0) die (of hunger/thirst/exposure), starve ~vati *v impf*

skel|a *nf* ferry ~ar *nm* ferryman ~e *nf pl* scaffolding

skepti|čan *adj* (*a*) sceptical ~k *nm* (*Npl* ~ci) sceptic

skic|a *nf* sketch, draft, outline ~irati *v* (što) sketch

skija *nf* ski ~nje *nn* skiing ~š *nm* skier ~ški *adj* ski, skiing ~ti *v* (0/se) ski

skin|uti *v* (*pres* ~em) 1 (koga/što) take down; take off; remove 2 (se) undress, get undressed

skit|ati *v* (0/se) wander; roam; rove; loaf ~nica *nf* tramp, vagrant; wanderer, rover ~nja *nf* wandering, roaming, roving; vagrancy *leg*

sklad *nm* harmony, accord, symmetry,

proportion **u** ~u **s(a)** in accordance/conformity/harmony/keeping/line with ~an *adj* (*a*) harmonious, well-proportioned; shapely ~atelj *nm* composer ~ati *v* (0/što) compose ~ba *nf* composition

skladišt|e *nn* warehouse, storehouse, depot; (vojno) dump na ~u in stock

sklapa|ti *v impf* → sklopiti na ~nje folding

sklek *nm* press-up *GB*; push-up *US*

sklepan *adj coll* jerry-built

sklero|tičan *adj* (*a*) sclerotic ~za *nf* sclerosis

skli|zak *adj* (*f* ~ska) slippery ~zati *v* (se) (*pres* ~žem) slide ~nuti *v* (0) (*pres* ~znem) slip; slide; skid

sklon *adj* 1 inclined, disposed 2 prone 3 apt, liable; likely to, tending to 4 favourable

skloni|šte *nn* shelter; cover; refuge; hiding place ~ti *v* 1 (koga/što) put away, remove, take away; hide 2 (se) hide, find refuge/shelter 3 (se) get away, make way

sklonost *nf* 1 inclination, liking, partiality; favour 2 tendency; bent

sklop *nm* complex; structure ~iti *v* (što) 1 fold 2 conclude, contract, make, sign 3 assemble, put together ~iti oči close one's eyes ~iti ruke fold one's hands ~iti sporazum enter into/conclude/make an agreement ~iv *adj* collapsible, folding ~ka *nf* (*Dsg* ~ci) switch, circuit breaker

sklupčati *v* (se) curl up, coil/roll oneself into a ball

skljokati *v* (se) *coll* collapse, flop

skoč|iti *v* (0) 1 jump, leap, hop, spring 2 go up, rise prvo ~či, pa onda reci hop! don't count your chickens before they're hatched ~k *nm* 1 jump, leap, hop 2 *fig* rise ~k uvis high jump ~ udalj long/broad *US* jump ~kovi u vodu diving kud ja okom, tud on ~kom he's at my beck and call ~knuti *v* (0) (*pres* ~knem) run/slip down to; pop, nip (in/out/over/off/round) *coll*

skončati *v* (0) die, meet one's end

skorbut *nm* scurvy

skoro *adv* 1 → nedavno; uskoro 2 almost, nearly

skorojević *nm* upstart, parvenu

skorup *nm* cream **skinuti ~** skim (off) the cream

skotna *adj* big with young, pregnant

skotrljati *v* (se) roll down

skraćen *adj* shortened; abbreviated; abridged; summary

skrahirati *v* (0) go bankrupt; go bust *coll*

skrasiti *v* (se) settle down

skrati|ti *v* (što) shorten, make shorter; abbreviate; abridge; reduce **da ~m (priču)** to cut a long story short

skrb *nf* care **socijalna ~** social welfare **~iti** *v* (za koga/se o čemu) care for, look after **~nik** *nm* (*Npl* ~nici) guardian, tutor

skren|uti *v* (*pres* ~em) **1** (što) turn, direct; divert **2** (0) turn; (naglo) swerve; diverge, deviate **~uti pozornost** turn/call/draw sb's attention **~uti pameću** take leave of one's senses, go mad **~uti s puta a.** turn off a road **b.** *fig* go astray

skre|sati *v* (što) (*pres* ~šem) *coll* **~sati u brk/lice** tell sth to sb's face

skre|tati *v impf* (*pres* ~ćem) → **skrenuti ~tnica** *nf* switch **~tničar** *nm* signalman

skrha|n *adj* crushed, broken **~ti** *v* (što/koga) break, crush, smash

skripta *nf* (photocopied) course notes *pl*

skriva|č *nm* **igrati se ~ča** play hide-and-seek **~ti** *v* (koga/što) hide, conceal; keep from

skrivi|ti *v* (što) be guilty of, be responsible for, be to blame for; cause **on je to ~o** it's his fault, he is to blame

skrnaviti → **oskvrnuti**

skrojiti *v* (što) cut out

skrom|an *adj* (*α*) modest **~nost** *nf* modesty

skrovi|šte *nn* hiding place; hideout; refuge, shelter **~t** *adj* hidden, secret, concealed

skroz *adv coll* completely, totally

skrpati *v* (što) patch up

skršiti *v* (što) crush, break, shatter, wreck **~ otpor** crush resistance

skrupul|a *nf* scruple **~ozan** *adj* (*α*) scrupulous

skrušen *adj* contrite, penitent, repentant; humble **~ost** *nf* contrition

skucati *v* (što) *coll* scrape up/together, rake up

skučen *adj* **1** cramped, crowded **2** limited, restricted; narrow **~ost** *nf* limited space; restricted conditions

skuhati *v* (što) cook, make; boil **~ čaj** make/brew tea

skup (1) *nm* **1** rally; meeting, gathering, assembly **2** *math* set **3** cluster

skup (2) *adj* expensive, costly, dear

skup|a *adv* together, jointly **~ina** *nf* group; cluster; bunch; batch **~iti** *v* **1** (koga/što) gather, assemble, collect; rally; accumulate; muster; raise **2** (se) gather, assemble, rally; huddle together **3** (se) shrink **~ljač** *nm* gatherer; collector **~ni** *adj* collective, joint

skupo|cjen *adj* precious, valuable **~cjenosti** *nf pl* valuables **~ća** *nf* high prices, expensiveness

skupštin|a *nf* **1** assembly, parliament **2** meeting, conference **~ski** *adj* assembly, parliament(ary)

skuša *nf* mackerel

skut *nf* skirt **hvatati se za čije ~e** clutch at sb's skirts

skutriti *v* (se) coil, curl up

skvrčiti *v* (što/se) contort, twist; double up; shrink

slab *adj* **1** weak, feeble **2** poor; meagre **~a strana** weakness **~ina struja** low-voltage current **biti ~ na** have a weakness for **~ašan** *adj* (*α*) weak, sickly, thin **~ić** *nm* weakling, wimp **~iti** *v* (0) **1** weaken, get/grow weak(er) **2** abate, subside **~o** *adv* **1** weakly, feebly **2** poorly, badly **~o mi je** I don't feel well, I feel sick **~okrvan** *adj* (*α*) anaemic **~ost** *nf* weakness; frailty **~ouman** *adj* (*α*) feeble-minded

slabina *nf* flank, side

slad *nm* malt **~ak** *adj* (*f* slatka) **1** sweet (+ *fig*) **2** lovely, cute **~iti** *v* (što) sweeten, sugar **~okusac** *nm* (*Gsg* ~okusca, *Npl* ~okusci) gourmet **~oled** *nm* ice cream; ice *GB* **~oledar** *nm* ice-cream vendor **~ostrastan** *adj* (f ~ostrasna) sensuous, voluptuous, lustful ~unjav *adj* 1 sweetish 2 *derog* sentimental; corny, mushy, slushy, syrupy

slaga||lica *nf* (jigsaw) puzzle ~r *nm* compositor, typesetter

slagati (1) *v impf* 1 (što) → složiti 2 (se) get along 3 (se) match

slagati (2) *v* 1 (0) lie, tell a lie 2 (koga) lie to sb; fool

slam|a *nf* straw **mlatiti praznu ~u** talk nonsense ~**ka** *nf* (*Dsg* ~ci) straw **hvatati se za ~ku** clutch at straws **piti na ~ku** drink through a straw ~**nat** *adj* straw ~**nati krov** thatched roof

slan *adj* salty, salt ~**ina** *nf* bacon ~**oća** *nf* saltiness; salinity ~**utak** *nm* (*Gsg* ~utka, *Npl* ~uci) chickpea

slap *nm* waterfall, cascade

slas|t *nf* 1 sweetness 2 relish, delight, pleasure ~**tan** *adj* (*f* ~na) delicious, tasty ~**tica** *nf* (a piece of) cake, sweet, confectionery ~**tičar** *nm* confectioner ~**tičarnica** *nf* confectioner's, confectionery

slati *v* (koga/što) (*pres* šaljem) send; forward, dispatch, ship; transmit ~ **poštom** post; mail *US*

slat||kiš *nm* sweet *GB*; candy *US*; goody; sweetmeat *arch* ~**o** *nn* 1 preserve 2 dessert; pudding, sweet *GB* ○ *adv* 1 sweetly 2 heartily; with relish/gusto ~**oća** *nf* sweetness ~**orječiv** *adj* smooth-spoken/-tongued, glib ~**ovodni** *adj* freshwater

slav|a *nf* 1 glory 2 fame **živjeti na staroj ~i** rest on one's laurels ~**a mu!** may he rest in peace ~**an** *adj* (*a*) 1 glorious 2 famous, famed, renowned

slavina *nf* tap *GB*; faucet *US*

slav||iti *v* (koga/što) 1 celebrate; observe, mark 2 praise, glorify ~**lje** *nn* celebration; jubilation; triumph ~**odobitan** *adj* (*a*) triumphant ~**ohlepan** *adj* (*a*) ambitious ~**oluk** *nm* (*Npl* ~oluci) triumphal arch

slavuj *nm* nightingale

slediti *v* (se) freeze (+ *fig*)

slegn|uti *v* (*pres* ~em) 1 (0) ~**uti ramenima** shrug one's shoulders 2 (se) settle; sag, subside

slet|jeti *v* (0) (*pres* ~im) land, touch down; perch ~**jeti s ceste** run/skid/veer off the road ~**na** *adj* **staza** landing strip

slezena *nf* spleen

slič|an *adj* (*a*) similar, like; alike ~**iti** *v* (komu/čemu) resemble, be like, be similar to, bear resemblance to ~**no** *adv* similarly **i ~no** and the like ~**nost** *nf* similarity, resemblance, likeness

slijed *nm* sequence, succession; series ~**eći** *adj* → **sljedeći** ~**iti** *v* 1 (koga/što) follow 2 (0) come after, come next, follow **kao što ~i** as follows

slijep *adj* blind **potpuno ~** as blind as a bat, stone-blind ~**a ulica** blind alley, dead end ~**i putnik** stowaway ~**o crijevo** appendix ~**ac** *nm* (*Gsg* ~ca, *Npl* ~ci) blind man/person

slijepiti *v* 1 (što) glue/paste together, stick 2 (se) stick (together)

slijeva *adv* on the left, from the left; (brod) on the port side

slijevati *v* (se) 1 flow/run down 2 flow into, empty into 3 merge into

sli||ka *nf* (*Dsg* ~ci) 1 picture 2 painting 3 photo(graph), snapshot 4 illustration 5 image 6 scene, view, sight 7 figure **krvna ~ka** blood count ~**ka i prilika koga** the spitting/very image of sb ~**kar** *nm* painter, artist ~**karski** *adj* painting ~**karski stalak** easel ~**karstvo** *nn* (art of) painting ~**kati** *v* 1 (koga/što) paint, picture; photograph, take a photograph/picture of; X-ray 2 (se) have one's photograph taken; have an X-ray ~**kovan** *adj* (*a*) pictorial ~**kovit** *adj* 1 picturesque 2 figurative ~**kovnica** *nf* picture book

slin|a *nf* saliva ~**av** *adj* slobbering ~**avac** *nm* (*Gsg* ~avca, *Npl* ~avci) sniveller ~**avka** *nf* (*Dsg* ~avci) foot-and-mouth disease ~**iti** *v* (0) 1 slobber, slaver 2 *fig derog* snivel, whimper

slistiti *v* (što) *coll* eat up, polish off

sliti *v* (se) *pf* → **slijevati**

slitina *nf* alloy

sliv *nm* river basin

slivni|k *nm* (*Npl* ~ci) 1 sink 2 gutter; gully

slizati *v* (se) *coll* become as thick as thieves, be hand in glove with

slobod|a *nf* freedom; liberty **na ~i** at liberty, at large; on the loose **pjesnička ~a** poetic licence **~an** *adj* (*a*) 1 free 2 open; unobstructed 3 loose **~an dan** day off **~arski** *adj* freedom-loving **~no** *adv* 1 freely 2 openly, frankly **~no!** come in! **~no?** may I? **~njak** *nm* (*Npl* ~njaci) 1 *hist* yeoman 2 *coll* freelancer **~oljubiv** *adj* freedom-loving **~ouman** *adj* (*a*) liberal, freethinking

slog *nm* 1 syllable 2 type, typeface 3 *arch* style

sloga *nf* concord, harmony

slogan *nm* slogan

sloj *nm* layer; stratum; class **~an** *suffix* (*a*) -layered **~evit** *adj* 1 stratified, in layers, multi-layered 2 complex

slom *nm* 1 breakup, collapse, downfall, ruin; (burze) crash 2 breakdown **~iti** *v* 1 (koga/što) break; fracture; crush 2 (se) break (off/up); break down **~ljen** *adj* 1 broken; fractured 2 broken-hearted, heartbroken

slon *nm* elephant **~ u staklani** a bull in a china shop **~ova** *adj* **kost** ivory

sloviti *v* (0) (kao/za) have the reputation of, be reputed as/to be, rank as, be famous for

slovo *nn* 1 letter 2 *form* speech

slož|an *adj* (*a*) 1 harmonious 2 unanimous, in agreement **biti ~ni** stick together **~no** *adv* pjevati sing in unison

složen *adj* 1 → **složiti** 2 complex, complicated 3 compound **~enica** *nf* compound **~enost** *nf* complexity **~iti** *v* (što) 1 arrange 2 fold 3 pile up, stack up 4 assemble, put together; make 5 match 6 (se) agree; come to terms

slučaj *nm* 1 case; instance 2 event 3 incident **nesretan ~** accident **igra ~a/puki ~** a mere/pure/sheer coincidence **u svakom ~u** in any case, at any rate, at all events **ni u kom ~u** on no account **u krajnjem/najgorem ~u** at (the) worst, if the worst

comes to the worst **za ~ da** in case of, in the event of **prepustiti ~u** leave sth to chance **~an** *adj* (*a*) accidental, chance, fortuitous; random **~no** *adv* accidentally, by accident/ chance **~nost** *nf* chance, coincidence

sluga *nm* 1 (man)servant; valet; footman 2 *fig* henchman

slu|h *nm* 1 (sense of) hearing 2 *fig* ear **imati ~ha za** have a good ear for **~šač** *nm* student, attender **~šalica** *nf* 1 earphone 2 (telephone) receiver; earpiece **~šatelj** *nm* listener; hearer **~šati** *v* (koga/što) 1 listen (to) 2 obey 3 attend (classes); follow/take (sb's advice) **~šni** *adj* auditory

sluškinja *nf* maid, (maid)servant

slut|iti *v* (što) have an inkling (of sth/that), have a premonition; conjecture, surmise **~ti na dobro/zlo** well/ill **~nja** *nf* premonition, presentiment, foreboding, misgiving

sluz *nf* mucus; slime **~av** *adj* slimy; mucous **~nica** *nf* mucous membrane

služ|ba *nf* 1 service 2 post, job, employment **~ben** *adj* (*a*) 1 duty 2 *fig* formal, stiff **~benik** *nm* (*Npl* ~benici) 1 clerk, office worker, white-collar worker 2 officer; civil servant 3 employee **~iti** *v* (koga/što) 1 serve 2 attend, wait on 3 use, handle **čemu to ~i?** what is it for? what use does it have/serve?

sljedb|a *nf* sect **~enik** *nm* (*Npl* ~enici) 1 follower, adherent 2 sectarian

sljedeći *adj* following, next; subsequent **~ put** next time

sljep|ilo *nm*, **~oća** *nf* blindness **~ilo za boje** colour blindness **~oočnica** *nf* temple

sljez *nm* (marsh)mallow

smakn|uće *nn* execution **~uti** *v* (koga) (*pres* ~em) execute, put to death **~uti na električnoj stolici** electrocute sb; fry *US sl*

smanj|iti *v* 1 (što) reduce, cut down, diminish, lessen; (napetost) defuse 2 (se) decrease, diminish; shrink; abate, decline **~vati** *v impf*

smaragd *nm* emerald

smatra|ti *v* (koga/što) consider, regard, think, find, hold, view **~m da** I think/believe that

sma|zati *v* (što) (*pres* ~žem) eat up, polish off, gobble down/up, bolt down

smeće *nn* **1** rubbish *GB*; garbage, trash *US*; refuse **2** *fig* scum (of the earth) **kanta za ~** dustbin *GB*; garbage/trash can *US* **vreća za ~** bin-liner *GB*; garbage bag *US*

smeđ *adj* brown

smekšati *v* **1** (koga/što) soften up, mellow **2** (se) soften, mellow, mollify

sme|sti *v* (*pres* ~tem) **1** (koga) bewilder, confuse, nonplus, puzzle **2** (se) get bewildered/confused

smet → **zapuh**

smeta|ti *v* (kome) disturb; bother, interrupt; be in the way **ne ~** it doesn't matter, it's all right

smeten *adj* confused, bewildered, nonplussed

smetl|ar *nm* dustman *GB*; garbage collector *US* **~ište** *nn* rubbish heap/dump/tip

smetn|uti *v* (što) (*pres* ~em) **~o sam s uma** it slipped my mind

smetnj|a *nf* disturbance, interference; interruption; hindrance, impediment **~e** *nf pl* atmospherics, static **biti na ~u** impose on sb

smežurati *v* (se) shrivel up, wrinkle

smicalica *nf* trick, artifice, subterfuge

smij|ati *v* (se komu/čemu) (*pres* ~em) laugh (at) **tko se posljednji ~e, najslađe se ~e** *prov* he who laughs last, laughs longest **~eh** *nm* laughter, laugh **~ešak** *nm* (*Gsg* ~eška) smile **~ešan** *adj* (*a*) **1** funny, amusing; laughable **2** ridiculous; silly, absurd **~ešiti** *v* (se) smile **~uckati, ~uljiti** *v* (se) giggle, titter, chuckle **~urija** *nf* joke, laugh

smijeniti *v* (koga/što) remove, relieve, replace

smil|ovati *v* (se komu) (*pres* ~ujem) have mercy on; have/take pity on, feel compassion for

smion *adj* bold, brave, courageous, daring, audacious

smiraj *nm* sunset, twilight, dusk **~ dana** the close of the day

smir|en *adj* calm, cool, serene; tranquil **~iti** *v* (koga/što) **1** calm (down); soothe (down) **2** appease, tranquilize, pacify **3** (se) calm down; quieten down; abate, subside

smi|sao *nm* (*Gsg* ~sla) sense; meaning **imati ~sla za** have a talent/bent for **nema ~sla a.** it's useless, it's no use **b.** it doesn't make sense **u ~slu** in terms of **u pravom ~slu riječi** in the true/literal sense of the word **~slen** *adj* meaningful **~sliti** *v* (što) think out, devise; come up with **coll ~šljeno** *adv* deliberately, on purpose

smjelost *nf* boldness, courage, daring, audacity

smje|na *nf* **1** shift **2** relief; change **na ~nu** alternately, in turns, taking turns **~njivati** *v impf* → **smijeniti**

smjer *nm* direction; course; trend **~ati** *v* (0) intend, plan, have in mind, be up to **~nica** *nf* directive; guidelines *pl*

smjeran *adj* (*a*) modest, humble; self-effacing, meek

smjesa *nf* mixture, blend

smjesta *adv* at once, right away, straight off

smje|stiti *v* **1** (koga/što) accommodate, put up; place, put, locate **2** (se) find accommodation/lodging; lodge; settle down; find one's seat **3** (komu) frame, set sb up **~štaj** *nm* accommodation, lodging **~štati** *v impf*

smjeti *v* (što) (*pres* smijem) **1** be allowed/permitted, may **2** dare, venture **ne ~** must not, not be allowed **ne bismo smjeli** we shouldn't

smlačiti *v* (što) make lukewarm/tepid, warm (up) a bit

smlaviti *v* (koga/što) crush, smash; make mincemeat of sb *fig*

smočiti *v* (što) wet; drench, steep

smočnica *nf* larder, pantry

smo|ći *v* (što) (*pres* ~gnem) find, obtain, procure **~ći hrabrosti** take/pluck up/muster courage **~ći snage** summon up/gather strength

smoking *nm* dinner jacket; tuxedo *US*, tux *coll*

smokva *nf* fig

smola *nf* **1** resin **2** pitch **3** *coll* bad luck

smo|tak *nm* (*Gsg* ~tka, *Npl* ~ci) bundle; roll; scroll; packet **~tan** *adj* 1 rolled up; furled, coiled 2 *coll* mixed up, muddled, jumbled up **~tati** *v* 1 (što) roll up, wrap up, fold 2 (koga) *coll* sweet-talk 3 (se) curl up, coil

smotra *nf* 1 festival 2 review; inspection

smožditi *v* (koga) crush

smračiti *v* (se) darken, become/grow dark

smrad *nm* stench, bad/foul smell/-odour

smrča → smreka

smrd|jeti *v* (0) (*pres* ~im) stink, smell **~ljiv** *adj* stinking, smelly

smreka *nf* 1 spruce 2 juniper

smrkn|ut *adj* gloomy, dejected **~uti** *v* se (*pres* ~em) 1 get dark, darken 2 become dejected/gloomy/sombre

smrskati *v* (što) crush, smash, demolish

smršav|jeti *v* (0) (*pres* ~im) lose weight, become thin; slim

smrt *nf* death **prirodna ~** death from natural causes **umrijeti prirodnom/nasilnom smrću** die a natural/violent death **~an** *adj* (*a*) mortal, deadly; fatal **~a kazna** capital punishment **~na presuda** death sentence **~ni grijeh** deadly sin **~nik** *nm* (*Vsg* ~niče, *Npl* ~nici) mortal; human **~nost** *nf* mortality; death rate **~onosan** *adj* (*a*) deadly, lethal, mortal **~ovnica** *nf* death certificate

smrviti *v* 1 (što) crush, crumble 2 (koga) crush

smrz|nuti *v* (*pres* ~nem) 1 (što) freeze 2 (se) freeze, become frozen, freeze to death **~avati** *v* (se) *impf*

smucati *v* (se) gad about, loiter, roam; prowl

smućkati *v* (što) *coll* 1 shake up 2 botch up, bungle; (jelo) whip up

smuđ *nm* perch

smuk *nm* **pijan kao ~** as drunk as a newt

smuljati *v coll* 1 (što) botch (up); goof *US coll* 2 (koga) fool, snow

smušen *adj* confused, muddle-headed, mixed up

smut|iti *v* 1 (što) mix, stir 2 (koga)

confuse, bewilder, puzzle 3 (se) become confused **~ljivac** *nm* (*Gsg* ~ljivca, *Npl* ~ljivci) intriguer; spoilsport, troublemaker, wheeler-dealer **~nja** *nf* 1 intrigue, discord 2 confusion **kamen ~nje** bone of contention

sna|ći *v* (*pres* ~đem) 1 (se) cope, get on *fig*; find one's way (around sth) 2 (koga) befall

sna|ga *nf* (*Dsg* ~zi) 1 strength, energy 2 power 3 force **radna ~ga** manpower, workforce **stupiti na ~gu** take effect **~gator** *nm* strongman **~žan** *adj* (*a*) strong; powerful

snaha *nf* daughter-in-law

snajper *nm* rifle with a telescopic sight **~ist** *nm* sniper, sharpshooter

snala|ziti *v impf* → **snaći ~žljiv** *adj* resourceful

snije|g *nm* snow **pada ~g** it is snowing **~žiti** *v* (0) snow

snijeti *v* (*pres* snesem) lay

snim|atelj *nm* cameraman; photographer; (zvuka) sound engineer **~ati** *v impf* **~iti** *v* (koga/što) record, tape; shoot, film **~ka** *nf* (*Dsg* ~ci) 1 (zvuk) recording 2 (snap)shot

sni|ziti *v* (što) lower, reduce, cut **~žavati** *v impf*

snob *nm* snob **~ovski** *adj* snobbish

snop *nm* sheaf; bundle **~lje** *nn* sheaves

sno|siti *v* (što) bear **~siti odgovornost** take/bear responsibility **~siti posljedice** accept/bear the consequences **~siti troškove** cover the costs **~šaj** *nm* (sexual) intercourse **~šljivost** *nf* tolerance

snov|ati *v* (što) (*pres* snujem) plan, plot **~i** *nm pl* → **san**

snubiti *v* (koga) court,woo

snužditi *v* (se) become depressed

snje|gović *nm* snowman **Snjeguljica** *nf* Snow White **~žan** *adj* (*a*) snow **~žna pahuljica** snowflake

sob *nm* reindeer

sob|a *nf* room **spavaća ~a** bedroom **dnevna ~a** living/sitting room **radna ~a** study **~ar** *nm* valet **~arica** *nf* (chamber) maid **~ni** *adj* room **~oslikar** *nm* decorator

socijal|an *adj* (*a*) social **~no osiguranje** social security **~izam** *nm* (*Gsg*

~izma) socialism

sociolo|g *nm* (*Npl* ~zi) sociologist

sočan *adj* (*a*) juicy (+ *fig*), succulent

soda *nf* soda ~ **bikarbona** *coll* bicarb, baking soda *coll*; bicarbonate (of soda)

sofa *nf coll* sofa, settee

soj *nm* 1 kind 2 strain, race

soja *nf* soya (bean)

sok *nm* juice; (biljke) sap ~**ovnik** *nm* (*Npl* ~ovnici) juicer, juice extractor

sokna *nf coll* sock

sokol *nm* falcon

so|l *nf* salt **kuhinjska ~** table salt **imati ~i u glavi** be smart ~**liti** *v* (0/što) salt, add salt to ~**liti komu pamet** tell sb what to do ~**lni** *adj* salt ~**lna kiselina** chloric acid ~**ljenka** *nf* salt cellar

solid|an *adj* (*a*) 1 solid 2 *fig* reliable ~**arnost** *nf* solidarity

solist *nm* soloist

solsticij *nm* solstice

som *nm* catfish

sond|a *nf* 1 sounding line 2 *med* probe, sound ~**irati** *v* (što) probe (into *fig*)

sonet *nm* sonnet

sopran *nm* soprano

sos *nm coll* sauce **biti u ~u** *fig* be in a fix

sotona *nm* satan

sova *nf* owl

spakirati *v* (što/se) pack (up)

spadati *v* (kamo) belong

spaja|ti *v impf* → **spojiti** ~**lica** *nf* paper clip

spa|liti *v* (koga/što) burn; incinerate ~**ljivati** *v impf*

spar|an *adj* (*a*) sultry, muggy ~**ina** *nf* oppressive heat

spariti *v* 1 (koga s kim/što s čim) match, mate 2 (se) couple

spas *nm* salvation; rescue ~**avati** *v impf* ~**itelj** *nm* 1 life guard 2 Saviour ~**iti** *v* 1 (koga/što) save, rescue 2 (se) save oneself, survive

spava|ćica *nf* nightgown ~**ća** *adj* **soba** bedroom ~**onica** *nf* dormitory ~**ti** *v* (0) sleep

spaziti *v* (koga/što) spot

specifi|cirati *v* (što) specify ~**čan** *adj* (*a*) specific; peculiar ~**čnost** *nf* specific feature, peculiarity ~**kacija** *nf* specification

specijal|an *adj* (*a*) special ~**izirati** *v* (se za što) specialize (in) ~**ka** *nf coll* racer ~**nost** *nf* speciality

spektakl *nm* (*Gsg* ~a) spectacle, sight

spekt|ar *nm* (~ra) spectrum

sperma *nf* sperm; come *sl*

spetlja|ti *v* 1 (što) tangle 2 (se) get confused/all mixed-up 3 (se s kim) *coll* get involved with

spiker *nm coll* announcer; presenter, newscaster

spilja *nf* cave

spirala *nf* 1 spiral 2 *coll* intra-uterine device; IUD *coll*

spis *nm* document, paper ~**atelj** *nm* writer

spiskati *v* (što) squander, blow

spjev *nm* canto

splačine *nf pl* (pig)swill

splasn|uti *v* (*pres* ~em) (0) go down, shrink

splav *nf* raft

sple|sti *v* (*pres* ~tem) 1 (što) braid 2 (se) get all mixed-up ~**t** *nm* **okolnosti** set/combination of circumstances ~**tka** *nf* intrigue, scheme ~**tkariti** *v* (0) plot, scheme

spljoštiti *v* (što/se) flatten

spodoba *nf* freak

spoj *nm* 1 connection, junction, joint; (kemijski) compound **kratki ~** short circuit 2 *coll* date ~**iti** *v* (što) join, couple, link ~**ka** *nf* clutch

spokojan *adj* (*a*) serene

spol *nm* sex ~**ni** *adj* 1 sexual 2 genital ~**na bolest** venereal desease; VD *coll* ~**ovilo** *nn* genitals *pl*; sexual organ

spom|en *nm* 1 memory ~**en-ploča** memorial plaque **u ~en** in memory of 2 mention ~**enica** *nf* memorial medal ~**enik** *nm* (*Npl* ~enici) monument ~**enuti** *v* (*pres* ~em) 1 (što) mention 2 (se) remember ~**injati** *v impf*

spona *nf* link, bond

spontan *adj* spontaneous

spopa|sti *v* (koga) (*pres* ~dnem) seize **što te je ~lo?** *coll* what's come over you?

spor (1) *nm* dispute **~an** *adj* (*a*) debatable, controversial

spor (2) *adj* slow

sporazum *nm* agreement **sklopiti ~** reach/conclude an a. **~an** *adj* (*a*) (s čim) in agreement with, agreeable **~ijevati** *v impf* **~jeti** *v* (se) (*pres* **~ijem**) 1 manage to understand each other 2 reach an agreement **~no** *adj* by mutual consent

sporedan *adj* (*a*) secondary, of less importance; auxiliary; (cesta) ancillary

sport → **šport**

sposob|an *adj* (*a*) 1 fit, able (to do sth) 2 capable, clever **~nost** *nf* ability, capacity, talent

spot|aknuti *v* (se) (*pres* **~aknem**) stumble **~icati** *v impf* **kamen ~ica-nja** stumbling block

sposna|ja *nf* 1 (proces) cognition 2 insight **~ti** *v* (što) comprehend; realize

sprati *v* (što) (*pres* **sperem**) wash away, clear

sprava *nf* device, gadget, implement

sprda|čina *nf* mockery, farce **~ti** *v* (se iz koga/čega) mock, ridicule

sprečavati *v impf* → **spriječiti**

sprega *nf* collusion **povratna ~** feedback

sprem|a *nf* qualification **~an** *adj* (*a*) ready, prepared, willing **~ati** *v impf* **~iti** *v* 1 (što) put (aside), prepare 2 (što) prepare 3 (što) tidy up, clean 4 (se) get ready, prepare oneself **~ište** *nn* warehouse; repository **~nik** *nm* (*Npl* **~nici**) tank **~nica** *nf* pantry

spretan *adj* (*a*) clever, skilful

spre|zati *v* (što) (*pres* **~žem**) *gram* conjugate

sprijatelj|iti *v* (se s kim) make friends with sb

spriječiti *v* (koga/što) prevent, obstruct

sprijeda *adv* 1 ahead 2 on the front, in front, at the front 3 from the front

sprovod *nm* funeral

sprtljati *v* (što) botch up, mess up

sprud *nm* sand bank

spržiti *v* (što) burn, scorch

spu|st *nm* 1 descent 2 *sport* downhill

~stiti *v* 1 (koga/što) put down; take sb/sth down, lower; (cijene) cut, reduce; (jedra) strike **~stiti sidro** drop anchor 2 (se) come down, get down, descend; (zrakoplov) land **~štati** *v impf*

sputa|ti *v* (koga) fetter, bind (+ *fig*) **~vati** *v impf*

spuzn|uti *v* (0) (*pres* **~em**) slide down, slip

spužva *nf* sponge **~st** *adj* spongy

sra|čka *nf vulg* the runs/trots/shits **~nje** *nn vulg* shit **~ti** *v* (0) (*pres* **serem**) 1 shit, have/take a shit 2 talk shit, bullshit

sram *nm* shame **~ me je** I am ashamed **~ te bilo!** shame on you! **~an**, **~otan** *adj* (*a*) shameful **~žljiv** *adj* shy, bashful **~iti** *v* 1 (0) be shy 2 (koga/čega) be ashamed of sb/sth **~ota** *nf* shame, disgrace **~otiti** *v* 1 (se) disgrace oneself 2 (koga/što) disgrace

srast|i *v* (0) (*pres* **~em**) grow into one, coalesce

sravniti *v* (što) **~ sa zemljom** raze to the ground

sraz *nm* collision; clash

sr|ce *nn* 1 heart (+ *fig*) 2 sweetheart **~čan** *adj* brave **~čani** *adj* heart; cardiac **med ~čani udar** heart attack **~dačan** *adj* (*a*) cordial, warm **Uz ~dačan pozdrav** (u pismu) Kind regards

srdela *nf* pilchard

srdobolja *nf* diarrhoea, dysentery

sr|dit *adj* angry **~diti** *v* 1 (koga) make sb angry 2 (se) be angry **~džba** *nf* anger

srebr|n *adj* silver **~nast** *adj* silvery **~nina** *nf* silverware **~o** *nn* silver

sre|ća *nf* 1 luck, fortune 2 happiness, serenity **imati ~će** be lucky **na ~ću** fortunately **kamo ~će!** if only! **~ćom** *adv* luckily **~ćka** *nf* (*Gpl* **~ćaka**/**~ćki**) lottery ticket **~tan** *adj* (*a*) 1 lucky, fortunate 2 happy **~tan put!** bon voyage! have a nice trip! **~tan Božić!** Merry Christmas! **~tnik** *nm* (*Vsg* **~tniče**, *Npl* **~tnici**) lucky man **~tno!** *int* good luck

sred|ina *nf* 1 middle; centre; (aritmetička) mean **zlatna ~ina** golden mean 2 environment **~išnji** adj central **~išnjica** nf head office, headquarters **~ište** nn centre; (mete) bull's eye **~njak** nm (Npl **~**njaci) middle finger **~nje** adv so-so **~nji** adj 1 middle, medial 2 central 3 average **~nja škola** secondary school; high school US **~nji vijek** the Middle Ages **~nja Europa** Central Europe **~nji rod** neutral gender **~njoškolac** nm (Gsg **~**njoškolca) secondary/high school student **~njovjekovni** adj medieval **~ovječan** adj middle-aged **S~ozemlje** nn the Mediterranean

sre|diti v (što) 1 fix, arrange; sort out; settle 2 (koga) coll take out; (pretući) do sb over; (ubiti) do sb in **~đivati** v impf

sredstv|o nn means **~o za čišćenje** clean(s)ing agent **~a** pl funds **ne birati ~a** use every means at one's disposal, be ruthless

sre|sti v (koga/se) (pres **~**tnem) meet **~tati** v iter

sri|cati v (što) (pres **~**čem) 1 read slowly 2 spell (out)

srijeda nf Wednesday

sr|kati v (što) (pres **~**čem) slurp **~knuti** v (što) sip

srljati v (0) rush

srn|a nf doe **~dać** nm roebuck **~netina** nf venison

sro|čiti v (što) formulate, word **~k** nm rhyme

srodan adj (a) similar, akin; (duša) kindred

srozati v (se) go down, stoop, degrade oneself

srp nm sickle

srp|anj nm (Gsg **~**nja) July

srušiti v 1 (koga/što) knock down; (zgradu) pull down; (studenta) fail; (zrakoplov) down, shoot down 2 (se) fall down, collapse; (zrakoplov) crash

srž nf marrow, core; essence fig

stabilan adj (a) stable

stab|lo nn trunk; (cijelo drvo) tree **~ljika** nf (Dsg **~**ljici) stalk

stadij nm stage

stadion nm stadium

stado nn (krava) herd; (ovaca) flock

staja nf stable, cowshed

staja|lište nn 1 standpoint 2 stop **~ti** v (0) (pres stojim) 1 stand 2 (komu) suit, fit 3 cost

stakl|en adj glass **~enik** nm (Npl **~**enici) hothouse, greenhouse **~o** nn glass

stal|ak nm (Gsg **~**ka, Npl **~**ci) stand; (čaše) stem **slikarski ~ak** easel

stalan adj (a) 1 permanent 2 fixed 3 steady

stalež nm 1 class 2 profession

staložen adj calm, composed

stamben|i adj housing **~a zgrada** apartment building, block of flats

stan (1) nm flat GB; apartment US **~i hrana** board and lodging **namješteni ~** furnished flat **glavni ~** headquarters **~ar** nm 1 tenant 2 lodger **~arina** nf rent **adresa ~ovanja** place of residence **~ovati** v (0) (pres **~**ujem) live, reside (in/at) **~ovnik** nm (Npl **~**ovnici) inhabitant, resident

standard nm standard **životni ~** standard of living **~an** adj (a) standard

stanica (1) nf coll 1 stop 2 (kolodvor/radio/policijska) station

stani|ca (2) nf cell **~čevina** nf cellulose

staniol nm coll tinfoil

stanka nf pause, break; (kazalište) intermission

stanj|e nn state, condition, situation **imovno ~e** financial position **bračno ~e** marital status **biti u drugom ~u** be pregnant

stapati v impf → **stopiti**

star adj old; (kruh) stale **~i vijek** antiquity **~ac** nm (Gsg **~**ca, Vsg **~**če) old man **~ački** adj senile **~ački dom** old people's home; nursing home **~iji** adj senior; elder **~inar** nm junk dealer **~etinarnica** nf junk shop, second-hand shop **~i** nm old man (+ otac) **~ina** nf 1 antiquity 2 antique **~inar** nm antique dealer **~inarnica** nf antique shop **~inski** adj 1 antique 2 old-fashioned, quaint **~ješina** nf head, superior **~jeti** v (0) (pres **~**im) grow old, age **~kelja** nm derog old geezer **~mali** adj precocious

~omodan *adj* (*a*) oldfashioned, outdated **~osjedilac** *nm* (*Gsg* ~osjedioca, *Vsg* ~osjedioče) aboriginal, native **~ost** *nf* old age **~udija** *nf* junk

stas *nm* stature, build **~it** *adj* wellbuilt

sta|ti *v* (0) (*pres* ~nem) **1** stand, assume the position **2** stop, cease **3** start **~ti plakati** burst into tears **4** hold *u torbu ~nu dvije knjige* this bag can carry two books *u kazalište ~ne tisuću ljudi* this theatre seats 1,000 people

stati|čan *adj* (*a*) static **~ka** *nf* (*Dsg* ~ci) statics **~rati** *v* (0) be an extra **~st** *nm* extra **~stika** *nf* (*Dsg* ~stici) statistics

stativa *nf* goal-post

status *nm* status, rank

statut *nm* statute

stav *nm* **1** posture, bearing **2** attitude, stance *zauzeti ~ fig* take a stand

stav|ak *nm* (*Gsg* ~ka, *Npl* ~ci) movement

stav|iti *v* (što *u* što) put; place **~iti na kocku** risk **~iti komu do znanja** let sb know **~ljati** *v impf*

stavka *nf* item

staza *nf* path, track; lane *sport*

staž *nm* length/years of service; (liječnika) internship **~ist** *nm* houseman *GB*; intern *US*

stečaj *nm* bankruptcy *otići pod ~* go bankrupt **~ni** *adj* **upravitelj** receiver

steći *v* (*pres* stečem) (što) acquire, gain, earn

steg|a *nf* discipline; restraint **~ovni** *adj* disciplinary **~nuti** *v* (što) (*pres* ~nem) tighten

stenografija *nf* shorthand

stenjati *v* (0) moan, groan

stepeni|ca *nf coll* stair **~šte** *nn* staircase

stereotip *nm* stereotype **~an** *adj* (*a*) stereotypical

steril|an *adj* (*a*) sterile **~izator** *nm* sterilizer **~izirati** *v* (što) sterilize

stetoskop *nm* stethoscope

ste|zaljka *nf* clamp **~zati** *v* (*pres* ~žem) **1** (što) *impf* → **stegnuti 2** (koga) (cipele) pinch **~že me oko srca** it breaks my heart **~znik** *nm*

(*Npl* ~znici) corset

stići *v* (*pres* stignem) **1** (0) arrive **2** (što) manage to do sth **3** (koga) catch up with sb **stigla ga je kazna** he got due punishment

stid *nm* shame **~ me je** I am ashamed **~jeti** *v* (se) (*pres* ~im) **1** (čega) be ashamed **2** (0) be shy **~ljiv** *adj* shy **~na** *adj* **uš** crab (louse) **~nica** *nf* vulva, pudendum

stih *nm* verse

stijeg *nm* standard

stijen|a *nf* rock **~ka** *nf* (*Dsg* ~ci) wall

stijesniti *v* (koga/što) squeeze

stil *nm* style **~ski** *adj* **1** stylistic **2** period, antique

stimul|acija *nf* stimulation; incentive; (novčani iznos) incentive bonus **~ans** *nm* stimulant **~irati** *v* (koga/što) stimulate, promote; arouse

stipendija *nf* fellowship, scholarship, grant

stis|ak *nm* (*Gsg* ~ka) squeeze **~ka** *nf* crowd, crush **biti u ~ci s vremenom/novcem** be pressed for time/money **~kati** *v impf* **~nuti** *v* (*pres* ~nem) **1** (što) squeeze **~nuti (komu) ruku** shake (sb's) hand **2** (koga) *fig* exert pressure on sb **3** (se) huddle; (odjeća) shrink

stišati *v* **1** (koga) quiet **2** (što) turn down **3** (se) (osobe) fall silent; (buka) subside

stjec|aj *nm* concurrence **~ajem okolnosti** by coincidence **~ati** *v impf* → **steći ~ište** *nn* meeting place; junction

stjegonoša *nm* standard-bearer (+*fig*)

stjenica *nf* **1** bedbug **2** *fig* bore

stjenovit *adj* rocky

stjerati *v* (koga/što) chase down **~ koga u kut** corner sb

stjuardesa *nf* flight attendant, stewardess

sto *num* one/a hundred (100) **~godišnjica** *nf* centenary **~ljeće** *nn* century **~ljetni** *adj* **1** one-hundred-years-old **2** *fig* age-old **~noga** *nf* centipede **~posto** *adv* for sure, positively **~postotni** *adj coll* complete **~ti** *num ord* hundredth **~tina** *num* one/a hundred

~tinka nf one hundredth

stoč|ar nm cattle breeder; rancher **~arstvo** nn cattle breeding **~ni** adj cattle **~ni fond** livestock

stog nm haystack

stoga adv therefore

stoi|čki adj stoical **~k** nm (Npl ~ci) stoic

stojéće adv standing (up), on one's feet

sto|ka nf (Dsg ~ci) cattle, livestock

stol nm table **pisaći ~** desk **~ac** nm (Gsg ~ca) chair **~ar** nm carpenter **~arija** nf 1 carpentry 2 woodwork **~ica** nf 1 chair **Sveta S~ica** the Holy See **sjediti na dvije ~ice** sit on the fence 2 med stool, bowel movement **~ni** adj table **~na crkva** cathedral **~ni tenis** table tennis, ping pong **~njak** nm (Npl ~njaci) table cloth **~ovati** v (0) (pres ~ujem) reside, hold court

stomatolog nm stomatologist, dental surgeon/practitioner **~ija** nf stomatology

stop|a nf 1 foot **slijediti u ~u a.** trail, dog **b.** follow in one's footsteps 2 rate **~a rasta** growth rate **~alo** nn foot

stopiti v (se s čim) merge with sth, blend together/with sth

stornirati v (što) cancel

sto|žac nm (Gsg ~šca) cone **~žast** adj conical

stožer nm pivot; mainstay, pillar fig **glavni ~** headquarters **~ni** adj 1 central, pivotal 2 mil staff

stradati v (0) 1 fall victim, suffer 2 (poginuti) die

straga adv at/in the back

strah nm fear **~ me je** I am afraid **~opoštovanje** nn awe, reverence **~ota** nf horror **~ovati** v (pres ~ujem) 1 (0) worry, be anxious 2 (da) fear (that) **~ovit** adj terrible, tremendous **~ovlada** nf reign of terror

stran adj foreign, alien **~ac** nm (Gsg ~ca, Vsg ~če) foreigner, alien; stranger **~putica** nf wrong path **zaći na ~puticu** fig go astray

stran|a nf 1 side **slaba ~a** weak point **~a svijeta** point of the compass

desna ~a righthand side **na desnu ~u** to the right **šalu na ~u** joking aside **~a u sukobu** party to the conflict **stati na čiju ~u** side with sb, take sb's part 2 (~ica) page **~ački** adj party **~ka** nf (Dsg ~ci, Gpl ~aka) party pol, leg; client, customer

strast nf passion **~ven** adj passionate

straš|an adj (a) 1 horrible 2 coll fig great **~ilo** nn scarecrow **~iti** v (koga) scare **~ljiv** adj faint-hearted, cowardly

strate|g nm (Npl ~zi) strategist **~gija** nf strategy **~ški** adj strategic

stratište nn scaffold

strav|a nf horror, dread **~a i užas** horror **~ičan** adj (a) dreadful

straža nf guard, watch **počasna ~** guard of honour **tjelesna ~** bodyguard **~r** nm sentry, guard **~riti** (0) v stand guard; be on guard duty **~rnica** nf sentry box

stražnji adj back, rear **~ca** nf behind, bottom, rear

streha nf eaves

stre|lica nf arrow **~ličar** nm archer **~ličarstvo** nn archery **~lovit** adj swift, rapid **~ljački** adj **vod** firing squad **~ljana** nf shooting range/gallery **~ljivo** nn ammunition

stremen nm stirrup

stres|ti v (pres ~em) 1 (koga/što) shake (down/off) 2 (se) shake, shudder

stri|c nm (Vsg ~če, Npl ~čevi) uncle **~na** nf aunt

strići v (koga/što) (pres ~žem) shear

strije nf pl stretchmarks

strije|la nf arrow **~lac** nm (Vsg ~lče, Npl ~lci) 1 marksman **dobar ~lac** good/crack shot 2 archer 3 astrol Saggitarius **~ljati** v 1 (koga) execute by firing squad 2 (0) shoot

strip nm comic (book); (novinski) comic strip, strip cartoon

str|ka nf (Dsg ~ci) scramble, rush

strm adj steep **~ina** nf steep slope **~oglaviti** v 1 (koga) precipitate 2 (se) fall headfirst, plunge down

strofa nf stanza

strog adj (comp stroži) strict, severe **~o** adv **povjerljivo** top secret, classified

stroj *nm* 1 machine **pisaći** ~ typewriter ~ **za pranje rublja** washing machine 2 engine ~**ar** *nm* machinist ~**arnica** *nf* engine room ~**arski** *adj* machine; mechanical ~**arstvo** *nn* mechanical engineering ~**ni** *adj* machine ~**nica** *nf* machine gun ~**opis** *nm* typing ~**ovođa** *nf* engine driver *GB*; engineer *US*

strop *nm* ceiling

stropoštati *v* (se) tumble down, collapse

strovaliti *v* (se) fall down, plummet; slump

strpati *v* (što u što) stuff sth into sth

strpljeti *v* (se) (*pres* ~im) be patient, have patience ~**ljiv** *adj* patient ~**ljivost** *nn* patience

stršati *v* (0) stick out, protrude

stršljen *nm* hornet

struč|ak *nm* (*Gsg* ~ka, *Npl* ~ci) bunch, posy

struč|an *adj* (*a*) expert; professional ~**na sprema** qualification ~**nost** *nf* skill ~**njak** *nm* (*Npl* ~njaci) expert, authority

stru|g *nm* plane; lathe ~**gati** *v* (što) (*pres* ~žem) scrape, grate ~**gotina** *nf* shavings *pl*

struj|a *nf* 1 current, stream 2 (electric) current **jaka/slaba** ~**a** high/low voltage current ~**ni** *adj* electric ~**ni krug** circuit ~**ni udar** (electric) shock ~**ati** *v* (0) (*pres* ~im) flow, stream

struk *nm* waist

stru|ka *nm* (*Dsg* ~ci) profession ~**kovni** *adj* professional

struktura *nf* structure

struna *nf* 1 string 2 horse hair

strunjača *nf* sport mat

strusiti *v* (što) (piće) knock back

stub|a *nf* step, stair ~**ište** *nn* staircase

stubokom *adv* radically

studen *nf* cold • *adj* cold, chilly ~**ac** *nm* (*Gsg* ~ca) well ~**i** *nm* November

stud|ent *nm* (university) student ~**entski** *adj* student ~**ij** *nm* course (of study) ~**irati** *v* (što/o) study, read

stup *nm* column, pillar, post ~**ac** *nm* (*Gsg* ~ca) column

stup|anj *nm* (*Gsg* ~nja, *Npl* ~njevi)

degree; grade

stupati *v* (0) march, step

stupica *nf* trap

stupiti *v* (0) 1 step (in), enter 2 join ~ **na snagu** enter into force ~ **u vezu** get in touch

stvar *nf* 1 thing, object ~**i** *pl* stuff *coll* 2 matter; affair; business; issue; cause ~**alački** *adj* (*a*) creative ~**an** *adj* real ~**ati** *v* *impf* → **stvoriti** ~**atelj** *nm* creator ~**no** *adv* really

stvor *nm* being, creature ~**enje** *nn* creature ~**itelj** *nm* creator; Maker *rel* ~**iti** *v* 1 (koga/što) create 2 (se) appear

stvrdn|uti *v* (se) (*pres* ~em) harden

su- *prefix* 1 co-, fellow- 2 ublaživanje, umanjivanje: *supijan* tipsy, *sulud* foolish

subjekt *nm* subject ~**ivan** *adj* subjective

subota *nf* Saturday

subvenci|ja *nf* subsidy ~**onirati** *v* (koga/što) subsidize

subverzija *nf* subversion

sučeli|ce *adv* face to face, facing, opposite ~**ti** *v* (koga s kim/čim) bring sb face to face with

sućut *adj* sympathy **izraziti** ~ convey/offer one's condolences

sud *nm* 1 court, tribunal **vrhovni** ~ supreme c. **općinski** ~ municipal c. **ratni** ~ court-martial ~ **prvog stupnja** court of first instance 2 (postupak) trial 3 judg(e)ment ~**ac** *nm* (*Gsg* suca, *Vsg* suče) 1 judge, justice; magistrate 2 *sport* (nogomet) referee; (tenis) umpire ~**ački** *adj* judicial ~**beni** *adj* legal; judicial ~**iti** *v* 1 (kome) try in court, put on trial 2 (koga/što) judge 3 (0) administer justice ~**nica** *nf* court(room) ~**nji** *adj* judgement ~**ski** *adj* court, legal, forensic ~**ska medicina** forensic medicine ~**ski postupak** legal proceedings *pl* ~**stvo** *nn* the judiciary

sudar *nm* collision ~**ati** *v* *iter* ~**iti** *v* (se) collide, crash, run into

sudb|ina *nf* fate, destiny ~**onosan** *adj* (*a*) fateful; momentous

sudioni|k *nm* (*Npl* ~ci) participant

sudjel|ovati *v* (u čemu) (*pres* ~ujem))

participate in, take part in

sudoper *nm* sink

suđe *nn* dishes *pl* **oprati ~** wash/do the dishes; wash up *GB*

suficit *nm* surplus

sufler *nm* prompter

suge|rirati *v* (što kome) suggest sth to sb **~stija** *nf* suggestion **~stivan** *adj* suggestive

suglas|an *adj* (a) in agreement **~na sam** I agree **~iti** *v* (se) agree **~nik** *nm* (*Npl* ~nici) consonant **~nost** *nf* accord, consent **~je** *nn* consonance

sugovorni|k *nm* (*Npl* ~ci) interlocutor *form*

sugrađan|in *nm* (*Npl* ~i) fellow-citizen

suigrač *nm* team-mate

suh *adj* dry **~omesnata** *adj* roba delicatessen **~onjav** *adj* scrawny **~oparan** *adj* (a) dry, tedious

suklad|an *adj* congruent **~no tomu** consequently

sukljati *v* (0) pour, gush

sukno *nn* cloth

suknja *nf* skirt

sukob *nm* conflict, clash **doći u ~ sa zakonom** fall foul of the law **~iti** *v* (se s kim) 1 clash 2 *mil* engage (in combat)

sukriv|ac *nm* (*Gsg* ~ca) accomplice

sukrvica *nf* pus mixed with blood

sulica *nf* arrow, dart

sumaglica *nf* mist

sumanut *adj* frantic

suložnica *nf* mistress, concubine

sulud *adj* crazy, foolish

sumnj|a *nf* doubt; suspicion **bez (svake) ~e** without (any/a shadow of) doubt, undoubtedly **~ati** *v* 1 (na koga) suspect 2 (što) suspect, have a suspicion 3 (0) doubt **~ičav** *adj* suspicious **~ičiti** *v* (koga za što) suspect sb of sth **~iv** *adj* 1 dubious, doubtful 2 suspect, suspicious

sumoran *adj* (a) gloomy

sumpor *nm* sulphur **~ni** *adj* sulphuric

sumrak *nm* dusk, twilight

sunarodnja|k *nm* (*Vsg* ~če, *Npl* ~ci) fellow-countryman

sun|ce *nn* (*Gpl* ~aca) sun; sunshine **na ~cu** in the sun **~cobran** *nm* sunshade, parasol **~cokret** *nm* sunflower **~costaj** *nm* solstice **~čan** *adj* sunny **~čani**, **~čev** sun, solar **~čani sat** sundial **~čanica** *nf* sunstroke **~čati** *v* (se) sunbathe, sun oneself

sunovrat *nm* daffodil **~iti** *v* (se) plunge

suoč|iti *v* 1 (se s kim/čim) face/confront sb/sth 2 (koga s kim/čim) confront, bring face to face **~avati** *v* *impf*

suoptuženi|k *nm* (*Vsg* ~če, *Npl* ~ci) codefendant

suosjećaja|n *adj* (a) sympathetic, compassionate **~ti** *v* (s kim) sympathyze

sup *nm* vulture **bjeloglavi ~** griffon

suparni|k *nm* (*Vsg* ~če, *Npl* ~ci) rival; adversary **~štvo** *nn* rivalry

supatni|k *nm* (*Vsg* ~če, *Npl* ~ci) fellow sufferer

superioran *adj* (a) superior

superlativ *nm* superlative

superoksid *nm* peroxide

supotpi|s *nm* countersignature **~sati** *v* (što) (*pres* ~šem) co-sign, countersign **~snik** *nm* (*Npl* ~snici) countersignatory

suprot|an *adj* (a) contrary (to), opposite **~no** *adv* 1 contrary 2 on the contrary **~nost** *nf* opposite **~staviti** *v* 1 (se komu/čemu) oppose 2 (koga komu; što čemu) pit sb against sb **~stavljati** *v* *impf*

supru|g *nm* (*Npl* ~zi) spouse, husband **~ga** *nf* (*Dsg* ~zi) spouse, wife **~žnici** *n pl* husband and wife

suptilan *adj* (a) subtle

suputni|k *nm* (*Npl* ~ci) 1 (u istom prometalu) passenger 2 travelling companion

sura|dnik *nm* (*Vsg* ~dniče, *Npl* ~dnici) associate, colleague **~dnja** *nf* collaboration, co-operation **~đivati** *v* (s kim) collaborate, cooperate, work (together)

surla *nf* trunk

surogat *nm* surrogate

surov *adj* cruel, brutal **~ost** *nm* brutality

surutka *nf* whey

survati *v* (se) plunge

susjed *nm* neigbour ~**an** *adj* (*α*) neighbouring, adjacent ~**stvo** *nn* neighbourhood

susnježica *nf* sleet

suspendirati *v* (koga) suspend

suspre|gnuti *v* (što/se) (*pres* ~gnem) hold back, restrain ~**zati** *v impf*

susre|sti *v* (koga/što/se) (*pres* ~tnem) meet ~**t** *nm* encounter **izaći u** ~**t** oblige sb ~**tati** *v impf* ~**tljiv** *adj* helpful, co-operative

susta|jati *v* (0) (*pres* ~nem) lose steam/energy/momentum, abate

sustanar *nm* flatmate, co-tenant

sustav *nm* system ~**an** *adj* systematic

suste|gnuti *v* (*pres* ~gnem) 1 (kome što) withold, deduct 2 (se) refrain ~**zati** *v impf* ~**zljiv** *adj* reserved

susti|ći *v* (koga/što) (*pres* ~gnem) catch up with

suš|a *nf* drought ~**an** *adj* dry ~**ica** *nf* tuberculosis, consumption ~**ičav** *adj* consumptive ~**iti** *v* 1 (što) dry; (meso) cure 2 (se) dry up ~**ilo** *nn* dryer

suština *nf coll* essence

suteren *nm* basement

suton *nm* dusk

sutra *adv* tomorrow ~**dan** *adv* the following day ~**šnji** *adj* tomorrow's ~**šnjica** *nf* the future, tomorrow

suučesni|k *nm* (*Npl* ~ci) leg accomplice

suvenir *nm* souvenir

suveren *adj* sovereign • *nm* sovereign

suvisli *adj* coherent, logical, lucid

suviš|ak *nm* (*Gsg* ~ka, *Npl* ~ci) surplus, excess ~**an** *adj* (*α*) superfluous, excess ~**e** *adv* too much, excessively

suvlasni|k *nm* (*Npl* ~ci) joint owner

suvozač *nm* 1 co-driver 2 passenger

suvremen *adj* modern, contemporary ~**ik** *nm* (*Vsg* ~iče, *Npl* ~iče) contemporary

suz|a *nf* tear ~**an** *adj* (*α*) tearful ~**avac** *nm* (*Gsg* ~avca) tear gas, CS gas ~**iti** *v* (0) water

suzbi|ti *v* (što) curb, have/put under control ~**jati** *v impf*

suzdrž|ati *v* 1 (koga) restrain, curb 2 (se) restrain oneself ~**ljiv** *adj* reticent

suziti *v* (2) 1 (što) narrow; (odjeću) take in 2 (se) become narrow(er); (odjeća) shrink

suž|anj *nm* (*Gsg* ~nja) slave, prisoner ~**anjstvo** *nn* captivity, bondage

sužavati *v impf* → **suziti**

Sv. (Sveti) abbrev. St. (Saint)

svačiji *adj* everybody's

svadb|a *nf* wedding ~**eni** *adj* marriage, wedding

sva|diti *v* (se) quarrel ~**dljiv** *adj* quarrelsome ~**đa** *nf* quarrel

svagda *adv* always **jednom za** ~ once and for all ~**šnji** *adj* daily

svak *pron* everybody ~**akav** *adj* (*α*) of all sorts ~**ako** *adv* by all means ~**i** *adj* every; each; (bilo koji) any ~**odnevica** *nf* daily life, everyday life ~**odnevni** *adj* daily

svali|ti *v* 1 (što) shift ~ **krivnju na drugoga** lay/put the blame on sb else 2 (se) drop, flop (down)

svan|uće *nn* daybreak, dawn ~**uti** *v* (0) (*pres* ~em) dawn

svastika (1) *nf* swastika

svasti|ka (2) *nf* (*Dsg* ~ci) mother-in-law

svašta *pron* (*Gsg* svačega) everything, various things ~! *int iron* well, I never! ~**r** *nm* 1 junk dealer 2 Jack-of-all-trades 3 eclectic

svat *nm* 1 *arch* wedding guest 2 fellow ~**ovi** *n pl* wedding (party)

svatko *pron* (*Gsg* svakoga) everybody, everyone

sve *adj* everything, all

svečan *adj* 1 festive 2 formal, ceremonial ~**ost** *nf* celebration, ceremony

svećen|ik *nm* (*Vsg* ~iče, *Npl* ~ici) priest, clergyman ~**stvo** *nn* clergy

svejedno *adv* still ~ **mi je** it is all the same to me, it makes no difference

svek|ar *nm* (*Gsg* ~ra) father-in-law ~**rva** *nf* mother-in-law

svemir *nm* (outer) space, universe ~**ski** *adj* space

svemoć *nf* omnipotence ~**an** *adj* (*α*) omnipotent, all-powerful

svemoguć *adj* almighty **S~i** *nm* the Almighty

sveobuhvatan *adj* (*α*) comprehensive

sveopći *adj* general, universal

svesrd|an *adj* (*α*) wholehearted ~**na**

pomoć willing help

svesti v (pres svedem) 1 (što na što) reduce sth to sth 2 (se na što) boil down to

svestran adj versatile, all-round

svet adj holy; sacred S~o pismo (Holy) Scripture S~i Ivan Saint/St. John ~ac nm (Gsg sveca, Vsg sveče) 1 saint 2 (dan) holiday, feast ~ac zaštitnik patron saint ~ački adj saintly ~ak nm (Gsg ~ka, Npl sveci) holiday, feast ~ica nf saint ~inja nf sacred thing ~ište nn sanctuary, shrine ~kovati v (što) (pres ~kujem) celebrate; observe (a holiday) ~kovina nf feast ~ogrđe nn sacrilege ~ohranište nn tabernacle ~ost nn holiness

sveučiliš|ni adj university ~te nn university

sveukupan adj (a) total, complete, overall

Svevišnji adj, n (the) Almighty

sve|za nf connection; association u ~zi (s čim) in relation to sth, as regards sth, concerning/regarding sth ~zak nm (Gsg ~ska, Npl ~sci) volume ~zati v (koga/što) (pres ~žem) tie (up)

svezna|jući adj omniscient ~lica nm/f know-it-all; smartarse coll tab

svež|anj nm (Gsg ~nja) bundle

svib|anj nm (Gsg ~nja) May

svi|djeti v (se komu) (pres ~dim) please, charm ~đati v impf on mi se ~đa I like him

svijati v impf → svinuti

svijeć|a nf candle ~njak nm (Npl ~njaci) candlestick

svijest nf consciousness (+ fig); awareness fig izgubiti ~ lose c. stvoriti ~ o problemu raise c./a. of the problem

svijet nm (Npl svjetovi) 1 the world iz cijelog ~a from all over the world na cijelom ~u world-wide, around the world 2 crowd, people

svijet|ao adj (~la f) bright, light ~liti v (0) shine, give light ~ložut adj light yellow

svil|a nf silk zubna ~a dental floss ~en adj silk, silken ~enkast adj silky

svin|uti v (što/se) (pres ~em) twist, bend

svinj|a nf pig; hog US; swine divlja ~a wild boar ~ac nm (Gsg ~ca) pigsty (+ fig) ~ar nm swineherd ~arija nf disgrace ~etina nf pork ~ski adj 1 pig 2 pork

svir|ač nm musician, player ~ala nf flute, pipe na vrbi ~ala pie in the sky ~ati v (0/što) play ~ka nf music

svisoka adv condescendingly gledati koga ~ patronize sb

svisn|uti v (0) (pres ~em) die of sorrow

Svi sveti nm All Saints' Day, All Hallows' Day

svita nf suite, retinue, entourage

svi|tak nm (Gsg ~tka, Npl ~ci) scroll

svi|tati v (0) (pres III sg ~će) dawn

svjećica nf 1 (small) candle 2 mot spark plug

svjedo|čanstvo nn testimony ~čiti v (0) testify, give evidence, bear witness ~džba nf certificate ~k nm (Npl ~ci) witness

svjes|tan adj (~na f) 1 (pri svijesti) conscious 2 aware

svjet|iljka nf lamp džepna ~iljka torch; flashlight US ~ionik nm (Npl ~onici) lighthouse ~lati v (što) polish, shine ~losni adj light ~lost nf light ~lucati v (se) glitter ~lucav adj glittering

svjetina nf mob, rabble

svjet|ovni adj secular, lay ~ski adj world, global ~ski čovjek fig man of the world. ~ski rat World War 1, the 1st World War

svjež adj fresh ~ina nf freshness

svlači|onica nf locker room ~ti v impf → svući

svlada|ti v 1 (koga/što) overpower, overcome 2 (se) restrain oneself 3 (što) master ~vati v impf

svod nm vault, arch nebeski ~ the firmament

svodni|k nm (Vsg ~če, Npl ~ci) pimp

svoditi v impf → svesti

svoj pron one's own, personal uzmi ~u knjigu take your book pozvao je svoje ljude he called his men biti ~ na svome be one's own master ~atati v (koga/što) claim, usurp ~**edobno** *adv* at one time ~**eglav** *adj* stubborn ~**evoljan** *adj* 1 capricious 2 voluntary ~**evremeno** *adv* at one time ~**ski** *adj* with all one's might ~**stven** *adj* peculiar ~**stvo** *nn* 1 property 2 capacity

svota *nf* sum

svrab *nm* scabies

svraka *nf* magpie

svra|tište *nn* inn ~**titi** *v* 1 (kamo) pay a visit to, drop by 2 (što) divert ~**titi** (čiju) **pozornost** draw sb's attention ~**ćati** *v iter*

svrb|ež *nm* itching ~**jeti** *v* (0) (*pres* ~im) itch ~**e ga tabani** his feet are itching ~**i ga jezik** he is dying to spill his guts

svrdlo *nn* gimlet, drill

svrgn|uti *v* (koga) (*pres* ~em) depose, remove from power, oust

svr|ha *nf* purpose, goal ~**sishodan** *adj* (*a*) appropriate, suitable

svrsta|ti *v* 1 (koga/što u/među koga/što) classify sb/sth with sb/sth 2 (se) line up 3 (se u/među koga/što) be classified/ranked among ~**vati** *v impf*

svrš|iti *v* 1 (što) finish 2 (0) *coll* come *coll*, reach an orgasm ~**avati** *v impf* ~**etak** *nm* (*Gsg* ~etka, *Npl* ~eci) end, conclusion

svu|ći *v* (*pres* ~čem) 1 (što) take/pull sth off 2 (koga/se) undress

svuda *adv* everywhere

svugdje *adv* everywhere

Š

Š, š 25th letter of Cro. alphabet

š-š-š *int* (s)sh, shush

šablon|a *nf* 1 stencil 2 *fig* pattern, model; routine **~izirati** *v* (što) stereotype **~ski** *adj* mechanically, routinely

šačica *nf* 1 *dim* → **šaka** 2 handful

šafran *nm* saffron, crocus

šah *nm* 1 (igra) chess 2 (upozorenje) check **~-mat** checkmate 3 (vladar) shah **~ist** *nm* chess player **~ovnica** *nf* 1 chessboard 2 *coll* Croatian coat of arms **~ovski** *adj* chess **~ovske figure** chessmen

šak|a *nf (Dsg* šaci) 1 hand 2 (stisnuta) fist 3 *fig* handful **~a u oko** eyesore **~om i kapom** open-handedly **ako/kad mi dopadne ~a** if/when I lay my hands on him/her **imati (koga) u šaci** have (sb) in one's pocket **~ač** *nm* boxer **~anje** *nn* boxing **~ati** *v* (se) box

šakal *nm* jackal

šal *nm (Npl* šalovi) scarf; shawl

šal|a *nf* joke; trick; jest; fun **~u na stranu** joking aside, seriously **kao od ~e** standing on one's head, easily **odnio je vrag ~u** things have become serious **~iti** *v* (se) 1 joke, kid; play tricks 2 (s čime) be flippant about sth

šalabahter *nm sl* crib notes

šalica *nf* cup; mug

šalter *nm coll* 1 counter, desk 2 switch

šaljiv *adj* funny, humorous **~ac** *nm (Gsg* ~ca, *Npl* ~vci), **~čina** *nm* joker

šamar *nm* → **pljuska**

šampanj|ac *nm (Gsg* ~ca, *Gpl* ~aca) champagne

šampinjon *nm* mushroom

šampion *nm* champion **~at** *nm* championship

šampon *nm* shampoo

šank *nm* bar, counter

šansa *nf* chance

šapa *nf* paw

šap|at *nm* whisper **dramski ~at** stage whisper **~(a)tom** *adv* in a whisper **~nuti** *v* (što komu) whisper (sth to sb) **~tač** *nm* prompter **~taonica** *nf* prompt box **~tati** *v impf* **~utati** *v impf*

šapirograf *nm* duplicator; mimeograph *US*

šar|a *nf* line, pattern; marking **~ac** *nm (Gsg* ~ca, *Gpl* ~aca) dappled horse **~ati** *v* (0) 1 draw lines/figures, doodle 2 (u braku) *sl* play around with other women **~en** *adj* 1 colourful; patterned; multicoloured 2 (životinja) dappled, mottled, speckled **~enilo** *nn* 1 colourfulness 2 *fig* variety, diversity, medley **~eniti** *v* (se) be colourful; display a wide range of colours

šarada *nf* charade

šaraf *nm coll* → **vijak ~iti** *v* 1 (što) *coll* screw 2 (koga) *sl* put the screws on sb

šaran *nm* carp

šarenica *nf* iris

šarka *nf* hinge

šarlah *nm* scarlet fever

šarlatan *nm* charlatan, quack

šarm *nm* charm, attraction **~antan** *adj* (*a*) charming, attractive **~irati** *v* (koga) charm

šarolik *adj* motley; diverse **~ost** *nf* diversity

šaržer *nm* clip

šasija *nf* chassis

šaš *nm (Npl* ~evi) sedge

šašav *adj* daft, silly, crazy

šator *nm* tent **postaviti ~** pitch a tent

šatr|a *nf* slang **~ovački** *adj* slang

šav *nm (Npl* ~ovi) 1 seam 2 stitch

ščepati *v* (što/koga) grab, get hold of, snatch

šćućuriti *v* (se) shrink, cower; snuggle up

šećer *nm* sugar **kristal ~** granulated s. **~ u prahu** caster s. **piješ li kavu/čaj** *sa* **~om**? do you take sugar (in your coffee/tea)? **~ana** *nf* sugar refinery **~aš** *nm coll* diabetic **~iti** *v* (što) sugar, put s. in sth **~ni** *adj* sugar **~na bolest** diabetes

šef *nm* (*Npl* ~ovi) boss; manager, chief, head **~ovati** *v* (0/komu) *coll* 1 be (the) boss 2 (ponašanje) boss sb around **~ovski** *adj* boss's

šegrt *nm* apprentice

šenuti *v* (0) *coll* go crazy

šepa|ti *v* (0) *coll* 1 limp 2 be weak in/at sth **~v** *adj* lame

šepuriti *v* (se) strut

šeprtlja *nm/f* bungler, fumble-foot **~ti** *v* (0) fumble, bungle **~v** *adj* clumsy; awkward

šesnaest *num* sixteen (16) **~erac** *nm* (*Gsg* ~erca) *sport* penalty area/box

šest *num* six (6) **~erokut** *nm* hexagon **~i** *num ord* sixth **~orica** *nf* six men **~ina** *nf* sixth

šestar *nm* compasses *pl*

šešir *nm* hat

šet|ač *nm* walker **~alica** *nf* pendulum **~alište** *nn* promenade **~ati** *v* (0/se) walk, go for a walk, stroll **~nja** *nf* walk, stroll

ševa (1) *nf* (sky)lark

šev|a (2) *nf sl vulg* screw **~iti** *v* (koga/se) *sl vulg* screw

šezdeset *num* sixty (60) **~i** *num ord* sixtieth

šib|a *nf* cane, rod **~alo** *nn* lash, whip **~ati** *v* 1 (koga/što) lash, flog 2 (0) belt along **~ica** *nf* 1 *dim* → **šiba** 2 match **~lje** *nn* brush(wood) **~nuti** *v pf*

šic *int* shoo

šifon *nm* chiffon

šifr|a *nf* code **~irati** *v* (što) code

šihta *nf coll* shift

šija *nf* scruff (of the neck)

šik *adj* chic

šikanirati *v* (koga) harass

šikara *nf* thicket

šik|ljati *v* (0) gush, spout, spurt **~nuti** *v pf*

šilo *nn* awl **~ za ognjilo** tit for tat

šilt *nm coll* peak (of a cap)

šilj|ak *nm* (*Gsg* ~ka, *Npl* ~ci) point, sharp end, spike **~ast** *adj* pointed **~ilo** *nn* pencil sharpener **~iti** *v* (što) sharpen

šindra *nf* shingle(s)

šip|ak *nm* (*Gsg* ~ka, *Npl* ~ci) 1 (rose)hip 2 (nar) pomegranate 3 *sl* (sweet) fanny adams, nothing **~kov** *adj* (rose)hip

šipka *nf* bar, crowbar, pole, stick

šipražje *nn* thicket

šir|ina *nf* width, breadth **zemljopisna ~ina** latitude **~itelj** *nm* propagator **~iti** *v* 1 (što) spread; disseminate; propagate 2 (se) spread; gain ground **~ok** *adj* (*comp* širi) wide; broad **~okogrudan** *adj* (*a*) broad-minded **~om** *adv* wide

šišarka *nf* pinecone

šiša|ti *v* 1 (što) cut 2 (koga) cut sb's hair 3 (se) have one's hair cut, have a haircut **tko te ~** *sl vulg* screw you

šiške *nf pl* fringe *GB*, bangs *US*

šišmiš *nm* bat

šištati *v* (0) hiss

šiti *v* (*pres* šijem), **šivati** *v* (*pres* šivam) sew **šivaći** *adj* **stroj** sewing machine

šiziti *v* (0) *coll* 1 have a fit, flip (the lid), rage 2 (za kim) be crazy about sb

šizma *nf* schism

šizofreni|ja *nf* schizophrenia **~čar** *nm* schizophrenic

šjor *nm coll dial* mister

škaf *nm* pail

škakljati *v* (koga) tickle **~iv** *adj* ticklish (+ *fig*)

škalja *nf* gravel

škampi *nm pl* scampi

škare *nf pl* scissors

škarpina *nf* scorpion fish

škart *nm* reject **~irati** *v* (što) reject

škiljiti *v* (0) squint

škljoc *int* click **~aj** *nm* click **~ati** *v* (0) click

škod|iti *v* (0/komu/čemu) harm, do harm, damage **~ljiv** *adj* harmful

školļa *nf* school **u ~i** at s. **osnovna ~**
primary s. *GB*, elementary s. *US*
srednja ~ secondary s. *GB*, high s.
US **~arac** *nm* (*Gsg* **~arca**) school
child **~arina** *nf* tuition fee **~ica** *nf* 1
dim → **škola** 2 (igra) hopscotch
~ovati *v* (koga) educate, school, put
through school **~ski** *adj* school **~stvo**
nn education

školjka *nf* 1 shell 2 (ušna) auricle 3
(WC) toilet bowl **~š** *nm* crustacean

škopiti *v* (koga) geld, castrate

škorpion *nm* 1 scorpion 2 *astrol*
Scorpio

škrabati *v* (0/što) scribble

škrabica *nf* collection box

škrapa *nf* escarpment, scarp

škrba *nf* missing/broken tooth, stump
~v *adj* with one's teeth missing, gap-
toothed

škrebetaljka *nf* (zvečka) rattle

škrge *nf pl* gills

škrgut *nm* gnashing/grinding of teeth
~ati *v* (0/čime) gnash/grind one's
teeth

škriljļac *nm* (*Gsg* **~ca**) slate

škrinja *nf* 1 chest, trunk 2 *coll* chest
freezer

škripļa *nf* creak(ing) **~av** *adj* creaky
~iti *v* (0) creak **~nuti** *v pf*

škripļac *nm* (*Gsg* **~ca**) 1 vice 2 *fig*
tight corner/spot

škrob *nm* starch **~iti** *v* starch

škropiļonica *nf* font **~ti** *v* sprinkle

škrt *adj* mean, stingy, tight(fisted),
niggardly **~ac** *nm*, **~ica** *nm/f* miser,
niggard; skinflint *coll* **~ariti** *v* (0)
skimp; be stingy **~ost** *nf* stinginess,
meanness

škvadra *nf sl* 1 gang, crowd, posse 2
people, folks

šlag *n coll* 1 cream 2 stroke

šlager *nm* pop/hit song

šlajer *nm coll* veil

šlampav *adj coll* sloppy

šlapa *nf coll* slipper **prost kao ~** common, vulgar

šlep *nm coll* 1 barge 2 (haljine) train
~ati *v coll* (koga/što) tow, haul, tug
~er *nm coll* 1 tug(boat) 2 articulated
lorry *GB*; semi *US*

šlic *nm coll* 1 (raspor) slit 2 (na hlača-

ma) fly

šlif *nm coll* refinement, breeding

šljakļa *nf* 1 slag 2 *sl* graft, work **~ati** *v*
(0) *sl* graft, work **~er** *nm* worker

šljam *nm coll* scum

šljapkati *v* (0) squelch, squish

šljem *nm* → **kaciga**

šljivļa (1) *nf* 1 plum **suha ~a** prune 2
plum tree 3 *sl* black eye **~arstvo** *nn*
plum growing **~ik** *nm* (*Npl* **~ici**)
plum orchard **~iti** *v* (koga) *sl* give a
damn about sb **~ovica** *nf* slivovitz,
plum brandy

šljiva (2) *nf sl* freezing cold

šljokati *v* (što) *sl* guzzle, swig, swill,
booze

šljokica *nf* spangle, sequin

šljuka *nf* woodcock

šljunļak *nm* (*Gsg* **~ka**) gravel, pebbles
pl **~čan** *adj* gravelled, pebbly

šminkļa *nf* make-up **~ati** *v* 1 (koga)
make up 2 (se) put on make-up **~er**
nm 1 *film, theat, TV* make-up artist 2
coll trendy **~erski** *adj* trendy

šmirgl *nm coll* **~ papir** sandpaper

šmokljan *nm* dickhead *GB*; jerk,
schmuck *US*

šmrcati *v* (0) sniff, sniffle

šmrk *nm* (*Npl* **~ovi**) *coll* hose(pipe)

šmrkļalj *nm* (*Gsg* **~lja**, *Gpl* **~alja**) snot
~ati *v* (0) sniff **~nuti** *v pf*

šmugnuti *v* (0) sneak out, slip out

šnicla *nf coll* → **odrezak**

šofer *nm coll* → **vozač**

šogor *nm* brother-in-law **~ica** *nf* sister-in-law

šojka *nf* jay

šok *nm* shock **u ~u** in a state of shock
~irati *v* 1 (koga) shock 2 (se) be
shocked

šonjo *nm* sissy, wimp

šovinļist *nm* chauvinist; (nacionalni)
jingoist **~istički** *adj* chauvinist; jin-
goistic **~izam** *nm* (*Gsg* **~izma**) chauvinism; jingoism

špagļa *nf coll* string, cord **~erice** *nf pl*
espadrilles

špageti *nm pl* spaghetti

špajza *nf coll* larder, pantry

španga *nf coll* hairpin

šparoga *nf* asparagus

špeceraj *nm coll* groceries

špediter *nm coll* haul(i)er

špekula *nf coll* marble

špekul|acija *nf* speculation ~**ant** *nm* speculator ~**irati** *v* (0) speculate

šperploča *nf* plywood

špica (1) *nf* (koštica) stone; pip

špi|ca (2) *nf coll* 1 (šiljak) point 2 rush hour 3 (filmska) credits 4 (glazbena) signature tune 5 (sezone) peak ~**cast**, ~**čast** *adj* pointed

špijun *nm* spy ~**aža** *nf* espionage ~**irati** *v* (koga) spy (on sb) ~**ka** *nf* 1 (žena) spy 2 (na vratima) peephole ~**ski** *adj* spy

špil *nm coll* deck (of cards)

špilja *nf* cave

špinat *nm* spinach

špinčiti *v* (se) *sl* show off, flaunt, brag

špirit *nm* (methylated) spirits *pl*, meths *coll*

šport *nm* sport(s) ~**aš** *nm* sportsman, athlete

špotati *v* (koga) *coll* scold

špranja *nf coll* splinter

šprica *nf* syringe

špricer *nm* spritzer **hladan kao ~** cool as a cucumber

šrapnel *nm* shrapnel

štab *nm* 1 general staff 2 (stožer) headquarters **krizni ~** crisis centre

štafelaj *nm coll* easel

štafeta *nf* 1 (palica) baton 2 (utrka) relay race

štagalj *nm* barn, shed

štaka *nf* crutch

štakor *nm* rat ~**ski** *adj* rat-like, rat's

štal|a *nf coll* stable; cowshed ~**ica** *nf coll* Nativity scene/set

štambilj *nm coll* stamp

štampa *nf* → **tisak žuta ~** yellow journalism, gutter press

štancati *v* (što) *coll* 1 churn out 2 (voznu kartu) punch

štand *nm* stand, stall

štap *nm* stick, cane; staff; (biljarski) cue **ne bih ga ni ~om** I wouldn't touch him with a barge pole/ten-foot pole **spasti na prosjački ~** go bankrupt, lose everything ~**ić** *nm* 1 (dirigentski) baton 2 (za grickanje) pretzel **čarobni ~ić** magic wand **sladoled na ~iću** ice lolly; popsicle

štavi|lo *nn* tannin ~**ti** *v* (što) tan

šted|ionica *nf* savings bank ~**jeti** *v* (pres ~**im**) 1 (što) save 2 (koga) spare 3 (se) spare oneself ~**ljiv** *adj* thrifty, economical ~**ni** *adj* savings ~**nja** *nf* saving

štednjak *nm* (Npl ~**njaci**) cooker; stove US

štek|tati *v* (pres ~**ćem**) (0) yap, yelp

šten|ara *nf* kennel ~**e** *nn* puppy

štet|a *nf* 1 damage **nanijeti ~u** inflict damage (up)on 2 pity ~**an** *adj* (a) harmful ~**iti** *v* (0/komu/čemu) damage, harm, be bad (for sth/sb) ~**očinja** *nm/f* pest

štićeni|k *nm* (Npl ~**ci**) ward; protege

štihača *nf coll* spade

štih-proba *nf coll* spot check

štikla *nf coll* (high) heel

štimung *nm coll* mood, atmosphere

štip|aljka *nf* 1 (za rublje) peg 2 (raka) claw ~**ati** *v* (koga) pinch; nip ~**avac** *nm* scorpion ~**nuti** *v pf*

štir|ak *nm* (~**ka** *nf*) starch ~**kati** *v* (što) starch

štit *nm* shield ~**iti** *v* (koga/što/se) protect (oneself); shield, screen ~**na** *adj* **žlijezda** (~**njača** *nf*) thyroid gland ~**nik** *nm* (Npl ~**nici**) screen; visor ~**onoša** *nm* shield bearer, esquire

štivo *nn* reading matter, text

što *pron* (G **čega**, D **čemu**, A **što**, I **čime**) 1 what 2 which; who; that 3 something; anything 4 **~ prije** as soon as possible **~ prije, to bolje** the sooner the better 5 since **~ god** whatever ~**god** *pron* something ~**kavski** *adj* štokavian ~**šta** *pron* all sorts of things ~**više** *adv* what's more, moreover, furthermore, indeed

štof *nm coll* cloth, fabric

štok *nm coll* jamb

štop|ati *v* (što) *coll* 1 (vrijeme) time 2 (čarape) mend ~**erica** *nf* stopwatch

štos *nm coll* 1 trick, joke 2 pile, heap, stack

štova|telj *nm* admirer, lover ~**ti** *v* (koga/što) respect, admire, honour, hold in high esteem **Š~ni gospodine/gospođo** Dear Sir/Madam ~**nje** *nn* respect (**bilježim se**) **sa ~njem**

Yours Sincerely/Faithfully/ Truly

štrajk *nm* strike ~ **glađu** hunger strike ~**ač** *nm* striker ~**ački** *adj* strikers' ~**ačka** *adj* picket ~**ati** *v* (0) strike, go/be on strike ~**olomac** *nm* strikebreaker; blackleg, scab *coll*

štrapac *nm coll* exertion, effort

štrc|aljka *nf* sprinkler, sprayer ~**ati** *v* squirt ~**nuti** *v pf*

štreb|ati *v* (što) *sl* swot (up) *GB*, grind *US* ~**er** *nm* swot, grind; nerd

štrik *nm coll* rope, line

štrkljast *adj* lanky

štropot *nm* clatter, rumble

štrudl *nm coll* strudel

štuc|ati (1) *v* (0) hiccup, hiccough, have hiccups ~**avica** *nf* hiccups

štucati (2) *v* (što) trim, clip, prune

štuka *nf* pike

štula *nf coll* stilt

štur *adj* meagre, sparse, scanty

šubara *nf* fur cap

šuga *nf* mange ~**v** *adj* mangy

šuknut *adj coll* daft, gaga, batty

šuljati *v* (se) sneak, slink

šuljevi *nm pl* piles

šum *nm* **1** noise **2** (šuštanje) rustle **3** (vode) murmur ~ **na srcu** heart murmur ~**an** *adj* (a) noisy ~**iti** *v* (0) **1** (lišće) rustle **2** (radio) crackle ~**i mi u ušima** my ears are buzzing

šum|a *nf* forest (+ *fig*), woods ~**ar** *nm* forester ~**arak** *nm* (*Gsg* ~arka, *Npl* ~arci) grove ~**arski** *adj* forestry ~**arstvo** *nn* forestry ~**ovit** *adj* wooded ~**ski** *adj* forest

šund *nm* trash • *adj* pulp

šunka *nf* ham

šunjati *v* (se) sneak

šupa *nf* shed

šup|ak *nm* (*Gsg* ~ka, *Npl* ~ci) *vulg tab* asshole

šup|alj *adj* (a) hollow, empty ~**ljikav** *adj* porous ~**ljina** *nf* cavity

šupiti *v* (koga) *coll* hit, slap

šurja|k *nm* (*Npl* ~ci) brother-in-law ~**kinja** *nf* sister-in-law

šurovati *v* (0/s kim) plot, conspire, be in cahoots (with)

šuša *nf* svaka ~ any fool

šuš|anj *nm* rustle, noise ~**kati** *v* **1** (0/čime) rustle **2** (što) rumour ~**nuti** *v pf* što je to ~nulo? what was that noise? ~**tati** *v* (*pres* ~tim) (0) rustle

šut *nm coll* shot, kick ~**irati** *v* (što) kick ~**nuti** *v pf*

šuta *nf coll* rubble

šut|jeti *v* (*pres* ~im) (0) be/keep silent/quiet, say nothing, hold one's tongue ~**ljiv** *adj* quiet ~**nja** *nf* silence, quiet, hush

Švabo *nm coll* Kraut, Jerry

švedsk|e *adj* ~ **ljestve** wall bars ~**i stol** buffet

švelja *nf* seamstress

šverc *nm* black marketeering; smuggling ~**ati** *v* **1** (što) smuggle **2** (se) fare-dodge ~**er** *nm* **1** black marketeer; spiv *GB coll* **2** smuggler **3** (u prijevozu) fare dodger

švig|nuti *v* (0/čime) crack (a whip) ~**alo** *nn* lash

švorc *adj sl* broke, skint

švrljati *v* (0) loiter, roam (around)

T

T, t (te) 26th letter of Cro. alphabet

ta *pron* → **taj**

taban *nm* sole (of the foot) **imati ravne ~e** have flat feet, be flat-footed

tabati *v* (što) stamp (down), tread

tabelaran *adj* (*a*) tabular

tabernakul *nm* tabernacle

tablica *nf* table; chart

tabloid *nm* tabloid

tabor *nm* camp (+ *fig*), encampment **~ište** *nn* campsite

tabu *nm* (*Npl* ~i) taboo **~ tema** taboo subject

tač|ke *nf pl* (*G* ~aka/~ki) (wheel)barrow

tad(a) *adv* 1 then, at that/the time 2 afterwards, next, thereupon **~ašnji** *adv* the then, of that time

taj (ta, to) *dem pron* (*Gsg* toga (te), *Dsg* tomu/tome (toj), *Isg* tim (tom), *Npl* ti (te, ta), *Gpl* tih, *Dpl* tima) this (one/here), that (one) *ja sam taj* I am the one *toga i toga dana* on such and such a day **pored toga (uz to, k tome)** besides, in addition (to that)

taj|lac *nm* (*Gsg* ~ca) hush, silence

tajanstven *adj* 1 mysterious; enigmatic 2 secretive; hush-hush *coll*

tajfun *nm* typhoon

taj|iti *v* (što) keep secret/dark, hide, conceal, suppress **~na** *nf* 1 secret 2 mystery **javna ~na** open secret **~ni** *adj* 1 secret; clandestine 2 hidden, concealed **~nik** *nm* (*Vsg* ~niče, *Npl* ~nici) secretary **glavni ~nik** secretary-general **~nica** *nf* secretary **~ništvo** *nn* secretary's office **~nost** *nf* secrecy **~novit** → **tajanstven**

tak|av (takva, takvo) *adj* such (a), of such kind/sort; such as this, that kind/sort of, like that **~av kakav** such as

takmičar → **natjecatelj**

takn|uti *v* (koga/što) (pres ~em) touch (+ *fig*)

tako *adv* 1 in such a way, in this/that way/manner, thus 2 so **~ da** so (that) **(isto) tako ... kao** as ... as **ne tako ... kao** not so ... as **i ~ dalje** and so on/forth **~ reći** so to speak **~ ~** so-so, middling **~ je!** that's right **~ mu i treba** serves him right **~ mi Boga** by God

također *adv* also, too, as well; besides, likewise

takozvani *adj* so-called

taksa *nf coll* stamp duty/tax; duty; tax; fee; toll

taksi *nm* taxi, cab **~st** *nm* taxi driver; cabby *coll*

takt (1) *nm* time, measure; beat; rhythm, tempo **davati/udarati ~** beat time

takt (2) *nm* tact **imati ~a** have/show tact **izbaciti iz ~a** upset, make sb lose their temper **~ičan** *adj* (*a*) atactful **~ički** *adj* tactical **~ika** *nf* tactics *pl;* ploy, tack **~ika odugovlačenja** delaying/stalling tactic **~izirati** *v* (0) temporize; manoeuvre

tal|ac *nm* (*Gsg* ~oca, *Npl* ~oci) hostage

talent *nm* talent **~iran** *adj* talented, gifted

tali|onica *nf* foundry, smelting works **~šte** *nn* melting point **~ti** *v* 1 (što) smelt 2 (se) fuse, melt

talo|g *nm* sediment; dregs, grounds *pl* **~žiti** *v* 1 (što) deposit 2 (se) settle, be deposited

tama *nf* dark(ness); gloom

taman (1) *adj* (*a*) dark; gloomy

taman (2) *adv coll* 1 just 2 just right 3 even if **~ posla!** no way!

tamaniti *v* 1 (koga/što) exterminate 2

(**što**) *coll* devour, eat up

tamjan *nm* (frank)incense

tamni|ca *nf* dungeon, prison **~čar** *nm* jailer; gaoler *GB*

tam|niti *v* (**što**) darken, obscure **~noprefix** dark **~njeti** *v* (0) (*pres* ~nim) 1 darken, get dark/dim 2 (srebro) tarnish 3 *fig* fade, lose lustre

tamo *adv* there, in that direction ~ **prijeko** over there **amo** ~ to and fro, back and forth **tu i** ~ **a.** here and there **b.** sometimes, now and then/again **~šnji** *adv* of that place, local

tampon *nm* tampon ~ **država/zona** buffer state/zone

tan|ak *adj* (*α*) (*comp* tanji) thin **~ko crijevo** small intestine **~an** *adj* 1 thin 2 delicate, subtle **u ~čine** *nf pl* in detail

tandr|kati *v* (0) (*pres* ~čem) clatter; rattle (along), rumble

tanker *nm* tanker

tankoćutan *adj* (*α*) sensitive, susceptible

tanjiti *v* 1 (**što**) (make) thin 2 (se) get thin; taper off

tanjur *nm* plate **duboki** ~ soup plate **plitki** ~ dinner plate **leteći** ~ flying saucer **na ~u** *fig* on a plate **~ić** *nm dim* saucer

tape|cirati *v* (**što**) *coll* upholster **~cirung** *nm coll* upholstery **~ta** *nf* wallpaper **~tar** *nm* 1 upholsterer 2 paperhanger

tapirati *v* (**što/se**) backcomb (one's hair)

tapiserija *nf* tapestry

tapkati *v* (0) patter; grope/feel one's way

tapš|ati *v* (**koga**) (*pres* ~em) pat (on the back), tap (on the shoulder)

tara *nf comm* tare

tarifa *nf* rate, tariff

tartuf *nm* truffle

tast *nm* father-in-law

tastatura *nf* keyboard

tašt *adj* vain, conceited **~ina** *nf* vanity, conceit

tata *nm* dad(dy), pa; pop(pa) *US coll*

tava *nf* frying pan; skillet *US*

tavan *nm* attic, loft **~ica** *nf* roof beam

~ski *adj* attic **~ski prozor** skylight **~ska soba** garret

tavoriti *v* (0) live miserably, eke out a living

te *conj* 1 and; also, as well 2 so (that), and so **jedno** ~ **isto** always the same, one and the same thing

teat|ar *nm* (*Gsg* ~ra) → **kazalište ~ralan** *adj* (*α*) theatrical

tebe, **te** *pron* (*Gsg/Asg*) → **ti**

tečaj *nm* 1 course 2 *econ* rate; exchange rate, rate of exchange

teč|an *adj* (*α*) 1 fluent 2 tasty, savoury, appetizing **~nost** *nf* fluency

tečevina *nf* heritage, inheritance

te|ći *v* (0) (*pres* ~čem) 1 flow, run, stream 2 pass 3 *fig* progress, proceed

tegla *nf* 1 flower pot 2 jar

teg|leći *adj* draught **~lenica** *nf* barge **~liti** (**što**) tow, haul, lug **~ljač** *nm* 1 articulated lorry *GB*; semi *US*; trailer truck 2 tug(boat)

tegoba *nf* 1 difficulty; hardship; trouble 2 discomfort **~n** *adj* (*α*) arduous

tehn|ičar *nm* technician **~ički** *adj* technical **~ika** *nf* (*Dsg* ~ici) 1 technology 2 technique **~ologija** *nf* technology **~ološki** *adj* technological

tek (1) *adv* 1 only, just; as late as, not until; but 2 hardly, scarcely ~ (**što**) ... **kad** no sooner ... than, hardly ... when, as soon as ~ **što a.** almost **b.** be about to ~ **tako** for no reason, just like that

tek (2) *nm* 1 appetite 2 relish, gusto 3 taste, flavour, savour

te|ka *nf* (*Dsg* ~ci) *coll* exercise book, notebook

teklić, **teklič** *nm* messenger, courier, runner; errand boy

tekovina *nf* achievement

tekst *nm* 1 text 2 (pjesme) lyrics

tekstil *nm* textile(s) **~an** *adj* (*α*) textile

tekuć|i *adj* 1 flowing, running 2 fluid, liquid 3 current **~a voda** running water **~a vrpca** assembly line **~i račun** current account *GB*; checking account *US* **~ina** *nf* liquid, fluid

tel|ad *nm* calves *pl* **~e** *nn* (*Gsg* ~eta) calf **~eći** *adj* veal **~etina** *nf* veal

tele- *prefix* tele- **~dirigiran** *adj* remote-controlled **~fon** *nm* telephone;

phone *coll* ~**fonirati** *v* (0/komu) telephone; phone, ring (up), give a ring/bell/buzz *coll* ~**fonist** *nm* telephonist, telephone/switchboard operator ~**fonski** *adj* telephone ~**fonska govornica** (tele)phone box *GB*/booth *US* ~**fonska centrala a.** telephone exchange **b.** (kućna) switchboard ~**fonski imenik** telephone directory; phone book *coll* o *adv* by telephone ~**graf** *nm* telegraph ~**grafirati** *v* (što komu) telegraph, wire ~**gram** *nm* telegram; wire *US*; cable *form* ~**komunikacije** *nf pl* telecommunications ~**ks** *nm* telex ~**objektiv** *nm* telescopic lens ~**printer** *nm* teleprinter; teletype TM ~**skop** *nm* telescope ~**skopski** *adj* telescopic ~**vizija** *nf* television, TV; telly *coll* ~**vizijski** *adj* television, TV **prenositi** ~**vizijski** televise ~**vizor** *nm* television/TV set

tema *nf* subject, topic, theme ~**tika** *nf* (*Dsg* ~tici) subject matter ~**tski** *adj* thematic

temelj *nm* foundation, base; basis **do** ~**a** to the ground **na** ~**u** based on; on the basis/grounds of **iz** ~**a** fundamentally, radically ~**ac** *nm* (*Gsg* ~ca, *Npl* ~ci) (juha) stock **kamen** ~**ac** foundation stone, cornerstone ~**ni** *adj* basic, fundamental; elementary ~**it** *adj* 1 thorough, radical; sweeping 2 (znanje) profound, solid ~**iti** *v* 1 (što) base on, found on 2 (se) be based on/founded on, rest on

tempera *nf* poster paint/colour, tempera

temperament *nm* 1 temperament 2 temper ~**an** *adj* (*a*) temperamental

temperatur|a *nf* temperature **imati** ~**u** have a fever, have/run a temperature **mjeriti** ~**u** take one's temperature

tempirati *v* (što) time ~ **bombu** set a time bomb

tempo *nm* 1 pace, rate 2 tempo

ten *nm coll* complexion

tenda *nf* awning

tendencij|a *nf* 1 tendency 2 inclination, bent 3 trend ~**ozan** *adj* (*a*) tendentious, biased

tenis *nm* tennis **stolni** ~ table tennis

~**ač** *nm* tennis player ~**ice** *nf pl* trainers *GB*; sneakers *US*; tennis shoes, running shoe; plimsolls s ~**ki** *adj* tennis ~**ko igralište** tennis court

tenk *nm* tank

tenkirati *v* (0/što) (auto) *coll* fill up

tenor *nm* tenor

teologija *nf* theology, divinity

teor|etičar *nm* theoretician ~**etizirati** *v* (0) theorize ~**etski** *adv* theoretically, in theory ~**ija** *nf* theory

tepati *v* (0) use baby talk, coo

tepi|h *nm* (*Npl* ~si) *coll* carpet, rug

terap|eut *nm* therapist ~**eutski** *adj* therapeutic ~**ija** *nf* therapy

terasa *nf* terrace

teren *nm* ground; terrain; field; turf *sl* ~**ac** *nm* (*Gsg* ~ca) field worker ~**ski** *adj* field ~**sko vozilo** jeep

teret *nm* 1 burden, load, weight 2 cargo, freight ~**ana** *nf* gym ~**ni** *adj* cargo, freight ~**ni vlak** freight/goods train ~**ni brod** cargo ship, freighter ~**iti** *v* (koga/što) 1 press/weigh down 2 (optužiti) charge with 3 debit ~**njak** *nm* (*Npl* ~njaci) truck; (s prikolicom) articulated lorry *GB*; semi *US*

teritorij *nm* territory; turf *sl* ~**alan** *adj* (*a*) territorial

termin *nm* 1 term, expression 2 term, time, slot, period **udarni** ~ *TV* prime time

termit *nm* termite, white ant

termo|centrala, termoelektrana *nf* thermoelectric power plant, thermal power plant ~**for** *nm* hot-water bottle ~**metar** *nm* (*Gsg* ~metra) thermometer ~**s boca** (~**sica** *coll*) *nf* thermos (flask) *TM*

teror *nm* terror ~**ist** *nm* terrorist ~**istički** *adj* terrorist ~**izam** *nm* (*Gsg* ~izma) terrorism ~**izirati** *v* (koga) terrorize; bully, harass

te|sar *nm* carpenter ~**sati** *v* (što) (*pres* ~šem) cut, hew

test *nm* test ~**irati** *v* (koga/što) test, put/subject to the test

testament *nm* testament, last will

teško *adv* 1 heavily 2 badly, seriously, severely 3 (jedva) hardly, scarcely ~ **raditi** work hard ~ **njemu** woe betide him **~ća** *nf* difficulty; trouble; hardship

te|ta *nf* aunt **~tak** *nm* (*Gsg* ~tka, *Npl* ~ci) uncle

tetiva *nf* 1 tendon, sinew 2 (na luku) string 3 *math* chord

tet|ka *nf* (*Gpl* ~aka/~ki) aunt

tetošiti *v* (koga) pamper

tetov|irati *v* (koga/što) tattoo **~aža** *nf* tattoo

tetrapa|k *nm* (*Npl* ~ci) carton

tetrijeb *nm* grouse

teturati *v* (0) stagger, totter, wobble

teza *nf* thesis

tež|a *nf* sila **~e** the force of gravity, gravitation

teža|k (1) *nm* (*Npl* ~ci) farm labourer/hand

tež|ak (2) *adj* (teška) (*comp* teži) 1 heavy, weighty 2 *fig* hard, difficult; laborious 3 *fig* grave; serious **~ina** *nf* 1 weight; gravity 2 burden, load 3 difficulty **~ište** *nm* 1 *fig* emphasis 2 centre of gravity **~iti** *v* (0) 1 weigh, scale 2 (za kim/za čim/čemu) aspire after/to, crave for, strive for **~nja** *nf* aspiration, ambition

ti *pron* (*G* tebe/te, *D* tebi/ti, *A* tebe/te, *L* tebi/ti, *I* tobom) you biti **na ~ s kim** *coll* be on first-name terms with

ticalo *nn* antenna, feeler

ti|cati (se) *v* (koga/čega) (*pres* ~čem) concern **što se mene ~če** as far as I am concerned, as for me **što se toga ~če** for that matter

tifus *nm* trbušni ~ typhoid pjegavi ~ typhus

tig|ar *nm* (*Gsg* ~ra, *Npl* ~rovi) tiger **~rica** *nf* tigress

tih *adj* (*comp* tiši) 1 still 2 quiet, tranquil; silent 3 (glas) low **T~i ocean** the Pacific (Ocean) **~a voda brijege dere** *prov* still waters run deep **~o** *adv* 1 still 2 quietly; silently; softly 3 in a low voice **~!** (be) quiet!

tijek *nm* course; progress biti **u ~u** be in progress, be under way **~om** *adv* (čega) during, in the course of

tijel|o *nn* body (+ *fig*) **dušom i ~om** body and soul

tijesan *adj* (a) tight; narrow

tijesto *nn* 1 dough, pastry ~ za

palačinke batter 2 *coll* pasta

tik (1) *adv* **~ do** close to, next to; next door to

tik (2) *nm* *med* tick

tik|va *nf* (*Gpl* ~ava/~vi) 1 pumpkin, gourd, marrow 2 *coll* head; noddle *coll* **~van** *nm* blockhead **~vica** *nf* 1 courgette *GB*; zucchini *US* 2 (laboratorijska) flask

tili *adj* *coll* **u ~ čas** in no time, in a jiffy, in a trice *coll*

tim (1) *nm* team **~ski** *adj* team

tim (2) *pron* *Dsg* → **to ~ bolje** so much the better **~ više** all the more so **što/čim prije ~ bolje** the sooner the better

timariti *v* (konja) groom

tinta *nf* ink **~rnica** *nf* inkstand

tinjati *v* (0) smoulder

tip *nm* 1 type 2 type, character; guy *coll*; bloke *GB* *coll* **~ičan** *adj* (a) typical

tip|feler *nm* *coll* typing error **~ka** *nf* (*Gpl* ~aka/~ki) key **~kač** *nm* typist **~kati** *v* (što) type **~kati naslijepo** touch-type **~kovnica** *nf* keyboard

tiranlija *nf* tyranny **~n** *nm* tyrant **~zirati** *v* (koga) tyrannize; bully

tiraža *nf* 1 circulation 2 edition; printing

tirkiz *nm* turquoise **~an** *adj* (a) turquoise

tis|ak *nm* (*Gsg* ~ka) 1 the press 2 printing, impression **~kanica** *nf* form; printed matter **~kar** *nm* printer **~kara** *nf* printing office **~karski** *adj* printing **~karska pogreška** printing error, misprint **~karski stroj** printing press **~kati** *v* 1 (što) print, impress 2 (koga) (cipela) pinch 3 (se) crowd, throng **~kovna** *adj* **konferencija** press conference

tisuć|a *num* a/one thousand **~godišnji/~ljetni** *adj* thousand-year-old **~godišnjica** *nf* thousandth anniversary **~lječe** *nn* millenium

tišina *nf* silence, stillness, quiet(ness), hush **grobna ~** dead silence

tišt|ati *v* (koga/što) (*pres* ~im) depress, lie heavy on

titl *nm* subtitle

titrati *v* (0) 1 oscillate, vibrate 2 flicker

titul|a *nf* title **~ar** *nm* (vlasništva) legal owner

tj. *abbrev* (to jest) i.e., that is

tjed|an *nm* (*Gsg* ~na, *Npl* ~ni) week **dva ~na** two weeks; fortnight *GB* **~ni** *adj* weekly **~nik** *nm* (*Npl* ~nici) weekly **~no** *adv* weekly, a/per week

tjel|esan *adj* (*a*) bodily, corporal, physical **~esna kazna** corporal punishment **~esna straža** *nf* security, bodyguards **~esni odgoj** physical education/training **~ohranitelj** *nm* bodyguard **~ovježba** *nf* gymnastics, callisthenics *pl*, physical training

tjeme *nn* crown/top of the head **~njača** *nf* parietal bone

tjera|lica *nf* arrest warrant; wanted poster **~ti** *v* (koga/što) 1 chase, pursue 2 drive, force, urge 3 drive, propel, run 4 (mladice) put out, sprout 5 (se) be on/in heat **~ti svoje** want one's own way

tjeskoba *nf* anxiety, apprehension **~n** *adj* (*a*) anxious, apprehensive

tjesnac *nm* 1 strait(s) 2 *fig* dire straits, squeeze

tjestenina *nf* pasta

tješiti *v* (koga) comfort, console

tka|lac *nm* (*Gsg* ~lca, *Npl* ~lci) weaver **~lački** *adj* **stan** loom **~lja** *nf* weaver **~nina** *nf* textile, fabric; cloth **~ti** *v* (što) weave

tkivo *nn* 1 tissue 2 fabric

tko *pron* who **~ god** who(so)ever **malo ~** hardly anyone, very few **ako se ~ javi** if anyone/someone calls

tla|čitelj *nm* oppressor **~čiti** *v* 1 (koga/što) oppress, tyrannize 2 (što) compress, press **~k** *nm* pressure **krvni ~k** blood pressure **~komjer** *nm* 1 barometer 2 pressure gauge

tlapnja *nf* illusion, delusion; fancy

tlo *nn* ground; soil **plodno ~** fertile soil (+ *fig*) **~crt** *nm* ground plan

tm|ina *nf* dark(ness), gloom **~uran** *adj* (*a*) 1 (vrijeme) gloomy, sombre, dull; overcast 2 *fig* downcast, low-spirited

to *pron* (→ **taj**) this, that, it **k ~me** in addition, besides; moreover **radi se o ~me da** the point is that **što brži ~ bolji** the faster the better

toalet|a *nf* 1 evening dress 2 toilet **~ni** *adj* toilet

tobogan *nm* slide **~ na tračnice** roller coaster, big dipper

tobol|ac *nm* (*Gsg* ~ca, *Npl* ~ci) 1 quiver 2 (životinja) pouch **~čar** *nm* marsupial

tobož|e *adv* ostensibly, allegedly **~nji** *adj* 1 ostensible; so-called 2 alleged

toč|an *adj* (*a*) 1 exact, accurate; precise 2 punctual; prompt 3 point; correct, right **~no vrijeme a.** exact time **b.** (telefonsko) speaking clock **~no** *adv* **u 10 sati** at 10 o'clock sharp

toč|en *adj* draught, on tap **~ionica** *nf* bar, pub **~iti** *v* (što) 1 pour 2 sell (alcoholic drinks)

toč|ka *nf* (*Dsg* ~ki, *Gpl* ~aka) 1 (rečenična) full stop *GB*; period *US* 2 (na slovu; uzorak) dot 3 point; item; clause, provision 4 (programska) act, number **~ka zarez** semicolon **mrtva ~ka** standstill, deadlock, impasse **~ka gledišta** point of view, viewpoint **~kast** *adj* dotted

tok (1) *nm* 1 flow, current; course 2 → **tijek nisi u ~u** you're not in the swim/with it

tok (2) *nm* sheath, scabbard

tokar *nm* turner; lathe operator **~ski** *adj* **stroj** lathe

toki-voki *nm* walkie-talkie

toler|antan *adj* (*a*) tolerant **~irati** *v* (koga/što) tolerate, put up with

toli|ki *adj* 1 such (a)/so (big, large, tall, high, etc.) 2 so many/much **dvaput ~ki** twice as big/large etc., as big again **~ko** *adv* so many/much, this/that much, such a number/quantity of **dvaput ~ko** twice as much, as much again **~ko ... koliko** as much/many ... as **ne ~ko ... koliko** not so much/many ... as **u ~ko što** in so far as, inasmuch as

toljaga *nf* club, cudgel

tom *nm* volume

tombola *nf* tombola; bingo

ton *nm* 1 tone, note, sound 2 voice 3 shade, tint

tona *nf* ton **metrička ~** metric ton, tonne **registarska ~** register ton **~ža** *nf* tonnage

toni|k nm (Npl ~ci) tonic

ton|uti v (0) (pres ~em) **1** sink, founder, go down **2** (tlo) sag, subside

top nm cannon, gun **gluh kao ~** stone-deaf **spavati kao ~** sleep like a log/top

top|ao adj (~la f) warm **~lana** nf heating plant **~lice** nf pl thermal springs; spa **~lina** nf warmth (+ fig), heat **~linski** adj thermal, heat **~lo** adv warmly **~lomjer** nm thermometer

topiti v **1** (što) melt; dissolve; (mast) render **2** → **taliti 3** (se) melt, thaw (+ fig)

top-lista nf the charts pl

topni|čki adj artillery **~k** nm (Vsg ~če, Npl ~ci) gunner **~štvo** nn artillery; guns pl

topola nf poplar

topot nm stamping, trample

tor nm fold, pen

tor|anj nm (Gsg ~nja, Npl ~njevi) **1** tower **2** (šiljati) spire, steeple **3** (zvonik) belfry **kontrolni ~anj** control tower

torb|a nf **1** bag **2** case **3** satchel **4** pouch **~ica** nf handbag, purse

torped|ni adj torpedo **~o** nm torpedo

torta nf cake

total|an adj (a) total, complete **~ni rat** all-out/full-scale war **~itaran** adj (a) totalitarian

tovar nm load, cargo, freight; shipment **~iti** v (što) load **~ni** adj lading, loading **~ni list** bill of lading

toviti v **1** (stoku) fatten **2** (se) fatten, grow fat

trabunjati v (0/što) coll drivel on (about)

trač nm gossip **~ati** v (0/koga) gossip, tattle (about)

trač|ak nm (Gsg ~ka, Npl ~ci) **1** beam, ray **2** fig trace **~ak nade** ray of hope

tračnic|a nf rail **~e** nf pl rails, track

tradici|ja nf tradition **~onalan** adj (a) traditional

trafostanica nf transformer station, substation

trag nm track, trail; trace; (stopa) footprint **bez ~a** without (a) trace **ući u ~ a.** track down **b.** fig find a clue **zamesti ~(ove)** cover one's tracks pas

~ač nm tracker dog **~ati** v (za kim/čim) track, trail; trace; search for

trag|edija nf tragedy (+ fig); tragic event **~ičan** adj (a) tragic

traj|an adj (a) **1** lasting, permanent **2** (biljka) perennial **3** (boja) fast **~ati** v (0) (pres ~em) **1** last, endure **2** continue, go on **~no** adv permanently, continually **~nost** nf durability, permanence

trajekt nm ferry(boat)

tra|k nm (Npl ~ci/~kovi) **1** beam, ray **2** ribbon, strip **~ka** nf (Dsg ~ci) **1** band, ribbon, strip; tape **2** lane **pokretna ~ka a.** assembly line **b.** conveyer belt

trakavica nf **1** med tapeworm **2** sl derog soap (opera)

trakt nm anat tract

traktat nm treatise

traktor nm tractor

traljav adj **1** shabby **2** bad, poor

tramp|a nf barter **~iti** v (što za što) barter (for)

tramvaj nm tram(car) GB; streetcar, trolley US

trans nm trance

transformator nm transformer

transparent nm banner, placard

transport nm **1** transport; transportation US **2** carriage; haulage; trucking US **~irati** v (koga/što) transport **~ni** adj transport; cargo **~no poduzeće** forwarding agent; trucking company US

tranzit nm transit **~ni** adj transit

trap nm **stajni ~** landing gear

trapav adj clumsy

traperice nf pl jeans

trapez nm **1** trapeze **2** math trapezium GB; trapezoid US **~hlače** coll flares

tras int bang! slam!

tras|a nf route **~irati** v (što) **1** mark out **2** (mjenicu) draw on

tratin|a nf lawn **~čica** nf daisy

tratiti v (što) waste, squander

trauma nf trauma **~tološki** adj trauma-tological **~tološka bolnica** casualty hospital

trav|a nf grass **ljekovite ~e** medicinal herbs **~ka** nf (Dsg ~ci, Gpl ~ki) blade of grass ~**nat** *adj* grassy ~**njak** *nm* (*Npl* ~njaci) 1 lawn 2 grassland; meadow

trav|anj *nm* (*Gsg* ~nja) April

traž|iti *v* (koga/što) 1 look for, seek; search for 2 ask (for), request, petition; apply for 3 call for, demand; claim ~**ilo** *nn* viewfinder

trbu|h *nm* (*Npl* ~si) belly; abdomen, stomach **ići ~hom za kruhom** look for a better livelihood ~**hozborac** *nm* (*Gsg* ~hozborca) ventriloquist ~**šast** *adj* 1 potbellied 2 bulging ~**ščić** *nm* tummy ~**šina** *nf* potbelly ~**šni** *adj* abdominal, belly ~**šni tifus** typhoid ~**šnjaci** *nm pl coll* sit-ups

trč|ati *v* (0) (*pres* ~im) run; race ~**ećim korakom** *mil* at/on the double ~**karalo** *nn* errand boy ~**ka** *nf* partridge ~**karati** *v* (0) run (around)

treba|ti *v* 1 (što) need, require, want 2 (0) be necessary/needed to ~ **učiniti** this should be done **nije kako** ~ it's not as it should be ~*ju mi nove cipele* I need new shoes ~*t će mu dva sata* it will take him two hours *tako mu i* ~ serves him right

treć|i *num ord* third ~**i korijen** cube root ~**a sreća** third time lucky ~**ina** *nf* a/one third

tref *nm* club ~ **kralj** the king of clubs

trema *nf* stage fright

tren *nm* instant, moment **u ~ oka** in no time ~**utačan**, ~**an** *adj* (a) momentary; instantaneous ~**utak** *nm* (*Gsg* ~utka, *Npl* ~uci) moment, instant

tren|er *nm sport* coach, trainer ~**ing** *nm sport* training ~**irati** *v* 1 (koga/što) train; coach 2 (0) train ~**irka** *nf* (*Dsg* ~irci) tracksuit

trenje *nn* friction

trep|avica *nf* eyelash ~**eriti** *v* (0) 1 flutter 2 blink, flicker, twinkle ~**et** *nm* 1 flutter(ing) 2 flicker(ing), twinkle **strah i ~et** holy terror ~**nuti** *v* (0) (*pres* ~nem) wink **ne ~nuvši a.** without batting an eyelid **b.** without wincing ~**taj** *nm* wink ~**tati** *v impf*

tres *int* bang! crash! slam! ~**ak** *nm* (*Gsg* ~ka) bang, crash *vrata su se zatvorila s* ~**kom** the door banged/slammed shut ~**nuti** *v* (*pres*

~nem) 1 (što/koga/čime) bang, crash, slam; hit, whack 2 (0) *coll* fall with a bump/thud

tres|ti *v* (*pres* ~em) 1 (koga/što) shake 2 (se) shake, shiver, tremble, quiver

treš|nja *nf* (*Gpl* ~anja/~nji) cherry

trešt|ati *v* (0) (*pres* ~im) blare

tret|irati *v* (koga/što) treat ~**man** *nm* treatment

trezor *nm* safe, strong room, vault

trezvenja|k *nm* (*Npl* ~ci) teetotaller

trg *nm* square

trg|ati *v* 1 (što) tear; rip 2 (voće) pick 3 (se) *sl* fight, struggle for sth ~*a me u leđima* I have shooting pains in the back ~**nuti** *v* (*pres* ~nem) 1 (što) draw, pull (out); jerk 2 (što) knock back (a drink) *coll* 3 (koga) rouse, give a start 4 (se) rouse oneself; be startled; pull oneself together; snap out of it ~**nuti se iz sna** wake with a start

trgov|ac *nm* (*Gsg* ~ca, *Vsg* ~če, *Npl* ~ci) 1 shopkeeper; dealer; businessman 2 (na malo) retailer; tradesman 3 (na veliko) wholesaler; merchant ~**ački** *adj* commercial, business, merchant, mercantile ~**ački centar** shopping centre/mall ~**ački putnik** sales representative, travelling salesman ~**ački pomoćnik** shop assistant ~**ačka mornarica** merchant navy/marine *US* ~**ati** *v* (čime) (*pres* ~ujem) trade in, deal in ~**ati na malo** retail ~**ati na veliko** buy/sell wholesale ~**ina** *nf* 1 trade, commerce 2 shop; store *US* ~**ina mješovitom robom** grocer's, grocery ~**inski** *adj* commercial, trade ~**inska komora** chamber of commerce

tri *num* (*G* ~ju, *D/L/I* ~ma) three **T~ kralja** Epiphany

tribina *nf* 1 stand 2 speaker's platform, rostrum 3 forum, panel

trica *nf* (košarka) three-point shot, three-pointer

tri|ce *nf pl* trifles ~**čarija** *nf* trifle ~**čav** *adj* trifling, trivial

trideset *num* thirty ~**i** *num ord* thirtieth

trijem *nm* porch

triješće *nn* kindling

trijezan *adj* (*a*) sober (+ *fig*)

trijumf *nm* triumph, exultation **~alan** *adj* (*a*) triumphant **~irati** *v* (0) triumph (over)

trik *nm* trick, ruse

triko *nm* leotard **~taža** *nf* knitwear

triler *nm* thriller

trinaest *num* thirteen **~i** *num ord* thirteenth

triper *nm coll* the clap *sl*

tristo *num* three hundred **~ti** *num ord* three hundredth

trk *nm* run **~kom** *adv* a. at a run b. double-quick **~ka** *nf* (*Dsg* ~ci) 1 running 2 race **~ka s vremenom** race against time **~kač** *nm* runner, racer **~kaći** *adj* race, racing **~kalište** *nn* racecourse, racetrack

trkn|uti (1) *v* (koga/što) (*pres* ~em) push; knock down, run down

trkn|uti (2) *v* (kamo/do čega/koga) (*pres* ~em) *coll* run/pop down/over to

trljati *v* (što) rub; massage, chafe

trn *nm* thorn **~ u oku** thorn in one's flesh/side **~ci** *nm pl* pins and needles; gooseflesh, goose pimples **~okop** *nm* pick(axe) **~ovit** *adj* thorny (+ *fig*)

trn|uti *v* (0) (*pres* ~em) get/grow numb, lose feeling

trnje *nm* thorns *pl*; brambles *pl*

tro|bojka, trobojnica *nf* (*Dsg* ~bojci) tricolour **~jka** *nf* (*Dsg* ~jci) 1 number/figure three 2 (ocjena) C 3 three people; trio **~jke** *nf pl* triplets **~jni** *adj* tripartite **~jstvo** *nn* trinity **~katnica** *nf* three-storey(ed)/-storied *US* building **~kut** *nm* 1 triangle 2 (pribor) setsquare; triangle *US* **~list** *nm* 1 trefoil 2 *fig* trio **~međa** *nf* tripartite border **~mjesečan** *adj* (*a*) quarterly **~mjesečje** *nn* quarter **~mjesečnik** *nm* (*Npl* ~mjesečnici) quarterly **~nožac** *nm* (*Gsg* ~nošca, *Npl* ~nošci) 1 tripod 2 three-legged stool **~skok** *nm* (*Npl* ~skoci) triple jump **~stran** *adj* three-sided; trilateral; three-way **~struk** *adj* threefold; three-ply; triple **~struko** *adv* three times as much **~zubac** *nm* (*Gsg* ~zupca, *Npl* ~zupci) trident

trofej *nm* trophy

trolejbus *nm* trolleybus

trom *adj* sluggish, slow, tardy

tromblon *nm* rifle-launched grenade

trop|i *nm pl* the tropics **~ski** *adj* tropical

troš|ak *nm* (*Gsg* ~ka, *Npl* ~kovi) expense, expenditure, cost **snositi ~ak** bear the cost **putni ~kovi** travelling expenses **baciti se/dati se u ~ak** go to a lot of expense **~an** *adj* (*a*) dilapidated **~arina** *nf* excise (tax/duty) **~iti** *v* 1 (što) (novac/vrijeme) spend 2 (što) consume 3 (što) use 4 (se) wear out; be spent **~kovnik** *nm* (*Npl* ~kovnici) estimate, quotation

trovati *v* (koga/što) (*pres* trujem) poison (+ *fig*)

trpak *adj* (*a*) bitter, tart, acrid

trpati *v* (što) stuff, cram

trp|eljiv *adj* tolerant **~eljivost** *nf* tolerance **~jeti** *v* (*pres* ~im) 1 (koga/što) bear, stand, tolerate, put up with 2 (0) suffer **šuti i ~i** grin and bear it **~ni** *adj gram* passive

trs *nm* vine

trsiti *v* (se) try hard, strive

trs|ka *nf* reed; cane **šećerna ~ka** sugar cane **~tika** *nf* (*Dsg* ~tici) reed

trtica *nf* rump

trub|a *nf* 1 trumpet 2 (auto) horn, hooter 3 (vojnička) bugle **~iti** *v* 1 (0) trumpet 2 (0/kome) hoot (at sb)

trućati *v* (0) babble; talk nonsense

trud *nm* effort, exertion **dati sebi ~a** make efforts, take pains, exert oneself **~na** *adj* pregnant **~iti** *v* (se) 1 take pains, exert oneself 2 (nastojati) try **~nica** *nf* pregnant woman **~noća** *nf* pregnancy **~ovi** *nm pl* labour pains, contractions

truliti → trunuti

trun *nm*, **trunka** *nf* bit, jot, mite; mote **ni ~a istine** not a grain/jot/iota of truth

tru|nuti *v* (0) (*pres* ~nem) rot, decay, putrefy, decompose **~o** *adj* (~la *f*) rotten, putrid

trup *nm* 1 trunk 2 torso 3 body 4 (broda) hull

trupa *nf* 1 *mil* troop 2 (glumačka) troup, company

trup|ac *nm* (*Gsg* ~ca, *Npl* ~ci) log

truplo *nn* 1 dead body, corpse 2 (životinje) carcass

trut *nm* drone (+ *fig*)

trvenje *nn* 1 friction (+ *fig*) 2 strife

trzalj *nm* 1 jerk, pull, tug, twitch 2 convulsion, spasm 3 flinch, wince 4 (oružja) recoil, kick ~lica *nf* plectrum; pick *coll* ~ti *v* (0) 1 jerk, tug, twitch 2 (se) flinch, wince 3 (se) recoil ~vice *nf pl fig* friction

tržišni *adj* market ~ište *nn* market ~nica *nf* market(place)

tu *adv* here ~ i tamo a. here and there b. now and then

tuberkuloza *nf* tuberculosis; TB *coll*

tucanik *nm* gravel ~ti *v* (što) pound, crush ~ti kamen break rocks ~ti orahe crack nuts

tuce *nn* (*Gsg* ~ta) a dozen veliko ~ gross

tuča *nf* hail

tučak *nm* (*Gsg* ~ka, *Npl* ~ci) (cvijeta) pistil

tučen *adj* ~o vrhnje whipped cream

tučnjava *nf* fight, brawl, scuffle, scrap

tući *v* (*pres* ~čem) 1 (koga/što) beat; thrash ~ći iz topova shell, bombard, pound 2 (se) fight, scuffle, scrap

tuđ *adj* 1 somebody else's, other people's 2 strange; foreign; alien ~ica *nf* loanword ~ina *nf* u ~ini abroad, in a foreign country ~inac *nm* (*Gsg* ~inca, *Npl* ~inci) stranger; foreigner; alien ~inski *adj* foreign; alien

tuga *nf* 1 sorrow, sadness 2 grief; mourning ~ovati *v* (0/za kim/za čim) (*pres* ~ujem) mourn (for), grieve; be in mourning

tulipan *nm* tulip

tuliti *v* (0) wail, howl

tulum *nm sl* party, bash, do *coll* ~ariti *v* (0) *sl* party

tuljan *nm* seal

tumač *nm* interpreter sudski ~ official interpreter ~enje *nn* interpretation; explanation ~iti *v* (što) interpret; explain; comment ~iti ulogu play a role

tumarati *v* (0) roam, ramble, rove, wander

tuna *nf* tuna

tunel *nm* tunnel

tunika *nf* (*Dsg* ~ci) tunic

tup *adj* 1 blunt, dull, obtuse 2 dull(-witted), slow 3 (pogled) blank ~iti *v* 1 (što) blunt, dull, make blunt/dull 2 (koga) *sl* badger, nag ~av, ~oglav *adj* dull; dim *GB*; dumb *US*; thick, slow-witted ~oglavac *nm* (*Gsg* ~oglavca, *Npl* ~oglavci) dimwit, nitwit *coll*

tur *nm* 1 rear, bottom; buttocks *pl* 2 (hlača) seat

tura *nf coll* 1 tour 2 round

turati *v impf* → **turnuti** ~ nos u što poke one's nose into sth

turbina *nf* turbine

turirati *v* (što) rev up

turist *nm* tourist; holidaymaker ~stički *adj* tourist ~zam *nm* (*Gsg* ~zma) tourism; tourist industry

turneja *nf* tour na ~i on tour; on the road

turnir *nm* tournament

turnuti *v* (što) (*pres* ~em) thrust; shove; slip

turoban *adj* (*a*) sad; gloomy

tust *adj* fat, obese; plump

tuš (1) *nm* Indian ink

tuš (2) *nm* shower ~irati *v* (se) have/take a shower, shower

tuš (3) *nm mus* fanfare, flourish

tutnjava *nf* boom, roar, rumble, thunder

tutor *nm* guardian ~stvo *nn* guardianship

tuzemni *adj* domestic, home, internal

tužakalo *nn* telltale; tattletale *US*; sneak *GB sl* ~ti *vt* (koga/0) tell on; sneak

tužaljka *nf* (*Dsg* ~aljci) lament; dirge ~an *adj* (*a*) sad, sorrowful, melancholy

tužba *nf* 1 charge; indictment 2 complaint podići ~bu press charges against, indict ~ibaba *nf* → tužakalo ~itelj *nm* plaintiff javni ~itelj public prosecutor *GB*; district attorney *US* ~iteljstvo *nn* public prosecutor's office ~iti *v* (koga/što za što) 1 charge with 2 sue, prosecute 3 report 4 (se) complain about

tvar *nm* matter, substance, stuff ~an *adj* (*a*) material, real

tvoj *pron* your; yours
tvor *nm* polecat, skunk
tvor|ac *nm* (*Gsg* ~ca, *Npl* ~ci) creator, maker, originator ~**ba** *nf* creation, formation, making ~**evina** *nf* creation, product; entity ~**iti** *v* (što) constitute, form, make up ~**ni** *adj* **napad** *leg* assault and battery ~**nica** *nf* factory, plant, mill, works ~**ničar** *nm* manufacturer, factory owner ~**nički** *adj* factory, industrial, manufactured

tvrd *adj* hard; firm; solid
tvrd|iti *v* (što) **1** claim, assert, maintain, declare **2** allege ~**nja** *nf* **1** assertion, statement, claim **2** allegation
tvrdo *adv* hard ~ **spavati** be fast/sound asleep ~**glav** *adj* obstinate, stubborn, headstrong ~**koran** *adj* (*a*) hardcore, die-hard; hardened, inveterate
tvrđava *nf* fortress; citadel
tvrtka *nf* firm, company; house

U

U, u 27th letter of Cro. alphabet

u *prep* **1** (gdje?) in, at ~ *inozemstvu* abroad ~ *biti* essentially **2** (kamo?) to, into **3** (vrijeme) *u petak* on Friday *u pet sati* at five o'clock ~ *roku do dva tjedna* within two weeks **4** ~ *ime (čega)* in the name of ~ *(čije) ime* on behalf of

u- *prefix* glagol + into, in *uploviti* sail in(to)

ubaci|ti *v* **1** (što u što) throw into; insert **2** (koga u što) *fig* infiltrate sb into, smuggle ~**vati** *v impf*

ubijati *v impf* → ubiti

ubilježiti *v* (što/koga u što) enter, register

ubir|ati *v impf* → ubrati (što) (*pres* ~**em**) collect

ubitačan *adj* (*a*) deadly, murderous

ubi|ti *v* (*pres* ~**jem**) **1** (koga/što) kill, murder **2** (se) kill oneself, commit suicide

ublaž|iti *v* (što) alleviate, relieve, ease ~**avati** *v impf*

ubod *nm* prick, sting; (nožem) stab

uboj|ica *nf/m* killer, murderer ~**it** *adj* lethal ~**stvo** *nn* murder, homicide ~**stvo iz nehata** manslaughter ~**stvo s predumišljajem** premeditated murder

ubo|sti *v* (koga/što) (*pres* ~**dem**) prick; sting; (nožem) stab

ubrajati *v impf* → ubrojiti

ubrati *v* (što) (*pres* uberem) gather, collect; (cvijet, plod) pick

ubrizgati *v* (što komu) inject sth into sth/sb, inject sb with sth

ubrojiti *v* (koga/što u koga/što, među koga/što) count among, include in

ubrus *nm* napkin, serviette

ubrz|an *adj* fast, speedy ~**ani tečaj** crash course ~**ati** *v* **1** (što) quicken, speed up, accelerate; push **2** (0/se) quicken, pick up/gather speed ~**o** *adv* soon

ubuduće *adv* in future

uc|ijeniti *v* (koga) blackmail ~**ijeniti čiju glavu** put a price on sb's head ~**jena** *nf* blackmail; reward **lovac na** ~**jene** bounty hunter ~**jenjivati** *v impf*

ucmekati *v* (koga) *sl* bump off, waste *sl*

ucviljen *adj* bereaved

uč|en *adj* learned ~**enica** *nf* schoolgirl, pupil, student ~**enik** *nm* (*Vsg* ~**eniče**, *Npl* ~**enici**) schoolboy, pupil, student ~**enjak** *nm* (*Npl* ~**enjaci**) scholar ~**enje** *nn* **1** learning, study **2** teaching ~**ilište** *nn* school **vojno** ~**ilište** military academy ~**ilo** *nn* teaching aid ~**ionica** *nf* classroom ~**itelj** *nm* teacher ~**iti** *v* **1** (0) study **2** (što) learn, study **3** (koga) teach

učesta|o *adj* (~**la** *f*) frequent

učetverostručiti *v* (što/se) quadruple

učin|ak *nm* (*Npl* ~**ci**) effect; performance; output ~**iti** *v* **1** (što) do; make **2** (se) ~**ilo mi se** it seem to me ~**kovit** *adj* effective, efficient

učlaniti *v* (se) become a member, join

učma|o *adj* (~**la** *f*) lethargic; (mjesto) sleepy

učvr|stiti *v* (što) **1** *fig* strengthen; consolidate **2** fasten, fix, secure ~**šćivati** *v impf* (*pres* ~**šćujem**)

uči *v* (0) (*pres* uđem) enter, go in, come in(to), get in ~ **u trag** track down ~ **u stranku** join the party

ud *nm* limb, extremity **spolni** ~ penis, member, sexual organ

udahn|uti *v* (0/što) (*pres* ~**em**) breathe in, inhale **duboko** ~**uti** take a deep breath

uda|lja *nf* marriage ~**ti** *v* (se za koga) marry sb ~**vati** *v impf*

udalj adv **skok ~** long/broad US jump **~en** adj distant **~enost** nf distance **~iti** v 1 (se) move away, withdraw; drift apart, grow away from **~iti se od teme** stray from a subject 2 (koga) expel **~avati** v impf

udar nm 1 shock 2 (napad) strike 3 (vjetra) gust **biti na ~u** come under attack **podnijeti ~** bear the brunt **državni ~** coup (d'état) **moždani ~** stroke **srčani ~** heart attack **toplinski ~** heat stroke **~ac** nm (Gsg ~ca, Npl ~ci) 1 blow (+ fig); knock; (nogom) kick 2 sport shot **~ac groma** thunderbolt **kazneni/slobodni ~ac** penalty/free kick **~aljke** nf pl percussion **~ati** v impf beat **~iti** v (koga/što) hit, strike, (nogom) kick, (šakom) punch **~iti žig** affix a seal **~iti temelj** lay the foundation **~iti u oči** strike one **~iti u plač** burst into tears **~iti u bijeg** take (to) flight **~ni** adj shock; assault mil **~ni termin** TV prime time

udav nm boa (constrictor), python

udaviti v 1 (koga) strangle, throttle 2 (se) drown

udebljati v (se) put on/gain weight

udesno adv right, on/to the right

udic|a nf hook **progutati ~u** swallow/take the bait

udijeliti v (komu što) grant, confer on; (milostinju) dole out

ud|io nm (Gsg ~jela) 1 share, portion 2 part **imati ~jela** take part, participate, share in

udi|sati v (0/što) (pres ~šem) breathe in, inhale

udjen|uti v (što) (pres ~em) thread (a needle)

udlaga nf splint

udob|an adj (a) comfortable; cosy, snug **~nost** nf comfort

udolina nf valley, dell

udomaćiti v (se) 1 feel at home 2 acclimatize, become naturalized

udostojiti v (se) deign

udov|ac nm (Gsg ~ca, Npl ~ci) widower **slamnati ~ac** grass w. **~ica** nf widow

udovolj|iti v 1 (komu) satisfy; please, humour, indulge 2 (čemu) meet, comply with **~avati** v impf

udru|ga nm (Dsg ~zi) association, society, union **~žiti** v (se) join, unite; merge; team up with coll **~žiti sredstva** pool resources/funds

udubina nf recess, niche, dent

udvara|č nm suitor **~ti** v (se komu) court sb

udvoje adv together, in twos/pairs

udvor|an adj (a) courteous, civil **~ica** nf/m sycophant

udvostručiti v (što/se) double

udžbeni|k nm (Npl ~ci) textbook

ufa|nje nn hope **~ti** v (se) hope

ugađati v impf → **ugoditi**

ugan|uti v (što) (pres ~em) sprain

ug|ao nm (Gsg ~la) corner

ugas|iti v 1 (što) (vatru) put out, extinguish; (svjetlo, uređaj) turn/switch off; (žeđ) quench 2 (se) go out **~li** adj (vulkan) extinct

ugaziti v 1 (što) trample down 2 (u što) step into

ugibalište nn lay-by GB; rest stop US

ugi|nuti v (0) (pres ~nem) die **~bati** v impf

uglađen adj well-bred, polished

uglavnom adv chiefly, mainly

uglazbiti v (što) set sth to music

ugled nm reputation, good name, prestige **~an** adj reputable, respectable, eminent **~ati** v 1 (koga/što) catch sight of, set eyes on, spot 2 (se u koga) follow sb's example **~nik** nm (Npl ~nici) notable, VIP

uglj|en adj coal **drveni ~en** charcoal **~eni** adj coal, carbon **~enokop** nm coal mine/pit; colliery GB **~ični** adj carbonic **~ični dioksid** carbon dioxide **~ik** nm carbon **~ikohidrat** nm carbohydrate; starch coll **~ikovodik** nm hydrocarbon

ugnjetavati v (koga) oppress

ugo|da nf pleasure **~dan** adj (a) pleasant; (osoba) nice **~diti** v 1 (komu) humour/indulge sb 2 (što) tune **~đaj** nm mood, nm atmosphere

ugostit|elj nm caterer; hotel-keeper, restaurant owner **~eljstvo** nn hotel industry, catering **~i** v (koga) entertain

ugov|arač nm negotiator **~arati** v impf

(što) negotiate (terms of the contract); **~or** *nm* contract, agreement; treaty **sklopiti/raskinuti ~or** enter into/terminate an agreement **~orni** *adj* contractual **~oriti** *v* (što) agree on, arrange for

ugrabiti *v* 1 (što) seize, snatch 2 (koga) kidnap, abduct

ugraditi *v* (što u što) build in(to), install

ugrijati *v* (*pres* ~em) 1 (što/koga) warm up 2 (se) get warm, warm oneself

ugri|sti *v* (koga) (*pres* ~zem) bite **~sti se za jezik** bite one's tongue **~z** *nm* bite

ugro|ziti *v* (koga/što) 1 imperil, jeopardize 2 threaten, menace **~žavati** *v impf* **~žena** *adj* **vrsta** endangered species

ugruš|ak *nm* (*Gsg* ~ka, *Npl* ~ci) clot

ugurati *v* 1 (što u što) push/shove/cram into 2 (se) force one's way into

ugušiti *v* 1 (koga/se) suffocate 2 (što) *fig* repress, supress

uhi|ćenik *nm* (*Npl* ~ćenici) arrested person, detainee **~dbeni** *adj* **nalog** arrest warrant **~titi** *v* (koga) arrest, apprehend

uho *nn* (*Npl* uši) ear **naćuliti uši** prick up one's ears **sjediti na ušima** be inattentive **srednje ~** middle ear **~laža** *nf* earwig

uhod|a *nm* spy **~iti** *v* (koga) spy on

uhoda|ti *v* (se) get into one's stride **~n** *adj* well-established; up and running

uhra|niti *v* (koga) fatten up **~njen** *adj* well-fed/-nourished

uhvatiti *v* (koga/što) catch, seize, capture; get hold of **~ na djelu** catch red-handed **~ korijen(a)** take root 2 (se za što) grip sth **~ se čega** take up **~ se posla** get down to work **~ se za ruke** join hands

uistinu *adv* really, indeed

uj|ak *nm* (*Npl* ~aci) uncle **~na** *nf* aunt

ujedi|niti *v* (što/se s čim/kim) 1 unite 2 merge; join forces; team up with **coll ~njenje** *nn* unification; merger *econ*

ujednačiti *v* (koga/što s kim/čim) standardize, make uniform

ujedno *adv* at the same time

ujutro *adv* in the morning **sutra ~** tomorrow morning

ukalupiti *v* (što) mould; mold *US*

ukaljati *v* (koga/što) soil; sully

uka|z *nm* decree **~zati** *v* (*pres* ~žem) 1 (što) show 2 (na što) point to; draw attention to 3 (se) appear, arise **~zivati** *v impf*

uki|nuti *v* (*pres* ~nem) (što) abolish, annul, suspend, revoke; (zakon) repeal, rescind; discontinue, cancel **~dati** *v impf*

ukipiti *v* (se) be/stand rooted to the spot/ground

ukiseliti *v* 1 (što) pickle; (mlijeko) sour 2 (se) go sour

uklanjati *v impf* → **ukloniti**

uklapati *v impf* → **uklopiti**

uklet *adj* haunted; damned **~i** *v* (koga/što) (*pres* ukunem) curse

ukliještiti *v* (se) get stuck; impact

ukloniti *v* (koga/što) remove, eliminate

uklopiti *v* (koga/što/se u što) fit into; dovetail with

uključ|iti *v* 1 (što) turn/switch on; plug in 2 (koga/što) include 3 (što) comprise, include **~ujući, ~ivo** *adv* **~ivo do nedjelje** till Sunday inclusive **~ujući napojnicu** including the tip, tip included

uknjižiti *v* (što) enter, register

ukočen *adj* stiff (+ *fig*) **~iti** *v* (se) become stiff, stiffen

ukoliko *adv* if, provided

ukop *nm* burial **~ati** *v* 1 (koga/što) bury 2 (se) entrench, dig in

ukor *nm* reprimand **~iti** *v* (koga) reprimand

ukorič|iti *v* (što) bind **meko ~en** *adj* paperback **tvrdo ~en** hardback, hard-cover

ukorijeniti *v* (se) take root

ukosnica *nf* hair-pin

ukoštac *adv* **uhvatiti se ~** come/get to grips with, grapple with

ukras *nm* ornament, decoration, trimming **~iti** *v* (što) decorate, ornament, deck, trim **~ni** *adj* (*a*) ornamental, decorative

ukra|sti *v* (*pres* ~dem) (što) steal

ukrašavati *v impf* → **ukrasiti**

ukratko *adv* in brief/short, briefly

ukrcati *v* **1** (se) embark, go aboard, board **2** (koga) take on **3** (što) load

ukriž *adv* crosswise

ukrotiti *v* (koga) tame, break in

ukrutiti *v* (se) stiffen

ukućani|n *nm* (*Npl* ~) member of the household

ukup|an *adj* (*a*) total, overall, whole, entire ~**no** *adv* in all ~**no iznositi** total

ukus *nm* taste **o** ~**ima se ne rasprav-lja** there's no accounting for taste ~**an** *adj* (*a*) (odjeća) tasteful; (hrana) tasty

ulagati *v impf* → **uložiti**

ulag|ivati *v* (se komu) (*pres* ~ujem) ingratiate oneself with sb, curry favour with sb; suck up to sb *coll*

ular *nm* halter

ulaštiti *v* (što) polish

ula|z *nm* entrance; entry; (pristup) admission **zabranjen** ~**z** no entry/admittance ~**zak** *nm* (*Gsg* ~ska, *Npl* ~sci) entry ~**ziti** *v impf* → **ući** ~**zni** *adj* entrance ~**znica** *nf* ticket, entrance fee, admission

ulekn|uće *nn* dent, depression ~**uti** *v* (se) (*pres* ~em) droop, sag

ulet|jeti *v* (0) (*pres* ~im) fly into; burst into *fig*

uli|ca *nf* street **na** ~**ci** in/on the street **glavna** ~**ca** main road, highstreet **sli-jepa** ~**ca** blind alley ~**čar** *nm* street arab ~**čarka** *nf* street-walker, prostitute ~**čni** *adj* street

ulijeniti *v* (se) become lazy

ulijetati *v impf* → **uletjeti**

ulij|evati *v* **1** *impf* **2** (se) flow into, empty into ~**ti** *v* (što) (*pres* ~jem) **1** (u što) pour into **2** (u koga) *fig* inspire sb with, inspire sth in sb ~**ti komu strah** strike fear into sb ~**ti povjerenje** inspire confidence ~**ti nadu** instil hope

ulijevo *adv* left, on/to the left

uliz|ivati *v* (se komu) curry favour with sb; brown-nose *tab sl* ~**ca** *nm/f* toady

ulog *nm* **1** (štedni) deposit **2** investment; stake; interest

ulo|ga *nf* (*Dsg* ~zi) role, part **igrati ve-liku** ~**u** *fig* play an important part/a crucial role

ulom|ak *nm* (*Gsg* ~ka, *Npl* ~ci) fragment, passage

ulov *nm* catch ~**iti** *v* (koga/što) catch

ulo|žak *nm* (*Gsg* ~ška, *Npl* ~šci) **1** (olovke) refill **2** (cipele) insole **3** (higijenski ~žak) sanitary towel/napkin; panty pad *coll* ~**žiti** *v* (što u što) **1** insert **2** (novac i sl.) invest **3** (u banku) deposit **4** (molbu) file, submit, lodge ~**žiti napore** take pains, make an effort

ultimatum *nm* ultimatum

ultrazvu|čan *adj* (*a*) ultrasonic; ultrasound ~**k** *nm* ultrasound

uludo *adv* in vain

ulj|ani *adj* oil ~**anica** *nf* oil lamp ~**arice** *nf pl* oil crops ~**e** *nn* oil **biljno** ~**e** vegetable oil **riblje** ~**e** cod-liver oil ~**e za loženje** heating/fuel oil

uljepšati *v* **1** (se) smarten up, doll up *coll* **2** (koga) make more attractive **3** (što) embellish; (prikazati boljim) whitewash

ulješura *nf* spermwhale

uljez *nm* intruder

uljud|an *adj* (*a*) polite, civil ~**ba** *nf* (*Gpl* ~aba/~bi) civilization ~**nost** *nf* politeness

uljulj|ati *v* (se) *fig* lull oneself

um *nm* mind, intellect *ne pada mi na ~ da to učinim* I wouldn't dream of doing it **smetnuti s** ~**a** forget **imati/držati na** ~**u** have/keep in mind ~**an** *adj* (*a*) sage ~**no pore-mećen** *adj* mentally deranged ~**njak** *nm* (*Npl* ~njaci) wisdom tooth

uma|či *v* (0/komu/čemu) (*pres* ~knem) escape

uma|k *nm* (*Npl* ~ci) sauce ~**kati** *v impf* → **umočiti**

umalo *adv* almost, nearly

umanjjenica *nf* diminutive ~**iti** *v* **1** (što) lessen, reduce, diminish, decrease; play down **2** (se) decrease, decline

umarati *v impf* → **umoriti** (1)

umatati *v impf* → **umotati**

umet|ak *nm* (*Gsg* ~ka, *Npl* ~ci) insert; inset ~**ati** *v impf* ~**nuti** *v* (što) insert

umijeće *nn* skill, art

umiješati *v* 1 (što u što) mix in, fold in 2 (se u što) *fig* interfere, intervene, meddle in, get involved in

umilja|t *adj* sweet, lovable **~vati** *v* (se komu) fawn on sb

umirati *v impf* → **umrijeti** ~ **od gladi** be starving

umiri|ti *v* 1 (koga) calm, soothe, pacify 2 (se) calm down, quiet down, abate **~vati** *v impf*

umirov|iti *v* 1 (koga) retire, pension off 2 (se) retire **~ljenik** *nm* (Npl ~ljenici) (old age) pensioner; retiree *US*

umišlj|aj *nm leg* premeditation **~ati** *v* (što) imagine **~en** *adj* conceited; big-headed *coll* **~eni** bolesnik hypochondriac

umi|ti *v* (koga/što/se) (*pres* ~jem) wash (one's face) **~vaonik** *nm* (Npl ~vaonici) wash basin **~vati** *v impf*

umjeren *adj* moderate; reasonable **~i pojas** temperate zone

umjes|tan *adj* (~na f) fitting, appropriate, fortuitous

umjesto *adv* (koga/čega) instead of

umješan *adj* (а) skilful, clever

umjet|an *adj* (а) artificial; (zubi) false; (koža) imitation, fake **~no gnojivo** fertilizer **~i** *v* (što) know how, be able (to) **~nički** *adj* art, artistic **~ničko klizanje** figure skating **~nik** *nm* (Npl ~nici) artist **~nina** *nf* work of art, objet d'art **~nost** *nf* art

umnožiti *v* (što) (photo)copy

umočiti *v* (što u što) dip

umor *nm* 1 fatigue, weariness 2 biti na **~u** be dying **~iti** (1) *v* 1 (koga) tire out 2 (se) tire, get tired

umor|iti (2) *v* (koga) murder **~stvo** *nn* murder

umotati *v* (koga/što/se) wrap up

umrijeti *v* (0) (*pres* umrem) die ~ **prirodnom smrću** die a natural death

umr|jati *v* (se/što) stain, smudge, smear

umrtviti *v* (što/se) make/become numb, deaden

umuk|nuti *v* (0) (*pres* ~em) fall silent

~**i!** shut up!

unajmiti *v* (što komu) rent, lease, hire

unaka|ziti *v* (koga/što/se) disfigure **~žen** *adj* disfigured, misshapen

unakrsn|i *adj* cross **~a vatra** crossfire **~o ispitivanje** cross-examination

unaprijed *adv* in advance, beforehand **~ijediti** *v* 1 (što) advance; further 2 (koga) promote **~eđivati** *v impf*

unatoč *prep* (čemu) in spite of, despite, notwithstanding

unatrag *adv* backwards **plaćanje** ~ back payment, payment in arrears

unazaditi *v* (što) cause to deteriorate/degenerate/worsen

unedogled *adv* indefinitely

unesrećiti *v* 1 (koga) cause grief to sb 2 (se) have an accident

uniforma *nf coll* uniform

unijeti *v* (što u što) 1 bring/carry/take in 2 (upisati) enter, input

uništ|iti *v* (koga/što/se) destroy sb/sth/oneself, ruin **~avati** *v impf*

univerzalan *adj* (а) 1 universal 2 *coll* all-purpose

unos *nm comp* input **~iti** *v impf* → **unijeti**

unosan *adj* (а) lucrative, profitable

unovačiti *v* (koga) recruit, enlist, conscript; draft *US*

unovčiti *v* (što) 1 cash (in), realize 2 *fig* capitalize on, cash in

unu|k *nm* (Npl ~ci) grandson **~ka** *nf* (Dsg ~ci) granddaughter **~ci** *pl* grandchildren

unut|ar *prep* within, inside • *prefix* intra- **~arnji** *adj* internal; (promet) domestic **~ra** *adv* inside **~rašnji** *adj* inland, interior **Ministarstvo ~arnjih poslova** the Ministry of the Interior **~rašnjost** *nf* 1 inside, interior 2 *fig* the interior

uobičaj|en *adj* habitual, customary, usual **~iti** *v* (se) become customary

uoč|i *adv* on the eve of, ahead of **~iti** *v* (što/koga) notice, see, spot **~avati** *v impf* **~ljiv** *adj* noticeable, visible

uokviriti *v* (što) frame

uopćavati *v* (što) generalize, put in general terms **~e** *adv* at all

uostalom *adv* after all, anyway

uozbiljiti *v* (se) become serious, stop joking

upad *nm* invasion, intrusion, incursion, inroad ~ati *v impf* → **upasti** ~ica *nf* interruption

upa|la *nf* inflammation ~la pluća pneumonia ~la slijepog crijeva appendicitis ~liti *v* (što) 1 ignite, set on fire 2 *coll* switch/turn on 3 (vatru) light 4 (šibicu) strike ~ljač *nm* 1 (cigarette) lighter 2 detonator ~ljiv *adj* (in)flammable

upamtiti *v* (koga/što) memorize, remember

upa|sti *v* (u što) (*pres* ~dnem) 1 fall in(to) 2 (napasti) raid, invade 3 (ući) dash in, burst into ~sti u riječ butt in, cut in ~sti u oči notice, be struck by

upecati *v coll* 1 (koga/što) catch (+ *fig*) 2 (se na što) fall for sth

uperiti *v* (što na što/koga) aim at, point at

up|eti *v* (se) (*pres* ~nem) try hard, exert oneself, do sth with all one's might

upetljati *v* (se) get involved/entangled

upicaniti *v* (se) *sl* dress/doll up

upi|jač *nm* blotting pad ~jati *v impf* ~ti (što) absorb (+ *fig*)

upinjati *v impf* → **upeti**

upirati *v impf* → **uprijeti**

upi|s *nm* 1 (škola) enrolment, registration 2 (uplata) subscription 3 (podataka) entry, input ~sati *v* (*pres* ~šem) 1 (što) write in, enter 2 (koga/se) register, enrol ~sivati *v impf*

upišati *v* (se) *tab* piss oneself

upit *nm* enquiry ~ati *v* (koga što) ask ~ni *adj* 1 questioning 2 *gram* interrogative ~nik *nm* (*Npl* ~nici) 1 question mark 2 questionnaire

uplaćivati *v impf* → **uplatiti**

uplakan *adj* tearful

uplašiti *v* 1 (koga) scare, frighten 2 (se čega/koga) become frightened of, take fright at

upla|ta *nf* payment ~titi *v* (što) pay, make a payment ~nica *nf* money order

upl|esti *v* (*pres* ~etem) 1 (što u što)

weave into; (kosu) braid into 2 (koga u što) entangle, involve in 3 (se u što) interfere, meddle; get entangled ~esti se u razgovor cut in ~itati *v impf* (*pres* ~ićem)

uploviti *v* (0) enter a harbour, come into/reach port, put in (at)

upola *adv* (by) half

upljesniviti *v* (se) go mouldy

uporaba *nf* use

uporan *adj* (a) persistent, stubborn

uporište *nn* 1 foothold, footing; purchase *form* 2 *mil* stronghold

upotr|eba *nf* use ~ebljavati *v impf* ~ebljiv *adj* usable ~ijebiti *v* (što) use, employ

upozna|ti *v* 1 (koga s čim) acquaint sb with sth, inform sb of sth 2 (koga s kim) introduce sb to sb 3 (se s čim) familiarize oneself with sth, learn about sth 4 (se s kim) meet sb, get acquainted with sb; (prvi puta) be introduced to sb ~vati *v impf*

upozor|enje *nn* warning, caution ~iti *v* (koga na što) warn sb of sth, caution ~avati *v impf*

uprav|a *nf* management, administration, direction prisilna ~a receivership ~itelj *nm* director; administrator ~iti *v* (što na koga/što) direct sth at/to sb/sth ~ljač *nm* steering wheel daljinski ~ljač remote control ~ljati *v* (čim) 1 (ustanova) run, manage, govern, administer 2 (auto) drive; (zrakoplov) fly; steer ~ni *adj* administrative ~ni govor direct speech ~o *adv* just ~o tako precisely

upre|gnuti *v* (koga/što) (*pres* ~gnem) harness; enlist *fig* ~zati *v impf*

upr|ijeti *v* (*pres* ~em) 1 (što) (pogled) fix; (prstom) point ~ijeti svim snagama do one's utmost, make an all-out effort 2 (se o što) lean on/against, push against

uprljati *v* (što/se) soil, stain, dirty

upropa|stiti *v* (koga/što) ruin, wreck, spoil ~štavati *v impf*

upuca|ti *v* (koga/se) *coll* shoot sb/oneself (dead) ~vati *v* (se kome) *sl* chat sb up, make a pass at

upuć|en *adj* (u što) well-informed, knowledgeable (about sth) ~ivati *v* *impf* → **uputiti**

upu|stiti *v* (se u što) engage in, get involved in

uput|a *nf* instruction; guideline ~**an** *adj* (*a*) advisable, expedient ~**iti** *v* 1 (koga u što) instruct sb about sth ~**iti u tajnu** let sb in on a secret 2 (koga na koga/što) refer sb to sb/sth 3 (se kamo) set off for ~**nica** *nf* (novčana) money order; (liječnička) referral sheet

ura *nm* 1 clock, watch 2 hour ~**r** *nm* watchmaker

uračun|ati *v* (što u što) count in, include ~**ljiv** *adj* of sound mind **smanjena ~ljivost** *nf* diminished responsibility

uragan *nm* hurricane

uraniti *v* (0) 1 be up early 2 come early

uras|ti *v* (u što) grow into ~**tati** *v impf* ~**li** *adj* **nokat** ingrown nail

uravnotežen *adj* balanced

urazumiti *v* 1 (koga) bring sb to their senses, bring sb to reason, make sb see reason 2 (se) come to one's senses

urban|i *adj* urban ~**stički** *adj* city/town/urban planning ~**zam** *nm* (*Gsg* ~**zma**) city/town/urban planning

ure|ći *v* (*pres* ~**knem**) (koga) curse

ured *nm* office ~**ba** *nf* (*Gpl* ~**aba**/~**bi**) decree, act ~**ovati** *v* (0) (*pres* ~**ujem**) 1 be on duty 2 act ~**ovno** *adj* **vrijeme** office hours ~**ski** *adj* office ~**ski pribor** stationery

ure|dan *adj* (*a*) tidy, neat ~**diti** *v* 1 (što) tidy up; arrange; (tisak) edit 2 (se) dress up ~**dnik** *nm* (*Vsg* ~**dniče**, *Npl* ~**dnici**) editor **glavni (i odgovorni)** ~**dnik** editor-in-chief ~**dništvo** *nn* editorial staff/board ~**đenje** *nn* organization, structure, system ~**đivati** *v impf*

uređaj *nm* device, appliance; gadget **coll** ~**i** *n pl* equipment, facilities

ure|z *nm* cut, nick ~**zati** *v* (*pres* ~**žem**) (što u što) 1 incise, cut into 2 engrave, carve ~**zati se komu u pamćenje** be imprinted on one's mind

url|ati *v* (0/što) howl, holler ~**ik** *nm* (*Gsg* ~**ici**) howl ~**ikati** *v* (*pres* ~**ičem**) → **urlati**

urna *nf* urn

urnebes *nm* **coll** uproar, hullabaloo ~**an** *adj* (*a*) uproarious; hilarious

urod *nm* crop, yield ~**iti** *v* (čime) result in ~**iti plodom** bear fruit

urođen *adj* congenital **med**; innate ~**ik** *nm* (*Vsg* ~**iče**, *Npl* ~**ici**) native; (australski) Aborigine

uro|k *nm* (*Npl* ~**ci**) spell, curse ~**kljivo** *adj* **oko** evil eye

uroniti *v* (što) immerse, dip

urot|a *nm* conspiracy, plot ~**iti** *v* (se) conspire (+ *fig*), plot ~**nik** *nm* (*Vsg* ~**niče**, *Npl* ~**nici**) conspirator, plotter

uruči|ti *v* (što komu) hand, deliver ~**ti sudski poziv** serve a summons on sb ~**vati** *v impf*

urudžbeni *adj* ~ **zapisnik** registry ~ **broj** reference number

urušiti *v* (se) fall/cave in

us *nf* whalebone

usa|diti *v* (što u što) put in, embed; implant, instil *fig* ~**đivati** *v impf*

usahn|uti *v* (0) (*pres* ~**em**) wilt, whither

usamljen *adj* lonely, solitary; lone; isolated

usavrš|iti *v* 1 (što) perfect, improve 2 (se) improve oneself/one's skill ~**avati** *v impf*

usekn|uti *v* (se) (*pres* ~**em**) blow one's nose

use|liti *v* (0/se/u što) move in; (u zemlju) immigrate ~**ljavati** *v impf* ~**ljenik** *nm* (*Npl* ~**ljenici**) immigrant, settler

ushi|t *nm* rapture, elation ~**titi** *v* (koga) enrapture, thrill, delight ~**ćivati** *v impf*

usidjelica *nf* **derog** spinster, old maid

usidriti *v* (što/se) anchor

usij|an *adj* red/white-hot ~**ana glava** hothead ~**ati** *v* (što) heat (until sth is red-hot)

usiljen *adj* forced, affected

usiriti *v* (se) curdle

usisa|ti *v* (što) 1 suck in 2 (usisačem) vacuum; hoover *GB* ~**(va)č** *nm* vacuum cleaner; hoover *GB* ~**vati** *v impf*

usitniti *v* (što) chop into pieces

usje|ći v → **urezati** ~**k** nm (Npl ~ci) **1** ravine, gorge **2** notch

usjevi nm pl crops

uskakati v impf → **uskočiti**

uskip|ljeti v (0) (pres ~im) **1** come to the boil **2** fig boil (over) with rage

uskladišt|iti v (što) store ~**avati** v impf

uskladiti v (što s čim) bring sth into line with sth; coordinate, harmonize, match sth with sth; adjust sth to sth; reconcile

uskli|čnik nm (Npl ~čnici) exclamation mark ~**k** nm (Npl ~ci) exclamation, cry ~**knuti** v (0/što) (pres ~knem) exclaim, cry out

usko adv closely ~**grudan** adj (α) narrow-minded

uskočiti v **1** (u što) jump into **2** (0) coll stand in, fill in for

uskomešati v (se) become agitated

uskoro adv soon

uskra|titi v (što komu) deny sb sth/sth to sb, deprive sb of sth ~**ćivati** v impf

Uskrs nm Easter **u~avati** v impf ~**ni** adj Easter **u~nuće** nn resurrection **u~nuti** v (pres ~nem) **1** (0) rise from the dead **2** (koga/što) resurrect, raise from the dead

uslijed prep due to ~**iti** v (0) ensue, follow

uslišati v (što) grant; (molitvu) answer

uslu|ga nf (Dsg ~zi) favour; service **dobre ~ge** good offices **biti kome na ~zi** be at sb's service/disposal **učiniti (kome) ~gu** do sb a favour ~**žan** adj (α) obliging, helpful

usmeni adj oral; verbal

usmjeriti v (što) direct, aim

usmrd|jeti v (se) (pres ~im) go rotten, go bad, begin to stink

usmrtiti v (koga/što) kill

usn|a nf pl ~**i** adj labial ~**ica** nf lip

usn|uti v (0) (pres ~em) fall asleep

uso|liti v (što) salt ~**ljen** adj corned

uspaničiti v (se) panic

uspav|anka nf lullaby ~**ati** v (koga) lull sb to sleep ~**ljivati** v impf ~**ljujući** adj soporific, hypnotic

uspeti v (se) (pres ~nem) climb up

uspijevati v (0) **1** impf → **uspjeti 2** (biljke) grow, thrive

uspinja|ča nf funicular (railway) ~**ti** v → **uspeti**

uspljeh nm (Npl ~jesi) success ~**ješan** adj (α) successful ~**jeti** v (0/u čemu) (pres ~ijem) succeed (in), be successful, manage

usplahir|en adj agitated, in a flutter ~**iti** v (se) become agitated, get into a tizzy

uspomena nf **1** remembrance, memory **2** souvenir

uspon nm ascent

usporavati v impf → **usporiti**

uspore|dan adj (α) parallel ~**dba** nf comparison ~**diti** v (što sa čim/koga s kim) compare sth/sb to sth/sb ~**dni-ca** nf parallel ~**do** adv parallel to/with; abreast with ~**đivati** v impf

usporiti v (0/koga/što) slow down

uspostav|a nf establishment ~**iti** v (što) establish; (ponovno) restore ~**ljati** v impf

usprav|an adj (α) erect, upright ~**iti** v (se) stand up straight

usprkos prep (čemu) despite, in spite of

usprotiviti v (se čemu) oppose, resist sth

usput adv in passing; casually ~ **rečeno** by the way ~**ni** adj incidental

usrati v (se) (pres userem) tab shit oneself; (od straha) be scared shitless

usrdan adj (α) ardent, fervent

usreć|iti v (koga/se) make (sb/oneself) happy ~**vati** v impf

usred adv in the middle of, amid(st)

usredotočiti v (se) concentrate, focus

usta nn pl mouth **govoriti na sva ~** shout from the rooftops

ustaja|lo adj (~la f) stale, stagnant ~**ti** (1) v (se) go stale

ustajati (2) v impf → **ustati**

usta|liti v (se) become established ~**ljen** adj habitual, settled

usta|nak nm (Gsg ~nka, Npl ~nci) uprising, insurrection **dići se na ~nak** rise up in arms ~**nik** nm (Vsg ~niče, Npl ~nici) rebel, insurgent ~**ša** nm hist Ustasha ~**ti** v (0) (pres ~nem) **1** get up, stand up, get on one's feet **2** (iz kreveta) get up **3** (protiv koga) rise up, rebel (against)

ustanov|a *nf* institution ~**iti** *v* → **utvrditi; osnovati**

ustav *nm* constitutional ~**nost** *nf* constitutionality ~**otvoran** *adj* (α) constituent

ustava *nf* sluice, dam, floodgate, lock

uste|gnuti *v* (*pres* ~gnem) **1** (što od čega) stop out, deduct **2** (se) refrain; (od glasovanja) abstain ~**zati** *v impf*

ustoličiti *v* (koga/što/se) inaugurate, install

ustraja|n *adj* (α) persistent, tenacious ~**ti** *v* (0) persist, persevere

ustrebati *v* (što) (happen to) need

ustremiti *v* (se na koga/što) turn on

ustrijeliti *v* **1** (koga/što) shoot **2** (se) shoot oneself

ustroj *nm* organization, system, structure, setup ~**iti** *v* (što) organize, set up

ustručavati *v* (se) hesitate, hold back

ustukn|uti *v* (0) (*pres* ~em) **1** flinch **2** give in, yield

ustup|ak *nm* (*Gsg* ~ka, *Npl* ~ci) concession ~**ati** *v impf* ~**iti** *v* (komu što) relinquish, yield, cede ~**ati** *v impf*

ustvrditi *v* (što) assert

usud *nm* fate, destiny

usuditi *v* (se) dare, venture

ususret *adv* ići kome ~ go towards sb **izaći** (komu) ~ *fig* oblige sb

usvojiti *v* (koga/što) adopt (+ *fig*) ~**ajati** *v impf*

uš *nf* louse ~**ljiv** *adj* lousy (+ *fig*); lice-infested

uš|i *nn pl* → **uho** ~**ni** *adj* auricular ~**na školjka** outer ear, auricle

ušće *nn* (river) mouth

ušećeriti *v* (što) candy

ušica *nf* eye (of a needle)

uši|tak *nm* (*Gsg* ~tka, *Npl* ~ci) dart, **kaputić s** ~**cima** tailored jacket ~**ti** *v* (što) (*pres* ~jem) sew in

uškopiti *v* (koga) castrate, geld

uštap *nm* full moon

uštaviti *v* (što) tan

ušte|da *nf* saving ~**djeti** *v* (što) (*pres* ~dim) save ~**đevina** *nf* savings *pl*

uštipn|uti *v* (koga/što) (*pres* ~em) pinch

uštip|ak *nm* (*Gpl* ~ka, *Npl* ~ci) doughnut

uštrb *nm* na ~ to the detriment of

uštrcati *v* (što u što) inject into

ušuljati *v* (se u što) sneak into

ušut|jeti *v* (0) (*pres* ~im) fall silent, stop talking ~**kati** *v* (koga) silence

utabati *v* (što) stamp

utaboriti *v* (se) set up/pitch camp, encamp, camp

utaj|a *nf* fraud, embezzlement ~**a poreza** tax evasion ~**iti** *v* (što) embezzle; (porez) evade ~**ivač** *nm* embezzler; tax evader ~**ivati** *v impf*

utakmica *nf* **1** match, game **2** competition

utakn|uti *v* (što u što) (*pres* ~em) stick into

utamničiti *v* (koga) imprison, incarcerate

utapati *v impf* → **utopiti**

utažiti *v* (što) (žeđ) quench, slake

ute|ći *v* (*pres* ~čem/~knem) (0/komu) run away (from), make good one's escape, flee

ute|g *nm* (*Npl* ~zi) weight

utemelj|it|elj *nm* founder ~**i** *v* (što) found, institute, establish

uti|cati *v impf* (*pres* utičem) → **utaknuti** ~**čnica** *nf* socket ~**kač** *nm* plug

utihn|uti *v* (0) (*pres* ~em) fall silent; become quiet

utir|ati *v impf* (*pres* ~em) → **utrti**

utis|ak *nm* (*Gsg* ~ka, *Npl* ~ci) → **dojam** ~**nuti** *v* (*pres* ~nem) **1** (što u što) press/squeeze into **2** (što na što) stamp, impress ~**kivati** *v impf*

utišati *v* **1** (koga/što) silence; calm, quiet; (radio) turn down **2** (se) fall silent; abate, subside

utjeca|j *nm* influence, impact **vršiti/imati** ~**j** (na koga) exert influence on sb **pasti pod** ~**j** come under the influence ~**jan** *adj* (α) influential, powerful ~**ti** *v* **1** (u što) flow into, empty into **2** (na koga/što) influence; affect **loše** ~**ti** affect

utje|ha *nf* (*Dsg* ~si) comfort, consolation, solace ~**šan** *adj* (α) consoling ~**šna nagrada** consolation prize ~**šiti** *v* **1** (koga) comfort, console **2** (se čime) find solace (in)

utjelov|iti *v* **1** (koga/što) embody, per-

sonify 2 (se) become incarnate ~lja-
vati *v impf* ~ljenje *nn* incarnation;
embodiment

utjerati *v* (koga/što) drive into ~ dug
collect/recover a debt ~ komu strah
u kosti strike fear into sb's heart

utočište *nn* sanctuary, refuge

uto|k *nm* (*Npl* ~ci) *leg* appeal uložiti
~k lodge an a.

utoliko *adv* ~ bolje so much the better

uton|uti *v* (u što) (*pres* ~em) sink into,
sink down ~uti u misli be immersed
in thoughts

utopija *nf* Utopia

utop|iti *v* 1 (koga/što/se) drown 2 (što)
fig sl flog, sell ~ljenik *nm* (*Npl*
~ljenici) drowning/drowned man

utopliti *v* (se) put on warm clothes,
keep warm

utor *nm* groove

utor|ak *nm* (*Gsg* ~ka) Tuesday

utovar *nm* loading ~iti *v* (što) load
~ivač *nm* lift truck ~ivati *v impf*

utoviti *v* (koga) fatten

utrč|ati *v* (u što) (*pres* ~im) run/rush
into

utr|ka *nf* (*Dsg* ~ci) race ~kivati *v* (se s
kim/čim) race (against) sb/sth

utrn|ulost *nf* numbness, pins and nee-
dles ~uo *adj* (~ula *f*) 1 numb, asleep
2 extinguished 3 expired ~uti *v* (*pres*
~em) 1 (što) (vatru) extinguish, put
out; (svjetlo) switch off 2 (se) (vatra)
go out; (isprava) expire, become null
and void 3 (0) go numb

utroba *nf* intestines, entrails majčina
~ womb

utrostručiti *v* (što/se) treble, triple

utroš|ak *nm* (*Gsg* ~ka) consumption;
(novac) expenditure ~iti *v* (što) consume, use, spend

utrpati *v* (što u što) cram/stuff into

utr|ti *v* (što) (*pres* ~em) 1 clear the way
2 *fig* pave the way, blaze a trail

utr|žak *nm* (*Gsg* ~ška) takings *pl*, pro-
ceeds *pl*

utu|čen *adj* dejected; down in the
dumps *coll* ~ći *v* (*pres* ~čem) 1
(koga) beat to death 2 *fig* depress ~ći
vrijeme kill time

utuviti *v* (komu što) beat into sb, impress on sb ~ si u glavu take it into

one's head

utvara *nf* hallucination, vision; (duh)
apparition ~ti *v* (sebi što) imagine,
delude oneself

utvr|da *nf* fort(ress), fortification ~diti
v (što) 1 (grad) fortify 2 (činjenicu)
establish, ascertain 3 (gradivo) review, revise ~đivati *v impf*

uvala *nf* cove

uval|iti *v* 1 (koga/se) ~ u nepriliku
land in trouble ~ se u dugove run
into debt ~ se u stolicu flop into a
chair 2 (komu što) *coll* flog

uvaž|iti *v* (što) accept, take into con-
sideration ~avati *v* 1 *impf* 2 (koga)
respect

uvečer *adv* in the evening

uveća|ti *v* (što) enlarge; (fotografiju)
blow up, enlarge ~vati *v impf* (*pres*
~vam)

uveličati *v* (što) lend importance to;
grace with one's presence

uvelike *adv* largely, to a considerable
extent

uven|uo *adj* (~ula *f*) withered ~uti *v*
(0) (*pres* ~em) wither, wilt

uvertira *nf* overture

uvese|liti *v* (koga) cheer up ~ljavati *v*
(koga) amuse

uve|sti (1) *v* (*pres* ~dem) 1 (što) intro-
duce; install 2 (koga) lead into, usher
in(to) ~sti u društvo introduce into a
circle ~sti djevojku u društvo bring
out

uve|sti (2) *v* (što) (*pres* ~zem) import

uve|z *nm* binding, cover ~zati *v* (što)
(*pres* ~žem) bind ~zivati *v impf*

uvi|d *nm* inspection, access imati ~da
have full knowledge/all information
at one's disposal ~djeti *v* (što) (*pres*
~dim) realize ~dati *v impf*

uviđavan *adj* (*a*) considerate

uvijač *nm* hair curler

uvijek *adv* always još ~ still još ~ nije
došao he has not come yet

uvijen *adj* *fig* implied, indirect

uvis *adv* up skok ~ *sport* high jump

uvjer|enje *nn* conviction ~iti *v* 1
(koga) convince; (nagovoriti) persuade 2 (se) convince oneself, be sat-
isfied, see for oneself ~avanja *nn pl*
assurances *pl* ~avati *v* 1 *impf* 2

(koga) try to convince ~ljiv *adj* convincing

uvjet *nm* condition ~an *adj* (α) conditional, tentative ~na kazna suspended sentence ~no *adv* pušten iz zatvora released on parole ~ovati *v* (što) (*pres* ~ujem) 1 lead to 2 stipulate 3 (čime) make sth conditional on sth ~ovan *adj* conditioned

uvježba|ti *v* (koga/što/se) drill, train ~vati *v impf*

uvlačiti *v* 1 (što/se/koga) *impf* → **uvući** 2 (se kome) *coll* curry favour with sb ~ se kome u guzicu *tab* kiss ass, brown-nose

uvod *nm* introduction ~iti *v impf* → **uvesti** (1) ~ni *adj* introductory ~ni članak, ~nik *nm* (*Npl* ~nici) editorial, leading article, leader

uvoj|ak *nm* (*Gsg* ~ka, *Npl* ~ci) lock, curl

uvoz *nm* import ~iti *v impf* → **uvesti** (1) ~nik *nm* (*Npl* ~nici) importer

uvr|eda *nf* insult, offence bez ~ede no offence (meant) ~edljiv *adj* 1 (koji vrijeđa) insulting, abusive 2 (koji se lako vrijeđa) touchy ~ijediti *v* 1 (koga) offend 2 (se na što) take offence (at)

uvrijeđiti *v* (se) become habitual/established, take root

uvrstiti *v* (koga/što) include; classify

uvrt|jeti *v* (što) (*pres* ~im) ~jeti si što u glavu take it into one's head

uvu|ći *v* (*pres* ~čem) 1 (koga/što) pull in, draw in; (dim) inhale 2 (koga u što) entangle, involve 3 (se) crawl in, sneak in

uz(a) *prep* 1 at, by, beside, near, next to 2 along ~ rijeku up the river ~ brdo up the hill ~ popust at a discount biti ~ koga *fig* stand by sb, support sb ~a sve to nevertheless ~a sve probleme for/despite all the problems

uzajam|ni *adj* mutual, reciprocal ~no *adv* ~no si pomagati help each other ~mnost *nf* reciprocity

uzak *adj* (uska *f*) narrow; (odjeća) tight

uzalud *adv* in vain, to no avail ~an *adj* (α) futile, useless

uz|ao *nm* (*Gsg* ~la, *Npl* ~lovi) knot

uzastop|ce *adv* 1 successively, in succession tri dana ~ce on three consecutive days, three days in a row tri puta ~ce three times running 2 slijediti koga ~ce shadow, dog sb('s heels) ~ni *adj* successive, consecutive

Uzašašće *nn* Ascension

uzbrd|ica *nf* incline, acclivity; uphill road/path ~o *adv* uphill

uzbu|diti *v* 1 (koga) agitate, excite, stir; (seksualno) arouse; (uzrujati) upset 2 (se) get excited/aroused ~dljivost *nf* thrill, excitement ~đenje *nn* excitement, stir; arousal ~đivati *v impf* (*pres* ~đujem) ne ~đuj se! keep your cool/hair on *coll*

uzbun|a *nf* alarm; alert zračna ~a air-raid alert oglasiti ~u sound the alert prestanak ~e all-clear ~iti *v* (koga) cause a stir, alarm

uzburkati *v* (se) (more) become choppy/rough

uzda *nf* rein (+ *fig*)

uzda|h *nm* (*Npl* ~si) sigh ~hnuti *v* (0) (*pres* ~hnem) sigh, breathe/give a sigh

uzda|nica *nf* mainstay, pillar of strength ~ti *v* (se u koga/što) trust in; put one's trust/faith in

uzdi|ći *v* 1 (što) lift, raise 2 (se) rise; ascend ~zati *v* (*pres* ~žem) 1 *impf* 2 (koga) praise, extol

uzdisati *v impf* → **uzdahnuti**

uzdrž|ati *v* (se od čega) (*pres* ~im) abstain from ~avati *v* 1 *impf* 2 (koga) support ~ljiv *adj* disciplined ~ljivost *nf* restraint

uzduh *nm* air

uzduž *prep* along ~ i poprijeko far and wide, in all directions, all over ~ni *adj* longitudinal

uzemljiti *v* (što) earth GB; ground US

uz|et *adj* paralysed ~eti *v* (*pres* ~mem) 1 (koga/što) take ~eti maha spread, gain impetus/momentum ~eti na znanje take note of ~eti pod ruku take sb's arm ~eti u obzir take into consideration ~eti u najam rent ~eti u službu employ ~eti u zakup lease ~eti u zaštitu stand up for ~eti za

ruku take sb by the hand **~eti (komu što) za zlo** take sth amiss **~eti za ženu** take as a wife, marry **~mimo da...** suppose/let us assume that... **2** (se) get married **~etost** *nf* paralysis

uzgajat|i *v* (što) **1** (biljke) grow, raise **2** (životinje) breed; keep **~elj** *nm* breeder

uzglavlje *nn* headboard

uzgoj *nm* (životinja) breeding; (biljka) growing

uzic|a *nf* **1** string **2** (za psa) leash (+ *fig*); lead **držati na kratkoj ~i** keep on a tight leash

uzidati *v* (što) build in(to)

uzimati *v impf → uzeti*

uzja|hati *v* (koga/0) (*pres* **~šem**) mount

uzlazni *adj* rising, upward

uzl|et *nm* take-off **~etište** *nn* **1** runway **2** airfield **~etjeti** *v* (0) (*pres* **~etim**) (avion) take off; fly up **~ijetati** *v impf*

uzma|ći *v* (0) (*pres* **~knem**) retreat, draw back, fall back **~k** *nm* retreat

uzmanjka|ti *v* (komu čega) run out of sth, be short of sth

uzmicati *v impf → uzmaći*

uzmo|ći *v* (što) (*pres* **~gnem**) manage

uznemiri|ti *v* **1** (koga) upset, worry, alarm; disturb **2** (se) get upset, become alarmed, be troubled **~vati** *v impf*

Uznesenje *nn* Assumption

uznojiti *v* (se) work up a sweat

uznosit *adj* proud, haughty

uzoholiti *v* (se) become arrogant

uzor *nm* model; ideal **po ~u na** on the model of **~ak** *nm* (*Gsg* **~ka**, *Npl* **~ci**) sample; pattern **~an** *adj* (*a*) model, exemplary **~itost** *nf* eminence

uzrast *nm* **1** stature **2** age

uzrečica *nf* saying

uzro|čan *adj* causative **~čni veznik** *gram* causal conjunction **~čno-posljedična veza** cause and effect **~čnik** *nm* (*Npl* **~nici**) cause **~kovati** *v* (što) (*pres* **~kujem**) cause

uzruja|n *adj* upset **~ti** *v* **1** (koga) upset **2** (se) get upset **~vati** *v impf* **ne ~vaj se!** keep your hair on!

uzurp|ator *nm* usurper **~irati** *v* (što) usurp

uzvani|k *nm* (*Npl* **~ci**) guest

uzver|ati *v* (se) (*pres* **~em**) clamber/climb up

uzvik|nuti *v* (što/0) (*pres* **~nem**) shout, exclaim, cry **~ivati** *v impf*

uzvi|sina *nf* elevation, rise, high ground **~siti** *v* (koga) *fig* exalt **~sivati** *v impf* **~šen** *adj* sublime, exalted, most high

uzvitlati *v* (što/se) stir up **~ prašinu** kick up dust

uzvodno *adv* upstream

uzvra|titi *v* (komu što) return; repay **~titi novac** give change **~titi udarac** strike back **~titi istom mjerom** repay in kind, give tit for tat **~t** *nm* return **za ~t** in return (for) **~ni** *adj* **susret** *sport* return match/game **~ćati** *v impf*

uzvrpoljiti *v* (se) become fidgety, get the fidgets

už|ad *nn pl* rigging; ropes **~e** *nn* (*Gsg* **~eta**) rope; line; (debelo) cable

užar|en *adj* hot; red-hot **~iti** *v* **1** (što) heat **2** (se) become red-hot

užas *nm* horror; (djelo) atrocity **na moj ~** to my horror/dismay **~an** *adj* (*a*) horrible; dreadful, revolting **~avati** *v* **1** *impf* **2** (se čega/koga) abhor sth/sb, dread **~nuti** *v* (*pres* **~nem**) **1** (koga) horrify, terrify **2** (se) be shocked/terrified

užežen *adj* (mast) rancid

užina *nf* snack; lunch; brunch *US coll*; (odmor) lunch-break; (popodnevna) tea

uži|tak *nm* (*Gsg* **~tka**, *Npl* **~ci**) pleasure, joy, thrill **~vatelj** *nm* **1** connoiseur **2** user **3** holder **~vatelj mirovine** pensioner **~vati** *v* **1** (u čemu) enjoy, take pleasure in **2** (što) (povlasticu) have; (drogu) take drugs, be on drugs, abuse drugs

uživ|jeti *v* (se u što) (*pres* **~im**) **1** become familiar with, get into the role of **2** emphatize with **~ljavati** *v impf*

užurba|n *adj* hurried, bustling **biti ~n** be in a rush **~ti** *v* (se) be in a hurry, bustle (around)

V

V, v (ve) 28th letter of Cro. alphabet

vabiti *v* (koga/što) decoy (+ *fig*)

vadi|čep *nm* corkscrew ~**ti** *v* (što) take out, draw, pull out

vaga *nf* (*Dsg* vagi/vazi) 1 scales *pl*, scale *US*, balance **vodena ~** (spirit) level 2 *astrol* Libra ~**ti** *v* (koga/što/se) (*pres* važem) weigh (sb, sth, oneself) (+ *fig*)

vagon *nm* (railway) carriage *GB*, car *US* **teretni ~** goods waggon/van *GB*, box/freight car *US* ~-**restoran** dining/restaurant car; diner *US*

vakuum *nm* vacuum (+ *fig*)

val *nm* (*Npl* ~ovi) wave ~**ni** *adj* wave ~**na duljina** wave length ~**ovit** *adj* wavy; undulating; (brežuljci) rolling

valcer *nm* waltz **plesati ~** waltz

valencija *nf* valency *GB*, valence *US*

valoriz|acija *nf* valuation ~**irati** *v* (što) value

valuta *nf* currency **konvertibilna ~** hard c.

valj|ak *nm* (*Gsg* ~ka, *Npl* ~ci) roller ~**ak za tijesto** rolling pin **parni ~ak** steamroller ~**kast** *adj* cylindrical ~**ati** (1) *v* (što/se) roll ~**ati gluposti** *sl* talk nonsense

valja|n *adj* 1 valid 2 decent, honest 3 proper ~**nost** *nf* validity ~**ti** (2) *v* (*f*) be valid **ništa ne ~** it's no good ~**lo bi...** we should...

valjda *adv* probably, I guess, I suppose

valjuš|ak *nm* (*Gsg* ~ka, *Npl* ~ci, *Gpl* ~aka) dumpling

vampir *nm* vampire

van *adv* out ~**i** *adv* 1 out(side) 2 *coll* abroad

vanilija *nf* vanilla

vanjski *adj* 1 outer 2 foreign **Ministarstvo ~h poslova** Foreign Ministry; Foreign Office *GB*, Department of State *US*

vap|aj *nm* cry (of pain/for help), moan, wail; *fig* plea ~**iti** *v* (0) (*pres* ~**im**/~**ijem**) cry, moan, wail; plead

vapn|enac *nm* (*Gsg* ~**enca**, *Npl* ~**enaca**) limestone ~**o** *nn* lime **živo ~o** quicklime

var *nm* (*Npl* ~**ovi**) weld ~**itelj**/~**ilac** *nm* (*Gsg* ~**ioca**, *Gpl* ~**ilaca**) welder ~**iti** *v* (što) 1 weld (together, to) 2 cook ~**ivo** *nn* stew ~**jača** *nf* wooden spoon

vara|lica *nm* cheat; swindler; impostor ~**ti** *v* 1 (koga) cheat; deceive, fool, swindle 2 (0) cheat 3 (se) be wrong ~**v** *adj* deceptive, illusory, illusive ~**ljiv** *adj* 1 illusive 2 changeable ~**ka** *nf* deception, deceit, trick

varija|bilan *adj* (ɑ) variable ~**bla** *nf* variable ~**cija** *nf* variation ~**nta** *nf* (*Gpl* ~**nata**) variant, variety

vaš *pron poss* your; yours

vat *nm* watt

vata *nf* cotton wool

vaterpol|o *nm* water polo ~**ist** *nm* water polo player

vatr|a *nf* 1 fire **dati ruku u ~u** vouch for (sb/sth) **dolijevati ulje na ~u** add fuel to the flames **gdje ima dima ima i ~e** there's no smoke without fire **između dvije ~e** between the devil and the deep blue sea **otvoriti/prekinuti ~u** open/cease fire **pasti u ~u** lose one's temper **skočiti** (za koga) **u ~u i vodu** go through fire and water (for) 2 (za cigaretu) light ~**en** *adj* hot, hot-blooded; heated ~**ogasac** *nm* (*Gsg* ~**ogasca**, *Vsg* ~**ogašče**, *Gpl* ~**ogasaca**) fireman, firefighter ~**ogasno** *adj* **društvo** fire brigade *GB*, fire department *US* ~**omet** *nm* firework (display) ~**ostalan** *adj* (ɑ) heatproof; (zdjela) ovenproof

vau(-vau) *interj* bow-wow, woof

vaza *nf* vase

vazal *nm* vassal

Vaz|am *nm* (*Gsg* ~ma) Easter **vazmeni** *adj* Easter, paschal

vazda *adv* forever, always

vazelin *nm* *TM* Vaseline

važ|an *adj* (*a*) important, significant, prominent **praviti se ~an** put on airs, show off **vrlo ~no!** *coll* big deal **~nost** *nf* importance, significance

večer *nf* evening; night **dobra ~!** good evening **Badnja ~** Christmas Eve **~a** *nf* supper; dinner **Posljednja ~a** Last Supper **~as** *adv* tonight, this evening **~ati** *v* 1 (0) have supper/dinner **~ati u restoranu** dine, eat out 2 (što) have (sth) for supper/dinner **~njak** *nm* (*Npl* ~njaci) evening newspaper **~nji** *adj* evening **~nja služba** vespers

već (1) *conj* but

već (2) *adv* already, before **~ dva sata čekam** I've been waiting for two hours

većin|a *nm* majority (of); most **golema ~a** vast/overwhelming majority **~ski** *adj* majority **~om** *adv* mostly

ved|ar *adj* (*a*) 1 (nebo) clear; bright, sunny 2 (osoba) cheerful, light-hearted **~rina** *nf* 1 clearness, serenity; brightness **~riti** *v* (što/se) clear (up) **~riti i oblačiti** call the shots

vedro *nn* (*Npl* vedra, *Gpl* vedara) pail

veget|acija *nf* vegetation, plant life **~arijanac** *nm* (*Gsg* ~arijanca) vegetarian; veggie *coll* **~arijanski** *adj* vegetarian **~irati** *v* (0) vegetate

velebilje *nf* belladonna, deadly nightshade

velečasni *nm, adj* Reverend, Father

velegrad *nm* city **~ski** *adj* city

veleizdaj|a *nf* high treason **~nik** *nm* (*Vsg* ~niče, *Npl* ~nici) traitor

veleposjedn|ik *nm* (*Vsg* ~iče, *Npl* ~ici) landowner **~ici** *pl* landed gentry

veleposlan|ik *nm* (*Vsg* ~iče, *Npl* ~ici) ambassador (to) **~stvo** *nn* embassy

veleprodaj|a *nf* wholesale **~ni** *adj* wholesale

velesaj|am *nm* (*Gsg* ~ma, *Npl* ~movi) fair

veležupa *nf* canton

veličanstv|en *adj* magnificent, majestic, grand **Vaše/Njegovo V~o** Your/His Majesty

veli|čati *v* (koga/što) praise, exalt **~čina** *nf* size; quantity **~k** *adj* (*comp* veći) 1 big, large 2 *fig* great **~kan** *nm* great man, giant **~kaš** *nm* peer, lord, noble **~kodušan** *adj* (*a*) generous, magnanimous

velim *v defect* (što) say

veljača *nf* February

ven|a *nf* vein **~ski** *adj* venous

Venera *nf* Venus

veneričn|i *adj* venereal

ventil *nm* *coll* vent, valve **~acija** *nf* ventilation **~ator** *nm* fan, ventilator

venuti *v* (0) wilt, wither, languish (+ *fig*)

veo *nm* (*Gsg* vela, *Npl* velovi) veil

veoma *adv* very

vep|ar *nm* (*Gsg* ~pra, *Npl* ~rovi) wild boar

ver|ati *v* (se) (*pres* ~em) climb, clamber (up)

verbal|an *adj* (*a*) verbal

vergl *nm* *coll* barrel/hand organ **~aš** *nm* organ-grinder **~ati** *v* 1 (0) play a barrel organ 2 (što) *coll* reel off, rattle off

verifi|kacija *nf* verification **~cirati** *v* (što) verify, attest

vertikala *nf* vertical **~n** *adj* (*a*) vertical

verzal *nm* block letters/capitals

verzija *nf* version

verziran *adj* (well) versed

vese|ljak *nm* (*Gsg* ~ljaka, *Vsg* ~ljače, *Npl* ~ljaci) jolly/jovial person **~lje** *nn* cheer(fulness), joy, high spirits **~o** *adj* (~la *f*) cheerful, blithe, joyful, merry, bright, sunny

vesl|ač *nm* rower; oarsman **~ački** *adj* rowing **~anje** *nn* rowing **~ati** *v* (0) row **~o** *nn* oar **nisam ni ja ~o sisao** I'm not that stupid

vesta *nf* jumper, pullover

vestern *nm* western

vesti *v* (što) (*pres* vezem) embroider

veš *nm* *coll* → **rublje ~mašina** *nf* *coll* washing machine

veteran *nm* veteran; vet *coll*

veterinar *nm* veterinary surgeon *GB*,

veterinarian US; vet coll

veto nm (Gsg veta) veto **staviti ~ (na)** veto; put a veto (on)

vez (1) nm (Npl ~ovi) embroidery

vez (2) nm berth **~a** nf 1 connection, link 2 relationship 3 mil communications pl **časnik za ~u** liaison officer **stupiti u ~u** get in touch **~ati** v 1 (povezati) (koga/što s kim/čim) connect, link 2 (zavezati) (koga/što) tie, fasten 3 (se) fasten (one's) seat belt, buckle (up) 4 (se) fig make a commitment; get married **~ica** nf (shoe)lace **~ivati** v impf (pres ~ujem) **~ivni** adj connective **~nik** nm (Npl ~nici) conjunction

vezir nm vizier

veža nf hall(way)

vi pron Npl you

vibr|acija nf vibration **~e** nf pl sl vibes **~irati** v (0) vibrate

vic nm (Npl ~evi) joke **pričati ~eve** tell/crack jokes

vice- prefix vice-

vičan adj (a) versed, skilled, experienced

vid nm (Npl ~ovi) 1 sight 2 aspect **~no** adj polje field of vision **~ik** nm (Npl ~ici) view, sight **na ~iku** in sight **proširiti ~ike** broaden (one's) horizons **~ikovac** nm (Gsg ~ikovca, Gpl ~ikovaca) gazebo **~jelac** nm (Gsg ~ioca, Gpl ~jelaca) visionary, seer **izaći na ~jelo** nn come to light, be discovered **~jeti** v (koga/što) (pres ~im) see **ne mogu ga (živa) ~jeti** I can't stand him **~ljiv** adj visible **~ljivost** nf visibility **~okrug** nm (Npl ~okruzi) horizon **~ovit** adj clairvoyant, visionary **~ovitost** nf clairvoyance, second sight **~ovnjak** nm (Vsg ~ovnjače, Npl ~ovnjaci) clairvoyant

vida|r nm healer **~ti** v (koga/što) heal, cure

video nm video **~kaseta** nf v. tape/cassette **~rekorder** nm video (cassette) recorder, VCR **~teka** nf video rental(s)

vidra nf otter

vid|ati v impf (koga/se s kim) see sb/each other (from time to time, regularly) **~en** adj prominent, distin-

guished **iz ~enja** nn by sight

vihor nm 1 gale, whirlwind 2 fig storm

vijača nf skipping rope GB, jump rope US

vijaduk|t nm (Gpl ~ata) viaduct

vijak nm (Gsg vijka, Npl vijci) screw

vija|ti v 1 (0) blow hard, rage 2 (žito) winnow 3 (zastavu) fly **~vica** nf blizzard, snowstorm

vijeć|ati v (0) confer, be in session; deliberate **~e** nn council **V~e sigurnosti** Security Council **~nica** nf council chamber; city/town hall **~nik** nm (Vsg ~niče, Npl ~nici) councillor

vijek nm (Npl vjekovi) 1 age(s), era **srednji ~** the Middle Ages **životni ~** lifespan 2 → stoljeće

vijen|ac nm (Gsg ~ca) wreath **lovorov ~ac** laurel w. **položiti ~ac** lay a w.

vije|st nf (Isg ~sti/~šću) (a piece/item of) news; story **~sti** pl news sg

vijoriti v (0, čime, se) wave, flutter

viju|ga nf (Dsg ~zi) 1 (moždana) convolution 2 twist, whorl **~gati** v (0) twist, snake, wind **~gav** adj twisting, winding

vik|a nf (Dsg vici) shouts pl, clamour, tumult, uproar **mnogo ~e ni za što** much ado about nothing **~ač** nm loudmouth coll **~nuti** v pf (pres ~nem) **~ati** v impf (pres vičem) shout, cry (out), yell; holler US

vikar nm vicar

vikend nm weekend **~ica** nf weekend cottage, summer house

vikler nm coll hair roller/curler

vil|a (1) nf fairy, sprite **dobra ~a** fairy godmother **~enjak** nm (Vsg ~enjače, Npl ~enjaci) fairy, elf, sprite, pixie **~inski** adj fairy

vila (2) nf villa

vile nf pl (hay)fork, pitchfork sg

vilica (1) nf fork

vilica (2) nf → čeljust

viličar nm forklift

vime nn (Gsg ~na, Npl ~na) udder

vin|ar nm vinter, wine merchant **~arija** nf wine cellar **~arstvo** nn wine business **~o** nn wine bijelo/crno **~o** white/red wine **~ograd** nm vineyard **~ogradarstvo** nn wine production, viticulture **~ogradski** adj vineyard

~oteka nf wine shop **~ova** adj **loza** (grape)vine **~ski** adj wine

vinuti v (se) soar, fly up, take off

vinja|k nm (Npl ~ci) brandy

viol|a nf viola **~ina** nf violin **~inist** nm violinist **~inski** adj **ključ** treble clef **~ončelo** nn (violon)cello

vir nm (Npl ~ovi) whirlpool, vortex

vir|iti v (0) 1 stick out, protrude 2 (gledati) peep **~nuti** v pf peek

virman nm transfer

virtuoz nm 1 virtuoso 2 fig coll expert, dab hand

virus nm virus **~an** adj (a) viral

vis nm (Npl ~ovi) height **~ina** nf 1 height, altitude **nadmorska ~ina** elevation **gledati koga s ~ine** look down on sb 2 (glasa) pitch **~očje** nn highlands **~ok** adj (comp → **viši**) high; tall **imati ~oko mišljenje o kome** hold sb in high esteem **živjeti na ~okoj nozi** lead a life of luxury **~oko** adv high, highly **~oko-prefix** high(ly) **~okogradnja** nf construction (industry) **~okoparan** adj (a) highbrow **~oravan** nf (Gsg ~oravni) plateau **~ost** nf highness **Vaša Visosti** Your Highness

vis|ak nm (Gsg ~ka) plumb line **~eći** adj dangling, suspended **~eći most** suspension bridge **~ibaba** nf snowdrop **~iti/~jeti** v (0) hang (down)

viski nm whisk(e)y

viskoza nf viscose **~n** adj (a) viscose

viš|ak nm (Gsg ~ka, Npl ~kovi) 1 excess 2 econ surplus **~e** (1) adv more; plus **~e-manje** more or less **ni manje ni ~e** (nego) no less (than) **~e ovdje ne radi** he doesn't work here any more/longer **to ~e** particularly **sve ~e** increasingly, more and more **~e-** prefix multi-, poly- **~ekratan** adj (a) repeated, reiterated **~ekratnik** nm (Npl ~ekratnici) math multiple **~estran** adj many-sided **~estruk** adj multiple, manifold **~i** adj comp higher; taller **~a sila** leg act of God, force majeure

viš|e (2) adv over, above; beyond

višnj|a nf sour cherry; marasca **~ev** adj sour-cherry **~evac** nm (Gsg ~evca, Npl ~evci, Gpl ~evaca) cherry

brandy

vit|ak adj (comp ~kiji) slim, slender; lean **~kost** nf slimness; slim figure

vital|an adj (a) 1 (osoba) vital, lively 2 vital, essential **~nost** nf vitality

vitamin nm vitamin **~ski** adj vitamin

vite|ški adj chivalrous **~štvo** nn chivalry, knighthood **~z** nm (Vsg ~že, Npl ~zovi) knight

viti v (pres **vijem**) 1 (što/se) wind, twist, twine 2 (zastavu) fly 3 (se) blow in the wind **~ca** nf 1 tendril 2 (kose) curl 3 flourish, curl **~časta** adj **zagrada** brace(s)

vitlati v 1 (0, čime) brandish 2 (što) hurl

vitlo nm 1 windlass 2 reel GB, spool US

vitraj, vitraž nm stained glass window

vitrina nf cabinet; showcase

viv|ak nm (Gsg ~ka, Npl ~ci, Gpl ~aka) lapwing

viz|a nf visa **ulazna/izlazna ~a** entry/exit v. **dati ~u** grant a visa

vizij|a nf vision **~onar** nm visionary

vizir nm hist visor

vizit|a nf coll rounds

vizualan adj (a) visual

viž|l(j)ast adj agile, nimble

vječ|an adj (a) eternal, endless, infinite, undying **~no** adv eternally, for ever **~nost** nf eternity

vjeđa nf eyelid

vjenča|nica nf wedding gown **~nje** nn wedding **~ti** v (se s kim) wed, marry, get married

vjenčić nm dim coronet, small wreath

vjer|a nf faith, belief **~an** adj (a) faithful, true **~nik** nm (Vsg ~niče, Npl ~nici) believer **~nici** pl the faithful **~no** adv faithfully **~odajnica** nf 1 credentials pl 2 econ letter of credit **~odostojan** adj (a) authentic, credible **~odostojnost** nf authenticity, credibility **~oispovijed** nf religious denomination, confession, faith **~ojatnost** nf probability, likelihood **~ojatan** adj (a) probable, likely **~ojatno** adv probably, (most) likely **~onauk** nm religious instruction, Sunday school, catechism **~oučitelj** nm religion teacher, catechist **~ova-**

nje *nn* 1 belief 2 (molitva) Creed **~ovati** *v* (*pres* ~ujem) 1 (što/komu/u što) believe (in) 2 (komu) trust **~ovnik** *nm* (*Vsg* ~ovniče, *Npl* ~ovnici) creditor **~ski** *adj* religious

vjes|nik *nm* (*Vsg* ~niče, *Npl* ~nici) herald

vješa|la *nf pl* gallows **~lica** *nf* (coat) hanger **~ti** *v* (koga/što/se) hang

vješt *adj* skillful, adroit, dexterous, deft **~ačenje** *nn* leg expert opinion **~ačiti** *v* (0) *leg* give an expert opinion (in court); expertise *US* **~ak** *nm* leg expert witness **~ina** *nf* skill **~o** *adv* skillfully

vješti|ca *nf* witch lov **na ~ce** witchhunt (+ *fig*) **~čji** *adj* witch's

vjet|ar *nm* (*Gsg* ~ra, *Npl* ~rovi) wind pustiti **~ar** break wind **~renjača** *nf* windmill **~rić** *nm dim* breeze **~riti** *v* (što) air **~robran** *nm* windscreen *GB*, windshield *US* **~rogonja**, **~ropir** *nm* gadabout **~rokaz** *nm* weather vane **~rometina** *nf* windward side **~romjer** *nm* wind gauge **~rovka** *nf* (*Dsg* ~rovci) windbreaker

vjeverica *nf* squirrel

vježb|a *nf* exercise; drill; practice; training **~alište** *nn* exercise grounds **~aonica** *nf* gym **~ati** *v* (0/što) exercise; drill; practise; train 2 (0) workout **~enica** *nf* exercise book **~enik** *nm* (*Npl* ~enici) trainee

vlada *nf* government, administration **~nje** *nn* behaviour, demeanour, conduct **~r** *nm* ruler, sovereign **~ti** *v* 1 (0/čime) govern, rule, reign (over) 2 (se) behave **~vina** *nf* reign, rule

vlaga *nf* damp(ness), humidity

vlak *nm* (*Npl* ~ovi) train **~ovođa** *nm* guard *GB*, conductor *US*

vlak|nast *adj* fibrous **~no** *nm* (*Gpl* ~ana) fibre

vlas *nf* hair **~ište** *nn* scalp **~ulja** *nf* wig

vlas|ac *nm* (*Gsg* ~ca) chives *pl*

vlas|nički *adj* proprietary **~nik** *nm* (*Vsg* ~niče, *Npl* ~nici) owner, proprietor **~ništvo** *nn* ownership; property **~t** *nf* power, authority **na ~ti** in power **~ti** *pl* authorities **~tela** *nf collect* landed gentry **~telin** *nm* squire **~tit** *adj* proper, own **~todržac** (*Gsg*

~todršca, *Gpl* ~todržaca) *derog* dictator **~toljubiv** *adj* thirsty for power **~toručan** *adj* (α) personal

Vlašići *nm pl* Pleiades

vlat *nf* blade (of grass)

vlaž|an *adj* (α) 1 damp; moist 2 (zrak) humid **~iti** *v* (što) moisten, damp(en) **~nost** *nf* moisture, humidity

voajer *nm* voyeur; peeping Tom *coll*

voć|ar *nm* 1 fruiterer, fruit seller 2 fruiter, fruit grower **~arstvo** *nn* fruit growing **~e** *nn* fruit **~ka** *nf* (*Gpl* ~aka/~ki) fruit tree **~ni** *adj* fruit **~njak** *nm* (*Npl* ~njaci) orchard; grove

vod (1) *nm* (*Npl* ~ovi) *mil* platoon **~nik** *nm* (*Vsg* ~niče, *Npl* ~nici) corporal **stožerni ~nik** staff corporal

vod (2) *nm* (*Npl* ~ovi) lead **~ati** *v impf* **~eći** *adj* leading **~ič** *nm* 1 guide 2 guide book **misao ~ilja** *nf* guiding thought **zvijezda ~ilja** guiding star **~itelj** *nm TV, radio* presenter, host **~iti** *v* (koga/što) lead; guide, conduct **~iti rat** wage war **~iti ljubav** make love **~iti brigu** take care **~ljivost** *nf* conductivity **~stvo** *nn* (*Gpl* ~stava) *nm* leadership; guidance

vod|a *nf* water **pitka ~a** drinking w. **tekuća ~a** running w. **~en** *adj* water **~ene boje** watercolours **~ena para** water vapour **~eni žig** watermark **~enast** *adj* watery **~enica** *nf* watermill **~enkonj** *nm* hippo(potamus) **~enjak** *nm* (*Npl* ~enjaci) 1 *astrol* Aquarius 2 water sprite 3 *med* amnion **~ik** *nm* hydrogen **~njikav** *adj* watery, watered-down **~oderina** *nf* gully **~oinstalater** *nm* plumber **~ootporan** *adj* (α) watertight; (tkanina) waterproof **~opad** *nm* waterfall, cascade **~oprivreda** *nf* water resources management **~oravan** *adj* (α) horizontal, level **~oskok** *nm* (*Npl* ~oskoci) fountain **~ostaj** *nm* water level **~otoranj** *nm* (*Gsg* ~otornja, *Npl* ~otornjevi) water tower **~ovod** *nm* waterworks, water supply (system) **~ozemac** *nm* (*Gsg* ~ozemca, *Npl* ~ozemci, *Gpl* ~ozemaca) amphibian

vodvilj *nm* vaudeville

vođa *nm* leader

vojjačiti v (koga) enlist, conscript; draft US ~**arna** nf barracks ~**evati** v (pres ~ujem) (0) wage war ~**na** nf 1 campaign 2 war ~**ni** adj military ~**ni obveznik** conscript; draftee US ~**na osoba** serviceman ~**na policija** military police (MP) ~**nički** adj soldierly, military ~**nik** nm (Vsg ~niče, Npl ~nici) soldier; private, enlisted man ~**ska** nf (Dsg ~sci) 1 army, the military 2 armed forces ~**skovođa** nm military leader, commander

vojvo|da nm duke ~**dina** nf duchy ~**dstvo** nn dukedom ~**tkinja** nf duchess

vokabular nm vocabulary

vokal nm vowel ~**an** adj (ā) vocal

vokativ nm vocative

vol nm (Vsg ~e, Npl ~ovi) ox ~**ovski** adj ox

volan nm coll 1 (upravljač) steering wheel za ~**om** at the wheel 2 (na odjeći) flounce

volej nm sport volley

volont|er nm volunteer ~**irati** v (0) volunteer

volt nm volt ~**aža** nf voltage

volumen nm volume

volj|a nf will, volition **dobre/loše** ~**e** in a good/bad mood/humour **drage** ~**e** willingly **preko** ~**e** unwillingly **učini to meni za** ~**u** humour me **to mi je po** ~**i** it's to my liking **do mile** ~**e** to one's heart's content **nemam** ~**e za to** I don't feel like it, I'm not in the mood for it ~**an** adj (ā) willing, voluntary ~**no** adv willingly

voljeti v (pres volim) love; like, be fond of **više** ~ prefer

vonj nm smell ~**ati** v (0) smell

vos|ak nm (Gsg ~ka, Npl ~kovi) wax **premazan** ~**om** waxed

vošt|an| adj wax ~**anica** nf candle ~**iti** v (što) wax

votka nf vodka

voz|ač nm driver ~**ar** nm carter ~**arina** nf fare ~**ati** v impf 1 (koga/što/se) drive around 2 (koga) fig cheat, lead on ~**ilo** nn vehicle ~**iti** v 1 (koga/što) drive 2 (se) ride ~**ni** adj red timetable ~**ni park** car pool

vožnja nf drive; ride

vra|bac nm (Gsg ~pca, Vsg ~pče, Npl ~pci) sparrow

vrač nm (Npl ~evi) witch doctor, medicine man, shaman ~**ara** nf fortune-teller ~**ati** v (0) cast spells

vraćati v impf → vratiti

vrag nm (Vsg vraže, Npl ~ovi/vrazi) devil, Satan ~**olan** nm rogue, little devil ~**ol(j)ast** adj roguish, mischievous ~**olija** nf prank, mischief

vran adj raven black ~**a** nf crow **bijela** ~**a** an exception ~**ac** nm (Gsg ~ca, Vsg ~če, Gpl ~aca) black horse

vraški adv devilishly, horribly, terribly

vrat nm (Npl ~ovi) neck **skinuti** (što/koga) **s** ~**a** get sth/sb off one's back **sjediti/stajati kome za** ~**om** breathe down sb's neck ~**ni** adj neck ~**oloman** adj (ā) breakneck, reckless ~**olomija** nf reckless undertaking

vrat|a nf pl 1 door(s) 2 (vrtna, fig) gate, gateway **buljiti kao tele u šarena** ~**a** gape 3 sport goal ~**ar** nm 1 doorkeeper, doorman 2 gatekeeper 3 sport goalkeeper; goalie GB coll ~**arnica** nf gatehouse ~**nica** nf gatepost

vratiti v 1 (koga/što) return, give back, bring back; restore 2 (se) return, come back, be back, get back

vražji adj 1 (god)damn, bloody, blasted 2 mischievous, naughty

vrb|a nf willow (tree) **žalosna** ~**a** weeping willow **kad na** ~**i rodi grožđe** pigs might fly; never

vrbovati v (koga) recruit

vrcati v (što) extract (honey)

vrckast adj lively

vrč nm (Npl ~evi) jug GB, pitcher US

vrći v (što) thresh

vrdati v (0) dodge, evade

vrebati v (koga/što) lurk, prowl

vreć|a nf bag **mačak u** ~**i** pig in a poke ~**a bez dna** bottomless pit ~**ica** nf dim (plastic/paper) bag

vrel|ište nf boiling point ~**o** (1) adv → **vreo**

vrelo (2) nn well, spring

vreme|nski adj 1 temporal 2 weather ~**šan** adj (ā) aging

vrenje nn 1 fermentation 2 fig commotion, seething

vreo *adj* (vrela *f*) boiling hot, sizzling, scalding

vreten|ast *adj* spindle-shaped ~o *nn* spindle

vreti *v* (*pres* vrijem) 1 boil 2 ferment 3 *fig* seethe

vreva *nf* hustle and bustle

vrganj *nm* cep

vrh (1) *nm* (*Npl* ~ovi) top, peak, summit **na ~u jezika mi je** it's on the tip of my tongue **sastanak na ~u** summit **razgovori na ~u** top-level talks ~**ovni** *adj* supreme, chief ~**ovni zapovjednik** supreme commander, commander in chief ~**ovnik** *nm* (*Vsg* ~ovniče, *Npl* ~ovnici) sovereign; supreme commander ~**ovništvo** *nn* leadership ~**unac** *nm* (*Gsg* ~unca, *Gpl* ~unaca) climax, culmination, peak ~**unski** *adj* top; supreme, superb ~**uška** *nf derog* powers that be

vrh (2) *adv* above

vrhnje *nn* cream **kiselo ~** sour(ed) c. **tučeno ~** whipped c.

vrijed|an *adj* (*a*) (*comp* vredniji, vrjedniji) 1 valuable, worthy **nije toga ~no** it's not worth it **zlata ~an** worth its weight in gold 2 → **marljiv ~iti** *v* (0) 1 be valuable 2 be valid; be in effect 3 (što) be worth sth **ne ~i ni pišljiva boba** it's worthless ~**nost** *nf* value, worth **neprocjenjive ~nosti** invaluable, priceless ~**nosni** *adj* papiri securities

vrijeđati *v* 1 (koga/što) insult, offend, call names, hurt 2 (se) insult each other, exchange insults 3 (se) take offence

vrijeme *nn* (*Gsg*, *Npl*, *Gpl* vremena) 1 time **čitavo/cijelo ~** all the time **gubiti ~** waste time **radno ~** working/opening hours **sve u svoje ~** all in good time **od vremena do vremena** from time to time **za ~** during 2 weather **kakvo je ~?** what's the weather like? **prognoza vremena** weather forecast 3 *gram* tense

vrijes(ak) *nm* heather

vri|sak *nm* scream ~**snuti** *v* (0) scream (out) ~**štati** *v impf*

vriština *nf* moor(s)

vrlet *nf* steep/rocky/rough ground,

crag ~**an** *adj* (*a*) craggy

vrli *adj* virtuous ~**na** *nf* virtue

vrlo *adv* very, highly

vrludati *v* (0) ramble (about), roam, wander (about)

vrp|ca *nf* (*Gpl* ~ci/~ca) 1 ribbon; band, strip 2 tape

vrpoljiti *v* (se) fidget

vrsnoća *nf* quality, excellence

vrsta *nf* 1 kind, sort 2 species 3 (red) line-up ~**n** *adj* (*f* vrsna, *comp* vrsniji) excellent, quality, choice

vrša *nf* fish trap

vrš|ak *nm* (*Gsg* ~ka, *Npl* ~ci/~kovi) tip

vršalica *nf* threshing machine ~**idba** *nf* threshing ~**iti** (1) *v* (žito) thresh

vrši|lac, ~**telj** *nm* doer, performer ~**telj dužnosti** (v.d.) acting ~**ti** (2) *v* (što) carry out, perform, execute; commit, perpetrate

vršnja|k *nm* (*Npl* ~ci) person of the same age, peer

vrt *nm* (*Npl* ~ovi) garden ~**ić** *nm* kindergarten ~**lar** *nm* gardener ~**larski** *adj* gardening ~**larstvo** *nn* gardening ~**ni** *adj* garden

vrt|jeti *v* (*pres* ~im) (koga/što/se) whirl (around), spin, twirl ~**log** *nm* (*Npl* ~lozi) whirlwind (+ *fig*) ~**ložiti** *v* (se) whirl ~**oglav** *adj* vertiginous, giddy, dizzy ~**oglavica** *nf* vertigo, dizziness ~**uljak** *nm* (*Gsg* ~uljka, *Npl* ~uljci) merry-go-round *GB*, car(r)ousel *US*

vruć *adj* hot **željezo se kuje dok je ~e** strike while the iron is hot ~**ica** *nf* fever ~**ina** *nf* heat

vrulja *nf* submarine spring

vru|tak *nm* (*Gsg* ~tka, *Npl* ~ci, *Gpl* ~taka) spring, well

vrvjeti *v* (0, čime) (*pres* vrvim) swarm with, teem with, crawl with, be alive with

vrzin *adj* ~**o kolo** 1 fairy ring 2 *fig* vicious circle

vrzmati *v* (se) loiter, hang around

vucarati *v* (se) *derog* wander around

vucibatina *nm, nf derog* tramp, bum

vuč|a *nf* drag, tow, traction ~**ni** *adj* traction

vuč|ica *nf* she-wolf ~**jak** *nm* 1 wolfhound 2 *coll* German shepherd, Alsatian ~**ji** *adj* wolf's, wolfish

vući *v* (*pres* vučem) **1** (što/koga) drag, draw, haul, tow **2** (se) drag, move slowly

vuk *nm* (*Vsg* vuče, *Npl* vuci/~kovi) wolf ~ **u janjećoj koži** a wolf in a sheep's clothing **mi o ~u, a ~ na vrata** talk of the devil ~**odlak** *nm* (*Vsg* ~odlače, *Npl* ~odlaci) werewolf

vulgar|an *adj* (α) vulgar
vulkan *nm* volcano ~**ski** *adj* volcanic
vulkaniz|er *nm* tyre repairer ~**irati** *v* (što) **1** (gumu) repair **2** *chem* vulcanize
vun|a *nf* wool **šećerna** ~**a** candy floss *GB*, cotton candy *US* ~**ast** *adj* woolly ~**en** *adj* woollen

Z

Z, z (ze) 29th letter of Cro. alphabet

za *prep* 1 (~ vrijeme) during ~ **života**
during/in one's lifetime 2 for ~ **mene**
for me ~ **sada** for now, for the time
being 3 at ~ **stolom** at the table 4 by
uzeti ~ **ruku** take by the hand **dan** ~
danom day by day 5 after **jedan** ~
drugim one after another ~ **mnom**
follow me 6 in ~ **pola sata** in half an
hour 7 behind **meni** ~ **leđima** behind
my back 8 **imenovati koga** ~ **pred-
sjednika/predstavnika** appoint sb
president/(as a) representative 9 **ar-
gumenti** ~ **i protiv** the pros and cons
10 **šalica** ~ **kavu** coffee cup 11 **jezik**
~ **zube!** hold your tongue! keep your
mouth shut!

zaba|citi *v* (što) throw back ~**čen** *adj*
remote, isolated, far-flung

zabadati *v impf* ~ **zabosti** ~ **nos u
tuđe poslove** poke one's nose into
other people's affairs/business;
snoop *coll*

zabadava *adv coll* 1 free (of charge),
gratis 2 in vain

zabašuriti *v* (što) hush up, cover up,
suppress

zabat *nm* gable

zabav|a *nf* 1 amusement, entertain-
ment, fun 2 party ~**an** *adj* (*a*) amusing, entertaining ~**na glazba** pop
music, easy-listening music ~**iti** *v* 1
(koga) amuse, entertain 2 (koga)
keep occupied 3 (se) amuse oneself;
have fun, have a good time ~**ljač** *nm*
entertainer ~**ljati** *v impf*

zabezekn|uti *v* (se) (*pres* ~**em**) be
dumbfounded/flabbergasted

zabijati *v impf* → **zabiti**

zabilje|ška *nf* (*Dsg* ~**šci**, *Gpl*
~**žaka/~ški**) note ~**žiti** *v* (što) 1 (zapisati) note, make a note; jot down 2
register, record

zabit *nm* remote/isolated place ~**an** *adj*
(*a*) remote, isolated

zabi|ti *v* (*pres* ~**jem**) 1 (što)
drive/ram/run/hammer in(to) ~**ti
čavlima** nail down/up ~**ti gol** score a
goal 2 (se) run/crash into

zablatiti *v* 1 (što) muddy, dirty, soil
(se) get dirty

zablen|uti *v* (se) (*pres* ~**em**) gape,
stand agape

zabli|ještiti *v* 1 (0) flash, glisten 2
(koga/što) dazzle ~**stati** *v* (0) (begin
to) glisten, sparkle

zablud|a *nf* error, mistake; fallacy,
misconception, false belief **biti u** ~**i**
be mistaken **dovesti u** ~**u** mislead
~**jeti** *v* (0) (*pres* ~**im**) go astray

zaboga *int* for God's/goodness' sake

zabolje|ti *v* (koga) 1 (begin to) hurt
~**la me glava** my head began to ache
2 grieve

zaborav *nm* oblivion ~**an** *adj* (*a*) for-
getful ~**iti** *v* 1 (koga/što) forget 2 (se)
forget oneself ~**ljati** *v impf*

zabo|sti *v* (što) (*pres* ~**dem**)
stick/drive/pin in(to)

zabra|na *nf* 1 ban, prohibition 2 em-
bargo ~**niti** *v* (što) 1 ban, forbid, prohibit 2 embargo 3 (novine) supress
~**njen** *adj* **ulaz** no admittance ~**nji-
vati** *v impf*

zabraviti *v* (što) lock

zabri|nut *adj* worried, anxious ~**nuti** *v*
(*pres* ~**nem**) 1 (koga) trouble, worry,
disturb 2 (se) worry, fret ~**nutost** *nf*
concern; anxiety ~**njavati** *v impf*

zabrljati *v* (što) *coll* botch up, bungle,
blow, mess up

zabrtviti *v* (što) choke up, plug up,
stop up

zabuljiti *v* (se) (u koga/što) stare at

zabun|a *nf* 1 error, mistake 2 confu-
sion **unijeti** ~**u** cause confusion ~**om**

adv by mistake, erroneously **~iti** *v* (se) make a mistake

zabundati *v* (se) bundle (oneself) up

zabuša|nt *nm coll* shirker; skiver *GB sl* **~vati** *v* (0) shirk, skive

zabušiti *v* (se) *coll* crash into, run into

zacijeliti *v* (0) heal

zacijelo *adv* certainly, surely, very likely

zacrniti *v* (što) blacken

zacrtati *v* (što) map out; draw up, outline

zacrve|njeti *v* (se) (*pres* ~nim) redden, turn red; (lice) blush

zacviliti *v* (0) squeak, squeal

začara|n *adj* enchanted **~ni krug** vicious circle **~ti** *v* (koga/što) enchant, bewitch, cast a spell on

začas *adv* in a moment/minute, in a little while

začeće *nn* conception

začelje *nn* rear

začepiti *v* (što) plug/stop/choke up; (bocu) cork; (usta) gag; (probavu) constipate

začešljati *v* (što) comb back

začetak *nm* (*Ggs* ~etka, *Npl* ~eci) beginning, start, outset; origin **spriječiti u ~etku** nip in the bud **~eti** *v* (pres ~nem) **1** (koga/što) conceive **2** (0) become pregnant **~etnik** *nm* (*Npl* ~etnici) originator, progenitor

začin *nm* **1** spice(s); condiment *form* **2** dressing, seasoning **~iti** *v* (što) season, spice (+ *fig*); (salatu) dress

začkoljica *nf coll* catch, snag, hitch

začu|dan *adj* (*α*) amazing, remarkable **~diti** *v* **1** (koga) amaze, astonish, surprise **2** (se) be amazed, wonder at **~do** *adv* surprisingly/curiously enough **~den** *adj* amazed, astonished

za|ći *v* (*pres* ~đem) **1** (za što) go/get behind **~ći za ugao** turn the corner **2** (u što) go/get into **~ u godine** be getting on in years **3** (0/za što) set, go down, sink; disappear

zaćoriti *v* (0) *sl* fall asleep; nod off *coll*

zadaća *nf* task, assignment; mission, job

zada|h *nm* (*Npl* ~si) unpleasant/bad/foul smell, stench **~h iz usta** bad breath

za|dak *nm* (*Gsg* ~tka, *Npl* ~tci) abdomen

zada|tak *nm* (*Gsg* ~tka, *Npl* ~ci) **1** task, assignment; job, mission **2** problem **~ti** *v* (što) (zadatak) give sb an assignment, assign/give/set sb a task; (udarac) deal; (riječ) give, pledge; (bol) cause, inflict; (brige) cause; (pitanje) ask sb a question, put a question to sb **~vati** *v impf*

zadaviti *v* **1** (koga) strangle, throttle **2** (se) choke to death

zader|ati *v* (se) (*pres* ~em) cry out, (give a) shout, yell

zadesi|ti *v* **1** (koga) befall, happen to sb **~la nas je nesreća** we met with/were overtaken by misfortune **2** (se) happen to be, find oneself

zadign|uti *v* (što) (*pres* ~em) hitch up

zadi|han *adj* out of breath, breathless **~hati** *v* (se) (*pres* ~šem) gasp for breath, puff, pant

zadijevati *v impf* → **zadjenuti**

zadim|iti *v* (što) fill with smoke **~ljen** *adj* smoky

zadirati *v* (u što) encroach (up)on

zadirk|ivati *v* (koga) (*pres* ~ujem) tease

zadiviti *v* (koga) amaze

zadjen|uti *v* (što) (*pres* ~em) stick in(to), insert

zadjevica *nf* disagreement, quarrel, squabble

zadnj|i *adj* **1** last; final, ultimate **2** back, rear **u ~e vrijeme** *coll* recently, in recent times, lately **~ica** *nf* buttocks *pl*, bottom, rear

zadobi|ti *v* (što) (*pres* ~jem) **1** get, obtain, receive **2** (povjerenje) gain, win **3** (ozljede) sustain

zadojiti *v* (koga) imbue

zadovolj|an *adj* (*α*) content(ed), satisfied **~avajući** *adj* **1** satisfactory, satisfying **2** sufficient **~enje** *nn* satisfaction; fulfilment **~iti** *v* **1** (koga/što) content, satisfy, gratify **2** (što) fulfil, meet **3** (se) be satisfied (with); settle for **~stvo** *nn* content(ment), satisfaction; pleasure **~avati** *v impf*

zadrijemati *v* (0) doze off, nod off, take a nap/snooze

zadrt *adj* die-hard, dyed-in-the-wool,

set in one's ways

zadruga *nf* cooperative **poljoprivredna ~** cooperative farm

zadrž|ati *v* (koga/što) (*pres* ~im) 1 keep 2 hold (up), stop, keep from 3 delay, detain, hold back 4 keep back, withhold, retain 5 (se) be detained; stay, stop, spend time **~vati** *v impf*

zadubiti *v* (se) be absorbed/engrossed in

zadugo *adv* for long

zadušnica *nf* (misa ~) requiem, memorial service

zadužen *adj* 1 indebted, in debt 2 (za što) in charge of, responsible for **~enje** *nn* duty, obligation, responsibility, task **~iti** *v* 1 (koga) put in charge of, entrust with, make responsible for 2 (se) get/run into debt, run up/incur a debt **~nica** *nf* promissory note; IOU *coll*; bond **~ivati** *v impf*

zafrkavati *v coll* 1 (koga) tease, pull sb's leg 2 (se) kid, joke; have fun, fool around

zaga|diti *v* (što) contaminate, pollute **~đen** *adj* contaminated, polluted, foul **~đivati** *v impf*

zagasit *adj* dark, deep

zagasiti *v* 1 (što) extinguish, put out; turn/switch off 2 (se) go out

zagaziti *v* (u što) 1 (u rijeku) wade into 2 tread on, step into ~ **u dugove** run into debt

zaglaviti *v* 1 (što) jam, wedge 2 (0) meet one's end, lose one's life 3 (se) jam, get stuck

zaglavlje *nn* head(ing); letterhead(ing)

zagledati *v* (se) 1 (u što) gape at, stare at 2 (u koga) take a fancy to sb

zaglibiti *v* (0) sink into the mud/mire, get bogged down (+ *fig*)

zaglup|iti *v* (koga) make stupid **~ljivati** *v impf*

zaglušan *adj* (α) deafening, ear-splitting

zagnojiti *v* (se) suppurate, fester

zagnjuriti *v* 1 (koga/što) immerse, dip, plunge 2 (se) dip, dive

zagolicati *v* (koga/što) tickle (+ *fig*)

zagone|tan *adj* (α) enigmatic, mysterious, puzzling **~tka** *nf* (*Dsg* ~tki/~ci) riddle, puzzle, enigma,

mystery

zagorča|ti *v* (što) make bitter **~ti kome život** make sb's life miserable **~vati** *v impf*

zagor|jeti *v* (0) (*pres* ~im) burn

zagospodariti *v* (kim/čim) establish/ impose one's rule; take over

zagov|arati *v* (što) advocate, argue for, support **~ornik** *nm* (*Npl* ~ornici) advocate, proponent

zagrabiti *v* (što) scoop out/up

zagrad|a *nf* 1 (uglata) (square) bracket 2 (okrugla) (round) bracket, parenthesis 3 (vitičasta) brace 4 (kosa) oblique, slash, solidus **~iti** *v* (što) fence in, enclose; (zidom) wall in

zagrcn|uti *v* (se) (*pres* ~em) choke (on)

zagrij|ati *v* (*pres* ~em) 1 (što) warm (up) (+ *fig*), heat 2 (koga za što) *fig* stir up/arouse sb's interest in 3 (se) warm (up), warm oneself 4 (za što) *fig* warm to, become keenly interested in

zagri|sti *v* (što) (*pres* ~zem) 1 bite (in/into), take a bite 2 *fig* bite, swallow **~žen** *adj* die-hard, bigoted **~žljiv** *adj* caustic

zagr|liti *v* 1 (koga/što) embrace, (give sb a) hug, put one's arms around 2 (se) embrace **~ljaj** *nm* embrace, hug **pasti u ~ljaj** fall into sb's arms

zagrm|jeti *v* (0) (*pres* ~im) thunder (+ *fig*); roar (out) *fig*

zagrn|uti *v* (*pres* ~em) 1 (što) cover (with) 2 (koga/što/se čime) put/slip/throw sth over sb's/one's back/shoulders

zagrobni *adj fig* sepulchral ~ **život** afterlife

zagroziti *v* (se komu/čime) threaten sb (with sth)

zagrtati *v impf* → **zagrnuti**

zagubiti *v* (što) mislay, misplace

zaguljen *adj coll* pigheaded, difficult do deal with ~ **problem** knotty problem

zagust|jeti *v* (0) (*pres* ~im) *fig* come to a critical point, get hot

zaguš|iti *v* 1 (koga/što) suffocate, smother, stifle, choke; (tel. liniju) jam 2 (se) suffocate, choke (to death)

~ljiv adj stifling, stuffy, close

zahlad|njeti v (0) (pres ~nim) become/get/turn cold

zahod nm toilet, lavatory, water closet (WC); bathroom; public convenience GB; loo GB coll; bog GB sl; john US sl; rest room, washroom US muški ~ gents GB; men's room US ženski ~ ladies GB; ladies room US

zahr|kati v (0) (pres ~ćem) 1 (begin to) snore 2 fall fast asleep

zaht|ijevati v (što) demand, claim, require; call for, insist on ~jev nm demand; request; requirement ~jevan adj (α) demanding

zahuk|tati v (se) (pres ~ćem) fig be in full swing

zahvaćati v impf → zahvatiti

zahva|la nf thanks pl; acknowledgment ~lan adj (α) grateful, thankful ~liti (se) v 1 (komu) thank 2 (na čemu) acknowledge ~liti na dužnosti resign from office ~liti na pozivu decline an invitation ~lnost nf gratitude, thankfulness; appreciation ~ljujući adv thanks to, owing to ~ljivati v impf

zahvat nm hold, grip, grasp kirurški ~ surgery, surgical operation ~iti v (što/koga) 1 grab, grasp, grip, take hold of, seize 2 scoop out/up 3 affect, reach, spread over/to

zaigra|ti v 1 (0) (begin to) play 2 (se) be absorbed in play srce mi je ~lo od veselja my heart leapt with joy

zainteresirati v 1 (koga) interest sb in sth 2 (se za što/koga) show/take an interest in

zaista adv really, indeed, surely, truly, certainly

zaja|hati v (što/koga) (pres ~šem) mount, get on

zajam nm (Gsg ~ma, Npl ~movi) loan, credit

zajamčiti v (što) guarantee

zajapuriti v (se) go red/purple (in the face)

zajeb|ati v (koga/što) (pres ~em) tab fuck/screw up tab ~avati v tab 1 (koga) take the piss out of sb tab sl 2 (se) fool around coll; fuck around tab sl 3 (se s kim) fuck with sb tab sl

zajedljiv adj caustic

zajedn|ica nf 1 community 2 (organizacija) union, association, society bračna ~ica marriage, matrimony ~ički adj common, joint; shared; mutual ~ištvo nn unity, togetherness ~o adv together

zajmo|davac nm (Gsg ~davca, Npl ~davci) creditor, lender ~primac nm (Gsg ~primca, Npl ~primci) borrower, debtor

zaju|trak nm (Gsg ~tarka) form breakfast

zakapati v impf → zakopati

zaka|sniti v (0/na što) be/come late (for); be overdue ~šnjenje nn delay, late arrival doći sa ~šnjenjem od dva sata be two hours late/overdue ~šnjavati v impf

zaka|zati (1) v (što) (pres ~žem) call, convene, schedule

zaka|zati (2) (0) (pres ~žem) fail

zaki|nuti v (koga/na čemu/u čemu) (pres ~nem) stint (on); cheat ~nuti na vagi give short weight ~dati v impf

zakip|jeti v (0) (pres ~im) (begin to) boil, come to the boil

zaklad|a nf foundation, endowment ~nik nm (Npl ~nici) founder

zaklanjati v impf → zakloniti

zak|lati v (koga) (pres ~oljem) cut/slit sb's throat; kill, slaughter

zak|let adj sworn ~leti v (pres ~unem) 1 (koga) swear sb in 2 (se) swear, swear/take an oath ~letva nf oath ~linjati v (se) impf

zaklon nm shelter ~iti v 1 (koga/što) shelter, guard, protect 2 (se) shelter, find/take shelter/refuge ~iti pogled block the view

zaklopiti v (što) close, shut

zaključ|ak nm (Gsg ~ka, Npl ~ci) 1 conclusion 2 deduction, inference 3 resolution, decision ~iti v (što) 1 conclude 2 deduce, infer 3 (ugovor) sign 4 decide ~iti slučaj close a case ~ni adj final, definite ~no adv inclusive ~no do petka until Friday inclusive ~ivati v impf

zaključati v 1 (što/koga) lock (in/up) 2 (se) lock oneself in

zakočiti v (što) 1 brake 2 (oružje) slip on the safety catch

zakolutati v (čime) ~ očima roll one's eyes

zakon nm law (+ fig); act, code, legislation, statute **nacrt** ~a draft bill **prijedlog** ~a bill **kazneni** ~ penal code **krivični** ~ criminal code/law **donijeti** ~ pass/enact a law **krojiti** ~ lay down the law ~**ik** nm (Npl ~ici) code ~**it** adj legitimate, legal ~**itost** nf 1 legality, legitimacy 2 law, rule ~**odavac** nm (Gsg ~odavca, Npl ~odavci) legislator, lawmaker ~**odavni** adj legislative ~**odavstvo** nn legislature ~**ski** adj legal, statutory

zakopati v (što/koga) bury, inter

zakopčati v 1 (što) button (up); buckle; clasp 2 (se) button; button oneself (up)

zakoračiti v (0) make/take a step

zak|ovati v (što) (pres ~ujem) 1 nail down 2 rivet ~**ovica** nf rivet

zakrabuljiti v (se) disguise oneself

zakratko adv in a short while, soon

zakrčiti v (što) block; jam, crowd

zakre|nuti v (pres ~nem) 1 (što/čime) ~**nuti komu ruku** twist sb's arm ~**nuti komu vratom** wring sb's neck 2 (0) turn; swerve ~**nuti za ugao** turn/round the corner ~**tati** v impf

zakriliti v (koga/što) take under one's wing, protect, shield

zakrpa nf patch ~**ti** v (što) patch (up); darn; mend

zakrvav|iti v (što) stain with blood ~**ljen** adj (oči) bloodshot

zakržljati v (0) become stunted

zakucati v 1 (što) hammer in, nail down 2 (što) knock, tap 3 (loptu) sport sl dunk, slam-dunk (a basketball)

zakučast adj convoluted, intricate

zakuhati v 1 (što) boil, bring to the boil 2 (što) fig stir up 3 (0) boil, come to the boil

zakulisni adj behind-the-scenes, secret, underhand(ed)

zakup nm lease, tenure **dati u/pod** ~ lease (out), rent (out) **uzeti u** ~ take a lease on, rent ~**ac** (Gsg ~ca, Npl ~ci), ~**nik** (Npl ~nici) nm leaseholder, tenant, renter ~**iti** v (što) lease, rent ~**nina** nf rent(al) ~**ljivati** v impf

zakuriti v (0) coll come down with a fever, get a temperature

zakus|ka nf (Dsg ~ci, Gpl ~aka/~ki) refreshment(s), snack, buffet

zakvačiti v 1 (što) hook/hitch on/up, fasten 2 (se) get hooked/hitched/caught 3 (se) fig come to grips, grapple; (oko čega) quarrel about/over sth

zalaga|onica nf pawnshop ~**oničar** nf pawnbroker ~**ti** v 1 (što) pawn 2 (se za što/koga) support, advocate, intercede with sb for sb/on sb's behalf 3 (se u radu) work conscientiously

zala|z, **zala|zak** (Gsg ~ska, Npl ~sci) nm ~**zak sunca** sundown, sunset **na** ~**zu** fig on the wane ~**ziti** v (0) 1 impf → **zaći** 2 (kamo) frequent, be a regular visitor of

zale|điti v 1 (što) freeze (+ fig), ice 2 (se) freeze (up), ice over/up ~**đivati** v impf

zaleđe nn 1 back, rear 2 fig backing, support 3 hinterland

zalemiti v (što) solder

zalet nm run-up **skok sa** ~**om** running jump ~**jeti** v (se) (pres ~im) 1 dash, rush, make a dash at 2 (u što) crash/run/slam into 3 fig blab, let slip ~**avati** v impf

zaliha nf stock, supply, reserve(s); supplies, provisions pl

zalihost nf redundancy

zaliječiti v (što) heal, cure

zalijepiti v 1 (što) stick, glue, paste (up/down/together) ~ **kuvertu** seal an envelope 2 (se) stick

zalijetati v (se) impf → **zaletjeti se**

zalijevati v impf → **zaliti**

zali|sci nm pl (G ~zaka) whiskers; sideboards GB, sideburns US **srčani** ~**stak** nm (Gsg ~ska) heart valve

zaliti v (što) water ~ **vinom** wash down with wine

zali|zati v (što) (pres ~žem) slick down

zalo|g nm pawn, pledge; security ~**žiti** v pf → **zalagati**

zalogaj nm mouthful, bite; morsel

zalu|diti v (koga) turn one's head ~**đen** adj (čim/kim) crazy about, infatuated with sb

zalupiti v (što/se) slam (shut)

zalutati v (0) lose one's way

zaljev nm bay, gulf

zaljub|iti v (se) fall in love with **~iti se preko ušiju/glave** fall head over heels in love **~ljenik** nm (Npl ~ljenici) (čega/u što) lover, aficionado **~ljivati** v (se) impf

zamagli|ti v 1 (što) mist up, fog, blur 2 (se) mist over, fog up, steam up; become misty/hazy (+ fig) **~lo mi se pred očima** my head is swimming

zama|h nm (Npl ~si) 1 swing; stroke 2 fig momentum, impetus **u punom ~hu** in full swing **~hnuti** v (0/čime) (pres ~hnem) (take a) swing

zam|ak nm (Gsg ~ka, Npl ~ci/~kovi) castle

zamakn|uti v (0/za što) (pres ~em) disappear behind **~uti za ugao** turn the corner

zamalo adv almost, nearly

zamaman adj (α) enticing, seductive, alluring

zamarati v impf → zamoriti

zamastiti v (što) smear, stain (with grease)

zamatati v impf → zamotati

zama|zan adj dirty **~zati** v (pres ~žem) 1 (što/koga) (make) dirty, soil, smear **~zati kome oči** pull the wool over sb's eyes 2 (se) get dirty

zame|sti v (što/koga) (pres ~tem) snow in/up **~sti tragove** cover up tracks **~o mu se svaki trag** he vanished without a trace **~t** nm snowdrift

zame|tak nm (Gsg ~tka, Npl ~ci) embryo **uništiti u ~tku** nip in the bud

zametn|uti (1) v (što) (pres ~em) mislay, misplace

zamet|nuti (2) v (što) (pres ~nem) start, engage in **~nuti svađu** pick a quarrel **~ati** v impf

zamijeniti v 1 (što/koga) exchange; swap coll 2 (što) barter, trade (off) 3 (koga/što za koga/što) mistake sb/sth for sb/sth, confuse sb/sth with sb/sth 4 (koga) represent, act for/on behalf of 5 (koga/što) replace, substitute 6 (stražu) relieve **~ mjesta** switch positions

zamijesiti v (što) knead **~ kruh** make bread **~ komu kašu** cause trouble for sb

zamijetiti v (koga/što) notice, observe

zamirati v impf → zamrijeti (2)

zami|sao nf (Gsg ~sli, Npl ~sli) 1 idea, notion, conception 2 plan **~sliti** v (što) imagine, think of, fancy, picture; conceive 2 (se) be absorbed in one's thoughts; muse, ponder **~šljen** adj thoughtful, pensive **~šljati** v impf

zamjećivati v impf → zamijetiti

zamje|na nf 1 exchange; swap coll 2 barter 3 replacement, substitution 4 substitute 5 relief **u ~nu za** in exchange/return for **~nica** nf gram pronoun **~nik** (Vsg ~niče, Npl ~nici) 1 deputy, vice- 2 representative 3 replacement, substitute **~njivati** v impf

zamjer|iti v 1 (komu što) resent, bear a grudge, hold sth against sb, blame; find fault with **ne ~iti** take in good part 2 (se komu) incur sb's disfavour **~ka** nf (Dsg ~ci) objection, reproach

zamjet|ljiv adj noticeable **~no** adv markedly

zam|ka nf (Dsg ~ci) trap, snare (+ fig) **uhvatiti u ~ku** (en)trap, (en)snare

zamol|ba nf request **~iti** v (koga/što) ask, request

zamor nm fatigue **~an** adj (α) 1 tiring, weary 2 tiresome **~iti** v 1 (koga) tire out, weary, make tired/wearied 2 (se) tire/weary of

zamor|ac nm (Gsg ~ca, Npl ~ci) 1 guinea pig (+ fig) 2 green monkey

zamo|tak nm (Gsg ~tka, Npl ~ci) bundle **~tati** v (koga/što) wrap up, envelop **~tati u pelene** swaddle

zamračiti v (što) darken, dim, obscure; black out

zamr|lijeti v (0) (pres ~em) 1 fall into a coma 2 die out; die down

zamrljati v (što) stain, smear, soil

zamr|siti v 1 (što) (en)tangle 2 (se) get tangled up/entangled; become intricate fig **~šen** adj intricate, complicated

zamrziti v (koga/što) begin to hate, take a dislike to

zamrzn|uti v (pres ~em) 1 (što) freeze 2 (se) freeze (over/up), be frozen

zamuck|ivati *v* (0) (*pres* ~ujem) stammer, stutter

zamukn|uti *v* (0) (*pres* ~em) fall silent, hush

zamutiti *v* (što) 1 make turbid, cloud 2 *fig* stir up (trouble) 3 stir, mix ~ jaja whisk eggs 4 (se) become turbid/clouded

zanat *nm* (handi)craft, trade **ići u/izučiti/ispeći** ~ learn a trade **dati u/na** ~ apprentice sb ~**stvo** *nn* handicrafts

zanemari|ti *v* 1 (koga/što) neglect; ignore, disregard 2 (se) neglect one's appearance ~**v** *adj* negligible

zanese|n *adj* 1 carried away 2 elated ~**njak** *nm* (*Npl* ~njaci) dreamer; enthusiast

zanije|kati *v* (što) (*pres* ~čem) deny

zanijemiti *v* (0) 1 become mute 2 be dumbfounded, be struck dumb, be speechless

zan|ijeti *v* (*pres* ~esem) 1 (koga) *fig* enrapture, enthrall 2 (se) swerve, skid, veer 3 (se čim) get carried away, be ecstatic 4 (0) conceive, become pregnant

zanim|acija *nf* coll hobby ~**anje** *nn* 1 occupation, profession 2 interest ~**ati** *v* 1 (koga) interest **to me ne** ~**a** it doesn't interest me, I'm not interested in it ~**a me idete li** I'd like to know/I wonder whether you are going 2 (se za koga/za što) show/take an interest in ~**ljiv** *adj* interesting ~**ljivost** *nf* 1 interest 2 interesting event/detail/thing 3 ~**ljivosti** *pl* sights; attractions

zanoktica *nf* hangnail

zanos *nm* enthusiasm, rapture, ecstasy, elation ~**an** *adj* (*a*) captivating, fascinating ~**iti** *v* 1 *impf* → **zanijeti** (1,3) 2 (se) delude oneself, labour under the delusion

zanovijeta|lo *nn* grumbler, nag ~**ti** *v* (0/kome) grumble; nag (at)

zao *adj* (zla *f*) bad, evil, wicked, mean; vicious **u** ~ **čas** in an evil hour ~ **glas** bad name/reputation **zla sreća** ill luck **zlo mi je** I feel sick

zaobi|ći *v* (koga/što) (*pres* ~đem) 1 go (a)round, bypass, make a detour 2

circumvent 3 *fig* leave out, overlook ~**lazak** *nm* (*Npl* ~lasci) detour, bypass ~**lazan** *adj* (*a*) roundabout, indirect; circuitous *form* ~**laznica** *nf* bypass; ring road *GB*; beltway *US* ~**laziti** *v impf*

zaob|liti *v* 1 (što) (make) round 2 (se) become round, round out ~**ljen** *adj* round(ed)

zaogrn|uti *v* (*pres* ~em) 1 (koga) wrap (up) 2 (se) wrap up; slip/throw sth over one's shoulders

zaokre|nuti *v* (0/se) (*pres* ~nem) turn (round); swerve ~**t** *nm* 1 turn; aboutturn (+ *fig*) 2 *fig* reversal ~**tati** *v impf*

zaokružiti *v* 1 (što) circle; (svotu) round up 2 (se) round out

zaokupiti *v* (koga) absorb, engross

zaosta|lost *nf* backwardness; underdevelopment ~**o** *adj* (~la *f*) 1 backward, underdeveloped 2 (umno) retarded ~**tak** *nm* (*Gsg* ~tka, *Npl* ~ci) 1 remnant, remainder, rest 2 arrears *pl* ~**ti** *v* (0) (*pres* ~nem) 1 lag (behind) 2 be/fall/drop behind 3 be behindhand; be in arrears with 4 be backward ~**jati** *v impf*

zaoštriti *v* 1 (što) sharpen 2 (što) *fig* intensify; strain; worsen 3 (se) become strained/tense; intensify; worsen; deepen; escalate

zaova *nf* sister-in-law, husband's sister

zapad *nm* 1 the west 2 *fig* the West **na** ~ west, to the west, westward(s); due west **na** ~**u** in the west ~**ati** *v impf* → **zapasti** ~**ni** *adj* west, western, westerly ~**no** *adv* (to the) west of; westward(s) ~**noeuropski** adj Western European ~**njački** *adj* western; western-style ~**njak** *nm* (*Npl* ~njaci) 1 westerner 2 west(erly) wind

zapahn|uti *v* (koga) (*pres* ~em) assail, sweep over ~**uo nas je smrad trulog mesa** the smell of decaying meat overpowered us

zapa|liti *v* 1 (što) set fire to, set on fire; light (up), kindle, ignite; rouse *fig*; (vatru) light, start; (šibicu) strike; (svjetlo) turn/switch on; (motor) start 2 (se) catch fire, start to burn, ignite 3 (se za što) become crazy about ~**ljiv** *adj* 1 (in)flammable; incendiary (+ *fig*) **2** *fig* inflammatory **~ljiva bomba** incendiary bomb

zapamtiti *v* **1** (koga/što) remember, keep/bear in mind **2** (što) memorize, commit to memory

zapanj|iti *v* **1** (koga) amaze, astound, dumbfound, strike dumb, flabbergast, stun **2** (se) be amazed/taken aback **~ujući** *adj* amazing

zapapriti *v* **1** (što) pepper **2** (komu) make it hot for sb

zapa|sti (*pres* ~dnem) **1** (0) (sunce) set, go down; (snijeg) fall **2** (u što) fall/get into, get stuck in **~sti u dugove** run into debt **3** (koga) devolve on/to **~lo me da** it fell to my lot to

zapa|ziti *v* (koga/što) notice, observe, perceive; see **~žanje** *nn* observation **~žen** *adj* **1** noticed **2** marked, prominent **~žati** *v impf*

zapečatiti *v* (što) seal (up)

zape|ći *v* (što) (*pres* ~čem) **1** brown; overdo; burn **2** *fig* sting

zapešće *nn* wrist

zap|eti *v* (*pres* ~nem) **1** (0) be/get stuck, stick (fast) **~eti za oko a.** catch one's eye **b.** catch one's fancy **2** (o/za što) stumble over; hitch on, catch in/on **3** (0) come to a standstill **4** (0) try hard; get down to work **~eti iz petnih žila** try with all one's might **5** (za što/0) insist

zapetljati *v* **1** (što) (+ *fig*) entangle, tangle up, enmesh **2** (se) get entangled/enmeshed, be in a tangle **3** (se) *fig* get all mixed up

zapiljiti *v* (se) stare (fixedly) at

zapinjati *v impf* → **zapeti** ~ **u govoru** stumble over one's words, falter

zapi|s *nm* **1** (što) entry, note, record **2** ~**si** *pl* memoirs **~sati** *v* (*pres* ~šem) **1** (što) write/put/note down; record, register, enter **2** (što) (policija) book **~sničar** *nm* recording secretary **~snik** *nm* (*Npl* ~snici) (sastanka) minutes *pl*; report **voditi ~snik** take minutes

zapit|ati *v* **1** (koga što/koga o čemu) ask sb sth **2** (se) ask oneself, wonder **~kivati** *v* (0/koga) keep asking questions

zapi|ti *v* (što) (*pres* ~jem) **~ti novac** drink one's money away

zapjeniti *v* (se) foam, froth **~ se od bijesa** foam with rage, foam/froth at the mouth

zapjevati *v* (0/što) (begin to) sing, burst into song

zapla|kan *adj* tearful, in tears **~kati** *v* (0) (*pres* ~čem) (begin to) cry/weep, burst into tears

zaplašiti *v* (koga) frighten, (give sb a) scare

zaple|sati *v* (0/što) begin to dance

zaple|sti *v* (*pres* ~tem) **1** entangle, tangle (up), enmesh; ravel (up) **2** (se) (+ *fig*) get entangled/enmeshed, entangle oneself; get mixed up/involved; stumble over one's words, get stuck **~t** *nm* **1** entanglement, tangle **2** complication, confusion **3** plot

zaplijeniti *v* (što) confiscate, seize; impound, sequestrate *form, leg*

zaplotnjački *adj* underhand(ed), treacherous

zaploviti *v* (0) set sail, put (out) to sea

zapljena *nf* confiscation, seizure; sequestration *leg*

zaplju|snuti *v* (koga/što/čime) (*pres* ~nem) **1** splash **2** dash; hit **~kivati** *v impf* (*pres* ~kujem) (more) wash, lick

započ|eti *v* (što) (*pres* ~nem) **1** begin, start; commence *form* **2** launch, initiate, open; embark (up)on **~injati** *v impf*

zapodjen|uti *v* (što) (*pres* ~em) begin, start; commence *form*; engage in **~uti razgovor** strike up a conversation **~uti svadu** pick a quarrel

zapoma|gati *v* (0) (*pres* ~žem) cry for help

zapon|ac *nm* (*Gsg* ~ca, *Npl* ~ci) **1** bolt **2** catch, clasp, hasp

zaposjesti *v* (što) (*pres* ~dnem) occupy, engage, take; seize, take control of

zapo|sliti *v* **1** (koga) employ; keep busy/occupied, occupy; set sb to work **2** (se) find work, get a job **~šljavati** *v impf*

zapostaviti *v* (koga/što) neglect, disregard

zapov|ijed *nf* command, order **deset ~ijedi** the Ten Commandments **~ije-dati** *v* 1 (kim/čim) command, be in command/charge of, be in authority 2 (0/komu) order around; boss around *coll* **~jediti** *v* (koga što) order, command **~jedni, ~jednički** *adj* commanding, imperious **~jedni način** *gram* imperative mood **~jed-nik** *nm* (*Vsg* ~jedniče, *Npl* ~jednici) commander **vrhovni ~jednik** commander-in-chief **~jednik broda** captain, master; skipper *coll* **~jedništvo** *nn* command; headquarters *pl*

zaprašiti *v* 1 (koga/što) make dusty 2 (cvijeće) dust, spray 3 (se) get dusty

zapravo *adv* in fact, as a matter of fact, actually

zapre|ga *nf* (*Dsg* ~zi) wagon, cart

zapre|ka *nf* (*Dsg* ~ci) 1 obstacle, barrier 2 *sport* hurdle

zaprem(n)ina *nf* volume, cubic capacity

zaprepastiti *v* 1 (koga) amaze, appal, shock 2 (se) be amazed/flabbergasted

zapriječiti *v* (što) block, obstruct

zaprijetiti *v* (komu čime) threaten sb with sth

zapr|jati *v* 1 (koga/što) (make) dirty, soil 2 (se) get dirty

zaprositi *v* (koga) propose to sb; pop the question *coll*

zapr|ška *nf* (*Dsg* ~šci) browned flour **~žiti** *v* (što) brown

zapi|ti *v* (što) (*pres* ~jem) spend sth on drink/booze, drink away

zapuč|ak *nm* (*Gsg* ~ka, *Npl* ~ci) buttonhole

zapu|h *nm* (*Npl* ~si) snowdrift

zapu|hati *v* (0) (*pres* ~šem) begin to blow, come/spring up

zapu|stiti *v* 1 (koga/što) neglect 2 (se) neglect one's appearance, let oneself go **~šten** *adj* (osoba) neglected; (zgrada) dilapidated

zaputiti *v* (se) set off/out for, start for

zar *adv* ~ **doista**? really? *on je bogat,* ~ **ne**? he is rich, isn't he? *ne želite ga,* ~ **ne**? you don't want it, do you?

zaračunati *v* (komu što) charge, include in the charges

zaraćen *adj* warring, belligerent

zara|da *nf* 1 earnings *pl*; income 2 profit **~diti** *v* (što) earn (+ *fig*), make (money); make a profit **~diti batine** *coll* get a licking **~đivati** *v impf*

zarana *adv* 1 early, at an early hour 2 at an early age, early in life

zarast|i (1) *v* (0) (*pres* ~em) heal

zarast|i (2) *v* (u što) (*pres* ~em) be overgrown with

zaratiti *v* (0/se s kim) declare war (on), go to war (against)

zarav|an *nf* (*Gsg* ~ni) plateau

zaraz|a *nf* 1 infection, contagion 2 epidemic **~an** *adj* (α) infectious, contagious, catching (+ *fig*) **~iti** *v* 1 (koga) infect (+ *fig*) 2 (se) become infected, contract a disease

zarđati → **zahrđati**

zare|ći *v* (se) (*pres* ~čem/~knem) 1 swear, give one's word 2 blab, blurt out

zaredati *v* (0) follow (in succession), come one after the other

zarediti *v* 1 (koga) ordain 2 (se) be ordained, take holy orders

zarez *nm* 1 *gram* comma 2 cut, notch

zaribati *v* (što) *coll* blow, mess up; screw up *coll*

zari|nuti (*pres* ~em), **~ti** (*pres* ~jem) *v* (što) drive, thrust, sink, plunge

zarob|iti *v* (koga/što) 1 take captive/prisoner; capture, seize, take 2 *fig* captivate **~ljenički** *adj* logor prisoner-of-war camp **~ljenik** *nm* (*Npl* ~ljenici) captive, prisoner **~ljeništvo** *nn* captivity

zaroniti *v* (0) dive, dip, sink, go under

zaru|čiti *v* (se) (s kim) get engaged (to) **~čni** *adj* **prsten** engagement ring **~čnica** *nf* fiancée **~čnik** *nm* (*Vsg* ~čniče, *Npl* ~čnici) fiancé **~ke** *nf pl* engagement

zarume|njeti *v* (se) (*pres* ~nim) 1 redden, turn red 2 blush, flush

zaružiti *v* (0) *sl* stay out late, go (out) boozing

zasad(a) *adv* for the time being, for now

zasada *nf* (basic) principle

zasaditi *v* (što) plant

zaseban *adj* (α) 1 separate; individual

2 special

zase||lak *nm* (*Gsg* ~oka/~lka, *Npl* ~oci/~lci) hamlet

zasićenost *nf* 1 saturation 2 satiety

zasigurno *adv* undoubtedly, for sure, surely

zasij|ati (1) *v* (što) (*pres* ~em) sow

zas|ijati (2) *v* (0) (*pres* ~ijam), **~jati** (*pres* ~jam) (0) (begin) to shine

zasit|an *adj* (*a*) (hrana) rich **~iti** *v* 1 (koga) satiate 2 (što) saturate 3 (se) be satiated, have enough

zas||jeći *v* (što) (*pres* ~iječem) cut (into)

zasjed|a *nf* ambush **čekati u ~i** wait in ambush, lie in wait **napasti koga iz ~e** ambush sb

zasjeda|nje *nn* session, meeting **~ti** *v* (0) be in session, be sitting

zasjeniti *v* 1 (što) shade, screen 2 (koga/što) *fig* overshadow, eclipse

zasje|sti *v* (0) (*pres* ~dnem) 1 plant oneself (in a chair) 2 stay too long

zaskočiti *v* (koga) take sb by surprise; (napasti) jump *coll*

zasladiti *v* (što) sweeten, put sugar in

zaslijepiti *v* (koga/što) blind (+ *fig*), dazzle

zaslon *nm* screen, shade

zaslu|ga *nf* (*Dsg* ~zi) merit, credit **~žan** *adj* (*a*) deserving, meritorious **~žiti** *v* (što) 1 deserve, merit, be worthy of 2 earn 3 have it coming

zasn|ovati *v* (što) (*pres* ~ujem) 1 establish, found 2 design, conceive **~ivati** *v* 1 (što) *impf* 2 (se) be based on

zasoliti *v* (što) 1 salt, add salt to 2 *fig* exaggerate, embellish

zasp|ati *v* (0) (*pres* ~em) go to sleep, fall asleep; drop off *coll*

zastajk|ivati *v* (0) (*pres* ~ujem) stop (from time to time/every now and again)

zastar|a *nf* expiration **odredbe o ~i** statute of limitations **~io** *adj* (~jela *f*) 1 obsolete, antiquated; archaic 2 old-fashioned, out of date **~jeti** *v* (0) (*pres* ~im) 1 become obsolete/old-fashioned; go out of fashion 2 expire

zasta|ti *v* (*pres* ~nem) pause, stop

zastav|a *nf* flag; colours *pl*; (brodska)

ensign **~a na pola koplja** flag at half-mast **istaknuti/izvjesiti/podignuti/razviti ~u** display/fly/hoist/unfurl a flag **~ica** *nf* pennant **~ice** *nf pl* bunting **~nik** *nm* (*Vsg* ~niče, *Npl* ~nici) 1 standard bearer 2 (čin) second lieutenant

zastenj|ati *v* (0) (*pres* ~em) (give a) groan

zastoj *nm* standstill, stoppage; stagnation **prometni ~** traffic jam; (kolona) tailback

zastor *nm* curtain; drape *US*; drapery

zastraš|iti *v* (koga) frighten, scare **~ivati** *v impf* (*pres* ~ujem) intimidate

zastup|ati *v* 1 (koga) represent 2 (koga) act for 3 (što) support **~ljenost** *nf* representation **~nički** *adj* dom house/chamber of representatives **~nik** *nm* (*Vsg* ~niče, *Npl* ~nici) 1 deputy, representative 2 agent **ovlašteni ~nik** authorized agent/dealer **pravni ~nik** attorney, counsel **~ništvo**, **~stvo** *nn* 1 representation 2 agency; office

zasu|kati *v* (što) (*pres* ~čem) roll up **~kati rukave** *fig* gird up one's loins

zasun *nm* bar, bolt

zasuti *v* (koga/što) (*pres* ~pem) 1 cover, fill up 2 *fig* shower

zasvinjiti *v* (što) *coll* mess up, muck up

zasvirati *v* (0/što) begin to play, strike up

zašarafiti *v* (što) *coll* screw (down/on/to)

zašećeriti *v* (što) sugar, put sugar in

zašiljiti *v* (što) sharpen

zaši|ti *v* (što) (*pres* ~jem) sew up

zašted|jeti *v* (što) (*pres* ~im) save (up)

zaštit|a *nf* protection **~iti** *v* (koga/što) protect; safeguard; shelter **~ni** *adj* protective **~ni znak** trademark **~nik** *nm* (*Vsg* ~niče, *Npl* ~nici) 1 protector 2 patron **svetac ~nik** patron saint

zašto *adv* why, what for

zašut|jeti *v* (0) (*pres* ~im) fall silent, stop talking

zatajiti *v* 1 (što) keep secret, suppress 2 (0) fail; (oružje) misfire; (motor) stall

zatakn|uti   *v*   (što)   (*pres*   ~em)

stick/tuck (in/into)

zataškati *v* (što) cover/hush up

zate|ći *v* (*pres* ~čem/~knem) **1** (koga/što) find; catch sb in the act of doing sth **~ći na djelu** catch sb red-handed **2** (se) find oneself

zate|gnut *adj* (odnos) strained **~gnuti** *v* (što) (*pres* ~gnem) tighten, pull tight **~gnutost** *nf* tension; strain **~zati** (*pres* ~žem) *v* **1** *impf* **2** (što) delay, procrastinate **3** (0) (u govoru) drawl **~zna** *adj* **kamata** penalty interest

zatim *adv* then, after that, afterwards, subsequently **malo ~** soon/shortly after

zatirati *v impf* → **zatrti**

zatišje *nn* lull **~ pred buru** the calm before the storm

zato *adv* therefore, for that reason, that's why; hence **~ da** in order to, so that **~ što** because

zatoč|enik *nm* (*Npl* ~enici) captive **~eništvo** *nn* captivity **~iti** *v* (koga) confine, imprison

zatomiti *v* (što) suppress, stifle

zaton *nm* bay

zatopliti *v* (0) (vrijeme) become warmer, grow warm

zatravljen *adj lit* bewitched, enchanted

zatražiti *v* (što/od koga) ask for, call for, request, demand, claim

zatrebati *v* (što) (happen to) need

zatres|ti *v* (što/čime/se) (*pres* ~em) shake **~ti mrežu** *sport* net the ball

zatr|ovati *v* (što) (*pres* ~ujem) poison (+ *fig*)

zatrpa|ti *v* (koga/što) cover; fill (up) **~n čime** *fig* flooded/swamped with sth

zatr|ti *v* (*pres* ~em) **1** (koga/što) exterminate **2** (se) die out

zatrud|njeti *v* (0) (*pres* ~nim) become pregnant

zatucan *adj* hidebound, narrow-minded **~a osoba** stick-in-the-mud

zatu|ći *v* (koga) (*pres* ~čem) beat sb to death

zatupiti *v* **1** (što) blunt **2** (koga) *coll* bore, bother

zatv|arač *nm* **1** (boce) cap **2** (oružja)

breech **patentni ~arač** zip fastener; zip *GB coll;* zipper *US coll* **~or** *nm* **1** prison, jail, gaol **2** (kazna) imprisonment, custody **3** *med* constipation **~orenik** *nm* (*Npl* ~orenici) prisoner, convict, inmate **~oriti** *v* **1** (što) close, shut; (tvornicu) close/shut down **2** (koga) put in prison, imprison, lock up/away **3** (se) close/shut (oneself) **~arati** *v impf*

zaudarati *v* (0/na što) smell/stink (of)

zaustav|iti *v* **1** (koga/što) stop, halt; (vozilo) pull up **2** (što) bring to a stop/halt/standstill, put a stop to **~iti krvarenje** staunch the blood **3** (se) stop, come to a stop/halt/standstill; (vozilo) pull up **~ljati** *v impf*

zauš|nica *nf* box/clip on the ears **dati kome ~nicu** box sb's ears **~njaci** *nm pl* mumps

zauvijek *adv* for ever, for good **jednom ~** once and for all

zauzdati *v* (koga/što) bridle, rein (+ *fig*); curb *fig*

zauz|et *adj* **1** busy (with/doing sth), engaged (in), occupied (with/in) **2** (vojno) occupied, captured **3** (sjedalo) taken, occupied **4** (tel. linija) engaged *GB;* busy *US* **~eti** *v* (što) (*pres* ~mem) **1** capture, seize, take (control of), occupy **~eti stav** take a stand **2** (se za koga) intercede with sb for sb/on sb's behalf, plead for **3** (se za što) support, advocate **~imati** *v impf*

zavad|a *nf* feud; quarrel **biti u ~i** be at loggerheads with **~iti** *v* **1** (koga) antagonize **2** (se) fall out, quarrel; start a feud

zavaliti *v* (se) sit back, slump; sprawl (out), loll

zavapiti *v* (0) cry out

zavara|ti *v* (koga) deceive, delude; trick, hoodwink, hoax **~vati** *v* **1** (koga) *impf* **2** (se) labour under the delusion, kid/fool/delude oneself

zavariti *v* (što) weld (together)

zave|sti *v* (*pres* ~dem) **1** (koga) seduce, lead astray; mislead **2** (što) enter, record **~sti red** establish/restore order

zave|zati *v* (koga/što) (*pres* ~žem) tie/bind (up/together); (cipele) lace up ~zati komu oči blindfold sb ~ži! shut up! ~žljaj nm bundle

zavičaj nm native country/land/place; home(land) čeznuti za ~em be homesick

zavid|an adj (α) 1 envious 2 (uspjeh i sl.) enviable ~jeti v (komu na čemu) (pres ~im) envy sb sth, be envious of sb

zavijati (1) v (0) howl, whine, wail

zavijati (2) v (0) turn, bend, curve, meander

zaviri|ti v (u što) peep/peer into ~vati v impf

zavis|an adj (α) dependent (on) ~na rečenica subordinate clause ~iti v (o kome/o čemu) depend on ~no adv od depending on ~nost nf dependence

zavist nf envy

zavi|ti v (što) (pres ~jem) wrap up, envelop; shroud fig

zavjer|a nf conspiracy, plot skovati ~u hatch a c./p. ~enik nm (Npl ~nici) conspirator, plotter

zavjesa nf curtain; hangings pl

zavjet nm vow Stari/Novi ~ the Old/New Testament ~ni adj votive ~ovati v (se) (pres ~ujem) (make a) vow

zavjetrina nf lee

zavlačiti v (što/0) delay, procrastinate

zavlada|ti v (0) 1 begin to rule, assume rule 2 become predominant/prevalent/fashionable ~la je panika there was a panic, panic spread

zavod nm institute; bureau, office nakladni ~ publishing house ~ za zapošljavanje employment agency; job centre GB

zavod|iti v impf → zavesti ~ljiv adj seductive, alluring, enticing ~nica nf seducer, temptress ~nik nm (Vsg ~niče, Npl ~nici) seducer; womanizer, lady-killer

zavoj nm 1 bend, turn, curve 2 (za ranu) bandage, dressing ~it adj winding ~nica nf spiral, coil

zavojevač nm aggressor, conqueror

zavo|ljeti v (pres ~lim) 1 (koga/što) become fond of, come/get to like, take to 2 (se) fall in love

zavor nm brake

zavrijediti v (koga/što) deserve, merit, be worth

zavrn|uti v (što) (pres ~em) roll up ~uti ruku twist sb's arm ~uti vratom wring sb's neck

završ|etak nm (Gsg ~etka, Npl ~eci) 1 end; close 2 gram ending ~iti v 1 (što) finish, end, complete, close, terminate; bring to an end/a close; wrap up coll 2 (0) finish, end, terminate; come to an end; end up (in) ~ni adj final, closing, concluding ~ni račun balance sheet ~nica nf sport finish, final(s); (šah) end game

zavrtaj nm turn

zavrt|jeti v (što/koga/se) (pres ~im) spin, twirl, whirl ~jeti komu glavom turn sb's head ~jelo mi se u glavi I felt dizzy/giddy, my head swam

zavrzlama nf tangle, confusion

zavu|ći v (se) (pres ~čem) creep/crawl into

zazele|njeti v (se) (pres ~nim) become/turn green; shine green

zazidati v (što/koga) wall in/up

zaz|irati v (od čega) (pres ~irem) abhor, shrink from; shy away from ~or nm aversion

zaziv|ati v (koga/što) (pres ~am/~ljem) 1 invoke 2 cry out for sb

zazubice nf pl rastu joj ~ her mouth waters

zazvižd|ati v (0) (pres ~im) whistle

zazvoniti v (0) ring (the bell)

zažariti v (se) 1 become red hot 2 (lice) flush

zaže|ljeti v (pres ~lim) 1 (što) wish, express a desire for; make a wish 2 (se koga/čega) miss very much; long for

zaživ|jeti v (0) (pres ~im) become viable

zažmiriti v (0) 1 close one's eyes; screw up one's eyes 2 (na što) turn a blind eye to, wink at

zažut|jeti v (0) (pres ~im) become/turn yellow

zažvaliti v (koga/se) sl kiss, smooch

zbaciti v 1 (koga/što) throw/cast off 2 (vladu) topple, overthrow

zbijati v impf (što) → zbiti (1) ~ šalu joke, poke fun at

zbilj|a nf reality • adv really, truly, indeed **~ski** adj real, true, veritable

zbir|ka nf (Dsg ~ci) 1 collection 2 miscellany **~ni** adj collective

zbi|ti (1) v (što) (pres ~jem) compress, condense, press together; pack tightly **~ti redove** close the ranks

zbi|ti (2) v (se) (pres zbude) happen, occur, take place **~vanje** nn happening **~vanja** pl events, developments

zbjeg n exodus; m refugees pl

zbližiti v 1 (se) come together; grow close 2 (koga) bring together

zbog prep because of, owing to, due to, on account of, for **~ toga** therefore, for that reason

zbogom int goodbye, farewell, adieu

zbor nm 1 gathering; meeting; convention 2 (pjevački) choir, chorus 3 (diplomatski) corps **~ište** nm meeting place **~nica** nf staff room **~ski** adj choir; choral **Z~ narodne garde** Croatian National Guard

zboriti v (0) speak

zborni|k nm (Npl ~ci) 1 papers and studies, symposium 2 proceedings

zbrajati v 1 (što) impf → **zbrojiti** 2 (0) do sums

zbratimiti v (se) fraternize (with sb)

zbrčkati v (što) botch up, mess up

zbrda-zdola adv higgledy-piggledy, topsy-turvy

zbrin|uti v (koga) (pres ~em) provide for, take care of

zbri|sati v (pres ~šem) 1 (što) wipe off, rub out, erase 2 (0) coll clear off, run off, escape, do a bunk, give sb the slip

zbr|ka nf (Dsg ~ci) confusion; mess, muddle **~kati** v (što) confuse, mix up, muddle up, jumble up

zbroj nm sum (total), total amount **~iti** v (što) add/sum up, add to

zbu|niti v 1 (koga) confuse, bewilder, puzzle, baffle, mystify; embarrass 2 (se) get confused/mixed up

zdanje nn building, edifice

zden|ac nm (Gsg ~ca) well

zdepast adj stocky, squat

zder|ati v (što) (pres ~em) tear off

zdesna adv from the right; on the right, on/to one's right; (brod) on the

starboard side

zdimiti v (0) coll disappear, clear off, run off

zdipiti v (što) sl nick, pinch

zdjel|a nf bowl, dish **~ica** nf 1 dim 2 anat pelvis **~ični** adj pelvic

zdrav adj healthy, sound; wholesome **~ razum** common sense **živ i ~ safe and sound** **~ica** nf toast **održati ~icu** propose/drink a toast to sb **~lje** nn health **duševno ~lje** sanity **dom ~lja** health (care) centre **u~lje!** to your health! here's to you! **na~lje!** bless you! **~o! a.** hi! hello! **b.** bye! **~stven** adj 1 health 2 sanitary **~stvena knjižica** health insurance card **~stveno osiguranje** health insurance **~stvo** nn health care system, public health

zdrmati v (koga/što) shake

zdrobiti v (što) crush; pulverize

združiti v 1 (koga/što) unite, join, integrate, bring together; combine, merge **~ sredstva** pool resources 2 (se) unite; ally oneself with, join forces with; merge

zdušan adj (a) wholehearted

zdvojnost nf despair

zeba nf chaffinch, finch

zebnja nf anxiety, apprehension

zebra nf 1 zebra 2 zebra crossing GB; pedestrian crossing US

ze|c nm (Npl ~čevi) hare **praviti ražanj dok je ~c u šumi** count one's chickens before they are hatched **u tom grmu leži ~c** there's the rub **~čja** adj usna harelip **~ko** nm bunny

zelj|ast adj herbaceous **~e** nn cabbage **kiselo ~e** sauerkraut

zem|aljski adj 1 earthly, worldly, terrestrial **~aljska kugla** the globe 2 national **Z~lja** nf 1 Earth; the earth 2 land; ground; soil **kao nebo i ~lja** like night and day **laka mu ~lja** may he rest in peace 3 country **~ljak** nm (Vsg ~ljače, Npl ~ljaci) compatriot, fellow countryman **~ljan** adj earthen, earthy **~ljano posuđe** earthenware **~ljarina** nf land tax **~ljišna** adj knjiga land register **~ljište** nn 1 plot; building site 2 terrain **~ljopis** nm geography **~ljopisna** adj karta map

~ljoposjednik nm (Npl ~ljoposjedni-ci) landowner **~ljoradnja** nf → **poljodjelstvo ~ljovid** nm map **~ni** adj **plin** natural gas **~unica** nf mil dugout

zenit nm zenith (+ fig)

ze|psti v (0) (pres ~bem) **~bu me ruke** my hands are freezing

zerdav nm ermine

zet nm son-in-law

zez|ati v sl 1 (koga) kid, pull sb's leg, take the mickey out of sb, wind sb up 2 (se) crack jokes; have fun **~nuti** v (pres ~nem) sl 1 (koga) trick, hood-wink, con 2 (što) blow, screw/muck up 3 (se) make a mistake

zgaditi v (0) (komu što) be/feel disgusted with, be sickened by

zgarište nn burnt-out ruins

zgaziti v (što/koga) trample down, stamp; stamp out fig

zglob nm 1 joint 2 (prsta) knuckle; (ruke) wrist **upala ~ova** arthritis

zgnječiti v (što/koga) crush, squash, mash

zgod|a nf 1 occasion; opportunity; chance **jednom ~om** on one occa-sion **prvom ~om** at the first opportu-nity 2 event **~e i nezgode** adventures **~an** adj (ɑ) 1 convenient; favourable; suitable 2 advisable; ex-pedient 3 (privlačan) attractive, good-looking, nice; handsome; pret-ty

zgodi|tak nm (Gsg ~tka, Npl ~ci) 1 prize **glavni ~tak** first prize, jackpot 2 sport goal **postići ~tak** score a goal

zgorega adv **ne bi bilo ~** it would not come/go amiss

zgotoviti v (što) (jelo) get ready, pre-pare 2 finish; make

zgrabiti v (koga/što) grab

zgrad|a nf building, structure, edifice **~urina** nf augm big (ugly) building

zgran|uti v (pres ~em) (se/biti ~ut) be amazed/aghast/taken aback/shocked

zgraža|nje nn disgust, outcry **~ti** v (se) impf → **zgroziti se**

zgrbiti v (se) stoop

zgrčiti v (što/se) contort, screw up, twist; (šaku) clench

zgrij|ati v (pres ~em) 1 (koga/što) warm/heat (up) 2 (se) get warm

zgriješiti v (0) 1 (commit a) sin 2 err; commit an offence

zgr|nuti v (što) (pres ~nem) rake up **~nuti velike novce** coll rake in a for-tune **~tati** v impf

zgromiti v (koga) fig destroy

zgroziti v (se) be disgusted/shocked/scandalized

zgrušati v (se) coagulate, congeal, clot; (mlijeko) curdle

zguliti v (što) peel off, strip off; scrape off; skin

zgurati v 1 (koga/što) push, cram, crowd 2 (se) crowd/squeeze in

zguriti v (se) cower, cringe

zgusn|uti v (što/se) (pres ~em) con-dense, thicken

zgužvati v (što/se) crumple, crease

zibati v 1 (koga/što/se) rock, sway 1 (se) roll

zid nm wall **zvučni ~** sound barrier **živi ~** human shield **htjeti glavom kroz(a) ~** bang one's head against the wall **~ar** nm bricklayer; mason **slobodni ~ar** freemason **~arstvo** nn bricklaying; masonry **~ati** v (što) build, construct **~ina** nf (thick) wall **~ni** adj wall; mural

ziherica nf coll safety pin

zijati v (0) gape

zijev nm gram hiatus

zijev|ati v (0) 1 impf → **zijevnuti** 2 gape **~nuti** v (0) (pres ~nem) (give a) yawn

zim|a nf 1 winter(time) 2 cold **~a mi je** I'm cold **~i** adv in winter **~nica** nf winter provisions/stocks pl **~ogrozan** adj (ɑ) sensitive to cold **~ovalište** nn winter resort **~ski** adj winter; wintry **~ski san** hibernation **~us** adv last winter

zimzelen nm 1 periwinkle 2 evergreen • adj evergreen

zin|uti v (0) (pres ~em) open one's mouth **~uti od čuda** be agape, stare openmouthed

zip|ka nf (Dsg ~ci) cradle

zirkati v (0) peek (at)

zjake nf pl coll **prodavati ~** lounge, dawdle

zjapiti v (0) gape

zjenic|a nf pupil (of the eye) **on je čuva/pazi kao ~u oka svog** she is the apple of his eye

zla|ćan adj golden, gold-like **~tan** adj (α) 1 gold 2 fig golden **~tna sredina** the golden mean 3 fig kind, sweet **~tar** nm goldsmith **~tica** nf buttercup **krumpirova ~tica** potato beetle **~tnik** nm (Npl ~tnici) gold coin **~tni-na** nf jewellry **~to** nm 1 gold **nije ~to sve što sja** all that glitters is not gold 2 fig darling, honey, sweetheart **~tokos** adj golden-haired

zlikov|ac nm (Gsg ~ca, Vsg ~če, Npl ~ci) villain **~ački** adj criminal, villainous

zlo nn 1 evil 2 harm **nužno ~** necessary evil **nisam mislio ništa zla** I meant no harm **uzeti za ~** take amiss **poći po zlu** go wrong **po zlu poznat** notorious **od zla nagore** from bad to worse **svako ~ ima svoje dobro** every cloud has a silver lining • adv → **loše ~ mi je** I feel sick **~ nam se piše** woe betide us

zlob|a nf malice, spite, rancour **~an** adj (α) malicious, spiteful **~nik** nm (Vsg ~niče, Npl ~nici) malicious person

zločest adj 1 wicked 2 naughty, mischievous

zločin nm crime **~ac** nm (Gsg ~ca) criminal **~ački** adj criminal

zloća nf wickedness

zloćudan adj (α) 1 evil-minded 2 med malignant

zlodjelo nn crime; misdeed form

zlodu|h nm (Npl ~si) evil spirit

zloglasan adj (α) infamous, notorious

zloguk adj ominous

zlokoban adj (α) ominous, portentous, sinister, baleful

zlonamjeran adj (α) malevolent

zlopamtilo nn vindictive person **nisam ~** I'm not one to bear a grudge

zlopatiti v (se) suffer, have a hard time

zlorabiti v (što/koga) abuse, misuse

zloslutan adj (α) ominous, portentous, sinister

zlosretan adj (α) unfortunate

zlostavljati v (koga) maltreat, manhandle

zlotvor nm evildoer

zloupotr|eba nf abuse, misuse **~eba položaja** misuse of office **~ijebiti** v (što/koga) abuse, misuse **~ebljavati** v impf

zlovoljan adj (α) ill-tempered, sullen, peevish

zlurad adj malicious, spiteful, malignant

zmaj nm 1 dragon 2 (igračka) kite 3 hang glider

zmij|a nf snake **~olik** adj snaky, serpentine **~ski** adj snake **~ski otrov** venom **~ski zub** fang

znač|aj nm 1 coll → **značenje** (2) 2 lit character, disposition **~ajan** adj (α) significant, important, notable, major **~ajka** nf (Dsg ~ajci) characteristic, feature, mark **~enje** nn 1 meaning, sense 2 significance, importance **~enjski** adj semantic **~iti** v (što) mean; signify; (kratica) stand for **~i ne idete?** so you're not going?

znač|ka nf (Dsg ~ki, Gpl ~aka/~ki) badge

zna|k nm (Npl ~ci/~kovi) 1 sign; symbol; mark; token 2 signal 3 indication 4 symptom **dobar/loš ~k** good/bad omen **~kovit** adj indicative

znal|ac nm (Gsg ~ca, Npl ~ci) expert, specialist; connoisseur **~ački** adv knowingly

znamenit adj famous, renowned **~ost** nf 1 fame, renown 2 cultural monument **razgledavati ~osti** see the sights, go sightseeing

znamen|ka nf (Dsg ~ci) figure, digit, numeral **~kast** suffix -digit

znamenje nn 1 insignia; sign, symbol 2 omen, portent

znan|ac nm (Gsg ~ca) (~ica f) acquaintance

znan|ost nf science **~stven** adj scientific **~stvenik** nm (Npl ~stvenici) scientist, scholar; research worker, researcher

znanj|e nn knowledge **dati/staviti do ~a/na ~e** bring sth to sb's attention, make known to, inform **primiti/uzeti k ~u/na ~e** take note of

znatan *adj* (α) considerable, substantial

zna|ti *v* (što/koga) (*pres* ~m/~dem) know **koliko ja ~m** as far as I know, to my knowledge **to se ~** that goes without saying **~o sam ići tamo** *coll* I used to go there **otkad ~m za sebe** in my born days **nije ne ~m što, nije bog~ što/kakav** it's not much, it's nothing to write home about

znatiželja *nf* curiosity **~n** *adj* (α) curious, inquisitive

znoj *nm* sweat; perspiration *form* ~**an** *adj* (α) sweaty ~**iti** *v* (se) sweat, perspire ~**nica** *nf* 1 sweat gland 2 *coll* sweatband

zob *nf* oats *pl* ~**en** *adj* oat ~**eno brašno** oatmeal ~**ena kaša** oatmeal porridge

zobati *v* (što) 1 (zrnje) peck at 2 (grožđe) eat

zona *nf* zone, area **industrijska ~** industrial district/estate/zone **pješačka ~** pedestrian precinct **slobodna trgovinska ~** free trade zone/area

zoološki *adj* zoological **~ vrt** zoo

zor|a *nf* dawn, daybreak **u cik ~e** at the crack of dawn **u ranu ~u** at first light ~**nica** *nf* matins

zoriti (1) *v* (0) dawn

zoriti (2) *v* (0) ripen, mature

zorno *adv* in graphic detail

zov *nm* call ~**nuti** *v* (koga) call

zra|čan *adj* (α) air ~**čni prostor** air space ~**čenje** *nn* radiation ~**čiti** *v* (što) 1 air 2 (koga/što) irradiate; X-ray 3 (što/čime) *fig* radiate sth ~**čnica** *nf* 1 inner tube 2 *coll* airgun ~**k** *nm* air **dići u ~k** blow up **visjeti u ~ku** *fig* be in the air ~**ka** *nf* (Dsg ~ci) ray, beam ~**koplov** *nm* aircraft, airplane ~**koplovac** *nm* (Gsg ~koplovca, Npl ~koplovci) aviator, flier ~**koplovstvo** *nn* 1 aviation 2 (ratno) air force ~**koprazan** *adj* (α) **prostor** vacuum

zrcal|iti *v* (se) be mirrored; glitter ~**o** *nn* mirror, looking glass

zre|lost *nf* ripeness; maturity **ispit ~losti** *fig* school-leaving examination ~**o** *adj* (~la *f*) ripe; mature ~**ti** *v* (0) (*pres* ~m/zrim) ripen; mature

zri|kati *v* (0) (*pres* ~čem) chirp ~**kav** *adj* cross-eyed ~**kavac** *nm* (Gsg ~kavca, Npl ~kavci) cricket

zrn|ast *adj* granular; granulated ~**at** *adj* full of grains ~**ce** *nn dim* small grain, granule **krvna ~ca** blood cells ~**o** *nn* 1 grain (+ *fig*) 2 bullet, shot, shell

zub *nm* (Gpl ~i/~a) tooth **~ vremena** the ravages of time **naoružan do ~a** armed to the teeth **imati koga na ~a** have it in for sb **stisnuti ~e** keep a stiff upper lip **jezik za ~e!** hold your tongue! ~**ac** *nm* (Gsg zupca, Npl zupci) (češlja) tooth; (zupčanika) cog; (vilice) prong ~**alo** *nn* 1 teeth 2 false teeth, dentures ~**ar** *nm* dentist ~**at** *adj* toothed ~**atac** *nm* (Gsg ~aca, Npl ~aci) dentex ~**ni** *adj* dental ~**no meso** gums *pl* ~**na pasta** toothpaste ~**obolja** *nf* toothache ~**otehničar** *nm* dental technician

zucn|uti *v* (što/o čemu) (*pres* ~em) *coll* **ni ~uti** not breathe a word

zuj|ati *v* (0) (*pres* ~im) buzz, hum

zumbul *nm* hyacinth

zupčani|k *nm* (Npl ~ci) cog(-wheel); gear

zuriti *v* (0/u što/u koga) stare (at)

zva|nje *nn* calling, vocation ~**ti** *v* (*pres* zovem) 1 (koga) call; (u goste) invite ~**ti u pomoć** call/cry for help ~**ti u vojsku** conscript; call up *GB*; draft *US* 2 (se) be called/named **kako se zoveš?** what's your name? **zovem se Richard** my name is R. **zovu me Dick** they call me D.

zvecka|ti *v* (0/čime) clink, jingle, tinkle ~**nje oružjem** sabre-rattling

zveč|arka *nf* rattlesnake ~**ati** *v* (0) (*pres* ~im) resound, jar ~**ka** *nf* (Dsg ~ki, Gpl ~aka/~ki) rattle

zveka|n *nm* nincompoop, simpleton ~**st** *adj* daft, nutty

zveke|tati *v* (0/čime) (*pres* ~ćem) clang, clank, clink

zvijer *nf* 1 beast (of prey), wild animal 2 *fig* beast, brute

zvije|zda *nf* 1 star (+ *fig*) 2 *sport* cartwheel **morska ~zda** starfish ~**zda repatica** comet ~**zda vodilja** lodestar **kovati/dizati u ~zde** praise to the skies **vidjeti sve ~zde** see stars

~žđe *nn* constellation

zvizn|uti *v* (koga/što) (*pres* ~em) *coll* whack, sock

zvižd|aljka *nf* (*Dsg* ~aljci) whistle ~ati *v* (0) (*pres* ~im) whistle ~uk *nm* (*Npl* ~uci) whistle ~ukati *v* (0) (*pres* ~učem) whistle

zvjer|ad *nf* wild animals/beasts *pl* ~injak *nm* (*Npl* ~injaci) menagerie ~ka *nf* wild animal **velika** ~ka *coll* big shot/wheel ~okradica *nf* poacher ~ski *adj* beastly, brutal, bestial o *adv* brutally, savagely ~stvo *nn* brutality, atrocity

zvjerati *v* (0) stare, gape

zvjezd|an *adj* starry, starlit ~arnica *nf* observatory ~ica *nf dim* 1 small star 2 asterisk ~oznanac *nm* (*Gsg* ~oznanca, *Npl* ~oznanci) astronomer, stargazer ~oznanstvo *nn* astronomy

zvocati *v* (0/kome) *coll* nag (sb)

zvo|nar *nm* sexton, sacristan ~nast *adj* bell-shaped ~nce *nn* bell ~nik *nm* (*Npl* ~nici) belfry, bell-tower; steeple ~niti *v* (0) ring (the bell); chime; (za mrtve) toll ~niti na uzbunu sound the alarm ~no *nn* bell udarati u velika ~na/na sva ~na shout sth from the rooftops ~njava *nf* ringing, chiming, peal

zvrcn|uti *v* (koga/što) (*pres* ~em) *coll* ring sb (up), give sb a ring/bell/buzz

zvrk *nm* top

zvrndati *v coll* 1 (0/kome) nag (sb) 2 (0) buzz, whirr

zvu|čan *adj* (*a*) 1 resonant, sonorous; ringing 2 *gram* voiced ~čni film sound film ~čno ime high-sounding name ~čati *v* (0) (*pres* ~čim) sound, ring ~či poznato it rings a bell ~čnik *nm* (*Npl* ~čnici) loudspeaker ~čnost *nf* resonance, sonority ~k *nm* (*Npl* ~ci/~kovi) sound

Ž

Ž, ž (že) 30th letter of Cro. alphabet

žab|a *nf* frog **~a krastača** toad **ljudi ~e** frogmen **~ac** *nm* (*Gsg* žapca, *Npl* žapci) frog **~lji** *adj* frog('s) **~okreči-na** *nf fig* backwater

žac|ati *v* (se čega) shrink from **~nuti** *v* (*pres* ~nem) **1** (se) start, wince **2** (koga) *coll* nettle, sting

žad *nm* jade

žagor *nm* chatter

žal *nm* strand

žal|ac *nm* (*Gsg* ~ca) sting

žal|ba *nf* **1** complaint **2** *leg* appeal **uložiti ~bu** file/lodge an appeal **~iti** *v* **1** (koga) pity, feel sorry for **2** (što) regret **3** (se) complain **4** (za kim/čim) miss **ne ~iti truda** spare no effort **~oban** *adj* (*a*) mournful **~opojka** *nf* lament, dirge **~ost** *nf* sorrow, grief **na ~ost** unfortunately **na moju (ve-liku) ~ost** to my regret **biti u ~osti** be in mourning **~ostan** *adj* (~osna *f*) sad **~osna vrba** weeping willow **~ostiti** *v* **1** (koga) sadden, grieve **2** (se) be sad, grieve

žamor *nm* chatter, murmur

žanr *nm* genre

žao *adv* **~ mi je** I am sorry **~ mi ga je** I feel sorry for him

žar *nm* **1** glow **2** *fig* ardour **3** live coals **meso na ~u** grilled meat **~ač** *nm* poker **~išni** *adj* focal; central **~ište** *nn* focus **krizno ~ište** hot/trouble spot **~iti** *v* **1** (0) burn **~iti i paliti** *fig* rule with an iron hand **2** (se) glow **~ki** *adj* **1** hot, torrid **2** bright, dazzling **3** *fig* ardent

žara *nf* urn

žargon *nm* jargon, parlance **novinarski ~** journalese *coll*

žbica *nf* spoke

žbir *nf* **1** police agent **2** *coll* police officer; cop *coll*

žbuka *nf* mortar, plaster **~ti** *v* (0/što) plaster

žbun *nm* bush

žder|ati *v* (*pres* ~em) **1** (što) devour, gorge oneself (on sth) **2** (se) *fig* fret **~onja** *nm derog* glutton

ždral *nm* crane

ždrebica *nf* filly

ždrijeb *nm* lot **izabrati ~om** choose by lot **~ati** *v* (0) cast lots

ždrije|bac *nm* (*Gsg* ~pca) stallion **~be** *nn* foal

ždrijelo *nn* **1** pharynx **2** *fig* crater; abyss

že|ći *v* (koga/što/0) (*pres* ~žem) burn, scorch

že|dan *adj* (*a*) thirsty (+ *fig*) **prevesti koga ~dnog preko vode** lead sb up the garden path **~đa** *nf* thirst **~đati** *v* (0) be thirsty; thirst

žega *nf* scorching/sweltering heat

žele *nm* jelly **~-bombon** *nm* jelly-bean

želu|čani *adj* gastric, stomach **~dac** *nm* (*Gsg* ~ca) stomach **boli me ~dac** I have a stomach ache

želj|a *nf* **1** wish, desire **2** (glazbena) request **ispunila mi se ~a** my wish came true **ispuniti kome ~u** fulfil sb's wish, make sb's wish come true **~an** *adj* (*a*) (čega) keen (on), avid (for) **~eti** *v* (*pres* želim) **1** (što) wish (for), want; like **2** (koga) want **~eti komu dobro/zlo** wish sb well/ill **~ela bih vam reći** I would like to tell you **~ela bih da to mogu** I wish I could do it **~ela bih da sam mlađa** I wish I were younger **~no** *adv* eagerly

željez|an *adj* (*a*) iron (+ *fig*) **~ara** *nf* **1** ironmongery *GB*; hardware store *US* **2** ironworks **~nica** *nf* railway; railroad *US* **podzemna ~nica** the underground/tube *GB*; subway *US* **Britanske ~nice** British Rail **~ničar**

nm railwayman; railroad worker *US* **~nički** *adj* railway; railroad *US* **~nički nasip** railway embankment; permanent way *GB* **~nički prag** sleeper; tie *US* **~nička pruga** railway line **~nička postaja/stanica** *coll* railway station **~o** *nn* iron **kovano/lijevano ~o** wrought/cast iron **staro ~o** scrap iron

žemička, žemlja *nf* roll

žen|a *nf* **1** woman **2** (supruga) wife **~idba** *nf* marriage **~ik** *nm* (*Vsg* ~iče, *Npl* ~ici) bridegroom **~iti** *v* **1** (koga) marry **2** (se) get married **~ka** *nf* female **~omrzac** *nm* (*Gsg* ~omrsca, *Vsg* ~omršče) misogynist **~ska** *nf* **1** *derog* female; bird *GB*; broad *US* **2** *coll* girlfriend **~skar** *nm* womanizer, lady-killer **~ski** *adj* **1** woman's, women's **2** ladies' **3** female **4** gynecological **~ski rod** a. womanhood b. *gram* feminine gender **~skast** *adj derog* effeminate **~stven** *adj* feminine, womanly

žeravica *nf* embers *pl*

žest|a *nf* spirit(s) **~ina** *nf* intensity **~iti** *v* **1** (koga) make sb angry **2** (se) be furious, rage **~ok** *adj* violent, intense; severe; fierce; (bol) acute **~oko piće** spirits

žet|elac *nm* (*Gsg* ~eoca) reaper, harvester **~elica** *nf* harvester **~i** (što) (*pres* žanjem) reap, harvest **kako siješ tako češ i ~i** as you sow so shall you reap **~va** *nf* harvest **rekordna ~va** bumper harvest/crop

žeton *nm* coll token

žezlo *nn* sceptre

žganci *nm pl* polenta; maize porridge; mush *US*

žgaravica *nf* heartburn

žgoljav *adj* skinny

ži|ca *nf* **1** wire **2** string, chord **3** *sl* bent **bodljikava ~ca** barbed wire **~car** *nm* cadger **~cati** *v* (0/koga što) bum, cadge (sth from/off sb), panhandle *US coll* **~čan** *adj* wire **~čara** *nf* cable-car, cable railway

Židov *nm* Jew **ž~ski** *adj* Jewish

žig *nm* stamp, seal; brand **poštanski ~** postmark **vodeni ~** watermark **udariti ~** stamp, seal; brand

žiga|ti *v* (koga) **~ me u leđima** I feel stabbing pain in my back

žigica *nf* match

žila *nf* blood vessel, vein **~ kucavica** artery **zlatna ~** vein of gold **iz petnih ~** for all one's worth **~v** *adj* **1** sinewy **2** (meso) tough **3** *fig* stubborn, tenacious

žilet *nm* coll razor blade

žir *nm* acorn

žirafa *nf* giraffe

žiri *nm* coll jury

žiroračun *nm* bank account

žit|arica *nf* cereal **~o** *nn* corn *GB*; grain **~nica** *nf fig* granary

žitki *adj* liquid, viscous

živ *adj* **1** living, live, (samo u predikatu) alive **2** lively, vivacious; brisk **nitko ~ ne zna** nobody on earth knows that **~ pokopan** buried alive **~a istina** plain truth **nema ni ~e duše** there is not a living soul **~i pijesak** quicksand **~i zid** human shield **~o biće** living being **~o vapno** quick lime **~a** *nf* mercury, quicksilver **~ac** *nm* (*Gsg* ~ca) nerve **pogoditi u ~ac** *fig* touch to the quick **ići komu na ~ce** get on sb's nerves **~ahan** *adj* (α) lively **~cirati** *v coll* **1** (koga) get on sb's nerves **2** (se) fret **~čan** *adj* nervous **~ež** *nm* food, victuals **~ežne namirnice** food, foodstuffs **trgovina ~žnim namirnicama** grocer's *GB*; grocery store *US* **~ica** *nf* hedge **~ina** *nf* beast (+ *fig*) **~inče** *nn* animal **~jeti** *v* (0) (*pres* ~im) live **~io!** *int* long live ...! **~jeli!** *int* cheers! **~nuti** *v* (0) spring to life, liven up **~opisan** *adj* (α) picturesque, colourful **~ot** *nm* **1** life; lifetime **2** living; livelihood **borba na ~ot i smrt** mortal combat **pitanje ~ota i smrti** a matter of life and death **zarađivati za ~ot** earn one's livelihood **način ~ota** way of life, lifestyle **troškovi ~ota** cost of living **~otariti** *v* (0) live from hand to mouth **~otinja** *nf* animal **~otinjski** *adj* **1** animal **2** *fig* brutal **~otni** *adj* **1** life; vital **2** of a lifetime **~otni standard** standard of living **biti u ~otnoj opasnosti** a. be in mortal danger b. be in critical/life-threatening condition ~otopis nm biography

ži|žak nm (Gsg ~ška) **1** burner **2** (kukac) weevil

žli|ca nm (table)spoon ~ca **brašna** a spoonful of flour ~ca **za cipele** shoehorn **zidarska** ~ca trowel ~**čica** nf teaspoon

žličnja|k nm (Npl ~ci) dumpling

žlijeb nm **1** groove **2** (krova) gutter

žlijezda nf gland

žmarci nm pl goose-flesh **podilaze me** ~ my flesh creeps

žmiga|ti v (očima kome) wink at sb ~vac nm (Gsg ~vca) coll indicator

žmir|iti v (0) keep one's eyes closed, close one's eyes ~kati v (0) blink, flicker

žniran|ac nm (Gsg ~ca) coll shoe-lace

žohar nm cockroach

žongler nm juggler

žrtv|a nf (Gpl žrtava) **1** (Bogu) sacrifice **2** victim; casualty **3** (prevare) prey (to) **podnijeti** ~**u** make/offer a sacrifice ~**eni** adj sacrificial ~**eno janje a.** sacrificial lamb **b.** fig scapegoat ~**enik** nm (Npl ~enici) altar ~**ovati** v (koga/što/se) (pres ~ujem) sacrifice (sb/sth/oneself)

žrv|anj nm (Gsg ~nja) millstone

žubor nm murmur, babble ~**iti** v (θ) babble

žuč nm gall, bile (+ fig) ~**an** adj **1** bilious (+ fig) ~**ni kamenac** gall-stone ~**ni mjehur** gall-bladder ~**ni vod** bile duct **2** fig bitter ~**ljiv** adj fig bitter

žućkast adj yellowish; (put) sallow;

fawn

žud|jeti v (za kim/čim) (pres ~im) yearn/crave/lust (for), covet ~**no** adv eagerly, hungrily ~**nja** nf lust

žulj nm callus; blister **stati kome na** ~ fig tread on sb's corns ~**evit** adj calloused ~**ati** v (koga) pinch ~**aju me cipele** my shoes pinch me

žumanj|ak nm (Gsg ~ka, Npl ~ci) (egg)yolk

žuna nf woodpecker

žup|a n parish ~**ljanin** nm (Npl ~ljani) parishioner ~**ni** adj parish ~**ni ured** parish priest's office ~**nik** nm (Vsg ~niče, Npl ~nici) parish priest; rector, vicar, parson

župan nm County Head ~**ija** nf county ~**ijski** adj county ~**ijski dom** Chamber of Counties

žur|an adj hasty, hurried; quick; urgent ~**ba** nf haste, hurry **biti u** ~**bi** be in a hurry ~**iti** v (0/se) be in a hurry; rush

žust|ar adj (a) brisk, quick, agile ~**rina** nf agility, briskness

žut adj yellow ~**anjak** nm (Gsg ~anjka, Npl ~anjci) (egg)yolk ~**ica** nf jaundice ~**jeti** v (0) (pres ~im) turn yellow ~**okljun** adj fig green ~**okljunac** nm (Gsg ~okljunca, Vsg ~okljunče) greenhorn

žva|kati v (što) (pres ~čem) chew ~**kaća guma** coll chewing gum

žval|e nf pl bit ~**iti** v **1** (što) (konja) bridle **2** (koga/što/se) coll vulg French-kiss, smooch

Hrvatske kratice
Croatian abbreviations

a.a.   ad acta, među spise
AVNOJ   *pov* Antifašističko vijeće narodnog oslobođenja Jugoslavije

BiH   Bosna i Hercegovina
b.o.   *med* bez osobitosti, nalaz uredan
br.   broj

cm   centimetar
CZ   civilna zaštita

Č. (čit.)   čitaj (pronounced)
čl.   članak

DA   *pol* Dalmatinska akcija (political party)
dcl   decilitar
dipl.   diplomirani (bachelor's degree or equivalent)
dm   decimetar
dr.   doktor
DZ   dom zdravlja

EEZ   Europska ekonomska zajednica
EU   Europska unija

fra   fratar, franjevac

g   gram
g.   **1** (gosp.) gospodin **2** (god.) godina
gđa   gospođa
gđica   gospođica

HAK   Hrvatski autoklub
HAZU   Hrvatska akademija znanosti i umjetnosti
HBZ   Hrvatska bratska zajednica
HDZ   *pol* Hrvatska demokratska zajednica
HINA   Hrvatska izvještajna novinska agencija
HKD   Hrvatsko kulturno društvo
HKDU   *pol* Hrvatska kršćansko-demokratska unija
HND   *pol* Hrvatski nezavisni demokrati
HNK   Hrvatsko narodno kazalište
HNL   Hrvatska nogometna liga
HP   Hrvatske pošte
HRM   Hrvatska ratna mornarica
HRT   Hrvatska radiotelevizija
HRZ   Hrvatsko ratno zrakoplovstvo
HSLS   *pol* Hrvatska socijalno-liberalna stranka

HSP	*pol* Hrvatska stranka prava
HSS	*pol* Hrvatska seljačka stranka
HT	Hrvatske telekomunikacije
HTZ	higijensko-tehnička zaštita
HUS	Hrvatska udruga sindikata
HV	Hrvatska vojska
HVEP	Hrvatsko vijeće europskog pokreta
HVIDRA	Hrvatsko vijeće invalida domovinskog rata
HVO	Hrvatsko vijeće obrane
HŽ	Hrvatske željeznice
I	istok
i. d.	i dalje
INA	Industrija nafte (name of oil company)
ing.	inženjer (graduate engineer)
i sl.	i slično
i dr.	i drugo
IDS	*pol* Istarski demokratski sabor (political party)
itd	i tako dalje
J	jug
JAR	Južnoafrička Republika
JI	jugoistok
JZ	jugozapad
KBC	Kliničko-bolnički centar
kg	kilogram
kl.	klasa
kn	kuna
KS	konjska snaga
KUD	kulturno-umjetničko društvo
l	litra
lp	lipa
m	metar
MH	Matica hrvatska
ml	mililitar
mm	milimetar
MMF	Međunarodni monetarni fond
MORH	Ministarstvo obrane Republike Hrvatske
MP	mjesto pečata
mr.	magistar; magistrica
MUP	Ministarstvo unutarnjih poslova
NDH	*pov* Nezavisna Država Hrvatska
NK	nogometni klub

NKV	nekvalificiran (unskilled)
NLO	neindetificirani leteći objekt
N.N.	netko nepoznat (John Doe)
npr.	na primjer
NSB	Nacionalna i sveučilišna biblioteka
NSS	niža stručna sprema (first level education)
Nj. Eksc.	Njegova ekscelencija
Nj. V.	Njegovo/Njezino Veličanstvo
o. g.	ove godine
o. mj.	ovog mjeseca
o.	**1** otac **2** otok
OŠ	osnovna škola
OTV	Otvorena televizija
PIK	poljoprivredno-industrijski kombinat
p. Kr.	poslije Krista (A.D.)
p. p.	poštanski pretinac (P. O. box)
PKV	polukvalificiran (semiskilled)
pr. Kr.	prije Krista
prof.	profesor
red. br.	redni broj
RH	Republika Hrvatska
rkt.	rimokatolik
S	sjever
SAD	Sjedinjene Američke Države
SDP	*pol* Socijaldemokratska partija
SI	sjeveroistok
SNS	*pol* Srpska narodna stranka
SRCE	Sveučilišni računski centar
SSS	srednja stručna sprema (second level education)
st.	**1** stoljeće **2** stavak
str.	stranica, stranice
sv.	svezak
SZ	sjeverozapad
šk. god.	školska godina
t	tona
TBC	tuberkuloza
tj.	to jest
tzv.	takozvani
UN	Ujedinjeni narodi

ul.	ulica
usp.	usporedi
uz.	u zamjenu
v.	vidi
VBR	višecijevni raketni bacač
v. d.	vršitelj dužnosti (acting)
vlč	velečasni
v. r.	vlastitom rukom (signed)
VKV	visokokvalificiran (highly-skilled)
VP	Vojna policija
VSS	visoka stručna sprema (third level education)
Z	zapad
ZAP	Zavod za platni promet
ZET	Zagrebački električni tramvaj (name of company)
ZNG	Zbor narodne garde
ZV	Zagrebački velesajam

BASIC CROATIAN GRAMMAR
Word formation

OSNOVE HRVATSKE GRAMATIKE
Tvorba riječi

Croatian Letters and Sounds

The Vowels

There are six vowels in Croatian indicated by the letters

a, e, i, o, u and **r**.

a is pronounced as **a** in father: alat *tools*, dan *day*
e is pronounced as **e** in pet: ep *epic*, esej *essay*, polje *field*
i is pronounced as English **ee** or **ea** in *meet, meat, tea*: iskra *spark*
o is pronounced as **o** in for: okolo *around*, brdo *hill*
u is pronounced as **oo** in root: usta *mouth*, ruka *arm*
r is similar to Scots trilled **r** in heart: ruski *Russian*

The Croatian vowels appear as either long or short depending on the word in which they occur.

Sometimes the difference in meaning is signalled by the length of the vowel:

pas *dog* - pas *belt*   pitati *ask* - pitati *feed*

The distinction in meaning appears occasionally in the declension (of nouns and adjectives) although the forms of words are spelt identically:

žena (Nsg) *woman* - žena (Gpl) *of the women*

The Consonants

The following letters appear both in Croatian and English and stand for approximately similiar sounds in both languages:

b, d, f, g, h, k, l, m, n, p, s, t, v, z.

The sounds represented by the following Croatian letters have to be learned in comparison with similar sounds or sound patterns in English.

š = **sh** in shirt – škola *school*, šaš *sedge*
ž = **z** in azure or **s** in vision – žaba *frog*
c = **ts** in pits, *rats, tse–tse* – car *emperor*, jarac *billy goat*
č = **ch** in charge – čast *honour*
ć – (for practical reasons similar to **č**, but articulated with the tip of the tongue behind the lower teeth) ćup *jug*
dž = **j** in juice – džep *pocket*
đ – (similar to **dž**, but articulated with the tip of the tongue behind the lower teeth) dak *pupil*
j = **y** in youth, pay – jastog *lobster*
lj = **lue** in value – ljiljan *lily*, žulj *blister*
nj = **n** in new – njegov *his*

Accent

The accent in Croatian is melodic and philologically interesting but for practical reasons it may help to note:

– the stress can fall on any syllable except the last (with a few exceptions)

– in a two syllable word the stress will be regularly on the first syllable – voda *water*, vatra *fire*, sunce, *sun*

– in a three syllable word the stress may be on the first or on the second – dvorana *hall*, hladnoća *cold*

– long vowels occur only under stress.

The influence of *j* sound on the preceding consonants

It occurs in the comparative, the instrumental case, the passive participle and in nouns formed with –je suffix.

p – plj tup *dull* – tuplji *duller*, grabiti *to take hold of* – grablje *rake*
b – blj grub *coarse* – grublji *coarser*, ljubiti *to love* – ljubljen *loved*
v – vlj kriv *crooked* – krivlji *more crooked*, krv *blood* – krvlju (instr.)
m – mlj bezuman *mad* – bezumlje *madness*, mamiti *to lure* – mamljen *lured*
t – ć smrt *death* – smrću (instr.), vratiti *to return* – vraćen *returned*
d – đ mlad *young* – mlađi *younger*, glad *hunger* – glađu (instr.)
s – š iznositi *to wear out* – iznošen *worn out*, visok *high* – viši *higher*
z – ž brz *fast* – brži *faster*, gaziti *to trample upon* – gažen *trampled*
k – č jak *strong* – jači *stronger*, peku *they bake* – pečen *baked*
h – š duh *spirit* – duša (duh–ja) *soul*, tih *quiet* – tiši *quieter*
g – ž blag *mild* – blaži *milder*, drag *dear* – draži *dearer*
st – šć gust *dense* – gušći *denser*, radost *happiness* – radošću (instr.)
zd – žd grozd *bunch of grapes* – grožđe *grapes*, zabrazditi *to plow a furrow* – zabražđen *furrowed*

Other sound patterns and changes

A) The sounds g, h and k are replaced by č, ž, š before the vocative ending –e:

Bog *God* – Bože!
Vlah *Vlach* – Vlaše!
junak *hero* – junače!

and before –e endings of the present tense:

oni strigu *they clip* – on striže *he clips*
oni vrhu *they thresh* – on vrše *he threshes*
oni peku *they bake* – on peče *he bakes*

B) The sounds **k, g** and **h** are replaced by **c, z, s** in the declensions of nouns and the conjunctions of verbs:

bubreg *kidney* – bubrezi *kidneys*
duh *spirit* – dusi spirits
vojnik *soldier* – vojnici *soldiers*

noga *leg* – na nozi (loc.)
epoha *epoch* – u eposi (loc.)
ruka *arm* – u ruci (loc.)

strigu *they clip* – strizi!
vrhu *they thresh* – vrsi!
peku *they bake* – peci!

The "movable" *a* sound

Combinations of consonants that cluster in nonfinal position usually appear in final position separated by the vowel **a**:

–mk– : -mak momka (gen. sg.) momak – *lad*
–rc– : -rac starca (gen. sg.) starac – *old man*
–br– : -bar dobri (def. adj.) dobar (indef.) – *good*
–dn– : -dan hladni (def. adj.) hladan (indef.) – *cold*
–zm– : -zam liberalizma (gen. sg.) liberalizam – *liberalism.*

Sign (*a*) in the Dictionary marks the movable **a** sound in adjectives.

Syntax and morphology

Nouns – Imenice

Gender

Each noun in the dictionary carries the indication of masculine **m**, feminine **f** or neuter **n** gender. This category (which is also found in adjectives, pronouns and verb participles) is important in selecting the form of words accompanying the noun as they must be of the same gender. Most nouns ending in –a (žena, škola) are feminine, those ending in a consonant (grad, prozor, učenik) are masculine, and those ending in –o and –e (pero, more) are neuter. Grammatical gender in Croatian does not necessarily correspond to sex as both žena (woman) and kuća (house) are feminine.

Case

The various functions that nouns have in the sentence (subject, direct object and indirect object, possessives, etc.) are signalled by their endings called **cases**. The same functions are recognized in English sentences by the position of the noun or by the use of prepositions – žene *of the woman*; ženi *to the woman*; žena gleda *a woman is watching*; ženu gleda *he/she is watching a woman*.

Croatian nouns have a seven case paradigm: **nominative, genitive, dative, accusative, vocative, locative** and **instrumental**, for which endings vary according to gender, but sometimes coincide (nominative and accusative of masculine inanimates; genitive and accusative of masculine animates; dative and locative, etc.).

Some examples:

	masc.	fem.	neut.
sg.			
N	jelen *deer*	koza *goat*	selo *village*
G	jelena	koze	sela
D	jelenu	kozi	selu
A	jelena	kozu	selo
V	jelene	kozo	selo
L	jelenu	kozi	selu
I	jelenom	kozom	selom
pl.			
N	jeleni	koze	sela
G	jelena	koza	sela
D	jelenima	kozama	selima
A	jelene	koze	sela
V	jeleni	koze	sela
L	jelenima	kozama	selima
I	jelenima	kozama	selima

Besides these, there are other types of paradigms with somewhat different endings. Alternative endings are sometimes due to consonant modifications as when **k, g, h** followed by **e** change into **č, ž, š** or into **c, z, s** when followed by **i**.

eg. Nsg. masc. vuk *wolf*, Vsg vuče, Npl vuci (or vukovi) etc.

Adjectives – Pridjevi

Adjectives have a seven case declension which varies according to gender and number. In addition, there are two sets of forms for most adjectives: **definite** and **indefinite**. Here is the masculine declension:

	def.	indef.	
sg.			
N	mudri	mudar	*wise*
G	mudroga	mudra	
D	mudromu	mudru	
A	mudroga	mudra	
V	mudri	mudar	

L	mudrom	mudru
I	mudrim	mudrim

pl.

N	mudri
G	mudrih
D	mudrima
A	mudre
V	mudri
L	mudrima
I	mudrima

The use of the two sets of forms is sometimes comparable to that of the definite and indefinite article in English.

The comparison of adjectives

The comparative is derived from the masculine indefinite forms by adding:

1. –**iji** for masculine, –**ija** for feminine, and –**ije** for neuter

  star *old* – stariji, starija, starije

2. –**ji, –ja, –je** (often with the alteration of the preceding consonant)

  drag *dear* – draži, draža, draže

3. –**ši** (for three adjectives only)

  lak *light*   – lakši, lakša, lakše
  lijep *beautiful* – ljepši, ljepša, ljepše
  mek *soft*   – mekši, mekša, mekše

4. There are **irregular comparatives**:

  dobar *good* – bolji, bolja, bolje   zao *ill* – gori, gora, gore

The superlative is formed by prefixing **naj–** to the comparative form:

  najdraži, najdraža, najdraže
  najbolji, najbolja, najbolje
  najjači, najjača, najjače

Adverbs – Prilozi

Adverbs may be formed from adjectives in one of the following ways:

1. by using the neuter singular form of the adjective:

staro *old*, dobro *well*, drago *dearly*, meko *softly*.

2. by using the masculine singular nominative form of adjectives in –**ski** (with alterations in –**ški** and –**čki**):

hrvatski *Croatian*, ženski *womanly*, gospodski *gentlemanly*, junački *heroically*, muški *manly*.

Adverbs also exist as simple or compound words.

eg. jučer *yesterday*, sutra *tomorrow*, danas *today*, ovdje *here*, zaista *indeed*.

Verbs – Glagoli

Aspect

Most verbs in the dictionary appear in two forms: **perfective** and **imperfective**. That is because Croatian requires, besides person, gender and number, that verb forms show aspect, ie. whether the action of the verb is in progress (imperfective) or has been completed (perfective). The contrast in aspect is signalled by means of prefixes or infixes:

čitati – pročitati *read*, pisati – napisati *write*
bacati – baciti *throw*, skakati – skočiti *jump*

The infinitive, ending in -**ti**: raditi *work*, and in -**ći**: peći *bake*, appears as the main entry in the dictionary, but also the first person singular of the present tense is listed in the cases when the infinitive stem is considerably different from the present tense one. There are four types of endings for the present tense (personal pronoun subjects are not compulsory because the person is recognized from the verb form itself):

tresti *shake*	čuti *hear*	čuvati *guard*	nositi *carry*

sg.

1. tres-**em**	ču-**jem**	čuv-**am**	nos-**im**
2. tres-**eš**	ču-**ješ**	čuv-**aš**	nos-**iš**
3. tres-**e**	ču-**je**	čuv-**a**	nos-**i**

pl.

1. tres-**emo**	čuj-**emo**	čuv-**amo**	nos-**imo**
2. tres-**ete**	čuj-**ete**	čuv-**ate**	nos-**ite**
3. tres-**u**	čuj-**u**	čuv-**aju**	nos-**e**

There are four **past tenses**:

perfekt (the general past tense formed from the present tense of the auxiliary verb biti *be* and the active participle of the verb):

ja sam baci-**o**   (masc.)
ja sam baci-**la**   (fem.)

aorist (the completed past tense formed mostly from the infinitive stem of perfective verbs):

baciti: baci-**h**, baci, baci, baci-**smo**, baci-**ste**, baci-**še**

imperfekt (the durative past tense formed mostly from the present tense stem of imperfective verbs):

bacati: bac-**ah**, bac-**aše**, bac-**aše**, bac-**asmo**, bac-**aste**, bac-**ahu**

pluskvamperfekt (the pluperfect formed from the perfect or imperfect of the auxiliary "be" and the active participle):

ja **sam bio** baca-**o** or **bijah** baca-**o** (masc.)
ja **sam bila** baca-**la** or **bijah** baca-**la** (fem.)

There are two **future tenses:**

futur I (formed from the enclitic present tense of the auxiliary htjeti *want* and the infinitive of the verb):

ja **ću bacati**   or   **bacat ću**

futur II (the before future, most frequently formed from perfective verbs with the perfective prresent tense of the verb "be" and the active participle):

ja **budem bacio**

There are three **moods:**

conditional (formed from the aorist of the auxiliary "be" and the active participle):

ja **bih bacio**

past conditional (formed from the conditional of the auxiliary "be" and the active participle):

ja **bih bio bacao**

imperative (formed from the present tense stem):

	perfective	imperfective
2nd pers. sg.	bac-**i**	bac-**aj**
1st pers. pl.	bac-**ime**	bac-**ajmo**
2nd pers. pl.	bac-**ite**	bac-**ajte**

The third person sg. and pl. are formed from the particle **neka** and the third person present tense sg. and pl. respectively:

neka baci - *let him throw*
neka bace - *let them throw*

Passive shows all the tenses, moods and participles as the active state. The present tense of the passive is formed by the imperfective or perfective present tense of the auxiliary "be" plus passive participle of the verb:

ja sam bačen   **bivam bačen**

Note: Passive is used considerably less in Croatian than in English.

The active participle (mentioned in connection with the construction of the perfekt, pluskvamperfekt, futur II and kondicional) is formed from the infinitive stem with the addition of the endings for masculine, feminine and neuter:

-o, -la, -lo: baciti: baci-**o**, baci-**la**, baci-**lo**; or
-ao, -la, -lo: tresti: tres-**ao**, tres-**la**, tres-**lo**

The passive participle (necessary in the construction of the passive) is mostly formed from the infinitive stem of transitive verbs and a series of endings:

tresti: tres-**en**, tres-**ena**, tres-**eno**
nositi: nos-**jen** nošen, nos-**jena** nošena, nos-**jeno** nošeno
čuvati: čuva-**n**, čuva-**na**, čuva-**no**

The present participle is formed from imperfective verbs by adding **-ći** to the third person plural of the present tense:

tresu-**ći**, čuju-**ći**, čuvaju-**ći**, nose-**ći**

The past participle is formed from the infinitive stem of perfective verbs by adding the endings **-vši** or rarely **-v** (ču-**vši**, ču-**v**) or **-avši**, **-av** (istres-**avši**, istres-**av**).

The present tense of the auxiliary verbs biti and htjeti

stressed/unstressed forms

biti		**htjeti**	
1. jesam, sam	1. jesmo, smo	1. hoću, ću	1. hoćemo, ćemo
2. jesi, si	2. jeste, ste	2. hoćeš, ćeš	2. hoćete, ćete
3. jest, je	3. jesu, su	3. hoće, će	3. hoće, će

Pronouns – Zamjenice

The **personal pronouns** paradigm:

sg.

N	ja (I)	ti (you)	on (he)	ono (it)	(ona)
GA	mene, me	tebe, te	njega, ga	njega, ga	nje, je
DL	meni, mi	tebi, ti	njemu, mu	njemu, mu	njoj, joj

I	mnom	tobom	njime	njime	njom
pl.					

N	mi (we)	vi (you)	oni (they)	ona (they)	one (they)
GA	nas	vas	njih, ih	njih, ih	njih, ih
DLI	nama	vama	njima	njima	njima

It is to be noted that personal pronouns show stressed and unstressed (shorter) forms the use of which is subject to certain grammatical and stylistic rules, eg. the stressed forms always follow a preposition: **govori o meni** (he speaks about me), and may produce a contrast as in **daj meni** (give it to me and not to someone else) and **daj mi** (give me).

Possessive pronouns
sg.

N	moj, -a, -e	*my, mine*
	tvoj, -a, -e	*your, yours*
	njegov, -a -o	*his, her, hers, its*

pl.

N	naš, -a, -e	*our, ours*
	vaš, -a, -e	*your, yours*
	njihov, -a, -o	*their, theirs*

A special possessive pronoun **svoj, -a, -e** (one's own) helps to avoid ambiguity:

on gradi svoju kuću - *he is building his own house*
on gradi njegovu kuću - *he is building his (other person's) house*

Relative and interrogative pronouns

tko (G koga, D komu, A koga, L komu, I kim)	*who*
što (G čega, D čemu, A što, L čemu, I čim)	*what*
koji, -a, -e	*who, which, that, what*
kakvi, kakva, kakvo	*what kind of, as*

Demonstrative pronouns

ovaj, ova, ovo	*this one*
taj, ta, to	*that one*
onaj, ona, ono	*that one there*

Possessive, relative-interrogative and demonstrative pronouns show the three genders and full singular and plural declensions.

Interjections

Interjections express emotions and are outside syntactic relations in a sentence.

Their meanings are flexible within a certain semantic field depending on context. Here are some Croatian interjections with their approximate meanings and English equivalents:

o, oh (surprise)	*oh*
uf (disgust)	*ugh*
fuj (disgust)-	*yuck*
jao, joj (pain)	*ouch, woe*
avaj (pain, worry)	*alas*
ch (satisfaction, recognition)	*ah*
(h)ajde (encouragement)	*come on, move on*

Conjunctions – Veznici

Conjunctions are unchangeable parts of speech some of which function only as conjunctions, some others as both conjunctions and other parts of speech as eg. adverbs.

Some conjunctions are semantically limited to one type of function:

ali *but*; čim *as soon as*; jer *because*; premda, makar *although*; dakle *therefore*; kao, kao što *as, like.*

Other conjunctions are semantically empty and understood pragmatically from the context ie. they may have several types of function:

da *that, so that, if*; kako *as, that, how*; kad *when, because, since, as.*

Some usual **coordinating conjunctions** (joining words, phrases and independent clauses) are:

i, pa, te - *and*; ni, niti - *no, neither*; ili *or*; a *but, and*; ali, no, nego, već *but*; dakle, stoga, zato *therefore*; samo *only*; osim *except.*

Some **subordinating conjunctions** (introducing dependent or subordinate clauses) are:

expressing **purpose** - da, kako, neka *in order*
temporal - dok *while, till, when*; čim, tek što *as soon as, no sooner*; pošto *after*; kako *as*; prije nego *before*
expressing **manner and comparison**: kako *as, like*; kao da *as if, as though*; koliko *as much as*; nego *than*
introducing **indirect discourse**: da *that*
expressing **reason**: jer, što, kako *because*
result or consequence: da, te *that*
conditional: ako, da, kad *if*
concessive: iako, makar, premda, da *although*

Prepositions – Prijedlozi

Prepositions in the Dictionary are marked by the case or cases in which the following noun must appear. Some prepositions are followed by:

genitive - bez *without*; blizu *near*; do *as far as, till*; iz *from*; oko *around*
dative - k *towards*; nasuprot *against*; unatoč *in spite of*
accusative - kroz *through*; niz *down*; uz *up*
locative - pri *at*; prema *towards*

Some prepositions governing more than one case:

genitive and instrumental: s *with*
accusative and locative: na *on*; o *about, concerning*
genitive, accusative and locative: u *in, into*

(following T. F. Magner)

Numerals – Brojevi → Osnove engleske gramatike

Tvorba riječi
Word formation

Tvorba imenica
Noun formation

I. Osobe
    Persons

a) muška osoba
    male

Glagol + nastavak
Verb + ending

-ac	kositi - kosac	reaper, haymaker
	suditi - sudac	judge
-ač	jahati - jahač	rider
	kovati - kovač	blacksmith
-ar	slikati - slikar	painter
	zidati - zidar	bricklayer
-lac	misliti - mislilac	thinker
	roniti - ronilac	diver
-nik	potpisati - potpisnik	signatory
	predsjedati - predsjednik	president
-telj	čitati - čitatelj	reader

izvijestiti - izvjestitelj   reporter

Imenica + nastavak
Noun + ending

-ar	dimnjak - dimnjačar	chimneysweep
	mlijeko - mljekar	milkman
-aš	nogomet - nogometaš	footballer, football player
	orgulje - orguljaš	organist, organ player
ist	bicikl - biciklist	cyclist
	gitara - gitarist	guitarist

Pridjev + nastavak
Adjective + ending

-ac	kriv - krivac	culprit
	pijan - pijanac	drunkard
-ak	čudan - čudak	strange fellow
	lud - luđak	lunatic
	veseo - veseljak	cheerful/jovial fellow
-ik	jadan - jadnik	poor person/soul
	ranjen - ranjenik	wounded person

b) ženska osoba
  female

-ica	krojač - krojačica	dressmaker
	student - studentica	(female) student
-inja	junak - junakinja	heroine
	rođak - rođakinja	female relative, kinswoman
-ka	bolničar - bolničarka	nurse
	novinar - novinarka	(woman) journalist
-kinja	aristokrat - aristokratkinja	(woman) aristocrat
	stranac - strankinja	foreign woman

c) etnici
  ethnics

muška osoba
male

-ac	Alžir - Alžirac	Algerian (man)
	Zagorje - Zagorac	Zagorje man
-anac	Afrika - Afrikanac	African (man)

-anin	Amerika - Amerikanac	American (man)
	Beč - Bečanin	Viennese man
	Europa - Europljanin	European (man)
	Zagreb - Zagrepčanin	Zagreb man

ženska osoba
female

-ica	Hrvat - Hrvatica	Croatian (woman)
	Mađar - Mađarica	Hungarian (woman)
	Nijemac - Njemica	German (woman)
-inja	Čeh - Čehinja	Czech (woman)
	Poljak - Poljakinja	Polish woman
-ka	Slovenac - Slovenka	Slovenian (woman)
	Talijan -Talijanka	Italian (woman)
-kinja	Danac - Dankinja	Danishwoman
	Englez - Engleskinja	Englishwoman
	Francuz - Francuskinja	Frenchwoman

II. Apstraktne imenice
   Abstract nouns

Pridjev + nastavak
Adjective + ending

-ilo	lud - ludilo	madness
	zelen - zelenilo	greenery
-oća	lak - lakoća	ease
	sam - samoća	solitude
-ina	brz - brzina	speed
	cijel - cjelina	a whole
-ost	grub - grubost	roughness
	jednak - jednakost	equality
-ota	dobar - dobrota	goodness
	grozan - grozota	atrocity
	lijep - ljepota	beauty

Imenica + nastavak
Noun + ending

-stvo, -tvo	novinar - novinarstvo	journalism
	prijatelj - prijateljstvo	friendship
	vitez - viteštvo	knighthood

       zdravlje - zdravstvo   health system

III. Glagolske imenice
Verbal nouns

-ba	narediti - naredba	order
	posuditi - posudba	loan
	tvoriti - tvorba	formation
-će	čeznuti - čeznuće	yearning
	porinuti - porinuće	launch
-nje	hodati - hodanje	walking
	letjeti - letenje	flying
	ljubiti - ljubljenje	kissing
	pjevati - pjevanje	singing
	sjediti - sjedenje	sitting

IV. Zbirne imenice
Collective nouns

-ad	bure - burad	barrels
	tele - telad	calves
-je	biser - biserje	pearls
	klas - klasje	ears (of grain)
	otok - otočje	archipelago
	šiprag - šipražje	thicket
-stvo, -tvo	gledatelj - gledateljstvo	audience, viewers
	radnik - radništvo	workers, working class(es)
	svećenik - svećenstvo	clergy

V. Umanjenice
Diminutives

a) imenice muškoga roda
masculine nouns

-ak	cvijet - cvijetak	small flower
	smijeh - smiješak	smile
	trak - tračak	glimmer (of hope)
-čić	dječak - dječačić	little boy
	obraz - obraščić	little cheek
	prozor - prozorčić	small window
-ić	cvijet - cvijetić	small flower
	nož - nožić	small knife, penknife
	pijetao - pjetlić	cockerel

b) imenice ženskoga roda
feminine nouns

-čica	cijev - cjevčica	small tube
	grana - grančica	twig
	stvar - stvarčica	small thing

-ica	crkva - crkvica	little/small church
	knjiga - knjižica	booklet
	zvijezda - zvjezdica	small star, starlet; asterisk

c) imenice srednjega roda
neuter nouns

-ašce	gnijezdo - gnjezdašce	little nest
	mjesto - mjestašce	(nice/cosy) little place
	sunce - sunašce	sweet little sun

-ce	jezero - jezerce	pond
	stablo - stabalce	small tree
	staklo - stakalce	slide
	zvono - zvonce	bell

VI. Uvećanice
Augmentatives

| -čina | šamar - šamarčina | violent slap |
| | vojnik - vojničina | big soldier |

| -etina | baba - babetina | old hag |
| | torba - torbetina | big bag |

-ina	junak - junačina	big hero
	rep - repina	big tail
	trbuh - trbušina	potbelly

| -urina | kosa - kosurina | long (unkempt) hair |
| | trava - travurina | wild grass, weed |

Tvorba pridjeva
Adjective formation

I. Opisni pridjevi
Descriptive adjectives

| -an (-ni) | blato - blatan (blatni) | muddy |
| | mrak - mračan (mračni) | dark |

-an (-ani)	lanac - lančan (lančani)	chain
	pijesak - pješčan (pješčani)	sandy
	zvijezda - zvjezdan (zvjezdani)	starry
-ast	igla - igličast	needle-like
	kuka - kukast	hooked
-at	krilo - krilat	winged
	rep - repat	tailed
-av	pjega - pjegav	freckled
	znoj - znojav	sweaty
-en	borba - borben	combative; combat
	glazba - glazben	music, musical
-ičan	ironija - ironičan	ironic
	realist - realističan	realistic
-kast, -ičast	crven - crvenkast	reddish
	plav - plavičast	bluish
-ljiv	crv - crvljiv	wormy
	uš - ušljiv	lousy
-nat	papir - papirnat	paper
	slama - slamnat	straw
-ovan, -evan	duh - duhovan	spiritual
	duša - duševan	mental, psychic
	mir - mirovan	peace
-ovit, -evit	brdo - brdovit	hilly
	sloj - slojevit	layered, stratified

II. Posvojni pridjevi
Possessive adjectives

-ački, -ički	Zagreb - zagrebački	Zagreb
	turist, turizam - turistički	tourist
-aći	jahati - jahaći	riding
	kupati - kupaći	bathing
-ašnji, -nji, -šnji	jučer - jučerašnji	yesterday's
	sinoć - sinoćnji	last night's
	sutra - sutrašnji	tomorrow's
-ev	bratić - bratićev	cousin's
	stric - stričev	uncle's

-in	mama - mamin	Mum's
	tata - tatin	Dad's
-ji, -i	Bog - Božji	God's
	pas - pasji	dog('s), canine
-ni	država - državni	state, national
	ruka - ručni	hand; manual
-ov	brat - bratov	brother's
	direktor - direktorov	director's
-ski, -ki	grad - gradski	city, town, urban
	klub - klupski	club
	krojač - krojački	tailor's, dressmaker's

Tvorba priloga
Adverb formation

Pridjev + nastavak
Adjective + ending

-o, -e	brz - brzo	fast, quickly
	divlji - divlje	wildly
	loš - loše	badly, poorly
	ružan - ružno	badly, nastily

Tvorba glagola
Verb formation

Imenica + nastavak
Noun + ending

-ati	bubanj - bubnjati	drum
	komad - komadati	cut to pieces, carve
	veslo - veslati	row
-iti	carina - cariniti	charge customs duty
	grijeh - griješiti	sin; err; make mistakes
	noć - noćiti	spend the night
	snijeg - sniježiti	snow
-irati	analiza - analizirati	analyze
	bankrot - bankrotirati	go bankrupt
	telefon - telefonirati	(tele)phone
-ovati,	dar - darovati	give a present; donate
-evati	mač - mačevati	fence
	put - putovati	travel

	stupanj - stupnjevati	grade
-jeti	stid - stidjeti se	be ashamed; be shy
	vid - vidjeti	see

Pridjev + nastavak
Adjective + ending

| **-ati** | jak - jačati | strengthen |
| | mahnit - mahnitati | rave |

-iti	bogat - bogatiti se	get rich
	suh - sušiti	dry
	truo - truliti	rot
-jeti	crven - crvenjeti	redden
	živ - živjeti	live
	žut - žutjeti	become yellow

| **-ovati** | gladan - gladovati | starve |
| | lud - ludovati | rave; be crazy |

Usklik + nastavak
Interjection + ending

-ati	kukuriku - kukurikati	crow
	srk - srkati	slurp
	škljoc - škljocati	click

-kati	fiju - fijukati	whizz
	mjau - mjaukati	mew, miaow
	mljac - mljackati	slurp

Glagolska osnova
Verb base

Vid
Aspect

a) svršeni
  perfective

nesvršeni glagol + nastavak
imperfective verb + ending

-nuti	kucati - kucnuti	knock, give a knock
	šaptati - šapnuti	whisper
	bliještati - bljesnuti	flash
	drečati - dreknuti	scream

b) nesvršeni

imperfective
svršeni glagol + nastavak
perfective verb + ending

-(j)avati	kazniti - kažnjavati	punish
	opravdati - opravdavati	justify
	prilagoditi - prilagođavati	adjust
-(j)ivati	dobaciti - dobacivati	remark; make catcalls; heckle
	naslutiti - naslućivati	have a presentiment
	uspavati - uspavljivati	lull to sleep; make sleepy
-iti	donijeti - donositi	bring
	dovesti - dovoditi	bring
	izaći - izlaziti	go out
	obući - oblačiti	dress
-ati	dići - dizati	lift
	izgristi - izgrizati	eat away
	pasti - padati	be falling
	pomoći - pomagati	help
	posuti - posipati	sprinkle
	umrijeti - umirati	be dying
	baciti - bacati	throw
	lupiti - lupati	bang, beat
	roditi - rađati	deliver, give birth
	skočiti - skakati	be jumping
-jati	javiti - javljati	inform, report
	opaziti - opažati	observe
	platiti - plaćati	pay

APPENDIX
DODATAK

Christian holidays
Kršćanski blagdani

(in chronological order – kronološki kroz kršćansku godinu)

Advent	Došašće
Immaculate Conception (of the Blessed Virgin Mary)	Bezgr(j)ešno Začeće
Christmas Eve	Badnji dan ili Badnjak
Christmas Day	Božić
St. Stephen's Day (Boxing Day *GB*)	Sv. Stjepan (Stjepanovo)
Epiphany (Twelfth Day)	Tri kralja ili Bogojavljenje
Candlemas or Presentation	Svijećnica ili Prikazanje Gospodinovo
Ash Wednesday	Pepelnica ili Čista srijeda
Lent	Korizma
Annunciation Day or Lady Day	Blagovijest
Palm Sunday	Cvjetnica
Holy Week	Veliki tjedan
Holy (or **Maundy**) **Thursday**	Veliki četvrtak
Good Friday	Veliki petak
Holy Saturday	Velika subota
Easter (Sunday)	Uskrs
Easter Monday	Uskrsni ponedjeljak
Ascension Day	Uzašašće ili Spasovo
The Body and Blood of Christ or **Corpus Christi**	Tijelovo
The Sacred Heart of Jesus	Srce Isusovo
The Transfiguration of the Lord	Preobraženje Gospodinovo
Assumption Day	Velika Gospa
Birth of Our Lady	Mala Gospa
All Saints' Day	Svi Sveti
All Souls' Day	Dušni dan
Christ, the King	Krist Kralj

Chemical elements
Kemijska počela

Ac	*actinium*	aktinij
Ag	*silver*	srebro
Al	*aluminium*	aluminij
Am	*americium*	americij
Ar	*argon*	argon
As	*arsenic*	arsen
At	*astatine*	astat
Au	*gold*	zlato
B	*boron*	bor
Ba	*barium*	barij
Be	*beryllium*	berilij
Bi	*bismuth*	bismut
Bk	*berkelium*	berklij
Br	*bromine*	brom
C	*carbon*	ugljik
Ca	*calcium*	kalcij
Cd	*cadmium*	kadmij
Ce	*cerium*	cer
Cf	*californium*	kalifornij
Cl	*chlorine*	klor
Cm	*curium*	kirij
Co	*cobalt*	kobalt
Cr	*chromium*	krom
Cs	*caesium*	cezij
Cu	*copper*	bakar
Dy	*dysprosium*	disprozij
Er	*erbium*	erbij
Es	*einsteinium*	ajnštajnij
Eu	*europium*	europij
F	*fluorine*	fluor
Fe	*iron*	željezo
Fm	*fermium*	fermij
Fr	*francium*	francij
Ga	*gallium*	galij
Gd	*gadolinium*	gadolinij
Ge	*germanium*	germanij
H	*hydrogen*	vodik
Ha	*hahnium*	hanij
He	*helium*	helij
Hf	*hafnium*	hafnij
Hg	*mercury*	živa
Ho	*holmium*	holmij
I	*iodine*	jod
In	*indium*	indij
Ir	*iridium*	iridij
K	*potassium*	kalij
Kr	*krypton*	kripton
La	*lanthanum*	lantan

Li	*lithium*	litij
Lu	*lutetium*	lutecij
Lw	*lawrencium*	lorensij
Md	*mendelevium*	mendelevij
Mg	*magnesium*	magnezij
Mn	*manganese*	mangan
Mo	*molybdenum*	molibden
N	*nitrogen*	dušik
Na	*sodium*	natrij
Nb	*niobium*	niobij
Nd	*neodymium*	neodim
Ne	*neon*	neon
Ni	*nickel*	nikal
No	*nobelium*	nobelij
Np	*neptunium*	neptunij
O	*oxygen*	kisik
Os	*osmium*	osmij
P	*phosphorus*	fosfor
Pa	*protactinium*	protaktinij
Pb	*lead*	olovo
Pd	*palladium*	paladij
Pm	*promethium*	prometij
Po	*polonium*	polonij
Pr	*praseodymium*	prascodim
Pt	*platinum*	platina
Pu	*plutonium*	plutonij
Ra	*radium*	radij
Rb	*rubidium*	rubidij
Re	*rhenium*	renij
Rh	*rhodium*	rodij
Rn	*radon*	radon
Ru	*ruthenium*	rutenij
S	*sulphur*	sumpor
Sb	*antimony*	antimon (stibij)
Sc	*scandium*	skandij
Se	*selenium*	selen
Si	*silicon*	silicij
Sm	*samarium*	samarij
Sn	*tin*	kositar
Sr	*strontium*	stroncij
Ta	*tantalum*	tantal
Tb	*terbium*	terbij
Tc	*technetium*	tehnecij
Te	*tellurium*	telur
Th	*thorium*	torij
Ti	*titanium*	titan
Tl	*thallium*	talij
Tm	*thulium*	tulij
U	*uranium*	uran
V	*vanadium*	vanadij
W	*tungsten*	(wolfram) volfram

Xe	*xenon*	ksenon
Y	*yttrium*	itrij
Yb	*ytterbium*	iterbij
Zn	*zinc*	cink
Zr	*zirconium*	cirkonij

Planets
Planeti

Mercury	Merkur
Venus	Venera
Earth	Zemlja
Mars	Mars
Jupiter	Jupiter
Saturn	Saturn
Uranus	Uran
Neptune	Neptun
Pluto	Pluton

Military ranks
Vojnički činovi

British Army

Field Marshal (FM)
General (Gen)
Lieutenant-General (Lt-Gen)
Major-General (Maj-Gen)
Brigadier (Brig)
Colonel (Col)
Lieutenant-Colonel (Lt-Col)
Major (Maj)
Captain (Capt)
Lieutenant (Lieut)
Second Lieutenant (2nd Lieut)
Warrant Officer 1st Class (WO 1)
Warrant Officer 2nd Class (WO 2)
Staff Sergeant (S/Sgt)
or Colour Sergeant (C/Sgt)
Sergeant (Sgt)
Corporal (Cpl)
Lance-Corporal (L-Cpl)
Private (Pte)

United States Army

General of the Army (GEN)
General (GEN)
Lieutenant General (LTG)
Major General (MG)
Brigadier General (BG)
Colonel (COL)
Lieutenant Colonel (LTC)
Major (MAJ)
Captain (CAPT)
First Lieutenant (1 LT)
Second Lieutenant (2 LT)
Chief Warrant Officer (CWO)
Warrant Officer (WO)
Command Sergeant Major (CSM)
Staff Sergeant Major (SSM)
1st Sergeant (1 SG)
Master Sergeant (MSG)
Sergeant 1st Class (SFC)
Staff Sergeant (SSG)
Sergeant (SGT)
Corporal (CPL)
Private First Class (PIC)
Private (PVT)

Hrvatska vojska

stožerni general
general zbora
general-pukovnik
general-bojnik
stožerni brigadir
brigadir
pukovnik
bojnik
satnik
natporučnik
poručnik
zastavnik
časnički namjesnik
stožerni narednik
narednik
stožerni vodnik
vodnik
desetnik
razvodnik
pozornik

Weights and measures
Mjere

Length – Dužina

1 centimetre (cm) = 0.394 inch (in)
1 metre (m) = 39.4 inches or 1.094 yards (yd)
1 kilometre (km) = 0.621 mile (m)

1 inch (in) = 2.54 cm
1 foot (ft) = 12 in = 30.48 cm
1 yard (yd) = 3 ft = 0.914 m
1 mile (m) = 1.609 km

Weight – Težina

1 gram (g) = 15.43 grains
1 kilogram (kg) = 2.205 pounds
1 tonne (metric ton) = 2204.62 pounds

1 grain (gr) = 0.065 g
1 ounce (oz) = 28.35 g
1 pound (lb) = 12 oz = 0.454 kg
1 stone (st) = 14 lb = 6.356 kg

Capacity – Mjere za tekućinu

1 litre (l) = 1.76 pints (2.1 US pints)

1 pint (pt) (1.201 US pints) = 0.568 l
1 quart (qt) (1.201 US quarts) = 2 pt = 1.136 l
1 gallon (gal) (1.201 US gallons) = 4 qt = 4.546 l

Temperature – Temperatura

Celsius or centigrade (C)	Fahrenheit (F)
100	212
50	122
40	104
30	86
20	68
10	50
0	32
–10	14
–17.8	0

$$C = \frac{5}{9}\left(F - 32\right) \qquad F = \left(\frac{9}{5}\,C\right) + 32$$

Geographical names
Zemljopisna imena

Noun	Adjective; person	Imenica; pridjev; osoba
Afghanistan /æf'gænistɑːn; -stæn/	Afghan /'æfgæn/, Afganistani /æf'gænistɑːnɪ; -stæni/	Afganistan; afganistanski; Afganistanac, -nka
Africa /'æfrikə/	African /'æfrɪkən/	Afrika; afrički; Afrikanac, -nka
Albania /əl'beɪnɪə/	Albanian /əl'beɪnɪən/	Albanija, albanski; Albanac, -nka
America /ə'merɪkə/	American /ə'merɪkən/	Amerika; američki Amerikanac, -nka
Andorra /ɒn'dɔːrə/	Andorran /ɒn'dɔːrən/	Andora; andorski; Andorac, -rka
Angola /æŋ'gəʊlə/	Angolan /æŋ'gəʊlən/	Angola; angolski; Angolac, -lka
(the) Antarctic /ɒn'tɑːktɪk/	Antarctic	Antarktik; antarktički
(the) Arctic /'ɑːktɪk/	Arctic	Arktik; arktički
Argentina /ˌɑːdʒən'tiːnə/, the Argentine	Argentinian /ˌɑːdʒən'tɪnɪən/, Argentine	Argentina; argentinski; Argentinac, -nka
Armenia /ɑː'miːnɪə/	Armenian /ɑːːmiːnɪən/	Armenija; armenski; Armenac, -nka
Asia /'eɪʃə; 'eɪʒə/	Asian /'eɪʃən; 'eɪʒən/	Azija; azijski; Azijac, jka
(the) Atlantic /ət'læntɪk/	Atlantic	Atlantski ocean, Atlantik; atlantski
Australia /ɒ'streɪlɪə; 'ɔːs-/	Australian /ɒ'streɪlɪən; 'ɔːs-/	Australija; australski; Australac, -lka

Austria /'ɒstrɪə; 'ɔ:s-/	Austrian /'ɒstrɪən; 'ɔ:s-/	Austrija; austrijski; Austrijanac, -nka
Azerbaijan /ˌæzəbaɪ'dʒɑ:n/	Azerbaijani /ˌæzəbaɪ'dʒɑ:nɪ/	Azerbajdžan; azerbajdžanski; Azerbajdžanac, -nka
(the) Bahamas /bə'hɑ:məz; -'heɪm-/	Bahamian /bə'heɪmɪən/	Bahamsko otočje, Bahama; bahamski; Bahamac, -mka
(the) Balkans /'bɔ:lkənz/	Balkan /'bɔ:lkən/	Balkan; balkanski
(the) Baltic /'bɔ:ltɪk/	Baltic	Baltik; baltički
Bangladesh /ˌbæŋglə'deʃ/	Bangladeshi /ˌbæŋglə'deʃɪ/	Bangladeš; bangladeški
Barbados /bɑ:'beɪdɒs/	Barbadian /bɑ:'beɪdɪən/	Barbados; barbadoški
Belarus /ˌbeləʳ'ru:s/	Belarussian /ˌbeləʳ'rʌʃən/	Bjelorusija; bjeloruski; Bjelorus, -kinja
Belgium /'beldʒəm/	Belgian /'beldʒən/	Belgija; belgijski; Belgijanac, -nka
Benin /be'ni:n/	Beninese /ˌbenɪ'ni:z/	Benin; beninski; Beninac, -nka
Bermuda /bə'mju:də/	Bermudan /bə'mju:dən/	Bermuda; bermudski
Bhutan /bu:'tɑ:n/	Bhutani /bu:'tɑ:nɪ/; Bhutanese /ˌbu:tɑ:'ni:z/	Butan; butanski Butanac, -nka
Bolivia /bə'lɪvɪə/	Bolivian /bə'lɪvɪən/	Bolivija; bolivijski; Bolivijac, -jka
Bosnia and Herzegovina /'bɒznɪə ənd ˌhɜ:tsəgəʊ'vi:nə/, Bosnia-Herzegovina	Bosnian /'bɒznɪən/	Bosna i Hercegovina; bosanskohercegovački
Brazil /brə'zɪl/	Brazilian /brə'zɪlɪən/	Brazil; brazilski; Brazilac, -lka
Bulgaria /bʌl'geərɪə/	Bulgarian /bʌl'geərɪən/	Bugarska; bugarski; Bugarin, -rka

Burma /'bɜ:mə/	Burmese /ˌbɜ:'mi:z/	Burma; burmanski; Burmanac, -nka
Burundi /bʊ'rʊndi/	Burundian /bʊ'rʊndiən/	Burundi; burundijski; Burundijac, -jka
Cameroon /ˌkæmə'ru:n/	Cameroonian /ˌkæmə'ru:niən/	Kamerun; kamerunski; Kamerunac, -nka
Canada /'kænədə/	Canadian /kə'neidiən/	Kanada; kanadski; Kanađanin, -anka
Cape Verde /keip vɜ:d/	Cape Verdean /keip 'vɜ:diən/	Zelenortski otoci; zelenortski
(the) Caribbean /ˌkæri'bi:ən/	Caribbean	Karibi; karipski
Central African Republic /ˌsentrəl ˌæfrikən ri'pʌblik/		Centralnoafrička Republika
Chad /tʃæd/	Chadian /'tʃædiən/	Čad; čadski; Čađanin, -đanka
Chile /'tʃili/	Chilean /'tʃiliən/	Čile; čileanski; Čileanac, -nka
China /'tʃainə/	Chinese /ˌtʃai'ni:z/	Kina; kineski; Kinez, -neskinja
Colombia /kə'lɒmbiə/	Colombian /kə'lɒmbiən/	Kolumbija; kolumbijski; Kolumbijac, -jka
Congo /'kɒŋgəʊ/	Congolese /ˌkɒŋgə'li:z/	Kongo; kongoanski; Kongoanac, -nka
Costa Rica /ˌkɒstə 'ri:kə/	Costa Rican /ˌkɒstə 'ri:kən/	Kostarika; kostarikanski; Kostarikanac, -nka
Croatia /krəʊ'eiʃə/	Croatian /krəʊ'eiʃən/; Croat /'krəʊæt/	Hrvatska; hrvatski; Hrvat, -ica
Cuba /'kju:bə/	Cuban /'kju:bən/	Kuba; kubanski; Kubanac, -nka
Cyprus /'saiprəs/	Cypriot /'sipriət/	Cipar; ciparski; Cipranin, -anka
(the) Czech Republic /tʃek ri'pʌblik/	Czech /tʃek/	Češka; češki; Čeh, -inja

Denmark /ˈdenmɑːk/ — Danish /ˈdeɪnɪʃ/; Dane /deɪn/ — Danska; danski; Danac, -nkinja

Djibouti /dʒɪˈbuːtɪ/ — Djiboutian /dʒɪˈbuːtɪən/ — Ðibuti; dibutski

(the) Dominican Republic /dəˈmɪnɪkən rɪˈpʌblɪk/ — Dominican /dəˈmɪnɪkən/ — Dominikanska Republika; dominikanski; Dominikanac, -nka

Ecuador /ˈekwədɔː(r)/ — Ecuadorian /ˌekwəˈdɔːrɪən/ — Ekvador; ekvadorski; Ekvadorac, -rka

Egypt /ˈiːdʒɪpt/ — Egyptian /ɪˈdʒɪpʃən/ — Egipat; egipatski; Egipćanin, -anka

El Salvador /el ˈsælvədɔː(r)/ — Salvadorean /ˌsælvəˈdɔːrɪən/ — Salvador; salvadorski; Salvadorac, -rka

England /ˈɪŋglənd/ — English /ˈɪŋglɪʃ/; Englishman /ˈɪŋglɪʃmən/, Englishwoman /ˈɪŋglɪʃwʊmən/ — Engleska; engleski; Englez, -gleskinja

Estonia /eˈstəʊnɪə/ — Estonian /eˈstəʊnɪən/ — Estonija; estonski; Estonac, -nka

Ethiopia /ˌiːθɪˈəʊpɪə/ — Ethiopian /ˌiːθɪˈəʊpɪən/ — Etiopija; etiopski; Etiopljanin, -ljanka

Europe /ˈjʊərəp/ — European /ˌjʊərəˈpɪən/ — Europa; europski; Europljanin, -ljanka; Ev-

Fiji /ˌfiːˈdʒiː, ˌfiːˈdʒiː/ — Fijian /ˌfiːˈdʒiːən; ˈfiːdʒɪən/ — Fidži; fidžijski

Finland /ˈfɪnlənd/ — Finnish /ˈfɪnɪʃ/; Finn /fɪn/ — Finska; finski; Finac, -nkinja

France /frɑːns; US fræns/ — French /frentʃ/; Frenchman /ˈfrentʃmən/, Frenchwoman /ˈfrentʃwʊmən/ — Francuska; francuski; Francuz, -cuskinja

Gabon /gæˈbɒn/ — Gabonese /ˌgæbəˈniːz/ — Gabon; gabonski; Gabonac, -nka

Gambia /'gæmbɪə/	Gambian /'gæmbɪən/	Gambija; gambijski; Gambijac, -jka
Germany /'dʒɜːmənɪ/	German /'dʒɜːmən/	Njemačka; njemački; Nijemac, Njemica
Ghana /'gɑːnə/	Ghanaian /gɑːˈneɪən/	Gana; ganski; Ganac, -nkinja
Gibraltar /dʒɪˈbrɔːltə(r)/	Gibraltarian /dʒɪbrɔːlˈteərɪən/	Gibraltar; gibraltarski
Georgia /'dʒɔːdʒə/	Georgian /'dʒɔːdʒən/	Gruzija; gruzijski; Gruzijac, -jka
Great Britain /ˌgreɪt ˈbrɪtn/	British /'brɪtɪʃ/; Briton /'brɪtn/, US Britisher /'brɪtɪʃə(r)/, coll Brit /brɪt/	Velika Britanija; britanski; Britanac, -nka
Greece /griːs/	Greek /griːk/	Grčka; grčki; Grk, -inja
Guatemala /ˌgwɑːtəˈmɑːlə/	Guatemalan /ˌgwɑːtəˈmɑːlən/	Gvatemala; gvatemalski; Gvatemalac, -lka
Guinea /'gɪnɪ/	Guinean /'gɪnɪən/	Gvineja; gvinejski; Gvinejac, -jka
Guyana /gaɪˈænə/	Guyanese /ˌgaɪəˈniːz/	Gvajana; gvajanski; Gvajanac, -nka
Haiti /'heɪtɪ/	Haitian /'heɪʃn/	Haiti; haitski; Haićanin, -ćanka
Honduras /hɒnˈdjʊərəs; -dʊə-/	Honduran /hɒnˈdjʊərən; -dʊə-/	Honduras; honduraški; Hondurašanin, -šanka
Hungary /'hʌŋgərɪ/	Hungarian /hʌŋˈgeərɪən/	Mađarska; mađarski; Mađar, -rica; Mađžar-
Iceland /'aɪslənd/	Icelandic /aɪsˈlændɪk/; Icelander /'aɪsləndə(r)/	Island; islandski; Islanđanin, -đanka
India /'ɪndɪə/	Indian /'ɪndɪən/	Indija; indijski; Indijac, -jka

Indonesia /ˌɪndə'niːzɪə; -'niːʒə/ | Indonesian /ˌɪndə'niːzɪən; -'niːʒn/ | Indonezija; indonezijski; Indonežanin, -žanka

Iran /ɪ'rɑːn/ | Iranian /ɪ'reɪnɪən/ | Iran; iranski; Iranac, -nka

Iraq /ɪ'rɑːk/ | Iraqi /ɪ'rɑːkɪ/ | Irak; irački; Iračanin, -čanka

Ireland /'aɪələnd/ (the) Irish Republic /ˌaɪrɪʃ rɪ'pʌblɪk/ | Irish /'aɪərɪʃ/; Irishman /'aɪərɪʃmən/, Irishwoman /'aɪərɪʃwʊmən/ | Irska; irski; Irac, Irkinja

Israel /'ɪzreɪl/ | Israeli /ɪz'reɪlɪ/ | Izrael; izraelski; Izraelac, -lka

Italy /'ɪtəlɪ/ | Italian /ɪ'tælɪən/ | Italija; talijanski; Talijan, -ka

Ivory Coast /ˌaɪvərɪ 'kəʊst/ | Ivorian /ˌaɪˌvɔː'rɪən/ | Obala Bjelokosti

Jamaica /dʒə'meɪkə/ | Jamaican /dʒə'meɪkən/ | Jamajka; jamajkanski; Jamajkanac, -nka

Japan /dʒə'pæn/ | Japanese /ˌdʒæpə'niːz/ | Japan; japanski; Japanac, -nka

Jordan /'dʒɔːdn/ | Jordanian /dʒɔː'deɪnɪən/ | Jordan; jordanski; Jordanac, -nka

Kazakhstan /ˌkɑːzɑːk'stɑːn; -'stæn/ | Kazakh /kə'zɑːk/ | Kazahstan; kazaški; Kazah, -inja

Kenya /'kenjə; 'kiːnjə/ | Kenyan /'kenjən; 'kiːnjən/ | Kenija; kenijski; Kenijac, -jka

Kirghizia /kɜː'gɪzɪə/ | Kirghiz /'kɜːgɪz/ | Kirgizija; kirgiski; Kirgiz, -giskinja

(North/South) Korea /kə'rɪə/ | Korean /kə'rɪən/ | (Sjeverna/Južna) Koreja; korejski; Korejac -jka

Kuwait /kʊ'weɪt; -waɪt/ | Kuwaiti /kʊ'weɪtɪ; -waɪtɪ/ | Kuvajt; kuvajtski; Kuvajćanin, -ćanka

Laos /'lɑːɒs/ | Laotian /'lɑːɒʃn; leɪ'əʊʃn/ | Laos; laoski; Laošanin, -šanka

Latvia
/'lætvɪə/

Latvian
/'lætvɪən/

Latvija; latvijski;
Latvijac, -jka

Lebanon
/'lebənən; -nɒn/

Lebanese
/ˌlebə'ni:z/

Libanon; libanonski;
Libanonac, -nonka

Liberia
/laɪ'bɪərɪə/

Liberian
/laɪ'bɪərɪən/

Liberija; liberijski;
Liberijac, -jka

Libya
/'lɪbɪə/

Libyan
/'lɪbɪən/

Libija; libijski;
Libijac, -jka

Liechtenstein
/'lɪktənstaɪn/

Liechtenstein;
Liechtensteiner
/'lɪktenstaɪnə(r)/

Lihtenštajn;
lihtenštajnski

Lithuania
/ˌlɪθjʊ'eɪnɪə/

Lithuanian
/ˌlɪθjʊ'eɪnɪən/

Litva; litvanski,
litavski; Litvanac,
-nka, Litavac, -vka

Luxemb(o)urg
/'lʌksəmbɜ:g/

Luxemb(o)urg
Luxemb(o)urger
/'lʌksəmbɜ:gə(r)/

Luksemburg; luksemburški;
Luksemburžanin, -žanka

Macedonia
/ˌmæsɪ'dəʊnɪə/

Macedonian
/ˌmæsɪ'dəʊnɪən/

Makedonija; makedonski;
Makedonac, -nka

Malaysia
/mə'leɪzɪə;
-'leɪʒə/

Malaysian
/mə'leɪzɪən;
-'leɪʒn/

Malezija; malezijski;
Malezijac, -jka

Mali
/'mɑ:lɪ/

Malian
/'mɑ:lɪən/

Mali; malijski;
Malijac, -jka

Malta
/'mɔ:ltə/

Maltese
/mɔ:l'ti:z/

Malta; malteški;
Maltežanin, -žanka

Mauritania
/ˌmɒrɪ'teɪnɪə;
ˌmɔ:r-/

Mauritanian
/ˌmɒrɪ'teɪnɪən
ˌmɔ:r-/

Mauritanija; mauritanski;
Mauritanac, -nka

Mauritius
/mə'rɪʃəs; mɔ:-/

Mauritian
/mə'rɪʃn; mɔ:-/

Mauricijus; mauricijski

Mexico
/'meksɪkəʊ/

Mexican
/'meksɪkən/

Meksiko; meksički;
Meksikanac, -nka

Moldavia
/mɒl'deɪvɪə/

Moldavian
/mɒl'deɪvɪən/

Moldavija; moldavski;
Moldavac, -vka

Monaco /ˈmɒnəkəʊ/	Monegasque /ˌmɒnəˈgæsk/	Monako; monegaški
Mongolia /mɒŋˈgəʊlɪə/	Mongolian /mɒŋˈgəʊlɪən/; Mongol /ˈmɒŋgl/	Mongolija; mongolski; Mongol, -golka
Montenegro /ˌmɒntɪˈniːgrəʊ/	Montenegrin /ˌmɒntɪˈniːgrɪn/	Crna Gora; crnogorski; Crnogorac, -rka
Morocco /məˈrɒkəʊ/	Moroccan /məˈrɒkən/	Maroko; marokanski; Marokanac, -nka
Mozambique /ˌməʊzæmˈbiːk/	Mozambiquean /ˌməʊzæmˈbiːkən/	Mozambik; mozambički; Mozambikanac, -nka
Namibia /nəˈmɪbɪə/	Namibian /nəˈmɪbɪən/	Namibija; namibijski; Namibijac, -jka
Nepal /nɪˈpɔːl/	Nepalese /ˌnepəˈliːz/	Nepal; nepalski; Nepalac, -lka
(the) Netherlands /ˈneðələndz/	Dutch /dʌtʃ/; Dutchman /ˈdʌtʃmən/, Dutchwoman /ˈdʌtʃwʊmən/	Nizozemska; nizozemski; Nizozemac, -mka
New Zealand /ˌnjuː ˈziːlənd/	New Zealand; New Zealander /ˌnjuːˈziːləndə(r)/	Novi Zeland; novozelandski; Novozelanđanin, -đanka
Nicaragua /ˌnɪkəˈrægjʊə; -ˈrɑːgwə/	Nicaraguan /ˌnɪkəˈrægjʊən; -rɑːgwən/	Nikaragva; nikaragvanski; Nikaragvanac, -nka
Niger /niːˈʒeə(r)/	Nigerien /niːˈʒeərɪən/	Niger; nigerski; Nigeranin, -ranka
Nigeria /naɪˈdʒɪərɪə/	Nigerian /naɪˈdʒɪərɪən/	Nigerija; nigerijski; Nigerijac, -jka
Northern Ireland /ˌnɔːðən ˈaɪələnd/	Northern Irish /ˌnɔːðən ˈaɪrɪʃ/	Sjeverna Irska; sjevernoirski
Norway /ˈnɔːweɪ/	Norwegian /nɔːˈwiːdʒən/	Norveška; norveški; Norvežanin, -žanka
Oman /əʊˈmɑːn/	Omani /əʊˈmɑːnɪ/	Oman; omanski; Omanac, -nka

(the) Pacific /pə'sɪfɪk/	Pacific	Tihi ocean, Pacifik; pacifički
Pakistan /ˌpɑːkɪ'stɑːn; 'pækɪstæn/	Pakistani /ˌpɑːkɪ'stɑːnɪ; pæki'stænɪ/	Pakistan; pakistanski; Pakistanac, -nka
Palestine /'pæləstaɪn/	Palestinian /ˌpælə'stɪnɪən/	Palestina; palestinski; Palestinac, -nka
Panama /'pænəmɑː/	Panamanian /ˌpænə'meɪnɪən/	Panama; panamski; Panamac, -mka
Papua New Guinea /ˌpæpʊə ˌnjuː 'gɪnɪ; -ˌnuː/	Papuan /'pæpʊən/	Papua Nova Gvineja; papuanski; Papuanac, -nka
Paraguay /'pærəgwaɪ; -gweɪ/	Paraguayan /ˌpærə'gwaɪən; -'gweɪən/	Paragvaj; paragvajski; Paragvajac, -jka
Peru /pə'ruː/	Peruvian /pə'ruːvɪən/	Peru; peruanski; Peruanac, -nka
(the) Philippines /'fɪlɪpiːnz/	Philippine /'fɪlɪpiːn/; Filipino /ˌfɪlɪ'piːnəʊ/	Filipini; filipinski; Filipinac, -nka
Poland /'pəʊlənd/	Polish /'pəʊlɪʃ/; Pole /pəʊl/	Poljska; poljski; Poljak, -inja
Polynesia /ˌpɒlɪ'niːzɪə; -'niːʒə/	Polynesian /ˌpɒlɪ'niːzɪən; -'niːʒn/	Polinezija; polinezijski; Polinežanin, -žanka
Portugal /'pɔːtʃʊgl/	Portuguese /ˌpɔːtʃʊ'giːz/	Portugal; portugalski; Portugalac, -lka
Puerto Rico /ˌpwɜːtəʊ 'riːkəʊ/	Puerto Rican /ˌpwɜːtəʊ 'riːkən/	Portoriko; portorikanski; Portorikanac, -nka
Qatar /kʌ'tɑː(r)/	Qatari /kʌ'tɑːrɪ/	Katar; katarski
Romania, R(o)umania /ruː'meɪnɪə/	Romanian, R(o)umanian /ruː'meɪnɪən/	Rumunjska; rumunjski; Rumunj, -njka
Russia /'rʌʃə/	Russian /'rʌʃn/	Rusija; ruski Rus, -kinja

Rwanda
/rʊ'ændə/

Rwandan
/rʊ'ændən/

Ruanda; ruandski;
Ruanđanin, -nka

Samoa
/sə'məʊə/

Samoan
/sə'məʊən/

Samoa; samoanski

San Marino
/ˌæn mə'ri:nəʊ/

San Marinese
/ˌsæn ˌmærɪ'ni:z/

San Marino;
sanmarinski

Saudi Arabia
/ˌsaʊdɪ ə'reɪbɪə/

Saudi /'saʊdɪ/;
Saudi Arabian
/ˌsaʊdɪ ə'reɪbɪən/

Saudijska Arabija;
saudijski; Saudijac, -jka

Scotland
/'skɒtlənd/

Scottish /'skɒtɪʃ/
Scotch /skɒtʃ/;
Scot /skɒt/, Scotsman
/'skɒtsmən/ Scotswoman
/'skɒtswʊmən/

Škotska;
škotski;
Škot, -kinja

Senegal
/ˌsenɪ'gɔ:l/

Senegalese
/ˌsenɪgɔ'li:z/

Senegal; senegalski;
Senegalac, -lka

Serbia
/'sɜ:bɪə/

Serbian /'sɜ:bɪən/;
Serb /sɜ:b/

Srbija; srpski,
srbijanski;
Srbin, Srpkinja,
Srbijanac, -nka

(the) Seychelles
/seɪ'ʃelz/

Seychellois
/seɪʃel'wa:/

Sejšeli; sejšelski

Sierra Leone
/sɪ'erə lɪ'əʊn/

Sierra Leonean
/sɪ'erə lɪ'əʊnɪən/

Sijera Leone;
sijeraleonski

Singapore
/ˌsɪŋə'pɔ:(r)/

Singaporean
/ˌsɪŋə'pɔ:rɪən/

Singapur; singapurski

Slovakia
/sləʊ'vækɪə/

Slovakian
/sləʊ'vækɪən/;
Slovak
/'sləʊvæk/

Slovačka;
slovački;
Slovak, -inja

Slovenia
/sləʊ'vi:nɪə/

Slovenian
/sləʊ'vi:nɪən/;
Slovene
/sləʊ'vi:n/

Slovenija;
slovenski;
Slovenac, -nka

Somalia
/sə'mɑ:lɪə/

Somali
/sə'mɑ:lɪ/

Somalija; somalski;
Somalac, -lka

South Africa /ˌsaʊθ 'æfrɪkə/	South African /ˌsaʊθ 'æfrɪkən/	Južnoafrička Republika; južnoafrički; Južnoafrikanac, -nka
Spain /speɪn/	Spanish /'spænɪʃ/; Spaniard /'spænɪəd/	Španjolska; španjolski; Španjolac, -lka
Sri Lanka /ˌsriː'læŋkə/	Sri Lankan /ˌsriː'læŋkən/	Šri Lanka; šrilanski
Sudan /suː'dɑːn/	Sudanese /ˌsuː də'niːz/	Sudan; sudanski; Sudanac, -nka
Surinam /ˌsʊərɪ'næm/	Surinamese /ˌsʊərɪnæ'miːz/	Surinam; surinamski
Sweden /'swiːdn/	Swedish /'swiːdɪʃ/; Swede /swiːd/	Švedska; švedski; Šveđanin, -danka
Switzerland /'swɪtsələnd/	Swiss /swɪs/	Švicarska; švicarski; Švicarac, -rka
Syria /'sɪrɪə/	Syrian /'sɪrɪən/	Sirija; sirijski; Sirijac, -jka
Ta(d)jikistan /tɑːˌdʒɪkɪ'stɑːn/	Ta(d)jik /tɑː'dʒɪk/	Tadžikistan; tadžikistanski; Tadžikistanac, -nka
Tahiti /tɑː'hiːtɪ/	Tahitian /tɑː'hiːʃn/	Tahiti; tahićanski; Tahićanin, -nka
Taiwan /taɪ'wɑːn/	Taiwanese /ˌtaɪwə'niːz/	Tajvan; tajvanski; Tajvanac, -nka
Tanzania /ˌtænzə'nɪə/	Tanzanian /ˌtænzə'nɪən/	Tanzanija; tanzanski; Tanzanac, -nka
Thailand /'taɪlænd/	Thai /taɪ/	Tajland; tajlandski; Tajlanđanin, -đanka
Tibet /tɪ'bet/	Tibetan /tɪ'betn/	Tibet; tibetanski; Tibetanac, -nka
Togo /'təʊgəʊ/	Togolese /ˌtəʊgə'liːz/	Togo; togoanski; Togoanac, -nka

Tunisia /tju:'nızıə; tu:'nıʒə/	Tunisian /tju:'nızıən; tu:'nıʒən/	Tunis; tuniski; Tunižanin, -žanka
Turkey /'tɜ:kı/	Turkish; /'tɜ:kıʃ/ Turk /tɜ:k/	Turska; turski; Turčin, -rkinja
Turkmenistan /,tɜ:kmenı'sta:n/	Turkmen /'tɜ:kmen/	Turkmenistan; turkmenistanski; Turkmenistanac, -nka
Uganda /ju:'gændə/	Ugandan /ju:'gændən/	Uganda; ugandski; Ugandanin, -nka
Ukraine /ju:'kreın/	Ukrainian /ju:'kreınıən/	Ukrajina; ukrajinski; Ukrajinac, -nka
United Arab Emirates /ju:'naıtıd 'ærəb 'emırəts/	Emirian /ı'mıərıən/	Ujedinjeni Arapski Emirati
(the) United Kingdom (of Great Britain and Northern) Ireland → Great Britain		Ujedinjeno Kraljevstvo Velike Britanije i Sjeverne Irske
(the) United States of America /ju:,naıtıd ,steıts əv ə'merıkə/	American, /ə'merıkən/ U.S.	Sjedinjene Američke Države; američki; Amerikanac, -nka
Uruguay /'juərəgwaı; -gweı/	Uruguayan /,juərə'gwaıən; -'gweıən/	Urugvaj; urugvajski; Urugvajac, -jka
Uzbekistan /,ʊzbekı'sta:n/	Uzbek /'ʊzbek, 'ʌz-/	Uzbekistan; uzbekistanski; Uzbekistanac, -nka
the Vatican /'vætıkən/, Vatican City	Vatican	Vatikan; vatikanski
Venezuela /,venı'zweılə/	Venezuelan /,venı'zweılən/	Venezuela; venezuelanski; Venezuelanac, -nka
Vietnam /,vjet'næm; -nɑ:m/	Vietnamese /,vjetnə'mi:z/	Vijetnam; vijetnamski; Vijetnamac, -mka

Wales /weɪlz/	Welsh /welʃ/; Welshman /'welʃmən/, Welshwoman /'welʃwʊmən/	Vels; velški; Velšanin, -anka
(North/South) Yemen /'jemən/	Yemeni /'jemənɪ/	(Sjeverni/Južni) Jemen; jemenski; Jemenac, -nka
Yugoslavia /ˌjuːgəʊ'slɑːvɪə/	Yugoslavian /ˌjuːgəʊ'slɑːvɪən/; Yugoslav /'juːgəʊslɑːv/	Jugoslavija; jugoslavenski; Jugoslaven, -nka
Zaire /zɑː'ɪə(r)/	Zairean /zɑː'ɪərɪən/	Zair; zairski; Zairac, -rka
Zambia /'zæmbɪə/	Zambian /'zæmbɪən/	Zambija; zambijski; Zambijac, -jka
Zimbabwe /zɪm'bɑːbwɪ, -weɪ/	Zimbabwean /zɪm'bɑːbwɪən/	Zimbabve; zimbabveanski; Zimbabveanac, -nka

¶ Imena stanovnika i pridjeve nismo naznačili tamo gdje za njih nismo našli potvrdu

Cities
Gradovi

Noun	Adjective	Imenica; pridjev
Athens /ˈæθɪnz/	Athenian /əˈθiːniən/	Atena; atenski
Belgrade /belˈɡreɪd, ˈbelɡreɪd/	Belgrade	Beograd; beogradski
Brussels /ˈbrʌsəlz/	Brussels	Bruxelles; briselski
Bucharest /ˌbuːkəˈrest, ˌbjuː-/	Bucharest	Bukurešt; bukureštanski
Budapest /ˈjuːdəˈpest/	Budapest	Budimpešta; budimpeštanski
Cologne /kəˈləʊn/	Cologne	Köln; kelnski
Copenhagen /ˌəʊpənˈheɪɡən, -hɑː-/	Copenhagen	Kopenhagen; kopenhaški
Florence /ˈflɒrəns/	Florentine /ˈflɒrən,taɪn/	Firenza; firentinski
Geneva /dʒɪˈniːvə/	Genevan /dʒɪˈniːvən/	Ženeva; ženevski
Genoa /ˈdʒenəʊə/	Genoese /ˌdʒenəʊˈiːz/	Genova; đenoveški
Glasgow /ˈɡlɑːzɡəʊ, ˈɡlæz-/	Glaswegian /ɡlæzˈwiːdʒən/	Glasgow; glazgovski
The Hague /heɪɡ/	Hague	Den Haag; haški
Lisbon /ˈlɪzbən/	Lisbon	Lisabon; lisabonski
Liverpool /ˈlɪvə,puːl/	Liverpudlian /ˌlɪvəˈpʌdlɪən/	Liverpool; liverpulski
Manchester /ˈmæntʃɪstə(r)/	Mancunian /mæŋˈkjuːnɪən/	Manchester; mančesterski
Milan /mɪˈlæn/	Milanese /ˌmɪləˈniːz/	Milano; milanski

Moscow /ˈmɒskəʊ/	Moscow; Muscovite /ˈmʌskə‚vaɪt/	Moskva; moskovski; Moskovljanin
Munich /ˈmjuːnɪk/	Munich	München; minhenski
Naples /ˈneɪpəlz/	Naples	Napulj; napuljski
Paris /ˈpærɪs/	Parisian /pəˈrɪzɪən/	Pariz; pariški
Prague /prɑːg/	Prague	Prag; praški
Rome /rəʊm/	Roman /ˈrəʊmən/	Rim; rimski
Sofia /ˈsəʊfɪə/	Sofia	Sofija; sofijski
St Petersburg /ˈpiːtəz‚bɜːg/	St Petersburg	Sankt Petersburg; sanktpetersburški
Trieste /triːˈest/	Trieste	Trst; tršćanski
Turin /ˈtʊərɪn/	Turin	Torino; torinski
Venice /ˈvenɪs/	Venetian /vɪˈniːʃən/	Venecija; venecijanski
Vienna /vɪˈenə/	Viennese /‚vɪəˈniːz/	Beč; bečki
Warsaw /ˈwɔːsɔː/	Warsaw	Varšava; varšavski
Zurich /ˈzjʊərɪk/	Zurich	Zürich; ciriški

Izdavač / Published by:
© **Naklada C**, Zagreb
4. izdanje

Kompjutorska obrada / Computor Prepress:
ANDROMEDA d.o.o. Rijeka

Za izdavača / For Publisher:
Sarija Mahmić

Tisak i uvez / Print and Binding:
Grafički zavod Hrvatske d.o.o. Zagreb

Naklada / Printed: 3000

Distributeri:
ANDROMEDA d.o.o. Braće Cetina 2, Rijeka,
tel: 051/684-761, 01/6555 825,
e-mail: prodaja@andromeda.hr

TRSAT POLO d.o.o. J. Žerjavića 16, Zagreb,
tel: 01/48-55-005, e-mail: trsatpol@inet.hr

CIP - Katalogizacija u publikaciji
S V E U Č I L I Š N A K N J I Ž N I C A
R I J E K A

UDK 811.111(038)=163.42
811.163.42(038)=111

ČENGIĆ, Nata
Englesko-hrvatski i hrvatsko-engleski
moderni rječnik / sastavili Nata Čengić,
Vojo Micak, Nataša Pavlović. - 4. izd. -
Zagreb : Naklada C, 2003

Na spor. nasl. str.: English-Croatian and
Croatian-English dictionary.

ISBN 953-6088-03-7

1. Micak, Vojo 2. Pavlović, Nataša
100901091

ISBN 953-6088-03-7